Race, Poverty, and Domestic Policy

THE INSTITUTION FOR SOCIAL AND POLICY STUDIES
AT YALE UNIVERSITY

THE YALE ISPS SERIES

EDITED BY C. MICHAEL HENRY
FOREWORD BY JAMES TOBIN

Race, Poverty, and Domestic Policy

Yale University Press
New Haven &
London

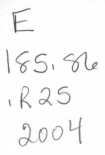

"Dedicated to the impoverished residents of the inner city and to the memory of Professor James Tobin, who advocated policies for poverty alleviation in the inner city."

Set in Sabon type by Keystone Typesetting, Inc.
Printed in the United States of America.

ISBN: 0-300-09541-4 (cloth)
Library of Congress Control Number: 2004041409

A catalogue record for this book is available from the British Library.

The paper in this book meets the guidelines for permanence and durability of the Committee on Production Guidelines for Book Longevity of the Council on Library Resources.

10 9 8 7 6 5 4 3 2 1

Contents

Foreword

James Tobin

In his time at Yale, Michael Henry was the entrepreneur most responsible for organizing and maintaining interdisciplinary discussion of contemporary issues of United States social policies, in particular those relating to poverty and related disadvantage of inner-city minorities. Yale was fortunate that
Michael took this initiative. The many scholars at Yale concerned with these
difficult issues of professional social science are scattered — among economics,
political science, sociology, public health, medicine, law, African-American
studies, and women's studies. As in other universities, it takes conscious effort
and concentration on common interests to bring them together. Yale's long-
established Institution for Social and Policy Studies was the natural administrative home for Michael's six-year series of multidisciplinary seminars, many
led by local scholars, many featuring leading authorities and practitioners
from all over the nation. The series covered diverse disciplines, "schools,"
ideologies, and policy advocacies. This book contains twenty-six essays that
grew out of the sixty-one seminars, representing a fair share of the best work
on these crucial subjects in the 1990s.

It is always difficult to bring together contributions so diverse in disciplines
and methodologies, as well as in the value judgments and interests of the
authors. We all recognize the need for interdisciplinary approaches, but they
are hard to achieve in practice. Languages and assumptions differ. There is no

agreed overarching social science methodology. In its absence, the best cross-disciplinary work is probably the result of focus on common practical problems of knowledge and action.

The immense scope of the subjects of this book is obvious from the table of contents and includes poverty, inequality, education, crime, health, AIDS, addictions, drug trade, racial discrimination, affirmative action, entrepreneurship, crime and punishment, immigration, welfare, taxes and transfers. Just to publish chapters on all these together — by the leading authorities in the fields and representing the major agreements and disagreements over findings, facts, diagnoses and prescriptions, is a major achievement. In his introductory essay, Michael has tried valiantly to do more, to bring some synthesizing organization to the field.

Though incredibly prosperous, the United States faces many problems — poverty, family instability, illegitimacy, unemployment, illiteracy, educational failures, health, crime, discrimination, and so on. There is a strong temptation to select one of them as a sovereign source of the others, for individuals, families, communities, regions, and society as a whole. If only X were solved, then W, Y, Z, etc., would be remedied too. For example, marriage is alleged to be the key to career success, or maybe marriage plus completion of high school plus staying off drugs is the key to good jobs. All of these propositions are convincing in some degree, and statistical correlations can be mobilized to support cause-and-effect assertions. Is the source of the underclass a culture of poverty, leading to self-defeating behavior by the poor? Is it instead the denials of opportunity by the larger and more prosperous society? Must the answer be one or the other?

The trouble is that causation is elusive and complex in the areas of interest and concern, maybe often meaningless. Usually there is no one variable or no simple set of social institutions or circumstances that is determinative. More likely all or most variables are both causes and effects, both independent and dependent. If its schools are good, a community is likely to have higher employment, better jobs, and less crime. But these phenomena themselves make schools better.

I think it is useful to think of both macro (community-wide) variables and micro (individual) outcomes and how they are connected. The prospects and outcomes for one individual depend on his or her family genetics and environment. They also depend on neighborhood circumstances (crime, schools, drugs, jobs, networks). The macro-micro connections generate the system's dynamics. Yesterday's macro environment determines the characteristics of today's individuals, children and adolescents, and their composition results in tomorrow's macro environment, and so on. In these dynamics, there may be vicious circles or virtuous circles. In a vicious circle, bad macro states worsen the outcomes for new individual members of the community, making the next set of macro variables still worse. A virtuous circle exploits positive feedbacks and obtains successively better results, macro and micro. The necessary but difficult task is to intervene in ways that will replace vicious with virtuous dynamics, strengthening the connections between good social institutions and constructive behaviors of individuals. Doubtless positive interventions will work better if combined.

This is a sketch of an idea stimulated by the multitude and variety of the diagnoses and prescriptions in the chapters of this book. This is a way to think about it. Now, if only Michael's next book will perform the task of integration.

Editor's Preface

The chapters in this volume are updated and revised versions of faculty seminar papers on Inner City Poverty, sponsored by the Institution for Social and Policy Studies (ISPS), the center for interdisciplinary enquiries at Yale. When I joined ISPS in 1991, the intense poverty in inner-city New Haven and, indeed, inner cities nationwide — the society of poverty — where the impoverished create their own survival structures and rationale, reminded me of poverty in less developed countries (LDCs), where suffering is more real than comfort. Clearly, evidence of poverty and inequality is also found beyond inner cities. In fact, it is the view of many scholars that, nationwide, income and economic inequality are growing worse, as CEOs of many corporations earn more in a day than a significant portion of the corporation's employees earn in a year. But owing in large measure to historical racism, racial and familial hardships make poverty in inner cities considerably more intense. I proposed to the then director of ISPS, Joseph La Palombara, that ISPS offer a multidisciplinary faculty seminar on inner-city poverty to bring to bear the enormous intellectual capital at Yale to stimulate university-wide interdisciplinary scholarship that would contribute to analysis and formulation of effective antipoverty policy. At that time, a very small part of the research undertaken at Yale focused on domestic poverty, let alone poverty in inner cities. Thus, the seminar papers presented were primarily by faculty and leading scholars from distinguished academic institutions across the nation. I served as faculty coordinator of the seminars, which were attended by faculty and graduate students from departments in the Faculty of Arts and Sciences as well as from the graduate and professional schools and, occasionally, by policy makers from New Haven and state governments.

The essays in this volume address inequality, poverty, discrimination, and attendant racial hardship, and, antipoverty policy and all that, spanning the period from the mid-1960s to 2000. The introduction places contemporary inner-city poverty in historical context, providing answers to questions such as: how did these problems arise; and, why have they persisted, over time, with such brutalizing effect?

A number of colleagues provided considerable support to this ISPS endeavor. These include Brad Gray, who succeeded Joe La Palombara as director of ISPS, James Tobin, Doug Rae, Rogers Smith, and Jerry Mashaw. In addition, I should like to thank the present director of ISPS, Don Green, for his encouragement and for ISPS financial support for publication of this volume. I should also like to express my appreciation to Bill Brainard who, during his term as chair of the economics department, extended secretarial assistance from the department in compilation of the essays. Editing of the final draft of the manuscript was done while I was Visiting Research Fellow at Queen Elizabeth House, University of Oxford.

I am personally grateful to the authors of these chapters for their cooperation, and to those who submitted their essays and revisions early for their patience in awaiting final compilation of all. Three anonymous referees selected by Yale University Press made useful suggestions. Additionally, I should like to thank Sanjay De Silva for excellent research assistance and Nora Wiedenback for her patient typing and retyping on the computer. And finally, I should like to thank John Kulka, Noreen O'Connor, Margaret Otzel, and Mary Traester of the editorial staff at Yale University Press for their efforts.

All royalties from the volume will be used to found a program to train and place rehabilitated drug abusers from New Haven in enterprises established to provide goods and services to the Greater New Haven community.

Introduction

Historical Overview of Race and
Poverty from Reconstruction to 1969

C. MICHAEL HENRY

This introductory essay focuses on historical factors that effected the straitened circumstances of African Americans. Race and poverty are placed in historical context to shed light on the link between race and poverty in the historical past and contemporary problems of black penury.

For analytical purposes, African American history is divided into four periods: pre–Civil War, 1865 to 1940, 1941 to 1969, and 1970 to the present. The pre–Civil War period encompasses slavery, which is not of immediate relevance here, although the problems of race and poverty are a significant part of the damning legacies of slavery. Chapters in this volume address issues of race and poverty in the contemporary period,[1] spanning 1970 to the present. And, in this introduction, I focus on the period between 1865 and 1970 to examine historical factors that explain race and poverty in the contemporary period. To readers knowledgeable of African American history, much of this introduction may cover familiar ground.

Subsequent to Reconstruction, a disproportionately large number of black Americans have lived in appalling poverty relative to their white counterparts. This impoverishment was well documented by noted scholars in the late nineteenth century as well as in the twentieth century.[2] But awareness of the severity of black impoverishment never gave rise to any large-scale alleviation, let alone eradication of racial and economic hardship. Notwithstanding the Fourteenth

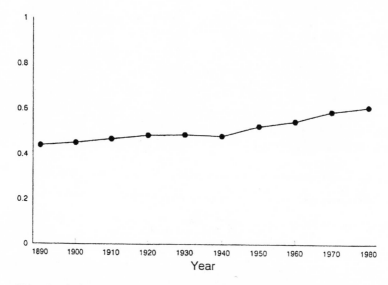

Figure I.1 Black-to-White Earnings Ratios: Males, Ages 20 to 64, 1890–1980
Source: Smith (1984), cited in Robert A. Margo, *Race and Schooling in the South, 1880–1950* (Chicago: University of Chicago Press, 1990), p. 2.

Amendment, historically, these Americans have always been arbitrarily excluded from the moral imperatives of the Declaration of Independence owing to racism and its derivative, racial discrimination, formally institutionalized in society and deeply embedded in the "national" ethos. Such socially contrived circumstances spawned black impoverishment and attendant racial economic inequality. These adversities prevailed in both the north and south.

Economic Stagnation and Retrogression

In the south, during the period of government-sanctioned racial segregation (from the end of Reconstruction (1866–77) to the close of the civil rights movement), blacks made little economic "progress," measured by the racial wage gap, prior to 1940.[3] Between 1940 and 1980 this earnings gap was reduced some 13 percent (Figure I.1).[4] Scholars have offered several explanations for this lack of black progress.[5] The first explanation emphasized deficiency in supply of labor brought about by differences between black and white students in "quantity" (number of years in school) and "quality" (the rate of illiteracy, test scores, etc.) of elementary and high school education. This deficiency was reflected by black-white ratios in per capita school expenditure, which was approximately equal shortly after Reconstruction, declined

Table I.1. School Attendance and Parental Illiteracy: Southern Black Children, Ages Five to Twenty

	Number of Observations	Attending School (%)
Both parents illiterate	2,147	36.8
Father literate, mother illiterate	1,046	45.1
Father illiterate, mother literate	909	45.5
Both parents literate	2,308	56.8

Source: Robert A. Margo, *Race and Schooling in the South, 1880–1950* (Chicago: University of Chicago Press, 1990), p. 13.

from the late nineteenth to early twentieth century, remained relatively stable between 1910 and 1940, then rose somewhat after 1940.[6] A second explanation emphasized deficiency in demand for labor brought about by racial discrimination and segregation in the labor market, creating a "dual labor market," effectively trapping most blacks in low-wage jobs. Given this labor market duality, blacks — whether extravagantly gifted, very good, average, or mediocre — could not overcome the barriers of skin color, whatever their level of education. The third explanation encompasses the above deficiencies in demand and supply along with what Robert Margo termed "intergenerational drag" — that is, high rates of adult illiteracy among blacks, resulting in black children being kept on the farm and out of school. In short, literacy gaps between black and white students over generations are attributed to black family background disadvantages, such as poverty, lower occupational status, and, in particular, parental illiteracy. For example, in a sample from the 1910 census, approximately 63.2 percent of the students whose parents were both illiterate did not attend school, as opposed to 43.2 percent of students whose parents were both literate (Table I.1).

Thus, "withholding" literacy, which began during slavery, fostered a mind-set that was perpetuated through generations of school discrimination, has had a major adverse impact on black educational achievement over the decades to the present.

Educational Failure

Significant qualitative and quantitative differences in schooling between black and white students were not peculiar to the south. Indeed, such differences also prevailed in the north, albeit, not to the same degree. A crude measure of the minimum acceptable quantity of schooling is the percentage of individuals, at least twenty-five years of age, who completed five or more years of schooling.[7] In 1960, 24 percent and 7 percent, respectively, of blacks and whites in the north, had less than five years of schooling, whereas, in the south, 35 percent of blacks did.[8] Qualitatively, schooling provided to blacks in the north was also inferior to that of whites. This was especially evident during World War II in the national experience with a standardized written test given to all registrants by the Selective Service System. Nationwide, 4 percent of all registrants were rejected as deficient on the basis of the test. Rejection rates were 5 percent for blacks in the north and west, and 18 percent for blacks in the south, while rejection rates were 2.5 percent for all whites and 5 percent for southern whites.[9]

The 1960 Coleman Report, based on a large-scale national survey, found low levels of educational achievement by blacks in every region of the country.[10] For example, in verbal ability, twelfth-grade blacks in the metropolitan northeast and midwest averaged 3.3 grades below twelfth-grade whites; whereas twelfth-grade blacks in the metropolitan south averaged 4.2 grades below whites in the metropolitan northeast. Although the findings for blacks in the north are more favorable than those for blacks in the south, the record in the north is found equally wanting. These racial differences persisted despite the 1954 ruling by the Supreme Court in *Brown v. Board of Education* that "separate but equal" facilities in education were a violation of the Fourteenth Amendment.[11] Small wonder, therefore, that over generations, blacks have bemoaned socially contrived barriers to educational opportunities, which created a disproportionately large number of blacks who floundered while their white counterparts savored emphatic economic success.

Dearth of Employment Opportunities

Subsequent to manumission, poverty-stricken blacks constituted a significant portion of residents in the Black Belt (Georgia, Alabama, Mississippi, and Louisiana) of the south comprising some three hundred counties.[12] County residents were segregated by race and class, but, in the main, blacks were domiciled in rural areas, where they worked as sharecroppers for a pittance. Stern[13] reports an extremely high level of poverty among blacks residing in these counties. In fact, in 1939, about 82 percent of black families in the Black Belt were impoverished, greatly exceeding poverty rates in present-day "inner cities." Margo notes that the fundamental factor behind black poverty was racial discrimination according to prevailing white social norms.[14] Thus, prior to 1940, even though most blacks in the labor force were gainfully employed, their earnings were low.

Table I.2. *Racial Differences in Unemployment Rates in the United States, 1890–1965*

	White	Black	Difference	Unemployment Rate Ratio
1890	4.41%	4.07%	0.34	0.92 to 1
1900	6.47	7.57	1.10	1.17 to 1
1930	6.59	6.07	0.52	0.92 to 1
1940[a]	9.50[a]	10.89[a]	1.39	1.15 to 1
1950	4.90	9.0	4.10	1.84 to 1
1955	3.9	8.7	4.8	2.23 to 1
1960	5.0	10.2	5.2	2.04 to 1
1965	4.0	8.1	4.0	1.98 to 1

Note: [a] Counting government emergency workers as employed; counting them as unemployed increases white unemployment to 14.15%, black unemployment to 16.87%, and the black-white unemployment ratio to 1.19.

Source: Warren C. Whatley, "Is There a New Black Poverty?" (unpublished papers, 1992).

Given the dearth of opportunities, poverty, and degradation in the south, many blacks went north in search of what Claude Brown termed "the promised land."[15] But they were in for a rude awakening, for they remained largely mired in poverty and political repression, working at low-paying, menial and dirty jobs. In the north, they suffered ill effects of employment discrimination and wage inequality. In fact, prior to 1940, blacks were excluded from most industrial jobs as well as from subsets of other jobs reserved for whites.[16] Prior to World War II, aggregate data show black and white labor having approximately equal rates of unemployment (Table I.2). But when these data are disaggregated, unemployment rates among blacks in the northeast are more than double the rates for whites. After the war, however, aggregate data show rates for blacks as twice those for whites.

Labor Market Discrimination

Labor market discrimination against blacks has been virtually ubiquitous and takes a variety of forms. First, in some firms, contrived barriers (to hiring, apprenticing, promotion, etc.) militate against employment of blacks, while in others, blacks are employed only in low-skilled, low-paying jobs with no opportunities for advancement. Second, some firms recruit only in areas far removed from black neighborhoods or in areas not frequented by blacks. And third, as elaborated below, it is highly likely that some firms maintain tacit

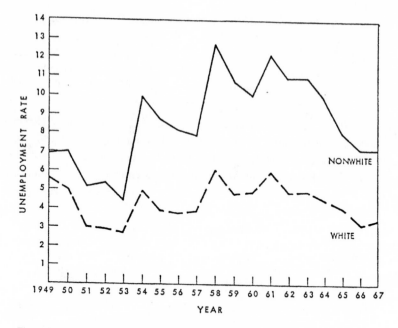

Figure I.2 Nonwhite and White Unemployment Rates, 1949–1967
Source: Bureau of Labor Statistics and Bureau of the Census, "Social and Economic Conditions of Negroes in the United States" (October 1967), cited in John F. Kain, ed., *Race and Poverty: The Economics of Discrimination* (Englewood Cliffs, N.J.: Prentice-Hall, 1969), p. 4.

agreements with unions to discriminate against blacks. Thus, subsequent to World War II, the unemployment rate for blacks is invariably some multiple of that for whites, in large measure, because blacks were "eligible" for employment only in a subset of available jobs (see Table I.2). The gap between white and nonwhite unemployment rates grew wider circa 1954 and began to shrink around 1963; it should be noted that these rates exclude unemployed workers who were no longer actively seeking work, many of whom are nonwhite. Furthermore, blacks experience considerable barriers to training and apprenticeship programs, which are requisite for entry into certain trades, occupations, or skilled jobs.[17]

Such discriminatory practices are commonplace in the north as well as in the south, although they are somewhat less overt in the north than in the south. A 1953 study of employment practices by enterprises in Pennsylvania reported that nine-tenths of the firms surveyed practiced some form of discrimination against blacks with respect to hiring, apprenticing, and promoting. A 1958 study of firms in Ohio reported similar findings of discrimination against blacks.[18]

Union Barriers to Gainful Employment and Skill Development

Historically, unions played a significant role in limiting employment opportunities for blacks. Over the period 1886–1935, the dominant labor union, the American Federation of Labor (AFL), was committed to organizing workers without regard to race. Under the stewardship of Samuel Gompers and subsequent leadership, this policy was maintained until circa 1895 when machinists (who discriminated against blacks) were admitted to the federation. Over time, however, the AFL leadership acquiesced to the practice of racial discrimination by local affiliates and, rather than refuse to organize workers in their localities, organized blacks and whites as segregated locals. In 1935, the other major union, the Congress of Industrial Organizations (CIO), was established within the AFL. The CIO practiced less racial discrimination primarily because its workers were in mass production industries where large numbers of blacks were employed as "unskilled" labor; hence, the CIO did not control the supply of jobs. In short, these industrial unions, unlike the craft unions that dominated the AFL, had little control over the racial composition of the membership and thus far less opportunity to discriminate.

Nonetheless, antidiscriminatory policies of the unions conflicted with practices of locals, especially in the AFL. Since 1943, however, the number of unions excluding blacks has declined significantly. Railway trainmen and locomotive firemen removed prohibitions against black membership in 1960 and 1965, respectively. Thus, formal barriers to black membership were removed, but many local affiliates continue to exclude blacks by "informal" means, which are difficult to eliminate.

Barriers to entry into apprenticeship programs have always been the principal means of excluding blacks from skilled trades, thereby restricting them to low-wage unskilled employment from which they eked out a meager living. Low wage inevitably equals bad housing, poor diet and deteriorating health. Indeed, nationwide, black apprentices have been few relative to whites. For example, the census of 1960 reported that there were 2,191 black apprentices nationally, approximately 2.5 percent of all apprentices. Small though this proportion may seem, it represents an improvement over the proportion of black apprentices in 1950, 1.9 percent.[19] Hence, the relatively small proportion of blacks employed in the highly remunerated skilled trades.

Traditionally, craftsmen hailed primarily from one of the European ethnic groups such as Irish, Polish, Italian, German. Invariably, these craftsmen exercised a kind of proprietary right over their crafts and the unions, restricting entry to apprenticeship programs to their sons, nephews, other relatives, and sons of close friends who, most likely, were from the same ethnic group. They therefore prevented entry of "strangers." Moreover, even if individuals outside the ethnic group were considered, the likelihood was very small that blacks would be among those having close rapport with these craftsmen, given widespread residential racial segregation. In addition, lack of information about opportunities for apprenticeships and the distance between union halls and black communities placed apprenticeship and training programs beyond the reach of many blacks.

These circumstances created an employment access problem and illustrate how one form of discrimination may be enforced by another. That is, housing market discrimination confines blacks to certain residential communities, and suburbanization of employment increases the distance between inner-city communities and employment centers. Moreover, blacks who secure employment in the suburbs may spend a great deal of time and money commuting to and from a low-wage job.[20] The relatively high ratio of weekly commuting and related costs to the low weekly wage may discourage workers from seeking employment in distant suburbs — the "discouraged worker" hypothesis. In short, housing market discrimination significantly reduces black employment, as well as earnings after subtracting transportation and other costs, and engenders black impoverishment.

Housing Segregation

As noted in the foregoing, black poverty and racial segregation were commonplace in both the north and south. Notwithstanding the Fourteenth Amendment, which guaranteed the rights of citizenship, the 1898 Supreme Court ruling in *Plessy v. Ferguson* provided the constitutional basis for segregation. Segregated facilities for blacks and whites were deemed constitutional as long as they were "separate but equal."[21] In northern cities, residential segregation by race (and class) began in the period between World Wars I and II. Blacks who migrated northward during World War I and in the 1920s were segregated into large and growing urban ghettos from which they were unable to escape owing to the dearth of employment opportunities. Furthermore, wage policies of the New Deal era militated against expansion of employment opportunities for blacks. The Civil Rights movement of subsequent decades focused, primarily, on integration of the black middle class into mainstream political and social life, and not the escape of blacks from penury.[22] Moreover, the hardships of black impoverishment were exacerbated by federal policy after 1933, when the government institutionalized statistical discrimination in the mortgage market.[23] Federal credit guarantors considered black residential areas to be declining neighborhoods and labeled them high-risk "red" zones to be avoided.[24] Such a policy effectively depressed the value of residential and other property in black neighborhoods, making it difficult for blacks to accumulate wealth through home ownership.[25] Accordingly, the market value of residential homes in black neighborhoods is invariably lower than that of comparable homes in white communities. Depressed market values reduce home equity, thereby denying these families a source of funds to defray costs of, for example, their children's college education.

The large inner-city ghettos in the north represent the prototype model of residential segregation. Using census data for city blocks, Taeuber and Taeuber computed segregation indices for a number of cities in 1940, 1950, and 1960 in which zero indicates an even distribution of blacks on each block and 100 indicates that each block contains no blacks or no whites — complete segregation. Indices computed for 207 cities ranged from 60.4 in San Jose, California, to 98.1 in Fort Lauderdale, Florida. Half of the cities had segregation indices greater than 88, and only eight had indices lower than 70.[26] In short, a great degree of segregation of blacks is the hallmark of U.S. cities.

A number of reasons have been offered for prevalence of segregated residential housing, the most important of which is the marked difference in income between blacks and whites (see discussion of these issues in Chapter 8). But empirically, only a relatively small proportion of black residential segregation is explained by low income (Table I.3). The data presented below do not support the hypothesis that concentration of blacks in inner cities and paucity of blacks in the suburbs are due to low income. Indeed, a significant proportion of low-income whites reside in the suburbs, while only a small proportion of middle- and high-income blacks are part of the suburban residentiary.

Historically, racial zoning had been an effective legal means of excluding blacks from white neighborhoods. The prototype ordinance passed in Louisville, Kentucky, stated that a given block containing a disproportionately large number of whites should be deemed a white residential block, and the same holds for blacks.[27] Hence, blacks *may* not move into white areas and vice versa. In 1917, the Supreme Court declared this ordinance a violation of the Fourteenth Amendment; however, notwithstanding this ruling, the practice was continued somewhat unobtrusively and was tacitly sanctioned by authorities in many cities. For example, in a 1958 survey of the attitude and behavior of Philadelphia officials, a builder informed the interviewer that he was willing to sell suburban homes to blacks, but if he were to do so he would be ruined economically by local building inspectors.[28]

Another important measure used to maintain racial segregation is restriction of deed. Race restrictive covenants were widespread during the 1920s; such covenants were used by homeowners' associations, real estate boards,

Table I.3. White and Black Families Residing in the Suburban Ring of the Ten Largest Urbanized Areas, by Income, 1960*

	White			Black		
	All Families	Under $3,000	Over $10,000	All Families	Under $3,000	Over $10,000
1. New York	27.8%	16.3%	39.2%	9.4%	8.2%	13.9%
2. Los Angeles–Long Beach	59.5	53.5	57.7	25.1	20.7	28.5
3. Chicago	47.6	37.2	54.7	7.7	5.9	9.0
4. Philadelphia–Camden	47.7	32.7	42.2	11.5	10.1	13.8
5. Detroit	58.9	44.9	63.3	12.1	11.3	12.6
6. San Francisco–Oakland	57.8	48.8	60.8	29.2	25.8	31.5
7. Boston	74.3	64.0	82.4	19.2	13.9	37.7
8. Washington	75.7	59.6	77.3	9.8	10.4	8.4
9. Pittsburgh	70.5	63.3	73.6	29.4	27.1	29.4
10. Cleveland	59.2	39.3	75.2	3.1	2.4	4.3

Note: For New York and Chicago the suburban ring is the difference between the SMSA and the urban place (central city). For all other cities it is the difference between the urbanized area and central city. San Francisco–Oakland, Los Angeles–Long Beach, and Philadelphia–Camden are counted as two central cities.

Source: U.S. Bureau of the Census, U.S. Census of Populations: 1960, vol. I, Characteristics of the Population. Cited in John F. Kain, ed., Race and Poverty: The Economics of Discrimination (Englewood Cliffs, N.J.: Prentice-Hall, 1969) p. 23.

and the Federal Housing Authority. Indeed, although racial zoning was ruled illegal by the courts, for decades the practice of racial covenants continued without abatement, legally sanctioned, as a "private matter." In 1948, however, the Supreme Court ruled that legal enforcement of such restrictive covenants to prohibit sale of private residential properties to blacks was unconstitutional. But, by that time, the damage had already been done; most homes sold to whites over past decades were still covered by such covenants. But officially the practice was illegal.[29]

It is important to note that even though the Court removed sanction of the law from such practices, these practices continued, albeit illegally. To be sure, those who desired continued exclusion of blacks from white neighborhoods resorted to private agreements among real estate agents, financial institutions, and homeowners as well as by use of extralegal and illegal means. These formidable barriers have discouraged many blacks from buying homes in white neighborhoods.

Outlawing residential segregation by race would augur well for blacks. In the north, housing market desegregation is the key to school desegregation, thereby making better schools available to blacks. Elimination of residential segregation has important implications for eradication of black poverty because, as noted above, housing market discrimination limits employment opportunities for blacks. Furthermore, blacks are compelled to spend more than nonblacks to obtain housing of equal quality as a result of housing market discrimination. Over past decades, considerable efforts at desegregation have been attempted, but to no avail. Effective countervailing measures taken by whites, including most sinister human rights abuses (of blacks), were the signature of the period covered in this chapter (see Chapters 6 and 8).

Black Poverty

Accordingly, one of the hallmarks of the black historical experience has been limited employment opportunities, which restricted them to low-wage menial jobs. Thus, opportunities open to blacks for economic betterment through advancement on the job were practically nonexistent: hence the paucity of skills, high unemployment rates, relatively low incomes, and abject poverty among a disproportionate number of these citizens. Over generations, material deprivation and racial hardship created a growing economic distance between blacks and whites.[30] Yet, despite the fullness with which these hardships were documented in works of merit, these findings resonated neither in the minds of policy makers nor in the hearts of employers to permanently ameliorate conditions of blacks. For the most part, these works were either ignored, treated like a jeu d'esprit, or drew cavils from segments of society, giving credence to the words of Harvard's Duncan Kennedy that, "judgements of merit are inevitably culturally, racially and ideologically contingent." In a similar vein, proponents of critical race theory argue that people's perspectives on events are overwhelmingly determined by their racial (or ethnic) background. These are quite persuasive views, given the historical record. Indeed, the severity of black poverty was not officially appreciated until the civil rights movement effected qualms of conscience in some quarters by poignantly dramatizing the gravity of racial hardship, coupled with publications by Michael Harrington and Dwight MacDonald that described the wretched conditions of the poor.[31] In the wake of these realizations, poverty was defined and federal antipoverty policy was designed to pull the poor from the mire.

Anti-Poverty Policy

Initially, poverty was defined in absolute terms, but this was supplanted by a relative definition (see Chapter 3). Under the absolute definition, individuals whose incomes fell below an absolute dollar magnitude considered necessary to maintain a minimally acceptable living standard were considered poor. In the relative case, individuals whose incomes fell below half the median income were considered poor.[32] Policy makers thought that absolute poverty could be eradicated by rapid economic growth and munificent income maintenance policies, but they failed to realize that problems of social isolation and inequality would be impervious to such measures. And, as noted by James Tobin in the Foreword, problems of inequality and social isolation must also be addressed if relative poverty is to be eradicated. Over time, relative poverty became the assumed policy objective and almost "every report on poverty issued by the Federal Government contains the direct or implicit caveat that poverty is relative and that an absolute standard loses its meaning and validity over time."[33]

To enhance efficacy of policy, the poor were treated as a dichotomous group, of which one subset was the target of discretionary fiscal measures and the other of nondiscretionary measures. One subset comprised the steadily working poor continuously attached to the labor market, and the other comprised those incapable of or unable to find work owing to ill health or family problems, and those struggling with imperatives beyond their control. Over time, the usefulness of this dichotomy diminished. Consequently, a second bifurcation was used, which comprised the permanent and temporary poor. The permanent poor refers to those trapped in poverty — an underclass as Sundquist first described it[34] — whether employed, unemployed, or out of the labor force, whether healthy or unhealthy, capable or incapable of work. The temporary poor comprised those whose incomes fell below the poverty line owing to cyclical or random causes, but which could be expected to rise above the line as economic conditions improved. Discretionary fiscal policy was considered the appropriate instrument to address problems of the working or temporary poor through measures promoting economic growth that would lift this subset out of poverty — the "backwash hypothesis." In contrast, public assistance and Social Security were considered appropriate for problems of the permanent poor or those unable to find work owing to barriers beyond their control.

Munificent income maintenance programs were implemented to increase income and consumption of poor blacks. Such programs included increased welfare payments and broadened eligibility, negative income tax and family allowances, low-income housing, and various employment and training initiatives to increase earnings of the poor. Subsequently, some experts suggested that these programs should be modified because what the poor needed most was money and not services; therefore, emphasis in welfare programs shifted from provision of services to provision of income. But there was considerable division of sentiment about the desirability of income transfers to "able-bodied males," especially blacks. It was argued that such transfers created disincentives to work and that, therefore, government should guarantee employment. In a word, government should be the "employer of last resort." Proponents of income transfers, however, argue that employment guarantee programs would be more costly. In fact, they argued that income transfer can be designed to produce strong work incentives through measures such as the negative income tax, which would provide a minimum income floor for all groups and improve work incentives.[35] (See Chapters 20 and 21 on issues of welfare reform, eligibility, and job availability for welfare recipients.)

Daniel Patrick Moynihan, who proposed a set of policies to create opportunities for blacks, presented a mandarin view of dispossessed blacks. Moynihan argued for job creation for unemployed blacks with an attendant program of income allowances for children. This antipoverty policy to ameliorate conditions of the poor was based on his identification of the deterioration of the black family as the main cause of black disadvantage. The weakness of the black family, he argued, was due to unemployment among black males. But given the black historical experience reviewed above, this proposal seems seriously wanting. To be sure, providing employment to blacks may strengthen the black family, but such a policy may merely mask continued racial discrimination. Moynihan's policy recommendation was of enormous importance to increase opportunities for blacks, but discriminatory practices remained untouched, leaving black males continuously subject to low wages, menial jobs, underemployment, and job instability.

Policies designed to increase opportunities for blacks and to eradicate discrimination have only some measure of overlap; for example, lowering barriers to employment, education, housing, and other areas enhance opportunity. Programs that increase opportunities without directly attacking discrimination include various education, training, and other human capital programs to enhance the abilities and skills of blacks to help them secure better jobs, but not necessarily in the face of continued discrimination. In short, antidiscrimination policies are a prerequisite for socioeconomic betterment of blacks. These policies, and policies to increase opportunities, are both required to improve the socioeconomic well-being of blacks.

Attention of experts and policy makers was trained on the underemployed. A rather narrow economic measure, the unemployment rate, was used to define and measure labor market problems at both the micro and macro levels. Policies were therefore formulated to expand employment opportunities. Manpower policies were introduced to assist workers who remained unemployed when the unemployment rate was low. But initially these policies focused only on problems of workers in "depressed areas" — effectively helping white blue-collar, semi-skilled workers by training them for new kinds of jobs.[36] Thus, consistent with their historical experience, black underemployed workers were excluded from the cadre of workers selected for retraining. In fact, it was the civil rights movement, ghetto riots, and threats of more mayhem in the future, which gave rise to some measure of change, forcing attention to employment difficulties of blacks, especially those residing in inner cities.

Experts and policy makers finally became aware that unemployment rates in inner cities remained intolerably high in the midst of prosperity, and a new approach debuted, coupling a number of other labor market characteristics with unemployment as symptoms of labor market disadvantage. As indicated above, for blacks, unemployment was a relatively small part of a much broader picture. Many depended on public assistance or simply "hustled" for extra cash. Others were in and out of work, and, owing to the relatively debilitating and "culturally deprived" environment, many were poorly motivated. Moreover, their attitude toward work was often similar to those of their employers. As Elliot Liebow observes, "With few exceptions, jobs filled by streetcorner men are at the bottom of the employment ladder in every respect, from wage level to prestige. Typically, they are hard, dirty, uninteresting and underpaid. . . . [The worker] has little vested interest in such a job and learns to treat it with the same contempt held for it by the employer and society at large. From his point of view, the job is expendable; from the employer's point of view, he is."[37] Problems such as job instability, menial work, low-level skills, poor worker motivation, racial discrimination, and an inadequacy of both job information and access to jobs all seemed to warrant considerable attention. Each of these problems seemed causally related to others. In fact, some of these perceptions emerged from results of government programs when it became clear that efforts to remedy one disadvantage required simultaneous and complementary efforts to remedy others.[38]

In the light of this, a new measure — underemployment, which embraced most of the foregoing aspects of labor market disadvantage — supplanted unemployment as the basis for design of manpower policy. In 1966, a composite statistical measure, subemployment, was used in some national and local surveys. The subemployed included the unemployed, part-time workers seeking full-time work, along with "heads of household under 65 working full time and earning less than $65 per week, half the number of labor force 'nonparticipants' among men between ages twenty and sixty-four (the disguised unemployed), and half the estimated 'missing males' or 'census undercount.' "[39] In the latter case, the percentage of subemployed workers in inner cities exceeded the unemployment rate by a factor of three or four.[40]

This new measure led to revision of manpower programs and the focus of government policy encompassed additional aspects of employment problems.[41] These included the worker's attitude — to induce a more positive attitude toward work and greater job stability. In addition, programs were designed to provide specific skills through institutional training, improve opportunities for prevocational remedial training and on-the-job-training, and encourage job creation in the private sector to satisfy the needs of underemployed workers. Furthermore, attempts were made to correct those labor market imperfections which engender increasing ghetto unemployment — such as employer and union discrimination, inadequate labor market information, and suburbanization of primary employment. And finally, policy makers began to promote ideas of black capitalism and ghetto economic development. But with respect to black capitalism, programs to develop black entrepreneurs were actually designed to fail (see Chapter 25).

Over the past century, desegregation has been as attainable as the Holy Grail. Indeed, results of endeavors to integrate have always been well adrift of the objectives, in large measure because meaningful integration has been militantly resisted. As noted above, however, housing segregation explains a great deal of unemployment and concomitant poverty among blacks because it distances blacks from employment and educational opportunities. The latter is denied to blacks because many whites still cling to the absurd illusion that blacks are incapable of achieving the highest ideals of humanity. If desegregation is an unattainable objective, the second-best policy, therefore, is socioeconomic development of black communities.[42] Persuasive arguments in this regard were advanced in the 1960s by Robert F. Kennedy and Richard Nixon. According to Kennedy, "This nation faces many problems. . . . But of all our problems, none is more immediate — none is more pressing — none is more omnipresent — than the crisis of unemployment in every major city in the Nation."[43] Kennedy considered ghetto economic development the sine qua non of racial integration. Education and economic uplift of blacks would apparently dwarf whites' feelings of revulsion and repugnance toward the color of their skin. And, according to President Nixon, "What we have to do is to get private enterprise into the ghetto, and get the people of the ghetto into private enterprise — not only as workers, but as managers and owners."[44] In similar vein, Samuel Myers, Jr., argues for black entrepreneurial development and economic opportunities for blacks so that they may utilize their entrepreneurial skills and ingenuity in socially "acceptable" economic activities rather than illegal drug transactions and the like in the underground economy (see Chapter 23). Similarly, I apply a social accounting system to show that inner city development may be effected through government-led development of black entrepreneurs and skilled labor, specifically to supply goods and services to public institutions and to inner-city households — a large and growing market (see Chapter 26). Over time, significant increases in the number of black employers will partially insulate a subset of black labor from employment discrimination and provide them with opportunities for advancement as well as benefits on the job.

Pecuniary Costs of Discrimination

The costs of racial discrimination may be considered from two perspectives: the cost to the economy as a whole and the cost to blacks. Racial discrimination gives rise to economic losses to the national economy owing to failure to develop and utilize existing and potential skills of blacks. Based on data developed by Becker, in 1962, Denison estimated that national income would be augmented by 0.8 percent if labor market discrimination against blacks were eliminated. In addition, Denison pointed out that if blacks were provided educational qualifications comparable to whites and if employment discrimination were eliminated, these changes would effectively raise the national product by approximately 4 percent. He concludes that "disadvantages faced by the average Negro child in developing his work potential are, by comparison with those of the average white child, huge. They relate to home and neighborhood environment, schools and incentives, in a complex and mutually re-enforcing manner. Job discrimination against well-qualified adult Negroes dulls the incentive for the young to prepare themselves for the better jobs."[45] In 1965, the Council of Economic Advisers estimated that if discrimination were eliminated, national income would increase by $12.8 billion, and that if blacks were provided education equivalent to that of whites, national income would increase by an additional $7.8 billion. Thus, elimination of discrimination in employment and education would increase gross domestic product by an estimated 3.7 percent.[46] Siegel estimated the economic cost to victims of discrimination — blacks — as being $1,000 per year, which seems rather low given estimates by Denison and the Council of Economic Advisers.[47]

The foregoing estimated costs of discrimination are, at best, only partial. To begin with, estimates of costs to the national economy omit costs incurred by society owing to ill effects of discrimination. As pointed out hitherto, historically, discrimination was legally sanctioned; presently, it is illegal but nonetheless still commonly practiced, and invariably, with impunity. One of its ill effects is growth and expansion of extralegal and illegal activities (petty crimes and so forth), which are costs to the national economy. Owing to lack or inadequacy of income, many individuals are driven to participate in the underground economy to earn extra cash, giving rise to "crime" and to greater outlays for policing and law enforcement. In addition, taxes are collected on neither such income nor goods and services in the underground economy. Furthermore, in those cases where individuals earn extra cash from sale of illegal drugs, greater expenditures are incurred not only for policing, but also for the "war" against illegal drugs and drug rehabilitation. Second, with growth of illegal activities (from dearth of employment opportunities owing to discrimination) and more policing, more arrests are made, and felons are prosecuted and convicted for "crimes" perpetrated. Thus, the courts must increase personnel to deal with more cases, and owing to a larger number of incarcerations more prisons must be built to accommodate the growing prison population. Third, employment discrimination and unemployment may give rise to mental and physical afflictions such as hypertension, coronary disease, and depression but the cost of treatment is usually borne by society (Medicaid) because the afflicted individuals can ill afford costs of their health care and usually do not have access to other insurance. Hence, in addition to reduction in output owing to failure to utilize potentially skilled manpower, society incurs other costs to deal with the adverse impact of discrimination. David R. Williams provides an interesting analysis of the effects of discrimination on the health of blacks (see Chapter 11).

Human Costs of Antiblack Violence and White Antipathy

Having addressed pecuniary costs of segregation and racial discrimination to the economy, we turn to the human costs of the most heinous abrogation of human rights between 1866 and 1943. During this period antiblack feelings were as endemic as they were second nature, and blacks were killed indiscriminately by whites. I focus on the human costs of lynching and of antiblack riots, which were quite common. Lynching and other forms of mob violence against blacks did occur subsequent to 1943 and prior to 1880, but according to Tolnay and Beck, "radical racism and mob violence peaked during the 1890s in a surge of terrorism that did not dissipate until well into the twentieth century."[48]

Lynching arose from the lynch laws—a set of arbitrary rules for social control of blacks through mob violence. These "laws" originated during the

American Revolution from activities by vigilante Col. Charles Lynch (Charles the Terrible) and his Virginia Associates.[49] From the 1880s, vigilantism or "summary justice" reflected white America's contempt for other racial, ethnic, and cultural groups. Blacks bore the brunt of vigilantism and the fury of white mobs, which comprised scores to hundreds of individuals. Invariably, thousands of blacks died from unspeakably brutal violence (mental and physical) for some presumed "crime," real or imagined, serious or trivial.[50] Indeed, according to Walter White, executive director of the NAACP, "Their crime was that their skins were black." In short, the question of guilt or innocence of blacks was of no importance. Lynching was practiced mainly, but not exclusively, in the Black Belt of the south. Between 1882 and 1930, there were approximately 2,500 documented lynchings of blacks by white mobs, of which 2,177 occurred in the Black Belt.[51] In all likelihood, however, lynchings between 1882 and 1930 must have exceeded 2,500 by a considerable measure. John Hope Franklin writes, "In the last sixteen years of the nineteenth century there had been more than 2,500 lynchings."[52] In a word, "The scale of this carnage means that on the average, a black man, woman or child was murdered once a week, every week, between 1882 and 1930 by a hate-driven white mob."[53]

Recorded fatalities by white lynch mobs in southern states do not document fully the number of victims (Tables I.4, I.5). Lynching included burning, torture, hanging, and dismemberment to prolong the agony of victims as well as to extend the thrill and exhilaration of spectators. In fact, it involved a "festive atmosphere" with many spectators, including women and children, from the local community and distant towns.[54] Various ostensible reasons were given for lynching, but the main objectives were to) maintain the social order that preserved the social status of whites and suppressed blacks, and prevent competition from blacks for economic, political, and social rewards.[55] For example, lynching successful black farmers provided new economic opportunities to local whites who simply appropriated the farms of victims at once, reaffirming their place in the social hierarchy. In consequence, lynching depopulated black communities, incapacitated many blacks through serious physical injury, and impoverished a preponderant number by dispossessing them of their property, which was appropriated by whites.[56]

By 1921, lynching was so common that, at the behest of the National Association for the Advancment of Colored People (NAACP), Representative L. C. Dyer of Missouri introduced a bill that would have made lynching a federal crime. The bill was passed only in the House, because southern senators filibustered and prevented a vote. Hence, the law was not passed. These senators had argued that it is the responsibility of each state to deal with extralegal mob actions. But the states had always refused "to protect us [blacks] against the mob and the Federal Congress has washed its hands of all anti-lynching legislation. Lynchers are free to prowl the earth and butcher any Negro who gets in their path."[57] Vigilantism, therefore, continued without abatement. Indeed, in 1921, fifty-one blacks were reported lynched. Despite untiring efforts by Walter White of the NAACP and other well-meaning citizens, an antilynching law was never enacted.[58] Such a law would have saved blacks from the consequences of conventional white antipathy and violence.

Widespread antiblack riots represent the second aspect of the inhuman and amazingly fierce assault on blacks that accounted for substantial human costs. Above, Walter White observed that inhuman treatment was constantly meted out to blacks owing to the color of their skin. Therefore, since they had been always held in contempt by whites, what was it about blacks during this period that riled whites to the point of turning against blacks with such ferocity? Some insights may be gained from a brief review of the sociopolitical and economic milieu in the north and south, including perceptions and attitudes of whites toward blacks, during this period. To facilitate analysis of the human costs and how these riots effected black penury, we analyze selected antiblack riots that occurred in three distinct periods: 1898 to end of World War I, the period between the wars, and World War II.[59]

To begin with, at this time, measures were being taken to revive the Ku Klux Klan (KKK) which had been rendered ineffective and nearly nonexistent in the 1870s. Revival of the Klan reflected racial concerns of whites in the north and south. For example, the 1915 movie *Birth of a Nation*[60] generated considerable interest among whites in activities of the Klan, giving great impetus to its revival. The movie, shown for forty-seven weeks in New York, glowingly portrayed the Klan in terms of courageous fortitude and ready resolution. In its conclusion, the Klan is depicted riding to save southern civilization from a black militia, which is found wanting in courage. After seeing the movie, President Woodrow Wilson expressed his approval, stating that "It is like writing history with lighting and my only regret is that it is all terribly true." Notwithstanding the president's endorsement, the movie grossly distorted the reality of Reconstruction, but it was compatible with white concerns about black migration northward and with the growing hostility of whites toward those in society who were from different racial or ethnic backgrounds. Furthermore, wherever the movie was shown, race relations deteriorated and racial violence frequently erupted.[61]

Membership of the Klan grew rapidly in the south as well as in many northern communities, where it was often associated with the police and sheriff's deputies; indeed, many police and sheriff's deputies moonlighted as Klansmen.

Table I.4. Time Series of Victims of Lynchings in Ten States in the South, 1882–1930[a]

Year	All Victims	Black Victims	Black Victims of Black Mobs	Black Victims of White Mobs	White Victims of White Mobs
1882	44	34	1	33	9
1883	55	47	4	43	7
1884	59	43	6	37	14
1885	62	47	5	42	15
1886	71	56	8	48	9
1887	62	49	9	40	9
1888	67	58	5	53	7
1889	81	58	5	53	20
1890	64	53	7	46	10
1891	121	89	6	83	28
1892	129	106	14	92	16
1893	116	103	4	99	11
1894	117	94	8	86	11
1895	89	74	5	69	14
1896	80	63	2	61	15
1897	79	72	1	71	2
1898	81	77	4	73	4
1899	82	70	6	64	12
1900	76	74	2	72	2
1901	94	86	10	76	8
1902	62	59	1	58	3
1903	73	68	7	61	5
1904	61	58	4	54	3
1905	42	40	3	37	2
1906	49	47	0	47	2
1907	48	45	3	42	3
1908	77	73	6	67	4
1909	55	54	0	54	1
1910	55	50	2	48	4
1911	52	50	1	49	2
1912	54	53	1	52	1
1913	43	43	2	41	0
1914	38	37	0	37	0
1915	58	50	0	50	6
1916	40	39	2	37	1
1917	26	26	1	25	0
1918	39	38	0	38	0

Table I.4. Continued

Year	All Victims	Black Victims	Black Victims of Black Mobs	Black Victims of White Mobs	White Victims of White Mobs
1919	63	60	1	59	2
1920	36	35	1	34	1
1921	51	45	0	45	6
1922	37	32	0	32	5
1923	25	23	1	22	2
1924	14	14	0	14	0
1925	13	13	0	13	0
1926	24	20	0	20	4
1927	12	12	0	12	0
1928	7	7	0	7	0
1929	9	6	0	6	3
1930	13	12	0	12	1
Total	2,805	2,462	148	2,314	284

[a] Alabama, Arkansas, Florida, Georgia, Kentucky, Louisiana, Mississippi, North Carolina, South Carolina, and Tennessee.

Source: Stewart E. Tolnay and E. M. Beck, *A Festival of Violence: An Analysis of Southern Lynchings, 1882–1930* (Urbana: University of Illinois Press, 1992), pp. 271–272.

Membership and active participation of law enforcement officers aided the hooded order in its intimidation of blacks into acceptance of segregation with equanimity.[62] Moreover, Klansmen included political, economic, and religious leaders, giving the group renewed legitimacy. In fact, members often held publicly advertised parades through the center of towns.[63]

Second, considerable spatial and social dislocation occurred in both the north and south during the mobilization effort for World War I, and gave rise to increased contact between blacks and whites. This seemingly new arrangement unsettled whites, and the arming and training of black soldiers in the south intensified their fears. Whites were afraid that black soldiers would use military skills to repulse the fierce assaults by which they frequently terrorized blacks and left black communities in ruin. Moreover, having fought in the war to make the world "safe for democracy," black military personnel returning home expected to be accorded the same treatment as their white counterparts. When such treatment was not extended, many black soldiers expressed their resentment vociferously.[64]

Table I.5. State Summary of Lynching Victims, 1882–1930

State	Total Victims	Black Victims	Black Victims of White Mobs[a]	White Victims of White Mobs[a]	Other Victims[b]
Deep South					
Alabama	300	273	262	24	3
Georgia	458	435	423	21	2
Louisiana	360	304	283	52	3
Mississippi	538	509	462	21	7
South Carolina	156	148	143	5	2
Subtotal	1,812	1,669	1,573	123	17
Border South					
Arkansas	241	184	162	48	9
Florida	250	224	212	19	7
Kentucky	191	128	118	43	20
North Carolina	97	82	75	15	0
Tennessee	214	175	174	36	2
Subtotal	993	793	741	161	38
Total	2,805	2,462	2,314	284	55

[a] Mobs presumed to be white.

[b] Includes victims whose race is unknown.

Source: Tolnay and Beck, *Festival of Violence*, p. 273.

Third, mobilization for World War I increased demand for labor in war factories. Both white and black labor were recruited in the south for jobs in northern cities. In the south, blacks as a people remained permanently under siege. Indeed, they sensed that their existence in the south was but a "confiscated life" and, that destiny beckoned them northward. Hence, while whites migrated northward, primarily for better economic opportunities, blacks did so for better economic opportunities as well as for better treatment. But much to their surprise, in the north the depth of white antipathy toward them was no different than in the south. Furthermore, the influx of blacks led to additional demand for housing, transportation, education, and recreational facilities, which—coupled with competition between whites and blacks for jobs—gave rise to greater white hostilities toward blacks. In fact, it was not uncommon for blacks to be battered daily by antagonistic whites in their determination to assert their supremacy and to belittle blacks.[65]

Fourth, southern whites resented any activities that contested their privileges, threatened their political leadership, or hindered their domination of blacks. Thus, when the well-meaning southerners and carpetbaggers from the north brought blacks into the political fold, they formed a biracial coalition to wrest political power from whites. But local whites desired to maintain terrorist social control over blacks and to preserve the social order.[66] Thus, they responded to perceived threats by brutally assaulting blacks, destroying or confiscating their property, effecting an exodus of blacks to the north.

Finally, it was always socially acceptable for black females to have affairs willy-nilly with white males, yet white males always objected to any affinity between a black male and a white female. Thus, any alleged assault, real or imagined, on the sanctity of southern women, led to vigilantism. Any perceived provocation of a white woman aroused anger and inspired determination of whites to disregard the justice system and brutally assault alleged black culprits. Moreover, newspapers in the north and south constantly added to white fears by publishing daily recitals of alleged racial attacks and rapes of white women. In fact, a day seldom passed in which such an incident was not reported in headlines on the front page. Violent retribution was the *norm* for alleged crimes against white women, especially in the south, but also in the north.[67]

Against this sociopolitical and economic environment, in which the antiblack riots occurred, whites' primary objective was preservation of the social order. Understanding this background also sheds light on why blacks were driven from their communities, suffered from the pangs of dispossession, progressively marginalized and endured the unendurable as this virulent form of terrorism continued, year after year, without abatement.

ANTIBLACK RIOTS, 1898 TO WORLD WAR I

Four major antiblack riots occurred between 1898 and World War I: the Wilmington, North Carolina, riot of 1898; the Evansville, Indiana, riot of 1903; the Atlanta riot of 1906; and, the Springfield, Illinois, riot of 1908.

The Wilmington riot: Relative to the south and other regions of the nation, Wilmington, North Carolina, was one of the last beacons of hope for biracial government. In 1894, a coalition of Populists and Republicans won control of the state legislature and two years later, Daniel Russell, a white Republican, won the gubernatorial race.[68] Russell extended to blacks the same employment opportunities accorded to the white citizenry, and blacks were appointed as registrars, magistrates, deputy sheriffs, and county commissioners, and employment of black professionals increased notably.[69] But as a thriving black *middle class* developed, Democrats played the race card to regain political control of the state in the 1898 elections. Democrats resented encouragement by Republicans of perceived liaisons between white women and black males, whom the Democrats deemed rapists. However, in an editorial in the *Wilmington Daily Record*, a black-owned newspaper, the editor, Alexander Manly, scoffed at the charge. In the article, Manly averred that white women "are not more particular in the matter of clandestine meetings with coloured men than the white men with coloured women." Manly was quite familiar with interracial liaisons because he was a direct descendant of Charles Manly, governor of North Carolina from 1849 to 1851. Further, Manly wrote "Every Negro lynched is called a Big Burly Black Brute, when, in fact, many of these who have been thus dealt with had white men for their fathers, and were not only not black and burly, but were sufficiently attractive for white girls of culture and refinement to fall in love with them, as is well known by all."[70]

Manly's editorial incensed Democrats, and armed white vigilantes campaigned to discourage (if not prevent) blacks from voting in 1898, which led to an emphatic Democratic victory. Two days after the election a white mob took revenge on Wilmington. Ostensibly, their objective was to expel Manly from the city, although it was well known that he had already left. Therefore, to satisfy their thirst for revenge, the mob burned the offices of the *Wilmington Record*, then moved on to the black residential section where they destroyed black homes and businesses.[71] Blacks fled Wilmington and North Carolina in large numbers, and whites took their jobs and appropriated their land. This riotous behavior fostered further development of a large class of dispossessed blacks. And finally, in order to disenfranchise blacks, in 1900, a constitutional amendment imposed a poll tax and literary test (with a grandfather clause) for "exclusion of all Negroes from participation" in elections.[72] In fact, notwithstanding the Fifteenth Amendment, from circa 1898 until passage of the Civil Rights Act in 1964, white rule in North Carolina remained virtually unchallenged.

The Evansville riot: The Evansville riot of 1903 erupted because a black man, Lee Brown, had fatally shot police officer Lewis Massey. Apparently, Brown had a heated altercation with a saloon porter and was so incensed that when he left the saloon he threatened to return "to deal further with the matter." Brown's threat was reported to patrolman Massey, who located him. In a shoot-out between the two, both Massey and Brown were wounded, but Massey died the following day.[73] This incident was reported in the local daily paper, the *Evansville Courier,* in rather incendiary language with the caption, "Negro Bullet Plows Through Body of Patrolman Massey." Brown was arrested and incarcerated, but the incident inflamed passions of racial hatred among whites, and on the following day, a white mob of approximately 1,000 stormed the jail to lynch Brown. Sensing the mob's bent for revenge, law enforcement authorities secretly moved Brown to another jail in Vincennes, Indiana.[74]

Having failed to lynch Brown, the mob trained its fury on blacks in general. They destroyed all homes in the black community as well as black-owned businesses. Blacks fled in droves to neighboring communities where they were unwelcome. This riotous behavior put a brake on development of the black business and professional community in Evansville. Needless to say, this experience coupled with wrongful appropriation of black property discouraged skilled and professional blacks from considering Evansville as a place to settle.

The Atlanta riot: Once again, incendiary reporting in the local papers, the *Atlanta Constitution, Atlanta Journal, and Atlanta News* about alleged sexual assaults by black males against white women sparked the Atlanta riot of 1906.[75] An important contributing factor, however, was the 1906 gubernatorial campaign between Hoke Smith, advocate of "ruthless suppression of the Negro" and Clark Howell, editor of the *Atlanta Constitution.* Smith had allied himself with former populist leader, Thomas Watson, who on the hustings taunted, "Niger, niger niger." Watson was "especially effective among the cotton mill workers and other poor whites in and near Atlanta" informing them "that their own interests were best served by . . . hating nigers."[76]

Concurrently, a new daily, the *Atlanta News,* was being launched. In attempting to gain a significant share of the afternoon market from the *Atlanta Journal,* the new daily followed the lead of candidates on the campaign trail by publishing daily eight-column stories of raping of white women by blacks. Subsequently, none of these stories was found to be true. This sinister strategy increased the market share of the *Atlanta News* as newsboys shouted the inflammatory headlines. With respect to race relations, however, this made Atlanta "a tinder box."[77]

Accordingly, these events inflamed the passions of the white masses, and white mobs moved through the city in search of the alleged rapist, destroying black-owned homes. At least ten blacks were reported killed, but the police did nothing to protect black citizens. In fact, the police confiscated guns from blacks while whites were left armed. The latter simply aided whites to dispense further vigilante justice and dispossess blacks of their property.[78]

The Springfield riot: In 1908, Springfield, Illinois, was a growing industrial center with a rapidly growing population, a significant proportion of which were southern black migrants and European immigrants, both of whom competed with local whites for factory and coal mining jobs, which were in short supply. Job competition disgruntled local whites. Actually, many blacks were brought to Springfield as scabs, which fueled white antipathy toward blacks.

The Springfield riots of 1908 were caused by two allegations of sexual assault of white women by black men.[79] In one case, a white man, Clergy Ballard, pursued Joe James, who was alleged to have attempted to sexually assault his daughter. Ballard was wounded in a scuffle with James and died the following day. The press reported, in rather inflammatory language, that Ballard's death was the result of a failed sexual assault. About two fortnights later, an article captioned, "Dragged from Her Bed and Outraged by Negro,"[80] reported that Mabel Hallam, a twenty-one-year-old housewife, was allegedly snatched sleeping from her bed and sexually assaulted by a black man, whom she identified as George Richardson. These reports further infuriated whites already peeved about job competition from blacks, although it was the alleged sexual assault of Mabel Hallam that led to riotous behavior. The two suspects, Joe James and George Richardson, were arrested and incarcerated. Whites assembled a mob and proceeded to the jail to seize the prisoners and lynch the men. For their own safety, the prisoners were secretly transferred to another jail in Bloomington, Indiana. Having failed to mete out vigilante justice, the mob moved on to a restaurant owned by Harry Loper, whom they were informed had aided authorities in secret transfer of the James and Richardson to Bloomington. Loper fled his restaurant and the mob consumed the liquor on the premises, destroyed the restaurant, and burned his car. Abetted by shouts of "Women desire protection and this seems the only way to get it," the inebriated mob went to Levee, the black commercial district where they destroyed black-owned businesses and the dreams of the owners. The mob then moved on to Badlands, the black residential district and, on the way, they fatally shot a black barber, hanging him from a tree, and riddling his body with bullets.[81]

On arrival in Badlands, the mob destroyed the homes in the community. Property damage was said to be in excess of $200,000 (1908 dollars). Some displaced blacks found places to hide in Springfield, but about two to three thousand were forced to flee and take refuge in other towns where they were welcomed by signs that read, "All niggers are warned, out of town by Monday 12 Sharp." The following day, the mob lynched a prosperous and distinguished octogenarian who had been a cobbler to Abraham Lincoln, because his wife of thirty-two years was white. Interracial marriage was anathema to local whites.[82]

Finally, at the end of all the riotous behavior, murder and mayhem, Mabel Hallam, the white woman who had claimed that Richardson raped her, withdrew her charge. Hallam confessed to authorities that she had concocted the story to conceal an affair she was having. Richardson was therefore released from jail while Joe James was tried and convicted for the murder of Ballard. No charges were brought against Mabel Hallam for peddling a canard, and it is not known whether Richardson was ever compensated for wrongful arrest. Once again, however, droves of blacks were dispossessed of their property contributing to creation of a growing class of impoverished blacks.

RIOTS DURING THE INTERWAR PERIOD

The Houston riot: We now turn to antiblack riots that occurred during the inter-war period. We begin with the Houston riot of 1917. In the spring of that year, the army ordered the Third Battalion of the black Twenty-fourth United States Infantry to Houston, Texas, to guard the construction site of two military installations. Local whites grew rather uneasy about the presence of black soldiers in the community because they thought that their presence would threaten the social order and "racial harmony." Ultimately, this threat led to the Houston riot of 1917.[83]

Subsequent to arrival in Houston, the black contingent suffered racial discrimination whenever they left the base to visit the city. This mistreatment incurred their displeasure because they expected the same treatment accorded to fellow white soldiers. City officials thought that if black soldiers were accorded the same treatment as whites, local blacks would expect similar treatment, which would upset the social order. Additionally, in the city the police harassed black soldiers, and at the military construction site white workers frequently hurled insults at them. Most local blacks suppressed the anger they felt from white belittlement, but the soldiers openly expressed their indignation. This response added considerably to racial tension that traditionally prevailed in the community.

On August 17, a black soldier was arrested for interceding in the arrest of a black woman, and when Cpl. Baltimore, a military policeman, inquired about the soldier's arrest, he was physically assaulted and arrested. It was rumored, however, that Cpl. Baltimore was fatally shot and that a white mob was approaching the camp. Armed black soldiers marched from the barracks to the city to inquire about the whereabouts and well-being of Cpl. Baltimore, considered a model of decorum by his colleagues. On their way, the mutinous soldiers killed fifteen whites, including four policemen. Four black soldiers were killed. And, in the winter of 1917–18, the army court-martialed and indicted 118 black enlisted men of I company and found 110 guilty. Nineteen of the mutinous soldiers were hanged and sixty-three were given life sentences in federal prison. Two white officers faced courts-martial but were released. No white civilians were brought to trial.[84]

The East St. Louis riot: The East St. Louis, Illinois, antiblack riot of 1917 stemmed largely from burning white resentment of employment of blacks in war factories. As pointed out hitherto, many blacks migrated from the South,

in part, to escape lynching and daily degradation and, in part, for greater employment opportunities and human decency. This competition from blacks for
"white" jobs ignited a fierce antiblack riot during which blacks were lynched
and their homes destroyed by fire. Whites attacked blacks "indiscriminately
stabbing, clubbing and hanging them."[85] Six thousand blacks were forced to
flee their homes of which three hundred homes (valuing more than $500,000)
were burned to the ground. Throughout the riot, shouts were heard of "Burn
'em out."[86] President Woodrow Wilson denounced the riot against blacks as
well as lynchings, of which there were 54 in 1916 and 35 in 1917. But the
president never took steps to prevent reoccurrence of such violence in any part
of the nation. The NAACP also vigorously protested the flagrant violations of
human rights of the black citizenry, but the federal government did nothing.

James Weldon Johnson termed May to October 1919 "Red Summer," after
the streets of many black communities were bloodied with the hatred of whites.
During this summer, approximately 25 antiblack riots erupted in three south-
ern and two northern states as well as in Washington, D.C. In this chapter,
I focus on antiblack riots that occurred in Longview, Texas; Chicago, and
Washington, D.C.

Washington, D.C.: In Red Summer, the population of Washington, D.C.
was approximately 75 percent white. An influx of blacks from the south,
however, changed the racial composition of the city considerably with a substantially growing black middle class. Many black migrants to the city had
secured employment in low-level government jobs. But, from the perspective
of whites, this created job scarcity that was bitterly resented by unemployed
whites. In addition, the white community opposed "invasion" by blacks of previously segregated communities. Furthermore, thousands of returning black
war veterans hoped that their military service would "earn" them human rights
to which all citizens were entitled.[87] Despite the Fourteenth Amendment, black
soldiers (and, indeed, blacks in general) were never treated as full citizens. In
fact, race relations grew worse during Woodrow Wilson's administration,
which was dominated by southern whites. In his campaign, Wilson had promised "New Freedom" in a perfidious bid to win black support. In fact, he won
more black votes than any democrat previously, but he did not keep his word.
Instead of "New Freedom," previously integrated government departments
now had "Jim Crow corners" with separate facilities for "colored only," as
southerners replicated social conditions prevailing in the south.[88] At the same
time, the Ku Klux Klan and attendant racial hatred were revived in neighboring Maryland and Virginia. Concurrently, there was resurgence, across the
country, of lynching of blacks including black war veterans wearing their
military uniforms. Finally, daily papers, the *Evening Star,* the *Times,* the *Her-*

ald, and the *Post* exacerbated racial tensions with sensational stories of alleged sexual assaults of white women by unidentified black men.[89]

The Washington antiblack riot of 1919 stemmed from release by police of a black suspect who was questioned about an attempted sexual assault of the wife of a navy man. Rumors of the alleged assault spread to pool halls and other areas downtown. Later that evening, a white mob assembled to take justice into their own hands. The mob grew to about four hundred and moved toward Southwest, the black residential section of the city. The chief executive of the city appealed for public calm: "The actions of the men who attacked innocent Negroes cannot be strongly condemned, and it is the duty of every citizen to express his support for law and order." The riotous behavior might have been short-lived,[90] but the *Washington Post* published an article with the incendiary headline "Mobilization for Tonight." In response to the article, white rioters assembled and blacks began arming themselves.[91] Over four days, the mob unleashed a wave of violence that swept over the city. The rampage by whites drew only scattered resistance from blacks, among whom 39 were killed and more than 150 were shot. After a long delay, the police arrived, but the white officers arrested mainly blacks, providing a clear indication of their partiality. The NAACP requested a formal federal inquiry into the violence against blacks, but Southern congressmen blocked the inquiry.

Chicago riot: Another riot that occurred during "Red Summer" was in Chicago. Between 1910 and 1920, the black population of Chicago rose from 44,000 to 119,000, which led to inadequate housing, job competition from blacks, and overcrowding in the ghetto. Underpinning white antipathy to blacks were stereotypes and misconceptions. In his study of the Chicago race riot of 1919, Tuttle wrote that whites believed that blacks "were mentally inferior, immoral, emotional, and criminal. Some secondary beliefs were that they were innately lazy, shiftless, boisterous, bumptious, and lacking in civic consciousness."[92] Belief in these stereotypes was reinforced by newspapers, which published stories that depicted immoral behavior and real or imagined crimes by blacks. Whites held blacks in such low esteem that they were prepared to treat them most inhumanely whenever they felt threatened by them. In addition, black World War I veterans who had fought to make the world "safe for democracy" showed greater resistance to racial discrimination. Such militant insistence on fundamental human rights intensified racial friction in the city.[93]

In July 1919, whites fatally stoned a black youth swimming in Lake Michigan when he drifted into the area tacitly "reserved" for whites. The police, however, refused to arrest the perpetrators and this greatly angered blacks. Crowds of blacks began to gather and a riot ensued. For thirteen days,

Chicago was without law and order. Twenty-three blacks and 15 whites died, 537 blacks were injured, and the homes of many blacks were destroyed leaving one thousand homeless.[94] Once again, President Wilson castigated whites as "the aggressor" and efforts were initiated to establish racial harmony, but to no avail.

The Longview riot: During "Red Summer," racial tension waxed in Longview, Texas. Two prominent black leaders, Samuel Jones and Dr. Calvin Davis, had recommended that black cotton farmers bypass local white cotton brokers and sell their cotton directly to buyers in Galveston, reducing farmers' costs as well as the price to Galveston buyers. Shortly thereafter, an article in the *Chicago Defender,* a national black newspaper, described a white mob's murder of a black man, Lemuel Walters, who was romantically involved with a white woman from Kilgore, Texas. The article quoted the woman as saying that she and Walters would have married if they had resided in the north. Jones, a local correspondent of the *Defender,* was held responsible for the article and was beaten by brothers of the Kilgore woman. News of the article and the attack on Jones inflamed racial passions. A mob of whites attempted to attack Jones's home. Failing that, they set fire to black homes, including that of Dr. Davis, and a dance hall used by blacks. The following day, Marion Bush, father-in-law of Dr. Davis, was murdered. The National Guard was called out and the city and county were placed under martial law. Twenty-one blacks were arrested and sent to Austin temporarily for their own protection, and nine whites were charged with arson. However, none of the blacks or whites was ever tried. Shortly thereafter, tension subsided and martial law was lifted.[95]

The Ococee riot: Newspapers added to white fears by publishing daily allegations of racial attacks and alleged rapes of white women. The customary response to such allegations was violent retribution, in the north and south, for crimes, real or imagined, against white women. Ococee, Florida, was a victim of this frenzied violence. During the riot, in addition to lynching forty-seven blacks, the Klan attacked the black community in Ococee, destroying a number of black homes when two black citizens attempted to vote. Approximately six blacks and two whites were killed, and twenty-five black homes, two churches, and a lodge were destroyed.[96]

The Tulsa riot: In 1921, Tulsa, Oklahoma, included viable black businesses and residential homes in a large black community, referred to as Black Wall Street or Little Africa. The community encompassed thirty-six blocks including twenty-three churches, twenty-one restaurants, thirty grocery stores, two movie theaters, libraries, schools, various shops, law offices, a hospital, a bank, and six private planes. By way of marriage to native Indians, some blacks acquired the promised forty acres and a mule. The thriving business district of Black Wall Street undertook local, national, and international transactions.[97]

Residents of Little Africa were fully aware that whites on the other side of town envied their affluent community. They knew the time would come when whites would act on their impulse. Blacks therefore prepared for such an eventuality with guns and an adequate store of ammunition.[98]

The insurrection against blacks occurred ostensibly because a black man, Dick Rowland, allegedly assaulted a white girl, Sarah Page, in an elevator. This allegation was reported in sensational terms in the local newspaper. And, in the evening of May 21, 1919, planes dropped nitroglycerin bombs on the black community and, coupled with a white mob, destroyed Black Wall Street. The mob burned and looted homes and businesses killing hundreds of blacks. More than three thousand blacks were killed, buried in mass graves, or thrown into the river. The terror against blacks that evening dwarfed the terror of 9/11. Indeed, approximately three thousand blacks were killed and more than one thousand homes were destroyed, leaving many black families homeless.[99] But much to the chagrin of blacks, insurance companies never paid any claims submitted by black families and businesses. Blacks were effectively dispossessed.

Finally, the alleged sexual assault (that sparked the riot) for which Dick Rowland was charged was dismissed because Sarah Page refused to press charges. What remains unclear, however, is whether the alleged assault ever occurred, and was merely used as a ploy to destroy the black community. In fact, in a thirty-one-page confession a former police officer, Van B. Hurley, named city officials who met in downtown Tulsa to plan the air attack on the community. In addition, the Ku Klux Klan was said to be part of the conspiracy.[100]

The Perry riot: In December 1922, an escaped convict allegedly murdered a schoolteacher in Perry, Georgia. The suspect, Charlie Wright, and an alleged accomplice were arrested and jailed.[101] Local whites, together with whites from other parts of Georgia and from as far away as South Carolina, seized the prisoners from the custody of the sheriff and his deputies. And, in the hope of extracting a confession from Wright to determine the involvement of others in the alleged crime, the mob tortured him. Much to their surprise, Wright had no information to disclose, and he was therefore lynched. Additionally, two other black men suspected of involvement in the crime were shot and hanged. Following these murders, the mob turned against the black community, burned their homes, church, Masonic lodge, amusement hall, and school.[102]

The Rosewood riot: In 1923, Rosewood, Florida, was a relatively prosperous black community. Since 1870, the community supplied cedar, oranges, vegetables, and cotton to distant states, including New York. The community included residences and prosperous black businesses, among them M. Groins and Brothers' Naval Store, a large enterprise that distilled turpentine and rosin obtained from large tracts of pine trees grown in the community.[103]

The Rosewood riot stemmed from a claim by a white woman, Frances Taylor, that a black man had sexually assaulted her. The alleged assault was reported sensationally in newspapers across the nation inflaming racial hatred in white communities. A white mob lynched and hanged Sam Carter because he failed to provide satisfactory answers about the suspect, Jesse Hunter. The mob then turned on the black community as a whole, burning homes and indiscriminately killing blacks. Many blacks fled into the woods nearby, where they hid for days and received food and other assistance from friends who knew their hideout. Most whites participated in the riotous behavior, but a few whites aided many blacks in their efforts to escape to Gainesville. The large black firm Goins and Brothers' Naval Store was forced to move from Rosewood to Gainesville, owing to a number of lawsuits from competing white firms over land rights in the community.[104]

Finally, after the riots ended, it was reported that Frances Taylor, the white housewife who had claimed that a black man assaulted her, had misled authorities. It was contended that Taylor was actually having a long-term passionate clandestine affair with a white man, John Bradley, who had frequently visited her at home when her husband was at work. Apparently, on that day, Taylor and her lover had an altercation during which he physically abused her. In order to conceal the affair from her husband, she reported that a black man had sexually assaulted her.[105] This false accusation was apparently made with impunity, for there is no record that she was charged with a crime. But the consequences were enormous. Blacks were not only forced to flee their communities, but they were dispossessed of their land as well as those homes that were not destroyed by fire. These heinous acts created the seeds of widespread black impoverishment that has prevailed for many decades.

The Detroit riot: In 1943, Detroit was among the northern cities that provided employment opportunities in war factories, and many southern blacks migrated to Detroit in search of jobs and freedom from discrimination. Much to their surprise, blacks found white bigotry in Detroit every bit as pervasive and virulent as in the south.[106]

The influx of migrant labor was claimed by whites to have placed a strain on housing, transportation, and educational and recreational facilities. To be sure, times were relatively difficult for all, but the hardships were considerably greater for blacks, who were excluded from all public housing except the Brewster projects. Many blacks lived in homes without indoor plumbing, yet they paid rent two or three times more than families in white districts. In addition, blacks experienced discrimination in public accommodations and unfair treatment by the police.[107]

In one war factory, three black workers were promoted and their white counterparts went on strike in protest. In fact, the whites' hatred of blacks was so deep that a striking worker shouted, "I'd rather see Hitler and Hirohito win than work beside a nigger on the assembly line." This protest coupled with burning white resentment of blacks residing in the Sojourner Truth housing project, originally an exclusive white neighborhood, led to riots.[108]

Thirty-six hours of violence ensued and took the lives of thirty-four people, twenty-five of whom were black. Police killed seventeen blacks, yet the police were criticized for using too much restraint in dealing with blacks. Thurgood Marshall of the NAACP assailed the city's handling of the riot. Marshall noted that 85 percent of those arrested were black, while white policemen did nothing to whites who overturned and burned cars. In the words of Marshall, "This weak-kneed policy of the police commissioner coupled with the anti-Negro attitude of many members of the force helped to make a riot inevitable."[109]

The human costs of violence against blacks during this period were enormous. The estimated number of lives lost and homes destroyed are those accounted for immediately after the lynchings and antiblack riots, but does not include subsequent deaths from injuries sustained in the violence. Moreover, the human costs detailed here do not include families and professional careers destroyed owing to death of breadwinners and destruction of property. This violence played a major role in the creation of the class of impoverished blacks who constitute a significant portion of the underclass in contemporary America.

The primary reason given for violence against blacks was to preserve the social order, of which black impoverishment was an important part since it ensured continued subjugation of blacks. Hence, the *Kansas City* (Kansas) *Call* remarked, "It has been proven time and again that the desire to eliminate Negroes from industrial competition, to acquire Negroes' property without paying a fair price, and other similar *mercenary reasons have been the real cause of race riots*."[110] But perhaps most important, by failing to restrain white mobs and preserve law and order, the federal, state, and local governments willingly participated in wanton violence against black citizens.

Summary and Conclusion

We have noted that historically, inimical circumstances — socially contrived by antiblack violence and by denial of access to employment and educational opportunities — have conspired to create conditions that generate poverty associated with squalor, violence and crime in black communities. Discrimination continues to be practiced with unfortunate regularity, hence, the disparity between blacks and whites remains depressingly wide. This is disheartening because it makes us feel like Rip Van Winkle, awakening to the same appalling poverty-stricken conditions that a disproportionate number of blacks suffered in the historical past. Policy makers have made some progress, albeit, less than has been hoped for. Many employers still hold the same negative views of blacks as were held by their forebears.[111] Gilens reports that many whites consider the U.S. a "land of opportunity" for *all,* and that lack of progress on the part of blacks is due to sloth (see Chapter 12). Until these convictions are stilled, racial economic inequality will remain significant. And, so far, antipoverty policy has been ineffective in achieving its fundamental aims: elimination of racial discrimination in employment, housing, health-care, education, and other aspects of American life.

In conclusion, racial discrimination not only gives rise to poverty, squalor, and degradation, its perpetration is a serious contravention of basic human rights of blacks. It is my supposition that lynching and antiblack riots are fundamental causes of contemporary black poverty. Indeed, the riots and destruction of homes and businesses over the forty-five-year period account for significant black poverty. Families had to flee their homes, sometimes following the death of the breadwinner. Loss of breadwinners may have made it difficult for children of those families to receive adequate schooling. In addition, violence prevented development of a large black professional class. Second, destruction of businesses prevented development of a growing viable black business sector, which would have provided employment to blacks. In fact, one of the reasons for development of Black Wall Street in Tulsa was the large demand by blacks for goods and services, which were supplied by black enterprises. And, in order to supply these commodities firms had to employ labor to produce goods and services. In Tulsa this sector was destroyed, and with it the dreams and aspirations of black entrepreneurs and, indeed, black consumers in general. But this destruction occurred not only in Tulsa, but also in Chicago, Wilmington, Detroit, and other cities. Furthermore, it occurred over nearly half a century. In fact, at the same time the Nazis were perpetrating some of the most horrendous crimes of the twentieth century, destroying Europe and Jews, blacks were being destroyed in America in the same horrendous manner. But this did not give rise to the revulsion of feelings, universally, that is characteristic of the Nazi crimes against Europe as well as Jews. In fact, German prisoners were treated more humanely than African American soldiers who fought against the Germans. And, as noted above, during the events that gave rise to the Detroit riot, one worker stated, "I'd rather see Hitler and Hirohito win than work beside a nigger on the assembly line."

Having being made helpless by death, destruction, and dispossession, blacks were then made dependent on predominantly white institutions — firms, banks, unions and, state, local and federal governments. These institutions were all under the stewardship of whites who endeavored to keep blacks at the bottom of the social hierarchy. Hence, they were not given opportunities to overcome past destruction to develop educational institutions and skills with the same quantum of resources made available to their white counterparts. Given the predisposition of private and public institutions and the white populace as a whole, heroic efforts by blacks and a small number of fair-minded whites were doomed to failure.

This contravention of basic human rights belies the embrace by whites of universal human rights. In fact, many endeavors by blacks to secure basic rights — such as the right to live in a neighborhood of choice — are resisted by whites with no little menace. Indeed, such truculent resistance is characteristic of enemies rather than champions of human rights. Yet human rights may be considered the flagship of U.S. foreign policy. But, clearly, in the presence of such flagrant human rights violations, the world community may no longer be lulled into thinking of the U.S. as a sort of Mecca of human rights. What has the period of focus taught us? Is it that the U.S. has been a monstrous deception with appalling human consequences? And, does behind the sunny triumphalism of white life lie a great lie formalized as a free democratic society?

In plural societies, no single group *may* usurp absolute freedom. To be sure, absolute freedom *is* incompatible with absolute equality. Hence, if the desideratum of society is absolute political equality, the state must restrain the liberties of whites from disturbing it when they subjugate and dominate blacks. On the contrary, however, whites have used the state as an instrument for maintenance of a social order created in the eighteenth century for economic subjugation of blacks and, so far, these forces have prevailed (see Chapter 6). In the absence of fundamental social change or innovative and effective antidiscrimination and antipoverty policies, there will always be a tragic inevitability about the fate of blacks. In short, whites will continue to rule the roost and society will always be awash with growing material impoverishment of blacks as well as socially undesirables among victims and perpetrators of racial injustice. In *Leviathan*, Thomas Hobbes described human life as "solitary, nasty, brutish and short" — not a bad description of the lot of most American blacks over the period covered in this chapter. Has there been any significant progress in the lives of a significant portion of blacks since 1965? The answer to this question may be found in the chapters of this volume, which focus on the circumstances of blacks from 1965 to the present.

Overview of the Book

The volume is divided into eight conceptual parts. The first part addresses the notion of inequality, focusing specifically on a distinction between income inequality and economic inequality, including racial economic inequality; followed by Part II, which examines issues in measurement of inequality and poverty. Part III addresses structural causes of poverty among African Americans; followed by Part IV, in which focus is given to the devilment, arising from the prevailing inimical structure, which militate against achievement of significant black progress; while the ensuing section, Part V, examines the relationship between skill endowment and earnings and the incommensurate impact of skill endowment and training on earnings of blacks and whites. Part VI focuses on racial and familial hardship addressing issues on welfare and welfare reform; while Part VII examines communal hardship in African American residential areas, focusing on issues of crime and law enforcement. Finally, Part VIII examines reasons for past failure of minority business development, in the light of which, a policy framework is proposed for socioeconomic development of viable black communities.

PART I: ECONOMIC INEQUALITY AND INCOME INEQUALITY

To begin with, the following question is addressed: Can we be indifferent to a significant distinction between income inequality and economic inequality? According to Amartya Sen and William Darity, the answer is in the negative. Indeed, in Chapter 1, Sen argues for acknowledgment of the significant difference between income inequality and economic inequality. Indeed, achievement of economic equality may militate against the principle of income equality, as in the case of the disabled to whom a larger quantity of resources must be transferred owing to greater need effected by the disability. Sen points out the deficiencies of income inequality as a measure of well-being and demonstrates why economic equality is a broader and more all-encompassing measure of quality of life. In short, the greater the economic equality in a given society, the better the quality of life. In an international comparison, between African Americans, Chinese, and citizens of the Indian state of Kerala, Sen shows that even though black Americans earn substantially higher average incomes than their Chinese and Indian counterparts, African Americans have a considerably lower life expectancy relative to the Chinese and Indians.

While Sen sheds light on the distinction between income inequality and economic inequality, William Darity, Jr. (Chapter 2), examines racial/ethnic economic inequality in seven countries (Brazil, United States, Israel, South Africa, India, Malaysia, and Trinidad and Tobago). He attempts to explain persistence of racial/ethnic economic inequality generated by employment discrimination in markets worldwide. Darity argues that the neoclassical school can explain observed differences in economic outcomes across groups only if the groups have different endowments of human capital. However, groups with similar productive capacities have experienced widely disparate economic outcomes, a phenomenon that the neoclassical model is unable to explain. For example, he cites the patterns of discrimination, regardless of qualifications, seen in audit studies of behavior of employers, mortgage lenders, and real estate agents in the United States, Britain, and Australia.

The author therefore turned to classical and Marxist models to formulate an economic theory of discrimination. He uses the concept of noncompeting groups, groups that exclude individuals on the basis of race or ethnicity from economic and social outcomes, to explain the induced deficiency theory of discrimination. By admitting these groups, the neoclassical view that discrimination is purely a premarket or extramarket phenomenon can be emphatically refuted.

Darity finds that racial/ethnic discrimination in the market is not only the provenance of income inequality between racial/ethnic groups; but the perpetrators enshrine and perpetuate this inequality, which, over time, induces economic inequality (elucidated by Sen). Moreover, this inequality obtains regardless of the competitiveness of markets, the level of economic development or rate of economic growth.

From his analysis, he draws the following conclusions. First, mean incomes across racial groups don't seem to converge (New Zealand, United States, Malaysia). Second, there is little evidence of decline in discrimination over time (Brazil). Third, discrimination is endogenous and functional (New Zealand, Malaysia, Guyana, United States, South Africa). Fourth, plural societies do not fit neatly into the Kuznets relationship. And, finally, discrimination is persistent in economic outcomes.

PART II. ISSUES IN MEASUREMENT OF INEQUALITY AND POVERTY

This section examines issues in measurement of poverty, commencing with Chapter 3, in which Daniel H. Weinberg focuses on problems of measurement of poverty and gives a brief historical account of proposed remedies.[112] He relates problems encountered when household income was used to measure poverty thresholds. Such problems include: underreporting and underestimation of noncash income such as food stamps and Medicare;

non-market income from extralegal and home production activities; measurement error, arising from underreporting that undermines the reliability of income data; and, failure to account for the effect of differences in tax brackets on disposable income. Mollie Orshansky introduced a number of changes in the early 1960s, the most significant of which was the notion of per capita income, which took into account differences in household size. But per capita income treats all individuals identically, ignoring differences in basic needs across age, gender, and culture. Weinberg examines shortcomings of the per capita measure and use of equivalence scales (expressing each individual's needs in terms of a numeraire) to account for demographic differences. In his review of steps taken to remedy these and other shortcomings of current measures of poverty, he discusses proposals advanced by the National Academy of Sciences Committee on National Statistics.[113]

Issues in measurement of poverty are further examined in Chapter 4 by Gary Burtless and Sarah Siegel, who focus on inclusion of health care expenditures. If household expenditures on medical care are accounted for in poverty measurement, poverty rates of the disabled and aged would be significantly affected owing to their relatively large expenditure on health care. According to Burtless and Siegel, although current treatment of health spending needs represents a significant deficiency in measurement of poverty, there are no simple approaches incorporating medical spending in poverty measurement that are acceptable to a wide range of economists and policy makers. The authors propose alternative approaches to incorporate household medical spending and health care needs in poverty measurement. Their analysis concludes that inclusion of medical spending in the definition of poverty has a significant effect on the level and composition of those individuals defined as living in poverty.

PART III. STRUCTURAL CAUSES OF AFRICAN AMERICAN POVERTY

This section commences with Chapter 5, in which Tukufu Zuberi provides a critical reexamination of the "underlying theoretical orientation" of *An American Dilemma*[114] by Gunnar Myrdal, who writes that the African-American problem is due to lack of assimilation into white American culture. According to Myrdal, assimilation would eradicate racial discrimination and, by extension, black poverty. Zuberi suggests two fundamental flaws in the argument: it is based on the premise that white American culture is the standard that others should adopt; and it treats the problem of African Americans akin to problems of European immigrants. He eloquently demonstrates that attempts by blacks to assimilate have always encountered enormous political and social obstacles, and, virulent opposition from whites. Additionally, in the ethos of white society, blacks are considered inferior beings; therefore, for blacks to assimilate into such a culture would be problematic and potentially psychologically damaging for the assimilated.

Douglas S. Massey provides a general framework in Chapter 6 that depicts how institutional barriers created racial inequality between inner cities and suburbs nationwide. His principal focus is the urban-suburban divide, where, on the one hand, there is a concentration of affluence in suburbs, populated primarily by whites, and on the other, a concentration of poverty in inner cities, populated mainly by blacks. And of the latter, there is a significant portion of female-headed households, 50 percent of whom are unemployed, and 26 percent of whom are low-income recipients. Massey argues that the principal forces, which give rise to the two self-perpetuating spirals of affluence in the suburbs and poverty in the inner cities, are political, fiscal, and legal. These measures are used by whites to institutionalize segregation and isolation of blacks, to limit economic and educational opportunities for blacks, and to create widespread affluence for whites and extensive deprivation among blacks. Furthermore, he argues that demarcation of inner cities and suburbs as distinct governmental units prevents use of the rich property tax base of the suburbs for benefit of the crumbling infrastructure and educational system in inner cities. This inequality, he concludes, exacerbates the effects of poverty and unemployment such as crime and drug abuse. In order to break the downward spiral of gloom and doom in inner cities, Massey suggests reorganization of urban government to end political and fiscal segregation, substantial investment in education in inner cities, and desegregation of the housing market to end historical discrimination. But the author entertains little hope that such measures will be implemented.

In chapter 7, George Galster, Ronald Mincy and Mitch Tobin provide a critical examination of the impact of restructuring of the US economy in the decades of the 1980s and 1990s on communities populated primarily by African Americans relative to white communities. Significant in their findings is that restructuring had effected significant increases in poverty rates in black communities relative to predominant white communities. The authors' findings hold with regard to metropolitan and nonmetropolitan residential communities.

PART IV. CRITICAL FACTORS MILITATING AGAINST BLACK PROGRESS: RETROSPECT AND PROSPECT

This section addresses factors arising from the inimical socioeconomic and political structure and preventing black progress. The section commences with (Chapter 8) Jennifer Hochschild and Michael N. Danielson's case study of white resistance to attempts at racial integration in Yonkers, New York, which corroborates the salient point made by Zuberi and elaborated on by Massey — the African-American problem is due to social and political obstacles created by whites. First, in the early 1960s, the Board of Regents envisaged school desegregation to be implemented, without legislative enforcement, by the state education department, a relatively weak institution. Second, housing desegregation was attempted by the Urban Development Corporation (UDC), a relatively strong institution with unprecedented powers. Both efforts were to no avail; whites pressured lawmakers to pass legislation preventing desegregation and to curtail funding of extant programs by the state education department. Notwithstanding these measures, the education department persisted in its objective of desegregation, but again, whites prevailed by persuading lawmakers to replace membership of the Board of Regents of Education and to reduce the powers of the Board. Financial and administrative support for the department collapsed. Furthermore, the state legislature took away the UDC's powers and discontinued its funding, and by 1975 the corporation was bankrupt.

Gary Orfield provides further evidence in Chapter 9 that housing segregation is fundamental to the structure of racial, income, and economic inequality. He addresses the growing cleavage in metropolitan areas where resources are shifted to haves from the have-nots and "minority communities are battered by economic trends and hostile policies." This was brought about by suburban land policies that prevent low-income families from seeking jobs in the suburbs and racial discrimination that keeps minority families out of conveniently located, affordable housing. Moreover, the legislative and executive branches of government have been of little assistance, and the Supreme Court recognized local autonomy as a right "more important than achieving successful remedies for intentional segregation and discrimination." Because the most important legal case took place in Mount Laurel, New Jersey, Orfield examined the sociopolitical structure of the cities to better grasp the success and failure of the Mount Laurel reforms in the 1970s and 1980s.

In light of the civil rights movement's seemingly significant positive impact on virtually all social and economic variables in the 1960s, Reynolds Farley investigates whether gains achieved during this era have been sustained. In Chapter 10 he graphically depicts a very clear pattern of moderate racial convergence in the 1960s, but little or no convergence in the 1970s and 1980s. The data on high school and college education show clear racial differences even in the era of "immigration and diversity."[115] Farley suggests a number of reasons for lack of racial convergence since the 1960s. First, negative stereotypes still prevail, as seen in a recent survey of white attitudes (elaborated on in Chapter 12 by Gilens) that prevent blacks from obtaining employment and economic opportunities. Second, segregation still persists as observed in the high average dissimilarity index of 65 even in the 1990s. Third, economic stagnation in the 1970s and 1980s led to less benevolent white attitudes toward affirmative action and an erroneous belief that blacks were not worse off than whites.

In Chapter 11, David R. Williams focuses on the uneven distribution of health outcomes between blacks and whites. He examines three possible explanations — biological, lifestyle, and social structures — and concludes that the last of the three is the crucial determinant of racial differences in health. The author maintains that health outcomes and lifestyles are functions of residential and work environment, education, income, poverty, and political and social factors. He supports this view with data on self-assessed health status from the *National Health Interview Survey* conducted in 1985–87. Williams dismisses biological explanations and blames the racist sociopolitical structure for historical discrimination against blacks. For example, after migrating to the north, blacks were concentrated in the least desirable inner city neighborhoods and were exposed to high-risk employment, industrial pollution, and other environmental hazards. Furthermore, blacks have relatively poor access to treatment for life-threatening conditions. Using the same data on self-assessed ill-health, he shows that those living in inner cities, both black and white, are less healthy than suburban residents, but because blacks are more concentrated in inner cities, as related by Massey, they are more likely to be affected by these adverse conditions.[116] In final analysis, however, Williams notes that it is racist policies that gave rise to income, economic, and educational racial inequality, which have led to relatively poorer health of blacks.

In chapter 12, Martin Gilens provides a lucid and thorough analysis of a very interesting question — do the American news media contribute to the widespread public misconception about race and poverty nationwide? His work is based on empirical observations that both the public and news media tend to exaggerate the proportion of blacks among the poor and portray the black poor more negatively than the nonblack poor. Moreover, whites who hold such exaggerated perceptions tend to oppose welfare. The author provides an explanation of these misrepresentations based on the model by Gans (1979) where news content is determined by availability (i.e., accessibility, time constraints) and suitability (which is a function of the medium and the interests of the audience and the news agency) of news items. He finds suitability as the most significant explanatory factor of misrepresentation.

Journalists, even if committed to "accuracy" and "objectivity" in reporting, are guided by the same perception of reality as the general public.[117] This is as expected since the general ethos of the people to whom they provide news shape and foster perceptions of the journalists.

PART V. THE DIFFERENTIAL IMPACT OF SKILLS ON EARNINGS

This section examines the effect of skill endowment on earnings of blacks relative to whites. The section begins with chapter 13 in which James J. Heckman critically evaluates proposals made by a growing "new consensus" to reduce rising wage and income inequality by eradicating the seemingly principal cause of the problem — the large inequality in skill levels. This remedy involves investments in human capital, especially on-the-job training and apprentice programs that smooth the transition from school to work. Heckman does admit the "desirable ends" of these proposals, but contend that there are more cost-efficient paths to their achievement.

The author uses a common measure of 10 percent rate of return to human capital investment to show that it is prohibitively costly to increase earnings of low-skilled workers on par with highly skilled workers. To simply restore 1979 earnings ratio between high- and low-skilled workers, he estimates an investment of $1.66 trillion in 1989. And, at the same rate of return, an investment of $426 billion is required to bring unskilled workers to their 1979 real earnings level. Such enormous costs suggest that one-time nationwide investments in human capital are prohibitive.[118]

Heckman recommends the following alternatives: (1) substantial improvement in primary and secondary education, especially for blacks, to give all segments of the population sufficient general skills that are complementary to firm-specific skill enhancement; (2) more emphasis on improving incentives for individuals to invest in their human capital by removing credit and information constraints; and (3) rigidities, in terms of minimum wage and job tenure, must be removed from the unskilled labor market; public sector programs, where they exist, should be limited to adults, especially women, and focus on job search assistance etc. Until equity in general education can be achieved through improvements in primary and secondary education, he recommends use of job subsidy schemes to keep the low-skilled employed along with income transfers from high skilled workers who currently benefit from firm-specific job training in the private sector

Massey emphasized institutional factors as the principal cause of racial inequality that gave rise to income and economic inequality. In Chapter 14, Richard Murnane, John B. Willett, and Frank Levy examine the importance of cognitive skills, proxied by scaled mathematics test scores, in wage determination. They use two large surveys of twenty-four-year-old high school graduates to show that cognitive skills were a significantly more important predictor of real wages in 1986 than in 1978. Their approach represents a significant improvement over previous literature, which relied on indirect evidence that skills have become increasingly important in industry owing to increasing returns to schooling and to increasing dispersion among workers of similar age, education, gender, and race. They consider this earlier evidence inconclusive, flawed, and contradictory.

Samuel Bowles, Herbert Gintis, and Robert Szarka argue in Chapter 15 that cognitive skills explain neither rising returns to schooling nor rising income inequality. They contend that neither the link between cognitive skills and schooling, nor that between schooling and inequality is clearly established. The authors report various estimates of income equations with regressors (schooling, cognitive skills, and socioeconomic background), and rightly point out that studies which use instrumental variables to account for endogeneity of regressors, especially schooling, are more reliable. Contrary to earlier works, they conclude that cognitive skill inequality explains only a small fraction of the residual inequality. Indeed, they find little direct evidence that association of schooling and economic returns can be attributed to development of skills. Furthermore, they show that including cognitive skills in earnings equations reduces the schooling effect by only 25 percent, an estimate considerably lower than that of Murnane, Willett, and Levy. From their empirical analysis and critical survey of the existing literature, they conclude that the causes of residual inequality, often identified as increasing demand for cognitive skills, are in fact unknown.

In Chapter 16, Philip Gleason and Glen Cain examine the relationship between employment of youth and their family income and poverty status. They analyze historical trends of youth employment and family poverty by race, nationwide, from 1955 to 1995. The racial gap in the ratio of civilian youth employment to civilian youth population (E/P) increased for both males and females. Among males, the ratio was approximately coincident for blacks and whites in 1955; however, in 1995 the ratio for whites remained constant while that for blacks *fell sharply*, widening the racial gap by as much as 24 percent for sixteen- to nineteen-year-olds. The relationship between E/P and family poverty was negative for whites for the entire period, but, for blacks, it has been negative only in the period 1981–95. Gleason and Cain argue that youth unemployment has widened income and poverty gaps between blacks and whites and the income gap between rich and poor families.

But unlike the earlier literature, they focus here on the effect of youth employment on poverty.

PART VI. RACIAL AND FAMILIAL HARDSHIP: WELFARE BENEFITS AND WELFARE REFORM

This section addresses familial hardship focusing on welfare benefits and welfare reform. In Chapter 17, Arline T. Geronimus challenges conventional wisdom, which holds teenage childbearing as irresponsible misuse of welfare benefits and thus seeks to amend eligibility requirements to exclude teen mothers from the dole. She provides a forceful argument, iconoclastic in conception and rich in insight, why punitive measures against teen mothers overlook fundamental causes of teen pregnancy and, hence, have adverse effects on disadvantaged blacks.[119] The author also addresses important cultural and racial aspects that caution strongly against considering teen childbearing as a social evil. She argues that the effect of teen childbearing can be dramatically different in extended families of blacks, where resources are pooled and child bearing is shared, in contrast to the "standard" nuclear family that still forms the basis of America's social and political thinking.

Clearly, the decision to bear a child must be made in the context of the socioeconomic environment. The African American teenager, although resident in one of the most affluent nations, by and large, makes the same choice as her distant counterpart in remote villages of India, to bear children early if the expected life span is short, educational and employment prospects bleak, and support for childbearing is available within the kinship system. In short, even if there is evidence that teen childbearing is harmful, the social, economic, and cultural context in which fertility decisions are made must be taken into account in order to identify true irresponsibility and misuse of welfare resources without penalizing all teenage mothers from all types of background.

Geronimus argues that more state-of-the-art analyses are needed before causes and consequences of teen childbearing are established and used for policy. In Chapter 18, Harold Pollack attempts to fill this breach with an empirical analysis to determine whether public assistance programs, such as Aid to Families with Dependent Children (AFDC), encourage teen mothers to establish independent households rather than live with their parents. This is an important issue since it is thought that establishing independent households, as opposed to co-residence with parents, may be harmful to the well-being of teen mothers as well as to the public interest. But, according to Pollack, little is known about long-term consequences of residential choice on mothers and children, and the few studies that have been undertaken suffer from selection bias because residential choice can be determined by a vector of characteristics, such as family background, that also independently affect long-term outcomes such as poverty and education.

In his empirical results, Pollack confirms that AFDC benefits encourage teen mothers to set up independent households, But he questions the widespread belief that setting up independent households is necessarily detrimental to teen mothers, although the children, who fare much worse than others with respect to grade repetition, seem to be somewhat ill-affected.

In Chapter 19, Cecilia Conrad examines the relationship between income support policies and poverty among female-headed families in the United States relative to other developed nations. This is a rather important subject, given relatively higher poverty rates among female-headed households and the growing number of such households in developed nations. Unlike other developed nations, however, the risk of extreme poverty is highest in the United States. Moreover, the United States is the only developed nation without a universal child allowance scheme, relying instead on means-tested transfers. Is the absence of universal child assistance schemes the main cause of higher relative poverty?

The author draws on the literature of child support schemes in the United States, Canada, and Europe to determine if a more generous European-style system were introduced in the United States, whether the positive direct income effect may be offset by the leisure substitution effect of transfers.[120] She finds that the French, German, and British systems would not reduce poverty, but that the Swedish family allowance system, along with the advanced maintenance program, would eliminate extreme poverty in the United States.

She estimated an income function to determine whether transformation of life-style by elimination of single parenting and teenage parenting would be more effective than providing child allowances. Although reducing family size and mother's age reduces poverty in female-headed households, she finds that these gains are less effective than adopting a Swedish-style allowance scheme.

In Chapter 20, LaDonna Pavetti examines comparative work experiences of welfare recipients and nonrecipients to estimate the amount of additional work that welfare mothers may be expected to do, if they followed the same employment paths as nonrecipients with similar characteristics. Her analysis shows a 30 percent increase in work time of nonrecipients, which nonetheless represents a substantial period of joblessness. Lower employment rates of recipients are due, in part, to the fact that women with least favorable characteristics comprise a disproportionate part of welfare recipients. Pavetti's analysis shows that between ages eighteen and twenty-seven, women who have ever received welfare work only about 60 percent of the time worked by nonrecipients who never received welfare. She estimates that if recipients followed the same employment paths as nonrecipients with similar characteristics, their current employment would increase by about 30 percent. Women with low levels of education, low basic skills, and more children would realize the greatest employment gains, since they currently spend the least amount of time working. Even if recipients were to follow the same employment paths as nonrecipients, however, Pavetti finds that they would continue to experience substantial periods of joblessness.

In Chapter 21, Jeffrey Lehman and Sheldon Danziger focus on the Personal Responsibility and Work Opportunity Reconciliation Act of 1996, which they characterize as a regressive step that compromises the basic right of a safety net because employment opportunities are not available to most welfare recipients. Efficacy of the AFDC program depended on achievement of its two goals: providing a safety net to the needy (e.g., cash, food stamps, Medicaid) and ensuring that welfare recipients move from welfare to work. The authors acknowledge, however, that failure of the AFDC program was due to its not achieving the latter goal, owing to lack of employment opportunities, inadequacy of job skills as well as job training programs, and inability to restrict reentry into the program. Under the welfare reform act, the AFDC program was supplanted by block grants to state governments, substantial reductions in federal and state funding requirements, strict time limits on cumulative participation in the program, and stringent work requirements. The authors propose time-limit experiments, job opportunities provided or found by government, a safety net for those who need it, health care for low pay workers, child care for single parents, child support enforcement and, finally, a willingness to spend money for the social good.

In Chapter 22, Rebecca Blank addresses important behavioral changes observed in low-income families in the 1990s, exemplified by significant reduction in use of public assistance and substantial increases in labor force participation, an interesting contrast to preceding chapters by Pavetti and by Lehman and Danziger. She examines the role played by the macro economy and policy in engendering these behavioral changes. In addition to decline in welfare and increases in work, she also addresses decline in poverty rates that occurred throughout the decade. The decline in welfare was greater than decline in poverty. The strong macro economy is found to be important in decline of welfare, increased labor force participation, and falling poverty rates, which implies that in absence of a strong economy, the observed changes may no longer obtain to the same degree.

PART VII. COMMUNAL HARDSHIP IN BLACK RESIDENTIAL AREAS:
CRIME AND LAW ENFORCEMENT

This section investigates communal hardships endured by black communities, focusing on crime and law enforcement. The section begins with chapter 23, in which Samuel Myers, Jr., addresses the relationship between crime and lack of entrepreneurial opportunities in impoverished inner cities, the latter of which, he believes, has been "utterly ignored in recent discussions." In the conventional literature, low-wage "blue-collar" jobs are the suggested solution to poverty and welfare dependence. But this solution, inadequate though it may be, does not include inner-city residents with entrepreneurial and managerial talents who find legitimate, low-wage menial work unappealing, and resort to extralegal activities such as drug dealing and prostitution to make best use of their managerial, risk-taking, and problem-solving skills.[121]

The author uses prison data from California, Michigan, and Texas to examine the relationship between self-admitted drug dealing and labor force behavior. Quantitative measures of criminal preferences and motivations are used to assess their economic effects on employment and crime. Approximately 40 percent of offenders believed that legitimate activities helped them socially and psychologically while an equal proportion thought crime helped them "become their own man," interpreted by Myers to mean, an independent entrepreneur. Only about 20 percent thought that crime pays economically, while less than 5 percent were criminals by preference.

Why are blacks with significantly lower legal-to-illegal earnings ratios less likely to engage in drug dealing? Myers addressed this question by simulating the probability of drug dealing by blacks, assuming that they have the same backgrounds, experiences, and perception of whites. He finds that a white "drug dealer" image would raise black drug dealing by 15 percent, but white criminal perceptions do not change black drug dealing at all. However, relative earnings of whites would have a substantial reduction in black drug dealing, a decline of 90 percent.

These results suggest that equitable employment opportunities would reduce drug dealing among blacks. But the results also raise an important question to which no answer is provided. Counter to the standard economic model, and modifications introduced by Myers, whites are considerably more likely to deal in drugs than blacks, even though drug use problems are assumed to be more widespread among blacks in inner cities. Hence, attempts to provide work and entrepreneurial opportunities to black drug dealers would not be adequate to stem the flow of drugs to inner cities. Attention must also be directed at reducing demand for drugs in poor inner-city communities by providing residents with more rewarding and creative ways to live their lives and improving their self-respect and value to society.

Elijah Anderson examines the underlying mechanism by which violence and aggression have become characteristic of inner cities in Chapter 24. He attributes the propensity to violence broadly to "the circumstances of life among the ghetto poor — lack of jobs that pay a living wage, the stigma of race, the fallout from rampant drug use and drug trafficking, and the resulting alienation and lack of hope for the future." In the light of this, he explains how poverty, race, and crime are essential links in the vicious cycle that has cast inner cities in a downward spiral of violence, despair, and anarchy.[122] According to Anderson, poverty and racial stigma (or feelings of social injustice) have given rise to "street culture," where respect or social recognition are earned only by physical force. Residents are left with little choice but to use violence and aggression as the only way to assert themselves and demand the respect they deserve from society at large. This is due to uncertainty about life in a society plagued with the vicious cycle of poverty, race, and violence, the frighteningly low value on human life, lack of faith in law enforcement and the judicial systems, and the utter hopelessness and socioeconomic isolation of inner-cities.

Anderson argues that two distinct cultures, "street" culture and "decent" culture, coexist in inner cities. Violent behavior is advocated by the "code of the streets," established and enforced by "street" people, but often followed and accepted by "decent" people as a defensive method of survival in a hostile environment. The code is based on the idea of respect that introduces a structure and homespun justice to inner-city society, which suffers from a profound lack of faith in mainstream political, legal, social, and judicial institutions. Establishing respect through physical strength, control, or violent means is fundamentally motivated by the need to ensure one's safety in a community devoid of a functional police and judicial systems. The author summarizes the quest for respect as a zero-sum game, but clearly, when negative social costs of violence are accounted for, this quest is really a negative-sum game.

PART VIII. ECONOMIC DEVELOPMENT OF BLACK COMMUNITIES TO ALLEVIATE POVERTY

This section addresses obstacles to development of minority enterprise and derives policies from a model of socioeconomic development, implementation of which will effect socioeconomically viable black communities. In Chapter 25 Timothy Bates provides a critique of minority enterprise assistance programs in which he argues that the strategy of geographic targeting — flow of assistance to low-income inner-city minority communities — is conceptually flawed.

The Small Business Administration (SBA) provided financial assistance specifically targeted to poor inner city minority communities in the 1960s and 1970s to encourage entrepreneurship. But this program, he notes, by its very design was flawed because assistance was targeted to a group that lacked not only financial capital, but also the necessary entrepreneurial skills, education, and experience. The inevitable results were business failures, substantial rates of loan default, and continued poverty and decay in minority urban communities.

Bates analyzes the minority enterprise small business investment company (MESBIC) program to show that even if conceptually sound, this attempt may fail if implementation is flawed. MESBICs are privately owned small business investment firms established to finance minority business investments chartered and funded on preferential terms by the SBA. MESBICs were designed to provide business assistance on competitive terms and were not required to carry out any targeted goals. Of the 141 MESBICs chartered in the first decade, however, only 32 were in operation by 1994. In short, they have failed to function as "viable sources of financial capital for the minority business community." Small business development, in Bates's view, can be effectively achieved only in areas with high purchasing power, robust local markets, and abundant entrepreneurial talent and skill.

In the light of the failures depicted by Bates, Henry presents a social accounting matrix (SAM) model to provide an alternative policy for enhancement of the economic well-being of residents of inner-city New Haven. In place of the hopelessly inadequate prevailing policy that includes empowerment and enterprise zones to provide employment to blacks, Henry uses the SAM to show that comparatively greater and widespread benefits would accrue to these citizens if an alternative policy were implemented. The prevailing policy subsidizes traditional firms to establish branches on the periphery of inner cities and to employ a workforce comprising at least 30 percent black labor. However, in the SAM model, the federal government would enable inner-city workers and entrepreneurs to acquire skills specific to provision of services utilized by the government, and award long-term procurement contracts for these services to black entrepreneurs. These business owners would, in turn, employ inner-city labor to supply these services to federal institutions, with immeasurable benefits. Indeed, the effects devolve not only to the inner city, but to the state and the nation as a whole. The proposed policy posits an outflow of services from and considerable financial inflow to the inner city.

This significantly enhances inner-city employment and income, reduces public assistance to inner-city citizenry, enhances the occupational distribution of the workforce, and transforms the skill structure of the labor force.

Notes

1. With exception of Chapter 5, in which Tukufu Zuberi critically appraises Gunnar Myrdal's *An American Dilemma: The Negro Problem and Modern Democracy* (New York: Harper and Row, 1944).

2. Among these are Myrdal, *An American Dilemma*; E. Franklyn Frazier, *The Negro Family in the United States*, rev. ed. (Chicago: University of Chicago Press, 1966); C. Vann Woodward, *The Strange Career of Jim Crow* (New York: Oxford University Press, 1955); W. E. B. DuBois, *The Philadelphia Negro: A Social Study* (New York: Schocken Books, 1899); St. Clair Drake and Horace R. Cayton, *Black Metropolis: A Study of Negro Life in a Northern City* (New York: Harcourt, Brace, 1945).

3. According to Margo, it showed an improvement of about 3 percent. See Robert A. Margo, *Race and Schooling in the South, 1880–1950* (Chicago: University of Chicago Press, 1990).

4. Thus, in 1940, average earnings of black males were about 48 percent of their white counterparts, but by 1980, relative average earnings rose to 61 percent. See Margo, *Race and Schooling in the South*.

5. Ibid., pp. 1–32.

6. For details, see ibid., pp. 23–28.

7. With the advent of computer technology and widespread use of computers in firms, the minimum now may be the twelfth grade.

8. See John F. Kain, ed., *Race and Poverty: The Economics of Discrimination* (Englewood Cliffs, N.J.: Prentice-Hall, 1969), p. 15.

9. See Eli Ginzberg and Douglas W. Bray, *The Uneducated* (New York: Columbia University Press, 1953), p. 42.

10. Commonly known as the Coleman Report, see James S. Coleman et al., *Equality of Educational Opportunity* (Washington, D.C.: Government Printing Office, 1967).

11. See M. E. Dudley, *Brown v. Board of Education, 1954* (New York: Twenty-First Century Books, 1994).

12. See Warren C. Whatley, "Is There a New Black Poverty?" unpublished paper, 1992.

13. See Mark J. Stern, "Poverty and Family Composition Since 1940" in *The "Underclass" Debate: Views From History*, ed. Michael B. Katz (Princeton: Princeton University Press, 1993), pp. 220–53. The percentage of impoverished black families residing in the Black Belt is given on p. 234.

14. See Margo, *Race and Schooling in the South, 1880–1950*.

15. According to Brown, blacks who migrated to the North prior to World War II were filled with high hopes and expectations that their lot would be improved. These expectations induced them to accept and tolerate all sorts of menial jobs. See Claude Brown, *Manchild in the Promised Land* (New York: Macmillan, 1965), pp. 7–8.

16. Whatley, "Is There a New Black Poverty?"

17. The discussion in this section draws on the work of Kain, ed., *Race and Poverty: The Economics of Discrimination*.

18. See Paul H. Norgren and Samuel F. Hill, *Toward Full Employment* (New York: Columbia University Press, 1964).

19. Ray Marshall, *The Negro and Organized Labor* (New York: John Wiley and Son, 1965).

20. See John F. Kain and John R. Meyer, "Transportation and Poverty," *Public Interest* 18 (Winter 1970).

21. The "separate but equal" doctrine was extended to all areas of public life.

22. The movement did articulate the plight of the black poor, but this was not the essence of its mission.

23. See Stern, "Poverty and Family Composition Since 1940."

24. See Howard Birnbaum and Rafael Weston "Home Ownership and the Wealth Position of Black and White Americans," *Review of Income and Wealth* (1974), and Whatley, "Is There a New Black Poverty?"

25. See Henry S. Terrel, "Wealth Accumulation of Black and White Families: The Empirical Evidence," *Journal of Finance* 26 (1971).

26. See Taeuber and Taeuber in Kain, ed., *Race and Poverty,* 100–11.

27. May 11th 1914, the date on which the ordinance became effective. Date was provided by Professor Thomas L. Owen of the University of Louisville. It is based on a paper by his former undergraduate student, Margaret B. Pennington. The paper is titled, "What was the Ordinance of May 11, 1914?" University of Louisville (1980).

28. According to the builder, "If I sold just one suburban home to a Negro the local building inspectors would have me moving pipes three-eighths of an inch every afternoon in every one of the places I was building; and moving a pipe three-eights of an inch is mighty expensive if you have to do it in concrete." Quoted by Morton Grodizins in "The Metropolitan Area as a Racial Problem," in *American Race Relations Today*, ed., Earl Raab (Garden City, N.Y.: Anchor Books, 1962) p. 94 and cited in *Race and Poverty: The Economics of Discrimination* by John Cain ed., (Englewood Cliffs, N.J.: Prentice-Hall, 1969), p. 25.

29. See Kain, ed., *Race and Poverty*.

30. The term *economic distance* is taken from Victor Fuchs, "Comments on Measuring the Low-Income Population," in Lee Soltow, ed., *Six Papers on the Size Distribution of Wealth and Income,* Studies in Income and Wealth 33 (New York: National Bureau of Economic Research, 1969), pp. 198–99.

31. The government was alerted to the hardships and enduring difficulties of the poor by Michael Harrington, *The Other America* (New York: Macmillan, 1962), and Dwight MacDonald, "Our Invisible Poor" *New Yorker* (January 1963).

32. Fuchs, "Comments on Measuring the Low-Income Population."

33. See S. M. Miller and Pamela A. Roby, *The Future of Inequality* (New York: Basic Books, 1970), p. 171.

34. See James L. Sundquist, "Jobs, Training and Welfare for the Underclass," in K. Gordon, ed., *Agenda for the Nation* (Washington, D.C.: Brookings Institution, 1968), pp. 49–76.

35. Details of these programs may be found among recommendations made by the Kerner Commission, *Report of the National Advisory Commission on Civil Disorders* (New York: Bantam, 1968), pp. 146–52.

36. In this respect, Thurow offers some interesting suggestions. See Lester C. Thurow, "Raising Incomes Through Manpower Training Programs," in A. H. Pascal, ed., *Contributions to the Analysis of Urban Problems* (Santa Monica, Calif.: RAND, 1968).

37. See Elliot Liebow, *Tally's Corner: A Study of Negro Streetcorner Men* (Boston: Little, Brown, 1967).

38. This section draws on the work of David M. Gordon, *Theories of Poverty and Unemployment* (Lexington, Mass.: D. C. Heath, 1972).

39. For details, see *Manpower Report of the President* (Washington, D.C.: Government Printing Office, 1967), pp. 74–75.

40. Ibid.

41. They built and improved on the 1962 Manpower Development and Training Act.

42. In this respect, see Chapter 26 of this volume. Parallels were drawn with development of less developed countries (LDCs) and strategies were proposed similar to those for LDCs. See William Tabb, *The Political Economy of the Ghetto* (New York: Norton, 1970), and Thomas Vietorisz and Bennett Harrison, *The Economic Development of Harlem* (New York: Praeger, 1970).

43. See Kain, ed., *Race and Poverty*, p. 154.

44. Ibid., p. 166.

45. See Edward F. Denison, *The Sources of Economic Growth in the United States and the Alternatives Before Us* (Washington, D.C.: Committee for Economic Development, 1962), p. 197.

46. Drawn from a staff memorandum of the Council of Economic Advisers. See Kain, ed., *Race and Poverty*, pp. 58–59.

47. In estimating this cost, Siegel accounted for differences in education, occupation and residential location. See ibid., pp. 60–67.

48. See Stewart E. Tolnay and E. M. Beck, *A Festival of Violence: An Analysis of Southern Lynchings, 1882–1930* (Urbana: University of Illinois Press, 1992), p. 17. Prior to 1880, such barbarity was common during Reconstruction when unavailing attempts were made to extend voting rights to blacks.

49. See James E. Cutler, *Lynch Law* (New York, 1905); and NAACP, *Thirty Years of Lynching in the United States, 1889–1918* (New York, 1919)

50. See Tolnay and Beck, *Festival of Violence*, p. 17.

51. Ibid., p. 17. Undocumented deaths are not included in these data. A total of 2,805 victims was documented, of which 300 were white men and women.

52. See John Hope Franklin, *From Slavery to Freedom: A History of Negro Americans*, 4th ed. (New York: Alfred A. Knopf, 1974).

53. See Tolnay and Beck, *Festival of Violence*, p. xi.

54. "Communities had grown so violent that public notices were placed in newspapers inviting whites to come and watch the burning of a live black." Furthermore, "parents took their children to view lynchings because, in those formative years, such an experience creates another generation from whom hatred poured out like bird-song from a bird." In essence, "it is in childhood that we acquire the repertoire of emotions that accompanies us for the rest of our lives. It is then that we slowly build up the stock of characteristics (the loving and the mean, the trustworthy and treacherous, the bullies and the bully-able), which we recognize in later life." Ibid.

55. Ibid., pp. 18–19.

56. See the *Reader's Companion to American History,* ed. Eric Foner and John A. Garraty (Boston: Houghton Mifflin, 1991); and Robert L. Zangrando, *The NAACP Crusade Against Lynching, 1900–1950* (Philadelphia: Temple University Press, 1980).

57. Drawn from the *Pittsburgh American,* an African American newspaper.

58. See Walter White, *Rope and Faggot: A Biography of Judge Lynch* (New York: Knopf, 1929), and Zangrando, *The NAACP Crusade Against Lynching.*

59. There were additional antiblack riots during these periods, but I have selected those riots with relatively great human costs.

60. The movie was based on Thomas Dixon's book *The Clansman,* cited in *The Rosewood Report (1993): A Documented History of the Incident Which Occurred at Rosewood, Florida,* January 1993 (submitted to the Florida Board of Regents, December 22, 1993).

61. See Dixon, *The Clansman,* cited in *Rosewood Report.*

62. *Rosewood Report.*

63. Ibid.

64. See Robert Haws, *The Age of Segregation: Race Relations in the South, 1890–1945* (Jackson: University of Mississippi, 1978), and C. Vann Woodward, *The Strange Career of Jim Crow,* 3rd rev. ed. (New York: Oxford University Press, 1974).

65. See Tolnay and Beck, *Festival of Violence,* p. 8.

66. Ibid.

67. See Haws, *The Age of Segregation,* and Walter White, *The Fire and the Flint* (London: A. A. Knopf, 1924).

68. See David Cecelski and Timothy Tyson, eds., *Democracy Betrayed: The Wilmington Race Riot of 1898 and Its Legacy* (Chapel Hill: University of North Carolina Press, 1998), and Jules Archer, *Riot: A History of Mob Action in the United States* (New York: Hawthorn, 1974).

69. Cecelski and Tyson, eds., *Democracy Betrayed.*

70. Ibid.

71. Ibid.

72. Ibid.

73. See *Evansville Courier* (1995), 150th anniversary special section; and Archer, *Riot.*

74. *Evansville Courier* (1995), 150th anniversary special section.

75. See White, *Fire and the Flint,* pp. 5–12.

76. Ibid.

77. Ibid.

78. Ibid.

79. See Allen D. Grimshaw, *Racial Violence in the United States* (Chicago, 1969), and Irwin J. Sloan, *Our Violent Past* (New York, 1970).

80. Grimshaw, *Racial Violence in the United States,* and Sloan, *Our Violent Past.*

81. Grimshaw, *Racial Violence in the United States,* and Sloan, *Our Violent Past.*

82. See *Illinois State Journal* cited in Sloan, *Our Violent Past.*

83. See Grimshaw, *Racial Violence in the United States;* Sloan, *Our Violent Past;* and Tolnay and Beck, *Festival of Violence.*

84. See Grimshaw, *Racial Violence in the United States;* Sloan, *Our Violent Past;* and Tolnay and Beck, *Festival of Violence.*

85. See Rudwick Elliot, *Race Riot in East St. Louis* (Carbondale: Southern Illinois University Press, 1964).

86. Ibid.

87. *Washington Post,* 1 March 1999.

88. *Washington Post,* 1 March 1999.

89. *Washington Post,* 1 March 1999.

90. *Washington Post,* 1 March 1999.

91. *Washington Post,* 1 March 1999.

92. See William Tuttle, *Race Riot: Chicago in the Red Summer of 1919* (New York: Atheneum, 1970).

93. Ibid.; Carl Sandburg, *The Chicago Race Riots, July, 1919* (New York: Harcourt, Brace & World, 1969); Lee E. William and Lee E. William II, *Anatomy of Four Race Riots: Racial Conflict in Knoxville, Elaine (Arkansas), Tulsa and Chicago, 1919–21* (Hattiesburg: University and College Press of Mississippi, 1972).

94. Tuttle, *Race Riot;* Carl Sandburg, *The Chicago Race Riots;* William and William, *Anatomy of Four Race Riots.*

95. Kenneth R. Durham, "The Longview Riot of 1919," *East Texas Historical Journal* 18 (1980), and William Tuttle, "Violence in a Heathen Land: The Longview Race Riot of 1919," *Phylon* 33 (1972).

96. See John Higham, *History of Florida Past and Present* (Chicago, 1923).

97. The community was reported to have a relatively large transaction velocity of circulation of thirty-six. See Scott Ellsworth, *Death in the Promised Land: The Tulsa Race Riot of 1921* (Baton Rouge: Louisiana State University Press, 1982); Ed Wheeler, "It Happened in Tulsa," *Impact* (June–July 1971); Ed Wheeler, "Profile of a Race Riot," *Oklahoma Impact Magazine* 4 (June–July 1971); Walter White, "The Eruption of Tulsa," *Nation* 112 (June 29, 1921); Jonathan Larsen, "Tulsa Burning," *Civilization* (February 1947); R. Halliburton, Jr., "The Tulsa Race War of 1921," *Journal of Black Studies* 20 (March 1972); and Connie Cronley, "That Ugly Day in May," *Oklahoma Monthly* 2 (August 1976).

98. Ellsworth, *Death in the Promised Land;* Wheeler, "It Happened in Tulsa"; Wheeler, "Profile of a Race Riot"; White, "The Eruption of Tulsa"; Larsen, "Tulsa Burning"; Halliburton, "The Tulsa Race War of 1921"; Cronley, "That Ugly Day in May."

99. See Ellsworth, *Death in the Promised Land;* Wheeler, "It Happened in Tulsa"; Wheeler, "Profile of a Race Riot"; White, "The Eruption of Tulsa"; Larsen, "Tulsa Burning"; Halliburton, "The Tulsa Race War of 1921"; Cronley, "That Ugly Day in May."

100. See Ellsworth, *Death in the Promised Land;* Wheeler, "It Happened in Tulsa"; Wheeler, "Profile of a Race Riot"; White, "The Eruption of Tulsa"; Larsen, "Tulsa Burning"; Halliburton, "The Tulsa Race War of 1921"; Cronley, "That Ugly Day in May."

101. See Higham, *History of Florida Past and Present,* and Haws, *Age of Segregation.*

102. Higham, *History of Florida Past and Present,* and Haws, *Age of Segregation.*

103. See *Rosewood Report.*

104. Ibid.

105. Ibid.

106. See Earl Brown and George Leighton, *Why Race Riots? Lessons from Detroit* (New York, 1944), and Robert Shogun and Tom Craig, *The Detroit Race Riot: A Study in Violence* (Philadelphia, 1964).

107. Brown and Leighton, *Why Race Riots?* and Shogun and Craig, *Detroit Race Riot.*

108. Brown and Leighton, *Why Race Riots?* and Shogun and Craig, *Detroit Race Riot.*

109. Cited in Shogun and Craig, *The Detroit Race Riot.*

110. See *The Rosewood Report.* Italics my own.

111. See Tuttle, *Race Riot.*

112. Remedies proposed to problems of measurement by the Committee on National Statistics.

113. The report is titled "Measuring Poverty: A New Approach" (1995).

114. Myrdal, *An American Dilemma.*

115. With respect to completion of high school, Asians show a consistent advantage over other racial groups, even though all racial groups (except foreign-born Hispanics) appear to have made significant progress in this regard. But the gap between Asians and whites, and between whites and other racial groups, is even wider in regard to completion of college. American-born Asians were four times as likely, and whites were three times as likely, to graduate from college relative to blacks, Hispanics, or Native Americans. Subsequent to the labor market changes in the 1970s, this racial gap in college education has greatly influenced the persistence of racial differences in such economic variables as earnings and unemployment.

116. The differences between inner city and suburban residents are still small, especially among the poor, relative to income and education effects. For example, more affluent blacks living in inner cities are about twice as healthy as poor suburban blacks. Hence inner cities per se do not seem to have a devastating impact on blacks.

117. The "availability" view argues that news reporters are typically located in large cities where the poor are predominantly black and tend to be concentrated in more visible "poor neighborhoods," and where most of the "extreme poor" are black. Although only 32 percent of the urban poor are black (compared to 29 percent nationwide), about 47 percent of those in poor "neighborhoods" are black, and about 60 percent of the "extreme poor" are black. Therefore it could be argued that journalists continually present black poor in their coverage because the extremely poor, mainly black, inner city neighborhoods are most accessible to them. However, if accessibility is the only issue, there should not be any systematic patterns of misrepresentation, such as the strange underrepresentation of the black elderly. Systematic underrepresentation of certain "sympathetic groups" such as the elderly and employed suggests that "suitability" plays an important role, especially in selection of photographs by photo editors.

118. There has been a surprising consensus across the political spectrum on these reforms, which are seen not only as an attempt to restore proper economic incentives in the welfare system but also an attempt to reform the "American moral order."

119. Geronimus highlights the fact that the U.S. has the least generous social safety not for FHHs, and as much as 90 percent of U.S. assistance is in the form of means-tested allowances targeted at the poor; to many critics these programs act as a disincentive to mothers to earn wages.

120. In presenting such pessimistic prognosis on human capital investments, the

authors overlook several factors. (1) Structural changes in human capital programs can be undertaken to improve the rate of return (ROR). Indeed, it is important to make the ROR endogenous to the process of choice and emphasize OJT programs which are known to yield higher RORs. (2) Population-wide projections inflate the investment required over time to reduce the inequality. To be sure, a one-time investment should never be expected to restore real wage inequality across the entire population. A more meaningful approach would be to target human capital investments at sections of the population whose real wages are at a low ebb, but whose incomes are relatively responsive to such investments. If properly targeted, managed, and phased out, OJT and apprentice programs can raise real wages of low-skilled workers without increasing income inequality or requiring trillions of dollars.

121. In addition, certain criminal activities can be used to raise capital to finance legitimate entrepreneurial activities.

122. He recognizes the fact that racial stigma, or the feeling of social injustice, explains the unprecedented degree to which violence has been ingrained in the black culture.

PART I

Economic Inequality and Income Inequality

From Income Inequality to Economic Inequality

AMARTYA K. SEN

I begin by recounting a true story — a rather trivial and innocuous story, as it happens, but one with something of a lesson. Some years ago, when I went to give a lecture at another campus, I chose "Economic Inequality" as the title of my talk. On arrival, I found the campus covered with posters announcing that I was speaking on "Income Inequality." When I grumbled about it slightly, I encountered gentle, but genuine, amazement that I wanted to fuss about such "an insignificant difference." Indeed, the identification of economic inequality with income inequality is fairly standard, and the two are often seen as effectively synonymous in the economic literature. If you tell someone that you are working on economic inequality, it is quite commonly assumed that you are studying income distribution.

This implicit identification can be found in the philosophical literature as well. For example, in his interesting and important paper "Equality as a Moral Ideal," Harry Frankfurt (1987), the distinguished philosopher, provides a closely reasoned critique of what be calls economic egalitarianism, defining it as "the doctrine that there should be no inequalities in the distribution of money" (p. 21).

The distinction, however, is important. Many criticisms of economic egalitarianism as a value or a goal apply much more readily to the narrow concept of income inequality than they do to the broader notions of economic inequality. For example, giving a larger share of income to a person with more needs — say, due to a disability — may be seen as militating against the principle of equalizing incomes, but it does not go against the broader precepts of economic equality because the greater need for economic resources due to the disability must be taken into account in judging the requirements of economic equality.

The subject of this chapter is precisely the difference between economic inequality and income inequality. It will be argued that we ought to pay much more attention than we conventionally do to economic inequality in an appropriately broad sense, taking note of the fact that income inequality, on which economic analysis of inequality so often concentrates, gives a very inadequate and biased view of inequalities, even of those inequalities that can be powerfully influenced by economic policy. There is a serious gulf here, and the distinction, I would argue, is of considerable importance for economic practice as well as for economic theory. I shall also present some empirical examples, involving the United States as well as other countries, to illustrate the force of this distinction. The more difficult issue concerns the problems involved in having an appropriately broad notion of economic inequality that is both theoretically adequate and empirically usable. This question, too, I shall briefly try to address.

The Need for Going Beyond Income Inequality

A convenient point of departure is A. B. Atkinson's (1970) pioneering move in the measurement of inequality.[1] He assessed inequality of incomes by bringing in an overall social objective function and measured inequality of an income distribution through the social loss (in terms of equivalent income) from that distribution in comparison with a corresponding equal distribution. However, he took the individuals to be symmetrical and also did not explicitly consider what the individuals respectively get out of their incomes and other circumstances.[2]

There is a case for going beyond this structure and for examining the nature of individual advantages themselves as the constituent elements of social welfare (or, more generally, of social objectives). In this context, we have to take note of the heterogeneities of the individuals and of their respective non-income circumstances.

The important point to note is that the valuation of income is entirely as a means to other ends and also that it is one means among others. A more inclusive list of means has been used by John Rawls in his theory of justice through his concentration on primary goods, which include rights, liberties and opportunities, income and wealth, and the social bases of self-respect (Rawls 1971, pp. 60–65).[3] Income is, of course, a crucially important means, but its importance lies in the fact that it helps the person to do things that she values doing and to achieve states of being that she has reasons to desire. The worth of incomes cannot stand separated from these deeper concerns, and a society that respects individual well-being and freedom must take note of these concerns in making interpersonal comparisons as well as social evaluations.

The relationship between income (and other resources), on the one hand, and individual achievements and freedoms, on the other, is not constant. Different types of contingencies lead to systematic variations in the conversion of incomes into the distinct functionings we can achieve (i.e., the various things we can do or be), and that affects the lifestyles we can enjoy. There are at least five important sources of parametric variation.

Personal heterogeneities: People have disparate physical characteristics connected with disability, illness, age, or gender, making their needs diverse. For example, an ill person may need more income to fight her illness than a person without such an illness would need. While the compensation needed for disadvantages will vary, some disadvantages may not be correctable even with more expenditure on treatment or care.

Environmental diversities: Variations in environmental conditions, such as climatic circumstances (temperature ranges, rainfall, flooding, and so on), can influence what a person gets out of a given level of income.

Variations in social climate: The conversion of personal incomes and resources into functionings is influenced also by social conditions, including public health care and epidemiology, public educational arrangements, and the prevalence or absence of crime and violence in the particular location. Aside from public facilities, the nature of community relationships can be very important, as the recent literature on social capital has tended to emphasize.[4]

Differences in relational perspectives: The commodity requirements of established patterns of behavior may vary between communities, depending on conventions and customs. For example, being relatively poor in a rich community can prevent a person from achieving some elementary functionings (such as taking part in the life of the community) even though her income, in absolute terms, may be much higher than the level of income at which members of poorer communities can function with great ease and success. For example, to be able to "appear in public without shame" may require higher standards of clothing and other visible consumption in a richer society than in a poorer one (as Adam Smith [1776] had noted more than two centuries ago).[5] The same parametric variability may apply to the personal resources needed for the fulfillment of self-respect. This is primarily an intersocietal variation rather than an interindividual variation within a given society, but the two issues are frequently linked.

Distribution within the family: Incomes earned by one or more members of a family are shared by all, nonearners as well as earners. The family is thus the basic unit for consideration of incomes from the point of view of their use. The well-being or freedom of individuals in a family will depend on how the family income is used in furtherance of the interests and objectives of different members of the family. Thus, intrafamily distribution of incomes is quite a crucial parametric variable in linking individual achievements and opportunities with the overall level of family income. Distributional rules followed within the family (e.g., related to gender or age or perceived needs) can make a major difference to the attainments and predicaments of individual members.[6]

Illustrations of Contrasts

I have presented elsewhere empirical examples of different types that illustrate the variability of the relation between incomes and achievements (Sen 1981, 1985a, 1995a, 1998). I shall take the liberty of dwelling on a few such illustrations to indicate what kind of contrasts may be involved. Figure 1.1 presents the gross national product (GNP) per head and life expectancy at birth of six countries (China, Sri Lanka, Namibia, Brazil, South Africa, and Gabon) and one sizable state (Kerala) within a country (India).[7] The income-poor people of Kerala or China or Sri Lanka enjoy enormously higher levels of life expectancy than do the much richer populations of Brazil, South Africa, and Namibia, not to mention Gabon. Since life expectancy variations relate to a variety of economic influences, including epidemiological policies, health care, educational facilities, and so on, the reach of economic opportunities is much broader than that of income alone. I have had the occasion to discuss elsewhere how public policies in particular have been quite crucial in influencing the quality of life and longevity of different populations (see Sen 1981; Drèze and Sen 1989). In terms of inequality analysis, even the direction of the inequality points oppositely when we compare Kerala, China, and Sri Lanka on one side with Brazil, South Africa, Namibia, and Gabon on the other.

Figures 1.2 and 1.3 make a related but differently focused comparison, bringing in the United States itself. Even though the income per capita of African Americans is considerably lower than that of the American white population, African Americans are of course a great many times richer in income terms than the people of China or Kerala (even after correcting for cost-of-living differences). In this context, it is interesting to compare the survival prospects of African Americans vis-à-vis the immensely poorer Chinese

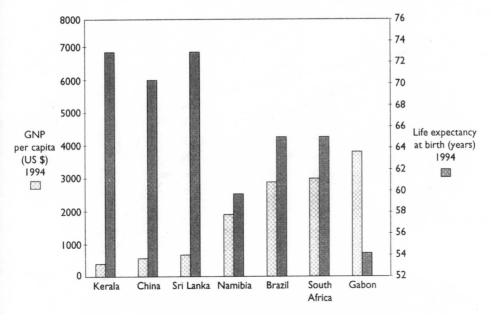

Figure 1.1 GNP per Capita (US $) and Life Expectancy at Birth, 1994
Sources: World Bank (1996); Kerala data, life expectancy, 1989–1993, sample registration system reported in Government of India (1997a); domestic product per capita, 1992–1993, Government of India (1997b)

or Indians in Kerala. American blacks do much better in terms of survival at low age groups (particularly in terms of infant mortality), but the picture changes over the years.

It turns out that, in fact, the Chinese and the Keralites decisively outlive American black men in terms of surviving to older age groups. Even American black women end up having similar survival patterns for high ages as the Chinese and decidedly lower survival rates than the Indians in Kerala. So it is not only the case that American blacks suffer from relative deprivation in the income space (vis-à-vis American whites); they are also absolutely more deprived than the much poorer Indians in Kerala and the Chinese (in the case of men) in terms of living to a ripe old age. In explaining these differences between living standards judged by income per capita and that judged by the ability to survive to higher ages, a number of causal issues are relevant (including medical insurance, public health care, elementary education, law and order) that are not unrelated to economic policies and programs.[8]

Figure 1.4 compares, for different states within India, the values of gross domestic product (GDP) per capita, literacy (female and male), life expectancy

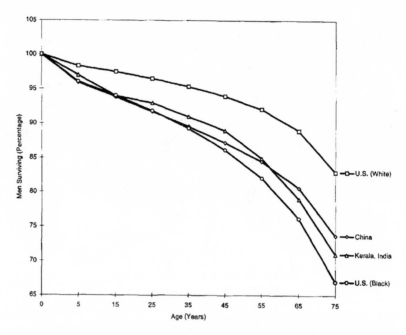

Figure 1.2 Variations in Male Survival Rates by Region
Sources: United States, 1991–1993, U.S. Department of Health and Human Services (1996); Kerala, 1991, Government of India (1991); China, 1992, WHO (1994)

at birth (female and male), and total fertility rate. The last has eventual importance for population growth, but its inclusion here is mainly for its immediate role, at high levels, as a major restraint that continual bearing and rearing of children imposes on the freedom and well-being of young women. Since continual child bearing and rearing are viewed as a negative influence on the quality of life, it is measured in the opposite (downward) direction from the zero line.

It is readily seen (as can also be confirmed by standard measures of statistical relations) that the relative values of GDP per capita figures are much at variance with the nonincome indices of aspects of quality of life (female literacy, male literacy, female life expectancy, male life expectancy, and low fertility rate), which all move very closely together. For example, the GDP figures would put Haryana and Punjab very much higher than Tamil Nadu and Kerala, but in terms of aspects of quality of life, exactly the opposite is the case.

As these illustrations exemplify (Figures 1.1 to 1.4) and as can be confirmed by other statistics (see, e.g., Sen 1985a, 1995a, 1998, and literature cited

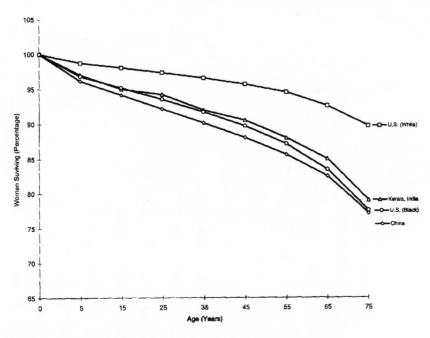

Figure 1.3 Variations in Female Survival Rates by Region
Sources: United States, 1991–1993, U.S. Department of Health and Human Services (1996); Kerala, 1991, Government of India (1991); China, 1992, WHO (1994)

there), there are substantial differences between the income-based view and the nonincome indicators of quality of life. Inequality comparisons will yield very different results depending on whether we concentrate only on incomes or also on the impact of other economic and social influences on the quality of life.

A further issue, which I shall not take up in this chapter (but that I have addressed elsewhere, particularly in Sen 1997), concerns the severely negative impact of unemployment, especially persistent unemployment, on the lives that people can live.[9] This is an especially important issue for the assessment of quality of life and inequality in contemporary Europe. Although unemployment benefits and social security may reduce the impact of the extraordinary levels of high unemployment on European income inequality in particular, the persistence of unemployment leads to many other kinds of deprivation (see Sen 1997 and literature cited therein) that are not reflected at all in the income statistics. An overconcentration on income inequality alone has permitted greater social and political tolerance of unemployment in Europe (and even some economic smugness vis-à-vis the achievement of low unemployment

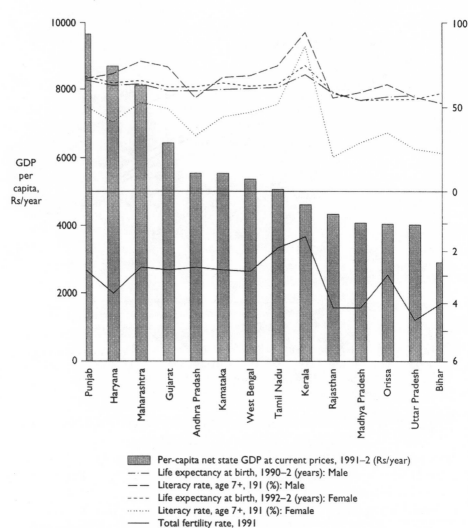

Figure 1.4 Selected Indicators for Indian States
Source: Drèze and Sen (1995), table A.3

levels in the U.S.) that cannot be justified if a broader view of economic inequality is taken.

Interpersonal Utility Comparisons and Inequality

The illustrations just presented of contrast between income and achievement deal with particular classes of indicators of quality of life (longevity, survival, literacy, fertility, and employment status).[10] Illustrations can also be provided to exemplify variability in the relation between income and other substantive achievements such as being healthy, being well-nourished, taking part in the life of the community, and so on. The acceptance of variability between income and achievement is not, however, an adequate ground for a definitive rejection of income inequality as the center of our attention in inequality assessment — without considering whether an alternative approach would be workable and satisfactory. Practical economics, no less than politics, is the art of the possible, and that issue remains, even when the need for going beyond income inequality is well accepted. Can we devise an alternative, practical approach based on the broader concentration on functionings rather than incomes?

Before taking on this issue fully, I would like to examine a related question, proposing a different alternative to the focus on incomes. Are we not likely, it may be sensibly asked, to be served better by opting for a more familiar notion, like utility, in shifting away from income inequality? Why not the inequality of utilities as the central focus of attention for inequality analysis? Indeed, just such a focus has been proposed and elegantly explored already by James Meade (1976) in his exploration of "the just economy." So the utility-based evaluation of inequality should be examined first, before stepping on to the less tried, and perhaps more hazardous, field of functionings (or the freedom to function).

The possibility of interpersonal comparisons of utilities was, of course, famously challenged by Lionel Robbins (1938) and others in the high days of simple positivist criticism of utilitarian welfare economics. Certainly, the claim to a high scientific status of utility comparisons is compromised by many practical difficulties in relating observations to firm and indisputable conclusions regarding interpersonal rankings of utilities and utility differences. In contrast, comparisons of pleasures and happiness are made in our day-to-day reflections and discourse, and there is considerable discipline in the making of such comparisons. Indeed, as Donald Davidson (1986) has pointed out, the nature of our understanding and communication regarding intrapersonal comparisons of states of happiness and desires are not radically different from the corresponding interpersonal exercises. Also, interpersonal comparison of utilities need not take an all-or-nothing form, and it is possible to have "partial interpersonal comparability" with a rigorous analytical structure (see Sen 1970a, b).

The difficult issue in basing inequality analysis on interpersonal comparisons is not so much the impossibility of making such comparisons but the possibility of being misled by such comparisons (particularly about important differences in the substantive deals that people get and the real predicaments from which they suffer). Our ability to take pleasure in very adverse circumstances tends to adapt to the hardship of circumstances so that the badly placed underdogs do not typically spend their lives weeping over what they have missed. People learn to make the most of small opportunities and to cut desires to size, that is, to levels that are realistic under the circumstances. Thus, in the scale of pleasures and desire fulfillment, the deprivation of the persistent underdog finds rather muffled and muted expression. Deprived people, varying from subjugated housewives in sexist societies to the hopelessly poor in strongly stratified economies, come to terms with their deprivation, and the psychological indicators of pleasure or desire fulfillment may fail to reflect the extent of real deprivation that these people suffer.[11]

There is, I believe, force in this criticism of relying on interpersonal comparison of pleasures and desire fulfillment for making judgments about inequality or injustice. However, this critique does not touch at all the more modern definition of utility as a numerical representation of individual choice behavior. In this interpretation, to say that a person gets more utility from x than from y is not essentially different from saying that, given the straightforward choice between x and y, the person would choose x.[12] The malleability or adaptation of pleasure-taking ability need not compromise the perspective of utility as real-valued representation of preference.

However, if we see utility only as a numerical representation of each person's choice behavior, there is, then, no basis here for interpersonal comparisons of utility since each person's choice behavior is a distinct and separate entity. My choices may well reveal that I prefer a banana to an apple, but no choice of mine would, in any obvious sense, reveal whether I prefer to be someone else. Interpersonal comparisons deal with objects of comparison that are not objects of actual choice.[13]

This point is often missed when it is presumed that similarity of choice behavior over commodity space must reveal a congruence of utilities. It is often presumed that, when two persons are observed to have the same demand function, then they must be seen as having the same level of interpersonally comparable utility for any given commodity bundle. Indeed, much of real-income comparison proceeds on the basis of identifying individual advantages with the commodity basket enjoyed, evaluated by a shared preference relation, and that procedure is not illegitimate for making situational comparisons of different persons' opulence.[14] But to interpret them as utility comparison, going beyond opulence, would be a complete non sequitur.[15] If instead of assuming that each person gets the same utility as others do from the same commodity bundle, it were assumed that one gets exactly one-tenth of the utility that another gets from each respective bundle, then that too would be perfectly consistent with all the behavioral observations (including the shared demand function). Congruent demand functions tell us nothing about the congruence of utility functions, and this follows generally from the fact that the observations on which demand functions are based do not lend themselves to any presumption about interpersonal comparisons of well-being (only of commodity holdings and opulence).

This must not be seen as just a fussy difficulty of theoretical interest; it can make a very big difference in practice as well. Even if a person who is disabled or ill or depressed happens to have the same demand function as another who is not disadvantaged in this way, it would be quite absurd to assume that she is having exactly the same utility or well-being from a given commodity bundle as the other can get from it. To attribute the same utility function to each and to treat that as the basis of interpersonal comparison for the analysis of inequality or injustice would be both epistemologically unsound and ethically unfair.

Utility cannot, therefore, serve as a satisfactory basis for interpersonal comparison for inequality analysis, and this holds no matter whether we interpret utility as pleasure or as desire fulfillment or as a numerical representation of choice behavior. Indeed, as I have tried to discuss, attempts to make that use arbitrarily can be pernicious for judgments of equity and justice.

Quality of Life, Functionings, and Capabilities

The choice of nonutility variables in terms of which inequality can be judged has been a matter of some interest in recent years, and such concepts as the quality of life or freedom of living and other such notions have been invoked.[16] It is, however, important to emphasize that focusing on the quality of life rather than on income or wealth or on psychological satisfaction is not new in economics. Indeed, the origin of the subject of economics was strongly motivated by the need to study the assessment of and causal influences on the conditions of living.[17] The motivation is stated explicitly, with reasoned justification, by Aristotle, but it is also strongly reflected in the early writings on national accounts and economic prosperity by William Petty, Gregory King, François Quesnay, Antoine Lavoisier, Joseph Louis Lagrange, and others. While the national accounts devised by these pioneers established the foundations of the modern concept of income, the focus of their attention was never confined to this one concept. They were also very aware of the basic issue that the importance of income is instrumental and circumstantially contingent rather than intrinsic and categorical.[18]

In traditional welfare economics, there has been interest both in individual utilities and in individual incomes. When individuals are taken to be symmetrical, the two are closely linked. John Rawls has pointed to the important issue that income is not the only versatile means that facilitates a person's pursuit of his or her respective objectives. He has focused instead, as was stated earlier, on the broader category of primary goods, which are general-purpose means that help anyone to promote his or her ends (including "rights, liberties and opportunities, income and wealth, and the social bases of self-respect" [see Rawls 1971]).

The concentration on primary goods in the Rawlsian framework relates to his accounting of individual advantage in terms of the opportunities they enjoy pursuing their respective objectives.[19] Rawls's Difference Principle, which is part of his theory of justice as fairness, assesses efficiency as well as equity in terms of the respective holdings of primary goods, represented by an index.

The broadening of the narrow concentration on incomes alone involved in this move is significant, but this widening of the informational focus from incomes to primary goods is not adequate to deal with all the relevant variations in the relationship between resources and functionings. Primary goods themselves are mainly various types of general resources, and the use of these resources to generate the capability to do things is subject to distinct types of variations (as has been already discussed), including personal heterogeneities, environmental diversities, and variations in social climate, and differences in relational perspective. We can have complete equality of the chosen index of primary goods, and yet some people may be immensely more deprived than others because of age, disabilities, proneness to illness, epidemiological conditions, and so on.

I have tried to argue for some time now (Sen 1980, 1985a, b, 1992) that, for many purposes, the appropriate space is neither that of utilities (as claimed by welfarists) nor that of primary goods (as demanded by Rawls). If the object is to concentrate on the individual's real opportunity to pursue her objectives, then account would have to be taken not only of the primary goods the person holds but also of the relevant personal characteristics that govern the conversion of primary goods into the person's ability to promote her ends.[20] For

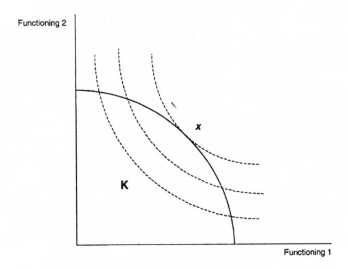

Figure 1.5 Functioning Vectors and the Preference Map

example, a person who is disabled may have a larger basket of primary goods and yet have less chance to lead a normal life (or to pursue her objectives) than an able-bodied person with a smaller basket of primary goods. Similarly, an older person or a person more prone to illness can be more disadvantaged in a generally accepted sense even with a larger bundle of primary goods.[21]

The concept of functionings, which has distinctly Aristotelian roots, reflects the various things a person may value doing or being. The valued functionings may vary from such elementary ones as being adequately nourished and being free from avoidable disease to very complex activities or personal states, such as being able to take part in the life of the community and having self-respect.[22] The extent of each functioning enjoyed by a person may be represented by a real number and, when this is the case, a person's actual achievement is given by a functioning vector in an *n*-dimensional space of *n* functionings (presuming finiteness of distinct functionings). When numerical representation of each functioning is not possible, the analysis has to be done in terms of the more general framework of seeing the functioning achievements as a functioning *n*-tuple and the capability set as a set of such *n*-tuples in the appropriate space (this will, then, not be a vector space). The set of alternative functioning vectors available to her for choice is called her capability set. While the combination of functionings (strictly, *n*-tuples) a person undertakes reflects her achievements, the capability set represents the freedom to achieve: the alternative functioning combinations from which this person can choose.

Figure 1.5 illustrates a functioning space (two dimensional), with the capability set of person being given by region K, and from this capability set K, the person chooses one functioning vector x (though this need not necessarily be unique). It may be useful to think of choice in this space in terms of an indifference map of valued living defined over the functioning vectors, and x can then be seen as belonging to the highest reachable indifference curve (as indicated).[23] The focus of this capability approach could be either on the realized functionings (what a person is actually able to do) or on the set of alternatives she has (her real opportunities).

I shall not go into the details of the approach here (which I have tried to present elsewhere [Sen 1985a, 1992, 1993]). But it is useful to ask whether the focus on capability is likely to be very different from that on functionings. The capability approach can be used either with a focus on what options a person has — given by the whole capability set — or on the actual functioning combination she chooses — given by the chosen functioning vector. In the former procedure, what may be called the options application, the focus can be on the entire K, whereas in the latter, the choice application, the concentration is more narrowly on x. The options application is directly concerned with the freedom to choose over various alternatives, whereas the choice application is involved with the alternative that is actually chosen. Both the versions of the capability approach have been used in the literature, and sometimes they have been combined.[24]

By a well-established tradition in economics, the real value of a set of options lies in the best use that can be made of them and, given maximizing behavior and the absence of uncertainty, the use that is actually made. The use value of the opportunity, then, lies derivatively on the value of one element of it (to wit, the best option or the actually chosen option).[25] In this case, the focusing on chosen functioning vector coincides with concentration on the capability set. With this type of elementary evaluation, the two uses of the capability approach share not only the identification of a relevant space (that of functionings) but also the focal variable in that space (the chosen functioning vector).[26]

However, the options application can be used in other ways as well since the value of a set need not invariably be identified with the value of the best, or the chosen, element of it. It is possible to attach importance to having opportunities that are not taken up. This is a natural direction to go if the process through which outcomes are generated is of significance of its own. Indeed, choosing itself can be seen as a valuable functioning and having an x when there is no alternative may be sensibly distinguished from choosing x when substantial alternatives exist.[27] The importance of this type of consideration lies more in drawing attention to broader concerns than in offering a quick resolution of interpersonal comparison of freedoms (and thus of overall individual advantages that take note of the significance of freedom).

Weights, Valuations, and Explicitness

I turn now to a crucial methodological issue that has received much attention in recent discussions involving the capability approach and related proposals. The heterogeneity of functionings involves the need to weigh them against one another. This would apply to all approaches geared to functionings, whether the concentration is on realized functioning vectors x (as with the choice application) or on the capability sets K (as with the options application).[28]

Is this weighting requirement a special difficulty associated with the capability approach? This cannot be the case since heterogeneity of factors that influence individual advantage is a pervasive feature of actual evaluation. While we can decide to close our eyes to this issue by simply assuming that there is something homogeneous (e.g., income or utility) in terms of which everyone's overall advantage can be judged and interpersonally compared (and that variations of needs, personal circumstances, etc., can be, correspondingly, assumed away), this does not resolve the problem — it only evades it.

Comparisons of real income involve reduction of bundles of different commodities into points on a real line and judgment of comparative individual advantages; there is the further problem of interpersonal comparisons taking note of variations of individual conditions and circumstances. As was discussed above, even when each person's preference is taken to be the ultimate arbitrator of well-being for that person and even when, to take a very special case, everyone has the same demand function or preference map, the comparison of market valuations of commodity bundles (or their relative placing on a shared system of indifference map in the commodity space) may tell us rather little about interpersonal comparisons of well-being.

In evaluative traditions involving fuller specification, considerable heterogeneity is explicitly admitted. For example, in Rawlsian analysis, primary goods are taken to be constitutively diverse (including "rights, liberties and opportunities, income and wealth, and the social bases of self-respect"), and Rawls (1971) deals with them through an overall index of primary goods holdings.[29] While a similar exercise of judging over a space with heterogeneity is involved both in the Rawlsian approach and in the use of functionings, the former is informationally poorer, for reasons discussed already, because of the parametric variation of resources and primary goods vis-à-vis the opportunity of achieving high quality of living.

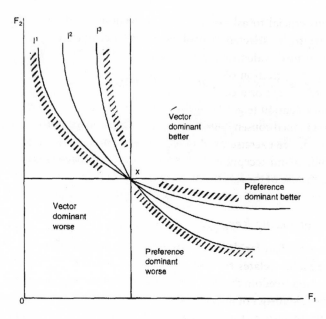

Figure 1.6 Functioning Vectors and Dominance

The problem of valuation is not, however, one of an all-or-nothing kind. Some judgments, with incomplete reach, follow immediately from the specification of a focal space. When some functionings are selected as significant, such a focal space is specified, and the relation of dominance itself leads to a partial ordering over the alternative states of affairs. If person i has more of a significant functioning than person j and at least as much of all such functionings, then i clearly has a higher valued functioning vector than j has. This partial ordering can be extended by further specifying the possible weights. A unique set of weights will, of course, be sufficient to generate a complete order, but it is typically not necessary. Given a range of weights on which there is agreement (i.e., when it is agreed that the weights are to be chosen from a specified range, even without any agreement as to the exact point on that range), there will be a partial ordering based on the intersection of rankings (Figure 1.6). This partial ordering will get systematically extended as the range is made more and more narrow. Somewhere in the process of narrowing the range, possibly well before the weights are unique, the partial ordering will become complete.[30] But even with an incomplete ordering, many decision problems can be adequately resolved, and even those that are not fully resolved can be substantially simplified (through the rejection of dominated alternatives).

It is thus crucial to ask, in any evaluative exercise of this kind, how the weights are to be selected. This judgmental exercise can be resolved only through reasoned evaluation. For a given person who is making his or her own judgments, the selection of weights will require reflection rather than inter-personal agreement or a consensus. However, in arriving at an agreed range for social evaluation (e.g., in social studies of poverty), there has to be some kind of a reasoned consensus on weights or at least on a range of weights. This is a social choice exercise that requires public discussion and a democratic understanding and acceptance.[31] It is not a special problem that is associated only with the use of the functioning space.

A Concluding Remark

The argument for shifting our attention from income inequality to economic inequality relates to the presence of causal influences on individual well-being and freedom that are economic in nature but that are not captured by the simple statistics of incomes and commodity holdings. The case for such broadening of informational focus also entails the need to pay evaluative attention to heterogeneous magnitudes and calls for the derivation of partial orderings based on explicit or implicit public acceptance. The normative force of this acceptance rests substantially on the quality and reach of public discussions on matters of central social concern. The subject of this essay, though nominally about inequality, is ultimately as much about the nature and importance of public discussion on social evaluation.

In matters of public judgment, there is no real escape from the evaluative need for public discussion. The work of public valuation cannot be replaced by some "super clever" assumption. Some assumptions that give the appearance of working very well operate through hiding the choice of values and weights in some constructed opaqueness. For example, the assumption, often implicitly made, that two persons with the same demand function must have the same relation between commodity bundles and well-being (no matter whether one is ill and the other not, one disabled and the other not, etc.) is basically a way of evading the consideration of significant influences on well-being. That evasion becomes transparent, as I have tried to illustrate, when we supplement income and commodity data by information of other types (including matters of life and death).

The exercise need not, however, be as exacting as it may first appear and as it certainly would be if we were not to settle for anything less than getting complete orderings of interpersonal advantages and inequalities. Our values about inequality aversion are not typically of the fine-tuning variety, getting the level of inequality "just right," taking note of all its pros and cons. Rather, the engagement is mainly about the avoidance of substantial inequalities and serious injustice.

As material for public discussion and for informed consensus or acceptance, the need is not so much for a complete ordering of interpersonal advantages and of levels of inequality (which would be inevitably based on some crude assumptions and evasions) but for usable partial orderings that capture the big inequalities in a clear way, taking note of the various significant concerns that go well beyond the commodity space. The focus has to be on the reach and relevance of partial orderings that can be cogently derived and used. Insistence on completeness can be an enemy of informed and democratic decision making.

Notes

This chapter draws on my work in a research project on "Inequality and Poverty in Broader Perspectives," with support from the MacArthur Foundation. For helpful comments, I am grateful to Sudhir Anand, Fubrizio Barca, Andrea Brandolini, Anne Case, Angus Deaton, James Foster, Christina Paxson, and Ben Polak.

1. See also Dalton (1920) and Kolm (1969).

2. While Atkinson used the utilitarian form whereby social welfare was seen as the sum total of individual components that he called u, there is no need to identify u_1 specifically with individual utilities. The social objective function is, however, assumed in this Atkinsonian formulation to be additively separable (on individual incomes), and this limiting assumption can be readily dispensed with in a generalized form of the Atkinson approach (see Sen 1973; Blackorby and Donaldson 1978, 1980).

3. For a further broadening of the resources that we use, or can use, as means for pursuing our respective ends, see Dworkin (1981).

4. See particularly Coleman (1986) and Putnam, Leonardi, and Nanetti (1993).

5. See also Runciman (1966) and Townsend (1979) for sociological analyses of the relativist aspects of well-being and achievements.

6. See Sen (1990) and the literature cited therein.

7. While Kerala is merely a state rather than a country, nevertheless, with its population of 29 million, it is larger than the majority of countries in the world.

8. On this, see Sen (1993) and also the medical literature cited therein. See also the discussion that American black men from the Harlem district of rich New York fall (in terms of survival) not only behind the Chinese or the Indians in Kerala but also behind the famished population of Bangladesh.

9. See Darity and Goldsmith (1993), Goldsmith, Veum, and Darity (1996), and the literature cited therein.

10. These variables have played substantial roles, under the visionary leadership of Mahbub ul Haq (and now Richard Jolly), in *Human Development Reports* of the United Nations (see, for example, UNDP 1990, 1995, 1997), with which I have been privileged to be associated; see also Anand and Sen (1995, 1997).

11. I have discussed this issue more fully in Sen (1984, 1985a, b).

12. The formulation can be made more complex through considering nonbinary choices, but the basic understanding of utility as preferred choice remains similar (see Sen 1982).

13. It is, of course, possible to think of hypothetical choices in which becoming someone else may be imaginatively involved (see, e.g., Harsanyi 1955). Such comparisons may be enlightening as a thought experiment, but they are unlikely to become practical methods for interpersonal comparisons.

14. I have discussed the welfare-economic reasoning underlying such comparisons in Sen (1976, 1979).

15. Explanations as to why this is an error have been helpfully discussed by several authors, including Samuelson (1947), Graaff (1957), Gintis (1969), and Fisher and Shell (1972). Evidently, this has not prevented regular recurrence of the error.

16. See the literature considered in Nussbaum and Sen (1993).

17. See Sen (1987).

18. On these and related matters, see Sen (1987). The focus of attention of William Petty, who had experimented with both the income method and the expenditure method in estimating national income, included "the Common Safety" and "each Man's particular Happiness." Petty's explicitly stated objective for undertaking his study related directly to the assessment of the condition of living of people and combined scientific investigation with a motivating dose of seventeenth-century politics ("to show" that "the King's subjects are not in so bad a condition as discontented Men would make them").

19. In a related line of argument, Dworkin (1981) has argued for equality of resources, broadening the Rawlsian coverage of primary goods to include insurance opportunities to guard against the vagaries of brute luck.

20. A person does have some opportunity of changing the conversion relations, for example, by cultivating special tastes or by learning to use resources better. But, nevertheless, there are limits that constrain the extent to which such shifts can be brought about.

21. On the nature and pervasiveness of such variability, see Sen (1980, 1985b, 1992). The problem of different needs considered in *OEI-1973* relates to this general issue. On the relevance of taking note of disparate needs in resource allocation, see also Doyal and Gough (1991), Ebert (1992, 1994), Balestrino (1994, 1997), Chiappero Martinetti (1994, 1997), Fleurbaey (1994, 1995a, b), Granaglia (1994), Balestrino and Petretto (1995), Shorrocks (1995), Nolan and Whelan (1996), among other contributions.

22. See Sen (1984, 1985a, 1987, 1992). This approach has clear linkages with Adam Smith's (1776) analysis of necessities (see Sen 1981, 1984) and with Aristotle's discussions of well-being in *Nicomachean Ethics* and in *Politics* (see Nussbaum 1988, 1993). See also Mill (1859) and Marx (1875). The conceptual broadening has powerful implications on practical procedures for assessing advantage and deprivation; see also Crocker (1992), Nussbaum and Sen (1993), Nussbaum and Glover (1995), and Nolan and Whelan (1996).

23. The use of such an indifference map in explaining valuation of functionings may be of considerable pedagogic value, especially in moving from the familiarity of the commodity space to the unaccustomed functioning space. It is, nevertheless, important to recognize that the nature of the indifference map in the functioning space may not altogether

mirror what we standardly presume in the case of commodity space. In particular, there may be considerable areas of incompleteness as well as fuzziness (see Sen 1985a). The recent literature on fuzzy set theory can be helpful in analyzing the valuation of functioning vectors and capability sets (see, among other contributions, particularly Chiappero Martinetti 1994, 1997; Delbono 1989; Cerioli and Zani 1990; Balestrino 1994; Balestrino and Chiappero Martinetti 1994; Ok 1995; Casini and Bernetti 1997).

24. See the rather extensive literature on this referred to in Foster and Sen (1997).

25. This approach is called elementary evaluation of the capability set; on the nature and scope of elementary evaluation, see Sen (1985a).

26. Cohen's (1989, 1990, 1995) arguments for concentrating on what he calls midfare also lead to this particular focus; see also Arneson (1989, 1990).

27. See Sen (l985a, b). There remains the more difficult issue of determining how this process considered should be incorporated. For various alternative proposals and also axiomatized formulas, see Suppes (1987), Pattanaik and Xu (1990), Sen (1991a), Foster (1993), Arrow (1995), Herrero (1995), Puppe (1995), among others.

28. In the latter case, there is the further task of comparing sets rather than points in this space, and it involves the additional issue that the importance of freedom can stretch well beyond the value of the particular element that is chosen (except in the special case of elementary evaluation).

29. In analogy with Arrow's (1951) impossibility theorem and its single-profile extensions, various impossibility theorems have been presented in the literature about the existence of satisfactory overall indices of Rawlsian primary goods (see Plott 1978; Gibbard 1979; Blair 1988). Informational limitations play a crucial part in precipitating these results (as in the case of Arrow's theorem). The case against imposing such informational limitations is discussed in Sen (199lb), which reduces the rub of these alleged impossibility results, applied to Rawlsian procedures.

30. Analytical correspondences between systematic narrowing of the range of weights and monotonic extension of the generated orderings have been explored in Sen (1970a, 1970b, 1982), Blackorby (1975), Fine (1975), and Basu (1980). The use of the intersection approach (see Sen 1973; Foster and Sen 1997) relates directly to this procedure. The approach of intersection quasi-orderings can be combined together with "fuzzy" representation of the valuation as well as measurement of functionings (see Casini and Bernetti 1997; Chiappero Martinetti 1994, 1997).

31. This issue and its connection with both social choice theory and public choice theory are discussed in my presidential address to the American Economic Association (Sen 1995b).

References

Anand, S., and A. K. Sen. 1995. Gender inequality in human development: theories and measurement. Working Paper No. 95.05, Center for Population and Development Studies, Harvard University, Cambridge, Mass.

———. 1997. Concepts of human development and poverty: A multidimensional perspective. Working Paper, Center for Population and Development Studies, Harvard University, Cambridge, Mass.

Arneson, R. 1989. Equality and equality of opportunity for welfare. *Philosophical Studies* 56:77–93.

———. 1990. Liberalism, distributive subjectivism, and equal opportunity for welfare. *Philosophy and Public Affairs* 19: 158–94.

Arrow, K. J. 1993. *Social choice and individual values.* 2nd edition. New York: Wiley.

———. 1995. A note on freedom and flexibility. In *Choice, welfare and development: A Festschrift for Amartya K. Sen,* edited by K. Basu, P. Pattanaik, and K. Suzumura. Oxford, UK: Clarendon Press.

Atkinson, A. B. 1970. On the measurement of inequality. *Journal of Economic Theory* 2:244–63.

Balestrino, A. 1994. Poverty and functionings: Issues in measurement and public action. *Giornale degli Economisti e Annali di Economia* 53:389–406.

———. 1997. A note on functioning: Poverty in affluent Societies. *Notizie di Politeia* 12:97–105.

Balestrino, A., and E. Chiappero Martinetti. 1994. Poverty, differentiated needs, and information. Mimeographed, University of Pisa and University of Pavia.

Balestrino, A., and A. Petretto. 1994. Optimal taxation rules for "functioning": Inputs. *Economic Notes* 23:216–32.

Basu, K. 1980. *Revealed preference of government.* Cambridge, UK: Cambridge University Press.

Blackorby, C. 1975. Degrees of coordinality and aggregate partial ordering. *Econometrica* 43:845–52.

Blackorby, C., and D. Donaldson. 1978. Measures of relative equality and their meaning in terms of social welfare. *Journal of Economic Theory* 18:59–80.

———. 1980. A theoretical treatment of indices of absolute inequality. *International Economic Review* 21:107–36.

Blair, D. H. 1988. The primary-goods indexation problem in Rawls' *Theory of justice. Theory and Decision* 24:239–52.

Casini, L., and I. Bernetti. 1997. Environment, sustainability, and Sen's theory. *Notizei di Politeia* 12:55–78.

Cerioli, A., and S. Zani. 1990. A fuzzy approach to the measurement of poverty. In *Income and wealth distribution, inequality and poverty,* edited by C. Dagum and M. Zenga. New York: Springer.

Chiappero Martinetti, E. 1994. A new approach to evaluation of well-being and poverty by fuzzy set theory. *Giornale degli Economisti e Annali di Economia* 53:367–88.

———. 1997. Standard of living evaluation based on Sen's approach: Some methodological suggestions. *Notizie di Politeia.* 12:37–53.

Cohen, G. A. 1989. On the currency of egalitarian justice. *Ethics* 99:906–44.

———. 1990. Equality of what? On welfare, goods and capabilities. *Recherches Economiques de Louvain* 56:357–82.

———. 1995. *Self-ownership, freedom, and equality.* Cambridge, UK: Cambridge University Press.

Coleman, J. S. 1986. *Individual interests and collective action: Selected essays.* Cambridge, UK: Cambridge University Press.

Crocker, D. 1992. Functioning and capability: The foundations of Sen's and Nussbaum's development ethic. *Political Theory* 20:584–612.

Dalton, H. 1920. The measurement of the inequality of incomes. *Economic Journal* 30:348–61.

Darity, W., Jr., and A. Goldsmith. 1993. Social psychology and the theoretical foundations of unemployment hysteresis. *Journal of Post Keynesian Economics* 16:55–72.

Davidson, D. 1986. Judging interpersonal interests. In *Foundations of social choice theory,* edited by J. Elster and A. Hylland. Cambridge, UK: Cambridge University Press, pp. 195–211.

Delbono, F. 1989. Poverta come incapacita: Premesse teoriche, identificazione e misurazione. *Rivista Internazionale di Scienze Sociali* 97.

Doyal, L., and I. Gough. 1991. *A theory of human need.* New York: Guilford Press.

Drèze, J., and A. K. Sen. 1989. *Hunger and public action.* Oxford, UK: Clarendon Press.

———. 1995. *India: Economic development and social opportunity.* Oxford, UK: Clarendon Press.

Dworkin, R. 1981. What is equality? Part 1: Equality of welfare, and What is equality? Part 2: Equality of resources. *Philosophy and Public Affairs* 10:185–246; 283–345.

Ebert, U. 1992. On comparisons of income distributions when household types are different. Economics Discussion Paper No. V-86–92, University of Oldenberg.

———. 1994. Social welfare when needs differ: An axiomatic approach. Unpublished paper, Department of Economics, University of Oldenberg.

Fine, B. 1975. A note on interpersonal aggregation and partial comparability. *Econometrica* 43:169–72.

Fisher, F. M., and K. Shell. 1972. *The economic theory of price indices.* New York: Academic Press.

Fleurbaey, M. 1994. On fair compensation. *Theory and Decision* 36:277–307.

———. 1995a. Three solutions for the compensation problem. *Journal of Economic Theory* 65:505–21.

———. 1995b. Equality and responsibility. *European Economic Review* 39:683–89.

Foster, J. E. 1993. Notes on effective freedom. Paper presented at the Stanford Workshop on Economic Theories of Inequality, sponsored by the MacArthur Foundation.

Foster, J. E., and A. K. Sen. 1997. *On economic inequality after a quarter century.* Oxford, UK: Clarendon Press.

Frankfurt, H. 1987. Equality as a moral ideal. *Ethics* 98:21–43.

Gibbard, A. 1979. Disparate goods and Rawls's difference principle: A social choice theoretic treatment. *Theory and Decision* 11:267–88.

Gintis, H. 1969. Alienation and power: Toward a radical welfare economics. Ph.D. diss., Harvard University, Cambridge, MA.

Goldsmith, A., J. R. Veum, and W. Darity, Jr. 1996. The psychological impact of unemployment and joblessness. *Journal of Socio-Economics* 25:333–58.

Government of India. 1991. *Sample registration system. Fertility and mortality indicators.* New Delhi.

———. 1997a. *Women in India: A statistical profile.* New Delhi: Department of Education.

———. 1997b. *Economic survey, 1996–97.* New Delhi: Ministry of Finance.

Graaff, J. van de. 1957. *Theoretical welfare economics.* Cambridge, UK: Cambridge University Press.

Gragnalia, E. 1994. More or less equality? A misleading question for social policy. *Giornale degli Economisti e Annali di Economia* 53:349–66.

Harsanyi, J. C. 1955. Cardinal welfare, individualistic ethics and interpersonal comparisons of utility. *Journal of Political Economy* 63:309–21.

Herrero, C. 1995. Capabilities and utilities. Unpublished paper, University of Alicante and Lyle, Spain.

Kolm, S. C. 1969. The optimal production of social justice. In *Public economics,* edited by J. Margolis and H. Guitton. London: Macmillan.

Marx, K. 1875. *Critique of the Gotha program.* English translation, New York: International Publishers, 1938.

Meade, J. E. 1976. *The just economy.* London: Allen and Unwin.

Mill, J. S. 1859. *On liberty.* Republished, Harmondsworth: Penguin Books, 1974.

Nolan, B., and C. T. Whelan. 1996. *Resources, deprivation, and poverty.* Oxford, UK: Clarendon Press.

Nussbaum, M. 1988. Nature, function, and capability: Aristotle on political distribution. *Oxford Studies in Ancient Philosophy,* Supplementary volume.

——. 1993. Non-relative virtues: An Aristotelian approach. In Nussbaum and Sen (1993).

Nussbaum, M., and J. Glover. 1995. *Women, culture, and development: A study of human capabilities.* Oxford, UK: Clarendon Press.

Nussbaum, M., and A. K. Sen, eds. 1993. *The quality of life.* Oxford, UK: Clarendon Press.

Ok, E. 1995. Fuzzy measurement of income inequality: A class of fuzzy inequality measures. *Social Choice and Welfare* 12:111–36.

Pattanaik, P., and Y. Xu. 1990. On ranking opportunity sets in terms of freedom of choice. *Recherches Economiques de Louvain* 56:383–90.

Plott, C. 1978. Rawls' theory of justice: An impossibility result. In *Decision theory and social ethics,* edited by H. W. Gottinger and W. Leinfellner. Dordrecht: Reidel.

Puppe, C. 1995. Freedom of choice and rational decisions. *Social Choice and Welfare* 12:137–53.

Putnam, R., R. Leonardi, and R. Y. Nanetti. 1993. *Making democracy work: Civic traditions in modern Italy.* Princeton, N.J.: Princeton University Press.

Rawls, J. 1971. *A theory of justice.* Cambridge, Mass.: Harvard University Press.

Robbins, L. 1938. Interpersonal comparisons of utility: A comment. *Economic Journal* 48:635–41.

Runciman, W. G. 1966. *Relative deprivation and social justice.* London: Routledge.

Samuelson, P. A. 1947. *Foundations of economic analysis.* Cambridge, Mass.: Harvard University Press.

Sen, A. K. 1970a. *Collective choice and social welfare.* San Francisco: Holden-Day. Republished Amsterdam: North-Holland, 1979.

——. 1970b. Interpersonal aggregation and partial comparability. *Econometrica* 38:393–409.

——. 1973. *On economic inequality.* Oxford, UK: Clarendon Press.

——. 1976. Real national income. *Review of Economic Studies* 43:19–39.

——. 1979. The welfare basis of real income comparisons: A survey. *Journal of Economic Literature* 17:1–45.

——. 1980. Equality of what? In *Tanner lectures on human values,* edited by S. McMurrin. Cambridge, UK: Cambridge University Press.

——. 1981. Public action and the quality of life in developing countries. *Oxford Bulletin of Economics and Statistics* 43:287–319.

——. 1982. *Choice, welfare and measurement.* Oxford: Blackwell.

——. 1984. *Resources, values and development.* Oxford: Blackwell.

——. 1985a. *Commodities and capabilities.* Amsterdam: North-Holland.

——. 1985b. Well-being, agency and freedom: The Dewey lectures 1984. *Journal of Philosophy* 82:169–221.

——. 1987. *The standard of living,* edited by G. Hawthorn, and with comments from K. Hart, R. Kanbur, J. Muellbauer, and B. Williams. Cambridge, UK: Cambridge University Press.

——. 1990. Gender and cooperative conflict. In *Persistent inequalities,* edited by Irene Tinker. New York: Oxford University Press.

——. 1991a. Welfare, preference and freedom. *Journal of Econometrics* 50:15–29.

——. 1991b. On indexing primary goods and capabilities. Unpublished paper, Harvard University, Cambridge, Mass.

——. 1992. *Inequality reexamined.* Oxford: Oxford University Press

——. 1993. The economics of life and death. *Scientific American* 268 (May): 40–47.

——. 1995a. Demography and welfare economics. *Empirica* 22:1–21.

——. 1995b. Rationality and social choice. *American Economic Review* 85:1–24.

——. 1997. Inequality, unemployment and contemporary Europe. Paper presented at the Calouste Oulbenkian Conference on A Joint Europe, May 1997. *International Labour Review* 136 (2).

——. 1998. Mortality as an indicator of economic success or failure. *Economic Journal* 108 (446): 1–25.

Shorrocks, A. F. 1995. Inequality and welfare comparisons for heterogeneous populations. Unpublished paper, Department of Economics, University of Essex, UK.

Smith, A. 1776. *An inquiry into the nature and causes of the wealth of nations,* edited by R. Campbell and A. S. Skinner. Oxford: Clarendon Press.

Suppes, P. 1987. Maximizing freedom of decision: An axiomatic analysis. In *Arrow and the foundations of economic policy,* edited by G. R. Feiwel. London: Macmillan.

Townsend, P. 1979. *Poverty in the United Kingdom.* London: Penguin Books.

UNDP. 1990. *Human development report.* New York: Oxford University Press.

——. 1995. *Human development report.* New York: Oxford University Press.

——. 1997. *Human development report.* New York: Oxford University Press.

U.S. Department of Health and Human Services. 1996. *Health, United States 1995.* Hyattsville, Md.: U.S. Department of Health and Human Services.

World Bank. 1996. *World development report.* New York: Oxford University Press.

World Health Organization (WHO). 1994. *World health statistics annual 1994.* Geneva: World Health Organization.

Racial and Ethnic Economic Inequality
A Cross-National Perspective

WILLIAM A. DARITY, JR.

Orthodox economic theory denies the persistence of employment discrimination in markets. Neoclassical microeconomics really cannot be massaged to produce a convincing story of why members of productively equivalent but ascriptively different groups experience widely disparate economic outcomes. Even the best story modern marginalists have to offer, the statistical discrimination hypothesis, does not wash well.

If members of two groups — call them group A and group B — share the same frequency distributions of ability to perform a job, employers should learn this is the case over time. Conventional theory would then lead us to conclude that employers should become indifferent between the prospects of hiring persons from either group. In contrast, if members of each group come from populations with different frequency distributions of ability to perform a job, then the statistical theory of discrimination does not actually offer a theory of market-based, group-linked discrimination at all. The assumption of similarity in ability or productivity is suspended. Sustained observed differences in economic outcomes can be attributed either to an induced or to an inherent deficiency in the group with inferior outcomes. In the jargon of orthodoxy, the laggard group has a comparative deficiency in human capital.

But the empirical record displays widespread evidence of a gap in treatment of members of ascriptively distinct groups even after controlling for productivity-linked differences — evidence of raw discriminatory differentials across groups, across countries, and across time. Moreover, there is no consistent evidence that the discriminatory differentials necessarily decline in magnitude over time, even in market-based economies.

The strongest cross-national evidence of discrimination can be found in direct results of audit studies. These are studies designed and executed to detect explicit instances of discriminatory behavior by employers, mortgage lenders, and real estate agents. Tests have been administered in the United States of America, Britain, and Australia (see Riach and Rich 1991–1992, Mincy 1993, Fix et al. 1993). The tests have involved both the use of the correspondence technique and trained actors of different races or ethnicities who make direct contact with potential employers or other economic agents. The evidence from these tests demonstrates clear patterns of racial and ethnic preference by the agents in question, regardless of the comparative qualifications of the applicants. Indeed, significant rates of discrimination against nonwhites were detected in both the private and public sectors in these countries, despite the presence of antidiscrimination legislation in all three (see Riach and Rich 1991–1992: 341–342).

Therefore, the theoretical task in economics is to develop a convincing story that explains why discrimination can remain a force in market-based economies with profit-seeking employers. The thrust of a major phase of my own research (Darity and Williams 1985, Darity 1989, Darity and Mason 1998), in conjunction with other "outcast economists" such as Patrick Mason (1992) and the late Rhonda Williams (1997), has been to reconsider the concept of competition on a non-neoclassical basis as the pivot for reconstruction of the economic theory of discrimination. We have turned instead to the classical and Marxist traditions and have built a theoretical framework that emphasizes the functional role that discrimination plays in preserving place and privilege for the dominant group. We also have developed a theory of sustained discrimination applicable to market-based economies that is not plagued by the theoretical inconsistencies of the neoclassical approach.

Our framework is open to the induced deficiency hypothesis by restoring a variant of the old notion of "noncompeting groups." A noncompeting group can be produced by the actions of a rival group that seeks to exclude them on the basis of race or ethnicity from preferred jobs, quality schooling, credentials, and, in general, higher social status (Lewis 1979). Recognition of the idea of noncompeting groups and their genesis blurs the line orthodox economics has sought to draw so intensely between discriminatory mechanisms that shape human capital as purely premarket or extramarket phenomena and economic discrimination as a market-based phenomenon. Orthodox theory patently denies the persistence of the latter. But a theory that incorporates the idea of produced noncompeting groups admits both types of discrimination into the same picture.

A still evolving body of works that is comparative and cross-national is providing information and evidence consistent with the proposition that inter-racial/interethnic discrimination in markets is a general and sustained con-dition across time and space. The assembly of this body of work began in an undergraduate course on intergroup economic disparity that I taught at the University of North Carolina at Chapel Hill (UNC) in 1994–1995. During the following academic years, I directed a faculty-graduate student seminar at UNC under the auspices of the Center for International Studies that ex-plored ethnic and racial economic disparity across countries. The seminar met twenty-one times. A representative session would be the one held May 24, 1996, on the theme of remedies for intergroup disparity. There were three presenters at that session: Marc Galanter, a University of Wisconsin law pro-fessor, who examined the application of the compensatory discrimination or "reservations" scheme on behalf of the scheduled castes in India; Cecilia Con-rad, an economist at Pomona College, who reported on her research measur-ing the aggregate benefits and costs of affirmative action in the United States and on the projected effects of the retreat from affirmative action in the Cali-fornia and Texas systems of higher education; and Karen Gibson, then a fellow with the seminar and an urban planner, who critically assessed the racial impact of policies advanced in the United States ostensibly intended to address the plight of the urban underclass.

Throughout the year numerous scholars reported on their research on a variety of cases of intergroup disparity across the globe. These included: Mari-lyn Lashley and Arthur Goldsmith who addressed the status of aboriginal peoples in New Zealand and Australia, respectively. John Choonoo and Fred-erick Kustaa who examined the relative economic status of black and colored peoples in pre- and postapartheid South Africa. Kustaa also provided a histor-ical perspective on education of blacks throughout southern Africa, particu-larly the role of missionary schools. James Stewart, Rhonda Williams, and Patrick Mason provided a comprehensive analysis of competing economic theories of discrimination. Stephanie Lawson explored the political dimen-sions of ethnic animosities in the Fiji Islands between the native Fijians and the ethnic East Indian Fijians.

Mahmood Mamdani and Catherine Newbury analyzed the roots of geno-cidal violence between the Hutus and Tutsis in Rwanda and Burundi. Iren Omo-Bare discussed the spatial dimensions, political patronage effects, and economic consequences of ethnic divisions in Nigeria. Lydia Lindsey presented her findings on the historical experience of West Indian immigrants to Britain, while Suzanne Model presented her research on Caribbean immigrants to the United States. Francisco Rivera-Batiz presented his work on immigration from Latin America to Puerto Rico and on ethnic economic inequality on the island. Herman Kurthen and Ira Gang described the nature of division and disparity between native-born and foreign-born workers in Germany.

Subsequently, I continued to offer the course both at the undergraduate and graduate levels at both UNC and Duke University. During the 1999–2000 academic year I also directed a seminar at UNC more broadly on the topic of race itself which provided a vehicle to examine the work not only of social scientists but also physical anthropologists, cultural anthropologists, literary critics, historians, political scientists, geographers, sociologists and evolutionary biologists. In this context, additional research was presented that contributed to the catalogue of international work on intergroup disparity. For example, the anthropologists France Twine and Jonathan Warren provided rich insights about the construction of race and patterns of social stratification in Brazil. Twine also examined the education of West Indian youths in Britain as a noncompeting group via the operation of the system of schooling in the context of her broader study of white birth mothers of black children in that country. Another anthropologist, Karla Slocum, provided a critical review of the literature on immigration, group mobility, and social stratification. Economist Ashwini Deshpande presented her research on caste disparity in India using data from the most recent National Family Health Survey and the National Sample Survey. Geographer Minelle Mahtani presented her hypotheses about racism and occupational stratification in the news media sector of Canada, and Patrick Mason provided the most substantial empirical examination of the role of culture and family values on economic outcomes available to date using data from the Panel Study of Income Dynamics.

Several important questions emerged from the two seminars and the classes. Two major questions were prompted by the conditions in Rwanda, Burundi, and the former Yugoslavia were the following: First, what are the precise circumstances under which ethnic and racial divisions descend into civil war or genocidal measures by one group toward another, and second, to what extent does economic disparity play an important role as a precipitant of such intergroup hostilities? Further questions that emerged included the following: Does intergroup disparity cause intergroup animosity, or does intergroup animosity lead to intergroup disparity? Does intergroup disparity tend to widen or narrow over time, that is, do groups that comprise a society tend to diverge or converge? For the United States, the latter question is partially addressed in work by George Borjas (1992), using data primarily on white ethnic immigrants from the National Longitudinal Survey of Youth (NLSY). Borjas seeks to identify the cross-generational effects of what he terms "ethnic capital." He provides a pessimistic answer for the United States. Convergence will be slow, if it occurs at all, since he finds evidence of substantial intergenerational drag. Borjas demonstrates that ethnic affiliation can affect economic performance favorably or unfavorably across several generations. The characteristics an ethnic group possessed two and three generations past can influence outcomes for their descendants today. In a new study Jason Dietrich, David Guilkey, and I (Darity, Dietrich, and Guilkey forthcoming), using decennial U.S. census data spanning 1880 through 1990, have found enormous adverse effects on the contemporary occupational status of members of a given ethnic or racial group of the discrimination faced by their ancestors a century earlier. This, again, is not salutary evidence of convergence.

Whether one perceives a trend suggestive of convergence or divergence frequently depends upon the measure chosen to assess relative progress for the lagging group. For example, the case for dramatic black economic progress in the United States since the 1940s, enunciated so forcefully by the Thernstroms (1997), is contingent on a focus limited to individual wage and earnings data by race and on ignoring the disproportionately higher presence of zero-earners among blacks. If one chooses to look instead at relative family incomes, a much less salutary picture emerges; black family incomes have hovered around 60 percent of white family incomes throughout the post–World War II era. More astonishing still is the evidence that the black-white per capita income ratio was virtually the same in 1990 as it was in 1880. And no scholar can make a serious claim that blacks are closing the wealth gap with nonblacks in the United States.

Furthermore, there is at least one country, New Zealand, where intergroup disparity unambiguously has widened over the past twenty-five years. This is ironic since New Zealand may have had the lowest degree of measured intergroup inequality of any country in the world in the early 1970s. At the time average Maori incomes were roughly on a par with Europeans, and Pacific Islanders had slightly higher mean and median incomes than both of the other two groups. By the 1990s a significant gap had opened favoring New Zealanders of European ancestry.

What happened? First, at the behest of the International Monetary Fund, New Zealand adopted a stringent austerity program in the mid-1980s that led to sharp reductions in social transfer payments. The Maori community, relative to Europeans, had relied disproportionately on transfer payments as a source of income due to their higher poverty rate (Martin 1995). Second, the austerity program led to higher unemployment, which had a sharper adverse impact on the Maori (as well as the Pacific Islanders) than the Europeans. Third, the educational discrepancy between Europeans and the other two groups widened between the 1970s and 1990s (Lashley 1995a). Fourth, the situation was compounded by pronounced evidence of ongoing discrimination against the Maoris; their "human capital is not compensated equally" with that of the Europeans (Lashley 1995b: 15).

In contrast, official statistics provide evidence of closure of the interracial gap in income and wealth between ethnic Malays and Chinese in Malaysia. The first phase of Malaysian affirmative action under the New Economic Policy (NEP) directed specifically at the native Malay spanned the years 1971–1990. During that period, government statistics indicate that the Malay/Chinese monthly income ratio rose from 0.46 in 1957–58 to 0.57 in 1984. The Malaysian economy grew rapidly, also, at a 4.6 percent rate between 1975 and 1994. It would appear that the combination of the NEP and rapid economic growth contributed to closure of the gap between the two groups.

However, retrospective work histories provided in the independently gathered Second Malaysian Family Life Survey (MFLS2) completed in 1989 suggest the opposite. Malay men appear to be falling significantly behind Chinese men in earnings and slightly behind Indian men (Gallup 1997). Furthermore, there is strong evidence of private sector discrimination against Malay men, despite Malay control over the state sector and civil service (Gallup 1997). And, even based upon government statistics, the intragroup distribution of income did not improve in Malaysia. The officially reported Gini index for Malay household income rose from .34 to .47. Sundaram and Shari (1986: 6) conclude that this rise in intragroup inequality was not unique to the ethnic Malays; it also occurred for ethnic Chinese and ethnic Indian households as well. But they conclude that the pattern for ethnic Malays "may have been primarily due to the relatively rapid growth of the Malay-dominated bureaucracy (with the 'Malayanization' of the civil service after independence) and the miniscule Malay capital-owning class."

Typically a small proportion of the adults in an ethnic/racial group will fill civil service positions. If there is a sharp wedge between the income afforded by public sector employment and the income afforded by private sector employment for members of the group, the initial entry of the group's members into the bureaucratic apparatus will have an unequalizing effect. Intragroup inequality will be compounded if the spoils of bureaucratic control are allocated narrowly to civil service employees, their relatives, and their personal friends. Indeed, Sundaram and Shari (1986) assert that gains from the NEP were concentrated excessively among a small ethnic Malay elite with direct links to the state bureaucracy. There are strong reasons to believe that this was especially true of the wealth redistribution component of the NEP. While the ethnic Malays, the numerical majority in a country with a parliamentary system of government, controlled the state bureaucracy, historically, the ethnic Chinese dominated the commercial sector. Ethnic East Indians have long been the odd man out. The NEP included a policy of redistribution of ownership shares of Malaysian corporations toward ethnic Malays.

Mobilization of the state to execute redistributive measures on behalf of a specific ethnic or racial group is not unique to Malaysia. In the most extreme case, the apartheid regime in South Africa practiced a venomous form of racialized socialism on behalf of the white minority, a mere 13 percent of the population, for about half a century. Group targeted social policies are evident in the switch back and forth from Afro-Guyanese to Indo-Guyanese control over Guyana's government, in the precoup spoils system conducted by the Americo-Liberians in Liberia, and in preindependence Tutsi dominance and postindependence Hutu dominance of Rwanda's state bureaucracy.

Ethnic control over the military also is important in these contexts. In all of these cases high degrees of interethnic tension typically prevail, but there is less explosive relevance for economists interested in the alleged stylized facts of growth and development. Harewood and Henry (1982) has hypothesized that in racially or ethnically plural societies, where the state can become a direct instrument for intergroup redistribution, Kuznets' familiar inverted U relationship between per capita income and inequality will suffice no longer. According to Henry, there could be a series of inverted U's. As a country experiences economic growth its overall size distribution of income will be affected by changes in the intragroup distributions which, in turn, will be influenced by which group is best able to mobilize the state as its redistributive agent.

Easterly and Levine (1997) have proposed, as a general principle, that the greater the degree of ethnic diversity in a country, the lower the growth rate. They build their argument around the ethnic struggles to control the state and the associated rent-seeking which they contend produces inefficiencies. Hence, their claim is the more diverse a country the worse it will do economically. They argue that this is especially pertinent to countries in Africa where growth has been slow, on a continent which they contend is characterized by the highest degree of ethnic diversity internationally. Robert Bates (2000) has challenged their position. What may reduce growth, he argues, is not ethnic diversity per se or ethnic tension per se but political violence. He demonstrates empirically that political violence does not follow lockstep from ethnic diversity or tension. Nor does political violence follow from intergroup disparity, that is, sharp racial differences in economic outcomes in Brazil have not translated into antiracist political movements of any significance. Indeed, political violence may not require much ethnic diversity, if any. Thus, for Bates, there is no systematic relationship between ethnic diversity or disparity and economic growth.

In another recent study, Jessica Nembhard and I (Darity and Nembhard 2000) examined twelve countries "where we could find data of a reasonable quality that measure the gap between economically subaltern and dominant groups" to address the reverse causal question. We wanted to see whether countries with higher levels of economic development or higher rates of economic growth tended to have lower or falling levels of intergroup disparity. We found no connection between economic development or economic growth and reduced racial or ethnic economic inequality. In fact, in at least one case, South Africa, very slow economic growth was accompanied by reduced intergroup disparity, obviously attributable to the dismantling of apartheid.

In contrast, economic growth did facilitate the redistribution of wealth that took place in Malaysia. Best estimates of the increase in the ethnic Malay share in ownership of Malaysian corporations indicate a rise from about 2 percent in 1970 to about 20 percent in 1990. Surprisingly, the same estimates indicate there was a slight rise in the ethnic Chinese share over the same interval. How could the ethnic Malays achieve a tenfold increase in their ownership share and the ethnic Chinese still experience a mild increase in their proportion of holdings? Part of the answer is the fact that Malaysia underwent a period of marked economic prosperity. Corporate valuation rose sharply as did the number of enterprises making public issues. Therefore, the ethnic Malays could attain a large gain in wealth without reducing the relative wealth of the ethnic Chinese. The pie grew sufficiently to permit a much larger slice to go to the ethnic Malays without reducing the slice going to the ethnic Chinese. The other part of the answer is one group did experience a significant reduction in their ownership share in Malaysian corporations over the two decades of the NEP. These were foreign owners, in all likelihood, primarily British owners of claims on Malaysian corporations.

The assets newly acquired on behalf of the native Malays initially have been held in a government trust, and their disbursement across the ethnic Malays has been the object of much controversy. The entire process can be viewed as a means of enrichment of a minority of ethnic Malays, rather than the entire ethnic Malay community. But it is not clear that there is any instance where group advance also has been accompanied by a more equal distribution of income within the group.

In virtually all countries where statistical investigations have been conducted to estimate the degree of discrimination against a subaltern group, market-based discrimination has been found. The list of countries includes

Brazil, Israel, South Africa, India, Malaysia, Trinidad and Tobago, and the United States (Darity and Nembhard 2000). In the limited number of cases where there are studies taken at different points in time, little evidence supports the view that discrimination necessarily tends to decline over time.

Perhaps most disturbing among these studies is George Sherer's (2000) finding that although the South African racial wage gap has closed modestly, the portion of the gap that can be attributed to discrimination has increased in the postapartheid era. U.S. data suggests that the sharpest decrease in discrimination against blacks took place during the ten years following the passage of the Civil Rights Act of 1964. Thereafter, the most careful studies indicate that the degree of discrimination stabilized up through the mid-1990s, costing black men 12–15 percent in earnings (Darity and Mason 1998).

Nelson do Valle Silva's (1985) study using surveys taken in 1960 and 1976 was intended to address two propositions widely held among Brazilians. First is the proposition that Brazil is a "racial democracy," a society where race is irrelevant to social mobility and where only class matters. Second is the proposition that Brazil possesses a "mulatto escape hatch" or, through amalgamation, that "lightening" or "whitening" will occur. Mulatto Brazilians ostensibly face a more open opportunity structure than black Brazilians. Of course, the idea that Brazil is a "racial democracy" is oddly inconsistent with the "mulatto escape hatch" proposition. Why would an escape hatch be needed in a society where race (or color) is irrelevant?

What does Silva discover? First, both blacks and mulattos received much lower earnings than whites in 1960 and 1976. Furthermore, a significant portion of the gap could be attributed to differential treatment or discrimination. Thus, Silva rejects the notion that Brazil is a racial democracy. Second, economic outcomes for blacks and mulattos were so similar in both years that Silva concluded that it would be legitimate to cluster the two groups together as nonwhites. Paradoxically, his research suggested that there was slightly more discrimination against mulattos than blacks in Brazil. Therefore, Silva also rejects the "mulatto escape hatch" proposition.

While I am convinced that Silva's findings demolish the "racial democracy" proposition, I am more skeptical that he has eliminated the "mulatto escape hatch" proposition. Both he and Peggy Lovell (1993) consistently find that Brazilians who self-report their race as mulatto earn somewhat more than Brazilians who self-report themselves as black. But Telles and Lim (1997) also report results from a 1995 urban survey that provides both interviewer (self) and interviewee (social) classification of race. They find that self-identification underestimates white income and overestimates black and brown incomes relative to interviewer classification. Mulattos still earn more than blacks, but

Telles and Lim find that the relative discriminatory differentials are more costly for blacks than mulattos. It is possible that the relative degree of discrimination against blacks and mulattos has changed since the 1960s and 1970s versus the 1990s. Silva used a 1.27 percent subsample of the 1960 Brazilian census to look at racial inequality in Rio de Janeiro. He found that 14.6 percent of the gap in income between blacks and whites was due to discrimination while 17.6 percent of the gap in mulatto and white incomes was due to discrimination. The loss in income for mulattos and blacks due to discrimination — Silva's estimate of the cost of being nonwhite in Rio de Janeiro in 1960 — was 955 cruzeiros or about $181 U.S. per month at the time. Silva's 1976 data were drawn from the National Household Survey (PNAD). Silva finds that the gap in income between nonwhites and whites narrowed, but a larger proportion of the gap was due to discrimination. The cost of being nonwhite in Brazil had fallen to 566 cruzeiros, but 32.9 percent of the mulatto-white income gap and 26.3 percent of the black-white income gap was due to discrimination. However, the 1976 findings are not strictly comparable with the 1960 results, since the latter were limited to Rio de Janeiro while the former were based upon nationwide data. In addition, the PNAD survey included questions about father's occupation and schooling. These variables were included in the underlying regressions Silva estimated to generate his statistical estimates of discrimination for 1976 but not for 1960, since they were not available in the 1960 census. Peggy Lovell's (1993) study using the 0.8 percent subsample of the 1980 Brazilian census provides further evidence on the magnitude of discrimination in earnings specific to the Rio de Janeiro region. She finds that close to 50 percent of the gap in earnings for mulattos and 41 percent of the gap in earnings for blacks in Rio was due to discrimination. If anything, the Brazilian data are suggestive of an intensification of discrimination over time, perhaps even going hand in hand with a narrowing of the interracial earnings gap. Indeed, roughly speaking, in 1980 in those regions of Brazil where the nonwhite-white gap in average annual earnings was smallest and where nonwhites were less represented in the population, Lovell's estimates of the portion of the earnings gap due to discrimination were the highest. For example, in Salvador, the region with the greatest relative concentration of Afro-Brazilians, less than 1 percent of the black-white earnings gap could be assigned to discrimination, while in predominantly Euro-Brazilian Porto Alegre, 70 percent of the black-white earnings gap could be assigned to discrimination (Lovell 1993: 93). While Lovell's primary objective was to demonstrate the racially disparate impact of national Brazilian development policy, that is, development policy that promoted industrialization of the south (the relatively whiter regions of Brazil), her evidence on discrimination suggest the functionality hypothesis: discrimination is exercised most forcefully when it is "needed" by the dominant group. The largest absolute income gaps between nonwhites and whites are found in Salvador, but there one also finds the widest interracial gap in human capital endowments. Whites hardly need to discriminate at the point of employment if the human capital characteristics of blacks and mulattos are so systematically depressed relative to whites that blacks and mulattos are not competing for the same tier of jobs.

A study using 1970 survey data in Delhi, India, by Dhesi and Singh (1989) is also suggestive of the functional endogeneity of discrimination for the discriminators. From this perspective, discrimination is much more than a matter of mere "taste"; it is a serviceable method of preserving advantage and rewards for members of a particular group. Dhesi and Singh find comparatively low levels of measurable discrimination against members of the Hindus scheduled castes, the strata of Delhi's population predominantly consisting of the untouchables. The highest relative levels of discrimination appear to go against the Sikhs, while Hindu Brahmins actually appear to receive nepotistic advantage, or positive discrimination, from their position at the top of the Hindu scheme of social stratification.

My interpretation is the Hindu upper castes in Delhi in 1970 had no reason to execute strong discriminatory measures against members of the Hindu scheduled castes because the latter had been so severely deprived educationally that they were rarely in the running for many of the positions preferred by upper-caste Hindus. The Sikhs, on the other hand, did possess the credentials to compete for similar positions regularly; hence they would be subject to more direct forms of exclusion.

Finally, a study using data from the 1880, 1900, and 1910 U.S. censuses (Darity, Dietrich, and Guilkey 1997) provides further reinforcement for the functional endogeneity of discrimination. Using Duncan's socioeconomic status index as the outcome variable, we find a rise in lost status for black males ages 25–64 from discrimination during the period. Simultaneously, the literacy rate among black men rose dramatically from about 25 percent to more than 60 percent. A straightforward interpretation is that employment discrimination hardened precisely while black men were becoming less distinguishable from other American males in terms of their human capital endowments.

What can we conclude? The cross-national data does not indicate that incomes of ascriptively differentiated groups necessarily converge over time in the modern world. Nor is a higher level of economic development or a higher rate of economic growth necessarily associated with lower levels of intergroup inequality. The presumption in orthodox economics is that discrimination should decline over time in market-based economies. But the available cross-national evidence does not support this presumption either. Evidence from India, Brazil, and the United States points toward recasting discrimination as both functional and endogenous rather than being a matter of an exogenously held "taste" or "preference."

The state can play a fundamental role in shaping both the interracial and intraracial distributions of income and wealth. The dynamics of growth and inequality in ethnically plural societies obviates the basis for the conventional Kuznets' inverted U hypothesis. Discrimination, unfortunately, is a persistent and ongoing phenomenon on a global scale.

References

Bates, Robert H. "Ethnicity and Development in Africa: A Reappraisal." *American Economic Review: Papers and Proceedings* 90:2 (May 2000): 131–134.

Borjas, George J. "Ethnic Capital and Intergenerational Mobility." *Quarterly Journal of Economics* (February 1992): 123–150.

Darity, William A., Jr. "What's Left of the Economic Theory of Discrimination?" in Steven Shulman and William Darity, Jr. (eds.), *The Question of Discrimination: Racial Inequality in the U.S. Labor Market.* Middletown, Conn.: Wesleyan University Press, 1989, 335–374.

Darity, William A., Jr., Jason Dietrich, and David Guilkey. "Persistent Advantage or Disadvantage? Evidence in Support of the Intergenerational Drag Hypothesis." *American Journal of Economics and Sociology* 60:2 (2001): 435–470.

———. "Racial and Ethnic Inequality in the United States: A Secular Perspective." *American Economic Review: Papers and Proceedings* 87:2 (May 1997): 301–305.

Darity, William A., Jr., and Jessica Nembhard. "Racial and Ethnic Economic Inequality: The International Record." *American Economic Review: Papers and Proceedings* 90:2 (May 2000): 308–311.

Darity, William A., Jr. and Rhonda Williams. "Peddlers Forever? Culture, Competition, Discrimination." *American Economic Review: Papers and Proceedings* 75:2 (May 1985): 256–271.

Deshpande, Ashwini. "Caste at Birth? Redefining Disparity in India." *Review of Development Economics* 5:1 (2001): 130–144.

Dhesi, A., and Harbhajan Singh. "Education, Labour Market Distortions and Relative Earnings of Different Religion-Caste Categories in India (A Case Study of Delhi)." *Canadian Journal of Development Studies* (1989): 75–89.

Easterly, William, and Ross Levine. "Africa's Growth Tragedy: Policies and Ethnic Divisions." *Quarterly Journal of Economics* 112:4 (November 1997): 1203–1250.

Fix, Michael, George C. Galster, and Raymond J. Struyk. "An Overview of Auditing for Discrimination," in Michael Fix and Raymond Struyk (eds.), *Clear and Convincing Evidence: Measurement of Discrimination in America.* Washington, D.C.: Urban Institute Press, 1993, 165–186.

Gallup, John Luke. "Ethnicity and Earnings in Malaysia." Development Discussion Paper No. 593, Harvard Institute of International Development, July 1997.

Harewood, Jack, and Ralph Henry. "Inequality in a Postcolonial Society: Trinidad and Tobago, 1956–1981." University of the West Indies at St.Augustine: Institute of Social and Economic Studies, 1982.

Lashley, Marilyn. "Balanced Budgets, Social Welfare Policy Reform and Unbalanced Costs: The Americanization of New Zealand in the Wake of the Great 'Experiment.'" Unpublished manuscript, 1995a.

——. "No Tangible Assets." Keynote address for the Population Association of New Zealand, University of Canterbury, New Zealand, 1995b.

Lewis, W. Arthur. "The Dual Economy Revisited." *Manchester School* 47:3 (1979): 211–229.

Lovell, Peggy. "Development and Discrimination." *Development and Change* 24 (1993): 83–101.

Martin, Barry. "The New Zealand Family and Economic Restructuring in the 1980s." Population Studies Centre Discussion Paper No. 4, University of Waikato, New Zealand, May 1995.

Mason, Patrick. "The Divide-and-Conquer and Employer/Employee Model of Discrimination: Neoclassical Competition as a Familial Defect." *Review of Black Political Economy* 20:4 (Spring 1992): 73–89.

Mincy, Ronald B. "The Urban Institute Audit Studies: Their Research and Policy Context," in Michael Fix and Raymond J. Struyk (eds.), *Clear and Convincing Evidence: Measurement of Discrimination in America*. Washington, D.C.: Urban Institute Press, 1993, 165–186.

Riach, Peter A., and Judith Rich. "Measuring Discrimination by Direct Experimental Methods: Seeking Gunsmoke." *Journal of Post Keynesian Economics* 14:2 (Winter 1991–92): 143–150.

Sherer, George. "Intergroup Economic Inequality in South Africa: The Post-Apartheid Era." *American Economic Review: Papers and Proceedings* 90:2 (May 2000): 317–321.

Silva, Nelson do Valle. "Updating the Cost of Not Being White in Brazil," in Pierre Michel-Fontaine (ed.), *Race, Class and Power in Brazil*. Los Angeles: CAAS, 1985, 25–40.

Sundaram, Jomo K., and Ishak Shari. *Development Policies and Income Inequality in Peninsular Malaysia*. Kuala Lumpur: Institute of Advanced Studies, 1986.

Telles, Edward, and Nelson Lim. "Does Who Classify Race Matter? Self vs. Social Classification of Race and Racial Income Inequality in Brazil." Unpublished manuscript, Department of Sociology, UCLA, April 25, 1997.

Thernstrom, Abigail, and Stephan Thernstrom. "The Real Story of Black Progress," *Wall Street Journal*, September 3, 1997, A20.

Williams, Rhonda M. "Capital, Competition and Discrimination: A Reconsideration of Racial Earnings Inequality." *Review of Racial Political Economics* 19:2 (1987): 1–15.

PART **II**

Issues in Measurement of Inequality and Poverty

Measuring Poverty
Issues and Approaches

DANIEL H. WEINBERG

History

The official poverty thresholds used presently by the U.S. Census Bureau to measure poverty have their basis in seminal papers by Orshansky (1963, 1965). At that time, the major attempt to quantify the number and distribution of the poor was given by tabulations published from the 1960 Census. In addition, several 1960s reports from the Current Population Survey (CPS) that provided the number of families with incomes below $3,000 and unrelated individuals with incomes below $1,500 (see U.S. Census Bureau, 1965, 1969).

The key problem with the concept used in the Census and CPS tabulations was that both small and large families with, say, $2,900 of income were assumed to be poor. There was no explicit relationship to any measure of need. In contrast, Orshansky's method had thresholds that increased with family size so that to be out of poverty, larger families needed more income than smaller ones.

Orshansky started with a set of minimally adequate short-term food budgets calculated for families of various sizes and composition by the U.S. Department of Agriculture for 1961. Based on evidence from the 1955 Household Food Consumption Survey, she determined that, for the typical family, food represented about one-third of after-tax income. This relationship yielded a "multiplier" of three, that is, the minimally adequate food budgets were multiplied by a factor of three to obtain 124 poverty thresholds that differed by family size, number of children, age and sex of head, and farm or nonfarm residence (adjustments were made for families of size one and two). These proposed thresholds were viewed as reasonable partly because the threshold for a family of four (close to the median family size at the time) was $3,130, close to the $3,000 figure used in the 1960 Census tabulations and the 1965 CPS publication.

As President Lyndon Johnson's "War on Poverty" was just beginning, there was a great interest in measuring its progress, hence, Orshansky's measure of poverty was widely used by policy makers at the Council of Economic Advisers and other researchers. Attempts to update the poverty scale to account for inflation in the 1960s used increases in the price of food to inflate the minimal food budget, maintaining the multiplier of three. In 1969, the U.S. Bureau of the Budget (now the Office of Management and Budget) adopted Orshansky's measure as the government's standard measure of poverty, mandating that inflation be measured using the Consumer Price Index (CPI), published by the U.S. Bureau of Labor Statistics (BLS). With only minor modifications since then (mostly reducing the number of categories, now 48), the Orshansky thresholds still form the basis of the official poverty statistics.[1]

The U.S. Census Bureau publishes statistics annually using the CPS, a household survey of roughly 50,000 households conducted monthly mainly to determine the nation's unemployment rate. The Annual Social and Economic Supplement (ASEC) provides the income data necessary to determine poverty statistics. Official poverty rates show a steady decline from 1959 to 1973, decreasing from 22.4 percent to 11.1 percent.[2] The poverty rate remained at roughly that level until 1978. From 1978 to 1983, the poverty rate increased by roughly one-third, rising from 11.4 percent to 15.2 percent. From 1983 to 1989, the poverty rate declined, reaching 12.8 percent in 1989. The peak since then was 15.1 percent in 1993, declining to 11.3 percent in 2000, statistically equal to the 1973 level. The poverty rate increased to 11.8 percent in 2001 (Proctor and Dalaker, 2001).

Current Issues

Serious examinations of the poverty thresholds were undertaken in 1969, 1976, 1980, 1990, and 1995. One of the most thorough was the work of a 1976 government task force, the findings of which (and 17 background working papers) were published in a series of volumes titled *The Measure of Poverty* (U.S. Department of Health and Human Services, 1976). Some minor changes in the methodology of measurement resulted, but there was no comprehensive redefinition. The 1990 interagency task force had a much less broad mandate than the 1976 group. It developed a draft research agenda and recommendations that would review current and alternative measures of income and poverty.[3] The most recent is an examination of the concept of poverty by the Committee on National Statistics of the National Academy of Sciences.[4] Their recent report will be discussed in detail below.

When considering the adequacy of official poverty thresholds, it is important to realize that we cannot separate the issue of income measurement from the definition of poverty. When we define the level of resources required to be nonpoor, we must also determine which resources are to be counted. Hence, the discussion that follows covers both income measurement and poverty definition issues.

The first decision involves whether to use an absolute or relative measure of poverty. A relative measure sets the poverty standard at a fixed fraction, say 50 percent, of some measure of the population's well-being such as median family income. Thus, with a relative measure poverty declines only if incomes of families at the bottom of the income distribution improve relative to the rest of the distribution. In 1965, the poverty threshold for a family of four was 45.0 percent of median income; by 1989 this percentage had fallen to 37.0 percent (and was 28.9 percent for a family of three).[5] By 1994, the percentages had returned roughly to its 1965 level — 46.9 percent for a family of four (and 36.6 percent for a family of three).

The European Community often uses relative thresholds to facilitate cross-national comparisons since absolute income levels differ markedly among member countries (see O'Higgins and Jenkins, 1990). Use of relative thresholds within an individual country is less common, as relative thresholds provide a moving target. In good economic times income rises, raising relative thresholds, and making a specific level of poverty reduction harder to achieve. In addition, economic slowdowns may produce what the public perceives as perverse results — poverty declining during a period of recession (as median income falls, usually faster than incomes of those at the bottom end). Only the United Kingdom publishes a relative poverty measure — Households Below Average Income — on a regular basis; Canada publishes households with incomes below "Low Income Cutoffs" from time to time (Burtless and Smeeding, 2000).

The alternative method of measuring poverty and the one currently in use in the United States (at least in theory) is more or less an absolute one (the U.S. is the only country other than the United Kingdom that publishes a poverty estimate on a regular basis). When constructing an absolute measure, one attempts to measure minimal consumption levels of as many goods as possible. The cost of that consumption bundle is then increased to account for necessary goods not included by use of a "multiplier." Orshansky measured only the cost of a minimally adequate diet. Other proposals have suggested adding shelter, clothing, and medical care to the list. We limit our discussion here to absolute measures; most observers expect the U.S. poverty concept to retain this feature.

In reality, the poverty thresholds chosen are ultimately arbitrary — reasonable social scientists and politicians will always disagree about their appropriate levels. Whatever level is chosen should be the result of a carefully specified process that cannot be changed arbitrarily from year-to-year, and should be capable of being updated at reasonable intervals as the economic circumstances of society and the behavior of its demographic and economic components change. If such a method were adopted, the level, in itself, will be less important — it is changes from year to year and comparisons among demographic groups that should matter to policy makers.

Income Measurement

There are three important issues of income measurement for the U.S.: (1) valuation of noncash income; (2) measurement of disposable income (the role of taxes and work expenses); and (3) reduction of survey under reporting and nonsampling errors. Two additional issues addressed below are the choice of an appropriate measure of resources (the role of wealth and consumption-based measures) and measurement of nonmarket income. Further interest is generated by considering whether publication of official estimates based on the CPS should be continued, or, whether to adopt a newer survey designed to collect better income information, the Survey of Income and Program Participation (SIPP).

NONCASH INCOME

The issue of valuation of noncash income spans the income distribution. A more comprehensive income measure would place a value not only on noncash government transfers, such as food stamps (coupons used as cash for qualified food purchases), which typically go to low-income families, but also place a value on elements of nonwage compensation (from employer-provided health insurance to company cars) that typically go to earners at all income levels.

Noncash income to U.S. families has grown substantially in the past 25 years. In the 1980s, over half of government transfer spending for the poor was in the form of noncash benefits (U.S. Census Bureau, 1995). This growth of benefits to the poor has been paralleled by a growth of nonwage compensation to wage earners, induced in part by tax laws exempting such compensation from income and payroll taxes. By 1990, employer costs of nonwage compensation had grown to over one-quarter (27.6 percent) of total compensation costs, up from 19.4 percent in 1966.[6] Furthermore, 67 percent of families and unrelated individuals own homes, which provide them with additional noncash income in the form of housing services.

The Census Bureau began publishing estimates of the value of many of these noncash benefits in 1982 (the latest is DeNavas-Walt et al., 2003). This experimental series values food, housing, government medical transfer benefits, and employer-provided health insurance. Each of these areas needs further developmental work to improve measurement methods.

Currently, food stamps are valued at their coupon value, that is, their full dollar value. This appears widely acceptable as research shows recipients are unconstrained in their food choices by the requirement to use coupons. The imputed value of public and subsidized housing is derived by means of a crude methodology involving a statistical match between the CPS and the American Housing Survey (AHS).

Of key concern to understanding well-being is the valuation of medical benefits, both the government health programs — Medicare (medical aid to the elderly) and Medicaid (medical aid to the poor) — and employer-provided health insurance. Valuation of medical benefits is particularly difficult since coverage of high medical expenses for the sick does nothing to improve his or her poverty status (although the benefits clearly make him or her better off). Even if one imputes the value of an equivalent insurance policy to program participants, these benefits (high in market value owing to large medical costs for the fraction who do get sick) cannot be used by recipients to meet other needs of daily living. Accordingly, the Census Bureau developed a not-altogether-satisfactory method, termed fungible value, to avoid giving too high a value of these benefits to those at the low end of the income scale.[7]

Because these medical programs are so large, determining a better measure of the value of medical benefits or a better way of accounting for the presence of adequate health insurance should be a high priority. Ellwood and Summers (U.S. Census Bureau, 1986) argued that there is little theoretical foundation for including medical benefits as income, on the one hand but then not adjusting income for other medical expenditures, such as insurance premium costs, for those who must buy their own insurance and out-of-pocket expenditures for medical care, on the other. To treat all medical costs consistently, they concluded that it is preferable to exclude all medical care costs from income because: (1) there are large variations in medical need and more medical needs do not leave the individual better off; (2) medical benefits are not fungible, especially for the poor; and (3) there are many difficult measurement problems in trying to value medical benefits. The poverty thresholds would also presumably be adjusted to exclude medical costs.

Aaron (U.S. Census Bureau, 1986) suggested (a suggestion attributed to Gary Burtless) that if a person was not poor on the basis of income, he could still be classified as poor if he did not have health insurance coverage. He argued that medical care is not fungible, so medical benefits should not be added to income.

Work should also be undertaken on valuation of employer-provided benefits other than health insurance. Should employer contributions to retirement pensions be included in nonwage compensation of current earners or as paid out to pension recipients (as is now done)? And, what about other benefits, such as life insurance, subsidized meals, etc.? Much could be learned about nonwage compensation from a study matching household data with data from their employers on nonwage compensation.

Ownership of assets clearly promotes well-being. Homeownership provides the largest noncash flow of services not counted in family income. The Census Bureau estimated the imputed income from homeownership at 5.6 percent of cash income in 1994. Beyond measuring the flows from assets is the question whether someone with even modest assets should even be considered poor. Indeed, many government transfer programs exclude those with low income from participation if their asset holdings are relatively high.[8]

DISPOSABLE INCOME

Even though Orshansky's original calculations were based on posttax income, poverty has always been calculated for official statistics using pretax income because of the limited information collected on the CPS. Census Bureau estimates of after-tax income are based on a model of the likely taxes a family of given circumstances would pay. While the model is reasonably accurate at an aggregate level, additional research could be carried out to improve its accuracy at the household level. Also important is the advisability of deducting work expenses for wage earners such as child care and transportation costs in calculating disposable income.

UNDERREPORTING AND NONSAMPLING ERRORS

Research matching household survey responses to federal income tax returns relative to national income accounts has revealed substantial areas where the level and receipt of certain income sources are underreported (see U.S. Census Bureau, 1991, appendix C; Roemer, 2000). Attempts were made to reduce underreporting by revising CPS questionnaire language for the SIPP when it was launched. This was only partially successful. Response errors remain and questionnaire changes continue to be tested to reduce this problem; a new SIPP questionnaire is being introduced in February 2004.

While current Census Bureau procedures reweight the data for full interview nonresponse and impute appropriate income responses for individual unanswered questions (item nonresponse), these are inadequate to fully correct the problem. Procedures to enhance the data through microsimulation, matching to administrative records, or other means should be investigated, along with continued improvement in imputation for nonresponse.

OTHER ISSUES

In most societies, "underground," "nonmarket," or "black market" income from legal or illegal activities is typically omitted from official income statistics. This income ranges from barter transactions to home production (e.g., home gardens) to illegal income. Researchers are a long way from measuring this activity, so including this income into official statistics would be quite difficult.

It has been suggested that consumption is a better measure of well-being than income (see Cutler and Katz, 1991, and Slesnick, 1993). If a family can maintain its consumption through judicious use of assets when income falls, is it truly poor? Unfortunately, it is difficult to collect accurate annual data on consumption or even expenditures Furthermore, consumption reflects choices of how to allocate resources, rather than need. Nevertheless, fuller investigation of a consumption-based measure would be useful; see U.S. Census Bureau, 2003, for some forays into this area.

The final issue of income measurement addressed is the choice of surveys on which to base income measurement. The CPS is a cross-section survey of housing units, while the SIPP is a longitudinal household survey, following the same individuals for 3 or 4 years, regardless of residence. Consequently, even though the SIPP questionnaire was designed to reduce income underreporting, relative to the CPS, by collecting greater income detail more often (every 4 months), apparently successfully for almost all income sources.[9] Nevertheless SIPP has several drawbacks relative to the CPS. SIPP has historically had a smaller sample size (now 36,700 households versus 78,000 for the CPS ASEC) and slower data release (inconsistencies between successive interviews must be resolved). Another drawback in obtaining a consistent time series of annual national poverty estimates from the SIPP will be sample attrition (as households are lost from the sample) and time-in-sample bias (as households get conditioned by repeated interviewing), as only one SIPP panel is now in the field during any one three-year period.

While we can never envision timeliness being resolved fully in SIPP's favor, SIPP can provide a preliminary estimate on nearly the same schedule as CPS. Still, it is desirable to view the surveys complementarily. If modeling with administrative records can correct under reporting errors in both surveys, they would give the same aggregate statistics. The CPS could be used for a quick snapshot, consistent with data collected since 1947 (the SIPP began in 1983). On the other hand, SIPP would be used for more detailed estimates, for sub-annual and multiyear estimates, and for understanding other dimensions of poverty (assets, disability, gross flows and other dynamic aspects, and so forth); see for example Iceland (2003).[10] Furthermore, the Census Bureau has proposed to Congress an overlapping panel design of two additional smaller three-year panels, which would alternate with the large panel to provide a reasonably reliable annual SIPP poverty estimate.

Poverty Thresholds

In developing an absolute measure of poverty, there are key decisions to be made in determining the appropriate level. The key research issues addressed are: (1) determination of the relationship between minimal commodity consumption levels and minimal income; (2) adjustment for differences in family size and composition; and (3), adjustment for cost-of-living differences over time and between areas.

MINIMAL CONSUMPTION STANDARDS

Minimal consumption standards for all necessary commodities could, in theory, be established, perhaps by an expert panel, but doing so would raise difficult ethical issues in respect to commodities to be included (e.g., is a telephone a necessity?). One alternative would be to define minimal consumption standards for a limited number of necessities and obtain a poverty threshold by using a multiplier to account for necessities not measured. This has been done by Renwick and Bergmann (1993), who developed a full "Basic Needs Budget" that requires no multiplier for single-parent families.[11]

EQUIVALENCE SCALES

The relationship embodied in current U.S. poverty thresholds among families of different sizes (termed the equivalence scale) is meant to represent the different relative costs of supporting those families at minimally adequate levels. In fact, the relationship is based solely on relative food costs as they extant in 1961 and, which, unfortunately, include some anomalies (see Ruggles, 1990, pp. 64–68). While it is possible to develop minimal budgets for every type and size of family separately and thus obviate the need for equivalence scales entirely, in practice it is difficult to do so. Presently, there is no single scale that is generally accepted. Issues in developing equivalence scales include: (1) choice of distinctions in family circumstances (e.g. owner vs. renter), which lead to different thresholds; (2) apportionment of resources within the family; and (3), whether a more useful basis for determining poverty is the household (those living in one housing unit) rather than the family (those in one household related by blood or marriage), or some other, such as cohabitors, or cohabitors with children in common.

COST-OF-LIVING DIFFERENCES

In as large and diverse a country as the U.S., there are significant differences in the cost-of-living among localities. Unfortunately, there are no currently available data on which to reliably estimate interarea price differences for all commodities reliably. Furthermore, such data are difficult to collect. In addition, were such data to be incorporated into poverty thresholds, it would give rise to questions about whether government transfer program benefits (or even tax exemptions) should differ by area as well.[12] Only if some practical alternative cost-of-living index were developed, such as rental housing prices for relatively large areas (suggested in Citro and Michael, 1995), would geographic variation be possible in the thresholds. Substantial research is required before adoption is implemented (see Kokoski et al., 1992, and Moulton, 1992, for some work in this area).

A related price issue is adjustment for inflation. The U.S. poverty thresholds now use the CPI to adjust thresholds over time. If the measurement of minimal consumption is used as the basis for new thresholds, presumably this basis should remain unchanged from year to year, with components, prices, and multipliers reestimated as often. A reasonable compromise might be to re-specify and reestimate the minimal consumption bundle at prespecified intervals as market baskets become outdated, say every ten years, and use the CPI for interim adjustments. The market basket used for the CPI itself is typically reviewed and respecified at least once every ten years.[13]

The National Academy of Sciences Report and Subsequent Developments

In a recent (1995) report (*Measuring Poverty: A New Approach*), the National Academy of Sciences (NAS) Committee on National Statistics recommended that the federal government redefine the way it measures poverty. The key changes recommended are: change the income measure; change the poverty thresholds; and change the survey used. To change the income measure from the current money income definition, they propose addition of non-cash benefits, subtraction of taxes, work expenses, child care expenses, child support paid, and medical out-of-pocket expenses (MOOP). The poverty thresholds are to be based on food, clothing, shelter, and "a little bit more" (78–83 percent of median expenditures on these items multiplied by 1.15–1.25), a new equivalence scale (a two-parameter equivalence scale of the form [#Adults + a*#Children]^b), and given geographic variation, an allowance, based on growth in median expenditures, which is updated annually. Finally, the panel recommended that the government use the SIPP instead of the CPS ASEC to collect basic income and poverty-related data.

Under the guidance of a technical working group on poverty measurement, convened by the Office of Management and Budget (OMB), experts from the Census Bureau and other agencies, using the NAS report as a point of departure, have been examining technical methods for revising the way the U.S. measures poverty. Their first report, based on the CPS (Short et al., 1999), presents six illustrative measures designed to inform public debate on the issues. A subsequent report investigated additional technical issues (Short, 2001) and working papers have used SIPP (Short, 2003) to examine the effects of using the new measure on our understanding of the distribution of poverty. Alternative measures of poverty are now published regularly as part of the Census Bureau's annual report on poverty (for example, Proctor and Dalaker, 2003). The key findings from the work to date are:

- "All the experimental measures showed a different profile of the poor population than did the official measure."
- "Each of the experimental measures yielded lower poverty rates than the official measure for people in families with a female householder and no husband present, whereas the opposite was true for people in married-couple families and male householder families."
- "People under 18 [children] had lower [experimental] poverty rates than under the official measure, while those ages 18 to 64 had higher rates than under the official measure, and those 65 years and over had differences that were higher still."
- "The experimental measures yielded slightly higher poverty rates for non-Hispanic Whites and lower rates for Blacks than the official measure. Among Hispanics (who may be of any race), the experimental measures all showed higher poverty rates than the official measures, but the geographically adjusted measures produced higher rates for Hispanics than those with no geographic adjustment." (Proctor and Dalaker, 2002, pp. 17–18)

Progress is being made toward a new consensus. In August 2000, an open letter on revising the official measure of poverty from a number of prominent academics and researchers, was sent to the then OMB Director, Lew, and the then Census Bureau Director, Prewitt, urging expeditious adoption of an alternative measure, based on work to date by the NAS panel and the Census Bureau.[14]

There are a number of technical and policy issues that must be debated and resolved before a new measure is adopted. These include:

- Medical costs and benefits. The NAS panel recommended excluding MOOP, employer contributions to health insurance, and medical transfer program benefits from resources. Continuing current (experimental) practice would require revising the current method for valuing medical transfer program benefits and updating the methodology for imputing employer contributions to health insurance. One alternative being explored is inclusion of MOOP in the thresholds, (adjusted for health insurance coverage) along with food, clothing, and shelter, and exclusion of medical transfer program benefits entirely.
- Basing thresholds on a pre-specified fraction of median expenditures. How might the public and Congress react to a new poverty threshold, which shows additional millions of poor people than is shown in the current measure? Are we confident about the quality of (i.e. lack of biases in) the Consumer Expenditure Survey data that are used to determine the thresholds? It may be that the likely acceptance of any new definition would be enhanced if the new index were "chained" to the old by matching the overall rate obtained (allowing the distribution to vary); this proposal is included in the early Census Bureau work (Short et al., 1999), as "standardized" measures.
- Developing geographical cost-of-living variations. It is clear that the cost-of-living differs substantially from place to place, and different choices of methodology have different implications. If geographic variation is to be incorporated, some method of measuring all cost differentials (rather than just for housing) and periodically updating the thresholds for relative price changes among areas should be established.
- Annual inflation updating. The panel proposed using the rate of growth in median expenditures to index the thresholds. This is an attempt to introduce some deliberate "relativity" into the measure (if, as was true in the past, median expenditures grow faster than inflation). The alternative is to use the Consumer Price Index.
- Choosing the equivalence scale. The panel recommended a two-parameter equivalence scale; the Census Bureau also investigated a three-parameter

Table 3.1. *Standardized Poverty Rates (percent poor), 1997*

	Official Measure	Experimental Measures						
		NAS[b]	DCM1[c]	DCM2[d]	DES-DCM2[e]	NGA[f]	DES-DCM2-NGA[g]
All individuals[a]	13.3	13.3	13.3	13.3	13.3	13.3	13.3
Children	19.9	17.6	17.9	17.7	17.3	17.4	17.2
Nonelderly adults	10.9	11.1	11.0	11.0	11.2	11.1	11.2
Elderly	10.5	15.0	14.5	14.9	14.9	15.3	15.2
White	11.0	11.5	11.5	11.5	11.5	11.5	11.6
Black or African American	26.5	23.3	23.5	23.2	23.5	23.2	23.1
Other race	16.1	17.0	16.7	16.9	16.9	16.3	15.9
Hispanic origin (of any race)	27.1	27.0	27.1	26.9	26.5	24.9	24.6
No workers	36.3	34.4	33.8	34.4	34.5	34.9	34.7
One or more workers	9.5	9.8	9.9	9.8	9.8	9.7	9.7
Family type							
Married couple	6.4	7.8	7.7	7.8	7.3	7.8	7.3
Male householder	16.1	15.6	15.6	15.6	16.6	15.3	16.2
Female householder	31.5	27.8	28.1	27.8	28.7	28.0	28.7

	a	b	c	d	e	f	g
Geographic region							
Northeast	12.6	14.1	14.1	14.0	14.2	12.0	11.8
Midwest	10.4	10.0	10.0	10.0	10.0	10.8	10.8
South	14.6	13.1	13.3	13.3	13.2	14.8	15.1
West	14.6	16.1	15.9	16.0	16.0	14.4	14.2
Metropolitan area							
Central city	18.8	18.5	18.5	18.5	18.4	17.2	17.2
Not central city	9.0	10.2	10.2	10.2	10.3	9.7	9.7
Nonmetropolitan area	15.9	13.1	13.2	13.2	13.0	16.5	16.4

[a] Standardized to match the official rate for all individuals.

[b] Matches National Academy of Sciences (NAS) recommendations (Citro and Michael, 1995).

[c] Different childcare method based on estimates from the Survey of Income and Program Participation.

[d] Different childcare method based on Aid to Families with Dependent Children (AFDC) program allowances.

[e] Different (three-parameter) equivalence scale and childcare method based on AFDC program allowances.

[f] NAS measure with no geographic adjustment.

[g] Childcare method based on AFDC program allowances, three-parameter equivalence scale, and no geographic adjustment.

Source: Short et al. (1999), Table B1a; based on U.S. Census Bureau tabulations of March 1998 Current Population Survey.

Table 3.2. *Distribution of the Poverty Population Under Alternate Poverty Measures: 1997*

			Poverty Population					
					Experimental Measures			
	Total Population	Official Measure	NAS[b]	DCM1[c]	DCM2[d]	DES-DCM2[e]	NGA[f]	DES-DCM2-NGA[g]
All individuals[a]	100.0	100.0	100.0	100.0	100.0	100.0	100.0	100.0
Children	26.5	39.7	35.1	35.8	35.3	34.5	34.8	34.3
Nonelderly adults	61.6	50.8	51.4	51.1	51.3	52.0	51.4	52.0
Elderly	12.0	9.5	13.5	13.1	13.4	13.4	18.8	13.7
White	82.4	68.6	71.4	71.2	71.4	71.2	71.7	71.9
Black	12.8	25.6	22.5	22.8	22.5	22.7	22.5	22.3
Other	4.8	5.8	6.1	6.0	6.1	6.1	5.9	5.7
Hispanic origin (of any race)	11.4	23.4	23.3	23.4	23.1	22.8	21.4	21.2
No workers	14.2	38.8	36.8	36.2	36.8	36.9	37.3	37.1
One or more workers	85.8	61.2	63.2	63.9	63.2	63.1	62.7	62.9
Family type								
Married couple	65.5	31.5	38.3	37.8	38.4	36.0	38.3	36.3
Male householder	11.6	14.1	13.7	13.6	13.7	14.5	13.4	14.2
Female householder	22.9	54.4	48.0	48.6	48.0	49.6	48.3	49.6

Geographic region							
Northeast	19.1	18.2	20.3	20.2	20.2	20.4	17.3	16.9
Midwest	23.3	18.3	17.6	17.6	17.5	17.5	18.9	19.0
South	35.1	38.7	34.7	35.2	35.1	34.9	39.2	39.9
West	22.6	24.9	27.4	27.0	27.2	27.2	24.6	24.2
Metropolitan area								
Central city	29.8	42.2	41.6	41.6	41.5	41.5	38.8	38.8
Not central city	50.7	34.5	39.1	39.1	39.1	39.3	36.9	37.1
Nonmetropolitan area	19.5	23.3	19.3	19.4	19.4	19.2	24.3	24.2

[a] Standardized to match the official rate for all individuals.

[b] Matches National Academy of Sciences (NAS) recommendations (Citro and Michael, 1995).

[c] Different childcare method based on estimates from the Survey of Income and Program Participation.

[d] Different childcare method based on Aid to Families with Dependent Children (AFDC) program allowances.

[e] Different (three-parameter) equivalence scale and childcare method based on AFDC program allowances.

[f] NAS measure with no geographic adjustment.

[g] Childcare method based on AFDC program allowances, three-parameter equivalence scale, and no geographic adjustment.

Source: Short et al. (1999), Table B1b; based on U.S. Census Bureau tabulations of March 1998 Current Population Survey.

scale (allowing the cost of the first child in a one-adult family to be higher than for other children). Choice of the scale will inevitably alter the distribution of the poor. Related to this decision is the choice of income-sharing unit (e.g. family, cohabitors plus children, households, or something else).

- Underreporting. Should the income statistics from the survey be adjusted for underreporting based on administrative data and modeling?
- Review and revision. Should any new definition include a regular cycle of review and revision based on pre-specified criteria (NAS recommended once a decade)?

As these issues are resolved in open debate, over time, this may offer the best opportunity for OMB to approve and other policymakers to accept a revised methodology for improvement of the way the United States measures poverty.

Notes

This essay reports the results of research and analysis undertaken by Census Bureau staff. It has undergone a more limited review than official Census Bureau publications. This analysis is released to inform interested parties of research and to encourage discussion. The author would like to thank Enrique Lamas, Charles Nelson, and Kathleen Short and for their comments and suggestions.

1. See Fisher (1992) for more historical detail on the development of the poverty thresholds.

2. Ross, Danziger, and Smolensky (1987), using 1950 Census data, have estimated the poverty rate for 1949 to be 40.5 percent.

3. The author participated in the deliberations of that task force. This chapter does not necessarily represent the views of the other task force members.

4. A report issued by the committee was based on this examination, which was made at Congressional request and funded by the Census Bureau, the Bureau of Labor Statistics, and the Administration for Children and Families in the Department of Health and Human Services.

5. The average family size was 3.70 in 1965 but only 3.16 in 1989.

6. Data are from the Compensation and Working Conditions Branch, Bureau of Labor Statistics. The 1966 percentage is not strictly comparable to the 1990 figure.

7. Fungible value is a crude estimate of the value of medical benefits to a family. Medicare and Medicaid benefits are counted as income to the extent that they free up resources that could have been spent on medical care. Neither has any income value if the family is unable to meet basic food and housing requirements.

8. See Fitzgerald and David (1987) for further discussion of this issue.

9. Exceptions are wages and salaries (due to a failure to always collect gross instead of net earnings) and workers' compensation (payments for injuries on the job).

10. The Committee on National Statistics panel on the future of the SIPP recommended

moving toward the use of the SIPP for official income and poverty measurement (Citro and Kalton, 1993).

11. A full review of budget-based approaches is in Watts (1993).

12. I am indebted to Mollie Orshansky for this point.

13. There is also an issue about whether to use the official CPI-U (urban consumers), an experimental CPI created to correct for errors in the official CPI in its measurement of housing costs prior to 1983 (CPI-U-X1), or a yet newer CPI-U-RS (research series) designed to incorporate all CPI methodological improvements made since 1978.

14. For the letter see http://www.ssc.wisc.edu/irp/povmeas/povlet.htm.

References

Burtless, Gary, and Timothy M. Smeeding. 2000. "The Level, Trend, and Composition of American Poverty: National and International Perspectives." Conference paper, April.

Citro, Constance F., and Graham Kalton (eds.). 1993. *The Future of the Survey of Income and Program Participation*. Washington, D.C.: National Academy Press.

Citro, Constance F., and Robert T. Michael (eds.). 1995. *Measuring Poverty: A New Approach*. Washington, D.C.: National Academy Press.

Cutler, David M. and Lawrence F. Katz. 1991. "Macroeconomic Performance and the Disadvantaged." Brookings Papers on Economic Activity No. 2, pp. 1–74.

DeNavas-Walt, Carmen, Robert W. Cleveland, and Bruce H. Webster, Jr. 2003. "Income in the United States: 2003." U.S. Census Bureau, Current Population Reports P60–221, September.

Fisher, Gordon M. 1992. "The Development and History of the Poverty Thresholds." *Social Security Bulletin* 55, no. 4 (Winter), pp. 3–14.

Fitzgerald, John, and Martin David. 1987. "Measuring Poverty and Crisis: A Comparison of Annual and Subannual Accounting Periods Using the Survey of Income and Program Participation." Institute for Research on Poverty Discussion Paper No. 843–87, November.

Iceland, John. 2003. "Dynamics of Economic Well-Being: Poverty, 1996 to 1999." U.S. Census Bureau, Current Population Reports, P70–91, July.

Kokoski, Mary, Patrick Cardiff, and Brent Moulton. 1992. "Interarea Price Indices for Consumer Goods and Services: An Hedonic Approach Using CPI Data." U.S. Bureau of Labor Statistics, January.

Moulton, Brent R. 1992. "Interarea Indexes of the Cost of Shelter Using Hedonic Quality Adjustment Techniques." U.S. Bureau of Labor Statistics, October.

O'Higgins, Michael, and Stephen Jenkins. 1990. "Poverty in the EC: Estimates for 1975, 1980, and 1985." In Rudolph Teekens and Bernard M.S. van Praag (eds.), *Analysing Poverty in the European Community: Policy Issues, Research Options, and Data Sources*. Luxembourg: Office of Official Publications of the European Communities. Pp. 187–212.

Orshansky, Mollie. 1963. "Children of the Poor." *Social Security Bulletin* 26 (July), pp. 3–13.

———. 1965. "Counting the Poor." *Social Security Bulletin* 28 (January), pp. 3–29.

Proctor, Bernadette D., and Joseph Dalaker. 2002 "Poverty in the United States: 2001." U.S. Census Bureau, Current Population Reports P60–219, September.

——. 2003. "Poverty in the United States: 2002." U.S. Census Bureau, Current Population Reports P60–222, September.

Renwick, Trudi J., and Barbara Bergmann. 1993. "A Budget-Based Definition of Poverty." *Journal of Human Resources* 28, no. 1 (Winter), pp. 1–24.

Roemer, Marc I. 2000. "Assessing the Quality of the March CPS and SIPP Income Estimates, 1990–1996." Census Bureau Working paper, Washington D.C.

Ross, Christine, Sheldon Danziger, and Eugene Smolensky. 1987. "The Level and Trend of Poverty in the United States, 1939–1979." *Demography* 24, no. 4, (November), pp. 587–600.

Ruggles, Patricia. 1990. *Drawing the Line.* Washington, D.C.: Urban Institute Press.

Short, Kathleen. 2001. "Experimental Measures of Poverty: 1999." U.S. Census Bureau, Current Population Reports P60–216, October.

——. 2003. "Alternative Poverty Measures in the Survey of Income and Program Participation: 1996." U.S. Census Bureau staff paper, January.

Short, Kathleen, Thesia Garner, David Johnson, and Patricia Doyle. 1999. "Experimental Poverty Measures: 1990 to 1997." U.S. Census Bureau Current Population Report P-60–205.

Slesnick, Daniel T. 1992. "Gaining Ground: Poverty in the Postwar United States." *Journal of Political Economy* 101, no. 1 (February), pp. 1–38.

U.S. Census Bureau. 1965. "Low Income Families and Unrelated Individuals in the U.S.: 1963." Current Population Report P-60–45, June.

——. 1969. "Year-Round Workers with Low Earnings in 1966." Current Population Report P-60–58, April.

——. 1986. "Conference on the Measurement of Noncash Benefits. Proceedings. Volume 1."

——. 1991. "Money Income of Households, Families, and Persons in the United States: 1988 and 1989." Current Population Report P-60–172.

——. 1995. "Income, Poverty, and Valuation of Noncash Benefits: 1994." Current Population Report P-60–189.

——. 2000a. "Money Income in the United States: 1999." Current Population Report P-60–209.

——. 2000b. "Poverty in the United States: 1999." Current Population Report P-60–210.

——. 2003. "Supplemental Measures of Material Well-Being: Expenditures, Consumption, and Poverty, 1998 and 2001." Current Population Reports P-23–201, September.

U.S. Department of Health and Human Services. 1976. *The Measure of Poverty: A Report to Congress.*

Watts, Harold W. 1993. "A Review of Alternative Budget-Based Expenditure Norms." Paper prepared for the Panel on Poverty Measurement and Family Assistance of the Committee on National Statistics, revised (May).

Medical Spending, Health Insurance, and Measurement of American Poverty

GARY BURTLESS AND SARAH SIEGEL

Controversy has swirled around the measurement of U.S. poverty for at least three decades. Unlike other economic indicators, such as the gross domestic product or the unemployment rate, the poverty rate arouses such intense controversy that government statisticians have been unable to make fundamental improvements in its calculation. The consumer price index is the only other economic indicator that receives a comparable degree of public scrutiny. Political controversy surrounding the measurement of price change has not prevented the Bureau of Labor Statistics from implementing major improvements in measuring inflation over the past two decades, however. Indeed, the political controversy over price measurement probably hastened a technical revision process in the late 1990s that might otherwise have stretched out over several years.

One of the most controversial aspects of poverty measurement is the appropriate treatment of personal spending on health care. Patterns of medical care use and of paying for health care have changed significantly since the current poverty measure was developed in the 1960s. In addition, the total resources devoted to health care consumption have also risen steeply, in part because modern medical practice delivers a much improved level of care. The way the government measures poverty has not changed to reflect these developments, however. The current measure of poverty takes no explicit account of consumer medical spending or of the subsidized health insurance that families receive as a result of participating in employer-sponsored or government insurance plans. Critics are divided on how health insurance and medical expenses should be included in poverty measurement.

In 1960 medical spending accounted for just 5 percent of national income, but by 1999 this fraction had risen to 13 percent. Medical care now represents a large fraction of all consumption, and many observers believe it has become a necessity at least as important as food and shelter. They believe the poverty definition should accurately reflect this development. If poverty measurement took full account of households' expenditures on medical care, the poverty rates of the disabled and aged would be particularly affected because of their heavy spending on care.

On the other hand, relatively little of the health spending increase was financed directly out of household budgets. Between 1960 and 1999, the proportion of health spending paid out of public budgets more than doubled, and the fraction financed through third-party payments from private health insurers rose almost 60 percent. The actual percentage of health care costs paid as out-of-pocket payments by households fell from 55 percent to 18 percent between 1960 and 1999 (Health Care Financing Administration, 2000). In spite of the dramatic increase in medical care consumption, a smaller percentage of household expenditures is now devoted to health care than was the case in 1960.[1] Many critics of the current poverty measure believe the consumer value of subsidized health insurance should be included when counting the income available to American households. Depending on how the subsidy is included in income, the resources of many households could be substantially increased and poverty rates reduced. On the other hand, U.S. health insurance coverage is very uneven. More than one in seven Americans, or 42 million people, lacked health insurance coverage during all twelve months of 1999.

This chapter examines the effects of three basic methods of including household spending on health care in the measurement of poverty. The first is the method embodied in the official poverty statistics. The other two are based, directly or indirectly, on the recommendations of the National Academy of Sciences (NAS) Panel on Poverty and Family Assistance (Citro and Michael, 1995). That panel argued that the nation's poverty statistics should be revamped to reflect a new measure of family need and an improved measure of family resources. Its recommendations for treating health insurance and medical spending have not won wide acceptance in the research community, but they offer a starting point for analysis.[2]

The chapter is organized as follows. In the next section we review the definition of poverty and describe alternative approaches to treating household medical spending in an assessment of family needs and resources. This section describes the theoretical approach proposed by the NAS poverty statistics panel, and it outlines alternatives to this approach that have been suggested since publication of the panel's report. In the next section we describe the alternatives implemented in this chapter and outline our methods for calculating household medical spending and health care needs. The last substantive section presents and discusses our statistical results. The chapter ends with a brief conclusion.

Medical Spending and Poverty

Most social scientists that have studied poverty believe the official U.S. poverty definition does a poor job of distinguishing between the nation's poor and nonpoor. The official measure is deficient in a number of respects, a fact that has long been recognized by specialists. These defects can pose problems both for policymaking and for social science. For example, trends in the number of people who are officially classified as poor are often used to decide whether public policies have been effective in reducing poverty. If poverty is mismeasured, this kind of assessment can produce seriously misleading results.

OFFICIAL POVERTY DEFINITION

The Census Bureau's current estimate of the official poverty rate is based on poverty thresholds and definitions of countable income developed in the early 1960s by the Social Security Administration and modified by the Council of Economic Advisers. The official poverty thresholds were originally developed by determining the minimum cost of an adequate diet and then multiplying a family's minimum food budget by a multiplier believed to cover other consumer necessities. This multiplier, in turn, was derived from a 1955 food consumption survey, which showed that families on average spent about one-third of their budgets on food. Part of the remaining two-thirds of spending was devoted to purchasing medical products and services, so in one sense the poverty thresholds reflect Americans' medical consumption behavior in the mid-1950s. The poverty thresholds vary by family size, under the assumption that large families require more income than small ones to enjoy the same standard of living.

In order to determine whether a family is poor, its resources are compared with the poverty threshold. The family resource measure used by the Census Bureau is gross money income. It includes before-tax cash income from all sources except gains or losses on the sale of property. This definition includes gross wages and salaries, net income from the operation of a farm, business, or partnership, pensions, interest, dividends, and government transfer payments that are distributed in the form of cash, including social security and public assistance benefits. The measure is not comprehensive, because it ignores all sources of noncash income, including food stamps, housing subsidies, and government- and employer-provided health insurance. The resource measure is also inappropriate for measuring poverty, because some of the noncash income sources, which are ignored, can be used to pay for basic necessities, such as food and shelter.

NAS PANEL RECOMMENDATIONS

The official poverty estimates have been subject to intense criticism over the past three decades. Specialists have offered a variety of technical criticisms, and politicians and journalists have offered critiques of their own. The most comprehensive evaluation of the official poverty statistics was published by the National Academy of Sciences in 1995 when it presented the recommendations of the Panel on Poverty and Family Assistance (Citro and Michael, 1995). The NAS panel described flaws of the official measure and suggested methods for reducing or eliminating them. It described the pros and cons of different methods for dealing with problems of the current measure, and it made specific recommendations for improvement. Some of the most important problems identified by the panel were the following:

- The official poverty measure excludes in-kind benefits, including food stamps and housing assistance, when counting family resources.
- It ignores the cost of earning wage income, including childcare costs, when calculating the net income available to families containing working members.
- It disregards regional variations in the cost of living, especially the cost of housing, in determining a family's consumption needs.
- It ignores direct tax payments, such as payroll and income taxes, when measuring family resources. By the same token, it ignores the contribution to family resources provided by refundable income tax credits, such as the Earned Income Credit (EITC).
- Differences in health insurance coverage are ignored in determining family resources, and differences in medical spending are disregarded in determining family consumption needs.
- The official thresholds have never been updated to reflect the changing consumption levels or patterns of American households.

To remedy these defects, the NAS panel recommended a complete overhaul of the procedures and data used to measure poverty. Its core recommendations can be summarized briefly:

- The poverty thresholds should be based on the budget needed for food, clothing, shelter, and a small additional amount for other needs (personal care, non-work-related transportation, etc.). These budgets in turn should be based on actual spending patterns observed in surveys of representative American households, and the budget amounts should be updated each year based on spending patterns over the previous three years. (In other words, the budget amounts should be updated on a regular basis to reflect the society-wide trend in actual consumption; they should not be fixed for all time based on a fixed market basket of goods and services.)
- Family resources should be defined as the sum of money income from all sources plus the value of near-money income, such as food stamps, that are available to buy goods and services in the budget, minus expenses that cannot be used to buy these goods and services.
- The expenses subtracted from available family resources should include: payroll and income taxes; childcare and other work-related expenses; child support payments to another household; and out-of-pocket medical care costs, including payments for health insurance premiums.
- The equivalence scale that reflects differences in consumption needs according to family size and composition should be revised. The panel's suggested scale reflects a higher estimate of the anticipated cost of supporting a couple and a lower estimate of supporting a single person than are reflected in the existing scale, for example.
- The poverty thresholds should be adjusted to reflect differences in the cost of housing across geographical areas of the country. The panel recommended that the Census Bureau make estimates of the cost of housing for the nine census regions and, within each region, for several population-size categories of metropolitan areas.
- Assistance provided to the family in the form of near-money nonmedical in-kind benefits — specifically, food stamp benefits, subsidized housing, school lunches, and home energy assistance — should be directly added to net cash income to determine family resources.
- Work-related expenses should be subtracted from cash income using the following procedures:
  for each working adult, a flat amount per week worked should be subtracted from net cash income (up to a limit of after-tax earnings) to reflect transportation and other miscellaneous expenses connected to work;
  for families in which there is no nonworking parent, actual childcare costs per week worked (up to a limit of the net earnings of the parent with lower earnings or a standard weekly limit, whichever is lower) should be subtracted from net cash income.

- The Survey of Income and Program Participation (SIPP) should replace the March Current Population Survey (CPS) as the source of survey data used to estimate the poverty rate.

The NAS panel made no recommendation for including the flow of housing services from owner-occupied homes in its new definition of family resources. Families of the same size which live in the same communities would be assigned the same budget for housing regardless of whether they rented an apartment, made monthly loan payments on a home mortgage, or owned their homes free and clear of mortgage debt. While public housing subsidies would be treated as resources available to pay for a family's housing costs; the flow of services from an owner-occupied home would not be treated in an equivalent way.

If the panel's proposals were fully implemented there would be a substantial effect on the level and distribution of poverty across groups and regions and important changes in the eligibility standards for some federal programs. For this reason, the NAS panel report attracted close scrutiny from scholars interested in poverty measurement. Burtless, Corbett, and Primus (1997) proposed a sequence of studies to examine the statistical and policy implications of adopting part of the panel's entire proposal. They also urged publication of micro-census data sets containing the resource and threshold data necessary to calculate the poverty rate under the definition suggested by the NAS panel as well as under plausible alternatives to the panel's definition. Garner et al. (1998) and Short et al. (1999) performed careful analyses of the panel's proposals to determine how they would affect the poverty rate if adopted either alone or in combination. The Census Bureau has subsequently made available public-use files that allow researchers to reproduce the calculations described in Short et al. (1999). (These Census files are the source of some of the tabulations reported in this paper.)

Although many of the NAS panel's recommendations enjoy wide support among poverty specialists, some have aroused opposition. Thomas Corbett (1999) has summarized a discussion among poverty experts of many aspects of the NAS panel's proposal. Corbett reports overwhelming support for the panel's recommendations that near-cash in-kind benefits should be included in the definition of resources and income and that payroll tax payments and estimated work-related expenses should be subtracted. He also reports wide acceptance of a new equivalence scale to replace the one in the current poverty thresholds. Corbett reports far less agreement with the panel's proposal that poverty thresholds should reflect regional differences in the cost of housing and should be updated from year to year in proportion to recent changes in median consumption. As noted above, only a minority of conference participants accepted the panel's recommendation for treating health insurance and out-of-pocket medical expenses.

The remainder of this chapter focuses on the treatment of health insurance and health care expenses in the definition of poverty. This issue is almost certainly the most difficult and controversial one that remains in defining an appropriate measure of U.S. poverty. Although our estimates of poverty are based in part on many of the NAS panel's recommendations, we will discuss in detail only those that relate to measuring health care expenses.[3]

HEALTH CARE EXPENSES AND POVERTY MEASUREMENT

The measurement of poverty involves the comparison of some index of household well-being or economic resources with household needs. When command over economic resources falls short of needs, a household (or person or family) is classified as poor. Economic well-being refers to the material resources available to a household. The definition of poverty in the United States usually begins with the assumption that households must have command over at least enough resources to purchase a basket of basic necessities. The original poverty thresholds were derived by estimating the cost of a minimally adequate diet and then multiplying this estimate by a factor large enough to cover other necessities. The NAS panel on poverty and family assistance included food, clothing, and shelter in its short list of consumer necessities.

Most Americans would include adequate medical care within the core set of basic needs. The architects of the original poverty thresholds and members of the NAS poverty panel probably agreed with this judgment. However, they chose radically different approaches to recognizing medical care expenditures in their definitions of poverty. The official thresholds implicitly treat medical care expenditures in the same way as they treat expenditures on all other necessities. Some portion of the poverty budget is implicitly set aside for each basic need, with one-third of the budget assigned to food consumption and perhaps 7 percent of it set aside for medical spending.[4] This approach to poverty measurement made sense in an era when most families paid for almost all their consumption with cash income, but it makes less sense when a large fraction of consumption is financed with in-kind transfers and third-party insurance payments.

In attempting to define a more comprehensive definition of household resources, the NAS panel explicitly recognized the growing importance of in-kind transfers to the low-income population. It proposed adding near-cash in-kind benefits to after-tax cash income when determining household resources.

Near-cash benefits clearly include food stamps and probably include most housing subsidies. The NAS panel did not treat third-party payments for medical care or the insurance value of a third-party-provided health plan in the same way as food stamps, however, for two reasons. First, all noninstitutionalized households must devote some resources to purchasing food. This implies that food stamps directly help to pay for necessary consumption, freeing up part of the household's other income to be spent on other basic necessities. Moreover, food stamp allotments are intentionally set at a modest level, so it can be safely assumed that every dollar in food stamp benefits frees up one dollar of the household's remaining income for spending on other necessities.[5] The second problem with treating health insurance subsidies in the same way we treat food stamps is that households of the same size and composition have similar food requirements but widely varying requirements for medical care. As the panel notes, "Everyone has a need to eat and be sheltered throughout the year, but some people may need no medical care at all while others may need very expensive treatments" (Citro and Michael, 1995, p. 224). Thus, a free insurance policy that has an average cost of $6,000 per year for an average household with two members might be worth only $500 to a household containing two young, healthy adults. That is, this healthy household might reasonably expect that coverage by the insurance plan will only reduce its out-of-pocket spending on medical care by $500. If the young family has only $10,000 in net income aside from the health insurance plan, the way we count their insurance plan in measuring household resources could be crucial in determining whether the household is classified as poor.

The Census Bureau has tried to resolve these two problems by calculating the "fungible cash value" of Medicare and Medicaid insurance. The insurance is converted into a cash value equal to the amount of resources that are freed up to pay for necessities other than food and shelter.[6] Rather than place a value on the subsidy value of insurance received by households, however, the NAS panel proposed subtracting from other resources households' spending on medical care, including the premiums they pay for health insurance. This treatment of medical spending is fundamentally different from the implicit treatment in the official poverty standards because it does not include an estimate of necessary medical spending in the poverty thresholds. Instead, it treats *actual* medical spending as a subtraction from other family resources. Thus, spending on medical care is given special priority over other spending on basic necessities in the measurement of *resources*, though medical care is not explicitly recognized as a necessity in the definition of thresholds.

Although the NAS panel's proposed treatment of medical spending is logical and internally consistent, it raises two issues that disturb some observers.

First, because medical care is not explicitly included as a necessity in the definition of poverty thresholds, some households may be classified as nonpoor even though they do not have command over enough resources to obtain adequate health care. Consider a household with net income just slightly above the NAS panel's proposed poverty threshold but with no health insurance. If the household spends no money to purchase medical care, it would be classified as nonpoor under the panel's proposed definition. But the household may have failed to receive necessary medical care precisely because its resources are strained and it lacks minimal health insurance. Households with adequate command over resources should have better access to medical care. This problem with the NAS definition may cause some households to be classified as nonpoor even though they do not have enough resources to obtain adequate care, which implies that they are poor if adequate care is a necessity.

A second problem with the panel's proposal is that all medical spending receives privileged treatment in the determination of household resources, regardless of whether the spending is necessary. This issue was highlighted in John Cogan's dissent to the NAS panel report (Citro and Michael, 1995, pp. 388–90). Cogan notes that medical spending, like spending on other kinds of goods and services, is responsive to both prices and family income. Subtracting expenditures on this one item from family resources, while setting fixed thresholds for spending on other kinds of necessities, is inconsistent with the basic theory of consumer choice. People who elect to receive expensive medical treatments or use the services of high-priced health providers should not be classified as poor as a result of their own consumption choices. Such a procedure makes no more sense than classifying households as poor if they choose to live in expensive apartments or purchase costly designer clothes. This problem with the NAS panel's treatment of medical spending could cause poverty rates to be overstated. Well-off households that voluntarily chose to spend lavishly on health care could be classified as poor even though their health insurance and incomes give them command over enough resources to live comfortably.

The second criticism of the NAS panel's recommendation may seem unduly harsh. Most Americans believe their medical spending is devoted to insurance and care that are needed to protect or restore their health. People who are sick or injured may think they have little alternative but to pay for prescribed medical care, unless they are covered by a free and exceptionally generous insurance plan. Little medical spending seems voluntary. This was essentially the position adopted by the NAS panel. A problem with this view is that different groups in the population spend widely differing amounts on medical care, even if we hold constant their net incomes and insurance coverage.[7]

The resource definition proposed by the NAS panel requires that much more spending be subtracted from the resources of some groups than of others, even though the extra spending may contribute to greater well-being in the high-spending groups. This difference in average well-being might not be apparent at a single point in time, when it is plausible to assume that both high- and low-spending groups are spending whatever is needed to maintain or protect their health. Over long periods of time, however, it is difficult to believe that systematically faster increases in spending by a particular group fail to translate into systematically faster improvements in that group's relative well-being. Perversely, however, the NAS panel's resource definition would produce the result that a faster rate of increase in health spending causes an increase in the poverty rate of groups in which expenditures increase fastest.

According to the 1999 Consumer Expenditure Survey, consumer units with a family head under age 55 devoted 3.9 percent of their total expenditures to out-of-pocket health costs. Among families headed by someone between ages 55 and 64, the proportion of expenditures devoted to health care was 5.7 percent. For families headed by a person age 65 or older, the fraction devoted to medical care was 12.0 percent, or more than three times the percentage spent on health care by families headed by people under 55.[8] These spending patterns imply that much larger amounts must be subtracted from the net incomes of aged households than from the net incomes of nonelderly households in order to calculate household resources under the proposed NAS definition. David Betson and Jennifer Warlick (1998) show that these subtractions from household resources have a sizable impact on trends in relative poverty among aged and nonaged households. Under the official definition of poverty, the poverty rate of the elderly fell from 13.8 percent to 11.7 percent between 1983 and 1994, while the poverty rate in the population at large fell much more modestly from 15.2 percent to 14.6 percent. Using the more comprehensive definition of resources suggested by the NAS panel, but subtracting medical spending from resources, the poverty rate of the aged increased between 1983 and 1994 while the poverty rate of the general population fell. Out-of-pocket medical spending among the lower-income elderly apparently increased faster than after-tax incomes. Instead of falling sharply below the poverty rate in the population at large, the elderly poverty rate under the NAS definition remained significantly higher than the rate in the general population (Betson and Warlick, 1998, Table 1).

There is some evidence that the increases in out-of-pocket medical spending by the elderly (and the far larger increases in third-party expenditures on health consumption of the elderly) produced tangible benefits for the aged. The death rate of men between 65 and 84 years old fell 1.2 percent a year from

1982 and 1994, while the death rate of men between 14 to 64 years old fell just 0.6 percent a year. There was a much smaller difference in the mortality rate improvements of women younger and older than age 65. Women between 65 and 84 experienced mortality rate reductions of 0.6 percent a year, while women between 14 and 64 enjoyed reductions of 0.7 percent a year (Bell, 1997, table: Historical Average Annual Percentage Reductions in Age-Adjusted Central Death Rates). The mortality statistics nonetheless suggest that older Americans enjoyed relatively rapid gains in life expectancy during much of the period in which their out-of-pocket medical spending was rising. If the spending increases produced faster gains in the well-being of the low-income aged than were enjoyed by low-income but nonaged Americans, some people might be skeptical of a poverty index that shows destitution among the elderly has worsened in comparison with that among the nonaged.

AN ALTERNATIVE TO THE NAS PROPOSAL

The NAS panel considered alternative methods for including health expenditures in the measurement of poverty (Citro and Michael, 1995, pp. 223–37). Later analysts have also proposed alternatives. We consider variants of the NAS panel proposal which add estimates of necessary medical spending to the poverty thresholds rather than subtract actual spending amounts from household resources. The basic idea is to treat spending on medical care as a necessity in the basic poverty thresholds. An estimate of how much money should reasonably be devoted to this necessity is obtained by measuring the actual out-of-pocket medical spending of selected (mostly nonpoor) members of the population and then adjusting these estimates to reflect the health insurance status of families. This alternative was suggested by an informal working group of academic and government analysts interested in improving the nation's poverty statistics. While researchers have found no ideal method of including health care spending in the definition of poverty, the two general approaches we consider offer contrasting views of the problem.

Methodology

As implemented by the Census Bureau, the NAS panel's approach to measuring family resources involves making an estimate of each family's spending on medical care and then subtracting this amount from the family's other after-tax cash and near-cash income. An ideal data set to implement the NAS poverty definition would be one that combines accurate and timely information about family income, tax payments, and work-related expenses with reliable reports of family spending on medical care and health insurance. No large and nationally representative data set combines all of these features. The data source used to estimate the official poverty rate is the Annual Demographic Survey supplement to the March Current Population Survey (CPS), but this survey contains no questions concerning family medical spending and very limited information about health insurance coverage. To compensate for the lack of information about medical spending on the CPS, the Census Bureau has imputed predicted medical expenditure amounts to families and unrelated individuals surveyed in the CPS.

The Bureau's imputation procedure is performed in three steps.[9] In the first step, the Bureau predicts whether a family incurs any medical expenses during the relevant year. This prediction is made on the basis of a statistical model estimated with data from the 1987 National Medical Expenditure Survey (NMES), which contains information on family medical spending, health insurance coverage, income, and individual demographic data (Short et al., 1999, Table C13). Since similar data, except for medical expenditures, are contained in the March CPS file, the statistical model estimated with the NMES can be used to predict out-of-pocket health spending for families in the CPS file. The second step of the Bureau's procedure imputes actual medical spending amounts, including premiums for most health insurance, to the families that were predicted to incur medical expenses in the first step. The statistical model used in this step was also estimated with data from the 1987 NMES, although the data were aged to reflect medical prices and spending patterns in the calendar year covered by the CPS file. That is, the Census Bureau adjusted the predictions of family medical spending to ensure that the weighted sum of spending was equal to an aggregate total estimated in an independent source. In the final step, the Census Bureau imputed Medicare Part B premiums to people insured under Medicare who did not have their premiums reimbursed by the Medicaid program.

Significantly, the Census Bureau's imputation method attempts to impute actual medical spending amounts rather than the expected amount of spending given the family's characteristics. In other words, the medical spending amounts imputed to CPS respondents reflect the full distribution of health expenditures observed in the NMES sample. Because annual medical spending may vary greatly, even among families with identical characteristics, some families are predicted to have extremely high health outlays. This point is illustrated in Figure 4.1, which shows the cumulative percentage distribution of out-of-pocket medical spending for two kinds of families. The top panel shows the distribution of spending among families without an aged member which contain either two or three members. To make the sample even more homogenous, we restrict it to families in which every member has health

Nonaged families containing two or three members with at least one member in "poor" or "fair" health

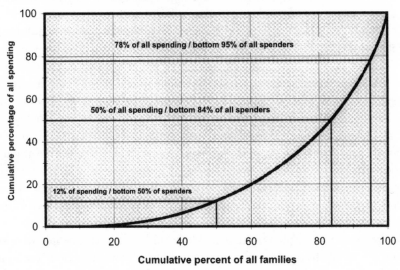

Aged unrelated individuals who are in "poor" or "fair" health

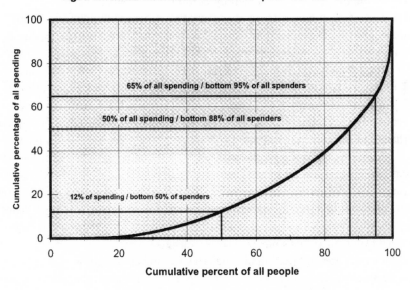

Figure 4.1 Cumulative Distribution of Out-of-Pocket Medical Spending, 1987
Source: Authors' tabulations of 1987 National Medical Expenditure Survey

insurance and in which at least one family member reports "poor" or "fair" health. Note that only half of all spending in this sample is incurred by the 84 percent of families with smallest spending amounts. Only 78 percent of spending is incurred by the 95 percent of families with lowest spending. In other words, the top 5 percent of families accounts for 22 percent of all out-of-pocket expenditures. The distribution of out-of-pocket spending is even more skewed among elderly unrelated individuals who are in "fair" or "poor" health (bottom panel of Figure 4.1). The top 5 percent of spenders in this group accounts for 35 percent of out-of-pocket expenditures.

A striking feature of the Census Bureau's predictions is that family out-of-pocket spending among people with low income is 61 percent of the amount of average out-of-pocket spending among all people, poor and nonpoor (Short et al., 1999, Table C5). What makes this result remarkable is that 43 percent of persons classified as poor under the official poverty definition are receive free health insurance through the Medicaid program. One-quarter of the poor are insured under some plan other than Medicaid.[10] Obviously, people who are insured by Medicaid do not receive completely free health care, for some medical goods and services are not covered, and many in the insured population do not receive insurance in every month of the year. It is nonetheless surprising that the low-income population is predicted to spend such a large fraction of the average amount of out-of-pocket expenditures, even though many low-income Americans receive free health insurance and the remainder have cash incomes that are only a small percentage of those received by the nonpoor population.[11] It follows that many uninsured and poorly insured low-income families are predicted to face (and to pay) large medical bills.

Under the alternative treatment of medical spending considered here, an estimate of "reasonable" health spending is added to each family's poverty threshold to reflect the expected cost of obtaining necessary medical care.[12] We derive our estimates of reasonable health spending with the NMES medical spending data used by the Census Bureau when it estimated the poverty rate under the NAS panel's proposal. We also follow the Census Bureau's practice and update the expenditures reported in the 1987 NMES to reflect medical price inflation and estimates of aggregate out-of-pocket spending provided by an individual source (see Appendix).

Our estimates of "reasonable" health spending are based on spending patterns among a subset of families on the NMES file. To ensure that our estimates do not reflect spending on unnecessary or excessively costly care, we usually restrict our estimation sample to families with income-to-needs ratios no higher than the median income-to-needs ratio in the population. (The income-to-needs ratio is defined as the family's Census money income divided by its

official poverty threshold.) To ensure that families are not excessively constrained by low income in their consumption of health care, we usually restrict
the sample used to measure reasonable medical spending to families that have
at least one-half the median income-to-needs ratio in the population.[13]

Once these income restrictions are imposed on the analysis sample, we
calculated the average out-of-pocket health expenditures of families within
cells defined by four characteristics:

- Age of head of household: (1) under 65 (2) 65 or older.
- Number of persons in family: If the family head is under 65, the categories
  are (1) one; (2) two or three; (3) four or more. If the family head is 65 or
  older, the categories are (1) one; (2) two; (3) three or more.
- Health of family members: (1) all family members report health as "good,"
  "very good," or "excellent"; (2) at least one family member reports health as
  "fair" or "poor."
- Health insurance status: (1) the family is fully insured but is not insured
  under the Medicaid program; (2) the family is fully insured and at least one
  family member is insured under Medicaid; (3) one or more family members
  are not covered by health insurance.

In principle, we could estimate "reasonable" health spending within each cell
by calculating the average amount spent by families within that cell. It is
possible, however, that families which are uninsured or only partially insured
may consume less medical care than is warranted by the health needs of family
members. If they had adequate insurance, they might receive a more appropriate level of care. How much on average would it cost uninsured families to
obtain an appropriate level of care? If this average spending amount were
known, we could impute it to families in the uninsured cell. Because this
hypothetical spending amount is unknown, however, our research strategy is
to perform a sensitivity analysis in which alternative estimates of "reasonable"
medical spending are calculated and then imputed to families whose members
are uninsured or only partly insured. In our basic sensitivity analysis, we
derive three estimates of reasonable spending corresponding to "high," "medium," and "low" assessments of the medical spending needs of uninsured or
partly insured families.

- High assessment of needs: uninsured and partly insured families will purchase an individual health insurance plan and spend the same average
  amount for out-of-pocket medical costs (including health insurance premiums) as families which purchase individual plans.
- Medium assessment of needs: uninsured and partly insured families will pay

health insurance premiums and pay out-of-pocket medical costs that are the same as out-of-pocket spending of all families which have health insurance, including families enrolled in either individual or group plans.
- Low assessment of needs: (a) uninsured and partly insured families that are eligible for Medicaid but which report that they are not insured by Medicaid are assigned the same average out-of-pocket medical costs as families that are insured by Medicaid;[14] (b) uninsured and partly insured families that are ineligible for Medicaid are assigned the same average out-of-pocket medical costs as families that are insured by a private insurance plan.

Ideally, the high, medium, and low estimates of "reasonable" medical outlays would be measured using a sample with at least one-half of median income and no more than the median income. This proved impractical for two of our estimates. Only a small percentage of Americans obtain health insurance coverage outside of a group insurance plan. To estimate average out-of-pocket medical spending of families covered by individual health insurance plans, we therefore use the average spending levels of all families covered by individual plans, regardless of the family's income. In addition, very few families with incomes greater than one-half median income are covered by the Medicaid program. To estimate average out-of-pocket medical spending of Medicaid-insured families, we measured the average spending levels of all families covered by Medicaid, regardless of whether the family had income above or below one-half the median income. (Our estimates of "reasonable" medical spending for different classes of families are presented in the Appendix.)

The three alternative estimates of "reasonable" medical spending may span the plausible range of spending requirements for families which do not have insurance for most of their members — under the assumption that lower-income families should expect to face average out-of-pocket spending requirements. The out-of-pocket spending of persons or families who purchase individual health insurance plans is an upper-bound estimate of "reasonable" medical spending for two reasons. First, some families that are uninsured probably have access to a group health insurance plan that is less expensive and more advantageous than a private, individual plan. The imputed cost of health insurance premiums thus is higher than the amount that some uninsured families would actually have to pay. Second, families that purchase private, individual plans probably expect to incur higher average medical costs than similar families that do not purchase such plans. One reason that people choose to become insured under an individual health plan is that they expect to incur above-average medical expenses. If families which purchase individual plans use more medical care services than average, while families which do not purchase insurance would consume less care than average if they were insured, then we would overstate the likely spending of uninsured families by assuming they would consume as much care as families that purchase an individual policy.

Similarly, our low assessment of medical spending of the uninsured and partially insured is intended to represent a lower-bound estimate of their expected spending if they had adequate access to medical care and anticipated paying average out-of-pocket amounts for care. Some of the people whom we predict could become eligible for a free Medicaid insurance plan may not be eligible for Medicaid during every month of the year. In months when they are uninsured, their out-of-pocket medical spending may be higher than that of people who are actually insured under Medicaid. It is possible, of course, that many families that are eligible for Medicaid remain uninsured because they do not expect to incur large medical expenses. If they faced a medical emergency, they would apply to become insured under Medicaid. In this case, we might be overstating the likely medical spending of these families by assuming they will spend as much as families which actually become insured under Medicaid.

To derive our smallest estimate of "reasonable" medical spending, we performed one last sensitivity test. As illustrated in Figure 4.1, the medical expenditures of apparently similar families are very unequal. Families with the largest medical bills account for a high percentage of aggregate out-of-pocket health costs. It is conceivable that most low-income families remaining uninsured are in good enough health so that they do not expect to incur extremely large medical bills. Such families may also anticipate that if a severe medical episode occurred, they would become insured under a means-tested insurance plan, such as Medicaid or emergency medical assistance. If this expectation is valid, uninsured families would not need to provide for the contingency of facing extremely large medical bills, because such bills would be paid by a public insurance program or absorbed by health care providers as an unreimbursable expense. To embody this idea in our estimate of "reasonable" medical outlays, we top-code the spending amounts of families which have medical expenditures in the top 5 percent of the medical spending distribution when calculating average medical spending in each cell.[15] In particular, we calculate medical spending at the 95th percentile and convert all values of medical spending larger than this amount to 95th-percentile amount. Because the distribution of medical spending is so skewed, top coding can significantly lower our estimate of "reasonable" medical spending. For example, among nonaged families with two or three members in which all members are insured and in which at least one member has "poor" or "fair" health, top-coding reduces the estimate of "reasonable" spending by 16 percent. Among aged unrelated individuals who are in "poor" or "fair" health, top coding reduces estimated "reasonable" spending 20 percent. If we top-coded respondents' expenditure reports at a lower value, such as the 90th or the 80th percentile, in our estimates of "reasonable" medical outlays would be smaller still.

Our estimates of "reasonable" medical expenditures were added to one variant of the NAS panel's recommended poverty thresholds. The NAS panel recommended that the thresholds provide enough income to cover the cost of food, clothing, and shelter and something extra to cover other common needs (except medical care). This basic threshold is calculated for a reference family consisting of two adults and two children. The panel proposed that the reference family's threshold be set equal to some plausible percentage of the median spending on food, clothing, and shelter of all families of that type, as measured in the Consumer Expenditure Survey. Members of the panel believed a plausible range would be 89.7 percent of median spending up to 103.75 percent of median spending on food, clothing, and shelter. Our basic threshold represents the midpoint of this range, or 96.725 percent of median spending. (For a more detailed discussion of how the basic threshold is estimated using the Consumer Expenditure Survey, see Short et al., 1999, pp. 4–5 and C-2).

To calculate poverty thresholds of families with different sizes and compositions, we used the three-parameter equivalence scale proposed by Betson (1996) as implemented by Short et al. (1999, pp. C-1–C-3). The three-parameter equivalence scale is defined as follows:

1. For single parents: $[A + 0.8 + 0.5 * (K - 1)]^{0.7}$
2. All other families: $[A + 0.5 * K]^{0.7}$
3. Ratio of the scale for 2 adults compared to 1 adult is 1.41

where A = number of adults in family, and K = number of children in family.

To adjust our alternative thresholds for successive years between 1990 and 1998, we increased the thresholds in line with the annual percentage change in the CPI-U. The same procedure is used to adjust the official poverty thresholds. (The NAS panel recommended, however, that the thresholds be increased in line with changes in median spending on food, clothing, and shelter.) We used a single set of poverty thresholds for the entire nation, the same procedure used to develop the official poverty thresholds. (The NAS panel recommended that thresholds be adjusted across geographical regions and, within geographical regions, across different sizes of metropolitan areas to reflect differences in shelter costs.)

When we implemented our new treatment of medical spending in the definition of poverty we took the poverty thresholds described above and added an estimate of the family's "reasonable" medical spending.[16] In the empirical section below, we show poverty rates estimated fewer than six variants of this new poverty definition. Each variant uses a different estimate of "reasonable" out-of-pocket medical spending, with the alternative estimates calculated using the procedures described above.

FAMILY RESOURCES

Except when estimating the poverty rate under the official poverty definition, we use a variant of the comprehensive definition of family income proposed by the NAS panel. Our definition of family income consists of the sum of the following elements:

pre-tax cash income (the measure of income used in the official poverty definition);
near-cash in-kind benefits (except health insurance) at market value (food stamps, school lunches, energy assistance, housing subsidies);
net capital gains;
refundable tax credits (Earned Income Tax Credit, or EITC)

minus the following elements:

estimated payroll and income taxes (federal income taxes, state income taxes, and FICA contributions); and
work-related expenses.[17]

This definition of family resources is used to evaluate families' poverty status under the alternative definitions we examine, except the alternative that is directly based on the NAS panel's recommended treatment of medical spending. To calculate poverty under the NAS panel recommendation, we subtract from resources as defined above the family's out-of-pocket medical spending, including spending on insurance premiums.[18]

Estimated Poverty Rates

Table 4.1 contains our estimates of poverty rates in 1998 under the official poverty definition and eight alternatives to the official definition. Poverty rates are shown for the entire CPS population as well as a variety of subgroups within the noninstitutionalized population. The estimates in column 1 were obtained using the official poverty definition. That is, family resources were measured as pretax money income and were compared to the official poverty threshold to determine whether each family is poor.

The second column implements all of the NAS panel's recommendations except its proposed treatment of out-of-pocket medical spending. Out-of-

Table 4.1. Percentage of Population That Is Poor Under Alternative Poverty Definitions, 1998

	Official (1)	NAS (a) (2)	NAS (b) (3)	Mean spending not top-coded			Mean spending top-coded at 95th percentile		
				(4a)	(4b)	(4c)	(5a)	(5b)	(5c)
All persons	12.7	12.0	16.1	16.4	16.6	19.4	16.0	16.2	19.0
Race and ethnicity									
White non-Hispanic	8.2	7.9	11.5	11.5	11.6	13.3	11.1	11.3	13.0
White	10.5	10.0	14.0	14.2	14.4	16.8	13.8	14.0	16.5
African American	26.1	23.6	28.8	30.0	30.5	35.0	29.4	29.9	34.5
Asian or Pacific Islander	12.5	12.8	16.3	15.8	15.9	18.1	15.8	15.8	18.0
Hispanic[a]	25.6	24.0	30.0	31.4	32.2	39.4	31.0	31.8	39.0
Member of immigrant household[b]									
Yes	20.3	19.5	25.1	25.9	26.5	32.8	25.5	26.1	32.4
No	11.6	10.8	14.7	14.9	15.2	17.3	14.5	14.8	17.0
Age group									
Children (under age 18)	18.9	17.0	21.2	21.1	21.2	25.0	20.7	20.9	24.8
Nonelderly adults (age 18 to 64)	10.5	10.4	13.5	13.8	14.2	16.9	13.6	13.9	16.6
Elderly (age 65 and older)	10.5	8.9	17.7	19.2	19.3	19.7	17.9	18.1	18.5
Family structure									
In all families	11.2	10.7	14.6	14.6	14.9	17.8	14.3	14.6	17.5
In married-couple families	6.2	6.0	9.3	9.1	9.3	11.6	8.9	9.1	11.4
In families with a female householder, no spouse present	33.1	31.1	37.4	37.9	38.8	43.4	37.4	38.2	43.1
Unrelated individuals	19.9	17.4	22.9	24.9	24.9	26.6	23.9	23.9	25.5

	Definition 1	Definition 2	Definition 3	Definition 4a	Definition 4b	Definition 4c	Definition 5a	Definition 5b	Definition 5d
Residence									
In metropolitan areas	12.3	11.5	15.1	15.4	15.7	18.3	15.1	15.3	18.0
In central cities	18.7	17.0	21.6	22.2	22.6	18.7	21.7	22.1	18.7
In suburbs	8.6	8.2	11.3	11.5	11.6	8.6	11.2	11.4	8.6
Outside metropolitan areas	14.4	14.0	19.5	20.0	20.3	14.4	19.4	19.7	14.4
Region									
Northeast	12.3	10.7	14.6	14.6	14.8	12.3	14.2	14.5	12.3
Midwest	10.3	9.8	13.5	13.8	14.0	17.0	13.4	13.6	16.6
South	13.7	13.5	17.9	18.5	18.8	15.9	18.1	18.4	15.6
West	14.0	13.0	17.1	17.2	17.5	22.0	16.8	17.2	21.7
Head of family or spouse works									
Yes	8.7	8.6	11.9	11.8	12.1	20.9	11.6	11.8	20.5
No	31.6	28.0	35.9	38.0	38.4	40.0	36.9	37.2	38.8

Note: Definition 1: Official poverty measure; Definition 2: Modified NAS definition, ignoring the impact on net income of medical out-of-pocket spending; Definition 3: Modified NAS definition, subtracting medical out-of-pocket spending from household income. Definitions 4a, 4b, 4c, 5a, 5b, and 5d: Six different alternative measures using the fixed averages method for medical out-of-pocket spending. For details see text.

[a] Persons of Hispanic origin may be of any race.

[b] Member of a family headed by an immigrant or an unrelated individual who is an immigrant.

Sources: U.S. Census Bureau and authors' tabulations of March 1999 CPS file.

pocket health expenditures are not subtracted from other net cash and near-cash in-kind income in this column to determine family resources. However, this column implements the NAS panel's other recommendations with regard to defining the poverty thresholds and measuring family resources. The third column implements all of the NAS panel's recommendations including its proposed treatment of family medical spending.

If out-of-pocket medical spending is not subtracted from available resources, the poverty rates under the official definition and the NAS panel definition are very close. The estimated poverty rate under the two definitions is within 1 percentage point over the entire period since 1979 (Burtless and Smeeding, 2002). The most striking feature of the tabulations in the first three columns of Table 4.1 is the much higher rate of poverty if out-of-pocket medical expenses are subtracted from household resources. In comparison with a definition that ignores household medical spending, a definition that subtracts such spending adds 3.4 to 4.1 percentage points to the national poverty rate.

Subtraction of health expenditures also significantly changes the apparent composition of the nation's poor. Many of the people who are pushed into poverty have high spending on medical care because they are old or chronically disabled. Thus, the choice of a poverty definition makes a big difference in the relative poverty rates of different age groups. Under the official poverty definition, both elderly and nonelderly adults had the same poverty rates in 1998. The rate among children was 80 percent higher than that of adults (18.9 percent versus 10.5 percent). Under the second definition of poverty, the rate among children and the elderly falls while the rate among nonelderly adults is virtually unaffected (column 2). Under this definition, the elderly face the lowest risk of poverty (8.9 percent). Under the alternative definition that subtracts out-of-pocket medical spending, the poverty rate among the elderly almost doubles, rising to 17.7 percent (column 3). The rates among children and nonelderly adults rise more modestly, to 21.2 and 13.5 percent, respectively. Because the elderly face the biggest medical bills, their relative income position suffers the most under the third poverty definition.

As noted above, the high and rising medical spending of the elderly has also provided genuine improvements to their well-being. As older Americans' spending has increased over time, their average health has improved and their risk of dying at a given age has declined (Wolfe and Smeeding, 1999, Table 2). Under a definition of income that subtracts medical spending from household income, the upward trend in out-of-pocket spending could yield an increase in their measured poverty, even though it has also produced a real enhancement to their health, especially among the people who are spending the largest amounts.

The next six columns display poverty rates estimated using several variants of the poverty thresholds that include estimates of "reasonable" health outlays. The first three of these columns contain poverty estimates under "low," "intermediate," and "high" estimates of reasonable medical spending, where the estimates of reasonable spending were obtained without top-coding of NMES respondents' health expenditure reports (columns 4a, 4b, and 4c). The last three columns contain poverty estimates obtained using somewhat lower estimates of reasonable medical spending. In particular, the estimates of reasonable spending were calculated with top-coded values of health expenditure reports (columns 5a, 5b, and 5c).

The estimated poverty rates in columns 4b, 4c, and 5c are uniformly higher than those shown in column 3. The estimates in column 4a and 5a are usually slightly below those displayed in column 3, while those in column 5b are usually a bit above those in column 3. Thus, only our lowest estimates of "reasonable" out-of-pocket medical spending produce a set of poverty thresholds that results in a lower poverty rate estimate than the one obtained under the NAS panel's recommendation. The other four estimates of poverty thresholds produce a higher poverty rate than the poverty definition proposed by the NAS panel.

All six variants of the new poverty definition produce a substantially higher estimate of poverty than the official poverty definition. The poverty rate under the new definition is 2.8 percent to 6.7 percent higher than the official poverty definition, depending on the variant of "reasonable" medical spending that is included in the poverty threshold. The jump in the poverty rate occurs because the poverty thresholds under all variants of the new definition are substantially higher than the thresholds in the official definition. Even using the lowest estimate of "reasonable" medical needs, the average poverty threshold in 1998 was 17 percent higher than the average poverty threshold under the official poverty definition (compare the first and third rows in Table 4.2). For families headed by a person aged 65 or older, the discrepancy is even larger. The addition of "reasonable" medical needs to the NAS-recommended poverty thresholds yields an average threshold that is 40 percent higher than the official poverty line. Even though the NAS-recommended measure of income used in the new poverty definition results in a much higher estimate of family resources at the bottom of the income distribution, the increase in the poverty thresholds produces the bigger impact on poverty. As a result, inclusion of medical needs in the thresholds greatly increases the estimate of poverty.

Why is the estimated poverty rate typically higher when reasonable medical spending is added to the poverty thresholds than when actual medical spending is subtracted from family resources? When we add an intermediate estimate of reasonable medical spending to the poverty thresholds, the overall

Table 4.2. Average Poverty Thresholds Under Alternative Threshold Definitions, 1998

Threshold definition	Families headed by person under 65	Families headed by person age 65 or older
Official poverty threshold	$14,840	$10,660
NAS-recommended threshold	14,960	11,520
NAS threshold plus "reasonable" medical expenses[a]	17,390	14,970

[a] Lowest estimate of "reasonable" medical expenses (see text).

Source: Authors' tabulations of March 1999 CPS files.

poverty rate is 16.6 percent (column 4b). Under the preferred NAS poverty measure, the rate is just 16.1 percent (column 3). In part, the higher poverty rate under the alternative poverty definition is explained by the fact that our intermediate estimate of reasonable medical spending includes a higher estimate of average spending than the actual average observed for some families. In particular, we assume that families which lack health insurance will spend as much as lower-middle-income families which are covered by an insurance plan, even though on average uninsured low-income families spend less than this amount. Under the NAS definition, only the actual amount of out-of-pocket spending is subtracted from other family resources to determine net family resources.

The most important reason for the higher poverty rate under our alternative definition, however, is that actual medical spending is very unevenly distributed in the population (see Figure 4.1). Among lower-middle-income nonaged families with health insurance containing two or three members, at least one of whom is in fair or poor health, average out-of-pocket medical spending is $3,545. This estimate of reasonable medical spending is added to the NAS panel's recommended poverty thresholds for all families with the indicated characteristics. However, two-thirds of all families in the category spent less than $3,545; one-third of all families spent less than half of $3,545; and 15 percent spent less than $500 on medical care. Thus, compared with the NAS panel's recommended procedure, our alternative procedure includes a higher provision for medical spending for the great majority of families. In a minority of cases, the NAS panel's procedure includes a bigger provision for medical spending than our alternative procedure, but these cases represent a small proportion of the families counted as poor.

As noted above, the NAS panel did not endorse a single set of poverty thresholds. Instead, it described a method for estimating thresholds that would cover the cost of minimal food, clothing, and shelter consumption, plus a small extra allowance for other necessary items except for medical care. It suggested that an appropriate threshold should fall in the range between 89.7 percent and 103.75 percent of median spending on food, clothing, and shelter. In deriving the thresholds used to estimate poverty rates under alternative definitions, we have used a multiplier at the mid-point of this range (96.725 percent of median spending). If instead we used the NAS panel's lowest multiplier, 89.7 percent of median spending, the thresholds and estimated poverty rates under the alternative definitions would fall. Under any of the variants we examined, however, the estimated poverty rate would remain above the rate measured using the official poverty definition. For example, if we combined our lowest estimate of "reasonable" medical spending with the NAS panel's lowest multiplier on food, clothing, and shelter needs, the estimated poverty rate would be 13.9 percent, or 1.2 percentage points above the official estimate.

In order to reproduce the official estimate of poverty using the new poverty definition, it is necessary either to scale back the NAS panel's minimum estimate of spending needs for food, clothing, and shelter (plus a little extra) or to reduce our lowest estimate of "reasonable" medical spending. Assuming that all of the adjustment is made in the NAS panel's estimate of minimum food, clothing, and shelter requirements, we could reproduce the official estimate of the poverty rate by assuming that minimum spending requirements for food, clothing, and shelter (plus a little extra) are equal to about 85.4 percent of median spending on food, clothing, and shelter. This spending level is about 5 percent lower than the minimum proposed poverty thresholds suggested by the NAS panel. On the other hand, the new poverty threshold makes an explicit allowance for spending on medical care, with different medical spending allowances for families with differing health needs and health insurance coverage. In contrast, the poverty thresholds recommended by the NAS panel included no provision for medical spending. Under these circumstances, it is not obvious whether a threshold that provides enough resources for families to obtain 85.4 percent of median spending on food, clothing, and shelter plus an allowance for "reasonable" medical spending should be judged too parsimonious.

Relative poverty rates across subgroups in the population. Table 4.3 presents estimates of the relative poverty rates of different population subgroups under the competing poverty definitions. In each case, the poverty rate of the indicated group is measured as a percentage of the total poverty rate under that definition. For example, persons who are white and non-Hispanic have a

Table 4.3. *Relative Poverty Rates of Population Subgroups Under Alternative Poverty Definitions, 1998*

| | Percent of population that is poor under definition number— | | | | | | | | |
| | Official (1) | NAS (a) (2) | NAS (b) (3) | Mean spending not top-coded | | | Mean spending top-coded at 95th percentile | | |
Group or characteristic				(4a)	(4b)	(4c)	(5a)	(5b)	(5c)
All persons	100	100	100	100	100	100	100	100	100
Race and ethnicity									
White non-Hispanic	65	66	71	70	70	69	70	69	68
White	83	83	87	86	87	87	86	86	87
African American	206	197	179	183	183	181	184	184	182
Asian or Pacific Islander	98	107	102	97	96	94	99	98	94
Hispanic[a]	202	200	187	192	193	204	194	196	205
Member of immigrant household[b]									
Yes	160	163	156	158	159	169	160	161	170
No	91	90	91	91	91	90	91	91	89
Age group									
Children (under age 18)	149	142	132	129	128	129	130	128	131
Nonelderly adults (age 18 to 64)	83	87	84	84	85	87	85	86	88
Elderly (age 65 and older)	83	74	110	117	116	102	112	111	97
Family structure									
In all families	88	89	91	89	89	92	89	90	92
In married-couple families	49	50	58	56	56	60	56	56	60

In families with a female householder, no spouse present	261	259	233	232	233	224	234	235	227
Unrelated individuals	157	145	143	152	149	137	150	147	134
Residence									
In metropolitan areas	97	96	94	94	94	95	94	94	95
In central cities	147	142	134	135	136	97	136	136	99
In suburbs	68	68	71	70	70	44	70	70	45
Outside metropolitan areas	113	117	121	122	122	74	122	121	76
Region									
Northeast	97	89	91	89	89	63	89	89	64
Midwest	81	82	84	84	84	88	84	84	87
South	108	113	112	113	113	82	113	113	82
West	110	108	106	105	105	114	105	106	114
Head of family or spouse works									
Yes	69	72	74	72	72	108	72	73	108
No	249	233	223	232	231	206	231	229	204

Notes: Poverty rate as a percentage of the overall poverty rate under the definition

Definition 1: Official poverty measure; Definition 2: Modified NAS definition; Definition 2: Modified NAS definition, ignoring the impact on net income of medical out-of-pocket spending; Definition 3: Modified NAS definition, subtracting medical out-of-pocket spending from household income. Definitions 4a, 4b, 4c, 5a, 5b, and 5d: Six different alternative measures using the fixed averages method for medical out-of-pocket spending. For details see text.

[a] Persons of Hispanic origin may be of any race.

[b] Member of a family headed by an immigrant or an unrelated individual who is an immigrant.

Sources: U. S. Census Bureau and author's tabulations of March 1999 CPS file.

poverty rate using the official poverty definition that is 65 percent of the overall official poverty rate. African Americans have a rate that is 206 percent of the official poverty rate for the population as a whole. In each column we show the relative poverty rates calculated under a different definition of poverty or using a different estimate of "reasonable" medical needs.

Although relative poverty rates are usually similar under all of the definitions we consider, there are some notable exceptions. Relative poverty rates are most similar under the definitions that include medical spending either in the measure of family resources or in the poverty thresholds. The biggest differences in relative poverty rates are between the two definitions that exclude any explicit treatment of medical spending (columns 1 and 2) and the remaining seven definitions that include such spending either in the measure of family resources (column 3) or in the poverty thresholds (columns 4a through 5c).

This important difference is highlighted in Table 4.4, which shows relative poverty rates under the official poverty definition (column 1) and under an alternative definition that includes "reasonable" medical spending allowances in the poverty thresholds (column 5a'). In this case we have used our lowest estimates of "reasonable" medical spending (used to estimate poverty rates in column 5a of Tables 4.1 and 4.3), but we have reduced our estimate of family spending requirements for food, clothing, and shelter to just 85.4 percent of median spending on food, clothing, and shelter reported in the Consumer Expenditure Survey. This estimate of the poverty thresholds yields an estimated poverty rate of 12.7 percent, exactly the same as the official poverty rate in 1998. Thus, the relative poverty rates displayed in Table 4.4 reflect relative poverty differences when the overall poverty rate estimated by the two definitions is exactly the same.

Including an estimate of necessary medical spending in the 1998 poverty thresholds increases the relative poverty rate of the elderly and reduces the relative poverty rate of children. It leaves the relative poverty rate of nonelderly adults virtually unchanged. The reason for the increased relative poverty of the elderly has already been mentioned. Older Americans spend larger amounts on medical care. Whether this fact is reflected in the poverty thresholds, as it is in the second column of Table 4.4, or in the measure of family resources, as it is in the poverty definition proposed by the NAS panel, the old-age poverty rate will increase. On the other hand, the relative poverty rate of children is reduced by inclusion of medical spending in the definition of poverty. Under the official poverty definition, the child poverty rate is nearly 1.5 times the poverty rate of the entire population. Under the alternative definition examined in Table 4.4, the child poverty rate is just 1.28 times the overall poverty rate. Two factors account for the improvement of the measurement of

Table 4.4. Relative Poverty Rates of Population Subgroups Under Alternative Poverty Definitions, 1998

Group or characteristic	Poverty definition[a]	
	Official	(5a')
All persons	100	100
Age group		
Children (under age 18)	149	128
Nonelderly adults (age 18 to 64)	83	86
Elderly (age 65 and older)	83	109
Family structure		
In all families	88	87
In married-couple families	49	50
In families with a female householder, no spouse present	261	244
Unrelated individuals	157	162
Residence		
In metropolitan areas	97	94
In central cities	147	137
In suburbs	68	70
Outside metropolitan areas	113	121
Region		
Northeast	97	89
Midwest	81	83
South	108	115
West	110	104

Notes: Poverty rate as a percentage of the overall poverty rate under the definition
[a]Definition 5a': Alternative poverty definition that yields same estimate of poverty rate as official poverty definition (see text).

Sources: U.S. Census Bureau and authors' tabulations of March 1999 CPS file.

the relative condition of children under the new poverty definition. First, since few families containing children also contain elderly members, average health spending is somewhat lower among families with children than it is in the population as a whole. Second, many low-income families containing children receive free or nearly free health care as a result of enrollment in the means-tested Medicaid program. This program has been gradually expanded over the past decade, allowing a larger fraction of low-income children to obtain free or inexpensive care. Moreover, in the implementation of the alternative poverty threshold examined in Table 4.4, we have assigned relatively low medical spending thresholds to many low-income families with children. Children who are reported to be uninsured are sometimes assigned out-of-pocket spending amounts characteristic of families that are insured by the Medicaid program. This is done in cases where the income and other characteristics of the family suggest it is eligible for Medicaid.

This method of assigning medical spending thresholds to families that appear to be eligible for Medicaid, even if they do not report they were insured by Medicaid, also helps explain changes in the relative poverty rate of families with a single-female head. These families have a lower relative poverty rate under the alternative definition than they do under the official poverty definition. Many of these families are insured by Medicaid or have income and other characteristics that suggest they are eligible to be insured, even if they report they are uninsured.

Note that the relative poverty rate of central city residents is reduced by including medical spending in the poverty threshold. On the other hand, the relative poverty rate of residents of nonmetropolitan areas increases when medical spending is included in the thresholds. Residents of rural areas, small towns, and small cities tend to be older and hence to face larger medical bills. Table 4.4 also shows that the alternative poverty definition would have a noticeable impact on the regional distribution of poverty. People living in the south face a relatively higher risk of poverty under the alternative definition; people in the northeast face a significantly lower relative risk under that definition. Of course, some of these changes in relative poverty rates are due to the different measures of family resources under the two poverty definitions. Nonetheless, the poverty differentials displayed in Table 4.4 show that adopting alternative ways of measuring poverty can subtly alter common perceptions of poverty.

Conclusion

Critics of U.S. poverty measurement have long complained that the official poverty definition has serious defects. These deficiencies are most apparent in its treatment of health spending needs. Unfortunately, there are no simple approaches to incorporating medical spending in poverty measurement that command wide support among economists or policy analysts. Neither social scientists nor policymakers have defined a basic bundle of health care "necessities" as opposed to less essential health care "luxuries." The same medical procedure may save one person's life, ameliorate pain for another, and be unnecessary for another. Welfare evaluation of either medical consumption or medical need is notoriously difficult.

Some people have tried to implement simple fixes in our existing measures of family deprivation or household resources. For example, several early researchers proposed adding the monetary value of health insurance subsidies to other components of cash and noncash income to estimate a family's total spendable resources. This procedure greatly reduces measured poverty in population groups, such as the elderly, which have both generous health insurance subsidies and heavy medical utilization. A drawback of this procedure is that it assumes an unrealistic substitutability between health insurance protection and ability to consume other goods. Because households cannot easily use their health insurance coverage to pay for nonmedical necessities, such as food and shelter, adding the cash value of health insurance subsidies to other household income overstates its value to most households, especially households with modest incomes.

A panel of the National Academy of Sciences proposed a radically different approach toward accounting for medical spending in the measurement of poverty. It suggested that health care expenses be integrated into poverty measurement by subtracting out-of-pocket spending on medical care from other elements of household income. In effect, all health care expenses, including those on health insurance premiums, would be treated as a "tax" on incomes. Under this procedure, the benefits provided by health care subsidies are assumed to be incommensurate with benefits generated by other consumption expenditures. The procedure treats two families as equally poor (or equally well off) if each has income of X, and one receives a free health insurance plan and the other does not, if their expenditures on health care are the same. Many economists do not find the implications of the NAS panel's procedure very appealing. Are two families with the same income and the same medical spending, but different medical insurance plans, both equally well off, even if one family has no insurance and the other is very generously insured?

Subtracting health care expenses from other income also produces a resource measure that does not directly address the problem of households' differing health care needs. Actual expenses reflect differences in health status and insurance coverage to some extent, because out-of-pocket spending is higher for those who are seriously ill and lower for those who are covered by a generously subsidized insurance plan. But actual medical spending provides no clear indication of the adequacy of health care available to individuals or households or of the appropriateness of the health services they receive.

In this chapter, we have examined a procedure for measuring poverty that includes an estimate of the "reasonable" medical spending in the poverty thresholds. Instead of subtracting actual medical spending from other family income to measure net family resources, as proposed by the NAS panel, we obtain plausible estimates of expected medical spending requirements faced by different classes of families. The estimates take account of the number, age, and health of family members as well as their coverage under a health insurance plan. For families that lack insurance coverage, we attempt to estimate their expected spending to gain insurance coverage as well as to pay their medical bills after insurance coverage has been obtained. Because we do not have enough evidence to calculate "reasonable" health spending with much precision, we examine the sensitivity of poverty rates to the use of different estimates of "reasonable" medical spending.

Two conclusions stand out in this analysis. First, the inclusion of medical spending in the poverty definition has a large effect on the level and composition of poverty. Groups that are heavy users of medical care, such as the aged and disabled, appear to suffer relatively worse poverty when explicit account is taken of the burden of medical spending. This is true whether medical spending is subtracted from family resources — as proposed by the NAS panel — or approximations of "reasonable" spending levels are added to the poverty thresholds. Under either of these procedures, groups with high out-of-pocket expenditures on health care appear to suffer worse poverty rates than revealed by the official poverty statistics. Second, the level and composition of poverty is comparatively unaffected by the decision to add "reasonable" medical spending to poverty thresholds rather than subtract actual medical spending from family resources. By judiciously selecting estimates of "reasonable" health spending, analysts can derive estimates of poverty thresholds that nearly duplicate the level and pattern of poverty found when actual medical spending is subtracted from family resources. The choice between these two methods of measuring poverty then largely depends on theoretical preferences and convenience of estimation, for both approaches to including health spending can produce virtually identical pictures of the nation's poor.

Appendix 4.1. *"Reasonable" Out-of-Pocket Medical Spending and Its Relation to Family Characteristics, Measured in 1998 Prices*

			Healthy Family[b] Family Size[f]			Less Healthy Family[c] Family Size		
			1	2	3	1	2	3
High Estimate[a]								
Non-elderly family head,[d]	Not fully insured,	Not receiving Medicaid	$3,346	$6,938	$7,525	$4,349	$7,668	$7,104
		Receiving Medicaid	3,346	6,938	7,525	4,349	7,668	7,104
	Fully insured,	Not receiving Medicaid	1,382	2,862	2,935	2,896	3,544	3,518
		Receiving Medicaid	512	580	953	332	1,200	1,903
Elderly family head,[e]	Not fully insured,	Not receiving Medicaid	2,409	4,201	4,843	2,696	5,011	4,134
		Receiving Medicaid	2,409	4,201	4,843	2,696	5,011	4,134
	Fully insured,	Not receiving Medicaid	1,987	2,968	3,146	2,549	4,421	4,482
		Receiving Medicaid	485	1,372	1,388	1,670	1,230	2,962
			Healthy Family[b] Family Size[f]			Less Healthy Family[c] Family Size		
			1	2	3	1	2	3
Middle Estimate[a]								
Non-elderly family head,[d]	Not fully insured,	Not receiving Medicaid	$1,382	$2,862	$2,935	$2,896	$3,544	$3,518
		Receiving Medicaid	512	580	953	332	1,200	1,903
	Fully insured,	Not receiving Medicaid	1,382	2,862	2,935	2,896	3,544	3,518
		Receiving Medicaid	512	580	953	332	1,200	1,903
Elderly family head,[e]	Not fully insured,	Not receiving Medicaid	1,987	2,968	3,146	2,549	4,421	4,482
		Receiving Medicaid	485	1,372	1,388	1,670	1,230	2,962
	Fully insured,	Not receiving Medicaid	1,987	2,968	3,146	2,549	4,421	4,482
		Receiving Medicaid	485	1,372	1,388	1,670	1,230	2,962

Appendix 4.1 Continued

Low Estimate[a]		Healthy Family[b] Family Size			Less Healthy Family[c] Family Size		
		1	2	3	1	2	3
Non-elderly family head,[d]	Not fully insured, Not eligible for Medicaid[g]	$1,382	$2,862	$2,935	$2,896	$3,544	$3,518
	Eligible for Medicaid	512	580	953	332	1,200	1,903
	Fully insured, Not eligible for Medicaid	1,382	2,862	2,935	2,896	3,544	3,518
	Eligible for Medicaid	512	580	953	332	1,200	1,903
Elderly family head,[e]	Not fully insured, Not eligible for Medicaid	1,987	2,968	3,146	2,549	4,421	4,482
	Eligible for Medicaid	485	1,372	1,388	1,670	1,230	2,962
	Fully insured, Not eligible for Medicaid	1,987	2,968	3,146	2,549	4,421	4,482
	Eligible for Medicaid	485	1,372	1,388	1,670	1,230	2,962

Source: Authors' tabulations of NMES as explained in the text.

[a] All calculations are based on the untruncated distribution of medical spending observed in the NMES updated to spending amounts for 1998.

[b] All family members report health as "good," "very good," or "excellent."

[c] At least one family member reports health as "fair" or "poor."

[d] Under 65.

[e] 65 or older.

[f] If the family head is under 65, the categories are (1) one member; (2) two or three members; (3) four or more members. If the family head is 65 or older, the categories are (1) one member; (2) two members; (3) three or more members.

[g] Our imputations of eligibility for Medicaid are based in part on descriptions and analysis described in Broaddus and Ku (2000). Eligibility criteria were found in Hoffman and Schlobohm (2000) and the 1998 and 2000 editions of *The Green Book*.

Notes

We gratefully acknowledge the substantial research assistance of Patricia Powers and Molly Fifer and the helpful comments of David Betson, Nancy Birdsall, Jan Blakeslee, Carol Graham, Timothy Smeeding, and Barbara Wolfe. We also acknowledge the financial support of the Annie E. Casey Foundation provided through the University of Wisconsin's Institute for Research on Poverty. The opinions and conclusions are solely those of the authors and should not be attributed to the Annie E. Casey Foundation, the Institute for Research on Poverty, or the Brookings Institution.

1. In the 1960–61 Consumer Expenditure Survey, 6.7 percent of household expenditures was devoted to health care consumption; in the 1999 Survey, the share devoted to health care was just 5.3 percent (Jacobs and Shipp, 1990, p. 21; and ftp://ftp.bls.gov/pub/special.requests/ce/standard/y9399/multiyr.txt, downloaded March 16, 2001).

2. After attending a two-day conference on poverty measurement, forty-four social scientist specialists and public policy students were asked to evaluate the recommendations of the NAS panel. Only 40 percent of voting participants — and just 27 percent of all participants at the conference — approved of the panel's recommendation for treating household medical spending. This is a far lower level of agreement than reported for other elements of the panel's proposal (Corbett, 1999, p. 53). See also Bavier (2000) and the response by Betson (2000).

3. We describe below the basic procedures used to measure family resources and estimate poverty thresholds for families with different sizes and compositions.

4. Roughly 7 percent of household expenditures were devoted to health care spending when the original poverty thresholds were adopted. See note 1.

5. This reasoning clearly does not apply in the case of a household for which an overwhelming percentage of household resources is received in the form of food stamps. In this case, however, the family would be classified as poor regardless of the treatment of food stamp benefits, because the basic food coupon allotment is far below any plausible poverty threshold. Thus, the NAS panel's proposal makes a difference in measuring poverty status only where the household's resources, aside from food stamps, bring the household reasonably close to the threshold. The panel's proposed treatment of near-cash in-kind benefits is more problematical in the case of housing subsidies. In some parts of the United States, the market value of this subsidy can be very high; it may even approach the poverty threshold. Yet households occupying subsidized apartments may have limited ability to use the housing subsidy to pay for other necessities, such as food or medical care. This is particularly true in the case of households with few other resources aside from the housing subsidy.

6. The Census Bureau describes fungible value as follows: "The fungible approach for valuing medical coverage assigns income to the extent that having the insurance would free up resources that would have been spent on medical care. The estimated fungible value depends on family income, the cost of food and housing needs, and the market value of the medical benefits. If family income is not sufficient to cover the family's basic food and housing requirements, the fungible value methodology treats medicare and medicaid as having no income value. If family income exceeds the cost of food and housing requirements, the fungible value of medicare and medicaid is equal to the

amount which exceeds the value assigned for food and housing requirements (up to the amount of the market value of an equivalent insurance policy (total cost divided by the number of participants in each risk class)." http://www.census.gov/hhes/income/histinc/ redefs.html [downloaded March 19, 2001].

7. Another problem is that, contrary to the popular view, an important fraction of medical spending *is* discretionary. Two people who have identical health and health insurance plans may choose to visit doctors, dentists, and physical and mental therapists on differing schedules, depending on their taste for medical services. It is extremely unlikely that every visit to a doctor or therapist is equally necessary to the maintenance of good health.

8. Authors' tabulations of Bureau of Labor Statistics data from the 1999 Consumer Expenditure Survey.

9. Procedures for developing estimates of household medical spending are described in Betson (1997) and Betson (1998) and in Short et al. (1999), pp. C-16–C-19.

10. The Census Bureau estimates the 1997 poverty population consisted of 35.6 million people. http://www.cache.census.gov/hhes/hlthins/hlthin97/hi97t1.html, downloaded March 19, 2001. Of these, 15.4 million (or 43.3 percent) were insured by Medicaid and 8.95 million (or 25.2 percent) were insured by some other plan. Some people who are insured under a government or private insurance plan are not insured during all twelve months of a calendar year.

11. Our tabulations of the March 1999 CPS files show that the average income-to-needs ratio of people below the official poverty threshold was about one-ninth of the ratio among people above the poverty line. These calculations are performed using the Census Bureau's definition of pre-tax money income.

12. The term *family* is used loosely. Our analysis is performed for families and unrelated individuals as defined by the Census Bureau. For purposes of this discussion, a family may be either a Census-defined family or may include an unrelated individual.

13. While it might seem plausible to expect lower average spending in a sample restricted to families with income-to-needs ratios between 0.5 and 1.0 times the median income-to-needs ratio than in a sample containing all families, regardless of income, this expectation is not always realized in the NMES. In about one-third of the sample cells, average health spending was actually higher in the income-constrained sample than in the full sample. This may reflect the sensitivity of the estimated sample mean to spending among families at the extreme upper tail of the distribution. High-expenditure families are almost as likely to be found in the income-constrained sample as in the full sample.

14. Our imputations of eligibility for Medicaid are based in part on descriptions and analysis described in Broaddus and Ku (2000). Eligibility criteria were found in Hoffman and Schlobohm (2000) and the 1998 and 2000 editions of *The Green Book*. It is likely we slightly overestimated the number of children who would be eligible for Medicaid or SCHIP in 1998, for our data sources estimated insurance eligibility rates using the 2000 State Children's Health Insurance Program rules.

15. Another approach suggested and analyzed by Richard Bavier (2000) is to include an estimate of 80 percent of the *median* out-of-pocket health spending in the basic poverty thresholds. Because of the highly unequal distribution of medical expenditures (see Figure 4.1), this method would clearly produce a lower set of thresholds than the

methods we examine here. In light of the very skewed distribution of medical spending, some observers might wonder whether median medical spending provides families with a reliable cushion for paying for the medical care episodes they can anticipate over the course of their lifetimes — or even over the space of a few years.

16. Because our estimates of "reasonable" medical spending increase from year to year in line with changes in actual medical spending, this part of the poverty threshold would on average increase faster than the change in the CPI-U.

17. We use the "SIPP median method" of estimating childcare expenses and other work-related expenses. Essentially, a small weekly allowance is made for work-related expenses except for childcare expenses. Childcare expenses are imputed to a family only when all parents are working. In that case, the imputed childcare expense can be no larger than the wages of the lower paid parent. SIPP panel "median childcare expense" values are taken from Short et al. (1999), Table C12 (p. C-13). The procedures used by the Census Bureau to implement the National Research Council panel's recommendations with respect to childcare and other work-related expenses are described in Short et al. (1999, pp. C-11–C-14).

18. Estimates of out-of-pocket spending are derived using the MOOP imputation method as described by Short et al. (1999, pp. C-16–C-19). We took the imputed spending amounts directly from the Census Bureau's data files posted in the Bureau's web site. For 1998, see http://ftp.census.gov/housing/povmeas/pov98/.

References

Bavier, Richard. "Medical Out-of-Pocket Spending in Poverty Thresholds." Mimeo. Washington, D.C.: U.S. Office of Management and Budget, 2000. *http://www.cen sus.gov/hhes/poverty/povmeas/papers/altmoop.html.*

Bell, Felicitie C. *Social Security Area Population Projections: 1997.* Baltimore: Social Security Administration, Office of the Chief Actuary, 1997. *http://www.ssa.gov/OACT/NOTES/AS112/as112cov.html.*

Betson, David M. "Is Everything Relative? The Role of Equivalence Scales in Poverty Measurement." Mimeo. South Bend, Ind.: Department of Economics, University of Notre Dame, 1996. *http://aspe.os.dhhs.gov/poverty/papers/escale.pdf.*

———. "In Search of an Elusive Truth: How Much Do Americans Spend on Their Health Care?" Mimeo. South Bend, Ind.: Department of Economics, University of Notre Dame, 1997. *http://aspe.os.dhhs.gov/poverty/papers/moop.pdf.*

———. "Imputation of Medical Out-of-Pocket (MOOP) Expenditures to CPS Analysis Files." Mimeo. South Bend, Ind.: Department of Economics, University of Notre Dame, 1998.

———. "Response to Bavier's Critique of the NRC Panel's Recommendations." Mimeo. South Bend, Ind.: Department of Economics, University of Notre Dame, 2000. *http://www.census.gov/hhes/poverty/povmeas/papers/comonbavier.pdf.*

Betson, David M., and Jennifer L. Warlick. "Reshaping the Historical Record with a Comprehensive Definition of Poverty." Mimeo. South Bend, Ind.: Department of Economics, University of Notre Dame, 1998.

Broaddus, Matthew, and Leighton Ku. "Nearly 95 Percent of Low-Income Uninsured Children Now Are Eligible for Medicaid or SCHIP: Measures Need to Increase Enrollment Among Eligible but Uninsured Children." Mimeo. Washington, D.C.: Center on Budget and Policy Priorities, 2000. *http://www.cbpp.org/12–6–00schip.htm.*

Burtless, Gary, Thomas Corbett, and Wendell Primus. "Improving the Measurement of American Poverty." Mimeo. Madison: Institute for Research on Poverty, University of Wisconsin, 1997.

Burtless, Gary, and Timothy M. Smeeding. "The Level, Trend, and Composition of Poverty." In Sheldon Danziger, Robert Haveman, and Barbara Wolfe (eds.), *Understanding Poverty: Progress and Problems.* Cambridge, Mass.: Harvard University Press, 2002.

Citro, Connie F., and Robert T. Michael (eds.). *Measuring Poverty: A New Approach.* Washington, D.C.: National Academy Press, 1995.

Corbett, Thomas. "Poverty: Improving the Measure After Thirty Years — A Conference." *Focus* 20, no. 2 (Spring 1999), pp. 51–55.

Garner, Thesia I., Kathleen Short, Stephanie Shipp, Charles Nelson, and Geoffrey Paulin. "Experimental Poverty Measurement for the 1990s." *Monthly Labor Review* (March 1998), pp. 39–68.

Health Care Financing Administration. "1999 National Health Expenditures Tables," Table 4, *http://www.hcfa.gov/stats/nhe-oact/tables/Tables.pdf,* 2000.

Hoffman, Catherine, and Alan Schlobohm. "Uninsured in America: A Chart Book." 2nd ed. Washington, D.C.: Kaiser Commission on Medicaid and the Uninsured, 2000.

Jacobs, Eva, and Stephanie Shipp. "How Family Spending Has Changed in the U.S." *Monthly Labor Review* (March 1990), pp. 20–27.

Short, Kathleen, Thesia I. Garner, David Johnson, and Patricia Doyle. *Experimental Poverty Measures, 1990–1997,* U.S. Bureau of the Census, P-60-205. Washington, D.C.: U.S. Government Printing Office, 1999.

Wolfe, Barbara, and Timothy M. Smeeding. "Poverty, Health and Health Care Utilization: The Health Needs of the Poor." Mimeo. Syracuse, N.Y.: Center for Policy Research, Syracuse University, 1999.

PART **III**

Structural Causes of African American Poverty

5

The Dynamic Racial Composition of the United States

TUKUFU ZUBERI

A Racially Divided Society

In revisiting Gunnar Myrdal's *An American Dilemma: The Negro Problem and Modern Democracy*, it is appropriate to reconsider the underlying theoretical orientation of that work. Myrdal and his collaborators reduced the "Negro problem" to a problem of assimilation or amalgamation into white America. *An American Dilemma* presents the racial conflict in American society as a moral problem, a problem of the resistance to African amalgamation by European Americans.[1] Myrdal viewed the cultural and physical amalgamation of immigrants as the solution to their social isolation. But Myrdal and his colleagues were not aware at the time they were writing of the dramatic changes in the immigrant population that were about to occur. They could not have foreseen the increase in migrants from Asia and Latin America.

Myrdal saw the antiamalgamation attitude of whites as the obstacle to African American assimilation. In *An American Dilemma*, race is presented as a special case of ethnicity; the problems of African Americans are considered in the same context as the problems of immigrants from Europe.[2] This confounding of race and immigrant status, or ethnicity, in the study of race relations has in origins in the Chicago School's early, pre-1940s study of urban conditions within the United States.

Myrdal presents the European American standard of behavior as that which

African Americans and other immigrants should emulate. This view has its own built-in biases. For example, it suggests that the "Negro problem" would be solved *if* African Americans adopted standards of behavior set by European Americans. This view also dictates that the removal of barriers to assimilation would facilitate both an improvement in the behavior of African Americans and access for them to the fruits of modern democracy. In addition, it is thought that assimilation would eliminate the discrepancy between the ideal of American egalitarianism and the reality of racial discrimination. Thus, racism and discrimination are not problematic if assimilation is allowed.

According to Myrdal, a group's racial problems are caused by that group being unassimilable. Such an approach assumes that racial discrimination is a contradiction rather than an integral part of the American system of stratification, and it has led to a kind of economic reductionism in the study of race relations in the United States. Herman Hoetink was one of the first to criticize this aspect of *An American Dilemma* in his work *Caribbean Race Relations: A Study of Two Variants:*[3] "if, in other words, the Negro group were spread over the higher and the whites on the lower rungs in proportion to their numbers, and the socio-economic gap separating whites and Negroes were to disappear — the race problem would cease to be a problem."[4]

Hoetink argued that populations show a proclivity for racial group attachments. There is a tendency for individuals to consider the interests of their group to be more important than those of other groups. Sociologists generally maintain that racial identity arises as a result of invidious intergroup distinctions and competition,[5] which result from individuals having a biosocial predisposition to consider members of their group to be more important than other people. Individuals seek to increase the position of their race at the expense of other races. When different populations come into contact, conflict will result. Recent research supports Hoetink's earlier formulation of the problem. Lawrence Bobo and James Kluegel suggest that in the United States, "the strongest aspect of group self-interest seems to be a straightforward calculation by whites that members of their own group will not benefit."[6] Even if we are not prepared to view racial problems as natural for human populations, we should consider the role of race in group conflict. In a multiracial society, conflict between racial groups may be a result not only of the struggle over resources but also of a struggle over standards of appropriate behavior and the legacy of difference. In the United States, behavioral differences such as athletic ability and performance on intelligence tests have been connected to phenotypic differences. Race and behavior are thought to interact, thus racial classification is one of the ways that individuals are placed within the system of social stratification.

In generic terms, race refers to social relations among "distinct" peoples. Accordingly, a race may be defined as a group of people living competitively in a relationship of superordination or subordination with respect to some other group or groups of people within a state, country, or economic area. The degree to which individuals can be assimilated depends largely on whether they are ethnically or racially different. For example, European immigrants to the United States are ethnically classified as foreign if they are born abroad and have foreign-born parents. The descendants of these immigrants, starting with the third generation, lose their identity as foreigners and merge into the mainstream, native-born white population. For immigrants from Africa and Asia, however, separate racial categories have been maintained irrespective of how many generations have lived in the United States. In this sense, race is distinct from ethnicity. The United States has many ethnic groups, but it is race not ethnicity that characterizes the divisions within this society. Particularly important in these divisions are physical differences, especially skin color. Africans did not come to America as Africans, they came as Alcan, Yoruba, Ibo, and Wolof. Europeans did not come as Europeans, they came as Englishmen, Scots, Frenchmen, and Irishmen. Likewise, Asians do not come to the United States as Asians, they arrive as Chinese, Japanese, and Indians. And, migrants from Latin America do not come to the United States as Hispanic or Latinos, they come as Mexicans and Cubans.

Race is generally thought of in historical terms. That is, a racial classification is usually applied based on the belief that different racial groups originate from different geographical locations, which are thought to have given each, group its dominant characteristics. From a sociological point of view, geographical locations are thought to have given each racial group its dominant cultural origins, the source of its ethos. Thus, although Europeans originate from a variety of nations and cultures, in the United States their whiteness is what identifies them. Likewise, the physical distinction of blackness, or Africanness, identifies the African American.

As a concept, race requires that two or more distinct races be in existence. Thus, racial groups are always part of a system of race. In a racial system, individuals are classified on the basis of culture and physical distinguishability. Although race may have a biological aspect, racial classification depends on social interaction.

"Race relations" refers to the contact between different racial groups. Ethnic relations are a special case of race relations, like race relations, ethnic relations refer to the social interaction of two populations which are distinguishable on the basis of their physical appearance and culture. Although the contact between two distinct ethnic groups may initially be governed by race relations, given time and favorable social conditions the physical differences are given decreasing significance and the subordinate group's culture is assimilated into that of the superordinate group.

In the United States this process has been extremely important in the creation of the "white race." In the racial assimilation of *an* ethnic group, physical distinctions are overshadowed by the myth of cultural and historical similarities. Assimilation requires that the subordinate group recognize myths of historical similarities and accept the dominant group's culture and historical predisposition. The assimilation of the Irish in the United States is the classic example of this process.[7]

A similar exercise took place in regard to African immigrants to the United States. African slaves were in no position to perpetuate their own national/tribal identity, and they were forced by their social conditions within the Americas to accept their designation as blacks or Africans. However, unlike the Irish, the African population continues to be unassimilable within the United States. In fact, the unassimilability of the African-derived population continues to be a major element of racial classification within American society.

Symbols of social status are an independent factor in the creation of racial prejudice.[8] Every racial group has a complex of physical characteristics that are accepted by the group as its norm.[9] In the United States, skin color is the most salient racial characteristic. For example, the rejection of blackness by mainstream society is seen as a question of social power, and this rejection has had negative consequences for the African American population, especially those with darker skin.[10] The African phenotype, blackness, has a significant negative effect on the occupational status and income of African and Mexican Americans.[11]

The Dynamic Racial Composition of the United States

Changes in the racial composition of the United States result from a combination of differential fertility, differential mortality, and net immigration. In the United States all births, deaths, and migrations are racially classified. Thus, racial classification and immigration have had a direct impact on the social conception of race in the United States. Figure 5.1 presents the changing racial composition of the United States from 1810 to 1990. Variations in fertility and mortality determine to a disproportionate degree the absolute size of past and future populations in the United States. The racial composition of the population of the United States has been dominated by immigration from Europe, Asia, and Africa. Historically, the most distinguishing feature of the changing racial composition of the United States was the

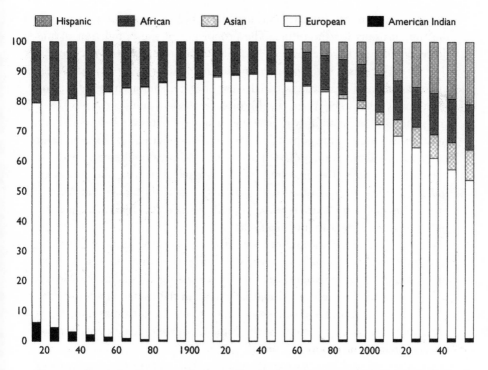

Figure 5.1 Population Percentages by Race, 1810–2050

growth of the African and European populations and the decline of the American Indian population. Equally important, however, is the growth of the Asian and Hispanic populations from 1950 onward. The sudden appearance of the Hispanic population is a result of that classification being introduced in contemporary debates about race and ethnic difference in the U.S. Census Bureau. It is difficult, perhaps impossible, to estimate the actual size of the Hispanic population for the period before 1950.[12]

Figure 5.1 shows the population proportions by race from 1810 to 1990. In 1810 the European population accounted for about 73 percent of the total population. By 1930 the European population accounted for more than 88 percent of the total. In 1990, however, the European population accounted for less than 80 percent of the total. The early rise of the European population resulted from extensive immigration between 1810 and 1930. The European immigrant population began to decline substantially following the Great Depression. The subsequent decline in the proportion held by the European population was in large part caused by the increased migration of Asians and Hispanics (particularly Mexicans).

The racial composition, past and current, of the U.S. population has important implications for the future. The proportion of the population that is
descendants from Europe has been declining since the 1940s. This decline and
the relative increases in the proportion of individuals who are of Asian, African, Hispanic and American Indian descent have tremendous implications for
what it will mean to be American.[13] Projections show that over the next sixty
years the U.S. population will grow more slowly than ever before and the
racial distribution of the population will change dramatically. Nonwhite and
Hispanic populations are projected to dominate future population growth.

Figure 5.2 shows the projected Hispanic, Asian, African, and American
Indian populations up to the year 2050. The American Indian and African
proportion of the population declined until the 1940s. (This decline is most
notable for the American Indian population.)

For the most part, these declines in relative size were the result of European
migration and exceptionally high rates of mortality within the American Indian and African populations. Another reason for the decline in the African
population was the end of the legal slave trade in the United States in 1808.
Around 1950 the Hispanic and Asian populations began to substantially increase their relative proportions of the population, with die Hispanic population experiencing the most growth.

From the fifteenth century to the beginning of the nineteenth century there
was a massive transfer of populations from Africa and Europe to North America. In the nineteenth century and the first half of the twentieth century this
transfer continued for European derived populations. At the same time, the
immigration of large numbers of Africans to North America was substantially
reduced. The past fifty years have witnessed a massive new transfer of populations to North America, particularly the United States, from Asia, Latin America, and the Caribbean.

The diversity within the so-called minority population is complicated by the
problems of racial classification. How racial groups are classified has a tremendous impact on racial composition. The Hispanic and Asian populations
continue to confound the dominant conception of race. Hispanics, Asians,
and other immigrant groups are increasing in numbers and are not fitting into
the traditional racial groups. In the 1990 Census, close to ten million people
chose the "Other, Not Specified" race category. This makes racial classification of the population difficult.

If the current demographic trends and racial conceptions hold, minority
groups will account for over 45 percent of the population. In addition, the
contribution of the different racial groups to the overall population will be
much more diverse than in the past. African Americans will comprise about 14

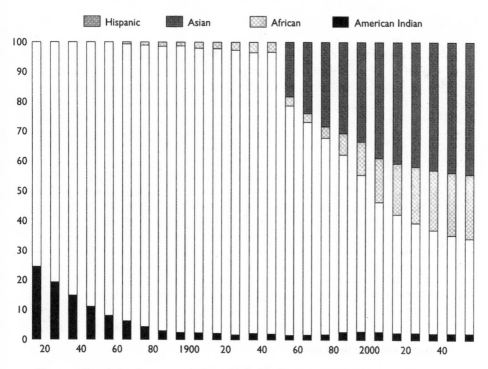

Figure 5.2 Population Percentages by Race (Excluding European), 1810–2050

percent of the U.S. population, with Hispanics accounting for about 22 percent of the total population.[14] However, racial classifications tend to change and population projections rarely hold for more than five or ten years.[15] As in the past, immigration will continue to have a profound impact on the racial composition of the United States.

Race, region of origin, and ethnicity have always been fundamental aspects of the selection of immigrants permitted to enter and settle in the United States. Following the termination of the slave trade, the U.S. Congress attempted to regulate the racial and ethnic composition of the immigrant population as part of its national immigration policy.[16] The major policy objective seems to have been to maintain the racial composition of the population, or to preserve the white majority. This policy found its fullest expression in the national-origin system for the allocation of immigration quotas. It excluded certain populations from immigration on the basis of region of origin. For example, the Asiatic Barred Zone Act of 1917 excluded Asians of various nationalities from U.S. citizenship. This exclusion did not end until 1952, when quotas for Asians were established on the basis of race or ancestry rather

Table 5.1. Percentage of Population by Race and Nativity, 1960–1990

Race	1960	1970	1980	1990
African American				
Foreign-born	1%	1%	3%	4%
Native-born	99	99	97	96
Hispanic				
Foreign-born	32	28	36	41
Native-born	69	72	64	60
European American				
Foreign-born	5	5	4	3
Native-born	95	95	96	97
Asian				
Foreign-born	32	37	61	63
Native-born	68	63	39	37
American Indian				
Foreign-born	1	2	2	1
Native-born	99	98	98	99

Source: 1960–1990 Public Use Microdata files.

than birthplace. Another less drastic example was the selective policy used to curb Southern and Eastern European immigration.

The Hart-Celler Immigration Act of 1965 attempted to eliminate the racially preferential nature of immigration legislation. The stated purpose of the bill was "the elimination of the national-origins system as the basis for the selection of immigrants to the United States."[17] Before the Hart-Celler Immigration Act, the vast majority, over 80 percent, of legal immigrants to the United States were from Europe.[18] Since 1965, the proportion of immigrants from Europe has substantially declined, while the proportions from the Americas and Asia have substantially increased. In addition, the magnitude of undocumented immigration is substantial, and most illegal immigrants come to the United States primarily from Latin America.

Immigrants from Asia, Latin America, and the Caribbean have different conceptions of racial identity.[19] For example, Mexicans have a racial continuum that runs from white to red, not from white to black as in Puerto Rico. Furthermore, the Puerto Rican continuum from white to black is different from the bipolar conception in the United States. The Puerto Rican racial continuum may have more to do with culture than skin color.[20] Racial identification for Asians may not be based on a color continuum and may have

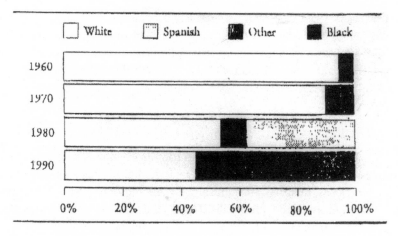

Figure 5.3 Racial Classification of Latin American Immigrants, 1960–1990

more to do with social and political exigencies.[21] For immigrants from the non-Hispanic Caribbean, Africa, and Europe, racial identification within the United States is defined by the history of the United States. For example, when black immigrants from the Caribbean and Africa enter the United States, they are treated as African Americans. European immigrants at the turn of the century experienced a transformation in racial conception: they entered the United States as Poles, Greeks, or Irishmen but were assimilated into the white race. European ethnic groups, unlike Africans, Asians, American Indians, and Hispanics, employ their ethnic identity as an option rather than as an ascribed status.[22]

We may get a better picture of the racial classification of immigrants by examining the racial self-classification of the foreign-born. Table 5.1 presents a cross-tabulation of race by birth status for the period from 1960 to 1990. As shown in Table 5.1, the majority of Asians and a large percentage of Hispanics are foreign-born.

Most Asians classify themselves as Asian, but the racial classification of the Hispanic population is problematic. Figure 5.3 shows the dynamic character of the racial classification of immigrants from Latin America. The two principal problems in racially classifying Hispanics arise from the large immigrant population and the different racial classifications within the countries of origin. Many Hispanics who immigrate to the United States would be classified as whites in their countries of origin. In fact, prior to 1980 most Hispanics classified themselves as racially white within the United States. In 1960 and 1970 over 95 percent of the immigrants from Latin America were classified as white. In 1980 the Census Bureau broadened its racial classifications to allow the Hispanic population to indicate their "Spanish" origin. In 1990, however, the Census Bureau eliminated the "Spanish" origin category, but the immigrants from Latin America continued to classify themselves as other than black or white.

The Limits of Racial Assimilation

The classical model of assimilation is the melting pot.[23] This model assumes that immigrants arrive with a relative disadvantage vis-à-vis European Americans, that they are culturally distant and disdained, and that they lack communication and other skills. Thus, immigrants are initially clustered/segregated near the core of the city. However, the passage of time brings a withering of ethnic differences, and socioeconomic advancement translates into residential mobility/assimilation. This model assumes that the immigrant group will become like the majority population. In the United States the three principal forms of assimilation are residential integration, intermarriage, and the racial classification of children. In each of these types of assimilation the African American has been uniquely excluded.

African Americans are by far the most segregated racial group within the United States.[24] Compared with Asians and Hispanics, among whom higher levels of education and income have been associated with lower levels of segregation, African Americans show a tendency to be residentially isolated regardless of level of income, education, or occupation. Thus, residential segregation may be mote related to racial stratification than to class inequality. Residential segregation is a reflection of the racial separation within the United States. The significance of this separation is rooted in how the members of a given society see themselves and what they want to see in the future.

Ethnic and racial ancestry are attributes that parents transmit to their children within the constraints of socially prescribed rules. Thus, racial and ethnic classifications depend heavily on the family. There is a very high rate of intermarriage among European ethnic groups within the United States.[25] Thus, the children of such marriages could be classified as ethnically mixed, but they are racially white.[26]

The issue of racial heredity is complicated by the tendency for bipolar racial categorizing. Recent research suggests that in marriages between whites and African Americans the children are usually classified as African Americans.[27] Furthermore, Native Americans and Asians in mixed marriages with whites classified their children as white almost twice as often as did African American parents in mixed marriages.

The tendency for children of mixed races to be classified as white except when one parent is African American is further complicated by the patterns of interracial or interethnic marriage. Though the rates of intermarriage of African Americans and whites increased over the past two decades, African American-white intermarriage rates continue to be low compared to those of other nonwhite groups. For example, about 40 percent of Japanese and more than 50 percent of Native American women are interracially married whereas only about 1 percent of African American women and 3 percent of African American men are interracially married. Female outmarriage of African Americans is lower than for all other racial and ethnic groups.

American Indians and Asians are not only assimilating culturally, they are also assimilating physically via intermarriage and residential integration. African Americans, however, are not being assimilated culturally, residentially, or physically. Children from African American mixed marriages are classified as African American; African Americans are not intermarrying as often as other groups; and residential segregation may be increasing. Race continues to be a salient issue in American life.

Conclusion

Immigration has been and continues to be an important factor in the proportional differences in the racial composition of the population of the United States. The American Indian population experienced a dramatic decline in size as a result of the formation of the United States of America. The African and European populations increased proportionally both because of this decline and because of their continued immigration. Immigration continues to be a central issue in race relations in the United States. Racial conflict and competition have been hallmarks of American society from the moment the European settlers encountered established Native American populations in the fifteenth century. The reception of immigrants into the United States to a great degree reflects the interest of the racial groups that compose the population, especially the majority population. In the first half of the twentieth century, European immigrants to the northern United States "provided new supplies of cheap labor that competed with Negro labor for even the lower jobs such as domestics and common laborers."[28] Africans have historically felt that European immigrants displaced African workers and contributed to their continued poverty.[29] Recently, however, African Americans have begun to see their stance on immigration in racial/political terms. This new perspective is apparent in their views about the different treatment given Haitian versus Cuban immigrants to the United States. The older concern with displacement has not died, but it is becoming more politically motivated.

Following immigration, white ethnic groups intermarried and reduced their own ethnic classification to a social option. Given the recent rise in levels of intermarriage among Asians, Hispanics, and American Indians, the importance of homogamy as a factor in racial classification is being called into question. The majority of children produced by these interracial marriages are classified by their parents as whites, which reinforces the polarized definition of race. However, over half of the Hispanic population racially classified itself as "other" in the 1990 decennial census. This has led some scholars to argue that some Hispanics are racially intermediate between white and black.[30] Others have argued that groups like Puerto Ricans view race as culture regardless of the physical types within the culture.

Recently, both Asians and Hispanics have sought racial classification specific to their own historical and cultural experiences. Only time will tell whether this is the beginning of a new system of racial classification within the United States. Still, the patterns of assimilation cannot be denied. Asians and Hispanics have successfully residentially integrated within European American communities.[31]

Racial classification is a unique form of social exclusion. "Majority and minority," "black and white," are formulations of the collective self and the collective other. These distinctions remain important because they facilitate social differentiation and exclusion. These classifications of social difference reconfirm the social inequality of different populations within the society.

Racial isolation and antagonism have stimulated complacency and indifference to racism. Individual and group physical differences are often associated with beauty, culture, and intellectual ability. These associations are the hallmark of racial intolerance and conflict. The social rejection of blackness has helped maintain a social order in which social opportunities and equality are preferentially offered to some and denied to others on the basis of race. Skin color continues to be a major factor in housing, education, and employment. By not confronting the problem of racial stratification socially and economically, we prolong racial conflict.

The social exclusion and marginalization of the African American and American Indian populations have always been confounded by the low economic class position of their average member and the low social prestige ascribed to their racial status. In a multiracial society like the United States conflict results from a legacy of social difference.[32] The assimilationist tradition embodied in *An American Dilemma* stresses the idea that African Americans and other racial groups are below whites socially and morally because of certain values and behaviors. The phenotypic characteristics of different groups are viewed as surface manifestations of inner realities, such as values and behaviors. For African Americans these deviant values and behaviors are thought to have resulted from their endurance of modal, political, and economic marginalization. The idea of race has been important in sustaining this view of social difference. Overcoming the shortcomings of this perspective requires a program of research and action which recognizes race as an integral part of American society, and seeks to change the society. It is not simply a change in African American values and behaviors which is needed. White behaviors and values also require modification if we are to move beyond the trap of race relations.

Little is gained from a discussion of the racial makeup of the United States, which diverts our attention from the issues of racial conflict and competition. To understand the nature of racial conflict in the United States it is necessary that we understand the demographic transformations, which have accompanied the social construction of racial differences and racial acceptance. Race is more a relationship than a group classification. Racial classification places individuals within the system of racial conflict. The United States was born in the racial conflict among European and African immigrants and the American Indians, and today this tradition of conflict continues to live among the descendants of these and newer racial groups from Asia and Latin America.

Notes

1. Gunnar Myrdal, *An American Dilemma: The Negro Problem and Modern Democracy* (New York: Harper and Row, 1962; originally published in 1944), chap. 3.

2. See Robert E. Park and Ernest W. Burgess, and R. D. McKenzie, eds., *The City* (Chicago: University of Chicago Press, 1967, originally published in 1925); Louis Wirth, *The Ghetto* (Chicago: University of Chicago Press, 1923); and Franklin Frazier, *The Negro Family in Chicago* (Chicago: University of Chicago Press, 1932).

3. Herman Hoetink, *Caribbean Race Relations: A Study of Two Variants* (London: Oxford University Press, 1962). Also see Oliver C. Cox, *Caste, Class, and Race: A Study in Social Dynamics* (New York: Doubleday, 1948), chap. 23.

4. Hoetink, *Caribbean Race Relations*, 88.

5. See Milton Gorgon, *Human Nature, Class, and Ethnicity* (New York: Oxford University Press, 1978). Also see Katherine O'Sullivan See and William J. Wilson, "Race and Ethnicity," in Neil Smelser, ed., *Handbook of Sociology* (New York: Sage Publications, 1988), 224–26, for an excellent summary of the arguments on this issue.

6. Lawrence Bobo and James R. Kluegel, "Opposition to Race-Targeting: Self-Interest, Stratification Ideology, or Racial Attitudes?" *American Sociological Review* 58 (4) (1993): 443–64.

7. Audrey Smedley, *Race in North America: Origin and Evolution of a Worldview* (Boulder, Colo.: Westview Press, 1993), and Theodore W. Allen, *The Invention of the White Race*, volume 1: *Racial Oppression and Social Control* (New York: Verso, 1994).

8. Frantz Fanon, *Black Skin, White Masks* (New York: Grove Press, 1967; originally

published as *Peau Noire, Masques Blancs* in 1952); Herman Hoetink, *The Two Variants in Caribbean Race Relations: A Contribution to the Sociology of Segmented Societies* (London: Oxford University Press, 1967).

9. Hoetink, *The Two Variants in Caribbean Race Relations*, pp. 120–60.

10. Fanon, *Black Skin, White Masks*, pp. 190–91. Also see Edward B. Telles and Edward Murguia, "Phenotypic Discrimination and Income Differences among Mexican Americans," *Social Science Quarterly* 71 (4) (1990): 682–96; Verna M. Keith and Cedric Herring, "Skin Tone and Stratification in the Black Community," *American Journal of Sociology* 97 (3) (1991): 760–78; and Clara B. Rodriguez and Hector Cordero-Guzman, "Placing Race in Context," *Ethnic and Racial Studies* 15 (4) (1992): 523–42.

11. See Telles and Murguia, "Phenotypic Discrimination and Income Differences among Mexican Americans"; and Verna M. Keith and Cedric Herring, "Skin Tone and Stratification in the Black Community," *American Journal of Sociology* 97 (3) (1991): 760–78.

12. The majority of the pre-1950 Hispanic population has been counted as white. Therefore, in Figure 5.1 they are included in the pre-1950 European population. The common ancestral ties to Spain and Latin America do not imply an underlying cultural unity among peoples of Hispanic origin. See Frank D. Bean and Marta Tienda, *The Hispanic Population of the United States* (New York: Russell Sage Foundation, 1990), chaps. 1 and 2, for an excellent discussion and summary of the issues surrounding the historical and contemporary problems of classifying the Hispanic population. Mexicans, Puerto Ricans, and Cubans are distinct population with discernable characteristics. Also see JoAnne Willette et al., "The Demographic and Socioeconomic Characteristics of the Hispanic Population in the United States: 1950–1980," Report to the Department of Health and Human Services by Development Associates, Inc. and Population Reference Bureau, 18 January 1982.

13. Future population depends on many factors, which are not necessarily taken into account in population projections. The actual future population is never identical to the projected population. For a discussion of these projections and their limitations see Dennis A. Ahlburg, "The Census Bureau's New Projections of the U.S. Population," *Population and Development Review* 19 (1) (1993): 159–74.

14. As Figure 5.3 suggests, the projections presented in Figures 5.1 and 5.2 may be deceptive. Many members of the Hispanic population feel that they are members of the white race, and a smaller number feel they are members of the black race. If these attitudes are built into our projections, then what the future may look like becomes very different.

15. It is rare for population projections to anticipate actual demographic processes. See Samuel H. Preston, "Demographic Change in the United States, 1970–2050," in Kenneth C. Manton, Burton H. Singer, and Richard M. Suzman, eds., *Forecasting the Health of Elderly Populations* (New York: Springer-Verlag, 1993), 51–77.

16. Edward P. Hutchinson, *Legislative History of American Immigration Policy, 1798–1965* (Philadelphia: University of Pennsylvania Press, 1981), 478–91.

17. House of Representatives, 1965, in ibid.

18. U.S. Immigration and Naturalization Service, *Statistical Yearbook of the Immigration and Naturalization Service, 1988* (Washington, D.C.: U.S. Government Printing

Office, 1989), table 2; and U.S. Immigration and Naturalization Service, *Statistical Year-book of the Immigration and Naturalization Service, 1992* (Washington, D.C.: U.S. Government Printing Office, 1993), table 2.

19. Nancy A. Denton and Douglas S. Massey, "Racial Identity Among Caribbean Hispanics," *American Sociological Review* 54 (5) (1989): 790–808; and Herbert Barringer, Robert W. Gardner, and Michael Levin, *Asians and Pacific Islanders in the United States* (New York: Russell Sage, 1993), 3–8.

20. Rodriguez and Cordero-Guzman, "Placing Race in Context."

21. Yeu Le Espiritu, *Asian American Panethnicity: Bridging Institutions and Identities* (Philadelphia: Temple University Press, 1992), 31–41.

22. See Michael Hoot and Joshua R. Goldstein; "How 4.5 Million Irish Immigrants Became 40 Million Irish Americans: Demographic Americans," *American Sociological Review* 59 (1) (1994): 64–82.

23. K. Taeuber and A. F. Taeuber, *Negroes in Cities* (Chicago: Aldine, 1964); Ernest W. Burgess, "The Growth of the City," and Robert E. Park, "The City," in Robert B. Park, Ernest W. Surges, and R. D. McKenzie, eds., *The City* (Chicago: University of Chicago Press, 1967; originally published in 1925).

24. Reynolds Farley and Walter R. Allen, *The Color List and the Quality of Life in America* (New York: Russell Sage, 1987), 137–45; and Douglas S. Massey and Nancy C. Denton, *American Apartheid: Segregation and the Making of the Inter-class* (Cambridge, Mass.: Harvard University Press, 1993).

25. Gillian Stevens and Linda Owens, "The Ethnic and Linguistic Backgrounds of U.S. Children," paper presented at the annual meeting of the Southern Demographic Association, 1990.

26. Stanley Lieberson and Mary C. Waters, *From Many Strands: Ethnic and Racial Groups in Contemporary America* (New York: Sage, 1938), 258–60.

27. Mary C. Waters, "The Social Construction of Race and Ethnicity: Some Examples from Demography," Proceedings from the Albany Conference, "American Diversity: A Demographic Challenge for the Twenty-First Century," 1994.

28. Myrdal, *An American Dilemma,* 292.

29. Lawrence H. Fuchs, "The Reactions of Black Americas to Immigration," in Virginia Yans-McLaughlin, ed., *Immigration Reconsidered: History, Sociology, and Politics* (New York: Oxford University Press, 1990), 293–314. These fears may be unwarranted. Recent research finds little support for the notion that immigrants have had any significant negative impact on the employment situation of African Americans. See Robert D. Reischauer, "Immigration and the Underclass,"*Annals of the American Academy of Political and Social Science* 501 (1989): 120–31. Yet immigration may have a significant impact on the fiscal state of local governments. See Eric S. Rothman and Thomas J. Espenshade, "Fiscal Impacts of Immigration to the United States," *Population Index* 58 (3) (1992): 381–415. However, these conclusions themselves should be seen as tentative given the limitations of the available data and the questions addressed. This research has focused on wages, earnings, and unemployment, whereas the important effects may be in labor force participation, working conditions, and internal migration.

30. Rodriguez and Cordero-Guzman, "Placing Race in Context."

31. Farley and Allen, *The Color Line and the Quality of Life in America,* 145, table 5.8.

32. With African Americans comprising almost 50 percent of the prison population, the criminal justice system is a clear example of this conflict. The Los Angeles riot in April 1992 was multiracial and multiclass. More than anything, it reflected the sense of powerlessness that many nonwhite people feel. As Oliver C. Cox noted in 1948, four years after the publication of *An American Dilemma,* "There is here, then, an irreconcilable antithesis which must inevitably remain a constant source of social unrest. The 'lawlessness of judges' in deciding the law and the 'unlawful enforcement of the law' by policemen are pivotal in the racial system. The social anomaly is inherent." See Cox, *Caste, Class, and Race,* 435.

6

The New Geography of Inequality in Urban America

DOUGLAS S. MASSEY

The United States has become an increasingly stratified society. Over the past two decades, the distribution of income and wealth has grown progressively skewed, reversing a long postwar trend. During the 1980s, about one-fifth of the U.S. population experienced a sharp increase in real income; another fifth experienced a real decline in income; and those in the middle saw their incomes stagnate. Although these trends were at first questioned by critical observers, the shift toward greater income inequality is now widely accepted.

This growing inequality occurred within a geographic structure that was itself becoming more unequal. Affluent and poor Americans not only pulled apart in social terms; they separated spatially as well. Although the United States traditionally has been characterized by low to moderate levels of income segregation, this situation began to change during the 1970s. The affluent increasingly sought to live apart from the poor, and income segregation rose. As the poor got poorer, so did the neighborhoods where they congregated, and as the rich got richer, the places where they clustered also grew more affluent. As a result, poverty and affluence both became more concentrated geographically.

The causes of this new urban geography are complex and the consequences profound, and inevitably they are bound up in the politics of race, place, and class. In the ensuing sections, I attempt to establish what is known about

Table 6.1. Metropolitan Location of Americans, 1960–1980

	1960	1970	1980
Metropolitan area	66.7%	68.6%	74.8%
Central city	33.4	31.4	30.0
Suburb	33.3	37.2	44.8
Nonmetropolitan area	33.3	29.4	25.2
Total	179,323	203,323	226,323

Source: U.S. Census of Population, 1960–1980.

geographic inequality in the United States and to identify the root causes of spatially concentrated affluence and poverty. I then outline the consequences this new geography for individuals and the nation and discuss a set of actions need to be taken to redress the cleavages, social and geographic, that have opened up within American society.

Beyond the City-Suburban Divide

Geographic inequality in the United States is often reduced to a simple opposition between cities and suburbs. Although this is an oversimplification of a very complicated situation, it has a basis in fact. Table 6.1 shows the metropolitan distribution of Americans from 1960 to 1980. These figures reveal the remarkable transformation of U.S. society that has occurred over the past thirty years. In 1960, residents of the United States were about equally divided between central cities, suburbs, and nonmetropolitan areas. By 1980, however, the demographic balance had shifted decisively toward suburbs. In the intervening years, the percentage living in cities languished, the share in nonmetropolitan areas fell, and the percentage in suburbs surged. By 1980, nearly half of all Americans lived outside of central cities but within metropolitan areas.

For better or for worse, therefore, the United States has become a suburban society. The new spatial order is most clearly evinced among non-Hispanic whites. As Table 6.2 shows, by 1990 only one-quarter of the U.S. white population lived in central cities, while just over half lived in suburbs; another quarter lived in nonmetropolitan areas. Thus, three-quarters of white Americans have no direct experience of city living; the typical white experience now lies in the suburbs.

The situation is reversed for the nation's two largest minorities — blacks and

Table 6.2. Metropolitan Location of Americans by Race and Hispanic Origin, 1990

	Whites	Blacks	Hispanics	Asians
Metropolitan area	74.7%	83.5%	90.4%	93.8%
Central city	24.4	56.9	51.5	46.4
Suburb	50.3	26.6	38.9	47.4
Nonmetropolitan area	25.3	16.5	9.6	6.2
Total population	188,128	29,216	22,354	7,274

Source: U.S. Census of Population, 1990.

Hispanics. The most common experience for these groups is decidedly urban: 57 percent of blacks and 52 percent of Hispanics reside in a central city, whereas only 27 percent and 39 percent live in suburbs. Asians are about evenly distributed between the two locations, with 46 percent in cities and 47 percent in suburbs.

Increasingly, therefore, whites, blacks, and Hispanics inhabit very different social worlds. How different is suggested by Table 6.3, which presents selected socioeconomic and demographic characteristics for central cities, suburbs, and nonmetropolitan areas. The residential environment experienced by most whites — suburbs — is overwhelmingly white (82 percent), native born (92 percent), and nonpoor (94 percent). Unemployment rates are low and incomes are high. In contrast, the living environment of most minorities — central cities — is nonwhite, foreign, and disadvantaged: 41 percent of those living in central cities are black, Hispanic, or Asian; 13 percent are foreign born; and 14 percent are below the federal poverty line. City dwellers are twice as likely as suburbanites to live in female-headed families, 56 percent more likely to be unemployed, and their incomes are about 26 percent lower than those in the suburbs.

These figures suggest a fundamental geographic cleavage has arisen in the United States, yielding two distinct societies that are increasingly separate and unequal. One the one hand is affluent suburbs inhabited overwhelmingly by native-born whites; on the other hand are poor central cities populated increasingly by native minorities and immigrants. Calculations I have carried out to measure the degree of racial segregation across municipal boundaries confirm the existence of this cleavage and suggest that it is growing.

In collaboration with Zoltan Hajnal of the University of Chicago, I computed segregation indices to measure the degree to which blacks and whites

Table 6.3. Social and Demographic Composition of Different Metropolitan Locations

	City	Suburb	Central Nonmetropolitan Area
Race/Ethnicity			
White	59.0%	82.3%	85.1%
Black	21.3	6.8	8.6
Hispanic	14.8	7.6	3.8
Asian	4.3	3.0	0.8
Foreign-born	12.5%	7.7%	1.3%
Female-headed family	23.6%	12.6%	13.2%
Unemployment			
Male Rate	7.8%	5.0%	6.9%
Teen Male Rate	22.7	15.6	18.7
Median Family Income	$26,700	$36,300	$23,100
% in Poverty	14.0	6.0	13.0

Source: U.S. Census of Population, 1990

live in different municipalities, and we calculated isolation indices to determine the extent to which blacks are confined to predominantly black cities. Between 1950 and 1990, the black-white segregation index doubled, rising from 24 to 49, while black isolation increased by 84 percent, going from 19 to 35. These data suggest that over the past forty years black Americans grew increasingly isolated within cities that were themselves rapidly increasingly black (places such as Atlanta, Baltimore, Detroit, Gary, Newark, New Orleans, and Washington). Unlike segregation between neighborhoods, however, segregation across municipal boundaries brings political as well as social estrangement from American society.

Despite such growing contrasts, the city-suburb dichotomy is crude and obscures as much as it reveals. Suburbs vary greatly in their socioeconomic and demographic composition, as do neighborhoods within central cities. In addition, blacks and Hispanics, as well as whites, experience a wide range of residential conditions linked strongly to social class.

Although blacks have moved to the suburbs along with the rest of American society, their levels of suburbanization lag well behind those of whites and other minorities. Blacks are still less able than other groups to translate their socioeconomic achievements into suburban residence (Alba and Logan, 1991).

A combination of institutionalized discrimination in the banking and real estate industries, private prejudice on the part of individuals, and discriminatory public policies not only block access to suburbs, they also promote racial turnover within suburban neighborhoods and encourage racial resegregation. As a result, levels of black-white segregation remain quite high in suburbs as well as cities (Massey and Denton, 1993).

When Hispanics and Asians achieve suburban residence, in contrast, they generally experience significant integration and considerable neighborhood contact with non-Hispanic whites (Massey and Denton, 1988). Not only have Hispanics and Asians suburbanized at higher rates than blacks, they have also achieved higher levels of acceptance within suburbs. Few researchers have examined the specific neighborhood situations of these minority groups, but high levels of integration suggest that in suburbs, Hispanics and Asians can generally expect to experience living environments similar to those of suburban whites, although there are significant differences between specific national origin groups (e.g., Cubans versus Puerto Ricans, or Chinese versus Filipinos; see Alba, Logan, and Bellair, 1994).

There is a rather large literature on black suburbs, and the investigations universally show that black suburbanites do not gain access to the same range of benefits and amenities as their white peers. Black suburbs tend to be older areas of low socioeconomic status and high population density located near the central city. They are often older manufacturing suburbs with a weak tax base, poor municipal services, and a high level of debt. Compared to white suburbs, property values are lower and taxes are higher. Black suburbs spend a larger share of their revenues on social services and experience higher crime rates (Alba, Logan, and Bellair, 1994). Racial segmentation of suburban housing markets also restricts aggregate demand for housing in black suburbs, deflating housing values, lowering home equity, and generally undermining the ability of the black middle class to build wealth.

Because of persistent racial segregation, therefore, black suburbs display a striking tendency to replicate the problems of the inner city. Although much has recently been made of black suburbs and the benefits of segregated living in the popular press, and a growing number of articles and editorials have noted the retreat from integration in the black community, if historical patterns hold and residential segregation simply moves across the city line, then suburbanization will become yet another vehicle for perpetuation of black socioeconomic disadvantage and racial inequality.

The accumulated evidence suggests that racial segregation is a stark reality that cuts across the city-suburban boundary. Although levels of racial segregation have fallen in smaller metropolitan areas with low black percentages, notably in the south and west, the nation's largest black communities are as segregated as ever (Farley and Frey, 1994). In fact, levels of black residential segregation are so extreme that Nancy Denton and I coined the term *hyper-segregation* to describe the dire situation in some areas (Massey and Denton, 1993). As of 1990, twenty metropolitan areas containing 36 percent of the African American population were hypersegregated (Denton, 1994).

Thus, blacks and whites inhabit neighborhoods with divergent racial compositions; they also live in areas with very different social configurations. John Kasarda (1993) examined the degree to which whites, blacks, and Hispanics live in areas of extreme poverty and social distress. He defined an extreme poverty neighborhood as one with a poverty rate of 40 percent or more and a distressed neighborhood as one with high rates of poverty, joblessness, female-headed families, welfare receipt, and school dropouts, all at the same time. In the hundred largest central cities in 1990, he found that just 3 percent of whites lived in extreme poverty neighborhoods; but 24 percent of blacks and 15 percent of Hispanics did so. Moreover, whereas 30 percent of blacks and 13 percent of Hispanics lived in distressed areas, the figure was only 2 percent for whites.

The disparity between white and minority neighborhoods has grown more extreme over the past three decades. From 1970 to 1990 the percentage of blacks residing in extreme poverty areas rose from 16 percent to 24 percent while the share in distressed neighborhoods grew from 7 percent to 30 percent. Among Hispanics, the share in extreme poverty areas went from 10 percent to 15 percent and the percentage in distressed areas from 2 percent to 13 percent. The percentage of whites in extremely poor and distressed neighborhoods, in contrast, remained nearly constant at 3 percent or less over the entire period.

Kasarda specifically measured the degree to which poverty became more geographically concentrated in the hundred largest central cities. Consistent with earlier studies, he found a growing concentration of poverty that began in the 1970s and continued through 1990. Whereas 17 percent of all poor people lived in tracts that were more than 40 percent poor in 1970, the figure had risen to 28 percent by 1990. Likewise the percentage of poor people living in distressed areas rose from 7 percent to 28 percent.

Among blacks, the geographic concentration of poverty reached remarkable levels. By 1990, 42 percent of poor blacks in the nation's hundred largest cities lived in extreme poverty tracts, up from 28 percent two decades earlier; and the percentage of poor blacks living in distressed tracts exploded from 13 percent in 1970 to 47 percent in 1990. Thus, the experience of living in an area with multiple social and economic problems moved from being a rare situation affecting a small minority of the black poor to being the typical experience for a near-majority of poor blacks.

Poverty and its correlates have thus become more geographically concentrated during the 1970s and 1980s, and this growing concentration was highly structured along racial lines. Poor blacks, in particular, increasingly lived in extremely poor areas beset by a plethora of serious social and economic problems, all of which were escalating in intensity.

Massey and Eggers (1993) also uncovered a growing concentration of affluence in American cities, a trend even more pronounced and widespread than the ongoing concentration of poverty. Reflecting broader trends in American society, affluence was most strongly concentrated in metropolitan areas that displayed the sharpest increases in poverty concentration, such as Chicago, Detroit, Houston, New York, Newark, and Washington, D.C. In these metropolitan areas, the rich not only got richer and the poor poorer; increasingly these two income groups lived in different neighborhoods that were following very different socioeconomic trajectories.

Although the Massey-Eggers study was carried out before 1990 census data were available, Abramson and Tobin (1994) found that the level of segregation between poor and nonpoor individuals increased throughout the 1980s, with notably growing divergences observed in Milwaukee, Buffalo, Detroit, Philadelphia, Cleveland, and Chicago. Over the past several decades, therefore, the United States has divided increasingly on the basis of income, and this growing inequality has been expressed geographically.

Causes of the New Geography of Inequality

Several studies have been conducted to find out why poverty has become more geographically concentrated in recent years, particularly among blacks. The issue has been examined in some detail by Jargowsky and Bane (1990, 1991), Galster and Mincy (1993), and Massey and colleagues (Massey and Denton, 1993; Massey, Eggers, and Denton, 1994; Massey and Eggers, 1990, 1993; Eggers and Massey, 1991, 1992; Massey, Gross, and Shibuya, 1994). Massey and Eggers (1993) also studied the causes of concentrated affluence.

According to all of these investigations, a principal cause of concentrated urban poverty was the shift in the income distribution itself. Rising income inequality after 1970 meant a growing number of poor families with falling incomes and a rising number of affluent families with expanding incomes. Because the people who experienced these income trends tended to live in different areas, increases and decreases in aggregate income were spread unevenly around metropolitan areas. Working class and poor neighborhoods generally ended up with more poor families earning less money, while wealthy and upper-middle-class neighborhoods got more affluent families earning more money. The inevitable result was a geographic concentration of poverty and affluence.

In order to understand the causes of concentrated poverty, therefore, we must explain the shift in the U.S. income distribution itself. The ultimate cause appears to be the emergence during the 1970s and 1980s of a global market economy and the increasing integration of the United States within it. In a globalized economy, two classes of people can be expected to fare well and one poorly. Owners of financial and human capital (the wealthy and the educated) will do well because the things they offer on the global market (money, knowledge, skills) are in short supply. Owners of labor (workers) will not do well because what they have to offer (physical work effort) is cheap, plentiful, and oversupplied on a global scale.

Katz and Murphy (1992) found that the rapid growth of demand for highly educated workers was the driving force behind shifts in the structure of U.S. wages between 1963 and 1987, with wage premiums increasingly being paid to college graduates, compared with stagnant wages paid to those with less education. As a result, wage differentials by education steadily increased, particularly during the 1980s (see also Murphy and Welch, 1992).

Within specific metropolitan areas, these broad trends were expressed in terms of a decline in manufacturing employment, a rise in unemployment, an increasing concentration of jobs in the suburbs, and the growth of an occupational structure dominated by well-paid service jobs at the top and poorly paid service positions at the bottom. The shift toward inequality was most acute, therefore, in older manufacturing cities located in the northeast and midwest that were built up earlier in the century (see Massey and Eggers, 1990).

A second factor in the concentration of poverty was the shift toward higher levels of income segregation in U.S. cities. The general increase in poverty had some unfortunate by-products in the form of greater crime, violence, drug abuse, and dependency among the poor. The simultaneous increase in affluence, however, gave more people the means to insulate themselves from these undesirable conditions. During the 1970s and 1980s, therefore, we observed a modest but sustained increase in class segregation, as the affluent increasingly put distance between themselves and the problems of the poor.

Abramson and Tobin (1994) measured income segregation using an index unaffected by changes in the relative number of poor and nonpoor people and found that the extent of segregation between these groups increased steadily in most metropolitan areas between 1970 and 1990. As with other trends discussed so far, the shifts were sharpest in older industrial areas in the northeast and midwest, notably Milwaukee, Buffalo, Detroit, Philadelphia, Cleveland, and Chicago.

According to Massey and Eggers (1993), the trend toward greater class segregation interacted with a general increase in income inequality to drive up the geographic concentration of affluence and poverty. As additional poor and affluent families were created, and as levels of class segregation rose, poverty and affluence became spatially condensed. The concentration of poverty and privilege occurred to some extent in places where there was an increase in income inequality, and to some extent in places where class segregation rose, but it occurred most acutely in areas where class segregation and income inequality both rose.

Although growing income inequality and rising class segregation provide a general explanation for the new geography of inequality, these factors alone cannot explain why poverty becomes concentrated so disproportionately among blacks. The concentration of black poverty is partly attributable to the fact that blacks were less likely than whites to be college-educated and more likely to be employed in manufacturing, and therefore disproportionately affected by the global forces producing income inequality, but these factors alone cannot account for the remarkable concentration of black poverty during the 1970s and 1980s.

To explain the concentration of black poverty fully, we must introduce one additional variable: racial segregation. The degree of residential segregation between blacks and whites is considerably greater than the degree of segregation between poor and nonpoor people in U.S. metropolitan areas, and it therefore has a greater potential to interact with shifts in the black income distribution to produce geographically concentrated poverty. When rates of black poverty increased as a result of the forces of economic globalization, virtually all of the increase in poverty were absorbed by a small number of tightly packed, geographically isolated, and densely settled neighborhoods that were nearly 100 percent black. As black poverty rates rose, the increase was confined to a narrow segment of urban geography known as the ghetto. Massey and Eggers (1990, 1993) and Galster and Mincy (1993) have shown that racial segregation functioned powerfully to concentrate black poverty during the 1970s and 1980s.

One additional factor has been posited to explain the concentration of black poverty. Wilson (1987) hypothesized that black poverty concentration occurred because new civil rights laws allowed middle- and working-class blacks to leave the ghetto during the 1970s and 1980s, leaving behind poor blacks. This hypothesis, however, is contradicted by a variety of facts: black-white segregation does not decline as income rises; levels of income segregation are higher among Asians and Hispanics but poverty concentration is lower; nonpoor blacks living in poor ghetto neighborhoods are *less likely* to move out than poor blacks; and nonpoor black families who do leave poor ghetto areas tend to go to the same sorts of neighborhoods (see Massey, Gross, and Shibuya, 1994).

In sum, three ingredients appear to be important in explaining the new geography of inequality within U.S. metropolitan areas: (1) a sharp increase in income inequality that occurred as a byproduct of economic globalization; (2) rising levels of class segregation reflecting a desire among the affluent to escape the proliferating problems of the poor; and (3) the persistence of high levels of racial segregation, which interacted with trends toward greater income inequality to concentrate poverty uniquely among blacks. Metropolitan areas with large, segregated black populations that experienced increases in income inequality and class segregation generally displayed the highest levels and sharpest increases in the concentration of both poverty and affluence.

Consequences of the New Geographic Inequality

By subjecting poor people to a uniquely harsh and predatory social environment, geographically concentrated poverty exacerbates the handicaps imposed by individual income deprivation. As poverty is concentrated, so are the characteristics associated with it, leading to high concentrations of joblessness, welfare dependency, single parenthood, crime, violence, drug abuse, and school failure. Not only do poor families have to cope with the inevitable problems stemming from a lack of income, therefore; increasingly they must also cope with a range of external threats to their welfare stemming from the rising prevalence of poverty and its correlates in their neighborhoods.

The new geographic concentration of poverty has created a social environment that cultivates and supports high rates of antisocial behavior, leading to a self-reinforcing cycle of violence and social disintegration. Research suggests that growing up or living in a poor neighborhood substantially increases the odds of unwed and teenage childbearing (Hogan and Kitagawa, 1985; Massey, Gross, and Eggers, 1991), lowers the age of first intercourse (Furstenberg et al., 1987), decreases the odds contraceptive use (Hogan, Astone, and Kitagawa, 1985), and increases the probability of male unemployment and joblessness (Datcher, 1982; Corcoran et al., 1989; Massey, Gross, and Eggers, 1991). Racial segregation is also a strong predictor of the black homicide rate (Peterson and Krivo, 1993).

At the other end of the scale, living in an area of concentrated affluence generally reinforces the advantages of individual wealth and high income. The geographic concentration of affluence creates a social environment that is safe and secure, and which supports a range of resources and amenities that increase the odds of socioeconomic success. Living in a neighborhood of concentrated affluence has been shown to decrease the odds of unmarried childbearing, raise childhood intelligence, and lower the likelihood of dropping out of school (Crane, 1991; Brooks-Gunn et al., 1993).

Thus, the geographic concentration of affluence and poverty that occurred during the 1970s and 1980s appears to have exacerbated and deepened divisions that were already opening up in the United States because of the country's integration into the global economy. Poor families, especially poor black families, were subjected increasingly to a harsh, violent, and uniquely disadvantaged social environment that greatly increased the odds of socioeconomic failure above those attributable to individual characteristics alone. Meanwhile, affluent families, who were mostly white, enjoyed a social environment that was rich in resources and amenities, and which raised the odds of success above those attributable to their personal traits by themselves. Recent changes in urban geography, therefore, have made it harder for poor families to move up the economic ladder and easier to affluent families to stay on top.

Political Interests and Possible Solutions

At present the United States appears locked into a geopolitical structure that perpetuates inequality and widens the divisions of class and race. Affluent whites increasingly reside in racially homogeneous, affluent municipalities located outside of central cities. This concentration of wealth yields high property values, which means that residents can tax themselves at low rates to provide lavish services. Areas of concentrated affluence that happen to be in central cities increasingly opt out of public services altogether, voting down expensive tax levies that might benefit the entire polity and relying instead on private security forces, private schools, and private trash agencies to maintain a high level of service for themselves.

In contrast, poor minorities, and many poor whites as well, increasingly live in inner-city areas of concentrated poverty, in which municipal boundaries often serve as cages of fiscal and social isolation. On the one hand, the concentration of poverty creates low property values that require high tax rates to maintain services. On the other hand, the proliferation of social problems among the poor generates an escalating demand for services that puts a severe strain on municipal resources. Compared to the suburbs, central cities have greater needs and fewer resources.

As the problems of poor people and poor neighborhoods proliferate in self-reinforcing fashion, they inevitably spill over into the wider society; but rising income and growing spatial concentration among the affluent give the privileged new possibilities — both individual and collective — to insulate themselves from the burgeoning problems of the poor, which only exacerbates the latter's plight and perpetuates the downward spiral. In this new geography of inequality, the middle class struggles desperately to maintain itself as it is squeezed in a vice of rising mayhem from below and political withdrawal from above.

This geopolitical dynamic presents a formidable challenge to American leadership. The new geography of inequality is intractable because it is in the elite's narrow self-interest to perpetuate the status quo. Addressing the serious structural problems of the United States will inevitably require sacrifice, and the immediate path of least resistance for affluent people will always be to raise the walls of social, economic, and geographic segregation higher in order to protect themselves from the tide of social pathology and violence from below.

Unless rather drastic steps are taken, however, inequality can be expected to increase and racial divisions to grow, yielding an increasingly volatile and unstable political economy in the United States. Without some kind of forceful intervention in the near future, metropolitan America will experience steadily rising crime and escalating street violence punctuated by sporadic and destructive urban riots, such as the one that occurred in Los Angeles in 1992.

Whereas the poor will become increasingly disenfranchised and alienated from political and economic institutions, the middle class will grow angry, frustrated, and politically mobilized. The middle class will express its anger by castigating politicians blindly, imposing arbitrary term limits and rejecting them at the polls, and by demanding harsher and more repressive measures to control crime and social disorganization emanating from the underclass. The affluent elite will withdraw socially and seek to manage the situation politically by placating middle-class anger with quick fixes and demagogic excesses.

To avoid this alarming scenario, I believe the United States must accomplish three broad goals: (1) it must reorganize the structure of metropolitan government to end the fragmentation that promotes geographic inequality; (2) it must make greater investments in education to combat the bases of rising income inequality and accelerate economic growth; (3) and it must open housing markets to full participation by African Americans and other minorities, and thereby dismantle the system of segregation that has characterized metropolitan America for the past one hundred years.

The segmentation of metropolitan America into a patchwork of independent municipalities reinforces racial and class divisions and undermines the collective interests of American society. The segregation of classes and races across administrative and political boundaries creates disincentives for "us" to spend on "them," especially when the potential funds for social development lie in different administrative units from the areas needing investment.

If improvements are to be made in places where they are most needed, then broader, metropolitan-wide units of taxation and governance need to be created, joining central cities and suburbs into a collective entity whereby taxes and spending are both perceived to be for "us." Such a creation would recognize politically what is true in fact: that central cities and suburbs inevitably share a common fate, and that one cannot be healthy without the other.

The most important need for social spending in the United States is in the area of education. In a global economy, people who have nothing to offer to the world market but the physical power of their own labor will do poorly, and the only way for a nation simultaneously to reduce levels of income inequality and to promote economic growth is to invest in education. Yet the United States appears to be moving in the opposite direction.

At the primary and secondary level, a greater investment in education means greater spending on public schools, particularly those in central cities. Because students in these schools come from neighborhoods and families with a plethora of social problems that make them less prepared to learn, more money needs to be spent on them than on students in affluent areas if they are to learn the same amount. Money spent on education, especially higher education, will ultimately produce higher rates of economic growth as well as lower levels of income inequality. The key input in sustaining economic growth is no longer land, labor, or capital, but knowledge, and a country that supports a self-sustaining knowledge industry will perforce be an economic power; a nation that does not will sink to second-class status.

Finally, the federal government must undertake vigorous efforts to undo the legacy of American apartheid through the effective enforcement of open housing policies. Racial segregation is a leading force behind class segregation and the concentration of poverty in the United States. If racial segregation were eliminated, levels of poverty concentration and income segregation would fall dramatically (see Massey, Gross, and Shibuya, 1994). Few people appreciate the extent to which class divisions are actually caused by the continued segregation of Americans on the basis of race. Ending racial segregation does not require major new legislation, simply honest enforcement of the Fair Housing Act, the Home Mortgage Disclosure Act, and the Community Reinvestment Act.

In outlining these three broad areas for change, I do not underestimate the difficulty of the tasks involved. Progress in each area will require extraordinary leadership, courage, and ability on the part of American politicians, qualities that I frankly do not see in abundance at present. What I see instead is a facile willingness to pander to middle-class anger and racial prejudice for short-term political gain, to the long-term detriment of the nation. As a social scientist with an understanding of the forces that got us into our present state, I cannot be optimistic. The most likely scenario for the United States, I am afraid, is a path of increasing inequality, mounting class antagonism, growing racial division, and a long, drawn-out national decline.

References

Abramson, Alan J., and Mitchell S. Tobin. 1994. "The Changing Geography of Metro-politan Opportunity: The Segregation of the Poor in U.S. Metropolitan Areas, 1970 to 1980." Housing Policy Debate, 6 (1): 45–72.

Alba, Richard D., and John R. Logan. 1991. "Variations on Two Themes: Racial and Ethnic Patterns in the Attainment of Suburban Residence." *Demography* 28:411–30.

Alba, Richard D., John R. Logan, and Paul E. Bellair. 1994. "Living with Crime: The Implications of Racial/Ethnic Differences in Suburban Location." *Social Forces,* 395–434.

Brooks-Gunn, Jeanne, Greg J. Duncan, Pamela Kato Klebanov, and Naomi Sealand. 1993. "Do Neighborhoods Influence Child and Adolescent Development?" *American Journal of Sociology* 99:353–95.

Corcoran, Mary, Roger Gordon, Deborah Laren, and Gary Solon. 1989. "Effects of Family and Community Background on Men's Economic Status." Working Paper 2896, National Bureau of Economic Research, Cambridge, Mass.

Crane, Jonathan. 1991. "The Epidemic Theory of Ghettos and Neighborhood Effects on Dropping out and Teenage Childbearing." *American Journal of Sociology* 96:1226–59.

Datcher, Linda. 1982. "Effects of Community and Family Background on Achievement." *Review of Economics and Statistics* 64:32–41.

Denton, Nancy A. 1994. "Are African Americans Still Hypersegregated in 1990?" Pp. 49–81 in Robert Bullard, ed., *Race and Housing in the United States: An Agenda for the Twenty-first Century*. Berkeley: University of California Press.

Eggers, Mitchell L., and Douglas S. Massey. 1991. "The Structural Determinants of Urban Poverty: A Comparison of Whites, Blacks, and Hispanics." *Social Science Research* 20:217–55.

——. 1992. "A Longitudinal Analysis of Urban Poverty: Blacks in U.S. Metropolitan Areas between 1970 and 1980." *Social Science Research* 21:175–203.

Farley, Reynolds, and William H. Frey. 1994. "Changes in the Segregation of Whites from Blacks During the 1980s: Small Steps Toward a More Integrated Society." *American Sociological Review* 59:23–45.

Furstenberg, Frank F., Jr., S. Philip Morgan, Kristin A. Moore, and James Peterson. 1987. "Race Differences in the Timing of Adolescent Intercourse." *American Sociological Review* 52:511–18.

Galster, George C., and Ronald B. Mincy. 1993. "Understanding the Changing Fortunes of Metropolitan Neighborhoods: 1980 to 1990." *Housing Policy Debate* 4:253–302.

Hogan, Dennis P., Nan Marie Astone, and Evelyn Kitagawa. 1985. "Social and Environmental Factors Influencing Contraceptive Use Among Black Adolescents." *Family Planning Perspectives* 17:165–69.

Hogan, Dennis P., and Evelyn M. Kitagawa. 1985. "The Impact of Social Status, Family Structure, and Neighborhood on the Fertility of Black Adolescents." *American Journal of Sociology* 90:825–55.

Jargowsky, Paul A., and Mary Jo Bane. 1990. "Neighbourhood Poverty: Basic Questions." Pp. 45–67 in Laurence E. Lin and Michael G. H. McGeary, eds., *Inner City Poverty in the United States*. Washington, D.C.: National Academy Press.

———. 1991. "Ghetto Poverty in the United States, 1970–1980." Pp. 235–73 in Christopher Jencks and Paul E. Peterson, eds., *The Urban Underclass*. Washington, D.C.: Brookings Institution.

Kasarda, John. 1993. "Inner-City Concentrated Poverty and Neighborhood Distress: 1970–1990." *Housing Policy Debate* 4:253–302.

Katz, Lawrence F., and Kevin M. Murphy. 1992. "Changes in Relative Wages, 1963–1987: Supply and Demand Factors." *Quarterly Journal of Economics* 107:35–78.

Massey, Douglas S., and Nancy A. Denton. 1988. "Suburbanization and Segregation in U.S. Metropolitan Areas." *American Journal of Sociology* 94:592–626.

———. 1993. *American Apartheid: Segregation and the Making of the Underclass*. Cambridge: Harvard University Press.

Massey, Douglas S., and Mitchell L. Eggers. 1990. "The Ecology of Inequality: Minorities and the Concentration of Poverty, 1970–1980." *American Journal of Sociology* 95:1153–89.

———. 1993. "The Spatial Concentration of Affluence and Poverty During the 1970s." *Urban Affairs Quarterly* 29:299–315.

Massey, Douglas S., Mitchell L. Eggers, and Nancy A. Denton. 1994. "Disentangling the Causes of Concentrated Poverty." *International Journal of Group Tensions,* 24:267–316.

Massey, Douglas S., Andrew B. Gross, and Mitchell L. Eggers. 1991. "Segregation, the Concentration of Poverty, and the Life Chances of Individuals." *Social Science Research* 20:397–420.

Massey, Douglas S., Andrew B. Gross, and Kumiko Shibuya. 1994. "Migration, Segregation, and the Spatial Concentration of Poverty." *American Sociological Review* 59:425–45.

Murphy, Kevin M., and Finis Welch. 1992. "The Structure of Wages." *Quarterly Journal of Economics* 107:285–326.

Peterson, Ruth D., and Lauren J. Krivo. 1993. "Racial Segregation and Black Urban Homicide." *Social Forces* 71:1001–27.

Wilson, William Julius. 1987. *The Truly Disadvantaged: The Inner City, the Underclass, and Public Policy*. Chicago: University of Chicago.

7

The Disparate Racial Neighborhood Impacts of Metropolitan Economic Restructuring

GEORGE GALSTER, RONALD MINCY, AND MITCH TOBIN

The restructuring of the national economy during the past two decades has created profound strains in our metropolitan areas. The economic base has progressively shifted from production of goods to services, central cities to suburbs, and Northeast and North Central regions to the South and West (Castells, 1985; Kasarda, 1985; 1989). This restructuring has radically changed the type, numbers, locations, and skill requirements of jobs within most metropolitan areas. Although the ensuing adjustments have been difficult wherever they occurred, there is a growing belief that the effects of economic restructuring are not spread evenly across metropolitan space. In particular, many observers claim that economic restructuring has had disparate impacts on neighborhoods occupied by minority groups (Squires, 1982; Kasarda, 1985; Wilson, 1987). This is the issue we examine in this chapter.

Scholarly attention to the changing economic fortunes of metropolitan neighborhoods has grown dramatically during the past decade. This is, undoubtedly, because of concerns that population concentrations in neighborhoods with high poverty rates give rise to disproportionate social costs (cf. Hogan and Kitagawa, 1985; Mayer and Jencks, 1989; Massey, Gross, and Eggers, 1991; Crane, 1991; Clark, 1992; Brooks-Gunn, Duncan, Klebanov, and Sealand, 1993). Some observers have used the term "underclass" to focus attention on these concerns (Auletta, 1982; Lemann, 1986; Ricketts and Sawhill, 1988; Ricketts, 1992; Mincy, 1995).

The earliest studies, by Wilson (1987), Jargowsky and Bane (1990, 1991), and Massey and Eggers (1990), examined trends in neighborhood poverty during the 1970s. These studies concluded that growth of high-poverty neighborhoods was occurring almost exclusively in black-occupied neighborhoods outside Western metropolitan areas. Studies using data from the 1980s show that most metropolitan areas have experienced increasing numbers of high-poverty neighborhoods, especially those inhabited primarily by blacks. On average across 318 metropolitan areas, Jargowsky (1994) found a 54 percent increase in the number of census tracts with 40 percent or more poor black residents and an eight-point increase (from 37 percent to 45 percent) in the percentage of all black poor who live in such tracts.[1] Kasarda's (1993) data from the largest one hundred central cities revealed a 47 percent increase in the number of census tracts with 40 percent or more poor residents, although trends differed significantly among cities. From 1980 to 1990 the percentage of all black poor living in such high-poverty tracts rose from 34 percent to 42 percent; the comparable figures for all poor were 23 percent and 29 percent, respectively.

Mincy and Wiener (1993) found important shifts in the regional distribution and racial composition of high-poverty neighborhoods from the Northeast to the South and West and from blacks to nonblacks during the 1980s. In particular, the number of non-Hispanic whites living in neighborhoods with poverty rates of 40 percent or more grew by 141 percent between 1979 and 1989 while the number of non-Hispanic blacks in these neighborhoods grew by 49 percent. These changes increased the non-Hispanic white share of those living in high-poverty neighborhoods by 29 percent and reduced the black share of this population by 20 percent (Mincy and Wiener, 1995). Moreover, high-poverty areas have become more general metropolitan phenomena over time. During the 1970s, four major metropolitan areas (New York, Chicago, Philadelphia, and Detroit) accounted for 66 percent of the growth of the population living in high-poverty neighborhoods. During the 1980s, these metropolitan areas accounted for just 8.7 percent of the growth of this population (Mincy, 1997). Thus, during the 1980s pockets of poor, white-occupied neighborhoods grew in smaller metropolitan areas. Poverty growth in these neighborhoods may have had the same origins as poverty growth in black-occupied neighborhoods in large metropolitan areas (Mincy, 1997; O'Hare and Curry-White, 1992).

Studies attempting to explain the changing fortunes of neighborhoods in terms of economic restructuring of their metropolitan areas are limited and have focused on blacks almost exclusively. They have ignored growth in poverty rates in white neighborhoods and its causes (Mincy, 1995). For example, Hughes (1989) focused on a particular sort of "impacted ghetto" neighborhood: those predominantly black-occupied neighborhoods in which proportions of female-headed households, households receiving public assistance, teenage high school dropouts, and males detached from the labor force all were two standard deviations above the metropolitan area's median.[2] He modeled variations in the number of such tracts across a sample of thirty-eight large metropolitan areas in 1980. His explanatory variables included population and percentage black in the metropolitan area, the percentage change in central city manufacturing employment from 1972 to 1982, the difference between suburban and central county percentage change in manufacturing employment from 1972 to 1982, and a regional dummy variable. Deindustrialization and deconcentration of employment proved to be statistically significant predictors of impacted ghetto prevalence in the Middle Atlantic and East North Central regions;[3] racial composition of the metropolitan area was uncorrelated. Unfortunately, his dependent variable was the number of impacted ghetto neighborhoods in the metropolitan area. Therefore, Hughes could not test the central hypothesis that metropolitan-area variables have differential effects across neighborhoods and that these effects have disparate racial impacts.

This chapter examines the determinants of changing poverty rates in metropolitan neighborhoods across the United States during the 1980s. We focus on the role played by economic restructuring, its potential disparate racial neighborhood impacts, and the causes of such impacts. Specifically, we address the following research questions:

- Is there a relationship between economic restructuring of a metropolitan area and the changing poverty rates of neighborhoods within it?
- If so, is the relationship similar for predominantly white and black neighborhoods?

Building on our previous work (Galster and Mincy, 1993), which addresses the previous questions for four categories of neighborhoods distinguished by race and ethnicity, we ask:

- Do racial categories of neighborhoods differ in their poverty rate change because they are located in metropolitan areas with differing amounts of restructuring, or because they are differently affected by any given amount of restructuring?
- If the latter, what characteristics of neighborhoods render them more vulnerable to restructuring?

We begin with our conceptual framework for understanding how economic restructuring may have a disparate impact on predominantly white and black neighborhoods. Second, we present our sample, consisting of census tracts in all metropolitan statistical areas (MSAs) in 1980 and 1990, and describe the changes in poverty rates during this period for predominately white and predominately black tracts.[4] Third, we develop a summary indicator for economic restructuring, composed of changes in employment-population ratios, shares of employment in manufacturing, and shares of MSA manufacturing employment located in a tract's county. Fourth, we regress changes in tract poverty rates on this restructuring indicator, and conduct F-tests to determine whether the relationships are similar in predominantly black and white neighborhoods. Fifth, we use the parameters of these regressions to simulate what the subsamples' mean tract poverty rate change would have been in predominantly black neighborhoods had they been subjected to the mean restructuring experienced by predominantly white neighborhoods. Sixth, we develop a more robust regression model of tract poverty-rate changes. This model incorporates theoretically important social, demographic, and locational characteristics of tracts as explanatory variables and interacts these variables with restructuring. We close with a discussion of our findings, their limitations, and their implications.

A Conceptual Framework for Understanding the Disparate Impacts of Economic Restructuring on Metropolitan Neighborhoods

Besides the number of jobs, economic restructuring has affected several features of employment: wages, location, skill requirements, and distribution by industry and occupation. We see these features as important determinants of disparate impacts across metropolitan geography. The net effects of these changes have been a decline in high-wage, low-skill manufacturing jobs and growth in both low- and high-wage service-sector jobs. While high-wage service-sector jobs have increased, these generally have skill requirements that low-skilled workers cannot meet (Castells, 1985). From 1967 to 1987, for example, Chicago lost 60 percent of its manufacturing jobs; Detroit, 51 percent; New York City, 58 percent; and Philadelphia, 64 percent. These losses were a huge blow for low-skilled workers who had relied upon manufacturing jobs as their vehicle out of poverty. In these same central cities, service-sector job growth was dramatic (Kasarda, 1992); however, increased educational requirements of many such jobs has reduced the demand for low-skilled labor (Kasarda, 1989, 1990). Thus, workers in these cities who had a high school diploma or less, experienced severe reductions in employment (Kasarda, 1992). Finally, restructuring also shifted the remaining manufacturing jobs (and much of the service-job growth) to suburbs and small towns and generally toward the South and West (Kasarda, 1985).

Wilson (1987) popularized the notion that these changes disproportionately affected the black community. His analysis of Chicago described several dimensions of restructuring that occurred and the growth in poverty rates, especially in black neighborhoods. But neither he nor others specified the theoretical linkages between these phenomena or performed conventional statistical tests (Hughes, 1989). Restructuring may have triggered the poverty upsurge in black Chicago neighborhoods in at least two ways. First, these neighborhoods could have been concentrated in areas where many plant closings occurred and located distant from places of expanding employment. In this case, restructuring would have penalized whoever lived there. Second, neighborhood residents could have had traits that made them particularly vulnerable to restructuring. In this case, restructuring would have penalized these residents wherever they lived.

Both explanations are plausible. Manufacturing plant closings have been disproportionately concentrated in or near black-occupied neighborhoods (Squires, 1982; Soja, Morales and Wolf, 1983; Darden, 1987). The decentralization of new manufacturing jobs and the continuing concentration of blacks in neighborhoods near the urban cores could have created a spatial mismatch. As their proximity to jobs declines, black workers lose opportunities to learn about and commute to those jobs (Straszheim, 1980; Ihlanfeldt and Sjoquist, 1989; 1990; Kain, 1968; 1992). Blacks living in suburban neighborhoods apparently have overcome this mismatch problem. Evidence for this exists in the suburbs of the same Northeast and Midwest metropolitan areas we cite above. In these areas, the rate of joblessness among black males with no diploma actually decreased from 1980 to 1986 (Kasarda, 1992). The empirical significance of the mismatch hypothesis has been much debated (see Jencks and Mayer, 1989; Holzer and Vroman, 1992; Kain, 1992). Nevertheless, there seems little doubt that labor market opportunities are becoming more strongly differentiated over space in ways that place core neighborhoods in ever-more disadvantageous positions. Blacks disproportionately inhabit these neighborhoods (Galster, 1991).

Even if the locations of jobs were not changing, residential segregation may impose additional burdens on predominately black-occupied neighborhoods (Galster, 1993). One reason is behavioral; the other is tautological. The behavioral reason is that segregated black communities are likely to be more isolated from social networks that might expand their flow of information about employment opportunities (Fernandez and Harris, 1992; O'Regan and Quigley,

1993). Massey and his colleagues provided the tautological reason (Massey, 1990; Massey and Eggers, 1990; Massey and Denton, 1993). In a metropolitan statistical area with rising black poverty rates, segregation works to confine this increase to a few (predominantly black-occupied) neighborhoods. These neighborhoods, therefore, must have disproportionately higher rates of poverty.

Independent of location, however, certain household characteristics — disproportionately represented in black occupied neighborhoods — may make people more vulnerable to economic restructuring. Education, family structure, current industry of employment and, of course, race itself have been paramount in the literature. We consider each in turn.

Since, on average, blacks have lower educational attainment than whites, the burdens of rising educational requirements associated with industrial restructuring have fallen most heavily on blacks (Orfield, 1992).[5] This is illustrated by employment-rate declines for male workers between 16 and 64 years old, with a high school diploma or less. For example, in 1968–70, 81 percent of the black male workers in this age and education group who lived in large northeastern central cities were employed. By 1986–88 their employment rate fell to 66 percent. The comparable figures for white male workers were 86 percent and 67 percent, respectively.[6] In large Midwest central cities, the percentage of employed black males with no diploma fell from 76 percent in 1968–70 to 42 percent in 1986–88; the comparable figures for whites were 98 percent and 61 percent, respectively.[7]

The literature also cites marital status as a factor that potentially increases vulnerability to economic restructuring. If they experience a layoff, single adults are less likely to substitute the income of a spouse for their own. Compared to a single breadwinner, two spouses are better able to compensate for a breadwinner's loss of a higher-paying, full-time job, by working at lower-paying, perhaps part-time, jobs. Compared to single individuals, married couples may also have more extended kin networks. As a result, married couples have greater access to financial support for retraining or education. They also have a larger network from which to gain information about alternate employment opportunities. Married couples with children can also share childcare responsibilities and rely on a larger set of relatives to provide childcare. This will increase the likelihood that both family workers can accept jobs, even during weekends and other nonschool hours.

Finally, current dominant industry of employment will affect how an area responds to economic restructuring. A neighborhood occupied primarily by workers employed in growing industries — such as finance, insurance, real estate and services — clearly should be less vulnerable than one occupied primarily by workers employed in declining sectors like manufacturing (Blair and Fichtenbaum, 1992).

Race can play a role directly when employers use race as a screening device for hiring in slack labor markets (Price and Mills, 1985; Braddock and McPartland, 1987; Cross, 1990; Neckerman, 1991). To the extent that black workers have less seniority, restructuring-induced layoffs are likely to have a disproportionate impact on black workers and on black neighborhoods.

In summary, our conceptual framework suggests two broad explanations for the conventional view. The adverse effects of economic restructuring have been more severe for black-occupied neighborhoods because of the spatial features of these neighborhoods and the personal characteristics of their residents. Next, we turn to a description of the data we use in our empirical investigation of this issue.

Data and Sample

We use unpublished data from four sources: the 1980 and 1990 Census Summary Tape File (STF-3a); the USA County File; and the employment by detailed industry file of the Bureau of Economic Analysis Regional Information System (REIS). The STF-3a file contains aggregate counts of individuals and households across all census tracts and includes nearly the entire population of the United States. The file contains detailed information on 42,915 small geographic areas, census tracts, in 1980 and 61,258 in 1990. On average, census tracts include four thousand people and the Census Bureau designates tract boundaries so that people in a given census tract share similar socioeconomic characteristics. These data provide the substantial cross-sectional variation of neighborhood socioeconomic indicators we need to estimate our various empirical models. The REIS data contain aggregate counts of employment by detailed industry (from establishment surveys) across all counties. This is the most reliable source of establishment survey data on detailed employment by industry and is not available at scales below the county level.

After excluding tracts and counties for reasons noted below, our sample includes 37,218 tracts in 3,141 counties. We exclude tracts with populations less than 525 in 1980 because data on key variables would be suppressed in 1980. We also exclude tracts that represent a military vessel and tracts in which the nonhousehold population accounts for more than 29 percent of the population (that is, residents of homes for the aged, mental or other institutions, college dormitories, and group quarters).[8] We exclude tracts with missing or nonsensical values. These include tracts in the census where data converted to percentages is greater than one hundred or less than zero and tracts in counties with missing values in the REIS data (e.g., suppressed detailed industry data and tracts with boundary changes between 1980 and 1990). Finally, we exclude tracts (mainly in New England) located in counties in which less than 100 percent of the population resided in a single metropolitan area and tracts that were not part of an MSA. We adjusted the boundaries of all tracts that changed their boundaries from 1980 to 1990 to make them consistent with 1980 geography.

We stratified the 37,218 tracts into three subsamples depending on the race and ethnic mix of the tract's population. Our black subsample includes 4,115 tracts (11 percent of the sample) in which more than 50 percent of the population was African-American, but not Hispanic. Our white subsample includes 19,999 tracts (53 percent of the sample) in which more than 90 percent of the population was white, but not Hispanic. There was a great deal of racial stability in the subsamples over the decade. Over 93 percent of the tracts categorized as black in 1980 remained so in 1990; 76 percent of the tracts categorized as white in 1980 remained so in 1990. We did not analyze the remaining 13,215 tracts in our sample because we thought them too diverse to permit unambiguous interpretations of findings.[9]

TRENDS IN NEIGHBORHOOD POVERTY, 1979–1989

The neighborhood poverty variable is the growth from 1979 to 1989 (i.e., 1989 minus 1979 values) in the nonelderly poverty rate in a census tract: POVERTY CHANGE.[10] For both years, we calculate the poverty rate from data on the total number of persons under 65 for whom the Census Bureau determined poverty status.[11] We choose the nonelderly poverty rate because theoretically it is of more interest to analyze households whose heads society expects to participate in the labor force. POVERTY CHANGE is a measure of poverty including cash transfers, because the Census Bureau uses a household's total income to calculate the poverty status of its members.

Table 7.1 presents frequencies and descriptive statistics of POVERTY CHANGE for predominantly black and white neighborhoods.[12] These statistics strongly confirm the conventional view that predominantly black tracts disproportionately experienced neighborhood poverty growth during the 1980s. On average, predominantly black-occupied tracts had over a 3 percentage-point increase in their rates of poverty, over three times the average increase in predominantly white-occupied tracts. Poverty rates increased by at least 10 percentage points in 25 percent of the tracts in the black subsample. Only 4 percent of the tracts in the white subsample experienced this much poverty

Table 7.1. Distribution of Tract Poverty Rate Changes, 1979 to 1989, by Racial Category

Tract Racial Category Percentage-Point Change	Black Frequency	Percentage	White Frequency	Percentage
−15 and less	178	4.1	27	0.1
−15 to −10	226	5.2	93	0.5
−10 to −5	464	10.7	767	3.8
−5 to 0	798	18.5	8121	40.3
0 to 5	872	20.2	8361	41.5
5 to 10	699	16.2	1922	9.5
10 to 15	484	11.2	564	2.8
15 and more	600	13.9	272	1.4
Maximum	0.505		0.579	
Minimum	−0.689		−0.621	
Mean	0.033		0.01	
Median	0.026		0.004	
Standard deviation	0.109		0.046	

Note: Poverty rate based on postcash transfers, nonelderly poverty rate for census tract.

Source: Authors' analysis of U.S. Census data contained in the Underclass Database.

growth. Interestingly, the poverty rate was much more stable in the white subsample: the poverty change standard deviation was half that of the black subsample.

The Empirical Relationship Between Economic Restructuring and Neighborhood Poverty

THE MEASUREMENT OF RESTRUCTURING

As explained above, the literature suggests that restructuring has three key dimensions: changes in number, types, and location of employment. We measure changing aggregate employment prospects relative to the working-age population by JOB CHANGE: the 1980 to 1988 decline (i.e., 1980 minus 1988 value) in the ratio of the number of jobs located in the MSA to the MSA population.[13] We measure changing industrial composition by MFG. CHANGE: the 1980 to 1988 decline in the fraction of MSA employment in manufacturing. Finally, we measure the changing location of manufacturing jobs relative to the tract observed by MFG. LOCATION CHANGE: the 1980 to 1988 decline in the ratio of the number of manufacturing jobs located in the county (where the observed tract is located) to the total number of manufacturing jobs in the MSA. We use 1980 to 1988 changes because we assume that 1988 values affect poverty rates after a one-year lag. We expect that higher values for these restructuring variables (i.e., larger declines) would be associated with deteriorating economic fortunes of the tract being observed. Larger increases in tract poverty rates would result.

Before proceeding we should note some limitations of the above variables. First, while JOB CHANGE can proxy overall job availability; it cannot distinguish among jobs according to wages, industry, or skill requirements. Second, MFG. CHANGE measures only one dimension of changing industrial structure. We selected manufacturing because, as noted above, observers see manufacturing as crucial to the economic prospects of low-skill minority workers. Finally, we intend MFG. LOCATION CHANGE to measure the decline in the relative accessibility of manufacturing jobs from the perspective of residents in the observed tract. This measure is imperfect because a tract on the edge of a county may be closer to a manufacturing center in an adjacent county than one in its own. In principle, it would be possible, through a GIS, to compute a more robust measure of job accessibility for each tract based on weighted distances to various employment concentrations. However, this exercise was beyond the resources available for this project.

Using a somewhat different conceptual model, our previous research shows that these three dimensions of economic restructuring affect poverty growth differently in predominantly black, white, Hispanic, and mixed neighborhoods (Galster and Mincy, 1993). However, that research does not explore whether the disparate effects of restructuring occur because: (1) neighborhoods with different race and ethnic compositions are located in metropolitan areas that experienced differing amounts of restructuring or (2) because any given amount of restructuring differentially affects neighborhoods where these different race and ethnic groups concentrate. The latter would occur because of the spatial characteristics of these neighborhoods or the demographic characteristics of neighborhood residents. A full answer to this question would require interactions among each of our measures of economic restructuring and each of our variables measuring spatial and demographic characteristics. Our earlier work indicated that it would be difficult to distinguish and interpret this many interactions (Galster and Mincy, 1993).

To maintain a tractable model we limit the number of interactions by collapsing the three dimensions of restructuring into a single scalar. To do this we used a principal components analysis that produced one factor with an

Table 7.2. Distribution of Economic Restructuring, 1980–1988, by Racial Category and by Metropolitan Statistical Area (MSA)

Tract Racial Category Restructuring	Black	White
Maximum	.095	.095
Minimum	−.155	−.155
Mean	.011	−.006
Median	.013	−.008
Standard deviation	.031	.034

MSA Mean Values by Selected MSAs

Least Restructuring		Most Restructuring	
MSA	Mean	MSA	Mean
Elkhart, IN	−.155	Salisbury-Concord, NH	.057
Fall River, MA	−.091	Allentown, PA	.058
Atlantic City, NJ	−.088	Casper, WY	.058
Orlando, FL	−0.79	Sharon, PA	.058
Burlington, NJ	−.067	Houston, TX	.065
Columbia, MD	−.063	Tulsa, OK	.066
Tallahassee, FL	−.063	Waterloo-Cedar Falls, IA	.069
Champaign-Urbana, IL	−.061	Midland, TX	.074
Bloomington, IN	−.061	Odessa, TX	.083
Sarasota, FL	−.060	Gary-Hammond-E. Chicago, IN	.088
Other MSAs			
New York, NY	.001	San Francisco, CA	−.017
Los Angeles, CA	.008	Boston, MA	−.044
Chicago, IL	.025	St. Louis, MO	−.016
Philadelphia, PA	.002	Mean,* all MSAs	−.002
Detroit, MI	.007		

Note: Data based on full sample of metropolitan tracts; N=37,218

Source: Authors' analysis of U.S. Census data contained in the Underclass Database.

Eigenvalue exceeding one.[14] We used the standardized scoring coefficients of this vector to create our summary measure of economic restructuring:

RESTRUCTURING = .605 (JOB CHANGE) + .570 (MFG. CHANGE) + .511 (MFG. LOCATION CHANGE)

Within a MSA, tracts with higher values of RESTRUCTURING are tracts with larger declines in: overall employment opportunities, share of employment in manufacturing, and/or accessibility of manufacturing. Since we collapse the three dimensions into RESTRUCTURING, we cannot observe variation across subsamples due to the potentially distinct individual effects of JOB CHANGE, MFG. CHANGE and MFG. LOCATION CHANGE on poverty growth.

Table 7.2 presents descriptive statistics for RESTRUCTURING, including values for selected MSAs. For those who might find values for particular MSAs surprising, we reiterate that RESTRUCTURING (1) is the aggregation of three constituent variables, all with roughly equal weights; (2) uses changes, not levels, of all constituent variables; and (3) covers the period 1980–1990.

The Relationship Between Restructuring and Neighborhood Poverty Growth: Simple Model

Our central hypothesis is that our scalar measure of restructuring has different consequences upon metropolitan neighborhoods based on their racial composition. As an initial test we regressed POVERTY CHANGE on RESTRUCTURING, for both of the racial subsamples separately and for the combined sample. F-tests soundly rejected the null hypothesis that the full set of regression parameters was the same across the two subsamples, at extremely high levels of statistical significance (Zar, 1984: 347–348). We therefore present in Table 7.3 only the separate regressions estimated for the black and white subsamples.

The constant terms in Table 7.3 (and the F-tests, not reported) show that predominantly black tracts have an underlying growth rate of poverty that is over twice as large as that for white tracts. Further, the coefficients of RESTRUCTURING show that the poverty rates of predominantly black tracts are much more sensitive to any change in restructuring than are the poverty rates of white tracts. Indeed, any particular increment in restructuring is associated with an increment in white neighborhood poverty rates that is roughly one-third that in black neighborhoods (.29 versus .92). This provides strong support for the claim that restructuring does have disparate impacts on neighborhoods according to their predominant racial composition.[15]

These results allow us to explore why predominantly black tracts experienced so much more poverty rate growth than white tracts (see Table 7.1). How much of the more substantial growth in poverty in black tracts was due to concentration in MSAs with large amounts of restructuring (see Table 7.2)? How much was due to the greater vulnerability of black tracts to any given amount of restructuring (see Table 7.3)? To answer these questions we insert the mean value of RESTRUCTURING for the white subsample into the regression equation estimated for black subsample and then compute a predicted mean. This hypothetical figure shows what the average growth in poverty

Table 7.3. Results for Simple Regression of Poverty Rate Change on Restructuring

	Black	White
Restructuring	.916	.287
	(.053)[a]	(.009)[a]
Constant	.025	.012
	(.002)[a]	(.001)[a]
R-squared (adjusted)	.066	.045
F	293.7	931.3

Note: Standard errors are shown parenthetically.

[a] Coefficient is statistically significant at .1% level (one-tail test)

rates would have been in predominantly black tracts, if their cross-MSA distribution of economic restructuring had been the same (on average) as that observed for white tracts in 1980. The predicted value for the black subsample was .020 (compared to the actual value of .033). Thus, differences in the degree of metropolitan restructuring faced by blacks and whites explain 59 percent of the black-white gap in mean tract poverty rate growth. These results also suggest that tract-specific characteristics also have a large role to play in understanding the growth of neighborhood poverty for predominantly black tracts.

The Relationship Between Restructuring and Neighborhood Poverty Growth: More Robust Model

Following the conceptual framework above, we specify two sets of explanatory variables: one for geographic characteristics of the neighborhood; another for demographic-economic characteristics of the neighborhood's population. We use three measures of the spatial attributes of the census tract. All are proxies for the vulnerability of a tract to restructuring. The dummy variable CENTRAL CITY denotes location in the center city municipal jurisdiction. MFG. CENTRALIZATION denotes the proportional share of all manufacturing jobs in the MSA that are within the tract's county in 1980. Finally, we include a measure of racial residential isolation in the MSA of which any given predominantly black tract is a part. This measure is an exposure (P*)-based index of intraracial residential contact between black residents and their black neighbors (BLACK ISOLATION). We calculate BLACK ISOLATION as the proportion of the black metropolitan area population residing in the average black person's census tract in 1980, minus the proportion of blacks in the MSA population. Then we divide the result by the proportion of MSA population that is not black (see Appendix 7.A.1. for the formula). The entire variable assumes the (minimum) value of zero when the proportion of blacks in all tracts is identical to their overall proportion in the metropolitan area.[16] The variable assumes its (maximum) value of unity when all blacks live in tracts comprised entirely of other blacks.[17] White (1986) discusses the desirable properties of this isolation index.[18]

The characteristics of a tract's population that we include follow directly from the conceptual discussion above: education, family structure, race-ethnicity, and industry of employment. As with the geographic variables above, we specify demographic variables that would measure greater vulnerability to restructuring. We use EDUC. MISMATCH as a proxy for the degree of 1980 comparative educational disadvantage borne by adults in the tract. To calculate EDUC. MISMATCH, we take the ratio of (weighted) average educational attainment of the employees in the metropolitan area to the mean educational attainment of those aged 25 and older in the tract, as of 1980.[19] The numerator of EDUC. MISMATCH is a proxy for the overall skill level of the workforce in the metropolitan area and the denominator is a proxy for the skills possessed by residents in the tract. The more this ratio exceeds unity, the greater the comparative educational disadvantage of tract residents. In turn, the greater their degree of competitive inferiority, the more vulnerable they will be to changing metropolitan employment levels and industrial composition.

Definitions of the remaining demographic variables are simple :(1) the proportion of households that are not married, % NOT MARRIED; (2) the proportion of population that is non-Hispanic black, % BLACK; (3) the proportion of population that is Hispanic, % HISPANIC; and (4) the proportion of workers employed in manufacturing, transportation and public administration, % MFG. JOBS.

We regress changes in tract poverty rates on restructuring. As additional explanatory variables, we include characteristics of tracts and demographic-economic characteristics of their population. However, theory and our previous results suggest that the impact of metropolitan restructuring on poverty growth in a given neighborhood depends upon the characteristics of that neighborhood (Galster and Mincy, 1993). Therefore, we interact restructuring with all explanatory variables. The result is a fully interactive specification. Because we specify each of our explanatory variables to measure degrees of vulnerability, we predict positive signs for the coefficients of variables involving interactions with restructuring. Tables 7.4 and 7.5 present descriptive

Table 7.4. Model of Tract Poverty Rate Change, 1979–89: Descriptive Statistics, Regression Results and Standardized Impacts, Black Stratum of Census Tracts

	Coefficient	Standard Error	t-value	Mean	Standard Deviation (S.D.)	Standardized Coefficient* (@ Mean)	Standardized Coefficient* (@ Mean+S.D.)	Standardized Coefficient* (@ Mean−S.D.)
Dependent Variable								
Poverty change				.033	.109			
Independent Variables								
Constant	−.052	.021	−15.69[a]					
Restructuring	−.226	.585	−0.39[a]	.011	.031	2.160	3.90	.43
Educ. mismatch	.074	.016	4.48[a]	1.260	.117	.840	.80	.88
% Not married	−.002	.014	−.011	.610	.142	.000	.06	−.06
% Black	−.064	.026	−2.45[b]	.824	.150	−.104	−1.25	−.83
% Hispanic	−.174	.027	−6.38[a]	.045	.075	−1.22	−.99	1.45
% Mfg. jobs	−.049	.021	−2.32[b]	.343	.094	−.040	−.24	−.56
Central city mfg.	.010	.005	2.25[b]	.877	.329	.440	.70	.49
Centralization	.073	.011	6.48[a]	.608	.297	2.560	.66	1.47
Black isolation	.020	.039	0.51	.477	.153	.360	.53	.19

Interaction Terms (above variables x RESTRUCTURING)

Educ. mismatch	-.118	.485	-.24	.014	.040
% Not married	.142	.418	.34	-.007	.019
% Black	-.441	.584	-.76	-.010	.026
% Hispanic	.992	1.034	.96	-.001	.002
% Mfg. jobs	.547	.595	.92	.005	.011
Central city mfg.	.257	.149	1.72[c]	.012	.029
Centralization	1.187	.289	4.11[a]	.009	.022
Black isolation	.358	.743	.48	.007	.016

Adj. R-squared=.133

[a] = significance at .01 level, two-tailed test
[b] = significance at .05 level, two-tailed test
[c] = significance at .10 level, two-tailed test
* = multiplied by 100; see text for definition

Table 7.5. *Model of Tract Poverty Rate Change, 1979–89: Descriptive Statistics, Regression Results and Standardized Impacts, White Stratum of Census Tracts*

	Coefficient	Standard Error	t-value	Mean	Standard Deviation (S.D.)	Standardized Coefficient* (@ Mean)	Standardized Coefficient* (@ Mean+S.D.)	Standardized Coefficient* (@ Mean-S.D.)
Dependent Variable								
Poverty change				.010	.046			
Independent Variables								
Constant	−.050	.003	−15.69[a]					
Restructuring	−.747	.088	−8.45[a]	−.006	.034	.77	1.27	.28
Educ. mismatch	.048	.003	14.49[a]	1.091	.117	.49	.86	.11
% Not married	.031	.002	13.19[a]	.337	.137	.43	.40	.45
% Black	.144	.017	8.50[a]	.012	.017	.20	.43	−.01
% Hispanic	.073	.021	3.41[a]	.015	.016	.10	.18	.03
% Mfg. jobs	−.023	.004	−5.39[a]	.328	.102	−.21	.21	.14
Central city mfg.	.010	.001	15.82[a]	.406	.491	.49	.49	.49
Centralization	.001	.001	−.59	.561	.359	−.01	.09	.07

Interaction Terms (above variables x RESTRUCTURING)

Educ. mismatch	.955	.092	10.43[a]	−.006	.037
% Not married	−.057	.068	−.85	−.002	.012
% Black	3.903	.462	8.45[a]	−.000	.001
% Hispanic	1.378	.545	2.53[b]	−.000	.001
% Mfg. jobs	−.221	.110	−1.99[b]	−.001	.012
Central city mfg.	.001	.018	.02	−.000	.021
Centralization	−.070	.037	−1.88[c]	−.001	.022

Adj. R-squared=.108

[a] = significance at .01 level, two-tailed test
[b] = significance at .05 level, two-tailed test
[c] = significance at .10 level, two-tailed test
* = multiplied by 100; see text for definition

statistics of the variables in this more robust model for the black and white subsamples, respectively.

ECONOMETRIC ISSUES

Before proceeding to results, we must address the econometric issue of heteroskedasticity. Conventional regression models assume that errors in the estimating equation are (among other things) of constant variance and uncorrelated across observations. Our model may violate these assumptions and by that render ordinary least-squares estimates of parameters inefficient and their standard errors biased (Pindyck and Rubinfeld, 1981). Heteroskedasticity may arise in our model for two reasons. First, our census tract units of observation vary by population and, therefore, the size of the sample employed by the Census Bureau. Second, the estimating equation is a cross-sectional regression with a neighborhood's poverty growth on the left-hand side and several metropolitan-area variables on the right-hand side. Each metropolitan area contains many neighborhoods in the sample, so metropolitan-area variables affect all such component neighborhoods. If the variables included in the model do not capture all metropolitan-area characteristics that affect a neighborhood's poverty growth, some unmeasured metropolitan-area characteristics will be correlated with poverty growth in every neighborhood in a given metropolitan area. This implies that the error terms of the model are correlated across neighborhoods within a given metropolitan area. In such a grouped structure, ordinary least squares also produces inefficient parameter estimates and biased standard errors (Moulton, 1986).

To check for heteroskedasticity (arising from either source above), we used the chi-squared test developed by White (1980). The test provided strong evidence of heteroskedasticity in the black and white subsamples. As a correction, we employed the SAS routine developed by Moulton (1989) to estimate the variance components and obtain feasible generalized least squares estimates of the regression coefficients. Below we report the consistent and efficient parameters produced by this procedure.

ECONOMETRIC RESULTS

We note at the outset that conventional coefficients do not show the overall relationship between a particular independent variable and the dependent variable in our model. This relationship depends on the coefficient of the independent variable in question, but also on the coefficient and the values of interacted variables.[20] To fix representative values for the overall relationships, Tables 7.4 and 7.5 present three "standardized coefficients." Each shows the predicted changes in the nonelderly poverty rate, 1979 to 1989, associated with a (subsample) one-standard-deviation increase in the given independent variable, including all interaction effects. We calculate these standardized coefficients at three levels: (1) when all other variables with which the given variable is interacted assume their respective mean values; (2) when the other variables assume values of their respective means plus one subsample standard deviation; and (3) when the other variables assume values of their respective means minus one subsample standard deviation. These standardized coefficients are not comparable: (1) across variables within a given subsample because these variables are not all equally scaled, nor (2) across subsamples for the same variable because the standard deviations are not identical. Note also that sign reversals can occur in comparing three standardized coefficients of a given variable X. This can occur when the coefficients of X and the XZ interacted variable have opposite signs. It can also occur when standard deviation changes in the value of Z are sufficient to render the coefficient of XZ both less than and, alternatively, greater than X's coefficient.

In overview, the results of our more robust model (Tables 7.4 and 7.5) are far superior in explanatory power than the sample models shown in Table 7.3, although adjusted R-squares still are in the .11–.14 range. Many coefficients for both interactive and noninteractive terms are statistically significant in both subsamples, although signs and significance levels vary in provocative ways between subsamples.

Results for RESTRUCTURING *Variable*

Our central question for the more robust model is whether black neighborhoods have suffered from economic restructuring primarily because they were disproportionately located in MSAs having high levels of restructuring or because for any given level of restructuring they were more vulnerable than white-occupied neighborhoods. As indicated by our simple model, the more robust model suggests that the answer is "both." Both black and white estimated equations are similar. In both equations, standardized coefficients show that larger values of RESTRUCTURING are associated with larger increases in neighborhood poverty rates, regardless of the values assumed by the neighborhood characteristic variables (see Tables 7.4 and 7.5). For the black neighborhood equation, a subsample standard deviation increase in RESTRUCTURING was associated with a 67 percent (standardized coefficient at mean/POVERTY CHANGE MEAN, or .022/.033) higher growth of poverty, measured at the subsample means of all variables; the corresponding figure in the white neighborhood equation was 77 percent (.0077/.01).[21] For both these equations, larger values of the neighborhood characteristic variables were associated with larger standardized coefficients for RESTRUCTURING. That is, higher values of tract vulnerability measures did, as a whole, magnify the impact of RESTRUCTURING.

Another important question was whether any particular characteristics of tracts were related to their increased vulnerability to restructuring. The interactive variables in the bottom panels of Tables 7.4 and 7.5 provide the answer. For both subsamples, location in the central city was strongly associated with poverty rate growth. However, only in the black subsample did the association become stronger, the larger the value of RESTRUCTURING. White central city neighborhoods may be less sensitive to restructuring than black central city neighborhoods because residents of the former are not as isolated from job information networks (O'Regan and Quigley, 1993). For the white subsample, location in a county with a larger MSA share of manufacturing jobs (MFG. CENTRALIZATION) was associated with less poverty rate growth the larger the value of RESTRUCTURING; the relationship was the opposite for black tracts. Whites may have better access to jobs within the county of residence and elsewhere in the MSA because of race-specific residential patterns and may have better access to private modes of transportation (Ihlanfeldt, 1994). Finally, white tracts showed many statistically significant interactions with RESTRUCTURING that we did not observe in the black subsample: positive correlations with educational mismatch (EDUC. MISMATCH), black percentage (% BLACK), and Hispanic percentage (% HISPANIC).[22] This finding is disappointing. As shown above, black neighborhoods' poverty rates are much more sensitive to any given change in economic restructuring than are white neighborhoods' rates. Except for the central city and county share of manufacturing variables, however, we have been unable to identify any geographic or demographic characteristics of black neighborhoods through which this mechanism operates. It is tempting to argue that black residential predominance in these areas is responsible for the greater vulnerability to restructuring, because of all the problems individual blacks face in the labor market. The data do not support this argument, however, because the interaction effect between percentage black and restructuring is not statistically significant.

Other Salient Findings

Independent of restructuring, several characteristics of census tracts were related to their growth in poverty rates during the 1979–89 period. However, some results were unexpected and raise new questions. We touch on some more intriguing results here.

The results strongly support the position that the comparative educational standing of a tract crucially affects its future economic status. A tract with a population that is educationally mismatched given its MSA's occupational composition is much more likely to show more poverty growth in both black and white subsamples. A subsample standard deviation increase in EDUC. MISMATCH was associated with a 26 percent and 47 percent increase in tract poverty rates in black and white subsamples, respectively (measured at the subsample means of all variables). The apparent (and surprising) greater sensitivity of white tracts to this factor warrants further analysis.

Several findings were even more unexpected and difficult to explain. First, higher fractions of tract population employed in manufacturing in 1980 (% MFG. JOBS) were associated with smaller increases in tract poverty rates for both the white and the black subsamples. This finding may have resulted because % MFG. JOBS is a proxy for factors other than those we intended. Instead of measuring vulnerability to the loss of manufacturing base, MFG. JOBS may be serving as a proxy for a host of local institutions, informal associations, and kin networks that work to ameliorate the poverty-producing impacts of restructuring. Second, tract location in a county having a higher share of the MSA's manufacturing employment (MFG. CENTRALIZATION) was associated with larger increases in tract poverty rates for the black subsample. This finding may be related to the positive effect of the interaction of MFG. CENTRALIZATION and RESTRUCTURING on poverty growth. Both findings suggest that counties with predominant shares of their MSA's manufacturing had older, centralized, land-intensive industrial bases. These counties were least likely to remain competitive during the 1980s, yet were the main employers of black manufacturing workers. Finally, predominantly black tracts had smaller increases in poverty, the larger their 1980 fractions of either black or Hispanic residents (% BLACK, % HISPANIC). Because the tract's 1980 poverty rate was not used as a control variable, the 1980 percentage of black or Hispanic residents may be correlated with this omitted variable. Compared to tracts having, say, only 50–60 percent black residents, those that contain virtually all black residents may more likely be in a state of permanent depression. Further increases in poverty rates are unlikely in these tracts.

Conclusions, Caveats, and Implications for Metropolitan Opportunity Structures

This paper shows that, during the 1980s, metropolitan census tracts experienced vastly different changes in nonelderly poverty rates. Black tracts, in particular, experienced substantially higher growth in poverty rates, on average. Similarly, large cross-metropolitan differences in economic restructuring also abounded during the 1980s. What is the connection?

We have found that restructuring has had profound effects on growth in poverty rates in predominantly black neighborhoods. These effects appear significantly more powerful than those affecting predominantly white neighborhoods. Most of the increase of black neighborhood poverty rates during the 1980s occurred because of the severe restructuring experienced by the MSAs that contained these tracts. Beyond this, however, it appears that any given amount of MSA restructuring has more potent effects in black neighborhoods than in otherwise identical white ones. Two variables seem crucial in magnifying the impact of restructuring on poverty in black neighborhoods: location in a central city and in a county with large shares of the MSA's manufacturing base at the beginning of a period.

Cross-MSA variations in restructuring have much less effect on growth in poverty in white neighborhoods. Further, poverty growth in these neighborhoods seems much less sensitive to any given degree of restructuring. Nevertheless, some white neighborhoods were more vulnerable to restructuring than others. Lower educational levels, higher minority racial composition, lower employment share in manufacturing, and location in a county with a smaller share of the MSA's manufacturing all appear to make white neighborhoods more vulnerable to restructuring.

Thus, we conclude that economic restructuring does have significant disparate impacts on different neighborhoods classified by their predominant racial composition. Most metropolitan area black neighborhoods are more heavily affected by a given level of restructuring than comparable white neighborhoods. There is also evidence to suggest, however, that disparate restructuring impacts occur within both racial subsamples, depending on the particular demographic and geographic features of the neighborhoods. These features vary considerably between the two racial subsamples. Our exploratory study has only begun what we hope is a continued effort to clarify reasons for these provocative findings. Clearly we need to understand better the greater sensitivity of predominantly black tracts to economic restructuring.

Our findings are consistent with a growing body of research (see the review in Galster and Killen, 1995) that racial differences in the spatial opportunity structure are generating racial disparities in poverty. Put differently, racism is increasingly becoming "placism." Here we have contributed to this view by showing that blacks have had the misfortune of residing in: (1) MSAs with larger amounts of restructuring, (2) counties with larger shares of the MSA's manufacturing, and (3) neighborhoods that are overrepresented in central cities. These findings suggest that economic restructuring has created a spatial pattern of increasingly dissimilar economic opportunities for blacks and whites, both among and within metropolitan areas.

We close by suggesting some directions for future research that would build upon our work. First, our analysis is unable to distinguish changes in tract poverty rates due to differential in- and out-migration from changes in the income of the in-place population (cf. Gramlich, Laren, and Sealand, 1992; Massey, Gross, and Shibuya, 1994; Rosenbaum, 1995). Second, we focus on manufacturing, whereas changes in employment composition in other sectors may also produce important consequences for neighborhood poverty. Finally, future research needs to develop a richer measure of a tract's accessibility to various centers of employment before firm conclusions can be made about the effects of job-residence patterns.

Appendix 7.1. Variable Definitions, Sources, and Descriptive Statistics

Model Section	Name	Definition and Source
Dependent variable	POVERTY CHANGE	Nonelderly poverty rate in tract in 1989 − nonelderly poverty rate in tract in 1979; 1989: Table 117, 1979: Table 93
Restructuring	JOB CHANGE	(Ratio of jobs located in MSA/total population in MSA in 1980) − (ratio of jobs located in MSA/total population in MSA in 1988); job data: BEA[a]; population data: USA Counties[b]
	MFG. CHANGE	(Number of jobs in manufacturing located in MSA/total jobs in MSA in 1980) − (number of jobs in manufacturing located in MSA/total jobs in MSA in 1988); from BEA
	MFG. LOCATION CHANGE	(Number of jobs in manufacturing located in county/total jobs in manufacturing in MSA in 1980) − (number of jobs in manufacturing located in county/total jobs in manufacturing in MSA in 1988); from BEA
Summary restructuring variable	RESTRUCTURING	.605 (JOB CHANGE) + .570 (MFG. CHANGE + .511 (MFG. LOCATION CHANGE)
Demographic economic characteristics occupations, of people in tract	EDUC. MISMATCH	Educational attainment of employees in MSA (estimated by weighted average of national-median level of education for occupations, where weights are 1980 proportions of MSA employed in occupation)/mean educational attainment of those age 25 and older in tract; table 48

% NOT MARRIED	Proportion of households in tract in 1980 who are not married; table 20
% BLACK	Non-Hispanic Black share of tract population in 1980, tables 12, 14
% HISPANIC	Hispanic share of tract population in 1980, tables 12, 14
% MFG. JOBS	Proportion of tract workers employed in manufacturing, transportation, and public administration, 1980
BLACK ISOLATION	Minority isolation index for non-Hispanic Blacks in 1980: $[P-(M/T)]/[1-(M/T)]$ where t and m are total minority tract population, T and M are total and minority MSA population, respectively; P is $(m/M)*(m/t)$ summed over all tracts in MSA; tables 12, 14

Spatial characteristics of tracts

CENTRAL CITY	1 if tract located in center city municipality in 1990; zero otherwise.
MFG. CENTRALIZATION	Proportion of MSA manufacturing jobs located in tract's county; from BEA

Source: Unless otherwise identified, tables listed from U.S. Department of Commerce, *Census of Population and Housing: Census Tracts* (1980 and 1990).

[a] Bureau of Economic Analysis Division, U.S. Department of Commerce, Regional Economic Analysis Division.
[b] USA Counties on CD-ROM, prepared by the Bureau of the Census.

Notes

This chapter is a product of the Underclass Research Project, funded by the Rockefeller Foundation through a grant to the Urban Institute. The authors gratefully acknowledge the professional assistance of Sheila Bryant, John Douglass, Diane Hendricks, Martha Kuhlman, and Karen Thurman and the helpful suggestions of Rebecca Clark, Phil Clay, Craig Coelen, Paul Jargowsky, George Peterson, William Rogers, Robert Wilson, Doug Wissoker, and several anonymous reviewers.

1. Comparable estimates were not provided for other racial-ethnic groups.

2. These four characteristics were initially developed by Ricketts and Sawhill (1988) as a measure of the "underclass," but applied to black neighborhoods and neighborhoods with other racial or ethnic majorities.

3. Although it is not clear whether any additional region-specific interactions were attempted or why deindustrialization and deconcentration did not appear in the same regression.

4. Throughout we mean "non-Hispanic white" when we use the term "white," and "non-Hispanic black" when we use the term "black."

5. For a more complete review of the evidence, see Moss and Tilly (1991).

6. The cities were Boston, Newark, New York, and Philadelphia (Kasarda, 1992).

7. The cities were Cleveland, Chicago, Detroit, Milwaukee, and St. Louis (Kasarda, 1992).

8. Examination of the frequency distribution of the population living in such "group quarters" suggested 29 percent as a reasonable cutoff.

9. Tracts in which more than 50 percent of the population was Hispanic were also among those excluded from our estimation. These tracts were excluded because the Census category Hispanic includes Mexican Americans, Puerto Ricans, Cubans, and other groups who are diverse with respect to characteristics for which there are no controls in our data. Our earlier work (Galster and Mincy, 1993) confirmed that results for predominantly Hispanic tracts were inexplicable without recourse to the aggregation problem inherent in the "Hispanic" categorization.

10. We made no attempt to distinguish tracts that changed their racial identification during the decade.

11. Note that hereafter we will employ a variable name format where the name is denoted in small capital letters and is intended to convey a heuristic sense of the variable's meaning.

12. See the Appendix for a glossary and descriptive statistics for all variables.

13. We calculate this decline by subtracting the value of the variable in 1980 from the value of the variable in 1988. Therefore, if the former is larger, indicating that decline occurred, the difference is positive. We measure other variables that we label "decline" below in the same way.

14. The procedure employed the Varimax rotation and was conducted for the combined sample of white, black, and Hispanic tracts.

15. This claim is also supported when three dimensions of restructuring are employed as separate regressors (Galster and Mincy, 1993).

16. These percentages were computed by: 1 − (predicted black mean − actual white mean) / (actual black mean − actual white mean).

17. In this case, the numerator is zero.

18. In this case, both the numerator and denominator would equal the fraction of nonminorities in the MSA.

19. We recognize that our isolation indices do not vary across census tracts within any particular MSA, and thus empirically we estimate how a set of neighborhoods embedded in a more segregated MSA behaves relative to another set in a less segregated one.

20. The 1980 average educational attainment of employees in the MSA was computed as: (percent Professional/Technical * 16.504) + (percent Manager/Admin. * 13.765) + (percent Sales * 12.735) + (percent Clerical * 12.331) + (percent Craft * 12.386) + (percent Operators * 12.179) + (percent Nonfarm Labor * 12.049) + (percent Service * 12.113) + (percent Farm Labor * 11.558). The weights used are national averages for given occupations. The 1980 mean educational attainment of those aged 25 years old or more in the tract was computed as: (percent < 9 yrs. * 6.044) + (percent 9–11 yrs. * 10.03) + (percent high school grad. * 12) + (percent 1–3 yrs. college * 13.82) + (percent > 15 yrs. * 17.06). The weights used are national mean educational attainments for those in given category.

21. To illustrate, in the simple linear model $y = a + bx + cz + dxz + e$, the overall relationship between the dependent variable and the independent variable x is $b + dz$, the value of which will depend upon z.

22. Slightly higher values are estimated if only statistically significant coefficients are used to calculate standardized impacts.

23. Recall that, by construction the white tract subsample has a maximum of 10 percent black and Hispanic population combined.

References

Auletta, K. 1982. *The Underclass.* New York: Random House.

Blair, J., and R. Fichtenbaum. 1992. Changing black employment patterns. In *The metropolis in black and white,* edited by G. Galster and E. Hill, 72–92. New Brunswick, N.J.: CUPR/Rutgers University Press.

Braddock, J., and J. McPartland. 1987. How minorities continue to be excluded from equal employment opportunities. *Journal of Social Issues* 43:5–39.

Brooks-Gunn, J., G. Duncan, P. Klebanov, and N. Sealand. 1993. Do neighborhoods influence child and adolescent development? *American Journal of Sociology* 99: 353–95.

Castells, M. 1985. High technology, economic restructuring and the urban regional process in the U.S. In *High technology, space and society,* edited by M. Castells, 11–40. Beverly Hills, Calif.: Sage.

Clark, R. 1992. Neighborhood effects on dropping out of school among teenage boys. Washington, D.C.: Urban Institute, PSC-DSC-UI-13.

Crane, J. 1991. The epidemic theory of ghetto and neighborhood effects on dropping out and teenage childbearing. *American Journal of Sociology* 96: 1226–59.

Cross, H. 1990. *Employer hiring practices (Report 90–4).* Washington, D.C.: Urban Institute.

Darden, J. 1987. *Detroit: Race and uneven development.* Philadelphia: Temple University Press.

Eggers, M., and D. Massey. 1991. The structural determinants of urban poverty: A comparison of whites, blacks, and Hispanics. *Social Science Research,* 20:217–55.

Fernandez, R., and D. Harris. 1992. Social isolation and the underclass. In *Drugs, crime, and social isolation,* edited by G. Peterson and A. Harrell, 257–93. Washington, D.C.: Urban Institute Press.

Galster, G. 1991. Black suburbanization: Has it changed the relative locations of races? *Urban Affairs Quarterly* 21:621–28.

———. 1993. Polarization, place, and race. *North Carolina Law Review* 71:1421–62.

Galster, G., and S. Killen. 1995. The geography of metropolitan opportunity: A reconnaissance and conceptual framework. *Housing Policy Debate* 6 (1): 7–44.

Galster, G., and R. Mincy. 1993. Understanding the changing fortunes of metropolitan neighborhoods: 1980 to 1990. *Housing Policy Debate* 4:303–52.

Gramlich, E., D. Laren, and N. Sealand. 1992. Moving into and out of poor urban areas. *Journal of Policy Analysis and Management.* 11 (2): 273–87.

Hogan, D., and E. Kitagawa. 1985. The impact of social status, family structure, and neighborhood on the fertility of black adolescents. *American Journal of Sociology* 90:825–55.

Holzer, H., and W. Vroman. 1992. Mismatches and the urban labor market. In *Urban labor markets and job opportunities,* edited by G. Peterson and W. Vroman, 81–112. Washington, D.C.: Urban Institute Press.

Hughes, M. 1989. Misspeaking truth to power: A geographical perspective on the "underclass" fallacy. *Economic Geography* 65: 187–207.

Ihlanfeldt, K. 1994. The spatial mismatch between jobs and residential locations within urban areas. *Citiscape* 1:219–44.

Ihlanfeldt, K., and D. Sjoquist. 1989. The impact of decentralization on the economic welfare of central-city blacks. *Journal of Urban Economics* 16:110–30.

———. 1990. Job accessibility and differences in youth employment rates. *American Economic Review* 80:267–76.

Jargowsky, Paul. 1996. Take the money and run: Economic segregation in U.S. metropolitan areas. *American Journal of Sociology* 61 (6): 984–98.

———. 1994. Ghetto poverty among blacks in the 1980s. *Journal of Policy Analysis and Management* 13:288–310.

Jargowsky, P., and M. J. Bane. 1991. Ghetto poverty in the United States, 1970 to 1980. In *The urban underclass,* edited by C. Jencks and P. Peterson. Washington, D.C.: Brookings Institution.

Jencks, C., and S. Mayer, 1989. Residential segregation, job proximity and black job opportunities. In *Concentrated urban poverty,* edited by M. McGeary and L. Lynn. Washington, D.C.: National Academy Press.

Kain, J. 1968. Housing segregation, Negro employment and metropolitan decentralization. *Quarterly Journal of Economics* 82:175–97.

———. 1992. The spatial mismatch hypothesis: Three decades later. *Housing Policy Debate* 3:371–462.

Kasarda, J. 1985. Urban change and minority opportunities. In *The new urban reality,* edited by P. Peterson. Washington, D.C.: Brookings Institution.

———. 1989. Urban industrial transition and the underclass. *Annals of the American Academy of Political and Social Science* 501:24–47.

————. 1990. City jobs and residents on a collision course: The urban underclass dilemma. *Economic Development Quarterly* 4:313–19.

————. 1992. The severely distressed in economically transforming cities. In *Drugs, crime, and social isolation: Barriers to urban opportunity,* edited by A. Harrell and G. Peterson, 45–97. Washington, D.C.: Urban Institute Press.

————. 1993. Inner-city concentrated poverty and neighborhood distress, 1980–1990. *Housing Policy Debate* 4:253–302.

Lemann, N. 1986. The origins of the underclass. *Atlantic Monthly* 257 (June): 31–61.

Massey, D. 1990. American apartheid: Segregation and the making of the underclass. *American Journal of Sociology* 96:329–57.

Massey, D., and N. Denton. 1993. *American apartheid.* Cambridge, Mass.: Harvard University Press.

Massey, D., and M. Eggers. 1990. The ecology of inequality: Minorities and the concentration of poverty, 1970–1980. *American Journal of Sociology* 95:1153–88.

Massey, D., M. Eggers, and A. Gross. 1991. Segregation, the concentration of poverty, and the life chances of individuals. *Social Science Research* 20:397–420.

Massey, D., A. Gross, and K. Shibuya. 1994. Migration, segregation, and the geographic concentration of Poverty. *American Sociological Review* 59:425–45.

Mayer, S., and C. Jencks. 1989. Growing up in poor neighborhoods: How much does it matter? *Science* 243:1441–45.

Mincy, R. 1995. The Under class: Concept, controversy, and evidence. In *Poverty and public policy: What do we know, what can we do?* edited by S. Danzinger, D. Weinburg, and S. Sandefeur. Cambridge, Mass.: Harvard University Press.

————. 1997. Ghetto poverty: Black problem or harbinger of things to come? In *African American economic thought,* vol. 2, *Methodology and policy,* edited by D. Thomas. New York: Routledge.

Mincy, R., and S. Wiener. 1995. Concentrated poverty and the under class. In *Two views of urban America,* edited by M. J. Malbin, 5–13. Albany: Public Policy Institute of the State University of New York.

Moss, P., and C. Tilly. 1991. *Why black men are doing worse in the labor market.* New York: Social Science Research Council.

Moulton, B. 1986. Random group effects and the precision of regression estimates. *Journal of Econometrics* 32:385–97.

————. 1989. Using SAS to estimate a regression with two variance components. Washington, D.C.: Bureau of Labor Statistics, Division of Price and Index Number Research.

Neckerman, K. 1991. What getting ahead means to employers and disadvantaged workers. Paper presented to The Urban Poverty and Family Life Conference, University of Chicago, October 1991.

O'Hare, W., and B. Curry-White. 1992. The rural underclass: Examination of multiple-problem populations in urban and rural settings. Population Reference Bureau Working Paper. Washington, D.C.: Population Reference Bureau.

O'Regan, K., and J. Quigley. 1993. Family networks and youth access to jobs. *Journal of Urban Economics* 34:230–48.

Orfield, G. 1992. Urban schooling and the perpetuation of job inequality in metropolitan Chicago. In *Urban labor markets,* edited by G. Peterson and W. Vroman, 161–99. Washington, D.C.: Urban Institute Press.

Pindyck, R., and D. Rubinfeld. 1981. *Econometric models and economic forecasts.* New York: McGraw-Hill.

Price, R., and E. Mills. 1985. Race and residence in earnings determination. *Journal of Urban Economics* 17:1–18.

Ricketts, E. 1992. The nature and dimensions of the underclass. In *The metropolis in black and white,* edited by G. Galster and E. Hill, 39–55. New Brunswick, N.J.: CUPR/Rutgers University Press.

Ricketts, E., and I. Sawhill. 1988. Defining and measuring the underclass. *Journal of Policy Analysis and Management* 7:316–25.

Rosenbaum, E. 1995. The making of a ghetto: Spatially concentrated poverty in New York City in the 1980s. *Population Research and Policy Review* 14:1–27.

Soja, E., R. Morales, and G. Wolff. 1983. Urban restructuring: An analysis of social and spatial change in Los Angeles. *Economic Geography* 58:221–35.

Squires, G. 1982. Runaway plants, capital mobility, and black economic rights. In *Community and capital in conflict: Plant closings and job loss,* edited by J. Raines, L. Berson, and D. Gracie, 62–97. Philadelphia: Temple University Press.

Straszheim, M. 1980. Discrimination and the spatial characteristics of the urban labor market for black workers. *Journal of Urban Economics* 7:119–40.

White, H. 1980. A heteroskedasticity-consistent covariance matrix estimation and a direct test for heteroskedasticity. *Econometrica* 48:817–38.

White, M. 1986. Segregation and diversity measures in population distribution. *Population Index* 52:198–221.

Wilson, W. 1987. *The truly disadvantaged.* Chicago: University of Chicago Press.

Zar, J. 1984. *Biostatistical analysis.* 2d. ed. Englewood Cliffs, N.J.: Prentice-Hall.

PART IV

*Critical Factors Militating Against
Black Progress: Retrospect and Prospect*

The Demise of a Dinosaur
Analyzing School and Housing Desegregation in Yonkers

JENNIFER HOCHSCHILD AND MICHAEL N. DANIELSON

In October 1995, city officials of Englewood, New Jersey, appealed to Governor Christine Todd Whitman for help in resolving a controversy over whether Englewood and its two neighboring towns should embark on a program of mandatory school desegregation.[1] "The animosity is so strong now that the only way to get any kind of agreement — and I think it's possible — would be with the Governor or a very, very high state official acting as a mediator and facilitator," claimed Mayor Donald Aronson in a public hearing (Hanley 1995: B1). This mayoral plea is not unique. Citizens and politicians are increasingly turning to states to address problems that neither local nor federal governments can resolve; Congress's move to decentralize welfare through the creation of Temporary Aid to Needy Families (TANF) is an obvious, but not unique, example of this new focus. Politicians' turn to the states seems to be amply supported by the public. Almost half agree that the federal government has too much power, compared with only 6 percent who say the same about state governments. With regard to education in particular, the vast majority of Americans agree that local governments should have more power than states in setting policy, and that states should have more power than the federal government (*New York Times*/CBS News Poll 1995: q. 15; Johnson and Immerwahr 1994: 52–53; Hochschild and Scott 1998).

Are states eager and able to take on these new tasks? Not necessarily.

Governor Whitman and "top state education officials" responded to Mayor Aronson's overture with "little inclination to inject themselves into the dispute.... [They] apparently are waiting for the towns to act," according to the *New York Times* reporter. The governor of New York agrees on the virtues of educational localism; Governor George Pataki has "portrayed it [New York's Education Department] as a symbol of bureaucratic bloat, inefficiency, and aloofness. Like many Republican governors, Mr. Pataki favors returning more control to local school districts" (Dao 1995: B1). He has cut the department's budget drastically and sought to reduce its powers considerably.

Here, then, is one starting point for our research and for this chapter. What can states do to foster effective social policies (however they are defined), and what do they in fact do? Why and when do citizens and public officials turn to states for solutions to problems in education and housing; what happens when they make such an appeal? States are the almost-missing component in the study of — and frequently in the practice of — American federalism; for political, substantive, and analytic reasons, they warrant more attention than we have hitherto given them.

Our other starting point is race. More particularly, we seek to explain the demise of mandatory school desegregation and quasi-mandatory desegregation of public housing in the cluster of possible policy solutions to the problems of racial inequality and separation. In June 1995, the Supreme Court blocked perhaps the last remaining path to substantial school desegregation by curtailing the massive and expensive voluntary desegregation effort in Kansas City (in *Missouri v. Jenkins*). But few people minded; even many African Americans in Kansas City "don't think it's necessary to have a certain percentage of white students to achieve quality education" (Farney 1995: A1). In Yonkers, New York, the president of the local branch of the NAACP stated that court-ordered "school busing may have outlived its usefulness to achieve academic parity" (Jenkins 1995; Hernandez 1995: B1). (The national NAACP thereafter suspended him, but he remained unrepentant.)

The Yonkers suspension is especially noteworthy for our work because Yonkers is the site for our study of the role of the state in school and housing desegregation from 1950 to the present. We are focusing on the role of New York State, in the main, because the state government was a key actor in these efforts and because the history of interactions between New York State and Yonkers offers a wonderful opportunity to study how race affects federalism, the separation of powers, and the impact of democratic preferences — and vice versa.[2]

Our argument, in very brief compass, is as follows. The government of New York was powerful, officially committed to racial desegregation, and active on its behalf, on and off, for more than two decades. However, it was unable to overcome the obstacles of local opposition, bureaucratic and electoral politics, and structural complexity to achieve meaningful desegregation. Racial hostility was neither unimportant nor all-important in explaining the failure to desegregate Yonkers. Instead, it worked to magnify the nature of conventional political obstacles to substantial change so that desegregation efforts failed in Yonkers until the federal court stepped in.

To the degree that any locality can stand in for the whole, Yonkers is a microcosm of the United States on this issue. Its history demonstrates that, even with the best intentions and a lot of power, over the long term political actors cannot or will not extensively desegregate public schools and public housing. If Americans are serious about implementing the principles of equal opportunity and racial integration, they must find other means than the forms of desegregation with which our nation has been preoccupied since the 1960s. Mandatory school desegregation and quasi-mandatory public housing desegregation are dinosaurs — appreciated by many, laughed at by some, but doomed in any case to extinction.

School Desegregation — and the Lack Thereof — in Yonkers, 1950–1980

A brief history of efforts to promote, or stall, desegregation in Yonkers' public schools and public housing is essential for understanding what states can and cannot do to enhance racial equality. We begin with schools, and then move to housing, although it is important to keep in mind that the two tracks proceeded simultaneously and interactively.

THE STATE OF NEW YORK

The State Education Department (SED) of New York was established over a century ago in order to foster the image and practice of public education as a professional, rather than political, activity.[3] When our story started, the Board of Regents had staggered fifteen-year terms. Regents were appointed by the governor, often on the advice of a legislator from the district from which the appointee was to come, but without explicit (or usually implicit) political considerations. The Regents appointed the commissioner of education, who was answerable only to them. He had the responsibility of carrying out the Regents' broad policy mandates and enjoyed investigatory and quasi-judicial powers as well as standard administrative ones. (See discussion below on "310" petition powers.) SED dealt with all aspects of education, ranging from universities to museums to local school districts.

New York State's Education Law specified neither SED's nor the districts' role in ensuring racial balance, and racial segregation was only an issue of only intermittent concern throughout the 1940s and 1950s. Following the findings in *Brown v. Board of Education,* however, the Regents concluded on January 28, 1960, that segregated schools "damage the personality of minority group children" and "decrease their motivation and thus impair their ability to learn" (University of the State of New York 1960: 28). They therefore must be changed in the name of good educational practice. The Regents, like the law, did not allocate specific responsibilities between SED and local districts for identifying imbalances in schools or for remedying the imbalances.

Lacking guidance, Commissioner James Allen, Jr., began himself to define the roles of the state and localities. In 1960 he asked each district to begin eliminating segregation in its schools, and in 1961 he announced a racial census of every school "as the first step in a planned attack on segregation" (Buder 1961: A1). In early 1963, Allen directed each district with "racially imbalanced" schools (Dales 1963: A1) to inform the state by September of how it planned to achieve racial balance. The same day, the commissioner also responded to a "310 petition"[4] filed the previous year by the NAACP in Malverne School District on Long Island. His ruling required Malverne to desegregate an elementary school enrolling 75 percent black children (*Matter of Mitchell* 1963). It was the first time that New York State had required a local district to desegregate a school. Citizens and school boards (both mainly white) in many districts were appalled both with the 310 order in Malverne and with the commissioner's directive on racially imbalanced schools. Their resistance took several forms. Citizens formed pressure groups to protest directly the commissioner's efforts to integrate their schools. School boards, in turn, responded to protesters by refusing to implement Allen's orders and by legally challenging his authority to issue such directives. Although it was eventually overruled, one trial court did hold that the commissioner lacked authority to force Malverne to desegregate. Other districts began to cite the litigation as a reason to delay compliance with the commissioner's directives in their own districts (*Vetere v. Mitchell* 1963). In addition, the press covered extensively the politics of desegregation and resistance to it.

Previously neutral on the issue of integrated schools, state legislators began to react to the potent combination of constituents' protests, districts' defiance of SED, and media attention. By March 1964, legislators had introduced five bills in opposition to busing and any other compulsory measure to effect racial balance. Between 1965 and 1969, legislators introduced forty-five more such bills. In 1969, a bill to prohibit the assignment of students for desegregative purposes was passed, becoming Chapter 342 of the State Education Law. (A federal court later found the law unconstitutional.)[5] Legislators from districts with racially distinct schools also joined forces with long-term advocates of local rule to sponsor bills to limit the scope of, or even abolish, the commissioner's powers, and to create an office of inspector general to review the commissioner's 310 decisions.[6] Although few of these bills became laws, they fostered a legislative atmosphere that was suspicious of the commissioner and SED.

The legislature also inhibited SED's desegregative efforts through budgetary decisions. When Allen developed a statewide master plan for integrated education in 1967, the legislature refused to provide SED with enough money to enact the plan's measures. It underfunded SED's Division of Intercultural Relations (DIR), the office that administered the department's policies regarding integration and provided technical assistance to desegregating districts. (It eventually merged DIR into the Division of Nonpublic Schools.) It underfunded and later canceled the state's Racial Balance Fund, money earmarked for helping school districts to create and implement programs for achieving racial balance.[7] By 1970, lacking sufficient funds and the capacity to claim that "the state" was behind his policies, Allen's successor, Ewald Nyquist, could no longer battle effectively for desegregation on a statewide basis. Nyquist was reduced to pursuing integration through his 310 power, and even the invocation of that power was limited to occasions when a district or someone in it filed an official complaint.

Still frustrated that the commissioner continued to use his 310 power to pursue a policy opposed by a conspicuous majority of their constituents, legislators began to pressure the Board of Regents. Some legislators sent letters to the Regents, begging them to stop the commissioner from intervening in particular districts. Others called on the Regents to fire Nyquist. One senator, for example, urged the Regents to oust Nyquist because "citizens of this state and nation have repeatedly expressed their overwhelming opposition to busing of students for the purpose of forced racial integration." The commissioner should be replaced by someone "who is more sensitive and responsive to the will of the people" (Mason 1975). Legislators began to interview prospective Regents and to use an anti-busing "litmus test" in the appointment process, which had previously been prized as professional rather than political (Clark 1988).

Throughout the late 1960s, as the legislature was invoking one tool after another to rein in SED, the department continued to try to encourage or even mandate desegregation in local districts. Its efforts included setting up new divisions within SED, developing several "master plans," producing numerous research reports, working closely with the governor-appointed Fleischman

Commission on public schooling, writing a handbook on desegregation for local districts, and meeting with local educators and parents.[8]

The Board of Regents also stood firm behind its commitment to desegregation. Starting in 1960, and four times thereafter through 1972 (an unprecedented repetition), the Regents issued policy statements mandating desegregation as essential to good education for all of New York's students. The 1968 statement called for "more determined, more powerful, more energetic pursuit of the objectives set forth therein" by local districts and the state. It indicated that "where the solution to the problem [of racial integration of the schools] is beyond the capability of the local school districts, or where a district fails or refuses to act, then the responsibility for corrective action is clearly and inescapably that of the state" (State Education Department of New York 1968: 7, 12).

By the 1970s, however, the legislature succeeded. After several years of strenuous (and again unprecedented) effort, legislators removed most supporters of active policies to mandate desegregation from the Board of Regents and replaced them with strong opponents of busing and other mandatory desegregative techniques. (Observed one new Regent, "it breaks my heart to see those little bitsy things standing on the corner in ice, snow, and wind waiting for the bus" [Gershowitz 1974: 22].) New laws also shortened the terms of office of the Regents from fifteen to seven years and (with Regents' support) provided for stricter judicial review of the commissioner's 310 orders. The new set of Regents themselves revised their board's earlier strong policy statements on school desegregation, starting in 1974 and culminating in 1976 with inclusion of the dictum that desegregation did not necessarily include any arithmetic count of students by race.

By the mid-1970s, some Regents believed that as a matter of educational policy, mandatory desegregation was a mistake. Others were uncertain about or indifferent to the educational import of desegregation, but acutely aware of the political storms it induced. After all, as one Regent observed, "Education thinking is one thing and political thinking is another." After Nyquist persisted in issuing desegregative 310 orders through the first half of 1976, a majority of the Regents voted to fire him. The next commissioner, Gordon Ambach, no longer pursued the goal of integrated schools and issued no 310 rulings ordering schools to desegregate.[9]

YONKERS

In 1990, Yonkers had a population of 188,000. It is a medium-sized city of eighteen square miles, which encompasses a fading downtown area to the southwest, adjacent to older residential areas, and extensive newer sections of suburban housing and automobile-oriented commercial development to the east and northwest. Physical separation of the old and new is particularly sharp in Yonkers, with older commercial, industrial, and residential sections concentrated along the Hudson River in the southwestern part of the city, and separated from the newer and more attractive areas in the east by natural features and transportation corridors. Downtown residents are now almost entirely black and Latino; people of color are increasingly moving into the older residential areas; and the vast majority of those living in the suburbs and rural sections are white. Sectional interests have been vigorously represented in the Yonkers political system, with a ward-based city council that is highly responsive to constituent interests.

While the state was becoming less willing and able to help or require local districts to achieve racial balance, Yonkers was becoming more segregated. Although some Yonkers schools were racially distinct as early as 1961, racial balance was not much of an issue until the late 1960s when whites began to move out, and minorities began to move into the southwestern city, changing the demographics of the public schools. Because the new minorities settled in racially secluded neighborhoods (partly because of the location of public housing — see below), demographic changes reinforced the racial separation already present in Yonkers schools.

By late 1960s, SED officials had targeted Yonkers as one of the school districts most in need of prodding, or even of a plan written by the state, to deal with increasingly severe racial imbalance. Within Yonkers, however, citizens and municipal officials disagreed on what to do about their segregated schools. Some (mainly black) parents wrote letters to SED complaining of racial tension and imbalance; others (mainly white) formed protest groups similar to those in Malverne or altered the mission statements of extant neighborhood groups to oppose any school reorganization plan that involved busing.

Nevertheless, at two points local educational leaders were demonstrably willing to cooperate with the state to desegregate Yonkers schools. The first time of cooperation occurred in the late 1960s and early 1970 when Superintendent Paul Mitchell took steps toward improving the racial balance in his school district. He planned to open two racially integrated schools and to hire black staff, and he designed workshops to help personnel meet the distinctive needs of black students. He sought technical aid from DIR and money from the Racial Balance Fund, some of which he received. A DIR official, Morton Sobel, came to Yonkers and spoke to the PTA about the need for the district to desegregate its schools. He returned to Albany, however, wrote a memo about "rather heated" mothers with the "express intention of 'not letting my child be bussed for 45 minutes . . . all the way across town,'" and did nothing more

(Sobel 1970). This inaction is especially notable given that Sobel observed in the same memo that "we would not be faced with unsurmountable [*sic*] difficulties in assisting Yonkers to desegregate."

At about this point Superintendent Mitchell died suddenly. Lacking both his desire to integrate and any commitment from the state for supplemental funding, aid, or regulation, local school officials ceased efforts to desegregate Yonkers. Acting Superintendent James Gallagher later justified his reluctance to pursue Mitchell's plans by the community's resistance to desegregation. In its increasingly weakened position, SED did not push Gallagher to change his mind. Legislators had just eliminated the Racial Balance Fund, Nyquist was under growing political pressure, and the DIR was internally ineffective, focused on a contentious desegregation case in Buffalo and stymied by local opponents. Without state or local leadership, the momentum from Mitchell's efforts dissolved.

Almost a decade later, Superintendent Joseph Robitaille made the next major effort to desegregate Yonkers' schools. A severe budget crisis in 1977 combined with declining enrollments to make school closings seem essential, and school closings required redistricting. To Robitaille, a majority of the school board, and a newly energized NAACP, this was an excellent opportunity to improve racial balance as well. In fact, Robitaille had been hired largely on the strength of his success in desegregating a roughly comparable school district in Connecticut. Despite opposition from the mayor and many white citizens, the superintendent issued his "Phase II" reorganization plan on August 5, 1977.[10]

Yonkers, however, was in the midst of a citywide financial crisis and could not pay for desegregation on its own (Robitaille 1990). DIR officials promised technical assistance and came close to promising state funds to help develop and implement Phase II. But the now deeply weakened SED provided no technical assistance and delayed providing funds, and opponents to desegregation became well organized and energetic. By the time SED informed Yonkers that it could provide no additional money (it had became clear that the state could offer no technical or political assistance, either), Mayor Angelo Martinelli had completed his efforts to replace liberal, activist school board members with conservatives who rejected programs that would destroy "the tradition of neighborhood schools" (Guerney 1990).

No one in Yonkers perceived any state pressure to behave otherwise; as one neighborhood organization observed, "It is clear that busing for integration purposes is out of favor even at the state level, and that there is very little likelihood that the commissioner [Ambach] would mandate a forced busing program on the city of Yonkers. . . . [We] therefore again recommend . . . that the Board of Education reject Robitaille's plan without being intimidate[d] by fear of federal or state agency sanctions" (TONEY 1978: 1c; see also Lincoln Park Taxpayers 1977).

Proponents of desegregation diagnosed the same phenomenon but, not surprisingly, evaluated it differently. When the state did not provide the money or technical assistance it had offered, according to one former school board member, the loss felt like SED had "literally abandoned us and we found ourselves in the soup" (Jacobson 1990). The desegregative effort continued, but with less and less conviction of its efficacy. The following spring, the school board adopted the only two components of Phase II it ever considered: reorganizing the grade structure and transforming one middle school into a school for vocational education. Neither action affected racial balance, and Robitaille realized that the school board would never act on this part of his plan. Six months later, he resigned.

In 1980, the local chapter of the NAACP joined with the U.S. Department of Justice to sue the Yonkers Board of Education and the City of Yonkers for creating some discriminatory schools and allowing others to persist.[11] SED offered its aid to the district of Yonkers in responding to federal efforts to investigate the degree of segregation in Yonkers' schools, but it withdrew from all involvement when Yonkers decided to fight the federal desegregation order.

After another five years, a federal court found intentional segregation by the city and school board of Yonkers in the location of school boundaries, the siting of new schools, and the running of vocational and special education programs (*United States v. Yonkers Board of Education* 1985).

Public Housing Desegregation — and the Lack Thereof — in Yonkers, 1950–1980

The story of school desegregation, in short, is one of slow but steady growth in commitment and effort by one part of the state, combined with correspondingly increasing effort to reject that commitment by another part of the state. The legislature's control over budgets, lawmaking, and appointments eventually intimidated, hampered, and halted the actions of SED to desegregate Yonkers' schools; SED moved from a master plan to encourage or even require desegregation to a position on the opposite side of the table from the NAACP and U.S. Justice Department in the eventual desegregation suit. The story of public housing desegregation has the same outcome but follows a different path.

THE STATE OF NEW YORK

Since early in the twentieth century, New York State has played an extremely active role in the field of housing and urban development. It has been continuously involved in such activities in Yonkers directly and through local agencies empowered by the state. By the late 1960s, the state had financed, built directly, or authorized through local agencies about ten housing projects in Yonkers. With exception of one senior citizen project, all projects were built in increasingly or predominantly black areas of the community. Several projects were explicitly designed for "colored people," and all were located on "site[s] that would best preserve existing patterns of segregation" (*United States v. Yonkers Board of Education* 1985: 1313).

By 1968, Governor Nelson Rockefeller was strongly committed to a substantial state role in racial desegregation, housing development, and economic revitalization of cities. As a consequence, he created the New York State Urban Development Corporation (UDC), "perhaps the most powerful state housing and development agency ever created" (*United States v. Yonkers Board of Education* 1985: 32, paraphrasing testimony by Michael Danielson). UDC combined the functions of several agencies in its marriage of housing finance and project development and management. It also obtained unprecedented authority to override local building and land use controls and to exercise powers of eminent domain. In defense of UDC powers, Rockefeller argued that "sovereignty or home rule rights are a privilege" and that the state was responsible for intervening in any arena in which local governments were doing a poor job (Roberts 1968: 28). Its designer and first president, Edward Logue, specifically insisted on these sweeping powers in order to achieve effectiveness, bargaining leverage, an ability to avoid local vetoes, and the capacity to override race-based opposition.

Rockefeller and Logue explicitly intended for the state's new powers to mandate racial desegregation. Rockefeller presented the UDC bill to the legislature with the words, "we cannot live as a segregated people. The American dream is not divisible" (*Public Papers of Nelson A. Rockefeller* 1968: 204). Logue concurred, claiming that "the noble tool of zoning has been perverted to maintain the character of affluent lily-white suburbs" (*Business Week* 1970: 96). The legislature initially agreed with these goals; the mandate of UDC, according to the law that created it, was to "enable the State, in cooperation with private enterprise, to attack the root causes of poverty and slums" (New York State Urban Development Acts of 1968, section 1, chapter 174).

Once UDC began its work, however, opposition within the legislature grew. Resistance centered on the desire to strip UDC's power to override local authorities, and was fueled by UDC plans to build subsidized housing in the suburbs of Westchester County. In 1973, after the legislature threatened to deny UDC additional borrowing authority, Rockefeller reluctantly signed a bill giving villages and towns the right to veto proposed UDC projects. A bill to extend the override ban to cities followed, but did not pass. UDC then withdrew from projects in Westchester and Long Island. By 1975 it was bankrupt.

YONKERS

Even before UDC was created, the director of urban renewal in Yonkers notified the governor that a new agency with considerable power might aid in overcoming local resistance that had stymied the city's urban renewal program. As soon as UDC was in place, Yonkers officials urgently requested its help in relocating residents when a major employer threatened to leave town unless it could expand into the area of their homes.

The initial plan called for scattered-site housing for these one thousand mainly black families. Disclosure of the plan by a local newspaper touched off a political firestorm. Residents protested; the city council held public meetings; the Westchester County Board of Supervisors passed a resolution condemning UDC for proposing subsidized housing that would "completely destroy the residential character of the adjacent neighborhoods" (*United States v. Yonkers Board of Education* 1985: 1319). The UDC-friendly mayor and one council member lost their next elections.

Despite Yonkers' desperate need for federal urban renewal money, access to which was controlled by UDC, Logue chose not to bargain or maintain pressure on the city. Of its ninety-eight original proposed sites, seventy-six of which were outside Yonkers' urban core, UDC accepted the four sites chosen by the city council — all within the inner city — for its first housing projects. From that point on, UDC largely dropped its concern for spatial desegregation and focused only on its concern for "rapid development [of housing] . . . in sufficient quantity to meet the needs of both the state arterial program [and] the city's . . . redevelopment program" with "minimal disruption of community life" (Scher, 1985). That shift implied building projects where there would be least political opposition — that is, in the urban core. UDC wanted to show results, it wanted to develop a constituency, and it wanted to house people in better conditions. Desegregation gave way to these goals.

Like SED, UDC even ended up supporting the city of Yonkers against efforts by the federal government to insist on greater desegregative effort in policy choices. In 1968, HUD had conditioned its huge urban renewal grants on building scattered-site housing for families displaced from the inner city of Yonkers (and elsewhere). But once UDC agreed to the city council's choice of sites, its very power, ironically, relieved Yonkers of concern about HUD pressure. Because of the broad leeway HUD accorded UDC, Yonkers was able to proceed with a racially segregative program of relocation housing in southwest Yonkers larger than the relocation housing plans HUD previously had forbidden the City to undertake on its own because of their likely segregative impact. By 1972, UDC was successfully lobbying HUD to relax its rules conditioning further urban renewal funds on dispersal of new subsidized housing.

In the end, UDC sponsored 1,811 out of 2,647 units of family-oriented public housing built in Yonkers from 1968 to 1972. All seven of its projects were located in southwest Yonkers, the section of the city that is overwhelmingly poor, crowded, and peopled by African Americans and Latinos. In the words of Judge Leonard Sand, who presided over the Yonkers litigation, "for New York State like the City [of Yonkers], it is difficult to discern any plan at work in the . . . site selection process during these years, except for an apparent determination to avoid, at virtually any cost, a confrontation with community opponents of public housing" (*United States v. Yonkers Board of Education* 1985: 1310). Mayor Alfred DelBello was more partisan, but did not disagree: "The big threat had been . . . adequately controlled. The methods that the city administration used to produce housing . . . reflected a consideration for neighborhoods, [and] induced public participation in the process. I believe the public in Yonkers was no longer offended, as they were in prior years, by illogical approaches as to where housing should be built and where housing should not be built" (DelBello 1985: 95).

Race, Politics, and Policy Choices

What implications should we draw from these dismal histories? Let us suggest several, from the most crude but important, to the more subtle. First, mandating or even promoting racial desegregation is a difficult, if not impossible, policy goal. New York has been widely recognized as a powerful and innovative state, which pursued activist and liberal policies on a number of fronts during the 1960s and 1970s, especially in its school and housing agencies. SED was one of the most activist, powerful, and politically insulated state educational agencies in existence (Wirt 1977). UDC was explicitly designed to dominate local politics and policies. If any locality should have been able to avoid — or should have been forced to avoid — actions that led to a finding of intentional racial segregation by a federal court, it should have been a community in the state of New York. And yet, not only did New York fail to prevent Yonkers from engaging in segregative school and housing actions, but also the state contributed in important ways to those actions.

Of particular interest is the fact that New York failed to achieve its stated objectives with regard to desegregation in two quite different ways in the arenas of education and public housing. In some ways the two arenas were similar: both SED and UDC were powerful agencies headed by energetic individuals who were strongly committed to reducing racial segregation. Officials in both agencies were dealing with the same political forces in the other branches of state government and with the same demographic, economic, geographic, social, and political context in Yonkers. But the two agencies behaved differently. UDC responded to its challenge with intense activity, so that the state played a crucial, though not unilateral, role in developing subsidized housing in Yonkers. Between 1969 and 1973, when large amounts of federal funds were available for housing, almost all important decisions about subsidized housing in Yonkers were made by the state or required its approval and cooperation. In contrast, despite its proclamations in the early 1960s about the need for sweeping desegregation measures and its considerable activity on the issue later in the decade, SED was on the way to becoming a passive onlooker by the time Yonkers started to grapple with school segregation in the late 1960s. Even at its strongest, SED did not dare to use the power and resources it had authorized to alleviate school segregation; eventually the state, through the actions of the legislature, removed power and resources from its own officials who might have intervened in Yonkers.

The different behaviors of SED and UDC in Yonkers enable us to compare the causes and effects of powerful, direct action with indirect persuasion and passive accommodation to local desires. After all, some have argued that desegregative efforts failed because they were too authoritarian (Graglia 1976; Rossell 1990; Taylor 1986) and others because they were too weak (Hochschild 1984; Appendix to Brief in *Freeman v. Pitts* 1991). We have an example of each strategy, and can compare their relative effectiveness. We conclude that neither strategy was effective, nor would it have been effective if this or that policy lever or political incentive had been used more skillfully.[12] The issue of racial desegregation was simply too difficult for a democratic polity to handle.[13]

Why did both agencies, using very different strategies, fail equally to carry out their desegregation mandate? A simple and frequent answer is that racial hostility prevails, that governmental action to expand educational and housing opportunities for blacks fails in the face of determined white opposition. But that answer is too simple because it does not explain why white politicians in New York articulated and sought to put into practice policies that promised integrated schools and housing. After all, sophisticated and experienced government officials knew that many opposed these promises and that they were bound to become even more controversial when push came to shove in particular localities. So why did some of them brave hostility from their fellow whites — to the point of receiving death threats and losing their jobs — believing not only that it was the right thing to do but also that they could prevail?

As that question implies, racial hostility clearly was present and clearly contributed to the failure of the desegregative policies, but by itself neither completely explains the failure nor contributes anything to explaining the development of the policy itself. Thus we need additional explanations for both the rise and the fall of state desegregative efforts. Consider once again the trajectories we have described. SED was able to begin the 1960s as an active intervenor on school desegregation because of its distinctive structural characteristic of apparent isolation from popular preferences; its shift to passive spectator by the end of the 1970s reflected the ultimate responsiveness of even "insulated" executive officials and administrative agencies to the state legislature. More concretely, SED was initially empowered to act on school desegregation by legislative action. Later, the agency lost that power and even the desire to act through further legislative action as members of the state assembly and state senate responded to constituency concerns that SED would force local districts to desegregate. Similarly, gubernatorial and legislative action gave UDC its own initial ability to preempt popular preferences. But it too was eventually constrained by constant legislative challenges (some of them successful) to its powers — threats stimulated largely by legislators' fear that UDC would locate housing for blacks in white sections of the suburbs.

This dynamic of empowerment and disempowerment points to the signal importance of interactions among various branches of government, each with its own perspective, agenda, resources, and constraints (Danielson 1976; Failer et al. 1993). Each governmental actor — the governor, legislature, SED, UDC, mayor, city council, school board, and renewal agency — was following a different trajectory in response to different political and substantive stimuli, including but not limited to racial considerations. Although every student of American politics knows in general about the differences among the branches of government, surprisingly little has been written about how these various trajectories interact through law-making, budgeting, appointments, persuasion, vociferous protest, and so on.[14] This case illuminates these interactions spectacularly.

Along with interactions among branches of government go interactions among levels of government. In principle, New York could mandate desegregation of public schools and subsidized housing in Yonkers. The state had legal authority, budgetary control, and the weight of presumptive supremacy in conflicts with cities, school districts, and other local units. Commissioner Allen made just that point to the state school boards convention in 1963: "Responsibility for education in this country rests with the state. . . . The state delegates to local authorities power to administer local affairs. . . . This delegation of power in no way changes or lessens the state's responsibility" (Allen, 1963). In practice, the state was severely constrained in using its powers; it elected not to mandate desegregation, or backed down after its mandates encountered local opposition, or changed its mandates to make them more palatable to local actors. Examining these shifts offers leverage on the little-studied and under-theorized question of the relationship between formal hierarchies of political dominance and actual patterns of political negotiation and contestation (Pressman and Wildavsky 1979; Bardach, 1977).

New York's involvement in school and housing in Yonkers also was shaped by the tension within SED and UDC between the goals of racial integration and other objectives. Racial integration was not the primary concern of either agency. SED was responsible for a wide range of educational programs, as its mission was to oversee almost every aspect of public education in the nation's second largest state. UDC was created to build housing, renew cities, and stimulate economic development. Racial integration was a real but ultimately subsidiary goal for both agencies, commanding few resources and the direct responsibility of relatively few agency staffers. Moreover, racial integration was controversial, and thus a threat to the more central activities of each agency. Pushing racial integration risked stirring political opposition to the agency or losing local cooperation essential to implementing core programs. The path through this thicket that both agencies ultimately chose was to mute racial objectives through a revised understanding of priorities, passive indirection, or — ultimately — withdrawal.[15]

Timing also affected the ability of New York to fulfill its promise to desegregate schools and homes (Kingdon 1984; Kaufman 1991; Jones 1994; Baumgartner and Jones 1993). Strong state commitments were a product of the civil rights revolution of the 1960s and reflected a wide liberal consensus on the desirability and necessity of racial integration. In the case of UDC, the assassination of Rev. Martin Luther King, Jr., provided Governor Rockefeller with the leverage to overcome legislative resistance to the creation of a state agency empowered to override local controls in the pursuit of residential desegregation. But the coalitions that came together to advance residential integration were short lived; and their dissipation eroded support for state action to keep the promise of integrated neighborhoods. In the case of schools, at the point at which the Yonkers school board was ready to desegregate and the local NAACP was committed to keeping the pressure on, SED's weakness removed the possibility of state support that was essential to accomplishing that task. Thus the schools were not desegregated, and the NAACP sued.

In the end, the most democratically responsive actors turned out to be the most powerful. The elected governor and legislators overpowered the appointed agency bureaucrats, and the policies that were implemented fit the preferences of local more than of state officials (Hochschild 1984). To put the point more bluntly, the majority of citizens who resisted school and housing desegregation won more than did the minority who endorsed desegregation. The heart of our story lies in explaining how popular preferences won over professional judgments and purportedly dominant powers, and what the normative implications are of the fact that the most democratic institutions produced the most restrictive outcomes in terms of educational and housing opportunities. We are all, indeed, lost in Yonkers.

Notes

Our thanks for comments on earlier drafts to C. Anthony Broh, Nathan Scovronick, Clarence Stone, and participants in seminars at the University of Chicago, University of Pennsylvania, Rutgers University, and Columbia University. Thanks also go to the Center for Domestic and Comparative Policy Studies, Princeton University, and the Spencer Foundation for support in conducting this research.

1. We both worked as expert witnesses in a trial over the question of whether the state could be held "substantially" responsible for the *de jure* segregation of the Yonkers public schools. We thus have access to private and public documents, budgetary and demographic data, depositions and interviews with key state and local officials, transcripts from two complicated and extensive trials, and other material. The case on which we worked — *United States v. Yonkers Board of Education* — was tried in April 1994. We were both retained by the plaintiffs.

2. In fact, the 1985 federal court decision that found the schools to be segregated is notable in legal as well as policy terms because it insisted on the interdependence of schools and housing. Judge Leonard Sand concluded that housing policies had contributed to school segregation, and that racially inspired school policies had fostered residential segregation. The court ordered Yonkers to undertake housing as well as education remedies designed to reduce racial concentration in the city's schools and neighborhoods (*United States v. Yonkers Board of Education* 1985; Field 1986; Fried 1990; Galster and Keeney 1993; Zimmerman 1990).

3. This section is derived from Failer et al. 1993.

4. A 310 petition is an official complaint to which the commissioner must respond with "quasi-judicial proceedings designed to enforce state education policies." The com-

missioner may also initiate 310 actions on his own behest. (The term comes from Section 310 of the New York Education Law, which spells out the commissioner's responsibility and authority for these proceedings.) During the period that our study covers, substantive decisions could not be appealed; the only possible appeal to the courts was the procedural claim that the commissioner's decision was "arbitrary and capricious." The courts traditionally interpreted this standard very narrowly.

5. *Lee v. Nyquist* (1970). Chapter 342 did not prohibit elected school boards from reassigning students for desegregative purposes; its strictures reached only to SED and to appointed boards of education. Thus it can be described, and was so described by its supporters, as an endorsement of democratic reform.

6. Even after Chapter 342 was struck down by the courts in 1970, the legislature continued to debate and occasionally to pass anti-busing bills for the next few years.

7. In 1963, the Regents requested funds from the legislature to address "urgent problems of racial imbalance," and the plea continued through the 1970s (State Education Department of New York 1963). SED generally requested $10 to $15 million annually for this purpose; the legislature allocated $3 million in 1968, $1 million each of the succeeding two years, and nothing after that.

8. SED did not take other possible steps. Judge Sand's 1995 ruling pointed out that SED did not remove school officials who failed to comply with the commissioner's orders, withhold state funds under the same circumstance, initiate 310 investigations and rulings without waiting for a citizen's petition, issue regulations for desegregation and follow them with inspection and enforcement procedures, or deny approval for the construction of new schools in sites that would exacerbate segregation (*United States v. Yonkers Board of Education* 1995).

9. In fact, he delayed or watered down several of Commissioner Nyquist's remaining 310 orders. As an Assistant Commissioner concluded in 1985, "Our mission is limited, our purview is limited. We are a wonderful department, but we can't solve all of the problems of society."

10. In fact, even before the 1977 Phase II plan, inaction by the state had inhibited action by Yonkers. In 1975, the school board authorized a Task Force on Quality Education to design a desegregation plan. The task force urgently requested state funding; although SED promised money and aid, it produced no aid and very little money, very late. As a consequence, this group of volunteers took over a year to produce its plan, during which time opposition coalesced and the mayor started replacing liberal activist school board members with conservatives and/or political supporters.

11. The federal government had always pushed New York, albeit with little success, to mandate desegregation. As early as 1970, HEW had rejected New York State's application for Title IV funds on the grounds that the state had submitted no plan regarding desegregation of the "Big 6" school districts, which included Yonkers. Yonkers was denied Title IV money several times later in that decade because of its lack of a desegregation plan.

12. To put the contrast more schematically, it requires both political will and institutional capacity—and both over a very long term—to create such a change as meaningful racial desegregation. SED had the will for over a decade, but did not use its full capacity

and slowly lost what it had; UDC had the capacity but lost its will after a brief struggle. What would it take to create an agency with sufficient will and capacity for a sufficient period of time?

13. As one important supporter of the state senate's anti-busing bills observed in a reflective moment that school desegregation might have worked "if the communities . . . had extended a hand on the question of busing. . . . It did not happen . . . I am sorry to say — sometimes ashamed to say" (Bronston 1969: 2481). This raises the issue of local involvement, in both support and opposition to desegregation. Had there been more local support, could UDC or SED been more effective in their periodic interventions in Yonkers? We doubt it, but this is another issue for further exploration.

14. Among the few such analyses are Rebell and Block (1985) and Melnick (1994).

15. As one SED official pointed out in 1968, Commissioner Allen should take strong desegregative actions, but he must also "recognize the political . . . ramifications" (Nordos 1968a). Civil rights activists must in turn understand the semijudicial actions, with the goal of ensuring that state education policies are carried out (Nordos 1968b). More generally, see Wilson (1989) and Kaufman (1991).

References

Allen, James (1963) State Responsibility and Local Control. Statement Before State School Boards Convention, October 28.

Bardach, Eugene (1977) *The Implementation Game: What Happens After a Bill Becomes a Law.* Cambridge, Mass.: MIT Press.

Baumgartner, Frank, and Bryan Jones (1993) *Agendas and Instability in American Politics.* Chicago: University of Chicago Press.

Bronston, Jack (1969) Senate Debate on Concurrent Resolution Proposing an Amendment to Article Eleven of the Constitution, in Relation to Prohibiting the Assignment of Pupils to Public Schools on the Basis of Race, Color, Religion, or Place of National Origin. April 18: 2481.

Buder, Leonard (1961) "Racial Census Set in State Schools." *New York Times,* October 2: A1.

Business Week (1970) "A Superagency for Urban Superproblems." March 7, 1970, 96.

Clark, Kenneth (1988) Deposition, *Yonkers v. State of New York,* 60 Civ. 6761 (LBS), S.D.N.Y., 14.

Dales, Douglas (1963) "State Calling on Schools to End Racial Imbalance." *New York Times,* June 19: A1.

Danielson, Michael (1976) *The Politics of Exclusion.* New York: Columbia University Press.

Dao, James (1995) "Vermont Official Is Picked as State Education Chief for New York." *New York Times,* August 10: B1, B4.

DelBello, Albert (1985). Deposition in *United States v. Yonkers Board of Education.*

Failer, Judith, Anna Harvey, and Jennifer Hochschild (1993) "Only One Oar in the

Water: The Political Failure of School Desegregation in Yonkers, New York." *Educational Policy,* 7, no. 3: 276–96.

Farney, Dennis (1995) "Fading Dream? Integration Is Faltering in Kansas City Schools As Priorities Change." *Wall Street Journal,* September 26: A1, A8.

Field, Marcia Marker (1986) "Planners Guilty on Two Counts: The City of Yonkers Case." *Journal of the American Planning Association,* 52, no. 4: 387–88.

Freeman v. Pitts (1991) Appendix to Plaintiff's Brief, "School Desegregation: A Social Science Statement." June.

Fried, Mark (1990) "Residential Segregation: Where Do We Draw the Lines? A View of *United States v. Yonkers Board of Education* and Democratic Theory." *Columbia Journal of Law and Social Problems,* 23, no. 4: 467–85.

Galster, George, and Heather Keeney (1993) "Subsidized Housing and Racial Change in Yonkers." *Journal of the American Planning Association,* 59, no. 2: 172–81.

Gershowitz, Mike (1974) "New Regents Board Member Will Make Waves." *Long Island Press,* April 7: 22.

Graglia, Lino (1976) *Disaster by Decree: The Supreme Court Decisions on Race and the Schools.* Ithaca: Cornell University Press.

Guerney, Joseph (1990) Interview by Beth Lorenz, Steven Routh, and Monica Herk. November 1.

Hanley, Robert (1995) "Englewood Officials Ask Whitman for Desegregation Help." *New York Times,* October 24: B1, B6.

Hernandez, Raymond (1995) "NAACP Suspends Yonkers Head." *New York Times,* November 1: B1, B4.

Hochschild, Jennifer (1984) *The New American Dilemma: Liberal Democracy and School Desegregation.* New Haven: Yale University Press.

Hochschild, Jennifer, and Bridget Scott (1998) "The Trends: Governance and Reform of Public Education in the United States." *Public Opinion Quarterly,* 62, no. 1: 79–120.

Jacobson, Robert (1990) Interview by Jennifer Hochschild, Steven Routh, and Monica Herk. November 26.

Jenkins, Kenneth (1995) "The NAACP, Lost in Yonkers." *New York Times,* November 4.

Johnson, Jean, and John Immerwahr (1994) *First Things First: What Americans Expect from the Public Schools.* New York: Public Agenda.

Jones, Bryan (1994) *Reconceiving Decision-Making in Democratic Publics: Attention, Choice, and Public Policy.* Chicago: University of Chicago Press.

Kaufman, Herbert (1991) *Time, Change, and Organizations: Natural Selection in a Perilous Environment,* 2nd ed. Chatham, N.J.: Chatham House Publishers.

Kingdon, John (1984) *Agendas, Alternatives, and Public Policies.* Glenview, Ill.: Scott, Foresman.

Lee v. Nyquist (1970) 318 F. Supp. 710.

Lincoln Park Taxpayers Association Education Committee (1977) Unpublished report. March.

Mason, Edwyn (1975) Letter to Joseph McGovern, Chancellor of the Board of Regents. January 23.

Matter of Mitchell (1963) Decision No. 7240, 2 Ed. Dept. Rep. 501. June 17.

McGovern, Joseph (1975) Letter to Bishop Paul Moore. March 3.

Melnick, Shep (1994) *Between the Lines: Interpreting Welfare Rights.* Washington, D.C.: Brookings Institution.

Missouri et al. v. Jenkins et al. (1995) 115 S.Ct. 2038.

New York Times/CBS News Poll (1995) October 22–25.

Nordos, Wilbur (1968a) Memorandum to Ewald Nyquist Regarding Strategy for Mount Vernon. March 20.

—— (1968b) Memorandum to Ewald Nyquist. April 2.

Pforzheimer, Carl (1969) Regents Minutes. June 27.

Pressman, Jeffrey, and Aaron Wildavsky (1979) *Implementation,* 2nd ed. Berkeley: University of California Press.

Public Papers of Nelson A. Rockefeller (1968) Albany: State of New York.

Rebell, Michael, and Arthur Block (1985) *Equality and Education: Federal Civil Rights Enforcement in the New York City School System.* Princeton, N.J.: Princeton University Press.

Roberts, Steven V. (1968) "Governor Insists City Must Yield." *New York Times,* March 8, 28.

Robitaille, Joseph (1990) Interview by Jennifer Hochschild, Beth Lorenz, and Monica Herk. October 29.

Rossell, Christine (1990) *The Carrot or the Stick for School Desegregation Policy.* Philadelphia: Temple University Press.

Scher, Seymour (1985). Deposition in *United States v. Yonkers Board of Education.*

Sobel, Morton (1970) Memorandum to Yonkers File Regarding Title IV Technical Assistance. October 29.

State Education Department of New York (1963) The Regents Major Legislative Proposals for 1964, December.

—— (1968) *Integration and the Schools: A Statement of Policy and Recommendations by the Regents of the University of the State of New York.* Position Paper No. 3, January.

Taylor, D. Garth (1986) *Public Opinion and Collective Action: The Boston School Desegregation Conflict.* Chicago: University of Chicago Press.

TONEY (Taxpayers Organization of North East Yonkers Education Committee) (1978) *TONEY Report on School Reorganization Phase #2.* Printed in the *Herald Statesman,* March 5: 1–1d.

United States v. Yonkers Board of Education (1985) 624 F. Supp. 1276, S.D.N.Y.

University of the State of New York (1960) Regents Statement on Intercultural Relations in Education. *Journal of Regents Meeting,* January 27–28: 28–29.

Vetere v. Mitchell (1963) 41 Misc. 2d 200. *accord, Vetere v. Mitchell,* 21 A.D.2d 561 (1964), *aff'd,* 15 N.Y.2d 259 (1965), *cert. denied,* 382 U.S. 825 (1965).

Wilson, James Q. (1989) *Bureaucracy: What Government Agencies Do and Why They Do It.* New York: Basic Books.

Wirt, Frederick (1977) "School Policy Culture and State Decentralization," in Jay Scribner, ed., *The Politics of Education.* Chicago: National Society for the Study of Education. Pp. 164–87.

Yonkers Board of Education v. New York State (1995).

Zimmerman, Joseph (1990) "Federal Judicial Remedial Power: The Yonkers Case." *Publius,* 20, no. 3: 45–61.

9

Suburban Exclusion and the Courts
Can a Class-Based Remedy Reduce Urban Segregation?

GARY ORFIELD

Metropolitan housing segregation is a fundamental structure, a basic cause, of racial inequality in the United States. Martin Luther King's last major civil rights campaign was against housing segregation in Chicago, and it was there that he met the most relentless and successful opposition.[1] Not only were there violent attacks, but local political leaders defending local segregation patterns were able to escape with only symbolic change, in contrast to their southern counterparts. A third of a century later, Chicago and the other great centers of black migration remain intensely segregated. Sociologists Douglas Massey and Nancy Denton, in their massive statistical analysis *American Apartheid*, join numerous other social scientists who have found residential separation to be the bedrock of contemporary racial inequality.[2] Studies of the impact of moving very poor families from the inner city to subsidized housing in the suburbs have, on the other hand, shown life-transforming changes for these families and far richer educational opportunities, including college education, for their children.[3]

We have a metropolitan society characterized by growing social cleavages, in which resources are increasingly separated from those in need, and minority communities are battered by economic trends and hostile policies. Minority youths most in need of jobs are far from the suburban areas where new jobs are being created. Black and Latino students often must attend inferior schools because of housing segregation.

Major causes include suburban land-use policies that prevent lower-income families from following the jobs, and racial discrimination that keeps minority families out of well-situated, affordable housing. Civil rights litigators have urged the courts to counterbalance these forces since there has been very little success in obtaining remedies from the elected branches of government.

An Intractable Crisis?

More than three-fourths of Americans live in metropolitan areas, most of which are highly stratified by race and class and lack any institutions of metropolitan governance. Minority households are even more concentrated. Within metropolitan communities, suburbanites now greatly outnumber central city residents. We have created a new kind of urbanized society dominated by small communities fully embedded in large urban complexes, but given almost absolute power to outlaw housing for people with less income than the small community defines as desirable. By setting minimum lot sizes, prohibiting multifamily rental housing, and regulating types of buildings, communities can, in essence, dictate minimum housing costs and thus legislate the minimum income or wealth required to live there. Suburban communities devise policies to attract affluent people and desirable businesses from the city while excluding poor, working-class, and many middle-class families. Few suburbs seriously enforce civil rights.

The system gives planning choices mainly to the communities with the most exclusive housing markets in the most rapidly growing sectors of suburbia. It rewards localities that have permitted no affordable housing while systematically punishing the central city and older suburban communities that have large stocks of affordable housing and weak markets. Communities where low-cost housing provides homes for families with many needs and few resources are obligated to also provide expensive educational and social services and public safety. They must care for all who come even if the community is in a desperate economic downturn, caused in part by city employers who move out to receive suburban subsidies, thus further cutting into the tax base.

The system has a built-in momentum of increasing inequalities. The central city remains the educator and caregiver of last resort but has a constantly shrinking share of the region's job and tax resources. Unless there are growing transfer payments from higher levels of government, city institutions face the constant Hobson's choice between cutting essential services and further raising taxes on an increasingly low income and elderly population, thus further damaging the city's competitive position. These fundamental problems are not self-curing; to the contrary, they are self-reinforcing. They are built into the political institutions, and elected suburban officials have a powerful political incentive to perpetuate this system.[4]

There has been no major proposal to redress these problems by either political party for more than a quarter century; in fact, there have been many policy changes that make the consequences worse. Weak efforts at planning and regional cooperation have been dissolved in many metropolitan areas, and federal incentives for such efforts were eliminated during the Reagan Administration.[5] The scope of federal housing and urban development programs have shrunk drastically, limiting the tools available to local government to solve urban crises.[6] The Supreme Court has recognized local autonomy as more important than successful remedies for intentional segregation and discrimination.[7] Advocates seeking a solution to the intensifying isolation and inequality and the economic and social crises of many minority communities tend to primarily emphasize either "place-based" strategies to improve opportunity in the ghettos or mobility strategies aimed at connecting residents to opportunities where they are growing, often in suburbia. Place-based strategies for inner cities date back to early urban renewal and include a wide array of public and private efforts, particularly since the War on Poverty began in the mid-1960s.

After the Nixon Administration took power, place-based federal policies declined, particularly those providing housing and comprehensive neighborhood redevelopment. Mobility strategies assume that we've become a suburban society, that suburbanization is an irreversible process, and that it is more effective to use limited resources to enable as many as possible of those left behind to suburbanize and obtain suburban jobs and education. Strategies for pursuing this goal include enforcement of fair housing laws, certain forms of city-suburban school desegregation, the expansion of affordable suburban housing, lawsuits to force suburban access for public housing tenants (such as the Chicago *Gautreaux* case), and the "Moving to Opportunity" program of the U.S. Department of Housing and Urban Development during the Clinton Administration, which attempted to introduce pro-integration counseling into the housing voucher programs.

The strategies for breaking down the barriers to minority suburbanization start from two very different assumptions about the best way to solve the problem. Many experts, including William Julius Wilson and Theda Skocpol, have argued that it is better to emphasize class not race, avoiding polarization and creating the possibility of class-based alliances. This has been reflected in the supply-side solution of increasing affordable housing in suburban communities by outlawing economic exclusion. Since this can put suburban housing in the price range of many urban minority families who are very unhappy with city neighborhood and school conditions, some reformers believe that families will benefit without having to raise a directly racial issue. The racially explicit policy, on the other hand, has worked primarily with existing housing, providing rent certificates to supplement tenants' incomes, but is available only for those moving across racial lines. The basic assumption of this approach is that race-neutral policies will not work in racially defined markets.

Comparing the effects of these two approaches can help us understand both whether the suburban mobility policy is feasible and whether it can be accomplished without addressing the racial question directly. Since the late 1980s there has been a war in the courts and public opinion about the legitimacy of continuing race-based policies and the viability of class-based alternatives as solutions for social inequalities and discrimination. The suburban housing issue is an important test case.

Public interest law reformers in the 1960s and 1970s who confronted political resistance to suburban integration hoped that the courts might open up the suburbs as *Brown v. Board of Education* had helped open the path for black students to enter the white schools in the South. The problem of intensifying metropolitan separation and inequality was very apparent by the late 1960s.

The other major effort to force change in the pattern of suburban development was initiated within the U.S. Department of Housing and Urban Development in response to a growing urban crisis and the requirement of the 1968 Fair Housing Act that all federal programs be administered in a way that would support fair housing. Briefly during the early 1970s, before it was suddenly stopped by President Nixon, and then again during part of the Carter Administration in the late 1970s, there were both incentives and regulatory efforts to convince suburban communities to help provide affordable housing for the poor. The idea was to make federal planning and infrastructure and other grants conditional on provision of some affordable housing and to provide extra funds for communities with good plans and policies. Nixon's HUD Secretary, George Romney, proposed requiring suburbs to provide a fair share of regional housing needs. After angry protests in suburban Detroit, however, Nixon denounced "forced integration of the suburbs" and cancelled the policy.[8] Carter's policy incentives were rapidly abandoned by the Reagan Administration.

Administrators who attempted to force construction of subsidized housing in white areas, by threatening to cut off community development funds from resistant communities, thought that they would be opening very important new opportunities to low-income minority families, but no sustained policy was implemented and suburbs continued to receive a variety of subsidies for their development without any affordable or public housing. This led many advocates to turn to the courts.

A basic question for our society is whether our system of legal rights and independent courts can counterbalance the great forces pressing toward ever greater fragmentation and inequality among the communities in metropolitan America.

Reformers in the 1960s and 1970s who confronted political resistance to suburban integration hoped that the courts might open up the suburbs like Brown had opened southern schools. *Brown*'s initial goal, however, had been more modest—to force the schools of a deviant region to conform to the practices normal in the rest of the country. The reformers challenging suburb zoning, on the other hand, were challenging practices considered normal, legal, and desirable in local communities across the nation.

The most important legal battle took place in New Jersey. The case arose in Mt. Laurel, a rapidly growing suburban community outside one of the nation's poorest cities, Camden. In response to a 1971 lawsuit about the exclusionary practices of Mt. Laurel, the state Supreme Court limited zoning powers of the suburbs. The community's practice of forbidding affordable housing through its zoning authority was held to violate a fundamental right to housing. The New Jersey Constitution was held to create an obligation for each community to "plan and provide, by its land use regulations . . . for an appropriate variety and choice of housing, including, of course, low and moderate cost housing."[9] This ruling has been called the first major institutional reform order by a state supreme court.[10]

The *Mt. Laurel* case and its impact are at the center of two important and exceptionally well-written books on the New Jersey court's struggle to open up housing opportunities in the regions with the most resources, the most aggressive job growth, the best housing investments, and the strongest schools: *Suburbs Under Siege: Race, Space, and Audacious Judges* by Charles M. Haar and *Our Town: Race, Housing, and the Soul of Suburbia* by David L. Kirp, John P. Dwyer, and Larry A. Rosenthal.[11] Both books see this case as a test of whether or not the legal system is capable of dealing with what the authors view as the nation's most urgent social problem. A 1996 statistical report prepared by a research team at Seton Hall University, *The Impact of the Mt. Laurel Initiatives*, permits an assessment of what actually happened.[12]

Both books see the racial and economic fragmentation of metropolitan America as a fundamental social challenge that elected officials will not address. "No issue is more troubling to American society today," writes Haar, warning that we have become "two nations: one reserved for the haves and the other entrapping the have-nots."[13] Kirp, Dwyer, and Rosenthal speak of "the rise of a suburban majority, at once powerful and insecure, determined on separation and self-preservation" in a country where the triumph of the conservative political movement has been "accompanied by deep antagonism toward the nation's poor and minority citizenry."[14] The litigation is described as if it potentially held the key to overcoming the fundamental division within American society. Kirp, Dwyer, and Rosenthal speak of "a series of cases, designed to unlock America's suburbs."[15] Haar sees the case as the "indispensable" judicial response to metropolitan trends that have "split the country into two nations."[16]

The Mt. Laurel struggle provides important data on two basic questions about reform through the legal process. Do the courts have the capacity to manage resolution of very broad and complex social issues? This first question speaks to the workability of the whole idea of reform through litigation; if courts lack the tools to accomplish changes they believe are required by law, then only politics matters and the belief that we have legally enforceable unpopular rights is chimerical. The second issue is the central policy question being debated in the fight over the future of affirmative action, minority scholarships, minority voting districts, and other race-conscious civil rights remedies: Can a nonracial solution to racial inequality that focuses on poverty cure the effects of racial discrimination and segregation? More specifically, can ending exclusion of lower-income families from suburbs solve metropolitan racial polarization? The question about the workability of nonracial need-based remedies for resolving racial inequities is, of course, at the center of current debates in many other areas, including college admissions, voting rights, school desegregation, and minority contracting.

Two Ways of Framing the Issues

The two studies ask different questions. Haar focuses on statewide and national public policy issues while Kirp, Dwyer, and Rosenthal focus on the plaintiffs, the lawyers, and the decaying central city in Mt. Laurel. Haar devotes relatively little attention to the specific consequences for the Camden area and centers his analysis on the issues of judicial capacity to change the state's housing. When decisions about individual cases become the vehicle through which sweeping new interpretations of the meanings of constitutional provisions affecting entire large classes of people and institutions are developed in class action litigation, the court may declare principles different from and of far greater consequence than the resolution of the particular case.

Though the remedy that eventually emerged from the Mt. Laurel litigation had little impact on the plaintiffs or their community for a very long time, it did play a large and central role in the remaking of suburban housing development in the nation's most suburban state and influenced policy elsewhere.

The plaintiffs in Mt. Laurel were long-time black residents of an old suburban community caught in the midst of an exploding white suburb, whose community was threatened with elimination as part of economic "development." The heroic young law reform lawyers from Camden embodied the 1960s ideal of fighting a long uphill battle against the status quo to win a victory for their plaintiffs and reform the law in ways that would prevent similar abuses in the future.

The Mt. Laurel story, as presented in *Our Town,* begins with a bitter confrontation in a small black church between the mayor of the rapidly growing suburb and old black families working to build three dozen garden apartments to provide housing for their community. Mayor Bill Haines told the group that the community would not provide zoning for multifamily housing anywhere. "If you people can't afford to live in our town," he told them, "then you'll just have to leave."[17]

Ethel Lawrence, a housewife and worker on the housing plan, emerged as the kind of local hero that every civil rights lawyer dreams of. She is described as the Rosa Parks of the battle over exclusionary zoning, a determined fighter who would stick with the issue for the rest of her life.[18] Her cause was taken up by legal services lawyers from nearby Camden, the rapidly declining industrial city across the Delaware River from Philadelphia. The case, in the end, had little impact on Camden, which had two urban riots and lost the large majority of its white students and residents before the Mt. Laurel conflict. Its precipitous decline continued. Between 1960 and 1990 the town's population went from 52,000 to 34,000.[19] Almost all its major businesses left.

The three attorneys who took the case are described in *Our Town* as "children of the Warren Court era" who "regarded the law almost as a secular religion, and they had a faith in its power to undo injustice."[20] Their effective presentation of the outrageous facts in Mt. Laurel stirred the conservative trial judge, who was deeply offended by evidence of local discrimination, to overturn precedent. He noted that local blacks "were forced to leave their homes in a town where some of them had lived fifty years."[21] He found the town guilty of "economic discrimination" and set the stage for a Supreme Court test.[22] It is not surprising that this dramatic story should capture the attention of the authors of *Our Town*.

Haar's *Suburbs Under Seige* takes as its central issue the possibility of forging better policy for suburbia through the initiatives of "audacious judges" willing to take on the vast complexity of current land-use regulation. By comparing the results with the record in the rest of the country and showing major changes — though not necessarily the ones the plaintiffs worked for — he comes to a much more optimistic conclusion.

The Context and the First Mt. Laurel *Decision*

The public interest lawyers fighting for affordable housing in white suburbia filed the *Mt. Laurel* case in 1971, just three years after a Governor's Commission investigating very serious urban riots in Newark and elsewhere concluded that "suburban residents must understand that the future of their communities is inextricably linked to the fate of the city."[23] New Jersey politicians did not respond to this challenge and the courts were confronted with the issues.

At the time of *Mt. Laurel I*, the New Jersey supreme court faced exactly the kind of situation in which questions of constitutional rights are the most urgent and the most difficult. A basic right had been asserted — the right of less affluent and minority people to live in the areas where all the economic growth was occurring and where the best schooling and other opportunities were concentrated. This was asserted against the right of local governments to zone their land as they thought best. Social and racial polarization was deepening. The state's central cities were falling apart and erupting in riots. There was no evidence that the elected officials would solve these problems. It seemed clear, also, that the federal courts and the federal government would do little or nothing.

President Johnson's national commission on urban riots, the Kerner Commission, reported New Jersey had had the most extensive cluster of riots, with uprisings in fourteen cities.[24] The commission concluded that, "Powerful forces of social and political inertia are moving the country steadily along the course of existing policies toward a divided country."[25] The commission warned that the United States was fast approaching a time when isolated minority-controlled cities would be facing constantly growing needs with shrinking resources while demographic change would move more and more control to the suburbs. The growing suburbs would face rising costs of providing their own services and become less and less willing to transfer resources to the cities, trends that could "force simultaneous political and economic polarization" in metropolitan areas. The commission predicted that inaction would lead to a very rapid increase in segregated and declining central cities.[26]

The commission blamed subsidized housing for increasing the ghettoization of the poor and said that continuing such policies would "compound the conditions of failure and hopelessness."[27] It called for a greatly expanded housing subsidy effort using scattered site housing, pointing out that suburbs had "successfully restricted use of these programs outside the ghetto." The "main thrust," said the report, "must be in nonghetto areas, particular those outside the central city."[28]

The condition of zoning in New Jersey around the time of *Mt. Laurel I* was examined in Michael Danielson's 1976 book, *The Politics of Exclusion.* He notes that a state commission studying local government in 1970 found extraordinary exclusion and no inclination among local governments to cooperate in any way to solve the housing problems. In the booming New Jersey suburban area of Bergen County, less than half of 1 percent of the land was zoned for apartments in 1970.[29] In sixteen suburban growth counties more than 95 percent of the land was zoned for lots over a quarter acre by 1966, making construction of affordable housing impossible.[30] In 1970 twenty suburbs in the center of the state had zoned land for 1.2 million jobs but only about one-tenth as many housing units. A state study concluded that land use "cooperation is almost non-existent."[31]

New Jersey had no political will to address the issues. In fact, the state's reliance on local property taxes intensified the desire of each community to provide as little access as possible to nonaffluent families with children who would drive up local school costs and property taxes. The trends were leading toward ever more severe inequality.

Nor was the U.S. Supreme Court about to solve the problem. Even the liberal Warren Court had been unwilling to put any significant limit on suburban powers over land use. The year before *Mt. Laurel I* the U.S. Supreme Court had upheld restrictions on types of households who could live in a community.[32] President Nixon's four appointments turned it into a far more conservative court, even less likely to challenge suburban prerogatives.

Nixon blocked executive action. When John Ehrlichman, his domestic adviser, presented him with information about a proposed HUD strategy for suburban integration in 1970, the president directed, "Stop this one."[33] After the federal courts in the *Gautreaux* case ordered construction of subsidized housing in Chicago outside segregated areas to help repair the damage of generations of total intentional segregation, Nixon promised Mayor Richard Daley that nothing would be done by HUD.[34] Nixon fired his secretary of HUD over this matter and issued a presidential statement firmly opposing any requirements for what he called "forced integration of the suburbs."

Earlier, when President Lyndon B. Johnson proposed that the model cities program include a metropolitan coordinator and regional planning, the idea was shot down in Congress and stripped from the proposal.[35] There was no prospect of federal leadership. The judges facing the question in New Jersey could not expect any help from other levels of government.

The Law Evolves

Among the three major *Mt. Laurel* decisions, *Mt. Laurel I* is much like *Brown* — an extremely important statement of new legal principles without tools to actually change the institutions. In *Mt. Laurel II*, the court crafted a very dramatic judicial intervention that could and did overcome local resistance and rapidly began to change the reality of local housing practices. *Mt. Laurel III* was the high court's response to a broad reaction from the elected branches of government to take responsibility and limit the changes.

In its 1975 decision, *Mt. Laurel I*,[36] the New Jersey state supreme court was the first to rule that the exclusionary land use policies of many suburbs violate rights guaranteed by the state constitution. Housing was defined as a fundamental right and suburban exclusion as a violation of the state constitution. The sweeping conclusions of the New Jersey supreme court in *Mt. Laurel I* said nothing about any of the racial issues raised in the trial. The new right that the court found in the state constitution was a prohibition against local communities prohibiting all housing for lower-income households. The remedy was aimed at economic rather than racial exclusion and it was assumed that this would help excluded minorities. Communities were obliged to make it "realistically possible" for a "fair share" of low income families to live in the developing communities of suburbia. The decision offered very little specific direction on how to change them.

In New Jersey there was massive political mobilization against the decision and almost nothing happening on the ground, as the issue got lost in the minutiae of many local land-use skirmishes. Mt. Laurel officials, for example, proceeded to rezone a tiny share of their land in unworkable sites and no housing could be built. Their plan was accepted by the trial court.[37] Eight years later, the state supreme court realized that its first decision had not worked, and the court raised many issues about housing and residential patterns.[38] The court either had to accept transparent strategies to avoid compliance or to find ways to extend its authority. Its decision swept aside all the complexities and found Mt. Laurel guilty of enacting an ordinance "to exclude the poor," calling it a plan "papered over with studies, rationalized by hired experts." They decided that local authority was being systematically abused and that the necessary machinery and policies to enforce the law must be created by the court. The court crafted a policy that incorporated regional planning goals of the state government as well as the U.S. Department of Housing and Urban Development's definitions of housing need.

It is difficult to think of any issue of social policy that would involve greater complexity than housing and planning decisions about unique circumstances all over a rapidly developing state. If the courts are incompetent to manage such issues, however, and no one else will do it, housing exclusion becomes one of those fundamental issues, which cannot be solved. Haar clearly is convinced that the neoconservative attack on judicial capacity is wrong and that the *Mt. Laurel* cases show that courts have ample adaptive powers if they chose to use them.

Mt. Laurel II suspended the normal processes and created specialized courts to handle all enforcement across the state, arming them both with much clearer mandates and authorization to bring experts into the process in critical roles in advising the courts. The three judges drew on outside expertise and imposed dramatic deadlines. They were given sweeping authority to rewrite local housing policies.[39] Now the decisions were in the hands of courts with power, knowledge, and clear directions. A powerful "builders remedy" offered a massive financial incentive to developers to sue resistant suburban communities. (The value of developers' land could be increased greatly in many cases simply by allowing building at higher densities. Dividing the fixed cost of land among more housing units lowers the cost per unit and increases the number of buyers who can afford the housing as well as the number of units the developer has to sell.) The suburbs, said one lawyer, had become "Nice, fat, profitable targets."[40] The new courts could go beyond the particular dispute to force compliance by blocking other construction the suburb badly wanted, by suspending all or part of the local zoning code, by directly approving building permits rejected by the community, and by drastically limiting appeals. The state supreme court lowered the barriers to filing cases and required rapid implementation of decrees.[41] Within a year the courts, working with experts, had devised a methodology for solving the fundamental problem of determining what a community's "fair share" of affordable housing should be.[42] Haar concludes that "in a remarkably short period of time" the courts had devised policies and procedures "more than sufficient for settling disputes and providing guidelines."[43] He reports on progress after three years: "Twenty-two Mount Laurel suits had reached settlement, with over fourteen thousand units prescribed in fair share determinations. . . . A target for the production of moderate- and low-income housing had been established for the state. And ongoing litigation and negotiation were pushing the parties closer to statewide goals formulated in Mount Laurel II."[44]

Once policies were in place that threatened to actually change suburban communities rapidly, the intense attention of the state's political leaders focused on the issue. Before the *Mt. Laurel II* case it was inconceivable that the state legislature would overrule the suburbs and force them to make a significant response to the need for low income housing. With the exception of Massachusetts' "Anti-Snob Zoning" law no state had acted strongly on this issue.[45]

The court decisions brought an issue virtually nonexistent in politics to the center of political debate. In 1985, two years after *Mt. Laurel II,* the state legislature passed the Fair Housing Act to take control of zoning back from the courts and place it in the hands of an appointed Council on Affordable Housing. The legislation made the state government a major force in suburban land use decisions. But the legislation lowered the court's goal for affordable housing from 243,000 to 145,000, lowered the maximum requirement for any community, and allowed suburbs to pay cities to build up to half their required affordable housing back in the inner city.[46] On the positive side, the law took the onus off the courts and put it on executive agencies, substantially limiting suburban authority, and moved the legislated state affordable housing standard from zero to 145,000, and triggered suburban investment in city housing rehab and construction during a period in which federal housing programs were being drastically curtailed. In terms of the original goal of the plaintiffs, the law "shifted the rationale of the Mount Laurel doctrine away from the broad goal of ending geographic segregation . . . toward the raw provision of low-income housing, toward a pure class-based remedy, even though it lowered the obligations of the suburbs dramatically."[47] The Supreme Court said that it had only acted earlier because of the failure of the other branches of government and it welcomed the initiative of the legislature and the governor in responding to the problem. "This kind of response, one that would permit us to withdraw from the field, is what this Court has always wanted and sought." The court carried out a strategic retreat.[48]

The long-term evidence shows that a large change in land use policy was institutionalized, but it did not turn out to be a significant response to minority exclusion. Substantial affordable housing was constructed and the power of the state over local land use decisions was greatly increased, but almost all of the housing was for suburbanites.

The potential impact of the long legal struggle was weakened by allowing suburbs to produce more inner-city subsidized housing to fulfill part of their obligation, which was virtually certain to keep thousands of families living in inner-city areas with residential and educational segregation for decades to come, given their desperate need for affordable housing. Added to the record of white suburbanites getting the new affordable suburban units, the compromise meant that the net effect of Mt. Laurel on housing could actually increase metropolitan housing and school segregation, providing more subsidized housing for minority families in segregated cities and allowing some lower-income white families to live in expensive suburbs.

Part of the problem, according to Charles Haar, was that the New Jersey court failed to create an effective public justification for its rulings. The opinions tended to be long, to have unfocused language, and to lack clear and careful development and the kind of strong central statements of principles and obligations that are found in the most memorable judicial opinions. Haar criticizes *Mt. Laurel I* for failing to develop a powerful legal argument.[49] While admiring the decisive implementation requirements in *Mt. Laurel II*, he notes that the court "faltered in the equally critical task of expressing its opinion in a manner calculated to educate and persuade. . . . The lengthy and technical legal argument stripped the issues of the emotional appeal and obscured the essential link between local administrative actions and the rule of law under the constitution."[50] Although critics of race-based remedies often argue that class-based remedies would have a stronger appeal the truth may be that they are harder to explain and have less basis in American political and legal rhetoric and history. Unequal housing and neighborhoods for poor people have always been the norm.

The Fair Housing Act did involve a substantial change in the role of the state. After the court showed that it was prepared to impose sweeping judicial control, the legislature found a bipartisan compromise that was more acceptable to the suburbs but far beyond what existed before the court acted. Evaluated in comparison with state policy before Mt. Laurel, this was a massive step forward. Evaluated against the plan and goals of *Mt. Laurel II*, it was a major step backward. Evaluated in terms of solving the low-income housing crisis in the state or in breaking up urban ghettos, its impact was modest, in part because the federal subsidies that were needed to make new housing developments for very poor families virtually disappeared under the Reagan Administration and did not return. So what was produced as "affordable housing" was usually within reach of many previously excluded families but not to the poor. Affordable housing for below average income families can be financed by internal subsidies and land use density bonuses to developers but housing for the poor requires much deeper construction subsidies and ongoing operating subsidies.

Assessing whether or not the land use and housing policies represent a successful case of reform through the judiciary depends to a considerable degree on what standard is used in assessing the production of affordable housing. The decisions did trigger substantial housing production (the decisions had produced more than 28,000 affordable new units by 2002), but only a modest share of the total goals was met by the mid-1990s and that has had very limited impact on housing for central city residents. Haar sees the accomplishments as evidence that the neoconservative critique that courts are incompetent to reform major institutions is wrong; in fact, he argues, courts are quite capable of making the needed adaptations in areas of the greatest complexity and their leadership clearly led to major accomplishments that would not have occurred otherwise, making a lasting change in state land use practices.

A generation later, it is important to assess whether or not a court can successfully alter suburban exclusion. The social and economic construction of communities through decisions about housing construction and marketing shapes neighborhoods. Housing creates strikingly different patterns of opportunity by creating access to different schools and labor markets.

The critical nature of the issue and the political void mean that Mt. Laurel is one of the only tests we have about the possibility of developing our metropolitan communities in a less segregated way.

Political power has been flowing to the suburbs for generations. One of the deepest ironies of the reapportionment decisions of the mid-1960s was that although celebrated as the belated triumph of the city constituencies over the rural areas, the decisions did not come until two decades into the period of mass suburbanization. Their principal effect has been to magnify the power of the suburbs to defend their autonomy. The 1992 national election was the first in which there was a suburban majority, and the "Contract with America" Congress elected in 1994 was the first clearly suburban Congress.[51]

The Democratic Party, described as the nation's urban party since the 1930s, followed a calculated suburban strategy in 1992 in its first successful Democratic presidential campaign since the Watergate scandal helped elect Jimmy Carter for one term.[52] The strategy — ignoring racial issues, promising help for the middle class, and praising the value of work — was explicitly set out by Clinton's pollster, Stanley Greenberg, and faithfully executed in the 1992 Clinton campaign.[53] Clinton's success in winning 8 percent more of the suburban vote than President George Bush played a crucial role in his 1992 victory.[54]

Since neither party dares significantly question the suburban status quo, the issues are virtually outside politics.[55] National and state election campaigns and many policy decisions between elections are now aimed at swing voters in the suburbs. As of 1980, the trend has been toward increasingly harsh policies blaming the urban poor and their leaders for their own problems and adopting sanctions. Since the Reagan Administration there have been sharp cuts in urban development funds and almost no federal funds for the construction of additional new housing for low-income families in the federal and state budgets.[56] National campaigns rarely mention urban policy.[57]

The suburbs are continuing to expand even where overall population is not growing; as urban densities thin, household size shrinks, and development of upscale suburban communities continues apace. There are powerful financial incentives for both the developers and the outer suburbs to continue this process, no matter what the costs may be to the rest of the area. This is the kind of politically intractable problem that inspires advocates to develop cases to bring the leverage of the courts into the process to force change. The problem appears to be as insoluble within the contemporary political system as those of the pre–civil rights South were within southern politics before the federal government abolished state requirements of segregation. The last major debate about federal action on suburban exclusion was when President Nixon created a new dominant political coalition of the South and the suburbs and then rejected and denounced requirements for integration of the suburbs.[58]

American political ideology is intensely individualistic and localistic, and very special political conditions are needed before political leaders will seriously debate fundamental problems of racial or economic discrimination.[59] Only during Reconstruction and the mid-1960s were there active majorities in Congress ready to act on structural racial issues. In both of those periods the main focus was on the unique problems of the South. There has never been a federal policy for metropolitan desegregation. Large majorities of Americans usually believe that government has done as much as it should about race.[60] Since the 1960s, politicians have made large political gains by exploiting fears of racial change and attacking "reverse discrimination" against whites.[61] For twenty-six years after the civil rights revolution all Supreme Court justices were appointed by presidents who had come to office as opponents of urban desegregation.[62] The Court ended the expansion of urban desegregation law by the 1974 Milliken decision (*Milliken v. Bradley,* 418 U.S. 717), which protected the suburbs from school desegregation. It was in this political and legal setting that the New Jersey court challenged the core of suburban power.

New Jersey epitomizes suburban exclusion. It is the most suburban state in the United States, a rich state whose impoverished cities include Newark and Camden. Newark is among the handful of the most segregated regions in the nation, with several other New Jersey metropolitan areas close behind.[63] New Jersey schools rank among the top four most segregated states for both African American and Latino students.[64] The state later took over three of its large urban districts — Newark, Paterson, and Jersey City — because of their profound and long-lasting failure.[65] New Jersey's central cities have been economically devastated.

David Kirp, John Dwyer, and Larry Rosenthal's study covers many of the same issues but poses a different basic question. It asks whether or not the *Mt. Laurel* decisions show that a litigation strategy could solve the urban racial crisis in New Jersey. Starting from the perspective of the black plaintiffs and the young public interest lawyers who brought the case, this book juxtaposes the overwhelming urban decline of the city of Camden and the fate of the threatened black enclave in Mt. Laurel against the legal and political machinations in the courts and the state government agencies. The authors conclude that little has changed and probably none of the suggested sweeping solutions are feasible. The underlying dilemma, they write, arises from the lack of any serious support for policies confronting the growing racial polarization of metropolitan America. The authors dismiss the ideas of the "policy wonks" and "policy mavens," note that there are no simple answers, discuss some interesting local experiments, and blame state politicians and the state supreme court for retreating in 1985 after *Mt. Laurel II* created the possibility of significant victories for the plaintiffs. Given these limitations, they held, "Real change, if it happens, will mainly take place town by town."[66]

The city of Camden continues its devastating downward spiral and a quarter century has elapsed since *Mt. Laurel I* by the time tenants move into the first major affordable development aimed at local blacks in the suburb. The role of the courts is a modest one in their narrative, a ripple in a much larger stream moving in the opposite direction. Even though the interventions have modified the destiny of Mt. Laurel in some ways, the impacts are far too small to halt the downward spiral of a central city, which has lost most of its economic functions.

Both *Our Town* and *Suburbs Under Siege* reflect an acute sense of the splitting apart of metropolitan society, and both are excellent in exploring the questions they pose but less effective in analyzing the policy outcomes, particularly the racial outcomes.

In assessing the possibility of change through litigation in a hostile setting, Charles Haar's general conclusion is that courts and litigators can take the initiative and make the necessary institutional adaptations. Furthermore, he argues, the courts took on big issues of urban development more effectively than any other part of government during the long period of conservative domination of social policy. Although his argument on this latter issue is well constructed and persuasive, what is missing in Haar's book is an analysis of the degree to which affordable suburban housing was actually related to the urban crisis and to racial segregation. That is presumed. Like the initial *Mt. Laurel* decision itself, Charles Haar tends to assume that limiting affordable housing exclusion alone will make a major difference. There is no sense of the vastness of the suburban need for affordable housing — of all the elderly, young, divorced, and temporarily low-income families in suburbia for whom no housing is available — nor is there a description of the conditions that would enable inner-city African American and Latino families to compete effectively with suburban whites for such housing when it was marketed by private developers. It is assumed that the increase in supply will solve the problem of the segregated markets.

Do Class-Based Housing Remedies Solve Race-Based Problems of Metropolitan Exclusion?

Advocates often assume that an aggressive policy dealing with exclusion of lower-income families from the suburbs would cut racial segregation. They assume, as many critics of race-specific policies explicitly argue, that solving the issue of class makes a major difference on racial outcomes.

For years the debate in New Jersey proceeded with no significant empirical evidence on such basic questions as who benefited from the housing. How much? Did it help a few families or were there community-wide impacts? How did the housing built in central cities actually work — what were the effects of the city and suburban housing opportunities on employment and education in the affected families? Was the net effect pro-integration through increasing minority access to white areas or toward entrenching more poor minority families in inner-city neighborhoods while aiding temporarily poor suburban whites to find suburban housing? What was known from other experiences in housing desegregation about what would be needed to actually increase residential integration and what the benefits from such efforts might be?

A basic reason why these books did not deal more effectively with the results was that neither the court decisions nor the legislation required the production of the kind of data needed to track the consequences. This is one of the typical failings of courts in implementing civil rights remedies. Courts engaged in institutional reform litigation need to require the production of specific types of information if they are to assess and refocus remedies. Without such data neither the court nor the plaintiffs can find out whether a remedy is working or how it needs to be changed. If class-based remedies produce no race data on beneficiaries then there is no way to know their impacts on racial problems.

Though there were strong reports of the absence of minority families in new suburban developments by the late 1980s,[67] more complete data were not available until 1996, two decades after the first *Mt. Laurel* decision.

The extensive data released in 1996, produced through a foundation-funded university research center project, starkly challenges the proposition that the *Mt. Laurel* cases had anything significant to do with race. Increasing the supply of affordable suburban housing could aid racial integration in New Jersey and elsewhere, but simply increasing the supply was not enough.

The 1996 study relied primarily on a database set up in the 1990s to qualify applicants for receipt of Mt. Laurel housing. It covered 7,500 occupants and 36,000 screened applicants.[68] Though far from comprehensive, the study provided a great deal of information about thousands of families affected by the program in the 1990s. It found that the units were being built and were going to families with genuine needs.[69] The vast majority of the residents moving into the housing, however, were either suburbanites moving to another suburban location or city residents moving to another city location, since many suburbs took advantage of the opportunity to build a substantial share of their affordable housing obligation in a city.

Qualified minority applicants were less likely than whites to find housing, suggesting discrimination in marketing of the housing.[70] Among the blacks in the program there was a net move from the city to the suburbs of only 15 people in the total sample, or 1.6 percent of the black occupants. Latinos were a much smaller part of the program, and had a net suburbanization of 2 people, or 1.1 percent of Latino participants. Among whites, in contrast, there was net migration of 121, or 9.2 percent from the city to the suburbs.

The program, in other words, produced almost no suburbanization for minorities but subsidized a long-established trend of white suburbanization. More than nine-tenths of the residents did not move across the city-suburban boundaries.[71] The program had no significant effect on the central city population; instead, its net effect was to very slightly increase the proportion of whites living in suburbia. As a solution to the metropolitan racial crisis, it was a bust.

There was an easy assumption that most people who needed affordable housing were nonwhite and lived in cities and that they would be the most likely to take advantage of any increased supply of affordable housing anywhere in the metropolitan area. Unfortunately these assumptions proved false when the New Jersey Supreme Court chose to define the problem strictly as a one of economics, saying nothing directly about the racial issues raised in the trial. The suburbs were found guilty of "economic discrimination" and using public funds "solely for the benefit of middle and upper income persons."[72]

Since it did not directly face the race issue, the court did not consider evidence on what was necessary to produce affordable housing for minority families in white areas. Even after removing legal barriers to construction of lower-income housing, evidence from studies of several federal housing programs shows that there are a series of other barriers. First, since 1981 there has been no significant federal or state program to finance construction and subsidize operation of housing for truly low income families; new commitments for family construction were substantially ended in the first Reagan budget. Thus it is impossible to create a supply of housing for truly needy families that require deep subsidies. Second, developers usually wish to maintain good relations with local officials and have strong incentives to give preference to local residents. That perpetuates segregation unless the building is constructed in an integrated community. Third, racial discrimination continues to be severe in the marketing and tenant selection of affordable buildings as shown by HUD's national studies of the housing markets.[73]

The experiences of relocation, public housing, and urban renewal programs of the 1950s and 1960s had shown that adding funds and subsidizing units was perfectly compatible with spreading segregation.[74] In 1971 a report by the U.S. Civil Rights Commission showed that the largest program of low income home ownership in American history was enabling whites to move out of interracial city neighborhoods to white suburbs while blacks were ending up in ghettos or racially changing communities.[75] Fourth, the stereotype that those needing affordable housing are urban and nonwhite is a vast oversimplification.[76] There are great numbers of people from the suburbs who need subsidized housing — people who have lost jobs, who have been divorced, who have health problems, who are aged, who are young and in part-time jobs, and so on — and suburban residents will always find out about new local affordable suburban housing much faster than minority outsiders from poor urban communities. Fifth, unless there are explicit efforts to show housing in different areas, many people will not consider moving across racial boundaries even though they have no preference for living in segregated communities.

The largest experimental study in U.S. history was the Nixon Administration's Housing Allowance Experiment, which tested the effect of vouchers in private markets and showed limited racial mobility.[77]

The federal study of the *Gautreaux* startup year,[78] when 7,000 black public housing tenants in Chicago were offered the chance to move to private apartments in the suburbs as the result of a 1976 Supreme Court decision, documents the fear and lack of knowledge of other communities that acted as a basic barrier to mobility for poor ghetto residents.[79] Until it became clear to city families that it was safe to move, few were willing to take the risk. (Later, after the program helped the first families move successfully, a very intense demand developed.) Systematic research showed that there were major benefits for the children and families who moved.[80]

Analysis of the rent subsidies and new suburban housing provided under the Section 8 program enacted in 1974, the largest federal subsidy program since that time, showed a tendency to reinforce residential segregation even when more buying power was introduced into the segregated markets.[81]

It was clear by the beginning of the 1980s that special outreach and personal counseling were critical to break down racial barriers, even if housing became affordable.[82] If the New Jersey court had seriously examined the racial dimension of suburban housing change, it would have found considerable evidence that a color-blind supply-side remedy would not produce integration and might well increase segregation by subsidizing movement of low income whites from interracial areas and subsidizing the racial steering of blacks into fragile desegregated neighborhoods where the sudden demand would push them into resegregation. Had the court reviewed the record, it might also have decided to require the kind of racial data that was only produced two decades later and that could well have led to specific fair housing strategies being incorporated in the succession of *Mt. Laurel* orders — strategies including counseling and providing escorts to show tenants broader ranges of housing choices, a practice that has had powerful effects in increasing mobility of minority families to the suburbs elsewhere.

Without major subsidy programs and an effort to break down lines of separation in the housing markets, the best that could be expected of a pure land use case of this sort is that it would open the way for affordable housing in areas where it had been excluded and that most of the beneficiaries would be white suburbanites. This is just what happened. Many thousands of units of more affordable housing were constructed in suburbia; thousands more were built or rehabilitated in cities. Communities have agreed to build many thousands more in the future.

The policy produced internal subsidies from developers for affordable units by permitting more dense and profitable development of land. It lessened modestly the extent of low density suburban sprawl. Builders' incentives took some of the enforcement burden off the courts and transferred it to private groups with deep pockets and considerable power.

This is an important judicial innovation, but it was something much different than the goals sought by the initial plaintiffs or ascribed to the case by the authors of *Our Town* and *Suburbs Under Siege*. The effectiveness of the courts in producing social change should be judged, however, in terms of what the court actually decided, not in terms of what those who filed the case wished it to decide.[83] In the area of race relations, particularly when dealing with a fundamental racial structure of urban society such as housing segregation, large successful changes without explicit goals and accountability are extremely unlikely.

The *Mt. Laurel* decisions are best understood as producing substantial numbers of affordable suburban housing units that would not otherwise have been built. Court approval of the state Fair Housing Act was a decision to let affluent suburbs deal with the obligation on their own terms, in part by building lower income housing in segregated cities. This has a segregatory effect by increasing available low-income units in ghetto and barrio areas where they are virtually certain to be occupied exclusively by minority families.

Although the case has not changed the racial status quo, which it never explicitly set out to do, it has created more affordable housing stock, which might make more integration possible in the future. Compared to the total housing needs of New Jersey, the contribution has been modest. However, compared to the record of most other states or of the federal government in this period, the accomplishment was a large one. An increased supply of affordable suburban housing is a necessary but far from sufficient condition for such a policy. The record shows, as Haar concludes, that courts do have the capacity to manage resolution of very broad and complex social issues that no one else will face and to change the politics of a very difficult issue. There was, however, no nonracial solution to metropolitan residential segregation.

To conclude from these depressing statistics either that the court order was a failure or that nothing can be done about metropolitan segregation would be incorrect. Housing research has repeatedly shown that racial segregation cannot be solved with a purely economic strategy. According to major studies by economist John Kain and sociologists Douglas S. Massey and Nancy Denton, economic differences explain only a relatively small part of the intense racial segregation in residence.[84] The findings in the *Mt. Laurel* remedy studies raise serious questions about the consequences of nonracial remedies being developed in other areas of civil rights policy. Creating a supply of affordable housing does not solve the problem because there is a vast unfilled need for such housing in the suburbs as well as the city and among whites as well as among minority households. Pumping more resources into a deeply rooted system of spreading segregation may well spread segregation more rapidly.

The *Mt. Laurel* experience proved something many would have thought impossible a generation ago — that a state court can force a substantial change in suburban land use practices and create policies to produce far more affordable housing in the state than all federal programs together. The court's success in creating an effective judicial mechanism for coping with complex planning and economic decisions suggests that the courts have major powers to enforce basic rights in an era of large bureaucracies and corporations and amid an extremely complex system of fragmented local governments.

Changing the Racial Impact of Mt. Laurel: Lessons from Another Major Housing Rights Case

The true lesson of the *Mt. Laurel* cases may be that land use reform is manageable under a court order, but that it is not enough. As the metropolitan Chicago *Gautreaux* remedies show, in order to go beyond the economic goals of the decisions and lower residential segregation by producing real access of minority city residents to suburban communities, however, there must be an explicit goal and concrete interventions to deal with current racial barriers and the effect of past residential isolation. If specific fair housing goals and mechanisms were added to the New Jersey plan and modifications were made in the 1985 state legislation, the results could certainly have been different. Even in retrospect, such policies could be applied to new units and to the many vacancies that arise over time in the existing *Mt. Laurel* units.

The *Brown* decision alone did not change the South, but it set the stage for a social movement and the development of legislative and administrative policy that did transform the South. After a decade, *Brown* appeared to be a failure, but that decade of struggle led to a transformation reflected in *Green* and in federal civil rights regulations, making the schools of the South the nation's most integrated by 1970.[85] *Brown* and the later cases left the North segregated, not because it was impossible to desegregate Northern metropolitan areas, but because the Supreme Court explicitly exempted suburban communities from desegregation plans in its 1974 *Milliken* decision, leaving the lower courts to struggle over the question of how to remedy intentional segregation without white students for desegregation.

The housing decisions do still retain the possibility of providing significant changes if the lessons of Mt. Laurel are combined with those learned in litigation which directly approached the goal of racial mobility and actually expanded housing choice. *Mt. Laurel*'s ability to increase the supply of affordable housing combined with *Gautreaux*'s ability to increase real housing choices for inner-city families could begin to move substantial numbers of minority families into the heartland of economic growth on the suburban periphery. Substantial progress on metropolitan racial segregation will require a direct attack on that issue. In the area of housing in suburbia, the class-based remedy failed to change the racial status quo but the lessons of a race-based remedy could change its impact.

Notes

1. Martin Luther King, Jr., *Where Do We Go from Here: Chaos or Community?* (New York: Harper and Row, 1967). Also see James R. Ralph, Jr., *Northern Protest: Martin Luther King, Jr., Chicago, and the Civil Rights Movement* (Cambridge, Mass.: Harvard University Press, 1993).

2. Douglas S. Massey and Nancy A. Denton, *American Apartheid: Segregation and the Making of the Underclass* (Cambridge, Mass.: Harvard University Press, 1993).

3. James Rosenbaum and associates, "Can the Kerner Commission's Housing Strategy Improve Employment, Education, and Social Integration for Low-Income Blacks?" in John Charles Boger and Judith Welch Wegner, eds., *Race, Poverty, and American Cities* (Chapel Hill: University of North Carolina Press, 1996), 273–308.

4. Gregory R. Weiher, *The Fractured Metropolis: Political Fragmentation and Metropolitan Segregation* (Albany: State University of New York Press, 1991).

5. Irene S. Rubin, *Shrinking the Federal Government: The Effect of Cutbacks on Five Federal Agencies* (New York: Longman, 1985), chapter 5. Also see Norman C. Amaker, *Civil Rights and the Reagan Administration,* chapter 5 (Washington, D.C.: Urban Institute Press, 1988).

6. When President Clinton sent Congress the first budget of a Democratic Administration in thirteen years in 1994, he called, for example, for a 75 percent cut in funds for new public housing and an 18 percent cut in funds for upgrading deteriorated buildings. See Gwen Ifill, "Clinton Budget Underscores Priorities in Lean Times," *New York Times,* February 8, 1994: B8. After the GOP Congress was elected in 1994 even the continued existence of HUD was placed in doubt. Housing programs were sharply curtailed. In the budget deal at the end of Congress, HUD took the largest cut and housing funds were reduced more than a fifth. See Jackie Calmes and David Rogers, "Historic Budget Battle Ends with a Whimper, as Congress Wraps up Work on Spending Deal," *Wall Street Journal,* April 26, 1996: A14.

7. *Milliken v. Bradley,* 418 U.S. 717 (1974): *Missouri v. Jenkins,* 115 S.Ct. 2038 (1995).

8. Congressional Quarterly, *Nixon: The Third Year of His Presidency* (Washington, D.C.: Congressional Quarterly Press, 1972), 23.

9. *Southern Burlington County NAACP v. Township of Mt. Laurel,* 67 N.J. 179 (1975) (*Mt. Laurel I*).

10. G. Alan Tarr and Mary Cornelia Aldis Porter, *State Supreme Courts in State and Nation* (New Haven: Yale University Press, 1988), 184.

11. Charles M. Haar, *Suburbs Under Siege: Race, Space, and Audacious Judges* (Princeton, N.J.: Princeton University Press, 1996); David L. Kirp, John P. Dwyer, and Larry A. Rosenthal, *Our Town: Race, Housing, and the Soul of Suburbia* (New Brunswick, N.J.: Rutgers University Press, 1995).

12. Naomi Bailin Wish and Stephen Eisdorfer, *The Impact of the Mt. Laurel Initiatives* (East Orange, N.J.: Seton Hall University, Centre for Public Service, October 1996).

13. Haar, *Suburbs Under Siege,* xi.

14. Kirp, Dwyer, and Rosenthal, *Our Town,* 4–5.

15. Ibid., v.

16. Haar, *Suburbs Under Siege,* xi, xiv.

17. Kirp, Dwyer, and Rosenthal, *Our Town,* 1–2.

18. Ibid., 3.

19. Ibid., 38.

20. Ibid., 70.

21. Ibid., 73.

22. Ibid., 79.

23. Governor's Select Commission on Civil Disorder, *Report for Action* (Trenton, N.J., 1968), xi.

24. National Advisory Commission on Civil Disorders, *Report of the National Advisory Commission on Civil Disorders* (New York: Bantam Books, 1968): 114–115.

25. Ibid., 396.

26. Ibid., 398–401.

27. Ibid., 474.

28. Ibid., 481–482.

29. Michael Danielson, *The Politics of Exclusion* (New York: Columbia University Press, 1976), 53.

30. Quoted in ibid., 61.

31. Ibid., 42.

32. *Village of Belle Terre v. Borass,* 416 U.S. 1 (1974). See Kirp, Dwyer, and Rosenthal, *Our Town,* 80. Within months of the *Mt. Laurel* case, the U.S. Supreme Court drastically limited the right to challenge suburban ordinances. (Ibid., 81, discussing *Warth v. Seldin,* 422 U.S. 490 [1975]).

33. President Nixon's notes on October 21, 1970, memo from Ehrlichman to the President. See John Erlichman, *Witness to Power: The Nixon Years* (New York: Simon and Schuster, 1982), 218.

34. Ehrlichman, *Witness to Power,* 222.

35. Bernard J. Frieden and Marshall Kaplan, *The Politics of Neglect: Urban Aid from Model Cities to Revenue Sharing* (Cambridge, Mass.: MIT Press, 1975), 58–64.

36. *Mt. Laurel I,* 67 N.J. 151.

37. Ibid., 92.

38. Ibid., 95–96.

39. Haar, *Suburbs Under Siege,* 44–46.

40. Kirp, Dwyer, and Rosenthal, *Our Town,* 105.

41. Haar, *Suburbs Under Siege,* 43–46.

42. Kirp, Dwyer, and Rosenthal, *Our Town,* 106–107; also see Haar, *Suburbs Under Siege,* 57–62.

43. Haar, *Suburbs Under Siege,* 70.

44. Ibid., 89–90.

45. Massachusetts in 1969 passed the "Anti-Snob Zoning" law, overriding total local control of zoning. (Massachusetts Acts of 1969, Chapter 774; 4-B, Mass. Gen. Laws Annotated, Sections 20–23 (approved August 23, 1969). See Karen J. Schneider, "Innovation in State Legislation: The Massachusetts Suburban Zoning Act," unpublished senior thesis, Radcliffe College, 1971. The act provided for state overrides of zoning when suburban communities excluded affordable housing and had less than 10 percent low or moderate housing or fell below the minimum annual provision of land for such housing.

See Richard F. Babcock and Fred P. Bosselman, *Exclusionary Zoning: Land Use Regulation and Housing in the 1970s* (New York: Praeger, 1973), 171–176.

46. Haar, *Suburbs Under Siege*, 102, 112–115.

47. Ibid., 114.

48. *Hills Development Co. v. Township of Bernards*, 103 N.J. 64 (1986), commonly referred to as *Mt. Laurel III.*

49. Haar, *Suburbs Under Siege*, 154.

50. Ibid., 28.

51. The Congressional Research Service reported that between 1966 and 1994 the number of majority suburban districts in the House of Representatives had risen from 92 to 212 while the number of predominantly urban districts dropped to 82. See Karen De Witt, "Have Suburbs, Especially in South, Become the Source of American Political Power?" *New York Times,* December 19, 1994.

52. William Schneider, "The Suburban Century Begins: The Real Meaning of the 1992 Election," *Atlantic Monthly,* July 1992: 33–44.

53. Stanley B. Greenberg, "From Crisis to Working Majority," *American Prospect,* 7 (Fall 1991): 104–117; Stanley B. Greenberg, *Middle-Class Dream: The Politics and Power of the New American Majority* (New York: Times Books, 1995).

54. Exit poll by Voter Research and Surveys, in *New York Times,* November 4, 1992.

55. Thomas Byrne Edsall with Mary D. Edsall, *Chain Reaction: The Impact of Race, Rights, and Taxes on American Politics* (New York: Norton, 1992).

56. Joseph B. Pechman, *Setting National Priorities: The 1983 Budget* (Washington, D.C.: Brookings Institution 1982), 119.

57. Ann Scales, "Cities Barely Figure as an Issue in National Campaign," *Boston Globe,* November 4, 1996: A12.

58. By the late 1960s it was clear to many civil rights leaders and urban experts that the most critical issues for the future of American society were issues about inequality within metropolitan areas. The Kerner Commission concluded that the fundamental problem was white discrimination. See U.S. National Commission on Civil Disorders, *Report of the National Commission on Civil Disorders,* 1968. On New Jersey's riots, see Governor's Select Commission on Civil Disorder, *Report for Action,* Trenton, N.J., 1968. Martin Luther King's last major campaign was the Chicago Freedom Movement. This frustrating effort to begin to break down the walls of exclusion in the metropolitan Chicago housing market left the century's greatest civil rights leader deeply pessimistic about the urban future. See Ralph, *Northern Protest.* King described the campaign and his realization that the white resistance to residential change in the north was more intense than white resistance in the South. See King, *Where Do We Go From Here?* 22. See also Gary Orfield, "Separate Societies: Have the Kerner Warnings Come True?" in Fred R. Harris and Roger W. Wilkins, eds., *Quiet Riots: Race and Poverty in the United States* (New York: Pantheon Books, 1988), 100–122.

59. James R. Kluegel and Eliot R. Smith, *Beliefs About Inequality: Americans' Views of What Is and What Ought to Be* (Hawthorne, N.Y.: Aldine de Gruyter, 1986). Also see Jennifer L. Hochschild, *Facing up to the American Dream: Race, Class, and the Soul of the Nation* (Princeton, N.J.: Princeton University Press, 1995), and Richard M. Merel-

man, *Making Something of Ourselves: On Culture and Politics in the United States* (Berkeley: University of California Press, 1984).

60. The basic trends are toward increased support for the principles of equal treatment but "relatively low levels of support for translating principles into practice." See Howard Schuman, Charlotte Steeh, and Lawrence Bobo, *Racial Attitudes in America: Trends and Interpretations* (Cambridge: Harvard University Press, 1985), 103–104.

61. Harry S. Dent, *The Prodigal South Returns to Power* (New York: John Wiley & Sons, 1978). Also see Wayne Greenhaw, *Elephants in the Cottonfields: Ronald Reagan and the New Republican South* (New York: Macmillan, 1982); Earl Black and Merle Black, *The Vital South: How Presidents Are Elected* (Cambridge, Mass.: Harvard University Press, 1992); Jack W. Germond and Jules Witcover, *Whose Broad Stripes and Bright Stars? The Trivial Pursuit of the Presidency 1988* (New York: Warner Books, 1989).

62. In the period of 1967 until the 1993 confirmation of Justice Ruth B. Ginsberg, President Nixon had four appointments, President Ford had one, President Reagan had three, and President Bush had two. Presidents Nixon and Reagan also had the opportunity to appoint Chief Justices.

63. Census computations by Nancy Denton, SUNY, Albany, prepared for Conference on Suburban Racial Change, Harvard Civil Rights Project, Cambridge, Mass., October 1996.

64. Gary Orfield, *The Growth of Segregation in American Schools: Changing Patterns of Separation and Poverty Since 1968*, with Sara Schley, Diane Glass, and Sean Reardon (Alexandria, Va.: National School Boards Association, 1993).

65. Kimberly J. McLarin, "New Jersey Prepares a Takeover of Newark's Desperate Schools," *New York Times*, July 23, 1994, 1. Also see Joseph L. Sullivan, "Improvement Lags After School Takeovers, State Says," *New York Times*, April 25, 1995, B6.

66. Kirp, Dwyer, and Rosenthal, *Our Town*, 168–173, quotation on p. 175.

67. Haar notes in passing a problem that "has dogged reform from the start: too few of the intended beneficiaries — African Americans and other minorities from the inner city — enjoy the benefits of the new housing." He blames the problem in part on problems of finding qualified applicants. (Haar, *Suburbs Under Siege*, 114). There had been reports by one of the state's leading newspapers, by a major Urban League chapter, by the Civic League of New Brunswick, and in a 1989 law review article that showed little minority access to the suburbs. (*Star Ledger*, November 17, 1992: 1; Civic League of Greater New Brunswick, *Final Report to the U.S. Department of Housing and Urban Development: Private Enforcement Monitoring Program*, 1991; M. Lamar et al., "Mt. Laurel at Work: Affordable Housing in New Jersey," 41 *Rutgers L. Rev.* 1197 [1989]. All of these sources are cited in Wish and Eisdorfer, *Impact of the Mt. Laurel Initiatives*, footnotes 53–55.)

68. Wish and Eisdorfer, *Impact of the Mt. Laurel Initiatives*, 26–32.

69. Ibid., 39, 47.

70. White applicants were overrepresented by 8 percent among those who succeeded in becoming occupants while black applicants were underrepresented by 50% and Latinos were underrepresented by 64 percent. See Ibid., tables 25–30).

71. Ibid., table 34.

72. *Mt. Laurel I.*

73. M. Turner, R. Struyk, and J. Yinger, *Housing Discrimination Study: Synthesis,* U.S. Department of Housing and Urban Development (Washington, D.C.: Government Printing Office, 1991).

74. By 1967, urban renewal had leveled about 400,000 units of housing, a great deal of it in black communities, replacing few units and forcing the residents into nearby communities where they created new ghettos. (U.S. National Commission on Urban Problems, *Building the American City* [Washington, D.C.: Government Printing Office, 1968], 163.)

75. U.S. Commission on Civil Rights, *Home Ownership for Lower Income Families* (Washington, D.C.: Government Printing Office, 1971).

76. In 1991 a fifth of white rental households had income below the poverty level. See J. M. Woodward, *America's Racial and Ethnic Groups: Their Housing in the Early Nineties* (U.S. Bureau of the Census, Current Housing Reports, Series H121/94–3, 1994), 27.

77. Daniel H. Weinberg, "Mobility and Housing Change: The Housing Allowance Demand Experiment," in W. A. V. Clark and Eric G. Moore, eds., *Residential Mobility and Public Policy* (Beverly Hills, Calif.: Sage, 1980), 68–193.

78. U.S. Department of Housing and Urban Development, *Gautreaux Housing Demonstration* (Washington, D.C.: Government Printing Office, 1979).

79. *Hills v. Gautreaux,* 425 U.S. 224. The *Gautreaux* experiment came out of a finding that the subsidized housing in Chicago had been intentionally segregated for decades. The remedy emphasized housing integration rather than increasing the supply of affordable housing. What turned out to be the most important part of the remedy was a contract between HUD and the nation's largest local fair housing group, for administering thousands of rent subsidy certificates through a program that encouraged black families to move from Chicago's housing projects to virtually all-white communities far out in suburbia. Some 7,000 households had moved under *Gautreaux* by 1996. Many critics believed at first that black public housing families strongly preferred to live in Chicago, close to relatives, welfare offices, clinics, etc. Only a tiny fraction of the eligible families—black public housing and public housing waiting list families—initially expressed interest in the program. The initial HUD report suggested that the strategy was not workable. What the Leadership Council staff learned, however, was that much of the resistance among black families was based on lack of contracts and fears of white hostility. Once a number of families moved, obtaining better housing, neighborhoods, safety, and better schools without facing severe white resistance, interest in the program exploded. Eliminating the need for painstaking efforts to contact a few dozen interested families, thousands applied immediately whenever registration was opened, overwhelming the capacity of the program. The key element was person-to-person counseling and individually showing outlying units and neighborhoods to young mothers who had no personal familiarity with them. Research led by Professor James Rosenbaum of Northwestern University shows substantial benefits for the education of the children and better college and job contacts for the mothers.

80. Leonard S. Rubinowitz and James E. Rosenbaum with Shirley Dvorin et al., *Crossing the Class and Color Lines: From Public Housing to White Suburbia* (Chicago: University of Chicago Press, 2000).

81. Robert Gray and Steven Tursky, "Local and Racial/Ethnic Occupancy Patterns for

HUD-Subsidized Family Housing in Ten Metropolitan Areas," in John Goering, ed., *Housing Desegregation and Federal Policy* (Chapel Hill: University of North Carolina Press, 1986), 235–252.

82. Gary Orfield, *Toward a Strategy for Urban Integration: Lessons in School and Housing Policy from Twelve Cities* (New York: Ford Foundation, 1981), 59–66.

83. An analysis comparing the results with the initial goals of those filing the case is an analysis of the effectiveness of the litigation strategy of the plaintiffs, not of the capacity of the court.

84. John F. Kain, "Housing Market Discrimination and Black Suburbanization in the 1980s," in Gary A. Tobin, ed., *Divided Neighborhoods: Changing Patterns of Racial Segregation* (Newbury Park, Calif.: Sage, 1987), 68–84.

85. Gary Orfield, *Public School Desegregation in the United States, 1968–1980* (Washington, D.C.: Joint Center for Political Studies, 1983).

IO

Civil Rights and the Status of Black Americans in the 1960s and the 1990s

REYNOLDS FARLEY

The accomplishments of the modern civil rights movement distinguish the 1960s from previous and later decades. The litigation strategy of the National Association for the Advancement of Colored People dating from the early twentieth century, the nation's growing commitment after World War II to the democratic ideal of equal opportunities for all, and the increasing educational attainment of the population laid a sturdy foundation for the eventually successful efforts of Dr. Martin Luther King, his collaborators, and his numerous followers. His oration at the Lincoln Memorial on August 28, 1963, will be one of the most frequently quoted speeches of the century, as it described the nation's highest principles and thereby hastened Congressional action. It also helped to strengthen an emerging national consensus supporting equal racial opportunities.

The following year, Congress enacted and President Johnson signed one of the most important laws of the twentieth century — an encompassing Civil Rights Act that banned racial discrimination in employment and in public accommodations, encouraged the integration of public schools, and put the Department of Justice on the side of plaintiffs in civil rights litigation. Although now seen as a crucial law that moved the nation toward racial justice, there was much opposition at that time. In the Senate, a filibuster blocked action for eighty-four days, and then twenty-seven senators, including the Republican nominee for the presidency that year, voted against this law.

The following year, after three deaths and several days of bloody rioting as voting rights advocates sought to march from Selma to Alabama's state capital in Montgomery, Congress passed and President Johnson signed the Voting Rights Act, finally making the Fifteenth Amendment effective in all states, ninety-five years after it was added to the Constitution. After James Earl Ray assassinated King in Memphis on April 4, 1968, Congress immediately put the third major civil rights bill of that decade on the law books; the Fair Housing Act that banned racial discrimination in the housing market. (For histories of this civil rights movement in the 1960s see Garrow, 1978, 1986.)

Changes of the 1960s and early 1970s were far more pervasive than just the addition of new laws. From the perspective of this first decade of the twenty-first century, it appears that all three branches of the federal government gradually moved toward providing equal opportunities for blacks. President Johnson established the Office of Federal Contract Compliance to ensure that firms doing business with the government treated blacks fairly in employment; that is, businesses had to submit reports about the racial composition of their workforces and could lose federal contracts if blacks were substantially and consistently underrepresented. President Nixon endorsed and supported his "Philadelphia Plan" to get African American men into high-paying construction jobs, a rewarding occupational niche from which they had been excluded. Importantly, the Supreme Court joined this effort, even when it meant changing traditional rules and terminating policies that had been firmly in place for decades. In 1971, the Supreme Court concluded that voluntary school integration plans seldom accomplished constitutionally mandated goals so they unanimously approved the use of busing and specific racial ratios to integrate previously segregated schools (*Swann v. Charlotte-Mecklenburg*). Six years later, in *Regents of the University of California v. Bakke,* they approved the use of race as one of several criteria for deciding who might be granted or denied admission to medical school. The next year, in *United Steelworkers of America v. Weber* (1979), they upheld a strong affirmative action plan that reserved job opportunities for black applicants even if they did not have the tenure and job histories required of white applicants. Then the Supreme Court's *Fullilove v. Klutznik* (1980) decision gave constitutional approval to a law Congress enacted reserving 10 percent of federal construction spending for minority contractors. The situation is strikingly different in the early 2000s. No civil rights laws have been removed from the books, but the social and legislative climate is not hospitable to programs that might rapidly provide equal outcomes for African Americans.

The election in 1980 marked a turning point. While few Americans wish to deny opportunities to blacks, affirmative action programs are now in disfavor and may soon disappear. President Reagan's appointment of Clarence

Pendleton to head the Civil Rights Commission and Clarence Thomas to head the Equal Employment Opportunity Commission portended a shift in the policies of the federal government. Both appointees presumably strongly supported equality of racial opportunity but opposed using the powers of the government to implement the many programs developed during the Johnson, Nixon, and Carter administrations. And then the Supreme Court reexamined their previous decisions that had upheld the constitutionality of programs designed to get more blacks into good jobs and into the best educational opportunities. This rethinking of racial issues — along with a drastic change in the composition of the federal bench — led courts to tone down many integration programs, perhaps a prelude to their elimination. The *Wygant* (1986), *Firefighters Local No. 1794 v. Stotts* (1984), and *Ward's Cove Packing* (1989) decisions put strict limits on what employers might do to overcome the discrimination that had kept blacks at the bottom of the occupational queue. *Richmond v. Croson* (1991) and *Adarand v. Pena* (1995) restricted those procedures that set aside a fraction of local governmental spending for minority contractors, while the *Missouri v. Jenkins* (1995) ruling minimized what state authorities must do to overcome racial segregation in public schools and the educational consequences of that segregation. By letting stand the *Hopwood v. Texas* ruling, the Supreme Court effectively challenged the use of race as one of many criteria for deciding who may be admitted to professional schools.

Why have these changes occurred and what are their implications? I will answer this question by looking at several dimensions of racial change since the 1960s.

Changes in the Nation's Racial Composition and the Meaning of Race

The meaning of race today is greatly different from what it was when Dr. King led the civil rights movement. Restrictive immigration laws dating from the post–Civil War era kept the Asian population small at the start of the 1960s — just about one million Asians out of the total U.S. population of 179 million. There were just one-half million American Indians in the United States, many of them living in rural areas of sparsely populated western states, and in 1960 no census question sought to identify the Spanish-origin population. Almost all congressional debate in the 1960s about civil rights and most Supreme Court decisions focused exclusively upon the grievances of blacks.

The nation is much more diverse, at least partially as a result of the successful civil rights movement. When Congress sought to eliminate discrimination on the basis of race, in addition to the Civil Rights Act of 1964, the Voting Rights Act of 1965, and the Housing Rights Act of 1968, they enacted a fourth major civil rights law: the Immigration and Nationality Amendments Act of 1965. This struck down those racially motivated provisions that permitted immigration from western Europe but sought to keep Asians, eastern Europeans, and southern Europeans out. After 1968, the United States began to receive, for the first time in the twentieth century, many migrants from Asia and Latin America. In the 1980s, those two areas continued to supply the majority of immigrants but, for the first time, numerous other nations from Africa, South America, the Middle East, and Southeast Asia — lands that had never before sent migrants — were common countries of origin. The Census of 1990 revealed that twenty-nine countries sent 50,000 or more migrants to the United States during the 1980s (U.S. Bureau of the Census, 1993). Each year in the 1990s about 800,000 legal and 300,000 undocumented immigrants arrived — a volume of immigration similar to that of the first decades of the century (Warren, 1990). One-third of the nation's population growth in the 1990s was due to immigration.

In addition to immigration, there has been an important change in demographic procedures, one that strongly influences how we describe the nation's racial composition. Through 1960, an enumerator visited every household to gather information, and thus racial identity depended primarily upon how people appeared to census takers. Since 1970, race has been self-reported: each person writes down his or her own identity or checks a category. While this change altered the counts for all races, it led to an especially rapid increase in the number of American Indians (Snipp, 1989: chap. 2), as people who previously seemed white to census takers marked Indian for their race.

The rapidly growing Spanish-origin population is also challenging old racial classification schemes, because Hispanics are often treated as if they were a racial group. In 1990, approximately 58 percent of those who said their origin was Spanish went on to identify with one of the traditional racial groups (white, black, or Indian), but 42 percent did not, indicating that their Spanish origin was equivalent to race. In 1990, the official count of whites was 199 million, but it was 10 million larger if those who used "Spanish" as if it were a racial category are included (U.S. Bureau of the Census, 1993).

The racial classification system is also influenced by the moderate to high rate of racial intermarriage. Among those who married recently, the majority of young people who say they are American Indians marry into another race, a proportion rivaled by native-born Asians. Even the black-white intermarriage rate doubled in the 1980s and, in the late 1990s, perhaps 8 to 10 percent of young black men who marry have white wives (Farley, 1999). This means that

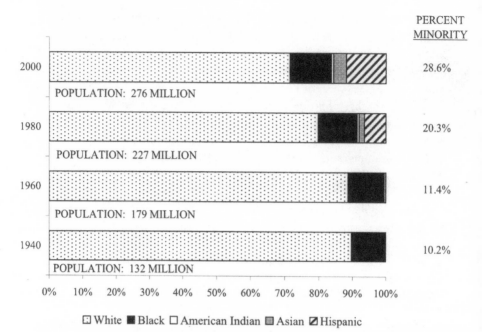

PERCENT
MINORITY

2000   28.6%

POPULATION: 276 MILLION

1980   20.3%

POPULATION: 227 MILLION

1960   11.4%

POPULATION: 179 MILLION

1940   10.2%

POPULATION: 132 MILLION

0%   10%   20%   30%   40%   50%   60%   70%   80%   90%   100%

⊡ White ■ Black ☐ American Indian ▨ Asian ▨ Hispanic

Figure 10.1 Population of the United States by Race, 1940–2000
Note: Hispanics not separately identified before 1970 Census. Data for racial groups in 1980 and 2000 refer to non-Hispanics.
Sources: U.S. Census Bureau, *Sixteenth Census of the United States: Population, 1940*, vol. II, table 4; *Census of Population: 1960*, vol. 1, part 1, table 44; *Current Population Reports*, P-25–1104 (November 1993), and www.census.gov/population/estimates.

an increasingly large fraction of children are born to parents from two races, making it less likely for some of them to identify with only one race. One of the most controversial changes in the census of 2000 was the decision of the Census Bureau and the Office of Management and Budget to allow individuals to mark as many races as they wished. Advocates of this procedure point out that high intermarriage rates imply we have a rapidly expanding mixed-race population. Preliminary examination of these new data suggest that between 1.5 and 2.6 percent of the national population will identify with two or more races (Farley, 2000).

Figure 10.1 shows the racial composition of the United States over a sixty-year span. In 1940 and again in 1960 it was reasonable to assume this was primarily a black-white nation, but that is no longer possible. After 1980, the non-Hispanic white population — with its older age composition and below replacement level birth rates — grew slowly at an average rate of only one-half of 1 percent each year; while the non-Hispanic black population increased by just over 1 percent each year. But the number of Hispanics grew by 4 percent annually, while the heterogeneous Asian population increased by 6 percent each year. At current rates, the Asian population will double every twelve years. As a result, a major change in racial composition is under way. Before 2005, Latinos will be more numerous than African Americans. The numerically dominant non-Hispanic white population will decline in relative size, although it is far from certain that whites will ever become a numerical minority since interracial marriages — especially those involving Asians — produce a disproportionately large number of children who are identified as white (Harrison and Bennett, 1995: table 4.4).

A Continued Liberalization of White Attitudes About Principles of Equal Racial Opportunity

The racial attitudes of whites changed, both before and after the civil rights decades as they increasingly endorsed equal opportunities. How do we know that attitudes have shifted? With the outbreak of World War II, the Defense Department undertook a domestic intelligence effort. They wanted to monitor racial attitudes because officials in Washington feared that rioting between blacks and whites on the nation's streets would undermine the highly successful efforts of the government to portray America's involvement in World War II as the fight of a righteous democracy against totalitarian dictators. Thus national samples of whites have been asked their attitudes about racial issues since the early 1940s.

Figure 10.2 reports the percentage of whites who gave the "equal racial opportunity" answer to questions about integrated schools and integrated public transportation and about equal opportunities for blacks in both the labor and housing markets. During the early years of World War II — just a little over two generations ago — only three whites in ten endorsed the idea of blacks and whites attending the same public schools. The majority of whites believed that whites should have the first chance at good jobs when they became available, and most whites endorsed the principle of segregated public transportation that Rosa Parks challenged so effectively on December 1, 1955.

By the 1960s, attitudes had changed, and for the first time, the majority of whites endorsed principles of equal opportunities for blacks. Many commentators speculated that with the outbreak of urban violence in the late 1960s, there would be a white "backlash" against blacks, suggesting that white support for equal racial opportunities would drop. That did not happen. Each successive generation of whites reported more egalitarian racial views, so

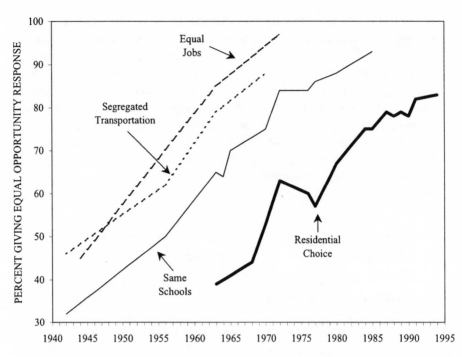

Figure 10.2 Percentage of Whites Giving the Equal Opportunity Response to Questions About Principles of Racial Equity

Questions:

Same Schools: Do you think that white students and (Negro/black) students should go to the same or separate schools? (Percentage saying "same schools.")

Equal Jobs: Do you think Negroes should have as good a chance as white people to get any kind of job, or do you think white people should have the first chance? (Percentage saying "as good a chance as white people.")

Segregated Transportation: Generally speaking, do you think there should be separate sections for Negroes on streetcars and buses? (Percentage saying "no.")

Residential Choice: Which statement on the card (showing four responses from "agree strongly" to "disagree strongly") comes closest to how you feel? White people have a right to keep blacks out of their neighborhoods if they want to, and blacks should respect that right. (Percentage disagreeing.)

Source: Schuman, Steeh, and Bobo, 1998, table 3–1; National Opinion Research Center, 1994.

much so that by the 1980s, more than nine whites in ten favored equal opportunities for African Americans in the housing market and in public education. Indeed, white approval for integrated public transportation and for equal job opportunities was so nearly unanimous that surveys stopped asking those questions in the 1970s. An analysis of racial attitudes by age reveals that younger whites in the 1990s endorsed equal opportunities to a greater degree than older ones, implying that the cohort replacement process will lead to even more egalitarian attitudes in the future. Although there is not, at present, racial equality in outcomes, nor extensive white support for affirmative action programs that might rapidly bring about black-white parity, racial attitudes, values, and norms have fundamentally shifted (Schuman et al., 1997: chapter 3). It is difficult to imagine that in the twenty-first century, a presidential candidate or twenty-seven senators will oppose legislation similar to the Civil Rights Act of 1964. There is no longer white support for those practices that kept African Americans home on election day, out of the jury box, or off the playing field in professional sports or that once limited black men to manual labor and black women to domestic service.

Racial Differences in This Era of Immigration and Racial Diversity

Many civil rights activists in the 1960s assumed that legal changes and shifts in racial attitudes would, within a generation or so, minimize black-white differences in social and economic status. Has that happened? Are racial discrepancies now much smaller than in the past?

Changes in immigration policy mean that a description of racial stratification in the 1990s cannot be limited to blacks and whites: the new immigrants and their descendants must be considered. When we then compare racial groups on the most important indicators of education, employment, and earnings, we find a consistent ranking. Whites and native-born Asians are at the top of the list, while American Indians and blacks are at the bottom. But that is not the complete story; gender makes a large difference, and African-American women fare just about as well as white women in terms of earnings and income.

Figure 10.3, from an investigation conducted by Robert Mare (1995), portrays seven decades of educational stratification. Birth cohorts are arrayed along the horizontal axis while data about seven racial groups are shown in the body of the figure, thereby describing trends in attainment across time. Among Asians and Hispanics, the native-born are distinguished from the foreign-born.

The findings are readily summarized. With regard to completing high school — data shown in the upper panel — Asians and whites have had a consistent and substantial advantage over other racial groups. There has been a steady trend toward much greater proportions obtaining high school diplomas or General Education Development certificates, but racial difference are evident in every birth cohort, including the youngest. Among the most recent

HIGH SCHOOL DIPLOMA OR GED

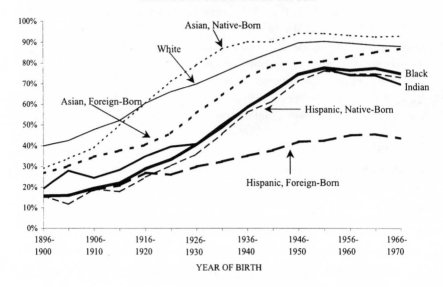

AT LEAST A BACHELOR'S DEGREE

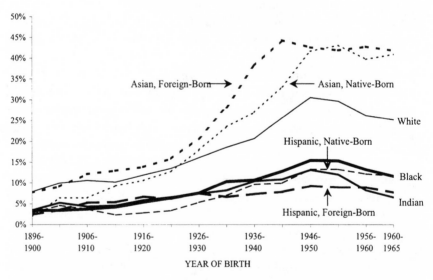

Figure 10.3 Percentage of Persons Completing at Least Twelve Years of School or at Least a
Bachelor's Degree, by Race and Year of Birth
Source: Mare, 1995, figures 4.8 and 4.9

cohorts, high school completion among foreign-born Hispanics lags far behind other groups, reflecting the in-migration of young adults from Mexico and Central American nations, where the absence of high schools and the shortage of employment encourage teenagers to migrate to the United States to fill those low-skill jobs that are now available in great numbers.

With regard to college completion — trends shown in the bottom panel of Figure 10.3 — Asians, both those born in the United States and those born overseas, are distinguished from other groups by the unusually great investments they make in higher education. They have a large advantage over whites who, in turn, have an advantage over those at the bottom of this racial ladder: blacks, Hispanics, and American Indians. Racial differences in college enrollment and completion remain troublingly large. Among those born during the civil rights decade, native-born Asians were four times as likely and whites were three times as likely to earn a four-year college diploma as blacks, Hispanics, or American Indians. Social and economic changes, as well as decreasing racial discrimination, have narrowed racial discrepancies in attainment at the high school level, but there is little evidence of any racial convergence at the college level. Thus, young Asians and whites now seem best poised to fill the jobs that are most rewarding.

When people enter the labor market, is there a net effect of race upon how they fare or are racial differences in employment and earnings largely accounted for by differences between groups in their demographic characteristics, especially their investments in education? Presumably, if Title VII of the Civil Rights Act of 1964 accomplished its aims, there might be gross racial differences in labor market outcomes, but they would be explained by factors other than race itself; that is, the net effect of race in the labor market would be close to nil. The census and Census Bureau surveys provide many indicators of success or failure in the labor market, only two will be considered here: unemployment and earnings.

Figure 10.4 considers unemployment rates by race for labor force participants aged 25 to 54 at the time of the 1980 and 1990 censuses. The odds of unemployment for minorities are compared to the odds of unemployment for native-born, non-Hispanic whites, taking into account those variables that influence whether a person is working or unemployed. These include his or her educational attainment, place of residence, reported ability to speak English, work disabilities, and marital status. For women, number of children ever born was also taken into account to get a better estimate of the net effects of race upon employment.

Examining the upper panel of Figure 10.4 — the relative unemployment rates of men — reveals how uniquely blacks and American Indians differ from

DATA FOR MEN

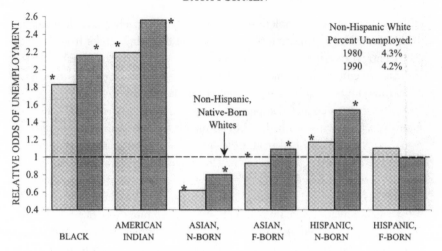

DATA FOR WOMEN

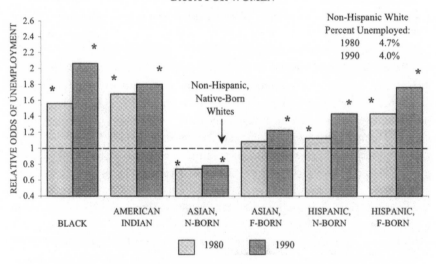

Figure 10.4 Odds of Unemployment for Racial Minorities Relative to Those of Native-Born, Non-Hispanic Whites Aged 25–54, 1980 and 1990, Net of Factors Accounting for Unemployment

* Difference in probability of unemployment from that of native-born, non-Hispanic whites is significant at the .01 level.

Note: These data refer to labor force participants. The bars show the net odds of unemployment for a racial group compared to those of native-born, non-Hispanic whites. These are estimated effects of race net of religion, metropolitan residence, age, educational attainment, reported ability to speak English, reported presence of a work disability, and marital status. For women, number of children ever born was also included as a control.

Source: U.S. Bureau of the Census, *Census of Population and Housing, 1980 and 1990.* Public Use Microdata Samples.

other races. At both dates, they were more than twice as likely to be searching for work, and not finding it, as non-Hispanic white men. Native-born Asian men, in contrast, were less likely to be out of work than white men. Hispanics had relative odds of unemployment between those of Asians and blacks. In all comparisons except one, the relative odds of unemployment for racial minorities compared to whites *increased* between 1980 and 1990. That is, taking into account human capital and demographic characteristics, minorities were less well off compared to white men in 1990 than a decade earlier with regard to employment.

The lower panel of Figure 10.4 describes the unemployment situation of adult women. Racial differences are similar to those among men, but the discrepancies are smaller. Black and American Indian women were about twice as likely to be unemployed than non-Hispanic, native-born white women, while native-born Asian women had significantly lower unemployment rates than white women once differences in their characteristics were entered in this model. Just as among men, differences in unemployment rates distinguishing minority women from non-Hispanic white women grew larger between 1980 and 1990. With regard to unemployment, the 1980s were not favorable years for minorities vis-à-vis whites, *since minorities fell further behind whites.*

A similar approach describes the net effects of race upon the hourly earnings of workers aged 25 to 54 who earned wages at some point during 1979 or 1989. The net effects of race are illustrated in Figure 10.5. Individual-level data from census samples were analyzed and a model was fit with the log of hourly earnings as its dependent variable. Race and a variety of human capital characteristics described in the figure were the independent variables. Note that this model controls for labor supply by focusing upon hourly earnings. If race made no difference in the labor market, then the earnings of minorities would be about the same as those of non-Hispanic, native-born whites once relevant characteristics were controlled.

Figure 10.5 reports that men and women in most minority groups had earnings that differed significantly from those of whites. That is, the net effect of race is reported by showing how the hourly earnings of a group compared to those of whites net of the other factors that determine earnings.

All groups of men — except native-born Asian men in 1989 — earned less per hour than white men. Black men, for example, experienced a loss of earnings equal to 13 percent of the wage rate of white men in 1979 and 15 percent in 1989. A black man with the same characteristics as the average native-born, non-Hispanic white man earned less for each hour spent on the job. And the racial discrepancy grew somewhat larger during the 1980s. (For an analysis of long-term trends, see Smith and Welch, 1989.) American Indian, Hispanic —

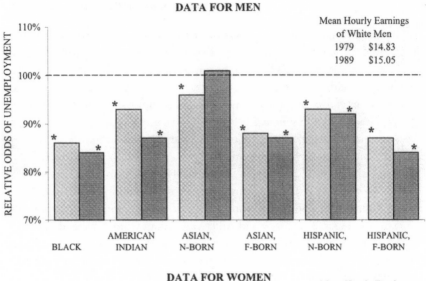

DATA FOR MEN

Mean Hourly Earnings
of White Men
1979 $14.83
1989 $15.05

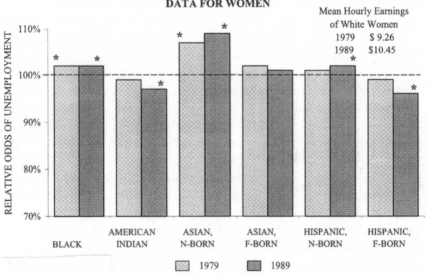

DATA FOR WOMEN

Mean Hourly Earnings
of White Women
1979 $ 9.26
1989 $10.45

1979   1989

Figure 10.5 Hourly Earnings of Racial Minorities as a Percentage of Those of Non-Hispanic Whites, Controlling for Factors Influencing Earnings, 1979 and 1989

* The difference between the hourly earning levels of this group and those of native-born, non-Hispanic whites is significant at the 0.1 level.

Note: These bars show the effect upon earnings of membership in a racial group net of region, metropolitan residence, age, educational attainment, reported ability to speak English, reported presence of a work disability, and marital status. For women, number of children ever born was also included as a control variable. The dependent variable in these models was the log of reported hourly earnings. Data are restricted to those who worked in the year prior to the census and reported positive earnings. Hourly earnings are shown in 1989 dollars.

Source: U.S. Bureau of the Census, *Census of Population and Housing, 1980 and 1990.* Public Use Microdata Samples.

both native and foreign born — and Asian men born abroad earned less than white men and, in every case, the racial gap widened in the 1980s. In terms of earnings, the cost of being a racial minority for men was larger at the end of that decade than at the start.

Before concluding that there is pervasive racial discrimination in the assignment of wages, consider the hourly earnings of minority women. Once those factors determining whether the pay rate is large or small were taken into account, in 1979, black women, native-born Asian women, and native-born Hispanic women also earned significantly *more* than white women: black and native-born Hispanic women about 1 percent more, but native-born Asian women, 8 percent more. In 1980, black, Asian, and native-born Hispanic women earned more per hour than white women.

To the extent that race or skin color affects wages, its consequences depend upon gender. Minority men apparently suffer in the labor market from their race, but there is no evidence from recent censuses that the earnings of minority women are reduced once because they were women and a second time because of their race. The relatively favorable earnings of minority women may come about because of racial differences in the duration of labor force attachment and job holding, factors not fully measured by the census. Whatever the cause, minority women are as successful as white women in translating their labor market characteristics into earnings.

The Economic Prosperity of the 1990s: Did It Close Racial Gaps?

The previous section described racial changes during in the 1980s. It was a discouraging picture. It is not so much that racial gaps got larger, rather there is little evidence of the racial convergence that might have been expected after the civil rights decade. The economic trends of the two decades leading to the 1990s were not so favorable. A capsule view would emphasize that the energy crisis of 1973 marked an important turning point leading to a restructuring of employment in the nation's labor markets. The unionized blue-collar jobs that once sustained much of the middle class — and provided attractive opportunities for black men in what were to become the Rust Belt states of the Midwest — decreased in number as durable goods manufacturing firms adopted more efficient technologies, shifted employment off-shore, or, in some cases, went out of business.

The eighteen years after 1973 were unsettling economic times. Late in the 1970s, unemployment rates soared along with the rate of inflation. Early in the 1980s, the jobless rate reached its highest levels since the Great Depres-

sion. Simultaneously, interest rates soared to such peaks that consumers drastically cut back on buying new homes and new cars while business could not
borrow money to modernize or expand. By the mid-1980s, a few signs of an
economic turn around appeared on the horizon but there was little confidence.
A brief and not-very-deep economic downturn in 1990 and 1991 played a key
role in presidential politics. Recall candidate Clinton's mantra: "It's the economy, stupid," and his defeat of President Bush.

Surprisingly strong economic growth characterizes the years since 1992.
Four important trends influenced opportunities for most Americans and, quite
likely, stimulated an increase in immigration flow from Asia and Latin America. First, employment itself grew rapidly. After 1991, the number of Americans employed went up by about two million every year—a considerably
larger annual increase than in 1970s and 1980s. As more Americans worked,
unemployment rates plummeted to low levels—4 percent in mid-2000, which
was the lowest since the Vietnam War years.

Second, this economic growth was sustained. The 1990s were not marked
by economic downturns followed by booms. Rather it was an era of steady
growth, the type of growth that apparently built confidence by convincing
many that the nation had moved beyond the doldrums of the 1970s and
1980s.

Third, after fluctuating in the 1970s and 1980s, inflation rates were steady
and moderate to low in the 1990s. Inflation averaged about 8 percent a year in
the 1970s, almost 5 percent annually in the 1980s, but was about 3 percent per
year in the 1990s.

Fourth, interest rates were moderate and fluctuated in a narrow range,
seemingly under the firm and beneficial control of the Federal Reserve Board.
Consumers could spend for major items and businesses could expand with the
assurance that they would not be damned by excessive interest payments.
Much more difficult to quantify are the possibly great beneficial economic
consequences in the 1990s of new technologies, especially the adoption of
computers throughout American society.

Was the economic expansion of the 1990s a tide that raised all boats? If so,
it would leave economic gaps pretty much unchanged, even if it improved the
economic lot of most Americans. Or was it an expansion that, when combined
with increasing support among whites for ideals of equal racial opportunities,
produced much smaller racial gaps?

It is important, at this point, to think about the nature of racial progress and
how such progress is measured. Some might herald trends showing that both
blacks and whites increasingly prospered during the 1990s while others might
argue that the most important progress will occur when the traditionally large

gaps in educational attainment, employment, earnings, and poverty decrease or disappear.

This section provides a first glance at what happened during the 1990s. To do so, data from the Census of 1990 were compared to information from a pooling of the Census Bureau's Current Population Surveys conducted in March, 1998 and March, 2000. These studies provide information about key economic indicators similar to those found in the decennial census, but the sample size — about 65,000 adults in each year's survey — is too small to permit simultaneous disaggregation by race, nativity, age, sex, place of residence, and educational attainment. The 1998 and 2000 surveys were pooled to insure no overlap of respondents. That is, one-half of those interviewed in March, 1998 were interviewed once again the following March. (Final revisions were made to this chapter in early 2001. A full analysis of recent racial trends demands those census data that provide information for detailed racial groups by nativity, by birth cohort and by educational attainment for local labor markets. The Census of 2000 released such information in 2002 but those data were not available to make comparisons similar to those based upon information from the censuses of 1980 and 1990.)

EMPLOYMENT-TO-POPULATION RATIOS

Because the focus is on the consequences of economic changes for the races in the 1990s, we first turn to indicators of labor force participation. The format for these figures is similar to that of the previous ones describing changes in the 1980s. In every case, the performance of minorities is compared to that of non-Hispanic, native-born whites controlling for sex. Figure 10.6 shows employment-to-population ratios of minorities as a percent of those of whites for persons aged 25 to 54 in 1990 and 1999. If all persons held jobs at the time of a census or survey, the employment-to-population ratio would equal 1,000.

The labor force trends of the 1990s were, generally, beneficial to minorities since they not only led to increases in the percentages who held jobs but also led to a narrowing of racial gaps. In April 1990 the employment to population ratio was a surprisingly low 682 for African American men — just 78 percent of the employment-to-population ratio for white men. At the end of the 1990s, the employment-to-population ratio for black men was up to 775 or 86 percent that of white men. There is still a large gap in employment, but the sustained growth of jobs in the 1990s shifted proportionally more black than white men onto payrolls. Similarly the employment-to-population ratio rose for African American women, both in absolute terms and relative to white women.

DATA FOR MEN

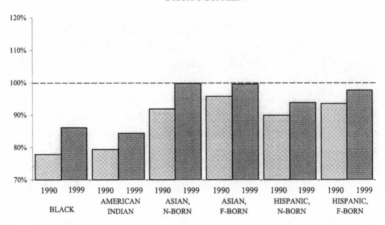

DATA FOR WOMEN

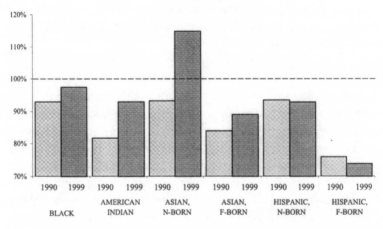

Figure 10.6 Employment-to-Population Ratios of Minorities as a Percentage of That of Native-Born, Non-Hispanic White for Persons Aged 25–54, 1990 and 1999
Note: These data describe the non-Hispanic white, black, American Indian, and Asian populations. For whites, blacks, and Indians, they refer to the native-born. The population-to-employment ratios for native-born, non-Hispanic whites in 1990 and 1999 were, respectively, for men, 877 and 900 (3 percent increase), and for women, 722 and 770 (7 percent increase).
Source: U.S. Bureau of the Census, Public Use Microdata Samples from Census of 1990 and Current Population Surveys of March 1998 and March 2000.

In terms of job holding, the 1990s were good years for all minorities since their population-to-employment ratios moved up—*higher proportions are working and gaps separating them from whites are smaller.*

HOURS OF EMPLOYMENT

Employment rates went up in the 1990s. However, employed minorities—especially black men—traditionally worked fewer hours than the majority population. Has there been a racial convergence in the 1990s in the number of hours people work? To investigate this, we determined per capita hours worked for adults in each racial group. Respondents answered questions about the number of weeks worked in the year before the census or survey and usual hours spent at work per week. From those numbers, per capita hours of employment were computed. Although focusing on adults aged 25 to 54, we include homemakers, early retirees, and the handicapped that may have worked no hours in a year.

Figure 10.7 shows the now often discussed trend of increasing time spent at the plant, in the office, or at the shop. For white men, per capita hours of employment rose by 56, or a little more than one hour each week of the year. For white women, the rise was 144 hours, or almost three hours per week.

During the 1990s, hours of employment increased for every minority group—and for both men and women. Without doubt, recent shifts in the labor market have not only drawn higher proportions of adults to work but have also increased the time they devote to employment. During the 1990s, racial gaps in per capita hours of male employment decreased but were not eliminated. At the end of the prosperous 1990s, black and American Indian men still lagged far behind white men in terms of employment—by about seven hours each week. All groups of minority women in 1990 reported working fewer hours than did non-Hispanic native-born white women but this changed. By 2000, African-American women averaged 1 percent more and native-born Asian women 8 percent more time on the job than white women. Foreign-born Hispanic women stand out. Their hours of employment rose, but much more slowly than those of white women.

HOURLY EARNINGS

In terms of employment itself, minorities moved closer to whites. The findings with regard to hourly wage and salary earnings are much more ambiguous. Many indicators of earnings may be derived for the census and the Current Population Survey, such as median earnings for all who worked, mean annual earnings, or average weekly earnings. To restrict this analysis to those who had a sustained involvement with employment, we considered the mean

DATA FOR MEN

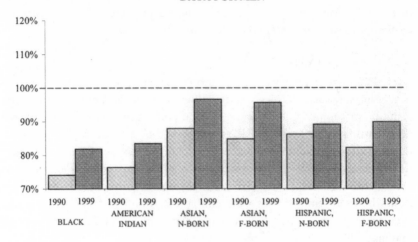

DATA FOR WOMEN

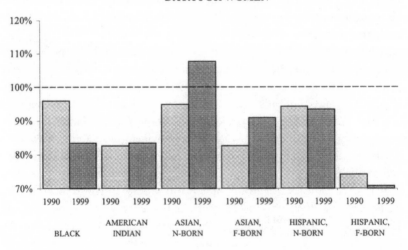

Figure 10.7 Per Capita Hours of Employment of Minorities as a Percentage of Those of Native-Born, Non-Hispanic Whites for Persons Aged 25–54, 1990 and 1999

Note: These data describe the non-Hispanic white, black, American Indian, and Asian populations. For whites, blacks, and Indians, they refer to the native-born. The per capita hours of employment for native-born, non-Hispanic whites in 1990 and 1999 were, respectively, for men, 2,045 and 2,101 (3 percent increase), and for women, 1,340 and 1,484 (11 percent increase).

Source: U.S. Bureau of the Census, Public Use Microdata Samples from Census of 1990 and Current Population Surveys of March 1998 and March 2000.

hourly earnings of persons who worked at least five hundred hours in the year before the census or survey. Comparisons are made using inflation-adjusted dollars shown in 1999 amounts.

The wages of men have stagnated or declined since the mid-1970s while those of women have increased slowly. The median earnings of men who worked full-time were 9 percent less in constant dollar amounts in 1998 than in 1973. The median earnings of women who worked full time went up 18 percent in the same interval (U.S. Bureau of the Census, 2001). A disaggregation by educational attainment reveals declines in the earning of those with limited educations and rises for those with advanced degrees. Data in Figure 10.8 suggest the trend dating from the 1970s was not reversed in the economic expansion of the 1990s. The mean hourly earnings of adult white men who worked at least five hundred hours fell by more than a dollar, while the average earnings of white women — in constant dollar amounts — went up by about forty cents.

Racial gaps in earnings changed only a little in the 1990s. The hourly earnings of African American men declined but slightly less rapidly than those of white men. Among women, the earnings of whites rose while those of blacks fell leading to a larger relative gap. Asians are distinguished from other races since the earnings of both men and women, native and foreign-born rose rapidly in the decade. By 2000, on an hourly basis, native-born Asian men earned 6 percent and native-born Asian women, 22 percent more than native-born non-Hispanic whites. At the other extreme, in terms of hourly earnings, the 1990s were not particularly good years for Hispanics since they fell further behind the earnings of whites. The changing composition of the immigrant population may help account for this finding, but a decline in relative hourly earnings was evident among Hispanics born in the United States.

A full explanation of what is happening to earnings and why requires an analysis of census data with the ability to control for differences in educational attainment, birth cohort, labor market experience, and place of residence. And it is possible that rises in employment might contribute to stagnation in wages since those drawn into the labor force may have fewer job skills than those who worked before. At this point, it is too early to conclude whether the economic boom of the 1990s did or did not narrow racial gaps in earnings.

PER CAPITA INCOME

The final economic indicator is the per capita income of adults. Adults 25 to 54 were considered and their incomes from all sources were summed. For most, their income is largely determined by how much time they spend on the job and their hourly wage rate, but many receive additional income from transfer payments, self-employment, dividends, or other sources.

DATA FOR MEN

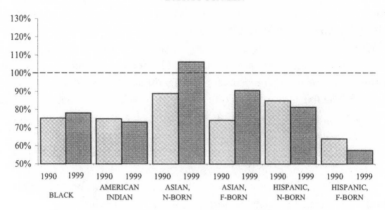

DATA FOR WOMEN

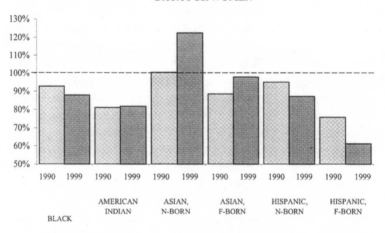

Figure 10.8 Median Hourly Earnings of Minorities as a Percentage of Those of Native-Born, Non-Hispanic Whites for Persons Aged 25 to 54 Who Worked at Least 500 Hours in the Years 1990 and 1999.

Note: These data describe the non-Hispanic white, black, American Indian, and Asian populations. For whites, blacks, and Indians, they refer to the native-born. The median hourly earnings of native-born, non-Hispanic whites who worked at least 500 hours in 1990 and 1999 were, respectively, for men, $16.51 and $15.39 (6.8 percent decrease), and for women, $11.42 and $11.78 (3.2 percent increase).

Source: U.S. Bureau of the Census, Public Use Microdata Samples from Census of 1990 and Current Population Surveys of March 1998 and March 2000.

DATA FOR MEN

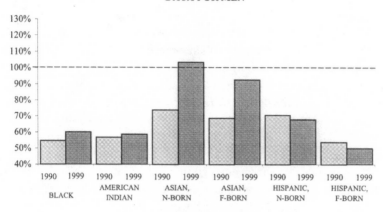

DATA FOR WOMEN

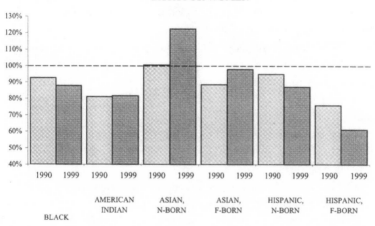

Figure 10.9 Per Capita Income of Minorities as a Percentage of That of Native-Born, Non-Hispanic Whites for Persons Aged 25–54, 1990 and 1999.

Note: These data describe the non-Hispanic white, black, American Indian, and Asian populations. For whites, blacks, and Indians, they refer to the native-born. The per capita incomes of native-born, non-Hispanic whites in 1998 dollars were, respectively, for men, $43,047 and $45,712 (6.2 percent increase), and for women, $19,634 and $24,405 (24.3 percent increase).

Source: U.S. Bureau of the Census, Public Use Microdata Samples from Census of 1990 and Current Population Surveys of March 1998 and March 2000.

The per capita income of adults rose in the 1990s, but increases were much more substantial for women than for men. Among men, the per capita incomes of blacks, American Indians, and Asians went up at a more rapid rate than that of white men, leading to smaller racial gaps. Native and foreign-born Asian men reported especially rapid rises in income. Despite the improvements for these minority men, their incomes lag quite far behind those of white men. At the end of the decade, African American and American Indian men reported earnings about 60 percent those of white men. Asian men were the exception since their incomes rivaled or exceeded those of native-born non-Hispanic whites.

Asian women saw their incomes go up very rapidly. For all other minority women, although there were gains in incomes, they were smaller than those of white women, so racial gaps among women grew somewhat larger in the 1990s. For instance, adult black women in 1990 reported per capita incomes 90 percent those of white women, but by the end of the decade, black women's incomes were 85 percent of white women's.

Recent educational trends imply that among white women now in their twenties, thirties, and early forties, a surprisingly large proportion invested in advanced education and are obtaining the earnings and occupational achievements commensurate with their schooling. It is possible that the cohort replacement process sharply increases the incomes of white women, a possibility that may be investigated with data from the census of 2000.

POVERTY RATES

The poverty rate rivals the unemployment rate as the most closely watched and frequently cited economic indicator. As an outcome of the beneficial economic trends, poverty declined throughout most of the 1990s. After the brief recession of 1990–91, the poverty rate climbed to 15.1 percent when based on income people received in 1993. By 1999, the poverty rate for the entire nation had fallen to 11.8 percent — not far above the all-time low of 11.1 percent recorded in 1973, the year when the first energy crisis prompted economic change. Among African Americans, the poverty rate sunk to a record low in 1999, but one black in four still lived in an impoverished household, compared to one in ten whites. For a household of four in 1999, a pre-tax cash income of $17,030 was necessary to leave the ranks of the impoverished.

Figure 10.10 compares the poverty rates of minorities to those of native-born non-Hispanic whites at the beginning and end of the 1990s. The format of this figure is identical to that of the previous ones. The difference is that in every comparison, the poverty rates of minorities were much higher than those of whites. The upper panel in Figure 10.10 shows changes in the decade for people of all ages, while the lower panel reports trends for children.

DATA FOR THE TOTAL POPULATION

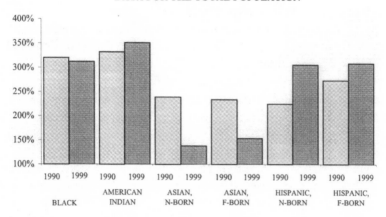

DATA FOR CHILDREN UNDER AGE 18

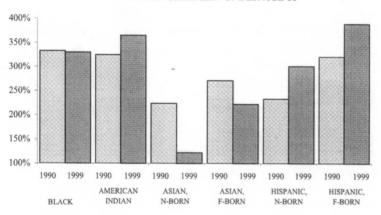

Figure 10.10 Poverty Rates of Minorities as a Percentage of That of Native-Born, Non-Hispanic Whites for Total Population and for Persons Under Age 18, 1990 and 1999.

Note: These data describe the non-Hispanic white, black, American Indian, and Asian populations. For whites, blacks, and Indians, they refer to the native-born. Poverty rates for native-born, non-Hispanic whites in 1990 and 1999 were, respectively, for all whites, 9.3 percentand 8.2 percent (12 percent decrease), and for whites under age 18, 12 pecent and 10.9 percent (9 percent decrease).

Source: U.S. Bureau of the Census, Public Use Microdata Samples from Census of 1990 and Current Population Surveys of March 1998 and March 2000.

Except for Asians — particularly native-born Asians — there is little evidence of a closing racial gap in poverty rates. The poverty rate of African Americans fell just a bit more rapidly than that of whites, but the relative change was miniscule. At the end of the decade, both adult blacks and African-American children were about three times as likely as whites to be impoverished. The decreases in poverty among Indians were somewhat smaller than those among whites, leading to larger gaps. Similarly, among Hispanics, drops in poverty were relatively smaller than those recorded for whites, so the ratio of Hispanic to white poverty increased.

Did the boom of the 1990s improve the economic lot of most races but leave gaps pretty much unchanged? Or was it a boom that reduced or eliminated the traditional discrepancies that have distinguished minorities from whites throughout the nation's history? One conclusion is that Asians are very different in this regard from blacks, Indians, and Hispanics. The economic trends of the 1990s apparently reduced or even eliminated the gaps that once distinguished Asians from native-born non-Hispanic whites.

Many more data will have to be examined to answer questions about other races. Certainly, the expanding labor market led to the employment of many minorities and thereby some declines in the racial gaps on indicators of employment itself. Declining gaps with regard to hourly earnings, overall income, and poverty rates are much more difficult to discern.

ECONOMIC POLARIZATION

When examining the implications of economic trends for racial differences, it is important to consider the nature of recent changes. In the past two decades, the labor market appears to most highly reward those with extensive educations and specialized training while offering fewer benefits to the unskilled. A significant change in the 1990s was the overall increase in employment at all skill levels but not necessarily higher wages for the unskilled. The result was a much larger gap between the earnings of those toward the top and the bottom of the earnings distribution. In 1973, the man at the 90th percentile point in the earnings distribution of men earned 3.85 times as much as the man at the 10th percentile point. By 1990, he earned 5.04 times as much, and, by 1999, 5.33 times as much. Among employed women, the parallel change was from the woman at the 90th percentile point earning 3.38 times as much as her 10th percentile counterpart in 1973 to 4.50 times as much as 1999. This new labor market, by placing a great premium on training and skills, widened the gap between the top and bottom of the economic ladder.

The increasing adoption of egalitarian racial attitudes and the emphasis upon diversity imply that minorities may face fewer barriers and less discrimination in getting hired and promoted, but a much higher proportion of whites than minorities may have the credentials to benefit from recent changes in the labor market. It may be that a substantial fraction of minorities are able to take advantage of new opportunities, but many others may not. The result would be greater economic polarization.

Figure 10.11 summarizes such trends by focusing upon black and white households in the era since the civil rights revolution. The top panel refers to households headed by an African American, the bottom to white households. Thin solid lines report the 80th percentile point in income distributions with amounts shown in constant 1999 dollars. Twenty percent of households reported incomes exceeding that amount, while 80 percent reported less. Among black households, the 80th percentile point rose steadily. In 1999, it was 18 percent greater than in 1990 and 59 percent greater than in 1967. Clearly, those at the top of the African-American household income distribution improved their status substantially, a change also encouraged by demographic shifts such as more two-earner households.

The 20th percentile point distinguishes the top four-fifths of the income distribution from the bottom one-fifth. Although the 20th percentile point for black households—shown as a dotted line in Figure 10.11—moved up sharply after 1995, the long-term trend was that of stability. In 1993, the 20th percentile point was at almost exactly the same dollar amount as in 1967, meaning the gap between the top and bottom had increased substantially. The difference between the incomes of those at the 20th and 80th percentile points in the black household distribution rose from $28,000 in 1967 to $41,000 in 1990 and then to $48,000 in 1999. The Gini Index—shown by the thick line in Figure 10.11—is the most widely understood and frequently cited summary index of income inequality. It would approach zero were every household to have roughly the same income and would approach 100 were almost all income received by just a few households. This index steadily rose, at least until the latter years of the 1990s.

Similar information for white households appears in the bottom panel of Figure 10.11, and the trends toward greater inequality are similar. In 1999, the 80th percentile point in the white household income distribution was 47 percent greater than in 1967, while at the 20th percentile point the 1999 value was just 25 percent larger than thirty-two years earlier. The economic status of low-income white households has improved but not nearly as much as that of white households toward the top.

The figure also reveals persisting and substantial racial differences. Those at the top of the black income distribution have much lower earnings and, presumably, smaller wealth holdings, than those at the top of the white income

DATA FOR BLACK HOUSEHOLDS

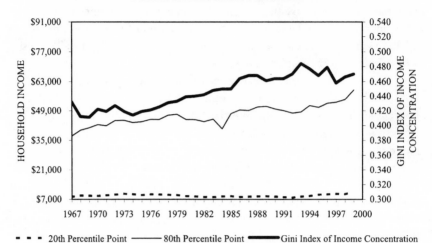

DATA FOR WHITE HOUSEHOLDS

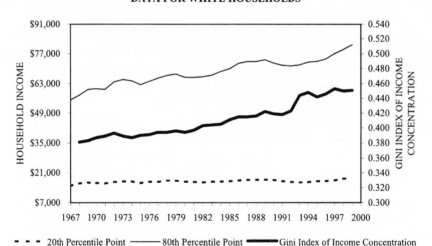

Figure 10.11 Twentieth and Eightieth Percentile Points in Household Income Distributions and Gini Indexes of Household Income Concentration, 1967–1999
Source: U.S. Bureau of the Census, www.census.gov/hhes/income/histinc

distribution. An income of $59,000 in 1999 placed an African-American household in the top one-fifth of their income distribution. Among whites, an income of $81,000 was needed.

Social Indicators: Recent Changes in the Status of Blacks

Social indicators often provide more optimistic information about change in the status of blacks. When we turn to indicators of racial residential segregation and interracial marriage, we find shifts in the recent past that are consistent with the ideals and programs of the civil rights revolution.

BLACK-WHITE SEGREGATION IN THE NATION'S NEIGHBORHOODS

The 1970 to 1980 span was the first decade in which transactions in the housing market came under scrutiny of the Fair Housing Act of 1968. Conflicting conclusions were drawn about the course of segregation during that interval. Focusing on the largest metropolises, Massey and Denton (1993: 83) observed that "the nation's largest black communities remained as segregated as ever in the 1980s." However, Jakubs (1986) found that segregation declined in the majority of the nation's 318 metropolises, especially in the younger locations that had grown rapidly in the decade.

To avoid ambiguity, we describe neighborhood change in the 1980s using all metropolises with substantial black populations. (Data to study segregation trends in the 1990s were not available when this chapter was revised.) There was a pervasive pattern of modest declines. Residential segregation has been assessed most often with the easily understood index of dissimilarity using data from the census showing the racial composition of neighborhoods. This index takes on its maximum value of 100 in a situation of total apartheid; that is, every neighborhood in a metropolis must be exclusively white *or* exclusively black. The index would approach its minimum of zero were individuals randomly assigned to their neighborhoods. In this unlikely case, all neighborhoods would have similar racial compositions.

Using data for block groups — areas defined by the Census Bureau for enumerating purposes containing about two hundred housing units — we measured black-white segregation in 1980 and 1990 for those 232 metropolises in which either at least 3 percent of the residents were black or there were at least 20,000 black inhabitants (Farley and Frey, 1994). In these metropolises, the average index of dissimilarity fell from 69 in 1980 to 65 in 1990. Segregation declined in 194 of the 232 places, and in 85 of them the decline was 5 points or more. In 1980, 14 metropolises had very high indexes (exceeding 85), whereas in 1990 only four metropolises were so thoroughly segregated. In 1980, 29 metropolises could have been classified as moderately segregated (an index of dissimilarity of less than 55). By 1990, the number of moderately segregated places more than doubled to 68. I emphasize that these indexes pertain to black-white neighborhood segregation and do not assess the segregation of either Latinos or Asians from blacks or whites.

Table 10.1 lists the most and least segregated metropolitan areas in 1980 and 1990. Of the fifteen most segregated in 1990, eleven were older midwestern industrial centers and two were retirement communities in Florida. A decade earlier, the list of most segregated included seven midwestern industrial centers but also seven retirement centers in Florida. Five of those Florida metropolises disappeared from the list as their populations grew rapidly and less segregated new housing was constructed.

The list of most residentially integrated metropolises was dominated in 1990 by places whose economic base was the military: Anchorage, Alaska (Elmendorf Air Base), Jacksonville, North Carolina (Camp Lejune), Lawton, Oklahoma (Fort Sill), and Fayetteville, North Carolina (Fort Bragg) appeared on the list both dates, while Ft. Walton Beach, Florida (Elgin Air Base), and Cheyenne, Wyoming (Warren Air Base) were on the list for 1990. The university towns of Lawrence, Kansas, and Charlottesville, Virginia, also had relatively integrated neighborhoods in 1990, while Columbia, Missouri, was among the most integrated a decade earlier.

New construction played an important role in accounting for changes in segregation during the 1980s, suggesting the Fair Housing Law of 1968 may have its intended impact. Decreases in segregation were more extensive in places with much new housing construction (e.g., Orlando, Phoenix, Dallas, and San Bernardino) than in metropolises where the housing stock changed little in the decade (e.g., Buffalo, Pittsburgh, and New York City). New housing construction was also linked to the finding that declines in segregation were greatest in the South and West. In several large metropolises in the West, neighborhoods are now quite integrated; that is, segregation scores were 45 or lower in Honolulu and Tucson, both areas with populations over 500,000; in San Jose, with its population in excess of one million; and in the Anaheim metropolis just south of Los Angeles with its 2.5 million residents.

The manner in which city limits were drawn is also a factor influencing segregation at the metropolitan level. Most older cities in the Northeast and Midwest had their boundaries established many generations ago, so since World War I they have been surrounded by independent suburbs, many of them well known for their hostility to blacks. But in the South and West, central cities annexed outlying land in the 1940s, 1950s, and 1960s so they now include much of what would be the suburban ring in the Midwest or East. Also, many governmental functions including public schools are organized on

Table 10.1. Indexes of Dissimilarity for the Fifteen Most Segregated and Least Segregated Metropolitan Areas: Black vs. Whites, 1980 and 1990

1980		1990	
Metropolitan Area	Index of Dissimilarity	Metropolitan Area	Index of Dissimilarity
Most Segregated			
Bradenton, FL	91	Gary, IN	91
Chicago, IL	91	Detroit, MI	89
Gary, IN	90	Chicago, IL	87
Sarasota, FL	90	Cleveland, OH	86
Cleveland, OH	89	Buffalo, NY	84
Detroit, MI	89	Flint, MI	84
Ft. Myers, FL	89	Milwaukee, WI	84
Flint, MI	87	Saginaw, MI	84
Ft. Pierce, FL	87	Newark, NJ	83
West Palm Beach, FL	87	Philadelphia, PA	82
Ft. Lauderdale, FL	86	St. Louis, MO	81
Naples, FL	86	Ft. Myers, FL	81
Saginaw, MI	86	Sarasota, FL	80
Milwaukee, WI	85	Indianapolis, IN	80
St. Louis, MO	85	Cincinnati, OH	80
Average	88	Average	84
Least Segregated			
El Paso, TX	49	Charlottesville, VA	45
Columbia, MO	49	Danville, VA	45
Victoria, TX	49	Killeen, TX	45
Charlottesville, VA	48	San Jose, CA	45
Clarksville, TN	48	Tucson, AZ	45
Colorado Springs, CO	48	Honolulu, HI	44
San Jose, CA	48	Anaheim, CA	43
Anaheim, CA	47	Cheyenne, WY	43
Honolulu, HI	46	Ft. Walton Beach, FL	43
Fayetteville, NC	43	Clarksville, TN	42
Lawton, OK	43	Lawrence, KS	41
Anchorage, AL	42	Fayetteville, NC	41
Danville, VA	41	Anchorage, AL	38
Lawrence, KS	38	Lawton, OK	37
Jacksonville, NC	36	Jacksonville, NC	31
Average	45	Average	42

Note: These indexes are based on block group data and pertain to persons reporting white or black as their race.

a county-wide basis in the South, thereby limiting the growth of suburban white enclaves.

Despite modest declines throughout the country, neighborhood segregation is still the rule in many of the older centers of black population such as Chicago, Detroit, Cleveland, Philadelphia, St. Louis, and New York. But the Census of 1990 was the first enumeration to report a pervasive pattern of declines in black-white residential segregation throughout the entire nation. In addition, new trends in the migration of blacks offer the hope that the Census of 2000 will reveal even less neighborhood segregation. Blacks are now moving away from the most highly segregated metropolitan areas of the Northeast and Midwest and into metropolises whose neighborhoods are somewhat more integrated: Orlando and Dallas in the South; San Diego, Sacramento, and San Bernardino in the West; and Minneapolis in the Midwest (Frey, 1995).

TRENDS IN BLACK-WHITE INTERMARRIAGE

Laws prohibiting interracial marriage and, sometimes, interracial sex, date from the seventeenth century with the emergence of slavery; whites feared a mulatto population that would not fit into the social hierarchy demanded by the American system of bondage. At first glance, one might think that the Fourteenth Amendment and the Civil Rights Act of 1866 ruled out anti-miscegenation statutes when they granted blacks all the legal prerogatives of whites, but that was not the case. State laws prohibiting intermarriage and the corresponding legal proceedings they required (specifying which offspring were black and which were white) were litigated from the 1880s to the civil rights decade. For eighty-four years, the *Pace v. Alabama* (1883) ruling established precedent. Just after Reconstruction, that state's legislature outlawed fornication, but interracial fornication was punished more severely than fornication between individuals of the same race. The U.S. Supreme Court upheld this act as constitutional since it applied equally to both races.

In the same year that Congress passed the most important civil rights bill of the twentieth century — 1964 — the Supreme Court upheld a Florida law that prohibited unmarried interracial couples from living together but included no such ban when the man and woman were of the same race. The civil rights revolution eventually ended such laws. In June 1958, a white Virginia man, Richard Loving, married a black Virginia woman, Mildred Jeter. Knowing that Virginia would not grant them a marriage license, they wed in the District of Columbia but later returned to Virginia. They were arrested, convicted, and sentenced to one year in jail, but the judge agreed to suspend their prison time if they would stay out of Virginia for twenty-five years. They moved back to Washington but, in 1963, perhaps prompted by the racial ethos of that era,

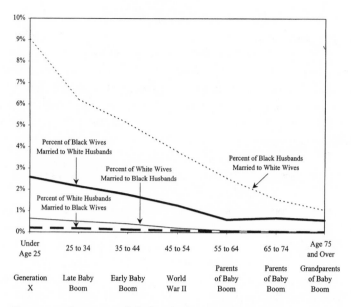

Figure 10.12 Percentage of Black and White Husbands and Wives Marrying Opposite Race; Black-White Comparison
Source: U.S. Bureau of the Census, *Census of Population and Housing, 1990.* Public Use Microdata.

filed a motion to vacate their conviction. Their litigation percolated slowly through the federal courts and, four years later, the Supreme Court ruled that Virginia's ban on interracial marriages involved an invidious racial classification prohibited by the Fourteenth Amendment, thereby invalidating such laws still on the books in fourteen states (*Loving v. Virginia, 1967*).

One of the important social changes apparently flowing from the civil rights revolution and the shift in racial attitudes is a rise in the frequency with which black and white intermarry. Using data from the Census of 1990, we considered married couples and classified both spouses by age, that is, by birth cohort, and by race. We then looked at shifts over time in the proportion of blacks who married whites and whites who married blacks. Note that this analysis is restricted to marriages that "survived" until 1990 and to marriages that involved whites and blacks. Figure 10.12 reports the findings.

Among the grandparents of the baby boomers — those aged 75 and over in 1990 — fewer than 1 percent of black husbands married white women. The norms of that era — and laws in many states — banned such marriages. Among the parents of the baby boomers, this increased to about 3 percent of black husbands marrying white women. Among younger cohorts there was a steady rise, and about 9 percent of the black husbands in Generation X (born between 1965 and 1974) who had married by April 1990 had white wives. Again we note that this excludes those who married Asians, Latinos, or American Indians and those who were divorced at the time of the census. A similar, albeit slower, rise is shown in the percentage of black wives who married white men: from fewer than 1 percent among the grandparents of the baby boomers to almost 3 percent among Generation X women. In every comparison, the proportion of black men marrying white wives greatly exceeded the proportion of black women marrying white husbands.

This figure suggests a fairly sharp rise in the proportion of blacks marrying whites but a more modest change in the proportion of whites marrying blacks. The relative size of the two populations comes into play. The *number* of black men marrying white wives necessarily equals the *number* of white women marrying black husbands. But a change from 2 percent of black husbands marrying white wives to 9 percent shows up as a larger change in this figure for blacks than for whites because the black population is much smaller than the white. The proportionate change over time in the rate of black-white intermarriage will be roughly identical for black men and for white women.

A further analysis of these data reveals that three variables were linked to interracial marriage among those who married in the 1980s. For blacks, college attendance was quite strongly related to the likelihood of marrying a white. Many young blacks who complete college have, presumably, more white classmates and friends than those blacks who finished their schooling at the secondary level where their school was more likely segregated. More than 10 percent of black men who graduated from college and married during the 1980s had white wives compared to about 5 percent for black men who failed to complete high school. And 5 percent of black women with college degrees had white husbands compared to less than 3 percent for high school dropouts. Among whites, however, educational attainment had no such impact upon intermarriage. It is likely that for whites, the racial composition of college classrooms is only marginally different from those of their secondary school classrooms.

For both races, there were important regional differences in intermarriage in the 1980s, net of the effects of other factors. Blacks and whites living in the South were least likely to intermarry. In California and other Pacific Rim states, rates of intermarriage were highest. It is unclear whether this comes about because of particularly liberal racial attitudes or the demographic diversity of the West. That is, a black person in Mississippi or Alabama will have a relatively large pool of other blacks from which to select a marriage partner, but a black living in Oregon or Washington will face a different "marriage market," one that likely includes relatively few blacks.

Finally, serving in the armed forces in the 1980s was strongly related to intermarriage for persons who married during that decade, presumably reflecting the thorough racial integration of the military. Approximately 14 percent of black men who served in the armed forces and married had white wives, compared to 7 percent for those who married but did not serve. Differences of a similar magnitude were observed among black women and among whites of both genders. For example, just under 9 percent of white women who served in the armed forces and married had black husbands, compared to 3 percent among those who did not serve in the military (Farley, 1999).

Conclusion

The most dramatic social changes in the United States in the late twentieth century flow from the civil rights revolution. White Americans came to support the principle of equal opportunities for African Americans, so laws were changed to provide opportunities for minorities. Few, if any, Americans now want to return to the era when blacks rode in the back of the bus, when the military was segregated, and when only whites could vote in the South. While the nation's laws were changed primarily in response to the civil rights grievances of blacks, immigration regulations were also rewritten to remove national origin quotas that dated from previous ages when there was consensus that race or ethnicity should determine who could enter the United States. After that change, the racial composition of the country started to shift and the meaning of race itself was, and continues to be, reexamined. Racial questions in the Census of 2000 are radically different from earlier questions since they allow the option of identifying with two or more races.

The first waves of recent Asian immigrants were either highly educated or came to obtain the advanced educations they needed to succeed in the restructured American economy. The Asian population flow is now more diverse and, while it includes many with exceptionally favorable credentials, it also includes poorly educated immigrants from the mountains of Indochina, south China, and the Indian subcontinent. In the aggregate, Asians invest heavily in education, work unusually many hours—especially Asian women—and do well in translating their human capital investments into earnings. They are more likely than whites to live in husband-wife families, thereby passing on crucial advantages to their children. It seems probable than many of the next generation of Asians born in this country will have the qualifications to excel in a job market that emphasizes technological sophistication and academic achievement.

The Hispanic population—soon to be the nation's largest minority—is also diverse. While many highly educated Latinos from around the world enter every year, there is an even larger stream of young immigrants from Mexico, Central America, and the Caribbean arriving with little schooling. Because there is a strong link between the educational attainment of parents and their children, it is possible that a sizable fraction of the next generation of Hispanic children born in the United States will enter the labor market lacking the credentials needed for success. In terms of years of school completed, they will fall far below whites and African Americans. Large Hispanic underclass neighborhoods may develop in New York, Los Angeles, Houston, and Miami. But it is also possible that the intergenerational link in education attainment will weaken and that Latinos born in this country will gradually close the gap that separates them from whites by remaining in high school, then enrolling in college.

What about African Americans? From the end of the Depression through the early 1970s, racial progress was recorded on most indicators as the economy's growth created millions of new jobs that could be filled by men and women with moderate educational attainments. Importantly, the racial attitudes of whites shifted. A continuation of those economic trends, that is, high rates of both employment and wage growth with a burgeoning of jobs in durable goods manufacturing, construction, and transportation would have brought the nation much closer to black-white parity in earnings and income. But several of the most important trends toward racial convergence came to an end in the early 1970s as the economy changed. Today the job market provides excellent opportunities for the educated elite and many lowly paid jobs for the unskilled (including those who arrive from abroad with little knowledge of English) but leaves a very large share of the blue-collar middle class challenged.

Why have black-white gaps not closed more rapidly since the early 1970s? There are four reasons. First, while whites consistently and almost universally endorse principles of equal racial opportunity, the legacy of slavery and Jim Crow fosters the retention of negative stereotypes about blacks. The National General Social Survey and the four-site Multi-City Study of Urban Inequality (MCSUI) asked representative samples of whites the modern stereotype questions. That is, whites are asked to rank whites as a race and then blacks as a race on seven-point scales with regard to five dimensions of stereotypes:

- tends to be intelligent versus tends to be unintelligent;
- tends to prefer to be self-sufficient versus tends to prefer to live off welfare;
- tends to speak English well versus tends to speak English poorly;
- tends to be involved in drugs and gangs versus tends not be involved in drugs and gangs; and
- tends to be easy to get along with versus tends to be hard to get along with.

Figure 10.13 uses MCSUI data to show how whites in metropolitan Atlanta, Boston, Detroit, and Los Angeles evaluated first their own race and then blacks with regard to each dimension. The first panel shows that whites assigned an average score of 5 points to whites on the "tends to be intelligent versus tends to be unintelligent" dimension using the scale where 7 was the most positive score, while 1 was the most negative score. Whites evaluated whites higher than blacks on this "tends to be intelligent versus tends to be unintelligent" dimension. Note that this question asks about "tends to be intelligent," not about educational attainment or test scores. Thus, these questions assess the endorsement of racial stereotypes.

Racial differences are even larger for other stereotypes. The biggest gap, in the view of whites, was regard to the tendency to rely on welfare rather than hard work. Whites ranked themselves toward the upper end of the "prefers to be self-sufficient versus prefers to live off welfare" scale (average score of 5.5). But whites gave blacks an average score of only 3.8, implying that whites see blacks as much more likely than whites as tending to prefer to live off welfare. Indeed, the majority of whites ranked blacks below the midpoint on this dimension.

Presumably, employers often wish to hire people who speak English competently, especially if the job involves meeting the public or teamwork. These modern stereotype questions report that whites, in general, think that whites rank much higher than blacks with regard to speaking English well. Whites, on average, ranked blacks one and one-half points below whites on this seven-point scale. Perhaps it is no surprise to find that whites also believe that blacks "tend to be involved in drugs and gangs" while whites "tend not be involved in drugs and gangs." More than one-half of the whites agreed that blacks "tend to be involved in drug and gangs," but only 18 percent of whites thought that whites do.

There is one stereotype item on which whites rated blacks and whites just about identically. That is, whites on average thought that whites and blacks were about equally easy to get along with. Thus there is no evidence that whites endorse the stereotype that blacks tend to have a chip on their shoulder.

While most whites strongly endorse principles of equal racial opportunities for blacks, many may also hold negative stereotypes — the kinds of stereotypes that may make it difficult or even impossible for African Americans to get jobs for which they are qualified or to move into white neighborhoods. After all, none of us want neighbors who are involved in drugs and gangs, nor do we wish to send our children to schools where many students speak English poorly, nor do we want employees who prefer to live off welfare rather than work for a living. One reason for persistent black-white differences in

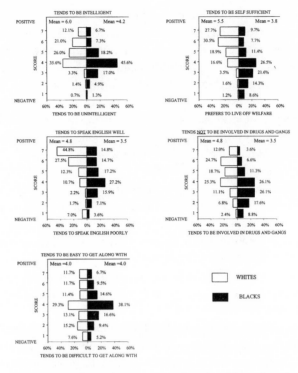

Figure 10.13 The Modern Stereotype Questions: How a Sample of Whites from Atlanta, Boston, Detroit, and Los Angeles Evaluate Whites and Blacks in Five Dimensions
Source: Data from the Multi-City Study of Urban Inequality, a sample of randomly selected adult respondents in four metropolises carried out in 1992–1994. The sample sizes: Atlanta, 692; Boston, 589; Detroit, 793; and Los Angeles, 861.

unemployment, in earnings, and in places of residence may be that quite a few whites still harbor doubts about the ability of blacks to do well on the job or to be highly desirable neighbors.

Second, although residential segregation scores fell moderately, most American neighborhoods still can readily be classified as either "black" or "white." As Myrdal (1944) argued a half-century ago and as Massey and Denton (1993) documented in their authoritative book, *American Apartheid,* numerous deleterious consequences result from isolating a negatively stereotyped racial group into its own neighborhoods, especially when the target of this exclusion is at the bottom of the economic ladder. Jim Crow schools and diminished labor market opportunities are attributable to segregated neighborhoods, and politicians elected by largely white districts can cut back on programs that benefit blacks, knowing that their own constituents will not suffer because of residential segregation. In the view of Andrew Hacker (1992), the United States remains a nation divided by race, with residential segregation being the major mechanism preserving that separation. Although Asians and Hispanics are residentially segregated from whites, they are much less isolated than blacks and are more likely than blacks to benefit from access to the schools, parks, shopping centers, resources, and facilities whites enjoy (Frey and Farley, 1996).

Third, in addition to rapid economic growth from 1940 through 1973, there was an awareness of the civil rights claims of blacks and the depth of the racial chasm. Recognizing the need for firm governmental actions to provide truly equal opportunities, laws were changed, new policies were put in place by several administrations, and federal courts issued innovative decisions seeking to end traditional practices of discrimination and segregation, with considerable federal courts ruling that it was permissible to take race into account in order to overcome the nation's history of racial discrimination. The situation is different now.

By the 1990s, the legislative, administrative, and judicial branches of government were moving in another direction. While there has been no diminution of support for the principle of equal racial opportunities, affirmative action programs designed to ensure opportunities for black Americans in schools and in the labor market are being challenged and may soon be dismantled.

Why is this happening? The cohort replacement process and the scarcity of high-paying jobs for workers lacking college educations account for the shrinking support for affirmative action. Parents of the baby boom remember the drinking fountains and toilets marked "colored" or "white"; they recall the stereotypical Hollywood portrayal of blacks as jesters or household servants. They grew up with Aunt Jemima syrup on their breakfast tables and listed to "Amos 'n' Andy" on the radio. They recall Birmingham Police Chief "Bull" Connor turning his attack dogs and fire hoses on black children who marched out of churches. Late baby boomers and Generation X learned about those events from history books or film clips, if they learned about them at all. Many younger whites have occasionally had a black classmate, have seen successful black politicians on the national scene, and have cheered for sports teams with black stars earning more in one year than they can hope to earn in their lifetimes. And if they live in a major metropolis, they probably grew up close to a city that elected a prominent black to the mayor's office. They know that African Americans can work their way up to the top jobs, so affirmative action appears to be a needless and illegal violation of a fundamental American ideal they were taught in school: skin color should not matter.

While great racial progress has been made since the civil rights decade, it is difficult to be optimistic about a rapid narrowing of black-white gaps on many indicators. Are there any current macro social, economic, political, or demographic trends now that will inevitably or quickly bring about equal outcomes for African Americans in schools or in the labor and housing markets? Thinking about the history of the last century, we observe that within two or three generations, descendants of the once-despised Catholic immigrants from southern Italy and equally despised Jewish immigrants from eastern Europe and Russia leapfrogged over those native-born, English-speaking black Protestants who arrived in the nation's metropolises at the same time (Lieberson, 1980; Perlman, 1988). A pessimist might speculate that this will happen once again, but this time the immigrants who leapfrog blacks will be those arriving from Asia and Latin America. A more optimistic view stresses that racial attitudes have fundamentally changed, that laws now condemn and severely punish racial discrimination, that there is the gradual emergence of a much larger black elite holding important positions in government and business, and that a rising rate of interracial marriage implies that the nation is slowly moving along a road of progress that will eventually lead to the color-blind society Justice John Harlan wrote about in his *Plessy* (1896) dissent more than a century ago.

Note

This chapter is an expanded and updated version of a presentation made at Yale University on February 1, 1995, "Racial Issues Thirty Years After the Civil Rights Decade." Some components of this essay were developed from chapter 6 of my *The New American Reality: Who We Are, How We Got Here, Where We Are Going* (New York: Russell Sage Foundation, 1996).

References

Adarand Construction v. Pena. 1995. Supreme Court Decision No. 93–1841 (June 12).

Firefighters Local Union No. 1794 v. Stotts. 1984. 467 U.S. 561.

Frey, William H. 1995. "The New Geography of Population Shifts." In *State of the Union: America in the 1990s*, vol. 2, edited by Reynolds Farley. New York: Russell Sage Foundation.

Frey, William H., and Reynolds Farley. 1996. "Latino, Asian and Black Segregation in U.S. Metropolitan Areas: Are Multi-Ethnic Areas Different?" *Demography,* 33, no. 1: 35–50.

Fullilove v. Klutznick. 1980. 448 U.S. 448.

Garrow, David J. 1978. *Protest at Selma: Martin Luther King, Jr. and the Voting Rights Act of 1965.* New Haven: Yale University Press.

——. 1986. *Bearing the Cross: Martin Luther King, Jr. and the Southern Christian Leadership Conference.* New York: William Marrow.

Hacker, Andrew. 1992. *Two Nations: Black and White, Separate, Hostile, Unequal.* New York: Scribner.

Harrison, Roderick J., and Claudette E. Bennett. 1995. "Racial and Ethnic Diversity." In *State of the Union: America in the 1990s,* vol. 1, edited by Reynolds Farley. New York: Russell Sage Foundation.

Hopwood v. Texas. 1996. Fifth Circuit Court of Appeals, No. 94–50664 (March 18).

Jakubs, John F. 1986. "Recent Racial Segregation in the U.S. SMSAs." *Urban Geography* 7: 146–163.

Lieberson, Stanley. 1980. *A Piece of the Pie: Black and White Immigrants Since 1880.* Berkeley: University of California Press.

Loving v. Virginia. 1967. 87 S.Ct. 1817.

Mare, Robert. 1995. "Changes in the Educational Attainment and School Enrollment." In *State of the Union: America in the 1990s,* vol. 1, edited by Reynolds Farley. New York: Russell Sage Foundation.

Massey, Douglas, and Nancy A. Denton. 1993. *American Apartheid: Segregation and the Making of the Underclass.* Cambridge, Mass.: Harvard University Press.

Missouri v. Jenkins. 1995. Supreme Court Decision No. 93–1823 (June 12).

Myrdal, Gunnar. 1944. *An American Dilemma.* New York: Harper.

Pace v. Alabama. 1883. 106 U.S. 583.

Perlmann, Joel. 1988. *Ethnic Differences: Schooling and Social Structure Among the Irish, Italians, Jews and Blacks in an American City, 1880–1935.* New York: Cambridge University Press.

Plessy v. Ferguson. 1896. 163 U.S. 537.

Regents of the University of California v. Bakke. 1978. 438 U.S. 265.

Richmond v. J. A. Croson Co. 1989. 488 U.S. 469.

Schuman, Howard, Charlotte Steeh, Lawrence Bobo, and Maria Krysan. 1997. *Racial Attitudes in America: Trends and Interpretations.* Cambridge, Mass.: Harvard University Press.

Smith, James P., and Finis R. Welch, 1989. "Black Economic Progress After Myrdal." *Journal of Economic Literature* 28 (2) June: 519–564.

Snipp, C. Matthew. 1989. *American Indians: The First of This Land.* New York: Russell Sage Foundation.

Spain, Daphne, and Suzanne M. Bianchi. 1996. *Balancing Act: Motherhood, Marriage, and Employment Among American Women.* New York: Russell Sage Foundation.

Swann v. Charlotte-Mecklenburg Board of Education. 1971. 401 U.S. 1.

U.S. Bureau of the Census. 1993. Public Use Microdata Samples from *1990 Census of Population and Housing.*

——. 2001. www.census.gov/hhes/income/histinc/p38ahtml.

United Steelworkers of America v. Weber. 1979. 43 U.S. 193.

Ward's Cove Packing v. Antonio. 1989. 490 U.S. 642.

Warren, Robert, 1990. "Annual Estimates of Nonimmigrant Overstays in the United States: 1985 to 1988." In *Undocumented Migration to the United States: IRCA and the Experience of the 1980s,* edited by Frank Bean et al. Washington, D.C.: Urban Institute Press.

Wilson, William Julius. 1978. *The Declining Significance of Race.* Chicago: University of Chicago Press.

Wygant v. Jackson Board of Education. 1986. 476 U.S. 267.

Poverty, Racism, and Migration
The Health of the African American Population

DAVID R. WILLIAMS

Health is an important and desirable personal and social resource. It determines the quantity and quality of life, and has an important effect on an individual's ability to capitalize on opportunities available in society. The health of the American population is distributed unevenly across race. In 1998, the life expectancy at birth in the United States was 77 years. However, it varied from 71 years for African Americans to 76 years for White Americans (National Center for Health Statistics 2000). Moreover, life expectancy for African Americans has worsened in recent years. For every year between 1985 and 1989 the life expectancy for both African American men and women declined from the 1984 level (National Center for Health Statistics 1993). These racial disparities in health are not new. In 1900, life expectancy at birth for White Americans was 48 years compared to 33 years for non-Whites, who at that time were mainly Blacks. Thus, over the course of the twentieth century the health status of both Blacks and Whites has improved, but a gap in health between the two groups has persisted.

Table 11.1 indicates how pervasive racial disparities in health are. It presents the death rates for Blacks and Whites, men and women, and the Black-White ratios for the fifteen leading causes of death in the United States, where a ratio greater than 1.0 indicates that the death rate for Blacks is higher than for Whites. With the exception of pulmonary disease, suicide, and Alzheimer's

Table 11.1. *Death Rates for the Fifteen Leading Causes of Death Per 100,000 Population by Race and Sex in the United States, 1998*

Cause of Death	Men			Women		
	Black	White	Black-White Ratio	Black	White	Black-White Ratio
Heart disease	231.8	162.3	1.43	146.8	88.1	1.67
Cancer	208.1	143.6	1.45	128.9	104.1	1.24
Cerebrovascular diseases (stroke)	46.8	24.5	1.91	37.2	22.0	1.69
Pulmonary disease	24.3	26.4	0.92	13.3	18.9	0.70
Accidents	54.4	42.2	1.29	19.6	17.7	1.11
Pneumonia and influenza	23.5	15.5	1.52	13.2	10.7	1.23
Diabetes	28.9	13.8	2.09	28.6	10.6	2.70
Suicide	10.5	18.3	0.57	1.8	4.4	0.41
Nephritis	11.4	4.8	2.38	8.6	3.2	2.69
Liver disease and cirrhosis	12.3	10.2	1.21	4.7	4.3	1.09
Septicemia (bacterial infection)	11.5	4.2	2.74	9.5	3.5	2.71
Alzheimer's disease	1.7	2.5	0.68	2.1	2.9	0.72
Homicide/legal intervention	43.1	6.4	6.73	8.6	2.2	3.91
Atherosclerosis	2.4	2.2	1.09	1.7	1.7	1.00
Hypertension	7.9	2.0	3.95	6.7	1.7	3.94

Source: *National Vital Statistics Reports*, vol. 48, no. 11, 24 July 2000.

disease, deaths of all types are higher for Blacks than for Whites. The differences are small for some conditions, such as atherosclerosis and liver disease, but substantial for others such as diabetes, homicide, hypertension, and AIDS.

Types of Explanations of Racial Disparities in Health

Traditionally, explanations for differences in health between the races have focused on biological differences between the two groups. In the nineteenth century, medical research attempted to document that Blacks were biologically inferior to Whites and, therefore, more susceptible to a host of illnesses (Krieger 1987). Most medical research is no longer so blatantly racist, but it still views most racial variations in disease as due to underlying differences in biology. However, attributing racial disparities in health to innate physical differences between the races maintains the historic implication of superiority and inferiority. More recently, a second type of explanation focusing on lifestyle or health behavior differences between African Americans and White Americans has gained considerable currency. Although they appear very different, the biological and lifestyle explanations share the common view that racial differences in health are due to factors that reside inside of the individual, and can therefore be successfully addressed by medical interventions that target individuals. In contrast, the view presented here sees racial variations in health as primarily due to differences in the social location of groups. Thus, effective solutions to reduce these social disparities depend on broad-based interventions in the social conditions that shape the daily reality of people's lives. Before reviewing the evidence for the social embeddedness of health, the limitations of the dominant types of explanation will be considered.

THE LIMITS OF BIOLOGICAL EXPLANATIONS

At the heart of the biological explanation for racial disparities in health is the conceptualization of what race is. The biological approach views racial taxonomies (Black, White, Asian, American Indian, and so on) as meaningful classifications of real genetic differences between human population groups. This approach assumes that race is a valid biological category, and that the same genes which determine what race an individual belongs to also determine the number and types of health problems that individual will have (Krieger and Bassett 1986).

This view is deeply entrenched in our society and reflected in the approach of much medical research, yet it is seriously flawed. First, the concept of race and its attendant racist beliefs about the superiority of some groups and the inferiority of others developed in the late eighteenth century, long before modern scientific theories of genetics existed. Classification of the human population into separate "races" developed in the historical context of slavery and imperialism, and served not only to classify human variation, but also to provide a rationale for the exploitation of groups that were regarded as inferior (Montagu 1965). Second, racial classification schemes are arbitrary and reflect changing social and political conditions across societies and in the same society over time. For example, a review of the racial classification schemes utilized by the U.S. Bureau of the Census between 1850 and 1980 indicated that no single set of racial categories had been used in more than two censuses during this period, with most used only once (Martin et al. 1990). Mexicans, for example, were classified as a separate race in the 1930 census, reclassified as White in the 1940 census, and designated as the "Spanish surnamed" population in the Southwestern states in the 1960 census.

Likewise, racial classification is arbitrary and inconsistent across and within societies (Davis 1991). The racial categories used in the United States are different from those of some other countries. In the United States, Blacks were defined according to ancestry by a legal standard that used the "one drop rule," which defined an individual as Black if any known ancestor was African. In contrast, racial definitions in the Caribbean and Latin America, where slavery and mixed marriages and unions also existed, reflected considerations of ancestry, social status, and phenotype. The resulting racial categories were more fluid and recognized gradations between Black and White. Many fair-skinned persons of mixed ancestry (such as Lena Horne, W.E.B. DuBois, A. Philip Randolph, and Booker T. Washington), who were classified as "Black" in the United States, would have received a different racial label elsewhere (Davis 1991).

Even more, our current views of race have been shown to be without scientific basis. There is more genetic variation within races than between races, and our current racial categories do not reflect biological distinctiveness. Regardless of geographic origin or race, all human beings are identical for 75 percent of known genetic factors (Lewontin 1982). Moreover, some 95 percent of human genetic variation exists within racial groups, with relatively small and isolated populations, such as Eskimos and Australian Aborigines, contributing most of the between group variation (Lewontin 1974). Stated another way, if an epidemic were to wipe out the entire population of the world except for Black persons in Africa, the world's population would then be entirely Black, but would still contain some 95 percent of all known genetic variation. Thus, our keen awareness of what racial group we belong to says much more about our society than about our biological makeup (Krieger and Basset 1986).

Proponents of biological explanations like to point to diseases that are clearly linked to the physical characteristics used to define race or that appear to be more frequent in some racial groups than others. An example of the former is the kind of skin cancer that more frequently affects light-skinned people; an example of the latter is sickle cell anemia, which is more common in blacks than in whites. However, sickle cell anemia is more prevalent not only in African Americans, but also in all peoples that lived in regions (the Mediterranean, Africa, and Asia) where malaria was endemic (Polednak 1989). Sickle cell anemia appears to be a protective, genetic adaptation to malaria produced by the interaction of biology with environmental conditions. Sickle cell anemia also illustrates that genetics is not static, but evolves over time as human groups adapt to environmental conditions. Thus, even when biological differences are found between two racial groups that live under different environmental conditions, these differences may not be due to innate physical differences, but to acquired ones that reflect the consequences of different living conditions over time.

Moreover, diseases that have a clear genetic component account for only a minuscule part of racial differences in health. Sickle cell anemia is the only potentially fatal disease that is linked to being Black, and Cooper and David (1986) indicate that only three-tenths of 1 percent of the total number of excess deaths among Blacks is clearly related to sickle cell anemia. Thus, differences in biology are not the primary cause of racial variations in health and disease.

THE LIFESTYLE EXPLANATION

Health practices — better nutrition and eating habits; diminished to-bacco, alcohol, and drug abuse; more exercise; and the use of conflict resolution strategies — play an important role in maintaining and improving health. It is estimated that almost half of all deaths in the United States are linked to unhealthy behavior or lifestyle (U.S. Department of Health, Education and Welfare 1979). In comparison, 20 percent are due to environmental factors such as exposure to toxic substances, 20 percent to genetics, and 10 percent to inadequate medical care. Research also indicates that the health of the population can improve more through increases in healthy behavior than if an over-night cure were found for heart disease or cancer (Olshansky 1985). If changes were made in risky health behaviors, the death rates for Black Americans would be substantially reduced (Department of Health and Human Services 1985).

Proponents of the lifestyle explanation tend to regard health practices as psychological in nature. Typically, health behaviors are assessed at the individual level, and only individual causes and consequences are attended to. John Knowles, a former president of the Rockefeller Foundation, illustrates this approach when he stated that we are "born healthy and made sick as a result of personal misbehavior" (1977: 58). He indicated that individuals are ulti-mately responsible for their own health and illness and are therefore under a "moral obligation" to preserve their health because one person's poorly cho-sen health practices can become another's "shackle in taxes and insurance premiums." This approach also has a tendency to "blame the victims" for the particular health problems they face.

THE PRIMACY OF SOCIAL STRUCTURE

In contrast to the biological and lifestyle explanations is a third ap-proach that views health as a product of the socioeconomic, political, and cultural situations of social groups (Williams, Lavizzo-Mourey, and Warren

1994). Racial differences reflect distinctive histories and specific conditions of life that affect the risk of disease. An adequate understanding of racial differences in health must consider these larger social structures and processes and identify the ways in which they affect the health of individuals and groups. Health behaviors and the risk of disease must be understood in the context of the living and working conditions in which they emerge. This approach is illustrated by considering the relationship between socioeconomic status and disease, the effects of racism on health, and the consequences that the massive migration of African Americans from the rural South to the urban North had on their health.

Socioeconomic Status and Health

Socioeconomic status, whether measured by poverty, earnings, wealth, education, or occupational status, is one of the strongest known determinants of variations in health. During the twentieth century, despite general improvements in health, social and economic change, advances in health care technology, and improvements in the delivery of medical services, the socioeconomic status differential has not much narrowed. For example, since the implementation of the National Health Service in Great Britain in the 1940s, the health of all groups in the society has improved, but the higher socioeconomic status groups have experienced greater improvement than their poorer peers, such that the gap in health status has actually widened (Wilkinson 1986; Marmot and McDowall 1986). These socioeconomic differences in health are fairly universal and have been documented in Western European countries, Australia, New Zealand, Japan, Canada, and throughout the Third World (Marmot, Kogevinas, and Elston 1987; Haan and Kaplan 1986; Williams, Wilson, and Chung, 1992). Trends in the social distribution of certain diseases over time provide a further illustration of the impact of socioeconomic status on adverse changes in health. In the history of many diseases, even when an illness was initially more common among the higher classes, over time it became more prevalent among the less affluent (Williams 1990). For example, in the 1950s the rates for heart disease were higher among the rich. But as the social conditions that led to greater risk of heart disease were identified and knowledge of them became widespread, persons of higher social status changed their behavior (quit smoking, reduced dietary fat, exercised regularly) more rapidly than their less prosperous peers. Thus, the relationship between social status and heart disease changed from a positive one to an inverse one. Similarly, most of the initial AIDS patients in the United States were White, middle-class men, but most new cases of AIDS are concentrated among impoverished

Table 11.2. Average Annual Percent of Persons Reporting to Be in Fair or Poor Health by Household Income, Respondent Education, and Place of Residence for Blacks and Whites in the United States, 1985–87

	Household Income			
	Less than $20,000		More than $20,000	
	Whites	Blacks	Whites	Blacks
Education				
Less than 12 years	33.1	38.8	16.1	20.5
12 years	15.2	17.9	6.8	9.6
More than 12 years	9.2	13.2	3.7	5.9
Total	16.6	19.0	5.1	7.6
Place of Residence				
Urban	15.8	18.1	5.0	7.4
Central city	16.3	18.7	5.5	8.5
Not central city	15.5	16.3	4.8	5.7
Rural/small town	18.3	22.7	5.5	9.1
Number (in thousands)	61,029	15,089	113,919	9,079

Source: P. Rica, "Health of Black and White Americans, 1985–87." National Center for Health Statistics. Vital Health Statistics 10 (171), 1990, table A, pg. 5, and table 16, p. 55.

Blacks and Hispanics. Persons of higher socioeconomic status are more aware of health risks and more likely to initiate behavioral change, because they command more resources to facilitate such change.

African Americans have lower levels of all socioeconomic status indicators than do White Americans. These differences are large and persist in spite of the progress that Blacks have made in recent years (Jaynes and Williams 1989). For example, one-third of all Blacks are poor, compared to only one-tenth of all Whites. Thus, the higher rates of ill health and mortality among African Americans must be understood as part of a universal phenomenon in which poverty is associated with higher rates of disease and death (Williams 1990). At the same time, it must be remembered that race is an imperfect indicator of poverty. Although Blacks are disproportionately poor, two-thirds of all Blacks are not poor, and two-thirds of all poor persons in the United States are white.

The top panel of Table 11.2 presents the relationship between two indicators of socioeconomic status (household income and years of formal education) and self-assessed health for Blacks and Whites in the National Health

Interview Survey between 1985 and 1987. The measure of health included here, the respondents' subjective report of their health, is one of the most robust indicators of health and is strongly related to objective measures of health. For example, persons who assess their health as "good" or "excellent" live longer than those who report it as "fair" or "poor." We can see that there are large disparities in self-assessed health by household income and level of education. For persons living in households with a total income of less than $20,000, 16.6 percent of Whites reported their health to be fair or poor, compared to 19 percent of Blacks, while in households with income greater than $20,000 the comparable numbers for Blacks and Whites are 5.1 and 7.6 percent, respectively. Thus, the differences by income and education are much larger than the differences by race. At the same time, it is instructive that even when education and income level are held constant, Blacks still have higher levels of ill health than Whites. This suggests that although most of the racial differences in health are accounted for by socioeconomic status, race also has an effect on health that is independent of its relationship with socioeconomic status. Racial discrimination is one critical factor that might operate independently of socioeconomic status, and/or interactively with socioeconomic status, to maintain an association between race and health.

Racism

As noted earlier, racist ideologies provided the rationale for differential treatment of social groups regarded as inferior. This treatment has also often been institutionalized as the consequence of organizational policies and procedures. Discrimination affects a broad range of social outcomes for individuals belonging to different racial groups, with those affected often unaware of it. Race, for example, transforms measures of socioeconomic status such that socioeconomic status indicators are not truly equivalent across race. On average, there are racial differences in the quality of education. Black students are disproportionately allocated or "tracked" into low-ability and non–college preparatory groups, which are characterized by a less demanding curriculum and lower teacher expectations (Jaynes and Williams 1989). Thus, the skills and knowledge that a student has upon completion of high school differ for high school graduates of different races. National data also consistently reveal that Whites have higher income returns on education than Blacks (Jaynes and Williams 1989). For both Blacks and Whites, the more years of formal education one has, the higher one's income. However, when Blacks and Whites are compared at the same educational level, Whites earn more than Blacks. For example, the average annual income of a Black male college graduate is 74 percent that of his White counterpart (Jaynes and Williams 1989).

In addition, the purchasing power of a particular level of income varies by race. Studies have documented that Blacks have higher costs of food, rent, automobiles, and auto insurance than Whites (Williams and Collins 1995). The prices of groceries at neighborhood stores, the cost per square foot of rental housing, and the premiums for auto insurance are all higher for residents of central cities (where Blacks are disproportionately concentrated) than for those who live in suburban locations. Moreover, a carefully executed study of auto dealerships found that compared to the purchase price of a new car offered to White men, White women had to pay a 40 percent mark-up, Black men a 200 percent mark-up, and Black women a 300 percent mark-up (Ayres 1991).

Institutionalized racism also affects the quality of services received across a broad range of institutions, including health care. Louis Sullivan, former Secretary of the Department of Health and Human Services, stated that, "There is clear, demonstrable, undeniable evidence of discrimination and racism in our health care system" (Sullivan 1991: 2674). A recent review of the available studies by the Council on Ethical and Judicial Affairs (1990) of the American Medical Association documents extensive racial disparities in the receipt of medical care. Compared to African Americans, White Americans are more likely to receive the following treatments: coronary angiography, bypass surgery, angioplasty, chemo dialysis, intensive care for pneumonia, and kidney transplants. These differences remain, even after adjustments are made for the severity of the illness, the income of the person, and his or her insurance status. The data on kidney transplants are especially compelling: Whites are more likely to be placed on waiting lists for kidney transplants (Council on Ethical and Judicial Affairs 1990) and wait only half as long as Blacks (Sullivan 1991).

Recently attention has also been given to environmental racism—that is, the disproportionate exposure of some racial groups to environmental toxic exposures. As it turns out, race is the strongest predictor of the location of hazardous waste facilities in the United States, even after adjustment for social class (Commission for Racial Justice 1987). Other evidence indicates that central city residents are five times more likely to be exposed to air and water pollution than their suburban peers, and that predominantly Black, poor, rural areas are also disproportionately exposed to health-threatening toxic materials from nearby industrial plants (Bullard and Wright 1987). Lead poisoning is also a major problem that disproportionately affects the health of minority children in the United States (Reed 1992). High levels of lead exist in the older buildings in impoverished neighborhoods where many African Americans are forced to live. Even after controlling for job experience and education, Blacks who are employed are more likely than their White peers to be exposed to occupational hazards and carcinogens (Robinson 1984).

A growing number of studies have examined how the experience of racism or racial discrimination affects health (Krieger 1999; Williams and Williams-Morris 2000). For example, in a study of Black and White women, Krieger (1990) found that Black women who passively experienced racial discrimination were four times as likely to have high blood pressure as those who talked with others about it or who took other action in response to the unfair treatment. Yet Black women were six times more likely than Whites to respond passively to unfair treatment, suggesting that they, probably accurately, perceived themselves as having little control over these encounters. A recent review documents that perceptions of discrimination are adversely related to mental health for African Americans as well as members of other racial groups (Williams and Williams-Morris 2000). Prior research suggests that at least two responses to the experience of racism may be especially predictive of adverse health consequences. An internalized denial of racial bias appears to have negative health consequences. Krieger (1990) found that Black women who reported that they had experienced no incident of racial or gender discrimination were two to three times as likely to have high blood pressure as those who said they had experienced unfair treatment. A second potentially health-damaging response is the oppressed minority's acceptance of the dominant society's racist ideology. Taylor and Jackson (1990) found in a study of Black women that internalized racism — belief in the innate inferiority of Blacks — was related to higher alcohol consumption. Other studies also suggest that endorsement of negative stereotypes about one's racial group is related to lower levels of well-being and physical health (Williams and Williams-Morris 2000).

Migration

The mass movement of African Americans from rural and urban centers in the South to the large industrial cities of the North was one of the greatest migrations in American history and was quantitatively larger than the migration of many other ethnic groups to the U.S. (Lemann 1992). This dramatic migration had a profound impact on the living conditions of the Black population. It also held important consequences for their health.

In 1940, 50 percent of all Black Americans lived in the rural areas of the South, and an additional 25 percent resided in more urban Southern communities (Jaynes and Williams 1989). Today's Black population is overwhelmingly urban and disproportionately represented in the central cities of the largest metropolitan areas. In 1990, 47 percent of African Americans lived outside of the South, 57 percent (17 million) were residents of central cities, and only 15 percent resided in rural areas (Wilson 1992). In the North and West, 77 percent of the Black population lives in central cities.

For each of the three decades between 1940 and 1970 there was a net out migration of 1.5 million Blacks from the South to the North (Jaynes and Williams 1989). As Blacks migrated to the cities, they were concentrated, by segregation and discrimination, into the least desirable neighborhoods (Massey and Denton 1993). A pervasive "web of discrimination" involving the actions and inactions of local and federal government, financial institutions, and real estate companies were used to entrap Blacks in inner-city ghettos (Jaynes and Williams). Municipal ordinances, restrictive covenants, and federal housing policies mandated segregation. Blacks were not allowed to buy or rent in certain White residential areas. Real estate agents steered Blacks out of White areas by quoting higher prices or directing them only to Black residential areas. Local banks routinely engaged in a practice called redlining, that is, denying a loan on the basis of race where the applicant was attempting to buy a house in an integrated neighborhood. This usually involved either charging higher rates to make a particular loan unattractive or cutting off all conventional mortgages in an entire area. School board policies often designated distinct attendance zones for White and Black children, and White neighborhood organizations were vigilant and sometimes violent in enforcing segregation.

Despite the reality of residential segregation and discrimination, Blacks who moved to the North were relatively successful, at least initially. These Black migrants were younger and had higher levels of education than those who remained in the South (Jaynes and Williams 1989). At the same time, they had lower levels of education than Northern-born Blacks. Newly arrived Black immigrants were charged more rent and paid lower wages than Whites in the North (Lemann 1992). Yet they earned considerably more even at low-level jobs in the manufacturing economy of the North than they had earned as tenant farmers and sharecroppers in the South. Thus, these Black migrants probably saw the glass as half full, rather than half empty and, compared to native-born Blacks in the North, they worked longer hours, had lower unemployment rates, more stable families, lower poverty rates, lower utilization of welfare, and higher income returns on their educational attainments (Farley and Allen 1989; Jaynes and Williams 1989). In fact, although Southern birth limited the achievement of White men who moved to the North, it appeared to have had the opposite effect for Blacks (Farley and Allen 1989).

Primarily due to this migration of African Americans from low-wage agricultural employment to higher wage manufacturing jobs, the economic status of the Black population as a whole improved considerably between 1940 and the 1960s. However, the economic gains from migration were relatively short lived, as by the late 1960s they had come to an end (Jaynes and Williams 1989). At least two reasons account for this. First, it appears that the children of Black immigrants did not achieve the same economic success as their parents. African Americans who migrated from the South to the North may eventually have experienced a considerable amount of frustration as their jobs provided them little opportunity for advancement, and racial segregation and discrimination in the housing market frequently kept them trapped in undesirable and deteriorating housing (Lemann 1992). This frustration may have been even more keenly felt by their children, whose reference group was not their Black counterparts who remained in the South, but their White peers in Northern cities. Discouraged by their restricted opportunities and truncated options, the children of Black migrants may have been less motivated than their parents to work hard at jobs that did not hold out any promise of real advancement.

A second and more important reason for the declining success of immigrants was the migration of jobs from the large metropolitan areas in the Northeast and Midwest. A major exodus has taken place of low-skill, well-paying blue-collar factory jobs from the inner cities to the suburbs (Wilson 1987). This has led to a concentration of poverty and high unemployment in large Northern industrial cities, trapping substantial portions of the African American population in the same geographic locations that attracted their parents or grandparents by the promise of economic opportunity (Massey and Eggers 1990).

EFFECTS OF MIGRATION ON HEALTH STATUS

The mass movement of African Americans in the twentieth century had profound implications for their health. First, the Black migration disproportionately distributed the African American population to areas where living conditions are hostile to life and health. The lower panel of Table 11.2 shows the relationship between health, as self-assessed, and place of residence by level of household income for Blacks and Whites. As we can see, irrespective of race or place of residence, higher income persons are less likely to be in poor health than their low-income counterparts. Also, at both income levels and in all residential settings, Blacks consistently have higher rates of poor health than Whites. However, for both Blacks and Whites, those who live in the central city have higher levels of ill health than those who live in the suburbs.

The higher level of ill health among those who live in rural areas may be a selection effect. Persons of all races who did not migrate are more likely to be older and in poorer health than the typical migrant who was young, adventurous, and in general good health.

The overall picture of the health of Blacks in central cities masks the ever-worsening conditions in some inner cities. A recent study of Harlem, one of the poorest areas of New York City, documented that, between the ages of 25 and 44, black males are six times more likely to die than White males in the United States (McCord and Freeman 1990). Cardiovascular diseases, cirrhosis of the liver, homicide, and cancer are the main causes of excess deaths—that is, deaths that occur for Blacks that would not occur if they had the same mortality experience as Whites. Moreover, the life expectancy of Blacks in Harlem is lower than that of persons in Bangladesh, which is currently categorized by the World Bank as one of the poorest countries in the world.

Life in poor inner-city environments can include poor nutrition, poor education, crime, traffic hazards, substandard and overcrowded housing, low-paying jobs, unemployment and underemployment, and a lack of health insurance and access to basic health services. The Black urban poor encounter these conditions more frequently than their White counterparts. The Black poor have been increasingly concentrated in depressed central city neighborhoods with bad living conditions, while the White urban poor are more evenly dispersed throughout the city, with many residing in relatively safe and comfortable neighborhoods away from the inner city (Wilson 1987). Thus the experience of stress, even in a given city, may be qualitatively different for Blacks and Whites.

Stress in poor urban environments can lead to illness. Harburg and colleagues (1973) characterized neighborhoods in Detroit as either high or low in stress. High-stress neighborhoods were those where the median level of income and years of formal education completed were low, and levels of residential instability (percentage of residents with less than five years tenure), marital break-up, and crime were high. Low-stress areas had the opposite conditions. Persons living in high-stress areas had higher levels of high blood pressure than those in low-stress areas, an association that was stronger among Blacks than Whites. Moreover, although national data reveal that Blacks are twice as likely as Whites to have high blood pressure, the blood pressure levels for Black and White males in low-stress neighborhoods did not differ.

Recent research has also indicated that community violence is damaging to health. Persons who live in inner-city housing projects are twice as likely to experience violence as other persons (Gabarino et al. 1992). This violence affects the victims, those who witness it, and those who are forced to live with the consequences. The repetitive nature of witnessing traumatic events may have a cumulative effect, especially on children. Each homicide also means fewer social and material resources to support children and families, and domestic violence often precedes homicide. Physical and sexual abuse are thus prevalent stresses in the lives of the urban poor, and persons who experience sexual and physical assault are more likely to develop substance abuse and mental health problems (Bell et al. 1988). Living in these conditions, in urban war zones where physical safety is not assured, can also lead persons to live in a state of heightened vigilance and also takes its toll on the human organism. A recent review noted that three studies of racial differences in blood pressure have documented that although average daytime blood pressure levels were similar for Blacks and Whites, blood pressure declined less among Blacks than Whites overnight, such that Blacks had higher blood pressure levels even while they were asleep (Williams, Lavizzo-Mourey, and Warren 1994).

CHANGE IN HEALTH BEHAVIORS

The internal migration of the African Americans also affected their health by changing their lifestyles in ways that lead to higher risks of disease and death. Health behaviors are important causes of the heavy burden of disease among Black Americans. The federal government estimates that there are 60,000 excess deaths in the African American population every year (U.S. Department of Health and Human Services 1985). The government also indicated that smoking cigarettes and drinking excessively played a large role as underlying causes of the excess deaths in the Black population.

Along with the great migration and urbanization of Black Americans came a dramatic rise in their use of alcohol and tobacco. The current rates of smoking and alcohol abuse among Blacks represent an important historic shift in the social distribution of these behaviors (Williams 1991). In the 1930s death rates from lung cancer were only 50 percent as high among Blacks as among Whites, and up through the 1950s Blacks were much less likely to smoke cigarettes than Whites (Cooper and Simmons 1985). Up through 1955, mortality rates from cirrhosis of the liver (an indicator of alcohol abuse) were higher for Whites than for Blacks. Since then, the increases in cirrhosis mortality rates have been higher for Blacks than for Whites. Moreover, ecological data reveal that the highest increases for Blacks occurred in urban areas with large migrant populations (Herd 1985). Some studies have also found that rates of alcoholism are higher among Blacks who migrated from the South (Boone 1985). The migration of Blacks may have affected their drinking and smoking behavior in a number of ways. First, the great migration of Blacks shifted a considerable portion of the Black population from the relatively "dry" rural South, where social life revolved around churches and family associations, to the "wet" areas of the urban north, where taverns, nightclubs, and associated alcohol use were an integral part of social life (Herd 1985). Second, the theologically conservative Protestant churches to which most Blacks belonged tended to frown on alcohol consumption, but their traditional authority and influence was reduced in the urban North (Frazier 1966).

Third, life in urban settings produced feelings of alienation, powerlessness, helplessness, and meaninglessness, thus creating the need for individuals to mask these feelings or obtain temporary relief from them by consuming tobacco and alcohol. Social and economic deprivation creates adverse working and living conditions from which people will attempt to escape. The amount of stress one experiences in work, neighborhoods, and family, as well as the resources to cope with it, vary with social status (Williams and House 1991). African Americans, like other persons of low socioeconomic status, face more stress and also have fewer options for dealing with it. People under stress are more likely to drink and smoke because these are socially approved ways that provide some temporary relief from the personal suffering that is induced by poor living conditions. Seeman and Anderson (1983) found that an individual's sense of powerlessness is directly related to how often and how much that person drinks and whether drinking problems develop. In addition, stressful life experiences also went hand in hand with increases in both powerlessness and drinking problems, setting off a vicious cycle. Not surprisingly, national data reveal that the sale of alcoholic beverages increases during economic recessions and during periods of increased unemployment (Singer 1986). By implication, efforts to reduce the consumption of alcohol should not just focus on the individual but should also seek to improve the conditions under which people live and work that give rise to the need for alcohol in the first place.

Finally, enterprising economic interests saw the newly arrived Black population as a potential market and heavily targeted this vulnerable population for advertising campaigns. One of the consequences of the rise in socioeconomic status of Black Americans in Northern cities was the development of a Black consumer market. Civil rights scholars have noted that White retail merchants frequently played a crucial role in prodding White-controlled social and political institutions to accommodate the demands of Black activists (Jaynes and Williams 1989). Since the 1950s African Americans have been special targets of the tobacco and alcohol industries (Levin 1988; Davis 1987; Singer 1986).

Hacker, Collins, and Jacobson (1987) provide an excellent description of the strategies used by the alcohol industry to target the African American community. Alcohol products have been closely tied to the music, sports, and cultural events that are important to the values and tastes of African Americans. Image advertisements promote education, fatherhood, Black history, and Black culture. The alcohol industry has also employed some of the best-known Black celebrities (such as Alex Haley, Lou Rawls, Wilt Chamberlain, and Patti Labelle) to promote their products. In addition, they provide substantial support for Black History Month and the United Negro College Fund, as well as a large number of social, religious, educational, athletic, and business programs for Black Americans. Some alcohol producers, such as Coors, have even linked continued economic support of the African American community to increased sales of the company's products.

The alcohol industry has also developed products exclusively for the African American market, such as malt liquors (beer with a higher alcohol content). Moreover, the saturation level of alcohol advertising in the Black community is higher than in the predominantly White market. This can be seen both in the advertising in the major Black magazines as well as in the outdoor media. Seventy percent of billboards in the United States contain advertisements targeted to Blacks, with cigarettes and alcohol, in that order, being the two most heavily advertised products. This bombardment of images that revolve around alcohol is combined with the greater availability of alcohol to African American urban communities, availability that also leads to greater alcohol consumption (Singer 1986). Retail establishments for the sale of alcohol are more common in minority neighborhoods than in more affluent communities (Rabow and Watt 1982), a concentration that reflects the cooperation of government with large-scale economic interests, because in every state retail outlets for alcoholic beverages are licensed.

The effects of the migration of Blacks to Northern cities on their health may not be all negative. The influx of large numbers of Blacks to northern industrial cities, combined with the successes of the civil rights movement, also provided a substantial political base and platform for representatives of the African American population to command national attention and influence in the halls of power. Since the differential distribution of power in our society affects the distribution of desirable goods, increased political power can lead to improvements in health. LaVeist (1992) has recently documented an inverse association between Black political power and post-neonatal mortality rates—that is, the more political power among Blacks, the better the survival of their newborn children. He suggests that the political empowerment of Black Americans may lead to more community-level political participation, increases in Black employment, and enhancement of the overall quality of life, which may in turn lead to improved levels of health and well-being.

Adaptive Resources: The Family and the Church

An analysis of the health of African Americans would be incomplete without consideration of their strengths and health-enhancing resources. An exclusive focus on vulnerability and risk gives a distorted view of the struggles of a disadvantaged group. The evidence on the mental health status of African Americans provides somewhat of a paradox. Compared to Whites, Blacks tend to have higher rates of the more mild indicators of mental health problems (psychological symptoms and distress), which tend to disappear when taking socioeconomic status into account (Vega and Rumbaut 1991), but they have similar or lower rates of the more severe indicators of mental illness (psychiatric disorders).

Table 11.3 presents both current and lifetime rates for Blacks and Whites of the most commonly occurring psychiatric disorders in the United States. These data come from the largest study of psychiatric disorders ever conducted in the country (Robins and Regier 1991). Conducted by researchers at five sites between 1980 and 1983, this study interviewed a sample of almost 20,000 Americans, including both treated and untreated persons. The overall pattern is consistent. Rates of depressive disorders and alcohol and drug abuse are very similar for Blacks and Whites. Rates of schizophrenia are slightly higher for Blacks, but the difference is not significant when differences in socioeconomic status are controlled for. Recent data from the first study to use a national probability sample to assess psychiatric disorders in the United States are even more striking (Kessler et al. 1994). In this study of more than 8,000 adults, Blacks had rates of mental illness that were similar or lower than those of whites. Lower rates for blacks than whites were particularly pronounced for the affective disorders (depression) and the substance use disorders (alcohol and drug abuse).

Thus, although African Americans confront a broad range of social conditions that are risk factors for mental illness, they do not have higher rates of suicide (as seen in Table 11.1) or higher rates of mental illness than Whites. These findings emphasize the need for renewed attention to identify the cultural strengths and health-enhancing resources of disadvantaged groups. All social groups have cultural resources that facilitate their efforts to gain control over their environment. In this respect, two social institutions — the family and the church — stand out as crucial in the African American community.

Strong family ties and an extended family system are important resources that may reduce some of the negative effects of stress on the health of Black Americans. A large body of data indicates that supportive social relationships are among the most powerful determinants of health (House, Landis, and

Table 11.3. Rates (per Hundred) of Psychiatric Disorder for Blacks and Whites

	Current		Lifetime	
	Black	White	Black	White
Affective disorders	3.5	3.7	63	8.0
Alcohol abuse	6.6	6.7	13.8	13.6
Drug use history	—	—	29.9	30.7
Drug abuse	2.7	2.7	5.4	6.4
Schizophrenia	1.6	0.9	2.1	1.4

Source: Lee N. Robins, and Darrel A. Regier (eds.), Psychiatric Disorders in America: The Epidemiological Catchment Area Study (New York: Free Press, 1991), table 4-3, p. 59; table 5-1, p. 85; table 6-3, p. 121; table 6-12, p. 133; table 3-6, p. 41.

Umberson 1988). This evidence indicates, for example, that social isolation is as bad for one's health as smoking. In addition to providing emotional support, social ties can provide information and practical assistance that enable individuals to share their resources for survival. An emphasis on the strength of the Black family contrasts with the more negative image of the weak or nonexistent Black family that is routinely presented in the U.S. media. This image focuses on the high rates of female-headed households. Currently, two out of three births to Black women are to unwed mothers, but being an unwed mother is not necessarily synonymous with being the head of the household. One small ethnographic study conducted at the time of the 1970 Census found that only 12 percent of officially classified "female-headed" households did not have a stable male cohabitant (Hainer et al. 1988). In this study, adult male cohabitants who were present in the majority of Black "female-headed" households and performed traditional domestic responsibilities were omitted in the enumeration of those households, because their presence was deliberately hidden from the Census enumerators. Residents may well have had what they perceived to be good reasons (such as protecting welfare benefits) for hiding the presence of these men.

Given the marginalized economic status of Black males and the low-wage jobs available to poor and working-class women, there is a strong relationship between poverty conditions and births to unwed mothers. Nonetheless, in the face of these serious social and economic challenges, the Black family is resilient and resourceful. For many Black persons, the concept of family is not restricted to individuals related by blood or to persons resident in the household. Families are composed of those who interact regularly in helping each other share resources, responsibilities, and crises (Stack 1974). These families operate across households and across generations to help each other survive. These patterns of supportive exchanges are not limited to the poor. Middle-class Blacks are also involved in the provision of material support to poorer members of their extended family.

It must be remembered that family structures and processes do not arise out of thin air or simply out of skewed family values; instead, they are shaped by the larger social environment. Marital status, for example, is linked to larger economic processes. Unemployment, declines in income, and high job turn-over are all associated with increased rates of marital dissolution; the number of female-headed households declines when male earnings go up and rise when male unemployment increases (Bishop 1977). The linkage between family structure and economic conditions is readily evident if the Black population of the United States is compared to the population of African ancestry in the English-speaking Caribbean. Both populations share a common heritage of slavery, but those outside of the United States currently face even more severe economic conditions. Not surprisingly, the percentage of births to unwed mothers of Black populations in these Caribbean countries is even higher than that of the Black population in the United States. For example, 85 percent of all births in Jamaica and 73 percent of those in Barbados are to unwed mothers (*Encyclopedia Britannica* 1993).

Recognition of the strengths of Black families should not be used to roman-ticize them as if they were a panacea for a broad range of adverse living conditions. While these networks of mutual aid and support do facilitate survival, they are also likely to provide stress. Moreover, it is likely that cut-backs in government-provided social services in recent decades have increased the burdens and demands on the support services provided by the black fam-ily. At the present time we do not know how well the black family is coping with these new challenges in the face of economic decline and worsening socioeconomic conditions.

The Black American church has been the most important social institution in the Black community. It emerged during the days of slavery as the only organization that was not controlled by the White power structure. These churches soon became centers of spiritual life as well as of social and political life. They provided a place for Blacks to carry out professional and adminis-trative roles that they were denied by the larger society, and were an impor-tant base of support for the civil rights movement. Recent studies of African American churches document that, as in the past, they are still involved in providing a broad range of social and human services to the African American community (Lincoln and Mamiya 1990; Caldwell, Green, and Billingsley 1992; Chang, Williams, Griffith, and Young 1994). They also serve as important conduits of material resources to the community.

The clergy of all races also play an important role as a provider of psychological and mental health support to their parishioners. A recent study of the African American clergy in New Haven, Connecticut, documented that Black ministers respond to a variety of needs that go beyond their role as spiritual adviser (Chang et al., 1994). This study found that most Black ministers spent much time counseling parishioners on issues ranging from sexual abuse to unemployment. The three most common problems that the clergy dealt with were marital and family problems, drug and alcohol-related problems, and financial problems. This study also documented that the scope of these Black ministers' counseling extends far beyond their own parishioners, with 85 percent reporting that they counsel persons from other religions and other religious denominations.

The New Haven study showed that the Black clergy also play an important role as a gatekeeper to the mental health system. Contrary to beliefs that religious leaders disparage professional models of counseling in favor of spiritual care, 47 percent of the African American clergy reported that they had referred parishioners to a community agency for mental health problems. Almost 44 percent of the clergy in this study reported that a referral had been made to them by an outside health professional or agency. Thus, at least some African American churches and mental health and social service agencies create networks of information and exchange in which institutional services are made accessible in church-based contexts of ongoing personal and community support.

The Black American church is also an important source of social integration and support. Congregation-based friendship networks function as a type of extended family and provide supportive social relationships to individuals as they go through the life cycle (Taylor and Chatters 1988). In addition, the African American population is arguably the most religious group in the industrialized world (Gallup Report 1985), and this high level of religious involvement on the part of Black Americans may also reduce the adverse consequences of stressful living conditions and promote their psychological well-being. Griffith and colleagues (Griffith, English, and Mayfield 1980; Griffith, Young, and Smith 1984) indicate that participation in Black church services can provide therapeutic benefits equivalent to those obtained in formal psychotherapy. The expression of emotion and active congregational participation that is characteristic of some African American churches can promote a collective catharsis that enhances the reduction of tension and the release of emotional stress (Gilkes 1990).

Conclusion

African Americans continue to suffer high levels of disease, disability, and death. As we have seen, health must be understood within its larger social context. Health is inextricably tied to the social, political, cultural, and economic conditions under which people live. Larger social structures create stressful living conditions and working environments and shape the nature of the response of social groups. The social distribution of health and disease reflect the convergence of a broad range of quality-of-life issues. As such, it is related to the struggle to make ends meet, to make sense out of life, and to cope with alienation and powerlessness.

The evidence presented here indicates that the health problems of African Americans are not primarily caused by underlying deficits in genetics or medical care. It follows that medical solutions alone will be limited in their capacity to improve health (Williams 1990). Thus, effective efforts to improve the health of groups, such as Black Americans, must consider changing the fundamental social conditions that created them in the first place.

References

Ayres, Ian. 1991. "Fair Driving: Gender and Race Discrimination in Retail Car Negotiations." *Harvard Law Review* 104 (4): 817–872.

Bell, C. C., K. Taylor-Crawford, E. J. Jenkins, and D. Chalmers. 1988. "Need for Victimization Screening in a Black Psychiatric Population." *Journal of the National Medical Association* 80:41–48.

Bishop, John. 1977. *Jobs, Cash Transfers, and Marital Instability: A Review of the Evidence*. Madison: Institute for Research on Poverty, University of Wisconsin.

Boone, Margaret S. 1985. "Social and Cultural Factors in the Etiology of Low Birthweight Among Disadvantaged Blacks." *Social Science and Medicine* 20:1001–1011.

Bullard, R., and B. H. Wright. 1987. "Environmentalism and the Politics of Equity: Emergent Trends in the Black Community." *Mid-American Review of Sociology* 12:21–38.

Caldwell, Cleopatra Howard, Angela Dungee Greene, and Andrew Billingsley. 1992. "The Black Church as a Family Support System: Instrumental and Expressive Functions." *National Journal of Sociology* 6:21–40.

Chang, Patricia, David R. Williams, Ezra E. H. Griffith, and John L. Young. 1994. "Church-Agency Relationships in the Black Community." *Nonprofit and Voluntary Sector Quarterly* 23 (2): 91–105.

Commission for Racial Justice. 1987. *Toxic Wastes and Race in the United States: A National Report on the Racial and Socioeconomic Characteristics of Communities with Hazardous Waste Sites.* New York: United Church of Christ.

Cooper, Richard S., and Richard David. 1986. "The Biological Concept of Race and Its Application to Public Health and Epidemiology." *Journal of Health Politics, Policy and Law* 11:97–116.

Cooper, Richard, and Brian E. Simmons. 1985. "Cigarette Smoking and Ill Health Among Black Americans." *New York State Journal of Medicine* 85:344–349.

Council on Ethical and Judicial Affairs. 1990. "Black-White Disparities in Health Care." *Journal of the American Medical Association* 263:2344–2346.

Davis, F. J. 1991. *Who Is Black? One Nation's Definition.* University Park: Pennsylvania State University Press.

Davis, Ronald M. 1987. "Current Trends in Cigarette Advertising and Marketing." *New England Journal of Medicine* 316: 725–732.

Encyclopedia Britannica. 1993. *Britannica Book of the Year.* Chicago: Encyclopedia Britannica.

Farley, Reynolds, and Walter R. Allen. 1989. *The Color Line and the Quality of Life in America.* New York: Oxford University Press.

Frazier, E. Franklin. 1966. *The Negro Church in America.* New York: Schocken Books.

Gabarino, James, Nancy Dubrow, Kathleen Kostelny, and Carole Pardo. 1992. *Children in Danger: Coping with the Consequences of Community Violence.* San Francisco: Jossey-Bass.

Gallup Report. 1985. *Religion in America — Fifty Years.* Princeton, N.J.: Princeton Religious Research Center.

Gilkes, Cheryl. 1990. "The Black Church as a Therapeutic Community: Suggested Areas for Research into the Black Religious Experience." *Journal of the Interdenominational Theological Center* 8:29–44.

Griffith, Ezra, Thelouizs English, and Violet Mayfield. 1980. "Possession, Prayer and Testimony: Therapeutic Aspects of the Wednesday Night Meeting in a Black Church." *Psychiatry* 43:12–128.

Griffith, Ezra, John Young, and Dorothy Smith. 1984. "An Analysis of the Therapeutic Elements in a Black Church Service." *Hospital and Community Psychiatry* 35:464–469.

Haan, Mary N., and A. George Kaplan. 1986. "The Contribution of Socioeconomic Position to Minority Health." Report of the Secretary's Task Force on Black and Minority Health 2:69–103. Washington, D.C.: U.S. Department of Health and Human Services.

Hacker, A., R. Collins, and M. Jacobson. 1987. *Marketing Booze to Blacks.* Washington, D.C.: Center for Science in the Public Interest.

Hainer, P., C. Hines, E. Martin, and G. Shapiro. 1988. "Research on Improving Coverage in Household Surveys." Fourth Annual Research Conference Proceedings. Washington, D.C.: U.S. Bureau of the Census.

Harburg, Ernest, John Erfurt, Catherine Chape, Louise Havenstein, William Scholl, and M. A. Schork. 1973. "Socioecological Stressor Areas and Black-White Blood Pressure: Detroit." *Journal of Chronic Disease* 26:595–611.

Herd, Denise. 1985. "Migration, Cultural Transformation and the Rise of Black Liver Cirrhosis Mortality." *British Journal of Addiction* 80 (4): 397–410.

———. 1990. "Subgroup Differences in Drinking Patterns among Black and White Men: Results from a National Survey." *Journal of Studies on Alcohol* 51 (3): 221–232.

House, James S., Karl R. Landis, and Debra Umberson. 1988. "Social Relationships and Health." *Science* 241:540–545.

Jaynes, Gerald D., and Robin M. Williams. 1989. *A Common Destiny: Blacks and American Society*. Washington, D.C.: National Academy Press.

Kessler, Ronald C., Katherine A. McGonagle, Shanyang Zhao, Christopher B. Nelson, Michael Hughes, Suzann Eshleman, Hans-Ulrich Wittchen, and Kenneth S. Kendler. 1994. "Lifetime and Twelve-Month Prevalence of DSM-III-R Psychiatric Disorders in the United States." *Archives of General Psychiatry* 51:8–19.

Knowles, John. 1977. "The Responsibility of the Individual." Pp. 57–80 in John Knowles (ed.) *Doing Better and Feeling Worse*. New York: W. W. Norton.

Krieger, Nancy. 1987. "Shades of Difference: Theoretical Underpinnings of the Medical Controversy on Black/White Differences in the United States, 1830–1870." *International Journal of Health Services* 17:259–278.

———. 1990. "Racial and Gender Discrimination: Risk factors for High Blood Pressure?" *Social Science and Medicine* 30:1273–1281.

———. 1999. "Embodying Inequality: A Review of Concepts, Measures, and Methods for Studying Health Consequences of Discrimination." *International Journal of Health Services* 29 (2): 295–352.

Krieger, N., and M. Bassett. 1986. "The Health of Black Folk: Disease, Class, and Ideology in Science." *Monthly Review* 38:74–85.

LaVeist, Thomas A. 1992. "The Political Empowerment and Health Status of African-Americans: Mapping a New Territory." *American Journal of Sociology* 97:1080–1095.

Lemann, Nicholas. 1992. *The Promised Land: The Great Black Migration and How It Changed America*. New York: Vintage Books.

Levin, Myron. 1988. "The Tobacco Industry's Strange Bedfellows." *Business and Society Review* 65 (Spring): 11–17.

Lewontin, R. 1974. *The Genetic Basis of Evolutionary Change*. New York: Columbia University Press.

———. 1982. *Human Diversity*. New York: Scientific American Books.

Lincoln, C. Eric, and Lawrence H. Mamiya. 1990. *The Black Church in the African American Experience*. Durham, N.C.: Duke University Press.

Marmot, M. G., M. Kogevinas, and M. A. Elston. 1987. "Social/Economic Status and Disease." *Annual Review of Public Health* 8:111–135.

Marmot, M. G., and M. E. McDowall. 1986. "Mortality Decline and Widening Social Inequalities." *Lancet* 2:274–276.

Martin, Elizabeth, T. J. DeMaio, and P. C. Campanelli. 1990. "Context Effects for Census Measures of Race and Hispanic Origin." *Public Opinion Quarterly* 54:551–566.

Massey, Douglas S., and Nancy A. Denton. 1993. *American Apartheid: Segregation and the Making of the Underclass*. Cambridge, Mass.: Harvard University Press.

Massey, Douglas S., and Mitchell L. Eggers. 1990. "The Ecology of Inequality: Minorities and the Concentration of Poverty, 1970–1980." *American Journal of Sociology* 95 (5): 1153–88.

McCord, Colin, and Harold Freeman. 1990. "Excess Mortality in Harlem." *New England Journal of Medicine* 322:173–177.

Montagu, A. 1965. *The Idea of Race.* Lincoln: University of Nebraska Press.

National Center for Health Statistics. 1991. *Vital Statistics of the United States, 1988,* vol. 2, *Mortality,* Part A. Washington, D.C.: Public Health Service.

———. 1993. *Health, United States, 1992 and Healthy People 2000 Review.* Hyattsville, Md.: Public Health Service.

———. 2000. *Health, United States, 2000 with Adolescent Health Chartbook.* Hyattsville, Md.: U.S. Department of Health and Human Services.

Olshansky, S. J. 1985. "Pursuing Longevity: Delay vs. Elimination of Degenerative Diseases." *American Journal of Public Health* 75:754–757.

Polednak, A. P. 1989. *Racial and Ethnic Differences in Disease.* New York: Oxford University Press.

Rabow, J., and R. Watt. 1982. "Alcohol Availability, Alcohol Beverage Sales and Alcohol-Related Problems." *Journal of Studies on Alcohol* 43:767–801.

Reed, Wornie L. 1992. "Lead Poisoning: A Modern Plague Among African American Children." In Ronald L. Braithwaite and Sandra E. Taylor (eds.), *Health Issues in the Black Community.* San Francisco: Jossey-Bass.

Ries, Peter W. 1990. *Health of Black and White Americans, 1985–87.* Data from the National Health Interview Survey 10 (171). Public Health Service publication 90–1599. Hyattsville, Md.: U.S. Department of Health and Human Services.

Robins, L. N., and D. A. Regier (eds.). 1991. *Psychiatric Disorders in America: The Epidemiologic Catchment Area Study.* New York: Free Press.

Robinson, James. 1984. "Racial Inequality and the Probability of Occupation-related Injury or Illness." *Milbank Memorial Fund Quarterly* 62:567–90.

Seeman, Melvin, and Carolyn S. Anderson. 1983. "Alienation and Alcohol: The Role of Work, Mastery, and Community in Drinking Behavior." *American Sociological Review* 48:60–77.

Singer, Merril. 1986. "Toward a Political Economy of Alcoholism." *Social Science and Medicine* 23:113–130.

Stack, Carol B. 1974. *All Our Kin: Strategies for Survival in a Black Community.* New York: Harper and Row.

Sullivan, Louis W. 1991. "Effects of Discrimination and Racism on Access to Health Care." *Journal of the American Medical Association* 266:2674.

Taylor, R. J., and L. M. Chatters. 1988. "Church Members as a Source of Informal Social Support." *Review of Religious Research* 30:193–203.

Taylor, Jerome, and Beryl Jackson. 1990. "Factors Affecting Alcohol Consumption in Black Women. Part II." *International Journal of Addictions* 25 (12): 1415–1427.

U.S. Department of Health, Education and Welfare. 1979. *Healthy People: The Surgeon General's Report on Health Promotion and Disease Prevention.* Washington, D.C.: United States Government Printing Office.

U.S. Department of Health and Human Services. 1985. *Report of the Secretary's Task*

Force on Black and Minority Health. Washington, D.C.: U.S. Government Printing Office.

Vega, William A., and Ruben G. Rumbaut. 1991. "Ethnic Minorities and Mental Health." *Annual Review of Sociology* 17:351–383.

Wilkinson, R. G. 1986. "Socioeconomic Differences in Mortality: Interpreting the Data on Their Size and Trends." Pp. 1–20 in R. G. Wilkinson (ed.), *Class and Health.* London: Tavistock.

Williams, David R. 1990. "Socioeconomic Differentials in Health: A Review and Redirection." *Social Psychology Quarterly* 52 (2): 81–99.

——. 1991. "Social Structure and the Health Behavior of Blacks" Pp. 59–64 in K. W. Schaie, James S. House, and D. Blazer (eds.), *Aging, Health Behaviors and Health Outcomes.* Hillsdale, N.J.: Erlbaum.

Williams, David R., and Collins, C. 1995. "U.S. Socioeconomic and Racial Differences in Health." *Annual Review of Sociology* 21: 349–386.

Williams, David R., and James S. House. 1991. "Stress, Social Support, Control and Coping: A Social Epidemiologic View." Pp. 147–172 in B. Badura and I. Kickbusch (eds.), *Health Promotion Research: Towards a New Social Epidemiology.* Copenhagen: World Health Organization.

Williams, David R., Risa Lavizzo-Mourey, and Rueben C. Warren. 1994. "The Concept of Race and Health Status in America." *Public Health Reports* 109 (1): 26–41.

Williams, David R., E. E. H. Griffith, J. Young, C. Collins, and J. Dodson. 1999. "Structure and Provision of Services in New Haven Black Churches." *Cultural Diversity and Ethnic Minority Psychology* 5 (2): 118–133.

Williams, David R., and Williams-Morris, R. 2000. "Racism and Mental Health: The African American Experience." *Ethnicity and Health* 5:243–268.

Williams, David R., Leon Wilson, and An-Me Chung. 1992. "Socioeconomic Status, Psychosocial Factors and Health in Urban Guyana." *Sociological Focus* 25 (4): 279–294.

Wilson, Frank H. 1992. "The Changing Distribution of the African American Population in the United States, 1980–1990." *Urban League Review* 15:53–74.

Wilson, William J. 1987. *The Truly Disadvantaged.* Chicago: University of Chicago Press.

The American News Media and
Public Misperceptions of Race and Poverty

MARTIN GILENS

> *The only feeling that anyone can have about an event he does not experi-*
> *ence is the feeling aroused by his mental image of that event. That is why*
> *until we know what others think they know, we cannot truly understand*
> *their acts.*
>
> — *Walter Lippmann*

As Walter Lippmann argued decades ago, our opinions and behavior are responses not to the world itself, but to our perceptions of that world. It is the "pictures in our heads" that shape our feelings and actions, and these pictures only imperfectly reflect the world that surrounds us. Just as importantly, our experience of the world is largely indirect. "Our opinions," Lippmann wrote, "cover a bigger space, a longer reach of time, a greater number of things, than we can directly observe. They have, therefore, to be pieced together out of what others have reported" (Lippmann 1960:79). Already in Lippmann's time, and even more so in our own, "reports about the world" come primarily through the mass media.

To understand the roots of American public opinion, we need to understand Americans' perceptions of the social and political world they inhabit, and the role of the media in shaping those perceptions. Survey data show that public perceptions of poverty are erroneous in at least one crucial respect: Americans substantially exaggerate the degree to which blacks compose the poor. Furthermore, white Americans with the most exaggerated misunderstandings of the racial composition of the poor are the most likely to oppose welfare.

This chapter investigates the portrayal of poverty in the national news, compares these images with the reality of poverty in America, and offers some preliminary evidence that media coverage of poverty shapes public perceptions and misperceptions of the poor. Examining weekly newsmagazines and, to a lesser extent, network television news shows, I find that news media distortions coincide with public misperceptions about race and poverty, and that both are biased in ways that reflect negatively on the poor in general, and on poor African Americans in particular.

I argue below that the correspondence of public misunderstandings and media misrepresentations of poverty reflects the influence of each upon the other. On the one hand, the media are subject to many of the same biases and misperceptions that afflict American society at large, and therefore reproduce those biases in their portrayals of American social conditions. On the other hand, Americans rely heavily on the mass media for information about the society in which they live, and the media shape Americans' social perceptions and political attitudes in important ways. Media distortions of social conditions are therefore likely to result in public misperceptions that reinforce existing biases and stereotypes.

Public Perceptions of Race and Poverty

African Americans account for 29 percent of America's poor (U.S. Bureau of the Census 1990a). But recent national surveys show that the public substantially overestimates the percentage of blacks among the poor. When one survey asked "What percent of all the poor people in this country would you say are black?" the median response was 50 percent (National Race and Politics Study 1991).[1] Another survey simply asked "Of all the people who are poor in this country, are more of them black or are more of them white?" Fifty-five percent of the respondents chose black compared to 24 percent who chose white, with 21 percent volunteering "about equal" (CBS/*New York Times* Survey 1994).[2]

The public's exaggerated association of race and poverty not only reflects and perpetuates negative racial stereotypes but it also increases white Americans' opposition to welfare. Whites who think the poor are mostly black are more likely to blame welfare recipients for their situation, and less likely to support welfare than are those with more accurate perceptions of poverty. In one national survey, 46 percent of the white respondents who thought African

Americans make up more than half of the poor wanted to cut welfare spending. In contrast, only 26 percent of those who thought blacks compose less than one-quarter of the poor wanted welfare spending cut (*Los Angeles Times* Poll 1985).[3]

Americans' views on poverty and welfare are colored by the belief that economic opportunity is widespread and that anyone who tries hard enough can succeed. For example, 70 percent of respondents to one survey agreed that "America is the land of opportunity where everyone who works hard can get ahead" (Kluegel and Smith 1986:44). For those who perceive abundant opportunities, poverty itself is presumptive evidence of personal failure. Thus Americans' exaggerated association of race and poverty perpetuates long-standing stereotypes of African Americans as poor and lazy. When social scientists began studying stereotypes in the early twentieth century, they found a widespread belief that blacks are lazy,[4] and this stereotype does not appear to have faded much over the years. In 1990, the General Social Survey asked respondents to place blacks as a group on a seven-point scale with "lazy" at one end, and "hard working" at the other. Forty-seven percent of whites placed blacks on the "lazy" side of the scale, and only 17 percent chose the "hard working" side (General Social Surveys 1972–90).

Negative stereotypes of African Americans as lazy, and misperceptions of the poor as predominantly black, reinforce each other. If poverty is a black problem, many whites reason, then blacks must not be trying hard enough. And if blacks are lazy in comparison with other Americans, and economic opportunities are plentiful, then it stands to reason that poverty would be a predominantly black problem. In sum, the public rather dramatically misunderstands the racial composition of America's poor, with consequences harmful to both poor people and African Americans.

Previous Research on Poverty in the News

The portrayal of poverty by the American news media has never been systematically studied. There have, however, been a number of studies of minorities in the news that have some relevance to the current project. The most common such studies have examined the proportion of ethnic or racial minorities appearing in news coverage, and have consistently found that blacks are underrepresented in the American news media, whether it be television (Baran 1973), newspapers (Chaudhary 1980), or newsmagazines (Stempel 1971; Lester and Smith 1990). The underrepresentation of African Americans has decreased over time, however. Lester and Smith (1990), for example, found that only 1.3 percent of the pictures in *Time* and *Newsweek* during the 1950s were of blacks, compared with 3.1 percent in the 1960s and 7.5 percent in the 1980s. Another study looked at the representation of African Americans in news magazine advertisements (Humphrey and Schuman 1984). Advertisements, of course, constitute a very different subject matter from news content, and we would not expect to find many poor people in advertisements. Nevertheless, 10 percent of the blacks in advertisements in *Time* magazine in 1980 were either Africans or Americans in poverty, while none of the whites in these ads were shown as poor.

Data and Methods

The primary data for this chapter consist of every story on poverty and related topics appearing between January 1, 1988, and December 31, 1992, in the three leading American newsmagazines, *Time, Newsweek,* and *U.S. News and World Report*. The *Reader's Guide to Periodical Literature* was used to identify stories related to poverty and the poor. In each year the "core categories" of *poor, poverty,* and *public welfare* were examined. Any cross-references listed under these topics were then followed.[5] In total, 182 stories related to poverty were found under 31 topic headings (the topic headings and number of stories indexed under each are found in the appendix).

Specifically excluded from the list of topics are references to blacks or African Americans. The stories identified thus represent only those that are primarily focused on some aspect of poverty or poor relief. To the extent that stories which focus on African Americans also discuss poverty, the body of stories examined here will *underestimate* the true degree to which poverty is presented as a black problem.

Once the poverty stories were identified, each accompanying picture (if any) was examined to determine if it contained images of poor people. Of the 214 pictures containing 635 poor people, the vast majority were photographs, but a few consisted of drawings, most often as part of a chart. Finally, the race of each poor person in each picture was coded as black, nonblack, or not determinable.

Of the 635 poor people pictured, race could be determined for 560 (88 percent). To assess the reliability of the coding, a random 25 percent sample of pictures was coded by a second coder. The intercoder reliability was .97 for percentage African American in each picture.[6] In addition to race, the age of each poor person pictured was coded as under 18 years old, between 18 and 64, or over 64 years old. For this coding both the picture and any accompanying textual information (often including the exact age of the person pictured) were used. Intercoder reliability for under or over 18 years old was .98, and reliability for under or over 64 years old was .95. Finally, each poor person between 18 and 64 years old was coded as working or not. Again, textual information accompanying the picture was used. Intercoder reliability for work status was .97.

In addition to newsmagazines, coverage of poverty by network television news was also examined. Stories on poverty and related topics were identified using the *Television News Index and Abstracts,* published by Vanderbilt University (see appendix for specific topics). During the five-year time frame for this study, the three weeknight network television news shows broadcast 534 stories on poverty and related topics, the equivalent of about one story every week-and-a-half per network. Although the differences among networks were not great, ABC broadcast the largest number of poverty stories (207), followed by NBC (173) and CBS (154). Of these 534 stories, 50 stories were randomly chosen for analysis. These 50 stories contained pictures of 1,353 poor people.

Television news stories typically include far more pictures of poor people than do magazine stories, but provide far less information about the individual poor people pictured. Consequently, only race of the poor was coded for the television stories on poverty. Of the 1,353 poor people in these stories, race could be coded for 1,100 (81 percent).[7] Intercoder reliability for percentage African American in each scene was .94.

Findings

During the five-year period examined, *Newsweek* published 82 stories on poverty and related topics, an average of about one story every three weeks (Table 12.1). Fewer stories on poverty were found in the other two magazines, with *U.S. News and World Report* publishing 56 poverty stories over this period, and *Time* only 44. Overall, African Americans made up 62 percent of the poor people pictured in these stories, more than twice their true proportion of 29 percent. Of the three magazines, *U.S. News and World Report* showed the lowest percentage of African Americans in poverty stories (53 percent, p < .02), but the differences between magazines were not great.[8]

A reader of these newsmagazines is likely to develop the impression that America's poor are predominantly black.[9] This distorted portrait of the American poor cannot help but reinforce negative stereotypes of blacks as mired in poverty and contribute to the belief that poverty is primarily a "black problem." Yet as problematic as this overall racial misrepresentation of the poor is,

Table 12.1. Stories on Poverty in U.S. Newsmagazines, 1988–1992

	Number of stories	Number of pictures	Number of poor people pictured[a]	Percent African American[b]
Time	44	36	86	65%
Newsweek	82	103	294	66%
U.S. News and World Report	56	67	180	53
Total	182	206	560	62%

[a] Excludes 75 people for whom race could not be determined.
[b] Difference in percentage African American across the three magazines is significant at p<.02 (see note 8).

we shall see that the portrayal of poor African Americans differs from the portrayal of the nonblack poor in ways that further stigmatize blacks.

AGE DISTRIBUTION OF THE "MAGAZINE POOR"

The public is more sympathetic toward some age groups of poor people than others. Working-age adults are expected to support themselves, and poverty among this group is viewed by many Americans as indicating a lack of discipline or effort. Children and the elderly are, to a large extent, not held to blame for their poverty, and these groups are looked upon much more favorably for government assistance. In one survey, for example, respondents gave the disabled elderly the highest priority for government financial assistance, followed by the poor elderly and poor children (Cook and Barrett 1992). Respondents were much less sympathetic toward the working-age poor, who were given the lowest priority for government help of the six groups examined. Yet as Cook and Barrett point out in their study, sympathy toward poor children is often not translated into support for government aid when providing that aid means helping their working-age parents. In terms of public policy, therefore, the elderly are the only unambiguously privileged age group among the poor.

Given the public's greater willingness to help the elderly poor, and to a lesser degree poor children, public perceptions of the age distribution of the poor are likely to have an impact on overall levels of support for government anti-poverty efforts. Although dramatically off base in terms of the racial composition of the poor, news magazine portrayals of poverty are fairly accurate in showing large numbers of children among the poor. Forty-three percent of the poor people pictured were coded as under 18 years old, compared with the

Table 12.2. Age Distribution of the American Poor and Age Distribution of the "Magazine Poor," by Race

	Total[a]	African American	Non-African American
True poor			
Under 18 years old	40%	47%	37%
18 to 64 years old	49%	45%	51%
Over 64 years old	11%	8%	12%
Total	100%	100%	100%
Magazine poor			
Under 18 years old	43%	52%*	35%
18 to 64 years old	55%**	48%	60%***
Over 64 years old	2%***	1%***	5%***
Total	100%	101%	100%
Number of magazine poor	635	345	215

[a] Includes 75 people for whom race could not be determined.
*p<.05; **p<.01; ***p<.001

true figure of 40 percent of America's poor (Table 12.2). And newsmagazines are also accurate in showing a somewhat larger number of children among the black poor than among the nonblack poor. The census bureau reports that 47 percent of poor African Americans are under 18, while newsmagazines show 52 percent. Similarly, children make up 37 percent of the nonblack poor, while newsmagazines show 35 percent.

With regard to the elderly, however, the magazine poor and the true poor differ substantially. In reality, those over 64 years old account for 11 percent of all poor people, but they are scarcely to be found at all in magazine poverty stories (see Table 12.2). If newsmagazine pictures reflected the true nature of American poverty, we would expect to find about 70 elderly people among the 635 poor people pictured; instead we find a mere 13 (2 percent). (In coding the age of the magazine poor, a very lax criterion was applied, so that any poor person who could at all plausibly be thought to be over 64 years old was so coded.)

The most sympathetic age group of poor people — the elderly — while a small proportion of the true poor, are virtually invisible among the magazine poor. Furthermore, of the 13 elderly poor shown over the five-year period under study, ten are white and only two are black (the race of one person could not be determined). According to census data, those over 64 constitute 12 percent of the nonblack poor and 8 percent of poor African Americans (Table 12.2); but in newsmagazines, the elderly represent only 5 percent of poor nonblacks, and a scant six-tenths of one percent of the black poor. Thus the most sympathetic age category of the poor is both underrepresented in general, and reserved almost exclusively for nonblacks.

WORK STATUS OF THE "MAGAZINE POOR"

For centuries, Americans have distinguished between the "deserving poor" who are trying to make it on their own, and the "undeserving poor" who are lazy, shiftless, or drunken, and prefer to live off the generosity of others (Katz 1989). More remarkable than the tenacity of this distinction is the tendency to place a majority of the poor in the "undeserving" category. In one survey, for example, 57 percent of the respondents agreed that "Most poor people these days would rather take assistance from the government than make it on their own through hard work" (National Race and Politics Study 1991). While the true preferences of the poor are hard to measure, the fact is that 51 percent of the working-age poor (and 62 percent of poor working-age men) are employed at least part-time (Table 12.3).

The magazine poor are much less likely to be employed than their real-world counterparts. Overall, only 15 percent of the working-age magazine poor hold a paying job (see Table 12.3). If we add in all those described as looking for work, or participating in some kind of vocational training program, or even just collecting bottles and cans, the number increases to only 21 percent. Thus the clearest indication of "deservingness" — preparing for or engaging in some form of employment — is rare indeed among the magazine poor. Whatever public sympathy might accompany the perception that the poor are trying to work their way out of poverty is unlikely to emerge from these newsmagazines.

Just as newsmagazines' underrepresentation of the elderly poor is greater for African Americans than for others, so is their underrepresentation of the working poor. In reality, poor African Americans are somewhat less likely to be employed than non-African Americans, but the difference is modest: 42 percent of poor African Americans work compared with 54 percent of the non-African American poor (see Table 12.3). But among the magazine poor, this difference is much greater. While 27 percent of the nonblack poor are shown as working, only 12 percent of the African American poor are portrayed as workers. Thus the true proportion of poor nonblacks who work is twice as high in real life as it is in these newsmagazines (54 percent vs. 27 percent), while the true proportion working among the black poor is three-and-one-half times that shown in *Time, Newsweek,* and *U.S. News and World*

Table 12.3. Work Status of the Working-Age American Poor and Work Status of the Working-Age "Magazine Poor," by Race

	Total[a]	African American	Non-African American
True poor			
Working	51%	42%	54%
Not working	49%	58%	46%
Magazine poor			
Working	15%***	12%***	27%***
Not working	85%***	88%***	73%***
Number of working-age magazine poor	351	165	129

[a] Includes 57 working-age poor for whom race could not be determined.
***$p<.001$
Note: Significance levels indicated differences between magazine portrayals and census figures for each category (see note 2). Working-age includes those 18 to 64 years old.

Source: U.S. Bureau of the Census, Current Population Reports, Series P-60, No. 171, *Poverty in the United States: 1988 and 1989.* U.S. Government Printing Office, Washington, D.C., 1990.

Report (42 percent vs. 12 percent). Once again, the misleadingly negative portrait of the poor presented in these news stories is even more misleading and more negative for poor African Americans.

THE "MAGAZINE POOR" BY TOPIC OF STORY

To examine portrayals of the poor by story topic, the thirty-one topics were grouped into nine major categories (including a residual "miscellaneous" category). The story topics shown in Table 12.4 relate to members of the poverty population that receive varying levels of public support or censure. For example, surveys show greater sympathy for the poor in general than for welfare recipients (Smith 1987). And we would expect more sympathetic responses to stories about poor children or poor people in employment programs than to stories about nonworking poor adults. Most of the topics shown in Table 12.4 are illustrated with approximately the same proportion of African Americans. These include "sympathetic" topics such as poor children (60 percent black) and education for the poor (65 percent black), and "unsympathetic" topics such as public welfare (57 percent black).

Of those topics that do differ substantially in percentage African American, however, fewer blacks are shown in stories on the more sympathetic topics of

Table 12.4. Percentage African Americans in Pictures of the Poor by Topic of Story

	Number of stories	Number of poor people pictured[a]	Percentage African American
Underclass	6	36	100%
Poor	33	147	69%
Housing/homelessness[b]	96	195	66%
Education for the poor[c]	4	17	65%
Poor children[d]	24	70	60%
Public welfare	25	97	57%
Employment programs for the poor[e]	9	52	40%
Medicaid	7	6	17%
Miscellaneous others[f]	14	13	43%
Total	182	560	62%

Note: Column entries exceed totals shown because stories may be indexed under more than one topic.

[a] Excludes 75 people for whom race could not be determined.

[b] Includes housing, [city/state]; U.S.; housing projects; housing, federal aid; housing vouchers; Department of Housing and Urban Development; homeless; poor, housing; welfare hotels; Habitat for Humanity; Covenant House.

[c] Includes Head Start; poor, education.

[d] Includes child welfare; children, homeless; runaways; socially handicapped children.

[e] Includes workfare; Job Corps; American Conservation Corps.

[f] Includes MadCAPP; LIFE program; I Have a Dream Foundation; refugees; economic assistance, domestic; legal aid; relief work; unemployment insurance; *Street News*; entitlement spending.

employment programs (40 percent black) and Medicaid (17 percent black), while stories on the underclass—perhaps the least sympathetic topic in Table 12.4—are illustrated exclusively with pictures of African Americans. While the underclass lacks any consistent definition in either popular or academic discourse,[10] it is most often associated with intergenerational poverty, labor force nonparticipation, out-of-wedlock births, crime, drugs, and "welfare dependency as a way of life" (Jencks 1991).

In fact, blacks do compose a large proportion of the American underclass, just how large a proportion depending on how the underclass is defined. But even those definitions that result in the highest percentages of African Americans do not approach the magazine portrait of the underclass as 100 percent black. One such definition counts as members of the underclass only poor residents of census tracts with unusually high proportions of (1) welfare recipients,

(2) female-headed households, (3) high school dropouts, *and* (4) unemployed working-age males (Ricketts and Sawhill 1988).[11] By this definition, 59 percent of the underclass is African American. However defined, it is clear that the American underclass contains substantial numbers of nonblacks, in contrast to the magazine underclass composed exclusively of African Americans.

With regard to topic of story, then, we find a tendency to portray a variety of subgroups of the poor as roughly similar in the proportion of African Americans. For those aspects of poverty that do differ in this regard, however, the more sympathetic groups among the poor are shown as relatively less black, while the least sympathetic element the underclass is shown as made up completely of African Americans.

RACE AND POVERTY IN TELEVISION NEWS STORIES

The three newsmagazines examined here have a combined circulation of over ten million (Folio 500 1994), and 20 percent of American adults claim to be regular readers of "newsmagazines such as *Time, U.S. News and World Report,* or *Newsweek.*"[12] In addition, these magazines influence how other journalists see the world. In one study, for example, magazine and newspaper journalists were asked what news sources they read most regularly (Wilhoit and Weaver 1991). Among these journalists, *Time* and *Newsweek* were the first- and second-most frequently cited news sources, far more popular than the *New York Times,* the *Wall Street Journal,* or the *Washington Post.*

Despite the broad reach of these weekly magazines, and their role as "background material" for other journalists, there can be little doubt that television is the dominant news source for most Americans. In recent surveys, about 70 percent of the American public identifies television as the source of "most of your news about what's going on in the world today" (Mayer 1993). If television news coverage of poverty were to differ substantially from that found in newsmagazines, the implications of this study would be severely limited.

Unfortunately, it is difficult to analyze television news in the way that newsmagazine coverage of poverty was analyzed above because television news typically provides far less information about the individuals pictured in poverty stories than do newsmagazines. The analysis of television news is therefore limited to the race of the poor people used to illustrate stories on poverty.

During the five-year period of this study (1988 through 1992), weeknight news shows on ABC, NBC, and CBS broadcast 534 stories on poverty and related topics, of which 50 stories were randomly selected for analysis. Of the 1,100 race-codable poor people in these stories, 65.2 percent were black — a slightly higher figure than the 62 percent black found in newsmagazine stories on poverty. Clearly, then, the overrepresentation of African Americans in stories on poverty found in weekly newsmagazines is not unique to this particular medium, but is shared by the even more important medium of network television news.

Do Media Portrayals of Poverty Influence Public Perceptions?

Although we lack the data to demonstrate directly the impact of media portrayals of poverty on public perceptions, a variety of evidence suggests that such portrayals are likely to be important influences. First, both experimental and nonexperimental studies have demonstrated the power of the media to shape public perceptions and political preferences. Media content can affect the importance viewers attach to different political issues (Iyengar and Kinder 1987; Rogers and Dearing 1988), the standards that they employ in making political evaluations (Iyengar and Kinder 1987; Krosnick and Kinder 1990), the causes they attribute to national problems (Iyengar 1989, 1991), and their issue positions and perceptions of political candidates (Bartels 1993).

None of these studies focused on the visual aspect of media content. Other evidence suggests, however, that visual elements of the news including the race of the people pictured are highly salient to viewers. In a study aptly titled "Seeing Is Remembering," Graber (1990) found that people were more likely to remember what they saw in a television news story than what they heard. With regard to viewers' use of race as a visual cue, Iyengar and Kinder (1987:41) presented subjects with television news stories about unemployment in which the unemployed individual pictured was either black or white. Following the unemployment story (which was included as part of a larger compilation of news stories), subjects were asked to name the three most important problems facing the nation. Of those white viewers who were randomly assigned the story about an unemployed white person, 71 percent said that unemployment was among the three most important national problems. Of those whites who saw a story about an unemployed African American, however, only 53 percent felt that unemployment was a pressing national concern.

Thus past research has shown that the mass media can exert a powerful influence on public perceptions and attitudes, that news pictures convey important information that viewers are comparatively likely to remember, and that the race of people pictured in news stories is a salient aspect of the story for many viewers. While past studies have focused largely on television news, there is no reason to think that the impact of pictures, or the salience of the race of those pictured, would be any less in newsmagazines.[13]

A second source of evidence concerning the plausibility that media portrayals shape public perceptions of the poor comes from the limited available longitudinal data. If the media drive public perceptions, then changes over time in media portrayals should be associated with changes in public beliefs. For many issues, this strategy for assessing media effects is complicated by the problem of "real-world" changes. That is, any association found between media coverage and public opinion could be due to the dependence of both upon some real change in social conditions. This is not a problem with regard to the racial composition of the poor, however, which has remained remarkably constant since the government started collecting official poverty data in the 1960s.[14]

Although the data gauging public perceptions of the racial composition of the poor are sparse, the patterns are consistent with the media effects hypothesis. Two questions asking about the racial composition of the poor are available from national surveys, each asked at two points in time. To assess the relationship between media portrayals and public perceptions, I examined the percentage black among the poor in the three magazines for the six-month periods prior to each survey. The median response to a straightforward question "What percent of the poor are black?" increased from 39 percent in 1985 to 50 percent in 1991; the percentage of African Americans in media portrayals of poverty also increased across this period, from 50 percent in 1985 to 63 percent in 1991. The second survey question asked whether most poor people in this country are white or black. This question elicited a larger "most are black" response in 1982 than in 1994 (63 percent versus 55 percent), and similarly the percentage of blacks among the magazine poor decreased from 34 percent to 26 percent.[15] These corresponding patterns of change in the media and public perceptions hardly constitute proof that the media is the causal agent, but they are consistent with that hypothesis.

A final indication that the media shape perceptions of the racial composition of the poor concerns the implausibility of the alternative hypotheses. If the media are not the dominant influence on public perceptions of the racial composition of the poor, then these perceptions must be shaped by either personal encounters with poor people or conversations about poverty with friends and acquaintances. Conversations with others might indeed be an important influence, but this begs the question of how an individual's conversation partners arrived at *their* perceptions. If personal encounters with poor people explain the public's perceptions, then variation in individuals' perceptions should correspond with variations in the racial mix of the poor people they encounter in everyday life.

Although the personal encounter thesis is plausible, survey data show that the racial makeup of the poor in an individual's state appears to have almost no impact on his or her perceptions of the country's poor as a whole. For example, residents of Michigan and Pennsylvania, where African Americans make up 31 percent of the poor, believe that 50 percent of America's poor are black.[16] In Washington and Oregon, blacks constitute only 6 percent of the poor, yet residents of these states believe that the American poor are 47 percent black. Finally, blacks make up only *1 percent* of the poor in Idaho, Montana, Wyoming, North Dakota, South Dakota, and Utah, yet survey respondents from these states think that blacks account for 47 percent of all poor people in this country. Thus, despite the large state-by-state differences in the percentage of blacks among the poor, personal experience appears to have little impact on public perceptions of the racial composition of poverty.

Not only do we find little variation in racial perceptions of the poor across states, but we also find little variation across other population groups. Although one might expect those with more education to hold more accurate understandings of current social conditions, differences in racial perceptions of the poor are fairly small and nonmonotonic. When asked whether most poor people are white or black, for example, 47 percent of respondents who lack a high school degree chose black, compared with 59 percent of high school graduates, 57 percent of those with some college education, and 48 percent of college graduates (p < .01). A similar pattern, but with smaller (and nonsignificant) differences, was found when respondents were asked the percentage of all poor people who are black. Nor do perceptions differ for blacks and whites. Fifty-two percent of blacks and 55 percent of whites said that most poor people are black, while the average estimate of the percentage of blacks among the poor is 51 percent for black respondents and 48 percent for whites.[17]

In sum, then, previous work on related issues shows that the media can have a significant impact on public opinion. Second, changes in media portrayals over time are associated with corresponding changes in public perceptions. And finally, as judged by the similarity in public perceptions across states, differences in personal exposure to poor people of different races appears to have little impact on perceptions of the poor as a whole. Taken together, this evidence strongly suggests that the portrayals of poverty in the media do matter. At least with regard to the racial composition of the poor, public perceptions appear to be shaped by the images offered by the mass media.

Explaining News Media Misrepresentations

Studies of the news process suggest a number of factors that might help to account for distortions in the news media's coverage of poverty. In his classic study of newsmagazines and network television news, Herbert Gans

(1979) identified "availability" and "suitability" as the most significant determinants of news content. By availability, Gans referred to the accessibility of potential news to a journalist facing a variety of logistical constraints and time pressures, while suitability concerns a story's importance and interest to the audience, and its fit within the framework of the news medium (whether newspaper, magazine, or television news).

Gans argued that availability is a product of both the news organization and the social world in which it operates. For example, the location of news bureaus in large cities lends an urban slant to the national news, while economically and politically powerful individuals and organizations use their resources to make themselves more easily available to journalists. Thus news "availability" reflects the social structure that exists outside of news organizations, as well as decisions made within those organizations.

With regard to the pictorial representation of poverty, the availability of different subgroups of the poor may shape the images captured by news photographers. Because news bureaus and the photographers they employ tend to be found in and around large cities, it should not be surprising that the poverty images produced by these organizations are dominated by the urban poor. And if African Americans make up a larger share of the urban poor than of the country's poor in general, then the "availability" of poor blacks to news photographers might explain their overrepresentation in newsmagazines and television news.

This "geographic" explanation for the overrepresentation of blacks in poverty news sounds plausible, but census data show that it is clearly wrong, at least in this form. Within the nation's ten largest metropolitan areas, blacks constitute 32.1 percent of the poverty population, only marginally higher than the 29 percent of all poor American's who are black.[18] Thus the poverty population that urban-based photographers have ready access to does not differ substantially in its racial composition from the American poor as a whole.

Another version of the "geographic" explanation may hold more promise in accounting for the overrepresentation of blacks in newsmagazine pictures of poverty. When an urban-based photographer receives an assignment for pictures of poor people, he or she is likely to look in those neighborhoods in which poor people are most concentrated. It is simply more efficient to look for poor people in neighborhoods with high poverty rates, than to seek out the relatively few poor people in more economically heterogenous neighborhoods.

To the extent that photographers look for poor people in poor neighborhoods, the racial mix of their photographs will reflect not the racial composition of poverty in the entire metropolitan area, but the composition of poverty in poor neighborhoods within the metropolitan area. Because poor blacks are more geographically concentrated than poor whites (Massey and Denton 1993), neighborhoods with high poverty rates are likely to be more disproportionately black than the percentage of blacks among the poverty population as a whole would suggest. In other words, poor whites tend to be "spread around" in both poor and nonpoor neighborhoods, while poor African Americans tend to live in neighborhoods with high poverty rates.

To gauge the extent to which the geographic concentration of African American poverty might lead to the misrepresentation of the poor in newsmagazines, I again examined the ten largest metropolitan areas, this time looking at the racial composition of only those poor people living in poor neighborhoods. Wilson (1987:46) identifies as "poverty areas" census tracts in which at least 20 percent of the population are poor. Using this criterion, about half (50.9 percent) of the poor people in these ten cities live in "poverty areas," and blacks constitute 46.5 percent of the poor people living in these neighborhoods—substantially higher than the overall proportion of 29 percent, yet still far below the proportion of blacks among portrayals of the poor in newsmagazines and on television news shows. But if photographers were even more selective in the neighborhoods they chose, they would encounter poverty populations with even higher percentages of African Americans. For example, in what Wilson (1987) calls "high poverty areas" (census tracts with at least a 30 percent poverty rate), blacks comprise 53.2 percent of the poor in these ten cities. And if photographers were to visit only Wilson's "extreme poverty areas" (with poverty rates of at least 40 percent), they would find that 60.7 percent of the poor are black.

In the ten largest metropolitan areas as a whole, then, just over 30 percent of poor people are black, but in the very poorest neighborhoods of these ten large cities, blacks comprise more than 60 percent the poor. For photographers working under deadline, the easier availability of poor African Americans might skew the images of poverty that appear in the national news. Although Gans focused on the forces that shape the substantive text of the news, the production of news pictures follows the same logic. Social structures outside of the newsroom influence the availability of news content. Because poor blacks are disproportionately available to news photographers, they may be disproportionately represented in the resulting news stories.

But the disproportionate availability of poor African Americans cannot explain all of the racial distortions in media images of poverty. First, only the very poorest neighborhoods come close to the extremely large proportions of poor blacks found in news stories on poverty. And by focusing exclusively on these neighborhoods, photographers would have to ignore the vast majority of urban poor, not to mention the millions of poor people living in smaller cities or rural areas. According to Jargowsky and Bane (1991), only 8.9 percent of all poor people live in "extreme poverty areas" as defined above, and as we saw, once the definition of poverty areas is broadened to include a larger percentage of the poor, the proportion of blacks declines significantly.

Furthermore, the residential concentration of black poverty can at best explain the racial mix of photographs that a newsmagazine photo editor has available to choose from. Because a photo editor typically has a vastly larger number of pictures available than will be used for publication, the racial composition of the photographs that ultimately appear in the magazine will reflect the selection criteria of the photo editor. A photographer will typically produce anywhere from 400 to 4,000 photographs for a single newsmagazine story.[19] Thus even if photographers submit, on average, three pictures of poor African Americans for every two pictures of poor whites, magazine photo editors have the ability to determine the racial mix of the few pictures that find their way into print.

The third and perhaps most important limitation of accessibility as an explanation for media portrayals of the poor is that racial distortions are not limited to the overall proportion of African Americans in news stories on poverty. As we saw above, there also exists a *pattern* of racial misrepresentation, such that blacks are especially overrepresented among the least sympathetic groups of the poor, and comparatively underrepresented among the most sympathetic poverty groups. Such a consistent pattern cannot be explained by the differential accessibility of the black and nonblack poor, and suggests instead that judgments of "suitability," rather than (or in addition to) accessibility, shape the pictorial representation of poverty in the national news.

Judgments of suitability enter into both the selection of news stories and the content of those stories (and of the pictures used to illustrate them). Perhaps the most fundamental aspect of suitability with regard to story content concerns the veracity of the news story. "Accuracy" and "objectivity" remain primary goals among news professionals (Fishman 1980; Gitlin 1980), yet as Gans argued, journalists cannot exercise news judgments concerning story accuracy and objectivity without drawing upon their own set of "reality judgments." Such judgments constitute the background understanding of society upon which a news story is built, and journalists' efforts to accurately portray the subject matter of their stories depend not only upon the specific information newly gathered for a particular story, but also upon this background understanding. While journalists' understandings of society derive in part from their professional work, they inevitably share as well the popular understandings (and *misunderstandings*) held by the larger society in which they live.

Most photo editors are as concerned with providing an accurate impression of their subject matter, as are the writers they work with. In interviews I conducted with photo editors at *Time, Newsweek,* and *U.S. News and World Report,*[20] most expressed a concern that their selection of photographs should faithfully reflect the subject of the story, and in particular, that the photographs of poor people should provide a fair portrayal of the demographics of poverty in the United States.[21]

Given the professed concern for accuracy of the photo editors I talked with, it is important to know whether these news professionals subscribe to the same stereotypes of the poor as the rest of the American public. If photo editors believe that most poor Americans are black, then their choice of pictures may simply reflect the world as they believe it truly is. To assess whether newsmagazine photo editors share the public's stereotypes of the poor, I asked each of the editors I contacted the same question that the public was asked in the 1991 National Race and Politics Study: What percent of all the poor people in this country would you say are black? As a group, these photo editors did share the public's misperceptions regarding the racial composition of the poor, but not to the same degree. On average, the photo editors estimated that 42 percent of America's poor people are black, somewhat less than the public's estimate of 50 percent, but still a good deal higher than the true figure of 29 percent.

Some part of the misrepresentation of poverty found in weekly newsmagazines may be attributable to the misperceptions of the photo editors responsible for selecting the pictures. However, a substantial gap still remains between the editors' perception that 42 percent of the American poor are black, and the pictures of poor people that appear in their magazines, consisting of 62 percent blacks.

One possible explanation for this remaining discrepancy is that in responding to my explicit query about the racial composition of the poor, these photo editors provided a "reasoned judgment" — a judgment that may differ from the "seat of the pants" intuition that in fact guides their selection of photographs. That is, given the opportunity to reflect upon the question, these editors conjecture that most poor Americans are nonblack; but in the everyday process of choosing news photographs, the unexamined, subconscious impressions guiding their ideas of "what the poor should look like" reflect a sense that blacks compose a majority of America's poor.

Social psychologists have demonstrated that even people who explicitly reject specific stereotypes often use those same stereotypes subconsciously in evaluating members of the relevant social group (Banaji et al. 1993; Devine 1989; Dovidio et al. 1986). Similarly, photo editors who consciously reject the stereotype of the poor as black may nevertheless subconsciously employ just that stereotype in selecting pictures to illustrate American poverty.

Alternatively, photo editors may be aware that popular perceptions of the poor as largely black are misguided, but may choose to "indulge" these misperceptions in order to present to readers a more readily recognized image of poverty. That is, if an editor wants a picture that is easily identified as a poor person, and believes that readers strongly associate poverty with blacks, he or she may feel that a picture of a poor African American would be more easily recognized as a poor person than a picture of a poor white. (This need not be a conscious process. An editor might sense that one picture is more easily recognized as a poor person than another without being aware of the importance of race in generating that recognition.)

The possibility that photo editors hold unconscious stereotypes, or that editors (consciously or unconsciously) indulge what they perceive to be the public's stereotypes, necessarily remains speculative. Yet it is clear that the other explanations for distortions in the portrayal of poverty cannot fully account for the very high proportions of blacks in news stories about the poor. More importantly, it is the *pattern* of racial misrepresentation that most clearly signals the impact of negative racial stereotypes on the portrayal of poverty. The absence of blacks among pictures of the working poor, the elderly poor, and poor people in employment programs, the abundance of blacks among pictures of unemployed working-age adults, and the association of blacks with the least favorable poverty topics, indicate the operation of a consistent prejudice against poor African Americans. As one photo editor I talked with acknowledged, it appears that only some kind of "subtle racism" can explain the racial patterning of poverty in American newsmagazines.

Summary and Conclusions

If 560 people were selected at random from among America's poor, we would expect 162 to be black. But of the 560 poor people of determinable race pictured in newsmagazines between 1988 and 1992, 345 were African American. In reality, two out of three poor Americans are nonblack, but the reader of these magazines would likely come to exactly the opposite conclusion.

Although the newsmagazines examined grossly overrepresent African Americans in their pictures of poor people as a whole, African Americans are seldom found in pictures of the most sympathetic subgroups of the poor. I found that the elderly constitute less than 1 percent of the black poor shown in these magazines (compared with 5 percent of the nonblack poor), and the working poor make up only 12 percent of poor blacks (compared with 27 percent of poor nonblacks).

I also found that stories dealing with aspects of antipoverty policy that are most strongly supported by the public are less likely to contain pictures of African Americans. Although 62 percent of all poor people pictured, African Americans make up only 40 percent of the poor in stories on employment programs, and only 17 percent in stories on Medicaid. In contrast, we find far too many African Americans in stories on the least favorable subgroup of the poor: the underclass. Every one of the 36 poor people pictured in stories on the underclass was black.

A number of explanations for the racial misrepresentation of poverty were considered in this chapter. First, the greater geographic concentration of poor blacks, in comparison with poor whites, might lead photographers to over-represent African Americans in their pictures of poor people. Second, photo editors' own misperceptions of the racial composition of American poverty can explain some of the overrepresentation of blacks among published photographs of the poor. But since neither of these factors can fully account for the dramatic distortions of the racial composition of the poor, however, two additional possibilities were considered. First, editors' conscious or unconscious indulgence of what they perceive to be the public's stereotypes could explain distortions in the portrayal of poverty. Alternatively, editors' own unconscious stereotypes concerning the nature of poverty in America could be at work. Although considerations of unconscious stereotypes must be somewhat speculative, the consistent pattern of racial misrepresentation (along with the consistently liberal nature of these editors' conscious beliefs about racial inequality)[22] strongly suggests that unconscious negative images of blacks are at work.

Perhaps the most disheartening aspect of the situation is that apparently well-meaning, racially liberal news professionals generate images of the social world that consistently misrepresent both black Americans and poor people in destructive ways. Whether these distortions stem from residential patterns, conscious efforts to reflect the public's existing stereotypical expectations, or editors' own unconscious stereotypes, these racial misrepresentations reinforce the public's exaggerated association of blacks with poverty.

Whatever the processes that result in distorted images of poverty, the political consequences of these misrepresentations are clear. First, the poverty population shown in newsmagazines as primarily black, overwhelmingly unemployed, and almost completely nonelderly is not likely to generate a great deal of support for government antipoverty programs among white Americans. Furthermore, public support for efforts to redress racial inequality is likely to be diminished by the portrait of poverty found in these newsmagazines. Not only do African Americans as a whole suffer from the exaggerated association of race and poverty, but poor African Americans (who are often the intended beneficiaries of race-targeted policies) are portrayed in a particularly negative light.

A more accurate portrayal of poverty would still, of course, include a large number of blacks. But rather than portraying poverty as a *predominantly* black problem, a true reflection of social conditions would show the poverty population to be primarily nonblack. The danger, perhaps, is that a more accurate understanding of current conditions might lead some to feel the problem of racial inequality is less pressing. But current misunderstandings may pose a greater danger: that whites will continue to harbor negative stereotypes of blacks as mired in poverty and unwilling to make the effort needed to work their way out. By implicitly identifying poverty with race, the news media perpetuate stereotypes that work against the interests of both poor people and African Americans.

Appendix 12.1. Number of Magazine Stories by Topic (stories can be indexed under multiple topics)

Poor, U.S. / Poor, statistics / Poor, [city or state] / Poor, taxation	33
Economic assistance, domestic	4
Public welfare / Public welfare, U.S. / Public welfare, [city or state] / Public welfare, law	5
Department of Housing and Urban Development	26
Homeless	47
Housing, [city or state] / Housing, U.S. / Housing projects / Housing, federal aid / Housing vouchers	10
Poor, housing	7
Welfare hotels	1
Habitat for Humanity	1
Covenant House	4
American Conservation Corps	2
Job Corps	1
Workfare	6
Head Start	3
Poor, education	1
Child welfare	12
Children, homeless	4
Runaways	1

Appendix 12.1. Continued

Socially handicapped children	7
Legal aid / Legal service	1
Medicaid	7
Old age assistance	2
Refugees	1
Relief work	1
Unemployment insurance	3
Underclass	6
MadCAPP	1
LIFE program	1
Street News	1
I Have a Dream Foundation	1
Entitlement spending	1

Total number of magazine stories = 182; total number of index entries = 221.

Number of Television Stories by Topic (stories can be indexed under multiple topics)

Appalachia	7
Children and youth, housing project	6
Children and youth, child care and support, low-income	1
Children and youth, medicine and health, homeless	15
Children and youth, medicine and health, hunger	2
Children and youth, poverty	40
Children and youth, runaways	2
Children and youth, welfare	1
Cities, homeless	249
Cities, inner cities	1
Covenant house	12
Employment, wages, working poor	7
Food stamps	8
Housing, programs, habitat for humanity	6
Head Start	20
Housing, programs, [city or state] / Housing, programs, low income / Housing, public housing / Housing, cities, tenements	68

Notes

Support for this research was provided by the Social Science Research Council's Program for Research on the Urban Underclass, and by the Block Fund at Yale University. I am grateful to Cathy Cohen, James Glaser, Michael Hagen, and Rogers Smith for their comments on earlier drafts of this paper, and to Linda Stork and Michael Ebeid for their exemplary research assistance. I am grateful to Guy Cooper and Stella Kramer at *Newsweek*, Richard L. Boeth and Mary Worrell-Bousquette at *Time*, and Richard Folkers and Sara Grosvenor at *U.S. News and World Report* for their time and cooperation. These interviews were conducted in October 1993. This chapter is reprinted from or adapted from Martin Gilens 1996, "Race and Poverty in America: Public Misperceptions and the American News Media," *Public Opinion Quarterly* 60 (4): 515–541.

Note to epigraph: Lippmann 1960, p. 13.

1. This datum is from the 1991 National Race and Politics Study, a nationwide random-digit telephone survey administered by the Survey Research Center at the University of California at Berkeley, and directed by Paul M. Sniderman, Philip E. Tetlock, and Thomas Piazza. Data were collected between February and November 1991 from 2,223 respondents, with a response rate of 65.3 percent (Survey Research Center 1991).

2. CBS/*New York Times* national telephone survey, conducted December 6–9, 1994. Comparing public perceptions of the poor with census bureau statistics implies that the public holds at least a roughly compatible understanding of who is included among the poor. According to census data, a decrease in the poverty threshold would result in a higher proportion of African Americans among the poor, while an increase in the poverty line would result in a lower proportion of blacks. Thus if the public has a lower implicit poverty threshold than the census bureau, public perceptions of the racial composition of the poor may not be as inaccurate as would otherwise appear to be the case. All evidence, however, suggests that if anything, the public has a higher (more inclusive) definition of poverty than is reflected in official government statistics. When a recent survey informed respondents that the federal poverty line for a family of four is now about $15,000 a year, 58 percent of respondents said the poverty line should be set higher, and only 7 percent said it should be set lower (Center for the Study of Policy Attitudes 1994). When asked in another survey what the level of income should be below which a family of four could be considered poor, the median response was about 15 percent higher than the official poverty line for a four-person family (General Social Survey 1993).

3. The association between perceptions of the racial composition of poverty and opposition to welfare spending does not, of course, prove that perceptions of poverty *cause* opposition to welfare. The causal influence might run in the opposite direction. That is, whites who oppose welfare for other reasons (such as its perceived cost to taxpayers) may come to view the poor as largely black. It is not clear, however, why such misperceptions of the poor should follow from welfare policy preferences. A more plausible alternative account of the association of perceptions of poverty and opposition to welfare is that both are consequences of a third factor. But when a number of such possible factors are controlled for, the relationship between perceptions of poverty and opposition to welfare is unaffected. In a regression equation predicting whites' opposition to welfare, the coefficient for perceived percentage black among the poor is 1.16

($\text{ß}=.19$) when percentage black is used as the only predictor. When age, sex, income, race, liberal/conservative ideology, and party identification are added to the model, the coefficient for percentage black barely declines to 1.08 ($\text{ß}=.18$).

4. In one early study (Katz and Braly 1933), Princeton students were given a list of eighty-four traits and asked to select the five which were "most characteristic" of blacks. Over 75 percent chose "lazy" as among these five traits (second in popularity only to "superstitious").

5. The *Reader's Guide* is inconsistent in citing cross-references to related topics. Therefore, when a cross-reference to another topic was found in a particular year, this topic was checked for all five years under study.

6. Intercoder reliability was calculated on the basis of percentage African American in each picture. This is because the picture, not the individual, is the unit of analysis in the computer data file. It is possible that the intercoder reliability for individuals would be slightly lower than the figures based on pictures. For example, two coders might agree that there are 5 blacks and 5 nonblacks in a picture, but disagree on which individuals are black and nonblack. Such a scenario is unlikely to occur often, however, and the picture-based intercoder reliability coefficient is therefore very close, if not identical, to what one would find using individuals as the unit of analysis. The reliability coefficients for age and work status are picture-based as well.

7. Race coding was done by first identifying individual "scenes" within each news story. A scene was defined as one or more camera shots of the same people in the same setting (or a subgroup of the same people in the same setting). Within each scene people were then identified as poor or nonpoor based on both the information contained in the text of the story and the visual information in the scene itself. Finally, the number of black, nonblack, and nonidentifiable poor people in each scene was recorded. To assess reliability of the race coding for the television news stories, a 10-percent random sample of news scenes was selected and independently coded by two coders.

8. As traditionally understood, significance tests and probability levels are not appropriate to the data on newsmagazine photographs. Since every photograph from every poverty story during the period of interest is included in the data set, these data do not constitute a sample drawn from a larger population. Nevertheless, the operation of producing and selecting photographs can be viewed as stochastic process (for example, a given photo editor might select pictures of African Americans for particular types of stories with some specific probability). Viewed this way, the resulting set of photographs can be understood as representative of a larger hypothetical population consisting of the universe of photographs that *might* equally likely have been published in these magazines during this time period. From this perspective, significance tests illuminate the question of how likely it is that similar results would have been found if a larger set of photographs — generated by the same processes that generated the actual photographs — were available for analysis (see Henkel 1976:85–86).

9. For the next stage of this research, the percentage black among the magazine poor has been coded for the period from 1950 through 1994. Since 1965, when these magazines began to include large numbers of African Americans in their pictures of the poor, the percentage black has averaged 54 percent. Thus it appears that for the period under study in this chapter — 1988 through 1992 — the magazine poor are somewhat "more

black" than average for the past three decades. In future analyses I will attempt to account for variation over time in the racial complexion of poverty in the news media.

10. Some argue that the very notion of an underclass is misguided at best and pernicious at worst (e.g., Reed 1991), but this is not the place to debate the utility of this concept. Because the media have adopted the term "underclass," those interested in understanding public attitudes must acknowledge its importance, irrespective of our feelings about the desirability or undesirability of the concept.

11. To qualify as an underclass area based on Ricketts and Sawhill's criteria, a census tract must be at least one standard deviation above the national average on *all* four of these characteristics. By this definition, 5 percent of the American poor live in underclass areas (Ricketts and Sawhill 1988).

12. A *Times Mirror* survey of February 20, 1992, asked "I'd like to know how often, if ever, you read certain types of publications. For each that I read tell me if you read them regularly, sometimes, hardly ever or never. . . . Newsmagazines such as *Time, U.S. News and World Report,* or *Newsweek.*" Twenty percent of respondents claimed to read such magazines regularly, 38 percent sometimes, 20 percent hardly ever, and 21 percent never.

13. In fact, the relative impact of pictures may be even greater in newsmagazines than in television news. In a newsmagazine, even those who do not read a story are likely to look at least briefly at the pictures as they browse through the magazine. In contrast, television viewers with little interest in a particular story are not likely to turn off the sound but may busy themselves with other things (like making or eating dinner) and may not bother to look at the pictures.

14. Between 1961 and 1995, the percentage of all poor people who are black fluctuated between 27 percent and 32 percent (U.S. Bureau of the Census 1993, 1996).

15. The two surveys asking for the percentage of blacks among the poor are the *Los Angeles Times* Poll 96, April 1985 (n=2,439) and the National Race and Politics Study, February–November 1991, (n=2,223; see note 1 for details). The surveys asking whether more of the poor are black or white are the CBS/*New York Times* Poll, March 1982 (n=1,545) and the CBS/*New York Times* Poll, December 1994 (n=1,147). The low percentage of blacks among the magazine poor prior to March 1982 and December 1994 (34 percent and 26 percent) are clearly anomalous. As note 9 indicates, an average of 54 percent of poor people in these magazines were African American for the period from 1965 through 1994.

16. Data on public perceptions come from the 1991 National Race and Politics Study (see note 1). Figures for the true percentage of blacks among the poor are from the 1990 census (U.S. Department of Commerce 1993c).

17. Figures for whether more poor people are black or white are from the CBS/*New York Times* Poll, December 1994; figures for the percentage of the poor who are black are from the 1991 National Race and Politics Study (see note 1).

18. The ten largest metropolitan areas (based on 1980 population) and the percentage of blacks among the poor are: New York, 34.9 percent; Los Angeles, 13.0 percent; Chicago, 49.9 percent; San Francisco, 19.3 percent; Philadelphia, 45.4 percent; Detroit, 52.9 percent; Boston, 15.7 percent; Washington, D.C., 51.4 percent; Dallas, 32.4 percent; Houston, 33.6 percent (1990 United States Census of the Population, Summary Tape File 3A).

19. Richard Folkers, associate director (photo staff), *U.S. News and World Report*, personal communication, October 8, 1993.

20. To better understand the media processes which produce the coverage of poverty news documented above, I interviewed the photo editors responsible for selecting pictures for stories on poverty at each of the three national newsmagazines. Poverty stories appear in two sections of these magazines, the national news section, which tends to contain hard news stories such as government poverty or unemployment statistics, and the society section, which contains softer news like stories on runaways, welfare hotels, and so on. (The exact titles of these sections differ somewhat among the magazines.) At each of the three magazines, I spoke with the senior photo editor responsible for the national news and the society sections. I asked each photo editor about the process of choosing photographs, about their own perceptions of the poor, and about the discrepancy between the racial representation of poverty in their magazine and the true nature of the American poor.

21. Not all of the photo editors I spoke with shared this concern about accuracy, however. Two of the editors responsible for "back-of-the-book" (i.e., softer news) stories stressed that the primary consideration was the "power" of the image, its human or emotional content. For these editors, the demographic characteristics of the poverty images were a distant consideration, when it was considered at all.

22. This characterization of the photo editors as racially liberal is based both on our general conversations about race and poverty and on their responses to survey-style questions about the causes of racial inequality. For example, when asked whether blacks or whites are primarily to blame for racial inequality, the photo editors either blamed whites alone or both blacks and whites together. In contrast, when the same question was asked of the public in the 1991 National Race and Politics Study, Americans were more likely to attribute blame for racial inequality to blacks rather than to whites.

References

Banaji, Mahzarin R., Curtis Hardin, and Alexander J. Rothman. 1993. "Implicit Stereotyping in Person Judgment." *Journal of Personality and Social Psychology* 65:272–281.

Baran, S. 1973. "Dying Black/Dying White: Coverage of Six Newspapers." *Journalism Quarterly* 50:761–763.

Bartels, Larry M. 1993. "Messages Received: The Political Impact of Media Exposure." *American Political Science Review* 87:267–285.

CBS/*New York Times* Survey. 1994. National telephone survey.

Center for the Study of Policy Attitudes. 1994. "Fighting Poverty in America." National telephone survey sponsored by the Center for the Study of Policy Attitudes, October 13–16.

Chaudhary, A. 1980. "Press Portrayals of Black Officials." *Journalism Quarterly* 57:636–641.

Cook, Fay Lomax, and Edith J. Barrett. 1992. *Support for the American Welfare State.* New York: Columbia University Press.

Devine, Patricia G. 1989. "Stereotypes and Prejudice: Their Automatic and Controlled Components." *Journal of Personality and Social Psychology* 56:5–18.

Dovidio, John F., Nancy Evans, and Richard B. Tyler. 1986. "Racial Stereotypes: The Contents of Their Cognitive Representations." *Journal of Experimental Social Psychology* 22:22–37.

Fishman, Mark. 1980. *Manufacturing the News.* Austin: University of Texas Press.

Folio. 1994. "Folio 500." *Folio: The Magazine for Magazine Management* 23 (12): 52.

Gans, Herbert J. 1979. *Deciding What's News.* New York: Pantheon.

General Social Survey. 1990. Machine readable data file. Conducted by the National Opinion Research Center; James Davis and Tom W. Smith, principal investigators.

——. 1993. National personal interview survey conducted by the National Opinion Research Center, February 5–April 26.

Gitlin, Todd. 1980. *The Whole World Is Watching: Mass Media in the Making and Unmaking of the New Left.* Berkeley: University of California Press.

Graber, Doris A. 1990. "Seeing Is Remembering: How Visuals Contribute to Learning from Television News." *Journal of Communication* 40:134–155.

Henkel, Ramon E. 1976. *Tests of Significance.* Sage University Paper series on Quantitative Applications in the Social Sciences, 07–004. Beverly Hills, Calif.: Sage.

Humphrey, Ronald, and Howard Schuman. 1984. "The Portrayal of Blacks in Magazine Advertisements: 1950–1982." *Public Opinion Quarterly* 48:551–563.

Iyengar, Shanto. 1989. "How Citizens Think About National Issues: A Matter of Responsibility." *American Journal of Political Science* 33:878–900.

——. 1991. *Is Anyone Responsible?* Chicago: University of Chicago Press.

Iyengar, Shanto, and Donald R. Kinder. 1987. *News That Matters.* Chicago: University of Chicago Press.

Jargowsky, Paul A., and Mary Jo Bane. 1991. "Ghetto Poverty in the United States, 1970–1980." Pp. 235–273 in *The Urban Underclass,* ed. Christopher Jencks and Paul E. Peterson. Washington, D.C.: Brookings Institution.

Jencks, Christopher. 1991. "Is the Americans Underclass Growing?" Pp. 28–100 in *The Urban Underclass,* ed. Christopher Jencks and Paul E. Peterson. Washington, D.C.: Brookings Institution.

Katz, D., and K. Braly. 1933. "Racial Stereotypes in One Hundred College Students." *Journal of Abnormal and Social Psychology* 28:280–290.

Katz, Michael B. 1989. *The Undeserving Poor.* New York: Pantheon Books.

Kluegel, James R., and Eliot R. Smith. 1986. *Beliefs About Inequality.* New York: Aldine de Gruyter.

Krosnick, Jon A., and Donald R. Kinder. 1990. "Altering the Foundations of Popular Support for the President Through Priming." *American Political Science Review* 84:497–512.

Lester, Paul, and Ron Smith. 1990. "African-American Photo Coverage in *Life, Newsweek* and *Time,* 1937–1988." *Journalism Quarterly* 67:128–136.

Lippmann, Walter. 1960 [1922]. *Public Opinion.* New York: Macmillan.

Los Angeles Times. 1985. Machine readable data file. Poll number 96, April.

Massey, Douglas S., and Nancy A. Denton. 1993. *American Apartheid.* Cambridge: Harvard University Press.

Mayer, William G. 1993. "Poll Trends: Trends in Media Usage." *Public Opinion Quarterly* 57: 593–611.

National Race and Politics Study. 1991. Machine readable data file. Conducted by the Survey Research Center, University of California, Berkeley. Paul Sniderman, Philip E. Tetlock, and Thomas Piazza, principal investigators.

Reed, Adolph L., Jr. 1991. "The Underclass Myth." *Progressive* 55:18–20.

Ricketts, Erol R., and Isabel V. Sawhill. 1988. "Defining and Measuring the Underclass." *Journal of Policy Analysis and Management* 7:316–325.

Rogers, Everett M., and James W. Dearing. 1988. "Agenda-Setting Research: Where Has it Been and Where is it Going?" In James A. Anderson, ed., *Communication Yearbook* vol. 11. Beverly Hills, Calif.: Sage.

Smith, Tom W. 1987. "That Which We Call Welfare by Any Other Name Would Smell Sweeter." *Public Opinion Quarterly* 51:75–83.

Stempel, G. 1971. "Visibility of Blacks in News and News-Picture Magazines." *Journalism Quarterly* 48:337–339.

Survey Research Center. 1991. "National Race and Politics Study." Machine-readable data file. Survey conducted by the Survey Research Center, University of California, Berkeley. Paul M. Sniderman, Philip E. Tetlock, and Thomas Piazza, principal investigators.

U.S. Bureau of the Census. 1990a. Current Population Reports, Series P-60, No. 168, *Money Income and Poverty Status in the United States: 1989.* Washington, D.C.: U.S. Government Printing Office.

——. 1990b. Current Population Reports, Series P-60, No. 171, *Poverty in the United States: 1988 and 1989.* Washington, D.C.: U.S. Government Printing Office.

——. 1993a. *Statistical Abstract of the United States.* Washington, D.C.: U.S. Government Printing Office.

——. 1993b. *1990 Census of Population and Housing, Summary Tape File 3A,* (CD90-3C-1).

——. 1993c. *1990 Census of Population and Housing, Summary Tape File 3c,* (CD90-3C-1).

——. 1996. *Census Bureau Web Page* http://www.census.gov/ftp/pub/hhes/income/povsum.html.

Wilhoit, G. Cleveland, and David H. Weaver. 1991. *The American Journalist: A Portrait of U.S. News People and Their Work.* Bloomington: Indiana University Press.

Wilson, William Julius. 1987. *The Truly Disadvantaged.* Chicago: University of Chicago Press.

PART V

The Differential Impact of Skills on Earnings

13

U.S. Education and Training Policy
A Reevaluation of the Underlying Assumptions
Behind the "New Consensus"

JAMES J. HECKMAN

The American labor market has undergone dramatic changes in the past fifteen years, and has particularly worsened for low-skilled workers. The wages of many groups of workers have declined. The ratios of the wages of college graduates to those of high school graduates and high school dropouts have increased and participation in the market by low-skilled workers has fallen.

Policy analysts have been quick to recognize these changes and to recommend policies designed to reverse them. Most of the proposed solutions entail increased investment in "human capital," that is, training and education, to upgrade the skill level of the workforce and to transform the American workplace. A new consensus has emerged in influential policy circles that the American labor market and educational system are unable to equip workers with sufficient skills. American youth are said to experience a disorderly transition from school to work characterized by too much job turnover and too little training on the job. In contrast, the German apprenticeship system has been held up as a model of order that produces smooth school-to-work transitions and provides workers with human capital directly related to their career interests in a format especially helpful for workers poorly served by formal schooling. Features of this system have been advocated as applicable to the U.S. labor market. Further proposals have been set forth to use taxes and subsidies to encourage firms to produce higher levels of training for their workers and to encourage them to shift to "high-wage" workplace environments.

This chapter examines the analytical and empirical foundations of the new consensus. We summarize the facts that motivate recent concerns about the labor market. We put the developments in the labor market in perspective by noting that under optimistic assumptions about the effectiveness of training programs, it would take a human capital investment of $1.66 trillion (in 1989 dollars) to restore the 1979 earnings ratios of less-skilled workers to workers with some college education, while holding workers with some college education at their 1989 levels of earnings.

Despite its widespread acceptance, the intellectual foundations of the new consensus consist largely of speculation and questionable interpretations of existing evidence on the U.S and German labor markets. For example, a key presumption of the new consensus is that job turnover among youth in the labor market is a wasteful activity. This view fails to recognize the value of job shopping in promoting efficient matches between workers and firms and fails to take account of the fact that most youth do not suffer long-term harmful consequences from frequent spells of early joblessness.

Similarly, there is no evidence that the widely acclaimed German apprenticeship system is especially effective in promoting skill formation, despite many claims to the contrary (see Hamilton, 1990; Commission on the Skills of the American Workplace, 1990). Lower youth unemployment in Germany compared to that in the United States results from regulations compelling young Germans to stay in school or participate in an apprenticeship program until age 18 if they seek any but the most menial job. Any positive effect that the German program has on youth employment is mainly due to the fact that apprentices are exempt from minimum wage laws and rigid employment protection laws that make it difficult to fire regular workers. The real lesson to be learned from this program is that flexible wages and work rules promote employment. Moreover, German apprentices leave the firms that train them at very high rates (Witte and Kalleberg, 1994). The current romance with German institutions is based on a myth that German labor is more productive than U.S. labor. In fact, it is less productive in many industries including beer production and automobile manufacturing, although this difference depends on a number of factors of which labor quality is only one (McKinsey, 1993).

Some proponents of the new consensus also claim that a significant transition is taking place in the methods of production and in the organization of work in the global economy. Firms in other highly developed countries are purported to be changing from the mass-production methods of the past to flexible technology and highly skilled methods. They hypothesize that these methods require apprenticeship-type institutions, credentialing and cooperation between employers and unions to prepare the workforce for more complicated and challenging tasks. These proponents presume that the reason American firms have been slow in adopting "flex-tech" methods is that these complementary institutions are not in place in the U.S. market, rather than because of deficiencies in the methods themselves. In fact, these advocates have failed to demonstrate that either flexible technology workplaces, or the additional educational training institutions they are said to require, actually increase productivity.

Another strong presumption of advocates of the new consensus is that U.S. government policy is biased toward formal schooling and away from vocational and on-the-job training. While some evidence suggests that current U.S. expenditure policies favor formal schooling over job training at the postsecondary level, the total body of evidence is far from clear on this matter. A deeper consideration of the issue reveals that tax policy favors on-the-job training over formal education. Furthermore, no theoretical or empirical evidence has been presented that equal expenditures on formal schooling and vocational or on-the-job training represent the optimal allocation of limited governmental funds for human capital investments.

Proposals to promote skill formation by establishing national skills certification tests fail to recognize the value of job-specific skills that cannot be certified by an exam. They exaggerate the ability of exams to measure the skills valued by employers. Tests that certify some skills, but not others, would tend to distort worker skill acquisition choices. General, easily measured skills would be emphasized at the expense of harder-to-measure firm-specific skills. In addition, tests that publicly reveal previously private information on worker skills may worsen the problem of financing worker investment in training. Firms will have less incentive to pay for the training of their workers if their skills can be easily identified by rival firms.

Finally, proposals to expand government training programs ignore the existing evidence on the ineffectiveness of these programs and on the comparatively greater effectiveness of private sector training programs. In the following sections, we explore each of these weaknesses in the theoretical and analytical foundations of the new consensus in greater depth. We find that these foundations lack the strength to support the edifice of taxes, subsidies, skill certification boards, and other policies constructed upon them by advocates of the new consensus. In our conclusion, we suggest a set of more limited policies, directed at the same targets but built upon a firmer understanding of the economics of the problem and a more realistic assessment of the functioning of the labor market in both the United States and abroad.

The New American Labor Market

Although many of the underlying assumptions of the new consensus are unfounded, there is much evidence to support the view that wage gaps have widened across skill levels. In purchasing-power-constant or deflated dollars, male high school graduates earned 4 percent less per week in 1989 than in 1979. Male high school dropouts earned 13 percent less per week than in 1979. In contrast, male college graduates earned 11 percent more per week (Blank, 1994). These comparisons widen further if we consider annual earnings. By any measure, labor incomes for men have become more unequally distributed. For women, the story is somewhat different. The real weekly earnings of female high school graduates have risen but the rise has been even greater for female college graduates.

Thus for both men and women, inequality of labor incomes has risen. The returns to schooling and skill have increased. The relative earnings of workers at the bottom of the skill distribution (less than high school graduate) have definitely declined for persons of each gender. Youth have been hit hardest in the shifting market for skills.

A corollary phenomenon is the decline in labor market activity, especially among the unskilled. A variety of labor force measures show increasing joblessness and longer unemployment spells for workers at all skill levels. Particularly problematic are less skilled youth (those with high school education or less), who appear to flounder in the market for years before they find stable jobs. These youth are a source of major social problems. Teenage pregnancy, crime, and idleness are important phenomena that are on the increase in most areas.

The problem of a deteriorating market for unskilled or semiskilled workers is not solely a problem of youth. Displaced adults, primarily factory workers, are also a major concern. Middle-age workers displaced from high-wage jobs are at a major disadvantage in the new market for labor that has emerged since many of these workers first took their jobs. Displaced workers constitute 10–20 percent of the unemployed, or roughly 1 to 2 million workers. Recent evidence on the patterns of earnings losses experienced by workers displaced by mass layoffs suggests that the losses are significant and long lasting, especially for those previously employed in unionized industries or occupations (Jacobson et al., 1993).

There have been many proposals for investments in human capital designed to increase the wage levels of the less skilled. An investment generally yields returns over many years after initial costs are incurred. For human capital, a round, and roughly correct, average rate of return is 10 percent. Thus, for each

$10 invested in a person, the expected annual return is $1. Some claim that this number is lower and some claim that it is higher, but most economists would accept a 10 percent return as a good starting point for estimating the aggregate investment needed to upgrade the skills of the low-skilled segment of the workforce.

At this rate of return, to add $1,000 in earnings per year to the average person it is necessary to make a one-time investment of $10,000 in that person. This is a large sum relative to the cost of most public and private training programs, but many college students make even greater investments each year. Using a 10 percent rate, the investment needed to reduce any wage gap is ten times the amount of the gap.

To put the magnitude of recent developments in the labor market in perspective, consider the following two questions:

> How much would we have to invest in our workforce in 1989 dollars to restore real earnings of male high school dropouts and graduates to their real 1979 levels?

This question is meaningful only for men because real weekly earnings for women have risen or remained roughly constant over the period 1979–1989. A second question is:

> How much would we have to invest in our workforce in 1989 dollars to restore 1979 earnings ratios between lower education groups and college graduates, without reducing the 1989 earnings of college graduates?

Using the 10 percent rate of return, it would require an investment of $25,000 in each high school dropout or a staggering $214 billion in 1989 dollars to restore male high school dropouts participating in the workforce to their 1979 real earnings level. To restore all high school graduates to their real 1979 levels would take an investment of $10,000 per high school graduate, or more than $212 billion 1989 dollars, for a total of $426 billion in 1989 dollars. To gauge the enormity of the required investment it is useful to compare these costs with those required to finance the Manhattan project that built the atomic bomb — only $15 billion dollars.

The cost of implementing the answer to the second question is even larger. Table 13.1 shows the amount needed to restore the 1979 earnings ratio between high school graduates or high school dropouts and college-educated full-time workers over age 25. To restore real earnings for both male and female workers over age 25 that are high school educated or less to their 1979 relative positions with respect to college graduates (holding the latter at 1989 real wage levels) would require an investment of more than $1.66 trillion.

Table 13.1. Investment in Human Capital Required to Restore Earnings to 1979 Levels and to Restore 1979 Relative Wage Ratios, Using a 10% Rate of Return (in billions of dollars)

To Restore Earnings to 1979 Levels	
Males	
Investment needed to restore average male high school dropout earnings in 1989 to average real earnings of male high school dropouts in 1979	$214
Investment needed to restore average male high school graduate earnings in 1989 to average real earnings levels of male high school graduates in 1979	$212
Total	$426
To Restore 1979 Earnings Ratios	
Males	
Investment needed to restore average male high school dropout earnings in 1989 to the level needed to achieve the 1979 high school dropout/college earnings ratio (holding 1989 college graduate wages fixed)	$382
Investment needed to restore average male high school graduate earnings in 1989 to the level needed to achieve the 1979 high school graduate/college earnings ratio (holding 1989 college graduate wages fixed)	$770
Females	
Investment needed to restore average female high school dropout earnings in 1989 to the level needed to achieve the 1979 high school dropout/college earnings ratio (holding 1989 college graduate wages fixed)	$136
Investment needed to restore average female high school graduate earnings in 1989 to the level needed to achieve the 1979 high school graduate/college earnings ratio (holding 1989 college graduate wages fixed)	$378
Total	$1.66 trillion

Source: Wages are from Blank (1994). We assume worker works 50 weeks a year. The figures on the education) breakdown for the labor force are from Table 5616, *Statistical Abstract of the United States, 1992*. We delete all persons out of the labor force and those less than age 25. On these criteria, our estimated investment casts are downward-biased.

These numbers are conservative because they do not consider persons below age 25 or persons who do not participate in the workforce at the current wage levels. They are conservative for another reason: few — if any — government training programs have returns anywhere near 10 percent. Zero percent is a much closer approximation of the true return.

One might wish to qualify these calculations in many ways. One might want to adjust down the rate of return as more difficult-to-train persons receive training. Or, one might wish to account for the fact that as persons have their skills upgraded, the real wages of the lower-skilled workers are likely to increase as they become scarcer and the real wages of those with higher skills are likely to decrease as their supply increases. Still, under most plausible scenarios, the costs of restoring skill parities to their 1979 levels are huge.

Investment in human capital may still not reduce income inequality. Raising the skills of a few need not reduce overall inequality. By moving some workers from low-skill to high-skill status, some standard measures of earnings inequality might actually increase. Many programs train only the high end among the low-skilled workers. Such training efforts could polarize the labor market. In addition, it takes skilled labor to produce skilled labor. A large-scale increase in training activity might therefore increase earnings inequality in the short run since it would further expand the demand for skilled labor to train the unskilled labor. It takes educated labor to produce educated labor.

Finally, the most efficient training policy may not be to train the unskilled. As first noted by Mincer (1962), there is strong evidence of universal complementarity between postschool investment and formal schooling. It may be economically efficient to invest in higher-skilled workers and to alleviate concerns about income and earnings inequality through income transfers. However, to the extent that working fosters socially desirable values among those who work, it may still be desirable to invest inefficiently in order to promote those values.

The New Consensus About the U.S. Labor Market

A consensus has emerged in certain circles about the ability of the current U.S. labor market, and the educational and training institutions that complement it, to produce the necessary skills for that labor market. It is negative in tone and looks abroad, especially to Germany and other Northern European countries, for advice on how to restructure the American labor market. The new view is stated most forcefully in the report of the Commission on the Skills of the American Workforce (CSAW), *American's Choice: High Skill or Low Wages!* and in numerous lectures and articles by Ray Marshall. Marshall and

Ira Magaziner, architect of President Clinton's health plan, were the principal authors of the CSAW report, along with former Secretary of Labor William Brock. This report had an enormous impact on the views of the Clinton Administration. Former Secretary of Labor, Robert Reich, elaborates the themes set forth in the CSAW agenda in his book *The Work of Nations*.

The following core ideas underlie the new consensus.

- The growing inequality in wages and incomes is a serious social problem. Especially troublesome is the decline in real earnings among young and unskilled workers.
- The quality of the labor force is not growing rapidly enough. Included in the notion of "quality" is the work ethic, or attitude, of employees. The United States is perceived to be facing a skills shortage exacerbated by the immigration of low-skilled workers. Productivity growth has declined in part because of the slow growth in the quality of American labor. The recent growth in output during the 1980s had more to do with expansion of inputs (primarily the surge of workers produced by the Baby Boom) than with workforce quality improvements.
- American schools have failed to produce high-quality students. They fail to motivate their students and leave them inadequately trained for academic or nonacademic alternatives. Most American education is only poorly connected in content or practicality with the demands of jobs. The low academic performance of Americans is manifest in poor test scores compared with those of other countries. (This comparison of levels overlooks recent improvements in trends, but the gap in test score achievement between the U.S. and other countries remains sizable.)
- The productivity of the workforce cannot be improved by investing in physical capital because, as the authors of *America's Choice: High Skills or Low Wages!* write, "low wage countries can now use the same machines and still sell their products more cheaply than we can." (This view is not held universally even within the group of scholars advocating the new consensus.)
- The CSAW blueprint for the future of the workplace claims that the key to enhanced productivity lies in a "Third Industrial Revolution" now taking place in the world. Henry Ford-style mass production and specialization is becoming obsolete, although it is still widely utilized in the United States. Instead, today's market requires "flexible technology," which allows the production of quality goods, sensitive to changing consumer tastes. This technology requires more highly trained — though not necessarily more highly specialized — workers. Participation in the global economy requires that we move toward high productivity work organizations built around highly trained workers.

- The authors of the CSAW report claim that the school-to-work transition in America is chaotic compared to the orderly, smoothly functioning transitions experienced by German youth. In Germany, youth apprenticeships, especially designed for nonacademically oriented youth, are said to motivate learning by making it tangible. They make learning relevant to market needs and foster achievement among nonacademically oriented youth. By granting nationally recognized credentials to apprentices upon successful completion of occupational skills tests, we could do for vocational training what we currently do for academic training by granting nationally recognizable and accepted degrees. Such certification would enhance incentives for the acquisition of skills in the workplace by guaranteeing an economic return to quality in a national market. In this way, the skill base needed for Americans to participate in the "Third Industrial Revolution" would be created.

The new consensus is a happy marriage of two recent lines of thought. One is the view that the craft economy, now called the "flexible technology" economy, is coming back after a century and a half of the triumph of mass production. This view was expounded by Michael Piore and Charles Sabel in their 1984 book, *The Second Industrial Divide,* and has fired the imaginations of many planners and policy makers. Though it has proven hard to document as a widespread phenomenon, "flex-tech" is widely trumpeted as the leading-edge technology. The other is the view that a return to the apprenticeship system that supported the old craft system will provide the incentives for workers to acquire the right skills. This view is most strongly espoused by Stephen Hamilton (1990). To these lines of thought has recently been adjoined a third argument, namely that flex-tech is best implemented in job environments in which firms and unions cooperate, and in which workers with general skills perform a multiplicity of tasks. It is claimed that by defying the law of comparative advantage and by forgoing the benefits of specialization in tasks in the workplace, worker and firm productivity will be enhanced. Unions are viewed as essential ingredients for fostering the cooperation needed to sustain the new workplace, even though it is well known that unions reduce firm profitability (see Mishel and Voos, 1992; Freeman, 1992). Coupled with the remarkable and unsupported claim that investment in physical capital cannot restore or boost American productivity in regard to other countries, the new consensus virtually dictates a cooperative strategy of workplace-based investment in human capital.

While earlier advocates of the new consensus saw adoption of the new technology as an inevitable consequence of progress, more recent advocates are less sanguine. Indeed, if this new technology had been adopted on a wide scale, this would explain why wage differentials among skill groups were growing. A shift in the demand for skills toward more-skilled workers would explain the recent trend in wage differentials found between and within sectors (see Murphy and Welch, 1992). However, it has been documented that very few firms have voluntarily adopted the "Third Industrial Revolution" technology and its associated training schemes (Osterman, 1993).

Instead of calling into question the arguments made about the superiority of the new technology, the advocates of the new view have criticized myopic American firms for failing to adopt an obviously superior technology.

Martin Baily, Gary Burtless and Robert Litan (1993) of the Brookings Institution endorse some—but by no means all—of the ideas in the new consensus. Burtless's chapter in this volume restates many of the main ideas in that work. Like the proponents of the new view, he and his colleagues emphasize the problems of growing wage inequality and declining real wages for unskilled workers. They claim that there are inappropriately low levels of investment in the workforce—especially among the unskilled—and they further claim that public policy is biased against such investment. They endorse features of the German apprenticeship system—especially skill standards, occupational certification and subsidized apprenticeship programs with firms for noncollege-bound youth. They propose payroll tax policies to finance training and "encourage" firms to organize training programs for their workers.

A central premise of their work is that the increased income inequality resulting from increased skill differentials is inequitable, and that this inequity justifies an active governmental response. They argue that the best way to reduce income inequality, and thereby to increase equity, is to invest in the skills of low-wage workers. They further claim that there is too little investment in human capital among workers at the low end of the skill distribution. They attribute this lack of investment to market failure, including borrowing constraints, and to the short time horizons of low-skill workers. While it may be that low-skill workers have short time horizons, the resulting lack of investment is not inefficient as this term is normally used in economics. These arguments confuse normative and positive statements regarding the amount of training undertaken at the low end of the skill distribution. It is important to disentangle the Brookings authors' concerns with equity *and* with the decision-making processes of the poor from their positive claims about the labor market. Claims about whether investment in unskilled workers is efficiently low and whether in-kind transfers in the form of human capital investments are an efficient way to reduce income inequality can and should be evaluated separately from these authors' normative concerns.

In this chapter, we evaluate arguments both from the Brookings authors and the new consensus group.

Weak Evidence Concerning Public Policy Bias Toward Formal Education and Against Employer-Based Training

One of the main tenets of new consensus authors and of the Brookings group is that improvements in the quality of the U.S. workforce, especially the less-skilled portion of that workforce, have not kept pace with improvements in other nations. Critics question the effectiveness of the postsecondary training options currently in place for noncollege-bound youth. Over 75 percent of youth still do not complete college, and many never attend. Baily, Burtless and Litan (1993), among others, claim that there is a dramatic imbalance between public expenditure on postsecondary schooling for youth who attend college and public expenditures on other forms of human capital acquisition for youth who do not attend college. This imbalance in public spending motivates their advocacy of expanded funding for apprenticeship programs and mandated training expenditures for firms to increase the amount of occupation-specific training acquired by noncollege-bound youth. In this section, we consider the evidence concerning the argument that current public policies for postsecondary education and training are biased toward formal academic education and away from vocational skills training.

Baily, Burtless and Litan state that noncollege-bound youth receive an inadequate amount of postsecondary school training. They cite as evidence a relatively higher level of public spending per college attendee compared to high school graduates and high school dropouts. They do not explain that a large part of public spending on college education is on community colleges, which provide both academic and vocational training. More than 40 percent of college students currently attend such schools, which receive substantial support from local, state, and federal sources. In 1991, 29 percent of the federal education budget was spent on community colleges (U.S. Bureau of the Census, 1992). Local governments devote considerable expenditure to these schools as well.

Moreover, federal student aid programs also support students in public and private vocational schools. Indeed, among students enrolled in the fall of 1989, the percentage of students enrolled in private vocational schools receiving federal support (82 percent, full-time; 60 percent, part-time) exceeded that among students in public four-year colleges (35 percent full-time, 18 percent part-time; U.S. Department of Education, 1993, table 311). Of the $5.7 billion given in Pell Grants, 24.3 percent went to students enrolled in community colleges and 20.7 percent went to students enrolled in proprietary schools (Hansen, 1994). State and local governments play an even larger role in supporting community colleges and vocational training.

A full accounting of the extent of governmental subsidies to different types of postsecondary education and training has not yet been done. It would require measuring subsidy contributions from all levels of government and determining the amount of expenditures on purely academic education versus vocational training.

Moreover, the level of governmental expenditures on formal education is not the best measure of the true scale of training activity *in* the U.S. economy. Baily, Burtless and Litan state that only 12 percent of youth report formal training on their first jobs and only 2 percent report receiving formal company training. These figures understate the true volume of training due to a basic bias in the way training is measured in the literature from which they draw. On-the-job training, especially learning-by-doing, is a major source of human capital investment. Much of this activity is not captured by surveys that record only formal training programs on which the Brookings authors rely so heavily. Mincer (1993) presents evidence from a variety of sources that there is a substantial amount of informal, hard-to-measure investment activity on the job. Omission of human capital acquired informally biases comparisons of the amounts of training acquired by youth attending and not attending college. The failure to adequately measure informal training activity underlies claims that there is an inadequate amount of training provided to noncollege-bound youth.

A more complete view of public policy toward training and education accounts for both tax and expenditure policy. Even if it were the case that current governmental educational spending favors formal education over other forms of training, current tax rules tend to operate in the other direction (see Quigley and Smolensky, 1990). Firms can immediately write off all of their training expenditures. They do not have to be amortized like investments in physical capital. This favors investment in human capital over physical capital. In addition, training expenditures can include tuition paid by employers for each employee up to $5,250 per year, though tuition support is restricted to undergraduate-level education (U.S. House of Representatives, Joint Committee on Taxation, 1992). As many community colleges qualify as undergraduate institutions, there is an incentive for firms to sponsor vocational training. The bias in the tax code favors vocational training and not academic education.

Because tuition paid by employers is exempt from federal personal income tax through educational assistance programs, individuals have an incentive to seek training on the job. Additionally, portable vocational or employer-based training can be sold to employees by firms and paid for by lower wages. The forgone higher earnings are de facto written off on personal income taxes. To the extent that direct costs of books and educational materials are paid for by lower wages, current tax laws favor on-the-job training activities over off-the-job training activities. Thus, they act to shift human capital investment activity away from formal schools and toward workplace environments.

Conversely, individuals cannot write off direct tuition costs for formal schooling if it is not expressly job-related. Write-offs are not given for training in skills useful in other jobs. Thus workers training to switch occupations cannot write off their educational expenses for this activity. Moreover, there is a floor level of training and education expenditures that must be met before persons can write off such self-investment activity. To be eligible for this tax break, it is necessary to itemize deductions and to incur training costs that exceed 2 percent of adjusted gross income. This tax policy likely biases human capital accumulation toward vocational over academic training, because vocational training is typically more narrowly defined and justifiable.

Since 1986, persons have been unable to deduct interest on educational loans from their taxable income. This removes an important incentive that promotes investment in human capital of all forms (Heckman, 1976). However, since mortgage interest is deductible, it is possible for persons with home equity to take out mortgages to finance their education or to rearrange their portfolios toward mortgage debt in order to finance educational loans.

The tax code for individuals favors human capital accumulation for higher income persons (and their children) who itemize and have equity in their homes. Low-income persons who pay no taxes receive little encouragement to invest in human capital from the current personal tax code. However, firms that employ them may write off training expenditures devoted to them. The personal tax code thus encourages low-skill workers to make training investments on the job. It does not encourage investment in general or academic education except for company tuition programs. Unfortunately, these programs (defined under section 127 of the 1988 Tax Code) have not received consistent treatment by the tax authorities. In recent years, companies have operated under uncertainty with regard to the likelihood that section 127 would apply to them in a given tax year.

Our examination of the claim that current tax and expenditure policies are biased against employer-based training reveals that it is necessary to examine specific tax and expenditure policies more closely. Simple comparisons of government expenditures on different types of training and education are irrelevant. First, such comparisons ignore the vast amount of informal private sector training and skill formation that is hard to measure but which appears to generate substantial wage growth after schooling (Mincer, 1993). Second, such comparisons typically ignore the vocational training portion of community college education. It is inappropriate to count expenditures on community colleges solely as spending on academic education.

At a deeper level, even if the public expenditure figures cited by Baily,

Burtless, and Litan were correct, they would still not reveal whether governmental training expenditures were divided between formal schooling and other types of training in the way best designed to increase social welfare. There is no reason why the expenditures required to produce the optimal levels should be equal absolutely or on a per capita basis in the two sectors. It might in fact be the case that the existing levels are correct, or that a reversal of the existing levels is appropriate. A complete discussion requires a full empirical and theoretical investigation of the reasons why the market and educational institutions fail to produce the correct levels of the two types of human capital investment and of the responsiveness of these training levels to government expenditures. In the absence of such a complete analysis, the evidence presented in Baily, Burtless, and Litan, even if correct, sheds little light on the questions they purport to address.

There is a widespread belief that markets for financing human capital are fragile and require help from governments to be sustained. The Brookings group claims that many young people have excessively high discount rates and that credit markets for financing training are imperfect. Evidence presented by Cameron and Heckman (1994) indicates that family income plays a powerful role in determining which young persons undertake on-the-job training, participate in schooling and work. This evidence is consistent with the importance of borrowing constraints, but it is also consistent with a strong role for family environmental factors. There is surprisingly little decisive evidence on this important issue. There is even less evidence that the discount rates of young persons are "too high," even though the Brookings group maintains that this is so. This blatantly paternalistic argument has not been subject to rigorous empirical scrutiny. The same can be said of claims that firms are "excessively" myopic in their training strategies for their workers.

Missing in this litany of market failures is any discussion of why the market for the provision of schooling may be inefficient. Schooling at the primary and secondary levels is primarily a government monopoly with little opportunity for choice by most parents. It would balance their discussion if the Brookings group recognized the possibility that introducing choice and competition in schools might be a fruitful policy option for improving the skills of young persons. In the next section, we document that the German apprenticeship program operates to enforce competition and improve choice in markets for the production of human capital.

Until the source of a market failure is found, the appropriate policy to address it cannot be formulated. Both the new consensus and Brookings policy recommendations are based on surprisingly weak empirical foundations. The new consensus is based on common beliefs and not hard evidence.

Background on the German Apprenticeship System

Based in part on the belief that there is too little public spending on the postsecondary vocational training of American youth, the new consensus looks to the German education and training system as a model that more appropriately balances formal and vocational education.

In this section, we examine the German system and provide some background on how it operates. In the next section, we consider what lessons should be learned from it. We stress at the outset that no one advocates wholesale adoption of the German system. However, features of it that stress learning on the job, skill certification, and early links between specific firms and students are widely advocated. Specific legislation has been passed to fund programs that incorporate these principles. We question whether the correct lesson has been learned from the German experience.

German youth move through three academic tracks. By grade 4 or 6 students are sorted into three schools: Hauptschule, where they continue until grade 9 or 10; Realschule, where they continue until grade 10; and Gymnasium, where they continue until grade 13. Hauptschule leads to apprenticeships, which are usually of three-year duration. Typically, one day a week of an apprenticeship is spent in academic schooling suitable to the occupation being trained for. The rest of the apprentice's time is spent learning and working on the job. Realschule qualifies students for further vocational schooling that eventually culminates in work and learning ("dual system") activities. Gymnasium leads to university preparation and is considered technically outside of the apprenticeship system, although in certain sectors, such as banking, students certified to go to the university instead take a form of professional apprenticeship. Hauptschuler become carpenters, auto mechanics, and office assistants. Realschuler become laboratory technicians, precision mechanics, and personnel managers. They are placed in higher level apprenticeships. Not all graduates of these schools become apprentices. (Only 38 percent of Realschuler and about 50 percent of Hauptschuler become apprentices.) Many youth, especially those from Realschuler, continue on in postsecondary vocational schools. The German government pays the full cost of this additional schooling, while apprentices pay part of the costs of their training by taking lower wages.

Apprenticeship wages range from 22–33 percent of full-time professional wages for experienced workers. The training wage varies by sector with larger firms paying more than smaller firms. In the hand crafts sector (retail trade and services), training wages are particularly low. Many apprentices live at home and are unable to support themselves with the apprenticeship wage. Only 10 percent of the firms in industry and commerce participate in these training programs, while 40 percent of the smaller crafts firms participate at the lower apprentice wage levels in that sector. (Rainer Winkelmann suggests that these figures may overstate the lack of participation of German firms in the apprenticeship programs because solo entrepreneurs, of which there are many in Germany, are required to register as firms but are unlikely to use apprentices.) These training wages thus operate like youth subminimum wages. Since the German economy is virtually 100 percent unionized, the variance from high union wage levels granted apprentices greatly facilitates their employment, given that their marginal productivity equals or exceeds the wages they receive. The apprenticeship system thus provides an escape route for firms from high union wages, and may be a mechanism for evading union-mandated minimum wage laws. In addition, apprentices are exempt from the rigid German laws that impose costs on firms that seek to terminate the employment of workers. This imparts a bit more flexibility to the German labor market for the group of apprentice workers.

Apprentices are tested for minimal knowledge of the basic skills of their trade at the end of their apprenticeships. The pass rate on these certification exams is 90 percent. Candidates may take the exam twice more if they fail it on the first attempt. Overall success rates in the exams thus tend to be quite high.

A German apprenticeship does not necessarily lead to lifetime employment at the firm training the worker (see, e.g., Witte and Kalleberg, 1994). Most apprentices move on to take full-time positions at other firms. This is especially true for trainees in the crafts sector, where firms are rather small. Apprentices often take jobs in different occupations than they are trained for. For example, the leading trainer of bakers in Munich is the Ford Motor Company. Recent evidence suggests that after five years, more than half of all apprentices are working in a different company than the one that trained them (see, e.g., Harhoff and Kane, 1993). Participation in apprenticeship programs postpones but does not eliminate job shopping.

Completion of an apprenticeship, like graduation from a school, often conveys more information about the tenacity of the trainee and his or her ability to finish a task than it does about the quality of the skills obtained. This information about the stamina and degree of socialization of the apprentice may be valued in the market. A recent study of the economic returns to the German apprenticeship program by Kenneth Couch (1993) suggests that they are low. The study by Dieter Haroff and Thomas Kane reveals that the rate of growth of earnings with work experience is the same for German and American youths. (The wage levels are different, of course.) The rate of growth of earnings with experience is often a reliable guide to the amount of human capital invested in workers. This evidence suggests that there is little difference in the amount of youth investment in human capital in the two societies, or that lower investment by American youth in formal training is compensated by better job matches resulting from higher levels of job shopping.

The very narrow technical training and rigid curriculum of the apprenticeship program may contribute to diminished options in later life. This observation goes part way toward explaining the current anomaly of low youth unemployment rates and higher adult unemployment rates found even in the former West Germany (see Schmidt, 1993).

Furthermore, the apprenticeship and schooling system in Germany has come under attack as rigid and unresponsive to developments in markets and to personal growth on the part of individuals. Students are tracked at an early age. There are many fewer second and third chance features in this system than are characteristic of schooling and training choices in the United States, a feature unlikely to be attractive in an American setting. Although some Realschuler become students at the universities, this occurs infrequently. It is often charged that minorities (especially natives of Turkey) are excluded from participation in the apprenticeship system because the informal nature of the workplace places a premium on personal ties as a basis for participating in work groups. Turkish participation rates among eligibles are only a third of ethnic German rates. These features of the German system would be unwelcome additions to the American workplace.

Lessons That Should Be Learned from the German Apprenticeship Program

Stripped to its essentials, the German apprenticeship system imparts some flexibility to an otherwise rigid labor market. The lesson to be learned from the German apprenticeship program is that reduced regulation of the employment relationship promotes employment. The German apprenticeship system provides relief from union-mandated minimum wage laws and regulations that make it difficult to terminate ordinary workers. It is no accident that those firms permitted to pay the lowest wages to apprentices (in the crafts sector) are more likely to train apprentices than firms in the industrial and commercial sectors, where the permitted reduction from the standard wage is not as great. Given that minimum wage laws in the United States prevent employers from training the low-skilled, an apprenticeship system would allow employers to circumvent the minimum wage laws and hire workers at a low wage, train them, and then give them higher wages later in their careers. Evidence presented by Cappelli (1993) indicates that when wage subsidies for youth were introduced in Britain, unemployment declined dramatically for youth in the subsidized age groups. During the period of the wage subsidy, the British youth unemployment rate was lower than the young adult rate, just as it is in Germany. Parenthetically, Cappelli's evidence should give pause to economists who argue that minimum wages have no disemployment effects on youth. Wage subsidies certainly produce employment effects.

The German apprenticeship system is also a device for permitting choice in schools in the sense that by selecting an occupation, a trainee also selects a school. He or she is thus able to shop around for better schools and better training, thus breaking the monopoly of public schools in Germany at the secondary level. This aspect of the German system could be useful in the U.S. market, where there is currently little choice among secondary schools, especially for children from lower-income households.

The Youth Labor Market in America

Comparing the United States and German labor markets, there can be no doubt that the latter is more orderly in the sense that a much smaller proportion of youth is not at work or not at school at age 17 in Germany than in the United States. This fact does not prove that the German system is the more efficient one. This is especially true in light of the fact that the compulsory schooling age is effectively 18 in Germany while it is 16 in most of the United States. In order to qualify for all but the most menial positions, German youth have to be in school or in an apprenticeship program two years later than most American youth are required to be in school. Most German youth are *required* to be "off the street" at the ages when many young Americans are making their transitions to full-time jobs.

Advocates of the CSAW report that has helped to produce the new consensus deny the value of the job shopping and job search that characterize the U.S. labor market. Joblessness and turnover are viewed as wasteful activities that are usefully curtailed. Yet a recent study documents the important role of job shopping in the career mobility of young male workers (over age 18) in the American labor market. During the first ten years of labor force attachment, a typical male worker holds seven jobs and achieves about one-third of his realized wage growth by changing jobs. (Career paths for young women have not been studied in similar detail.) Matching of workers to firms, which is characterized by the new consensus view as a time-intensive process that involves wasteful search and excessive turnover, is in fact a major source of productivity enhancement with important long-term economic and social consequences (Topel and Ward, 1992).

Such matching activity is productive because the worker skills utilized by firms are idiosyncratic. A bright person with an acerbic personality may not be suited for one firm but may be ideal for another. Diversity is an integral feature of the skills embodied in persons. Diversity of opportunities in firms is an essential feature of the American economy. Job shopping is a productive activity that reveals the suitability of worker-firm matches.

Finding a successful match is only the beginning of the investment process that characterizes most worker-firm relationships. There are match- or firm-specific investments that enhance productivity and are not portable elsewhere. The available evidence contradicts the technocratic view of youth job turnover as a wasteful activity. Job shopping promotes wage growth. Turnover is another form of investment not demonstrably less efficient than youth apprenticeships.

The concern about "inefficient" joblessness that is characteristic of recent proposals for youth apprenticeships also ignores some important features of the youth labor market summarized by Richard Freeman, David Wise, Martin Feldstein, David Ellwood, and Harry Holzer. First, most (83 percent) teenagers (men and women age 16–19) are either in school, working, or both. Most unemployed teenagers are either in school or seeking only part-time work. Only 6 percent of all teenagers are unemployed, out of school, and looking for full-time work. Most teenage unemployment spells are short. The bulk of teenage unemployment is experienced by a small group of teenagers with long spells of unemployment. These teenagers are concentrated in disadvantaged (minority, poor family background) groups with low levels of education. Unemployment and nonemployment problems are very acute for high school dropouts. They constitute, however, only a small portion of the total teenage population. Dead-end joblessness is a modal phenomenon for only a small minority of teenagers.

For youth as a whole, early employment experience has little effect on later employment chances controlling for age-invariant person-specific characteristics. Loss of work experience reduces wage growth, but such effects are transient in the life cycle. Even when teenagers hold dead-end jobs, most leave them by their early twenties. There appear to be few "permanent scars" (in the language of David Ellwood) from early "floundering" or job shopping during the teenage years. In the longer view, there is considerable evidence of wage growth resulting from job shopping.

None of this denies that there are disadvantaged groups that are not readily assimilated in labor markets. Special remedies such as apprenticeships and intensive job training programs may be appropriate for these groups. But in devising national strategies for revising education and training, it is important to keep in mind the broader picture of the youth labor market. "Churning" is a form of learning, and most youth who are in dead-end jobs work and search their way out of them. As noted below, this is true in both the U.S. and German labor markets.

Assessing the Impact of Turnover on Investment in Training by Firms

In the new consensus view, excessive job turnover characterizes the U.S. labor market, especially among younger workers. This excess turnover is said to lead firms to underinvest in both the general and firm-specific human capital of their workers by shortening the period over which they can realize the returns to such investment.

The standard economic theory of human capital investment (Becker, 1975) predicts that workers will bear the full costs of investments in general human capital. Such capital is by definition portable to other firms, so that workers can obtain the entire return to general training simply by switching jobs. Firms know this, and so will not finance investments in general human capital. In contrast, the theory predicts that the cost of investments in firm-specific human capital will be borne jointly by the firm and the worker, thereby providing both with an incentive to prolong the employment relationship so as to realize additional returns on these investments.

Little empirical evidence exists on the rules for sharing human capital investment costs that actually prevail in the labor market. If the theory is correct, turnover rates provide no information about the adequacy of investments in general human capital. Since workers bear the full cost (and receive the full returns to such investments), the level of investment in general human capital is unaffected by the expected tenure at particular firms and therefore unrelated to the rate of job turnover.

The actions of firms and workers in a competitive labor market jointly determine the level of firm-specific capital investment and the rate of job turnover. Though they claim that investment is too low and turnover is too high, Baily, Burtless, and Litan and advocates of the new consensus view provide no theoretical or empirical evidence as to why the levels resulting from market forces are not appropriate. To fully evaluate the suitability of the existing levels of investment and turnover would require estimates of the returns to job shopping, the returns to firm-specific human capital, and the responsiveness of investments in firm-specific human capital to changes in the rate of turnover. Such an analysis remains to be done.

The views advanced by the Brookings group combine and confuse efficiency arguments with equity arguments, although it would clarify the policy debate to separate these very distinct issues. Evidence that low-skilled workers receive low and declining real incomes does not bear on the issue of the efficiency of the existing levels of human capital investment in such workers. Concern over widening income inequality does not automatically imply that human capital investment is an efficient income transfer policy. Beliefs that low-skilled persons, their families and communities, and society at large are better served by having such individuals work — rather than receive welfare — do not necessarily justify human capital investment strategies for low-skilled workers.

There is an accumulating body of evidence that suggests that investments in low-skilled persons past a certain age — sometimes placed in the early twenties — have a very low return. Conditioning on measures of ability like the Armed Forces Qualifying Test administered in the late teens, scholars like Bill Johnson and Derek Neal (1994) find little evidence that additional years of schooling raise earnings. This evidence is consistent with the evidence summarized below that formal training programs for disadvantaged workers have little effect on the earnings of participants.

In thinking about policies to reduce income inequality, it is important to distinguish the question of the volume of resources to be transferred from the form the transfer should take. The evidence just reviewed suggests that skill investments may represent a very inefficient method for transferring resources to persons with low measured ability. Two important alternative methods for transferring resources to such persons are cash transfers and job subsidies. Neither alternative is perfect. Straight cash transfers have well-known, and well-documented, work disincentive effects. Job subsidies result in the creation of inefficient worker-firm matches, and, if funneled through employers, may have perverse distributional consequences. Nonetheless, transfers to low-ability persons through work subsidies may be the most politically palatable, and in the long run the most desirable, of the alternatives, given that they reward persons who demonstrate a willingness to conform to the work ethic of the larger society. Subsidized work may also promote the socialization of the poor, may lead to the accumulation of marketable skills, and may alter the preferences of subsidized workers so as to promote future work effort. (Heckman, 1981, presents some evidence supporting this position.)

Whether or not low-ability workers should receive resources from the rest of society is a separate question from whether or not they should receive more training. The universal complementarity of schooling and training emphasized by Mincer (1993) suggests that economically efficient investment strategies may entail more investment in the skilled and investment earlier in the life cycle. It has not been demonstrated by the Brookings group that investment in low-skilled workers is the efficient way to allay concerns over economic inequality.

The Economic Consequences of Using a Payroll Tax to Finance Training

Baily, Burtless, and Litan (1993) argue that "for reasons of their own, including shortsightedness, poor information, or inadequate access to credit, many workers do not invest enough in improving their own skills." They present no evidence on the empirical importance of these factors, but suggest that if workers are unwilling to invest in their own general human capital, firms should be induced to do so through a combination of tax policy and longer expected job tenure brought about by the introduction of an apprenticeship system. In particular, they advocate a payroll tax to finance training by firms. This idea is borrowed from France. Firms that spend less than a specified percentage of their payroll on training would be taxed, with the revenues devoted to a general training fund.

Except in certain extreme limiting cases, any tax has adverse consequences on employment and on the wages received by employees. If labor supply is perfectly inelastic (i.e., the number of workers is fixed), wages are simply reduced by the amount of the tax. If labor supply is perfectly elastic (e.g., the wages of workers are fixed), the tax reduces employment. The actual response of firms is an empirical matter and is not known with any precision. (see the evidence summarized in Hamermesh, 1993, p. 170). Either response worsens the labor market position of workers by reducing their wages or employment prospects.

For firms that already achieve the targeted level of worker training there are no adverse consequences. Indeed, employment might expand in such firms in response to the lower wages of workers in the market induced by the tax. For firms below the target level, the disemployment effects may be more severe than are predicted from the analysis of an ordinary payroll tax, because these firms are asked to spend resources in a certain way — by setting up a training program — which may or may not be an efficient use of their resources. Allowing firms the option to pay the tax instead of conducting training guarantees that the adverse disemployment and wage effects of the proposed training tax will be less than that of a general training tax because some firms will meet the target and be unaffected. Nonetheless, it is still expected that a training tax will have adverse employment and wage effects, although precise empirical magnitudes are not known.

Even if workers do underinvest in general training, blunt policy instruments like the payroll tax recommended by Baily, Burtless, and Litan might better be replaced by policies aimed more directly at providing information to workers and at overcoming financing constraints that impair the formation of human capital. Good policy requires good empirical foundations for the source of the policy problem. The Brookings group offers speculation in place of careful empirical analysis.

The Likely Ineffectiveness of a Testing System for Noncollege-Bound Youth

In addition to providing incentives for firms to invest in training their workers, the advocates of the new consensus recommend the implementation of a national credentialing scheme to provide incentives for workers to invest in their own training. A central tenet of the new consensus is that incentives within education can be restored by linking students' performance on tests to the quality of their job placements. The case for national testing and credentialing is based on the premise that tests measure job-relevant skills. The Brookings group strongly endorses this idea as well.

One test of general skill has recently been studied: the General Education Development test (GED). It is of interest in its own right because a major goal of many government job training programs is certification of participants as being equivalent to high school graduates through completion of the GED. The GED has become a major source of high school degrees in this country. One out of every seven new high school certificate holders achieves that status by a GED. In New York State and Florida the proportion is one out of four. High school completion levels, measured by the proportion of persons age 20–24 who have high school credentials or more, have not deteriorated in the last twenty years only because GED certification has been rising. Advocacy groups, in particular the American Council on Education which markets the GED, claim that it is easy to test for the job-relevant skills embodied in a high school diploma. Evidence on the earnings of GED recipients relative to high school dropouts indicates that a GED fails to provide information about the level of job-relevant skills of a worker. Except for a tiny upper tail, GED-certified high school equivalents earn roughly the same as high school dropouts. Controlling for their years of schooling completed, male GED certificate holders in their late twenties and early thirties earn the same as high school dropouts. For other groups of workers over the age range 20–60 there is little evidence that GED-certified workers earn the same wages or work the same hours as ordinary high school graduates (Cameron and Heckman, 1993).

These findings challenge both the wisdom of our current emphasis on GED certification and the folly of relying on tests of general skill to measure market-relevant skills. National tests that certify "skill" cannot capture the imagination, drive, or motivation of the person being tested, nor can they produce a score that will successfully rank its bearer in all firms in the economy, or even within a particular industry. Markets value, and humans possess, richer and more diverse skills and attributes than can be captured by standardized exams. While tests of general skill may have little value, tests of specific occupational skills may convey more information about the suitability of persons for particular tasks. They cannot, however, convey information about the motivation, personality, or fit of a person in a particular work environment.

Much occupational testing and credentialing already exists in the U.S. labor market. Currently, testing centers on skills that can be directly evaluated, such as typing or cutting hair. Other information sources, such as recommendations by coworkers and the reputation of the school or teacher providing training to a worker, formally or informally certify skills not readily measured.

Even if national skill certification were desirable, private firms could provide this information as least as well as public sector boards. It seems likely that private firms would also be more sensitive to changes in market demand for particular types of skills. If public goods problems prevent the generation of information about worker skills in the market, then general revenues could be used to subsidize private sector accreditation. Public goods are a class of goods and services that (a) cannot be withheld from one individual consumer without withholding them from all others, and (b) their consumption by one person does not reduce the amount available to other consumers. Public goods include national defense, lighthouses, clean air and television broadcasts that are not sponsored by advertisements. The inability of potential providers to exclude people who refuse to pay but who consume the good anyway means that many of the consumers of the good will act as free riders. Consequently, private production of such goods or services may prove unprofitable, and the good or service may not be provided at all by the free market, even if all consumers agree that they would be better off with some positive level of production of the good in question. This is known as a public goods problem. In the context of this paper, information that one firm generates about a worker that all firms can use is a public good.

One potential problem with a formal testing system for noncollege-bound youth is that teaching in vocational programs would quickly become directed toward performing well on a general standardized test rather than toward specific job-related skills needed in the current local labor market. It is unlikely that vocational tests can be changed quickly enough to keep up with the changing mix of skills needed in a vocation. "Teaching to the test" limits creativity and flexibility in a vocational training curriculum and may reduce its effectiveness. Tests also bias students toward investing in general skills measured by the test rather than investing in human capital that is relevant to their occupation.

Two untested implicit premises in the argument for credentialing are that individuals lack information about the skills needed to perform jobs and that the process of obtaining credentials provides such information. Information is scarce, and more information is preferred to less. But it has not been documented by advocates of skill standards that failure of students to know about the skills required in a particular occupation is a major cause of underinvestment in training.

Although the lack of incentives for firms to provide training to their workers is a major reason given in support of government intervention in the labor market, nationally recognizable measures of skill and vocational ability could further reduce existing incentives. In the presence of such certification, if a firm invests in training a worker in a specific skill, the worker can take a vocational test to certify the skills obtained and thereby become immediately marketable to other firms. As a result, the probability that the firm will lose its investment in the worker increases in the presence of such credentials and firms will become less willing to finance certifiable skills. Thus, a "successful" skill certification program could exacerbate the financing problem for skill acquisition.

Evidence on the Ineffectiveness of Public Training Programs

In addition to the policies already mentioned, a variety of public training programs have been proposed by advocates of the new consensus. Most are reworked versions of existing strategies already shown to be ineffective. In this section, we examine the evidence concerning the rate of return to government training. The evidence suggests that the 10 percent rate of return assumed in the calculations performed above is wildly optimistic.

THE SUMMER YOUTH EMPLOYMENT AND TRAINING PROGRAM

It has been proposed that the Summer Youth Employment and Training program under the Job Training Partnership Act be doubled in size. The stated purpose of this program is to preserve and upgrade the skills of low-income youth during the summers between school terms. The new twist on this program is that an "investment" argument has been given to support it. Barbara Heyns and her associates have argued that knowledge acquired in schools deteriorates through disuse during the summer (Heyns, 1987). The new proposals recognize this possibility and suggest that summer youth programs should be enhanced by learning enrichment activities. "Make work" has become an "investment" in the new vocabulary of Washington. Though the stated purpose of this program has been updated to reflect current fashions in educational theory, its activities and principles are similar to previous programs that have already been evaluated, and can therefore provide evidence on its likely rate of return. Predecessor programs like the Kennedy-Johnson Neighborhood Youth Corps were well known to be palliatives designed to keep inner-city youth off the streets. No firm evidence of any lasting effects of these programs on the employment, wages, or criminal or sexual behavior of their participants has ever been demonstrated.

What are the prospects for success of this program? An evaluation in 1992 of a similar effort, the Summer Training and Education Program (STEP), has been presented by Public/Private Ventures, a Philadelphia-based nonprofit corporation that evaluates and manages social policy initiatives aimed at helping disadvantaged youth. STEP offered two summers of employment, academic remediation, and a life skills program to low-achieving youth ages 14 and 15 from poor families. The objective of the program was to reach youth at the crucial ages at which they are deciding whether or not to drop out of school or become pregnant. Part-time summer work at the minimum wage was supplemented with remedial reading and math classes and courses on the long-term consequences of drug use, unprotected sex, and dropping out of school.

Using randomized trials, 4,800 youth in five cities were enrolled into or randomized out of the program. Both treatments and controls were followed for eight years. A high quality evaluation was conducted using state-of-the-art demonstration methods for three cohorts of participants. The findings from this evaluation are disappointing. STEP participants experienced measured short-term gains including increases of half a grade level in their math and reading competency test scores. These gains held up even after fifteen months, though gains in the second summer were less than those in the first. Especially large was short-term growth in knowledge of contraceptive methods.

This short-term promise did not translate into long-term gains. Three and a half years after the students' STEP experience, at the ages of 17 and 18, work rates and school completion rates were identical and low for those who had been in the program and those who had not. Some 22 percent of young women had children and 64 percent of these were receiving public assistance in some form (Walker and Viella-Velez, 1992).

Since STEP is, if anything, more intensive than the proposed summer youth programs, this evidence suggests that summer youth programs are not investments. There is no evidence that they have lasting effects on participants. They may protect the peace, prevent riots, and lower the summer crime rate, but there is no evidence of such effects.

EVIDENCE ABOUT CONVENTIONAL WORKFORCE TRAINING AND "WORKFARE" PROGRAMS

How effective are current programs in moving people from welfare to work and in increasing their employment and earnings? Our colleague, Robert LaLonde, addressed this question (LaLonde, 1992), and his evidence is summarized below along with our own evidence on the Job Training Partnership Act (JTPA).

Employment and training programs increase the earnings of adult female AFDC recipients. Earnings gains are modest, persistent over several years, arise from several different treatments, and are sometimes quite cost effective. Table 13.2 displays evaluation results for a variety of programs. For example, participation in an Arkansas job search program was required for AFDC recipients with children over age three. Participants attended a group job search club for two weeks and then were asked to search as individuals for an additional two months. A program in San Diego required all AFDC participants to take job search assistance and mandated work experience. The gains were high for participants in both programs. The National Supported Work program provided intensive training and job search assistance at a cost of about $16,550 per recipient. The estimated rate of return to this program was only 3.5 percent.

The results from the early 1990s experiment evaluating the Job Training Partnership Act (shown in Table 13.3) corroborate these findings. The largest impacts are for adult women, many of whom were collecting AFDC during their participation in JTPA. The impacts are not sufficiently large to move more than a tiny fraction of women out of poverty. As a general rule, conventional employment and training programs are often cost effective for adult women (especially if the opportunity cost of trainee time is ignored or is sufficiently low), but do not produce dramatic changes in participant earnings.

The evidence for adult men is consistent across programs. Returns are low but usually positive. Job search assistance is an effective strategy but produces only modest increases in mean earnings levels.

Evidence from the JTPA experiment indicates that this program produces only low or negative impacts on youth earnings. For male youth, the estimated negative effect is unbelievably strong. If taken seriously, participation in JTPA has a more negative impact on the earnings of male youth than participation in the Army, loss of work experience, or incarceration as measured by many studies.

Table 13.2. Experimental Estimates of the Impact of Employment and Training Programs on the Earnings of Female Welfare Applicants and Recipients

Services Tested/Demonstration	Net Cost Per Participant	Annual Earnings Gain (Loss)	
		After 1 Year	After 3 Years
Job Search Assistance:			
Arkansas	140	220**	410*
Louisville (WIN-I)	170	350**	530**
Cook County, IL	190	10	NA
Louisville (WIN-2)	280	560*	NA
Job Search Assistance and Training Services			
West Virginia	320	20	NA
Virginia Employment Services	520	90	330
San Diego I (EPP/EWEP)	770	600**	NA
San Diego II (SWIM)	1,120	430**	NA
Baltimore	1,160	190	630**
New Jersey	960	720*	
Maine	2,450	140	1,140
Work Experience and Retraining			
AFDC Homemaker-Health Care	11,550	460*	NA
National Supported Work	16,550	460**	810**

Note: All figures in the table are expressed in 1990 dollars.
*Significant at 10% level.
**Statistically significant at a 5% level.

Sources: Gueron and Pauly (1991), pp. 15–20; Bell et al. (1987), tables 3 and 4; Couch (1992), table 1.

Only the Job Corps has a demonstrated positive impact on earnings. It is an expensive program, costing around $20,000 per participant, with an estimated return of roughly 8–9 percent. There is same basis for supporting expansion of this program, but even here the evidence is weak. The primary existing evaluation of Job Corps is not experimental. A substantial portion of the high estimated return comes from the combination of a slightly lower rate of arrest for murder among Job Corp participants and a very large value imputed to human lives saved through reduced murder rates (see Donohue and Siegelman, 1994).

Table 13.3. Impacts on Total 18-Month Earnings and Employment: JTPA Assignees and Enrollees, by Target Group

	Adults		Out-of-School Youths	
Impact on:	Women	Men	Female	Male
Per assignee				
Earnings				
In $	$539aa	*$550*	$−182	$−854aa
As a %	7.2%	4.5%	−2.9%	−7.9%
Percentage employed	2.1%aa	2.3aa	2.8	1.5
Sample size (assignees *and* control group combined)	6,474	4,419	2,300	1,748
Per enrollee				
Earnings				
In $	$873	$935b	$−295b	$−1,355b
As a %	12.2%	6.8%	−4.6%	−11.6%
Percentage employed	3.5b	4.8b	4.5b	2.4b

Notes: At any time during the follow-up period.

b Tests of statistical significance were not performed for impacts per enrollee.

a Statistically significant at the .10 level, aa at the .05 level, aaa at the .01 level (two-tailed tat).

Source: Bloom, et al. (1993). Enrollee estimates obtained using the procedure in Bloom (1984).

WORKFARE AND LEARNFARE

How effective are the recent learnfare and workfare programs? An evaluation of two programs conducted in Wisconsin is of interest (see Pawasarat and Quinn, 1993). One program, the Community Work Experience Program (CWEP), required mandatory participation in unpaid community service jobs for nonexempt AFDC participants. A second program, Work Experience and Job Training, provided AFDC clients with assessment, job search activities, subsidized employment, job training, and community work experience. Participants who failed to find employment after completing their education and training were also required to participate in CWEP jobs.

Using randomized trials for one county and nonexperimental methods for the rest, researchers found *no effect* of these programs compared to existing program alternatives. The reduction in AFDC participation that is widely cited as a consequence of these programs is essentially due to the improvement in the Wisconsin economy during the time the programs were in place. These results are disappointing but consistent with previous studies of the efficacy of such programs by the Manpower Demonstration Research Corporation (Gueron and Pauly, 1991). Mandatory work experience programs produce little long-term gain. No cheap training solution has yet been found that can end the welfare problem. Lifting a female welfare recipient out of poverty by increasing her earnings by $5,000 per year ($100 per week) will cost at least $50,000. This is the scale of required investment. No quick-fix low-cost solution is in sight.

TRAINING PROGRAMS FOR DISPLACED WORKERS

As noted above, displacement of older workers with substantial experience in the labor market has become an increasingly important phenomenon in recent years. In response to this trend, Congress passed Title III of the Job Training Partnership Act in 1982 and the Economic Dislocation and Worker Adjustment Assistance Act in 1988.

Although studies evaluating these programs directly are not available as yet, evaluations of state-funded programs providing a similar mix of services have been conducted. Leigh (1990) summarizes the evidence on a variety of these programs. Results from some of these evaluations suggest small to moderate wages gains (8 percent for men and 34 percent for women) lasting about a year. A recent evaluation by Mathematica (see Corson et al., 1993) of training provided under the Trade Adjustment Assistance Act to workers displaced as a result of foreign trade finds no evidence of any effect of this long-term training program on the earnings and employment of recipients. Consistent with the other studies of government employment and training programs already discussed, the overall pattern for programs aimed at displaced workers is one of weak impacts for most groups.

Private Sector Training

Due to a lack of data and a bias in favor of funding studies of government training, the returns to private sector training are less well understood. Studies by Lynch (1992, 1993), Lillard and Tan (1986), Bishop (1994), and Bartel (1992) find sizable effects of private sector training. In comparison with studies of public sector training, most of these studies do not attempt to control for selection bias. The presence of selection bias would imply that if more able persons are more likely to take training, the estimated rates of return would overstate the true returns to training by combining them with the return to ability. Thus, part of the measured return may be due to more motivated and able persons taking training. Estimated initial returns range from 10 to 20 percent (Mincer, 1993), but they tend to decline after a few years as technical progress renders the training essentially obsolete. To the extent that rapid technical progress in many fields causes the knowledge obtained through training to lose its value after only a few years, fears about the detrimental effects of turnover in the labor market on the volume of human capital investment may be exaggerated.

An important feature of private sector training is that the more skilled do more investing even after they attain high skill levels. Different types of training and learning have strong complementarities with respect to each other. This universal complementarity of formal schooling and postschool investment is a key conclusion of Mincer's seminal study of postschool investment (1962). Even though the evidence is weak, the direction of the evidence is clear. To the extent that effective training can be produced on the job, it is produced in the private sector and not in the public sector. At the current state of knowledge, the only hope of getting reasonable returns from job training is to encourage private sector initiatives.

It is important to note, however, that private sector training typically excludes low-skilled persons. Firms can be exclusive in a way that government-training programs for disadvantaged workers are designed not to be. The lack of interest of private firms in training disadvantaged workers indicates the difficulty of the task and the likely low return to this activity. As previously noted, training is likely to be both an inefficient transfer policy and an inefficient investment policy for low-skilled workers.

The Conflict Between Economic Efficiency and the Work Ethic

To the extent that there are strong complementarities between different types of skill investments, there is a conflict between policies that seek to alleviate poverty by investing in low-skilled workers and policies that maximize the output of society. Taking the available evidence at face value, the best economically justified strategy for improving the incomes of the poor would be to invest more in the highly skilled, tax them, and then redistribute the tax revenues to the poor. However, many people view the work ethic as a basic value and would argue that cultivating a large class of transfer recipients would breed a culture of poverty and helplessness.

If value is placed on work as an act of individual dignity, and because of general benefits to families, communities, and society as a whole, then all individuals in society may be prepared to subsidize inefficient jobs. Job subsidies are not, however, the same as investment subsidies. The evidence points strongly to the inefficiency of subsidizing the human capital investments of low-skilled disadvantaged workers. Such investment may have some additional nonpecuniary returns. In this case, a purely economic evaluation of investment policies may be inappropriate. If, however, economically inefficient investments are to be made, the cost of reducing the skill gap grows beyond the already enormous sums presented in Table 13.1.

Alternative Policy Recommendations

The policies advocated by proponents of the new consensus target low skill levels as a fundamental problem in the current U.S. labor market. This section reviews these policy proposals in light of the evidence considered above, and suggests alternative policies with firmer theoretical and empirical foundations. In the long run, significant improvements in the skill levels of American workers, especially workers not attending college, is unlikely without substantial change and improvement in primary and secondary education. Mincer's (1993) evidence on universal complementarity demonstrates the value of early training in making subsequent training effective. Much of the current discussion about improving postsecondary education is misplaced when the value of early schooling is put in context.

Methods for improving primary and secondary education have received much attention in the general literature but very little attention by new consensus authors Baily, Burtless, and Litan (1993) or the Brookings scholars. Increasing the extent of consumer choice in the educational system would help to realign incentives in the right way to produce more effective schools. Choice among secondary training venues is an important aspect of the German apprenticeship system. It is odd that neither advocates of the new consensus nor the Brookings group consider the failure of government to provide adequate skills to students at the primary or secondary schooling levels as a major cause of the slowdown in labor force productivity growth.

The evidence in support of introducing a nationwide system of skill credentials based on formal tests is weak at best. New consensus advocates fail to address the problematic relationship between what tests can measure and what skills employers actually value. They ignore behavioral responses to the introduction of such tests in the form of incentives for vocational programs to "teach to the test" and incentives for workers to overinvest in the types of human capital captured on exams and to underinvest in other forms of job-relevant human capital. They fail to note that psychometrically based credentials may not arise in the market either because they are not needed or because alternative mechanisms for certifying workers are more effective.

Credentials developed or enforced by the government have a poor track record. As demonstrated by Cameron and Heckman (1993), the GED test of general skills fails miserably at its stated goal of certifying skills equivalent to those possessed by high school graduates. Other government credentials in the form of occupational certificates function in part as barriers to entry that reduce the supply of workers in the certified occupations, and limit opportunities to new entrants. Before taxing or threatening to tax firms into providing additional general training on the grounds that workers are unwilling or unable to purchase it for themselves, it is incumbent on advocates of new training policies to be more specific about the sources of market failure the policies are designed to correct. In particular, it should be demonstrated in a more rigorous way that credit market constraints or information costs prevent workers from undertaking valuable investments in general human capital. Policies aimed directly at empirically documented problems should result in fewer adverse consequences (and offer less scope for manipulation by interested parties) than imposition of another layer of taxation on every firm in the labor market.

In regard to the incentives facing firms to provide training to their workers, we note above that new consensus concerns about excess job turnover are likely to be overstated. This fact weakens the case for implementing an apprenticeship system designed to remove such turnover. To the extent that the German apprenticeship system does raise productivity, three aspects of that system have relevance to U.S. labor market policy. The first, which we previously noted, is that more choice among public schools may contribute to more productive investments. The second is that low apprentice wages stimulate employment and encourage firms to provide training. Similar results could be achieved in the United States by repealing the minimum wage laws, or by reducing the minimum wage level, thereby allowing firms to hire workers whose initial marginal product is worth less than the minimum wage but for whom training would be a worthwhile investment. Third, allowing greater flexibility to firms in discharging employees may make them more employable.

We note above that existing tax policy appears to favor human capital acquisition, but that this effect is strongest for high-income workers who already have substantial skills. Changes in the tax laws for firms and individuals designed to bring these incentives to bear at the low end of the skill distribution are worth much more consideration. Finally, support of cooperative activity among employers could allow firms within an industry to overcome free-rider problems by contracting to provide similar levels of industry-specific training or general training to their employees.

The evidence on government training programs suggests that they can make at best only a modest contribution to aggregate human capital formation. Evidence from existing evaluations suggests that such programs should be targeted primarily at adults, particularly adult women. The evidence further suggests a focus on job search assistance and wage subsidies as the strategies most likely to yield a small favorable return. Further research on more intensive training programs such as the Job Corps (the subject of a major experimental evaluation published in 2001) is required to reach a clear answer on whether or not they are worth the additional spending they require.

Finally, given the strong evidence of complementarity between schooling and training, it may be more efficient to focus training on high-skilled workers, and then use the tax system to transfer resources to the less skilled. If the goal is to raise their incomes, the extra surplus generated through more efficient investment can more than compensate low-skilled workers for the training they forgo. Investment may be more efficiently placed in the very young. Teaching children how to learn is likely to be a much more valuable activity than attempting to train unmotivated adults to learn new skills.

However, as noted earlier, work itself may have inherent social value that must be weighed against efficiency considerations. The appropriate form for the transfer is a separate issue. Job subsidies may be socially more desirable than welfare payments.

Conclusion

The American labor market has changed in recent decades with adverse consequences for low-skill workers. Our calculations reveal the enormous magnitude of the human capital investments required to restore 1979 wage differentials by skill groups in the 1989 labor market. In the current era of tight budgets, investments of this scale are unlikely at best.

Once we move beyond basic facts about the labor market, the evidence used to justify the proposed policies is weak. Policy advocates misread the lessons to be learned from the German apprenticeship program. A close look at how this program operates reveals that it builds flexibility in wages and employment into an otherwise inflexible German labor market. German apprentices turn over at a rapid rate and experience wage growth comparable to that experienced by American youth.

Informal training, job shopping and worker turnover among firms are viewed in the new consensus as pathologies, not as sources of productivity. Both new consensus advocates and the Brookings group place an emphasis on certifying certain easily-measured general skills rather than developing productive skills which contain an important hard-to-measure, firm-specific component. Certification exams are endorsed to foster and measure general skills at the expense of firm-specific skills.

Evidence on bias in government tax and expenditure policy toward education and training cited by the Brookings group is ambiguous at best. What is clear is that current tax policies encourage on-the-job training by higher income workers and by firms. New schemes designed to tax firms to pay for training will likely reduce employment and wages.

The evidence on the effectiveness of training programs reveals that publicly provided training is ineffective. Returns from private training programs are much greater. However, private training programs typically exclude disadvantaged workers because the private returns to their training are low. There is evidence that the highest payoff to training comes for highly educated workers. Economically efficient training strategies are likely to widen skill gaps, and not reduce them. There is a basic conflict between efficiency and the socially accepted value of the work ethic.

Rather than investing in high-skilled workers and then taxing them to pay for the consumption of low-skilled workers, many persons would favor redistribution through human capital investments because of the socializing value of work. This view — most strongly espoused by the Brookings group — confuses job subsidies with training subsidies. It may be inefficient to invest in low-skilled workers, but it may be socially useful to subsidize their employment. Given the universal complementarity among components of education and training, economically efficient programs would focus on early training and education at the primary and secondary schooling level rather than on postsecondary education and training as most of the recent discussion has done. In the short run, job subsidies may be the most palatable way to employ low-skilled workers. In the long run, investments in families and early childhood programs that boost skills for persons from disadvantaged families are likely to be much more economically efficient.

A broader portfolio of policies should be considered. Reducing the minimum wage, instituting choice in schools, creating tax subsidies for employing and/or training low-skill workers, and modifying the antitrust laws are alternative approaches to encouraging human capital formation that have received insufficient attention in current policy discussions.

Current discussions of human capital investment strategies ignore what cannot easily be measured and interpret productive turnover and job shopping as wasteful activities. This technocratic view favors a "planned" order in place of the "chaos" of market activities. It favors easily measured general skills over hard-to-measure, but productive specific skills. It ignores the perverse incentive effects of payroll taxes and national skill-certification exams. A richer, more factually informed view of how labor markets actually operate and how incentives affect choices is required before further intervention in labor markets is justified.

References

Baily, M., G. Burtless, and R. Litan, *Growth with Equity: Economic Policy Making for the Next Century,* Washington, D.C.: Brookings Institution, 1993.

Bartel, A., "Productivity Gains from the Implementation of Employee Training Programs," Cambridge, Mass.: NBER Working Paper no. 3893, 1992.

Becker, G., *Human Capital: A Theoretical and Empirical Analysis,* New York: NBER, 1975.

Bell, S., and C. Reesman, *AFDC Homemaker–Home Health Aide Demonstrations: Trainee Potential and Performance,* Washington, D.C., Abt Associates, 1987.

Bishop, J., "Formal Training and Its Impact on Productivity, Wages and Innovation," in Lisa Lynch, ed., *Training and the Private Sector: International Comparisons,* Chicago: University of Chicago Press, 1994.

Blank, R., "Employment Strategies: Public Policy to Increase the Work Force and Earnings," in S. Danziger, G. Sandfur, and D. Weinberg, eds., *Confronting Poverty: Prescription for Change,* Cambridge, Mass.: Harvard University Press, 1994, pp. 168–204.

Bloom, H., "Accounting for No Shows in Experimental Evaluation Designs," *Evaluation Review,* 8(2), 1984, pp. 225–246.

Bloom, H., L. On, G. Cave, S. Bell, and F. Doolittle, "The National JTPA Study: Title II-A Impacts on Earnings and Employment at 18 Months," Bethesda, Md.: Abt Associates, January 1993.

Burtless, G., "Meeting the Skill Demands of the New Economy," Washington, D.C.: Brookings Institution, 1993.

Cameron, S., and J. Heckman, "The Nonequivalence of High School Equivalents," *Journal of Labor Economics,* 11(1), January 1993, pp. 1–47.

——, "Determinants of Young Male's Schooling and Training Choices," in Lisa Lynch, ed., *Private Sector Skill Formation: International Comparisons,* Chicago: University of Chicago Press, 1994.

Cappelli, P., "British Lessons for School to Work Transition Policy in the U.S.," Philadelphia, Pennsylvania: National Center on the Educational Quality of the Workforce, no. WP19, 1993.

Commission on the Skills of the American Workforce (CSAW), "America's Choice: High Skill or Low Wages?" Rochester: National Center on Education and the Economy, 1990.

Corson, W., et al., *International Trade and Worker Dislocation: Evaluation of the Trade Adjustment Assistance Program,* Princeton, N.J.: Mathematica, 1993.

Couch, K., "New Evidence on the Effects of Employment Training Programs," *Journal of Labour Economics,* 10(4), October 1992, pp. 380–388.

——, "High School Vocational Education, Apprenticeship, and Earnings: A Comparison of Germany and the United States," *Applied Economics Quarterly Journal,* 1994.

Donohue, J., and P. Siegelman, "Is the United States at the Optimal Rate of Crime?" American Bar Foundation, Chicago, April 1994.

Feldstein, M. and D. Ellwood, "Teenage Unemployment: What Is the Problem?" in Richard Freeman and David Wise, eds., *The Youth Labor Market Problem: Its Nature, Causes and Consequences,* Chicago: University of Chicago Press, 1982.

Freeman, R., "Is Declining Unionization in the U.S. Good, Bad or Irrelevant?" in L. Mishel and P. Voos, eds., *Unions and Economic Competitiveness,* Armonk, N.Y.: M. E. Sharpe, 1992.

Freeman, R., and H. Holzer, *The Black Youth Employment Crisis,* Chicago: University of Chicago Press, 1986.

Freeman, R., and D. Wise, eds., *The Youth Labor Market Problem: Its Nature, Causes and Consequences,* Chicago: University of Chicago Press, 1982.

Gueron, J., and E. Pauly, *From Welfare to Work,* New York: Russell Sage Foundation, 1991.

Hamermesh, D., *Labor Demand,* Princeton, N.J.: Princeton University Press, 1993.

Hamilton, S., *Apprenticeship for Adulthood,* New York: Free Press, 1990.

Hansen, J., ed., *Preparing for the Workforce: Charting a Course for Federal Training Policy,* Washington, D.C.: National Academy Press, 1994.

Harhoff, D., and T. Kane, "Financing Apprenticeship Training: Evidence from Germany," National Bureau of Economic Research (NBER) Working Paper no. w4557, November 1993.

Heckman, J., "A Life Cycle model of Earnings, Learning and Consumption," *Journal of Political Economy,* August 1976, 84 (4) pp.SS11–44.

—— "Heterogeneity and State Dependence," in S. Rosen, ed., *Studies in Labor Markets,* Chicago: University of Chicago Press, 1981.

Heyns, B., "Schooling and Cognitive Development: Is There a Season for Learning?" *Child Development,* 58, 1987.

Jacobson, L., R. LaLonde, and D. Sullivan, "Earnings Losses of Displaced Workers," *American Economic Review,* 83(4), September 1993.

Johnson, W. and D. Neal, "The Role of Pre-Market Factors in Black-White Wage Differentials," unpublished paper, University of Chicago, April 1994.

LaLonde, R., "The Earnings Impact of U.S. Employment and Training Programs," unpublished manuscript, University of Chicago, January 29, 1992.

Leigh, D., *Does Training Work for Displaced Workers?* Kalamazoo, Mich.: W. B. Upjohn Institute for Employment Research, 1990.

Lillard, D., and H. Tan, *Private Sector Training: Who Gets It and What Are Its Effects?* Santa Monica, Calif.: Rand, March 1986.

Lynch, L., "Private-Sector Training and the Earnings of Young Workers," *American Economic Review,* 82(1), 1992.

McKinsey & Company, *Manufacturing Productivity,* Washington, D.C.: McKinsey Global Institute, 1993.

Mincer, J., "On the Job Training: Costs, Returns, and Some Implications," *Journal of Political Economy*, 70 (Suppl.), October 1962, pp. 50–79.

——, "Investment in U.S. Education and Training," Discussion Paper no. 671, Columbia University, New York, November 1993.

Mishel, L., and P. Voos, eds., *Unions and Economic Competitiveness*, Armonk, N.Y.: M. E. Sharpe, 1992.

Murphy, K., and F. Welch, "Industrial Change and the Rising Importance of Skill," in S. Danziger and P. Gottschalk, eds., *Uneven Tides: Rising Inequality in America*, New York: Russell Sage, 1992, pp. 101–132.

Osterman, P., "How Common Is Workplace Transformation and How Can We Explain It?" unpublished manuscript, Sloan School of Management, MIT, 1993.

Pawasarat, I., and L. Quinn, "Evaluation of the Wisconsin WEJT/CWEP Welfare Employment Programs," Milwaukee: Employment and Training Institute, University of Wisconsin, April 1993.

Piore, M., and C. Sabel, *The Second Industrial Divide*, New York: Basic Books, 1984.

Quigley, J. and E. Smolensky, "Improving Efficiency in the Tax Treatment of Training and Educational Expenditures," *Research in Labor Economics*, 11, 1990, pp. 77–95.

Reich, R., *The Work of Nations: Preparing Ourselves for Twenty-First-Century Capitalism*, New York: Knopf, 1991.

Schmidt, C., "Ageing and Unemployment," in P. Johnson and K. F. Zimmermann, eds., *Labour Markets in Ageing Europe*, Cambridge: Cambridge University Press, 1993.

Topel, R., and M. Ward, "Job Mobility and the Careers of Young Men," *Quarterly Journal of Economics*, 107, May 1992, pp. 439–480.

U.S. Bureau of the Census, *Statistical Abstract of the U.S.: 1992*, 112th edition, table 225, Washington, D.C.: U.S. Government Printing Office, 1992.

U.S. Department of Education, *Digest of Educational Statistics, 1993*, Washington, D.C.: U.S. Government Printing Office, 1993.

U.S. House of Representatives, Joint Committee on Taxation, *Description and Analysis at Tax Provisions Expiring in 1992*, Washington, D.C.: U.S. Government Printing Office, 1992.

Walker, G., and F. Viella-Velez, *Anatomy of a Demonstration*, Philadelphia: Public/Private Ventures, 1992.

Witte, J., and A. Kalleberg, "Matching Training and Jobs: The Fit Between Vocational Education and Employment in the German Labor Market," working paper, Carolina Population Center, January, 5, 1994.

14

The Growing Importance of Cognitive Skills in Wage Determination

RICHARD J. MURNANE, JOHN B. WILLETT,
AND FRANK LEVY

The past twenty years have witnessed a growing popular literature on transformation of U.S. industry. According to this literature, competitive pressures have forced rapid restructuring in manufacturing firms and, more recently, in service firms as well. The result is a rapid upgrading in occupational skill requirements, with important implications for the nation's schools (e.g., Marshall and Tucker, 1992). While this hypothesis has received enormous attention, there has been surprisingly little detailed empirical research supporting it.

The strongest evidence supporting the increased demand for skilled workers is the sharp rise since the late 1970s in the premium for increased schooling (Blackburn, Bloom, and Freeman, 1990; Katz and Murphy, 1992). A different kind of evidence is the twenty-year increase in wage dispersion *among* workers of a given age, education, gender, and race (Katz and Murphy, 1992). Some analysts have argued that this increase in within-group wage inequality reflects a rising price of dimensions of skill unobserved in the Current Population Survey data (Juhn, Murphy, and Pierce, 1989). To date, however, quantitative research has provided few clues about what skills might be in growing demand,[1] and the growth in within-group wage dispersion can be explained in many other ways (Levy and Murnane, 1992).

The evidence from case studies is equally ambiguous. Here, discussions of rising skill requirements usually involve "best practice firms." Employees in such firms rotate through a number of different jobs, are expected to exercise quality control, and suggest ways to solve problems and improve the production process. It is plausible that these employees exercise greater skill than employees in firms organized along Taylorist principles.[2] But estimates of the percentage of employers that have restructured work to take better advantage of employees' skills range from numbers too small to affect economy-wide wage patterns to numbers large enough to influence these patterns.[3]

In this chapter, we report a study that examines whether basic cognitive skills (as distinct from formal schooling) are becoming more important in wage determination on an economy-wide basis. We explore how mathematics skills of graduating high school seniors affect their wages at age 24.[4] We explore this relationship for two cohorts: for students who graduated from high school in 1972, and for students who graduated from high school in 1980. By examining how the mathematics score-wage relationship differs between the two cohorts, we can address two questions:

- Are basic cognitive skills becoming more important in determining wages on an economy-wide basis?
- How much of the increase in the college-high school wage premium during the 1980s stems from a widening of the skill gap between college graduates and high school graduates who did not go to college?

Data

We analyze data from two nationally representative databases that contain information on the labor market performance of students who graduated from high school in one of the last two decades. The *National Longitudinal Study of the High School Class of 1972* (NLS72) provides information on the labor market experiences of 22,652 students who were first surveyed in 1972, when they were seniors in high school. *High School and Beyond* (HS&B) provides information on the labor market experiences of 11,500 students first surveyed as high school seniors in 1980. Our analyses are based on men and women in the two data sets who had completed their formal education and were gainfully employed for pay six years after graduating from high school.

Table 14.1 provides estimates of sample means and standard deviations of the logarithm of hourly wages (in 1988 dollars) for males and females in the two data sets, grouped by highest educational attainment. To facilitate comparisons, the table also includes analogous data from the March CPS surveys of wages earned by 23- and 24-year-old males and females in 1978 and 1986. The average values of the log wage differ somewhat between our analysis

Table 14.1. Sample Means (and Standard Deviations) of the Natural Logarithm of Hourly Wage (in 1988 Dollars) Six Years After High School Graduation, by Highest Educational Attainment (Sample Weights Used in the Estimations)

	Males			
	NLS72	HS&B	CPS	CPS
Sample year to which wage pertains	1978	1986	1978	1986
Highest educational attainment				
High school graduate	2.25	2.07	2.14	1.85
	(0.38)	(0.43)	(0.45)	(0.48)
Some college	2.23	2.14	2.12	1.88
	(0.39)	(0.39)	(0.46)	(0.52)
Four-year college degree or more	2.22	2.21	2.16	2.08
	(0.38)	(0.39)	(0.48)	(0.55)
	Females			
	NLS72	HS&B	CPS	CPS
Sample year to which wage pertains	1978	1986	1978	1986
Highest educational attainment				
High school graduate	1.92	1.88	1.81	1.63
	(0.33)	(0.41)	(0.43)	(0.45)
Some college	2.02	1.97	1.87	1.79
	(0.35)	(0.33)	(0.45)	(0.44)
Four-year college degree or more	2.12	2.13	2.01	2.03
	(0.36)	(0.35)	(0.41)	(0.46)

Note: Since the year of high school graduation is not known for individuals included in the CPS samples, the CPS samples were drawn to include all 23- and 24-year-olds for whom a wage is recorded for the relevant year, 1978 or 1986.

samples and the CPS samples, in part because the wage questions in the surveys differ, but the wage patterns in our analysis samples generally reflect the now familiar patterns in CPS-based studies of earnings inequality.

For 24-year-old males whose highest educational attainment is high school graduation, the average wage was 16.5 percent lower in 1986 than in 1978.[5] For 24-year-old male college graduates, the average wage was only 1 percent lower in 1986 than in 1978. This pattern is consistent with CPS-based analyses showing that the college–high school wage gap for males widened during the 1980s, and that the increase stemmed primarily from a large decline in the real wages of male high school graduates (Levy and Murnane, 1992).

For 24-year-old females whose highest educational attainment is high school graduation, the average wage was 4 percent lower in 1986 than in 1978. For 24-year-old female college graduates, the average wage was 1 percent higher in 1986 than in 1978. This also fits the general pattern in CPS-based analyses, which show that women who did not go to college experienced less of a real wage decline than comparably educated men during the 1980s, but their wages lost ground relative to those of college-educated women.[6]

Table 14.1 also displays estimated standard deviations of the logarithm of wages for 24-year-old males and females in each data set, arrayed by highest educational attainment. For seniors who did not go past high school, the pattern follows that present in CPS data: within-group wage variance is larger in 1986 than in 1978. For both male and female college graduates in our analysis samples, there is little difference between the variation in wages six years after high school graduation for 1980 graduates and 1972 graduates. This is one respect in which our analysis samples differ from the CPS. While we have no explanation for this difference, we note that other researchers have reported differences between CPS samples and other nationally representative data sets in the distribution of wages (cf. Gottschalk and Moffitt, 1992).

With the single exception described above, the wage trends in the NLS72 and HS&B data sets follow closely the patterns present in CPS data. This suggests that relationships between measures of cognitive skills and wages in the NLS72 and HS&B data sets may help to explain patterns in CPS data that cannot be explored because the latter data lack direct measures of cognitive skills.

In their last year in high school, participants in the NLS72 and HS&B samples were administered tests of mathematics, reading, and vocabulary skills. Student responses on these tests were scaled by the Educational Testing Service using a three-parameter Item-Response Theory (IRT) model to ensure that scores on the same subject matter test could be compared across data sets. We chose the IRT-scaled mathematics score as our measure of cognitive skills because the results were consistently stronger than those using the other test scores.[7]

The mathematics test assessed students' skill in following directions, working with fractions and decimals, and interpreting line graphs. (Appendix 14.2 lists four of the items from the twenty-five-item test.) The test contained no items requiring knowledge of geometry or advanced algebra. Thus, the test measured mastery of elementary mathematical concepts, not knowledge of more advanced mathematics.

The average test scores for males and females grouped by educational attainment are displayed in Table 14.2 and show several interesting patterns. Score on the math test is a strong predictor of subsequent educational attain-

Table 14.2. Sample Means (and Standard Deviations) of the IRT-Scaled Mathematics Test Score, by Highest Educational Attainment (Sample Weights Used in the Estimations)

	Males		Females	
	NLS72	HS&B	NLS72	HS&B
Highest educational attainment				
High school graduate	10.48	9.87	9.82	8.93
	(6.45)	(6.58)	(6.31)	(5.75)
Some college	15.21	14.84	13.80	12.90
	(6.42)	(6.10)	(6.63)	(5.58)
Four-year college degree or more	18.94	19.67	17.79	17.19
	(5.39)	(4.89)	(5.52)	(5.44)
Full sample	13.94	13.28	13.09	12.10
	(7.12)	(7.21)	(7.02)	(6.46)

ment. For both males and females in the two data sets, the average math score for those who went on to graduate from college is almost twice that of those whose highest educational attainment was graduation from high school.

For both males and females, the average math score for the 1980 high school graduation cohort is lower than that for the 1972 cohort. This test score decline is frequently cited in critiques of U.S. schools, but sources of the decline are not well understood. Contributing factors appear to include the following. A decline over the 1970s in the proportion of students taking the academic curriculum as opposed to the general or vocational curriculum, a drop in the frequency with which students take traditional college preparation core courses, and a decrease in the amount of time spent doing homework.[8]

Finally, the decline over the 1970s in high school seniors' mathematics scores is concentrated among those who did not go on to graduate from college. Among females whose highest educational attainment was high school graduation, the average mathematics score for those graduating in 1980 is .89 points lower than the average score for those graduating in 1972. Among females who went on to graduate from college, the comparable difference is only two-thirds as large. For males, the pattern is even more striking. The average math score for 1980 male high school seniors who subsequently graduated from college is higher than the average score for the comparable group of 1972 male high school graduates. This pattern raises the possibility that a widening of the college–high school skill differential contributed to the widening of the college–high school wage gap during the 1980s. We address this question below.

Analyses

We replicated all of our analyses in four subsamples, treating men and women separately in the NLS72 and HS&B data sets. Each subsample, included information on the demographic characteristics and skill levels as of twelfth grade for each respondent, and longitudinal information on their post–high school educational attainment and work experience. We chose the natural logarithm of hourly wage six years after high school graduation (subsequently referred to as wage at age 24) because this is the only wage measure available for most participants in the HS&B survey.[9]

We were primarily interested in the impact of the direct measure of skill (the IRT-scaled mathematics score) on subsequent wages. We used Model B to estimate this impact. Model B controls for: (a) years of schooling completed as well as for race and ethnicity; (b) the respondent's attendance of high school in the South; (c) amounts of full-time and part-time labor force experience in the first six years after high school graduation; and (d) measurement of the dependent variable, wage, in a full-time or part-time job.[10] We also controlled for aspects of each respondent's family background, including the number of siblings, whether the family was headed by a single parent, and the highest grade each parent had completed.[11]

The regression coefficient associated with the direct skill measure provides an estimate of the impact of cognitive skills in explaining the variation in log wages among individuals with the same educational credentials and amount of labor force experience. For purposes of comparison, we also report the estimated coefficients of a conventional earnings model (Model A) that controls for years of completed schooling and family background variables, but does not include the mathematics score.

We considered the mathematics score and the number of years of completed schooling to be measured with error. As described in Appendix 14.3, we use conventional methods described by Fuller (1987) to deal with this problem.[12]

Results

Table 14.3 presents estimated regression coefficients and associated t-statistics for the fitted models in the two subsamples of males. Table 14.4 presents comparable estimates for the two subsamples of females.

FAMILY BACKGROUND AND CONTROL VARIABLES

The estimated relationships between family background predictors and log wages at age 24 are similar to patterns described in other research, although some relationships are weaker than those found in studies providing

Table 14.3. Estimated Coefficients (and t-statistics) from Models Relating Skill Measures to the Log of Hourly Wage Six Years After High School Graduation, for Males

| | NLS72 | | HS&B | |
	a	b	a	b
Education				
Years of completed schooling	0.022	0.013	0.044	0.021
	(3.63)	(1.85)	(5.72)	(2.22)
Mathematics score	—	0.004	—	0.011
	—	(3.13)	—	(5.06)
Family background				
Single parent household	−0.018	−0.017	−0.030	−0.031
	(−0.913)	(−0.882)	(−1.19)	(−1.25)
Number of siblings	−0.006	−0.006	−0.011	−0.010
	(−1.95)	(−1.97)	(−1.97)	(−1.84)
Mother's highest grade	−0.006	−0.007	0.006	0.004
completed	(−1.62)	(−1.81)	(1.10)	(0.777)
Father's highest grade	0.002	0.001	−0.008	−0.007
completed	(0.572)	(0.288)	(−1.50)	(−1.43)
Controls				
Went to high school in south	−0.071	−0.071	−0.045	−0.028
	(−5.49)	(−5.44)	(−2.22)	(−1.38)
Black	−0.066	−0.042	−0.116	−0.056
	(−2.97)	(−1.78)	(−4.48)	(−1.98)
Hispanic	−0.048	−0.031	0.015	0.062
	(−1.62)	(−1.02)	(0.640)	(2.46)
Years full-time work	0.045	0.043	0.022	0.020
experience	(8.08)	(7.68)	(2.89)	(2.63)
Years part-time work	−0.001	−0.002	0.017	0.015
experience	(−0.107)	(−0.218)	(1.55)	(1.37)
Wage is for part-time work	−0.067	−0.066	−0.032	−0.032
	(−1.84)	(−1.80)	(−0.572)	(−0.576)
Intercept	1.92	2.01	1.52	1.69
R^2	0.038	0.041	0.061	0.078
Number of observations	4114	4114	1980	1980

Table 14.4. Estimated Coefficients (and t-statistics) from Models Relating Skill Measures to the Log of Hourly Wage Six Years After High School Graduation, for Females

	NLS72		HS&B	
	a	b	a	b
Education				
Years of completed schooling	0.054	0.037	0.065	0.037
	(11.07)	(6.74)	(10.63)	(5.32)
Mathematics score	—	0.009	—	0.017
	—	(7.18)	—	(8.57)
Family background				
Single parent household	−0.017	−0.007	0.014	0.004
	(−1.07)	(−0.448)	(0.640)	(0.198)
Number of siblings	−0.002	0.002	−0.007	−0.007
	(−0.792)	(−0.744)	(−1.42)	(−1.55)
Mother's highest grade	0.008	0.006	0.015	0.014
completed	(2.47)	(1.86)	(3.20)	(2.97)
Father's highest grade	0.007	0.005	0.005	0.003
completed	(2.40)	(1.88)	(1.23)	(0.697)
Controls				
Went to high school in South	−0.041	−0.039	−0.094	−0.077
	(−3.47)	(−3.30)	(−5.51)	(−4.57)
Black	0.002	0.052	−0.025	0.057
	(0.086)	(2.67)	(−1.15)	(2.42)
Hispanic	0.008	0.045	0.047	0.105
	(0.291)	(1.57)	(2.26)	(4.91)
Years full-time work	0.026	0.023	0.049	0.042
experience	(5.25)	(4.57)	(7.44)	(6.57)
Years part-time work	−0.003	−0.005	0.022	0.013
experience	(−0.360)	(−0.579)	(2.66)	(1.60)
Wage is for part-time work	−0.041	−0.045	0.010	0.030
	(−2.26)	(−2.49)	(0.288)	(0.870)
Intercept	1.05	1.21	0.720	0.940
R^2	0.078	0.094	0.131	0.171
Number of observations	3925	3925	2163	2163

more detailed measures of family background. For example, family structure is not a statistically significant predictor of log-wages in our samples. However, our measure of family structure represents whether a student lived in a single-parent family as an adolescent, rather than the length of time spent in a single-parent family. Number of siblings is negatively related to subsequent wages, with the relationship stronger for males than females. Mother's and father's educational attainments are positively related to subsequent wages for females, but not for males.[13]

Controlling for family background and number of years of completed schooling (Model A), black males graduating from high school in 1972 had wages at age 24 that were approximately 6 percent lower than those of white males.[14] Among 1980 high school graduates with the same educational attainment, the comparable wage differential was 11 percent. Similar increases in the black-white wage gap for males during the 1980s are reported in studies based on the CPS (e.g., Bound and Freeman, 1992).

We do not find comparable wage gaps between black and white females with the same educational attainment, or between Hispanics and whites of either gender. In fact, controlling for educational attainment, Hispanic women graduating from high school in 1980 had a higher average wage at age 24 than their white female counterparts.

EDUCATIONAL ATTAINMENT

The estimated effects of educational attainment (years of completed schooling) on subsequent wages, as displayed in columns 1 and 3 of Tables 14.3 and 14.4, follow patterns that have become well known in recent years. The wage premium associated with postsecondary schooling was modest in the late 1970s, especially for men, but grew rapidly during the 1980s (cf. Blackburn, Bloom, and Freeman, 1990; Katz and Murphy, 1992).

Our estimate is that, among males graduating from high school in 1972, each year of completed college was associated with a wage premium in 1978 (at age 24) of 2.2 percent above the wage earned by high school graduates with no postsecondary education. For males graduating from high school in 1980, the corresponding wage premium in 1986 is 4.5 percent. Analogous wage premiums for 24-year-old women are 5.5 percent in 1978 and 6.7 percent in 1986.[15] Estimates of the college–high school wage differential computed from our results are lower than the premiums of 35–45 percent reported in other studies (cf. Levy and Murnane, 1992). The reason is that college graduates in our data sets had less than two years to complete on-the-job training and to move through the relatively steep experience-earnings profile of highly educated workers.[16]

The coefficient of years of schooling in Model A is a biased estimate of the wage increase, at age 24, that an individual could expect from going to college. The main reason for this is it does not take into account that high school graduates who go to college are more academically able, on average, than those who do not. The magnitude of the bias can be estimated by comparing the size of the coefficient of educational attainment in Model A with that in Model B, which contains the math score. Adding the math score to the model results in a decline of 41 percent in the coefficient of educational attainment for 1972 male high school graduates and a 52 percent decline for 1980 male high school graduates. The comparable figures for female graduates are 31 percent and 43 percent, respectively.

A striking aspect of our findings is that including the math score in the model completely eliminates the increase between 1978 and 1986 in the wage premium from college attendance for females and reduces its magnitude for males from 100 percent to 62 percent. In other words, for females, all of the increase in the return to college attendance is explained by the increase in return to cognitive skills. It is to this increase that we now turn.

MASTERY OF BASIC COGNITIVE SKILLS AND WAGE DETERMINATION

The test score measuring mastery of basic mathematics is more important in predicting subsequent wages among 1980 high school graduates with the same educational attainment than among 1972 graduates with the same attainment. The evidence comes from comparing the sizes of coefficients of mathematics score for the models displayed in columns 2 and 4 of Tables 14.3 and 14.4. For males, the coefficient of the mathematics score for the cohort graduating from high school in 1980 (.011) is almost three times as large as the comparable coefficient for the cohort graduating in 1972 (.004). For females, the coefficient of the math score for the later cohort (.017) is almost twice as large as the comparable coefficient for the earlier cohort (.009).[17]

To provide a sense of the impact on wages of differences in math scores, we used the coefficients in Model B for each sample to predict wages at age 24 (in 1988 dollars) for high school graduates with no postsecondary education who differed in their scores on the mathematics test. In each case, we set family background characteristics to the average values in each sample. Figure 14.1 pertains to males; Figure 14.2 to females. The end points of the line segments in each figure represent the predicted wage associated with a mathematics score of 6.25 points (the arithmetic average of the standard deviations of the math score in the four samples) above or below the mean.[18] In each figure the steeper slope of the line segment pertaining to 1980 high school graduates

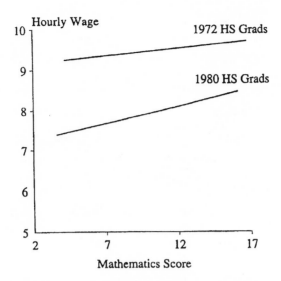

Figure 14.1 Fitted Relationship Between Hourly Wage at Age 24 (in 1988 dollars) and Mathematics Score for Males, by Year of High School Graduation

illustrates the central message of our chapter: basic cognitive skills were more important determinants of wage at age 24 for 1980 high school graduates than for 1972 graduates.

For males graduating from high school in 1972, a 6.25 point difference in the mathematics score is associated with a predicted wage differential six years later of $0.24 per hour (in 1988 dollars), a very modest impact. For males graduating in 1980, the same test score differential is associated with a larger wage differential six years later, $0.57 per hour. The same pattern is present for females, with the 6.25-point test score differential corresponding to a predicted wage differential of $0.39 per hour for 1972 high school graduates and $0.74 per hour for 1980 graduates.[19]

How important is increase in the role of basic cognitive skills in determining wages? The question matters politically because it bears on the debate about the relative importance of changes in schools and changes in firms in restoring real wages to their earlier levels. As illustrated in Figure 14.1, males who graduated from high school in 1980 with *strong* basic math skills (6.25 points or approximately one standard deviation above the mean) have a lower predicted real hourly wage at age 24 ($8.49) than that ($9.25) of 1972 high school graduates with *weak* math skills (6.25 points below the mean). Thus,

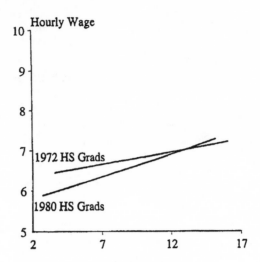

Figure 14.2 Fitted Relationship Between Hourly
Wage at Age 24 (in 1988 dollars) and Mathematics
Score for Females, by Year of High School
Graduation

helping a male graduating from high school in 1980 to improve his math skills
would contribute only modestly to the goal of increasing his wage level at age
24 to the level enjoyed by males graduating eight years earlier. It is possible
that other skills students learn in school or at home have grown in importance
in the labor market more than have basic math skills, but such skills have not
yet been identified.

At the same time, Figure 14.1 also illustrates that 1980 high school seniors
who lack basic math skills are at a greater disadvantage in the labor market
relative to their peers than was the case for 1972 seniors weak in basic math. In
fact, the predicted hourly wage ($7.40) for males entering the labor market
directly after graduating from high school in 1980 with weak math skills
corresponds to annual full-time (1,750 hours) earnings of $12,950, which is
just above the 1988 poverty line for a family of three.[20] As a comparison of
Figure 14.1 and Figure 14.2 illustrates, basic mathematical skills are more
important predictors of wages at age 24 for 1980 female high school graduates
than for male graduates. Thus, helping all students to acquire mastery of basic
cognitive skills is an important national goal.

One question readers may ask concerns how robust are the results relative
to alternative model specifications. We explored this question in some detail as
described in Appendix 14.4. As this appendix demonstrates, the bottom line
of our study—that basic cognitive skills play a stronger role in predicting

wages in the mid-1980s than in the late 1970s — is not sensitive to how we specified our statistical models.

CHANGING OCCUPATIONAL CONTENT OR OCCUPATIONAL SHIFTS

One potential explanation for the increase in importance of skills in determining wages is a decline between 1978 and 1986 in the percentage of young workers employed in occupations, such as machine operators, that paid relatively high wages but did not require mastery of basic math skills. To investigate the importance of such compositional effects, we reestimated Model B for each of our four samples, including a series of dummy variables for two-digit occupations. For males, inclusion of ten occupational indicators reduced the coefficient on the math score by less than 10 percent for both the 1978 and the 1986 samples of 24-year-olds. And, the estimated impact of the math score on wages in 1986 remained more than twice as large as the impact on wages in 1978. For women, inclusion of the occupational indicators reduced the coefficient on the mathematics score by less than 20 percent in the two samples, and the coefficient pattern was not affected. This suggests that increase in the importance of cognitive skills in wage determination primarily reflects increases in demand for skills within occupational groups rather than compositional effects.

GROWING SKILL GAPS AS AN EXPLANATION
FOR GROWING WAGE GAPS

As shown in Table 14.2, the average math score differential between high school seniors who subsequently graduated from college and those who did not go to college was larger for the 1980 high school graduation cohort than for the 1972 cohort — a supply-side phenomenon. Above, we noted that this increase in the college–high school skill gap could contribute to the increase in the college–high school wage gap. To test the quantitative importance of this supply side change, we estimated the college–high school skill differential in each sample, net of family background effects, and used the results to calculate the predicted increase between 1972 and 1980 in the college–high school skills differential. For males, the increase was 1.15 points; for females, 0.28 points. Then, for each gender, we multiplied the increase in the skill differential by the estimated total impact of a one-point difference in a 1980 high school senior's math score on the natural logarithm of wages six years later (.013 for males, and .022 for females).[21] The predicted increase in the college–high school wage gap stemming from the increase in the college–high school skills gap is .015 for males and .006 for females. Both of these are less than 18 percent of the increase in college-high school wage differentials reported above (.088 for

Table 14.5. Coefficients on Mathematics Score and Years of Completed Schooling from Versions of Model b with Different Predictor Reliability Specifications

Sample	Assumed Reliability of		Estimated Coefficients		Two-Way Interaction of Score and Schooling
	Math Score	Years of Completed Schooling	Math Score	Years of Completed Schooling	
1. NLS72 Males	0.87	0.89	.0041[a]	.0131[a]	
HS & B Males	0.86	0.89	.0110[a]	.0205[a]	
NLS72 Females	0.85	0.92	.0089[a]	.0372[a]	
HS & B Females	0.83	0.92	.0173[a]	.0370[a]	
2. NLS72 Males	0.92	0.89	.0038[a]	.0139[a]	
HS & B Males	0.91	0.89	.0098[a]	.0230[a]	
NLS72 Females	0.90	0.92	.0081[a]	.0388[a]	
HS & B Females	0.88	0.92	.0156[a]	.0398[a]	
3. NLS72 Males	1.0	1.0	.0035[a]	.0114[a]	
HS & B Males	1.0	1.0	.0087[a]	.0214[a]	
NLS72 Females	1.0	1.0	.0073[a]	.0346[a]	
HS & B Females	1.0	1.0	.0131[a]	.0388[a]	
4. NLS72 Males	0.87	0.89	−.0167	−.0142	.0016
HS & B Males	0.86	0.89	−.0342	−.0306	.0034[a]
NLS72 Females	0.85	0.92	−.0122	.0130	.0016[a]
HS & B Females	0.83	0.92	.0312[a]	.0495[a]	−.0010

5. Predicted impact on ln (wage) of a one point
   difference in IRT Math Score for a high
   school graduate who did not go to college,
   calculated from coefficients in model including
   the two-way math score by schooling interaction

NLS72 Males	.0025
HS and B Males	.0066
NLS72 Females	.0070
HS and B Females	.0192

[a] Significant at the 0.05 level in a two-tailed test

men, .044 for women).[22] These results support Katz and Murphy's (1992) conclusion that most of the increase in the college–high school wage differential stemmed from an increase in the demand for skills.

SKILLS, WAGE DETERMINATION, AND THE INCENTIVES TO LEARN

At first glance, the growing importance of skills in wage determination should increase the incentive for high school students to take the demanding courses that increase cognitive skills. A counterargument comes from the work of Bishop (1989a) and Rosenbaum and Kariya (1991) who argue that there is too little contact between U.S. employers and U.S. high schools. As a result, employers who hire high school graduates cannot judge their ability at entry and so student skills are not initially rewarded.[23] To test this counterargument in our data, we reestimated Model B with the logarithm of wage two years after high school, as the dependent variable. The estimated coefficients on math score for the different samples are displayed in row 3 of Table 14.5. To facilitate comparison, row 2 of Table 14.5 provides the analogous coefficients for identical subsamples, using the logarithm of wage six years after high school graduation as the dependent variable.[24] All coefficients in Table 14.5 were estimated using samples of high school graduates who did not go to college.

The results show that the timing of the wage measure matters. For males graduating from high school in either 1972 or 1980, the mathematics score is not positively related to wage two years later (row 3). It is, however, positively related to wage six years later, with the relationship stronger for 1980 graduates than for 1972 graduates.[25] For females, high school math score is positively related to wage two years later and to wage six years later. Among females graduating from high school in 1980, the math score is a much stronger predictor of wage six years after high school graduation than of wage two years after graduation.[26]

Summary

On an economy-wide basis, basic cognitive skills were more important predictors of wage six years after high school in the mid-1980s than in the late 1970s. This phenomenon is rooted in demand shifts and reflects primarily changes within occupational groups. It applies to persons of all educational levels, showing that a rising demand for basic skills is part of the explanation for the 30 percent increase since 1970 in within-group wage variation.[27] Our results indicate that the increased role of cognitive skills is not limited to a small set of best-practice firms, but is general enough to appear clearly in national random samples.

We emphasize that our findings concern the demand for *basic* cognitive skills, including the ability to follow directions, manipulate fractions and decimals, and interpret line groups. The mathematics test contains no items requiring knowledge of geometry or advanced algebra. Thus a high school senior's mastery of skills taught in American schools *no later than the eighth grade* is an increasingly important determinant of subsequent wages. This finding is surprising until one notes that only about half of the nation's high school seniors have mastered computation with decimals, fractions, and percents and recognize geometric figures (Mullis et al., 1991).

The restructuring literature usually ends in a call for better schooling. One would hope that the increased payoff to cognitive skills would lead to this call coming from students as well as policy experts. But as we have shown, the disjuncture between U.S. employers and U.S. schools undermines the incentive that might have arisen. The resulting market failure makes the necessary job of educational reform that much harder.

Appendix 14.1. Weighted and Unweighted Means and Standard Deviations[a] for Variables Used in Regression

	Males				Females			
	NLS72		HS&B		NLS72		HS&B	
	Wtd.	Unwtd.	Wtd.	Unwtd.	Wtd.	Unwtd.	Wtd.	Unwtd.
Log of wage six years after high school graduation	2.24	2.23	2.12	2.10	2.00	1.99	1.97	1.96
	(0.38)	(0.39)	(0.41)	(0.42)	(0.35)	(0.35)	(0.38)	(0.39)
Number of years of completed schooling	13.45	13.37	13.53	13.56	13.50	13.43	13.71	13.75
	(1.72)	(1.70)	(1.75)	(1.73)	(1.73)	(1.72)	(1.78)	(1.74)
Mathematics score	13.94	13.32	13.28	12.06	13.09	12.47	12.10	11.18
	(7.12)	(7.27)	(7.21)	(7.68)	(7.02)	(7.15)	(6.46)	(6.78)
Family background single-parent household	0.19	0.20	0.17	0.22	0.20	0.22	0.17	0.23
Number of siblings	3.04	3.16	2.99	3.17	3.09	3.19	2.85	3.09
	(2.14)	(2.21)	(1.67)	(1.76)	(2.11)	(2.21)	(1.67)	(1.76)
Mother's highest grade completed	12.27	12.20	12.73	12.47	12.33	12.23	12.68	12.40
	(1.97)	(2.00)	(2.09)	(2.10)	(2.07)	(2.08)	(2.09)	(2.10)
Father's highest grade completed	12.46	12.39	13.03	12.71	12.55	12.48	13.03	12.64
	(2.33)	(2.39)	(2.66)	(2.56)	(2.42)	(2.46)	(2.59)	(2.51)
Controls								
Went to high school in south	0.28	0.35	0.31	0.39	0.30	0.37	0.29	0.38
Black	0.06	0.10	0.09	0.22	0.09	0.13	0.09	0.22
Hispanic	0.03	0.04	0.09	0.25	0.03	0.04	0.07	0.22
Years full-time work experience	2.54	2.57	3.11	2.97	2.23	2.24	2.67	2.54
	(1.60)	(1.60)	(1.48)	(1.48)	(1.49)	(1.49)	(1.51)	(1.51)
Years part-time work experience	0.32	0.32	0.50	0.55	0.47	0.47	0.87	0.87
	(0.58)	(0.56)	(0.98)	(1.03)	(0.69)	(0.68)	(1.19)	(1.19)
Wage is for part-time work	0.03	0.03	0.03	0.03	0.11	0.11	0.06	0.06
Number of observations	4,114	4,114	1,980	1,980	3,925	3,925	2,163	2,163

[a] Standard deviations are not reported for dichotomous variables.

Appendix 14.2. Questions from Mathematics Exam Administered to Samples of American High School Seniors in 1972 and 1980

Directions: Each problem in this section consists of two quantities, one placed in Column A and one in Column B. You are to compare the two quantities and circle the letter

A   if the quantity in Column A is greater;
B   if the quantity in Column B is greater;
C   if the two quantities are equal;
D   if the size relationship cannot be determined
from the information given.

	Column A	Column B	
1.	Length represented by 3 inches on a scale of 4 feet to an inch	A length of 12 feet	A B C D

2.

$$\frac{1}{P} = \frac{4}{3}$$

$$\frac{1}{Q} = \frac{3}{4}$$

	P	Q	A B C D
3.	Cost per apple at a rate of $2.00 per dozen apples	Cost per apple at a rate of 3 apples for $0.50	A B C D
4.	245	$2(10)^3 + 4(10)^2 + 5(10)$	A B C D

Appendix 14.3

As is well known, measurement error in an explanatory variable tends to produce negative bias in the OLS parameter estimate associated with it, and due to predictor-predictor correlation, either a positive or negative bias in parameters associated with other predictors. For this reason, all regression models were fitted using the maximum likelihood methods of Fuller (1987) to correct our parameter estimates and goodness-of-fit statistics for the fallibility of these predictors. Conceptually, the Fuller correction procedure uses an estimate of a predictor's reliability to disattenuate the observed variance of the fallible predictor by removing measurement error variance from the appropriate diagonal element of the predictor-predictor covariance matrix prior to parameter estimation. The method has been well described in the literature, and has been implemented in commercially available computer software (Fuller, 1988).

We obtained an estimate of the reliability of the mathematics score for each sample from an Educational Testing Service publication.[28] For the male and female NLS72 samples, we estimated the reliability of the self-reported number of years of completed schooling using a method described in Kane and Rouse (1993). The estimated reliabilities for the schooling measure (.89 for men, .92 for women) are close to the value of .915 used by Bishop (1989b). We assumed that the reliabilities estimated from the NLS72 samples also pertained to the self-reported number of years of schooling for our HS&B samples.[29]

Appendix 14.4

While we believe that the coefficients on the math score reported in the previous section represent our best estimates, there are other plausible specifications of Model B. The first three sections of Table 14.5 list coefficients on the math score and the number of years of completed schooling obtained by estimating Model B with alternative values for the reliability of these key predictors. Section 1 repeats the estimates from Tables 14.3 and 14.4.[30] Section 2 presents estimates of the critical coefficients under the assumption that the reliability of the math score for each sample is five percentage points higher than the reliability reported in Rock (1985b). The logic for exploring the higher reliabilities is that the test scores for which reliability estimates are available (the formula scores) are not perfect linear transformations of the IRT scores used in our analyses. It is possible that the reliabilities of the IRT scores are slightly higher than those of the formula scores. To facilitate comparisons with studies that assume that all predictors are measured without error, section 3 of Table 14.5 presents coefficients estimated under the assumption of perfect reliability for the math score and years of completed schooling for all four samples.

As expected, increasing the assumed value of the reliability of the math score reduces somewhat the size of the coefficient associated with this variable. However, the basic message of the chapter, that the relationship between the math score and subsequent wages is stronger for 1980 high school graduates than for 1972 graduates, remains.

One other specification issue involves a potential interaction between the mathematics score and years of completed schooling. Blackburn and Neumark (1993) report that cognitive skills have a larger impact on subsequent earnings for males who complete college than for males who enter the workforce directly after high school graduation. We estimated models that included a two-way interaction between the mathematics score and the number of years of completed schooling under the assumption that both variables and their interaction are measured with error.

Consistent with Blackburn and Neumark, we find for men a positive interaction between skills and educational attainment in HS&B (i.e., the 1980s). The interaction is not present for men in NLS72 (the 1970s). By themselves, these results suggest that the economy changed in ways that made cognitive skills particularly

Table 14.6. Estimated Regression Coefficients, t-statistics, and Sample Size Associated with the Prediction of the Log of Hourly Wage by IRT-scaled Mathematics Score (Controlling for Family Background, Race, Ethnicity, and Work Experience) in Several Subsamples of High School Graduates Who Did Not Go to College

Subsample	Dependent Variable	Effect of Math Score on log-wage for Males who Graduated from High School in		Effect of Math Score on log-wage for Females who Graduated from High School in	
		1972	1980	1972	1980
All respondents with a wage value of the 6th year after high school graduation	Log-wage 6 years after high school graduation	0.004 (2.18) N = 1989	0.007 (2.37) N = 923	0.008 (5.05) N = 1818	0.019 (6.46) N = 868
All respondents with a wage value in both the 2nd and 6th year after high school graduation	Log-wage 6 years after high school graduation	0.003 (1.25) N = 1192	0.006 (1.52) N = 493	0.008 (3.90) N = 1006	0.019 (5.17) N = 455
All respondents with a wage value in both the 2nd and 6th year after high school graduation	Log-wage 2 years after high school graduation	−0.000 (−0.02) N = 1192	−0.004 (−1.20) N = 493	0.008 (4.13) N = 1006	0.009 (2.79) N = 455

important for college graduates. This conclusion is called into question, however, by the pattern for women: a positive interaction between skills and educational attainment in the 1970s, but no such interaction in the 1980s. There are a number of potential explanations for these opposing results. But the basic message is that the skills-education interaction must be interpreted with caution.[31]

To examine whether the fitted models that included the interaction term show a growing role for skills in predicting wages, we used these coefficients to estimate the impact of a one-point difference in math score on the natural logarithm of wage for high school graduates who did not go to college (years of completed schooling = 12). The estimates are presented in the last section of Table 14.5. The predicted impacts of skill differences on log wages calculated from the model with the skill-schooling interaction are smaller than the predicted impacts from the main effects model, especially for men. However, the estimates support the theme of the paper: skills are stronger determinants of subsequent wages for 1980 high school graduates than for 1972 graduates.

Notes

This chapter is a revised version of an article with the same title that appeared in *Review of Economics and Statistics* (May 1995).

1. Krueger (1993) reports a slight increase between 1984 and 1989 in the return to computer usage. Rivera-Batiz (1992) and Bishop (1989a, b) provide evidence about the importance of particular skills in explaining labor force outcomes *at one point in time*.

2. In explaining the sources of effective performance in best-practice firms, analysts differ in their judgments about the relative importance of hiring workers with relatively high skill levels and investing in training to develop workers' skills on the job. Compare, for example, Brown, Reich, and Stern (1992) and Packer and Johnston (1987).

3. Marshall and Tucker (1992, p. 64) report an estimate of less than 5 percent. Osterman (1994) reports an estimate of 35 percent, based on a survey of private sector establishments with fifty or more employees he conducted in 1992.

4. To be precise, wages are measured six years after high school graduation, a time when most, but not all, students are 23 or 24 years of age. For ease of exposition, we assume that all members of the four samples are aged 24 when their wages were measured.

5. Because of the nonlinear nature of the log transformation, we are referring to differences in the geometric mean, rather than the arithmetic mean. The 16.5 percent decline in the geometric average wage of male high school graduates was calculated as $(e^{-.18} - 1)$.

6. See, for example, Mishel and Bernstein (1992).

7. As reported in Rock et al. (1985a, p. 13), 18 of the 25 items on the mathematics test were either identical (12) or had minor editorial or format changes (6) between the 1972 and 1980 test administrations. See Rock et al. (1985b) for a description of the application of item-response theory that produced fully equatable scores for the 1972 and 1980 high school seniors. We would like to thank Donald Rock of the Educational Testing Service for making the IRT-based test scores available to us.

In note 19, we report the results of estimating models in which the vocabulary and reading scores were used as skill measures, both individually and along with the math score.

8. See Rock et al. (1985a) for a discussion of reasons for the test score decline. In a later publication, Koretz (1987) documented that the test score decline ended with the cohort of children born in 1962. The evidence for the cohort effect is that the approximate timing of the end of the decline was 1971 for 9-year-olds, 1975 for 13-year-olds, and 1979 for 17-year-olds.

9. The wage used in our analyses is the usual hourly wage in the primary job held at

the time the survey was conducted or, for individuals not working at the time of the survey, the hourly wage on the most recently held job (as long as it was held within the previous year). The survey questions ask for the current salary (before deductions) and for the time period (e.g., hour, week, month, year) to which the salary pertains. We then calculated the hourly wage to be the salary divided by the usual number of hours in the pay period.

10. We defined a part-time job as one in which the respondent worked fewer than thirty hours per week. The number of years of full-time work experience since high school graduation was calculated by dividing by twelve the number of months between high school graduation and the date of the survey six years later in which an individual worked for at least thirty hours per week for at least one week. An analogous method was used in calculating the number of years of part-time experience. As indicated in Appendix 14.1, the average values for these experience variables are quite low, especially since the variable includes work experience prior to postsecondary school completion. Part of the explanation is that many members of our samples had little recorded work experience while in college. Another part may be that some members of the sample did not answer correctly the complicated survey questions dealing with work experience.

11. We used the method described by Cohen and Cohen (1983) to resolve the problem of missing values. Under this strategy, missing values for a particular variable are replaced by a constant arbitrary value, and an additional dichotomous variable is included to distinguish, and hold separate, the replacement values.

12. The sampling designs for both the NLS72 and HS&B data sets result in overrepresentation of Black and Hispanic youth. To preserve the homoscedastic property of the error terms, we weighted all observations equally in fitting our models. However, we did test whether interactions between race/ethnicity and the measures of educational attainment and skill were predictors of the dependent variable and found that they were not. To illustrate the extent to which the sampling design influences the distribution of the variables used in the regressions, Appendix 14.1 presents sample means and (for nondichotomous variables) standard deviations for all variables used in the analysis, calculated both using the sampling weights, and weighting each observation equally.

Both males and females who went to high school in the South had lower subsequent wages than students who lived in other parts of the country. However, since we lack an indicator of the region in which an individual worked when the wage level was measured at age 24, we do not know whether this reflects regional wage patterns or differences in school quality not reflected in the skills measure.

13. The coefficients on the variables measuring years of full-time and part-time work experience are unstable because they are highly collinear with highest educational attainment.

14. Throughout the paper, the percentage wage differential associated with a one-unit difference in the value of an explanatory variable with a coefficient, b, is computed by the formula: $e^b - 1$.

15. When Model A is estimated without controlling for full-time and part-time work experience and for whether the individual was working full-time or part-time when the wage is measured, the coefficient on years of completed schooling is much smaller for each sample than the value reported in Table 14.3 or Table 14.4. In fact, the coefficient is

negative for the NLS72 sample of males. The reason is that individuals who enter the labor force directly have considerably more work experience than do individuals who graduate from college and this work experience is valued in the labor market.

16. Another possible explanation for why our estimates of the college–high school wage differential are lower than those of other researchers concerns our specification of educational attainment. We used a linear specification rather than a set of dichotomous variables (such as completed some college and four-year college graduate) because this is the only specification for which we could compute an estimate of reliability. In fact, however, our estimate of the size of the college-high school wage differential for each sample is not very sensitive to the specification of years of completed schooling. To explore this, we compared fitted models with both a linear specification and a general specification using dummy variables under the assumption that the number of years of completed schooling was measured without error. For all four samples, estimates of the college–high school wage differential from the general specification differed by no more than .005 from those obtained with the linear specification.

17. Bishop (1989b) found that a one standard deviation difference in test score was associated with a .19 standard deviation difference in earnings for household heads. This is larger than the effect sizes we report in this chapter, even for 1980 high school graduates.

18. The reason for choosing a common math score differential (6.25 points) in discussing the sizes of the associated wage differentials in the four samples, rather than using the standard deviations in the four samples, is that we wanted the magnitudes of the wage differentials to be directly comparable.

19. Each wage differential associated with a 6.25-point test score differential was calculated using the average wage for the relevant group as the starting point. We also fitted models in which high school seniors' scores on tests of reading and vocabulary were used as the skill measure. The pattern of results when the reading score is used as the skill measure is similar to the pattern using the math score, but the quantitative impacts on wages are smaller. For females, the vocabulary score is positively related to wages, with the coefficient approximately twice as large for 1980 graduates as for 1972 graduates. The vocabulary score is not a statistically significant predictor of wage for males in either sample.

When the math, reading, and vocabulary scores are included in the same model, the coefficients on the math score retain the pattern described in the text, but the coefficients on the reading and vocabulary scores become statistically insignificant for all four samples. This is due to the relative strength of the math score-wages relationship and the high correlations among the skill measures. Corrected for measurement error, the math-reading, math-vocabulary, and reading-vocabulary correlations are as follows: NLS72 males (.75, .67, .83); HS&B males (.81, .78, .90); NLS72 females (.76, .71, .87); and HS&B females (.81, .80, .89).

20. We use the 1988 poverty line because all wages are expressed in 1988 dollars.

21. The estimates of the total impact of the test score on subsequent wages came from estimating a model with the same specification as Model B in Tables 14.3 and 14.4, except that the indicator of educational attainment was excluded. Thus, the coefficient on the math score reflects not only the direct effect of math score on earnings, but also the

indirect effect stemming from the fact that students with higher math skills are more likely to participate in postsecondary education, which is itself rewarded in the labor market.

22. Had we done the calculation using the predicted total impacts of mathematics skills on the subsequent wages of males and females graduating from high school in 1972 rather than 1980, the predicted effects of the growth in the college–high school skill differential on the growth in the college–high school wage differential would have been only half as large as those reported in the text.

23. In Japan, in contrast, large employers maintain long-term recruiting relationships with selected high schools in which teachers recommend selected students for jobs (Rosenbaum and Kariya, 1991).

24. The coefficients reported in rows 2 and 3 of Table 14.6 were estimated using smaller subsamples than those used in estimating the coefficients reported in row 1 because the former subsamples included only individuals for whom a wage was available two years after high school graduation *and* six years after high school graduation.

25. While the positive coefficients on the math score are not significantly different from zero on conventional tests for the small subsamples used in estimating the results displayed in row 2 of Table 14.6, the coefficients are significantly different from zero when the identical model is estimated for the larger subsamples that include all males whose highest educational attainment is a high school diploma and who have a legitimate wage value six years after high school graduation (row 1).

26. These results are also consistent with the studies of Lillard (1977) and Bound et al. (1986) who show that the impact of ability on earnings increases with age.

27. See Levy and Murnane (1992) for a discussion of the determinants of within-group variation in earnings.

28. As reported in Rock et al. (1985b), the estimated reliabilities of the formula score on the vocabulary, reading, and math tests are as follows: NLS72 males (.78, .79, .87); NLS72 females (.78, .79, .85); HS&B males (.83, .80, .86); HS&B females (.82, .78, .83). These were obtained using Cronbach's coefficient alpha (Lord and Novick, 1968). We use IRT scores (as opposed to formula scores) in our analyses because the IRT scores are equatable across tests. In each of our four samples the correlation between the IRT score and the formula score was greater than .95. For this reason we took the advice of Donald Rock (of Educational Testing Service) and assumed that the reliabilities of the formula scores also pertained to the IRT scores. Below we examine the sensitivity of the results to the assumption that the reliabilities of the IRT scores are higher than those of the formula scores.

29. For each person in their NLS72 data set, Kane and Rouse (1993) have two indicators (S_1 and S_2) of the true number of years of completed schooling (S). The first (S_1) is a self-reported measure, which we also use in our research; the second (S_2) is a measure constructed from college transcripts. We are indebted to Tom Kane for providing us with the latter measure. Assuming that the measurement errors in the two indicators of schooling (ϵ_1 and ϵ_2) are independent and that both are independent of S, the variance in true schooling (σ^2) is estimated by the covariance of S_1 and S_2. The reliability of the self-reported measure of schooling is the ratio of the estimates of σ^2 and σ_1^2.

30. Table 14.5 presents the estimates with one more significant digit than is used in Tables 14.3 and 14.4 to facilitate sensitivity of the coefficients to model specification.

31. Another reason for interpreting the interaction cautiously is that Fuller's method of estimating the coefficient on a fallible interaction between two variables measured with error produces a slightly biased estimator of the impact of the interaction.

References

Bishop, John H., "Incentives for Learning: Why American High School Students Compare So Poorly to Their Counterparts Overseas," Working paper #89-09, Cornell University, Ithaca, N.Y, (1989a).

Bishop, John H., "Is the Test Score Decline Responsible for the Productivity Growth Decline?" *American Economic Review* 79 (March 1989b) 1, 178–197.

Blackburn, McKinley L., David E. Bloom, and Richard B. Freeman, "The Declining Economic Position of Less Skilled American Men," in Gary Burtless (ed.) *A Future of Lousy Jobs?* (Washington, D.C.: The Brookings Institution, 1990).

Blackburn, McKinley L., and David Neumark, "Omitted-Ability Bias and the Increase in the Return to Schooling," *Journal of Labor Economics* (1993).

Bound, John, and Richard B. Freeman, "What Went Wrong? The Erosion of Relative Earnings and Employment Among Young Black Men in the 1980s," *The Quarterly Journal of Economics* (February 1992), 201–232.

Bound, John, Zvi Griliches, and Bronwyn H. Hall, "Wages, Schooling and IQ of Brothers and Sisters: Do the Family Factors Differ?" *International Economic Review* 7 (February 1986)1, 77–105.

Cohen, Jacob, and Patricia Cohen, *Applied Multiple Regression/Correlation Analysis for the Behavioral Sciences* (second edition) (Hillsdale, N.J.: Lawrence Erlbaum Associates, 1983).

DuMouchel, William H., and Greg J. Duncan, "Using Sample Survey Weights in Multiple Regression Analyses of Stratified Samples," *Journal of the American Statistical Association* 78 (September 1983), 535–543.

Fuller, W. A., *EV Carp* (Ames, Iowa: Iowa State Statistical Laboratory, 1988).

Fuller, W. A., *Measurement Error Models* (New York: John Wiley & Sons, 1987).

Gottschalk, Peter, and Robert Moffitt, "Earnings and Wage Distributions in the NLS, CPS, and PSID," Part I of Final Report to the U.S. Department of Labor, Grant No. E-9-J-0047, "Earnings Mobility and Earnings Inequality in the United States," awarded to the National Bureau of Economic Research, (May 1992).

Johnston, William B., and Arnold E. Packer, *Workforce 2000, Work and Workers for the 21st Century* (Washington D.C.: Hudson Institute, 1987).

Juhn, Chinhui, Kevin M. Murphy, and Brooks Pierce, "Wage Inequality and the Rise in Returns to Skill," Paper presented at the Universities Research Conference "Labor Markets in the 1990s," (November 13, 1989).

Kane, Thomas J., and Cecilia E. Rouse, "Labor Market Returns to Two- and Four-Year College: Is a Credit A Credit and Do Degrees Matter?" Harvard University, Kennedy

School of Government, Faculty Research Working Paper Series, No. R-93-38, (December, 1993).

Katz, Lawrence F., and Kevin M. Murphy, "Changes in Relative Wages, 1963–1987: Supply and Demand Factors," *Quarterly Journal of Economics*, 107 (February 1992), 35–78.

Koretz, Daniel M., *Educational Achievement: Explanations and Implications* (Washington, D.C.: Congressional Budget Office, 1987).

Krueger, Alan B., "How Computers Have Changed the Wage Structure: Evidence from Microdata, 1984–89," *Quarterly Journal of Economics*, 108(February 1993) 1, 33–60.

Levy, Frank, and Richard J. Murnane, "U.S. Earnings Levels and Earnings Inequality: A Review of Recent Trends and Proposed Explanations," *The Journal of Economic Literature*, 30(September 1992), 1332–1381.

Lillard, Lee A., "Inequality: Earnings vs. Human Wealth," *American Economic Review*, 67 (March 1977) 2, 42–53.

Lord, Fred M., and Melvin R. Novick, *Statistical Theories of Mental Test Scores* (Reading, Mass.: Addison-Wesley, 1968).

Marshall, Ray, and Marc Tucker, *Thinking for a Living* (New York: Basic Books, 1992).

Mishel, Lawrence, and Jared Bernstein, "Declining Wages for High School and College Graduates: Pay and Benefits Trends by Education, Gender, Occupation, and State, 1979–1991," Briefing paper, Washington, D.C.: Economic Policy Institute, (1992).

Mullis, Ina V. S., John A. Dossey, Eugene H. Owen, and Gary W. Phillips, *The State of Mathematics Achievement*, Report Prepared by Educational Testing Service for National Center for Education Statistics, Washington, D.C. (June 1991).

Osterman, Paul, "How Common Is Workplace Transformation?" *Industrial and Labor Relations Review* 47 (January 1994) 2, 173–188.

Rivera-Batiz, Francisco L., "Quantitative Literacy and the Likelihood of Employment Among Young Adults," *Journal of Human Resources* 27 (Spring 1992) 2, 313–328.

Rock, Donald A. et al., *Factors Associated with Decline of Test Scores of High School Seniors, 1972 to 1980: A Study of Excellence in High School Education: Educational Policies, School Quality, and Student Outcomes* (Princeton, N.J.: Educational Testing Service, December 1985a).

Rock, Donald A. et al., *Psychometric Analysis of the NLS and the High School and Beyond Test Batteries: A Study of Excellence in High School Education: Educational Policies, School Quality, and Student Outcomes* (Princeton, N.J.: Educational Testing Service, September 1985b).

Rosenbaum, James E., and Takehiko Kariya, "Do School Achievements Affect the Early Jobs of High School Graduates in the United States and Japan?" *Sociology of Education* 64 (April 1991), 78–95.

15

Escalating Differences and Elusive "Skills"
Cognitive Abilities and the Explanation of Inequality

SAMUEL BOWLES, HERBERT GINTIS, AND ROBERT SZARKA

The increase in income inequality in the U.S. since the early 1970s, according to a virtual consensus among economists, policy makers, and the media, is the result of a long-term increase in the return to skilled labor, which in turn is said to reflect a shift in the structure of labor demand in favor of skilled workers.[1]

A reasonable, and often suggested, interpretation of the skill component in inequality is that much of it is associated with cognitive capacities. This interpretation is often combined with the view that cognitive skills are genetically transmitted, and that for this reason the distribution of cognitive skills in the population is only minimally susceptible to social policy interventions.[2] These views imply that because rising inequality results from the increased scarcity of a personal attribute that is difficult to produce or redistribute through social policy, increasing inequality in productivity cannot be altered, and the consequent increase in income inequality can be dampened only through tax and transfer programs.

There is an analogous implication concerning intergenerational inequality. If the main determinants of income inequality are genetically transmitted skill differences, then the intergenerational transmission of economic status within families is not susceptible to standard policies designed to ensure greater equality of opportunity, such as enhanced equality of educational opportunity or estate taxation. Furthermore if these genetically transmitted skills are becoming increasingly scarce and hence increasingly rewarded over time, then we may expect a long-term decline in intergenerational mobility.

In this chapter we do not address the logic of the above position, except to note that high levels of heritability do not necessarily imply the inefficacy of social policy interventions.[3] Nor do we address the factual claim that cognitive skills are highly heritable. We note, however, that current widely circulated heritability estimates, in particular those offered in Herrnstein and Murray (1994), are considerably reduced from those offered a generation ago by Jensen (1969) in his similar analysis of compensatory education. In addition, some respected geneticists, for instance Feldman et al. (2000), suggest coefficients of heritability about half the size of Herrnstein and Murray (1994), although they remain relatively large.

Rather, we question the factual basis of the above argument concerning productive skills, and particularly the presumed importance of cognitive skills in explaining economic differences. The importance of cognitive capacities in the production process is not at issue. However, we doubt that the relevant skills are sufficiently scarce and that their scarcity has been rising sufficiently rapidly to account for much of the recent trend toward greater inequality of income. In the penultimate section we suggest why individual earnings might be affected by traits unrelated to cognitive capacities and which may not even be considered skills might nonetheless affect individual earnings.

Elusive Skills

The main direct evidence for the skill interpretation of rising inequality is the increased inequalities between workers with different levels of schooling and experience (e.g., Murphy and Welch, 1993). It seems reasonably well established that the statistical association between schooling and earnings is not substantially attributable to the covariance of each with other influences on earnings such as ability or parental socioeconomic status.[4] But we know so little about how schooling enhances earnings that it seems unwarranted to attribute these differences to something called "skill" without more direct evidence.

First, the higher pay of the better educated can be accounted for by anything that contributes to expected profits and is education related, so skills need not be involved.[5]

Second, we would like to know *how much* of the increased inequality is attributable to the increased returns to schooling. If the "returns to schooling"

Table 15.1. Growth of Residual Inequality in the United States, 1979–1989

Decomposition	Men	Women
Change in inequality of wages (total)	.082	.094
Change in within-age/ schooling cells component	.043	.050
Change in between-age/ schooling cells component	.039	.044

Note: Data pertains to whites only and are based on 225 age-education cells for each gender. The wage measure is pretax hourly wages of individuals 16–64 years of age.

Source: Data from Card, Kranarz, and Lemieux (1995).

interpretation of rising inequality were true, it should account for the lion's share of the increase in inequality during the 1980s, the period of marked increases in the returns to schooling. But it does not. Table 15.1 provides evidence of the total increase in inequality, measured by the variance of the logarithm of wages (line 1), as well as the contribution of growing income differences among 225 groups classified by age and years of schooling (line 3). It is clear that for both men and women the largest contribution to growing inequality took place within these narrowly defined groups — that is, among people of similar schooling and age, not between different education groups. Gottschalk (1994) appears to be correct, referring to education/experience groups, in concluding that the "increase in within group inequality accounted for the majority of the increase in inequality." Moreover, where suitable data are available, the variance of the natural log of earnings between schooling/ experience groupings appears to account for no more of the variance in log earnings now than two decades ago.[6]

Third, if the variation in the returns to schooling explains the variation in inequality during the 1980s, and given that returns to schooling fell during the 1970s, we should have observed a reduction in inequality during that decade. Yet inequality rose during the 1970s, too.[7]

It thus appears that increased inequality *between* education/experience groupings contributes to the increase in overall inequality, but over the past quarter-century of increased inequality, the contribution of the component between education/experience groupings appears to be quite small.

It is not surprising, then, that the case that skills account for the increase in inequality is not based primarily on the direct evidence above, and that it hinges on the interpretation of the growing inequality within education/ experience groupings. Thus the importance attributed to "skill" stems from an interpretation of what is termed "residual inequality," according to which the unexplained variance of earnings within education/experience cells is held to be the result of "unobserved skill."[8]

It is uncontroversial that "residual inequality" is increasing; once the identification of residual inequality with "skill" is assumed the rest follows. In fact, as we have seen, most of the increase in inequality is due to increased residual inequality. Juhn, Murphy, and Pierce (1993) conclude, "The trend toward greater wage inequality is attributable primarily to increases in the premia on both unobserved and observed . . . dimensions of skill, . . . the majority of the increase over the period is due to the unobserved component" (p. 441).[9]

The skill most commonly said to explain residual variance is cognitive functioning. While other individual attributes, strength for example, are certainly skills at least in some jobs, few noncognitive skill-related traits have been measured. Thus we focus on cognitive skills. If the abilities measured on cognitive tests such as the Armed Forces Qualifying Test are deemed skills, we can answer three questions germane to the skills interpretation of growing inequality. First, what fraction of residual inequality is explained statistically by the variation of cognitive scores across individuals, and has this fraction changed over time? Second, are cognitive skills (as measured by the available tests) becoming increasingly scarce as measured by their market return? And third, to what extent are the economic returns to schooling explained by the contribution of schooling to cognitive skill? We will take up each in turn.

Differences in Cognitive Skill and Residual Inequality

Suppose that the income-generating structure for a given group is

$$y = y(s,b,a,c) + \alpha$$

where y, s, b, a, and c measure earnings or income, schooling, parental socioeconomic background, age, and cognitive skill level, and α measures stochastic influences on earnings uncorrelated with the other explanatory variables. Most estimates lack measures of cognitive skill and hence estimate

$$y = y'(s,b,a) + \alpha',$$

with α' representing the stochastic influences as above plus the influences of cognitive skill operating independently of age, socioeconomic background,

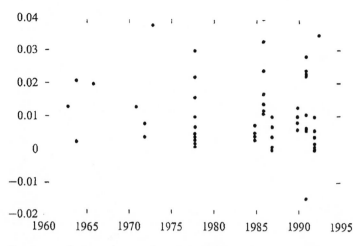

Figure 15.1 The Contribution of Cognitive Differences to Residual Inequality by Year: Fifty-seven Estimates from Twenty-four Studies

and schooling. If y is the natural logarithm of the income measure, its variance is a widely used measure of inequality, and $var\{\alpha'\}$ is then a measure of residual inequality. Where studies have estimated both of the above equations we can use $\Delta R^2 = var\{\alpha'\} - var\{\alpha\}$ as a measure of the amount of residual inequality explained by variation in cognitive skill. We have located fifty-seven of these estimates in twenty-four studies. The estimated values of ΔR^2 along with the years to which the income data pertain appear in Figure 15.1.[10] Methods of estimation differ, of course, and the demographic groups covered and the years for which the data apply vary considerably. We have surveyed these studies and selected what we considered to be the best specified estimates in each study. For example, we favored estimates using measurement error correction and instrumental variables estimation or other techniques to take account of endogeneity of the explanatory variables. We have included all studies available to us.

The mean value of ΔR^2 is 0.011, and regressing the estimates of ΔR^2 on the years to which they pertain, we find no time trend in its value. This result is robust to correcting for time trends in the demographic characteristics of the groups covered by the studies, and whether the estimate is based on the NLSY, the General Social Survey (GSS), or other data sources.[11]

It is evident that cognitive skills as measured on the tests used explain very little of the residual variance in most studies. This does not mean that cognitive skills are not important, but only that they add little explanatory power to an

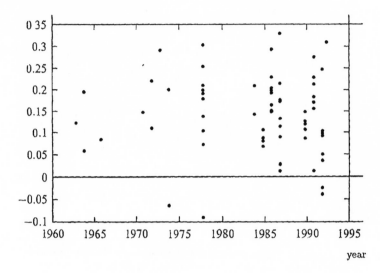

Figure 15.2 Normalized Regression Coefficient of Cognitive Score on the Logarithm of Income or Earnings by Year: Sixty-five Estimates from Twenty-four Studies

account of earnings differences based on the usual schooling, socioeconomic background, and demographic variables. We turn now to the importance of cognitive skills as determinants of earnings.

Increased Scarcity of Cognitive Skills?

The second question, whether cognitive skill is increasingly scarce or at least increasingly rewarded, is more difficult to assess on the basis of available studies. The relevant statistic is the change over time in the magnitude of a suitably normalized regression coefficient for the cognitive score in a well-specified earnings or income generating equation. Two problems arise.

First, it is far from clear how the relevant estimates should be normalized. The two obvious candidates represent answers to different questions. Assuming that the test scores are normalized to mean zero and unit standard deviation, we might want to know the effect of a unit change in cognitive ability on income expressed either in units of percentage change in income or in standard deviation units of the distribution of income. Thus the coefficient of the cognitive measure on the log of income (or earnings) gives us the effect on the level of income relative to mean incomes, while the normalized regression coefficient gives us the effect on income in units based on the distribution (rather than the level) of income.[12] We present estimates of the normalized regression coefficients.

A second problem is that we have few strictly comparable studies widely separated in time. A short time frame may be misleading if our interest is in long-term changes in inequality. Murnane, Willett, and Levy's (1995) careful study using two large surveys refers to earnings in 1978 and 1986. They find substantial increases over this eight-year period in the estimated coefficient of a mathematics score in predicting the log of the hourly wages. However, Huang's (1996) estimates using the GSS covering the period 1974–1994 yields no trend whatever. In Figure 15.2 we present the sixty-five estimates from twenty-four studies that we have been able to locate that represent the normalized regression coefficients for a cognitive measure in an income generating equation. In a regression of these estimates on time alone, on time and categorical variables measuring the age, race, and gender of the subjects, and on these plus the data source (NLSY, GSS, other), the time trend was very small and insignificant.

The evidence for an increase in the scarcity of cognitive skills appears to be remarkably weak; indeed, a consideration of all of the available evidence would caution against the conclusion of any trend.

Cognitive Skills and the Economic Returns to Schooling

There is no longer much doubt those with more schooling earn more at least in substantial measure *because* they are educated, and not solely because schooling covaries with ability, parental social status, and other traits rewarded in the labor market.[13] While schooling may also perform a credentialing function, the magnitude of the resulting diploma effects, where these have been identified, represent only a small proportion of the statistical association between years of schooling and earnings.[14]

Because schooling increases earnings, and because schooling imparts cognitive skills, many have supposed that the acquisition of cognitive skills is the mechanism whereby schooling increases earnings. Why else would employers pay the education premium? Tacitly accepting this argument, economists tend to equate differences in levels of schooling with skill differences.[15]

Yet it has proven remarkably difficult to give an adequate account of the skills that schools produce and to document their reward in labor markets. The most straightforward approach is to ask what schools teach and to consider the economic returns to the resulting curricular outcomes. It is simple to identify individual characteristics that are acquired through instruction and that also appear to raise earnings. But these characteristics typically explain only a small fraction of the observed economic return to schooling. Thus the economic contribution of the curricular content of schooling has proven elusive. Altonji (1995), for example, found that additional years of science, math, and foreign language in high school contribute to subsequent earnings, but that the value of courses taken in an additional year of high school is considerably less than the value of an additional year of high school.[16] Moreover, those school programs most deliberately designed to contribute to occupational skill enhancement — vocational programs — appear to have limited success.[17]

A more promising approach might be to define skills broadly as generic cognitive capacities, and to explore the contribution of schools to labor-market success via their teaching of the kinds of mental capacities required in employment. But if cognitive capacities are what explain the private return to schooling, it would be difficult to resolve an anomaly that has attracted considerable scholarly attention: most of the econometric analysis of educational production functions indicates that school inputs make limited contributions to students' cognitive levels, while earnings-functions estimates suggest significant contributions of school input measures to subsequent economic success.[18] If schools affect earnings primarily by their influence on noncognitive traits, of course, the anomaly is resolved.

The most direct test of the proposition that the contribution of schooling to the development of cognitive skills accounts for the effect of schooling on earnings is to ask if earnings covary with years of schooling in populations that are homogeneous with respect to level of cognitive skill. A positive answer in a well-specified model suggests that schools contribute to earnings by means other than their contribution to cognitive skill.

An approximation of this test is available. We can compare two estimated regression coefficients for a years-of-schooling variable, one in an equation like (1) above, in which a measure of cognitive skill also appears ($b_{sy.c}$) and another like (2) above in which the cognitive measure is absent (b_{sy}). Subject to a number of estimation biases that we address elsewhere (document available from the authors), the ratio of the first to the second is a measure of the contribution of noncognitive traits to the estimated return to schooling (Gintis, 1971). If schooling affected earnings solely through its contribution to cognitive skills (assuming these to be adequately measured by the test scores used), ρ would be zero, because the regression coefficient of years of schooling would fall to zero once the cognitive level of the individual is accounted for, there being (by hypothesis) no contribution of schooling to earnings beyond its effect on cognitive functioning. By contrast, if the contribution of schooling to cognitive skill explained none of schooling's contribution to earnings, ρ would be unity.

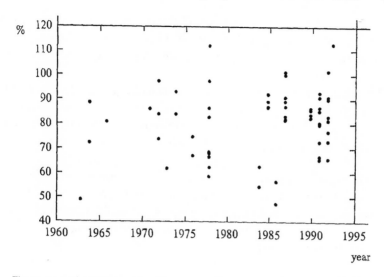

Figure 15.3 The Noncognitive Component (Percentage) of the Private Return to Schooling over Time: A Summary of Fifty-eight Estimates from Twenty-five Studies

We have been able to locate twenty-five studies allowing fifty-eight estimates of the relationship between b_{sy} and $b_{sy.c}$ and thus an estimate of ρ.[19] The mean value of ρ in our studies is 83, meaning that introducing a measure of cognitive skills into an equation using educational attainment to predict income reduces the coefficient of years of education by an average of 17. This suggests that a substantial portion of the returns to schooling are generated by effects or correlates of schooling substantially unrelated to the cognitive skills measured on the available tests. In Figure 15.3 we present these data, along with the year(s) to which the earnings data pertain. In a regression using categorical variables to take account of the demographic groups studied, there is an estimated two-thirds of a point negative time trend in the noncognitive component of the return to schooling, and this is significant at the 10 percent level. This evidence supports the conclusion that the role of cognitive traits in the contribution of schooling to earnings has increased over the past three decades.

However, a single study covering the years 1974 to 1994 uses the same cognitive test as well as earnings and schooling measures across time and thus allows a less noisy assessment of the secular movement of ρ. Huang presents estimates, based on the General Social Survey, of the returns to three levels of schooling among eight demographic groups using appropriate measures of family background as copredictors of the logarithm of earnings. Confining ourselves to the thirty-three cases where the estimated return to schooling is positive and significant at the 10 percent level, the mean estimates of σ are: 85 for 1974–1982, 90 for 1984–1989, and 95 for 1990–1994. There appears to be no tendency for the cognitive component in the returns to schooling to increase over time in these data.

These data do not indicate the unimportance of cognitive skills as an influence on earnings, or more narrowly on the returns to schooling. However, they do suggest that a major portion of the effect of schooling on earnings operates in ways independent of any contribution of schooling to cognitive functioning.[20]

Rather, we will suggest, schooling contributes to earnings in part by fostering the development of individual traits that contribute to labor discipline and hence are valuable to employers given the informational asymmetries between employer as principal and employee as agent, and the resulting incompleteness of the employment contract.

Productive Skills and Profitable Discipline

Sociological accounts frequently stress the noncognitive aspects of the contribution of schooling to the economy, often under the heading of "socialization for work."[21] Economists have widely ignored this literature, arguing that an employer would be no more willing to pay a premium for the services of a "well-socialized" worker than a shopper would be to pay a higher price for the fruit of a "well-socialized" grocer.

The economist's argument is reasonable if firms can write complete and cost-free enforceable contracts for the delivery of specific amounts of specific services with its employees. If employers know the characteristics of prospective employees, they will offer higher wages to more highly schooled workers in competitive equilibrium if and only if such workers have superior productive capacities in the sense that their labor enters the relevant production function in ways distinct from and superior to that of less schooled workers.

However, the employment relationship is generally contractually incomplete.[22] A cost-free enforceable promise of a wage is exchanged not for cost-free enforceable labor services but rather for the employees' agreement to accept the employer's authority during the hours of work.[23] This authority is then used to secure the flow of labor services that, when combined with other productive inputs, produces output. The employer's payment of a wage superior to the employee's next best alternative, coupled with the threat of termination of the contract, constitutes an essential part of the necessarily endogenous enforcement of the employer's objectives in the exchange.

In such a model employers choose to pay for nonskill inputs that assist in the exercise of the employer's authority.[24] Examples of such profitable individual traits are a predisposition to truth telling, identification with the objectives of the firm's owners and managers as opposed to the objectives of coworkers or customers, a high marginal utility of income, a low disutility of effort, and a low rate of time preference. We call these *affective* traits, and as is common in social psychology, we mean by this both emotional traits and other noncognitive behavioral characteristics.

Just as the employer's valuation of productive skills of employees will depend on the product mix and production functions in use, the valuation of such affective traits as described above will vary with the nature of the endogenous enforcement problem. Where monitoring is impossible, for example, the importance of truth telling might be heightened. Where one employee is expected to monitor other employees, employers might more highly value behavioral traits, demographic markers, or costly credentials contributing to the legitimacy of the exercise of authority.

By developing these valued affective traits in individuals and thus attenuating the costs of endogenous enforcement of the labor contract, schooling may have economic effects similar to, and perhaps complementary with, work norms and other shared values that often prove individually or collectively useful when individuals interact in the absence of complete contracting.

But do schools produce such affective traits? We know of only one study that has attempted to provide an answer. This study is not a satisfactory basis for generalization, but it is nonetheless worth reviewing. The study asked whether schools reward students who exhibit the specific personality traits valued by employers in the workplace. If they do, we might reasonably infer that schools foster the development of these traits, and the economic return to schooling might represent payments to individuals with these traits.

In one investigation conducted during the early 1970s, Richard Edwards (1976) used a peer-rated set of personality measures of members of work groups in both private and public employment to predict supervisor ratings of these workers. In a parallel investigation with a distinct sample, Peter Meyer used the same peer-rated personality variables to predict grade-point averages of students in a high school controlling for SAT (verbal and math) and IQ. Edwards found that being judged by their peers to be "perseverant," "dependable," "consistent," "punctual," "tactful," "identifies with work," and "empathizes with others" was positively correlated with supervisor ratings, while those judged to be "creative" and "independent" were ranked poorly by supervisors. Meyer found virtually identical results for the high school students in his grading study; independently of the student's cognitive level, schools reward with higher grades the same traits that Edwards found to predict favorable supervisor ratings. The simple correlations between grade-point average and the twelve identified personality traits are barely distinguishable from the analogous correlations in Edwards's study of employees.[25] Teachers and employers in these samples reward the same personality traits.

Conclusion

The interpretation of the returns to schooling as the return to the cognitive skills generated through the educational process has rendered public policy discussions misleading and reform efforts possibly misdirected. For instance, this interpretation has pushed to the forefront the issue of IQ in general, and genetic versus environmental determinants of intelligence and cognitive functioning. In fact, IQ differences make only a moderate contribution to the explanation of economic inequality, account for only a moderate portion of the returns to schooling, and are unlikely to be implicated in the explanation of recent increases in wage inequality. Similarly, assessments of the efficacy of the educational system have centered on cognitive achievement scores, rather than a comprehensive and logically defensible set of social outcomes of schooling.

Our conclusion that skills, and particularly cognitive skills, have been overrated in the discussion of inequality does not imply that adequate funding of high-quality schooling for all children should be abandoned as a policy priority. Efforts to raise cognitive functioning and to guarantee high-quality schooling to all children are valuable in their own right, and not simply as instruments for the reduction of income inequality.

Notes

We would like to thank Steven Durlauf for comments on an earlier draft and the MacArthur Foundation for financial support.

1. Juhn et al. (1993) write: "The net result of this divergence in earnings between the most skilled and the least skilled has been an enormous increase in wage inequality. . . . The variance of the log of weekly wages increased by about 72 percent from 1962 through 1989" (p. 411). Katz and Murphy (1992) write: "Rapid secular growth in the demand for more educated workers, 'more skilled' workers and females appears to be the driving force behind observed changes in the wage structure (from 1963 to 1987)" (p. 35). The source of the demand shift, in particular whether technology or international trade is the major influence, remains a matter of lively controversy.

2. Early statements of this view are Jensen (1969, 1975), Herrnstein (1971), and Eysenck (1971). More recent is Herrnstein and Murray (1994). Two of the authors evaluated the earlier statements of this view in Bowles and Gintis (1972, 1975), and Bowles and Nelson (1974).

3. This obvious point has been missed in much of the debate on heritability and social policy. The susceptibility to tuberculosis is genetically transmitted, but the incidence of TB shows substantial variation due to environmental differences. Height is one of the most heritable traits. Yet height varies over time for substantially environmental reasons. Perhaps more germane to this discussion, IQ, by which we mean the cognitive skills measured by IQ tests, has risen dramatically in many countries even over the course of two generations (Flynn, 2000).

4. Card (1998) provides a convenient survey of the major recent studies, all supporting the conclusion in the text.

5. See Bowles and Gintis (1997) for a formal model of the contribution of nonskill traits to the economic returns to schooling in competitive equilibrium, as well as some suggestive data. If hiring college graduates into management positions and paying them well either legitimates the authority structure of the workplace or inhibits collusion between monitors and those being monitored, for example, the economic returns to education might include an element unrelated to any reasonable conception of skill yet sustainable in competitive equilibrium. We do not mean to suggest that none of the return to schooling is skill-related, of course. For example, persuasive evidence that there is a technology-driven skill-related increase in the returns to schooling is presented in Krueger's (1993) study, which shows that the return to schooling is higher for those using computers.

6. Levy and Murnane (1992), table 4.

7. Moffitt's (1990) study shows that between 1979 and 1987 the fraction of a measure of male earnings inequality attributable to the usual income covariates such as schooling and experience fell, and that the growth in inequality among these covariates accounts for only 5 percent of the increased inequality in earnings. If the period 1969–1987 is considered the measure income covariates predict an equalizing trend. Calculations based on other studies attribute more of the increase inequality to the measured income covariates which might be measuring skill, but none, to our knowledge, can account for more than one-quarter to this source.

8. Thus Juhn et al. (1993) write: "We view this increase in within-group wage inequality as a trend toward higher skill prices" (p. 423). No reason is given for this view, unless the proposition that anything associated with higher earnings constitutes a skill can be counted as a reason. Katz and Murphy (1992) explain: "We use the dispersion of relative wages within our gender-education-experience cells as measures of the spread in relative wages across different skill levels within cells" (p. 43). Do they intend that an increase in racial differences in income would be explained as an increase in the return to a skill (whiteness apparently being the skill in question)? Their own reservations are evidenced by the quotation marks they place around the word "skill" throughout the paper. Indeed, at one point they remark that the "unskilled" in their framework might equivalently be called the "unlucky" (p. 44).

9. Aside from the groundless identification of the unexplained variance as a return to skill, they do not address the puzzle which their (and others') research points to: if technology or other factors have made skills more scarce, why are the patterns of returns to education and "unobserved skills" so different, with returns to education falling during the seventies and then rising, and what they call the returns to unobserved skills rising steadily over the period? Residual inequality appears to have risen steadily for both men

and women since 1970 (though it appears to have fallen or remained constant from 1963 to 1970), and it is considerably greater in every year for men than for women.

10. The data sources underlying this and the other figures in this paper are available from *http://www.unix.oit.umass.edu/gintis* or by writing to the authors.

11. Both measurement error and the transitory component in the income measure impart a downward bias to our estimate of ΔR^2 if this is to be interpreted (as would be appropriate) as the contribution of cognitive skills to the residual component in the inequality of permanent income. Measurement error in the cognitive scores is quite small, but the sum of the transitory and error components of the income variance is between a quarter and a third (Bowles, 1972; Zimmerman, 1992; Solon, 1992). Adjusting our estimate of ΔR^2 to take account of this bias would obviously not modify the conclusion in the text. There is also a possible downward bias in the time trend due the fact that later studies tend to use more regressors. We have not assessed the size of this bias.

12. If the relationship between the standard deviation of the income measure and its mean does not change much, these two measures will not diverge appreciably. But we know this has not been the case. Indeed, it is precisely the increase in the coefficient of variation of income that has motivated renewed interest in the determinants of income.

13. See Card (1998) for a survey of recent studies of the returns to schooling in the United States. Taking account of the endogenous determination of years of schooling appears, if anything, to raise the estimated returns to schooling in most cases. However, Altonji (1995) finds a substantial reduction in the estimated return to schooling associated with the introduction of adequate controls for both family background and ability measures. Moreover, Behrman (1990) finds compelling evidence in a number of poorer countries that failure to account for covarying family, ability, and other traits imparts a significant upward bias to estimates of the economic returns to schooling. None of these studies, however, suggests that the economic returns to schooling, properly estimated, are nonexistent.

14. Heckman et al. (1996), for example, identify statistically significant credentialing effects, but the economic return to years of schooling per se remains substantial even after accounting for these effects.

15. See, for example, Juhn et al. (1993) and Katz and Murphy (1992).

16. These results control for family background, aptitude, and participation in an academic program and are invariant to the use of OLS, OLS fixed effects, or instrumental variable estimation.

17. For instance, Altonji (1995) finds, both for OLS and instrumental variables estimates, lower than average returns to vocational programs.

18. Coleman et al. (1966) initiated the literature suggesting limited achievement score effects of school inputs. Hanushek (1986) extends this literature. Altonji and Dunn (1995), Card and Krueger (1996), and the works cited therein present evidence that school inputs affect subsequent earnings. Many studies purporting to show the limited effectiveness of schooling inputs in raising cognitive performance are seriously flawed; Bowles and Levin (1968) provide a critique of Coleman et al. (1966), for example. The work of Card and Krueger has been questioned by Heckman et al. (1996) on grounds of sensitivity to arbitrary functional form choices and identifying assumptions. See also

Speakman and Welch (1995). Altonji and Dunn (1996) present convincing evidence that school inputs affect labor market outcomes using a sample of siblings to control for family background effects.

19. See note 2 for sources. We have found five other studies, allowing an additional six estimates, where the dependent variable is a measure of occupational status rather than earnings: Bajema (1968), Conlisk (1971), Duncan (1968), Sewell et al. (1970), and Porter (1974). The mean value of ρ in these studies is 89 percent, and the lowest is 81. These results are not reported in Figure 15.3.

20. There is additional evidence that cognitive demands at work explain at least some of the returns to schooling. Alan Krueger (1993) found that increased use of computers explained a third to a half of the increased returns to schooling during the 1980s. However, Krueger's data do not indicate that the economic return to schooling derives substantially from the covariance of the level of schooling and the extent of computer use at work: the estimated coefficient of years of schooling in Krueger's main sample, when estimated without the computer-use variables in the equation, is reduced when the equation is estimated including a variable measuring computer use at work, but by only 9 percent for his 1984 sample and 13 percent for his 1989 sample. Moreover, Raphael and Toseland (1995) found that the estimated effect of schooling on log wages is reduced by only one-fifth when the extent of on-the-job use of eight distinct cognitive skills (including use of mathematics and use of computers) is measured and included in the estimating equation. Farkas et al. (1997) found that including a measure of the cognitive demands of the respondent's job in a log wage equation reduced the estimated return to schooling by an average of 26 percent for six estimated equations involving male and female whites, Mexican-Americans, and African-Americans (age, experience, mother's education, and rural residence were included in the equation). These data concern the U.S. alone, and we do not draw any inference from them about the returns to schooling in other economies. We suspect, and there is some evidence (Boissière et al., 1985) that in societies where schooling is more limited in its scope, the cognitive component in the returns to schooling may be considerably larger than in the U.S. However, according to Moll (1995), in a sample of black workers in South Africa, the value of ρ for returns to primary schooling is 0.73, for secondary schooling it is 0.67, while for higher education the value is 0.92. These are well within the range of estimates presented in Figure 15.4.

21. See Parsons (1959) and Dreeben (1967).

22. Indeed, the theory of social exchange (Blau, 1964), which underlies the sociological account of schooling as influencing individual preference structures, is recognizable to an economist as a theory of incomplete contracts.

23. Becker (1964) observed that in this case "any enforceable contract could at best specify the hours required on a job not the quality of the performance" (p. 6), but his work and the subsequent development of human capital theory did not take account of the important implications of this insight.

24. We formalize this model in Bowles and Gintis (1997).

25. These results are reported in Bowles and Gintis (1976). For the ten personality traits common to both studies, the simple correlations with grade-point average explain 96 percent of the variance in the simple correlations of these traits with supervisor ratings.

References

Altonji, Joseph G., "The Effects of High School Curriculum on Education and Labor Market Outcomes," *Journal of Human Resources* (Summer 1995): 410–438.

Altonji, Joseph G., and Thomas A. Dunn, "The Effects of School and Family Characteristics on the Return to Schooling," March 1995. NBER Working Paper No. 5072.

———, "The Effects of Family Characteristics on the Returns to Schooling," *Review of Economics and Statistics* 78, 4 (November 1996): 692–704.

Bajema, C. J., "A Note on the Interrelations Among Intellectual Ability, Education Attainment, and Occupational Achievement: A Follow-Up Study of a Male Kalamazoo Public School Population," *Sociology of Education* 41, 3 (Summer 1968): 317–319.

Becker, Gary, *Human Capital* (New York: Columbia University Press, 1964).

Behrman, Jere, *Human Resource Led Development? Review of Issues and Evidence* (New Delhi: International Labour Organization, 1990). World Employment Programme, Asian Regional Team for Employment Promotion; distributed by ILO, Geneva.

Blau, Peter, *Exchange and Power in Social Life* (New York: John Wiley, 1964).

Boissière, M., J. B. Knight, and R. H. Sabot, "Earnings, Schooling, Ability, and Cognitive Skills," *American Economic Review* 75, 5 (December 1985): 1016–1030.

Bowles, Samuel, "Schooling and Inequality from Generation to Generation," *Journal of Political Economy* 80, 3 (May–June 1972): S219–S251.

Bowles, Samuel, and Henry M. Levin, "The Determinants of Scholastic Achievement: An Appraisal of Some Recent Evidence," *Journal of Human Resources* (Winter 1968): 3–24.

Bowles, Samuel, and Herbert Gintis, "IQ in the U.S. Class Structure: A Statistical Analysis," *Social Policy* 3, 4–5 (November–December and January–February 1972).

———, "The Problem with Human Capital Theory," *American Economic Review* 65, 2 (May 1975):74–82.

———, *Schooling in Capitalist America: Educational Reform and the Contradictions of Economic Life* (New York: Basic Books, 1976).

———, "Labor Discipline and the Returns to Schooling," 1997. University of Massachusetts Working Paper.

Bowles, Samuel, and Valerie Nelson, "The 'Inheritance of IQ' and the Intergenerational Reproduction of Economic Inequality," *Review of Economics and Statistics* 56, 1 (February 1974).

Card, David, "The Causal Effect of Education on Earnings," in Orley Ashenfelter and David Card (eds.), *Handbook of Labor Economics, Vol. 3* (Amsterdam: North-Holland, 1998): 1801–1863.

Card, David, and Alan B. Krueger, "Labor Market Effects of School Quality: Theory and Evidence," in Gary Burtless (ed.), *Does Money Matter? The Effect of School Resources on Student Achievement and Adult Success* (Washington, D.C.: Brookings Institution Press, 1996), pp. 97–140.

Card, David, Francis Kramarz, and Thomas Lemieux, "Changes in the Relative Structure of Wages and Employment: A Comparison of the U.S., Canada, and France," December 1995. Unpublished.

Coleman, James, et al., *Equality of Educational Opportunity* (Washington, D.C.: GPO, 1966).

Conlisk, John, "A Bit of Evidence on the Income-Education-Ability Interaction," *Journal of Human Resources* 6, 3 (Summer 1971): 358–362.

Dreeben, Robert, *On what Is Learned in School* (Reading, Mass.: Addison-Wesley, 1967).

Duncan, Otis Dudley, "Ability and Achievement," *Eugenics Quarterly* 15, 1 (March 1968): 1–11.

Edwards, Richard C., "Personal Traits and 'Success' in Schooling and Work," *Educational and Psychological Measurement* 37 (1976): 125–138.

Eysenck, J., *The IQ Argument* (New York: Liberty Press, 1971).

Farkas, George, Paula England, Keven Vicknair, and Barbara Stanek Kilbourne, "Cognitive Skill, Skill Demands of Jobs, and Earnings Among Young European American, African American, and Mexican American Workers," *Social Forces* 75, 3 (March 1997): 913–940.

Feldman, Marcus W., Sarah P. Otto, and Freddy B. Christiansen, "Genes, Culture, and Inequality," in Kenneth Arrow, Samuel Bowles, and Steven Durlauf (eds.), *Meritocracy and Economic Inequality* (Princeton, N.J.: Princeton University Press, 2000), pp. 61–85.

Flynn, James R., "IQ Trends over Time: Intelligence, Race and Meritocracy," in Kenneth Arrow, Samuel Bowles, and Steven Durlauf (eds.), *Meritocracy and Economic Inequality* (Princeton, N.J.: Princeton University Press, 2000), pp. 35–60.

Gintis, Herbert, "Education, Technology, and the Characteristics of Worker Productivity," *American Economic Review* 61, 2 (1971): 266–279.

Gottschalk, Peter, "Policy Changes and Growing Earnings Inequality in Seven Industrialized Countries," February 1994. Luxemburg Income Study Working Paper 86.

Hanushek, Eric, "The Economics of Schooling: Production and Efficiency in Public Schools," *Journal of Economic Literature* 24, 3 (1986): 1141–1177.

Heckman, James, Anne Layne-Farrar, and Petra Todd, "Does Measured School Quality Really Matter? An Examination of the Earnings-Quality Relationship," in Gary Burtless (ed.), *Does Money Matter? The Effect of School Resources on Student Achievement and Adult Success* (Washington, D.C.: Brookings Institution Press, 1996), pp. 192–289.

Herrnstein, Richard J., "IQ," *Atlantic Monthly* 228, 3 (September 1971): 104–109.

Herrnstein, Richard J., and Charles Murray, *The Bell Curve: Intelligence and Class Structure in American Life* (New York: The Free Press, 1994).

Huang, Min-Hsiung, "Historical Changes in the Effects of Verbal Ability on Socioeconomic Success in the United States," March 1996. University of Wisconsin, Madison. Unpublished paper.

Jensen, Arthur A., "How Much Can We Boost IQ and Scholastic Achievement," *Harvard Educational Review* 39, 1 (1969):1–123.

——, *Educability and Group Differences* (New York: Harper and Row, 1975).

Juhn, Chinhui, Kevin Murphy, and Brooks Pierce, "Wage Inequality and the Rise in Returns to Skill," *Journal of Political Economy* 101, 1 (1993): 410–442.

Katz, Lawrence and Kevin Murphy, "Changes in Relative Wages, 1963–1987: Supply and Demand Factors," *Quarterly Journal of Economics* (1992):35–78.

Krueger, Alan, "How Computers Have Changed the Wage Structure," *Quarterly Journal of Economics* 108, 1 (1993): 33–60.

Levy, Frank and Richard Murnane, "U.S. Earnings Levels and Earnings Inequality: A Review of Recent Trends and Proposed Explanations," *Journal of Economic Literature* 30, 3 (September 1992): 1333–1381.

Moffitt, Robert, "The Distribution of Earnings and the Welfare State," in Gary Burtless (ed.), *A Future of Lousy Jobs?* (Washington, D.C.: Brookings Institution Press, 1990).

Moll, Peter, "Primary Schooling, Cognitive Skills and Wages in South Africa," June 1995. Unpublished.

Murnane, Richard, John B. Willett, and Frank Levy, "The Growing Importance of Cognitive Skills in Wage Determination," *Review of Economics and Statistics* 77, 2 (May 1995): 251–266.

Murphy, Kevin, and Finis Welch, "Inequality and Relative Wages," *American Economic Review* (May 1993): 104–109.

Parsons, Talcott, "The School Class as a Social System," *Harvard Educational Review* 29 (1959): 297–318.

Porter, James N., "Race, Socialization, and Mobility in Education and Early Occupational Attainment," *American Sociological Review* 39 (June 1974): 303–316.

Raphael, Steven, and Dennis Toseland, "Skills, Skill Breadth, and Wage Determination," October 1995. University of California, Berkeley.

Sewell, William H., Archibald P. Haller, and George W. Ohlendorf, "The Education and Early Occupational Status Achievement Process," *American Sociological Review* 35, 6 (December 1970): 1014–1027.

Solon, Gary R., "Intergenerational Income Mobility in the United States," *American Economic Review* 82, 3 (June 1992): 393–408.

Speakman, Robert, and Finis Welch, "Does School Quality Matter? A Reassessment," January 1995. Texas A&M University.

Zimmerman, David J. "Regression Toward Mediocrity in Economic Stature," *American Economic Review* 82, 3 (June 1992): 409–429.

Earnings of Black and White Youth and Their Relation to Poverty

PHILIP M. GLEASON AND GLEN G. CAIN

Economic analysis of the labor supply of young people who live with their parents traditionally includes attention to the effect of parental income on youth employment and earnings. In this chapter, we examine a particular aspect of the converse relation: the effect that work by young men ages 16 to 19 has on their family's income and poverty status. To address the question this way implies a reciprocal relation between youth employment and family income. Identifying causality is beyond our reach, but we can quantify the association of these two economic outcomes for black and white families with a rich source of data, the Survey of Income and Program Participation (SIPP), analyze the question of racial differences in youth employment in a historical context, and develop policy implications from our analysis.

Since the mid-1950s, employment rates of black youth (ages 16–24) declined relative to white youth. The second section of this chapter describes these trends and their causes and reports an unexpected positive relation between the income of parents and the employment of their teenage children. In the third section, SIPP data are used to examine the contemporaneous influence of youth employment on family income and on differences in the incidence of poverty between blacks and whites. We show that low employment for black youth and family poverty combine to create a depressing economic condition for a sizable minority of black families. The final section presents conclusions and policy implications.

Time Trends of Youth Employment and Family Poverty

YOUTH EMPLOYMENT

Table 16.1 and Figure 16.1 show time trends from 1955 to 1999 in ratios of civilian youth employment to the civilian youth population (E/P), by race and sex, for the age cohorts 16 to 19 and 20 to 24.[1] In 1999, the E/Ps for white men ages 16 to 19 and 20 to 24 were .49 and .79, respectively, but only .27 and .58 for black men of those age groups. Employment levels for blacks are lower despite their parents' lower incomes, which suggest a need for greater earnings, and despite their slightly lower enrollments in advanced schooling, a young person's main alternative activity to employment. The current racial gap in employment is the result of a sharp divergence in the time trends over the forty-four years under examination for the two groups: a pronounced declining trend for black young men and a fairly flat trend for whites. In 1955, the E/Ps for blacks were roughly the same as those for whites: about .52 for both white and black teenage males, and .80 and .78 for white and black men, respectively, ages 20 to 24.

A similar gap between the E/Ps of white and black young women increased during this period, although the direction of the women's trend lines differs from men's. The E/Ps for white women ages 16 to 19 rose from .37 in 1955 to .48 in 1999, while the E/Ps for black women of this age nudged from .26 to .29. Thus, the 11 percent gap in 1955, white-minus-black, became a 19 percent gap by 1999. For women ages 20 to 24, the E/P for whites rose from .44 in 1955 to .68 in 1996 and .69 in 1999; for blacks the rise was from .41 in 1955 to .53 in 1996 and .63 in 1999. The 3 percent gap in favor of whites in 1955 rose to a 15-point gap in 1996 and then narrowed to a 6-point gap in 1999. As discussed in more detail below, the sharp increase from .53 to .63 of the E/P for black women ages 20 to 24 during the period 1996 to 1999 is probably due to welfare reform in 1996, which virtually required women with dependent children who received income maintenance payments (from welfare programs) to secure gainful employment.

What were the economic and social forces behind these trends? Consider the rise in E/Ps for young white women and the nearly steady levels of E/Ps for young white men. The growth in parents' incomes led to *decreases in* these E/Ps from 1955 to 1999 and the associated rise in the proportion of 16-to 24-year-olds attending school. The rise in the market demand for youth labor induced an *increase in* the E/Ps was which was reflected in rising real wages. An important source of the increase in demand for young people's labor is growth in part-time jobs in the service industries, such as retail trade and fast-food restaurants, which accommodated combining employment with schooling.

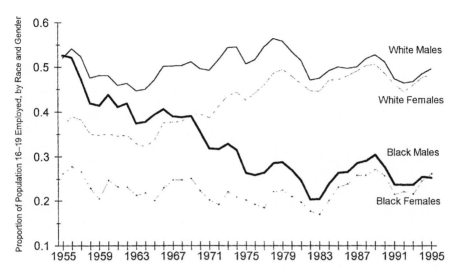

Figure 16.1 Employment-to-Population Ratios, 16- to 19-Year-Olds, 1955–1995
Source: Table 16.1

For young white men the incentives to work from the demand increase appears to have just offset the supply-side forces discouraging work (and encouraging education). For women, white and black, the increase in market demand appears greater than it was for men. Women's employment opportunities expanded relative to men's owing to technological changes that substituted mental for physical skills and by growth in demand for service relative to manufacturing goods. On the supply side, employment of young women was increased owing to their lower fertility and older ages of first marriages, although these changes surely reflect mutual causality; specifically, owing to rising wages and greater employment opportunities, women delayed their age of marriage and reduced their desired fertility rate.

The forces affecting the employment status of black youth are similar but more complex. In the early part of the forty-four years under analysis a substantial part of the black youth population lived in the rural South, where E/Ps were high, especially for males. Poverty and limited schooling opportunities were pervasive and causally related to a high E/P. These blacks were underemployed, but their unemployment rates were low. Migration of blacks to urban areas, especially to the North, where both their educational opportunities and rates of unemployment increased, explains some of the decline in their E/Ps from 1955 to the mid-1960s.[2] However, by 1965 most of the black population lived in urban settings, North and South, but declines in the E/Ps of black youth continued in the post-1965 period.

A related factor contributing to the widening racial gap in E/Ps from 1955

Table 16.1. Employment-to-Population Ratios (E/P) for Youth Ages 16–19, 20–24, by Race and Sex, 1955–1999

| | Men | | | | Women | | | |
| | 16–19 | | 20–24 | | 16–19 | | 20–24 | |
Year	White	Black	White	Black	White	Black	White	Black
1955	.520	.526	.804	.784	.370	.262	.435	.406
1956	.541	.521	.823	.781	.389	.278	.441	.384
1957	.524	.474	.805	.788	.382	.266	.434	.411
1958	.476	.419	.766	.714	.350	.229	.427	.392
1959	.481	.414	.808	.759	.348	.205	.414	.416
1960	.481	.438	.805	.784	.351	.247	.424	.413
1961	.459	.411	.788	.756	.346	.232	.430	.382
1962	.464	.419	.796	.763	.348	.231	.435	.398
1963	.447	.374	.791	.749	.329	.213	.438	.401
1964	.450	.377	.793	.781	.322	.218	.454	.436
1965	.471	.394	.802	.816	.337	.201	.461	.476
1966	.501	.406	.810	.829	.375	.230	.483	.476
1967	.502	.389	.805	.803	.377	.248	.499	.473
1968	.503	.387	.786	.780	.378	.248	.508	.512
1969	.511	.390	.787	.773	.395	.251	.533	.516
1970	.496	.355	.768	.729	.395	.223	.537	.490
1971	.492	.318	.754	.682	.386	.202	.531	.464
1972	.515	.316	.771	.704	.413	.192	.546	.469
1973	.543	.328	.802	.726	.436	.220	.574	.474
1974	.544	.314	.798	.699	.443	.209	.587	.476
1975	.506	.263	.743	.594	.425	.202	.581	.425
1976	.515	.258	.769	.613	.442	.192	.594	.441
1977	.544	.264	.787	.610	.459	.185	.615	.443
1978	.563	.285	.806	.622	.485	.221	.636	.486
1979	.557	.287	.811	.655	.494	.224	.650	.477
1980	.534	.270	.775	.609	.479	.210	.646	.462
1981	.513	.246	.770	.583	.462	.197	.650	.449
1982	.470	.203	.739	.539	.446	.177	.639	.423
1983	.474	.204	.743	.545	.445	.170	.647	.403
1984	.491	.239	.780	.580	.470	.201	.661	.451
1985	.499	.263	.780	.604	.471	.231	.675	.465
1986	.496	.265	.792	.613	.479	.238	.681	.487
1987	.499	.285	.796	.621	.490	.258	.693	.493
1988	.517	.290	.801	.639	.502	.258	.698	.507
1989	.526	.304	.789	.668	.505	.271	.679	.528

Table 16.1. Continued

	Men				Women			
	16–19		20–24		16–19		20–24	
Year	White	Black	White	Black	White	Black	White	Black
1990	.510	.276	.796	.612	.484	.257	.687	.501
1991	.472	.237	.766	.595	.460	.215	.669	.478
1992	.463	.236	.763	.569	.443	.221	.677	.467
1993	.466	.236	.772	.571	.458	.216	.680	.496
1994	.483	.254	.780	.596	.475	.245	.680	.518
1995	.494	.252	.784	.615	.481	.261	.670	.524
1996	.482	.249	.781	.593	.476	.271	.678	.532
1997	.481	.237	.789	.579	.472	.285	.692	.579
1998	.486	.284	.789	.588	.493	.318	.696	.587
1999	.493	.267	.794	.585	.483	.290	.694	.630

Source: U.S. Department of Labor, 1989, tables 3, 15, 16; and *Employment and Earnings,* January 1990–2000.

to the mid-1970s was growing convergence nationwide of the proportions of black and white youth attending high school. By the mid-1970s, the school-enrollment gap was nearly closed, but the continued relative decline in black youth E/Ps is not explained by schooling trends.[3] Once again, some reverse causation may be in effect, because poorer employment opportunities for black youth relative to whites may have given rise to decisions of black youth to stay in school longer.

Fertility rates of young black women are higher than those of whites, so this barrier to women's employment may be one explanation for the lower *level* of the E/Ps of young black women. The role of fertility in explaining the *trend* differences is less clear. From 1955 to 1999 both racial groups of women ages 20 to 24 showed sharp declines in fertility, while the trends for 15- to 19-year-olds were up for blacks and slightly down for whites.[4]

Related to childbearing in affecting employment of young women is a welfare system that has provided cash and noncash benefits to low-income families headed by a single parent (over 90 percent were women) with dependent children (18 years of age or younger). Until 1997, the largest welfare program for these families was Aid to Families with Dependent Children (AFDC), which discouraged employment by virtue of its income support payments and because earnings of recipients reduced welfare benefits. Mothers who had never married were particularly likely to be "on welfare." And, relative to whites, larger proportions of black women ages 15 to 24 who were never-married mothers[5] received welfare benefits.

In 1997, the AFDC program was replaced by the Personal Responsibility and Work Opportunity Reconciliation Act of 1996.[6] For our purposes, two important changes in the new welfare reforms, which vary across states, are (a) welfare mothers must seek and hold jobs and (b) provision of various forms of assistance to employment, such as subsidized daycare. As noted above, the E/P for black women ages 20 to 24 rose from .53 in 1996 to .63 in 1999, while the E/P for white women, who were much less affected by the welfare system, rose by only one percentage point, .67 to .68. We conclude that from 1955 to 1997, the welfare system played some role (probably minor) in determination of the relatively lower upward trend in the E/Ps for young black women.

From 1955 to 1996, the welfare system's disincentives to work could not have much affected young men, but the decline in E/Ps is much sharper for young black men than for young black women. Generally speaking, young men and young women were not eligible to receive welfare benefits if they lived in a two-parent family or in a family that was not poor. Young men living independently were rarely single parents with dependent children. Finally, if the young man or young woman was a dependent child in a family receiving welfare benefits, his or her earnings were usually exempt from reducing the family's welfare benefits (see Lerman, 1986, p. 412).

The foregoing discussion of the declining employment rate of black youth relative to white youth has emphasized supply-side factors; that is, factors that affect a person's offer of labor to the market. The demand side — job offers made by employers — has also received much attention. Although any hypothesis of long-run decline in market demand for labor of black youth is difficult to accept in the face of the overall rise in real wages during the 1955 to 1999 period,[7] the argument that the demand for black youth fell *relative to* whites has received considerable support.[8]

More could be said about the trends in youth employment, but our main concern is the relation between youth employment and family poverty. For this analysis we focus on men, ages 16 to 19, who, unlike 20- to 24-year-old men, usually live with their parents, which allows the relation between their parents' income and their employment status to be observed with data from household surveys. In addition, relative to 16- to 19-year-old women, 16- to 19-year-old men are less likely to be married and raising children. For example, in 1990, 3 percent of 18- to 19-year-old men were currently married,

Table 16.2. Five-Year Averages of Employment-to-Population Ratios for 16–19-Year-Old Men and Rates of Poverty for Families with Children Under Age 18: Whites and Blacks, 1959–1998

Years	Employment-to-Population		Family Poverty Rate	
	Whites	Blacks[a]	Whites	Blacks[a]
1959–63	.466	.411	14.9	55.2
1964–68	.485	.391	10.2	41.9
1969–73	.511	.341	8.4	34.2
1974–78	.534	.297	9.6	33.9
1979–83	.510	.242	12.1	37.3
1984–88	.500	.268	12.8	36.6
1989–93	.487	.258	13.3	38.0
1994–98	.485	.255	12.9	33.0

[a] Separate statistics for blacks for the years before 1967 were not reported by the Census Bureau. The figures shown for these years are for "nonwhite" persons and families. In 1967 black families were 91.4 percent of all nonwhite families and 96.5 percent of all nonwhite poor families, and in years before 1967 the black percentages of nonwhites are slightly larger. In 1967 the poverty rate for black families with children under 18 was 39.4; for corresponding nonwhite families, 37.4.

Source: See Table 15.1 for employment statistics. Poverty figures are from U.S. Bureau of the Census (1993, pp. 8–10); (1999b, pp. B-10–B-16).

compared to 10 percent of the women of that age (U.S. Bureau of the Census 1992, pp. 45, 71).

TRENDS IN POVERTY FOR FAMILIES WITH CHILDREN UNDER AGE 18

Table 16.2 shows family average poverty rates (the proportion of families with dependent children whose annual incomes fall below the official "poverty line" for eight five-year periods and the E/P for males 16 to 19, where poverty rates and E/P are given by the average for the period, 1959 to 1998. During this period, the average poverty rate for black families was 39 percent, more than three times the 12 percent poverty rate for white families. The use of five-year averages focuses attention on long-run trends and away from the year-to-year fluctuations that tend to be dominated by the business cycle. Poverty increases during recessions and decreases during prosperity, while E/Ps are affected conversely — decreasing during recessions and increasing during prosperity and low unemployment. Table 16.2 permits us to determine if a longer-run relation between youth E/P and family poverty is evident.

Among whites, there is evidence of a negative relation. Five of the seven changes in male teenage E/Ps from 1959 to 1998 are associated with opposite sign changes in family poverty. However, the change from 1969 to 1973 to 1974 to 1978 is positive for both the average E/Ps and the average poverty rate, and the E/P change from 1989 to 1993 to 1993 to 1998 is essentially zero while poverty decreased.

Among blacks, only three of the seven pairs of change in five-year-averages of E/Ps and poverty rates (1959 to 1998) have the opposite signs. In particular, the three pairs of changes from 1959 to 1979 are the same, all negative. This pattern is consistent with the hypothesis that declines in the poverty of black families during this period were associated with movement of black youth out of the rural South and into urban settings where their family incomes, school enrollments, and educational attainments increased. Indeed, in the century preceding 1960, a similar pattern held for white teenagers: a transition from rural to urban residence, decreasing rates of labor force participation, and increasing education, all associated with rising parental incomes and falling poverty rates. For reasons discussed above, E/Ps for whites ages 16 to 19 stopped declining around 1964.

In summary, teenage employment has not been, nor do we expect it to be, a major determinant of the poverty rate of families or of the black-white differences in family poverty. The time series do indicate, however, that youth employment has served to widen the income and poverty gap between white and black families and to widen the income gap between rich and poor families. The latter is addressed below.

A POSITIVE RELATION BETWEEN PARENTS' INCOME AND
EMPLOYMENT OF THEIR TEENAGE CHILDREN?

Using cross-sectional data, several researchers have found a positive relation between participation rates of young people and their parents' income (or family income excluding the income of the young person).[9] This relation holds despite the facts that: (a) conventional economic theory of labor supply assumes that leisure is a normal good, which implies that higher parental income leads, other things equal, to less gainful employment by their children;[10] (b) school enrollment among 16- to 19-year-olds is higher among high-income families;[11] and (c) young persons enrolled in school are less likely to be employed than those of the same age who are not enrolled.[12]

Among white families the positive cross-section relation between parental income and work by their children (ages 16 to 19 and living at home) is roughly consistent with the time-series relation observed from the mid-1960s to date. Parents' income and youth employment both increased from the mid-1960s until the mid-1970s, and declines and slowdown in white youth employment since the mid-1970s have been accompanied by stagnation of parents' incomes from that period until 1997. However, we are not arguing that the "pure" income effect on the labor supply of youth is positive, for that would imply that leisure and/or time spent in school are inferior goods. An alternative explanation for the time-series relation is simply that, for youth, rising market wages provided incentives to work that dominated the negative effect on work of the increase in their parents' income. An explanation for the positive cross-section relation between parents' income and the E/P of their 16- to 19-year-old children is that children in higher-income families can obtain better jobs, perhaps because of their parents' connections in the labor market and because more prosperous neighborhoods offer better employment opportunities for young people. Finally, there may be unobserved personal traits that cause low productivity among members of poor families, such as a lower quality of education for a given number of years of schooling completed. Whatever the underlying causes, the positive relation between parental income and their teenage children's employment generates greater income inequality between families and racially.

Using SIPP to Analyze the Relation Between the Employment of Young Men Ages 16 to 19 and Family Income

THE RELATION BETWEEN THE EMPLOYMENT OF TEENAGE MEN AND FAMILY POVERTY

SIPP is a nationally representative longitudinal (or panel) survey of households providing information on labor supply, income, and participation in government transfer programs. For each panel, a cohort of persons and families is followed for at most thirty-two months, with interviews taking place every four months. Table 16.3 shows the relation between employment of men, ages 16 to 19, living with their parents and poverty status of their families between late 1984 and early 1988, based on the 1985 and 1986 SIPP panels. Three levels of family income are used: below the poverty line (poor), between 1 and 1.5 times the poverty line (near poor), and above 1.5 times the poverty line (nonpoor). Family income is measured over a twelve-month span.[13]

As shown in Table 16.3, the incidence of poverty is high among black families with a teenage male and low among corresponding white families. Among black families, 38 percent are poor, 18 percent near poor, and 44

Table 16.3. Employment and Earnings of Young Men Ages 16–19 and Their Family's Poverty Status (1985–86 SIPP Data)

	White	Black	B/W Ratio
1. Poverty status of families (percentage distribution)			
Poor[a]	6%	38%	6.3
Near poor	7	18	2.6
Nonpoor	87	44	0.5
	100	100	
2. Percentage of months per year employed young men, ages 16–19			
Poor	27%	14%	.52
Near poor	35	20	.57
Nonpoor	52	38	.73
Total (all families)	49	26	.53
3. Average annual earnings of young men (workers and nonworkers)[b]			
Poor	$1,322	$717	.54
Near poor	1,671	943	.56
Nonpoor	2,928	2,532	.86
Total (all families)	2,750	1,553	.56
4. Hypothetical average annual earnings of the young men if worked twelve months[c]			
Poor	$4,897	$5,123	1.05
Near poor	4,777	4,716	.99
Nonpoor	6,504	6,664	1.02
Total (all families)	5,614	5,974	1.06
5. Number of families with a resident young man age 16–19 for 12 consecutive months	1,678	248	

[a] "Poor" refers to young men whose family income is below the poverty line; "near-poor" to between 1 and 1.5 times the poverty line; "nonpoor" to above 1.5 times the poverty line.
[b] To obtain the value of the dollar amounts in this table in 1998 dollars, multiply by 1.5, which is the inflation factor from 1986 to 1998.
[c] The hypothetical full-year earnings are calculated by dividing each earnings amount in item 3 by the decimal form of the percentages of months employed in item 2, cell by corresponding cell. See the discussion in the text concerning why these hypothetical annual earnings probably overstate the B/W ratio of all young men worked 12 months.

Source: Special tabulations from the 1985 and 1986 SIPP.

percent are nonpoor. Among the white families, 6 percent are poor, 7 percent are near poor, and 87 percent are nonpoor.

At all income levels, the employment proportions among 16- to 19-year-old men are lower among blacks than whites (item 2 in Table 16.3). Overall, young black males are employed in only 26 percent of the months in a year, relative to 49 percent for young white males. Differences in school enrollment do not explain this large difference in racial employment. White teenagers report enrollment in school for 79 percent of the months; the black teenagers, 75 percent.

Employment difference between the races is greater among poor families, where the months employed is 14 percent for black teenagers and 27 percent for whites, a black-white ratio of .52. For nonpoor families the black-white ratio is 38/52 = .73. The relation between the employment levels for young men and their family incomes is sharply negative, especially for blacks.[14] The large percentage of black families in poverty (38 percent, compared to 6 percent for whites), coupled with the low level of employment of young black men who are part of these families, presents a bleak picture, but one in which potential economic gains from improvements in their employment status have considerable scope.

The black/white ratios of earnings among 16- to 19-year-old men (item 3) are similar to their employment ratios (item 2), which implies that the labor market disadvantage of black youth is almost entirely a result of their lower employment levels. (Note that allowing for the rise in the Consumer Price Index from 1986 to 1998 would raise the earnings levels in item 3 by a factor of 1.5.) Also, as shown in item 4, the hypothetical average annual earnings obtained if the young men all worked twelve months would roughly equalize the earnings of black and white youth. The hypothetical full-year black-to-white earnings ratios in item 4 are, however, probably upwardly biased relative to what they would be if the same proportion of blacks and whites were actually employed. Such a bias would exist if, as seems reasonable, young men who are employed are selected from the higher end of the distribution of wage-earning abilities. Since the proportion of young black men employed is much smaller than the proportion of their white counterparts, employed blacks represent the higher end of the wage distribution to a greater extent than is the case for whites.

ESTIMATING THE DETERMINANTS OF THE
EMPLOYMENT OF YOUNG MEN AGES 16 TO 19

We use the 1985 and 1986 panels of SIPP to estimate the probability of employment in a given month for 16- to 19-year-old black and white men in relation to available personal, family, and labor market characteristics.[15] To examine the affect of the labor market of residence on a young man's employment, we restricted our sample to households living in standard metropolitan statistical areas (SMSAs) so that we could obtain such variables as the area's unemployment rate and its industrial structure. In 1990, 80 percent of the U.S. population lived in SMSAs. The panel survey provided up to thirty-two monthly observations for each person.

The dependent (or outcome) variable in our estimated model is categorical (or binary). It is given a value of one if working in the month and zero otherwise. Table 16.4 shows the independent (or determinant) variables, their means (in parentheses), and estimated "effects" of the independent variable — where "effect" denotes change in employment probability with respect to a specified (usually a unit) change in the independent variable.[16] We limit our discussion of Table 16.4 to personal and market variables that have potential policy implications for reducing family poverty by improving employment opportunities of young persons. Other variables, such as age, Hispanic ethnicity, and limitations of health on working, serve mainly descriptive purposes and as control variables.[17]

For both black and white men ages 16 to 19, the probability of employment is positively related to their family's income (excluding their own income), and this positive effect is stronger for black youth. An increase of $500 in monthly income for white families is estimated to increase the white youth's probability of employment by only .002, which is neither practically nor statistically significant.[18]

An increase of $500 in monthly income for black families is predicted to increase the employment probability of 16- to 19-year-olds by .018, which is both practically and statistically significant. Note that a $500 increase in the black family income is a 26 percent increase in their mean family income (shown in Table 4 to be $1,901 per month), but only a 15 percent increase in white mean family income (= $3,313).[19] For blacks, the larger size of the effect of family income is, however, demonstrated by the fact that even a 15 percent increase in black mean family income, which is $285, predicts an increase in the probability of the teenage males employment by .010, which is much larger than the white teenager's predicted increase of .002. Unfortunately, the policy implication of this finding is not clear, because the causal explanation for the positive relation between family income and the teenage male's employment is not well understood.

The categorical variable for nonlabor income has to do with a family that receives $100 or more per month of (mainly) property income, such as rents, dividends, interest payments, and capital gains. Transfer payments are not included. Only 4 percent of white families and 1 percent of black families received $100 or more of nonlabor income, and large amounts of this type of income tend to be concentrated in very wealthy families. Thus, the large negative effects of this variable on the probability of employment of the young person applies to less than 5 percent of the households.

Four other explanatory variables are related to family income: living in a one-parent family, living in a family that receives government cash transfer payments (mainly AFDC payments), living in public housing, and living in rent-subsidized housing. Each variable may be viewed, in part, as an indicator of low permanent (or normal) income, given that current income is observed and controlled for in the estimated model. In part, each variable also measures its own effect on labor supply; for example, the absence of a male role model for children in families with only a mother present, poor neighborhoods, limited employment opportunities where public housing is prevalent, and so on.

Fully 50 percent of black youths live in a one-parent household, relative to 22 percent of white youths, but the negative influence of this variable on the probability of employment is small and statistically insignificant for both white and black youth, −.03 and −.02, respectively. Welfare status, by itself, has a relatively large negative relation to youth employment of whites, −.10, which implies that a white 16- to 19-year-old who lives in a family receiving welfare benefits has a 10 percent lower probability of being employed than his counterpart whose family is not on welfare. This is a sizable effect, but only 10 percent of white families reported receiving welfare payments. The welfare coefficient for blacks is small, −.03, but 29 percent of the black families report receiving welfare payments.[20] Living in public housing has a statistically significant negative effect on the employment probability of black youth, −.10, and 13 percent of black families live in public housing. On the other hand, for whites, there is no effect. With respect to rent-subsidized housing only a very small percent of black and white families live in this housing, and thus, residence in this housing has no effect. While the separate effects of the four poverty-related variables are small, their cumulative negative effect on the youth's employment probability may be sizable (excluding living in rent-subsidized housing) living with a single parent, in public housing, and being on welfare given that each is arguably causally related to each other.

The effects of two personal variables, school enrollment and school attainment, must be interpreted with caution, because each variable may be a consequence of a youth's employment status rather than, or in addition to, a cause of that status.[21] Enrollment status is a categorical variable, and, as indicated by its mean value, young men in the sample were enrolled 75 percent of the months reported. School enrollment is, as expected, negatively related to employment, although increasing one's schooling is surely positively related to future earnings.

Table 16.4. *Estimated Marginal Effects of Independent Variables on the*
Probability of Employment in a Given Month Among Men 16–19, 1985 SIPP Data

Independent Variable	White Marginal Effect	(Mean)	Black Marginal Effect	(Mean)
Monthly family income[a]	.00	($3,313)	.02***	($1,901)
Hispanic	.11***	(.11)	−.20**	(.04)
Year: 1984	.00	(.05)	.04	(.06)
1986	.00	(.36)	−.00	(.34)
1987	−.03	(.17)	.02	(.15)
Summer month	.13***	(.20)	.05	(.20)
Age: 17	.20***	(.26)	.26***	(.27)
18	.25***	(.25)	.33***	(.25)
19	.33***	(.25)	.36***	(.24)
Parents on welfare	−.07**	(.10)	−.03	(.29)
Health limitation	−.07*	(.04)	.16	(.04)
Education: lagging behind[b]	−.17***	(.19)	−35***	(.29)
on track[b]	−.05	(.46)	−.23***	(.48)
some college[b]	−.10***	(.24)	−.24***	(.12)
Enrolled in school	−.17***	(.75)	−.10	(.72)
Proxy response[c]	−.10***	(.74)	−.16***	(.74)
Living alone[d]	.03	(.08)	−.01	(.15)
One parent[d]	−.03	(.22)	−.02	(.50)
Nonlabor income[e]	−.12***	(.04)	−.08	(.01)
Subsidized-rent housing	.05	(.01)	.05	(.03)
Public housing	.00	(.02)	−.10*	(.13)
Central city residence	−.05	(.35)	.00	(.53)
Segregation index	.01	(2.74)	.01	(2.59)

School attainment is specified by four categorical variables: (1) not enrolled and a high school graduate without any college experience (the omitted
variable); (2) having some college experience; (3) having completed less than
twelve years of schooling but being on track, in the sense that the number of
years of schooling is standard for the person's age; and (4) lagging behind, defined as having completed fewer years of schooling than that which is standard
for the person's age. The last category includes high school dropouts. School
attainment is positively related to gainful employment, with a relatively larger
coefficient for blacks than for whites. Being either a high school dropout or,
if in school, lagging behind, has a large negative effect on employment, −.35
for blacks and −.17 for whites. These values represent the largest changes

Table 16.4. Continued

Independent Variable	White Marginal Effect	White (Mean)	Black Marginal Effect	Black (Mean)
Log population[f]	.01***	(2.6M)	.00	(3.2M)
Percentage black	−.00	(16)	−.01***	(22)
1986 unemployment rate	.00	(6.5)	−.02**	(7.0)
1982 log per capita retail sales[g]	.01	($4,720)	.05***	($4,545)
Number (person-months)	10,871		2,081	
Employment-to-population ratio	.53		.30	

Note: The term "effect" in the headings of columns 2 and 4 does not necessarily imply a causal effect. See the text discussion of this point.

[a] Family income excludes the earnings of the 16–19-year-old male. The "marginal effect" is a response to a $500 increase in monthly income. To approximate the mean incomes in 1998 dollars, multiply by 1.5.

[b] The excluded education variable is "having a high school degree as the highest educational attainment."

[c] Respondent is someone other than the 16–19-year-old male.

[d] Living with two parents is the excluded variable. "Living alone" indicates living away from parents.

[e] Nonlabor income is a dummy variable: 1 if family received $100 or more of (mainly) rent, interest, dividend, or capital gains in the month; zero otherwise.

[f] The "marginal effect" is a response to an increase of one million in population.

[g] The "marginal effect" is a response to an increase of $750 (1985 dollars) in per capita retail sales.

Source: 1985 SIPP panel.

in probabilities of employment of any potentially policy-related variable in the model. Moreover, 29 percent of black youth are in this category, relative to 19 percent of white youth. Unfortunately, we cannot determine the extent to which the schooling effect is exogenous and indicative of a response to a policy change or the extent to which it is merely reflective of unobserved personal traits.

Of clearer policy significance are results for two variables that measure demand factors in the SMSA labor market where the youth resides. We assume that residence in a given SMSA is exogenous, which seems reasonable for male teenagers, almost all of whom live with their parents. Given this, the SMSA's unemployment rate (measured for 1986) and level of per capita retail sales (measured for 1982) may be considered exogenous determinants of the young person's employment status. Retail sales is selected as a proxy for market demand for youth labor because retail activity is the largest provider of jobs for teenagers. For white males ages 16 to 19, effects of these variables on the probability of employment are negligible, whereas for black youth the effects have the expected sign, are relatively large, and are statistically significant.[22]

Other SMSA characteristics have a small impact on youth employment. Living in an SMSA where a large fraction of the population is black has a statistically significant negative effect on the employment of black youth but no effect on employment of white youth. The effects of living in the central city (as distinct from the suburbs) and of segregation in an SMSA are also insignificant for both white and black youth.[23]

In summary, the results shown in Table 16.4 indicate that a number of factors are associated with, and arguably causally related to, low employment of black youth: high levels of unemployment in the area where the youth lives, low levels of teenage job availability, low educational attainment, low family income, and the combined negative effects on youth employment of three poverty-related variables — one-parent families, receipt of welfare payments, and living in public housing. These results suggest a role for policy intervention to increase employment opportunities of black youth and to increase income and improve living standards of black families.

SIMULATION ESTIMATIONS OF THE QUANTITATIVE EFFECT OF YOUTH EMPLOYMENT ON THEIR FAMILY'S POVERTY

Tables 16.5 and 16.6 show results of several types of simulation to measure effects on poverty, if youth employment and earnings were changed in specified ways. Table 16.5 shows change in poverty, if current earnings of 16- to 19-year-old males were excluded from current family income, on the assumption that no other changes in family income or in family composition occurred. The poverty rate rises, and the rise is larger among white than among black families. This is not surprising, because a larger proportion of white youth are employed than black youth. In Panel A of Table 16.5, which uses a twelve-month sample, the number of poor black families increases by 8 percent (from 95 to 103), the number of near poor does not change, and the number of nonpoor decreases by 7 percent (from 108 to 100). The incidence of poverty increases from .38 to .42.

Among white families, exclusion of earnings of 16- to 19-year-old males leads to an increase of 38 percent in the number of poor families (from 105 to 150), an increase of 27 percent in the number of near-poor families (from 118 to 145), and a decrease of 5 percent in the number of nonpoor families (from 1,455 to 1,383). The incidence of poverty increases from .06 to .09.

Table 16.5. Number of Families That Are Poor, Near Poor, and Nonpoor When Excluding or Including the Earnings of Young Men Ages 16–19, 1985–1986 SIPP Data

A. Number of families in the sample with a resident male age 16–19 for twelve consecutive months, under specified income conditions

| | Youth Earnings | | | | | |
| | White (n = 1,678) | | | Black (n = 248) | | |
Family Income[a]	Incl.	Excl.	%Chng.	Incl.	Excl.	%Chng.
Poor	105	145	38%	95	103	8%
Near poor	118	150	27	45	45	0
Nonpoor	1,455	1,383	−5	108	100	−7
Poverty rate	.063	.086	37	.383	.415	8

B. Number of families in the sample with a resident male age 16–19 for three consecutive months, under specified income conditions

| | Youth Earnings | | | | | |
| Family | White (n = 2,335) | | | Black (n = 332) | | |
Income[b]	Incl.	Excl.	%Chng.	Incl.	Excl.	%Chng.
Poor	178	252	42%	122	134	10%
Near poor	173	207	20	60	60	0
Nonpoor	1,984	1,876	−5	150	138	−8
Poverty rate	.076	.108	42	.367	.404	10

[a] "Incl." refers to family income that includes the earnings (if any) of the 16–19-year-old. "Excl." refers to family income that excludes the earnings (if any) of the 16–19-year-old, and assumes no other change in family income.
[b] In panel B the three-month earnings data are annualized.

Source: Special tabulations from the 1985 and 1986 SIPP.

Panel B of Table 16.5 is based on a sample which includes a 16- to 19-year-old male residing in the family for at least three consecutive months. Our main purpose is to obtain a larger sample size, especially for blacks, but the incidence of poverty based on a three-month accounting period (with the income adjusted to annualize the period) is of interest on its own. These samples, larger by 34 to 40 percent, show results similar to those based on twelve months of data.

In Table 16.6, nine simulated changes in earnings of black young men ages 16 to 19 are carried out to measure the effects change in the poverty rate and in

Table 16.6. Simulated Poverty Rates for Black Families Under Different Assumptions about Earnings of Black Males Ages 16–19, (1985–86 SIPP Data)

Simulation[a]	Mean Monthly Earnings Used ($)	Poverty Rate	Poverty Gap ($)
BASE: Poverty rates with actual earnings averaged over all black youth	$130	.383	−$5,586
S1. All black youth earn mean earnings of whites	230	.335	−3,975
S2. All black youth earn mean earnings of nonpoor black youth	211	.335	−4,209
S3. All black workers earn mean earnings of white workers	438	.379	−5,652
S4. All black workers earn mean earnings of nonpoor black workers	518	.371	−5,558
S5. All black youth earn mean earnings of white workers	438	.226	−1,896
S6. All black youth earn mean earnings of nonpoor black workers	518	.161	−1,451
S7. Black youth are randomly chosen to equal the employment percentage of white youth and earn the white workers' mean earnings	438	.323	−4,436
S8. Black youth randomly chosen to equal the employment percentage of white poor*, near poor[#], nonpoor[@] (32%, 42%, 53%) and earn the whites' mean earnings[b]	388* 390[#] 444[@]	.371	−5,202

the average poverty gap. The poverty gap is defined as the average of each poor family's income minus the family's poverty line. This measures changes in incomes of poor families whether or not the poverty line is crossed, and it is a more comprehensive measure of change in the economic well-being of families.

Again, increases in a young man's employment and earnings are assumed not to change his living arrangements or the earnings of his parents. For brevity, we do not show changes in the income status of the near-poor and nonpoor families in Table 16.6.

Table 16.6. Continued

Simulation[a]	Mean Monthly Earnings Used ($)	Poverty Rate	Poverty Gap ($)
S9. Employment percentage and earnings of black youth are determined as if their characteristics are rewarded the same as white characteristics[c]	593	.308	−5,155

[a] The simulation is based on a sample size of 248 black families.

[b] "Poor" refers to young men whose family income is below the poverty line; "near poor" to between 1 and 1.5 times the poverty line; "nonpoor" to above 1.5 times the poverty line. The percentages 32, 42, and 53 are those of white youth in poor, near poor, and nonpoor families, respectively.

[c] The employment status of black youth is determined by multiplying the values of their characteristics (age, etc.) by the coefficients of these characteristics from the employment probit model for white youth shown in Table 16.4. The earnings of black youth are determined analogously; that is, by multiplying the values of their characteristics by the coefficients from a regression for white youth with earnings as the dependent variable (regression not shown, see Cain and Gleason 1991). These simulations were conducted using only the 1985 SIPP panel. In the same type of simulation but with the estimated coefficients for black youth as well as the values of the characteristics of black youth, the resulting poverty rate is .346 and the poverty gap is −$6,451. See text for further discussion of these simulations.

Source: Special tabulations of the 1985 and 1986 SIPP.

Simulation 1, hereinafter S1, shows changes in the poverty rate and the poverty gap if *all* black youth earned the mean earnings of *all* white youth. S2 shows these changes if *all* black youth earned the mean earnings of *all* nonpoor black youth. The mean earnings of these assignments are shown in column (2) and are calculated using observations for those who worked and those who did not. S1 and S2 are based on changes that ought to be feasible policy goals. The impact on the poverty rate is modest, dropping to .34 from the base level of .38 in both cases. The reduction in the poverty gap is more impressive: the average poor family's gap is reduced in S1 from $5,586 to $3,975, a 29 percent reduction. The corresponding reduction in S2 is 25 percent. Interestingly, the reduction achieved by assigning the monthly earnings ($211) of black youth in nonpoor families to all black youth is about the same as the S1 reduction from an assignment of the monthly earnings ($231) of white youth. We will refer to the S1 type of change as a black/white difference and to S2 as a poor/nonpoor difference.

The next pair of simulations, S3 and S4, assign to young black workers the mean earnings of white workers (S3) or the mean earnings of nonpoor black workers (S4), but these have virtually no effect on the poverty rate or gap relative to the base levels. The reason for this is, among young men ages 16 to 19, nearly the entire source of lower earnings of blacks relative to whites stems from lower employment levels of the blacks, and not from lower earnings among those who have jobs.

Simulations S5 and S6 illustrate a particular version of an upper bound on the effect of increased earnings on poverty. In S5, black youths are assumed to have a 100 percent employment rate and to earn the mean earnings of whites ages 16 to 19. In S6, black youth are assumed to have a 100 percent employment rate and to earn the (higher) mean earnings of nonpoor black workers ages 16 to 19. The black poverty rate is virtually halved, but the rate is still almost three times that of whites, even though the assumption in the simulation is unrealistically beneficial to blacks.

Simulations S7 and S8 are different ways of allowing black youth employment and earnings to match those of white youth. In S7, a randomly chosen group of blacks is assumed to be employed and each is assigned the mean earnings of white workers. The random selection is done in such a way that the proportion of black youth employment matches that of white youth. The poverty rate resulting from this simulation declines from .38, the base rate, to .32, which is slightly lower than in S1. Note that this simulation removes not only differences in employment and earnings between blacks and whites but also the poor/nonpoor differences. Simulation S8 repeats the same random selection process so that the percent of black employment percentage and mean earnings matches the percent of white employment and mean earnings in each of the three income strata. Thus, this simulation does not remove differences in poor/nonpoor employment and earnings. It yields only a small reduction in black poverty, from .38 to .37. The reason for this is as follows: even though the employment proportion of the 16- to 19-year-olds in poor white families is about twice as high as among blacks, 27 percent compared to 14 percent, it is much lower than the employment proportion of 49 percent among all white youth, which was used in S7.

The final simulation, S9, is derived from the following background analysis. We have seen in Table 16.4 that various characteristics of young men ages 16 to 19 have certain effects on their employment probabilities. Elsewhere (Gleason and Cain, 1991) we have estimated how these variables (or characteristics) affect the earnings of young men. We, as have many other investigators, find that, on average, any given variable has a greater positive (or a smaller negative) effect on employment and earnings for white than for black young men. Indeed, such findings have provided economists with a definition and measure of labor market discrimination against black or other minority workers. In simulation S9, we assume that the personal and market characteristics used in the estimated models for employment and earnings are rewarded in the labor market equally for blacks and whites. Our operational procedure is to assign the white coefficients effects of the characteristics to the black values of the characteristics. By this device, we are able to estimate what these young black workers ages 16 to 19 would earn if they did not face labor market discrimination. The variables and their effects on employment are shown in Table 16.4. The earnings model is not shown, but the list of variables is the same.

We find that the incidence of poverty among blacks is reduced from .35 to .31, an 11 percent reduction, and that the poverty gap is reduced from $6,451 to $5,155, a 20 percent reduction.[24] Thus, black family incomes would rise and poverty would decrease if the labor market gave young black males the same employment and earnings rewards per characteristic (for example, per year of schooling) as those estimated for white males.

In summary, we refer to simulations 1 and 2. Simulation 1 assigned increases in earnings of the young black men to the levels attained by young white men, and this yielded a modest reduction of 12 percent in the black poverty rate and a substantial reduction of 29 percent in the poverty gap. Simulation 2, which assigned the average earnings of nonpoor black men, ages 16 to 19, to poor black men, ages 16 to 19, brought about a similar reduction in poverty, which shows that the lag in employment by black youth in poor families behind that of black youth in the relatively well-off families is another source of the high incidence of poverty in black families. A somber point is that the lag in youth employment of blacks relative to whites has been very large in recent years. As mentioned previously, employment, rather than earnings of those employed, is the main source of the black disadvantage in the youth labor market.

Conclusion

The relationship between youth employment and the poverty status of their families is a relatively small part of the larger problem of the white-black gap in youth employment performance. Most research has dealt with the latter problem because of the reasonable concern that the weaker employment performance of black youth compared with white youth portends a long-run prospect of earnings inequality between whites and blacks. In this chapter, we add an analysis of the immediate influence of youth employment on family income and on current black-white differences in the incidence of poverty.

We have found that improving the employment proportions among black young men ages 16 to 19 can reduce the amount of poverty in their families to a moderate but meaningful degree. Moreover, policies that improve the labor market opportunities of black youth would have larger effects than our calculations show, because the employment of young black women ages 16 to 19 and ages 20 to 24, blacks of both sexes would also increase — outcomes that we have not tried to calculate.

We also suggest that a small feedback relation between black youth employment and family income exists that would serve to magnify gains if either variable were increased. We doubt that parents would decrease their earnings if their children earned more, and higher family incomes might lead to residential moves to better neighborhoods and a local environment that offers more employment opportunities. Less speculative are the findings of the negative effects on youth employment of several variables that are also associated with poverty, such as marketwide unemployment, one-parent families, and low educational attainment. Improvements in these conditions would raise both youth employment and their family incomes.

Notes

Much of this research was carried out while the authors were research fellows of the American Statistical Association/National Science Foundation at the U.S. Bureau of the Census. We are grateful for assistance from Robert Fay and David McMillen and for research support from the Institute for Research on Poverty and the La Follette Institute of Public Affairs at the University of Wisconsin — Madison. IRP publications (discussion papers, special reports, and the newsletter *Focus*) are now available electronically at http://www.ssc.wisc.edu/irp/.

1. The E/P is similar to the more commonly used labor force participation rate, LF/P. In both ratios the civilian population of the demographic group under study is the denominator. The labor force, LF, is the employed plus the unemployed. We use E/P because it measures the fraction of the youth population that has been successful in obtaining a job. The E/Ps shown are the annual average of the twelve monthly surveys of the labor force activity of the civilian population at a point in time for each month. See Table 16.1 for sources.

2. The proportion of black youth ages 16 to 24 living in rural areas was 55 percent in 1940, 31 percent in 1960, and 15 percent in 1980. Almost all blacks living in rural areas were in the South. The trend for white youth ages 16 to 24 is 43 percent in 1940, 29 percent in 1960, and 25 percent in 1980 (U.S. Bureau of the Census 1943, table 7; U.S. Bureau of the Census 1964, table 155; U.S. Bureau of the Census 1983, Table 41).

3. The black-to-white ratios of school enrollment proportions for 16- to 17-year-olds

are: .90 (=.72/.80) in 1947, .94 (=.85/.90) in 1957, .94 (=.85/.89) in 1967, and 1.03 (=.91/.88) in 1977. The black-to-white ratios of school enrollment for 18- to 19-year-olds increased from .84 (=.407/.484) in 1967 to 1.06 (=.483/.455) in 1977, and have remained near 1 since 1977. It should be noted that if we measure success in high school by the proportion of 18- to 24-year-olds who have graduated, then the racial gap in this measure has been more prolonged. The black-to-white ratios of graduates in this age group were .72 (=.56/.78) in 1967 and .90 (=.75/.83) in 1997 (U.S. Bureau of the Census 1999a, p. 2; U.S. Bureau of the Census 1992, pp. A6, A12).

4. In 1959 the numbers of children ever born per 1,000 women (married and unmarried) ages 15 to 19 and 20 to 24 were 103 and 1,025, respectively, for whites; 179 and 1,426 for blacks (officially nonwhites). In 1995 the corresponding numbers of children ever born were 92 for white women ages 15 to 19, 518 for white women ages 20 to 24, 216 for black women ages 15 to 19, and 881 for black women ages 20 to 24 (U.S. Bureau of the Census 1961, table 1; U.S. Bureau of the Census, 1997, table 1).

5. Two sets of statistics provide evidence for this point. In 1996, among black women 17 percent of those ages 15 to 19 and 28 percent of those 20 to 24 were never-married mothers. The corresponding statistics for whites were 6 percent and 10 percent, respectively (U.S. Bureau of the Census, 1997, table 1). In another report of the Bureau of the Census (1995), 25 percent of black mothers and 7 percent of white mothers between the ages of 15 and 44 received payments from AFDC. Of course, not all never-married mothers with dependent children were on welfare, but in 1995 57 percent of welfare mothers had no marriage tie, which is twice the 28 percent who had divorced or separated from their husbands. Two-parent couples were only 12 percent of the recipient families, and other family arrangements made up the remaining 3 percent (U.S. Congress, 1998, p. 440).

6. See U.S. Congress, 1998, pp. 494–503, for a description of the provisions of the new welfare law.

7. Welch (1990) calculated the average increase in wages for employed young black workers from the 1960s to the 1980s and used the proportions of employed and not employed young blacks to argue that the overall average wage available to black youth rose during this period. It would be surprising if this were not the case, given the large overall rise in wages during this period. Between 1960 and 1990 real wages rose for all male workers by 27 percent and for all female workers by 50 percent (U.S. Bureau of Census, 1998, p. C-10).

8. A huge research literature deals with the issue of declining job opportunities for black youth during the 1970s and 1980s, primarily as a consequence of the exodus of businesses from inner cities to suburbs and the movement of businesses from areas with relatively large black populations (the "rust belt") to areas with relatively small black populations (the "sun belt"). See Moss and Tilly (1991) for a review of this literature.

9. Bowen and Finegan (1969, p. 387) show a weak positive relation between parents' income and the labor force participation rate of their children in the 1-in-1,000 sample of the 1960 census, especially evident over the parents' income range from $8,500 to $83,000 (in 1998 dollars), which covered about 80 percent of all families in their data. See also Cain and Finnie (1990), based on data from the 1980 census, and Cain and Gleason (1991).

10. Phrased another way, children may be assumed to prefer leisure to work, other things being equal, and children of richer parents have less need to work.

11. Using special tabulations from the 1980 decennial census, Cain (1987, p. 27) reports that in April 1980 approximately 80 percent of 17-year-old white men in families with incomes under $40,000 (in 1998 dollars) were enrolled in school, compared with 90 percent in families with incomes over $40,000. Among 17-year-old black men, the corresponding enrollment rates were 85 percent and 90 percent. Earnings, if any, of the 17-year-old sons were excluded from the family incomes for these calculations to permit a measure of family income that was mostly unaffected by the schooling and employment status of the son. See also the strong negative relation between family incomes and high school dropout rates shown for 1991 in data from the National Center for Education Statistics (McMillen et al., 1993). Other issues of this annual series of NCES also provide evidence for this relation.

12. Among 16- to 19-year-olds the negative relation between school enrollment and employment holds consistently only for males. See the November issues of *Employment and Earnings,* the labor force report of the U.S. Department of Labor. In 1991 the E/P for males ages 16 to 19 who were enrolled in school was 32.5; not enrolled, 67.3. For females the corresponding E/Ps were 36.2 and 33.1. Being married, bearing and raising children, and performing other household work are likely explanations for the low E/P for women ages 16 to 19 who are not enrolled in school.

13. We have also used samples of young men who were in the SIPP sample for as few as six months and three months to obtain larger sample sizes. In these trials we defined family poverty for a six- or three-month period. The results based on these larger samples were similar to the results based on the twelve-month sample and are not presented here.

14. As discussed in the next section, this negative relation remains when we exclude the earnings of the young men from their family incomes.

15. The labor market variables were appended to the original SIPP data set, using the *County and City Data Book, 1988* of the U.S. Bureau of the Census. Access to the city and county residence of the SIPP respondents is available to Census Bureau employees and was available to us during our period of research at the Census Bureau.

16. Our statistical method is probit estimation, which uses a nonlinear function that constrains the probability (of employment) to lie between zero and one. The "effect" that any given independent variable has in changing the probability of being employed depends on the point of evaluation, for which we use the estimated probability when the independent variables are set at their mean values. We use quotes around effects, because the term's implication that the coefficients measure causal impacts of changes in the determinant variables is not always warranted, as we discuss below.

17. For a more complete discussion of these estimations, as well as the results of a variety of other models of employment and earnings among white and black men ages 16 to 19 and 20 to 24, see Cain and Gleason (1991). We note here that one unexpected coefficient in the estimates for blacks is .16 for the binary variable indicating the presence of a health limitation. The coefficient is not statistically significant, and we have no explanation for its unexpected sign.

18. Statistical significance of the probit estimates in Table 16.4 is indicated to an approximation by the asterisks alongside the coefficients. Because we use person-months

as units of observation there is a person-specific source of nonindependence among the observations. In addition there is possible serial correlation, even though we control for the calendar year and whether the month was a summer month. Finally, SIPP's sample design is geographically clustered. To allow for the overstatement of statistical significance that results from these sources of nonindependence of our observations, we have applied a rule-of-thumb deflation factor to our reported t-ratios that we obtained from trial estimations of regression models that used a variance correction procedure developed by Robert Fay of the U.S. Bureau of the Census. We are indebted to Fay for his calculations for us of corrected standard errors, using his CPLX software program that incorporates a jack-knife procedure for computing the standard errors of estimated coefficients.

19. To scale these dollar amounts to 1998 price levels, they should be multiplied by 1.5.

20. As noted earlier, being on welfare before the welfare reform legislation of 1996 took effect carried a high implicit tax on the earnings of the head of the household, but this tax was generally not imposed on working children in these families. (The term *tax* is used because welfare payments were usually reduced as earnings increased.) Lerman (1986) did find a large negative effect of living in a welfare family on the probability that the young person is employed, despite the exemption of the young person's earnings from the welfare tax. However, it is difficult to argue that receiving welfare benefits, by itself, reduces the employment and earnings of the teenagers in the family, because (a) welfare families have very low incomes, and (b) the observed relation between parental income and youth employment is positive in the general population.

21. Living alone is another variable that may be caused by, rather than a cause of, the youth's employment. However, among the sample's 16- to 19-year-old men, only 8 percent of the whites and 15 percent of the blacks live alone, and this variable is insignificantly related to employment for each group.

22. In estimations (not shown) of the probability of employment of young men ages 20 to 24, the effect of unemployment is significantly negative for both whites and blacks, and the effect of retail sales is positive but insignificant for whites and positive and marginally significant for blacks.

23. In a specification not shown here, the coefficients of central city residence and the segregation index are both positive, and the coefficient on an interaction between them is negative and significant for black youth. This implies that in highly segregated cities, living in the central city has a negative influence on a black youth's chances of working. In cities that are less segregated, however, living in a central city is beneficial to a black youth's employment probability.

24. The base poverty rate and poverty gap used in S9 differ from those in the top row of Table 16.6 for two reasons. First, S9 is based on data from the 1985 SIPP panel, which we used for the estimations, but simulations S1 to S8 use both the 1985 and 1986 panels. Second, the base figures for S9 are calculated by using characteristics and coefficients of black youth to predict their earnings — and then adding predicted youth earnings to family income to determine whether the family is above or below the poverty line. By so doing we can attribute any changes in poverty rates and the poverty gap to the differences between the white and black coefficients, rather than to the method used to predict youth earnings.

References

Bowen, William G., and T. Aldrich Finnegan. 1969. *The Economics of Labor Force Participation.* Princeton: Princeton University Press.

Cain, Glen G. 1987. "Black-White Differences in Employment of Young People: An Analysis of 1980 Census Data." Institute for Research on Poverty, Discussion Paper No. 844–87, University of Wisconsin — Madison.

Cain, Glen G., and Ross E. Finnie. 1990. "The Black-White Difference in Youth Employment: Evidence for Demand-Side Factors." *Journal of Labor Economics* 8 (1, pt. 2): S364–S395.

Cain, Glen G., and Philip M. Gleason. 1991. "Using SIPP to Analyze Black-White Differences in Youth Employment." *Proceedings of the 1991 Annual Research Conference.* Washington, D.C.: U.S. Bureau of the Census.

Lerman, Robert. 1986. "Do Welfare Programs Affect Schooling and Work Patterns of Young Black Men?" In *The Black Youth Unemployment Crisis,* ed. Richard B. Freeman and Harry J. Holzer, pp. 412–441. Chicago: University of Chicago Press.

McMillen, M. M., P. Kaufman, E. G. Hausken, and D. Brady. 1993. *Dropout Rates in the United States, 1992.* Washington, D.C.: National Center for Education Statistics, Report No. 93–464.

Moss, Philip, and Chris Tilly. 1991. *Why Black Men Are Doing Worse in the Labor Market: A Review of Supply-Side and Demand-Side Explanations.* New York: Social Science Research Council.

U.S. Bureau of the Census. 1943. *1940 Census of the Population, Vol. II: Characteristics of the Population, Part 1, U.S. Summary.* Washington, D.C.

———. 1961. *Current Population Reports.* Series P-20. "Marriage, Fertility, and Childspacing." No. 108. Washington, D.C.

———. 1964. *1960 Census of the Population: U.S. Summary, Vol. 1, Part 1, Sec. D.* Washington, D.C.

———. 1983. *1980 Census of the Population: General Population Characteristics: U.S. Summary, PC80–1-B1.* Washington, D.C.

———. 1989. *County and City Data Book, 1988.* Washington, D.C.

———. 1992. *Current Population Reports.* Series P-20. "School Enrollment and Social and Economic Characteristics of Students." No. 460. Washington, D.C.

———. 1993. *Current Population Reports.* Series P-60. "Poverty in the United States: 1992." No. 185. Washington, D.C.

———. 1994. *Current Population Reports.* Series P-60. "Income, Poverty, and Valuation of Noncash Benefits." No. 189. Washington, D.C.

———. 1995. Statistical Brief 95–2. "Mothers Who Receive AFDC Payments: Fertility and Socioeconomic Characteristics." Washington, D.C.

———. 1996. *Current Population Reports.* Series P-20. "School Enrollment and Social and Economic Characteristics of the Students." No. 487. Washington, D.C.

———. 1997. *Current Population Reports.* Series P-20. "Fertility of American Women: June 1995 (Update: PPL-74)." No. 499. Washington, D.C.

———. 1998. *Current Population Reports.* Series P-60. "Measuring Fifty Years of Economic Change." No. 203. Washington, D.C.

——. 1999a. *Current Population Reports.* Series P-20. "School Enrollment and Social and Economic Characteristics of the Students." No. 516. Washington, D.C.

——. 1999b. *Current Population Reports.* Series P-60. "Poverty in the United States: 1998." No. 207. Washington, D.C.

U.S. Congress. 1998. *Background Material and Data in Programs Within the Jurisdiction of the Committee on Ways and Means.* Washington, D.C.

U.S. Department of Labor, Bureau of Labor Statistics. *Employment and Earnings.* January issues, 1989–2000.

——. 1989. *Handbook of Labor Statistics.* Bulletin 2340.

Welch, Finis. 1990. "The Employment of Black Men." *Journal of Labor Economics* 8 (1, pt. 2): S26–S74.

PART VI

Racial and Familial Hardship:
Welfare Benefits and Welfare Reform

Teenage Childbearing and Personal Responsibility

An Alternative View

ARLINE T. GERONIMUS

The nature and scope of the welfare reform debate resulting in the Personal Responsibility and Work Opportunity Reconciliation Act of 1996[1] (PRWORA) reflect a growing convergence toward the position that poverty is the result of poor people's values and behaviors.[2] Among examples of this convergence is a perspective on teenage childbearing that informed some provisions of PRWORA.[3] "Teenage childbearing" operates as a uniquely effective symbol of the failure to act responsibly. At first glance, everyone can agree that teenage childbearing is a "bad thing," unambiguously harmful to all involved — the young parents, the innocent children, and the larger society. Because of its perceived social costs and the fact that children are involved, the invocation of incentives and punishments to alter this behavior is now considered to be within the legitimate purview of public policy. This particular form of social engineering garners enthusiastic support from representatives of different political persuasions. To the extent that it represents concern for the well-being of vulnerable children it appeals to those with the desire to help the needy. And because to many the phenomenon represents extramarital sexuality it ignites the interests of those who seek to reaffirm social order. But if this apparent consensus siphons energy and resources away from searching debate about the nature of poverty, it presents a definite social danger.

In this chapter, I reopen discussion of widely shared assumptions about teenage childbearing. I begin with a brief discussion of its place in recent welfare reform proposals and legislation. I then argue that the scientific evidence of causal relationships between teenage childbearing and welfare dependence, or between teenage childbearing and the health and development of the children of teen mothers, is more modest and equivocal than conventional wisdom allows. I argue further that the current evaluation of teen mothers is crafted through the prism of middle-class nuclear family experience. This prism may ill-reflect the traditions or, more important, the environmental contingencies and life expectancy faced by members of poor families who hope to provide for children's well-being.

Based on these arguments, I question the merit of placing the reduction of teenage childbearing as an important goal of welfare reform. Teenage mothers and their children suffer from many disadvantages that public policy might address, as do all poor families. But current efforts to reduce teenage childbearing in the poor population may be ineffective, at best, or even harmful. Meanwhile energetic focus on reducing teen childbearing may distract from the development of more effective antipoverty policies.

Teenage Childbearing and Welfare Reform

One objective of welfare reform, shared by both political parties, is to reduce teenage childbearing.
— Representative Eva M. Clayton (D-North Carolina),
27 February 1996

In the recent national welfare reform debate, both Democrats and Republicans explicitly endorsed the view that successful welfare reform requires reducing teenage childbearing.[4] Furthermore, they both came to generally interpret teenage childbearing as "a bedrock issue of character and personal responsibility."[5] In June 1994, the Clinton administration offered the 103rd Congress a proposal for welfare reform that highlighted teenage pregnancy prevention. The proposal included provisions for a national campaign — sometimes referred to as a national mobilization[6] or crusade[7] — against teenage pregnancy. The 1994 proposal was unsuccessful, but the 104th Congress took up welfare reform with greater zeal and severity, including continued focus on teen childbearing.

As welfare reform was debated, some proposals highlighted the direct use of welfare regulations to discourage teenage childbearing, either by placing extra requirements on teen mothers who receive welfare benefits or by eliminating eligibility for welfare altogether among specified segments of the population of teenage mothers.[8] At the most extreme, conservative legislators floated the idea of enforced fosterage of children with financially needy teenage mothers.[9] The welfare bill signed into law by President Clinton in August 1996 singles out teen parents who hope to be welfare beneficiaries for extra requirements.[10] Except in special cases, states are prohibited from providing assistance to teen parents or their children if the parents fail to meet these requirements. The law also calls for the Secretary of Health and Human Services and the Attorney General to each implement programs aimed at teenage pregnancy prevention and for the former to implement a strategy by 1997 to assure that at least 25 percent of U.S. communities have teen pregnancy prevention programs in place.

In his 1996 State of the Union Address, President Clinton gave voice to the logic underpinning the link between teen childbearing and welfare reform. He argued that the "welfare system has undermined the values of family and work," and that "to strengthen the family we must do everything we can to keep the teen pregnancy rates going down." He announced that a group of prominent Americans had been convened to launch such a bipartisan national campaign. Its mission is "to reduce teenage pregnancy by supporting values and stimulating actions that are consistent with a pregnancy-free adolescence" and to do so by one-third by the year 2005.

Past arguments connecting teenage childbearing to welfare did not focus prominently on questions of values. Instead, they alleged a significant link between teenage childbearing and welfare costs as the rationale. In Congress, these arguments were more often made by family planning advocates than by advocates of welfare reform.[11] Family planners who sought to place teenage pregnancy on the national agenda advocated the view that teen pregnancy was often caused by (or was a symptom of) poverty (more than vice versa) and was an educational or medical problem to be solved by increased access to contraception, abortion, and sex education.[12] Now, reducing teenage childbearing is also seen as a measure of moral renaissance. Remedies include measures that can be seen as punitive — such as denial of welfare benefits and reinvigoration of statutory rape laws — and national discussion of religion, culture, and public values.[13] The legislation earmarks $400 million for abstinence-only education programs for teens, but eliminates the mandate making family planning available to welfare beneficiaries.

In terms of scientific evidence, either perspective is, at best, incomplete and oversimplified. Family planning advocates blur the distinction between teenagers at risk of pregnancy who avoid childbearing when given adequate information and technology and those who would bear children even provided the same. Meanwhile, welfare reformers focus narrowly on teenage childbearing and leave unexamined other important causes of persistent poverty. There is no doubt that teenage childbearing is *associated* with many social and public health problems. And, high rates of teen childbearing in socioeconomically disadvantaged communities likely result from the severe limits placed on the options available to the young for pursuing important goals. But none of these observations leads necessarily to the conclusion that reducing teenage childbearing itself, in the absence of other social changes, is either an attainable goal or one that would result in other social improvements. In targeting teen childbearing as a major activity for welfare reform, the basic question of cause and effect is consistently glossed over by policy makers and advocates.[14]

The Consequences of Teenage Childbearing

The question policy makers and social scientists need to answer is the following: Would social problems be alleviated *if the same women who become teen mothers postponed childbearing to older ages?* This question poses a serious challenge to scientific investigation, since the same women cannot have their first births twice. Nor can we do a controlled experiment and randomly assign women to their childbearing age. Instead, analysts must try to approximate an experimental approach by comparing teen mothers to older mothers who otherwise resemble them in every possible respect. But we know that those who will become teen mothers differ from the larger population in countless and consequential ways. For example, teen mothers are far more likely to have grown up in extremely impoverished circumstances and to have experienced prior school failure.[15] These disadvantages lead *both* to early motherhood *and* to the subsequent problems we now attribute to teen childbearing. To assess the effects of teen motherhood per se, we need to consider whether an already disadvantaged group is further disadvantaged by early motherhood. Without such reasoning, any conclusions about teenage motherhood are apt to be misleadingly dire.

TEENAGE CHILDBEARING AND WELFARE DEPENDENCE

My bill ensures that the responsibility of having a child belongs to the mother and father, rather than to the mother and U.S. taxpayers.
— *Representative Jan Meyers (R-Kansas), proposing the Welfare and Teenage Pregnancy Reduction Act, 10 March 1993*

Welfare payments are enormous when we talk about teenage pregnancy, which may be the greatest domestic social problem America faces today.
— *Senator Arlen Specter (R-Pennsylvania), on the issue of family planning, 27 July 1995*

Statements such as the above describe the simple statistical association between teen childbearing and poverty or welfare receipt and refer to public spending on women who had their first births in their teen years. However, this spending is incorrectly implied to represent the amount the government would save if teen mothers delayed their first births. That causal inference does not jibe with evidence from those studies on the relationship of teen childbearing to poverty or welfare dependence that most adequately control for the selection into teen childbearing of already disadvantaged teenagers. Simple associations may be easier to accept because they reinforce peoples' intuition that early childbearing is detrimental; yet the extent of measurable background differences between the teens most likely to become mothers and more typical teens nationwide suggest the importance of proceeding cautiously before relying on intuitions developed from experience with typical teens.

Many studies employ standard multivariate statistical techniques to control for specified, measurable background characteristics. These studies improve over simple statistical associations but are likely to overestimate the negative consequences of teen childbearing since there are many unmeasured factors that jointly determine a girl's likelihood of becoming a teen mother and of being poor in adulthood.[16] A subset of recent studies compares mothers of different ages who are similar on a fuller range of potentially important antecedents of teen childbearing than can be measured directly. For example, investigators have compared outcomes among national samples of *sisters* who had their first births at different ages.[17]

Unlike more typical studies, comparing sisters, in effect, controls for such factors as general access to resources throughout childhood (not simply income at a specific point in time), cultural environment, neighborhood, or school system. Sisters comparisons do not control for personal antecedents of early childbearing that can affect long-term economic success (such as low academic ability), but vary among teens in the same neighborhood, school or even family.[18] Sisters comparisons, then, can be seen as producing estimates of the effects of teen childbearing on subsequent economic success that remain upwardly biased, but illuminate the extent to which unobserved factors associated with family background account for the poor economic fortunes of teen mothers.

Another approach taken to account for unmeasured differences between teen and older mothers is to compare outcomes between teenage mothers and teenagers who became pregnant but *miscarried*.[19] Comparing teen mothers to those who would have become teen mothers, but for the accident of miscarriage, approximates random assignment to teen motherhood and, thus, yields estimates that approximate true effects.[20] This approach provides a more complete assessment of the full magnitude of upward bias in estimates produced by cross-sectional studies than do sisters comparisons, but does not offer evidence on what factors other than age-at-first-birth may be responsible for the economic difficulties associated with being a teen mother.

For key economic outcomes bearing directly on the question of long-term economic self-sufficiency, findings from studies using these methods challenge well-entrenched beliefs. As a group, they suggest substantially smaller effects of teen childbearing on economic outcomes than more typical studies, often reducing effects estimated by more traditional methods by at least one-half. Some findings suggest *no* independent effect of teen childbearing on important economic outcomes. For example, Geronimus and Korenman[21] reported no relationship between teen childbearing and high school graduation or subsequent family income in their analysis of sister pairs in the National Longitudinal Survey of Young Women. Using more recent data from the Panel Study of Income Dynamics, Corcoran and Kunz[22] found teen mothers to be no more likely to be welfare recipients after age 25 than their sisters who became mothers at older ages. So too, Hotz et al.,[23] comparing teens who gave birth to those who miscarried in recent data from the National Longitudinal Survey of Youth, concluded that a teen mother is no more likely to participate in welfare programs, to have her labor market earnings reduced, or to experience significant losses in spousal earnings than the same woman would have experienced if she had delayed childbearing.

Not all investigators using state-of-the-art methods conclude that teen childbearing has no independent effect on economic outcomes, although that possibility cannot be ruled out. There is general agreement that the alarmist view is unsubstantiated.[24] Yet those debating welfare reform accepted it uncritically. Even if one prefers a conservative interpretation of recent findings that teen mothers do pay some penalty in their future income — although lower than previously thought — this alone would not justify targeting teen childbearing prevention ahead of addressing other contributors to poverty as an important focus of welfare reform. And it is possible to imagine a scenario (as I will suggest below) where forgoing some income is a reasonable trade-off, if early childbearing were positive in other important respects.

TEENAGE CHILDBEARING AND CHILD HEALTH AND DEVELOPMENT

We need to make teens better understand that their actions have very serious consequences for which they are ultimately responsible. . . . Becoming a parent is a bad deal for children.
    — Representative Lee H. Hamilton (D-Indiana), 25 January 1995

Tragically, high pregnancy rates among adolescents take a toll not only on young parents but also on their children. Children born to teens are at greater risk of early death and are more likely to perform poorly in school and suffer abuse and neglect.

— President Bill Clinton, announcing
National Teen Pregnancy Prevention Month, May 1996

Teenage childbearing is believed to result in other negative outcomes for the children of teen mothers, in addition to long-term poverty or welfare dependence. These outcomes include child abuse or neglect by teen mothers, the propensity of children born to teen mothers to engage in antisocial acts such as crime in adolescence or young adulthood, infant poor health (indexed in terms, say, of low birth weight or infant mortality), and lower developmental or academic achievement. Does the research literature support these beliefs?

Regarding abuse or neglect of children, teen mothers are overrepresented in the population of maltreating parents in some samples, but not in others. Associations between teenage motherhood and maltreatment often persist after adjustment for simple demographic characteristics, such as race. However, several studies that employ more detailed multivariate analyses — for example, including a control for poverty — fail to show teen mothers to be at increased risk of abusing or neglecting their children.[25] No researcher of this topic has applied a research design to account for unmeasured factors. But, even based on her cross-sectional research findings, Massat concluded that the prevailing wisdom "that adolescent parents are more likely to maltreat their children than are older parents appears to be a myth entrenched in the popular culture . . . resources might better be used to cope with harms that research has shown to occur."[26]

There is very little evidence on the effect of teen motherhood on adolescent or young adult antisocial behavior. Moore, Morrison, and Greene[27] use standard cross-sectional techniques to analyze a national sample of 18–22-year-olds and find no association between one's probability of having a teen mother and having committed delinquent acts (such as assault, theft, arson, or prostitution) or used illegal drugs in the past year. They estimate an increased risk of running away from home in the previous year for 18–22-year-olds whose mothers were 18 or 19 at their birth, but not for sample members whose mothers were 17 years old or younger. On the specific outcome of incarceration, Grogger[28] tries to control for unmeasured background factors. His findings are difficult to interpret. Although he is speaking to the question of whether incarceration rates would be reduced if teen mothers delayed their

Table 17.1. Infant Mortality Rates by Age of Mother for U.S. Whites and African American Residents of Harlem

	U.S. Whites	Harlem
Infant Mortality Rate	7	26
Teen Mothers	10	14
Nonteen Mothers	6	33
Percent of First Births to Teenage Mothers	20	40

Note: Based on author's calculations using linked birth and infant death certificate data (1988 for U.S. whites; 1989–1991 for Harlem). Harlem refers to African American residents of the Central Harlem Health Center District in New York City. Infant mortality rate is per 1,000 live births; percent teen births are tabulated from birth certificates and rounded to nearest 10 percent.

first births, Grogger actually estimates the effect of maternal age, not the effect of maternal age-at-first-birth.[29] Grogger concludes, "Even large changes in young teen mothers' age at first birth would have a relatively modest effect on their sons' incarceration risk."[30] In the absence of strong causal evidence linking teen childbearing to child abuse, neglect, delinquency, or crime, one is left to assume that the firm belief that teen childbearing contributes to these problems is largely stereotypical.

On the relationship of teenage childbearing to infant health or outcomes in early childhood there is stronger evidence, much of which *refutes* the idea that the association between teenage childbearing and poor infant or child outcomes is due to maternal age per se.[31] The most robust evidence comes from studies on the health of African American infants. In contrast to President Clinton's comments, among African Americans, rates of low birth weight and infant mortality are *lowest* for babies whose mothers are in their mid- to late teens, and such risk among firstborns tends to increase with advancing maternal age from the teens through the twenties and early thirties.[32] There is some evidence that the increase in infant risk with advancing maternal age is steepest in poor communities. For example, in Harlem, infant mortality rates for teens are half those for older mothers (Table 17.1). So, too, among first births in the poorest African American communities in Michigan, infants with 15-year-old mothers are one-half as likely to be low birth weight than those whose mothers are 25, and one-third as likely as those whose mothers are 35. One reason for this is early deterioration in maternal health.[33] The health of poor African American women deteriorates in measurable ways as early as the mid-twenties, perhaps the consequence of long-term severe socioeconomic disadvantage.[34]

Empirical findings related to child development and school achievement also fail to provide consistent or strong endorsement for the political viewpoint that teen childbearing harms children. For example, in a national sample, Moore and Snyder[35] find no association between teen motherhood and young children's performance on the Peabody Picture Vocabulary Test among African Americans or Hispanics. Among whites, crude associations become insignificant once the researchers control for other maternal characteristics that antecede teen childbearing. In a multivariate, cross-sectional study of a wider range of child development indicators, Moore, Morrison, and Greene[36] arrive at conflicting estimates of the magnitude of any effects of teen childbearing depending on the outcome, the maternal age groups compared, or whether they focus on black or nonblack children. On balance, their evidence of negative effects is modest in comparison to the tenor of public concern. They even find some evidence of positive effects. Among black children in their sample of 4–14-year-olds, those whose mothers were 18 or 19 at their birth performed better in reading and math than those whose mothers had been in their early twenties. This finding is of particular interest given that black mothers in their late teens account for more than half of black and almost one-quarter of all unwed teen mothers.

The generally modest and conflicting estimates of Moore et al. were produced after control for measurable aspects of maternal family background, leaving open the question of their stability in the presence of more comprehensive controls. Evidence on this question is provided by Geronimus, Korenman, and Hillemeier[37] who also study the performance of preschool and elementary school-age children in a national sample on several standard tests of cognitive development and achievement by age of mother. To control for preexisting differences between teen and older mothers, they compare the test scores of the children of sisters who experienced their first births at different ages. Once maternal background characteristics are controlled by this method, the differences between children with teen versus older mothers are generally insignificant. Those tests where statistically significant differences are estimated usually *favor* the children of teen mothers: such assessments include indices of verbal ability and achievement in reading and math. And this general pattern of findings is suggested even when the teen birth group is restricted to young teen mothers (those under 18 years old).

Social Costs

Between 1985 and 1990, the public cost of births to teenage mothers under the AFDC program, the food stamp program, and the Medicaid program has been estimated at $120,000,000,000.
    — Personal Responsibility and Work Opportunity Reconciliation Act
of 1996

The problem of low-birth weight babies . . . constitutes a human trag-edy . . . because they carry scars for a lifetime. Frequently those lifetimes are not very long, but are very expensive to society, costing in the range of $200,000 a child and thousands more each year. It costs society multiple billions of dollars.
    — Senator Arlen Specter (R-Pennsylvania), 27 July 1995

I have argued that political statements of deleterious effects of teen child-bearing for teen parents and their children are out of line with the more mod-est and conflicting social scientific evidence. However, if there were demon-strably large social costs, policy aimed at reducing teen childbearing might still be justifiable.[38]

Although large numbers are quoted by politicians and advocacy organiza-tions have announced evidence of large social costs, in fact such figures are speculative. They are calculated using estimates of the effects of teen childbear-ing that are almost certainly exaggerated. In 1996, the Robin Hood Founda-tion released a summary report released at a White House press conference. It claimed enormous social costs resulting from teenage childbearing (ranging from $6.9 to $29 billion per year). Although the report's conclusions were widely publicized without qualification, the social cost estimates were arrived at by ignoring cautions offered by many of the investigators whose research formed the basis for the report.[39] In fact, the researchers studying the key question of government outlays for public assistance estimated that if all cur-rent teen mothers delayed childbearing, "the total expenditures on public assistance would *increase* slightly." Moreover, since they estimated that life-time earnings of teen mothers would *decrease* if they delayed childbearing, and, hence, so would their contribution to the tax base, they calculated "the *net* (of taxes) annual outlays by government for cash-assistance and in-kind transfers to these women would actually *increase* by 35 percent, or $4.0 bil-lion. This increase in net expenditures associated with delaying childbearing would amount to over $1,200 per teen mother."[40]

The possibility that delaying childbearing by teen mothers might, on balance, *increase* spending on public assistance was not considered in the debate over welfare reform. Instead, the presumption that preventing teen childbearing would result in substantial cost *savings* was taken as axiomatic. Yet a full and careful accounting of social costs remains to be performed. A prudent accounting would include sensitivity analyses based on the range of estimates produced by state-of-the-art evidence for economic and child health or developmental outcomes. Such accounting would likely result in social cost figures that are far lower than those quoted above to rationalize welfare reform. For example, the reviewed evidence suggests that if current teen mothers postponed childbearing, the social costs paid for income transfers or food stamps might be decreased only marginally — if they were decreased at all. Meanwhile the formidable expenses associated with low birth-weight babies — including for Medicaid, for funding of public hospitals, and for uncompensated care — might well increase.

Teenage Childbearing and Family Support

Senator Moynihan (D-New York) [has characterized teenage pregnancy] as a central problem in America today. It may well be the most important problem as we grapple with teenage pregnancy where we have a family coming into existence without any family structure at all.
            — Senator Arlen Specter (R-Pennsylvania), 25 May 1994

The dominant cultural ideal in the United States is for a baby to be born into a nuclear family. When that ideal is disregarded, it is common to assume that the alternative is no "family structure at all." Sociological and anthropological evidence suggest that categorizing families as either nuclear or nonexistent is overly simplistic, as I discuss below. However, the tendency to do so in the case of teen mothers has been reinforced by overdrawn popularized images. Because a teen mother is more likely to be unmarried now than in the past, the popularized image of teen parenthood is of an absent father and an immature, problem-prone girl raising her (unwanted) child alone. Given this image, common sense suggests that teen childbearing *must* jeopardize the health and well-being of children and be costly to society.

These nagging doubts might be assuaged by reconstructing this image to be more consistent with the literature. Teen mothers in the United States tend to be older (two-thirds of teen mothers are 18–19 years old; only 2 percent are under age 15), are more likely to be married (about 40 percent are married and teens constitute less than one-third of all unmarried mothers), or, if not married, to benefit from the support and guidance of others than the popularized image suggests. That is, welfare policy makers — along with many middle-class Americans — fail to distinguish between the *function* of providing stability, care, and economic support to children that is most often provided by married couples in the United States and the *form* of marriage itself.[41]

Within the United States, population-variation in family structure is well documented, both for the current period and historically.[42] Some scholarly theories that explain this variation take nonnuclear family structures as deficient, prima facie, while others attempt to appraise their strengths, weaknesses, and origins without prejudgment.[43] This latter academic tradition was ignored in the welfare reform debate. Yet, consistent with this tradition, some research suggests it may be more accurate to think of a poor teen mother (at least in African American communities that have been studied the most extensively) as an emerging adult participant in active multigenerational social networks than as a rebellious adolescent set apart from her elders, raising her baby alone.

Ethnographic observation and analyses of survey data provide evidence in African American communities that mothers, fathers (or father surrogates), grandmothers, aunts, uncles, and others from both maternal and paternal sides (regardless of parental marital status) actively contribute to the support and nurturance of the young.[44] This approach to shared childbearing, in effect, pools risk among poor families, providing social insurance against common risks. These include risks of severe income shortfall due to the unpredictability of wages, employment (or welfare benefits); risks of hunger, homelessness, or early adult disability; and risks of physical separation between children and any specific individual adult (due, for example, to inflexible work requirements, incarceration, or premature death). If we concern ourselves with family *function* rather than *form,* it is possible that in some circumstances greater stability, care, and economic support for children may be realized through family systems and forms of union that are not nuclear and that do not place high value on legal marriage, per se.[45]

Of course, theoretically, kin network participation and legal marriage are not mutually exclusive. Many teen mothers are married. But even among those who are not legally married, ethnographers have observed in specific poor, African American communities that a father and his kin often comprise an important segment of a mother's kin network, and further that the father's kin may remain as a resource to a mother and children even if the father is out of the city, out of the state, or out of the picture.[46] Empirical sociologists also find evidence to question the tendency to infer father absence from the lack of *legal* marriage. They argue that norms related to marriage and nonmarital fertility are and have been more fluid among African Americans than among U.S. whites.[47] In addition, based on his longitudinal analysis of a national sample of children, Mott[48] concludes that "the concept of a discrete discontinuity between father's presence and absence, particularly for black children, is singularly inappropriate whether used as an analytical tool or as a policy instrument."[49]

In addition to having kin support, a typical teen mother may be more mature and experienced in childcare than popular images suggest. As noted, the majority of teen mothers are 18 or 19 years old. Older teenagers in poor communities may be more mature than the typical American teenager. They are more likely to be economic contributors to their families and to have had to "grow up fast" and assume a range of responsibilities, including responsibilities for babies and young children in their social networks.[50] More generally, the relationship between late teen age and social maturity is variable.[51] Being a teenager and being an adolescent are not always synonymous. For example, although we now assume that teenagers are *never* developmentally ready to be responsible parents, many of our grandmothers bore their first children in their teen years.

The tendency to categorize poor teens in terms of their adolescent status instead of their socioeconomic group may also be misleading if it conceptually sets the individual teenager (or teenager and her boyfriend) as having impulses opposed to the viewpoints of more mature elders, taking risks and making pregnancy-resolution decisions in a vacuum apart from mature guidance. Yet, at least in specific socioeconomically disadvantaged local settings, there is evidence to suggest that teens generally decide how to resolve unplanned pregnancies in collaboration with elders.[52] In some instances, teens are *encouraged* to become mothers by elders who speak from life experience.[53]

Poor Teens and Life Prospects

Middle-class teens have opportunities stretching well beyond age 18 or 19 to become better educated, better skilled, and thus eventually more employable. If they bore children as teenagers, their childcare obligations might well conflict dramatically with their ability to utilize these opportunities. And, given such opportunities, middle-class youth have every reason to believe that they will be better providers for their children if they delay parenthood. But this is not true for the young women most likely to become teen mothers. Poor youth and minority youth in general, as well as those who have suffered early school failure, in particular, face more restricted educational or labor market opportunities.[54] Poor families do appear to mobilize to support those teenagers believed to possess the skills necessary to overcome chronic barriers to achievement and upward mobility, including discouraging them from engaging in the dating activities of their peers.[55] But other poor teens may have less to gain from postponing childbearing. Meanwhile, to the extent they have access to kin support for childcare, the trade-offs between school, work, and childcare may be diminished.[56] In targeting policy to address unequal opportunity among American youth, it is likely that social forces other than early childbearing constitute the major impediments to labor market success among poor teen mothers.

Differences in life prospects between poor and better-off teenagers are evident at their most basic and literal level. The most profound inappropriate assumption that leads us to believe that postponing childbearing well beyond the teen years is *always* in children's best interests is the assumption that teens from all social classes face a predictable future with death far off in its "logical position . . . at the close of a long life."[57] Yet, in the United States, one of the most disturbing expressions of social inequality is the variation across socioeconomic groups in rates of premature adult mortality.

For example, Table 17.2 shows the probability that a 15-year-old male or female will survive to age 45, 55, or 65 for U.S. whites and for African American residents of two poor communities: Harlem and Chicago's South Side. Ninety-five percent of white women, but less than 80 percent of Harlem or Chicago women, survive to their fifty-fifth birthday. More than one-third of Harlem or Chicago women die by age 65. For men, the statistics are more grim. Less than three-quarters of Harlem or Chicago men survive to age 45, compared to 94 percent of U.S. whites. Little more than half of Harlem or Chicago men can expect to survive to age 55, and almost two-thirds who reach their fifteenth birthday will not live to see their sixty-fifth. (This represents less than half the probability that the typical white 15-year-old-male nationwide will survive to age 65.) In Harlem and Chicago, 15-year-old men have less chance of surviving to age 45 than the typical white 15-year-old nationwide has of surviving to age 65. Deaths from chronic diseases, rather than the more publicized instances of homicide, are the primary reason.[58]

Lower but still strikingly high rates of early adult mortality for women and men have been described for other urban areas such as the Watts area of Los Angeles or Central City Detroit.[59] In predominantly African American poor urban populations — some of the same populations where early childbearing is common and engenders the most concern in the general population — the probability of premature mortality appears sufficiently high that, unlike the average American teenager, teens in these areas cannot confidently expect to survive through or even to middle adulthood.

Table 17.2. Probability of Surviving to Later Ages Conditional on Survival to Age 15 in Selected Populations, 1990

Age	U.S. Whites	Harlem	Chicago
	Women		
45	.98	.87	.88
55	.95	.78	.79
65	.87	.65	.63
	Men		
45	.94	.71	.73
55	.89	.55	.55
65	.77	.37	.37

Note: Harlem refers to African American residents of the Central Harlem Health Center District in New York City. Chicago refers to African American residents of highly impoverished southside community areas of Near Southside, Douglas, Oakland, Fuller Park, Grand Boulevard, and Washington Park. Mortality calculations based on data from the 1990 Census of the Population (adjusted for coverage error) and from death certificates for 1989–1991. See Geronimus et al. (1996) for general methods.

Without such confidence, to postpone central goals such as childbearing is to risk forgoing them. And if one believes that responsible parenthood includes maximizing the chance that a parent will survive to see and help her child grow up, then insecurity about one's own longevity would be a serious consideration when contemplating whether to defer parenthood.

When these aspects of life experience of the poor are ignored and teen mothers are viewed merely as youth, the state may appear justified in moving in, in loco parentis, to regulate the behavior of poor teens, whether through the "tough love" approaches advocated by conservatives or the paternalistically supportive approaches suggested by liberals. As Representative Linda Smith (R-Washington) argued on 23 March 1995: "The most compassionate thing we can do for these little kids and their kids is to not give them cash grants, to not go on and reward the wrong decisions, to not reward sometimes their mothers who encourage them in some tenement house to go get pregnant so they can get the welfare that they have learned to live on" (*Congressional Record*, 23 March 1995, p. 3718).

But if compassion is what we aim for, then this approach of constructing all sexually active teenage women as unsupervised adolescents and using that image to justify government policy as surrogate parent is deeply problematic. It pathologizes the role of elders in the decisions of poor teens. It definitionally attributes the same psychosocial developmental trajectories, opportunities, and human resources for helping to rear children (now or in the future) to all teenagers, although, as we have seen, there are marked variations across social groupings in all of these factors. Generalizing from middle-class to poor teens may lead to mistaken characterization of the motivations of unmarried, sexually active teens who are poor and of the opportunities and resources dependably available to them for realizing more socially approved goals than early childbearing. That is, it is not only incorrect in its premise that every teen, by definition, is unprepared to be a responsible mother, but also in its implication that every teen, by definition, will be in a better position to be one at a later date.

An Alternative View: The Rationality of Teen Childbearing

The perspective on teen childbearing that helped to inform the PRWORA is not only inconsistent with important empirical evidence, but it is also only one among several theoretical perspectives on the relationship of teenage childbearing to socioeconomic disadvantage. Here I outline one alternative perspective that is consistent with existing empirical evidence, but leads to a different conclusion regarding the rationality or "responsibility" of early fertility timing, at least among an important subset of teen mothers. I focus particularly on poor, urban African Americans for two reasons. First, there is more research evidence about this subset of the disadvantaged. And second, insofar as public concern about teen childbearing is now racialized,[60] teenage childbearing is construed as one in a constellation of pathological behaviors particularly engaged in by an urban, African American "underclass."[61] I argue instead that the generally earlier fertility exhibited in these communities relative to the national average has a quite different meaning. It does not represent the abandonment by teens or their elders of the mainstream "family value" that responsible parents strive to bring children into the world when they are most prepared to provide for their children's well-being, broadly defined. Instead, it expresses attempts to embrace this view of the appropriate time for childbearing within extremely adverse circumstances that constrain and qualitatively alter the routes available for achieving this goal.

What if a poor African American teen wants the following: to have two or three children who are healthy and continue to thrive, and who will be provided for materially and emotionally until they reach adulthood. Moreover, she (or he) wants to achieve this result, while minimizing the chance of needing government assistance in order to do so. If this is what she values, what age would she or the elders who advise her think would be the most appropriate to begin childbearing?

What if, as the literature suggests, in pursuing these goals, there are complicating factors. The poor teen might die at any time, might well not survive through middle age, and is likely to suffer from a chronic disease or disability starting at an even younger age. If she delays childbearing, this early health deterioration will jeopardize her chances of bearing normal-weight infants who survive infancy. If she does bear a low birth-weight baby, that child is at increased risk of long-term developmental deficits.[62] If she has a "special needs" child, that will be a drain on family resources and may depress the child's school performance and future economic prospects. The possibility of early death or disability also characterizes the people a poor mother depends on to support and care for her children — be they her baby's father or members of a broader social network. And a child with a disabled family member is more likely to exhibit behavior problems.[63] The research findings suggest that a poor mother faces particular uncertainty if she follows the nuclear family model and depends primarily on a husband for economic, practical, or emotional support. His chance of early death is distressingly high. Meanwhile, his earnings potential is likely to be low and unreliable.

In fact, whether or not she marries before her first birth, a poor mother must expect to contribute substantially to the financial support of her children. But her chances for labor market attachment are also unreliable.[64] If she finds employment, the wages and benefits she can command may not offset the costs of being a working mother.[65] She cannot expect paid maternity leave; nor is accessible or affordable daycare available that would free her from reliance on kin for childcare once she does return to work.[66] Moreover, she faces the social expectations that she must help to care for her kin as their health falters. Postponing childbearing increases the chance that her young children compete with ailing elders for her energies and decreases the chance that their father will survive through much of their childhood. Her greatest chance of long-term labor force attachment will be if her children's preschool years coincide with her years of peak access to social and practical support provided by relatively healthy kin. Her best chance of achieving her stated goals is by becoming a mother at a young age.

Note that, the kin-network approach to childrearing is motivated, among other reasons, by the community-level social expectation that adults work whenever they can, however they can, and that others pitch in to make this possible. Put another way, if the poor place value on economic self-sufficiency through gainful employment then they often must accept jobs that separate them from their children, sometimes for long periods. Low-skill jobs provide income and other practical and psychological rewards, but they may also exacerbate disease risk and the chance of early disability or mortality.[67] Working-poor parents may experience legitimate worries of becoming compromised in their capacity to provide for their children or of leaving them orphaned. If along with their work ethic, parents also value providing consistent emotional and material support for their children, then they must develop, invest in, and rely on informal social capital. By doing so they do their best to ensure that their children have caring adults willing and able to supplement or even substitute for parental support.

In sum, one need not assume the abandonment of personal responsibility to explain persistently high rates of early childbearing in poor communities. Instead, the scenario described here suggests the possibility that poor teens in collaboration with their elders may be making rational and "responsible" decisions. Instead of being a sign that their values place them apart from the mainstream, the behavior of teen mothers can be read as representing mainstream values whose phenotypic manifestations take different forms as suits the environmental contingencies that must be addressed. Of course, it is not being assumed that poor teens or their elders know the precise statistical odds they face of restricted opportunities, early death and disability, or infant mortality. But it is equally unreasonable to assume that their life experiences do not impress some version of these facts upon them.[68]

The perspective that teenage childbearing represents trade-offs made in order to maximize children's well-being in hard circumstances may also explain why early childbearing has persisted in extremely disadvantaged communities, despite increased access to contraceptive technology and abortion and in the face of very public disapproval of the behavior. And it would suggest that it may continue to persist in the face of welfare reform.

Implications for Social Policy

The harshest measures against teen childbearing proposed or adopted by welfare reformers are not supported by a careful review of the social scientific research on the costs and consequences of teen childbearing. The reviewed literature is sufficiently equivocal as to render radical policies or the conclusions on which they are based exceedingly premature. Nor does the literature justify the current equation of antipoverty policy with welfare reform. Indeed, the scenario I depict suggests that nonmarital teenage childbearing is sometimes a strategy for coping with economic uncertainty emanating from many sources, including, but not limited to, welfare generosity and can also be a strategy for insuring against the adverse health effects of poverty. To the extent this scenario applies, welfare policies meant to be disincentives to early childbearing would, at best, play a small role in reducing teen marital or birth rates.

If teen birth rates were reduced by welfare policy alone, we might witness some increase in other social problems as a result, such as low birth weight rates and their sequel, at least among African Americans. However, whether or not these policies will reduce teen birth rates is open to question. Despite two decades of active attempts to reduce teenage childbearing in poor communities, there has been little evidence of a successful targeted program. Meanwhile teen childbearing rates have fallen and risen along with secular trends in childbearing obtaining to greater or lesser extent among mothers of all ages.[69] Trends in nonmarital childbearing rates among teens also appear to mimic more general trends in nonmarital childbearing rather than be particularly responsive to expansions or retrenchments in welfare generosity.[70]

Like everyone else, poor teens and their elders respond to incentives when making fertility-related decisions. But the most important incentives to them may not be narrow carrot-and-stick incentives of the kind envisioned and manipulated by welfare reformers. Instead, they may derive from larger, more enduring aspects of their life experience. For example, faced with this trade-off, a woman might accept reduced welfare benefits, if by early childbearing she increases the chance that her child will be born healthy and have able-bodied caretakers who survive through his childhood.

My argument, then, is that the motivations underlying high rates of teenage childbearing in poor communities may be versions of exactly those values which many now believe the poor, generally, and African American residents of central cities, in particular, lack. These motivations can be understood in light of the problems that together form the larger context in which teen childbearing takes place. These problems merit policy attention. They include problems in educational systems, labor market opportunities, childcare, housing, and health that impede the productivity and shorten the lives of young through middle-aged adults in poor communities, making it difficult for them to escape the anxieties that accompany the profound uncertainties they face. These anxieties, in turn, may move responsible, future-oriented, and caring adults to arrange and invest in elaborate systems of social insurance, which in turn exert pressure toward earlier childbearing and away from marriage.

Through PRWORA, President Clinton and the 104th Congress have set policies in motion that are likely to exacerbate anxiety among the poor, perhaps providing indirect incentives *toward* early childbearing. Meanwhile, the Congress did little to improve job or educational prospects for the poor and appeared to be set on dismantling the public health service.[71] Increasingly stringent Medicaid and food stamp eligibility criteria included in provisions of PRWORA threaten the health and longevity of the poor and may effectively deny the option of nursing-home care to some segments of the poor population. In turn, young adults in these segments may be increasingly called upon to care for ailing elderly. If early childbearing reduces the stress of juggling this obligation with work and childcare responsibilities, and if ailing elders long to be grandparents, social expectation in these communities may move in the direction of teenage childbearing.[72]

How did this happen? Certainly, the so-called Republican Revolution contributed importantly to the configuration of the 1996 welfare reform bill. Yet some liberal advocacy organizations have been among the most industrious in their efforts to maintain a public misperception that was important for its success. The misperception is that irrefutable scientific evidence shows teenage childbearing to be highly costly to poor teens, their children, and society.[73] Liberal advocates may hope that the broad-based social consensus that teen childbearing is destructive can be used to funnel resources to poor women and children that they could not otherwise mobilize. Or they may hope to take advantage of this consensus — combined with the common failure to distinguish between teenage childbearing and teenage pregnancy — to protect the reproductive freedom of middle-class teens to avoid conception or childbirth. A full discussion of the pros and cons of such tactics is beyond the scope of this chapter. However, there is little evidence that any such strategy has succeeded. The premature consensus that teenage childbearing is a major social ill is now exploited to legislate abstinence education programs, while mandated support for family planning programs and abortion has eroded. And this consensus has been effectively used to help undercut support for the social safety net and other antipoverty programs.

For whatever reasons, liberals have played an active role in perpetuating myths about teen childbearing. These myths, alongside others, have been used to portray the poor as morally marred and helped justify proposals by radical Republicans to suspend rights and freedoms of poor teens and to direct resources away from their children. They have put Democrats in the position of making proposals and voting for or signing legislation that are now seen as compromises, but which in a different era would have been unthinkable by liberals or moderates. The result is antipoverty policy that may ultimately increase poverty.[74] And PRWORA is an act that is likely to intensify material hardship of the most severe forms including homelessness and infant and premature adult mortality once time limits are reached or a recession occurs, if not before. At this time, local governments will have limited resources to address expanding urgent needs. However, they must now commit some of these resources to developing political, administrative, and operational responses to devolution[75] as well as to activities whose success in reducing teen birth rates is highly speculative, such as conducting programs on the problem of statutory rape.

When the crusade against teen childbearing fails, will that failure be interpreted as evidence that the poor are morally even more far removed from the mainstream than they are already thought to be? Will that failure provide further ammunition for those who argue that public spending on social programs is wasteful? Or will we take the opportunity to learn that the poor continue to suffer from many compelling problems, problems that could be reduced by public intervention? Rather than being a cause of public problems, teenage childbearing may be emblematic of the price paid by the poor themselves — not by the larger society — as they work actively to fulfill the values of self-sufficiency, hard work, and responsibility to children and elders in a hostile environment that wears away their health and limits their life chances.

Notes

This work was undertaken while the author was a visiting scholar at the Russell Sage Foundation. The author gratefully acknowledges the support of the Russell Sage Foundation, the William T. Grant Foundation, and the Centers for Disease Control and Prevention, grant U83-CCU51249. I am indebted to Jim Caraley for encouraging me to write this essay. I thank Robert K. Merton, Sylvia Tesh, Alice O'Connor, Sherman James, James Rule, J. Phillip Thompson, Carol Stack, Mary Corcoran, John Bound, and two anonymous reviewers for helpful comments on previous drafts; Adam Becker for helpful discussions; Kimberly Giamportone and Marianne Hillemeier for research assistance and help with the production of the manuscript; and Jamie Taylor for editorial assistance.

   1. P.L. 104–193.

   2. Herbert J. Gans, *The War Against the Poor* (New York: Basic Books, 1995).

   3. Politicians and the public often fail to distinguish between teen childbearing, teen pregnancy, and illegitimacy. I use the term "teenage childbearing" because only those teen pregnancies that are carried to term can have the consequences most often cited as costing welfare dollars. In addition, the universe of nonmarital births includes more nonteenage than teenage mothers, while many teenage mothers are married. It should be noted, however, that these terms are used interchangeably in quotations from others.

   Elected representatives are also inconsistent about what ages constitute "teen mothers," sometimes they refer to mothers under 18, sometimes under 21, and sometimes under 23 years old. In Table 17.1, I define teenage mothers as those under 20 years old. In the text, my use of the concept is not tied to very specific ages, but to the generally earlier fertility-timing distributions characteristic of poor or minority communities relative to more advantaged communities or to the national average. In socioeconomically disadvantaged communities, first births tend to be concentrated in the mid- to late teens through the very early twenties. In more advantaged populations, first births are concentrated in the mid- to late twenties.

   4. For example, see comments of Representative Jolene Unsoeld (D-Washington), *Congressional Record*, 21 April 1993; Senator Joseph Lieberman (D-Connecticut), *Congressional Record*, 14 June 1994; Representative Linda Smith (R-Washington),

Congressional Record, 23 March 1995; Senator Arlen Specter (R-Pennsylvania), *Congressional Record,* 25 May 1994, 27 July 1995; Representative Joel Hefley (R-Colorado), *Congressional Record,* 21 March 1995; and Representative Eva M. Clayton (D-North Carolina), *Congressional Record,* 27 February 1996.

5. This quote is from the 1994 Clinton Administration proposal for welfare reform. For additional evidence that Republicans and Democrats now construe teenage childbearing as a question of personal responsibility, see GOP Contract with America, specifically the Personal Responsibility Act, which, among other provisions, seeks to "discourage illegitimacy and teen pregnancy by prohibiting welfare to minor mothers." See remarks of Republican representatives, e.g., Representative Jan Meyers, *Congressional Record,* 10 March 1993, on her introduction of the "Welfare and Teenage Pregnancy Reduction Act." See also remarks of Democratic representatives, e.g., Representative Lee H. Hamilton, *Congressional Record,* 25 January 1995, and Representative Lewis S. Payne, *Congressional Record,* 22 March 1995.

6. Clinton Administration 1994 welfare reform proposal.

7. Senator Joseph Lieberman on welfare reform, *Congressional Record,* 14 June 1994.

8. The 1994 Clinton Administration proposal included provisions to require every school-age parent or pregnant teenager who received or applied for welfare to finish school or enroll in a JOBS program; to live with a responsible adult, preferably a parent; and to cooperate in the effort to establish paternity. All welfare recipients under 23 years old would be required to search for a job during their first twelve weeks on the welfare rolls. Those who could not find a job would be required to attend school or undergo job training. A group of moderate Democrats offered a modified version of Clinton's plan that included a provision to deny all AFDC and food stamp benefits to unwed mothers under age 21 and to their children. The Welfare and Teenage Pregnancy Reduction Act introduced by Representative Jan Meyers (R-Kansas) would provide no AFDC benefits unless both the mother and the father are at least 18 years old and unless paternity is established. The provisions of the Republican Personal Responsibility Act would compel states to deny cash assistance to a child born out-of-wedlock to a teen parent, to reduce family assistance when paternity has not been established, and to deny family assistance when a parent has not cooperated in establishing paternity. A compromise advanced by a bipartisan coalition of governors in February 1996 would empower states to deny benefits to children born to unwed women under the age of 18. Massachusetts requested a waiver that would enable that state to deny cash assistance to a mother under age 20 unless she lives with a parent or other caretaker relative.

9. GOP House Speaker Newt Gingrich touted orphanages and adoption as solutions for the young and disadvantaged; see Michael Tanner, "Ending Welfare As We Know It," *USA Today Magazine,* vol. 123, no. 2598, p. 16, March 1995, or Fred Bayles and Sharon Cohen, "Nobody's Children: A Child Welfare System in Chaos," Associated Press, 1 May 1995.

10. The prohibitions and requirements for block grant assistance include that no assistance can be given to an unmarried minor with children over twelve weeks old who is not a high school graduate and is not participating in activities leading to a high school diploma or equivalent or an alternative educational program approved by the state; nor

can assistance be given to such individuals (whatever their children's age), if they do not reside in a residence maintained by a parent, legal guardian, or other adult relative, or some other form of adult-supervised living arrangement. A teen head of household who maintains satisfactory school attendance is deemed to be meeting workfare requirements. While not limited to teens, teens will be disproportionately affected by requirements that individuals cooperate with paternity establishment, with the minimum penalty for non-cooperation a 25 percent reduction in the family's grant.

11. Constance A. Nathanson, *Dangerous Passage: The Social Control of Women's Adolescence* (Philadelphia: Temple University Press, 1991).

12. Catherine K. Riessman and Constance A. Nathanson, "The Management of Reproduction: Social Construction of Risk and Responsibility," in Linda H. Aiken and David Mechanic, eds., *Applications of Social Science to Clinical Medicine and Health Policy* (New Brunswick, N.J.: Rutgers University Press, 1986).

13. See Personal Responsibility and Reconciliation Act of 1996, and the charge of the National Campaign to Prevent Teen Pregnancy, 2100 M Street, N.W., Suite 500, Washington, D.C. 20037.

14. Arline T. Geronimus, "On Teenage Childbearing and Neonatal Mortality in the United States," *Population and Development Review* 13, no. 2 (1987): 245–279; Kristin Luker, "Dubious Conceptions: The Controversy over Teen Pregnancy," *American Prospect* (Spring 1991): 73–83.

15. Allan F. Abrahamse, Peter A. Morrison, and Linda Waite, "Beyond Stereotypes: Who Becomes a Single Teenage Mother?" (Santa Monica, Calif.: Rand Corporation, 1988).

16. Arline T. Geronimus and Sanders Korenman, "The Socio-Economic Consequences of Teen Childbearing Reconsidered," *Quarterly Journal of Economics* 107 (1992): 1187–1214.

17. Geronimus and Korenman, "The Socio-Economic Consequences of Teen Childbearing Reconsidered"; Saul Hoffman, Michael Foster, and Frank Furstenberg, "Re-evaluating the Costs of Teenage Childbearing," *Demography* 30, no. 1 (1993): 1–13; Mary E. Corcoran and James P. Kunz, "Do Unmarried Births Among African American Teens Lead to Adult Poverty?" *Social Service Review*, 71, no. 2 (June 1997): 274–287.

18. There is evidence that such factors matter, although the magnitude of this bias is an empirical question. See Arline T. Geronimus and Sanders Korenman, "The Socio-economic Costs of Teenage Childbearing: Evidence and Interpretation," *Demography* 30 (No. 2, 1993): 281–290; and Christine A. Bachrach and Karen Carver, *Outcomes of Early Childbearing: An Appraisal of Recent Evidence.* Summary of a conference convened by the National Institute of Child Health and Human Development (Bethesda, Md., 1993).

19. Joseph V. Hotz, Susan W. McElroy, and Seth G. Sanders, "The Costs and Consequences of Teenage Childbearing for Mothers." *Chicago Policy Review* (Fall 1996): 55–94.

20. To the extent that miscarriages are random, comparing teen mothers to teens who miscarried eliminates heterogeneity more completely than sisters comparisons. In practice, there will be some misreporting of miscarriages in survey data that may be systematic. For example, if elective abortions are sometimes reported as miscarriages, then some

proportion of the women classified as having had miscarriages are teens who chose not to become mothers. Because miscarriages among teenagers are rarely related to chronic health problems, however, there is little reason to believe that the group who miscarried would suffer from health problems that would impede their chances for economic success. Hotz, Mullin, and Sanders perform tests of the validity of their method and conclude that it provides a valid approximation to their ideal conditions ("Bounding Causal Effects Using Contaminated Instrumental Variables: Analyzing the Effects of Teenage Childbearing Using a Natural Experiment," unpublished manuscript, 1996).

21. Arline T. Geronimus and Sanders Korenman, "The Socio-Economic Consequences of Teen Childbearing Reconsidered," *Quarterly Journal of Economics* 107 (1992): 1187–1214.

22. Mary E. Corcoran and James P. Kunz, "Do Out-of-Wedlock Births Among African American Teenagers Lead to Adult Poverty and Dependency?" *Social Service Review,* in press.

23. Joseph V. Hotz, Susan W. McElroy, and Seth G. Sanders, "The Costs and Consequences of Teenage Childbearing for Mothers," *Chicago Policy Review* (Fall 1996): 55–94.

24. For example, Hotz et al., "The Costs and Consequences," review studies that use various approaches to account for unobserved background factors that may confound the relationship between teenage childbearing and long-term economic outcomes. They conclude that selection bias "vastly" overstates the negative consequences of teenage childbearing estimated in cross-sectional studies. They find that the reviewed studies "provide no support that there are large, negative consequences." They further conclude that the range of uncertainty is over whether the effects of teenage childbearing are "slightly negative," "negligible," or "positive." See also Geronimus and Korenman, "The Socio-Economic Consequences of Teen Childbearing Reconsidered"; and, Christine A. Bachrach and Karen Carver, *Outcomes of Early Childbearing: An Appraisal of Recent Evidence,* summary of a conference convened by the National Institute of Child Health and Human Development (Bethesda, Maryland, 1993).

25. See, for example, reviews including Olle Sahler, "Adolescent Parenting: Potential for Child Abuse and Neglect?" *Pediatric Annals* 9, no. 3 (1980): 120–125; E. Milling Kinard and Lorraine Klerman, "Teenage Parenting and Child Abuse: Are They Related?" *American Journal of Orthopsychiatry* 50, no. 3 (1980): 481–488; H. Dubowitz, "Child Maltreatment in the United States: Etiology, Impact, and Prevention" (Washington, D.C.: Health Program, Office of Technology Assessment, 1987); and Ester Buchholz and Carol Korn-Bursztyn "Children of Adolescent Mothers: Are They at Risk for Abuse?" *Adolescence* 28, no. 110 (1993): 361–382. See also studies including Shelby Miller, "The Relationship Between Adolescent Childbearing and Child Maltreatment". *Child Welfare* 58 (No.6, 1984): 553–557; and Carol Rippey Massat, "Is Older Better? Adolescent Parenthood and Maltreatment," *Child Welfare* 74, no. 2 (1995): 325–336.

26. Massat, "Is Older Better?" 333–334.

27. Kristin A. Moore, Donna Ruane Morrison, and Angela Dungee Greene, "Effects on the Children Born to Adolescent Mothers," in Rebecca Maynard, ed., *Kids Having Kids* (Washington, D.C.: Urban Institute Press, 1997), chap. 5.

28. Jeff Grogger, "Crime: The Influence of Early Childbearing on the Cost of Incarceration," in *Kids Having Kids* (Washington, D.C.: Urban Institute Press, 1997), chap. 8.

29. Grogger's method for controlling for heterogeneity is likely to be inadequate. He tries to control for maternal background characteristics by controlling for whether or not each sample mother's first birth occurred during her early teens, and then estimating the effect on incarceration of her age at subsequent births. By using a dichotomous variable to control for maternal age-at-first-birth when estimating the effect of maternal age, he fails to control adequately for heterogeneity or even as well as he might have if he had instead used a continuous variable.

30. The statistical significance of Grogger's estimates varies depending on the specification he uses (see his table 8.3). The modest results he emphasizes are his strongest results.

31. Kristin A. Moore and Nancy O. Snyder, "Cognitive Attainment Among Firstborn Children of Adolescent Mothers," *American Sociological Review* 56 (1991): 612–624; Arline T. Geronimus, Sanders Korenman, and Marianne M. Hillemeier, "Does Young Maternal Age Adversely Affect Child Development? Evidence from Cousin Comparisons," *Population and Development Review* 20, no. 3 (1994): 585–609; Arline T. Geronimus and Sanders Korenman, "Maternal Youth or Family Background? On the Health Disadvantages of Infants with Teenage Mothers," *American Journal of Epidemiology* 137, no. 2 (1993): 213–225; Mark R. Rosenzweig and Kenneth I. Wolpin, "Sisters, Siblings, and Mothers: The Effect of Teen-Age Childbearing on Birth Outcomes in a Dynamic Family Context," *Econometrica* 63, no. 2 (1995): 303–326; and Arline T. Geronimus, "Black/White Differences in the Relationship of Maternal Age to Birthweight: A Population Based Test of the Weathering Hypothesis," *Social Science and Medicine* 42, no. 4 (1996): 589–597.

32. Arline T. Geronimus, "On Teenage Childbearing and Neonatal Mortality in the United States," *Population and Development Review* 13, no. 2 (1987); Arline T. Geronimus, "The Health of African American Women and Infants: Implications for Reproductive Strategies and Policy Analysis," in Gita Sen and Rachel C. Snow, eds., *Power and Decision: The Social Control of Reproduction* (Cambridge, Mass.: Harvard University Press, 1994); Geronimus, "Black/White Differences"; and Jennie Kline, Zena Stein, and Mervyn Susser, *Conception to Birth: Epidemiology of Prenatal Development* (New York: Oxford University Press, 1989).

33. Geronimus, "Black/White Differences."

34. Geronimus, "The Health of African American Women and Infants."

35. Moore and Snyder, "Cognitive Attainment Among Firstborn Children of Adolescent Mothers."

36. Moore et al., "Effects on the Children Born to Adolescent Mothers,"

37. Geronimus et al., "Does Young Maternal Age Adversely Affect Child Development?"

38. Of course, the documentation of large social costs alone is insufficient to implement policies — heavy-handed ones, in particular — intended to interfere with reproductive freedom. For example, we are unlikely to tolerate policies denying prenatal care to older socioeconomically advantaged mothers or neonatal intensive care to their infants, even though delayed childbearing is associated with increased risk of maternal morbidity,

c-section delivery, and neonatal intensive care use, all of which contribute to spiraling health insurance and medical care costs. Gertrud S. Berkowitz, Mary Louise Skovron, Robert H. Lapinski, and Richard Berkowitz, "Delayed Childbearing and the Outcome of Pregnancy," *New England Journal of Medicine* 322 (1990): 659–664.

39. See Arline T. Geronimus, "Mothers of Invention," *Nation*, 12/19 (August 1996): 6–7.

40. Hotz et al., "The Costs and Consequences," 85–86.

41. For a general discussion of the distinction between *form* and *function* of union types, see Robert A. LeVine and Susan C. M. Scrimshaw, "Effects of Culture on Fertility: Anthropological Contribution," in Rudolfo A. Bulatao and Ronald D. Lee, eds., *Determinants of Fertility in Developing Countries*, vol. 2 (New York: Academic Press, 1983).

42. S. Philip Morgan, Antonio McDaniel, Andrew T. Miller, and Samuel H. Preston, "Racial Differences in Household and Family Structure at the Turn of the Century," *American Journal of Sociology* 98, no. 4 (1993): 799–828.

43. Steven Ruggles, "The Origins of African-American Family Structure," *American Sociological Review* 59 (1994): 136–151; Antonio McDaniel, "Historical Racial Differences in Living Arrangements of Children," *Journal of Family History* 19, no. 1 (1994): 57–77.

44. Carol B. Stack, *All Our Kin* (New York: Harper & Row, 1974) and *Call to Home* (New York: Basic Books, 1996); Linda M. Burton, "Teenage Childbearing as an Alternative Life-Course Strategy in Multigeneration Black Families," *Human Nature* 1, no. 2 (1990): 123–143; Arline T. Geronimus, "Clashes of Common Sense: On the Previous Child Care Experience of Teenage Mothers-To-Be," *Human Organization* 51, no. 4 (1992): 318–329; Kari Sandven and Michael D. Resnick, "Informal Adoption Among Black Adolescent Mothers," *American Journal of Orthopsychiatry* 60, no. 2 (1990): 210–224; Marta Tienda and Jennifer Glass, "Household Structure and Labor Force Participation of Black, Hispanic, and White Mothers," *Demography* 22 (1985): 381–394; Dennis P. Hogan, Ling-Xin Hao, and William L. Parish, "Race, Kin Networks, and Assistance to Mother-Headed Families," *Social Forces* 68 (1990): 797–812; and Morgan et al., "Racial Differences in Household and Family Structure at the Turn of the Century."

45. Recent studies suggesting that children raised by single parents fare worse than those raised by two parents would appear to support policies to enhance the attractiveness of marriage. See Sara McLanahan and Gary Sandefur, *Growing Up with a Single Parent: What Hurts, What Helps* (Cambridge, Mass.: Harvard University Press, 1994). There are two general problems with this policy response in the context of teen mothers. First, the empirical findings are based on cross-sectional evidence and do not answer the key question of whether children of single parents would do better if their parents stayed together (if divorced) or married (if unmarried). Second, in the select populations where teen childbearing is common, premature mortality may be a major threat to a child's chance of being raised by two parents. Shotgun weddings are not responsive to this problem.

To the extent that welfare reformers are concerned that welfare rules themselves have served as a disincentive toward marriage, it would be reasonable to expand programs such as AFDC-UP and in-kind benefits for which two-parent families qualify or to change restrictions such as the "100-hour rule" that may encourage fathers with low-wage jobs to leave their families. Such an approach would remove welfare-driven disincentives toward marriage without, in effect, penalizing the poor or members of minority groups if they maintain multigenerational extended families.

46. Stack, *All Our Kin* and *Call to Home;* and Carol Stack and Linda Burton, "Kinscripts," *Journal of Comparative Family Studies,* 24, no. 2 (1993): 157–170.

47. Morgan et al., "Racial Differences in Household and Family Structure at the Turn of the Century"; and Deanna Pagnini and S. Philip Morgan, "Racial Differences in Marriage and Childbearing: Oral History Evidence from the South in the Early Twentieth Century," *American Journal of Sociology* 101, no. 6 (1996): 1694–1718.

48. Frank Mott, "When Is Father Really Gone? Paternal-Child Contact in Father-Absent Homes," *Demography* 27, no. 4 (1990): 514.

49. Conventional wisdom holds that kin network ties have weakened over time. The empirical basis for this view is anecdotal or inferred from declining marriage rates. However, census-based marriage rates reveal little about rates of participation in kin networks. There are certainly new assaults on kin networks resulting from the loss of prime-aged adults in some specific urban areas to AIDS or drug epidemics. And these threats to kin networks have arisen concurrently with increased housing costs, decreased value of real wages, and declining AFDC benefits, all of which leave families with fewer resources to spread across greater needs. Some have argued that specific urban planning policies have also disrupted or strained social networks. (See Roderick Wallace and Deborah Wallace, "Origins of Public Health Collapse in New York City: The Dynamics of Planned Shrinkage, Contagious Urban Decay and Social Disintegration," *Bulletin of the New York Academy of Medicine* 66 [1990]: 391–434; and J. Philip Thompson, "The Failure of Liberal Homeless Policy in the Koch and Dinkins Administration," *Political Science Quarterly* 111, no. 4 [1996–1997]: 639–660.) Increasing homelessness suggests increasing failure of kin networks to protect members from the worst forms of material hardship. And interest has been renewed in the inter- and intrapersonal tensions kin network participation invites (see Stack and Burton, "Kinscripts"; and Geronimus, "The Health of African American Women and Infants.") But the imperfections of kin networks and the new difficulties they face do not imply their absence as an important form of mutual support in poor populations. Recent ethnographic work suggests that kin networks continue to be critical sources of support and personal identity in some poor populations, and that they flourish, motivate, support, and pull across time and space, from generation to generation, from south to north. See Stack, *Call to Home.*

50. Stack, *All Our Kin*; Burton, "Teenage Childbearing,"; Arline T. Geronimus, "Clashes of Common Sense."

51. John Demos and Virginia Demos, "Adolescence in Historical Perspective," *Journal of Marriage and the Family* 31 (1969): 623–639; and Glen H. Elder, Jr., "Adolescence in Historical Perspective" in Joseph Adelson, ed., *Handbook of Adolescent Psychology* (New York: Wiley, 1980).

52. Mercer L. Sullivan, "Absent Fathers in the Inner City," *Annals of the American Academy of Political and Social Science* 501 (1989): 48–58.

53. Ethnographers have observed that those elders who sometimes encourage teen childbearing speak from life experience and know that members of poor families must rely on each other for caretaking as well as for economic support. As poor families

configure themselves, judgments are made about which teens are promising economic providers and which ones are better at caretaking. In communities where babies are highly valued, longevity is in question, and the experience of grandparenthood is longed for, elders may also encourage early childbearing. If, as the research suggests, in extremely disadvantaged communities, early childbearing maximizes the health and well-being of infants, a caring elder might encourage it. See Joyce Ladner, *Tomorrow's Tomorrow: The Black Woman* (New York: Doubleday, 1971); Burton, "Teenage Childbearing"; Stack, *All Our Kin;* Stack and Burton, "Kinscripts"; and Arline T. Geronimus, "What Teen Mothers Know," *Human Nature* 7, no. 4 (1996): 323–352.

54. Rebecca M. Blank, "Outlook for the U.S. Labor Market and Prospects for Low-Wage Entry Jobs," in D. Nightengale and R. Haveman, eds., *The Work Alternative: Welfare Reform and the Realities of the Job Market* (Washington, D.C.: Urban Institute Press, 1995).

55. Ladner, *Tomorrow's Tomorrow;* Burton, "Teenage Childbearing"; and Stack and Burton, "Kinscripts."

56. Stack, *All Our Kin*; and Geronimus, "Clashes of Common Sense."

57. Robert Blythe, *The View in Winter: Reflections on Old Age* (New York: Harcourt Brace Jovanovich, 1979); cited by Hagestad, "On-Time, Off-Time, Out of Time?" in V. H. Bengston, ed., *Adulthood and Aging: Research on Continuities and Discontinuities* (New York: Springer, 1996).

58. Arline T. Geronimus, John Bound, Timothy A. Waidmann, Marianne M. Hillemeier, and Patricia B. Burns, "Excess Mortality Among Blacks and Whites in the United States," *New England Journal of Medicine* 335 (1996): 1552–1558.

59. Ibid.

60. Nathanson, *Dangerous Passage.*

61. William Julius Wilson, *The Truly Disadvantaged* (Chicago: University of Chicago Press, 1987); and Christopher Jencks, "What Is the Underclass — And Is It Growing?" *Focus* (Special Issue: Defining and Measuring the Underclass), 12 (1989): 14–26.

62. Jeanne Brooks-Gunn, Cecilla M. McCarton, Patrick H. Casey, Marie C. McCormick, et al., "Early Intervention in Low-Birth-Weight Premature Infants," *JAMA* 272, no. 16 (1994): 1257–1262; Marie C. McCormick, Jeanne Brooks-Gunn, Kathryn Workman-Daniels, JoAnna Turner, et al., "The Health and Development Status of Very Low-Birth-Weight Children at School Age," *JAMA* 267, no. 16 (1992): 2204–2208.

63. Felicia B. LeClere and Brenda Marsteller Kowaleski, "Disability in the Family: The Effects on Children's Well-Being," *Journal of Marriage and the Family* 56 (1994): 457–468.

64. Blank, "Outlook for the U.S. Labor Market and Prospects for Low-Wage Entry Jobs."

65. Hotz et al., Susan W. McElroy, and Seth G. Sanders, "The Costs and Consequences," 85–86; and Kathy J. Edin and L. Lein, *Making Ends Meet: How Single Mothers Survive Welfare and Low-Wage Work* (New York: Russell Sage Foundation, 1997).

66. Sheila B. Kamerman and Alfred J. Kahn, *Starting Right: How America Neglects Its Youngest Children and What We Can Do About It* (New York: Oxford University Press, 1995).

67. Sherman A. James, David S. Strogatz, Steven B. Wing, and Diane L. Ramsey,

"Socioeconomic Status, John Henryism, and Hypertension in Blacks and Whites," *American Journal of Epidemiology* 126, no. 4 (1987): 664–673; Sherman A. James, "John Henryism and the Health of African-Americans," *Culture, Medicine and Psychiatry* 18 (1994): 163–182; Geronimus, "The Health of African American Women and Infants"; and Leith Mullings, "Minority Women, Work, and Health" in Wendy Chavkin, ed., *Double Exposure: Women's Health Hazards on the Job and at Home* (New York: Monthly Review Press, 1984).

68. Geronimus, "What Teen Mothers Know."

69. Among other explanations, the timing of changes in teen childbearing rates can be interpreted as reflecting the changing fortunes of the poor. For example, teen birth rates steadily declined through the 1960s and 1970s as opportunities for women and minorities increased and the desire to end poverty was a prominent part of the national political agenda. They rose somewhat for the first time in decades in the late 1980s at a time when the fortunes of the socioeconomically disadvantaged suffered reversals related to deep recessions and the threat to their well-being posed by the Ronald Reagan and George H. W. Bush administrations, including cuts in government-sponsored welfare programs. Teen birth rates again declined precipitously in the 1990s, a time when the United States experienced unprecedented economic expansion (see also Cynthia G. Colen, Arline T. Geronimus, and Maureen Phipps, "Getting a Piece of the Pie? Declining Teen Birth Rates During the 1990s," paper presented at the annual meeting of the Population Association of America, Minneapolis, 2003).

70. Nonmarital birth rates did begin rising in the 1960s when AFDC was relatively generous, but they continued to rise through the 1970s and 1980s when AFDC eligibility requirements became more stringent and the real value of benefits declined. See David Ellwood and Lawrence Summers, "Poverty in America: Is Welfare the Answer or the Problem?" in Sheldon Danziger and Daniel H. Weinberg, eds., *Fighting Poverty: What Works and What Doesn't* (Cambridge, Mass.: Harvard University Press, 1986); and Robert Moffitt, "Incentive Effects of the U.S. Welfare System," *Journal of Economic Literature* 30 (March 1992): 1–61. For a discussion of the effects of economic incentives on premarital childbearing among teens, see Shelly Lundberg and Robert D. Plotnick, "Adolescent Premarital Childbearing: Do Economic Incentives Matter?" *Journal of Labor Economics* 13, no. 2 (1995): 177–200.

71. John K. Inglehart, "Politics and Public Health," *New England Journal of Medicine* 334, no. 3 (1996): 203–207.

72. Burton, "Teenage Childbearing"; and Stack and Burton, "Kinscripts."

73. See Nathanson, *Dangerous Passage*, for a discussion of Planned Parenthood's role in constructing and publicizing the idea that teenage childbearing is a social problem of epidemic proportion. See Arline T. Geronimus, "Teenage Childbearing and Social and Reproductive Disadvantage: The Evolution of Complex Questions and the Demise of Simple Answers," *Family Relations* 40, no. 4 (1991): 463–471, for a discussion of the Children's Defense Fund's active public resistance to research findings challenging the conventional wisdom that were reported at the 1990 annual meeting of the American Association for the Advancement of Science. More recently, the Robin Hood Foundation has played a visible role proliferating the distortion that teen childbearing is known to have staggering social costs, through its highly publicized distribution of an alarmist

report. Of interest, Hotz et al.'s findings that teenage mothers gain *no* economic advantage by delaying childbearing formed part of the scientific base of the Robin Hood report. This was underplayed in the publicity, with no attempt to wrestle with the profound challenge to conventional wisdom Hotz et al.'s findings represented.

74. Estimate made by the Urban Institute, July 1996. David Super, Sharon Parrott, Susan Steinmetz, and Cindy Mann in "The New Welfare Law," Center on Budget and Policy Priorities, August 13, 1996, argue this is a conservative estimate.

75. See Thomas Corbett, "The New Federalism: Monitoring Consequences," *Focus* 18, no. 1 (1996): 3–6.

18

Where Should Teen Mothers Live?
What Should We Do About It?

HAROLD POLLACK

Many people believe that public aid creates incentives for young mothers to make choices detrimental to the public interest and their own long-term goals. One of the most important of these incentives concerns the ability of teen mothers on public aid to establish independent households rather than to reside with their parents or other relatives.

The prospect that welfare induces young mothers to prematurely establish independent households is disquieting for several reasons:

- This pattern suggests that welfare displaces informal support that parents, grandparents, and other relatives might otherwise provide. Generous public aid may therefore encourage friends and relatives of the needy to shift burdens onto the public fisc.
- "Coresidence" with parents or other adults produces economies of scale in consumption and permits young mothers and children to reside in safer and more prosperous neighborhoods than they otherwise could.[1] Coresidence also facilitates provision of child care and other important noncash transfers from family members to poor mothers and their children.
- Coresidence plausibly provides children with greater emotional and residential stability. Such stability is especially important in the light of evidence that frequent changes in both location and household composition are detrimental to children — even apart from the effect of these changes on family income or the quality of the neighborhoods in which children live.[2]

Perhaps most disquieting, public assistance that facilitates formation of separate households may lead teenagers to view pregnancy and welfare receipt as viable paths to adulthood and personal independence. For all of these reasons, both federal and state regulations require minor teen mothers to reside with their own parents or with other adults to remain eligible for cash aid. The Republican Contract with America included even stronger measures, though these provisions were not enacted into law.

Despite strong bipartisan support for such proposals, little is known about the long-run consequences of teen parents' residential choices. One widely cited study (Furstenberg, Brooks-Gunn, and Morgan 1987) suggests that teen mothers living with parents may be more likely than others to earn high school degrees. Coresiding teen mothers may also be less likely to form hasty marriages likely to end in divorce or poverty. Yet these authors add: "Residential arrangements following pregnancy also did not generally affect the outcomes examined, at least directly. Adolescents who lived with their parents immediately following birth did not on average do better in later life than those who immediately left their parents" (1987, p. 136).

Furstenberg et al. suggest that the great variation in teen mothers' values, opportunities and family circumstances defy easy generalization. Even within their small, inner-city Baltimore sample: "Not only was initial family support not strongly linked to an adolescent mother's fate in later life, a number of personal attributes and attitudes, often thought to be related to the adjustment to early childbearing, had little impact on a woman's later economic fortunes or fertility level . . . Indeed virtually none of the attitudes she or her parents expressed during the pregnancy or just after the birth of the child forecast how well she managed over the long term" (1987, p. 136).

Other researchers report equally negative findings. Moore and Snyder (1991) analyze the vocabulary skills of children born to young mothers. Controlling for mothers' prior academic skills and other variables, they find that coresidence has no significant impact on children's performance on standardized tests. Pavetti (1993) and others present hazard analysis of welfare receipt which finds no strong relation between coresidence and the duration of welfare spells.

Kellam et al. (1977) do find that children benefit from the presence of a stable grandmother figure within the household. Yet such recent studies as Chase-Lansdale, Brooks-Gunn, and Zamsky (1994) find little significant improvement for most children from such arrangements.[3] These authors find that coresiding grandmothers score lower on standardized assessments of parenting skill than do noncoresiding grandparents. Indeed, coresiding grandmothers appear quite similar in their economic resources and parenting styles to their daughters. All of these authors report that their findings are potentially sensitive to selection bias. Almost any individual or family characteristic that influences residential choice also has important direct effects on outcomes for both teen mothers and their children. Explicit efforts to model residential choices are therefore essential in examining the linkage to maternal and child outcomes.

This chapter examines these questions by investigating several important outcomes associated with teen mothers' residential choices. The first section describes the geocoded, 1979–1993 National Longitudinal Survey of Youth (NLSY) and other data used in the analysis. The second section presents the analytic framework used in the chapter. Following Lee (1983), this section presents a two-stage multinomial logit-OLS model of endogenous residential choice.

The third section presents corresponding empirical results on the determinants of residential choice. It is shown that public assistance significantly influences where and with whom teen mothers live. However, the impact of such aid varies greatly across the range of residential choices. Generous assistance and sharp benefit reductions for teen mothers living with their parents are more strongly associated with the establishment of independent households, shared living arrangements with other relatives, or the formation of other nonmarital living arrangements. Cash assistance has a smaller, statistically insignificant impact on the marital decisions of NLSY teen mothers. Point estimates suggest that the impact of such assistance is most pronounced in the ten most generous states.

The fourth section then applies the two-stage model to examine several concrete outcomes for teen mothers and their children. Although postpartum residential arrangements are correlated with important life outcomes, prebirth characteristics of teen mothers and their families play a much stronger role. Controlling for the endogeneity of residential choice, there is little evidence that postpregnancy residential arrangements strongly influence long-term outcomes for teen mothers themselves.

There is, however, evidence that such residential arrangements influence academic and behavioral outcomes among children. Continuous coresidence and teen marriage are associated with reduced risk of grade retention and academic suspension or expulsion among the children of teen mothers.

Data and Methodology

The principal data source is the linked, 1979–1992 child-mother National Longitudinal Survey of Youth (NLSY). This unique survey provides extensive longitudinal data on a national probability sample of young men and women between the ages of 14 and 22 at the beginning of the NLSY sample frame. Like other surveys such as the Panel Study of Income Dynamics and the Survey of Income and Program Participation, NLSY contains detailed data on the economic, educational, and household characteristics of survey respondents. Because this analysis exploits local and regional variation in market rents, it uses the geocoded version of the NLSY, which identifies city and county of residence.

Although the NLSY provides a smaller sample size than some other surveys, it incorporates superior data for examination of many academic and psychosocial outcomes associated with teen pregnancy. The NLSY also includes a rich battery of psychological and cognitive skill measures for both teen mothers and their children. For example, the NLSY includes teenagers' performance on the Armed Forces Qualification Test (AFQT), one of the best measures of academic and cognitive skill of young adults. The NLSY also includes detailed educational and psychosocial data regarding dependent children.

This analysis focuses on a sample of 689 mothers who gave birth to at least one child during their teen years. Teen mothers who gave birth to their first child before 1978 are excluded from the analysis, since their residential arrangements and educational attainment at the time of their first baby's birth cannot be accurately determined from the initial NLSY interview.

These NLSY data are then merged with two other data sources. Analysis such as Winkler (1992) and Haurin, Hendershott, and Kim (1993) suggest that local rental markets play an important role in mothers' residential choices. We therefore include median county rents as captured in the 1990 Census. These data are linked with teen mothers' reported state and county of residence in the year of their child's birth. In twenty-six cases, state and county measures were not available for the birth year. In these cases, rent measures are used for the state and county of the initial 1979 interview or the county in which the respondent lived when she was 14 years old.

Subtle features of public assistance policies also play an important role. Many states influence poor mothers' household choices by providing implicit penalties or bonuses to recipients who live with other adults. At one extreme, some states compute cash aid based upon the full income of every member of the recipient household. Such calculations effectively discourage recipients from living with their parents or with other legally employed adults. At the other extreme, some states have traditionally computed benefits based on the recipients' income alone — effectively ignoring income generated by other household members.

Many researchers report that state policies toward AFDC recipients in shared living arrangements are poorly described by official policies and regulations. Case workers often enjoy great discretion in detecting and classifying recipients' incomes in making allowances for the varying needs of individual household members.

We follow the general methodology suggested by Hutchens, Jakubson, and Schwartz (1989) to use individual-level administrative data to represent the implicit and explicit policies implemented by the states. In particular, we use the 1991 AFDC-Quality Control data set to construct fifty-one measures, one for each state and the District of Columbia. These measures seek to capture how AFDC monthly benefits vary in response to the presence of other adults in the recipients' household.

More formally, we estimate fifty-one state-specific regressions given in equation (1):

(1) $Log(Benefit_k) = vX_k + \gamma log(MAXBEN_j) + \beta_j {}^*SHARE_k + \epsilon_k$

Here k is an index of families, while j indicated the given state. $Benefit_k$ is the monthly benefit actually received by the family. X_k represents a vector of personal characteristics including an intercept term. $MAXBEN_j$ is the maximum allowable 1991 AFDC payment in state j for a family of two. In practice, most young AFDC mothers who live with no other adults receive very close to the maximum allowable amount.

The dummy variable $SHARE_k$ is of greatest immediate interest. This is set to one if the given recipient is listed as living rent-free from another person. The coefficients β_j, $j = 1, \ldots 51$ then provide one convenient measure of the effective penalty associated with coresidence. Appendix 18.1 includes the estimated parameter values for β corresponding to each state.

Table 18.1 below provides resulting summary statistics on the NLSY sample.

Analytic Framework

Where — and with whom — a teen mother will live is a complex decision involving the teenager herself, her family, the father of her children, and perhaps other adults. The young woman can live with her parents. She can marry or cohabitate with the father of her child. She and her children can establish an independent household. She can live with a roommate or with an older sibling or some other relative.[4]

These choices are most readily modeled using a two-stage framework following Lee (1983). Suppose that young woman i has a range of exogenous characteristics described by some vector X_i. This vector includes personal characteristics such as the young woman's age and ethnicity, her observed

Table 18.1. Summary Statistics of NLSY Sample

	Weighted Mean (1992 Sample Weight)	Standard Deviation
Age of mother at birth	17.9	1.15
Mother age 15 or younger at birth	0.035	0.18
Mother age 16 at birth	0.10	0.30
Mother age 17 at birth	0.21	0.40
Mother age 18 at birth	0.29	0.45
Mother age 19 at birth	0.38	0.49
First NLSY interview following birth	1981.0	1.6
Child is male	0.48	0.50
Mother's score on Armed Forces Qualification Test (AFQT)	536	190
Mother has GED certificate	0.20	0.40
Mother completed high school (not GED) by 1992 interview	0.59	0.49
Mother less than 9th grade at birth	0.10	0.305
Mother completed 9th grade at birth	0.14	0.35
Mother completed 10th grade at birth	0.21	0.41
Mother completed 11th grade at birth	0.21	0.41
Mother completed 12th grade at birth	0.33	0.47
Black	0.48	0.50
Latino	0.19	0.39
Married at 1992 interview	0.46	0.50
Child repeated grade in school	0.25	0.44
Child ever suspended or expelled	0.14	0.35
Mother's number of siblings in 1979 household	4.6	2.8
Mother with own parents at age 19	0.48	0.50
Mother with own parents at age 18	0.60	0.49
Mother with own parents at age 17	0.70	0.46
Mother with own parents at age 16	0.78	0.42
Mother with own parents at age 15	0.82	0.39
Mother lived with father and mother at age 14	0.51	0.50
Mother lived with her mother only at age 14	0.28	0.45
Mother lived with mother and stepfather at 14	0.11	0.31
Mother lived with relatives at 14	0.061	0.24
Mother lived with own Father (Not Mother)	0.021	0.14
Mother lived in other arrangement at 14	0.026	0.16
Mother had more children than initially desired	0.29	0.45

Table 18.1. Continued

	Weighted Mean (1992 Sample Weight)	Standard Deviation
Mother lived with own parents at second interview postpartum	0.28	0.45
Mother lived with other family members at second interview postpartum	0.019	0.14
Mother married at second interview postpartum	0.42	0.49
Mother cohabitated with opposite sex partner at second interview postpartum	0.07	0.25
Mother in independent household or in multiple arrangements by second interview postpartum	0.22	0.45
Median county rent	418	115
1990 AFDC benefit for family of two	311	154
In poverty for calendar year 1991	0.24	0.44
Mother living in urban SMSA 1979	0.82	0.39
East South Central Census Region	0.09	0.29
South Atlantic Census Region	0.209	0.41
New England Census Region	0.046	0.21
Mid-Atlantic Census Region	0.105	0.31
West South-Central Census Region	0.15	0.35
East North Central Census Region	0.18	0.38
West North Central Census Region	0.05	0.22
Mountain Census Region	0.05	0.213
Pacific Census Region	0.13	0.33
AFDC Coresidence "Penalty" (Log points)	0.17	0.26

academic skill and completed years of schooling. X_i also includes characteristics of local housing markets and available public assistance policies that are likely to influence her residential choice.

The young woman has available various residential arrangements s^*, $s = 1$, $2 \ldots$ M. To capture this variety of household choices, we model the young mother's residential decisions using a multinomial logit. She derives some utility $U_{i,s}$ from a given residential arrangement s in accordance with the linear relation

(2) $U_{i,s} = X_i \gamma_s + v_{i,s}$ s=1 ... M

The young woman then chooses the arrangement s^* that maximizes equation (2) above. In accordance with standard assumptions (Amemiya 1985, pp. 296–297), the error term $v_{i,s}$ is i.i.d, and governed by an extreme value distribution. This implies that the probability of choosing any particular arrangement s is given by

$$(3) \quad p_s = \frac{\exp(XX_i\gamma_s)}{\exp(X_i\gamma_1)+\exp(X_i\gamma_2)\dots+\exp(X_i\gamma_s)\dots+\exp(X_{igamma_M})}$$

This framework is widely used in empirical work, including at least one study of housing choices among teen mothers (Hilton and Shelton 1995). For simplicity, this framework presents teen mothers' residential arrangements as the outcome of utility maximizing choices of the young woman herself. This is clearly an oversimplification. The preferences and resources of other people play a critical role. Marriage is an option only when the potential husband agrees to take part. Strained family relations may preclude shared living with parents or other relatives.

Existing research suggests that teen mothers' living arrangements are the product of a more complicated interaction over time that involves the young woman, the father of her child, and other family members. Each arrangement brings its own costs and benefits to the young mother and to her children — costs and benefits difficult to characterize in a simple or tractable empirical model.[5]

Given any residential arrangement, the young mother experiences some outcome $y_{i,s}$ such as subsequent earnings or the acquisition of a high school degree. We model $y_{i,s}$ using the OLS regression

$$(4) \quad y_{i,s} = \alpha_s + X_i\beta + \epsilon_{i,s}$$

Here α_s is an intercept term that depends upon chosen residential arrangement. Again for simplicity, the error term $\epsilon_{i,s}$ is independent and normally distributed with mean zero and variance $\sigma_s 2$. In reality, the coefficients β will also depend upon s. For example, the characteristics of a teen mother's *own* parents may be more important when the young woman is living in the same home. However, because of the relatively small available sample size, β is constrained to be equal across residential choices.

We only estimate equation (4) for the residential arrangement, s^*, that is actually chosen. Both α_s and β are important for public policy. The vector β relates characteristics of the teen mother and her environment to subsequent outcomes. The intercept terms α_s capture the estimated impact of residential choice itself.

Teen mothers select residential arrangements given their own characteristics, their family prospects, and the wider social environment. Failure to properly model such endogenous choice may produce biased results. For example, the most academically motivated teen mothers may live with their parents because these young women need cheap and reliable child care to finish high school. Yet many of these young women would have graduated anyway, even if they had gotten married or moved in with friends. This suggests that the error term $\epsilon_{i,s}$ in equation (4) may be correlated with the residual $\nu_{i,s}$ from equation (2) that governs residential choice.

Under appropriate conditions, Lee (1983) demonstrates that a two-stage multinomial logit-OLS framework can provide consistent estimates of β_s and χ. In particular, equation (4) must be modified to include a selectivity term that depends upon the predicted probability that the observed residential arrangement would actually have been chosen:

$$(4')\quad y_{i,s} = \alpha_s + X_i\beta + \zeta_s\frac{\phi[\Phi^{-1}(\hat{p}_s)]}{\hat{p}_s} + \epsilon_{i,s}$$

Here $\phi(x)$ is the probability density function for the standard normal distribution. In like fashion, $\Phi(x)$ is the cumulative normal distribution. ζ_s is a parameter to be estimated from the data. Equation (4') is the fundamental equation controlling selection bias in this analysis.

Determinants of Household Choice

Using this empirical framework, one now estimates the multinomial logit model of teen mothers' residential choices. Depending upon the outcome of interest and the available data, one can model the timing and duration of such arrangements in many ways. This chapter focuses on residential choices of teen mothers during the first year of their child's life. This is the period during which many important outcomes are formed for both teen mothers and their children. This is also the period in which the most reliable data are most likely to be found.

An important limitation is that it is difficult to untangle the exact nature and timing of residential changes between NLSY interview dates. This analysis focuses upon teen mothers' status at the two NLSY interviews immediately following their child's birth. To obtain reliable results with the relatively small NLSY sample, residential choice is divided into four possible categories shown in Table 18.2 below.

Table 18.3 shows results of the multinomial logit analysis for selected coefficients. The complete specification is included in Appendix 18.2. To facilitate interpretation, results are reported as relative risk ratios, comparing a given outcome to continuous coresidence in the first year.

Table 18.2. Teen Mothers' Residential Choices

	Percent in Sample (Weighted by 1992 Sample Weight)
Coresident with parents at first two annual interviews following child birth	0.28
Married at second interview	0.42
Cohabitating or living with relatives at second interview	0.085
Established independent household or used multiple arrangements before second interview	0.22

Table 18.3. Multinomial Logit Model of Household Formation

Multinomial Logit Analysis of Household Choice (Omitted Category: Continuous Coresidence)	Relative Risk Ratio for Independent Household/Multiple Types (P-Value)	RRR for Marriage (P-Value)	RRR for Cohabitation/ Living with Relatives (P-Value)
Black	0.291***	0.086***	0.786
Latino	0.616	0.393***	0.609
1990 maximum AFDC benefit (standardized coefficient)	3.70***	1.11	1.463
[Standardized AFDC benefits]5	0.723	0.846	1.227
Coresidence penalty (log points)	0.663	1.68	10.81***
Standardized, median county rent	1.08	0.983	0.895
Urban SMSA	1.38	0.742	1.179
Percentage in category	22%	42%	8%
Observations		689	
Log likelihood		−685.8	

Note: Weighted by 1992 sample weight— *p<0.10, **p<0.05, ***p<0.01.

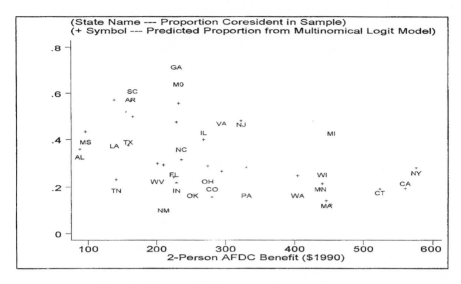

Figure 18.1 Actual and Predicted Coresidence by State

The multinomial logit model fits the data rather closely. Figures 18.1–18.4 illustrate model fit by showing the actual and predicted proportion of teen mothers in each residential arrangement. The figures are plotted for the thirty-five states that included at least ten teen mothers in the NLSY sample:

> There are major racial and ethnic disparities in household formation. African-American and Latino teen mothers are far more likely than whites to live with their own parents after giving birth, and are far less likely to get married. Fifty-seven percent of white mothers were married at the second interview postpartum. At the same point, 40 percent of Latino mothers, and only 18 percent of African-American mothers lived in married households.

These disparities are not appreciably reduced when one controls for differences in academic attainment, maternal age, geography, and other measures of social background. Nonwhite teen mothers are also less likely to cohabitate or to establish independent households once other sociodemographic characteristics were taken into account. Higher AFDC benefits do influence residential choice among teen mothers. The impact of public aid across the nation is illustrated in Figures 18.5–18.8 below.

In each figure, the multinomial logit model is used to compute the predicted impact of state policies on coresidence, marriage, and other residential arrangements. AFDC benefits in 1990 and the associated coresidence penalty are based on observed state policy. However, to focus on policy variables, all

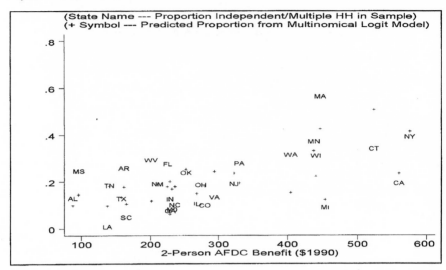

Figure 18.2 Actual and Predicted Rates of Independent/Multiple Household Formation by State

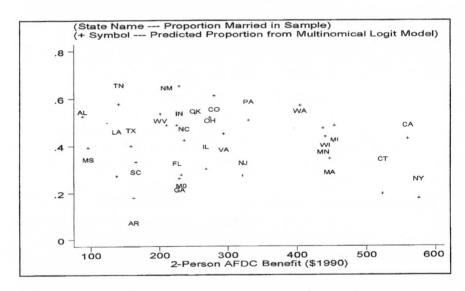

Figure 18.3 Actual and Predicted Marriage Rates by State

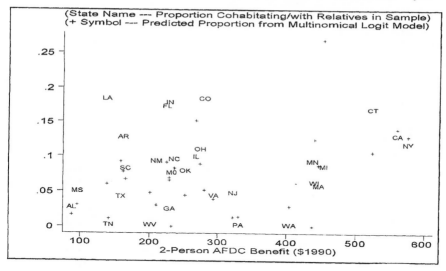

Figure 18.4 Actual and Predicted Rates of Cohabitation/Living with Relatives by State

personal characteristics such as race, educational attainment, and test scores are fixed at the NLSY sample mean. Regional dummy variables are also set to match the given state.

Figures 18.5 and 18.6 show an especially strong correlation between the generosity of state AFDC aid and residential choice. For an individual with mean characteristics, coresidence is more than twice as likely in Texas or Mississippi as in Wisconsin or New Hampshire, where cash assistance is most generous. The probability of establishing an independent household is predicted to double as monthly payments for a family of two rise from $250 to $400. Cohabitation and shared living with relatives are also responsive to public aid, though the resulting predicted probabilities are small in all but the ten most generous states.

The relationship between marriage and the generosity of public aid is less pronounced than for other choices. However, Figures 18.7 and 18.8 show signs of important nonlinear effects. The relationship between marriage rates and the level of AFDC payments appears strongest within the most generous quartile of states.

Public policies that implicitly penalize coresidence appear to play an important role, but the impact of such penalties differs sharply across residential arrangements. Policies that reduce cash aid to coresident teen mothers are associated with higher rates of cohabitation with boyfriends as well as shared living with other relatives. Such policies have a much smaller, statistically

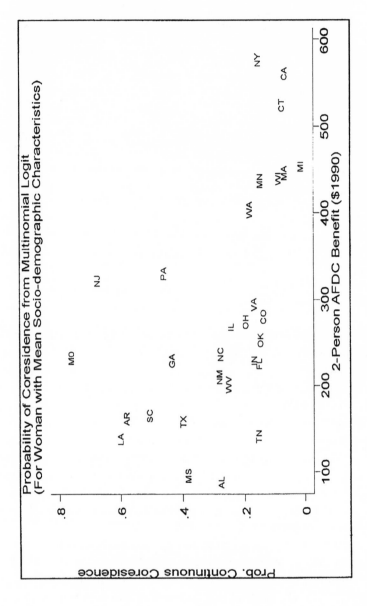

Figure 18.5 Predicted Coresidence Probability by State for Woman with Mean Sociodemographic Characteristics

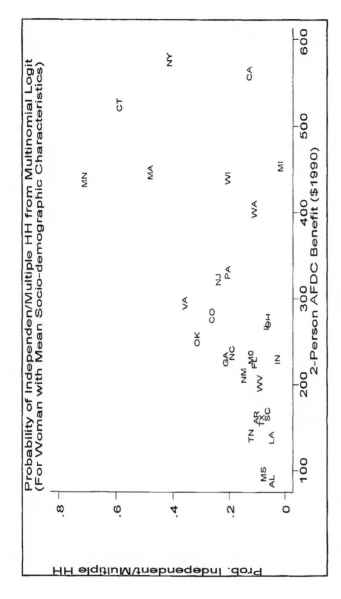

Figure 18.6 Predicted Probability of Independent Household Formation by State for Woman with Mean Sociodemographic Characteristics

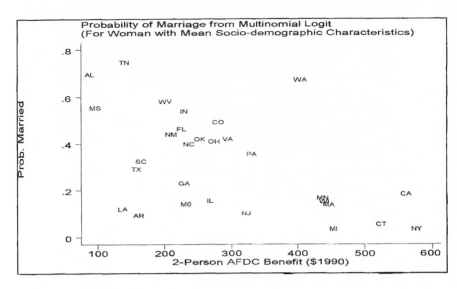

Figure 18.7 Predicted Marriage Probability by State for Woman with Mean Sociodemographic Characteristics

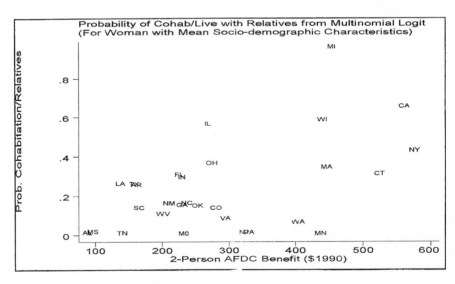

Figure 18.8 Predicted Probability of Cohabitation/Living with Relatives by State for Woman with Mean Sociodemographic Characteristics

insignificant impact on marriage rates and the establishment of independent households.

The impact of coresidence penalties appears greatest in states such as Vermont, Michigan, and New York that provide generous benefits and that also significantly reduce benefits associated with coresidence. These states are predicted to have the highest rates of alternative arrangements. They establish the strongest economic incentives for teen mothers to live apart from their parents. These states also provide large enough benefits to make possible other arrangements.

The observed patterns of Figures 18.1–18.8 are consistent with Bane and Ellwood (1985), who found that cash assistance had little impact on illegitimacy rates or fertility decisions. However, the generosity of state policies did influence rates of marital dissolution, coresidence, and other household choices. Recipients in the more generous states were more likely to establish independent households with public support. Converting their figures into 1996 dollars, their analysis implies that a national $2,000 increase in annual cash assistance payments would reduce the fraction of young unwed mothers in multigeneration homes by almost one-quarter.

The effects in this chapter are larger than those reported by Hutchens, Jakubson, and Schwartz (1989). Using 1984 data, these authors found roughly one-third the effect reported by Bane and Ellwood. One likely explanation for these differences is that Hutchens, Jakubson, and Schwartz examined a sample of predominantly older women.

From a life-course perspective, it is possible that the main impact of public aid is to accelerate or delay a recipient's trajectory in establishing her own independent household. If so, comparatively older mothers will appear less responsive to public aid in their household choices. Some have several children and therefore have limited options for shared living with other adults. Others are divorced or separated, and so may already have established independent households that they are reluctant to give up. Still others may wish to live with parents or other relatives but have reached an age where they are no longer welcome because their parents or others expect them to display greater independence.

The present results are also consistent with the contribution of Hilton and Shelton (1995). These authors also use a multinomial logit framework to explore the variety of single mothers' household choices. Using the Panel Study of Income Dynamics, these authors find that increased cash aid lowers the probability of coresidence, while raising the probability of alternative residential modes. Like Hutchens, Jakubson, and Schwartz, these authors focus mainly on the behavior of older mothers.

- Marriage rates among teen mothers declined over the period of the NLSY sample. The proportion of teen mothers in married households at the second post-partum interview declined by approximately 1.4 percentage points per year.
- Median county rents had little discernible impact on residential choice. This is surprising because some previous works (e.g., Winkler 1992) suggest that local rents play an important role in the housing arrangements of single mothers.

One possible explanation for the discrepancy is that teen mothers do not participate in commercial markets. Many teen mothers live in public housing. Others receive Section 8 certificates or other housing aid. Because of the prevalence of such housing aid, teen mothers who wish to obtain their own apartments may face distorted prices. Unfortunately, reliable data on the local supply of public housing are limited. A second possible explanation concerns housing resources available to other family members. Low regional rents may help a teen mother secure her own apartment. However, such low rents may also help her parents to rent a larger apartment that has room for her and her new children.

Residential Choice and Life Outcomes for Teen Mothers and Their Children

Results from previous sections suggest that public aid does influence residential arrangements of teen mothers. The policy implications, if any, of such findings depend upon the long-run consequences of such living arrangements for both teen mothers and their children. Unfortunately, little is known about such effects. Moreover, the great heterogeneity in teen mothers' resources and family circumstances suggests that no single policy is optimal for every family. Work such as Apfel and Seitz (1991) establishes that each residential arrangement brings its own combination of costs and benefits that play out differently in different families.

This section seeks to provide some guidance by using the same matched, child-mother NLSY data to examine several concrete outcomes for teen mothers and their children:

- mothers' acquisition of a high school diploma by the normal route;
- mothers' probability of exceeding their desired fertility;
- family poverty status at the end of the NLSY sample frame;
- mothers' probability of marriage at the end of the NLSY frame;
- children's probability of repeating at least one academic grade; and
- children's probability of being suspended or expelled from school.

Table 18.4. Educational Attainment of NLSY Teen Mothers, 1992

Age at First Birth	N	% Completed 12 Years of Schooling	% Receiving GED	% High School Dropout
15	25	36	24	40
16	75	36	31	33
17	149	46	29	26
18	203	58	16	26
19	268	71	13	15

This analysis focuses on outcomes among teen mothers' firstborn children. Less extensive data are available concerning younger siblings. Moreover, higher-order births raise empirical and analytic issues beyond the scope of the present analysis. Marriage and continuous coresidence are correlated with beneficial results in all six of these outcomes. Teen mothers who establish independent households or who live in multiple arrangements appear to display the worst outcomes on each of these measures. However, a more complete analysis indicates that most of the observed correlation reflects teen mothers' pre-birth human capital, race/ethnicity, and family characteristics. Postpartum residential choices appear to play a smaller causal role.

Teen mothers who marry are more likely than others to be married at the end of the NLSY sample frame. Married teen mothers are *less likely* to complete twelve grades of schooling. With exception of these two outcomes, OLS regression and more complex selection models fail to identify significant associations between teen mothers' residential arrangements and long-run adult outcomes.

Evidence is stronger concerning the academic and social skills of children. Controlling for potential selection bias, marriage and coresidence are associated with large reductions in the risk of grade repetition in school. Coresidence is also associated with a large (though statistically insignificant) decline in the risk of suspension or expulsion from school.

HIGH SCHOOL COMPLETION

High school graduation is an especially important outcome for both teen mothers and their children.[6] In part, because of the inherent difficulty of balancing parenting tasks, schooling, and paid work, one-quarter of NLSY teen mothers who gave birth during their high school years ultimately received General Education Development (GED) equivalency degrees (Table 18.4). This is worrisome, given evidence that GED certification does not provide a valued labor market signal of attitudes and skills associated with high school completion.[7]

Table 18.5. Residential Choice and High School Completion

Residential Choice and High School Completion (Linear Probability Model)	OLS Model (Standard Error)	Two-Stage Selection Model (Standard Error)
Continuous coresidence	0.076	0.124
	(0.071)	(0.529)
Married at second postpartum interview	−0.158**	−0.104
	(0.072)	(0.154)
Cohabitating/living with relatives at second postpartum interview	0.040	−0.341
	(0.098)	(0.267)
Selection correction — independent household at second postpartum interview	—	0.1095
		(0.134)
Selection correction — continuous coresidence	—	0.0875
		(0.129)
Selection correction — married at second postpartum interview	—	0.0891
		(0.105)
Selection correction — cohabitating/living with relatives at second postpartum interview	—	−0.138
		(0.161)
Joint significance of selection coefficients	Pr[>F]=0.837	
Observations	368	
R5	0.247	0.252

Note: Weighted by 1992 sample weight — *p<0.10, **p<0.05, ***p<0.01.

Early child bearing is associated with limited educational attainment. However, the direction of this causal pathway is unclear. Academic failure and poor cognitive skills are important risk factors for teen pregnancy. Pregnancy may then interrupt or forestall subsequent schooling. Table 18.5 explores the determinants of high school completion in greater detail.

The table is based upon the subsequent academic experiences of some 368 NLSY teen parents who first bore a child during the 1979–92 sample frame. Each woman gave birth before her nineteenth birthday, and none had graduated high school prior to May 1 in the calendar year of birth.

In both columns, the dependent variable represents the probability that a respondent graduated high school by the normal route before the 1992 wave. GED recipients were counted as nongraduates in the analysis below. This empirical strategy is open to question for the 20 percent of GED recipients who report some level of postsecondary education. Results are qualitatively unchanged if these twenty-five individuals are counted as having obtained high school degrees.

Not surprisingly, mothers' prior academic skill — as measured by their age-adjusted performance on the 1979 Armed Forces Qualification Test (AFQT) and prior grades completed — is an extremely powerful predictor of subsequent academic attainment.[8] A one-standard-deviation rise in AFQT performance is associated with a rise of some 0.07 in the absolute probability of high school graduation.

The most intriguing result is the *negative* association between teen marriage and high school completion. Among unmarried teen mothers, there are no statistically significant associations between residential choice and subsequent high school completion. Controlling for socio-demographic factors, married teen mothers are somewhat less likely to graduate high school than their counterparts in any other residential arrangement.

This is especially surprising because married teen mothers enjoy substantial human capital advantages relative to other teen mothers. Mean AFQT scores among teen mothers who marry are 0.5 standard deviations higher than comparable scores within the remainder of the NLSY sample. Moreover, 70 percent of married teen mothers are white, compared with 36 percent of the remaining sample. Controlling for these academic and social advantages, married teen mothers are significantly less likely to graduate high school by the normal route.

One reason for this pattern is that married teen mothers appear more likely to obtain GED certification. Twenty-two percent of married teens reported receiving a GED certificate, compared with 16 percent of the remaining sample.

The second column of Table 18.5 includes the two-stage selection model. The selection correction terms are jointly insignificant. Moreover, including these effects has little discernible impact on the magnitude of most coefficients.

The negative association between teen marriage and high school graduation persists in the two-stage specification. Standard errors are higher because the selection terms are highly correlated with the intercept terms β_s. However, pairwise F-test comparisons of the estimated coefficients indicate that married teen mothers are significantly less likely to graduate high school than their counterparts who live with other adults in different arrangements.

The estimated impact of teen marriage drops by one-third with the inclusion of selection effects. This suggests that negative selection may play some role. Young women who are not strongly committed to high school completion may be more willing to marry during their teen years.

CALENDAR YEAR 1991 POVERTY

Young mothers' ability to avoid poverty is a second outcome of obvious importance. Most teen mothers experience some hardship after a child's birth. However, for some teen mothers poverty is merely a temporary condition, while others experience prolonged poverty spells. To examine the effect of residential choice on poverty, this section examines whether a teen mother lived below the poverty line for calendar year 1991 — the last full year covered by the 1979–92 sample frame. Given the age distribution of teen mothers in the NLSY sample, this choice of timing examines teen mothers' economic status at least seven years after the birth of their first child. This variable therefore provides a plausible indicator of long-run outcomes rather than the transient dislocation occasioned by a teen birth.

Table 18.6 shows both OLS and two-stage results. (Again see Appendix 18.2 for the full specification.)

As in the case of high school completion, prior human capital measures such as AFQT scores and pre-birth years of schooling are powerful predictors of later poverty. Race, ethnicity, and urban social origins also play important roles. Black teen mothers are twice as likely as their non-Latino white counterparts to fall into 1991 poverty. Consistent with prior work, many race/ethnic disparities are mediated through marriage. Only 32 percent of African-American teen mothers were married at the end of the NLSY sample, compared with 50 percent of Latinos, and 57 percent of non-Latino whites.

It is striking that teen mothers' initial residential choices have a small, statistically insignificant impact on subsequent poverty. Married teen mothers are much less likely than other teen mothers to experience 1991 poverty. However, this correlation arises because married teen mothers are more likely than others to be white, to have higher AFQT scores, and to have other family and social characteristics associated with future economic success. Once these factors are controlled, the estimated impact of marriage is small and statistically insignificant.

As sensitively discussed in Furstenberg, Brooks-Gunn, and Morgan (1987), teen marriage is a high-risk, high-payoff strategy that brings its own complex mix of costs and benefits. Teen mothers who form successful marriages are the least likely group to experience 1991 poverty. Yet teen marriages that fail can be harmful when they lead to interrupted schooling, rapid childbearing, or

Table 18.6. Residential Choice and Calendar Year 1991 Poverty

Residential Choice and 1991 Poverty (Linear Probability Model)	OLS Model (Standard Error)	Two-Stage Selection Model (Standard Error)
Continuous coresidence	0.0398	−0.0415
	(.0467)	(0.170)
Married at second postpartum interview	−0.0287	0.0510
	(0.045)	(0.169)
Cohabitating/living with relatives at second postpartum interview	0.0519	−0.032
	(0.064)	(0.218)
Selection correction — independent household at second postpartum interview	−	−0.0184
		(0.104)
Selection correction — continuous coresidence	−	0.0526
		(0.0855)
Selection correction — married at second postpartum interview	−	−0.113
		(0.0821)
Selection correction — cohabitating/living with relatives at second postpartum interview	−	0.0408
		(0.117)
Joint significance of selection coefficients	Pr[>F]=0.702	
Observations	692	
R5	0.176	0.178

Note: Weighted by 1992 sample weight — $*p<0.10, **p<0.05, ***p<0.01$.

emotional trauma for young parents and children alike. At the margin, it is therefore unclear whether public policies or broader social norms ought to encourage teen parents to get married.

PROBABILITY OF 1992 MARRIAGE

A teen mother's life chances are markedly improved if she finds a stable marriage partner upon entering early adulthood. Table 18.7 below presents the estimated impact of residential arrangements on the probability that a

Table 18.7. Residential Choice and 1992 Marriage Rates

Residential Choice and 1992 Marriage (Linear Probability Model)	OLS Model (Standard Error)	Two-Stage Selection Model (Standard Error)
Continuous coresidence	−0.068	−0.0219
	(0.0617)	(0.247)
Married at second postpartum interview	0.203***	0.442*
	(0.0628)	(0.251)
Cohabitating/living with relatives at second postpartum interview	−0.0174	0.106
	(0.202)	(0.303)
Selection correction — independent household at second postpartum interview	—	0.239
		(0.159)
Selection correction — continuous coresidence	—	0.245**
		(0.115)
Selection correction — married at second postpartum interview	—	0.081
		(0.108)
Selection correction — cohabitating/living with relatives at second postpartum interview	—	0.120
		(0.157)
Joint significance of selection coefficients	Pr[>F]=0.027	
Observations	537	
R5	0.195	0.2181

Note: Weighted by 1992 sample weight — *p<0.10, **p<0.05, ***p<0.01.

recipient was married at the time of the 1992 interview. Because marriage at the second postpartum interview is such a critical variable in predicting later marriage, only OLS estimates are shown.

As expected, marriage at the second postpartum interview is highly correlated with 1992 marriage. AFQT scores also exert a strong effect. Very young teen mothers are less likely to be married at the end of the NLSY sample period, as are those from urban areas and those who grew up in single-parent homes.

Such variables capture almost all the observed racial and ethnic disparities in marriage rates. Although white teen mothers are almost twice as likely to be married as their African American counterparts, the race coefficient is small and statistically insignificant in a larger model which includes postpartum marriage rates and appropriate socio-demographic controls are included in the model. The coefficients corresponding to the generosity of state AFDC aid are also small and statistically insignificant. This suggests that much of the impact of cash aid on subsequent marriage occurs through its influence on the initial trajectory of teen mothers' residential choice.

CONTROLLING FERTILITY

The avoidance of rapidly repeated childbearing is an important predictor of a teen mother's long-run well-being and the well-being of her children. Furstenberg, Brooks-Gunn, and Morgen (1987) report that teen mothers who had two or more further children within five years were 72 percent less likely than other teen mothers to escape poverty seventeen years later. Longitudinal New Haven studies (Seitz and Apfel 1991, and Horwitz et al. 1991) also find deleterious effects of rapid subsequent fertility on the life chances of young women.

What constitutes "excess fertility" is an ambiguous and politically explosive matter. Such measures properly depend upon an individual's personal values, economic circumstances, and available sources of emotional and family support. Rather than to impose a unitary standard, this section uses respondents' self-reported preferences as one appropriate guide. The initial NLSY interview asks young women about their desired family size. Women who bear more than this number of children before the 1992 wave are counted as experiencing excess fertility. Alternative approaches — such as the probability of at least two subsequent births — yield similar results.

Age and education at first birth are the most powerful predictors of excess fertility. Young teens and those behind grade-level are substantially more likely to have high subsequent fertility than the population of teen mothers as a whole. These young mothers are therefore a natural target group for various intensive educational programs and support services aimed at avoiding prolonged welfare dependence and psychosocial distress.[9] African American and Latino teen mothers are also likely to report excess fertility.

Within the OLS specification, coresiding teen mothers are significantly less likely to report excess fertility over the sample frame. However, these results must be interpreted with caution. Sarah Horwitz notes (personal communication) that many coresiding young mothers are asked to leave their parents' homes if they bear another child. While such norms may have some desirable consequences, they also create simultaneity bias in interpreting these results.

Table 18.8. Residential Choice and Excess Fertility

Residential Choice and Excess Fertility (Linear Probability Model)	OLS Model (Standard Error)	Two-Stage Selection Model (Standard Error)
Continuous coresidence	−0.094*	0.116
	(0.050)	(0.182)
Married at second postpartum	0.015	0.180
interview	(0.0477)	(0.179)
Cohabitating/living with	−0.0246	−0.214
relatives at second	(0.0676)	(0.229)
postpartum interview		
Selection correction —	—	0.100
independent household at		(0.110)
second postpartum interview		
Selection correction —	—	−0.074
continuous coresidence		(0.090)
Selection correction — married	—	−0.0422
at second postpartum		(0.0860)
interview		
Selection correction —	—	0.208*
cohabitating/living with		(0.1212)
relatives at second		
postpartum interview		
Joint significance of selection coefficients	$Pr[>F]=0.36$	
Observations	653	
R5	0.1734	0.1759

Note: Weighted by 1992 sample weight — *p<0.10, **p<0.05, ***p<0.01. Appendix 18.2 includes the full specification.

Moreover, the associated coefficient reverses algebraic sign after inclusion of selection effects. This suggests that unobserved preferences and resources play an important role. For example, teen mothers with the strongest preferences to limit their fertility may move in with their parents to realize this goal. Because of such selection, simple comparisons between coresiding teen mothers and those in other arrangements likely overestimate the potential impact on family size of public policies that encourage or require teen mothers to live with their parents or other adults.

THE IMPACT OF RESIDENTIAL CHOICE ON
CHILDREN'S SOCIAL AND ACADEMIC SKILLS

It is well documented that children of teen mothers score poorly on standardized tests of academic knowledge and cognitive skill. This group of children also encounters a variety of psychosocial problems in adolescence and later life.[10] Improving social and academic outcomes among the children of teen mothers remains a central and elusive policy goal.

For many reasons, the quality and stability of teen mothers' residential arrangements may influence important child outcomes. The presence of mature adults helps to create a more secure and nurturing environment for young children. A large literature catalogues the many ways that grandparents provide critical guidance to teen mothers and their children.[11] Grandparents or other adult household members are available to provide childcare and other services to children. They provide financial resources and valuable in-kind services, and may provide emotional support to an adolescent who is learning a new and difficult parenting role. The role of teen mothers' residential arrangements in shaping child outcomes remains a topic of ongoing research. This section presents initial results concerning the impact of residential arrangements on children's academic performance in school. It explores the impact of teen mothers' living arrangements on children's grade retention in school and on the probability that a child will be suspended or expelled.

These measures capture important and concrete events in the lives of children.[12] Moreover, these adverse events are common among the children of teen mothers. More than 25 percent of first-born children born to NLSY teen mothers were retained at least one academic grade before 1992. Thirteen percent had been suspended or expelled. These figures are sobering when one considers that the mean age of sampled children was 11.6 years by the end of the 1992 wave.

As shown in Table 18.9, both coresidence and teen marriage have a large and statistically significant impact on grade repetition. Cohabitation and living with relatives have a similarly large impact once selection effects are controlled. The children of teen mothers in independent households appear to have markedly worse outcomes.

The estimated impact of residential arrangements is quite large in both OLS and the two-stage specifications. As shown in Table 18.10, coresidence appears to have a similar impact on the probability of school suspension or expulsion, though the coefficients are smaller and less statistically significant.

Here, too, there is some evidence of selection bias. Several coefficients

Table 18.9. Residential Choice and Grade Repetition Among Children

Residential Choice and Grade Failure Among Children (Linear Probability Model)	OLS Model (Standard Error)	Two-Stage Selection Model (Standard Error)
Continuous coresidence	−0.226***	−0.761***
	(0.067)	(0.265)
Married at second postpartum interview	−0.109*	−0.737***
	(0.0674)	(0.266)
Cohabitating/living with relatives at second postpartum interview	−0.131	−0.509*
	(0.095)	(0.319)
Selection correction — independent household at second postpartum interview	—	−0.462***
		(0.170)
Selection correction — continuous coresidence	—	−0.047
		(0.125)
Selection correction — married at second postpartum interview	—	0.0464
		(0.111)
Selection correction — cohabitating/living with relatives at second postpartum interview	—	−0.129
		(0.166)
Joint significance of selection coefficients		$\Pr[>F]=0.092$
Observations		398
R5	0.168	0.191

Note: Weighted by 1992 sample weight — *p<0.10, **p<0.05, ***p<0.01.
Appendix 18.2 includes the full specification.

reverse the algebraic sign with inclusion of selection effects. Unfortunately, the standard errors are roughly four times larger in the two-stage specification.

Investigating these results in greater detail remains the subject of future work. However, the results of this section suggest that coresidence may bring greater benefits to young children even if it does not significantly affect long-run outcomes for teen mothers themselves.

Table 18.10. Residential Choice and Academic Suspension/Expulsion Among Children

Residential Choice and Suspension/Expulsion of Children (Linear Probability Model)	OLS Model (Standard Error)	Two-Stage Selection Model (Standard Error)
Continuous coresidence	−0.140***	−0.306
	(0.0526)	(0.209)
Married at second postpartum	−0.0873*	0.137
interview	(0.0528)	(0.211)
Cohabitating/living with	0.0734	0.177
relatives at second	(0.075)	(0.253)
postpartum interview		
Selection correction —	—	0.0765
independent household at		(0.134)
second postpartum interview		
Selection correction —	—	0.250**
continuous coresidence		(0.098)
Selection correction — married	—	−0.117
at second postpartum		(0.088)
interview		
Selection correction —	—	−0.0178
cohabitating/living with		(0.1311)
relatives at second		
postpartum interview		
Joint significance of selection coefficients	Pr[>F]=0.136	
Observations	399	
R5	0.166	0.182

Note: Weighted by 1992 sample weight — *p<0.10, **p<0.05, ***p<0.01.
Appendix 18.2 includes the full specification.

Discussion

Public assistance policies influence young mothers' household choice. Although the power of the multinomial logit model is limited in the small NLSY sample, we establish several plausible and statistically significant patterns in the available data.

Some young mothers (and perhaps their families) prefer independent households when this is financially viable. Higher AFDC benefits have a large and statistically significant impact in the multinomial logit models estimated early in the paper. These patterns are similar to the decisions of the elderly, who have used much of their postwar increase in wealth to live independently from their children, escaping the tension and loss of privacy inherent in shared living.[13]

Policies that reduce benefits to recipients in multigeneration households also play a significant role. Policy makers wishing to encourage coresidence might examine the implicit incentives for independent households that are part of the cash assistance system in many states. These incentives apply not only to teen mothers, but to other needy individuals who might benefit from social support and economies of scale that accompany shared living.

Such incentives also apply to teen mothers themselves once they reach adulthood. A woman who gives birth at 16 might be compelled to live with her parents. Within a few years, however, she is likely to establish other household arrangements if there are strong economic incentives to leave her parents' home.

Such findings point to a dilemma at the heart of public aid. More generous public aid makes possible living arrangements that many citizens do not wish to support. Yet as Jencks and Edin (1990) describe, there is reason to believe that the current level of cash aid is already too low. In almost every state, cash benefits and food stamps to teen mothers remain far below the poverty line. The best argument for coresidence requirements for teen mothers may therefore be a political one. It is better to impose explicit requirements than to further reduce benefits in response to an angry public unwilling to subsidize undesired behaviors.

The analysis suggests that efforts to influence postpartum living arrangements will not significantly improve long-term maternal economic outcomes. Although teen marriage and continuous coresidence are correlated with several positive outcomes, these correlations do not imply a strong causal link. Pre-birth academic skills, race/ethnicity, and family circumstances are far more important in shaping economic, educational, and marriage outcomes among teen mothers.

The two-stage analysis also suggests the potential importance of selection bias. Straightforward comparisons of coresiding or married teen mothers with those in other residential arrangements are likely to overstate the benefits of such arrangements. For example, the OLS model suggests that coresidence is associated with restrained fertility. However, these results fail to hold when one controls for endogenous residential choices.

Influencing teen mothers' residential choice appears more promising as a means to improve outcomes among their young children. By themselves, continuous coresidence and early marriage do not ameliorate the chronic difficulties encountered by teen mothers. However, these arrangements may provide a stable and nurturing environment to shield children from some harms associated with social and economic distress. As Furstenberg, Brooks-Gunn, and Morgan (1987) observe, such arrangements may also discourage teen mothers from forming transient or destructive attachments in search of economic or emotional support.

It is also important to emphasize that some aspects of shared living may be detrimental to children. Coresidence may create ambiguous parenting roles that undermine teen mothers' confidence and authority with their children. Such arrangements may also exacerbate dysfunctional family relationships that started long before teen birth. In addition, coresidence may impose significant caregiving burdens on grandparents, siblings, and other family members.

Because of such complexity, one must be wary of any proposed policy that would impose rigid responses to the varied problems associated with teen pregnancy and welfare receipt. Proponents of coresidence requirements are right to emphasize the importance of creating a safe and supportive environment for teen mothers and their children. In many, but not in all cases, teen marriage or coresidence is helpful to achieve this goal. Finding other, more effective and lasting strategies remains an elusive task facing welfare reform.

Appendix 18.1. Estimated Coresidence Penalty by State

	Estimated Penalty	Standard Error
Alabama	−0.03	0.035
Alaska	0.20	0.068
Arizona	0.19	0.043
Arkansas	0.00	0.037
California	0.53	0.211
Colorado	0.12	0.123
Connecticut	0.12	0.107
Delaware	0.44	0.152
District of Columbia	−0.04	0.212
Florida	0.44	0.045
Georgia	−0.02	0.036
Hawaii	0.05	0.061
Idaho	0.31	0.082
Illinois	0.04	0.042
Indiana	0.02	0.040
Iowa	0.11	0.051
Kansas	0.11	0.072
Kentucky	0.02	0.030
Louisiana	0.05	0.033
Maine	0.05	0.067
Maryland	−0.04	0.150
Massachusetts	0.18	0.096
Michigan	0.80	0.042
Minnesota	0.00	0.049
Mississippi	0.02	0.037
Missouri	0.04	0.023
Montana	0.80	0.217
Nebraska	0.31	0.151
Nevada	−0.10	0.055
New Hampshire	0.68	0.213
New Jersey	−0.04	0.150
New Mexico	0.38	0.067
New York	0.54	0.081
North Carolina	0.06	0.063
North Dakota	0.12	0.133
Ohio	−0.05	0.053
Oklahoma	0.07	0.038
Oregon	−0.01	0.087
Pennsylvania	−0.02	0.211

Appendix 18.1. Continued

	Estimated Penalty	Standard Error
Rhode Island	0.08	0.088
South Carolina	−0.02	0.036
South Dakota	0.61	0.083
Tennessee	0.03	0.036
Texas	−0.04	0.029
Utah	0.18	0.083
Vermont	0.85	0.125
Virginia	0.08	0.038
Washington	0.25	0.122
West Virginia	0.01	0.044
Wisconsin	−0.03	0.042
Wyoming*	0.00	0.042
Sample Size	9,902	
R^2	0.7904	

Source: 1991 AFDC-Quality Control Data File.

Appendix 18.2. Multinomial Logit Model of Household Formation

Multinomial Logit Analysis of Household Choice (Omitted Category: Continuous Coresidence)	Relative Risk Ratio for Independent Household/ Multiple Types (P-Value)	RRR for Marriage (P-Value)	RRR for Cohabitation/ Living with Relatives (P-Value)
Black	0.291***	0.086***	0.786
Latino	0.616	0.393***	0.609
1990 Maximum AFDC benefit (standardized coefficient)	3.70***	1.11	1.463
[Standardized AFDC benefits]5	0.723	0.846	1.227
East South Central Census Region	12.47**	1.957	0.439
South Atlantic	4.468*	1.028	1.825
New England	1.921	0.674	1.859
Middle Atlantic	1.125	0.336**	0.336
West South Central	5.094	0.714	2.405
East North Central	1.726	0.801	4.66*
West North Central	2.08	0.433	0
Mountain	4.60*	0.658	1.922
Coresidence penalty (log points)	0.663	1.68	10.81***
Standardized, age-corrected AFQT	0.850	1.235	1.174
[Standardized, age-corrected AFQT]5	0.926	0.911	0.856
Mother age 15 or younger at birth	0.454	0.050***	0.058**
Mother age 16 at birth	1.04	0.382*	0.036***
Mother age 17 at birth	0.793	0.381***	0.181***
Mother age 18 at birth	0.709	0.689	0.600
Year of first interview following birth	1.03	0.864**	1.036
Standardized, median county rent	1.08	0.983	0.895
Urban SMSA	1.38	0.742	1.179
Mother completed 7th grade at birth	0.371	0.790	8.62
Mother completed 8th grade at birth	0.525	0.668	6.398
Mother completed 9th grade at birth	0.490	0.559	7.378
Mother completed 10th grade at birth	0.873	1.033	7.413*
Mother completed 11th grade at birth	0.548	0.656	4.628
Mother completed 12th grade at birth	0.795	1.049	0.837
Mother's number of siblings 1979	1.026	0.991	1.01
Teen mother lived with own mother only at 14	2.58***	0.959	2.68**
Teen mother lived with mother and stepfather at 14	1.992	1.623	4.75***

Appendix 18.2. Continued

Multinomial Logit Analysis of Household Choice (Omitted Category: Continuous Coresidence)	Relative Risk Ratio for Independent Household/ Multiple Types (P-Value)	RRR for Marriage (P-Value)	RRR for Cohabitation/ Living with Relatives (P-Value)
Teen mother lived with relatives (not parents) at 14	0.208*	0.860	0.846
Teen mother lived with father (not mother) at 14	2.22	1.968	2.831
Teen mother lived with neither parent at 14	12.66***	0.448	7.238*
Percentage in category	22%	42%	8%
Observations		689	
Log likelihood		−685.8	

Note: Weighted by 1992 sample weight — *p<0.10, **p<0.05, ***p<0.01

Appendix 18.3. Residential Choice and Calendar Year 1991 Poverty

Residential Choice and 1991 Poverty (Linear Probability Model)	OLS Model (Standard Error)	Two-Stage Selection Model (Standard Error)
Continuous coresidence	0.0398	−0.0415
	(.0467)	(0.170)
Married at second post-partum interview	−0.0287	0.0510
	(0.045)	(0.169)
Cohabitating / living with relatives at	0.0519	−0.032
second post-partum interview	(0.064)	(0.218)
Selection correction — independent	—	−0.0184
household at second post-partum		(0.104)
interview		
Selection correction — continuous	—	0.0526
coresidence		(0.0855)
Selection correction — married at second	—	−0.113
post-partum interview		(0.0821)
Selection correction — cohabitating / living	—	0.0408
with relatives at second post-partum		(0.117)
interview		
1990 maximum AFDC benefit	−0.0464	−0.051*
(standardized coefficient)	(0.0494)	(0.0508)
[Standardized AFDC benefits]5	0.0267	0.0315
	(0.0260)	(0.0264)
East South Central Census Region	−0.122	−0.145
	(0.144)	(0.148)
South Atlantic	−0.118	−0.127
	(0.0970)	(0.099)
New England	0.0477	0.0174
	(0.0756)	(0.0802)
Middle Atlantic	−0.0454	−0.0382
	(0.0644)	(0.0676)
West South Central	−0.0011	−0.0037
	(0.125)	(0.128)
East North Central	−0.0443	−0.0440
	(0.0816)	(0.0831)
West North Central	0.0643	0.0694
	(0.122)	(0.124)
Mountain	−0.0909	−0.0868
	0.103	0.106

Appendix 18.3. Continued

Residential Choice and 1991 Poverty (Linear Probability Model)	OLS Model (Standard Error)	Two-Stage Selection Model (Standard Error)
Black	0.148***	0.1856***
	(0.044)	(0.054)
Latino	0.0953**	0.111**
	(0.047)	(0.0496)
Standardized, median county rent	−0.0220	−0.0217
	(0.205)	(0.0207)
Urban SMSA	0.1032**	0.108**
	(0.0416)	(0.0428)
Standardized, age-corrected AFQT	−0.0960***	−0.1025***
	(0.0185)	(0.0192)
[Standardized, age-corrected AFQT]5	0.0202	0.0213
	(0.0134)	(0.0136)
Mother age 15 or younger at birth	0.0551	0.0892
	(0.103)	(0.110)
Mother age 16 at birth	0.0481	0.0641
	(0.070)	(0.0724)
Mother age 17 at birth	0.0315	0.0426
	(0.0517)	(0.0534)
Mother age 18 at birth	0.0040	0.00778
	(0.0410)	(0.0412)
Year of first interview following birth	−0.0045	−0.00164
	(0.0105)	(0.0108)
Mother completed 7th grade at birth	−0.1156	−0.1056
	(0.130)	(0.132)
Mother completed 8th grade at birth	−0.0273	−0.0178
	(0.116)	(0.118)
Mother completed 9th grade at birth	−0.1636	−0.1489
	(0.105)	(0.107)
Mother completed 10th grade at birth	0.0022	0.0090
	(0.0983)	(0.099)
Mother completed 11th grade at birth	−0.00308	−0.0154
	(0.0960)	(0.0973)
Mother completed 12th grade at birth	−0.0913	−0.0871
	(0.0920)	(0.0930)
Mother's number of siblings 1979	−0.0078	−0.00707
	(0.0058)	(0.0059)

Appendix 18.3. Continued

Residential Choice and 1991 Poverty (Linear Probability Model)	OLS Model (Standard Error)	Two-Stage Selection Model (Standard Error)
Teen mother lived with own mother only at 14	−0.0829**	−0.0771*
	(0.040)	(0.0406)
Teen mother lived with mother and stepfather at 14	0.0104	0.0114
	(0.052)	(0.0526)
Teen mother lived with relatives (not parents) at 14	−0.0669	−0.0351
	(0.119)	(0.126)
Teen mother lived with father (not mother) at 14	−0.0723	−0.0859
	(0.109)	(0.110)
Teen mother lived with neither parent at 14	0.1463	0.132
	(0.103)	(0.116)
Joint significance of selection coefficients	$\Pr[>F]=0.702$	
Observations	692	
R5	0.176	0.178

Appendix 18.4. Residential Choice and High School Completion

Residential Choice and High School Completion (Linear Probability Model)	OLS Model (Standard Error)	Two-Stage Selection Model (Standard Error)
Continuous coresidence	0.076	0.124
	(0.071)	(0.529)
Married at second post-partum interview	−0.158**	−0.104
	(0.072)	(0.154)
Cohabitating / living with relatives at	0.040	0.341
second post-partum interview	(0.098)	(0.267)
Selection correction — independent	—	0.1095
household at second post-partum		(0.134)
interview		
Selection correction — continuous	—	0.0875
coresidence		(0.129)
Selection correction — married at second	—	0.0891
post-partum interview		(0.105)
Selection correction — cohabitating / living	—	−0.138
with relatives at second post-partum		(0.161)
interview		
1990 maximum AFDC benefit	0.103	0.109
(standardized coefficient)	(0.0827)	(0.0848)
[Standardized AFDC benefits]5	−0.0552	−0.052
	(0.0449)	(0.045)
East South Central Census Region	0.363	0.405*
	(0.228)	(0.233)
South Atlantic	0.216	0.252
	(0.151)	(0.155)
New England	0.283**	0.306**
	(0.117)	(0.122)
Middle Atlantic	0.089	0.0905
	(0.109)	(0.111)
West South Central	0.215	0.260
	(0.195)	(0.197)
East North Central	0.1462	0.173
	(1.18)	(0.126)
West North Central	−0.042	−0.017
	(0.194)	(0.196)
Mountain	0.094	0.137
	(0.582)	(0.166)

Appendix 18.4. Continued

Residential Choice and High School Completion (Linear Probability Model)	OLS Model (Standard Error)	Two-Stage Selection Model (Standard Error)
Black	0.011	0.0148
	(0.072)	(0.0845)
Latino	−0.003	0.005
	(0.004)	(0.082)
Standardized, median county rent	−0.0237	−0.024
	(0.723)	(0.731)
Urban SMSA	0.0737	0.0755
	(0.068)	(0.070)
Standardized, age-corrected AFQT	0.0685**	0.0659**
	(0.030)	(0.031)
[Standardized, age-corrected AFQT]5	−0.0019	−0.0014
	(0.022)	(0.023)
Mother age 15 or younger at birth	0.209*	—
	(0.113)	
Mother age 16 at birth	—	−0.227*
		(0.119)
Mother age 17 at birth	0.084	−0.151
	(1.104)	(0.118)
Mother age 18 at birth	0.0287	−0.218*
	(0.083)	(0.128)
Year of first interview following birth	0.024	0.025
	(0.019)	(0.019)
Mother completed 8th grade at birth	0.167	0.159
	(0.134)	(0.137)
Mother completed 9th grade at birth	0.066	0.071
	(0.126)	(0.130)
Mother completed 10th grade at birth	0.0985	0.115
	(0.770)	(0.133)
Mother completed 11th grade at birth	0.428***	0.428
	(0.136)	(0.138)
Mother's number of siblings, 1979	−0.005	−0.0049
	(0.0089)	(0.539)
Teen mother lived with own mother only at 14	0.0164	0.020
	(0.059)	(0.062)
Teen mother lived with mother and stepfather at 14	−0.120	−0.113
	(0.079)	(0.08)

Appendix 18.4. Continued

Residential Choice and High School Completion (Linear Probability Model)	OLS Model (Standard Error)	Two-Stage Selection Model (Standard Error)
Teen mother lived with relatives (not parents) at 14	−0.382** (0.167)	−0.460** (0.180)
Teen mother lived with father (not mother) at 14	0.633** (0.293)	0.653** (0.295)
Teen mother lived with neither parent at 14	0.086 (0.138)	0.128 (0.169)
Joint significance of selection coefficients	Pr[>F]=0.837	
Observations	368	
R5	0.2474	0.2517

Note: Weighted by 1992 Sample Weight — *p<0.10, **p<0.05, ***p<0.01

Appendix 18.5. Residential Choice and 1992 Marriage Rates

Residential Choice and 1992 Marriage (Linear Probability Model)	OLS Model (Standard Error)	Two-Stage Selection Model (Standard Error)
Continuous coresidence	−0.068	−0.0219
	(0.0617)	(0.247)
Married at second post-partum interview	0.203***	0.442*
	(0.0628)	(0.251)
Cohabitating / living with relatives at second post-partum interview	−0.0174	0.106
	(0.202)	(0.303)
Selection correction — independent household at second post-partum interview	—	0.239
		(0.159)
Selection correction — continuous coresidence	—	0.245**
		(0.115)
Selection correction — married at second post-partum interview	—	0.081
		(0.108)
Selection correction — cohabitating / living with relatives at second post-partum interview	—	0.120
		(0.157)
1990 maximum AFDC benefit (standardized coefficient)	−0.0246	−0.0269
	(0.0693)	(0.071)
[Standardized AFDC benefits]5	0.0014	0.000989
	(0.0369)	(0.0373)
East South Central Census Region	−0.127	−0.0997
	(0.206)	(0.210)
South Atlantic	−0.0360	−0.159
	(0.132)	(0.134)
New England	−0.286***	−0.283**
	(0.107)	(0.114)
Middle Atlantic	0.0169	0.0488
	(0.0879)	(0.092)
West South Central	−0.104	−0.0578
	(0.172)	(0.174)
East North Central	−0.1309	−0.1224
	(0.1069)	(0.1075)
West North Central	−0.279*	−0.250
	(0.164)	(0.165)
Mountain	0.0002	−0.001
	(0.146)	(0.147)

Appendix 18.5. Continued

Residential Choice and 1992 Marriage (Linear Probability Model)	OLS Model (Standard Error)	Two-Stage Selection Model (Standard Error)
Black	−0.046	−0.0047
	(0.059)	(0.074)
Latino	0.037	0.0407
	(0.620)	(0.0657)
Standardized, median county rent	0.0027	0.0018
	(0.0276)	(0.067)
Urban SMSA	−0.107*	−0.093*
	(0.056)	(0.056)
Standardized, age-corrected AFQT	0.0644***	0.0705***
	(0.0247)	(0.025)
[Standardized, age-corrected AFQT]5	0.0039	0.007
	(0.0176)	(0.0177)
Mother age 15 or younger at birth	−0.119	−0.045
	(0.135)	(0.143)
Mother age 16 at birth	−0.160*	−0.169*
	(0.097)	(0.0987)
Mother age 17 at birth	0.039	0.0676
	(0.0719)	(0.0737)
Mother age 18 at birth	0.065	0.0688
	(0.055)	(0.0552)
Year of first interview following birth	0.0055	0.007
	(0.014)	(0.0146)
Mother completed 7th grade at birth	0.005	−0.021
	(0.179)	(0.180)
Mother completed 8th grade at birth	−0.191	−0.183
	(0.161)	(0.160)
Mother completed 9th grade at birth	−0.133	−0.174
	(0.141)	(0.141)
Mother completed 10th grade at birth	−0.195	−0.219*
	(0.130)	(0.129)
Mother completed 11th grade at birth	−0.222*	−0.239*
	(0.126)	(0.126)
Mother completed 12th grade at birth	−0.166	−0.135
	(0.120)	(0.121)
Mother's number of siblings, 1979	0.009	0.0108
	(0.0076)	(0.0076)

Appendix 18.5. Continued

Residential Choice and 1992 Marriage (Linear Probability Model)	OLS Model (Standard Error)	Two-Stage Selection Model (Standard Error)
Teen mother lived with own mother only at 14	−0.096* (0.054)	−0.105* (0.0556)
Teen mother lived with mother and stepfather at 14	−0.0048 (0.0672)	−0.0025 (0.067)
Teen mother lived with relatives (not parents) at 14	−0.004 (0.164)	−0.0708 (0.174)
Teen mother lived with father (not mother) at 14	0.048 (0.151)	−0.026 (0.151)
Teen mother lived with neither parent at 14	−0.038 (0.146)	0.008 (0.166)
Joint significance of selection coefficients	Pr[>F]=0.027	
Observations	537	
R5	0.195	0.2181

Note: Weighted by 1992 Sample Weight — *p<0.10, **p<0.05, ***p<0.01

Appendix 18.6. Residential Choice and Excess Fertility

Residential Choice and Excess Fertility (Linear Probability Model)	OLS Model (Standard Error)	Two-Stage Selection Model (Standard Error)
Continuous coresidence	−0.094*	0.116
	(0.050)	(0.182)
Married at second post-partum interview	0.015	0.180
	(0.0477)	(0.179)
Cohabitating / living with relatives at second post-partum interview	−0.0246	−0.214
	(0.0676)	(0.229)
Selection correction — independent household at second post-partum interview	—	0.100
		(0.110)
Selection correction — continuous coresidence	—	−0.074
		(0.090)
Selection correction — married at second post-partum interview	—	−0.0422
		(0.0860)
Selection correction — cohabitating / living with relatives at second post-partum interview	—	0.208*
		(0.1212)
1990 maximum AFDC benefit (standardized coefficient)	−0.0625	−0.0486
	(0.0523)	(0.0535)
[Standardized AFDC benefits]5	0.0088	0.004
	(0.027)	(0.0276)
East South Central Census Region	−0.206	−0.196
	(0.153)	(0.1559)
South Atlantic	−0.0507	−0.050
	(0.102)	(0.105)
New England	0.004	0.0085
	(0.079)	(0.084)
Middle Atlantic	−0.044	−0.045
	(0.0677)	(0.071)
West South Central	−0.104	−0.115
	(0.132)	(0.135)
East North Central	−0.0666	−0.078
	(0.086)	(0.087)
West North Central	0.085	0.0716
	(0.129)	(0.131)
Mountain	−0.188*	−0.189*
	(0.108)	(0.111)

Appendix 18.6. Continued

Residential Choice and Excess Fertility (Linear Probability Model)	OLS Model (Standard Error)	Two-Stage Selection Model (Standard Error)
Black	0.241***	0.232***
	(0.0479)	(0.059)
Latino	0.197***	0.200***
	(0.049)	(0.052)
Standardized, median county rent	0.013	0.011
	(0.021)	(0.021)
Urban SMSA	−0.008	0.00008
	(0.044)	(0.046)
Standardized, age-corrected AFQT	−0.044**	−0.0468**
	(0.0198)	(0.0206)
[Standardized, age-corrected AFQT]5	0.0442***	0.0420**
	(0.0142)	(0.0144)
Mother age 15 or younger at birth	0.2445**	0.220*
	(0.107)	(0.114)
Mother age 16 at birth	0.173**	0.164**
	(0.0752)	(0.077)
Mother age 17 at birth	0.0213	0.017
	(0.0553)	(0.057)
Mother age 18 at birth	−0.0040	−0.005
	(0.0434)	(0.0436)
Year of first interview following birth	−0.00690	−0.0053
	(0.011)	(0.011)
Mother completed 7th grade at birth	0.068	0.0486
	(0.139)	(0.141)
Mother completed 8th grade at birth	0.189	0.196
	(0.122)	(0.1232)
Mother completed 9th grade at birth	0.0719	0.0628
	(0.651)	(0.112)
Mother completed 10th grade at birth	0.1228	0.128
	(1.021)	(0.103)
Mother completed 11th grade at birth	0.041	0.0420
	(0.100)	(0.100)
Mother's number of siblings, 1979	0.0058	0.005
	(0.006)	(0.0062)
Teen mother lived with own mother only at 14	−0.0631	−0.0467
	(0.0416)	(0.0434)

Appendix 18.6. Continued

Residential Choice and Excess Fertility (Linear Probability Model)	OLS Model (Standard Error)	Two-Stage Selection Model (Standard Error)
Teen mother lived with mother and stepfather at 14	0.0895* (0.0542)	0.101* (0.055)
Teen mother lived with relatives (not parents) at 14	0.0522 (0.127)	0.0202 (0.135)
Teen mother lived with father (not mother) at 14	−0.088 (0.117)	−0.076 (0.119)
Teen mother lived with neither parent at 14	0.0878 (0.110)	0.168 (0.1233)
Joint significance of selection coefficients	Prob[>F]=0.36	
Observations	653	
R5	0.1734	0.1759

Note: Weighted by 1992 Sample Weight — *p<0.10, **p<0.05, ***p<0.01

Appendix 18.7. Residential Choice and Grade Repetition Among Children

Residential Choice and Grade Failure Among Children (Linear Probability Model)	OLS Model (Standard Error)	Two-Stage Selection Model (Standard Error)
Continuous coresidence	−0.226***	−0.761***
	(0.067)	(0.265)
Married at second post-partum interview	−0.109*	−0.737***
	(0.0674)	(0.266)
Cohabitating / living with relatives at second post-partum interview	−0.131	−0.509*
	(0.095)	(0.319)
Selection correction — independent household at second post-partum interview	—	−0.462***
		(0.170)
Selection correction — continuous coresidence	—	−0.047
		(0.125)
Selection correction — married at second post-partum interview	—	0.0464
		(0.111)
Selection correction — cohabitating / living with relatives at second post-partum interview	—	−0.129
		(0.166)
1990 maximum AFDC benefit (standardized coefficient)	−0.035	−0.063
	(0.070)	(0.0720)
[Standardized AFDC benefits]5	−0.008	−0.0019
	(0.0364)	(0.037)
East South Central Census Region	−0.104	−0.1754
	(0.212)	(0.214)
South Atlantic	0.05	0.0009
	(0.132)	(0.1338)
New England	0.032	−0.0213
	(0.105)	(0.114)
Middle Atlantic	0.0577	−0.0037
	(0.0901)	(0.0956)
West South Central	0.006	−0.0688
	(0.178)	(0.179)
East North Central	−0.136	−0.1665
	(0.104)	(0.104)
West North Central	−0.107	−0.1222
	(0.184)	(0.1836)
Mountain	−0.0532	−0.108
	(0.147)	(0.148)

Appendix 18.7. Continued

Residential Choice and Grade Failure Among Children (Linear Probability Model)	OLS Model (Standard Error)	Two-Stage Selection Model (Standard Error)
Black	−0.0995	−0.124
	(0.0624)	(0.080)
Latino	−0.0069	−0.0278
	(0.066)	(0.0697)
Standardized, median county rent	0.0217	0.0175
	(0.0291)	(0.0294)
Urban SMSA	0.003	−0.0068
	(0.059)	(0.060)
Standardized, age-corrected AFQT	−0.0518**	−0.050*
	(0.0256)	(0.0261)
[Standardized, age-corrected AFQT]5	−0.035*	−0.0323*
	(0.0183)	(0.0185)
Mother age 15 or younger at birth	0.136	0.0999
	(0.138)	(0.148)
Mother age 16 at birth	0.180*	0.173*
	(0.097)	(0.101)
Mother age 17 at birth	0.077	0.0472
	(0.074)	(0.0775)
Mother age 18 at birth	0.107*	0.0968*
	(0.057)	(0.0578)
Year of first interview following birth	−0.017	−0.020
	(0.018)	(0.0182)
Mother completed 7th grade at birth	−0.048	0.0236
	(0.18)	(0.187)
Mother completed 8th grade at birth	0.176	0.220
	(0.171)	(0.172)
Mother completed 9th grade at birth	0.158	0.232
	(0.145)	(0.146)
Mother completed 10th grade at birth	0.030	0.061
	(0.132)	(0.132)
Mother completed 11th grade at birth	0.0522	0.101
	(0.129)	(0.130)
Mother's number of siblings, 1979	−0.0039	−0.0076
	(0.0084)	(0.0085)
Teen mother lived with own mother only at 14	−0.087	−0.115*
	(0.057)	(0.0583)

Appendix 18.7. Continued

Residential Choice and Grade Failure Among Children (Linear Probability Model)	OLS Model (Standard Error)	Two-Stage Selection Model (Standard Error)
Teen mother lived with mother and stepfather at 14	0.0135 (0.072)	−0.0033 (0.072)
Teen mother lived with relatives (not parents) at 14	−0.0666 (0.236)	0.1919 (0.241)
Teen mother lived with father (not mother) at 14	−0.109 (0.170)	0.0401 (0.170)
Teen mother lived with neither parent at 14	−0.0819 (0.224)	−0.252 (0.235)
Joint significance of selection coefficients	Prob[>F]=0.092	
Observations	398	
R5	0.168	0.191

Note: Weighted by 1992 Sample Weight — *p<0.10, **p<0.05, ***p<0.01

Appendix 18.8. Residential Choice and Academic Suspension/Expulsion Among Children

Residential Choice and Suspension/ Expulsion of Children (Linear Probability Model)	OLS Model (Standard Error)	Two-Stage Selection Model (Standard Error)
Continuous coresidence	−0.140***	−0.306
	(0.0526)	(0.209)
Married at second post-partum interview	−0.0873*	0.137
	(0.0528)	(0.211)
Cohabitating / living with relatives at second post-partum interview	0.0734	0.177
	(0.075)	(0.253)
Selection correction — independent household at second post-partum interview	—	0.0765
		(0.134)
Selection correction — continuous coresidence	—	0.250**
		(0.098)
Selection correction — married at second post-partum interview	—	−0.117
		(0.088)
Selection correction — cohabitating / living with relatives at second post-partum interview	—	−0.0178
		(0.1311)
1990 maximum AFDC benefit (standardized coefficient)	0.030	0.0128
	(0.055)	(0.057)
[Standardized AFDC benefits]5	−0.0556*	−0.415
	(0.0287)	(0.0295)
East South Central Census Region	−0.0495	−0.067
	(0.167)	(0.170)
South Atlantic	−0.0797	−0.0667
	(0.104)	(0.106)
New England	−0.1450*	−0.083
	(0.083)	(0.0907)
Middle Atlantic	−0.0735	−0.0170
	(0.0711)	(0.0759)
West South Central	−0.124	−0.0977
	(0.881)	(0.143)
East North Central	−0.075	−0.053
	(0.0818)	(0.0829)
West North Central	−0.2206	−0.2096
	(0.145)	(0.146)
Mountain	−0.180	−0.1636
	(0.116)	(0.118)

Appendix 18.8. Continued

Residential Choice and Suspension/ Expulsion of Children (Linear Probability Model)	OLS Model (Standard Error)	Two-Stage Selection Model (Standard Error)
Black	0.117**	0.211***
	(0.0490)	(0.063)
Latino	−0.0396	0.0003
	(0.0528)	(0.0557)
Standardized, median county rent	0.0196	0.0162
	(0.0236)	(0.0238)
Urban SMSA	−0.0569	−0.0445
	(0.0472)	(0.0482)
Standardized, age-corrected AFQT	−0.0198	−0.026
	(0.0202)	(0.0206)
[Standardized, age-corrected AFQT]5	0.0066	0.011
	(0.0145)	(0.0147)
Mother age 15 or younger at birth	0.049	0.167
	(0.108)	(0.117)
Mother age 16 at birth	−0.0256	0.0250
	(0.077)	(0.080)
Mother age 17 at birth	−0.0539	−0.0073
	(0.058)	(0.0608)
Mother age 18 at birth	−0.0457	−0.0386
	(0.0456)	(0.046)
Year of first interview following birth	−0.0285**	−0.0251*
	(0.014)	(0.0143)
Mother completed 7th grade at birth	0.052	0.064
	(0.145)	(0.148)
Mother completed 8th grade at birth	0.1085	0.111
	(0.135)	(0.137)
Mother completed 9th grade at birth	0.149	0.144
	(0.114)	(0.115)
Mother completed 10th grade at birth	0.149	0.140
	(0.104)	(0.105)
Mother completed 11th grade at birth	0.218**	0.230**
	(0.102)	(0.103)
Mother completed 12th grade at birth	0.104	0.0982
	(0.0968)	(0.0971)
Mother's number of siblings, 1979	0.0034	0.0049
	(0.0065)	(0.0066)

Appendix 18.8. Continued

Residential Choice and Suspension/ Expulsion of Children (Linear Probability Model)	OLS Model (Standard Error)	Two-Stage Selection Model (Standard Error)
Teen mother lived with own mother only at 14	0.0295 (0.0448)	0.0315 (0.0464)
Teen mother lived with mother and stepfather at 14	0.076 (0.057)	0.0653 (0.0571)
Teen mother lived with relatives (not parents) at 14	−0.161 (0.186)	−0.136 (0.191)
Teen mother lived with father (not mother) at 14	−0.139 (0.134)	−0.166 (0.138)
Teen mother lived with neither parent at 14	0.194 (0.177)	0.168 (0.186)
Joint significance of selection coefficients	$\Pr[>F] = 0.136$	
Observations	399	
R5	0.166	0.182

Note: Weighted by 1992 Sample Weight — *p<0.10, **p<0.05, ***p<0.01

Notes

This chapter is a revised version of a 1996 paper. Comments from Nancy Apfel, David Boyum, Eric Feldman, Sarah Horwitz, Jerry Mashaw, Mark Schlesinger, T. Paul Schultz, Victoria Seitz, Mark Smith, Richard Weissbourd, and Richard Zeckhauser were quite helpful. Anne Green and Gerald Joireman helped acquire the AFDC-QC data. The Robert Wood Johnson Foundation Scholars in Health Policy program provided funding. The opinions expressed are mine alone.

1. See Hill (1990) and Furstenberg, Brooks-Gunn, and Morgan (1987).

2. On stability, see McLanahan and Sandefur (1994), chapter 7. Haveman, Wolfe, and Spaulding (1991) find that frequent moves during early childhood have a significant negative impact on subsequent educational attainment.

3. Also on multigeneration households, see Pearson, et al. (1990) and Tolson and Wilson (1990). For very young mothers, Chase-Lansdale et al. (1994) do find benefits associated with coresidence.

4. Since this chapter was written, several authors have examined single mothers' living arrangements and welfare participation. See, e.g., London (2000).

5. On these arrangements, see Apfel and Seitz (1991, 1996).

6. See, e.g., Horwitz, Klerman, Kuo, and Jekel (1991) on educational outcomes and teen pregnancy. On low-income women, see Cao, Stromsdorfer, and Weeks (1996).

7. Cameron and Heckman (1993) show that the earnings of male GED recipients do not significantly differ from non-GED holders who complete the same years of secondary schooling. Cameron 1994 reports the same findings among women, though the impact of GED certificates for teen mothers is not specifically explored.

8. AFQT scores rise with age over the teen years. We control for these age effects by subtracting actual scores from age-specific predicted values. These predicted values are calculated by regressing AFQT scores on a vector of dummy variables corresponding to respondents' year of birth.

9. Seitz and Apfel (1991) and Ellwood (1986) discuss these issues in greater depth.

10. See, e.g., Furstenberg, Brooks-Gunn, and Morgan (1987), Moore and Snyder (1991), and Horwitz et al. (1991).

11. See, e.g., Apfel and Seitz (1991), Furstenberg (1978), and Pearson et al. (1990).

12. For more recent analysis, see J. Levine, H. A. Pollack, and M. Comfort "Academic and Behavioral Outcomes Among the Children of Young Mothers," *Journal of Marriage and the Family*, May 2001, 63 (2), pp. 355–369.

13. See, e.g., Michael, Fuchs, and Scott (1980).

References

Amemiya, Takeshi, *Advanced Econometrics,* Harvard University Press, 1985.

An, Chong-Bum, R. Haveman, and B. Wolfe, "Teen Out-of-Wedlock Births and Welfare Receipt: The Role of Childhood Events and Economic Circumstances," *Review of Economics and Statistics,* May 1993, pp. 195–207.

Apfel, Nancy, and V. Seitz, "Four Models of Adolescent Mother-Grandmother Relationships in Black Inner-City Families," *Family Relations,* October 1991, pp. 421–429.

——, "African American Adolescent Mothers, Their Families, and Their Daughters: A Longitudinal Perspective over Twelve Years," in *Urban Adolescent Girls: Resisting Stereotypes,* Bonnie Leadbeater and N. Ways, editors, New York University Press, 1996.

Bane, Mary Jo, and D. Ellwood, "Single Mothers and Their Living Arrangements," mimeo, Harvard University, 1984.

Cameron, Stephen, "Assessing High School Certification for Women Who Drop Out," mimeo, Columbia University, 1994.

Cameron, Stephen, and J. Heckman, "The Nonequivalence of High School Equivalents," *Journal of Labor Economics,* January 1993, pp. 1–47.

Chase-Lansdale, P. Lindsay, J. Brooks-Gunn, and E. Zamsky, "Young African-American Multigenerational Families in Poverty: Quality of Mothering and Grandmothering," *Child Development,* 1994, pp. 373–393.

Ellwood, David, "Targeting the 'Would-Be' Long-Term Recipient: Who Should Be Served?" *Mathematica,* 1986.

Ellwood, David, and M. J. Bane, "The Impact of AFDC on Family Structure and Living Arrangements," in Ron G. Ehrenberg, editor, *Research in Labor Economics,* JAI Press, 1985, pp. 137–207.

Furstenberg, Frank, and A. Crawford, "Family Support: Helping Teenage Mothers to Cope," *Family Planning Perspectives,* November–December 1978, pp. 322–333.

Furstenberg, Frank, J. Brooks-Gunn, and S. Philip Morgan, *Adolescent Mothers in Later Life,* Cambridge University Press, 1987.

Haurin, Donald, P. Hendershott, and D. Kim, "The Impact of Real Rents and Wages on Household Formation," *Review of Economics and Statistics,* May 1993, pp. 284–293.

Haveman, Robert, B. Wolfe, and J. Spaulding, "Childhood Events and Circumstances Influencing High School Completion," *Demography,* February 1991, pp. 133–157.

Hill, Martha, "Shared Housing as a Form of Economic Support for Young, Unmarried Mothers," Mimeo, Institute for Social Research, 1990.

Horwitz, Sarah McCue, L. Klerman, H. Sung Kuo, and J. Jekel, "School-Age Mothers: Predictors of Long-term Educational and Economic Outcomes," *Pediatrics,* June 1991, pp. 862–868.

Hutchens, Robert, G. Jakubson, and S. Schwartz, "AFDC and the Formation of Sub-families," *Journal of Human Resources,* 24, no. 4, Fall 1989, pp. 599–628.

Jencks, Christopher, and K. Edin, "The Real Welfare Problem," *American Prospect,* 1, no. 1, 1990, pp. 30–50.

Kellam, S. G., M. Ensminger, and R. Turner, "Family Structure and the Mental Health of Children," *Archives of General Psychiatry,* 1977, pp. 1012–1022.

McLanahan, Sara, and G. Sandefur, *Growing Up with a Single Parent,* Harvard University Press, 1994.

Maddala, G. S., *Limited-Dependent and Qualitative Variables in Econometrics,* Cambridge University Press, 1983.

Michael, Robert, V. Fuchs, and S. Scott, "Changes in the Propensity to Live Alone: 1950–1976," *Demography,* 1980, pp. 39–56.

Moore, Kristin, and N. Snyder, "Cognitive Attainment Among Firstborn Children of Adolescent Mothers," *American Sociological Review,* October 1991, pp. 612–624.

Mott, Frank, and W. Marsiglio, "Early Childbearing and Completion of High School," *Family Planning Perspectives,* October 1985, pp. 234–237.

Pearson, Jane, A. Hunter, M. Ensminger, and S. Kellam, "Black Grandmothers in Multi-generational Households: Diversity in Family Structure and Parenting Involvement in the Woodlawn Community," *Child Development,* 1990, pp. 434–442.

Pindyck, Robert, and D. Rubinfeld, *Econometric Models and Economic Forecasts,* McGraw-Hill, 1981.

Seitz, Victoria, and N. Apfel, "Effects of an Intervention Program for Pregnant Adolescents: Educational Outcomes at Two Years Postpartum," *American Journal of Community Psychology,* 1991, pp. 911–930.

——, "Adolescent Mothers and Repeated Childbearing: Effects of a School-based Intervention Program," *American Journal of Orthopsychiatry,* 1993, pp. 572–581.

Tolson, Timothy, and M. Wilson, "The Impact of Two- and Three-Generational Black Family Structure on Perceived Family Climate," *Child Development,* 1990, pp. 416–428.

Winkler, Anne, "The Impact of Housing Costs on the Living Arrangements of Single Mothers," *Journal of Urban Economics,* November 1992, pp. 388–403.

19

Family Allowances and Poverty Among Lone Mother Families in the United States

CECILIA A. CONRAD

The feminization of poverty is not unique to the United States. Across industrialized countries, poverty rates are higher for families headed by women than for other families and the number of families headed by women is growing. However, by many measures, single mothers and their children face a higher risk of extreme poverty in the United States than in other western industrialized countries. Table 19.1 summarizes the results of four recent comparative studies of the economic status of lone mother families.[1] Although the studies rely on different indicators of economic well-being, they all reach a similar conclusion: lone mothers and their children face a greater risk of extreme poverty in United States than in Canada or Western Europe. Furthermore, over the past decade, other countries have succeeded in reducing the poverty rate among these families.

The United States has not. One explanation for the relative deprivation of lone mothers in the United States is the difference in income support policies. Research by Kamerman and Kahn, Blank and Blinder, and others has documented that the United States offers less income support for single mother families than do other countries (Kahn and Kamerman, 1983), that single mothers must rely more heavily on means tested transfers in the United States than in other countries, and that differences in public transfer income account for a significant portion of the difference in relative status (Smeeding et al.,

Table 19.1. *Poverty Rates of Lone-Mother Families, Findings from Luxembourg Income Study*

	Proportion of Persons in Households with Adjusted Incomes Below Standard Poverty Line, 1979–82	Proportion of Persons in Households with Adjusted Incomes Below Standard Poverty Line, 1984–87	Proportion of Persons in Households with Adjusted Incomes 50% of Standard Poverty Line, 1979–82	Proportion of Persons in Households with Adjusted Incomes 50% of Standard Poverty Line, 1984–87	Proportion of Children in Households with Incomes Below 50% of Median Household Income, 1979–82	Proportion of Children in Households with Incomes Below 50% of Median Household Income	Hauser's Relative Welfare Index (Ratio of Average Net Incomes Per Adult Equivalent Unit)	Net Disposable Income of Single Mother Families As Ratio of Net Disposable Income of Two-Parent Families
	Lone Mothers with Children	Lone Mothers with Children	Lone Mothers with Children	Lone Mothers with Children	Lone Parents with Children	Lone Parents with Children	Lone Mothers with Children	Lone Mothers with Children
United States	.60	.61	.23	.26	.59	.54	.57	.47
Canada	.50	.47	.13	.10	.51	.37	.66	.53
France	.69	.68	.21	.15	.31	.13	.78	.74
Federal Republic of Germany	.42	.76	.02	.18	.31	.16	.78	.75
Sweden	.64	.60	.08	.04	.08	.02	.87	.87
United Kingdom	.67	.78	.16	.11	.36	.09	.76	.65

Sources for data: Column 1, Blackburn, 1993 unpublished calculations from LIS data; column 2, Blackburn, 1993 unpublished calculations from LIS data; column 3, Blackburn, 1993 unpublished calculations from LIS data; column 4, Blackburn, 1993 unpublished calculations from LIS data; column 5, Smeeding et al. table 5.6, p. 102; column 6, Statistical Abstract of the United States, 1993; column 7, Richard Hauser, "Comparing the Relative Influence of Social Security Systems on the Relative Economic Positions of Selected Groups in Six Major Industrialized Countries," *European Economic Review,* 31 (1987), pp. 192–201. Hauser uses LIS data from 1979–81; column 8, Wong et al., table 1 p. 7.

1988). These findings have led some to suggest that lone mother families in the United States might be better off if the current welfare system was scaled back and replaced by a universal child allowance scheme similar to those in Canada and Western Europe. (Garfinkel and McClanahan,1986; Kahn and Kamerman, 1983).

However, there is a critical question that this research has not answered. These studies do not reveal whether a universal child allowance, if implemented in the United States, would be more successful at alleviating poverty than the current U.S. welfare system. The income transfer programs of Canada and Western Europe may not have the same impact in the United States if there are differences in demographic characteristics of recipients here and abroad or differences in the elasticity of wage and salary income with respect to public transfers. Accordingly, this paper explores three questions. One, to what extent do demographic differences account for the difference in the poverty rates of single mothers across countries? Two, what would be the impact on the poverty rates of single mothers and their children in the United States of scaling back the welfare system and adopting a European-style family allowance? Three, how does this policy compare with other strategies to reduce poverty among these families?

To answer the first question, this paper calculates hypothetical poverty rates for lone mothers in the United States if they had the age and marital status distributions of Canada and Western Europe. To answer the second, it simulates the effect on lone mothers in the United States of scaling back the Aid to Families with Dependent Children program and introducing a European style family allowance. To answer the third, I use regression analysis to study the relationship between wage and salary income and income from child support and various personal characteristics, including age, marital status, and education. I use the results of this analysis to calculate the effect on incomes (and hence on poverty status) of each of the following scenarios: (1) all never married mothers became ever married mothers; (2) all high school dropouts gained a high school diploma; (3) all lone mothers were at least 25 years old; and (4) all lone mothers had only one child.

The principal findings are as follows:

- The poverty rates of lone mothers in the United States would be lower if lone mothers had the age and marital distributions of those in Canada, France, Germany and the United Kingdom, but the reduction is small. Lone mothers in Canada and Great Britain look much like those in the United States. The hypothetical poverty rate if U.S. lone mothers had the age and marital status characteristics of those in Canada or Great Britain is no more than 0.01 percent smaller than the actual U.S. poverty rate. Although lone mothers in Germany are older and more likely to be ever married than in the United States, the poverty rate for U.S. lone mothers would be only 0.08 percent lower if they had the characteristics of lone mothers in Germany.

- Introduction of the Swedish family allowance system coupled with the advanced maintenance program could eliminate extreme poverty among lone mothers in the United States and dramatically reduce official poverty. France's pro-natalist family benefit is much less successful. The rate of extreme poverty among lone mother families increases if the French allowance system replaced welfare in the United States.
- Among alternative strategies to alleviate poverty, the most effective at reducing the overall poverty rate is reducing family size. The effect of a change in marital status is negligible.

Poverty and the Demographic Characteristics of Lone Mother Families

One explanation for the higher poverty rates of lone mother families in the United States is a difference in the demographic composition of these families. If there are differences among lone mother families in the risk of poverty and if characteristics associated with high poverty rates are more prevalent in the United States, it could explain the higher rates of poverty among lone mother families in the United States. This section conducts a simple decomposition exercise to ask what poverty rates would be for U.S. lone mothers if they had the age and marital status distributions of Canada and Western Europe.

The poverty rate of lone mother families can be expressed as a function of the poverty rates of the demographic subgroups and of their proportional representation in the population of lone mothers. An increase in the proportion of mothers from a subgroup at high risk of poverty will increase the poverty rate of lone mothers overall, ceteris paribus.

To investigate the importance of demographics in explaining the difference in poverty rates for lone mothers in the United States and in other countries, I offer a simple decomposition analysis. I calculate a hypothetical poverty rate for lone mothers in the United States with PRs constant and βs set at the values in the comparison country.

This decomposition analysis requires two pieces of information: the poverty rates of lone mothers in the United States by demographic subgroup and the distribution by age and marital status of lone mothers in the comparison countries.

Table 19.2. Poverty by Demographic Subgroup in the United States

Age	Official Poverty		Extreme Poverty	
	Never Married	Ever Married	Never Married	Ever Married
15 to 24	0.85	0.77	0.6	0.52
25 to 34	0.68	0.55	0.4	0.28
35 to 44	0.49	0.39	0.26	0.17
45 to 54	0.51	0.33	0.28	0.09
55 to 64	0.57	0.37	0.22	0.12

Source: Author's calculations using unpublished data from the U.S. Bureau of Census, March 1990, Current Population Survey.

Table 19.2 describes the poverty rates by demographic subgroup for the United States using data from the March 1990 Current Population Survey. It consists of all families meeting the following criteria: the family has a female head; the family includes never married children under 18 years of age without children of their own; the family head is younger than 65; and the family receives no income from self-employment and no rental income.[2] The poverty rates are based on the official U.S. poverty line. Extreme poverty is defined by a family income equal or less than 50 percent of the official poverty threshold. Poverty rates are higher for never married mothers than for lone mothers who are divorced or separated. Poverty rates tend to decrease as the age of the mother increases. Hence, if the United States has a high proportion of lone mothers under age 25 relative to other countries, it might explain the higher risk of extreme poverty among lone mothers in the United States.

Table 19.3 describes the distribution by age and marital status of lone mothers in the United States and in Canada and Western Europe.[3] Lone mothers are younger and more likely to be never married in the United States than in France[4] and Germany. They are more likely to be never married than in Canada and Great Britain, but the age distributions are similar. Sweden has a higher proportion of lone mothers who are never married but a smaller proportion less than 25 years old. The United States also has a greater proportion of lone mothers over 35 than any of the other countries.

Table 19.4 reports the hypothetical poverty rates in the United States if lone mothers had the age and marital status characteristics of the other countries. The first two columns report the poverty rate for lone mothers in the U.S. if they had the age distribution of lone mothers in each of the other countries. Columns three and four report the hypothetical poverty rate in the U.S. if the proportion of lone mothers divorced, widowed, or never married were the

Table 19.3. *Distributions of Lone Mothers by Age and Marital Status*

Canada, 1990

Age	Never Married	Divorced or Separated	All Marital Statuses
15–24	13.1	3.5	16.6
25–34	13.7	23.3	37.0
35–44	4.9	31.5	36.4
45–54	0.5	7.8	8.3
55–64	0.1	1.7	1.8
All ages	32.3	67.8	100

France, 1982

Age	Never Married	Divorced or Separated	All Marital Statuses
15–24	*	*	3
25–34	*	*	24
35–44	*	*	30
45–54	*	*	29
55–64	*	*	14
All ages	15	85	100

Germany, 1982

Age	Never Married	Divorced or Separated	All Marital Statuses
15–24	5.2	3.5	8.7
25–34	7.2	25.8	33.0
35–44	3.4	37.3	40.7
45–54	*	17.7	17.7
55–64	*	*	*
All ages	15.8	84.3	100

Sweden, 1988

Age	Never Married	Divorced or Separated	All Marital Statuses
15–24	10.9	0.6	11.5
25–34	34.2	7.8	42.0
35–44	17.5	19.5	37.0
45–54	1.8	7.0	8.8
55–64	0	0.6	0.6
All ages	64.4	35.5	100

United Kingdom, 1986–87

Age	Never Married	Divorced or Separated	All Marital Statuses
15–24	13.0	5.1	18.1
25–34	10.6	28.1	38.7
35–44	2.4	29.9	32.3
45–54	0.3	8.5	8.8
55–64	0	2.4	2.4
All ages	26.3	74.0	100

United States, 1990

Age	Never Married	Divorced or Separated	All Marital Statuses
15–24	12.4	3.9	16.3
25–34	13.6	24.2	37.8
35–44	4.0	26.7	30.7
45–54	9.8	1.0	10.8
55–64	0.5	3.9	4.4
All ages	40.3	59.7	100

Table 19.4. *Effect of Changes in Demographic Composition of Single-Mother Families*

Country	Age Distribution		Marital Status Distribution		Age and Marital Status	
	Proportion of Persons with Incomes Below U.S. Poverty Threshold	Proportion of Persons with Incomes Below 50% of U.S. Poverty Threshold	Proportion of Persons with Incomes Below U.S. Poverty Threshold	Proportion of Persons with Incomes Below 50% of U.S. Poverty Threshold	Proportion of Persons with Incomes Below U.S. Poverty Threshold	Proportion of Persons with Incomes Below 50% of U.S. Poverty Threshold
Canada	0.54	0.3	0.55	0.28	0.54	0.29
France	0.43	0.2	0.46	0.23	0.48	0.24
Germany	0.5	0.26	0.52	0.23	0.57	0.32
Sweden	0.53	0.29	0.62	0.37	0.54	0.29
United Kingdom	0.56	0.31	0.53	0.29	0.54	0.29
Actual U.S. Rate	0.56	0.31	0.56	0.31	0.56	0.31

same in the United States as in the other countries. Finally, the last two columns describe the hypothetical U.S. poverty rate with both the age and marital status distributions equal to those of another country.

The evidence in Table 19.4 corroborates findings from other studies. Differences in the demographic characteristics of lone mother families do not fully explain the differences in poverty rates. If lone mothers in the United States had the age and marital status distributions of those in Canada and Great Britain, poverty and extreme poverty would be slightly less prevalent. The smaller proportion of mothers never married in those countries accounts for the differential.

The poverty rates for lone mothers in the United States would increase if lone mothers had the demographic characteristics of lone mothers in Sweden. The proportion of lone mothers who are never married is higher in Sweden than in the United States. Sweden has a smaller proportion of lone mothers less than 25 years old, which would tend to reduce the poverty rate, but it also has a smaller proportion greater than 35, which tends to increase the poverty rate.

Even in the cases of Germany and France, two countries with a low proportion of young mothers and a low proportion of never married mothers, the predicted change in poverty rates is very small. If lone mothers had the age and marital status distribution of those in Germany, poverty rates would fall by .08 percent. Extreme poverty would fall by .07 percent.

Description of Family Allowance Schemes in Canada and Western Europe

An alternative explanation for the lower economic status of lone mothers in the U.S. is the difference in income support policies. The United States is unique among western industrialized countries in that it does not have a universal family or child allowance. The U.S. is also widely acknowledged to be less generous than other countries in the level (as well as the scope) of benefits offered. Kahn and Kamerman in their authoritative study conclude that this difference in social policy explains the difference in relative status between lone mothers here and abroad. More recent studies, using data from the Luxembourg Income Study, confirm their results.

This section summarizes the key differences between family policies in the United States and those in Canada, France, Germany, Sweden and the United Kingdom. This information will be useful for the simulation analysis reported below. Much of the material in this section is drawn from earlier comparative studies of social policies in industrialized countries. Kamerman and Kahn (1988) have detailed in several publications the benefits available to lone mothers and to working mothers in Western Europe. Hanratty and Blank (1992) compare the social safety nets in Canada and the United States. Hantrais (1994) compares family policies in France, Germany, and the United Kingdom. Information about the characteristics of the European policies is available in Dumon (1991).

Researchers who have compared the United States to other industrialized countries invariably reach the same conclusion. The United States provides one of the least generous social safety nets for families with children. It is one of the few industrialized countries that does not guarantee paid maternity/parental leave for mothers to be. It is one of the few industrialized countries that does not provide a universal family or child allowance. It does provide public funding for day care centers, but at a lower rate than in other countries and the bulk of the federal subsidy goes, not to poor families, but to those with middle incomes.

The only income support for poor families in the United States is the means-tested Aid to Families with Dependent Children program (AFDC).[5] Before 1998, only single parents with children were eligible for these benefits in most states.[6] In contrast, in Canada and Western Europe, all families are eligible for a monthly allowance regardless of income or family structure. Sweden also pays single mothers an advanced child maintenance payment. The government then collects the child support from absent fathers. Canada and the United Kingdom pay supplemental benefits to families with low incomes, but these means-tested transfers represent a much smaller component of family income than in the United States.[7] Means-tested transfers represented 90 percent of the public transfer income of single mothers in the United States; roughly 60 percent of the income in Canada; and 50 percent in Germany, France, Sweden, and the United Kingdom.

Table 19.5 describes the family allowance schemes of Canada, France, Germany, Sweden, and the United Kingdom. The second column reports the allowance for a single parent with two children, ages 8 and 10. It excludes means-tested supplemental benefits and it excludes the advanced maintenance payment in Sweden. Even without the advanced maintenance payment, Sweden is the most generous followed by the United Kingdom. (The UK allowance includes a special supplement for single parents.)

In the United States, this family would receive a benefit only if its family income fell below some specified threshold. Using data from the March 1990 CPS data in the United States, the average yearly income from public

Table 19.5. *Description of Family Allowance Benefits in Five Countries*

	1990 Allowance in U.S. Dollars for Single Parent and Two Children, Ages 8 and 10	Amounts Progressive by Age of Child?	Payment Per Child Increases As Number of Children Increases?	Benefits Taxable?	Definition of Dependent Child	Age Limited Extension for Students	Child Support Program	Special Allowance for Single Parents
Canada	1,027.36	No[a]	Yes[a]	Yes	Under 18	No	No	Yes
France	1,427.16	Yes	Yes	No	18 and under	Yes	No	Yes
Germany	1,124.40	No	Yes	No	Under 16	Yes	Yes[b]	No
Sweden	2,358.72	No	Yes	No	Under 16	Yes	Yes[c]	Yes
United Kingdom	1,933.88	No	No	No	Under 16	Yes	No	Yes[d]

[a] Provinces can choose to make benefits progressive.

[b] Government will pay court-awarded child support if father fails to do so.

[c] Swedish advanced maintenance program guarantees a minimum level of child support.

[d] United Kingdom supplements the basic allowance for parents, and there is also a means-tested supplemental benefit.

assistance for a lone mother family with two children was $1,335.63 (or roughly $111 a month). An AFDC recipient with two children is eligible for a payment of up to $577 a month in New York City plus an additional $232 a month in food stamps for a total of $809 a month or $9,708 a year. In Texas, this family would receive only $184 a month maximum from AFDC and food stamps equal to $292 a month for a yearly benefit of $5,712.

The fourth column describes whether the average allowance per child depends on the number of children. In some countries, the family allowance is part of a broader, pro-natalist strategy. In this case, the allowance for the third or fourth child is typically greater than the allowance for the first. For example, in France, a family does not receive an allowance for the first child. With two children, the allowance is $118.93 per month. For three children, it is $271.01 per month. As will become apparent in the following section, pro-natalist family allowance schemes are not very effective at reducing poverty among lone mothers in the United States because the majority of the women have only one or two children.

Canada's family allowance scheme differs from those of the European countries in several respects. Benefits are taxable in Canada and Canada does not extend benefits if a child is a full-time student or trainee. In France, a family can continue to receive a child allowance until a child is 20 if the child is a full-time student, apprentice, or invalid, or cares for younger siblings at home while the mother works. Germany, Sweden, and the United Kingdom also have extension policies.

Germany is the only country that does not offer a special supplement to single mothers.[8] It does have a child support assurance program. If a mother receives a child support award from the court, the government will pay the award if the father fails to do so. In Sweden, the government guarantees every child living with only one parent a minimum level of support from the absent parent. If the absent parent fails to make this payment, the government pays and collects from the absent parent. Two children would receive a minimum of $3,255 annually from the maintenance advance program. Child support assurance schemes are becoming more common in the United States, although they provide support only for AFDC recipients. The average child support received by lone mother families with two children in the March 1990 CPS sample was $1,142 annually.

The United States is clearly less generous to nonpoor lone mother families than the comparison countries. In the United States, they have no guaranteed income. In Canada and in Western Europe, they are guaranteed a yearly payment of at least $1,000. The question remains whether these family allowances could substitute for an antipoverty strategy.

Introduction of European-Style Family Allowances in the United States: A Simulation

The introduction of a European-style family allowance in the United States will have both direct and indirect effects on the income of lone mother families. Because these allowances coupled with means-tested supplements tend to be more generous than the Aid to Families with Dependent Children program, their introduction will have the direct effect of augmenting family income. This should reduce poverty. However, there is also an indirect effect of the family allowance scheme. It could cause a reduction in labor market earnings. An increase in government transfers increases the demand for nonmarket goods and reduces incentives for work. Hence, the increase in family income from one additional dollar of government transfer is likely to be less than one dollar. A simulation analysis requires first, the calculation of benefits for U.S. families under the rules of the family allowance schemes in other countries, second, estimation of the indirect effect of these benefits on wage and salary incomes, and finally, calculation of the net effect on total income and the poverty rate.

This section simulates the effect of introducing a European style-family allowance on the poverty rates of lone mother families. This analysis makes two assumptions about the effect of a family allowance on labor market earnings.

- It assumes wage and salary income of families with wage and salary income will fall by .15 multiplied by nonlabor income. (The .15 estimate came from a regression analysis of determinants of wage and salary income.)
- It assumes families without wage and salary income will continue to have zero wage and salary income.

Table 19.6 reports the basic results. Providing just the family allowances, with no means-tested supplement, leads to a reduction in poverty rates in the case of Canada and Sweden. The family allowances of France, Germany, and the United Kingdom do not reduce poverty rates. Although those countries are more generous to the average lone mother family than the United States, the family allowances are smaller than the average AFDC benefit received by poor women. Hence, they are less effective at lifting those women out of poverty. Replacing welfare with the Canadian basic allowance reduces the official poverty rate but increases the rate of extreme poverty among lone mothers. Only the Swedish system has a notable impact on the rates of extreme poverty.

The last two columns in Table 19.6 report the effect of implementing both the child allowance and a means-tested benefit. I am able to calculate the means-tested supplement for Canada, France (means-tested, single mother

Table 19.6. *Replacing Welfare and Public Assistance in the United States with Family Allowance Schemes of Other Countries*

If U.S. replaces welfare with family allowance scheme of country— Replacement Family Allowance Scheme	Basic Allowance Only		Basic Allowance + Income Tested Supplements	
	Predicted Proportion of Persons in Lone Mother Families With Incomes Below U.S. Poverty Threshold	Predicted Proportion of Persons in Lone Mother Families with Incomes Below 50% of U.S. Poverty Threshold	Predicted Proportion of Persons in Lone Mother Families With Incomes Below U.S. Poverty Threshold	Predicted Proportion of Persons in Lone Mother Families with Incomes Below 50% of U.S. Poverty Threshold
Canada	0.57	0.42	0.53	0.01
France	0.65	0.49	0.55	0.38
Germany	0.67	0.49	NC	NC
Sweden[a]	0.43	0.08	0.43	0.08
United Kingdom	0.66	0.48	0.28	0.00
U.S. Poverty Rate	0.58	0.32	0.58	0.32

[a] No income-tested supplement included in Swedish calculations. Advanced maintenance payment included if it exceeds child support income.

supplement), the United Kingdom, and Sweden. The family allowances coupled with a means-tested supplement are effective at reducing poverty rates of lone mother families. In some cases, this combination strategy eliminates extreme poverty.

According to the simulation, the most effective at reducing poverty is the Swedish family allowance coupled with the advanced maintenance payment. If U.S. lone mother families were guaranteed this minimum child support, the proportion living in extreme poverty would fall to zero. The explicitly pronatalist family allowance of France is much less successful. Implementation of the French scheme in the model increased extreme poverty among lone mothers and their children.

Other Strategies to Reduce Poverty

A universal family allowance is one proposal for reforming welfare, but the proposal attracts more academics than politicians. Politicians, especially those on the right of center, offer a different set of proposals. Most focus changes in behavior such as ending teenage motherhood and ending out-of-wedlock childbearing. This section examines the impact of these strategies on welfare. Using estimates from an analysis of the determinants of income, I calculate the effect on income and on poverty status of replacing lone mothers under the age of 25 with lone mothers over the age of 25; of replacing lone mothers who are never married with lone mothers who have been married; of replacing lone mothers with no high school diploma by lone mothers with high school diplomas; and finally, of replacing lone mothers with more than one child with mothers with only one child.

The results of the underlying regression analysis are available on request. The independent variables in the analysis of wage and salary income included occupational dummies, education (dropout, high school, college), marital status (never married, widowed, divorced or separated), family size (a categorical variable — one child, two children, three or more children), the number of children less than six, age (a categorical variable — less than 25, 25–34, 35–44, 45–54, 55–64), race, Hispanic origin, the average state wage, the AFDC maximum benefit in the state of residence, income from child support and alimony, income from employment-related transfers, and income from all other transfers. The signs on the coefficients were consistent with the predictions of economic theory. Notably, the maximum AFDC benefit, income from child support and alimony, and race appeared to have no effect on wage and salary income. Never married women have less wage and salary income than ever married women. Younger women have less income than older women.

Table 19.7. *Alternative Strategies to Reduce Poverty Rates of Lone-Mother Families*

Demo-graphic Change	Proportion of Population in Affected Group	Proportion of Persons in Affected Group with Incomes Below Official Poverty Threshold, Status Quo	Proportion of Persons in Affected Group with Incomes Below 50% of Official Poverty Threshold, with Status Quo	Proportion of Persons in Affected Group with Incomes Below Official Poverty Threshold, with Change	Proportion of Persons in Affected Group with Incomes Below 50% of Official Poverty Threshold, with Change	Reduction in Poverty Rate of Lone-Mother Families as a Result of the Change	Reduction in Extreme Poverty Among Lone-Mother Families as a Result of the Change
All lone mothers 25 and older	0.14	0.84	0.55	0.77	0.45	−0.01	−0.01
All lone mothers married at least once	0.30	0.75	0.46	0.72	0.44	−0.01	−0.1
All lone mothers with at least high school diploma[a]	0.30	0.84	0.52	0.80	0.45	−0.01	−0.02
No lone mother family with more than one child	0.67	0.66	0.36	0.63	0.29	−0.02	−0.04

[a] Estimate does not fully adjust for changes in labor force participation rates.

Income from child support depends on marital status, the number of children and race. A lone mother family with only one child receives less child support than one with three or more. Black women and Hispanic women receive less child support than other women. A never married woman receives less child support than an ever married woman. Women less than 25 receive less child support than those over 25.

Table 19.7 reports the results of the simulation analysis. By far, the biggest bang for the buck would come from reducing family size.[9] Sixty-seven percent of lone mother families have more than one child. Sixty-six percent of those families have income below the official poverty threshold. If those families all had only one child, the poverty rate of the group would be only 63 percent. The proportion of extremely poor drops by 0.07 percentage points. Because the population affected is rather large, this change translates into a decrease in the overall poverty rate for lone mothers of 0.02 and in the extreme poverty rate of 0.04. Transforming young lone mothers into older lone mothers has a more sizable effect on the poverty rate of the population affected. The extreme poverty rates drops by 0.10. However, this group represents a much smaller share of the population (14 percent) so the net effect on overall poverty is rather small.

Final Thoughts

The European-style family allowances have a bigger impact on poverty rates than any of the demographic changes considered in the preceding section. In addition, there are other arguments in favor of this approach. For starters, the family allowance schemes may rate less of a disincentive for marriage. Because AFDC has historically been available only to single mothers and their children, there is, in theory,[10] a monetary disincentive for marriage. The family allowances are available to all households with children regardless of the parents' marital status. Although most countries supplement the allowance for single mothers, the premium paid to those living alone is smaller and female-headed families form a smaller proportion of the population.

Second, the family allowance schemes are not means tested so the disincentives for work are likely to be smaller. The AFDC program reduces the benefits received one dollar for every dollar earned. This implicit tax creates a disincentive for work. The family allowance is independent of wage and salary income.

Finally, the family allowance scheme, because it is universal, might enjoy broader political support than the existing welfare system. The principal opposing argument is that a family allowance scheme is likely to be more expensive than the present system. Calculation of the expected costs of this program is the next logical step in this research.

Notes

1. A lone mother family consists of a mother and her related dependent children. The studies described in Table 19.1 all use data from the Luxembourg Income Study. This study defines as a lone parent family only those families with just one adult. Children must be under age 18. This chapter uses the same definition unless otherwise noted.

2. I exclude these families from the analysis to avoid problems with the reliability and compatibility of the data.

3. There are variations in the definitions of lone parent families across countries. The definitions are explained in the notes.

4. Cohabiting couples are counted as two-parent families in this data. The proportion of babies born to never married women in France is fairly high, but not all nonmarital births lead to the formation of a lone mother family. Cohabitation is more common in Europe than in the United States. There are also differences across countries in the definition of lone mother families that affect these percentages. France includes families with children over 18. For the other countries, the families must have a child (defined either as under 18 or as under 16). If families with children over 18 are included, the proportion of lone mothers under 25 decreases.

5. AFDC recipients are also eligible for a variety of other transfer programs, including food stamps, housing subsidies and Medicaid. However, the discussion in this chapter will focus on the basic cash grant.

6. Federal legislation passed in October 1990 mandated the creation of AFDC-UP programs in all states.

7. There are means-tested allowances in France and in Sweden, but they are administered by local authorities. In France, the means-tested allowance is discretionary.

8. In France, single parents are also eligible for a supplementary benefit — the single parent allowance. This allowance is a means-tested transfer and is available only for one year or until the youngest child reaches age three. The program is designed primarily to ease the transition to single parenthood. According to most sources, it is awarded with discretion of local case onlookers and is not a reliable source of assistance.

9. These results are preliminary. The methodology is likely to underestimate the effect of education on earnings.

10. The empirical evidence on the link between welfare and marital status reports mixed findings. For a recent survey, see Moffitt (1992).

References

Central Statistical Office. *Annual Abstract of Statistics*. London. Several years (book and microform).

Dumon, W. A. 1991. *National Family Policies in EC Countries in 1990*. Brussels: Commission of the European Communities.

Garfinkel, Irwin, and Sara S. McLanahan. 1986. *Single Mothers and Their Children: A New American Dilemma*. Washington, D.C.: Urban Institute.

Garfinkel, Irwin, and Patrick Wong. 1990. "Child Support and Public Policy," in *Lone-Parent Families: The Economic Challenge*. Ed. OECD. Paris: OECD.

Hanratty, Maria J., and Rebecca Blank. 1992. "Down and Out in North America: Recent Trends in Poverty Rates in the United States and Canada." *Quarterly Journal of Economics* 107, no. 1, pp. 233–254.

Hantrais, Linda. 1994. "Comparing Family Policy in Britain, France and Germany." *Journal of Social Policy* 23, no. 2, pp. 135–160.

Hauser, Richard. 1987. "Comparing the Relative Influence of Social Security Systems on the Relative Economic Positions of Selected Groups in Six Major Industrialized Countries." *European Economic Review* 31, pp. 192–201.

Kahn, Alfred J., and Sheila B. Kamerman. 1983. *Income Transfers for Families with Children: An Eight-Country Study*. Philadelphia: Temple University Press.

Kamerman, Sheila B., and Alfred J. Kahn. *Mothers Alone: Strategies for a Time of Change*. Dover, Mass.: Auburn House, 1988.

——. 1988. "What Europe Does for Single-parent Families." *Public Interest* 93 (Fall), pp. 70–86.

Les Services Statistiques des Ministères et L'INSEE. *Annuaire Statistique de la France*. Paris. Several years (book and microform).

Matheson, Jil, and Gill Trevor. 1989. *General Household Survey, 1987*. London: HMSO Books.

Millar, Jane. 1989. *Poverty and the Lone-Parent Family: The Challenge to Social Policy*. Avebury, England: Gower.

Statistisches Bundesamt. *Statisches Jahrbuch fur das Vereinte Deutschland*. Metzler Poeschel, Weisbaden. Several years (book and microform).

Statistics Canada. *Canada Yearbook*. Ottawa. Several years (book and microform).

Sveriges Officiella Statistik. *Statistick Arsbok: Statistical Abstract of Sweden*. Stockholm. Several years (book and microform).

Wong, Yin-Ling Irene, Irwin Garfinkel, and Sara McLanahan. 1992. "Single-Mother Families in Eight Countries: Economic Status and Social Policy." Institute for Research on Poverty Discussion Paper, University of Wisconsin — Madison.

20

How Much More Can They Work?

Setting Realistic Expectations for Welfare Mothers

LADONNA PAVETTI

In recent years, the social safety net for low-income families has been radically transformed. For sixty years, beginning in 1936, families with children and with limited income or assets were entitled to ongoing cash assistance from the program christened Aid to Families with Dependent Children (AFDC). Now, in most states, families with limited income or assets can receive cash assistance only if they agree to seek employment or work in exchange for government assistance (Pavetti, Holcomb, and Duke 1995; General Accounting Office 1997).

This transformation of the social safety net for low-income families with children began with implementation of numerous state welfare reform demonstration projects.[1] The shift was codified into federal law with passage of the Personal Responsibility and Work Opportunity Reconciliation Act (PRWORA) of 1996. PRWORA supplanted the AFDC program, which was replaced by block grants to states for establishment of the Temporary Assistance for Needy Families (TANF) program.

Although PRWORA provides states with considerable flexibility to decide what support they will provide to families in need of assistance, TANF is clearly intended to emphasize short-term, employment-related assistance. Families are eligible to receive TANF assistance for only sixty months in their lifetime, increasing the urgency for families to find employment or alternative means of support quickly. TANF recipients are also required to perform community service after receiving assistance for two months and to work once they are determined to be job-ready or after receiving assistance for twenty-four months. To ensure that state TANF programs emphasize work, PRWORA requires states to meet steadily increasing work participation rates to receive their full TANF allocation.

Widespread dissatisfaction with the old AFDC program and the dramatic increase in employment among all women and among mothers with children have generated broad-based support for requiring welfare recipients to work or look for work in exchange for receiving government assistance. Almost by definition, most welfare recipients are not employed, at least at the time they are receiving welfare benefits. Until recent changes, after four months of employment recipients who were employed lost welfare benefits dollar for dollar, making it difficult for mothers to work and receive assistance. Administrative data indicate that in any given month, only about 10 percent of the AFDC caseload reported income from employment (Zedlewski and Giannarelli 1997). However, when one takes into account the dynamic nature of the AFDC caseload, it becomes clear that work is more common among welfare recipients than this information suggests. Prior to welfare reform, research indicated that between 50 and 70 percent of recipients who first received welfare left the welfare rolls within a year. Furthermore, between half and two-thirds of these exits occurred when a recipient found employment or otherwise worked her way off welfare (Gritz and MaCurdy 1991; Harris 1993; Pavetti 1993).

Given that work was already common among at least some portion of the welfare caseload, when welfare reform legislation, which focused on increasing work among welfare recipients was enacted, it was not obvious how much more welfare recipients would need to work to mirror the work experiences of women in similar circumstances and with similar characteristics. Since a woman's welfare and employment status can change on a monthly basis, to obtain such an estimate one needs data on women's employment and welfare experiences over time. Fortunately, such data are available through several nationally representative longitudinal surveys. We examine the relative work experiences of welfare recipients and nonrecipients prior to the implementation of major work-related reforms. This was achieved by using data from the National Longitudinal Survey of Youth (NLSY) to construct complete employment and welfare histories for a cohort of women over a ten-year period, from age 18 to age 27. We developed a dynamic microsimulation model that predicts women's movement in and out of the labor market over the ten-year period. This model provided estimate of how much more women who ever received welfare would have worked if they followed the same employment paths as women with similar characteristics who never turned to welfare. This analysis shows that between ages 18 and 27, women who ever received welfare worked only about 60 percent as much as women who never received welfare. Though the majority of welfare recipients worked at some point in time, a substantial fraction spent minimal time in the labor market. About a third of recipients worked for less than 25 percent of the ten-year period; a third worked between 25 and 50 percent of the time, and the remainder worked for more than half of the ten-year period. Welfare recipients who spent the least amount of time in the labor market were primarily recipients with low education and skill levels and members of a minority group. Lower rates of employment in any given year and shorter periods of employment when they were employed contributed to welfare recipients spending less time in the labor force than nonrecipients.

I estimate that if welfare recipients would follow the same employment paths as nonrecipients with similar characteristics, their time in the labor market would increase by 30 percent. Women with low levels of education, low basic skills, and more children would realize the greatest employment gains, since they currently spend the least amount of time working. Even if welfare recipients were to follow the same employment paths as nonrecipients, they would continue to experience substantial periods of joblessness. I estimate that by age 27, fewer than half of recipients who had not completed high school would be employed steadily. These results suggest that a substantial fraction of welfare recipients are likely to continue to need a safety net to support them during periods when they are unable to find employment.

In this chapter, I begin by describing the level and type of work that is expected of welfare recipients under TANF, what we already know about the work experiences of women on welfare, and the data and methodology used for this analysis. In subsequent sections, I explain how women who received welfare prior to welfare reform differed from other women. I highlight differences that were likely to affect their employment prospects, describe how the work experiences of welfare mothers compared to nonrecipients, and examine characteristics of welfare recipients based on their level of labor force attachment. Finally, I estimate how much more we can expect recipients to work given their characteristics and circumstances — assuming recipients follow the same employment paths as women who never received welfare. I conclude with a discussion of the findings and their implications for transforming the current welfare system into a more work-oriented program.

Work Expectations Under TANF

PRWORA provides states with considerable flexibility in determining how they will use TANF funds, but it is quite specific with respect to work participation. Parents or caretakers receiving assistance under TANF must be gainfully employed once the state determines that the recipient is job-ready or if the recipient has received TANF assistance for more than twenty-four months. States may set shorter time limits for work participation and many have already done so (U.S. Department of Health and Human Services 1997). If a recipient is unwilling to work, TANF requires states to reduce the recipient's TANF grant, but states can also terminate assistance to recipients who do not comply with the work requirement. Medicaid coverage may also be terminated for an adult who refuses to work, although Medicaid coverage for children must remain intact.

The legislation sets forth explicit work participation rates that states must meet, including the minimum number of hours recipients must participate in a work-oriented activity (Table 20.1) and activities that satisfy the participation requirement. In 1997, the first year of full implementation, the law required states to have 25 percent of their mandatory TANF caseload participating in work activities for at least twenty hours per week. The percentage of mandatory TANF caseload required to participate in program activities increases by 5 percent each year, reaching a high of 50 percent in FY 2002. The level of participation required by each participant increases to twenty-five hours in FY 1999 and reaches the maximum level of thirty hours per week in FY 2000. With a few exceptions, these participation requirements apply to all TANF household heads, including teen mothers.[2] States have the option to exempt single-parent families with a child under the age of one from the work requirement, and may require single-parent families with a child under the age of six to work only twenty hours per week. TANF work participation rates are substantially higher than those required under the Job Opportunities and Basic Skills (JOBS) training program, the welfare-to-work program that states were required to operate prior to TANF. Owing to numerous exemptions from program participation, only about 10 percent of the AFDC caseload were required to participate in JOBS activities (Pavetti, Holcomb, and Duke 1995).

Participation requirements are also substantially different under TANF relative to those under the JOBS program. Under TANF, activities that count toward the participation rate have to do primarily with employment (e.g., on-the-job training, job search and job readiness, community service employment). With respect to JOBS they have to do mainly with employment preparation activities such as assessment or education and training. States are not

Table 20.1. TANF Work Participation Rate Requirements for All Families

Fiscal Year	Participation Rate	Required Hours per Week
1997	25%	20
1998	30	20
1999	35	25
2000	40	30
2001	45	30
2002	50	30

prohibited from placing recipients in these activities under TANF, but only activities specified in the law can count toward a state's work participation rate.

TANF work participation rates are structured so that states can meet them either by engaging recipients in allowable program activities while they are receiving assistance, or by reducing assistance caseloads below their 1995 level. The caseload reduction provision included in PRWORA allows states to reduce the required work participation rate by 1 percent for every 1 percent reduction in their assistance caseloads since 1995. The caseload reduction credit was included in PRWORA to reward states for getting recipients into private-sector jobs that would make them ineligible for program benefits. In the absence of bureaucratic hurdles that may discourage recipients from applying for assistance, states could reduce their TANF caseloads by increasing the employment requirement of recipients in several different ways. These include the following: helping recipients who would have gone to work anyway enter the labor market sooner than they might have done in absence of strict work requirements; second, getting recipients into the labor market who would not have done so on their own; and third, reducing the rate of return to the welfare system by helping recipients stay employed longer.

Work Experiences of Welfare Recipients

Most of our knowledge about work experiences of welfare recipients comes from studies of movement on and off the welfare rolls. The seminal work in this area (Bane and Ellwood 1983, 1994) found that although it was quite common for women to move on and off the welfare rolls, exits due to an increase in women's earnings accounted for only 21 percent of all exits from welfare. Subsequent research in this area found that Bane and Ellwood underestimated exits from welfare to work because the annual data used in their analysis failed to capture work exits that lasted for relatively short periods of time. Thus, studies using monthly rather than annual data find substantially higher rates of exit from welfare to work, ranging from 33 to 69 percent. Using monthly data from the Seattle/Denver Income Maintenance Experiment control group, Blank (1986) found that 33 percent of all completed welfare spells ended owing to an increase in the household head's labor market income. Using data from the NLSY, Gritz and MaCurdy (1991) and Pavetti (1993) estimated that about half of all welfare exits could be attributed to work. In a study using monthly data for 1984–1986 from the Panel Study of Income Dynamics (PSID), Harris (1993) found that 69 percent of all exits from welfare by women were due to work. In an analysis of self-reported reasons for welfare exits in Washington State, Weeks (1991) found that 54 percent of all recipients who exited the welfare system reported leaving welfare to enter the labor market.

Although studies using monthly data found much higher rates of women leaving welfare for work, they also found extremely high rates of return to the welfare system among women who had exited welfare for work. Pavetti (1993) found that 40 percent of all women who left welfare for work returned to welfare within twelve months and two-thirds returned within five years. Harris (1996) found somewhat lower rates of return, with 41 percent of women who left welfare for work returning to the welfare rolls within three years. In a comprehensive analysis of women's labor market involvement over a two-and-a-half year period, Spalter-Roth et al. (1995) found that 43 percent of the single mothers who ever received welfare during the period of their analysis were engaged in substantial hours of paid employment. Welfare recipients who were employed exhibited two different patterns of work: one group cycled back and forth between welfare and work, while another group combined work and welfare. Studies designed to evaluate the impacts of welfare-to-work programs show similar levels of employment among welfare recipients, including those who did not receive program services. For example, Riccio, Friedlander, and Freedman (1994) show that 57 percent of recipients who participated in California's Greater Avenues to Independence (GAIN) program and 51 percent of recipients who did not participate worked over a three-year period. Other welfare-to-work evaluation studies show employment rates ranging from 31 to 78 percent (Nightingale and Holcomb 1997).

Recent research based on interviews with single mothers to ascertain how they make ends meet shows that work among welfare recipients is not restricted to the time when they are off the welfare rolls. Edin (1991) found that just over half of a group of fifty welfare mothers she interviewed in Chicago engaged in part-time or full-time work that they did not report to the welfare department. Seven of the fifty welfare mothers worked at regular jobs under false Social Security numbers; twenty-two worked in regular or odd jobs and were paid in cash off the books, and ten worked in the underground economy. In a larger similar study of mothers in four cities, Edin and Lein (1997) found similar results: 46 percent of welfare mothers across the four cities reported earnings from reported work, unreported work, or work in the underground economy. Income from these sources accounted for an average of 15 percent of welfare mothers' total monthly income. In sum, this research suggests that work is common among welfare recipients, but most of it is short-term and relatively unreliable. In addition, few studies showed more than half of the AFDC caseload working, even over an extended period of time. Thus, the available evidence suggests that there is likely to be substantial room to increase work among welfare recipients, both by increasing the proportion of recipients who work and by increasing the duration of their employment.

The Data

The data used in this analysis come from the National Longitudinal Survey of Youth (NLSY), an annual survey of a nationally representative sample of young people between the ages of 14 and 21 as of January 1, 1979. The original sample of 12,686 members includes a cross-sectional sample, a supplemental sample designed to oversample Hispanic, African-American, and economically disadvantaged non-Hispanic, non-African-American youth, and a military subsample. About half (6,283) of the original survey were young women. Because this analysis examines women's work experiences over a fixed period of time, only women who are interviewed in every survey year (1979–1993)[3] and whose labor market experiences are observed from ages 18 to 27 are included. Women who report receiving welfare for at least one month between the ages of 18 and 27 are classified as previous recipients of welfare and all others are classified as never receiving welfare. This selection criteria yielded a total sample of 2,044 women, comprising 511 previous recipients of welfare and 1,533 nonrecipients. To examine work experiences of women over time, I initially constructed job histories for each of the women in my sample. This job file, created by linking jobs across all fifteen years of the survey, includes 13,665 jobs, of which women who were never recipients held 10,805 and previous recipients of welfare held 2,860. To facilitate this presentation, we examine mainly women's work and welfare experiences on a quarterly basis. When the data are collapsed in this manner, a woman who receives welfare in one month during the quarter is classified as receiving welfare during the quarter. Similarly, a woman who works at all during the quarter is classified as being employed during the quarter. For each of the forty sample quarters, we also distinguish between employment in a "bad" or a "good" job using the same criteria used by Pavetti and Acs (1997) in their analysis of transitions from bad to good jobs. Under this classification scheme, a quarter is classified as a good-job quarter if a woman works at least thirty-five hours a week and earns at least eight dollars an hour (in real 1993 CPI dollars). To qualify as a good job quarter, a woman has to work at least seventy hours in the quarter. If a woman works at all during the quarter but does not meet the good job criteria, the quarter is classified as a bad job quarter.

Conceptual Framework and Methods

There are many ways to examine how much additional work can be realistically expected from welfare recipients. For example, one could construct a behavioral economic model that attempts to capture work incentives and disincentives facing recipients under a reformed welfare system. Alternatively, one could construct estimates based on the results of previous welfare-to-work demonstration projects. However, given that current efforts to reform the welfare system differ dramatically from previous initiatives, both of these approaches would require numerous assumptions about recipients' likely response to a new set of incentives and penalties that may bear little resemblance to those they have faced in the past. Alternatively, one could use work experiences of women who have never used welfare as a starting point to estimate how much additional work may be expected from welfare recipients. If applied within a dynamic framework, this approach allows us to answer the question "How much additional work can be expected of welfare recipients if they follow the same employment paths as women who have never received welfare?" To employ such an approach, I develop a relatively simple dynamic microsimulation model to estimate women's movement in and out of jobs over a ten-year period, from age 18 to their twenty-seventh birthday. This period is a critical one in most women's lives. It is the time when most young women make their initial entry into the labor market. It is also a time when many women make important decisions about how much schooling they will pursue and whether and when they will marry and/or have children.

To capture the process of movement of young women in and out of employment, I use a multivariate framework known as a competing risk model, where competing risks are one of three employment states: (1) joblessness; (2) employment in a bad job; or (3) employment in a good job. I estimate a separate competing risk model to capture transitions from each of the three employment states. The models are based only on the experiences of women who never received welfare during the ten-year observation period. I then use the estimates from these models and the observed characteristics of women who previously received welfare to simulate the quarter to quarter employment transitions for welfare recipients.[4] The three competing risk models that form the heart of the microsimulation model provide a framework to estimate the effect of various characteristics. These include effect of demographics, parental status, education and mastery of basic skills, local labor market conditions, previous work experience (in good and bad jobs), and length of time in current employment on the probability of making the transition from one employment state to another, while holding other characteristics constant. These models allow us to address the following question: Holding all other factors constant, what is the impact of education or marital status or the presence of children or the condition of the local labor market on the likelihood that a woman who is jobless will become employed in a bad or a good job in the next quarter? The actual coefficients from the model are difficult to interpret and, therefore, are included in the appendix. However, the general pattern of the results provides important insight into the effects of characteristics and life circumstances of women who ever received welfare on their employment outcomes.

Not surprisingly, the amount of education a woman has had and whether or not she is in school significantly affect a woman's transition between employment states. While women are in school, their employment status is relatively unstable. However, once young women are within one to two quarters of completing their education, the likelihood that they will move from joblessness to a bad job or from a bad job to a good job increases substantially. Once a woman has completed her education, more schooling is associated with better employment outcomes. Women who have not completed high school are more likely to lose jobs once they become employed, while women who have completed college have a significantly better chance of making the transition to a good job, either directly from a state of joblessness or from a bad job. The presence of young children affects women's transitions in and out of the labor market in several important ways. Having a child under the age of five significantly reduces the likelihood that a woman who is jobless will make the transition to employment. Having a child under the age of one significantly reduces the likelihood that a woman will move from a bad to a good job and increases the likelihood that a woman employed in a good or bad job will make the transition to a state of joblessness.

The structure and condition of the local labor market affect the likelihood that a woman will find employment if she is jobless and will make the transition from a bad to a good job once she is employed. Women living in areas of low unemployment are more likely to find employment if they are jobless and to move from a bad to a good job than women living in areas with high unemployment. Women living in the Midwest and the South are less likely than women in the Northeast to make the transition from bad to good jobs. Good jobs in the Midwest and the South also tend to be less stable than in the Northeast. Employment outcomes are also somewhat better for women living in urban areas. Women living in or near cities are significantly more likely to find a job if they are without one and to move from a bad job to a good job than women in nonurban areas. A woman's transition from her current employment state is also significantly affected by the length of time she has been in her current state and her previous work history. A woman's previous work experience increases the stability of her current employment and increases the likelihood of moving from a bad to a good job. Time spent working in a bad rather than good job reduces a woman's employment stability by increasing the likelihood that she will lose her employment altogether or that she will move from a good to a bad job. In general, transitions from one employment state to another occur quite rapidly. Moreover, the longer a woman stays in a particular employment state, the less likely she is to leave it.

Who Turns to the Welfare System for Support?

Although stereotypes of welfare mothers abound, prior to welfare reform, welfare mothers were, in fact, a diverse group of women facing a wide range of life circumstances that led them to the welfare system for support. (It is likely that welfare mothers continue to be a diverse group; however, no information is currently available to document how the characteristics of welfare mothers have changed.) Mothers who completed high school or even some college may have found themselves seated in a welfare office or participating in a job search workshop alongside women who had less than a tenth-grade education. Mothers who had never been married, mothers whose marriages failed, and even a small number of mothers who were currently married all availed themselves of support provided by the welfare system. Even though there was considerable diversity within the welfare population, as a group welfare mothers differed substantially from women who never turned to welfare (Table 20.2).

On average, women who ever turned to the welfare system had substantially lower levels of education and basic skills, had more children to care for, and were more likely to be a member of a racial or ethnic minority than women who have never received welfare. Given these characteristics, one would expect welfare recipients to have greater difficulties finding and keeping employment than women in general. The low education levels and skill deficits

Table 20.2. Selected Characteristics of Young Women by Welfare Status at Age 27

	Ever Received Welfare	Never Received Welfare	All Women
Education at age 27			
Less than high school	44.5%	9.6%	15.7%
High school graduate	40.3	38.4	38.8
Education beyond high school	15.2	52.0	45.5
Basic skills (AFQT percentile rank)			
1st to 10th percentiles	32.8	6.2	10.8
11th to 25th percentiles	22.6	11.7	13.6
26th to 100th percentiles	44.6	82.1	75.6
Parental status at age 27			
One or more children	100.0	44.2	54.0
No children	0.0	55.8	46.1
Number of children (mothers only)			
1	32.2	52.9	46.2
2	36.2	36.6	36.5
3+	31.6	10.5	17.3
Age at first birth (mothers only)			
Before age 18	30.8	6.9	14.6
19–20	32.2	18.5	22.9
21–22	25.8	20.5	22.2
23+	11.3	54.2	40.3
Marital status (mothers only)			
Never married	34.0	6.8	15.6
Separated, divorced, or widowed	32.5	14.0	20.0
Currently married	33.5	79.2	64.4
Race/ethnicity			
White, non-Hispanic	54.6	84.1	79.0
Black, non-Hispanic	36.7	10.4	15.0
Other	8.7	5.5	6.1
Unweighted N	511	1533	2044

of welfare recipients are quite striking, as shown in Table 20.2. Forty-five percent of welfare recipients had not completed high school by age 27, relative to merely 10 percent of women who never received welfare. While more than half of nonrecipients had pursued some education beyond high school, only 15 percent of welfare recipients had done so. Furthermore, more than half of recipients' scores on the Armed Forces Qualifying Test (AFQT), an achievement test which has a strong relationship to higher levels of employment and earnings, fell in the bottom quartile of the AFQT distribution of all women. One out of every three recipients' scores was so low that they fell in the bottom decile of the AFQT distribution.

Early childbearing also distinguishes welfare recipients from other women. Sixty-three percent of welfare mothers had their first child by age 20, including 30.8 percent who gave birth to their first child before age 19. In contrast, only 10 percent of nonrecipient mothers gave birth to a child during their teens and 54.2 percent did not give birth to their first child until after their twenty-second birthday. Because many early births among welfare recipients are followed by subsequent births, by age 27, almost one-third of recipient mothers had three or more children, compared to just 11 percent of nonrecipient mothers. Although the majority of welfare recipients are white, blacks and other minority women are overrepresented among welfare mothers. Black, non-Hispanic women account for just 15 percent of this sample of women, but account for more than one-third of welfare recipients. The overrepresentation among other minority women is also evident, but far less dramatic. Hispanic and other minority women account for about 6 percent of the overall sample, but 9 percent of women who were ever welfare recipients.

How Do the Work Experiences of Recipients Differ from Nonrecipients?

Nearly all women spent some time in the labor market over this ten-year period, regardless of whether they ever received welfare. As shown in Table 20.3, about 95 percent of recipients and virtually all nonrecipients reported working during this ten-year period. Recipients entered the labor market at a somewhat slower rate than nonrecipients, possibly because their lower education and skill levels made it more difficult to find employment or because they were caring for young children. Nonetheless, most of those who would eventually enter the labor market had done so by age 20, with the majority (65 percent of recipients and 86 percent of nonrecipients) entering by age 18.

As the data in Table 20.3 show, even though recipients were almost as likely as nonrecipients to work during this ten-year period, on average, recipients

Table 20.3. Characteristics of Women's Labor Force Participation Ages 18 to 27 by Welfare Status at Age 27

	Ever Received Welfare	Never Received Welfare	Total
Percentage ever worked	94.8%	99.6%	98.8%
Percentage ever employed at age 18 (of those ever employed)	65.4%	85.9%	82.4%
Percentage ever employed by age 20 (of those ever employed)	86.7%	97.3%	95.5%
Average number of quarters with employment	18.9	31.9	29.7
Ever worked in two consecutive quarters	92.7%	99.2%	96.3%
Ever worked in four consecutive quarters	81.8%	98.0%	95.2%
Average length of employment spells (in quarters)	4.5	7.1	6.4
Average length of jobless spells (in quarters)	5.4	3.5	3.9
Average cumulative time in labor market (in weeks)	195.0	369.2	338.9

spent far less time working than nonrecipients. While nonrecipient mothers spent about 70 percent (369.2 weeks) of the total ten-year period working, nonrecipients worked for only about 38 percent (195.0 weeks) of the time period. This gap in the total time spent in the labor force results from shorter periods of employment and longer periods of joblessness among recipients compared to nonrecipients. On average, recipients' periods of joblessness were longer than their periods of employment, while the reverse was true for nonrecipients. Examining the experience of the "average" welfare recipient is useful in some respects, but the average masks the fact that some women who received welfare do reasonably well in the labor market while others do poorly.

Table 20.4 shows that welfare recipients can be divided into three groups, roughly equal in size, based on the time they spent working over the ten-year period. Approximately 36 percent spent 25 percent or less of the period working; 31.1 percent spent between 26 and 50 percent working and 33 percent spent more than half of the period working, but only 8.3 percent worked for 75 percent or more of the period.

In stark contrast, more than half of women who never received welfare worked for more than 75 percent of the ten-year period and an additional

Table 20.4. Selected Characteristics of Welfare Recipients by Level of Labor Force Involvement

	Level of Labor Force Involvement		
	Minimal (0–25%)	Moderate (26–50%)	High (51–100%)
Education at age 27			
Less than high school	62.1%	39.1%	30.5%
High school graduate	30.5	44.8	46.8
Education beyond high school	7.4	16.1	22.7
Basic skills (AFQT percentile rank)			
1st to 10th percentiles	59.0	22.3	14.4
11th to 25th percentiles	17.2	29.7	21.9
26th to 100th percentiles	23.8	48.0	63.7
Number of children (mothers only)			
1	18.9	32.6	46.3
2	32.7	36.7	39.4
3+	48.4	30.7	14.2
Age at first birth			
Before age 18	41.9	26.6	22.7
18–20	31.0	33.1	32.5
21–22	16.7	30.8	31.1
23+	10.5	9.6	13.7
Marital status (mothers only)			
Never married	45.2	22.7	32.6
Separated, divorced, or widowed	30.0	37.9	30.1
Currently married	24.8	39.4	37.3
Race/ethnicity			
White, non-Hispanic	41.7	59.3	64.2
Black, non-Hispanic	47.7	32.2	29.1
Other	10.7	8.5	6.7
Average quarters with welfare	19.0	9.7	7.1
Unweighted N	218	145	148

31 percent worked between 51 and 75 percent of that time. As the data in Table 20.4 show, recipients who spent the least amount of time in the labor force are overwhelmingly women who one would expect to have the least favorable economic prospects or for whom work may simply not pay. Almost two-thirds of recipients with minimal involvement in the labor market had not

completed high school and 59 percent had AFQT scores that fell in the bottom decile of the AFQT distribution. Almost three-quarters gave birth to their first child before age 20 and almost half also had three or more children. Minority women also accounted for the majority of recipients with minimal employment. Recipients with moderate levels of employment also had low levels of education and low basic skills although not to the extent of recipients with minimal employment. Almost one-third also had three or more children. Women with minimal employment received welfare in, on average, 19 out of the 40 quarters compared to 9.7 quarters for recipients with moderate employment and 7.1 quarters for recipients with high levels of employment.

How Much More Work Can We Expect?

The tabulations presented in Table 20.5 show that if women on welfare were to follow the same employment paths as women with similar characteristics who never received welfare, their employment would increase by 30 percent over the ten-year period. On average, I estimate that welfare recipients would work in 24.5 of the 40 quarters, up from the 18.9 quarters which they actually worked. While this increase brings welfare recipients' work experiences substantially closer to those of nonrecipients, because women who fare poorly in the labor market are overrepresented among welfare recipients, a substantial gap remains. In order to achieve complete parity with all nonrecipients, welfare recipients as a group would have to work 20 percent *more*, on average, than nonrecipients with similar characteristics. Recipients with the lowest levels of employment are predicted to experience the greatest gains in employment, primarily because they have the biggest gaps to close. Recipients who have not completed high school could potentially increase their employment by 41 percent, from 15.3 to 21.6 quarters.

The projected relative gains are even greater for women with the lowest basic skills. If women who score in the bottom decile of the AFQT distribution were to follow the same employment paths as their nonrecipient counterparts, I predict they would increase their employment by 48 percent, from 12.5 to 18.5 quarters. Recipients with three or more children would experience a somewhat larger gain of 48.6 percent, increasing their quarters of employment from 13.8 to 20.5. Not surprisingly, welfare recipients who spent only a minimal amount of time in the labor force could potentially experience the greatest gains, almost tripling the quarters they are employed, from an average of just 7 quarters to 20.4 quarters. Given that these recipients received welfare for far longer periods of time than other recipients, employment gains for women with a minimal attachment to the labor force could potentially have a

Table 20.5. Actual and Simulated Work Experience for Welfare Recipients with Selected Characteristics (Average Quarters with Work Experience)

	Quarters with Employment (out of 40 quarters over 10 years)			Steadily Employed by Ages 26/27
	Actual	Simulated	Percentage Change	
All women	29.7	—	—	
All welfare recipients	18.9	24.5	29.6%	61.0%
Education at age 27				
Less than high school	15.3	21.6	41.2	47.3
High school graduate	20.9	26.3	25.8	73.6
Education beyond high school	24.3	28.4	16.9	67.6
Basic skills (AFQT percentile rank)				
1st to 10th percentiles	12.5	18.5	48.0	40.6
11th to 25th percentiles	19.5	26.0	33.3	71.9
26th to 100th percentiles	23.5	28.3	20.4	70.2
Number of children (mothers only)				
1	23.3	28.9	24.0	79.3
2	19.4	24.2	24.7	59.7
3+	13.8	20.5	48.6	43.7
Level of labor force involvement				
Minimal (0–25%)	7.0	20.4	291.4	48.5
Moderate (26–50%)	19.9	25.4	27.6	62.1
High (51–100%)	30.9	28.2	8.7	73.4
Race/ethnicity				
White, non-Hispanic	21.0	26.5	26.2	65.1
Black, non-Hispanic	16.4	22.2	35.4	55.7
Other	16.1	22.3	38.5	57.4

substantial impact on a state's ability to meet the TANF work participation requirements, especially in later years.

These estimates suggest that there is considerable room to increase the amount of time welfare recipients spend working. It is important to note, however, that even if recipients were to follow the same employment paths as nonrecipients with similar characteristics facing similar circumstances, they would spend a substantial amount of time without employment. As shown in the second column of Table 20.5, on average, recipients are predicted to spend just 24 of 40 quarters working (61 percent of the ten-year period). Recipients who have not completed high school are predicted to work in 54 percent of the quarters, and women with the lowest basic skills are predicted to work in 46 percent of the quarters. The tripling of the labor force involvement among recipients who had only minimal involvement in the labor market is only sufficient to have them employed in half of the ten-year period. Some of the time spent jobless occurs while women are young and are about to make the transition to steady employment, but that is not always so. By the time they reach ages 26 and 27, only about 61 percent of all recipients are predicted to be working steadily, though there is substantial variation among recipients with different characteristics. At least 70 percent of women who completed high school have only one child to care for and have higher skills. These women are predicted to be working steadily, relative to less than half who have not completed high school, have the lowest basic skills, or have three or more children to care for.

These estimates assume that welfare recipients' work experiences will mirror those of nonrecipients. To the extent that unobserved characteristics associated with a young woman's reliance on welfare reduce the likelihood that she will find and keep employment, these estimates will overstate the employment outcomes for welfare recipients. Alternatively, if, when faced with no other alternatives, welfare recipients work more than nonrecipients, these estimates will understate their levels of employment.

Discussion and Conclusion

The foregoing analysis shows that even though the majority of welfare recipients spent some time working prior to the implementation of welfare reform, they worked substantially less than women who never turned to welfare for support. Lower levels of employment among welfare recipients are affected by shorter spells of employment and lower employment rates in any given year. If welfare recipients were to follow the same employment paths as nonrecipients with similar characteristics and similar family responsibilities, we would expect them to work 30 percent more. This represents a substantial increase over their current levels of employment, but recipients would still spend substantial periods of time jobless. The lower rates of employment among welfare recipients result, at least in part, from the fact that women with the least favorable employment prospects are overrepresented among the welfare population. In order to achieve complete parity with all nonrecipients, welfare recipients as a group would have to work 20 percent *more*, on average, than nonrecipients with the same characteristics.

The results presented here suggest that, even if states are successful in getting the most disadvantaged recipients into the labor market, these recipients are likely to continue to experience substantial periods of joblessness. Even if recipients with the lowest skill levels were to follow the same employment paths as nonrecipients, fewer than half of them would be steadily employed by the time they reach their late twenties. This suggests that, during these prolonged periods of joblessness, these families will continue to need access to a safety net for an extended period of time.

Notes

1. In 1992, through Section 1115(a) of the Social Security Act, Congress granted the U.S. Department of Health and Human Services authority to waive provisions of federal law for demonstration projects that would promote the objectives of the act. By the summer of 1996, thirty-three states had work-related waivers in place. These waivers included provisions to expand the fraction of the AFDC caseload required to participate in work activities and the types of allowable work or work-related activities, increase the incentives for recipients to find work, extend supportive services such as child care and Medicaid for recipients who find work, and strengthen the penalties for recipients who fail to meet work participation requirements (General Accounting Office 1997; U.S. Department of Health and Human Services 1997). With the implementation of these program changes, the primary emphasis of the AFDC program began to shift away from disbursing monthly benefit checks and toward helping recipients find employment.

2. States are also required to meet a two-parent work participation rate that is considerably higher than the rate for all families. In FY 1997, states are required to have 75 percent of their two-parent caseload working a minimum of thirty-five hours per week. Beginning in FY 1999, the rate increases to 90 percent, and the hour requirement remains the same.

3. Although federal welfare reform legislation passed in 1996, many states began implementing their own reforms after 1993. Thus, this data predates most recent welfare reform changes.

4. To simulate the employment paths of welfare recipients, I calculate the probability that a recipient stays in her current employment state or moves to a different state in each of forty quarters. If a woman is jobless, I calculate the probability that she stays jobless, moves to a bad job, or moves to a good job. In quarters when she is in a bad job, I calculate the probability she stays in a bad job, moves to a good job, or becomes jobless. Finally, if a woman is in a good job, I calculate the probability that she stays in a good job or moves to a bad job or becomes jobless. These calculations are made based on the results of the competing risk models and the actual characteristics of women who have never received welfare. To determine a recipient's employment status for the next quarter, this calculated probability is then compared to a number r between 0 and 1 that is drawn randomly from a uniform distribution. For transitions from joblessness, the likelihood of leaving joblessness for a bad job (p_{bad}) or a good job (p_{good}) are evaluated simultaneously. Thus, a recipient's status is determined according to the following:

Value of Random Number	Status in t+1:
$0 < r < = p_{bad}$	Transition to a bad job
$p_{bad} < r < = p_{bad} + p_{good}$	Transition to a good job
$p_{bad} + p_{good} < r < = 1$	Remain jobless

Transitions from bad and good jobs follow exactly the same logic.

References

Bane, Mary Jo, and David T. Ellwood. 1983. "The Dynamics of Dependence: The Routes to Self-Sufficiency." Report prepared for Assistant Secretary for Planning and Evaluation, Office of Evaluation and Technical Analysis, Office of Income Security Policy, U.S. Department of Health and Human Services. Cambridge, Mass.: Urban Systems Research and Engineering.

———. 1994. *Welfare Realities: From Rhetoric to Reform.* Cambridge, Mass.: Harvard University Press.

Blank, Rebecca M. 1986. "How Important Is Welfare Dependence?" Institute for Research on Poverty Discussion Paper 821–86, University of Wisconsin—Madison.

Edin, Kathryn. 1991. "Surviving the Welfare System: How AFDC Recipients Make Ends Meet in Chicago." *Social Problems* 38: 462–474.

Edin, Kathryn, and Laura Lein. 1997. *Making Ends Meet: How Single Mothers Survive Welfare and Low-Wage Work.* New York: Russell Sage Foundation.

General Accounting Office. 1997. *Welfare Reform: Three States' Approaches Show Promise of Increasing Work Participation.* Washington, D.C.: General Accounting Office.

Gritz, Mark R., and MaCurdy, Thomas. 1991. *Patterns of Welfare Utilization and Multiple Program Participation Among Young Women.* Washington, D.C.: U.S. Department of Health and Human Services.

Gueron, Judith M., and Edward Pauly. 1991. *From Welfare to Work.* New York: Russell Sage Foundation.

Harris, Kathleen Mullan. 1993. "Work and Welfare Among Single Mothers in Poverty," *American Journal of Sociology* 9(2): 317–352.

———. 1996. "Life After Welfare: Women, Work and Repeat Dependency." *American Sociological Review* 61 (4): 407–426.

Heckman James J., Lance Lochner, Jeffrey Smith, and Christopher Taber. 1997. "The Effects of Government Policy on Human Capital Investment and Wage Inequality." *Chicago Policy Review* 1 (2): 1–40.

Hershey, Alan, and LaDonna Pavetti. 1997. "Turning Job Finders into Job Keepers." *The Future of Children: Welfare to Work* 7 (1): 74–86.

Martinson, Karin, and Daniel Friedlander. 1994. *GAIN: Basic Education in a Welfare-to-Work Program.* New York: Manpower Demonstration Research Corporation.

Nightingale, Demetra, and Pamela Holcomb. 1997. "Alternative Strategies for Increasing Employment." *The Future of Children: Welfare to Work* 7 (1): 52–64.

Pavetti, LaDonna. 1993. *The Dynamics of Welfare and Work: Exploring the Process by*

Which Young Women Work Their Way Off Welfare. Cambridge, Mass.: Malcolm Wiener Center for Social Policy, Harvard University.

Pavetti, LaDonna A., Pamela Holcomb, and Amy-Ellen Duke. 1995. *Increasing Participation in Work and Work-Related Activities: Lessons from Five State Welfare Reform Demonstration Projects*. Washington, D.C.: Urban Institute.

Pavetti, LaDonna A., and Greg Acs. 1997. *Moving Up, Moving Out or Going Nowhere: A Study of the Employment Patterns of Young Women and the Implications for Welfare Mothers*. Washington, D.C.: Urban Institute.

Riccio, James, Daniel Friedlander, and Stephen Freedman. 1994. *GAIN: Benefits, Costs and Three-Year Impacts of a Welfare-to-Work Program*. New York: Manpower Research Demonstration Corporation.

Spalter-Roth, Roberta, Beverly Burr, Heidi Harman, and Lois Shaw. 1995. *Welfare That Works: The Working Lives of AFDC Recipients*. Washington, D.C.: Institute for Women's Policy Research.

U.S. Department of Health and Human Services, Office of the Assistant Secretary for Planning and Evaluation. 1997. *Setting the Baseline: A Report on State Welfare Waivers*. Washington, D.C.

Weeks, Gregory C. 1991. *Leaving Public Assistance in Washington State*. Olympia: Washington State Institute for Public Policy, Evergreen State College.

Zedlewski, Sheila, and Linda Giannarelli. 1997. "Diversity Among State Welfare Programs: Implications for Reform." *New Federalism: Issues and Options for States*, Series A, No. A-1 (Jan.) Washington, D.C.: Urban Institute.

21

Turning Our Backs on the New Deal
The End of Welfare in 1996

JEFFREY LEHMAN AND SHELDON DANZIGER

President Clinton campaigned on a platform "to make work pay" and to "end welfare as we know it." In *Putting People First* (1992) he declared, "It's time to honor and reward people who work hard and play by the rules. That means ending welfare as we know it — not by punishing the poor or preaching to them, but by empowering Americans to take care of their children and improve their lives. No one who works full-time and has children at home should be poor anymore. No one who can work should be able to stay on welfare forever."

Shortly after taking office, President Clinton created a high-level, inter-agency Welfare Reform Task Force to translate the campaign rhetoric into draft legislation. The task force sought to craft a reform of the program that most people know as "welfare" — Aid to Families with Dependent Children (AFDC) — that would resonate with "the basic American values of work, family, responsibility, and opportunity."[1] Despite the campaign rhetoric and an active task force, the first two years of the Clinton Administration ended without either house of Congress giving sustained committee consideration to any welfare reform bill. President Clinton's priorities were elsewhere (deficit reduction in 1993 and universal health coverage in 1994); while the task force did ultimately submit draft legislation to Congress during the summer of 1994, it came too late in the 103rd Congress to receive much attention.[2] In

1995, however, the new Republican Congressional majority placed welfare reform at the center of its Contract with America. After a year of heated legislative activity, Congress sent to the President's desk the Personal Responsibility and Work Opportunity Act of 1995,[3] which President Clinton promptly vetoed. Negotiations between the President and Congress continued through the presidential campaign of 1996, however, and during the summer of 1996 President Clinton agreed to sign a new bill, the Personal Responsibility and Work Opportunity Reconciliation Act of 1996 (PRWORA).[4] PRWORA totally abolished AFDC, replacing it with a system of block grants to state governments. Why didn't President Clinton veto PRWORA?

The President's explanation is that he was keeping his 1992 campaign promise: he had offered alternative ways to keep that promise, to no avail, and now the only way for him to avoid breaking his promise was to sign a law that he described as "flawed." Promise-keeping is, of course, a virtue. But President Clinton's "promise," as embodied in the quotation cited, surely should not have been understood to mean that he would sign anything that ended welfare. We interpret his promise instead to have had two components: (a) that he would, in good faith, submit his own legislative proposal to end welfare, and (b) that he would not veto legislation ending welfare as long as the legislation passed a minimalist test of public policy — namely, that, even if flawed, the legislation constituted an improvement over the status quo. Does PRWORA pass this minimal, incrementalist test? Is it likely to produce a better safety net and a better society than the one that existed when the President signed the law? We think not.

There were numerous ways to end welfare as we knew it. Many would have improved our welfare state, which was surely in need of repair. But we cannot view PRWORA as an improvement. We believe that, by signing it, the President broke the *other* promise quoted above — that welfare would be ended "not by punishing the poor or preaching to them, but by empowering Americans to take care of their children and improve their lives." In this chapter, we offer a structure for analyzing President Clinton's decision to sign PRWORA. We explain how it was possible to have used the most recent round of welfare reform as an opportunity to recalibrate the balance among some critical societal values. We argue that it was possible to replace welfare with a programmatic environment better suited to promoting the task force values of work, family, responsibility, and opportunity.

It was possible, but that is not what happened. PRWORA chose not to empower the poor, but rather to disidentify with their life circumstances. Rather than moving from a cash safety net to a work-based net, it chose to eliminate any nationwide net at all. It marked a radical departure from a half century's efforts to build cross-class social solidarity by expanding opportunity for all.

In the next section, we briefly describe how welfare operated in 1996. We then summarize the changes brought about by PRWORA. We then describe the economic context of welfare reform and present some empirical evidence on how welfare recipients are likely to fare in the labor market. The two subsequent sections focus on the four values identified by the task force — first work and opportunity, then family and responsibility. We consider how those values were expressed under AFDC and how they have been reconceptualized under PRWORA. The final section presents our views of what it would have taken for welfare reform in 1996 to have been consistent with our understanding of President Clinton's 1992 campaign rhetoric.

Welfare as We Knew It

Aid to Families with Dependent Children was an income support program that responded to immediate financial hardship. It embodied a commitment to support a subgroup of the poor that was, at one time, thought blameless: low-income families with young children and a missing or financially incapacitated breadwinner. To qualify for benefits, a family had to show that it had virtually no assets, that it had very low income (each state set its own eligibility ceiling), and that a child in the family was deprived of at least one parent's support because the parent was (a) not living with the child, (b) incapacitated, or (c) a recently unemployed primary breadwinner.

AFDC was primarily a program for single mothers and their children. A few single fathers participated, and a somewhat larger number of two-parent families satisfied the more stringent requirements for two-parent eligibility. But among the roughly 5 million families who received AFDC benefits in a typical month in fiscal year 1993, about 90 percent were fatherless.[5]

AFDC had two aspects: a safety net aspect and a transitional aspect. For eligible families, AFDC ensured a meager, but potentially vital, safety net. In 1994, a nonworking welfare mother with two children and no earnings received $366 in cash and $295 in Food Stamps (per month) in the median state, or about 69 percent of the poverty line. Importantly, AFDC recipients qualified for family health insurance in the form of Medicaid.

The transitional aspect of AFDC was embodied in JOBS, the Job Opportunities and Basic Skills training program created by the 1988 Family Support Act. Putting to one side special state options and some special requirements imposed on teenage high school dropouts, AFDC was a program of three-years-per-child-and-then-participate-if-you-can. Once the mother's youngest child reached age 3, she was required to participate for up to twenty hours per week in JOBS. Once that child reached age 6, she could have been required to participate for up to forty hours per week.

Participating in JOBS meant agreeing to a reasonable "employability plan" the state devised, as long as the state provided for childcare, transportation, and other work-related expenses. However, if the state did not appropriate sufficient funds to provide a JOBS slot (and many states did not), the recipient was not punished for the state's failure. Any recipient who complied with legitimately imposed JOBS requirements continued to receive a welfare check. Any recipient who failed to comply, without good cause, could have been sanctioned by having her monthly grant reduced to reflect a family with one fewer person. In 1995, each state was expected to provide JOBS slots for at least 20 percent of nonexempt participants or face the prospect of losing some federal funds.

This transitional aspect of AFDC imposed no time limits on its safety-net aspect. Recipients could enter AFDC, enroll in JOBS, find a job, lose that job, return to the rolls, and reenroll in JOBS. For most recipients, the program was not such an attractive alternative that they chose to make it a "way of life": half of all families that began a welfare spell left the rolls within one or two years.[6] Despite its flaws, however, the JOBS component of AFDC clearly embodied a commitment to mutual responsibility: recipients were expected to take advantage of training and work opportunities provided by the government.

Welfare as We Have Come to Know It

PRWORA begins by doing away with the entitlement to cash assistance. As of October 1, 1996, AFDC was replaced by the Temporary Assistance for Needy Families (TANF) block grant. Each state can now decide which categories of children are eligible for assistance and which are not, subject only to a requirement that families receive "fair and equitable treatment."

Next, PRWORA significantly reduces the total amount of money that the current system requires from the federal and state governments in support of poor children. The federal contribution to each state is essentially capped at its 1994 level of federal welfare payments.[7] Increased costs associated with population growth or economic downturns will be borne by the states, or else by the poor. Moreover, whereas states had to create and fund an entitlement to AFDC benefits within federal guidelines in order to receive matching funds from the federal government, PRWORA requires only that they continue to expend 75 percent of their 1994 level of expenditures on AFDC, JOBS, child-

care, and emergency assistance. These figures are not adjusted for future inflation or demographic or economic changes. Any state could, for example,
impose an immediate 25 percent cut in cash payments to welfare recipients
without any loss of federal funds, and it could freeze expenditures at 75 percent of the 1994 level for the foreseeable future.[8]

To be sure, some states that have both the funds and the political will may
choose on their own to go beyond the minimum and to provide a broader and
more supportive safety net than existed before. Each state can pursue whatever kind of reform it chooses, including the mutual responsibility reforms
outlined below. In practice, however, it is unlikely that any state will provide
an entitlement to cash assistance or an entitlement to a "workfare" position. In
our mobile society, income redistribution tends to take place at the federal
level or not at all.[9]

PRWORA not only eliminates the entitlement to cash assistance, it simultaneously *toughens* the conditions on participation. Programs funded by the
federal block grant and the state maintenance-of-effort funds may not provide
more than a cumulative lifetime total of sixty months of cash assistance to any
welfare recipient no matter how willing she might be to work for her benefits.
States have the option to grant exceptions to the lifetime limit to up to 20 percent of their caseload. In 1994, however, about half of recipient children lived
in families that had received benefits for more than sixty months. As we explain below, these recipients are likely to have great difficulty supporting their
families on their labor market income alone.

PRWORA also adds new conditions concerning parental participation in
work programs during the months in which the family may receive benefits.
Single-parent welfare recipients with no children under age one will have to
work at least 20 hours per week, rising to thirty hours per week by FY 2002
for families without children under 6 years old, in exchange for welfare. This
provision was phased in, rising to 50 percent of the total caseload in fiscal
year 2002.[10]

The Economic Context of Welfare Reform

It might be tempting to explain PRWORA as a simple policy response to
empirical evidence. After all, the early expectations of AFDC were that it
would "wither away" as the economy strengthened. It was hoped that ultimately the economy would be strong enough that AFDC would be unnecessary — the private market's demand for labor would be so strong that no
safety net would be needed.

In this section, we consider whether PRWORA can be justified in this manner. We look at descriptive evidence concerning the economy more generally. And we look at particularized data pertaining to welfare recipients. Neither set of evidence gives reason to believe that PRWORA was simply a natural step in the evolution of the economy.

In one sense, PRWORA could be seen as a predictable "next step." One of the most significant changes in America's welfare programs over the prior two decades was the decline in the level of cash benefits they provide.[11] Throughout that period, inflation eroded the effective purchasing power of a welfare grant. Moreover, during the 1990s, a number of states cut benefits in nominal terms. Thus, in the early 1990s in the median state, the combined AFDC and Food Stamp benefit was about 70 percent of the poverty line for a nonworking mother with two children, down from about 85 percent in the mid-1970s.[12] But the declining economic position of AFDC recipients did not correspond to a steady *improvement* in the quality of life of nonrecipients. Quite the contrary. The period from 1975 to 1995 was also characterized by economic distress for the middle class, the working poor, and the unemployed. There was relatively little economic growth over that generation, and the gains from growth were very uneven. In the two decades following World War II, "a rising tide lifted all boats" and most families gained — the poor as well as the rich, less-skilled workers as well as the most skilled. After the early 1970s, however, a rising tide became an "uneven tide," as the gaps in living standards widened between the most-skilled workers and the least-skilled workers.[13]

Economic hardship is now remarkably widespread. Popular portrayals of economic hardship tend to focus on inner-city poverty or single-mother families or displaced factory workers, and attribute poverty primarily to their behavior or lack of skills. But during the 1980s, inequalities increased within most socioeconomic groups as well. While white-collar workers fared better on average than blue-collar workers, and married-couple families fared better on average than mother-only families, many white-collar workers and many workers in married-couple families were also laid off or experienced lower real earnings. Not even the most educated groups were spared, so that a college degree no longer guarantees a high salary. In 1991, among 25-to-34-year-old college graduates (without post-college degrees), 16 percent of men and 26 percent of women worked at some time during the year but earned less than the poverty line for a family of four persons.[14]

Because economic hardship is this extensive, one should have been suspicious of claims that welfare reform could transform most recipients into self-sufficient workers. The "welfare problem" was part of a broader "poverty problem," which, in turn, was part of a broader economy-wide problem that resulted from two decades of slow economic growth and rising income inequality.

The primary source of this increased economic hardship has been a set of structural changes in the labor market. Less-educated workers have found it harder to secure employment, and those who are hired tend to receive low wages. Many factors moved the economy in the same direction. The decline in the percentage of the workforce that was unionized, reductions in the percentage that works in manufacturing, increased global competition, and the consequent expansion of the import and export sectors all lowered the wages of less-skilled workers. The automation which accompanied introduction and widespread use of computers and other technological innovations also increased demand for skilled personnel who could run more sophisticated equipment. Simultaneously, there was a decline in the demand for less-skilled workers, who either were displaced by the automated systems or had to compete with overseas workers producing the rising imports.

One would expect these changes in the structure of the labor market to have important implications for the labor market prospects of welfare recipients. Because most former welfare recipients have limited education and labor market experience, the economy offers them diminished prospects even when unemployment rates are low. The shift in the skill mix required in today's economy means that, even if an employer extends a job offer to a former welfare recipient with low skills and experience, one would predict that the employer would not be willing to pay very much.

To test those predictions, we chose to analyze a set of generally available census data. We began with the Public Use Microdata Sample from the 1990 Census of Population and drew a sample of single mothers between the ages of 18 and 45 who resided in the seventy-seven largest metropolitan areas.[15] (For these purposes, "single mothers" are defined as women who had at least one child under the age of 18 living with them and who did not have a husband residing in the same household.)

Compared to the average single mother who did not receive welfare, the typical welfare recipient had less education, was younger, had more children and was more likely to be never married. Following are a few examples. First, about one-quarter of nonrecipients, but half of recipients, were never-married. Second, about one-fifth of nonrecipients, but more than two-fifths of recipients, lacked a high school degree. Third, about one-sixth of nonrecipients, but one-quarter of recipients, were under 25 years of age. And, finally, about one-sixth of all nonrecipients, but one-third of recipients, had three or more children.

All of these observed characteristics suggest that welfare recipients, *ceteris*

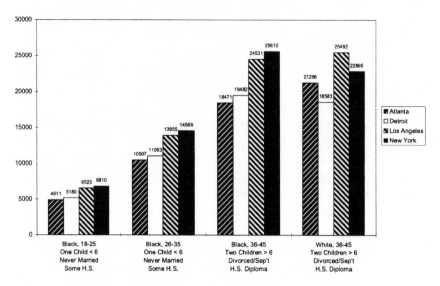

Figure 21.1 Predicted Annual Earnings for Selected Welfare Mothers (All Are Assumed U.S.-born living in Central City with No Disabilities)

paribus, were likely to have lower expected earnings capacities than non-recipients. Regression analysis confirms this suggestion. We first considered only those single mothers who did not receive welfare but who reported earnings during 1989. We regressed the natural logarithm of their annual earnings on a set of demographic characteristics. For each model we estimated separate regressions for single mothers who were white non-Hispanic, black non-Hispanic, Hispanic, or other non-Hispanic.[16] We then used the resulting set of regression coefficients to estimate how much each welfare recipient would have earned if she earned what observationally identical working single mothers earned.

Next, we estimated a second model in which the dependent variable was the probability that the single mother earned less than the poverty line for a family of three persons ($9,885 in 1989). The sample for this model included all 21,756 single mothers who did not report any welfare income—2,696 who reported no earnings and 19,060 who reported earnings in 1989. Thus, this model reflects both the probability that a single mother worked as well as her annual earnings. We then used the second set of regression coefficients to estimate for each welfare recipient the predicted probability that she could earn more than the poverty line for a family of three.

Examples of our estimates for welfare recipients with specific demographic characteristics are presented in Figures 21.1 and 21.2, for mean annual

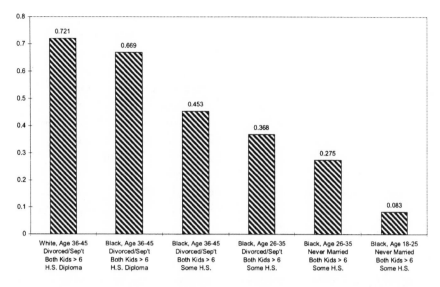

Figure 21.2 Probability of Earning More than the Poverty Line for a Family of Three (Selected Single-Mother Families with Two Children) in Central City Detroit

earnings and the probability of earning more than the poverty line, respectively. These estimates probably *overstate* the potential earnings of recipients because they might, for unobservable reasons, have worked fewer hours or have earned a lower hourly wage than observationally identical working single mothers. For example, consider two never-married single mothers with two children, neither of whom is a high school graduate. If one worked because she was more motivated or more skilled than the other who received welfare, then our estimates, which do not account for motivational or skill differences other than years of completed schooling, will be too high.

Nonetheless, our results, even if biased upward, suggest that former welfare recipients will have great difficulty in the labor market. Whereas the average earnings for working single women were $18,215 in 1989, our model predicts that the average recipient could have earned only about $13,000. Even more important, as Figure 21.1 shows, there is a wide variation in predicted earnings, depending on the characteristics of the welfare mother. The graph presents predicted earnings for native-born welfare mothers with no disabilities who resided in the central cities of Atlanta, Detroit, Los Angeles, and New York. The lowest earners, shown in the leftmost part of the graph (with predicted earnings below $7,000) were black, young, never married women who had not completed high school. As we proceed to the right, predicted earnings were higher for women between the ages of 26 and 35 than they were for those between the ages of 18 and 25, and higher for high school graduates than for high school dropouts. Race differences were smaller—in Atlanta and Los Angeles, white women had higher predicted earnings, but in Detroit and New York they had lower predicted earnings.

The second regression predicts that only 41.5 percent of welfare mothers could have earned more than the poverty line for a family of three in 1989, compared to 64.3 percent of the nonrecipient single mothers who earned that much. Figure 21.2 shows wide variation in the probability that a native-born, nondisabled welfare mother living with two children in the central city of Detroit would earn more than $9,885 as we varied her race, education, age, and marital status. For example, at the left of the graph, 72.1 percent of divorced or separated white women between the ages of 36 and 45 who were high school graduates with two children over the age of 6 are predicted to earn more than the poverty line. Each of the subsequent bars varies one characteristic, yielding a race effect of 5.2 percentage points, a high school diploma effect of 21.6 points, a "middle age" effect of 8.5 points, a marital status effect of 9.3 points, and a "young age" effect of 20.2 points. Thus, only 8 percent of black, never married mothers who were between the ages of 18 and 25 and lacked a high school diploma are predicted to have been able to earn enough to avoid poverty.

This evidence suggests that it is simply not the case that most former welfare recipients can obtain stable employment and work enough during the year to lift them and their children out of poverty.[17] Fear of destitution is a powerful incentive to survive; it will not, however, guarantee that an unskilled worker who actively seeks work will be able to earn enough to support her family. Changes in welfare mothers' economic incentives to search for work can increase the extent of labor force participation, but they are unlikely to make a large difference in their actual earnings unless they are accompanied by expanded opportunities.[18]

Consequently, PRWORA cannot be understood as a natural policy response to empirical data. In the absence of a fundamental shift in our society's norms and values, the data would have framed the policy debates differently. Two policy options would have been at the center of debate. Should we have continued to support some families *outside* the paid workforce? Or should we have set out to create a work-based safety net for those families?

Yet PRWORA debates were ultimately not framed in that manner. Moreover, President Clinton ultimately signed a bill that eliminated cash support for families without creating a work-based safety net in its place. PRWORA marked a shift in the nation's expression of certain fundamental values through its welfare state; in the next two sections, we attempt to understand and criticize the basis for that shift.

Two Fundamental Values: Work and Opportunity

As we noted at the beginning of this chapter, President Clinton's Welfare Reform Task Force cast its work in terms of fundamental societal values: the core values of "work, family, responsibility, and opportunity." Indeed, welfare reform debates have always been, at least implicitly, about such fundamental societal values. Ever since AFDC was created by the Social Security Act of 1935, each generation has changed the program to reestablish its understanding of what is required to respect those values while providing cash assistance for the "truly needy." Each round of statutory amendments has recalibrated the balance among (i) the interests of needy single parents, (ii) the interests of needy children, and (iii) the interests of the larger society in expressing its commitment to all four values. To be sure, it is not easy to forge a legislative consensus (much less a societal consensus) on how the balance should be recalibrated.

It is useful to divide the four enumerated values into two distinct axes: a family-responsibility axis and a work-opportunity axis. In this section, we shall concentrate our attention on the pull between the value of individual work and the value of having our society collectively offer opportunity to its citizens. To what extent should one precede the other? To what extent should our expectations that individuals will work to support themselves be dependent upon how well we have fulfilled a prior collective obligation to provide opportunities for work? Our aim here is to illuminate how the adoption of PRWORA reflected a significant change in the way such questions are resolved.

Perhaps the most widely discussed aspect of PRWORA was its time limit — its establishment of a cumulative lifetime maximum of sixty months in which a single parent may receive federal funds (through a state program) in return for caring for her own child. No provision of PRWORA more starkly indicates the legislative understanding of what it means for a mother to "hold up her end of the bargain" through "work." PRWORA time limit accelerates an important trend in welfare legislation: the change since 1935 in the implicit understanding of what it means for a single mother to "work."

In AFDC's early years, the implicit concept of work was linked to other markers of social status. A stylized interpretation of conditions during the 1930s and 1940s might run as follows: White widows "worked" vicariously through their late husbands and directly by maintaining a "suitable home" for their children. Over time, more white divorcees and unwed mothers claimed welfare benefits; they "worked" by satisfying the "suitable home" standard and, if the caseworker thought they were capable, by accepting "appropriate" work for wages. During that same time period, and especially in the south, black single mothers were expected to do whatever house or field work was demanded by local employers. In all cases, the mother, through her "appropriate behavior," justified public support for the fatherless child.

During the late 1960s, the federal AFDC statute began to embody a different notion of the kind of work required from single mothers in return for welfare. In response to growing public dissatisfaction over the rising welfare caseload (one which coincided with a rapid increase in married white women's participation in the paid labor force), Congress amended the statute to provide greater economic incentives for maternal labor force participation and to provide that some women (although, admittedly, few at first) would be required to participate in work training programs.

After 1967, the statutory expectation for workforce participation by single mothers steadily expanded. Traditionally, mothers of very young children were exempted. But over the next three decades the definition of a "very young" child fell from "under six" to "under three" (and at state option to "under one"). Under PRWORA, states are free to eliminate the "very young child" exception completely and some have chosen to shrink the exception to cover only the first thirteen weeks of a child's life. Thus, any lingering uncertainty about what is in the developmental interest of young children has all but disappeared as a policy consideration.[19]

The Family Support Act (FSA) of 1988 emphasized training, education, and work for AFDC recipients through the JOBS program. JOBS became a central feature of the FSA in part because of the favorable evaluations of many state "workfare" demonstration programs that were undertaken in response to the Reagan Administration's emphasis on work. In the early 1980s, many liberals opposed workfare programs and considered them to be punitive. When these programs were evaluated by the Manpower Demonstration Research Corporation, however, many were judged modestly successful in reducing welfare receipts and increasing earnings.[20] More important for liberals was the finding that many participants found the programs to be fair and helpful in connecting them to the workforce. The evaluation results were promising enough so that by the late 1980s, moving welfare recipients into employment had become a bipartisan "new consensus."

Liberals and conservatives still disagreed on other goals for welfare-to-work programs. Liberals thought welfare reform should offer opportunities for a welfare mother to receive training and work experience which would raise her family's living standard through increased work and higher wages. Conservatives emphasized work requirements, obligations owed by a welfare mother in exchange for the government's support, even if her family's income did not increase.

By the time of the most recent round of welfare debates, it seemed clear that the most liberal form of the argument had lost out in the popular mind. There was not majority support for the view that a mother should not have to move from welfare to paid employment unless she could show a net improvement in her economic situation. The contested terrain shifted rightward.

After 1988, it had become clear that a welfare mother could no longer simply count her labors on behalf of her own child as "work." And it had become clear that she could no longer expect that paid employment would enhance her economic position relative to that of a welfare recipient. The central issue was now whether her obligation to obtain paid work was in any way *dependent on* the availability of opportunity. Who has primary responsibility for identifying opportunities for paid employment? Is "responsibility" in this context mutual, or does it exist as a prior obligation of the mother?

David Ellwood, in his influential book *Poor Support: Poverty and the American Family* (1988), offered one set of answers. He proposed converting welfare into an explicitly transitional system that would provide cash support for a limited period of time. At the end of the transitional period, a recipient would be expected to earn wages in a regular job or a work opportunity provided by the government. Low wages would be supplemented by expanded tax credits, access to subsidized childcare and health insurance, and guaranteed child support. Ellwood's proposal captured the attention of candidate Clinton. It became the basis for Clinton's campaign promise to "end welfare as we know it." And once elected, Clinton appointed Ellwood to be one of the cochairs of his Welfare Reform Task Force.

From early on in the discussions that led to the enactment of PRWORA, it was clear that the notion of a time limit on receipt of welfare benefits held powerful political appeal. One can capture some of that appeal through an analogy to the world of insurance. The proposition that welfare should not be a way of life implies that the premium a family pays to society by rearing its own children is a limited one, one that will only allow it to collect a limited insurance benefit should it be struck by the calamity of poverty. Proposals to time-limit AFDC were thus proposals to make AFDC more like time-limited unemployment insurance, and less like Social Security, whose benefits continue indefinitely.

Yet such a metaphor cannot do all the work necessary to justify the draconian form of time limits adopted under PRWORA.[21] For let us assume that some welfare recipients are physically able and have marketable skills but are simply unwilling to take available low-paying jobs.[22] And let us also assume that some other welfare recipients who currently supplement their benefits (in violation of welfare's rules) by working off the books in low-wage jobs will simply move to more visible but higher paying employment.[23] The problem is that there will still remain substantial numbers of mothers who, for physical health, mental health, or other reasons, will not be able to find steady employment.[24]

PRWORA allows states to exempt as much as 20 percent of their caseloads from the strict sixty-month time limit. Unfortunately, the data we reviewed in the previous section indicate that many women who were on the pre-1996 welfare caseload were likely to have difficulty finding steady work without governmental intervention to expand job opportunities.

PRWORA reveals no sense of mutual responsibility or obligation on the government to help those "who want to help themselves." The time limit becomes a high wire with no safety net. PRWORA offers no opportunity to work-for-welfare, much less a job, at the end of sixty months, even though the evidence suggests that the employment prospects for many welfare recipients are not good. PRWORA offers no promise of health insurance for poor families who work, even though many hold jobs that do not offer health benefits. PRWORA evinces no willingness to spend new funds, even though the evidence suggests they are required to reduce economic hardship.

The message of the new statute is, quite simply, that in the aftermath of welfare reform, the American welfare state no longer recognizes any collective obligation to provide opportunities for paid employment to single mothers.[25] While the federal government may provide up to sixty months of cash "insurance" support, once the insurance money runs out the welfare recipient is on her own unless her state government intervenes with its own funds.[26]

Two Other Fundamental Values: Family and Responsibility

The other axis of values that has long been central to welfare reform debates links the value of parental responsibility to the value of two-parent families. Can welfare protect children from some of the economic costs of divorce without encouraging divorce? Can welfare protect children from some of the economic costs of being born out of wedlock without encouraging nonmarital births?

As we noted earlier, such questions were, until recently, an important but secondary issue in welfare policy discussions. During the 1980s and early 1990s, however, a broad political consensus emerged in which the dominant issue was work. The central reform goal was to maintain a social safety net while fighting the alienation of welfare recipients from the paid workforce.

In recent years, however, that changed, and family came to rival work as the central welfare question. After the November 1994 Republican Congressional victory, many conservative politicians rejected the work consensus and sought to shift the focus of debate to out-of-wedlock childbirth. In 1995, the first welfare reform bill passed by the House of Representatives would have denied AFDC benefits to children born out of wedlock. And in PRWORA, that possibility remains a state option under the general transformation of AFDC into a block grant to states.

Although there is disagreement concerning how welfare reform can support families, there is no disagreement that rapid changes in family structure have occurred. The number of young children who live with only one parent has skyrocketed since the early-1950s. In 1960, only 9 percent of children under 18 lived with one parent, and less than 0.5 percent lived with a single parent who had never married. In 1992, 27 percent of children under 18 lived with one parent, and 9 percent lived with a single parent who had never married.[27]

Because AFDC assisted low-income children in one-parent families, the demographics of recipient families have changed in tandem with the changes in society as a whole. In 1935, the typical AFDC family was headed by a widow; in the 1950s, by a divorced or separated mother. Since the mid-1980s, however, most AFDC-recipient children have lived with a never-married parent.[28]

Just as David Ellwood's book provided the intellectual rationale for time-limiting cash welfare benefits, Charles Murray's writings provided the rationale for denying benefits to unwed mothers. In 1993, Murray published a *Wall Street Journal* editorial page column under the headline, "The Coming White Underclass."[29] The column has proven to have a surprising amount of political influence; as Mickey Kaus has pointed out, after Murray's column appeared many Republicans abandoned the view that "work" was the primary welfare problem and adopted the view that "illegitimacy" was.[30]

In "The Coming White Underclass," Murray made effective use of the polemical style that he had deployed in *Losing Ground* a decade earlier and has used subsequently in *The Bell Curve*.[31] He constructed an argument with eight structural characteristics:

1. He presented a troublesome social fact. In *Losing Ground,* the troublesome fact was the increasing rate of pre-transfer poverty. In "White Underclass," it was the increasing rate of out-of-wedlock childbearing.
2. He presented the troublesome social fact in a variety of ways, using quantitative measures from several different data sets.

3. He speculated in apocalyptic terms about the future implications of the troublesome social fact.

4. He hinted darkly that the troublesome social fact had been concealed from the average American. While "headlines" reported one thing, Murray suggested that the "real news" had been suppressed.

5. He expressed his vision of society in quotable aphorisms. "In the calculus of illegitimacy, the constants are that boys like to sleep with girls and that girls think babies are endearing. . . . Bringing a child into the world when one is not emotionally or financially prepared to be a parent is wrong. The child deserves society's support. The parent does not."

6. He offered a simple account of how the troublesome social fact could (in theory) have resulted from the rational responses of self-interested individuals to government social welfare programs.

7. He insisted that the troublesome social fact would disappear if government disappeared (in this case, by eliminating many social welfare programs and denying an unwed mother any right to collect child support from the child's father). His proposal "does not require social engineering. Rather, it requires that the state stop interfering with the natural forces that have done the job quite effectively for millennia."

8. Finally, he offered assurances that the costs of his recommendation would be minimal because the world of private, voluntary exchange (families and charities) would be an effective substitute for the public safety net. "How does a poor young mother survive without government support? The same way she has since time immemorial."

Even after the enactment of PRWORA, it remains important to grapple with Murray's argument. Because even though AFDC has been abolished at the federal level, each state must now decide which families to help with the federal block grant funds. And the import of Murray's argument is that each state should decide to deny any assistance to young mothers who bear children out of wedlock.

An important part of what makes Murray's polemic effective is the clever way it baits academics. For the structural characteristics that we numbered (3), (4), and (5) in the list above seem calculated to goad professorial critics into making analytically sound, but politically unpersuasive, criticisms.

Consider an example. In Murray's argument, a key premise is that having a child out of wedlock is detrimental to both mother and child—a premise that would meet little resistance with the general public and that would seem to be supported by data showing a correlation between nonmarital births and unfavorable measured outcomes. To an academic reader of Murray, however, the claim evokes two responses. First, observed correlations between out-of-wedlock childbearing and, say, poverty might be "spurious." Nonmarital births might not *cause* poverty. Rather, nonmarital births could be the *consequence* when young people grow up in impoverished surroundings and see little potential for escaping their conditions. Alternatively, both nonmarital births and poverty might be caused by some other pernicious social force. Second, even a supposedly causal connection could be "contingent." In other words, even if out-of-wedlock childbearing is harmful to children under current conditions, it might not be so harmful if social programs or educational or economic opportunities were changed.

As a theoretical matter, these responses to Murray are completely sound. Social science methods are too limited to provide uncontrovertible proof of social causation. And social phenomena are virtually all contingent. Our point, however, is that, while such responses might expose *theoretical* weaknesses in Murray's argument, they do not present counterevidence to demonstrate that the relationship between out-of-wedlock births and poverty is in fact spurious. Nor do they demonstrate that American society could realistically be transformed to make the phenomenon benign. For policymakers, the knowledge that a social fact might not be *inevitably* troublesome is worth very little, especially if Murray's "troublesome" thesis (if not the "apocalypse" thesis) resonates with most people's intuitions about how the world works and is likely to continue to work.

It would be unfortunate if academic criticism of Murray's argument got bogged down in the logical failings of the way he used characteristics (3), (4), and (5). The danger is that the serious flaws reflected in characteristics (6), (7), and (8) of Murray's argument would remain unexposed. Accordingly, for purposes of discussion, let us stipulate that out-of-wedlock childbearing is a troublesome social phenomenon and that its recent rise is a troublesome social fact. Let us even stipulate that it might have been appropriate for the federal government to consider replacing the programs of the War on Poverty era with Murray's War on Illegitimacy. The problem is that Murray has not even remotely begun to make the case for the idea that the first step in his war should be to deny unwed mothers access to the social safety net.

Murray suggests, first, that the rise in nonmarital childbearing was caused by the growth of the welfare state; second, that eliminating the welfare state would reverse the trend; and third, that the side effects of eliminating the welfare state would be tolerable. These three propositions are independent. Even if the first were true, it would not necessarily imply the second; and the second would not necessarily imply the third.

Unlike his quasi-empirical discussion of the fact and consequences of nonmarital childbearing, Murray's discussion of the causes of the rise in nonmarital birth is purely theoretical. He attributes it to a change in the "calculus" of young boys and girls. He believes that the rise in nonmarital births has followed from a drop in their "costs." And he believes that eliminating welfare would, directly and indirectly, raise those costs enough to lead young girls (and maybe even young boys) to act differently.

Granting for the moment Murray's concern about the costs of nonmarital childbearing, is he right to target the welfare system as its cause? He is surely right that AFDC treated one-parent families better than two-parent families. Whereas a one-parent family needed only be poor to be eligible, two-parent families could receive AFDC benefits only if (a) one parent was incapacitated or (b) the primary earner had been recently employed and had become unemployed. Thus, it is not surprising that in 1991 only about 11 percent of AFDC children qualified for the program while living with both parents. Indeed, the fact that AFDC treated single-parent families better than two-parent families has been a concern of policymakers since at least the early 1960s.[32]

As a matter of pure theory, Murray could well have been right that the structure of AFDC eligibility brought about the rise in out-of-wedlock births. But it is just as easy to construct a story on the theoretical plane about why Murray's account of the rise in nonmarital childbearing is completely wrong. The key point, ignored by Murray in "White Underclass," is that merely knowing the *direction* of an economic incentive does not tell us anything about how big an *effect* the incentive actually has. When it comes to decisions to have sex, to bear a child, and to raise a child, a host of other factors can easily "dominate" or dwarf the effects of AFDC's benefit structure.[33]

One need not rely on theoretical speculation, however, because social scientists have attempted to measure the effects of welfare's incentives on family structure. In a comprehensive review of the literature, Robert Moffitt considered the time-series data.[34] He concluded, "the evidence does not support the hypothesis that the welfare system has been responsible for the time-series growth in female headship and illegitimacy." He then considered the econometric analyses of the effects of variations in the level of welfare benefits on the likelihood that a child lives with two parents.[35] Moffitt concluded that, while some of the most recent studies had begun to show some evidence of a detectable effect on rates of female headship, the magnitude of the effect was small. "The failure to find strong benefit effects is the most notable characteristic of this literature [on the relationship between welfare and female headship]." Summarizing the studies that looked specifically at the relationship between welfare benefits and nonmarital childbearing, Moffitt concluded that there was "mixed evidence" of any effect at all.[36]

In addition to eliminating welfare, Murray also proposed to reduce young men's and women's interest in bearing children out-of-wedlock by denying unwed fathers any legal right to have a relationship with their children, and by eliminating any obligation of unwed fathers to support their children. We have already challenged Murray's implicit assumptions about how such changes would affect young men's and women's perceptions of their own self-interest. Even more important, children who were born out-of-wedlock would find themselves, if his proposal were adopted, with no claims for financial support from *either* the father who was one cause of their predicament *or* the state that insulated him from responsibility.

In contrast, for the past twenty years Congress has steadily expanded the federal role in child support enforcement. A domain that was almost the exclusive province of state law as recently as 1974 is today subject to a complex and pervasive umbrella of federal regulation. The system is designed to enforce financial responsibility, not only on the part of fathers who never marry, but also on the part of fathers who divorce. Under federal law, even after the passage of PRWORA, each state is required to entrust its child support operations to a single agency. It must demand the Social Security numbers of both parents as a condition of issuing a birth certificate (unless it finds good cause for not doing so). It is given economic incentives to improve the technology used to establish paternity, and to increase the percentage of cases in which paternity is established (except in cases where doing so would be contrary to the best interests of the child).[37]

Having established paternity, states are also required by federal law to establish uniform presumptive guidelines for child support awards. In the case of AFDC recipient children, the state had a financial incentive to obtain support orders. Finally, the enforcement techniques for collecting child support, once it has been awarded, have been strengthened—states must maintain parent-locator services; they must cooperate with one another; they must utilize federal parent-locator services and even the federal courts, if necessary. Where necessary, states must use other enforcement mechanisms, including measures to withhold child support from fathers' tax refunds and unemployment compensation checks, and to impose liens on fathers' property. Since the beginning of 1994, states have been required to implement immediate withholding from fathers' paychecks (regardless of whether the father is behind) for all new child support orders. Nonetheless, despite these efforts, billions of dollars of potential child support payments remain uncollected.

In his January 1994 State of the Union Address, President Clinton suggested that he would press ahead even further. He said that we should "say to absent parents who aren't paying their child support, if you're not providing for your children, we'll garnish your wages, suspend your license, track you across state lines, and if necessary, make some of you work off what you owe. People who bring children into this world cannot and must not walk away from them." We have no way of knowing to what extent such measures would reduce the frequency of out-of-wedlock births, but they would have symbolic value. In addition, a prominent researcher has concluded that such reforms can reduce welfare dependency and poverty by increasing the amount of child support collected.[38]

We are not challenging Murray's concern about the increasing nonmarital birth rate. Rather, we reject his suggestion that denying all benefits to unmarried mothers and absolving unwed fathers of any child support responsibilities are the best ways to resolve this problem. Indeed, given the research data, we would conclude that any beneficial effects resulting from the small decline in nonmarital births that might occur would be greatly outweighed by the increased hardships that would have to be endured by the children who would still be born out of wedlock.

Nor do we reject Murray's assumption that young women, sometimes teenagers, are making rational decisions about whether to become single parents. Assume for the sake of simplicity that a young woman chooses between two options: (i) having a baby alone, and (ii) waiting until she has married. Assume also that there is a social concern that too many teens are now choosing option (i). Murray believes that if all welfare benefits and access to child support were eliminated, option (i) would suddenly become substantially less attractive than option (ii). He is almost certainly wrong to think that the effects would be so dramatic that the "War on Illegitimacy" would suddenly be won. But that should not prevent us from considering other policy interventions that could make option (ii) more attractive than option (i). Indeed, there is some evidence, for example, that, holding other characteristics constant, women are less likely to have a child before they graduate from high school if they attach a higher economic value to the diploma.

Anyone seriously concerned about out-of-wedlock births should carefully consider two possibilities: (1) that narrow, focused changes in the benefit structure might reduce the relative benefits (or increase the relative costs) of deferring childbearing, without significant attendant social harms; and (2), that other government interventions might raise the perceived "benefits" of deferring childbearing in ways that would influence behavior. For example, the government might subsidize higher education for any high school graduate who had not borne or fathered a child out of wedlock, or provide a guaranteed job, or do more to ensure that any "opportunity" provided for single mothers trying to get off welfare will be equally available to young women who avoided welfare by not having a child.

In sum, the statistical evidence fails to support Murray's strong historical claims that the current "crisis of illegitimacy" resulted from the structure of our welfare programs. It offers even less reason to believe Murray's suggestion that we could dramatically reduce out-of-wedlock births by denying unwed mothers access to public support.

Recalibrating Our Values

The package of normative and empirical assumptions that drove the Personal Responsibility and Work Opportunity Reconciliation Act is remarkable. If one were to put the proposal in its most favorable light, one would say that it reveals an astonishing degree of faith in the power of "shock therapy." Since the empirical evidence contradicts the view that welfare mothers could all find steady work if only they tried harder, supporters of PRWORA might believe that the prospect of starvation offers an unprecedented spur to entrepreneurial innovation, or at least to abstinence, abortion, or marriage.

One could also construct a somewhat darker rationale for PRWORA. One could say that it reflects a sense of deep despair and desperation about the future of America's poor children. Supporters of PRWORA might believe that children born out of wedlock pose such a grave threat to American society that we must take big chances, to make dramatic use of the symbolic power of government in an effort to change the behavior of individuals. They might even believe we should not invest too much energy in worrying about whether such dramatic moves injure some truly blameless mothers and children along the way.

A third rationale for PRWORA is simpler, and even more disturbing. The new law included a broad range of proposals for changes in the American welfare state. In addition to the AFDC repeal, it denied government benefits and services to legal resident aliens, cut back on SSI for some disabled children, and restricted Food Stamps for unemployed childless adults. It is surely possible that PRWORA reflects nothing more complicated than the narrow self-interest of a group that does not identify with other people who collect means-tested benefits.

Whatever the actual personal motivations of the proponents of PRWORA, we are unable to defend it by reference to any set of normative and empirical assumptions that we would find palatable. It would significantly increase hardship and absolve government of numerous responsibilities that it now attempts to fulfill. We have certainly ended welfare as we have known it. But, as we discuss in the next section, we missed an opportunity to do a much better job — one that would have ended welfare without punishing the poor.

The Reform That Might Have Been

During the 1960s and 1970s, the expert consensus was that the key to welfare reform was a "guaranteed minimum income." During the 1980s, the new consensus declared "work" to be the key. In the 1990s, two new "master keys" were pushed toward center stage: "reducing out-of-wedlock births" and, most recently, "devolution to the states."

Perhaps it is time to admit that there is no master key, no magic bullet. Welfare policy is about difficult choices and unsatisfying balances. And the devolution of responsibility to the states now serves only to shift the forum in which difficult policy choices must be made. We believe that there was room in the pre-1996 welfare system for a program of balanced reform. Changing social and economic conditions made it plausible to believe that America could have found a way to constructively recalibrate the balance among the values of work, family, responsibility, and opportunity. What would it have taken for Congress and the President to have a balanced reform of the welfare system that would have both ended welfare as it had been known and produced a national welfare state better attuned to the values of work, family, responsibility, and opportunity? In our opinion, such a reform package would have had the following features:

Time Limit Experiments. We are not opposed to experiments. While we would not have repealed AFDC nationwide, we would have allowed some states to experiment with a time limit on the period during which a parent could receive unconditional cash assistance.

Jobs. The best evidence suggests that the private market will fall far short of offering jobs to all welfare recipients who reach a time limit. For recipients who reached a time limit, we would have experimented with different forms of assurances of paid work — provided or subsidized by the government. Such experiments could have included the preservation of an entitlement to cash assistance beyond the time limit for any otherwise eligible parent who accepts a nominally unpaid community service (work-for-welfare) position.

Safety Net. Our reform would have maintained some entitlement to a minimal level of material support for deprived children.

Health Care. There is some evidence for the proposition that the loss of Medicaid is one of the biggest concerns of welfare recipients who enter the paid workforce. Under current law, people who leave welfare are entitled to retain transitional Medicaid benefits for a year. To make paid work more attractive than welfare, we would have been interested in further discussion of an entitlement to health care for the working poor. The 1997 Child Health Insurance Program (CHIP) moves in this direction, but it provides this insurance only for the children of the working poor.

Childcare. Any ambitious program of welfare reform rests on the premise that children's long-term interests are served by requiring their single mothers to participate in the paid workforce. That assumption about the long term is necessarily linked to some assumptions about the short term. In particular, it assumes that children who are currently being cared for by their mothers will receive adequate care once their mothers have jobs. But good childcare is expensive. Reformers must be willing to come to grips with that fact and account for it in their budgets. Otherwise, the presumed long-term benefits of reform are destined to be an unfulfilled promise. PRWORA gets good marks in this area. Federal funding for childcare was consolidated into a childcare and development block grant, and funding was increased by 25 percent over prior legislation. States have also shifted more of their own welfare spending from cash assistance to childcare in response to the post-1996 fall in caseloads.

Child Support Enforcement. Welfare reform cannot be just about women and children. No welfare reform plan can speak meaningfully about a "new commitment to enforcing parental responsibility" if it ignores fathers. Given the high rate of joblessness among the fathers of children on welfare, that probably means attention to fathers' opportunity sets as well. A comprehensive welfare reform package should include fathers paying child support within the scope of experimental public sector job programs that provide them opportunities.

Willingness to Spend Money. Any reform package that aspires to make a significant change along the dimensions of work, family, responsibility, and opportunity along the foregoing lines will be expensive. In the current economy, it will cost a lot to expand work opportunities for single parents who may lack marketable skills. But if welfare reform is to empower but not punish the poor, it must proceed on a principle of balanced responsibility: welfare recipients and prospective parents must take responsibility for themselves and their children; the government must take responsibility for providing meaningful employment opportunities for all.

To be sure, even a commitment to all these elements leaves open a great many choices about methods of implementation. Jobs could either be provided directly by government or be induced through subsidies to private employers. Health care and childcare could be provided directly by government, through subsidized purchases by employers on behalf of their employees, or through vouchers directly to the workers. A nonpoverty wage can be assured through a higher minimum wage or additional wage supplements to employees.

Any combination of approaches would have been more expensive than the current welfare system. But any combination could have been tried, as the price of ending welfare as we know it, in a manner that acknowledges the ongoing mutual responsibility that the poor and the rest of society owes one another.

Conclusion

The Great Depression taught Americans an important lesson: that individuals can be poor and unemployed through no fault of their own. The New Deal and the War on Poverty expressed a solidaristic commitment to help such individuals. Working Americans would pitch in to contribute, to help create opportunities for others, so that the country as a whole would be able to live out the values of productivity and compassion. PRWORA has rejected some of the values of the New Deal and the War on Poverty. It seems that the slow economic growth and greater widespread of economic inequality and insecurity of the early 1970s to the early 1990s merged with other social forces to undermine identification with the poor. Members of America's middle class now seem to have trouble seeing themselves, their parents, their children, or their friends standing in the shoes of the poor. If that has indeed happened, then much more than the well-being of single mothers and their children may be in jeopardy in the coming years.

Notes

This chapter draws together and expands upon arguments published by the authors in "The Road Not Taken: Ending Welfare Without Punishing the Poor," *Forum for Applied Research and Public Policy* (Winter 1997); "How Will Welfare Recipients Fare in the Labor Market?" *Challenge* (March–April 1996); and "Recalibrating the Balance: Reflections on Welfare Reform," *Law Quadrangle Notes* (Fall 1994). Edward Gramlich, Diane Lehman, Ann Lin, Theodore Marmor, Robert Moffitt, Sharon Parrott, Wendell Primus, Kristin Seefeldt, and Eugene Smolensky provided helpful comments on prior drafts.

1. Los Angeles Times, January 17, 1994.

2. Work and Responsibility Act of 1994, H.R. 4605, 103rd Cong., 2d Sess.

3. Personal Responsibility and Work Opportunity Act of 1995, H.R. 4, 104th Cong., 1st Sess.

4. Personal Responsibility and Work Opportunity Reconciliation Act of 1996, H.R. 3734, 104th Cong., 2nd Sess.

5. House Ways and Means Committee, 1994, WMCP 103–27, p. 325, Table 10–1, and pp. 401–402, Table 10–27. The 90 percent of families without a father subdivided as follows: in about 37 percent of cases a marriage was disrupted by death, divorce, or separation; in the other 53 percent the parents were never married. Ibid. at 401. In 1992, 39 percent of AFDC parents were white, 37 percent were black, 18 percent were Latino, 3 percent were Asian, 1 percent were Native Americans, and the remainder were of unknown race. Ibid. at 402.

6. Some of those who entered AFDC left after one or two years, but then returned to welfare later. As a result, about 70 percent of those who began a first welfare spell received benefits for more than two years during their lifetime. Ibid. at 440.

7. PRWORA also establishes special funds to provide supplemental grants to states with relatively low benefit levels or experiencing substantial population growth or high unemployment. But those funds give appropriations far below the level that would have been spent under AFDC in responses to changes in population, the poverty rate, and unemployment levels. PRWORA also creates "performance bonuses" for states that experience declines in the proportion of out-of-wedlock births without attendant increases in abortions.

8. PRWORA was implemented during a robust economic expansion. As a result, states did not cut back cash benefits in the period from 1996 to 2000. States did reduce the amount of their own funds devoted to cash assistance as caseloads fell dramatically after 1996. L. Jerome Gallagher, Megan Gallagher, Kevin Perese, Susan Schreiber, and Keith Watson, "One Year after Federal Welfare Reform: A Description of State Temporary Assistance for Needy Families (TANF) Decisions as of October 1997," published May 1, 1998, http://www.urban.org/url.cfm?ID=307472.

9. Howard Chernick and Andrew Reschovsky ("State Responses to Block Grants: Will the Social Safety Net Survive?" *Focus* [Madison, Wisc.: Institute for Research on Poverty], 18, pp. 25–29), drawing on econometric evidence, estimate that California will reduce its own spending dramatically under a block grant and that total federal and state welfare spending in 2002 would be 28 to 38 percent lower than 1994 spending (inflation adjusted). See also Howard Chernick and Therese J. McGuire, "The States, Welfare Reform, and the Business Cycle," pp. 275–303 in Sheldon H. Danziger, ed., *Economic Conditions and Welfare Reform* (Kalamazoo, Mich.: Upjohn Institute for Employment Research, 1999).

10. Individuals may not be sanctioned for failure to meet work requirements if their failure is based on the unavailability of childcare for a child under age 6.

11. It should be noted that per capita expenditures on Medicaid and subsidized housing increased during this period. That growth does not appear to reflect increased spending per recipient, only expansion of the class of eligible recipients.

12. In addition, a smaller percentage of poor children received welfare benefits in the 1980s and 1990s than in the 1970s. The ratio of children receiving AFDC benefits to the total number of poor children rose from about 20 percent in 1965 to about 80 percent in 1973 as a result of the program expansions set in motion by the War on Poverty and Great Society legislation. This ratio fell to about 50 percent in 1982 as the Reagan budgetary retrenchment went into effect, before rising to about 60 percent in 1991. Ways and Means Committee Proceedings 103–18, p. 688, Table 26.

13. See Sheldon Danziger and Peter Gottschalk, eds., *Uneven Tides: Inequality in America Rising* (New York: Russell Sage Foundation, 1993), and Sheldon Danziger and Peter Gottschalk, *America Unequal* (Cambridge, Mass.: Harvard University Press, 1995). The economy did boom in the late 1990s, and income inequality stopped rising. However, income inequality remains very high and the real wages of workers remain below the levels of the 1970s. See Sheldon Danziger and Deborah Reed, "The Era of Inequality Continues," *Brookings Review* 17, no. 4 (Fall 1999), pp. 14–17.

14. In 1991, the poverty line for a family of four was $13,924. College graduates do indeed fare much better than high school graduates. In 1991, 30 percent of male and 57 percent of female high school graduates earned less than $13,924.

15. Each of these seventy-seven metropolitan areas had a sample of at least one hundred single mothers in the 1 percent Census data file.

16. The regressions included these variables: whether or not the single mother resided in the central city; a dummy variable for her specific standard metropolitan statistical area; two dummy variables indicating her age cohort (18–25 or 26–35, with 36–45 the omitted category); whether or not she was born outside of the United States to noncitizen parents; four educational dummies (0–8 years of schooling, the omitted category; 9–11; 12; 13–15; and 16 or more years of schooling); two marital status dummies (never-married is the omitted category; divorced or separated; widowed); three number-of-children variables (one child is the omitted category; dummies for two, three, and four or more children); whether or not she had a child under the age of 6); and three disability variables (no disability is the omitted category; disability had limited previous work; disability limited current work effort; disability did not limit work but limited ability to care for self).

17. See also Judith M. Gueron and Edward Pauly, *From Welfare to Work* (New York: Russell Sage Foundation, 1991), documenting the difficulty that workfare program participants have in maintaining stable employment after the programs' end.

18. In the aftermath of PRWORA, caseloads have declined dramatically and the percentage of current and former welfare recipients who are employed has increased substantially. However, most of them remain poor. See Sheldon Danziger, "Approaching the Limit: Early National Lessons from Welfare Reform," in B. Weber, G. Duncan, and L. Whitener, eds., *Rural Dimensions of Welfare Reform* (Kalamazoo, Mich.: Upjohn Institute for Employment Research, 2002), 25–49.

19. The empirical literature on this issue is inconclusive. There is no reason to be confident that overall the effects on children will be distinctly positive or negative if mothers are forced to accept available work opportunities. We are aware of no studies that consider the effects of different forms of childcare (maternal or paid) on the children of welfare recipients. One can imagine that the two-year-old child of a disadvantaged welfare recipient might benefit from the stimulation of a daycare center; one could as easily imagine that she might suffer from disruption in her intimate relationships. Ultimately, the effects on children will reflect both (a) the quality of the AFDC recipient child's new daycare environment and (b) the extent to which increased experience in the paid workforce provides the mother with a transition to a higher standard of living and with a set of life opportunities that make her a more successful parent.

20. See Gueron and Pauly, *From Welfare to Work*.

21. As mentioned above, programs funded by the federal block grant and the state maintenance-of-effort funds may not provide more than a cumulative lifetime total of sixty months of cash assistance to any welfare recipient, no matter how willing she might be to work for her benefits.

22. For a discussion which seems to assume that such women dominate the welfare caseload, see Lawrence Mead, *The New Politics of Poverty* (New York: Basic Books, 1992). For an exploration of the reasons why some women might refuse work, and might even describe themselves as "too lazy" to work, see Lucie White, "No Exit: Rethinking 'Welfare Dependency' from a Different Ground," 81 *Georgetown Law Journal* 1961, June 1993.

23. Christopher Jencks and Kathryn Edin, "The Real Welfare Problem," *American Prospect,* Winter 1990.

24. See Sandra Danziger et al., "Barriers to the Employment of Welfare Recipients," February 2000, http://www.fordschool.umich.edu/poverty/pdf/wesappam.pdf.

25. Cf. Theodore Marmor, Jerry Mashaw, and Philip Harvey, *America's Misunderstood Welfare State* (New York: Basic, 1990) (arguing that America has an "insurance-opportunity" state); Jeffrey Lehman, "To Conceptualize, To Criticize, To Describe, To Improve: Understanding America's Welfare State," 101 *Yale Law Journal* 685–727 (December 1991).

26. Several states have announced that they will not automatically terminate recipients at sixty months, but will use their own funds to continue to provide cash assistance or vouchers. Gallagher et al., "One Year After Federal Welfare Reform."

27. House Ways and Means Committee, 1994, pp. 1112–1113.

28. House Ways and Means Committee, 1994, p. 401.

29. *Wall Street Journal,* October 23, 1993; see also Charles Murray, "Keep It in the Family," *Sunday Times (London),* November 14, 1993.

30. "Bastards: The Right Abandons Workfare," *New Republic,* February 21, 1994, pp. 17–19.

31. Charles Murray, *Losing Ground: American Social Policy, 1950–1980* (New York: Basic Books, 1984); Richard J. Herrnstein and Charles Murray, *The Bell Curve: Intelligence and Class Structure in American Life* (New York: Free Press, 1994).

32. One brief digression on terminology. This differential treatment was, for many years, described as an "incentive" to not marry, to have a baby, or to separate. Recently, writers like Murray speak less in terms of creating a positive incentive and more in terms of reducing a "natural" disincentive. This is sometimes expressed with metaphors such as "support systems" or "umbilical cords." The distinction is not purely semantic. There is some support in cognitive theory for the proposition that people do not think about economic incentives and economic disincentives equivalently. They often act as if they fear a punishment or loss more than they welcome a reward or gain. They are more likely to insure against an unlikely loss than they are to invest in a venture with the same probabilities and payoffs (see Daniel Kahneman and Amos Tversky, "Prospect Theory: An Analysis of Decision Under Risk," *Econometrica,* 1979). But as important as these differences may be, they do not alter the particular empirical prediction that is at stake—that the existence of AFDC led to more one-parent families and fewer two-parent families than there would have been in its absence.

33. If we offered an individual a dollar to jump off a building, the direction of the economic incentive would be clear, but we would not expect to see much of an effect in the real world. Likewise, we know that an increase in the tax on cigarettes will reduce the incentive to smoke, but it has not been shown that taxation is the most effective way to reduce smoking. For a review of the sociological, psychological, and economic factors affecting out-of-wedlock childbearing, see U.S. Department of Health and Human Services, *Report to Congress on Out-of-Wedlock Childbearing,* DHHS Pub. No. (PHS) 95–127.

34. Robert Moffitt, "Incentive Effects of the U.S. Welfare System: A Review," *Journal of Economic Literature,* 1992.

35. Much of that literature is based on interstate variations in the level of benefits. In 1992 the combined value of AFDC and Food Stamps for a family of three ranged from $456 to $798 in the contiguous forty-eight states.

36. After publishing "White Underclass," Murray finally confronted the data in "Does Welfare Bring More Babies?" *Public Interest* (Spring 1994). There, Murray suggests that welfare may have caused nonmarital births to increase but then, when welfare benefits fell, the rate of nonmarital births failed to decline because illegitimacy "took on a life of its own." Murray does not attempt to reconcile the idea that illegitimacy has taken on a life of its own with his theory that eliminating welfare benefits would reduce the rate of nonmarital births in the 1990s.

37. At present, paternity is established for only about one in three out-of-wedlock births.

38. Irwin Garfinkel, *Assuring Child Support: An Extension of Social Security* (New York: Russell Sage Foundation, 1992).

Fighting Poverty
Lessons from Recent U.S. History

REBECCA M. BLANK

In his 1964 State of the Union address, his first after assuming the presidency, Lyndon Johnson proclaimed: "This administration today, here and now, declares unconditional war on poverty in America." The result of Johnson's speech was a series of major legislative changes, whose success (or failure) is still hotly debated.

By the mid-1990s, the focus of policy concern had shifted from fighting poverty to reducing welfare dependence. One might argue, however, that the 1990s, rather than the 1960s, were truly the decade in which the United States fought a war on poverty. The 1990s were a time of substantial legislative change in programs designed to assist low-income families. At the same time, a remarkable change also occurred in the behavior of low-income families, with plummeting use of public assistance and substantial increases in labor market involvement. In this chapter, I document the magnitude and speed of these behavioral changes during the 1990s and then investigate the role of both the macroeconomy and policy in producing these outcomes. I end by discussing how these changes may or may not translate into improvements in long-term family well-being.

The Successes of the 1990s War on Poverty

The first and most obvious sign that something different happened in anti-poverty policy in the 1990s occurs in the data showing the number of households receiving public assistance. The dark line in Figure 22.1 shows the number of households receiving cash support, funded through the Aid to Families with Dependent Children (AFDC) program prior to 1996 and the Temporary Assistance for Needy Families (TANF) block grant after 1996. The dotted line in Figure 22.1 shows the changes in the number of households receiving food stamps over this period. The vertical line indicates the passage of the 1996 Personal Responsibility and Work Opportunity Reconciliation Act, a major welfare reform bill that produced a series of policy changes that are discussed further below. Caseloads rose rapidly in the early 1990s, but began to decline prior to the enactment of the welfare reform act, suggesting that legislation was not solely responsible for these changes.

Between January 1994 and June 1999, AFDC/TANF caseloads were cut in half, falling from 5 million to 2.5 million, while food stamp caseloads have followed a very similar trend. There are currently fewer people receiving cash support through public assistance than in any year since 1971. Strikingly, this statement is true even though the population of those most likely to be eligible for welfare—female-headed families with children—grew enormously over this period. The share of single mothers on welfare (based on administrative caseload counts divided by population numbers) rose from 38 percent in 1969 to 48 percent in 1980, but had fallen to 30 percent by 1998. These caseload changes are widespread, with every state in the country experiencing substantial caseload decline. This decline has been widely hailed by politicians as an indication that policies designed to reduce dependence on public assistance and move less-skilled adults into the labor market have been extremely effective.

The caseload information by itself provides little information on whether declines in receipt of public assistance have been matched by increased work effort. On the labor market side, however, there have indeed been remarkable increases in labor force participation. Figure 22.2 shows changes from 1979 to 1999 in the share of mothers with young children (women ages 20 to 65 with children under the age of six) participating in either the labor force or full-time schooling, which I will call the labor force participation/preparation rate. The dotted line in Figure 22.2 plots this rate among married mothers; the dashed line plots the same rate among widowed, divorced, or separated mothers; and the solid line plots the rate for never-married mothers.

Although married mothers with young children have experienced a steady

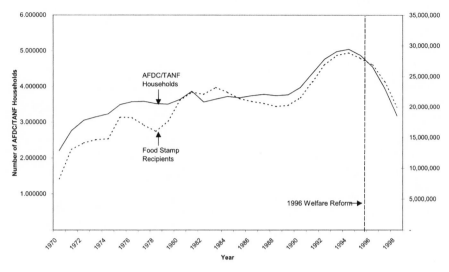

Figure 22.1 Total AFDC/TANF and Food Stamp Caseloads
Source: Agency for Children and Families, Department of Health and Human Services (www.acf.dhhs.gov/news/stats/3697.htm) and Department of Agriculture (www.fns.usda.gov/fns)

increase in their rate of labor force participation/preparation over this entire period, the rate of increase has slowed somewhat in recent years. In sharp contrast, never-married mothers and widowed, divorced, or separated mothers with young children have experienced sharp increases in their rates of participation/preparation in the 1990s, with particularly large increases occurring in the mid-1990s. Between 1989 and 1999, the rate of participation/ preparation rose by 20 percent among widowed, divorced, or separated mothers with young children, whereas it rose by 34 percent among never-married mothers. These are enormous changes within a relatively short period of time; in fact, they are comparable to the aggregate increases in female labor force participation in the 1960s and 1970s that generated so much comment.

These changes are even more striking when compared with labor force behavior by equivalent groups of women who have no children. There has been no increase in the rate of labor force participation/preparation among widowed, divorced, or separated and never-married women age 20 to 65 who do not have children. This suggests that the forces impacting mothers with young children are not the result of changes affecting the entire female labor market, but rather reflect changes unique to mothers with young children, and particularly single mothers.

The behavioral changes underlying the trends in Figures 22.1 and 22.2

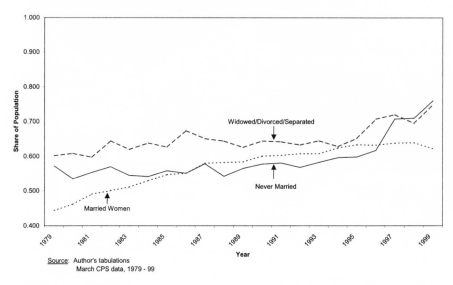

Figure 22.2 Share of Women with Children Under Age 6 Participating in Either Labor Force or Full-Time Schooling
Source: Author's tabulations, March CPS data, 1979–1999

constitute a revolution. The frequently stated goal of welfare reform efforts in the 1990s was to reduce welfare dependency and to move more women into work. This goal has been accomplished, at least in the short run, far more successfully than anyone would have predicted at the beginning of the decade.

Of course, declines in welfare and increases in work do not necessarily signal anything about poverty. It is possible that more people are working harder, but have only barely been able to replace welfare income with earnings. However, Figure 22.3 shows the steady decline in poverty rates that occurred throughout the decade. The solid line plots the poverty rate among all persons (the share of population living in a family whose income is below the official U.S. poverty line), while the dashed line plots the poverty rate among female-headed families. Poverty rates fell slowly following the economic slowdown in 1990–91, although they fell somewhat more rapidly among single mothers. By 1998, poverty was at its historical low point among single mothers. (Persons in single mother families with children under age 18 constituted 37 percent of all poor persons, and these families accounted for almost half of all poor families in 1998.) Alternative measures of poverty, which are based on disposable income and count in-kind transfers and tax payments, indicate that poverty among single mothers fell even faster than the official rate in the

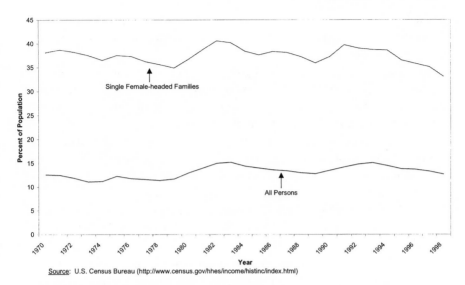

Figure 22.3 Official U.S. Poverty Rates, 1970–1998
Source: U.S. Census Bureau (www.census.gov/hhes/income/histinc/index.html)

1990s, largely because of the expansion of the Earned Income Tax Credit over the 1990s (U.S. Census Bureau, 1999).

These poverty counts are only one (relatively inadequate) way to measure changes in broader family well-being. Primus et al. (1999) note that the number of persons leaving public assistance is substantially higher than the number of people leaving poverty over the mid-1990s — that is, the fall in poverty is much more gradual than the decline in caseloads. This suggests that some group among the poor may have been made worse off by these changes, a topic I return to below.

The behavioral changes over this past decade are remarkable in both their speed and magnitude. I turn next to the causal factors behind these changes, asking what lessons we can draw for anti-poverty policy from 1990s.

Lesson 1: A Strong Macroeconomy Matters More than Anything Else

In February 2000, the current economic expansion set a record as the longest in U.S. history, lasting more than 106 months (the length of the expansion in the 1960s). Over this time period, investment growth has been strong, the federal government eliminated its annual deficits, productivity growth has been above trend, and inflation has remained low. All of these economic outcomes have benefited workers.

In the labor market, employment growth has been high, with more than 20 million new jobs created over the expansion by the end of 1999, while unemployment has been extremely low for several years. By the late 1990s, unemployment had returned to the low levels experienced in the 1960s. As I write this in early 2000, unemployment has been at or below 5 percent since April 1997 and at or below 4.5 percent since April 1998. Hispanic and black unemployment rates are at their lowest recorded levels since those numbers began to be tabulated. Female unemployment rates are lower than they have been since 1969. Even among high school dropouts — a group whose unemployment rates have long been in the double digits — unemployment in December 1999 stood at 6 percent.

Low unemployment has always disproportionately benefited less skilled workers. When employment grows, the previously unemployed, the part-time workers, the underemployed, and those out of the labor market are most able to benefit. A tight labor market also forces employers to turn to less traditional sources of labor, providing training and job opportunities to workers who might not have been considered for more skilled positions in a different economy.

These employment trends have been recently reinforced by substantial wage growth among workers of all skill levels. From the late 1970s through the early 1990s, wage inequality widened in the United States, with wages actually declining among less skilled workers at the same time as they rose among the more skilled. During the economic expansion from 1983 to 1990, less skilled workers worked more hours and their unemployment rate fell, but their wages fell at the same time, offsetting the earnings gains they would otherwise have experienced (Blank, 1993).

While there is little evidence of wage gains for less skilled workers in the early part of the 1990s expansion, wage increases among the less skilled have been quite strong since 1996 (although these gains have not been large enough to make up for the previous two decades of wage decline among this group). The Council of Economic Advisers (1999a) indicates that historically disadvantaged workers (blacks, young workers, immigrants) have shown particularly strong wage gains in the last few years. This means that both wages and employment have risen in recent years, so that the wage gains should have reinforced the employment gains, thereby providing greater income to low-income working households.

This strong economy has been important to all three of the trends documented above: declining caseloads, expanding labor force participation, and falling poverty rates. Depending on the study, between one-third and two-thirds of the caseload change in the early to mid-1990s appears due to economic factors. Wallace and Blank (1999) cite a variety of studies using state panel data which indicate that a one-point decline in unemployment produces about a 4 percent decrease in AFDC caseloads. Figlio and Ziliak (1999) estimate even larger effects. Schoeni and Blank (2000) use a similar panel data methodology and find that low unemployment rates and high employment growth rates increase work and reduce poverty rates.

My own past work on the role of the macroeconomy in reducing poverty documents changes in the relationship between unemployment and poverty. Blank and Blinder (1986) offered estimates of how lower unemployment should reduce poverty, but in Blank (1993), I noted that the expansion of the 1980s did not produce the predicted declines in poverty. I argued that the decline in unemployment over the 1980s (which should have lowered poverty) had been offset by the decline in real wages among less skilled workers (which should have raised poverty), producing a much more sluggish response of the overall poverty rate to economic expansion.

Table 22.1 updates this analysis using annual data from 1960 through 1998 to estimate the determinants of aggregate U.S. poverty rates. In column 1, U.S. poverty rates are regressed against a set of economic variables. I include a dummy variable running over the cycle of the 1980s (1980–89) and the cycle of the 1990s (1990–99), and interact this dummy variable with the unemployment rate as well. The results confirm that although the unemployment rate was significantly and positively associated with poverty in the 1960s and 1970s, its impact changed dramatically in the 1980s. The estimated effect in the 1980s actually suggests that decreases in unemployment *raised* poverty; that is, the regression indicates that a one-point decline in unemployment in the 1980s is associated with a 0.05 (0.27–0.32) rise in poverty rates.

For the 1990s, the relationship between unemployment and poverty is weaker than in the 1960s and 1970s, but stronger than in the 1980s. Particularly by the mid-1990s when wages began to rise, one might expect that the rising wages would have reinforced the decline in unemployment, leading to stronger effects of the economy on poverty. Consistent with this hypothesis, if one defines the 1990s dummy only over the expansion of the 1990s (1992–98), a stronger positive relationship between unemployment and poverty emerges (although still weaker than in the 1960s).[1]

Columns 2 and 3 investigate poverty rates among female-headed families and black families, groups that are highly likely to be receiving public assistance. Among these groups, the unemployment rate actually has a stronger

Table 22.1. The Effect of Macroeconomic Variables on Poverty Rates Among
Various Groups, 1960–1998

	All Persons	Female-Headed Families	Black Families
Poverty Rate	0.50**	0.07	0.26*
(lagged one period)	(0.10)	(0.15)	(0.15)
Unemployment	0.27**	0.24	−0.06
Rate	(0.07)	(0.19)	(0.27)
Unempl. Rate *	−0.32**	−0.25	0.17
1980s dummy variable	(0.12)	(0.31)	(0.44)
Unempl. Rate *	−0.19	0.74*	1.43**
1990s dummy variable	(0.16)	(0.43)	(0.61)
Consumer Price	−0.01	−0.24**	−0.09
Index	(0.04)	(0.10)	(0.09)
Poverty line/	0.35**	0.75**	0.71**
Mean income	(0.06)	(0.12)	(0.23)
Constant	−7.70**	8.89**	−1.07
	(1.12)	(3.38)	(6.60)
1980s dummy variable	3.39**	2.96	0.22
(1980–89 = 1)	(0.89)	(2.18)	(3.10)
1990s dummy variable	3.62**	−2.34	−7.08*
(1990–98 = 1)	(1.09)	(2.67)	(3.96)
Number of observations	39	39	32

Dependent variable equals officially reported U.S. poverty rates.
** Significant at 1 percent level; * Significant at 5 percent level.

effect in the 1990s than in any earlier decade (the combined coefficients on unemployment rates and unemployment interacted with the 1990s dummy variable are significant and more positive than is the coefficient on the unemployment rate alone). In short, Table 22.1 provides further evidence that the strong labor market helped decrease poverty in the 1990s among public assistance recipients.

While the strong economy appears to have been highly important in affecting outcomes among low-income families in the 1990s, it is difficult to measure these impacts precisely for several reasons. First, most of our economic measures reflect average economic effects (such as aggregate state unemployment rates) and do not measure the specific economic changes facing less skilled workers. Second, the strong economy has affected not only poverty but also economic policy, and it is especially hard to measure the magnitude of the effect on policy. For instance, the willingness of some states to enact their own earned income tax credits may be partially due to the flush situation of many state budgets in this economy. In addition, the strong economy and the availability of jobs has made it much easier for states to implement the program design and administrative changes required to reorganize their public welfare offices into work-oriented programs. Third, economists have a very poor understanding of how economic growth affects some of the more informal ways in which low-income families receive money. We know little about the relationship between economic growth and the underground economy. We know little about how many absent parents or boyfriends or other family members are more willing to share incomes with single mothers in good economic times and bad. There may be correlations between economic growth and family formation patterns which affect long-term economic well-being.

Ultimately, I believe that the first and most important lesson for antipoverty warriors from the 1990s is that sustained economic growth is a wonderful thing. To the extent that policies can help maintain strong employment growth, low unemployment, and expanding wages among workers, these policies may matter as much or more than the dollars spent on targeted programs for the poor. If there are no job opportunities, or if wages are falling, it is much more expensive — in terms of both dollars and political capital — for government programs alone to lift people out of poverty.

Lesson 2: Public Assistance Program Design Can Increase Work Incentives

It is unlikely that strong economic growth alone explains the striking movements in welfare caseloads and labor market participation in the 1990s. In fact, my own interpretation of the evidence is that large changes in behavior have occurred because economic forces have reinforced the direction of policy, and both policy and economics have worked together to change behavior much more strongly than either one alone would have been able to accomplish.

Welfare policies have evolved throughout the 1990s. In the early 1990s, the federal government granted a growing number of waivers, allowing states to experiment with alternative rules for the AFDC and food stamp programs. A variety of studies suggest that these waivers decreased caseloads overall (Wallace and Blank, 1999; Council of Economic Advisers, 1999b) and increased work and reduced poverty rates (Schoeni and Blank, 2000). In 1996 Congress passed the Personal Responsibility and Work Opportunity Reconciliation

Act, which fundamentally changed the public assistance system in the United States. This act abolished AFDC, which offered matching funds to states, and replaced it with the Temporary Assistance to Needy Families block grant to states. This change continued a stream of federal funding to state-run public assistance programs, but allowed states almost total discretion in setting the rules for eligibility and benefits. The 1996 welfare reform act also enacted time limits, which allow families to receive assistance from a TANF-funded program for no more than sixty months (cumulative) over a lifetime. In addition, the welfare reform act strengthened the incentives for states to increase their work-welfare efforts. Other changes in the bill abolished eligibility for most types of public assistance among noncitizens, limited food stamp eligibility for nonelderly adults without children, and removed a number of disability categories from Supplemental Security Income (the cash assistance program for low-income disabled and elderly persons).

In the aftermath of the 1996 welfare reform, states have implemented an increasingly diverse set of public assistance programs.[2] In comparison to the old AFDC program, states are more actively doing "diversion," which gives applicants one-time assistance without enrolling them in ongoing TANF-funded programs; they are experimenting with benefit programs that allow recipients to keep a higher level of public assistance benefits after going to work, which both increases work incentives and income among working low-income families; they are working to transform public assistance offices into employment assistance offices, where applicants are given constant incentives to seek and find work; they are doing more sanctioning, imposing penalties on those who do not respond to work incentives; and they are spending more money on work-related programs (such as childcare or transportation assistance) relative to cash benefits. While different states have opted for very different programs, it is accurate to say that most states are trying much harder to increase work among existing recipients, to support work among ex-recipients, and to encourage applicants to move into work rather than receive public assistance.

It is still early to measure the effects of these changes on low-income individuals' behavior. Most TANF-funded programs were not implemented until 1997, and often were not fully functioning until even later. This means that most currently available data comes from the transition period in which these programs were being implemented. Only a few papers have used post-1996 data to look at average effects of policy over the 1997–98 period (Council of Economic Advisers, 1999b; Schoeni and Blank, 2000). These papers, along with a wide variety of observers collecting case-study evidence, agree that the welfare policy changes have had a significant negative effect on the caseload. There is less research relating TANF changes to work behavior or poverty rates. Probably the best evidence comes from the timing of the labor force participation increases, as shown earlier in Figure 22.2, with very large increases in work among mothers with small children between 1995 and 1997. Schoeni and Blank (2000) — using admittedly crude techniques — indicate that TANF appears to reduce poverty but its effect on work behavior depends upon estimation strategy.

Given the magnitude of these welfare reform policy changes and the widespread publicity they have received, it would be astonishing if they did not have significant effects on behavior. However, these policy consequences are also hard to measure. First, it is hard to develop detailed characterizations of complex state programs that are usable in quantitative analysis. Second, it is hard to discern the difference between the legislation and regulations states have passed and what the states are actually doing in the field as they implement these new approaches. Third, the economic changes and the policy changes intermix in a variety of ways, as noted above, and the joint effects are hard to separate. States have almost surely been able to make faster and more fundamental changes to their programs because the strong economy provided both a more solid financial base and an easier environment in which to implement work-oriented welfare programs. Fourth, the mix of program options continues to evolve in almost all states, as states are experimenting with different approaches. In a period of such change and transition, it is almost impossible to measure the effects of any individual program component (because so much else is changing at the same time), and it is also difficult to reach any consensus about the long-term effects of these changes.

Although the overall effects of welfare reform writ large across the country are hard to pin down, a few states and cities have experimented with a particularly innovative type of financial incentive program designed to increase work behavior while not reducing income. Several of these financial incentive programs have been studied with experimental methods, in which participants were randomly assigned to different program models. The evidence from these new program experiments is quite striking to those who remember the negative income tax experiments of the 1970s, in which government assistance produced work reductions and a large transfer of government resources was required to raise incomes. In a review of the evidence from the negative income tax experiments, Burtless (1986) estimated that it took three dollars in government aid to raise family incomes by one dollar. In contrast, financial incentive programs result in increased employment *and* reduced poverty.

The new programs have focused on combining financial incentives to move into employment with work mandates. For instance, the Minnesota Family Investment Program (MFIP) substantially decreased the benefit reduction rate

Table 22.2. Impacts of Combined Financial Incentive/Employment Mandate Programs on Single-Parent Welfare Recipients

	SSP		MFIP	
	Applicants[a]	Long-term Recipients[b]	Applicants[c]	Long-term Recipients[c]
Employment				
Treatment Group	53.7	40.8	56.3	51.7
Control Group	41.8	29.0	52.1	36.1
Impact	11.9**	11.8**	4.2*	15.6**
Annual Earnings				
Treatment Group	$7,671	$3,435	$6,405	$4,207
Control Group	$5,638	$2,198	$6,631	$3,191
Impact	$2,033**	$1,237**	−$226	$1,016**
Annual Family Income				
Treatment Group	$18,438	$14,710	$15,167	$16,607
Control Group	$15,764	$12,730	$14,223	$14,676
Impact	$2,674**	$1,980**	$944*	$1,931**
Poverty Rates				
Treatment Group	57.2	77.5	67.5	71.4
Control Group	68.5	89.8	72.1	85.2
Impact	−11.3**	−12.2**	−4.6*	−13.8

Note: All data are reported in 1998 U.S. dollars, based on the Consumer Price Index. Canadian dollars are converted to U.S. dollars at the rate of 0.75 $U.S./$Can.

[a] From Michalopolous et al. (1999). Data are averages measured in quarters 8–9 after random assignment and are from a 30-month client survey (employment and earnings), as well as Income Assistance and SSP program records (income). Family income in both SSP columns equals earnings from all family members plus cash assistance less federal and provincial taxes. Poverty rate is calculated from the low-income cut off defined by Statistics Canada.

[b] From Lin et al. (1998). Data are averages measured over quarters 5–6 after random assignment and are from an 18-month client survey (employment and earnings), as well as Income Assistance and SSP program records (income).

[c] From Miller et al. (1997). Data are averages measured over quarters 5–7 after random assignment (employment and earnings) and are from Unemployment Insurance records (employment and earnings) as well as welfare program records (income). Family income in both MFIP columns equals earnings of head plus cash assistance, including cash value of Food Stamps. Poverty rate is calculated from the official U.S. poverty rate.

** Significant at 1 percent level; * significant at 5 percent level.

for public assistance recipients, thus allowing them to keep more public assistance income as they went to work, but mandated participation in work-welfare programs. An experiment in Canada called the Self-Sufficiency Project (SSP) provided substantial financial support to long-term public assistance recipients who went to work thirty hours or more per week.[3]

Table 22.2 summarizes some of the key results from these two experiments. The evidence suggests that employment, earnings, and family income increased substantially for program participants, while poverty fell. This is true for both new applicants as well as long-term recipients of public assistance in SSP; the strongest effects in MFIP were among long-term welfare recipients only. These programs were not money savers for the government, since they provided more assistance to low-income workers than did more traditional welfare programs. This is one reason many states have not followed Minnesota's lead in implementing such a program. For states that are particularly interested in both reducing poverty as well as increasing work behavior, however, these programs provide clear evidence that these two goals can be achieved together.[4] It is also worth noting that the Canadian economy was not nearly as strong as the U.S. economy over the 1990s, so that the SSP results demonstrate that such programs can work even in a higher unemployment environment.

Results from the MFIP program make it possible to decompose the effects of the financial incentives from the employment mandates. In this program, the employment mandates produced the work and earnings gains, and the financial incentives produced the antipoverty results. This finding emphasizes the importance of both of these program components — the carrot of financial incentives plus the stick of employment mandates work together to produce overall positive outcomes.

These experiments indicate that there is something new to be learned about policy in the 1990s. Financial incentive programs, linked to effective work requirements, can offer government assistance to reduce poverty without also reducing work behavior.

Lesson 3: Other Policies, Especially Wage Subsidies, Can Reinforce Welfare-to-Work Efforts

An enormous amount of research attention has been devoted to the effects of the 1996 legislation and the new TANF-funded state programs, but these are not the only policy changes of the 1990s. A variety of other policies have also acted to reinforce work incentives.

The minimum wage went up four times in the 1990s, from $3.35 at the beginning of 1990 to $5.15 in 1997, an increase of 17 percent in inflation-

Table 22.3. Effects of Changing Policy on Earnings of Single Mothers

	1989	1998	Percentage change
1. Minimum wage	$4.41	$5.15	16.8
2. Maximum EITC subsidy			
Single mother (1 child)	$1,197	$2,271	89.7
Single mother (2 children)	$1,197	$3,756	213.8
3. Earnings			
(Single mother working full-time at minimum wage)			
Single mother (1 child)	$9,856	$12,571	25.6
Single mother (2 children)	$9,856	$14,056	40.4
4. Ratio of earnings to U.S. poverty line			
Single mother (1 child)	0.89	1.16	
Single mother (2 children)	0.76	1.03	

Note: All numbers in 1998 dollars

adjusted terms, as shown at the top of Table 22.3. The very low unemployment rates among women and minority workers in recent years suggests that any disemployment effects from these recent minimum wage changes were swamped by the overall strength of the economy. More systematic evidence, which tries to adjust for aggregate macroeconomic factors, also suggests that the disemployment effects of these recent minimum wage increases were, at most, relatively small (Bernstein and Schmitt, 1998). The minimum wage increases disproportionately helped low-income families. Among persons earning between $4.25 and $5.15 an hour just prior to the 1996 and 1997 increases, 71 percent were adults, 58 percent were women, almost half worked full-time, and most lived in low-income families (Council of Economic Advisers, 1999a).

The minimum wage increases of the 1990s functioned in tandem with increases in the Earned Income Tax Credit, which provides wage subsidies to low-wage workers. The EITC was expanded several times in the 1990s, increasing the subsidy received by families and allowing families with more than one child to receive higher benefits. The result was a huge increase in the value of the EITC to those workers eligible to receive it. The second part of Table 22.2 indicates that the real maximum subsidy from the EITC rose by 90 percent for families with one child and by 214 percent for families with two or more children between 1989 and 1998.

The third part of Table 22.3 indicates how these minimum wage and EITC changes reinforced each other to increase the returns to work. A single mother with one child who worked full-time at the minimum wage earned $9,856 in 1989 (measured in constant 1998 dollars). With no changes in behavior, the same woman earned $12,571 in 1998, an increase of 26 percent. A single mother with two children experienced a 40 percent increase in her income. Clearly the value of employment rose significantly for those affected by these policy changes.

Several studies have indicated the importance of the EITC on work behavior. For example, about half of the increase in labor force participation among single mothers between 1984 and 1996 was due to the EITC expansions, according to Meyer and Rosenbaum (1999). Eissa and Liebman (1996) also find that the net effect of the EITC was to expand the work behavior of single mothers.[5]

Two final policy changes are also worth noting. First, there has been a substantial expansion in public childcare subsidies. From 1990 through 1998, federal support for childcare went from less than $7 billion to more than $11 billion annually (in 1998 dollars). Many states have also put more dollars into childcare as part of their welfare-to-work efforts. The elasticity of labor force participation among mothers with children under 13 to child care costs is between −0.05 and −0.35, with consistently larger estimates for less skilled mothers (Anderson and Levine, 2000), which suggests that the recent expansions in child care subsidies are another factor increasing labor supply among single mothers.

Second, health insurance coverage of low-income families by the Medicaid program has expanded steadily. Traditionally, women and children on public assistance have been automatically eligible for Medicaid, whereas most low-skilled jobs do not provide health coverage. As a result, moving from public assistance to work could mean the loss of health insurance, which would be a disincentive to work. While this problem is far from solved, it has gotten better. Throughout the 1990s, a growing number of children in low-income families (depending on the state, families between 135 and 185 percent of the poverty line) were automatically eligible for Medicaid. In addition, many welfare participants can now retain their Medicaid eligibility for at least a year after they go to work and leave public assistance. Lack of insurance remains a significant problem among the low-income population; however, a larger proportion of the problem is now due to eligible persons who do not take advantage of their benefits, particularly children, which is a very different problem from lack of coverage.

But Don't Declare Success Too Quickly

Back in 1990, nobody would have forecast as large a decline in caseloads or as large an increase in work behavior among single-mother families as has actually happened over the decade. In my opinion, this is the result of a conflux of events that all came together at the same time: a strongly expanding economy, substantial revisions in public assistance that emphasized work and reduced benefit eligibility, and major policy changes that increased the returns to work and the subsidies to support work, particularly among single mothers.

Before concluding that major gains in the war on poverty have been permanently won, however, I must note a number of caveats to these results.

First, it is not clear how sustainable these changes are in the long run or how reliant they are on the remarkably strong economy. Historical experience suggests that the past decade of low inflation and low unemployment is not typical. Although it is always tempting to be optimistic about the prospects for better future economic conditions, there is little reason to believe that the economy has solved the fundamental problem of business cycles. America's increasingly global economy is also more open to economic shocks from abroad. Nor is the Phillips curve tradeoff between unemployment and inflation dead, although it may have shifted to the left for a variety of both long-term and short-term reasons. State TANF programs are largely designed to work in an environment where jobs are readily available. When jobs become more scarce, states will either have to accept greater poverty among those to whom they refuse benefits, or revise their programs to provide longer-term assistance (such as public sector employment) to those unable to find jobs.

Second, the long-term effects of less public support and more hours of employment on the economic well-being of low-income families is still uncertain. Even though poverty has fallen overall, there are still subgroups that may have experienced losses. One report indicates that the bottom income quintile of single-mother families experienced a net income gain from 1993 to 1997, but an income loss between 1995 and 1997 (Primus et al., 1999). The bottom quintile of single-mother families is an extremely poor group, all of whom were below the official poverty line in all of these years, so this evidence suggests some of the poorest families may have lost ground. Such findings may not be surprising in a world where more and more persons are being "diverted" and refused access to public assistance or are being sanctioned for inadequate participation in work programs. In fact it is exactly those who are most disadvantaged and face the greatest barriers to employment that might not be able to take advantage of the employment expansion even in the face of increased welfare-to-work efforts. This includes persons with learning disabilities, a past history of drug abuse or domestic violence, or complex family needs.

Studies of people leaving welfare suggest that the majority of persons who have left the rolls—ranging from 55 to 85 percent in various studies—are employed at a future date. The scant evidence available in a few states suggests that between one-half and two-thirds report higher incomes post-welfare; Brauner and Loprest (1999) summarize these findings. But one might expect that—even in a strong economy—these policy changes would make life harder for some subset of women. In a weaker economy, the group that is made worse off by these changes would be even larger. It will be important over time to understand who is worse off and why.

It is also unclear exactly how to translate changes in official poverty rates and in income into measures of well-being. To the extent that employment involves childcare and other work expenses, aggregate income and earnings changes may seriously overstate the changes in disposable income.

Third, although this discussion has focused entirely on family income and women's behavior, there is another key issue facing these families: the well-being of their children. Little past research has addressed the effects of welfare-to-work programs on the children. Some believe that mothers will gain an increased self-confidence through work that will spill over in making them more positive role models for their children. Others worry that the reduced hours available for parenting because of increased work effort will put children at greater risk. One particular concern is that while previous welfare-to-work programs were focused on women with older children, many states now enforce work requirements on the mothers of infants and very small children, which in turn focuses attention on the quality of childcare available to low-income working mothers. A variety of studies are now in the field to examine the impact of strong work mandates on children. The results of these surveys will be important in evaluating the advantages and disadvantages of strong work-incentive programs aimed at single mothers.

Recent history demonstrates the extent to which both the macroeconomy and public policy can influence the behavior of low-income families, and reinforces the lesson that both work incentives and job availability do matter. However, economists and policymakers probably shouldn't take too much credit for designing and accomplishing these dramatic changes. As in most cases when a confluence of forces come together to create major economic and behavioral changes, chance is an important ingredient. As I read the economic evidence, America's good fortune in the 1990s was at least partly due to the luck of certain economic events and forces occurring in the right order and at the right time. Certainly the length and strength of the economic boom was not foreseen when welfare reform was passed in the mid-1990s. Nor were the large EITC expansions enacted in 1993 with the explicit idea of legislating time-limited public assistance a few years later.

In the absence of the robust economy, the legislated changes in 1996 would likely have had much weaker effects. But in the absence of the 1996 reforms, the magnitude of caseload decline and labor force increases is likely to have been much smaller. Having accomplished dramatic short-run changes in behavior during the 1990s, the ongoing challenge in today's war on poverty will be to build on these results. This means helping less skilled workers maintain the labor market connections they have developed in recent years, even if the economy slows down. It also means working to ensure that those employed at low wages are able to earn enough to build a stable economic life for their family and perhaps even experience improvements in their economic well-being over time if they persist in their employment and work efforts.

Notes

1. Haveman and Schwabish (1999) show similar regressions.

2. Nathan and Gais (1999) describe these changes. See also the working papers that are part of the Assessing the New Federalism Project at the Urban Institute, available at ⟨http://newfederalism.urban.org.⟩

3. For a more extended discussion of MFIP, see Miller et al. (1997). For Canada's SSP, see Lin et al. (1998).

4. Blank et al. (2000) discuss these issues at greater length.

5. Eissa and Hoynes (1999) find that the effect of the EITC is small and negative on the work behavior of married women.

References

Anderson, Patricia M., and Phillip B. Levine. 2000. "Child Care and Mothers' Employment Decisions," in *Finding Jobs: Work and Welfare Reform*, Rebecca M. Blank and David Card, eds. New York: Russell Sage Foundation.

Bernstein, Jared, and John Schmitt. 1998. *Making Work Pay: The Impact of the 1996–97 Minimum Wage Increase*. Washington, D.C.: Economic Policy Institute.

Blank, Rebecca M. 1997. "What Causes Public Assistance Caseloads to Grow?" National Bureau of Economic Research Working Paper No. 6343. Cambridge, Mass.: NBER.

———. 1993. "Why Were Poverty Rates So High in the 1980s?" in *Poverty and Prosperity in the USA in the Late Twentieth Century*, Dimitri B. Papadimitriou and Edward N. Wolff, eds. New York: Macmillan.

Blank, Rebecca M., and Alan Blinder. 1986. "Macroeconomics, Income Distribution and Poverty," in *Fighting Poverty: What Works and What Doesn't?* Sheldon H. Danziger and Daniel H. Weinberg, eds. Cambridge, Mass.: Harvard University Press.

Blank, Rebecca M., David Card, and Philip K. Robins. 2000. "Financial Incentives for Increasing Work and Income Among Low-Income Families," in *Finding Jobs: Work and Welfare Reform,* Rebecca M. Blank and David Card, eds. New York: Russell Sage Foundation.

Brauner, Sarah, and Pamela Loprest. 1999. *Where Are They Now? What States' Studies of People Who Left Welfare Tell Us.* Series A, No. A-32, Assessing the New Federalism. Washington, D.C.: Urban Institute.

Burtless, Gary. 1986. "The Work Response to a Guaranteed Income: A Survey of Experimental Evidence," in *Lessons from the Income Maintenance Experiments,* Alicia H. Munnell, ed. Boston: Federal Reserve Bank of Boston.

Council of Economic Advisers. 1999a. *Economic Report of the President, February 1999.* Washington, D.C.: U.S. Government Printing Office.

———. 1999b. *Economic Expansion, Welfare Reform, and the Decline in Welfare Caseloads: An Update* (Technical Report). August. Washington, D.C.: U.S. Government Printing Office.

Eissa, Nada, and Hilary W. Hoynes. 1999. "The Earned Income Tax Credit and the Labor Supply of Married Couples." University of California — Berkeley, Department of Economics Working Paper No. E99–267.

Eissa, Nada, and Jeffrey B. Liebman. 1996. "Labor Supply Response to the Earned Income Tax Credit." *Quarterly Journal of Economics* 111 (2): 605–37.

Figlio, David N., and James P. Ziliak. 1999. "Welfare Reform, the Business Cycle, and the Decline in AFDC Caseloads," in *Economic Conditions and Welfare Reform,* Sheldon Danziger, ed. Kalamazoo, Mich.: W. E. Upjohn Institute.

Haveman, Robert, and Jonathan Schwabish. 1998. "Macroeconomic Performance and the Poverty Rate: A Return to Normalcy?" Unpublished manuscript.

Lin, Winston, Philip K. Robins, David Card, Kristen Harknett, and Susanna Lui-Gurr. 1998. *When Financial Incentives Encourage Work: Complete Eighteen-Month Findings from the Self-Sufficiency Project.* Ottawa, Canada: Social Research and Demonstration Corporation.

Meyer, Bruce D., and Dan T. Rosenbaum. 1999. "Welfare, the Earned Income Tax Credit, and the Labor Supply of Single Mothers." National Bureau of Economic Research Working Paper No. 7363. Cambridge, Mass.: NBER.

Michalopoulos, Charles, Philip K. Robins, and David Card. 1999. *When Financial Work Incentives Pay for Themselves: Early Findings from the Self-Sufficiency Project's Applicant Study.* Ottawa, Canada: Social Research and Demonstration Corporation.

Miller, Cynthia, Virginia Knox, Patricia Auspos, Jo Anna Hunter-Manns, and Alan Orenstein. 1997. *Making Welfare Work and Work Pay: Implementation and Eighteen-Month Impacts of the Minnesota Family Investment Program.* New York: Manpower Demonstration Research Corporation.

Nathan, Richard P., and Thomas L. Gais. 1999. *Implementing the Personal Responsibility Act of 1996: A First Look.* Albany, N.Y.: Nelson A. Rockefeller Institute of Government.

Primus, Wendell, Lynette Rawlings, Kathy Larin, and Kathryn Porter. 1999. *The Initial Impacts of Welfare Reform on the Incomes of Single-Mother Families.* Washington, D.C.: Center on Budget and Policy Priorities.

Schoeni, Robert F., and Rebecca M. Blank. 2000. "The Effects of Welfare Reform and

Welfare Waivers on Welfare Participation, Employment, Income, Poverty, and Family Structure." Unpublished manuscript.

U.S. Census Bureau. 1999. *Experimental Poverty Measures: 1990 to 1997.* Current Population Reports P60–205. Washington, D.C.: U.S. Government Printing Office.

Wallace, Geoffrey, and Rebecca M. Blank. 1999. "What Goes Up Must Come Down? Explaining Recent Changes in Public Assistance Caseloads," in *Economic Conditions and Welfare Reform,* Sheldon Danziger, ed. Kalamazoo, Mich.: W. E. Upjohn Institute.

PART VII

Communal Hardship in Black Residential Areas:
Crime and Law Enforcement

23

Crime, Poverty, and Entrepreneurship

SAMUEL L. MYERS, JR.

Utterly ignored in recent discussions of poverty policy are strategies designed to enhance the managerial and entrepreneurial talents of inner-city residents. Poverty research has focused instead on welfare and work. We have tried, often with little success, to transform the poor into low-wage workers when perhaps we should be training them to be owners.

While many scholars persist in viewing participation in alternatives to legitimate employment as evidence of pathological behavior, there is a growing recognition that criminal participation may not be irrational.[1] It is often a very rational response to unappealing or unavailable job opportunities. Many criminal activities of past generations, like numbers running, hustling, and prostitution, appeared to have some of the characteristics of small-scale enterprises and embodied risk-tasking and problem-solving skills that are undervalued in low-wage jobs. Moreover, criminal activity has often served as the initial source of capital for the development of legitimate businesses in ethnic minority communities.[2]

Studies of the entrepreneurial opportunities for criminal offenders show that we trained these persons to be workers when they had all of the fundamental characteristics necessary to be Harvard MBAs.[3] The highly publicized trials of youthful drug kingpins in Washington, D.C., and elsewhere bear out the sophistication, business acumen, and financial savvy of these criminal entrepreneurs. These and other enterprising efforts provide at best anecdotal evidence of the presence of significant entrepreneurial talents in our inner cities and poverty-stricken neighborhoods.

Is this a highly romanticized view of the linkage between criminal behavior and economic well-being? Many would view the recent surges in criminal activity such as the crack-cocaine drug problem in inner-city communities as the source of these communities' destruction. And, given the dismal results over the past decade of rational models of crime[4] to explain or predict, one is led to question the reasoning behind the "crime as enterprise" perspective.

Furthermore, doubts arise in the labor market literature as to the rationality of the selective withdrawal from the labor force of those at greatest risk of being criminals: young black males.[5] There seems to be a growing consensus that labor force withdrawal by these persons is linked not simply to rational choice but to broader structural and macrosociological phenomena infrequently modeled in the economics of crime literature.[6]

Do noneconomic considerations dominate entry into drug dealing and withdrawal from the labor force? Do perceptions about the entrepreneurial benefits of criminal activities thwart entry into work and promote entry into drug dealing? Does the belief that "crime pays" in either the economic sense or the psychological sense confounds whatever objective measures there may be of the relative returns to work and crime? And could these beliefs about the payoffs from such criminal enterprises as drug dealing explain the apparent crisis of blatantly visible drug activity in black communities?

This chapter explores these themes by examining the connection between self-admitted drug dealing and labor force behavior. First, data on inmates in prisons and jails in California, Michigan, and Texas provide a basis for examining the characteristics of self-described drug dealers. Then, several measures of criminal preferences and motivations for engaging in crime are developed. Some of these measures capture the idea of crime as an entrepreneurial activity. I then expand the standard economic model of crime to include impacts of criminal preferences and motivations on both employment and crime.

Drug Dealing and Criminal Populations

The data for this investigation come from the Rand Inmate Survey, administered in 1978 and 1979 to convicted male inmates at twelve prisons and fourteen county jails in California, Michigan, and Texas. The survey examines three time windows to access criminal activities. The windows include the twelve-month period immediately before the arrest for which the inmate was incarcerated; the two-year period before that; and two additional years before that.[7] Basic background variables and a series of measures of attitudes about crime are available as well.

The background characteristics of the inmate sample mirror those of prisoners nationally: 45 percent were black; 19 percent Hispanics, Asians, and Native Americans; 22 percent completed less than the tenth grade; 35 percent completed some high school; 18 percent were high school graduates; 22 percent had completed schooling beyond high school, including college; and 20 percent were married. Inmates were asked if they used certain drugs before they were 18. Responses of frequent use of LSD, psychedelics, cocaine, uppers, downers, or heroin were recoded as "hard drug use." Twenty-five percent of the respondents admitted to frequent hard drug use before they were 18. Another 19 percent claimed that they never used any drugs, including marijuana, before they were 18. They were also asked about drug dealing (making, selling, smuggling, or moving drugs) in several time frames. Forty percent admitted to dealing drugs in the twelve months before their arrest. Of those, 68.4 percent claimed to have made eleven or more deals. Asked to describe themselves during the period before their arrests, 21 percent stated that they thought of themselves as drug dealers.[8] Of all respondents, 34 percent reported dealing hard drugs at some time in the twelve months before arrest. These data, drawn from the late 1970s, are consistent with more recent data.

Surveys of victims have found that about a quarter of the violent criminal incidents where the offender was under 20 were perpetrated by criminals perceived to be under the influence of alcohol or drugs.[9] While about three-quarters of jail and prison inmates admitted to ever using drugs in their lifetimes — a drug use prevalence that vastly exceeds reported use in the general population — only about 17 percent claimed they were under the influence of drugs at the time they committed the offense for which they were sentenced.[10] Among state prisoners in 1986, 19 percent admitted to using hard drugs daily in the month before their arrest.

The major difference between the self-reported data and other sources comes from the drug dealing end of the equation. Whereas self-reported drug use among criminal populations is gleaned from other data, self-reported drug dealing is considerably more prevalent than what emerges in the official data. Only about 26.1 percent of state prison inmates with no prior sentences were incarcerated for drug dealing in 1986, up somewhat from earlier years. Yet, in 1978–79 more than 40 percent of all inmates in our sample admitted that they had dealt drugs at some time in the twelve months before they were arrested. This suggests considerable undetected drug activity and is confirmed in our calculation of the ratio of drug arrests to admitted drug sales per month on the street. It is an astonishingly low .005 for those with drug sales. If this ratio is to be regarded as a measure of the riskiness of illegal drug activity, then one can only conclude that this is as risk-free a criminal enterprise as one can find.

Criminal Preferences and Entrepreneurship

A unique set of questions concerning attitudes about crime and the Criminal justice system was posed. Among other questions, inmates were asked to state how much they agreed or disagreed with the following statements:[11]

"It is possible to be so good at crime that you'll never get caught."
"Men who are really good at crime never seriously think about going straight."
"Crime is the easiest way to get what you want."

About 5 percent of the respondents agreed or strongly agreed with the above statements. We call these "type-A criminals." One might expect that "type-A" criminals are prone to criminal careers regardless of the relative risks and returns from crime and work. One might expect that these persons would persist in crime even if it were unprofitable or if legitimate alternatives were available. This is not the image of the legitimate entrepreneur since it overlooks one important rule of business ownership: hard work pays off. Or, at least, one would hope that legitimate businesspersons would not adopt this perspective, even if it does prove to be successful in their entrepreneurial activities.

Inmates were asked to rate the chances that certain things would happen as a result of doing crime. Those reporting an average of high or certain chance that the following would happen were labeled as believing crime pays (CRIME PAYS1): "Having money for necessities"; "High living"; "Owning expensive things"; "Having a lot of money."[12]

A second category of those believing that crime pays (CRIME PAYS2) included inmates who rated the following as having a high or certain chance on average: "Having friends"; "Being my own man"; "Having a family"; "Being happy."

The first of these perceptions about the payoff from crime measures economic benefits; the second captures social and psychological aspects. Inmates were asked to rate the chances that these same events would happen if they did not do crimes. Parallel measures were obtained to derive variables "Straight Pays 1" and "Straight Pays 2," the first being a measure of the perceived economic benefits of not doing crime and the second being a measure of the perceived social and psychological benefits of not doing crime. Table 23.1 records the means in the sample for these, the "type-A criminal" and the single

Table 23.1. Perceptions of Criminal Participation

Crime Pays 1	19.2%
Crime Pays 2	12.2%
Straight Pays 1	6.2%
Straight Pays 2	42.2%
Be Your Own Man	41.5%
Type-A Criminal	4.7%

response to the "be your own man" perception of doing crime. It shows that a significant minority of respondents believed that there are social and psychological benefits of going straight, while there are nontrivial economic benefits of doing crime. Yet, almost as many felt that there are high or certain chances of being your own man from crime as there were those who felt that there were high or certain chances of social and psychological benefits of going straight.[13] Only a handful were so sure of themselves that they might ignore the objective risks and returns altogether and persist to engage in crime.

The data suggest the possibility of a small, but nontrivial number of whose aspirations are geared to the economic trappings of the "high life" characteristic of entrepreneurial criminal activities. They want the social and psychological advantages of being their own men — something that assuredly is available if they go straight — but they also want to own expensive things and to have a lot of money. These things may be out of their reach in the legitimate labor market. These persons could make excellent legitimate entrepreneurs if offered the opportunities to do so. These persons who believe that crime pays might work less and engage in drug sales not simply because of higher relative returns to crime but because of the chance to be an owner rather than a worker. In contrast, type-A criminals, while perhaps entrepreneurial in their actions, are criminals by preference and might be criminals even if they were to own legitimate enterprises.

There are conventional means by which to have money for necessities, and even at times to have a lot of money. And, of course, there are conventional means by which to have friends, family, and happiness. Crime and drug dealing are but one route by which these economic and social psychological ends can be achieved. Employment is the conventional route.

Even though drugs and crime may be alternative routes by which to receive the economic and psychological benefits that normally accrue to legitimate labor market work, there is one crucial difference. In many instances drug dealing is more akin to running a small enterprise and less so to conventional "work." The choice is not between crime and work; the choice is between entrepreneurship and business (albeit illegal) and work. Since these need not be mutually exclusive — many customers may indeed be found where the drug seller works — there is no reason to believe that these two activities move in opposite directions. And, if they do move in opposite directions, it may be because they both are correlated with preferences for crime — drug dealing being directly related to these preferences and work being inversely related to them.

Employment Versus Drug Dealing

The conventional economic model of criminal participation posits a supply function that depends on the relative returns to crime. Criminal perceptions, however, may intervene, muting any expected impact that reduced relative returns to crime may have on participation in crime. Figure 23.1 shows that both criminal perceptions and expected returns to work and crime ought to influence drug selling and employment. Where both factors are operative, one would expect that increases in the relative returns to work will reduce participation in drug dealing and increase employment; perceptions about the economic or social-psychological benefits or crime ought to influence drug dealing and employment as well. However, the specification we have chosen does not demand an inverse relationship between employment and drug dealing. There are possible complementarities between the two: selling drugs, like running a consulting firm, can be done while one works.

The employment variables we examine relate to the year before the arrest. They are whether held a job, number of street months employed for those who worked, number of jobs held, and wage per month. For the entire sample the averages were 72.2 percent, 9.3 months, 2 jobs, and $700 per month, respectively.

Since wages are endogenous to labor supply, we estimate reduced form equations for the probability of receipt of wage income and log-income for those with positive earnings. We also estimate reduced form equations for the probability of receipt of illegal income and for log-monthly income for those with illegal earnings. We derive measures of the expected legal and illegal wages; the ratio of these two is a measure of the expected relative returns to work.[14] The results of these estimations yield a ratio of about .75, suggesting that for our sample legal wages were only about three-quarters of illegal wages.

Unless the impacts of criminal perceptions mitigate the economic returns to work and crime, one would expect increases in the expected relative returns to work to reduce entry into drug dealing, reduce drug deals among those engag-

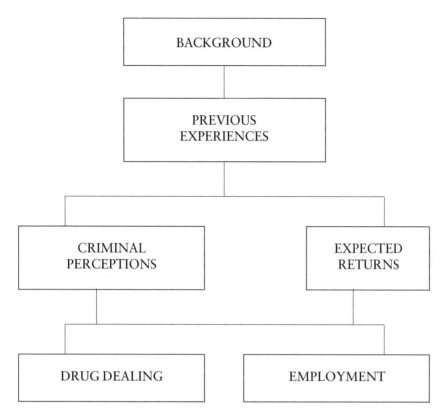

Figure 23.1 Criminal Perceptions and Expected Returns

ing in drug sales, increase employment probabilities, and increase months worked. The issues that might militate against these anticipated impacts of relative returns on employment and drug dealing include the offender's image as a drug dealer, the perceptions about the economic and social-psychological benefits of doing crime versus going straight, and the presence of "type-A" criminal personality. Since offenders who perceive of themselves as drug dealers may perceive of themselves as entrepreneurs and not simply wage earners, there may be stronger impacts of the relative returns to work on the behavior of criminals not engaged in such entrepreneurial activities as drug dealing. Moreover, perceptions about the rewards and benefits of doing crime versus going straight might dominate objective measures of the returns to these activities. And the sheer thrill of being an invincible criminal might outweigh the relative expected earnings from legitimate employment.

Table 23.2 presents the means of the key measures of criminal perceptions,

Table 23.2. Black-White Differences in Criminal Perception, Employment, and Drug Dealing

	Black Mean	White Mean	T-Statistic Probability
Be Your Own Man	0.4571	0.3231	5.810
Crime Pays 1	0.1970	0.1613	1.97
			0.049
Crime Pays 2	0.1478	0.0670	5.630
Going Straight Pays 1	0.0677	0.0392	2.7
			0.007
Going Straight pays 2	0.3577	0.4051	−2.06
			0.04
Type-A Criminal	0.0440	0.0435	0.05
			0.959
Successful in crime	0.0725	0.0965	−1.81
			0.071
Had job in window 3	0.6806	0.7803	−4.780
Street month employed in window 3	7.7364	7.7788	−0.08
			0.935
Number of drug deals per month on street	433.4347	148.1523	4.290
Image of drug dealer	0.1626	0.2544	−4.750
Probability of drug deals	0.1317	0.2956	−8.460
Expected wage ratio	0.33462	0.89234	−12.1335

employment and drug dealing, for blacks and whites in the sample. There are significant differences between the two groups. Blacks are more likely than whites to perceive of crime as an opportunity to "be your own man" and to believe that crime pays, in the economic as well as in the social-psychological sense.

In contrast, whites are more likely to believe that going straight pays. While there is no statistically significant difference in the incidence of "type-A" criminals between blacks and whites, whites are considerably more likely than blacks to view themselves as drug dealers and to admit to positive drug deals in the period before their arrests. This is despite the fact that blacks have lower relative legal wages and lower employment probabilities. The racial gap in drug dealing, indeed, is far larger than the racial gap in employment. White drug dealing probabilities are more than twice black drug dealing probabilities; white employment rates are not quite 15 percent higher than black rates.

We adopt a two-stage method to estimate the impacts of background variables, experiences, criminal perceptions, and the expected returns to work relative to crime on employment and drug dealing. First, probit equations are estimated for the probability of employment and for the probability of drug dealing. Then, the inverse of Mills ratio is computed and included as a right-hand-side variable in the log-earnings and log-drug-sales equations. The intent of this Heckman procedure is to correct for possible selection bias in employment and drug dealing.

Tables 23.3 and 23.4 present the results of these estimations for blacks and whites in the sample. Focusing on the impacts of experiences, preferences, and relative returns to work, one notices a common pattern: the ratio of legal to illegal monthly expected earnings is inversely related to the probability of drug sales, while the drug dealer image is positively related to drug sales and inversely related to employment. This pattern emerges for both blacks and whites. In addition, previous employment raises both black and white employment and drug sales probabilities.

With few exceptions, other aspects of criminal perceptions have no noticeable impacts on employment or drug dealing. The perception that crime pays, for example, whether in the economic context or in the social-psychological sense, fails to demonstrate a statistically significant impact on the probability of drug sales or the number of drug sales per street month among black or white offenders. Although black "type-A" criminals are less likely to be employed, there is no impact of this factor on drug sales or on white employment or drug dealing.

Thus, these results confirm that a significant aspect of rational calculus may be at work in drug dealing, while the impacts of a variety of criminal perceptions are minimal. Increases in the relative attractiveness of work will reduce appreciably the entry into drug dealing. There is an obvious entrepreneurial aspect of drug dealing, and those who imagine themselves to be businessmen do have lower employment rates and higher rates of participation in the drug trade. Yet, there are opposing impacts of the relative returns to work — which do not seem to affect black employment, although there are weak impacts on white employment. On the one hand, increased relative returns to work lower the probability of drug sales. On the other hand, however, higher relative returns to work, meaning lower returns to crime, require larger numbers of

Table 23.3. Heckman Estimates of Employment and Drug Dealing, Blacks

Independent Variables	P (Employment) coeff t-stat mean	Ln (Street Month Employment) coeff t-stat mean	P (Drug Sales) coeff t-stat mean	Ln (Drug Sales) coeff t-stat mean
Background				
Constant	0.999306	0.335606	−1.42864	3.2354
	2.076	0.825	−1.912	1.14
Age	−0.02878	0.076449	0.003499	0.191053
	−0.987	3.734	0.073	1.105
	26.491	26.163	26.491	25.943
Age squared	0.00026	−0.00788	−0.00036	−0.00309
	0.62	−2.658	−0.501	−1.125
	764.73	744.04	744.73	715.54
Some high school	−0.23791	0.173295	0.349799	−1.21006
	−1.742	1.343	1.802	−1.622
	0.44679	0.42987	0.44679	0.35753
High school graduate	0.005658	0.269219	0.530306	−1.25634
	0.034	2.441	2.29	−1.485
	0.15806	0.15637	0.15806	0.17206
College	0.119809	0.129791	0.833137	−1.17855
	0.748	1.279	3.904	−1.517
	0.23215	0.24209	0.23215	0.36712
California	−0.64562	−0.07444	−0.09231	0.459261
	−5.264	−0.344	−0.551	0.824
	0.24916	0.21292	0.24916	0.30502
Michigan	−0.70104	0.094786	0.220856	−0.32002
	−6.287	0.392	1.473	−0.65
	0.43499	0.37563	0.43499	0.43798
Experience				
Employment in	0.679814	0.127235	0.828341	−0.36287
window 2	4.211	0.543	4.355	−0.645
	0.65248	0.75942	0.65248	0.59474
Hard drugs	0.018219	—	−0.11445	—
	0.145		−0.726	
	0.2397		0.1397	
Ratio of legal to illegal	−0.15962	0.027175	−2.94492	2.16532
monthly earnings	−0.392	0.119	−5.771	1.418
	0.33462	0.3679	0.33462	0.24326

Table 23.3. Continued

Independent Variables	P (Employment) coeff t-stat mean	Ln (Street Month Employment) coeff t-stat mean	P (Drug Sales) coeff t-stat mean	Ln (Drug Sales) coeff t-stat mean
Preferences				
Image of drug dealer	−0.22547 −1.826 0.16509	—	1.17599 8.865 0.16509	—
Believes going straight pays (#1)	−0.29129 −1.469 0.058757	0.094318 0.595 0.064264	—	—
Believes going straight pays (#2)	0.223029 2.378 0.34018	0.53926 0.627 0.39231	—	—
Believes crime pays (#1)	—	—	0.14621 1.007 0.20008	0.541111 1.234 0.28774
Believes crime pays (#2)	—	—	−0.22414 −1.224 0.14913	0.438886 0.831 0.16475
Be your own man	−0.01456 −0.163 0.456795	—	0.06216 0.47 0.45795	—
Type-A criminal	−0.38778 −0.1839 0.044697	—	−0.15943 −0.553 0.044697	—
Lambda	—	−0.51571 −0.799 0.56741	—	0.4187
Chi-squared	143.67	—	182.08	—
Probability	3.22E-14	—	3.22E-14	—
% Correct classification	0.68601	—	0.864249	—
Adjusted r-squared	—	0.10348	—	−0.00695

Table 23.4. Heckman Estimates of Employment and Drug Dealing, Whites

Independent Variables	P (Employment) coeff t-stat mean	Ln (Street Month Employment) coeff t-stat mean	P (Drug Sales) coeff t-stat mean	Ln (Drug Sales) coeff t-stat mean
Background				
Constant	0.995051	1.30484	0.0328	5.92253
	1.947	4.949	0.041	2.438
Age	−0.04911	0.043504	0.02294	−0.13769
	−1.703	2.471	0.43	−0.766
	26.856	26.625	26.856	24.362
Age squared	0.000597	−0.00044	−0.00102	0.003506
	1.502	−1.837	−1.168	1.085
	801.67	789.27	801.67	622.46
Some high school	0.303624	−0.02625	0.369668	−0.96901
	2.236	−0.307	2.474	−2.91
	0.28104	0.28223	0.28104	0.3141
High school graduate	0.478031	−0.08243	0.506425	−1.00024
	3.077	−0.776	2.948	−2.566
	0.22028	0.22718	0.22028	0.21724
College	0.491168	−0.00689	0.526489	−1.18597
	3.345	−0.065	3.215	−3.372
	0.24866	0.26506	0.24866	0.2786
California	−0.5907	−0.03275	−0.91065	1.57785
	−3.367	−0.276	−5.05	3.608
	0.38228	0.33729	0.38228	0.44375
Michigan	−0.15411	−0.05955	−0.32569	1.23055
	−1.173	−0.925	−2.212	4.031
	0.35125	0.36941	0.35125	0.30851
Experience				
Employment in window 2	0.682408	−0.00255	0.504365	−0.86084
	5.207	−0.019	3.765	−2.825
	0.73346	0.7977	0.73346	0.61204
Hard drugs	0.153747	—	0.043204	—
	1.374		0.374	
	0.36693		0.36693	
Ratio of legal to illegal monthly earnings	−0.21015	0.108849	−1.21118	1.2121
	−1.446	1.691	−7.703	2.329
	0.86351	0.93548	0.86351	0.61204

Table 23.4. Continued

Independent Variables	P (Employment) coeff t-stat mean	Ln (Street Month Employment) coeff t-stat mean	P (Drug Sales) coeff t-stat mean	Ln (Drug Sales) coeff t-stat mean
Preferences				
Image of drug dealer	−0.34768 −2.925 0.25367	—	0.816212 7.056 0.25367	—
Believes going straight pays (#1)	0.393835 1.383 0.039282	−0.27465 −1.978 0.047622	—	—
Believes going straight pays (#2)	0.150068 1.49 0.40621	−0.05048 −0.019 0.7977	—	—
Believes crime pays (#1)	—	—	0.040529 0.417 0.16171	−0.45571 −1.717 0.19774
Believes crime pays (#2)	—	—	−0.14755 −0.662 0.067164	0.667895 1.627 0.06868
Be your own man	−0.00037 −0.004 0.3225	—	0.065602 0.535 0.3225	—
Type-A criminal	−0.02102 −0.09 0.043635	—	−0.0214 −0.087 0.043635	—
Lambda	—	−0.47358 −1.328 0.46181	—	−1.53581 −3.793 0.89446
Chi-squared	75.34	—	220.27	—
Probability	2.81E-12	—	3.22E-14	—
% Correct classification	0.723881	—	0.766169	—
Adjusted r-squared	—	0.06502	—	0.08346

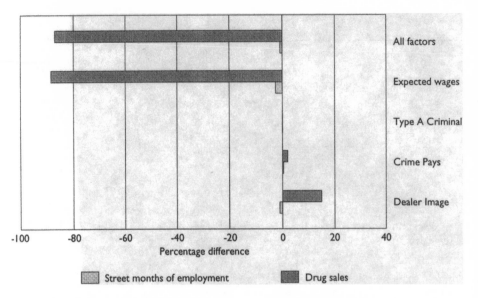

Figure 23.2 Impacts of Racial Differences in Opportunities and Perceptions

drug deals per month among those who deal drugs. This effect is more pronounced among white drug dealers, even though this group has considerably higher returns to work as compared to blacks, whether they deal drugs or not.

Despite the common conclusion that drug dealing among blacks and whites is driven by expected relative legal earnings and drug-dealing images, there remain conspicuous racial differentials in these and other variables. Blacks are much less likely than whites to view themselves as drug dealers; they can expect to receive lower legal wages relative to their illegal earnings.

What would happen to black employment and drug dealing if blacks had identical backgrounds, experiences, criminal perceptions, and expected relative earnings to whites? Figure 23.2 displays the results.[15] If blacks had white images of being drug dealers, black drug dealing would rise by about 15 percent, while black employment probabilities would fall slightly. If they had white criminal perceptions, blacks would experience little change in their employment or drug activities. However, if blacks had white relative wages (a huge upward adjustment in their relative earnings), blacks would reduce their participation in drug dealing by nearly 90 percent. The black drug dealing probability would drop from 13 percent to not much more than 1 percent. The consequence is that if blacks and whites had identical characteristics — and equal expected returns to work relative to crime — all but a small percent of blacks would remain in drug dealing. The cruel reality of these estimates, however, reveals that since crime and work are not assumed to be perfect substitutes, then employment would not necessarily increase when drug dealing declined.

The impact of rising relative legal earnings unambiguously reduces drug dealing; it may do so, however, by increasing labor force participation and not by increasing employment. The flip side of this equation, then, is that increases in illegal incomes may help to increase drug dealing and increase labor force withdrawal.

Conclusion

The inescapable conclusion of this analysis is that black and white offenders, while vastly differing in their perceptions about criminal opportunities and in their self-images as drug dealers, would face no major change in their relative work and drug dealing probabilities, even if these perceptions and criminal opportunities were equalized. It is the legitimate opportunities that would make a difference. Whites earn far more in legal wages relative to their illegal earnings than do blacks. Since there is such a strong inverse relationship between these relative earnings and participation in drug dealing, the natural effect of an increase in black wages is to reduce their drug involvement. If blacks earned the same legal and illegal wages as whites, the reduction in drug dealing would be nothing short of phenomenal: a 90 percent drop.

In other words, there is much more that can be said about the utility of examining drug dealing as a rational response to low wages in the labor market. Since another important variable, an individual's image of a drug dealer, also exhibits a strong impact on both employment and drug dealing, there are likely to be entrepreneurial attractions to drug dealing as well. However, given the strength of the expected wage impacts on drug dealing, it is not likely that the entrepreneurial motive dominates among those who deal drugs. A good possibility is that the entrepreneurial drug dealers are a distinct minority among all drug dealers. And since the "be your own man" motive for engaging in crime has negligible impacts on drug dealing and work in the aggregate, the entrepreneurship aspect of drug dealing must be more related to the earnings potential of drugs and not simply the aura of small business ownership.

These results, however, while confirming aspects of the rational calculus of drug dealing, challenge the often-heard notion that black communities are inundated with drug sellers. If the prison population is characteristic of the criminal population — and if the responses of criminals to surveys such as the Rand Survey are to be believed — then black offenders are less likely to deal drugs than whites. This raises troubling questions about the nature of the inner-city drug problem, questions that may challenge the conventional wisdom about the cocaine-crack epidemic in black communities. If blacks are less likely than whites to sell drugs, how or why does it appear that blacks are more likely to be regular customers of illicit drugs? Are there a few black sellers who make many, many sales per month? Are the sellers from other groups? And, relatedly, is there really a crisis of drug selling in black communities?

The good news is that one route toward reducing drug dealing is improved legitimate employment opportunities. Higher wages will reduce entry into the drug dealing market. Exits from the labor market, however, are likely to continue and pursuit of the lure of criminal enterprise in drug dealing will remain as long as a significant minority of offenders aspire to be dealers.

Notes

Research assistance was provided by Kevin Hart and Tish Crawford; computer programming was rendered by Dr. Tsze Chan. Portions of this chapter were presented at the first annual research conference of the Morehouse Research Institute. I am grateful to the participants for their comments and suggestions. The data used in this chapter were made available by the Inter-University Consortium for Political and Social Research. The data for the Survey of Jail and Prison Inmates, 1978, were originally collected by Mark Peterson, Jan Chaiken, and Patricia Ebener. Neither the collector of the original data nor the consortium bear any responsibility for the analyses or interpretations presented here.

1. Kip Viscusi, "Market Incentives for Criminal Behavior," in *The Black Youth Employment Crisis* ed. Richard Freeman and Harry Holzer (Chicago: University of Chicago Press, 1986), pp. 301–346.

2. Ivan Light, *Ethnic Enterprise in America* (Berkeley: University of California Press, 1972).

3. Samuel L. Myers, Jr., "Political Economy, Race and Morals," *Review of Black Political Economy* 18, no. 1 (1989): 5–15.

4. For a recent review see, Helen Tauchen et al., "Deterrence, Work and Crime: Revisiting the Issues with Birth Cohort," unpublished manuscript, August 1988.

5. Samuel L. Myers, Jr., "How Voluntary Is Black Unemployment and Labor Force Withdrawal?" in *The Question of Discrimination*, ed. William A. Darity, Jr., and Steven Shulman (Middletown, Conn.: Wesleyan University Press, 1990).

6. William Julius Wilson, *The Truly Disadvantaged* (Chicago: University of Chicago Press, 1987).

7. Mark Peterson et al., *Survey of Prison and Jail Inmates: Background and Method N-1635-NJ* (Santa Monica, Calif.: Rand Corporation, 1982).

8. The question was: "During the street months on the calendar, which of the following best describe the way you thought of yourself? (Check all that apply) Car thief, Booster, Thief . . ."

9. U.S. Department of Justice, *Drugs and Crime Facts, 1989* (Washington, D.C.: Government Printing Office, 1990), p. 4.

10. The latter statistic refers only to state prison inmates and was obtained from the 1986 census of state prison inmates. U.S. Department of Justice, *Drugs and Crime Facts, 1989*, p. 5.

11. All together there were sixteen statements ranging from "Whenever someone gets cut or shot there is usually a reason" to "When you've figured it out, doing prison time is not too hard."

12. Specifically, the responses to the questions were coded from 0 to 1, where 0 meant unlikely and 1 meant certain. The scores were averaged for the relevant questions. If the average exceeded .75, the "Crime Pays" measure was denoted by 1; otherwise, it was equal to 0.

13. About the same percentage felt that there were high or certain chances of being your own man by going straight.

14. Results of these reduced form equations are available from the author.

15. The method used to obtain the results is the following: Coefficients from the probit equations for the probability of employment and the probability of drug dealing were transformed into logit coefficients by dividing them by .625. This permits the calculation from the dosed form logistic function of the underlying probability evaluated at selected means of the independent variables. For all factors, the black means are replaced by white means of independent variables. For expected wages, type-A criminal, and drug dealer image, the black means are replaces by the white means, leaving the other independent variables unchanged at their black means. For crime pays, both CRIME PAYS 1 and CRIME PAYS 2 are replaced by their white means in the drug equation; STRAIGHT PAYS 1 & 2 are replaced by their white means in the employment equation. The impacts are measured by finding the percentage difference between (a) the values of employment and drug probabilities when the indicated white means are substituted for the black means and (b) the computed values of these probabilities at the black means only.

24

Violence and the Inner-City Street Code

ELIJAH ANDERSON

Of all the problems besetting the poor inner-city black community, none is more pressing than that of interpersonal violence and aggression. This phenomenon wreaks havoc daily on the lives of community residents and increasingly spills over into downtown and residential middle-class areas. Muggings, burglaries, carjackings, and drug-related shootings, all of which may leave their victims or innocent bystanders dead, are now common enough to concern all urban and many suburban residents. The inclination to violence springs from the circumstances of life among the ghetto poor — the lack of jobs that pay a living wage, the stigma of race, the fallout from rampant drug use and drug trafficking, and the resulting alienation and lack of hope for the future.

Simply living in such an environment places young people at special risk of falling victim to aggressive behavior. Although there are often forces in the community which can counteract the negative influences — by far the most powerful is a strong, loving, "decent" (as inner-city residents put it) family committed to middle-class values — the despair is pervasive enough to have spawned an oppositional culture, that of "the streets," whose norms are often consciously opposed to those of mainstream society. These two orientations — decent and street — socially organize the community, and their coexistence has important consequences for residents, particularly for children growing up in the inner city. Above all, this environment means that even youngsters whose home lives reflect mainstream values — and the majority of homes in the community do — must be able to handle themselves in a street-oriented environment.

This is because the street culture has evolved what may be called a "code of the streets," which amounts to a set of informal rules governing interpersonal public behavior, including violence.[1] The rules prescribe both a proper comportment and the proper way to respond if challenged. They regulate the use of violence and so supply a rationale which allows those who are inclined to aggression to precipitate violent encounters in an approved way. The rules have been established and are enforced mainly by the street-oriented, but on the streets the distinction between street and decent is often irrelevant; everybody knows that if the rules are violated, there are penalties. Knowledge of the code is thus largely defensive, and it is literally necessary for operating in public. Therefore, even though families with a decency orientation are usually opposed to the values of the code, they often reluctantly encourage their children's familiarity with it to enable them to negotiate the inner-city environment.

At the heart of the code is the issue of respect — loosely defined as being treated "right" or granted the deference one deserves. However, in the troublesome public environment of the inner city, as people increasingly feel buffeted by forces beyond their control, what one deserves in the way of respect becomes more and more problematic and uncertain. This situation in turn further opens the issue of respect to sometimes intense interpersonal negotiation. In the street culture, especially among young people, respect is viewed as almost an external entity that is hard-won but easily lost, and so it must constantly be guarded. The rules of the code in fact provide a framework for negotiating respect. Individuals whose very appearance — including their clothing, demeanor, and way of moving — deters transgressions feel that they possess, and may be considered by others to possess, a measure of respect. With the right amount, for instance, such individuals can avoid being bothered in public. If they are bothered, on the other hand, not only may they be in physical danger but they will have been disgraced or "dissed" (disrespected). Many of the forms that dissing can take might seem petty to middle-class people (maintaining eye contact for too long, for example), but to those invested in the street code, these actions become serious indications of the other person's intentions. Consequently, such people become very sensitive to advances and slights, which could well serve as a warning of imminent physical confrontation.

This hard reality can be traced to the profound sense of alienation from mainstream society and its institutions felt by many poor inner-city black people, particularly the young. The code of the streets is actually a cultural adaptation to a profound lack of faith in the police and the judicial system. The police are most often seen as representing the dominant white society and not caring to protect inner-city residents. When called, they may not respond, which is one reason many residents feel they must be prepared to take extraordinary measures to defend themselves and their loved ones against those who are inclined to aggression. Lack of police accountability has in fact been incorporated into the status system: The person who is believed capable of "taking care of himself" is accorded a certain deference, which translates into a sense of physical and psychological control. Thus, the street code emerges where the influence of the police ends and where personal responsibility for one's safety is felt to begin. Exacerbated by the proliferation of drugs and easy access to guns, this volatile situation results in the ability of the street-oriented minority (or those who effectively "go for bad") to dominate the public spaces.

This chapter is an ethnographic representation of the workings of this street code in the context of the socioeconomic situation in which the community finds itself.[2] The material it presents was gathered through numerous visits to various inner-city families and neighborhood hangouts and through many in-depth interviews with a wide array of individuals and groups; these interviews included sessions with adolescent boys and young men (some incarcerated, some not), older men, teenage mothers, and grandmothers. The structure of the inner-city family, the socialization of its children, the social structure of the community, and that community's extreme poverty, which is in large part the result of structural economic change, will be seen to interact in a way that facilitates the involvement of so many maturing youths in the culture of the streets, in which violence and the way it is regulated are key elements.

The Ethnographic Method

A clarifying note on the methodology is perhaps in order for those unfamiliar with the ethnographic method. Ethnography seeks to paint a conceptual picture of the setting under consideration, through the use of observation and in-depth interviews. The researcher's goal is to illuminate the social and cultural dynamics which characterize the setting by answering such questions as "How do the people in the setting perceive their situation?" "What assumptions do they bring to their decision making?" "What behavior patterns result from these choices?" "What are the consequences of those behaviors?" An important aspect of the ethnographer's work is that it be as objective as possible. This is not easy since it requires researchers to set aside their own values and assumptions as to what is and is not morally acceptable — in other words, to jettison that prism through which they typically view a given situation. By definition, one's own assumptions are so basic to one's perceptions that it may be difficult to see their influence. Ethnographic researchers, however, have been trained to recognize underlying assumptions, their own and those of their subjects, and to override the former and uncover the latter (see Becker, 1970).

"Decent" Families: Values and Reality

Although almost everyone in the poor inner-city neighborhood is struggling financially and therefore feels a certain distance from the rest of America, the decent and the street family in a real sense represent two poles of value orientation, two contrasting conceptual categories.[3] The labels decent and street, which the residents themselves use, amount to evaluative judgments that confer status on local residents. The labeling is often the result of a social contest among individuals and families of the neighborhood, and individuals of the two orientations can and often do coexist in the same extended family. Decent residents judge themselves to be so while judging others to be of the street, whereas street individuals may present themselves as decent, drawing distinctions between themselves and other even more street-oriented people. In any case, street is considered a highly pejorative epithet. In addition, there is quite a bit of circumstantial behavior among individuals — that is, one person may at different times exhibit both decent and street orientations, depending on the circumstances. Although these designations result from so much social jockeying, there do exist concrete features that define each conceptual category.

Generally, so-called decent families accept mainstream values more fully and attempt to instill them in their children. Whether a married couple with children or a single-parent (usually female) household, such families are generally working poor and so tend to be relatively better off financially than their street-oriented neighbors. The adults value hard work and self-reliance and are willing to sacrifice for their children. Because they have a certain amount of faith in mainstream society, they harbor hopes for a better future for their children, if not for themselves. Many of them go to church and take a strong interest in their children's schooling. Rather than dwell on the real hardships and inequities facing them, many such decent people, particularly the increasing number of grandmothers raising grandchildren, sometimes see their difficult situation as a test from God and derive great support from their faith and from the church community.

Intact families, although in the minority, provide powerful role models in the community. Typically, the husband and wife work at low-paying jobs; possibly, they are aided by the occasional financial contributions of a teenage child who works at a part-time job. At times, the man or woman may work multiple jobs. As the primary breadwinner, the man is usually considered the "head of household," with the woman as his partner and the children as their subjects. During bouts of unemployment, the man's dominance may be questioned, but the financially marginal black family with a decency orientation strongly values male authority. Typically, certain male decisions and behavior may be contested by the woman, but very rarely will they be challenged by the children. As they age, however, children, particularly males, may "try" (challenge) the authority of the father, which places some pressure on him to keep his children in line. In public, such a family makes a striking picture as the man appears to be in complete control, with the woman and the children often following his lead. This appearance is to some extent a practical matter, for the streets and other public places are considered dangerous and unpredictable, and it is the man who is most often placed in the public role of protector and defender against danger. In playing this role, the man may exhibit a certain exaggeration of concern, particularly when anonymous black males are near; through his actions and words, and at times speaking loudly and assertively to get his small children in line, he lets strangers know unambiguously, "This is my family, and I am in charge."

Extremely aware of the problematic and often dangerous environment in which they reside, decent parents tend to be strict in their childrearing practices, encouraging children to respect authority and walk a straight moral line. They have an almost obsessive concern with trouble of any kind and remind their children to be on the lookout for people and situations which might lead to such difficulties. When disciplining their children, they tend to be liberal in the use of corporal punishment, but unlike street parents, who are often observed lashing out at their children, they tend to explain the reason for the spanking. Outsiders, however, may not always be able to distinguish between parents who are using corporal punishment as a means to uphold standards of decency and those whose goal is to teach toughness and intimidation or who have no goal. Such confusion of decent motives with behavior that mainstream society generally disapproves of is a source of frustration for many black parents who are attempting to lead mainstream lives. Here is the experience of a 48-year-old man with an intact family:

> My boy and this other boy broke into this church, aw right? Stole this ridin' lawnmower, just to ride on, nothin' else. And when I found out, I whupped his behind. Now two weeks after that, he got suspended for fightin', which wasn't his fault — but they suspended him and the other boy. Now he scared to come home and tell me. Now this is two weeks after I done already talked to him. He's cryin' and carryin' on in school. So the school sends a 24-year-old black girl, a 24-year-old white girl to my house. Now the first thing I asked

them was did they have kids. None of 'em have kids. But I done raised seven kids. My oldest girl is 30 years old. I have nine grandkids. I'm 48. And I asked them how can they tell me how to raise my kids. And they don't have any of they own. I was so angry I had to leave. My wife made me get out of the house. But they did send me an apology letter, but the point is that I cannot chastise my child unless the government tells me it's OK. That's wrong. I'm not gon' kill my child, but I'm gonna make him know right and wrong. These kids today they know that whatever you do to 'em, first thing you know they call it child abuse. And they gon' lock us up. And it's wrong, it really is.

Consistent with this view, decent families also inspect their children's play-mates for behavior problems, and they enforce curfews. For example, they may require their young children to come in by a certain time or simply to go no farther than the front stoop of their house, a vantage point from which the children attentively watch other children play unsupervised in the street; the obedient children may then endure the street kids' taunts of "stoop children." As the children become teenagers, these parents make a strong effort to know where they are at night, giving them an unmistakable message of their caring, concern, and love. At the same time, they are vigilant in guarding against the appearance of any kind of delinquent or loose behavior, including violence, drug use, and staying out very late at night; they monitor not only their own children's behavior but also that of their children's peers, at times playfully embarrassing their own children by voicing value judgments in front of their children's friends.

A single mother with children may also form a decent family — indeed, the majority of decent families in the inner city are of this type — but she must work even harder at instilling decent values in her children. She may reside with her mother or other female or male relatives and friends, or she may simply receive help with child care from an extended family. She too may press for deference to her authority, but usually she is at some disadvantage with regard to young men who might "try" her ability to control her household, attempting to date her daughters or to draw her sons into the streets. The importance of having a man of the house to fill the role of protector of the household, a figure boys are prepared to respect, should not be underesti-mated. A mother on her own often feels she must be constantly on guard and exhibit a great deal of determination. A single mother of four boys, three of whom are grown, explains:

It really is pretty bad around here. There's quite a few grandmothers taking care of kids. They mothers out here on crack. There's quite a few of 'em. The drugs are terrible.

Now I got a 15-year-old boy, and I do everything I can to keep him straight.

'Cause they all on the corner. You can't say you not in it 'cause we in a bad area. They [drug dealers and users] be all on the corner. They be sittin' in front of apartments takin' the crack. And constantly, every day, I have to stay on 'em and make sure everything's O.K. Which is real bad, I never seen it this bad. And I been around here since '81, and I never seen it this bad.

At nights they be roamin' up and down the streets, and they be droppin' the caps [used crack vials] all in front of your door. And when the kids out there playin', you gotta like sweep 'em up.

It's harder for me now to try to keep my 15-year-old under control. Right now, he likes to do auto mechanics, hook up radios in people's cars. And long as I keep 'im interested in that, I'm O.K.

But it's not a day that goes by that I'm not in fear. 'Cause right now, he got friends that's sellin' it [drugs]. They, you know, got a whole lot of money and stuff.

And I get him to come and mop floors [she works as a part-time janitor] and I give him a few dollars. I say, "As long as you got a roof over yo' head, son, don't worry about nothin' else."

It's just a constant struggle tryin' to raise yo' kids in this time. It's very hard. They [boys on the street] say to him, "Man, why you got to go in the house?" And they keep sittin' right on the stoop. If he go somewhere, I got to know where he's at and who he's with. And they be tellin' him . . . He say, "No, man, I got to stay on these steps. I don't want no problem with my mama!"

Now I been a single parent for 15 years. So far, I don't have any problems. I have four sons. I got just the one that's not grown, the 15-year-old. Everyone else is grown. My oldest is 35. I'm tryin'. Not that easy. I got just one more, now. Then I'll be all right. If I need help, the older ones'll help me.

Most of the time, I keep track myself. I told him I'll kill him if I catch him out here sellin' [drugs]. And I know most of the drug dealers. He better not. I gon' hurt him. They better not give him nothin' [drugs or money]. He better not do nothin' for them. I tell him, "I know some of your friends are dealers. [You can] speak to 'em, but don't let me catch you hangin' on the corner. I done struggled too hard to try to take care of you. I'm not gon' let you throw your life away."

When me and my husband separated in '79, I figured I had to do it. He was out there drivin' trucks and never home. I had to teach my kids how to play ball and this and that. I said, "If I have to be a single parent, I'll do it."

It used to be the gangs, and you fought 'em, and it was over. But now if you fight somebody, they may come back and kill you. It's a whole lot different now. You got to be streetsmart to get along. My boy doesn't like to fight. I took him out of school, put him in a home course. The staff does what it wants to. Just work for a paycheck.

You tell the kid, now you can't pick their friends, so you do what you can. I try to tell mine, "You gon' be out there with the bad [street kids], you can't do what they do. You got to use your own mind." Every day, if I don't get up and say a prayer, I can't make it. I can't make it. I watch him closely. If he go somewhere, I have to know where he at. And when I leave him, or if he go to them girlfriends' houses, I tell the parents, "If you not responsible, he can't stay." I'm not gon' have no teenager making no baby.

There are so many kids that don't make 17. Look at that 16-year-old boy that got killed last week. Somebody was looking for his cousin. All this kinda stuff, it don't make sense. These kids can't even make 17. All over drugs. Drugs taken control. Even the parents in it. How a child gon' come home with a $100 sweatsuit on, $200 sneakers. Ain't got no job. A $1000 in they pocket. He ain't gon' come in my house and do that. Some parents use the money. Some of the kids'll knock they own parents out. The parents afraid of the kids. I've seen 'em knock the parents the hell down.

Probably the most meaningful word for describing the mission of decent families, as seen by themselves and outsiders, is that of instilling "backbone" in its younger members. In support of its efforts toward this goal, a decent family tends to be much more willing and able than the street-oriented family to ally itself with outside institutions such as school and church. The parents in such families have usually had more years of schooling than their street-oriented counterparts, which tends to foster in them a positive attitude toward their children's schooling. In addition, they place a certain emphasis on spiritual values and principles, and church attendance tends to be a regular family ritual, as noted earlier, although females are generally more so inclined than the males.

An important aspect of religious belief for the decent people is their conception of death. The intertwined ideas of fate, a judgment day, and an afterlife present a marked contrast to the general disorganization and sense of immediacy that is known to characterize street-oriented families and individuals. The situation of the street-oriented may then result in the tendency to be indifferent or oblivious to the probable consequences or future meaning of their behavior, including death. People imbued with a street orientation tend not to think far beyond the immediate present; their orientation towards the future is either very limited or nonexistent. One must live for the moment, for they embrace the general belief that "tomorrow ain't promised to you." For religious people, the sometimes literal belief in an afterlife and a day of reckoning inspires hope and makes life extremely valuable, and this belief acts to check individuals in potentially violent encounters. While accepting the use of violence in self-defense, they are less likely to be initiators of hostilities. Religious beliefs thus can have very practical implications. Furthermore, the moral feeling church-going instills in many people strengthens their self-esteem and underscores the sense that a positive future is possible, thus contributing to a certain emotional stability or "long fuse" in volatile circumstances.

In these decent families, then, there tends to be a real concern with and a certain amount of hope for the future. Such attitudes are often expressed in a drive to work to have something or to build a good life by working hard and saving for material things; raising one's children — telling them to "make something out of yourself" and "make do with what you have" — is an important aspect of this attitude. But the concern with material things, although accepted, often produces a certain strain on the young; often encouraged to covet material things as emblems testifying to social and cultural well-being, the lack the legitimate or legal means for obtaining such things. The presence of this dilemma often causes otherwise decent youths to invest their considerable mental resources in the street.

Involvement with institutions such as school and church has given decent parents a kind of savoir faire that helps them get along in the world. Thus, they often know how to get things done and use that knowledge to help advance themselves and their children. In the face of such overwhelming problems as persistent poverty, AIDS, or drug use, which can beset even the strongest and most promising families, these parents are trying hard to give their children as good a life — if not a better one — as they themselves had. At the same time, they are themselves polite and considerate of others, and they teach their children to be the same way. At home, at work, and in church, they work hard to maintain a positive mental attitude and a spirit of cooperation.

The Street

So-called street parents often show a lack of consideration for other people and have a rather superficial sense of family and community. Though they may love their children, many of them are unable to cope with the physical and emotional demands of parenthood, and they often find it difficult to reconcile their needs with those of their children. These families, who are more fully invested in the code of the streets than the decent people are, may aggressively socialize their children into it in a normative way. They believe in the code and judge themselves and others according to its values.

In fact, the overwhelming majority of families in the inner-city community try to approximate the decent-family model, but there are many others who clearly represent the worst fears of the decent family. Not only are the financial resources of these other families extremely limited, but what little they have may easily be misused. Often suffering the worst effects of social isolation, the lives of the street-oriented are often marked by disorganization. In the most desperate circumstances, people often have a limited understanding of priorities and consequences, and so frustrations mount over bills, food, and, at times, drink, cigarettes, and drugs. Some tend toward self-destructive behavior; many street-oriented women are crack-addicted ("on the pipe"), alcoholic, or repeatedly involved in complicated relationships with men who abuse them. In addition, the seeming intractability of their situation, caused in large part by the lack of well-paying jobs and the persistence of racial discrimination, has engendered deep-seated bitterness and anger in many of the most desperate and poorest blacks, especially young people. The need both to exercise a measure of control and to lash out at somebody is often played out in the adults' relations with their children. At the least, the frustrations of persistent poverty shorten the fuse in such people—contributing to a lack of patience with anyone, child or adult, who irritates them.

Many decent people simply view the street-oriented as lowlife or bad people. Even if they display a certain amount of responsibility, such "lowlife" people are generally seen as incapable of being anything but a bad influence on their neighbors. The following field note is germane:

> On the fringe of the Village, there are houses of the inner-city black community. On one street is the home of Joe Dickens, a heavy-set, 32-year-old black man. He rents the house and lives there with his three children, who range in age from about 3 ½ to 7. Dickens' wife is not around. It is rumored that the two of them were on crack together and his wife's habit got out of control. As has been happening more and more in this community, she gravitated to the streets and became a prostitute to support her habit. Dickens could not accept this behavior and so he had to let her go. He took over the running of the house and the care of the children as best he could. By doing what he can for his kids, he might be considered the responsible parent, but many of the neighbors do not see him as responsible. They observe him yelling and cursing at the children, as well as with his buddies, and allowing them to "rip and run" up and down the street at all hours. At the same time, Mr. Dickens lacks consideration of others, a lack which is a defining trait of street-oriented people. He often sits on his porch and plays loud music, either unaware of or insensitive to the fact that it disturbs the whole block. Sometimes the neighbors call the police, who do not respond to the complaint, leaving the neighbors frustrated and demoralized.
>
> In general, however, the decent people on the street are afraid to confront Mr. Dickens because they fear getting in trouble with him and his buddies. They know that like all street people, he subscribes to the belief that might makes right, and so he is likely to try to harm anyone who annoys him. In addition, it is believed that Dickens is a crack dealer. His house is always busy, with people coming in and out at all hours, often driving up in their cars,

running in and quickly emerging and driving off. Dickens' children, of course, are witnesses to all this activity, and one can only imagine what they see inside the house. They are growing up in a family, but it is a street-oriented family, and it is obvious to the neighbors that these children are learning the values of toughness and self-absorption from their father and the social environment in which he is raising them.

The decent people firmly believe that it is this general set of cultural deficits — that is, a certain fundamental lack of social polish and commitment to norms of civility, which they refer to as "ignorance" — which makes the street-oriented quick to resort to violence to resolve almost any dispute. To those who hold this view, such street people seem to carry about them an aura of danger. Thus, during public interactions, the decent people may readily defer to the street-oriented, especially when they are strangers, out of fear of their ignorance. For instance, when street people are encountered at theaters or other public places talking loudly or making excessive noise, many decent people are reluctant to correct them for fear of verbal abuse that could lead to violence. Similarly, the decent people will often avoid a confrontation over a parking space or traffic error for fear of a verbal or physical confrontation. Under their breaths they may utter disapprovingly to a companion, "street niggers," thereby drawing a sharp cultural distinction between themselves and such persons. But there are also times when the decent people will try to approach the level of the "ignorant" ones by what they refer to as "getting ignorant" (see Anderson, 1990). In these circumstances, they may appear in battle dress, more than ready to face down the ignorant ones, indicating they have reached their limit, or threshold, for violent confrontation. And from this, an actual fight can erupt.

Thus, the fact that generally civilly disposed, socially conscious, and largely self-reliant men and women share the streets and other public institutions with the inconsiderate, the ignorant, and the extremely desperate puts them at special risk. In order to live and to function in the community, they must adapt to a street reality that is often dominated by the presence of those who at best are suffering severely in some way and who are likely to resort quickly to violence to settle disputes.

Coming Up in Street Families

In the street-oriented family, the development of an aggressive mentality can be seen from the beginning, even in the circumstances surrounding the birth of the child. In circumstances of persistent poverty, the mother is often little more than a child herself and without many resources or a consistent source of support; she is often getting by with public assistance or the help of kin. She may be ambivalent with respect to the child: On the one hand, she may look at the child as a heavenly gift; but on the other hand, as she begins to care for it, she is apt to realize that it is a burden, and sometimes a profound burden. These are the years she wants to be free to date and otherwise consort with men, to have a social life, and she discovers that the child slows her down (see Anderson, 1989). Thus, she sometimes leans on others, including family members, to enable her to satisfy her social needs for getting out nights and being with male and female friends.

In these circumstances, a woman — or a man, although men are less consistently present in children's lives — can be quite aggressive with children, yelling at and striking them for the least little infraction of the rules she has set down. Often little if any serious explanation follows the verbal and physical punishment. This response teaches children a particular lesson. They learn that to solve any kind of interpersonal problem, one must quickly resort to hitting or other violent behavior. Actual peace and quiet — and also the appearance of calm, respectful children that can be conveyed to her neighbors and friends — are often what the young mother most desires, but at times she will be very aggressive in trying to achieve these goals. Thus, she may be quick to beat her children, especially if they defy her law, not because she hates them but because this is the way she knows how to control them. In fact, many street-oriented women love their children dearly. Many mothers in the community subscribe to the notion that there is a "devil in the boy" that must be beaten out of him or that socially "fast girls need to be whupped." Thus, much of what borders on child abuse in the view of social authorities is acceptable parental punishment in the view of these mothers.

Many street-oriented women are weak and ineffective mothers whose children learn to fend for themselves when necessary, foraging for food and money and getting them any way they can. These children are sometimes employed by drug dealers or become addicted themselves. These children of the street, growing up with little supervision, are said to "come up hard." In the interest of survival, they often learn to fight at an early age, sometimes using short-tempered adults around them as role models. The street-oriented home may be fraught with anger, verbal disputes, physical aggression, and even mayhem. The children observe these goings-on, learning the lesson that might makes right. They quickly learn to hit those who cross them, and the dog-eat-dog mentality prevails. In order to survive, to protect oneself, it is necessary to marshal inner resources and be ready to deal with adversity in a hands-on way. In these circumstances, physical prowess takes on great significance.

In some of the most desperate cases, a street-oriented mother may simply leave her young children alone and unattended while she goes out. The most irresponsible women can be found at local bars and crack houses, getting high and socializing with other adults. Sometimes a troubled woman will leave very young children alone for days at a time. Reports of crack addicts abandoning their children have become common in drug-infested inner-city communities. Neighbors or relatives discover the abandoned children, often hungry and distraught over the absence of their mother. After repeated absences, a friend or relative, particularly a grandmother, will often step in to care for the young children, sometimes petitioning the authorities to send her, as guardian of the children, the mother's welfare check, if the mother gets one. By this time, however, the children may well have learned the first lesson of the streets: Survival itself, let alone respect, cannot be taken for granted; you have to fight for your place in the world.

The Shuffling Process

As indicated earlier, in order to carry on their everyday lives in poor inner-city neighborhoods, children from even the most decent homes must come to terms with the streets. This means that they must learn to deal with the various and sundry influences of the streets, including their more street-oriented peers. Indeed, as children grow up and their parents' control wanes, they go through a social shuffling process that can undermine, or at least test, much of the socialization they have received at home. In other words, the street serves as a mediating influence under which children may come to reconsider and rearrange their personal orientations. This is a time of status passage (see Glaser and Strauss, 1972) when social identity can become very uncertain as children sort out their ways of being. It is a tricky time because a child can go either way. For children from decent homes, for example, the immediate and present reality of the street situation can overcome the compunctions against tough behavior that their parents taught them so that the lessons of the home are slowly forgotten and the child "goes for bad." Or a talented child from a street-oriented family may discover ways of gaining respect without unduly resorting to aggressive and violent responses — by becoming a rapper or athlete, for example, or rarely, a good student. Thus, the kind of home a child comes from becomes influential but not determinative of the way he will ultimately turn out.

By the age of ten, all children from both decent and street-oriented families are mingling on the neighborhood streets and figuring out their identities. Here they try out certain roles and scripts — which are sometimes actively opposed to the wishes of parents — in a process that challenges both their talents and their socialization and may involve more than a little luck, good or bad. In this volatile environment, they learn to watch their backs and to anticipate and negotiate those situations that might lead to troubles with others. The successful outcomes of these cumulative interactions with the streets ultimately determine every child's life chances.

Herein lies the real meaning of so many fights and altercations, despite the ostensible, usually petty, precipitating causes, including the competitions over girlfriends and boyfriends and "he say, she say" conflicts of personal attribution. Adolescents are insecure and are trying to establish their identities. Children from the middle and upper classes, however, usually have more ways to express themselves as worthwhile and so have more avenues to explore. The negotiations they engage in among themselves may also include aggression, but they tend to be more verbal in a way that includes a greater use of other options — options that require resources not available to those of more limited resources, such as showing off with things, connections, and so on. In poor inner-city neighborhoods, physicality is a fairly common way of asserting oneself. It is also unambiguous. If you punch someone out, if you succeed in keeping someone from walking down your block, "you did it." It is a *fait accompli*. And the evidence that you prevailed is there for all to see.

During this campaign for respect, through these various conflicts, those connections between actually being respected and the need for being in physical control of at least a portion of the environment become internalized, and the germ of the code of the streets emerges. As children mature, they obtain an increasingly more sophisticated understanding of the code, and it becomes part of their working conception of the world, so that by the time they reach adulthood, it comes to define the social order. In time, the rules of physical engagement and their personal implications become crystallized. Children learn the conditions under which violence is appropriate, and they also learn how the code defines the individual's relationship to his or her peers. They thus come to appreciate the give-and-take of public life, the process of negotiation.

The ethic of violence is in part a class phenomenon (see Wolfgang and Ferracuti, 1967). Children are more inclined to be physical than adults (because they have fewer alternatives for settling disputes), and lower-class adults tend to be more physical than middle- or upper-middle-class adults. Poor and lower-class adults more often find themselves in disputes that lead to violence. Because they are more often alienated from the agents and agencies of social control, such as the police and the courts, they are left alone more often to settle disputes on their own. And such parents, in turn, tend to socialize their kids into this reality.

But this reality of inner-city life is largely absorbed on the streets. At an early age, often even before they start school and without much in the way of adult supervision, children from such street-oriented families gravitate to the streets, where they must be ready "to hang," to socialize with peers. Children from these generally permissive homes have a great deal of latitude and are allowed to "rip and run" up and down the street. They often come home from school, put their books down, and go right back out the door. For the most severely compromised, on school nights, eight- and nine-year-olds remain out until nine or ten o'clock (and the teenagers come in whenever they want to). On the streets, they play in groups that often become the source of their primary social bonds. Children from decent homes tend to be more carefully supervised and are thus likely to have curfews and to be taught how to stay out of trouble.

In the street, through their play, children pour their individual life experiences into a common knowledge pool, affirming, confirming, and elaborating on what they have observed in the home and matching their skills against those of others. And they learn to fight. Even small children test one another, pushing and shoving others, and are ready to hit other children over circumstances not to their liking. In turn, they are readily hit by other children, and the child who is toughest prevails. Thus, the violent resolution of disputes — the hitting and cursing — gains social reinforcement. The child in effect is initiated into a system that is really a way of campaigning for self-respect.

There is a critical sense in which violent behavior is determined by situations, thus giving importance to the various ways in which individuals define and interpret such situations. In meeting the various exigencies of immediate situations, which become so many public trials, the individual builds patterns as outcomes are repeated over time. Behaviors, violent or civil, which work for a young person and are reinforced by peers whose reactions to such behavior come to shape the person's outlook, will likely be repeated.

In addition, younger children witness the disputes of older children, which are often resolved through cursing and abusive talk, and sometimes through aggression or outright violence. They see that one child succumbs to the greater physical and mental abilities of the other. They are also alert and attentive witnesses to the verbal and physical fights of adults, after which they compare notes and share their own interpretations of the event. In almost every case, the victor is the person who physically won the altercation, and this person often enjoys the esteem and respect of onlookers. These experiences reinforce the lessons the children have learned at home: Might makes right and toughness is a virtue, humility is not. In effect, they learn the social meaning of fighting. When it is left virtually unchallenged, this understanding becomes an ever more important part of a child's working conception of the world. Over time, the code of the streets becomes refined. Those street-oriented adults with whom children come in contact — including mothers, fathers, brothers, sisters, boyfriends, cousins, neighbors, and friends — help them along in forming this understanding by verbalizing the messages they are getting through experience: "Watch your back." "Protect yourself." "Don't punk out." "If somebody messes with you, you got to pay them back." "If someone disses you, you got to straighten them out." Many parents actually impose sanctions if a child is not sufficiently aggressive. For example, if a child loses a fight and comes home upset, the parent might respond, "Don't you come in here crying that somebody beat you up; you better get back out there and whup his ass. I didn't raise no punks! Get back out there and whup his ass. If you don't whup his ass, I'll whup yo' ass when you come home." Thus, the child obtains reinforcement for being tough and showing nerve.

While fighting, some children cry as though they are doing something they are ambivalent about. The fight may be against their wishes, yet they may feel constrained to fight or face the consequences — not just from peers but also from caretakers or their parents, who may administer another beating if they back down. Some adults recall receiving such lessons from their own parents and justify repeating them to their children as a way to toughen them up. Appearing capable of taking care of oneself as a form of self-defense is a dominant theme among both street-oriented and decent adults, who worry about the safety of their children. There is thus at times a convergence in their child-rearing practices, although the rationales behind them may differ.

The following field note graphically illustrates both the efficacy of these informal lessons and the early age at which they are learned:

> Casey is four years old and attends a local nursery school. He lives with his mom and stepfather. Casey's family is considered to be a street family in the neighborhood. At home, his mother will curse at him and, at times, will beat him for misbehavior. At times, his stepfather will spank him as well. Casey has attracted the attention of the staff of the nursery school because of his behavior. Of particular concern is Casey's cursing and hitting of other children. When Casey wants something, he will curse and hit other children, causing many there to refer to him as bad. He now has that reputation of "bad" around the center. He regularly refers to members of the staff as "bitches" and "motherfuckers." For instance, he will say to his teacher, "Cathy, you bitch" or "What that bitch want?" At times this seems funny coming from the mouth of a four-year-old, but it reflects on Casey's home situation. Around the center, he knows that such behavior is disapproved of because of the way the teachers and others react to it, though he may get reinforcement for it because of its humorous character. Once when his teacher upset him, Casey promptly slapped her and called her a "bitch."

Upon hearing of this incident, the bus driver refused to take Casey home, or even to let him on his bus. The next day, when Casey saw the bus driver again, he said, "Norman, you left me. Why'd you leave me? You a trip, man." When Casey desires a toy or some other item from a playmate, he will demand it and sometimes hit the child and try to take it. Members of the staff fear that Casey has a bad influence on other children at the center, for he curses at them "like a sailor," though "they don't know what he's talking about." In these ways, Casey acts somewhat grown up, or "mannish," in the words of the bus driver, who sometimes glares at him, wanting to treat him as another man, since he seems to act that way. Staff members at the center have found they can control Casey by threatening to report his behavior to his stepfather, to which he replies, "Oh, please don't tell him. I'll be good. Please don't tell him." It seems that Casey fears this man and that telling him might mean a beating for Casey. Other local decent blacks say his home life corresponds to that of the typical street family, which is rife with cursing, yelling, physical abuse of children, and limited financial resources.

Many of these parents do not want Casey to be a playmate for one of their own children. They think he would be a bad influence on their own children, particularly in encouraging them toward assuming a street identity. This is something most want to guard against, and children "like this one" worry them generally. They feel such children help to make their own children more unruly. They also feel that certain neighborhoods breed such children, and the decent children are at some risk when placed in an environment with the street kids.

In the minds of many decent parents, children from street families, because of their general ignorance and lack of opportunities, are considered at great risk of eventually getting into serious trouble.

Self-Image Based on Juice

By the time they are teenagers, most youths have either internalized the code of the streets or at least learned the need to comport themselves in accordance with its rules, which chiefly have to do with interpersonal communication. The code revolves around the presentation of self. Its basic requirement is the display of a certain predisposition to violence. Accordingly, one's bearing must send the unmistakable if sometimes subtle message to "the next person" in public that one is capable of violence and mayhem when the situation requires it—that one can take care of oneself. The nature of this communication is largely determined by the demands of the circumstances but can include facial expressions, gait, and verbal expressions—all of which are geared mainly to deterring aggression. Physical appearance, including clothes, jewelry, and grooming, also plays an important part in how a person is viewed; to be respected, you have to have the right look.

Even so, there are no guarantees against challenges, because there are always people around looking for a fight to increase their share of respect — or "juice," as it is sometimes called on the street. Moreover, if a male is assaulted, it is important, not only in the eyes of his opponent but also in the eyes of his "running buddies," for him to avenge himself. Otherwise, he risks being "tried" or "rolled on" (physically assaulted) by any number of others. To maintain his honor he must show he is not someone to be "messed with" or "dissed." In general, the person must "keep himself straight" by managing his position of respect among others; this involves in part his self-image, which is shaped by what he thinks others are thinking of him in relation to his peers.

Objects play an important and complicated role in establishing self-image. Jackets, sneakers, and gold jewelry, reflect not just a person's taste, which tends to be tightly regulated among adolescents of all social classes, but also a willingness to possess things that may require defending. A boy wearing a fashionable, expensive jacket, for example, is vulnerable to attack by another who covets the jacket and either cannot afford to buy one or wants the added satisfaction of depriving someone else of his. However, if a boy forgoes the desirable jacket and wears one that isn't hip, he runs the risk of being teased and possibly even assaulted as an unworthy person. A youth with a decency orientation describes the situation:

> Here go another thing. If you outside, right, and your mom's on welfare and she on crack, the persons you tryin' to be with dress [in] like purple sweatpants and white sneaks, but it's all decent, right, and you got on some bummy jeans and a pair of dull sneaks, they won't — some of the people out there sellin' drugs won't let you hang with them unless you dress like [in] purple sweatpants and decent sneaks every day. . . .
>
> They tease 'em. First they'll tease 'em and then they'll try to say they stink, like they smell like pig or something like that, and then they'll be like, "Get out of here. Get out. We don't want you near us. You stink. You dirty." All that stuff. And I don't think that's right. If he's young, it ain't his fault or her fault that she dressin' like that. It's her mother and her dad's fault.

To be allowed to hang with certain prestigious crowds, a boy must wear a different set of expensive clothes — sneakers and an athletic outfit — every day. Not to be able to do so might make him appear socially deficient. The youth may come to covet such items — especially when he sees easy prey wearing them. The youth continues:

> You can even get hurt off your own clothes: Like, say, I'm walkin' down the street and somebody try to take my hat from me and I won't let 'em take it and they got a gun. You can get killed over one little simple hat. Or if I got a gold ring and a gold necklace on and they see me one dark night on a dark street, and they stick me up and I won't let' em, and they shoot me. I'm dead and they hide me. I'm dead and won't nobody ever know [who did it].

In acquiring valued things, therefore, a person shores up his or her identity — but since it is an identity based on having something, it is highly precarious. This very precariousness gives a heightened sense of urgency to staying even with peers, with whom the person is actually competing. Young men and women who are able to command respect through their presentation of self — by allowing their possessions and their body language to speak for them — may not have to campaign for regard but may, rather, gain it by the force of their manner. Those who are unable to command respect in this way must actively campaign for it. The following incident, which I witnessed, is a good example of the way one's things can be used to establish status in a given situation:

> It was a warm spring day, and my twelve-year-old son and I were in a local Foot Locker shoe store about a mile north of the community. We were being waited on when a brand-new purple BMW pulled up in front of the store, music blaring out of its stereo system. Leaving the engine running, two young black males of about twenty-one or twenty-two jumped out and swaggered into the store. They were dressed in stylish sweatsuits, had close-cropped hair, and sported shades and gold chains and rings. One of them had an earring. Ignoring the two white salesmen, who deferred to them, they went straight to the wall where the shoes were stacked in boxes. In an obviously demonstrative way, they snatched three or four boxes of shoes, swaggered over to the counter, and threw down a few hundred dollars. Then, without waiting for their change or carrying on any verbal exchange, they walked out with their shoes.
>
> The most striking aspect of this episode was the way in which these young men exhibited control over the resource of money. By their appearance, which was dominated by expensive clothing and jewelry; by the aplomb with which they moved; by the ease with which they threw large bills around; by not only leaving their keys in the car but even keeping the engine running and the music playing enticingly, thus daring anyone to tamper with it — by all these means, they were demonstrating their total control over their possessions. And this display did make an impression. After the youths made their exit, they left a certain presence behind, a residue of their self-assurance. In their wake, the feeling in the store was, "What was that?" My son nodded knowingly, aware that these are the successful "homeboys." Indeed, these two unorthodox cus-

tomers exuded success, albeit a deviant sort of success. Their gaudy car roared off, and things in the store slowly drifted back to normal.

One way of campaigning for status is by taking the possessions of others. In this context, seemingly ordinary objects can become trophies imbued with symbolic value that far exceeds their monetary worth. Possession of the trophy can symbolize the ability to violate somebody — to "get in his face," to take something of value from him, to dis him, and thus to enhance one's own worth by stealing that which belongs to someone else. Though it often is, the trophy does not have to be something material. It can be another person's sense of honor, snatched away with a derogatory remark or action. It can be the outcome of a fight. It can be the imposition of a certain standard, such as a girl's getting herself recognized as the most beautiful. Material things, however, fit easily into the pattern. Sneakers or a pistol — even somebody else's boyfriend or girlfriend — can become a trophy. When individuals can take something from another and then flaunt it, they gain a certain regard by being the owner, or the controller, of that thing. But this display of ownership can then provoke other people to challenge him or her. This game of who controls what is thus constantly being played out on inner-city streets, and the trophy — extrinsic or intrinsic, tangible or intangible — identifies the current winner.

An important aspect of this often violent give-and-take is its zero-sum quality. That is, the extent to which one person can rise depends on his or her ability to put another person down. This situation underscores the alienation that permeates the inner-city ghetto community. There is a generalized sense that very little respect is to be had, and therefore everyone competes to get what little affirmation is actually available. The craving for respect that results often gives people thin skins. It is generally believed that true respect provides an aura of protection. Thus, shows of deference by others can be highly soothing, contributing to a sense of security, comfort, self-confidence, and self-respect. Transgressions by others that go unanswered diminish these feelings and are believed to encourage further transgressions. Hence, one must be ever vigilant against the transgressions of others; one cannot even allow the *appearance* of transgressions to be tolerated. Among young people, whose sense of self-esteem is particularly vulnerable, there is an especially heightened concern with being "disrespected." Many inner-city young men in particular crave respect to such a degree that they will risk their lives to attain and maintain it.

The issue of respect is thus closely tied to whether a person has an inclination to be violent, even as a victim. In the wider society people may not feel the need to retaliate physically after an attack, even though they are aware that they have been degraded or taken advantage of. They may feel a great need to defend themselves *during* an attack or to behave in such a way as to deter aggression (middle-class people certainly can and do become victims of street-oriented youths), but they are much more likely than street-oriented people to feel they can walk away from a possible altercation with their self-esteem intact. Some people may even have the strength of character to flee, without any thought that their self-respect or esteem will be diminished.

In impoverished inner-city black communities, however, particularly among young males and perhaps increasingly among females, such flight would be extremely difficult. To run away would likely leave one's self-esteem in tatters. Hence, people often feel constrained not only to stand up during and at least attempt to resist an assault but also to "pay back" — to seek revenge — after a successful assault on their person. This may include going to get a weapon. One young man described a typical scenario:

> So he'll [the victim] ask somebody do they got a gun for sale or somethin' like that. And they'll say yeah and they say they want a buck [a hundred dollars] for it or somethin' like that. So he'll go and get a hundred dollars and buy that gun off of him and then wait until he see the boy that he was fightin' or got into a argument [with] or something like that. He'll sneak and shoot 'im or somethin' like that and then move away from his old neighborhood. . . .
>
> Or if they already have a gun, they gonna just go get their gun and buy a bullet. And then they gonna shoot the person, whoever they was fightin', or whoever did somethin' to 'im. Then they'll probably keep the gun and get into a couple more rumbles and shoot people. And the gun'll probably have like nine bodies on it. Then they decide to sell the gun, and the other person'll get caught with it.

Or one's relatives might get involved, willingly or not. The youth continues:

> For instance, me. I was livin' in a projects [public housing] on Grant Street, right, and I think my brother is fightin' one of the other person's brother or cousin. Me and my brother look just alike — they thought I was my brother — and they try to throw me down the elevator shaft, but they threw me down three flights of steps. And I hit my face on a concrete rung, chipped my tooth, and got five stitches in my lip. And see, [later] my uncle killed one of them, and that's why he doin' time in jail now. Because they tried to kill me.

The very identity and self-respect — the honor — of many inner-city youths is often intricately tied up with the way they perform on the streets *during* and *after* such encounters. Moreover, this outlook reflects the circumscribed opportunities of the inner-city poor. Generally people outside the ghetto have other ways of gaining status and regard, and thus, they do not feel so dependent on such physical displays.

By Trial of Manhood

Among males on the street, these concerns about things and identity have come to be expressed in the concept of "manhood." Manhood in the inner city means taking the prerogatives of men with respect to strangers, other men, and women — being distinguished as a man. It implies physicality and a certain ruthlessness. Regard and respect are associated with this concept in large part because of its practical application: If others have little or no regard for a person's manhood, his very life and that of his loved ones could be in jeopardy. But there is a chicken-and-egg aspect to this situation: One's physical safety is more likely to be jeopardized in public *because* manhood is associated with respect. The "man" becomes the target of others who want to prove their own manhood. In other words, an existential link has been created between the idea of manhood and one's self-esteem, so that it has become hard to say which is primary. For many inner-city youths, manhood and respect are flip sides of the same coin; physical and psychological well-being are inseparable, and both require a sense of control, of being in charge.

The operating assumption is that a man, especially a real man, knows what other men know — the code of the streets. And if one is not a real man, one is somehow diminished as a person, and there are certain valued things one simply does not deserve. There is thus believed to be a certain justice to the code, since it is presumed that everyone has the opportunity to know it. Implicit in this presumption is the belief that everybody is held responsible for being familiar with the code. If the victim of a mugging, for example, does not know the code and so responds "wrong," the perpetrator may feel justified even in killing him and may feel no remorse. He may think, "Too bad, but it's his fault. He should have known better." At the same time, it is assumed that, if attacked, a victim is entitled to retribution and may feel no compunction about retaliating even with deadly force. According to one youth who tries to avoid such encounters: "They ain't got no conscience. They ain't got no kind of conscience. Like, say, what happens if you punch me, and I'm a devious person, and I'm mad and I see you again on the street and I got a gun. I'll shoot you and I won't have no kind of conscience because I shot you 'cause I'm payin' back for what you done did to me."

So when a person ventures outside, he must adopt the code — a kind of shield, really — to prevent others from messing with him. In these circumstances, it is easy for people to think they are being tried or tested by others even when this is not the case. In such a climate, it is sensed that something extremely valuable is at stake in every interaction, and people are thus encouraged to rise to the occasion, particularly with strangers. For people who are unfamiliar with the code — generally people who live outside the inner city — the concern with respect in the most ordinary interactions can be frightening and incomprehensible. But for those who are invested in the code, the clear object of their demeanor is to discourage strangers from even thinking about challenging them or testing their manhood. And the sense of power that attends the ability to deter others can be alluring even to those who know the code without being heavily invested in it — the decent inner-city youths. Thus, a boy who has been leading a basically decent life can, in trying circumstances, suddenly resort to deadly force.

Central to the issue of manhood is the widespread belief that one of the most effective ways of gaining respect is to manifest "nerve." Nerve is shown when someone takes a person's possessions (the more valuable, the better), messes with someone's woman, throws the first punch, gets in someone's face, or pulls a trigger. Its proper display helps on the spot to check others who would violate one's person and also helps to build a reputation that works to prevent future challenges. But since such a show of nerve is a forceful expression of disrespect toward the person on the receiving end, the victim may be greatly offended and seek to retaliate with equal if not greater force. A display of nerve, therefore, can easily provoke a life-threatening response, and the background knowledge of that possibility has often been incorporated into the concept of nerve.

True nerve exposes a lack of fear of dying. Many feel that it is acceptable to risk dying over the principle of respect. In fact, among the hard-core street-oriented, the clear risk of violent death may be preferable to being dissed by another. The youths who have internalized this attitude and convincingly display it in their public bearing are among the most threatening people of all, for it is commonly assumed that they fear no man. As the people of the community say, "They are the baddest dudes on the street." They often lead an existential life that may acquire meaning only when faced with the possibility of imminent death. Not to be afraid to die is by implication to have few compunctions about taking somebody else's life. Not to be afraid to die is the quid pro quo of being able to take somebody else's life — for the right reasons, if the situation demands it. When others believe this is one's position, it gives one a real sense of power on the streets. Such credibility is what many inner-city youths strive to achieve, whether they are decent or street-oriented, both because of its practical defensive value and because of the positive way it makes them feel about themselves. The difference between the decent and the street-oriented youth is that the decent youth makes a conscious decision to appear tough and manly; in another setting — with teachers, say, or at his part-time job — he can be polite and deferential. The street-oriented youth, on the other hand, has made the concept of manhood a part of his very identity; he has difficulty manipulating it — it often controls him instead.

Girls and Boys

Increasingly, teenage girls are mimicking the males and trying to have their own version of "manhood." Their goal is the same — to get respect, to be recognized as capable of setting or maintaining a certain standard. They try to achieve this end in the ways that have been established by the males, including posturing, abusive language, and the use of violence to resolve disputes; but the issues for the girls are different. Although conflicts over turf and status exist among the girls, the majority of disputes seem rooted in assessments of beauty (which girl in a group is the cutest?), competition over boyfriends, and the attempts to regulate other people's knowledge of and opinions about a girl's behavior or that of someone close to her, especially her mother.

A major cause of conflicts among girls is "he say, she say." This practice begins in the early school years and continues through high school. It occurs when "people," particularly girls, talking about others, thus putting their "business in the streets." Usually, one girl will say something negative about another in the group, most often behind the person's back. The remarks will then get back to the person talked about. She may retaliate or her friends may feel required to "take up for" her. In essence this is a form of group gossiping in which individuals are negatively assessed and evaluated. As with much gossip, the things said may or may not be true, but the point is that such imputations can cast aspersions on a person's good name. The accused is required to defend herself against the slander, which can result in arguments and fights, often over little of real substance. Here again is the problem of low self-esteem, which encourages youngsters to be highly sensitive to slights and to be vulnerable to feeling easily dissed. To avenge the dissing, a fight is usually necessary.

Because boys are believed to control violence, girls tend to defer to them in situations of conflict. Often, if a girl is attacked or feels slighted, she will get a brother, uncle, or cousin to do her fighting for her. Increasingly, however, girls are doing their own fighting and are even asking their male relatives to teach them how to fight. Some girls form groups that attack other girls or take things from them. A hard-core segment of inner-city girls inclined to violence seems to be developing. As one thirteen-year-old girl in a detention center for youths who have committed violent acts told me, "To get people to leave you alone, you gotta fight. Talking don't always get you out of stuff." One major difference between girls and boys is that girls rarely use guns. Their fights are therefore not life-or-death struggles. Girls are not often willing to put their lives on the line for their version of manhood. The ultimate form of respect on the male-dominated inner-city streets is thus reserved for men.

"Going for Bad"

In the most fearsome youths, such a cavalier attitude toward death grows out of a very limited view of life. Many are uncertain about how long they are going to live and believe they could die violently at any time. They accept this fate; they live on the edge. Their manner conveys the message that nothing intimidates them; whatever turn the encounter takes, they maintain their attack — rather like a pit bull, whose spirit many such boys admire. The demonstration of such tenacity shows "heart" and earns their respect.

This fearlessness has implications for law enforcement. Many street-oriented boys are much more concerned about the threat of "justice" at the hands of a peer than at the hands of the police. According to one young man trying to lead a decent life, "When they shoot somebody, they have so much confidence that they gonna get away from the cop, you see. If they don't, then they be all mad and sad and cryin' and all that 'cause they got time in jail." At the same time, however, many feel not only that they have little to lose by going to prison but that they have something to gain. The toughening-up one experiences in prison can actually enhance one's reputation on the streets. Hence, the system loses influence over the hard core who are without jobs and who have little perceptible stake in the system. If mainstream society has done nothing *for* them, they counter by making sure it can likewise do nothing *to* them.

At the same time, however, a competing view maintains that true nerve consists in backing down, walking away from a fight, and going on with one's business. One fights only in self-defense. This view emerges from the decent philosophy that life is precious, and it is an important part of the socialization process common in decent homes. A strategy strongly associated with hope, it discourages violence as the primary means of resolving disputes and encourages youngsters to accept nonviolence and talk as confrontational strategies. But if "the deal goes down," self-defense is greatly encouraged. When there is enough positive support for this orientation, either in the home or among one's peers, then nonviolence has a chance to prevail. But it prevails at the cost of relinquishing a claim to being bad and tough, and it therefore sets a young person up as at the very least alienated from street-oriented peers and quite possibly a target of derision or even violence.

Although the nonviolent orientation rarely overcomes the impulse to strike back in an encounter, it does introduce a certain confusion and so can prompt a measure of soul-searching — or even profound ambivalence. Did the person back down with his or her respect intact or did he or she back down only to be judged a "punk" — a person lacking manhood? Should he or she have acted? Should he or she have hit the other person in the mouth? These questions beset many young men and women during public confrontations. What is the right thing to do? In the quest for honor, respect, and local status — which few young people are uninterested in — common sense most often prevails, thus leading many to opt for the tough approach, in which they enact their own particular versions of the display of nerve. The presentation of oneself as rough and tough is very often quite acceptable until one is tested. And then that presentation may help individuals pass the test, because it will cause fewer questions to be asked about what they did and why. It is hard for people to explain why they lost the fight or why they backed down. Hence many will strive to appear to go for bad, while hoping they will never be tested. But when they are tested, the outcome of the situation may quickly be out of their hands, as they become wrapped up in the circumstances of the moment.

Conclusion

The attitudes of the wider society are deeply implicated in the code of the streets. Most people in inner-city communities are not totally invested in the code; but the significant minority of hard-core street youths who do embrace it have to maintain the code in order to establish reputations, because they have — or feel they have — few other ways to assert themselves. For these young people, the standards of the street code are the only game in town. The extent to which some children — particularly those who through upbringing have become most alienated and lack strong and conventional social support — experience, feel, and internalize racist rejection and contempt from mainstream society may strongly encourage them to express contempt for the more conventional society in turn. In dealing with this contempt and rejection, some youngsters will consciously invest themselves and their considerable mental resources in what amounts to an oppositional culture to preserve themselves and their self-respect. Once they do this, any respect they might be able to garner in the wider system pales in comparison with the respect available in the local system; thus, they often lose interest in even attempting to negotiate the mainstream system.

At the same time, many less-alienated young blacks have assumed a street-oriented demeanor as a way of expressing their blackness while really embracing a much more moderate way of life; they, too, want a nonviolent setting in which to live and raise a family. These decent people are trying hard to be a part of the mainstream culture, but the racism — both real and perceived —

that they encounter helps to legitimate the oppositional culture; and so, on occasion, they adopt street behavior. In fact, depending on the demands of the situation, many people in the community slip back and forth between decent and street behavior.

A vicious cycle has thus been formed. The hopelessness and alienation that many young inner-city black men and women feel, largely because of endemic joblessness and persistent racism, fuel the violence they engage in. This violence serves to confirm the negative feelings many whites and some middle-class blacks harbor toward the ghetto poor, further legitimating the oppositional culture and the code of the streets in the eyes of many poor young blacks. Unless this cycle is broken, attitudes on both sides will become increasingly entrenched, and the violence — which claims victims black and white, poor and affluent — will only escalate.

Notes

A version of this chapter appeared in the *Atlantic Monthly* 273, 5, (1994): 80–94. This chapter was originally published in *Violence and Childhood in the Inner City*, ed. Joan McCord (New York: Cambridge University Press, 1997), 1–30.

1. This phenomenon is to be distinguished from that described by Wolfgang and Ferracuti (1967), who identified and delineated more explicitly a "subculture of violence." Wolfgang and Ferracuti postulated norms which undergirded or even defined the culture of the entire community, whereas the code of the streets applies predominantly to situational public *behavior* and is normative for only a segment of the community.

2. The ethnographic approach is to be distinguished from other, equally valid, approaches, most notably the social psychological. A sensitive and compelling social psychological analysis of the phenomenon of murder is to be found in Jack Katz's *Seductions of Crime: Moral and Sensual Attractions in Doing Evil* (1988). Katz's purpose is to make sense of the senseless, that is, to explain the psychic changes a person goes through to become, at a given moment, a murderer. In contrast, the analysis offered here focuses on conscious behavior, which, in the circumstances of the inner-city environment, is sensible (makes sense). Katz explores the moral dimension of violence, whereas I explore its practical aspect.

3. For comparisons in the ethnographic literature, see Drake and Cayton's discussion of the "shadies" and "respectables" in *Black Metropolis* (1945). Also, see the discussion of "regulars," "wineheads," and "hoodlums" in Anderson (1978). See also Anderson (1991).

References

Anderson, Elijah. 1978. *A place on the corner.* Chicago: University of Chicago Press.

———. 1989. Sex codes and family life among poor inner-city youths. In *The ghetto underclass: Social science perspectives*, ed. William Julius Wilson. Special edition of *Annals of the American Academy of Political and Social Science* 501: 59–78.

———. 1990. *Streetwise: Race, class, and change in an urban community.* Chicago: University of Chicago Press.

———. 1991. Neighborhood effects on teen pregnancy. In *The urban underclass,* ed. Christopher Jencks and Paul Peterson. Washington, D.C.: Brookings Institution.

———. 1997. Violence and the inner city street code. In *Violence and Childhood in the Inner City,* ed. Joan McCord. New York: Cambridge University Press.

Becker, Howard. 1970. *Sociological work.* Chicago: Aldine.

Block, Fred, et al. 1987. *The mean season: The attack on the welfare state.* New York: Pantheon.

Cloward, Richard A., and Lloyd Ohlin. 1960. *Delinquency and opportunity: A theory of delinquent gangs.* Glencoe, Ill.: Free Press.

Coleman, James. 1988. Social capital in the creation of human capital. *American Journal of Sociology* 94: S95–S120.

Drake, St. Clair, and Horace Cayton. 1962. *Black metropolis.* New York: Harper and Row.

Glaser, Barney G., and Anselm L. Strauss. 1972. *Status passage.* Chicago: Aldine.

Katz, Jack. 1988. *Seductions of crime: Moral and sensual attractions in doing evil.* New York: Basic Books.

Katz, Michael B. 1989. *The undeserving poor: From the war on poverty to the war on welfare.* New York: Pantheon.

Kirschenman, Joleen and Kathy Neckerman. 1991. We'd like to hire them, but . . . In *The urban underclass,* ed. Christopher Jencks and Paul Peterson. Washington, D.C.: Brookings Institution.

Merton, Robert. 1957. Social structure and anomie. In *Social theory and social structure.* Glencoe, Ill.: Free Press.

Short, James F., Jr., and Fred L. Strodtbeck. 1965. *Group processes and gang delinquency.* Chicago: University of Chicago Press.

Simmel, Georg. 1971. In *George Simmel on individuality and social forms,* ed. Donald N. Levine. Chicago: University of Chicago Press.

Wacquant, Loic J. D., and William Julius Wilson. The cost of racial and class exclusion in the inner city. In *The ghetto underclass,* ed. William Julius Wilson. Special edition of *Annals of the American Academy of Political and Social Science* 501: 8–25.

Wilson, William Julius. 1987. *The truly disadvantaged.* Chicago: University of Chicago.

———. 1989. The underclass: Issues, perspectives, and public policy. In *The ghetto underclass,* ed. William Julius Wilson. Special edition of *Annals of the American Academy of Political and Social Science* 501: 183–92.

Wolfgang, M. E., and F. Ferracuti. 1967. *The subculture of violence.* London: Tavistock.

PART VIII

Economic Development of Black Communities

25

Minority Business Development Programs
Failure by Design

TIMOTHY BATES

Crippling Features of Government Aid to Minority-Owned Business

Minority enterprise assistance programs are largely flawed in intent, design, and implementation. Moreover, no fundamental rethinking or reorientation of these programs is in the offing: hence, ineffective policies have been implemented without brake (Bates, 2000). The language of minority enterprise assistance — helping "socially and economically disadvantaged firms" — reveals flawed premises that undermine minority business enterprise (MBE) programs: as long as minority entrepreneurs are thought of as the walking wounded of the small business world, efforts will be misdirected. Indeed, these minority business development programs fail frequently because they ignore the factors that shape small business viability.

Aid efforts often focus upon providing small amounts of debt capital to aspiring minority entrepreneurs. Yet these programs frequently target loan assistance to low-income persons who lack the education and skills that are prerequisites for success in most lines of self-employment. No serious studies of government or nonprofit sector microenterprise loan programs have demonstrated that small amounts of debt can overcome human capital deficiencies that otherwise minimize chances for business success (Bates and Bradford, 1979; Clark and Huston, 1993). In fact, available evidence overwhelmingly indicates that small loans, targeted to low-income individuals lacking the requisite skills for operating a business, very frequently become delinquent loans that are never repaid. Debt capital and proprietor human capital are complements, not substitutes, in the small business world (Bates, 1990; Bates, 1993).

This chapter is organized as follows: First, two closely interrelated and highly ineffective minority business enterprise assistance strategies are identified and discussed. The first ineffective strategy involves geographic targeting: aid flows into low-income, inner-city minority communities. The folly of this approach is often compounded by concentrating assistance efforts upon overcrowded, low-profitability lines of business possessing minimal economic development potential. Following this, we move to the second phase, in which a conceptually promising program — the Specialized Small Business Investment Company (SSBIC) program — is examined in detail and also found to be largely ineffective.

Choosing the Wrong Target:
Loan Assistance for Low-Income Minorities

Many thousands of minorities were encouraged by Small Business Administration (SBA) credit policies to become owners of nonviable firms in the 1960s and 1970s. After most of the firms failed, SBA dunned the owners, often for years. It is from these uninspiring beginnings that many MBE assistance programs continue to base their rationale and operating procedures. Practices that give rise to nonviable firms are sometimes undertaken for cynical political reasons, but more often they are rooted in noble intentions. One of the more destructive noble intentions is the notion that MBE assistance must be targeted to poor inner-city minority communities.

In the urban ghetto that typified America thirty years ago, many residents held well-paying jobs. The managerial and professional classes, along with the working class, the subemployed poor, and the underclass all resided in the ghetto. It was the racial trait — not poverty — that defined the black ghetto, which was comprised of both slum and nonslum areas. In recent decades, this heterogeneous class of residents in inner-city ghetto has been reduced to a class of dispossessed owing to a selective outmigration. As housing choices became broader and more varied, many in the managerial and professional classes left, leaving behind a poorer inner-city ghetto that, by the 1970s, was actually declining in population in many eastern and Midwestern urban areas. A significant factor in the growth of poverty of urban ghettos today is the exodus of labor, which has grown in intensity in recent years. The ghetto's chief resource is manpower, and its best workers have often left the neighborhood by way of the educational system and the high-wage economy. Drawn by opportunities outside poor urban areas, many of the most intelligent, capable, and imaginative young people have moved into the economic mainstream, where rewards are greater and opportunities wider. Meanwhile, the ghetto they leave behind gets poorer, the isolation of the ghetto and the drains of its talent and capital only grow worse.

Middle-income earners and working-class households still residing in inner-city ghettos have shown less and less inclination to shop in those environs. The suburban mall has captured a growing share of the purchases of central-city residents generally; older shopping districts in central cities have become less competitive, particularly so in ghetto areas experiencing depopulation of more affluent households. Declining middle-class population, a rising incidence of ghetto residents shopping outside of the community, and growing poverty typify most traditional ghettos in the United States, and it is not an environment that is conducive to small business creation and expansion. On the contrary, disinvestment is the norm. These trends have not encouraged area financial institutions to reverse their long-standing aversion to lending in inner-city minority communities (Bates, 1989; Bates, 1993).

During the 1960s and 1970s, loan assistance was the primary type of government aid provided to MBEs. The granddaddy of these programs was the Economic Opportunity Loan (EOL) program, administered by the Small Business Administration. EOL loan activity peaked in 1972, with SBA approving 5,791 loans to minority-business borrowers; median loan size was under $10,000 and loan recipients most commonly ran very small retail operations in inner-city minority communities (Bates, 1984). The guiding philosophy of the EOL program required most recipients to be bad credit risks. Loan recipients were primarily minorities and, by design, few possessed the skills, education, or work experience that successful business operation commonly requires.

A problem characteristic of loan programs, which target marginally viable and nonviable businesses, is that many of the borrowers do not repay their loans. For nearly a decade, SBA successfully concealed the fact that over half of MBEs receiving EOL loans defaulted on repayment obligations (Bates, 1981). According to one study, default rates among borrowers establishing new businesses exceeded 70 percent (Bates and Bradford, 1979). Many of those who actually repaid their EOL loans eventually closed down their businesses owing to their inability to make a decent living operating very small firms in the ghetto. In 1984, the EOL program was discontinued because its creditability was destroyed by its enormous ineffectiveness. Yet clones of the disastrous EOL program continue to be widespread today at all levels of government as well as in the nonprofit sector.

In the wake of the riots and rebellions in Los Angeles following the Rodney

King verdict in 1992, SBA reestablished a variant of the EOL program. This program was resumed so that ravaged urban areas, such as South Los Angeles, could once again receive federal loan dollars targeted to nonviable firms that had no potential to generate the sort of economic development so desperately needed in inner cities throughout the nation.

Facing declining purchasing power, redlined by financial institutions, increasingly stripped of entrepreneurial talent, the ghetto economy is most often the antithesis of an environment conducive to small-business development. How does a program targeting small loans to minority-owned retailers alter this situation? It is essential to understand why minority-owned businesses that serve a ghetto clientele are unlikely to alter the local landscape. Most fundamentally, the state of these enterprises reflects the economic circumstances of the clientele. Weak internal markets reflect the obvious fact that poor people possess minimal purchasing power. Declining local markets and lack of access to financial capital are not the sorts of lures that attract skilled and experienced entrepreneurs (Bates, 1993).

The mom-and-pop, zero employee-type small business continues to be common in low-income, inner-city minority communities. This sort of MBE often reflects, not economic development, but working poverty. Yet these are precisely the types of firms that are frequently targeted for lending assistance. The U.S. Commission on Minority Business Development's 1992 study of SBA loans to minority borrowers found that the greatest concentration of loans to MBEs was in the traditional retail fields in fiscal year 1991. Two essentially stagnant lines of minority business — restaurants and food stores — received 442 SBA loans, while three rapid growth areas — business services, construction, and wholesaling — received 357 loans (U.S. Commission on Minority Business Development, 1992). The commission concluded that SBA loan assistance to MBEs "perpetuates their relegation to areas of business endeavor that are among the most crowded and least profitable" (p. 24).

Successful loan programs assisting small minority (and nonminority) businesses have targeted higher income, better educated owners who possess appropriate skills and experience for operating viable small businesses. When assistance is provided to higher income entrepreneurs, the objection that invariably arises is "why help those who are already successful?" The response is straightforward: it is the viable firms that generate economic development and create jobs. Their profits support investments that permit future expansion and job creation. The alternative — supporting nonviable firms — simply creates mass loan default and business failure.

Who should be targeted as recipients of aid to MBEs — the most deprived minorities who (for that reason) need help most or those less in need of help personally, but whose prospects for business success are much better? This is one of the fundamental conflicts in goals that typify minority-business assistance programs. If minority-business assistance efforts genuinely seek to create strong firms capable of generating jobs for underemployed ghetto residents, then the conflict would be resolved by targeting entrepreneurs possessing the requisite resources for successfully building small businesses. Few of these entrepreneurs would be poor. Rather, most would be highly educated and earn above average incomes, and few would locate their business ventures in the poorest, most deprived ghetto areas. The thought of helping upper-middle-class minorities establish businesses located outside of poor ghetto areas is simply too much for the designers and implementers of most minority-business assistance programs. They prefer to aid the failure-prone MBEs that operate in the bleakest inner-city minority communities; these firms possess the least economic development potential. The result is predictable: such MBE assistance efforts produce high levels of business failure and little economic development. Such programs have been designed for failure.

Neither whites, blacks, Korean immigrants, nor any other group have been particularly successful at operating small businesses in urban ghetto areas in recent years (Bates, 1997). Korean immigrant-owned firms that have sprung up in many poor minority communities over the past fifteen years tend to be well-capitalized ventures run by highly educated owners who possess managerial or professional experience. These firms are typically earning very low rates of return on their human and financial-capital investments, and the survival rates of Korean firms serving minority clienteles are actually lower than those of similar African American small businesses (Bates, 1994). Given the harshness of the ghetto economy, how can welfare recipients, working poor, or the unskilled (possessing several thousand dollars in capital) make a living running a small business in the inner city? Very few do.

Targeting aid to the wrong potential entrepreneurs to run firms in the wrong geographic areas will not generate economic development. If economic development is the goal, it is counterproductive to target aid to poorly qualified entrepreneurs who plan to operate in a ghetto that provides an unattractive environment for running most types of small businesses.

The MESBIC Program: Promise Unfulfilled

Minority Enterprise Small Business Investment Companies (MESBICs, recently renamed Specialized Small Business Investment Companies or SSBICs) are privately owned small-business investment companies specializing in minority-business investments. Chartered by the SBA, MESBICs raise a large share of their funds by selling debentures and preferred stock to the SBA. These funds are provided on preferential terms, which are below the cost of borrowing incurred by the U.S. Treasury. For each dollar of private capital, MESBICs can raise as much as four dollars from the SBA, but leverage ratios, in practice, are commonly less than two to one. Created by executive order in 1969, the MESBIC program received statutory existence from Congress in 1972.

During the first ten years of the program's existence, 141 MESBICs were chartered. As of June 1994, 32 of those firms were still in operation: 65 had been forced into involuntary liquidation by the SBA, and 44 had voluntarily surrendered their charters. MESBICs, in practice, have most commonly failed to function as viable sources of financial capital for the minority-business community (Bates, 2000).

MESBICs were designed to fill some of the roles envisioned for the community development banks established by the Clinton Administration. The 1972 MESBIC legislation spoke of "establishing a program to stimulate and supplement the flow of private equity capital and long-term loan funds which minority-owned small business concerns need for the sound financing of their business operations" (quoted in Hansley, 1992, p. 1). Senator John Tower (Texas), co-sponsor of the 1972 MESBIC Act, envisioned MESBICs as a means "to facilitate capital formation in the minority community generally." MESBICs were a "self-help approach to curing poverty and unemployment in the minority community" (quoted in Hansley, 1992, p. 2).

Why have MESBICs failed to fulfill their envisioned role? This issue is addressed by analyzing a detailed ten-year time-series data file that includes annual balance sheets, income statements, and related information for every MESBIC/SSBIC operating in the U.S. from 1984 to 1993. Because this data file was plagued by errors and inconsistencies, my analysis focuses upon more recent years, for which there is clean data describing the performance of the individual SSBICs.

Viable and Nonviable SSBICS: Key Issues

MESBICs/SSBICs are profit-making entities (at least, by design) that are *not* required to target their investments in depressed geographic areas. Within broad constraints, SSBICs are free to invest in the larger scale minority businesses, including those headed by well-educated, experienced entrepreneurs whose incomes far exceed poverty levels. Within tight constraints, SSBICs can invest legally in nonminority-owned businesses, especially if these firms operate in poor minority communities. Our analysis of SSBICs proceeds along two lines: (1) costs, revenues, and profitability of SSBICs are investigated econometrically, utilizing data on all active SSBICs; (2) a subset of the most successful SSBICs is isolated and examined qualitatively as well as quantitatively.

MESBICs/SSBICs have always been promoted as vehicles for providing equity capital to the minority-business community. My analysis therefore stresses the problems SSBICs encounter in their attempts to function as venture-capital firms. Initial scanning of the time-series data generated or highlighted the following issues in need of analysis:

- Most SSBICs operate at a loss, quite apart from issues connected with generating capital gains (losses) from their venture-capital investments.
- Most SSBICs that make venture-capital investments in MBEs generate net capital losses over time on this type of investment.
- Most SSBICs specialized in small investments in traditional lines of minority business that possess little job creation potential: over half of all SSBIC investments in MBEs during 1993 were in three fields — restaurants, food stores, and taxicabs.
- The aggregate balance sheet of the SSBIC industry is highly liquid: cash assets such as bank CDs are much more widely held than equity investments in MBEs.
- After years of unprofitable operations, most SSBICs go out of business, primarily because they are forced by SBA into involuntary liquidation. The number of SSBICs in operation declined steadily throughout the 1990s.
- In the midst of this generally dismal, gradually liquidating industry, some SSBICs have operated profitably, grown substantially, and have achieved this success by actively investing in MBEs.

Problems in the industry are most clear-cut among the smaller SSBICs. Among 101 SSBICs active in 1993 that had investments in MBEs, 30 (hereby labeled "small" SSBICs) had total assets of under $2 million. Table 25.1 presents an aggregate 1993 balance sheet for these small SSBICs, along with an income statement summarizing operations for the twelve-month 1993 fiscal year. Balance sheet and income statement data are presented in two distinct ways: (1) mean absolute dollar amounts of assets and liabilities, income and expenses are listed for the 30 small SSBICs; (2) all balance sheet and income statement items are normalized, i.e., divided by total assets on a firm by firm basis. Method one of data presentation in Table 25.1 effectively allows the larger firms to dominate the statistics, while method two has the effect of weighting each SSBIC equally when means are calculated.

The average small SSBIC described in Table 25.1 has $821,153 invested in MBEs, and $575,169 invested in other assets, largely money-market

Table 25.1. *SSBIC Industry Balance Sheet, 1993 (SSBICs with assets of $2 million or less) (mean values)*

	$ Amount	% of total assets (calculated firm by firm)
Assets (uses of funds)		
Investments in small business		
Debt	$666,605	45.96%
Equity	124,439	8.58%
Receivables, assets acquired in liquidation	30,110	2.04%
Total business assets	821,153	56.58%
Other assets		
Cash, money market investments	532,266	40.59%
Misc. current assets	29,114	1.94%
Equipment	13,789	.89%
Total assets	1,396,322	100.00%
Liabilities + capital (sources of funds)		
Long-term debt		
Notes payable to SBA	$195,000	11.53%
Total long-term debt	214,667	12.73%
Other liabilities		
Payables, current	21,849	1.93%
Misc.	13,919	1.04%
Total liabilities	250,434	15.70%
Capital		
Capital stock	924,594	70.07%
3% preferred stock	480,760	34.83%
Unrealized gain (loss) on securities	−103,766	−6.73%
Undistributed earnings	−154,534	−13.87%
Total capital	1,146,055	84.31%
Total liabilities and capital	$1,396,322	100.00%
Revenue		
Interest on business loans, debt	$70,899	4.94%
Dividend income	2,167	.41%
Misc. business income	2,192	.15%
Total income derived from small business activities	75,258	5.50%
Interest on cash assets	16,512	1.29%
Other income	2,993	.30%
Total revenue	$94,763	7.09%

Table 25.1. Continued

	$ Amount	% of total assets (calculated firm by firm)
Expenses		
Cost of funds	$15,174	.91%
Labor costs	55,959	4.07%
Misc. operating costs	29,707	2.20%
Provision for loss on receivables	39,894	3.65%
Total expense	140,734	10.84%
Profit		
Net income before taxes	−45,972	−3.75%
Income taxes	449	−.02%
Net income after taxes	−46,421	−3.77%
Realized gain (loss) on securities	−12,847	−1.02%

Source: Internal SBA records

investments. These SSBICs rely very little upon debt as a source of funds, with private capital (averaging $923,594) exceeding SBA debt ($195,000) and SBA preferred stock ($480,760 mean). Private capital in the average small SSBIC has been eroded by $154,534 in past operating losses, as well as $103,766 in unrealized capital losses on holdings of securities, leaving a mean net private capitalization of $665,294. Operating losses as well as realized losses on disposal of securities holdings in 1993 did nothing to alter this pattern of capital erosion (see Table 25.1). The average small SSBIC reported an operating loss of $46,421 in 1993, along with realized capital losses of $12,847: capital erosion resulting from this performance therefore averaged $59,268 for the mean small SSBIC described in Table 25.1. Similar financial results typified the small SSBIC group over the entire 1987–1993 period. This pattern of losses from operations, losses from equity investments, and capital erosion — year after year — is an abysmal performance.

SSBICs with assets exceeding $2 million, described in Table 25.2, did much better than the small SSBICs; these SSBICs are hereafter referred to as "large." Of the 71 large SSBICs active in 1993, an average of $5.73 million was invested in MBEs, and $1.45 million was invested in other assets. An examination of the normalized means indicates that large SSBICs invest relatively less heavily in cash assets (which were 22.8 percent of total assets), in comparison to the small SSBICs (corresponding mean=40.6 percent). The average large

Table 25.2. SSBIC Industry Balance Sheet, 1993 (SSBICs with assets exceeding $2 million only) (mean values)

	$ Amount	% of total assets (calculated firm by firm)
Assets (uses of funds)		
Investments in small business		
Debt	$4,570,661	54.57%
Equity	926,761	16.0%
Receivables, assets acquired in liquidation	233,899	3.34%
Total business assets	5,731,321	73.93%
Other assets		
Cash, money market investments	1,235,424	22.82%
Misc. current assets	151,564	2.24%
Equipment	61,088	1.01%
Total assets	7,179,486	100.00%
Liabilities + capital (sources of funds)		
Long-term debt		
Notes payable to SBA	$1,664,322	22.33%
Total long-term debt	2,335,762	23.72%
Other liabilities		
Payables, current	783,529	5.37%
Misc.	128,951	2.96%
Total liabilities	3,248,242	32.05%
Capital		
Capital stock	2,105,057	37.15%
3% preferred stock	2,093,596	38.56%
Unrealized gain (loss) on securities	−99,481	−3.29%
Undistributed earnings	−167,927	−4.47%
Total capital	3,931,245	67.95%
Total liabilities and capital	$7,179,486	100.00%
Revenue		
Interest on business loans, debt	$551,208	6.06%
Dividend income	5,011	.11%
Misc. business income	9,312	.19%
Total income dividend derived from small business activities	565,531	6.36%
Interest on cash assets	33,422	.65%
Other income	27,963	.41%
Total revenue	$626,915	7.43%

Table 25.2. Continued

	$ Amount	% of total assets (calculated firm by firm)
Expenses		
Cost of funds	$204,371	1.80%
Labor costs	150,565	2.76%
Misc. operating costs	127,921	2.11%
Provision for loss on receivables	42,755	.75%
Total expense	525,612	7.42%
Profit		
Net income before taxes	101,304	.02%
Income taxes	4,118	.10%
Net income after taxes	97,185	−.08%
Realized gain (loss) on securities	−76,203	−1.73%

Source: Internal SBA records

SSBIC had invested 16 percent of its assets in equity forms, much higher than the 8.6 percent that small SSBICs devoted to equity investments in MBEs.

Thus, there are clear-cut differences in portfolio composition that appear to be related to SSBIC size, with the large SSBICs demonstrating less balance sheet liquidity as well as much more MBE venture-capital investing than the small SSBICs. These major differences are apparent in the sources of funds (liabilities plus capital) portion of the balance sheet. Large SSBICs rely on the SBA for more than 50 percent of their funds, with SBA debt accounting for an average of $1.66 million: their SBA preferred stock provided $2.09 million in funds for the average large SSBIC. Negative entries for undistributed earnings and unrealized capital losses are less burdensome for the large SSBICs, equaling 7.8 percent of normalized assets, versus 20.6 percent of the small SSBIC average total asset holdings. Finally, the 1993 income statement for large SSBICs is much stronger than the corresponding small SSBIC statement of operations: after-tax profits averaged $97,185 but this was reduced by average capital losses of $76,203. Thus, the average large SSBIC generated a very low net return on total capital in 1993. While this represents a low return on invested capital relative to small businesses generally, this performance is brilliant in comparison to the negative returns generated by small SSBICs.

What's wrong with the small SSBICs? Below a certain scale of operations, the viability of SSBICs as providers of equity and patient debt capital is

Table 25.3. SBA Licensing of MESBICS

	Number	Private Capital, total (thousands)	Private Capital, average (thousands)
1969	3	$750	$250
1970	19	3,541	186
1971	22	6,817	310
1972	14	4,982	356
1973	14	4,933	380
1974	10	4,600	460
1975	13	6,093	469
1976	9	6,571	730
1977	10	4,380	438
1978	20	13,838	691
1979	28	12,316	440
Total	161	$68,821	$428

Source: Internal SBA records

dubious. Small SSBICs cannot achieve sufficient portfolio diversification to cope with the risk inherent in providing equity capital to small firms. To achieve sufficient diversification in debt investments, loans must be small, and this limits the types of firms that such SSBICs can serve. From a cost of operations perspective, small SSBICs cannot achieve scale economies in the various kinds of paper processing that exist in small-business investment companies.

The pattern of small SSBIC nonviability (see Table 25.1) raises an important policy issue: why did the SBA charter so many tiny SSBICs? From 1969 through 1979, 161 MESBICs with an aggregate private capitalization of $68.8 million were chartered by the SBA (Table 25.3). While average private capitalization of MESBICs during this period was $427,500, median capitalization was lower and the median MESBIC began operations with less than $1 million in total resources. By 1979, only 18 of the 110 MESBICs then in operation possessed private capital exceeding $1 million. Even more remarkable than SBA's pattern of chartering overly small MESBICs was their inattention to whether the MESBICs being chartered were owned and operated by persons possessing the skill and experience needed to operate a small-business investment company successfully.

The long-run financial performance and viability of SSBICs cannot be judged solely on the basis of 1993 cost and revenue average figures. Large SSBICs

Table 25.4. Broad Patterns in SSBIC Total Revenue and Costs, Selected Years; Mean Values

	Small SSBICs	Large SSBICs
Total Revenues (expressed as a percentage of firm total assets)		
1987	8.4%	9.4%
1988	8.3%	8.4%
1989	9.0%	8.6%
1990	9.1%	8.8%
1991	9.1%	8.4%
1992	8.3%	8.0%
1993	7.1%	7.4%
Average, 7 years	8.5%	8.4%
Total Costs (expressed as a percentage of firm total assets)		
1987	9.0%	7.2%
1988	7.8%	6.8%
1989	8.2%	6.6%
1990	9.5%	7.1%
1991	10.9%	7.8%
1992	9.5%	7.2%
1993	10.8%	7.4%
Average, 7 years	9.4%	7.2%

have operated at a profit in recent years, and the small SSBICs collectively have managed to operate profitably in 1988 and 1989. Table 25.4 provides a broader perspective on SSBIC financial performance by summarizing average annual revenue and cost figures for large and small SSBICs over the 1987–1993 period. Normalized means suggest that small and large SSBICs report broadly similar revenue flows for the seven years ending in 1993: total revenues averaged 8.5 percent of total assets for the small SSBICs, versus 8.4 percent for the large SSBICs.

Regarding total costs, the small SSBICs report high and variable costs as a percent of total assets, while the large SSBICs clearly exhibit lower and more stable costs. Every year the small SSBICs report higher costs than the large SSBICs (see Table 25.4). Thus, relatively high costs (rather than low revenues) appear to be undermining the viability of the small SSBICs. Table 25.5 isolates the two largest cost components for SSBICs: labor costs, which include wages, salaries, directors' costs, fringe benefits, and advisory fees, and provision for loss on receivables (loan losses).

In both cost categories, the small SSBICs consistently report higher labor

Table 25.5. Key Cost Components That Are Particularly High for Small SSBICs;
Selected Years (Mean values)

	Small SSBICs	Large SSBICs
Labor Costs (expressed as a percentage of firm total assets/normalized means)		
1987	3.3%	2.5%
1988	3.7%	2.6%
1989	3.7%	2.4%
1990	4.2%	2.5%
1991	4.5%	2.7%
1992	4.3%	2.6%
1993	4.1%	2.8%
Average, 7 years	4.0%	2.6%
Loan Loss Provision (expressed as a percentage of firm total assets/normalized means)		
1987	1.4%	0.8%
1988	0.5%	0.4%
1989	1.1%	0.3%
1990	1.1%	0.4%
1991	2.3%	1.2%
1992	1.0%	0.7%
1993	3.6%	0.8%
Average, 7 years	1.6%	0.7%
*Loan Loss Provision (expressed as a percentage of firm total business assets/means are not normalized)**		
1987	2.5%	0.9%
1988	0.8%	0.5%
1989	1.6%	0.4%
1990	2.0%	0.4%
1991	3.0%	1.3%
1992	1.5%	0.8%
1993	4.9%	0.7%
Average, 7 years	2.3%	0.7%

Note: Normalized means are calculated by dividing cost components (such as loan loss provision) by total assets on a firm basis. Means that are not normalized are based upon absolute dollar for the entire group under consideration. When means are not normalized, the larger firms in the group tend to dominate the calculated values of means; when means are normalized, each SSBIC is weighted equally when the means are calculated.

costs and loan losses. Relative to total assets, loan losses over the 1987–1993 period are 1.6 percent for small SSBICs, in comparison to 0.7 percent for large SSBICs. The loss performance of the small SSBICs is actually worse than these figures suggest. Recall that small SSBICs invest much more heavily in cash assets than the large institutions. If losses are expressed relative to total investments in small businesses, loan losses average 2.3 percent of business investments over the 1987–1993 period for small SSBICs, versus 0.7 percent for the large SSBIC group. Repeating this calculation with normalized means raises the loan loss figure to 2.6 percent for small SSBICs. The results are the same (0.7 percent) for large SSBICs. Small SSBICs consistently do worse than their larger cohorts. These losses speak poorly for the quality of the manager who is operating a small SSBIC.

Labor costs are the largest single component of operating costs for SSBICs, and here again, the small institutions, averaging labor costs equal to 4 percent of total assets, are out of line relative to the large SSBICs. The presence of high labor costs is consistent with the presence of scale economies in the operations of SSBICs: small institutions cannot achieve efficiency in the routine aspects of operating an investment company.

The contrast between the cost structures of the large and small SSBIC groups is stark: over the 1987–1993 period, loan losses and labor costs absorbed 38.8 percent of total revenues of the average large SSBIC versus 66.5 percent of the total revenues of the typical small SSBIC. The group of small SSBICs incurred these very high costs while investing in a portfolio of assets that was top-heavy in bank CDs and other money-market investments.

The overall group of small SSBICs is not viable in the sense that they cannot cover their operating costs with the revenues they generate by investing in small businesses. Sale of equity investments produced capital losses for the group of small SSBICs in six of the seven years under consideration: 1987 was the exception, when their collective capital gains totaled 0.03 percent, relative to their capitalization. The problem of small SSBIC viability is their high costs of operation, while a secondary problem is their chronic inability to reap significant returns from their equity investments in small businesses.

Small SSBIC inefficiency rooted in high costs of operation is investigated in Table 25.6 by estimating statistically a cost function that shows the typical operating costs of different-size SSBICs. Table 25.6 investigates SSBIC operating costs only: loan losses and other nonoperating costs are excluded. The largest SSBIC operating cost is employee expenses, while other major cost categories include office expenses, travel expenses, legal and accounting expenses, and so forth. Operating costs per dollar of assets are prohibitively high for SSBICs with $1 million in total assets — 10.2 cents per asset dollar according to Table 25.6. Total operating costs are estimated to be $102,035

Table 25.6. Scale Economics in the Operation of SSBICs (annual costs)

I. SSBIC total assets	II. SSBIC operating costs	(II divided by I): Operating costs as a percent of total assets
Size and Cost		
0	$73,904	
$1,000,000	102,035	.102
2,000,000	129,990	.065
3,000,000	157,767	.053
4,000,000	185,367	.046
5,000,000	212,791	.043
10,000,000	347,251	.035
20,000,000	602,890	.030

Cost decomposition: (operating costs = fixed costs + variable costs − scale economy savings).

Fixed costs: operating costs incurred that are invariant with respect to SSBIC size = $73,904.

Variable costs: operating costs that vary in direct proportion to SSBIC size = .0282 dollars per dollar of SSBIC assets.

Costs that increase at a decreasing rate due to operating efficiencies that become more pronounced as the SSBIC gets larger:

at $1,000,000 in total assets, scale economy savings = $89
at $5,000,000 in total assets, scale economy savings = $2,213
at $20,000,000 in total assets, scale economy savings = $35,414

Ordinary least squares regression used to estimate and decompose operating costs for SSBICSs of various sizes (costs, assets measured in thousands of dollars).

Variable	Regression coefficient	Standard error
Intercept	73.904*	10.156
Total assets	.02822*	.0023
Total assets squared	−.0000000885*	.0000
$R^2 = .639$		
$F = 298.9$		

* Statistically significant, .01% significance level.

per year for a $1 million SSBIC, versus $347,251 per year for a $10 million SSBIC. A small SSBIC generating revenues of 9 percent annually on its assets would find that all of those revenues were immediately being taken by operating costs. At $1 million in total assets, the economics of this small SSBIC are to spend 10.2 cents in operating costs to generate 9 cents in gross revenues. This is the crux of nonviability. In contrast, the SSBIC with total assets of $10 million dollars spends 3.5 cents in operating costs to generate 9 cents in gross revenues. Its larger scale of operations holds down operating costs relative to its gross revenues.

Another way of portraying the viability of two SSBICs earning 9 percent gross returns on their assets — one SSBIC has assets of $1 million while the second has $10 million — is shown below:

1. Small SSBIC: total assets = $1,000,000
   a. Gross revenues at 9.0 percent = $90,000
   b. Operating costs at 10.2 percent = <u>$102,000</u>
                              Margin = $12,000
2. Large SSBIC: total assets = $10,000,000:
   a. Gross revenues at 9.0 percent = $900,000
   b. Operating costs at 3.5 percent = <u>$350,000</u>
                              Margin = $550,000

Which SSBIC would you prefer to invest in? The SBA's preference over most of the program's history has been for small SSBICs that lack sufficient size to achieve operating efficiencies. The cost figures used in these examples are not hypothetical. Rather, they were derived econometrically (see Table 25.6) and reflect the actual operating cost histories of all SSBICs that were functioning during 1991 through 1993. Below a $5 million scale of operations, small SSBICs are tremendously inefficient from a cost of operations perspective. Adding the high loan losses generated by the smallest SSBICs (see Table 25.5) to this element of nonviability, one observes a subset of SSBICs that is not efficient at the task of financing minority-owned businesses. That is why these tiny SSBICs are chronically unprofitable, and why most eventually either surrender their charters or end up being dismembered by the SBA's Office of Liquidations. No serious reform of the SSBIC industry can ignore the necessity of putting tiny SSBICs out of their misery.

SSBIC Viability: Further Analysis

SSBICs have differing portfolios of earning assets, and portfolio composition varies systematically with SSBIC size: SSBICs generally invest most heavily in loans to small businesses; small SSBICs invest more heavily in cash assets than others, and large SSBICs are more prone to make equity investments in small firms. How do these various portfolio mixes impact revenues, costs, and SSBIC profitability? Variations in SSBIC revenues and costs are related, in Table 25.7, to variations in loans to MBEs (debt); Equity investments in MBEs (equity); and investments in money-market instruments such as bank CDs (cash assets). These three types of assets account for nearly 94 percent of total SSBIC asset holdings (Tables 25.1 and 25.2) and explain over 98 percent of the variation in revenues generated by SSBICs over the 1991–1993 time period (Table 25.7).

Regression coefficients (see estimates in Table 25.7) are used to measure annual gross revenues associated with investing one dollar of SSBIC assets in debt (gross revenue = 13.3 cents), equity (gross revenue = 0.2 cents) or money-market assets (gross revenue = 8.2 cents). In terms of revenue generation potential, loans to small businesses yielded the highest gross returns to SSBICs during 1991, 1992, and 1993. SSBICs incur costs when they make loans, equity investments, or money-market investments. Attendant costs incurred by SSBICs in the (1991–1993) years associated with investing a dollar of assets in debt were 9.3 cents; corresponding figures for equity and cash assets were 2.9 cents and 3.8 cents, respectively (see Table 25.7). Comparing revenue and cost flows associated with these three types of SSBIC investments reveals that the most profitable type of investment is to be found in money-market forms such as bank CDs.

Debt turns out to be both the highest yielding (13.3 cents) and the most costly type of SSBIC investment (9.3 cents), yielding a net of 4 cents per dollar invested in small business debt. Small business equity investments produced expenses well above revenues; this calculation is measuring the dividend yield of equity holdings, not the capital gains that may be realized when the investment is sold.

The finding that small business debt is the most costly type of SSBIC asset holding seems reasonable, but the finding that equity is the least costly type of asset for SSBICs to acquire does not seem reasonable. Previous evidence indicated that large SSBICs are more likely than small ones to invest in equity forms, and vice versa for cash assets. If presence of equity investments is correlated to SSBIC size and large SSBICs are lower-cost operations than small SSBICs, then the equity coefficient in the total cost regression in Table 25.7 will be biased downward. For similar reasons, the cash-assets coefficient may be biased upward. Table 25.5 depicts low-cost large SSBICs and high-cost small SSBICs, which indicate that the cost per asset-dollar calculations, like those shown in Table 25.5, must be qualified. Across the board, larger SSBICs incur less expense per dollar invested than the small SSBICs. At small SSBIC

Table 25.7. Cost and Revenue Flows from SSBIC Holdings of Small Business Debt, Equity and Money Market Investments (1992–1993 data)

Overview	Annual revenue per asset dollar held	Annual costs per asset dollar held	Spread
1. Small business debt	.133	.093	.040
2. Small business equity	.002	.029	(.027)
3. Money-market investments	.082	.038	.044

Ordinary least squares regression used to estimate the above SSBIC revenue flows attached to debt, equity and money-market investments (all SSBICs, 1991–1993)

Variable	Regression coefficient	Standard error
Intercept	−33061.0*	9439.2
Debt, small bus.	.133*	.001
Equity, small bus.	.002	.006
Money-market inv.	.082*	.006
n = 338		
R^2 = .983		
F = 6271.2		

* Statistically significant, .05% significant level

Ordinary least squares regression used to estimate the above SSBIC cost flows attached to debt, equity, and money-market investments (all SSBICs, 1991–1993)

Variable	Regression coefficient	Standard error
Intercept	56,828*	23456
Debt, small bus.	.093*	.003
Equity, small bus.	.029*	.014
Money-market inv.	.038*	.015
n = 338		
R^2 = .812		
F = 481.2		

* Statistically significant, .05% significance level

Mean values of SSBIC holdings of small business debt, equity, and cash assets (in 1991 dollars: figures were taken from 1991, 1992, and 1993 SSBIC balance sheets)

1.	Small business debt	$3195.5 thousand
2.	Small business equity	$639.9 thousand
3.	Money-market investments	$844.9 thousand

size levels, money-market investments are clearly the most profitable use of SSBIC funds from the standpoint of generating annual revenues exceeding annual costs.

Do some SSBICs maintain viability by investing heavily in cash assets? The short answer is yes. The findings given in Table 25.7 show that SSBICs in the early 1990s were generating yields from cash assets well in excess of associated costs. Per dollar of such assets, the typical SSBIC produces 8.2 cents in revenues and incurs 3.8 cents in costs, yielding 4.4 cents. This resultant spread provides an attractive cash flow to the otherwise nonviable SSBIC. Table 25.1 revealed that small SSBICs collectively had invested 40.6 percent of their total funds in cash-asset forms. Cash and money-market investments exceeded 35 percent of total assets for small SSBICs in six of the seven years (1987–1993) studied.

SSBICs: Providers of Venture Capital?

Thus far, no evidence presented in this study suggests that SSBICs are successfully making equity-capital investments in minority-owned businesses. Balance sheets (see Tables 25.1 and 25.2) indicated that both small and large SSBICs were carrying net unrealized losses on their investments in securities (largely common stock issued by MBEs). The mean losses were $103,766 for small SSBICs and $99,481 for large SSBICs. Furthermore, income statements in Tables 25.1 and 25.2 for fiscal year 1993 operations indicate that large and small SSBICs realized average losses of $76,203 and $12,847, respectively, on their sale or disposal of securities. This pattern of realized and unrealized losses is not encouraging.

Pricing of equity positions held in small minority enterprises is rather arbitrary, however, suggesting that statistics on unrealized gains and losses may be unreliable. The pattern of realized losses taken in 1993, however, cannot be dismissed, because the value of venture-capital investments is determined when the assets are sold or disposed of. If such realized losses typify the SSBICs year after year, it is safe to assume that the industry is indeed losing money on its equity investments in MBEs. Here, again, the pattern varies: small SSBIC group does report realized losses on the sale of securities year after year, but large SSBICs do not.

An examination of realized gains and losses on securities, conducted by examining the aggregate annual income statements of large SSBICs, shows the following patterns:

Year	Net Gain or Loss as a Percentage of Total Assets
1987	1.43
1988	0.38
1989	0.03
1990	(1.32)
1991	1.03
1992	(0.27)
1993	(1.73)

Substantial capital losses from sale of securities typify the large SSBICs in two of these seven years, but these figures require qualification for two reasons. First, the above figures on capital gains and losses are normalized means, which means that the large SSBICs are each being weighted equally when the means are calculated. If nonnormalized means were reported, then the 0.27 loss figure reported above for 1992 would have been positive. The fact is that the large SSBICs are making money, over the long run, as venture-capital investors, but the larger of the large SSBICs have tended to be most successful. The most successful SSBIC venture-capital firms tend to have more than $10 million in total assets, and they invest much more heavily in equity forms than SSBICs in the $2 to $10 million asset range (Bates, 1996). Since these larger scale, more successful SSBIC venture-capital investors are a small group, they do not lend themselves to statistical analysis.

What kind of firm successfully invests equity capital in minority-owned businesses? An equity investment often generates no cash flow because of the extended period before dividends begin to be paid by the small firms in the investment portfolio. The real payoff comes (if it comes at all) only after the equity investment has stimulated sustained growth in the minority business; $1 million firms of today become $10 million firms seven years from now. At that point, the SSBIC sells its stake and realizes its gain. So how does the new SSBIC sustain a negative cash flow for the seven years while it waits for the opportune time to exit its equity investment? Those who provide the capital for the SSBIC simply must be prepared to wait for a return on investment that is many years down the road. Furthermore, the SSBIC must begin operations with sufficient capital to sustain a negative cash flow for many years. If these two elements are not in place, the new SSBIC cannot successfully make equity investments in minority businesses. Why would investors be willing to wait many years for their investments in SSBICs to start paying off? Such patience can exist only when it is matched by expectations of eventual high returns. Such high returns are most likely to be realized in larger scale minority-owned firms that are operating in growing lines of business. The successful equity-capital investments, furthermore, will accrue to minority entrepreneurs who are superbly qualified to create multimillion dollar ventures (Bates, 1996).

One could generously be called naive for believing, back in 1969, that a MESBIC possessing total resources of several hundred thousand dollars could successfully make equity investments in minority-owned businesses. Today, believers in such a scheme would, in addition to being naive, have to ignore the history of the MESBIC/SSBIC industry over the past thirty years.

One who applies for a SSBIC license today will not be successful in the realm of making equity investments in minority-owned firms unless those running the SSBIC have the skills and experience required to compete in the venture-capital industry; and the SSBIC is sufficiently large to achieve both portfolio diversification and operating efficiencies.

The Future of the SSBIC Industry

Bradford (1980) argued that the MESBIC industry collectively was highly liquid, not terribly active in the venture-capital realm, and many firms were consistently generating substantial operating and capital losses. The same characterization of the industry's weaknesses is appropriate today.

Simply stating goals for the SSBIC industry can be an empty exercise. Back in 1969, the industry was envisioned as a provider of equity and patient debt capital for black-owned businesses. Ten years later, nearly 50 percent of the industry's assets were held in money-market investments such as bank CDs and Treasury bills. Portfolios of many SSBICs today depict use-of-funds that typified small commercial banks in the 1950s: business lending focuses upon working capital needs of small firms and is predominantly short-term (SSBIC regulations notwithstanding). Furthermore, most SSBICs are much more likely to invest in money-market forms than to take equity positions in minority-owned businesses. Many years ago, these types of investment priorities caused SBA to identify a capital gap in the equity and long-term debt segments of the capital markets serving small businesses. One consequence of this was the creation of SSBIC industry. The fact is that most SSBICs have replicated the investment practices that produced the capital gap. Why? Most were simply not structured to cope successfully with the risks of investing equity and long-term debt capital (particularly subordinated debt) in minority-owned or any kind of small business. The very small SSBICs, in particular, have never been successful nor are they likely to perform any differently in the future.

If the SSBIC industry chooses to learn from the handful of industry veterans that operate profitably while providing equity and patient debt capital to MBEs, then the industry will focus upon an elite group of MBE clients (Bates,

1996). Most of these SSBICs will not target traditional lines of minority business that operate in ghetto areas. The fact that the total minority-business community suffers a capital gap is therefore not really a rationale for an SSBIC industry because this industry will finance elite MBEs, and not a broad cross-section of the minority-business universe. If the capital gap rationale has relevance, there must be a capital gap facing this elite targeted market. In fact, there is. Consider one concrete definition of "elite": about 10 percent of new business startups utilize equity capital of $25,000 or more to get under way (I am ignoring debt capital momentarily). Looking solely at these $25,000 plus firms, the average nonminority firm startup invested total financial capital of $202,067, versus $139,662 for Hispanic startups and $145,202 and $166,898, respectively, for blacks and Asian immigrants. Various definitions of the "elite" firm subset yield the same result: minorities lag far behind the nonminority business startups.

In a revitalized SSBIC industry, MBEs receiving loans and equity capital from these SSBICs will most often be owned by college graduates with above-average incomes, why should Congress support a SSBIC industry that invests in elite MBEs headed by high-income owners? Political reality requires an economic development rationale for this kind of a SSBIC industry. Congress must be convinced of a simple but profoundly important reality: programs that create strong companies capable of generating jobs for minorities must focus on entrepreneurs who possess the resources for successfully building small businesses. Most of those entrepreneurs would be highly educated and would have above-average incomes; rarely would they locate their business ventures in the poorest, most deprived ghetto areas, though they would draw workers from those areas (Bates, 1994b). As stated earlier, successful small businesses induce economic development and create jobs. Their profits also support investments that permit future expansion and job creation. Furthermore, their profits are the lifeblood of a viable SSBIC industry.

Perhaps the last line of defense for the traditional, small-scale SSBIC is the fact that such firms are sometimes run successfully by Asian immigrant owners who specialize in financing mom-and-pop firms, particularly in the New York City area (over 40 percent of all SSBIC investments in MBEs during 1993 were to New York City small businesses). A study comparing traits of Asian immigrants starting small businesses in the 1979–1987 period to nonminority and African American startups found that 57.8 percent of Asian entrepreneurs were college graduates (bachelor's degree holders), versus 37.5 percent of the nonminority business owners and 30.2 percent of the African Americans (Bates, 1997).

Higher rates of Asian immigrant business ownership coexist with a narrow industry base as well as annual sales that are low, on average, relative to those reported by the dominant nonminority small business sector. Waldinger (1986), for example, observes that Asian immigrants pursue self-employment less as a matter of preference and more as a matter of blocked mobility: impediments to more attractive alternatives include poor English language facility and inappropriate skills. Kim, Hurh, and Fernandez (1989) argue that American employers often do not recognize the education and work experience that immigrants have accumulated in their native countries.

The kinds of small-scale retail ventures that have attracted so many Asian immigrant entrants in recent years are precisely the types of firms that are frequently targeted for lending assistance. Like the SBA loan programs (which largely guarantee bank loans to minorities under the 7(a) program), SSBICs have very actively invested in the food store and restaurant niches. After taxicabs, restaurants and food stores ranked second and third as the most common lines of business attracting SSBIC investments in 1993. Over half of all SSBIC investments in minority businesses in 1993 financed restaurants, food stores, or taxi medallions. In both the SBA 7(a) loan guarantee program and the SSBIC industry, financing traditional lines of retailing increasingly means financing firms owned by Asian immigrants, particularly Chinese and Korean business owners. Whether this shift in emphasis is good or bad depends upon how one perceives the objectives of these programs. Asian Americans generally and Chinese and Koreans specifically are better educated, higher income, and wealthier than nonminorities (Bates, 1997). Native-born whites experience higher rates of poverty and unemployment, overall, than Asian Americans. This is not to deny that recent immigrants — including those as wealthy and highly educated as the average Korean business owner — face transition problems upon arrival in the United States. Aid from SSBIC and SBA loan programs helps to ease those transition problems for immigrants choosing self-employment.

Possessing substantial human-capital and financial-capital resources, Asian immigrants entering into small business are of course an ideal market for many SSBICs. Most of these SSBICs are too small to develop a portfolio of equity investments in minority business. Shorter term, working-capital loans to small firms owned by Asian immigrants make excellent economic sense (for the SSBICs). Lots of small loans to Asian immigrant-owned firms permit diversification of SSBIC's portfolio. Short-term working capital loans generate a steady stream of repayments, thus maintaining liquidity, a chronic problem among many SSBICs that have actually made equity and long-term subordinate debt investments in minority-owned businesses. The Bronx bodega, driven out of business by larger scale, better stocked Asian-owned competitors, may not appreciate this government-subsidized competition, but the decline of black- and Latino-owned mom-and-pop retail stores in places like Los Angeles and New York would have occurred anyway in the absence of 7(a) loans and SSBIC investments. The traditional mom and pops are weak competition for the well-capitalized firms headed by highly educated managers and professionals.

The tragedy of the SSBIC program is not the fact that so many of the industry investments accrue to zero-growth or very low-growth traditional lines of business. The tragedy is that so many of the licensed SSBIC are really capable of remaining viable only if they serve such niches. The program, to date, is simply not designed to emphasize the emerging lines of minority enterprise that hold the potential to grow rapidly. Lending to the college-graduate immigrant running the food store makes sense; investing equity capital in the emerging firm that has the potential to generate $20 million in sales does not make sense. We must ask whether a SSBIC program, thusly designed, makes sense.

A major determinant of the types of investments made by SSBICs is the size of the SSBICs: the smaller companies tend to make small debt investments in small businesses. The pattern of smallness is notable, as is the lack of equity investments. The larger SSBICs tend to invest in the largest of small businesses, and many of these larger SSBICs do indeed make equity investments.

If the provision of equity capital to minority-owned businesses is to be a high priority in a revitalized SSBIC industry, then the record to date indicates that this goal will not be achieved by chartering very small SSBICs. If provision of equity capital is a high priority, then a provocative model is offered by one sector of the Small Business Investment Company (SBIC) industry, the bank-owned SBICs. According to a study published by the Federal Reserve Bank of Chicago, bank-owned SBICs invested $2.807 billion into small businesses over the 1983–1992 time period: 51.1 percent of that sum represented straight equity investments, 25.1 percent was hybrid equity, debt financing, and the rest was debt/loan financing (Brewer and Genay, 1994). Examining the SBIC industry over the 1989–1991 period, Brewer and Genay further observed that the bank-owned SBICs were both larger and more profitable, on average, than nonbank SBICs. The bank-owned SBICs, finally, invested largely in manufacturing, skill-intensive services, and communications lines of small business. That is quite a contrast to the priority areas of the entire SSBIC industry — taxis, restaurants, and food stores.

The Brewer and Genay study cited above provided several insightful summary statistics, comparing 108 nonbank-owned SBICs to 68 bank-owned SBICs. First, the average SBIC had private capital of $3.8 million and $4.1

million in SBA funds in 1991. In contrast, the average bank-owned SBIC had $25.7 million in private capital and $1.9 million in SBA funds. While the bank average is skewed by a few large SBICs, it is nonetheless true that the bank-owned SBICs were clearly larger and less reliant upon SBA funding than the other firms. Thus, size of SBIC emerges, once again, as a determinant of portfolio composition; the larger SBICs (like the SSBICs) are the ones most likely to make equity investments in small firms. This pattern should be accepted as a premise in deliberations about the SSBIC industry: the large firms are the active equity investors; the very small SSBICs stick to debt investments in small firms.

The SBIC bank model offers another important lesson. Bank portfolios are very widely diversified and a large proportion of those assets are highly liquid. High liquidity makes it easy to pay one's bills day to day, month after month. SSBICs that truly do restrict investments in equity and long-term debt forms are likely to face cash-flow problems from time to time, even if their investments are profitable.

Investment firms need to be structured with their liquidity needs carefully considered. This has not been the case in the SSBIC industry. Banks achieve liquidity in their investments in a variety of ways. Inherently illiquid assets such as thirty-year mortgages can be made liquid by selling them in well-established secondary markets. Consumer loans, such as credit card balances, are often short-term, liquidating themselves in less than a year. Where are the short-term loans in the portfolio of the SSBIC? Where are the established secondary markets for their long-term illiquid loans?

The SSBIC program must be designed with greater attention to the fact that the SSBICs will not meet program objectives unless they are structured so that they can make a profit, pay their bills, *and* invest most of their funds into minority-owned businesses. The program can be structured to meet the liquidity needs of SSBICs by (1) designing straightforward ways for SSBICs to sell their small-business investments in secondary markets, and (2) permitting a percentage of SSBIC loans to be short-term in nature.

As an example of policies that would make secondary markets accessible, SSBICs should be permitted to qualify as participants in the SBA 7(a) loan-guarantee program. This would be particularly beneficial to the SSBICs that are at the low end of the industry capitalization spectrum. By selling the guarantee portion of SBA loans, the SSBICs can generate a much larger dollar volume of overall lending than would be possible utilizing only their own capital and SBA leverage. Liquidity would be enhanced; more loan dollars would flow to minority operations.

Liquidity would be further enhanced by permitting SSBICs to devote up to

20 percent of their assets to short-term debt forms such as revolving credit lines. Having the flexibility to lend short-term has many other potential benefits. A large client, for example, may win a major contract which requires a credit line that is tailored to the needs of that contract. By providing such credit, the SSBIC very likely enhances the value of its major investment (such as an equity stake) in that client. Bates and Williams (1995) have shown that minority vendors with government procurement contracts often suffer from liquidity crises when their clients are slow to pay bills. Such conditions can destroy otherwise viable minority-owned firms.

In a word, the SSBICs would better serve the financial needs of the minority business community if (1) the median SSBIC was a much larger firm than is the case today, and (2) all SSBICs operated in a more flexible environment. Portfolio diversification that permits some short-term lending will help to meet important liquidity needs of SSBICs. Access to secondary markets in which minority-business investments can be sold will enhance liquidity and expand the potential of SSBICs to finance minority-owned firms. Greater liquidity and greater flexibility may also enhance SSBIC profitability, reduce defaults on SBA debenture payments, and improve the overall survival rate among SSBICs. Finally, SSBICs that can achieve greater liquidity while actively financing small businesses are less likely to invest substantial assets in money-market investments.

Significant growth in the SSBIC industry can most easily be generated by luring private capital into the subset of stronger investment companies. Tax incentives could accomplish this. The 1993 Tax Act created a great precedent by passing tax breaks specifically targeted to SSBICs (the capital gains rollover), and more broadly targeted, but applicable to SSBICs (the 50 percent exclusion). The tax-free rollover of capital gains (from the sale of publicly traded securities) into SSBICs could, with modification, really attract private capital into the industry.

What's wrong with the existing rollover legislation? As an investment opportunity, SSBICs rank as illiquid, uncertain prospects to most investors. Most potential investors would have to spend a great deal of time learning about the industry, its prospects, which the strong players are, and so forth. Assume that an investor takes the time to identify an SSBIC or two that look like attractive investments. At this point, the potential investor has to figure out — most likely through extensive negotiation with the SSBIC — future prospects for SSBIC earnings actually being paid out as dividends (or whatever), and exit strategies. If the investor wants to get out, how does that occur? The learning process, the courtship, and the finalization of the investment are being motivated by a tax break that has a maximum value of $14,000 for an individual

(28 percent of $50,000). Further, the investor is not simply investing the capital gain; rather, the entire proceeds from the sale of the applicable publicly traded securities must go into the SSBIC.

What is needed? SSBIC owners and managers often seek private capital and they accept the fact that the process is tedious and very time consuming. If the potential capital infusion is $5 million from a large investor, the time and effort is worthwhile. But what amount of investment would be motivated by a tax break of $14,000 or less? It would be a small one — usually too small to be worth the effort (in a 60-day time frame no less). Raise the tax-free rollover ceiling from $50,000 to $2 million per year. To keep a lid on potential tax revenue losses to the U.S. Treasury, do not raise the lifetime ceiling proportionally: a $4 million lifetime ceiling certainly seems like a minimal reasonable increase. And, by all means, broaden the 60-day window for completing the investment to at least 180 days.

A $2 million capital gain, rolled over tax-free into a SSBIC, translates into an income tax saving of $560,000. A potential tax saving of that magnitude would certainly motivate investors in incur some search costs to become familiar with the SSBIC industry. More important, an intermediary might be lured into the picture. Purely for illustrative purposes, envision an intermediary called "SSBIC, Inc." (SI). SI could publicize the investment opportunities available in SSBICs, prepare appropriate profiles of attractive SSBICs for investors, and prepare some sort of standardized exit agreement that would allay investor concerns about the illiquidity of investments in SSBICs. This is not the only possible scenario for matching investors seeking to rollover capital gains into SSBICs with the SSBICs that can profitably invest substantial capital infusions.

Once the capital started flowing, SBA would find itself holding numerous applications for SSBIC licenses from blue-chip outfits. Straightforward restructuring of a tax break that is already on the books, in brief, could completely transform the SSBIC industry and unleash tremendous growth at the top end of the minority-business community nationwide.

Summary and Conclusions

In conclusion, I have found that public-sector programs designed to assist new and expanding minority-owned businesses are often ineffective. Government assistance efforts typically concentrate on low-profit lines of small business possessing minimal economic development potential. These government programs frequently fail because they pay inadequate attention to the factors that shape small business viability.

The Specialized Small Business Investment Company (SSBIC) program was an ambitious effort that potentially deviated from this pattern of ineffective business assistance. SSBICs are privately owned small-business investment companies that receive funds from the U.S. Small Business Administration (SBA) at subsidized rates. These funds are invested in minority-owned businesses, and they provide equity capital (venture capital) as well as long-term loans.

SSBICs are often chartered by the SBA in cases where their viability — in both financial and managerial realms — is dubious. Small SSBICs cannot achieve sufficient portfolio diversification to cope with the risk inherent in providing equity capital to small firms. Further, most lack sufficient capital to survive the negative cash flow that typifies new venture-capital investing firms during their first few years of operation. To achieve sufficient diversification in small business debt investments, loans must be very small, which limits the ability of SSBICs to finance the larger scale minority-owned firms. From a cost of operations perspective, small SSBICs cannot achieve scale economies in the various kinds of paper processing that exist in small-business investment companies. Most SSBICs begin operations as nonviable small-business investment companies, inherently limited in their ability to serve the range of capital needs of minority-owned firms in their target markets. Most of the SSBICs chartered over the past thirty years are out of business today. This study concludes by spelling out policies that would permit SSBICs to achieve greater effectiveness in their role of financing minority-owned businesses.

References

Bates, Timothy, "Effectiveness of the Small Business Administration in Financing Minority Businesses," *Review of Black Political Economy* (Spring 1981).

———, "Small Business Administration Loan Programs," in *Sources of Financing for Small Business,* ed. Paul Horvitz and R. Richard Pettit (Greenwich, Conn.: JAI Press, 1984).

———, "Small Business Viability in the Urban Ghetto," *Journal of Regional Science* (November 1989).

———, "Entrepreneurial Human Capital Inputs and Small Business Longevity," *Review of Economics and Statistics* (November 1990).

———, *Banking on Black Enterprise* (Washington, D.C.: Joint Center for Political and Economic Studies, 1993).

———, "Analysis of Korean Immigrant-Owned Small Business Startups with Comparisons to African American and Nonminority-Owned Firms," *Urban Affairs Quarterly* (December 1994).

——, "Self-Employment Entry Across Industry Groups," *Journal of Business Venturing* (March 1995).

——, *Race, Self-Employment, and Upward Mobility: An Illusive American Dream* (Baltimore: Johns Hopkins University Press, 1997).

——, "Financing the Development of Urban Minority Communities: Lessons of History," *Economic Development Quarterly* (August 2000).

——, "Michael Porter's Conservative Urban Agenda Will Not Revitalize America's Inner Cities: What Will?" *Economic Development Quarterly* (November 1996).

Bates, Timothy, and William Bradford, *Financing Black Economic Development* (New York: Academic Press, 1979).

Bates, Timothy, and Darrell Williams, "Preferential Procurement Programs Do Not Necessarily Assist Minority-Owned Businesses," *Journal of Urban Affairs* (February 1995).

Bradford, William, "The Effectiveness of the MESBIC Program: A Theoretical and Empirical Analysis" (unpublished manuscript, 1980).

Brewer, Elijah, and Hesna Ginay, "Small Business Investment Companies: Financial Characteristics and Investments," Working Paper Series: Federal Reserve Bank of Chicago (July 1994).

Clark, Peggy, and Tracy Huston, *Assessing Microenterprise as a Strategy for Boosting Poor Communities* (Washington, D.C.: Aspen Institute, 1993).

Hansley, James, "The Applicability of the Small Business Investment Company Model for Southern Africa," report to the Agency for International Development (January 1992).

Johnson, Douglas, "Urban Impact Analysis of the Small Business Administration 7(a) and Economic Opportunity Loan Programs," MIT Urban and Community Impacts Discussion Paper No. 7 (1980).

Kwang Chung Kim, Won Moo Hurh, and Marilyn Fernandez, "Intragroup Differences in Business Participation Rates: Three Asian Immigrant Groups," *International Migration Review* (1989).

U.S. Bureau of the Census, *Survey of Minority Business Enterprises: Summary* (Washington, D.C.: Government Printing Office, 1991).

U.S. Commission on Minority Business Development, *Final Report* (Washington D.C.: U.S. Government Printing Office, 1992).

Waldinger, Roger, *Through the Eye of the Needle: Immigration and Enterprise in New York's Garment Trades* (New York: New York University Press, 1986).

26

A Social Accounting Matrix Model of Inner-City New Haven
An Alternative Framework for Development

C. MICHAEL HENRY

In this chapter, I apply a social accounting system to demonstrate how positive policy interventions can considerably alleviate, if not eradicate, poverty and its concomitants in inner cities.[1] The inner city encompasses areas peopled primarily by impoverished black and Latino Americans. Perhaps in no other communities is despair as forlorn and morale as shattered as in inner cities. In these communities, unemployment looms large. Indeed, intolerably high levels of unemployment is characteristic of inner cities. Yet unemployment is treated by monetary policy authorities as a prophylactic against inflation,[2] a remedy which exacerbates and perpetuates inner-city hardship and, which may be worse than the disease.[3]

In our framework, poverty denotes "multiple deprivation" (in regard to jobs, food, housing, clothing, health care, education, equity in the courts, police protection, etc.), which may be measured, in part, either by income deficiency or by expenditure shortfall.[4] We focus on income enhancement because it enlarges the household's opportunity set. Civil rights legislation, affirmative action, and operations of the Equal Employment Opportunity Commission (EEOC) may have somewhat reduced direct effects of racial discrimination and attendant poverty (as well as indirect effects via unequal opportunities in education). But although the policy implications are clear in principle, experience suggests that they are not easily made effective. By and large, our primary objective is to replace a vicious cycle with a virtuous dynamic of inner-city existence.[5] However, our framework may leave untouched the social order which generates hardship and inequality,[6] and subsets of the impoverished who may have only a tenuous attachment to the labor force. The latter includes the aged, unemployables, and so on, whose prospects are dimmed by poverty as well as by incapacitating disabilities. Over the prolonged period from reconstruction to circa 1963, the cumulative adverse effects of political, economic, social and judicial forces were brought to bear, both officially and informally,[7] to institutionalize black abasement. A genuine commitment to black progress would have entailed a sort of domestic Marshall plan, for socioeconomic uplift of blacks to the level of their white counterparts.[8] But that was not to be. Consequently, in the lives of a disproportionately large number of blacks, every year may be an *annus horribilis*.

In our framework, replacement of the vicious dynamic is effected by development of inner-city residents through expansion of the range of choice available to them with respect to jobs, education, health care, etc. Thus, income enhancement is not considered an end in itself, but a means to effect "people development" by enlargement of their opportunity set through effective social policy. As suggested by A. K. Sen, it is not simply a matter of having, but of doing, more especially, of being *able* to do; "the focus has to be on what life . . . *they* lead and what . . . *they* can or cannot do, can or cannot be." What is important, therefore, is what blacks *can manage to achieve* with their material possessions and their *ability to achieve,* given the historically determined social order or circumstances of their lives.[9]

In the light of this, the central question addressed in this essay is as follows: How can federal fiscal units provide inner cities with an infusion of human and financial capital and "creative" access (for minority entrepreneurs) to the viable market for government procurement contracts, and thus effect significant enhancement of inner-city employment and income? Infusion of human capital is brought about by: (a) endowing inner-city entrepreneurs with organizational, managerial, and technical skills essential to provision of contractual services, and (b) endowing inner-city labor with specific and general skills for employment by these entrepreneurs. Financial capital, another indispensable requirement, may be satisfied by giving assistance to community development banks, which may be better placed to foster inner-city business development.[10] Alternatively, to facilitate implementation of the Community Reinvestment Act (CRA) on a broader scale (beyond consumer and mortgage loans), the Small Business Administration (SBA) may guarantee commercial bank loans (at below-market rates) to inner-city entrepreneurs who have successfully completed required courses.

In addition, this framework incorporates creation of cadres of competent and experienced enterprise extension officers to provide long-term technical assistance to recipients of procurement contracts. Indeed, extension officers and entrepreneurs can jointly determine the quantum of financial and human capital required for provision of specific contractual services.[11] To satisfy criteria of eligibility for access to financial capital, an entrepreneur must successfully complete requisite entrepreneurial development courses and be a current recipient of at least one government procurement contract. Provision of creative access by federal fiscal bodies to the market for procurement contracts is politically determined, but not necessarily problematic. For example, approximately $10.9 billion of federal contracts were set aside for minority entrepreneurs in 1996.[12] Hence, we argue that federal procurement contracts for services for which the time required to train entrepreneurs and labor does not exceed six months should be included under the rubric of setasides.[13] In fact, our application of the social accounting matrix model gives the following empirical results. Awarding substantial long-term contracts to minority entrepreneurs (whose workforce is made up, invariably, of at least 80 percent of minority labor)[14] significantly improves socioeconomic conditions for the inner-city populace through skill endowment and gainful employment. Moreover, this improvement obviates current practice of extending tax incentives mainly to nonminority entrepreneurs.

But considerable alleviation of inner-city poverty and, to some extent, racial economic inequality, can only be effected through legal and political challenges and not, as some are wont to think, by competitive market forces per se.[15] For example, because small inner-city enterprises may be unable to capture benefits of tax concessions offered by current policies for neighborhood development, these enterprises are at a competitive disadvantage via-à-vis larger established enterprises. Hence the importance of the direct role of government in this framework. In short, in the absence of *political will,* black poverty and racial inequality along with their unbearable concomitants will remain enduring and painful aspects of the national landscape.

Government institutions are required to award procurement contracts to the enterprise offering the lowest bid. But the proposed program for establishment of fledgling enterprises in the inner city to provide contractual services to public institutions should be considered a development program insulated from market forces during its first five years. In short, this is a program designed specifically to facilitate development of black Americans to the level of their white counterparts. Second, the current backlash against affirmative action after more than 125 years of black subjugation and systematic exclusion from opportunities accorded only to whites was sanctioned by local, state, and federal governments. In a word, private and public institutions and the white populace, as a whole, created the African American problem and therefore, special institutions must be created to bring about a meaningful solution.

At first blush, training entrepreneurs may be considered difficult because it requires a particular type of temperament along with a combination of imagination, self-confidence, and determination. These qualities have been evident among inner-city blacks over the years in their activities in the underground economy as well as in certain areas of entertainment, such as rap music. In our proposed framework, entrepreneurs in any walk of life are individuals who organize change. "They know a good idea when they see one . . . and they know how to make it work. They are the midwives of invention." But, in addition to private entrepreneurs, our framework requires social entrepreneurs who "spot gaps in the social fabric" and whose "aim is to enrich society, to bridge the gap between the powerful and powerless (whites and blacks) and to create a commonwealth of opportunities" for all Americans, black and white.[16]

Endowment of minority labor with skills specifically for employment by minority entrepreneurs to supply long-term services to government has the following effects. It changes: (a) composition of the inner-city workforce in terms of skilled relative to unskilled labor and (b) the occupational structure of this workforce in terms of white relative to blue collar workers. Skill formation includes general training, for example, development of behavioral traits (discipline, punctuality, etc.) appropriate to gainful employment as well as skills peculiar to a given activity. Similarly, entrepreneurial development addresses, *inter alia,* transmission to inner-city entrepreneurs of organizational, managerial, and technical skills specific to activities for provision of long-term contractual services to government.

In this chapter, I appraise recent policy measures taken for development of impoverished areas populated mainly by the racially disadvantaged. The impact of these measures has been rather anemic. Second, I develop the theoretical Social Accounting Matrix (SAM) model, which underpins alternative policies for inner-city development proposed in this chapter. Data for inner-city New Haven are applied to the SAM model to determine the impact of government procurement contracts to inner-city entrepreneurs on the socioeconomic well-being of the inner-city populace. Third, based on modesty of skill requirements, five industries are selected for evaluation of the proposed policy: janitorial service; laundry and cleaning; auto repair; maintenance and repair; and detective and protective service. Estimates are made of contribution of each of these industries to the inner city prior to provision of contractual services to government and the tax impact of current activity of these industries. Fourth, we evaluate the impact on the inner-city economy of skill formation *cum* annual provision of contractual services to government by inner-city entrepreneurs (in the selected industries) who employ inner-city labor to provide the services. Finally, we evaluate effects of implementation of these measures on (a) government tax revenues, (b) market and nonmarket monetary flows in inner-city New Haven, and (c), the distribution of income and the occupational distribution of employment created within the targeted area.

Appraisal of Current Policy: Enterprise Zones, Empowerment Zones, and Hub Zones

Initial measures for development of geographically targeted areas were based on the notion of enterprise zones, originally proposed by Sir Geoffrey Howe, as the means of revitalization of blighted and distressed areas of British cities by way of incentives exemplified by reduction in taxes and regulatory barriers.[17] According to Howe, zones defined impoverished areas spawned by "bureaucratic, tax and other obstacles. . . . The cumulative effect of which was that enterprise and social creativity were being stifled in the inner cities."[18] Over the past two decades (1980-2000), policymakers in the United States at the federal, state, and local levels, adapted the framework of enterprise zones to achieve economic development of geographically targeted urban areas,[19] by providing opportunities for enterprise through tax abatements and, to a lesser extent, reduction of regulatory barriers. In the 1993 Budget Reconciliation Act, these targeted areas were called empowerment zones, which, in addition to economic development, purport to bestow power on impoverished residents to enable them to forge their own destiny.

The focus of empowerment zones was on geographically defined areas to which incentives and other benefits were provided to effect development. This strategy involves building communities and empowering residents of the targeted area to enhance their standard of living. Tax incentives include a 20 percent reduction of payroll taxes for the first $15,000 of wages as well as tax breaks for certain kinds of training provided by firms that employed workers who reside in the zone. Reduction of the payroll tax is a useful means to foster labor intensity and, thus, increase employment, although, below some given rate, the tax may encourage labor hoarding. Furthermore, tax and financial incentives were provided to induce investment in the zone, and block grants were established to make funds available for social services to disadvantaged residents of the zone.

In subsequent legislation, the HUB Zone Act of 1997, passed as Title VI of the Small Business Reauthorization Act, was designed to bring about expansion and growth of business enterprises in distressed areas. This program allocates a portion of federal procurement dollars to businesses located in the zones and is implemented, in part, to enhance effects of previous federal, state, and local zone strategies, which emphasized tax concessions, included administrative expenditures, and provided housing in the zones. Firms eligible to participate in the program are mainly small enterprises located in HUB zones, where at least 35 percent of their employees must reside.

The objective of empowerment and HUB zones is economic revitalization of the community to maintain and strengthen its institutions and, ultimately, create gainful employment for zone residents and thus raise their standard of living. Indeed, according to Butler, these desiderata are based on the view that, "in a very meaningful sense people cannot be separated from place, and that an antipoverty strategy needs to treat individuals in the context of their community."[20] Moreover, given the relative social isolation of residents of the zone,[21] job creation in the zone reduces isolation of residents from the labor market. But gainful employment will be advantageous to zone residents only if they are endowed with requisite skills.Otherwise, jobs available to zone residents will be mainly of the unskilled type, hence, wages will be relatively low and there may be no break from dependence on the kind of public assistance commonly associated with the targeted zone.

Proponents of this strategy for poverty alleviation suggest incentives for a range of activities in the zone, so that the targeted area may contain residential, industrial, and commercial sectors. Such a variety will effect more rounds of household expenditure in the local market and give rise to a larger multiplier. Additionally, a range of activities would facilitate adaptability by residents to changing economic conditions, create more job opportunities, and thus reduce crime and other social problems inimical to local economic development.[22] Other advocates of sectoral diversification suggest that this mix of activities should be established primarily as small enterprises, which, according to Birch, generate more jobs relative to larger enterprises. Enterprises employing fewer than 20 workers account for about two-thirds of the jobs created.[23] But this finding by Birch has been challenged by Brown, Hamilton, and Medoff, whose work has shown that larger firms account for more significant job creation.[24] Nonetheless, participation of small firms is very important to community revitalization since firms in these zones are mainly small proprietorships and partnerships, a considerable proportion of which are owned by local residents who would have a relatively large stake in economic stability of the community.

Economic revitalization of targeted urban areas has been criticized by Kain and colleagues, who claim that racial discrimination in the housing market contributed to growth of inner-city ghettos and kept blacks in inner cities as jobs were moved to the suburbs. According to Kain, this led to a "spatial mismatch" between jobs and residential location.[25] Consequently, measures should be taken to facilitate relocation of inner-city residents to the suburbs. In an earlier work, Kain and Persky[26] argue against the present approach of increasing jobs in empowerment zones to effect economic development of the ghettos. They argue that residents should be assisted in leaving inner cities for the suburbs where they can obtain jobs along with better and cheaper housing in safer neighborhoods with good public schools. But this viewpoint does not take into account suburban residents' opposition to such relocation.[27] Another critic of zone policy, Mark Hughes, argues that suburban jobs should be made more accessible to ghetto residents.[28] Hughes' proposal includes job training, a restructured transportation system, daycare facilities, higher earned-income tax credits to supplement entry-level wages, and measures to reduce crime. Hughes' approach suggests that the culture of unemployment and welfare dependency in inner cities can be changed with access to jobs.[29] Such change can be enduring only if, in addition to acquiring a skill and securing gainful employment, workers are paid a livable wage along with adequate nonpecuniary benefits and have good long-term prospects for advancement on the job. But a cost-effective solution to the transportation problem is not soon forthcoming in most American cities.

Tax incentives are the main policy instruments employed to foster economic development of geographically targeted areas. Recent work by Erickson and Friedman[30] shows that most zones used tax incentives such as sales and tax credits, job creation and wage credits, selective hiring credits, investment credits, and property tax credits. But as Ladd points out,[31] given the emphasis on small firms, it is surprising that tax incentives are the main policy instruments employed since tax abatements per se are not particularly useful to small firms. For example, reduction in corporate taxes does not lend assistance to sole proprietorships and partnerships and reduction in property taxes does not aid small firms, which, in large measure, rent rather than own their sites. Second, few small fledgling enterprises have tax liabilities to benefit from such tax breaks.[32] In short, the type of tax break determines which firms will develop. And, in this case, small enterprises are not among the beneficiaries.

Furthermore, Gavelle observes that, given the objective of increasing employment of zone residents, it is subsidies to labor and not capital that are of relevance to zone policy.[33] Actually, a capital subsidy would induce firms to shift from labor to capital intensive methods, which militates against job creation. In fact, such a subsidy adversely affects job creation, except in the unlikely event that subsequent to a parallel parametric shift of the production function, in a perfectly competitive market, the firm maintains the same average costs of production, thus increasing output and employment. From a policy perspective, a more direct subsidy to labor would induce relatively labor intensive methods giving rise to greater job creation. Indeed, as shown by Papke,[34] who extended the work of Gavelle, the subsidy to labor, targeted to zone residents, would increase zone wages more than a general labor subsidy. This arises because the subsidy to labor targeted to zone residents, shifts the demand schedule for this labor and increases employment and wage income.

In a 1991 study, Elling and Sheldon[35] compared effects of supply-side policies and found direct government participation (interventionist)[36] considerably more effective than supply-side policies such as tax abatements. In fact, they reported that measures such as improvement of physical infrastructure and provision of technical assistance and administrative and other services to participating enterprises were considerably more effective than supply-side measures, which were effective only with respect to firms expanding in the zone. Elling and Sheldon found that tax and financial incentives have relatively insignificant impact on zone development. Levitan and Miller report similar findings.[37]

Most of the direct beneficiaries of zone programs are enterprises that were not originally located in the zones. Of course, incentive measures were meant to induce enterprises to establish branches or relocate to zones to increase employment opportunities locally. But to what extent have zone policies led to development of small enterprises owned and managed by zone residents? And, to what extent have zone policies led to significant change in composition of the labor force of the zone in terms of skilled relative to unskilled labor? What proportion of jobs created were skilled relative to unskilled and what proportion of zone residents held skilled jobs? To what extent was entrepreneurial development among zone residents fostered by zone policy? In the preceding, we noted that most of the small enterprises were unable to take advantage of tax concessions offered by zone policy. Indeed, "only sales tax exemptions were found to be useful to small businesses. Because small minority businesses normally receive their initial capital from friends and family, tax concessions on nonexistent stock and capital gains were inconsequential to them."[38] But enterprise zones are characterized by small enterprises most of which "could not use tax credits unless they were refundable."[39] In a word, zone policies fail to address the causes of deprivation, an essential aspect of development of economically deprived areas.

Moreover, change in the occupational distribution of zone residents is fundamental to development of zones peopled mainly by unskilled, racially disadvantaged groups. In short, a development program targeted to distressed areas such as inner cities must include measures to improve social, physical, and human capital, along with measures to stimulate establishment and development of small enterprises. To be sure, the focus of zone policies must be on the disadvantaged, but, at the same time, such policies must be comprehensive.

So far, we have seen that interventionist aspects of policy are most effective — for example, those policies implemented as joint public-private partnerships. An effective enterprise zone program requires direct government expenditure. That is, government must take measures which directly affect the disadvantaged. Education and training of zone residents require direct government expenditure and so do technical assistance and measures to make the community conducive to both enterprise and habitation. Our proposed framework addresses these and other aspects of policy to develop geographically targeted urban areas — inner cities.

The Social Accounting Matrix Model

The inner city characterizes an area with a relatively large cadre of homogeneous labor which is primarily unskilled, a significant portion of which is unemployed. By and large, annual output of the area comprises mainly services, the sales revenue from which gives rise to relatively meager monetary inflows into the community. In short, production of goods is insignificant, and residents of the community purchase most services supplied within the community. Moreover, the area is deficient in human, physical, and social capital. Relative to suburban communities, the inner city is an economic and social wasteland.

The model developed here reflects the reality of the inner-city economy. It captures the essence of economic activities within Greater New Haven, the community for which data were collected.[40] The model represents an extension of the inter-industry model developed by Leontief, which depicts market-based transactions among producers as buyers of each other's output, as users of scarce resources, and as sellers to final users.[41] However, in addition to these transactions, the social accounting matrix (SAM) model includes nonmarket financial flows, giving added emphasis to nonmarket transfers, such as public assistance to households, income-creation, and accumulation sectors, and their interaction with the processing sector (producers). In short, the SAM model includes transactions undertaken in the inner-city economy, in toto,[42] showing interdependence between the private and public sectors. For example, there are transfers, such as social security and unemployment benefits, from the public to the household sector as well as from the private to public

Table 26.1. Illustrative Transactions Between Producing and Using Sectors and Between Producers and "Final Users"

Producing Sectors	Using Sectors				Total Intermediate use (ω_i)	Final Use (y_i)	Total Use (z_i)
	J	L	B	O			
Janitorial services (J)	20	25	15	80	140	95	235
Laundry & cleaning (L)	10	25	35	120	190	110	300
Basic industry (B)	10	30	45	40	125	100	225
Other services (O)	15	20	35	80	150	320	470
Total purchases (u_j)	55	100	130	320	605		
Primary inputs (v_j)						625	
Labor	150	125	30	100			
Capital	30	75	60	50			
Total of output (χ_j)	235	300	220	470			1,230

sector, such as tax payments to government. These are referred to as inter-institutional transfers. In developing the SAM model, we begin with the simple and progress to the complex. Accordingly, we commence with simple inter-industry transactions.[43]

In Table 26.1, above, each sector or activity appears twice, as a producer of output and as a user of inputs. Final use comprises household, government, and investment expenditures on goods and services which are *not* resold. Elements of each row denote disposition of output of that sector for inter-mediate and final use, in a given period.[44] The role of the janitorial sector as purchaser of inputs is shown in column J. Total purchases by this sec-tor from all sectors is $55.[45] The remaining $180 consists of purchases of primary or nonproduced inputs, that is, inputs not produced by activities (industries)[46] in the processing sector. Direct payment for primary factors — labor and capital — comprises value added of the sector.[47]

In the simple Leontief model, distinction between final and intermediate use, and between produced and primary inputs gives rise to four transaction-types, each of which is captured by one of the four quadrants depicted in Table 26.2 below.

Quadrant I depicts the exogenous sector, from which final purchases of produced goods and services are made by households, government, and so on, while quadrant II represents the endogenous sector, which comprises the prin-cipal component of the inter-industry accounts. Each ξ_{ij} denotes quantity of good i purchased by sector j, measured in constant prices.[48] Quadrant III

Table 26.2. Schematic Depiction of Transaction Types in the Simple Inter-Industry Model

		Purchasing Sectors										
	Intermediate Use						Final Use				Supply	
Producing sector	Sector 1	...	j	...	n	Total inter-mediate Use	Household	Government	Investment	Total Final Use	Total Use = Total Supply	Imports	Production
1	ω_{11}	...	ω_{1j}	...	ω_{1N}	u_1	C_1	G_1	I_1	Y_1	Z_1	M_1	X_1
2	ω_{21}	...	ω_{2j}	...	w_{2N}		C_2	G_2	I_2	Y_2	Z_2	M_2	X_2
...	(Quadrant II)						(Quadrant I)						
i	ω_{i1}	...	ω_{ij}	...	ω_{iN}	u_i	C_i	G_i	I_i	Y_i	Z_i	M_i	X_i
...													
n	ω_{N1}	...	ω_{Nj}	...	ω_{NN}	u_N	C_N	G_N	I_N	Y_N	Z_N	M_N	X_N
Total production inputs	μ_1	...	μ_j	...	μ_N								
Primary inputs (Value-added)	v_1	...	v_j	...	v_N		v_C	v	v_I			V	V
					(Quadrant III)		(Quadrant IV)				V		
Total production inputs	x_1	...	x_j	...	x_N		C	G	I	Y	Z		X

Source: Adapted from Chenery (1967), p. 16.

encompasses use of "primary" (nonproduced) inputs, labor, payments for which measure value added in production — that is, the difference between the value of output and cost of inputs produced outside a given sector.[49] Quadrant IV includes direct payments to primary factors by final users, an example of which is government employment, say, by the U.S. postal service. However, none of the transactions in this quadrant is addressed in the inter-industry model. They are of analytical importance only in our SAM model.

Given the symmetry between producing and using sectors in Table 26.2,[50] the supply-demand balance equations for the productive system may be written as:

$$(1) \quad \begin{aligned} x_1 &= \omega_{11} + \omega_{12} + \ldots \omega_{1N} + f_1 \\ x_2 &= \omega_{21} + \omega_{22} + \ldots \omega_{2N} + f_2 \\ &\vdots \qquad \vdots \qquad \vdots \qquad \vdots \\ x_N &= \omega_{N1} + \omega_{N2} + \ldots \omega_{NN} + f_N \end{aligned}$$

where x_i denotes output of the ith sector, ξi_j is demand by the jth sector for output from the ith sector; and $_i$ is final demand for the ith sector.[51] And, since prices are suppressed,[52] each ξi_j is treated as a function of x_j alone and written as:

$$(2) \quad \omega_{ij} = f_{ij}(x_j)$$

Substitution of equation (2) into (1) gives a determinate system of n equations and n unknowns, provided that final demand, for example, household or government expenditure, is given exogenously.[53]

We assume a proportional relationship between intermediate inputs and output, and a nonproportional relationship between labor and output. To be sure, in regard to labor inputs, substantial evidence of economies of scale exists.[54]

Certain types of transfer payments loom large in inner-city economies. Indeed, in many cases, factor incomes are supplemented by various government transfer payments before being distributed to household accounts where they are spent, in large measure, on consumption goods. This additional expenditure induces larger increases in output, which further augments employment, incomes, and so on. In short, given our desiderata, this trajectory of output, employment, and income tells us that the foregoing inter-industry model is not a reasonable approximation of inner-city reality, because it excludes important activities that are characteristic of these economies. At this point, therefore, advantage of the SAM model becomes immediately evident.[55]

Let us consider an exogenous increase in government demand for say, janitorial services, in the activities account. This will induce repercussions in other sectors, primarily as complementary increases in output — the conventional multiplier effect in input-output analysis.[56] In our extended system, however, the effect of increased government demand for janitorial services will also be felt by accounts for factors and households, and their spending the extra income[57] will induce further increases in output by the activities account.[58] Finally, this impact on the activities' account will affect other accounts.[59]

Multiplier analysis is applied to inter-industry studies subsequent to an exogenous change, because in each "round" of the process leakages occur, the impact of each round is diminished, and the system converges. Such leakages comprise payments to primary inputs (labor), but households to whom these payments are distributed cannot be assumed to make no use of the receipts. Indeed, if they spend a relatively small part on goods and services, there will be further multiplier effects.

Accordingly, we can incorporate the impact of payments to households by means of SAM multiplier, which is tantamount to treating households as an endogenous activity.[60] That is, any given change in income is followed by changes in consumption and saving, and the change in consumption induces additional multiplier effects. A more comprehensive treatment of multipliers is therefore required.

In order to expand our treatment of multipliers, we turn to the SAM, presented in schematic form in Appendix 26.1, panel A, which distinguishes between production accounts, factor accounts and institution accounts. Hence, as previously indicated, and shown in panel B of this Appendix, $T_{1,1}$ denotes transactions between producing and using sectors, $T_{2,1}$ payments to factors by activities, and $T_{1,3,}$ payments to producers by households for goods and services. The SAM demonstrates how various flows originating from an exogenous change in, for example, the government account, have repercussions on all other accounts.

In the foregoing, we avoided a significant weakness of extended multiplier analysis, fixed coefficients, with the assumption of nonproportionality between labor and output. Another significant difficulty of fixed coefficients derived from the SAM model is that the average and marginal propensities must necessarily be the same. This may be a reasonable approximation to activities by producers[61] but inadequate when considering the consumption function for households, since equality of average and marginal propensities to consume require income elasticities of each household group to be unity. This will make for divergence between "accounting price" multipliers[62] and "fixed price" multipliers obtained when marginal and average propensities are not coincident and consumption behavior mirrors differences in income elasticity for specific goods at given prices. In our framework, the marginal and average propensities to consume are coincident.

Appendix 26.2 below portrays an idealized SAM. The production or activity account comprises ten activities of producing and using sectors considered typical in an inner-city economy. Each row (1 to 10) shows the distribution of output to using sectors as intermediate output, to the consumption account and, to capital account as inventory and net investment. The pattern of demand for goods and services produced in the community relates directly to the structure of production and the distribution of income. The consumption account, formerly exogenous to the demand driven production system in the simple inter-industry model, shows purchases of locally produced goods and services and receipt of income from institutional sources.

The remainder of activity output not purchased by using sectors as intermediate goods and not purchased by institutions (households, etc.) is paid for primary factors of production and for indirect taxes. These payments represent value added in the value-added or factor income account. In addition to income from the production account, factors of production also receive income from the institutions account (e.g., wages and salaries of government workers), while the occupation account shows the distribution of factor income according to occupational category. The institutions account shows disbursement to institutions of employee income received as wages and salaries in each occupation as well as inter-institution transfers such as dividends, interest, taxes, and public assistance. Finally, the capital account shows residential savings and investment by commercial and industrial enterprises. At this point, we apply inner-city data to our model to appraise the effects on the inner-city economy of annual infusions of human and physical capital into inner cities and, at the same time, awarding of substantial annual procurement contracts to inner-city entrepreneurs.

The Data

For empirical application of the model, inner-city New Haven is defined geographically by the zip codes within which the target population — disadvantaged black and Latino Americans — resides.[63] This area is graphically depicted in Appendix 26.5, below. Zip code 06511 is a special case that nonetheless does not undermine our findings. In addition to large number of racially disadvantaged residents, the area includes Yale University and two hospitals. These institutions and their more affluent faculty and staff could not be excluded from the data set, nor could zip code 06511 be excluded. In terms of size, inner-city New Haven covers a relatively large area of 20 square miles, with a population of 122,111 and 182 industries. The model includes all economic activities of significance.

The Minnesota Implan Group (MIG) provided industrial data.[64] The basic MIG database consists of two parts: (a) technology matrices at the national level; and (b) estimates of sectoral activity for final demand, industry output, and employment.[65] MIG also gathers data at the state, county, and subcounty (e.g., a city or its subset thereof) levels. The regional data are subdivided into two parts: (a) data on an industry basis, which include value added, output, and employment; and (b) data on a commodity basis, which include final demands and institutional sales. State-level data are balanced to national totals (using a matrix "ratio allocation system" or "RAS"), while county data are balanced to state totals.[66]

MIG's main source of data for generating zip code files is the Bureau of Census County Business Patterns (CBP) program, which provides four-digit Standard Industrial Classification Code (SIC) employment data at the zip code level. However, instead of employment counts, these data contain the number of firms in each of fourteen firm-size classes[67] for each four-digit SIC sector. By taking the product of the midpoint of each firm-size class and the number of firms associated with that size class, MIG obtains an estimate of employment for that sector by aggregating the product for each sector. Thus, given the zip codes specified for a region, employment estimates are determined based on the CBP data. Employment data for zip codes are aggregated for the counties, which contain the given region's zip codes. And, subsequent to aggregating the four-digit SIC data to the Implan sectors, ratios are created to distribute the county-level Implan data file to the desired zip code region.[68] These employment ratios are used to distribute all industry data: employment, output, employee compensation, proprietor's income, other property income, and indirect business taxes. All expenditures are converted to 1996 base year values. Productivity data for our targeted areas, measured by output per worker, earnings per worker and the ratio of value added to output, are the same as those for the county, which includes the zip code area. Estimated population for the area is based on the zip code areas' share of the county's 1990 census of population, which was applied to the respective county's 1993 population to obtain this estimate.

In addition to data for each inner city, MIG provides the Implan economic modeling software. Two models are constructed: a descriptive model, which shows transfers of money between all industries and institutions. This model contains input-output and social accounts. The second model predicts total activity in the inner city based on a given change in the vector of final demand or institutional disbursement. The predictive model represents the SAM model.

Furthermore, our model accounts for skill formation in the target area. In the model, the government defrays the cost of skill formation of inner-city labor and entrepreneurs. Acquisition of skills requires an average gestation period of ten months. Skill formation involves endowing 1,500 workers with low to middle level skills, 500 workers with middle to high level (managerial) skills, and 12 entrepreneurs with organizational, technical and managerial skills. Skill endowment of inner-city labor comprises (a) general training for job readiness, which involves development of behavioral traits (discipline, punctuality, etc.) appropriate to gainful employment; and (b) acquisition of skills specific to activities for provision of contractual services to government. During the training period, a stipend of $500 per worker per fortnight is paid to trainees mastering low to mid-level skills and, $750 per worker per fortnight are paid to trainees acquiring high level skills. The 12 entrepreneurs each receive a stipend of $1,500 per fortnight. During the gestation period, total stipend for 1,500 low to middle level skilled workers is $15 million, that for middle to high level skilled workers is $7.5 million, and that for the entrepreneurs is $360,000. These training costs are accounted for empirically in the model. We assume that annual earnings of workers with low to middle level skills will fall in the range of $20–30,000, those for workers with middle level skills will fall in the range of $30–40,000, and earnings of entrepreneurs in the range of $50–60,000.

With respect to access for minority entrepreneurs to the market for procurement contracts, we assume that the government awards annual contracts of $10 million to inner-city entrepreneurs endowed with the requisite skills. Contracts are awarded in each of the five selected sectors: laundry and cleaning; maintenance and repair; detective and protective services (security services); auto repair and services; and janitorial services. These sectors are selected because the skills required to supply these services efficiently are modest, that is, they can be acquired in a relatively short time period. Second, these are labor-intensive activities.[69] And third, services supplied by these sectors are all demanded by government institutions.

To assure enhancement of proficiency of skills from work experience, an *enterprise extension service* is established. This would be similar to an agricultural extension service,[70] where extension officers, like their counterparts in agriculture, command considerable knowledge of production and management of enterprises involved in these industrial activities. Any previous work (hands-on) experience in the activity by the officer is an added advantage. Officers execute their responsibilities by visiting and inspecting enterprises assigned to them at least once every fortnight to provide technical assistance and to ensure efficient management. The officer ensures that the entrepreneur manages his enterprise according to the principles imparted in entrepreneurial courses provided during skill formation, and corrects any mismanagement or technical and organizational blunders before they develop into significant impediments to enterprise. It is not necessary for the extension officer to be an expert in every aspect of production and management of the activity. However, officers must possess at least the skills to identify problems, which, if beyond their ken, can be referred to a "specialist" for a solution. The enterprise extension service is not formally included empirically in our model since it is meant to prevent depreciation of human capital, rather than its creation.

Since we are estimating a subset of the national economy, assumptions must be made about trade flows of goods and services between the inner city and the rest of the domestic economy. We use regional purchase coefficients (RPCs),[71] which predict the extent of local purchasing based on characteristics of the targeted area.

Empirical Results

First, we examine contributions of the five selected sectors to inner-city New Haven prior to skill formation and commencement of supply of contractual services. Second, we appraise the economic impact of skill endowment of inner-city labor, gainfully employed by inner-city entrepreneurs to supply long term contractual services to government institutions. Following these impact analyses, we evaluate the effect of these activities on government tax revenue, the distribution of income, and the occupational distribution of employment created. Table 26.3 summarizes the current impact of these industries on the respective inner-city economies. Detailed presentations of these results may be found in Appendix 26.4, below.

Prior to procurement contracts, industries with which these sectors are associated account for 3,748.3 employed workers (full-time and part-time), who produce a total output of $232.8 million, of which $116.7 million are value added. Labor income of $92.7 million, which comprises the sum of employee compensation and proprietor's income, is earned in production of this output. These are industry totals. With respect to the five sectors, 3,050.9 full-time and part-time jobs were created or, 81 percent of total job creation, accounting for 73 percent, 67 percent, and 72 percent, respectively, of output, value added, and labor income of the industry. Appendix 26.4 shows contributions to the local economy by the five selected sectors and their associated industries in terms of direct, indirect, and induced effects. Direct effects

Table 26.3. Contributions of Selected Sectors to the Economy of Inner-City New Haven, Prior to Policy Implementation

Jobs	Output*	Value-Added*	Labor Income*	Employee Compensation*
3,748.3	$232.8	$116.7	$92.7	$67.3

* In millions of dollars.

Table 26.4. Inner-City New Haven Induced Changes in Output, Income and Jobs

Output*	Jobs	Labor income*
Panel A Industry Level		
33.1	486.3	14.7
Panel B Sectoral Level		
1.4	25.5	.4

* In millions of dollars.

represent initial change in institutional (government) demand, the number of employees required to produce the initial change, and wages and salaries paid to produce the additional output. Indirect effects represent additional output produced by suppliers of inputs to the industry whose output increased owing to the initial impact. These effects are associated with "backward linkages," the relationship between suppliers of inputs and the enterprise, which uses these inputs in production. Induced effects represent change in institutional demand caused by changes in household income generated by direct and indirect effects of expanding output and employment. For example, in Table 26.4, panel A, at the industry level, the sum of direct and indirect effects induces an additional $33.1 million of output and 486.3 jobs in industries supplying additional goods and services demanded by households, owing to additional income of $14.7 million. Whereas, at the sectoral level (the five selected sectors), the sum of direct and indirect effects induces an additional $1.4 million of output and 25.5 jobs owing to additional income of $.4 million (panel B).

Table 26.5 summarizes the impact on tax revenue. We examine the impact on tax revenue of the 3,748.3 jobs generated industrywide, prior to provision of procurement services to the government.

These jobs yield total inner-city labor income of $93.7 million and total value added of $116.7 million. Industries generate $9.7 million of tax revenue to state and local government from all sources and $19.3 million of tax revenue to the federal government, of which 40 percent comprise personal income tax.

Table 26.5. Impact of Direct, Indirect and Induced Effects on Tax Revenue

Jobs	Labor Income*	Value-Added*	State and Local*	Federal*	Ratio
3,748.3	$93.7	$116.7	$9.7	$19.3	34.2

* In millions of dollars.

Table 26.6. Impact of Skill Transformation and Procurement Contracts on the Economy of Inner-City New Haven

Jobs	Output*	Value-Added*	Labor Income*	Employee Compensation*
5,380	$304.5	$157.3	$122.8	$88.6

* In millions of dollars.

The economic impact of skill formation of inner-city labor coupled with annual procurement contracts of $50 million to inner-city entrepreneurs in the selected sectors is also analyzed in terms of direct, indirect, and induced effects. The impact on the economy is summarized in Table 26.6, and detailed in Appendix 26.4.

With respect to employment and output, subsequent to supply of contractual services, the impact of the industry as a whole is as follows. Industrywide, 5,380 jobs (full-time and part-time) were created, which gives rise to labor income of $122.8 million, associated with an increase of $304.5 million of additional output (direct effects), of which $157.3 million are value added. These increases stimulated another $43.8 million of additional output, which results in creation of another 644.6 jobs within the enterprises supplying the five selected sectors (indirect effects). Direct and indirect effects together induce another $43.8 million of additional output and another 644.6 jobs in enterprises satisfying demand arising from increased household spending resulting from both direct and indirect effects. Thus, the total impact stemming from jobs and output changes in the five sectors gives rise to 6,598.9 jobs (full-time and part-time), over $304.5 million of additional output and $157.3 million of value added. With respect to the selected sectors, 4,962 jobs were created (78 percent of the industrywide total) producing additional output of $226.4 million (80 percent of industrywide incremental output) for which employee compensation is $110.7 (83 percent of industrywide compensation) and labor income $141.7 million (85 percent of industrywide labor income).

Let us turn to induced effects subsequent to procurement contracts. These effects, we may recall, represent changes in institutional demand brought

Table 26.7. Induced Changes in Output, Employment, and Income Subsequent to Procurement Contracts

Output*	Jobs	Labor Income*
Panel (a) Industry Level		
43.8	644.6	19.5
Panel (b) Sectoral Level		
1.8	32.4	.5

* In millions of dollars.

Table 26.8. Impact of Procurement Contracts on Tax Revenue

Jobs	Labor Income*	Value-Added*	State and Local*	Federal*	Ratio
5,380	$122.7	$157.3	$14.0	$25.3	.25

* In millions of dollars.

about by changes in household income generated by direct and indirect effects of expanding output and employment. Table 26.7, Panel (A), shows at the industry level, the sum of direct and indirect effects induces an additional $43.8 million of output and 644.6 jobs in the industries supplying additional goods and services demanded by households owing to their additional income of $19.5 million. In Panel B of Table 26.7, the sum of direct and indirect effects, induces an additional $1.8 million of output and 32.4 jobs owing to additional income of $.5 million.

Table 26.8 shows the impact of procurement contracts on tax revenue. In inner-city New Haven, 5,380 jobs were generated industrywide. These jobs yield total inner-city labor income of $122.7 million and total value added of $157.3 million. Industries generate about $14 million of revenue to state and local government from all sources and $25.3 million of revenue to the federal government, of which 40 percent are revenue from personal income tax. Tax payments to government as a proportion of value added are approximately 25 percent. Appendix 26.6 depicts disaggregated federal, state, and local government tax revenues.

Let us examine the "total effects" of job and output increases across the selected sectors. Within the "total effects," each job created by an enterprise supplying procurement services (the direct jobs effect) is associated with .16 of a job in the supplying firm[72] (the indirect jobs effect), and .16 of a job in enterprises,[73] which satisfy additional household spending (the induced jobs

Table 26.9. Industrywide Multipliers Subsequent to Procurement Contracts

Output	Employment	Income
1.43	1.32	1.42

Table 26.10. Regional Purchasing Coefficients for Sectors in Inner-City New Haven

Maintenance	.88
Laundry and Cleaning	.88
Janitorial Service	.47
Security Service	.52
Auto Repair	.88

effect). The Type (II) SAM employment multiplier for inner-city activities by this group of enterprises is thus 1.32.[74] Thus, for every ten jobs created (or retained) within the inner-city enterprise that satisfies procurement demand, three additional jobs are created elsewhere in the inner-city economy. Tables 26.9 and 26.10 depict "fixed price" multipliers (marginal and average propensities are unequal) for the inner-city and regional purchasing coefficients for selected sectors, respectively.

The multipliers are relatively small, whereas, with exception of janitorial and security services, the regional purchasing coefficients are quite large. About one-third of the "total effects" for output by all procurement firms is accounted for by maintenance and repair, which accounts for $100.6 million out of $304.5 million of total output. This enterprise accounts for about 26 percent of the total jobs impact on industries associated with the five selected enterprises. But that is not surprising since this enterprise accounts for the largest number of reported job changes (1,365.3 direct effects jobs). The smallest impact from procurement contracts is observed in security services, which accounts for approximately $4.5 million of additional output. We must note, however, that this degree of improvement may not occur in the absence of the enterprise extension service, which is absolutely essential to long-run efficacy of this policy.

Table 26.11 presents the occupational distribution of employment created in the inner city. Each row total gives employment created across all sectors from procurement contracts to inner-city entrepreneurs, Thus total employment of 335, row 1, represents employment created in all sectors and not

Table 26.11. Occupational Distribution of Employment Created in Inner-City New Haven

	Employment by Sector					
Occupational Categories	Maintenance and Repair	Laundry and Cleaning	Janitorial Services	Detective and Protective Services	Auto Repair Services	Total
I. Managerial and Administrative Occupations	102	53	23	26	55	335
II. Professional, Paraprofessional, and Technical Occupations	39	4	30	—	—	309
III. Sales and Related Occupations	24	200	10	86	52	522
IV. Clerical and Administrative Occupations	124	55	34	92	71	581
V. Service Occupations	—	87	581	197	8	1,059
VI. Agriculture and Related Occupations	27	—	—	—	—	44
VII. Production, Construction, Operating, Maintenance, and Material Handling Occupations	1,068	622	21	79	530	2,504
Total	2,761	2,033	1,353	988	1,434	

merely in the five sectors of focus in this chapter. Similarly, each column total represents employment created across all occupational categories in a given sector, and not merely the seven occupational categories of relevance here. For example, managerial and administrative occupations account for 77 percent of employment created in this occupational category across all sectors.

Each of the five sectors accounts for approximately 50 percent of total employment created, which is quite significant. And, with exception of professional, paraprofessional, and technical occupations, the five sectors account for at least 60 percent of employment created in each occupational category. This indicates significant transformation of the inner-city labor force. Occupational categories V and VII account for at least 80 percent of employment created in these categories across all sectors. This should not be surprising since the service sector looms large in inner cities, and occupational category VII includes a variety of activities, namely, production, construction, material handling, the last of which is mainly an unskilled activity.

Social Accounting Matrix of Inner-City New Haven

The social accounts track market and nonmarket monetary flows (in *millions* of dollars) between industry and institutions in the inner-city economy. Appendix 26.7 gives the aggregate SAM for the inner-city economy. For example, the first row shows industry transactions from which $5,128.2 million accrue to industry as income.[75] With this income, industry made payments to commodity, factors of production, and to foreign and domestic trade. The aggregated *use matrix*[76] in column 1, row 2, shows payments of $878.6 million to commodities. Industry makes payments of $3,179 million to factors of production, which represents receipt of income to employee compensation ($2,031.4 million), proprietors ($221.9 million), other property income ($771.3 million) and indirect business taxes ($154.4 million). Industry also makes payments for foreign ($85.4 million) and domestic ($985.1 million) commodity imports, which are used as intermediate inputs. We examine columns showing the distribution of employee compensation (column 3); distribution of proprietor's income (column 4); federal nondefense payments (column 8); and, the distribution of expenditures (noneducation) by state and local government (column 11).[77]

Commodity payments represent payments made by production of commodities. The first expenditure of $2,627.1, given in column 2, is payment to industries. This is an allocation of a part of commodity income to industries using commodities in production — the domestic industry make mix.[78] Institutions also produce commodities, which are treated here as institutional

Table 26.12. Precontract and Postcontract Wages, Profits, and Interest in Inner-City New Haven (in millions)

	Precontract	Postcontract
Wages	62%	62%
Profits	23%	23%
Interest	15%	16%

commodity sales. Institutional sales are made by households ($.1), the federal government ($.3), state and local government noneducation ($23.6). Other expenditures represent payments to capital ($6.3) and inventory ($1.9).

Column 3 gives the distribution of employee compensation. The first payment of $1,768.6 million goes to households, which represents a receipt of income to households. This payment to households includes wages and salaries as well as benefits and other nonwage compensation.[79] But these wages and salaries exclude employee contributions to social security.[80] Employee compensation also makes payments to institutions, which includes federal, state, and local governments. The payment of $226.9 million to federal government (nondefense) includes wage accruals less surplus, employee contributions to social security, and employer social security obligations. Similar payments ($34.1 million) are also made to state and local government (noneducation). The payment of $1.8 million to enterprises (corporations) represents wage accruals, that is, wages earned but not paid in the calendar year.

Column 4 gives the distribution of proprietor's income of $221.9 million. This income is distributed to households as self-employed income ($211.3 million) without social security and, to the federal government (nondefense) as employee payments of social security tax ($10.7 million). Household recipients of self-employed income pay income taxes to the federal, state, and local governments. Column 8 gives federal nondefense payments. The first expenditure of $25.7 million represents payment for goods and services. Payments to households include interest payments and transfers to households.[81] The latter includes public assistance. Payments to state and local government include federal grants-in-aid, whereas, payments to enterprises include subsidies and grants to corporations. Federal transfers of $2.3 million to the rest of the world include foreign aid. The federal payment of $1.6 million for domestic trade represents payment for purchase of commodities outside the local economy.

In column 11, we examine the distribution of expenditures by state and local government (noneducation). The first expenditure of $198.9 million is for goods and services (institutional demand). The disbursement of $127.3

Table 26.13. Pretax and Posttax Distributions of Income in Inner-City New Haven

Income Category	Posttax	Pretax
<5,000	.14%	.13%
5–10,000	3.0%	2%
10–15,000	3.0%	3%
15–20,000	4.0%	4%
20–30,000	10%	9%
30–40,000	11%	11%
40–50,000	13%	13%
50–70,000	27%	27%
70,000+	30%	31%

million to households includes interest (primarily for bond holding) and transfer payments, the latter of which are mainly state welfare payments and unemployment compensation. The transfer of $135.6 million to state and local government represents an allocation for education-related expenditures. Payments of $4.3 million and $52.7 million represent payments for foreign and domestic imports, respectively.

The functional distribution of income, before and after procurement contracts, is examined to determine whether these contracts affected labor's share of income. Table 26.12 shows the distribution of gross income among wages, profits, and interest prior and subsequent to procurement contracts. The relative distributions in the pre- and post-contract periods are not significantly different, but the absolute dollar value of wages and salaries increased considerably in the post-contract period, but the relative position of labor is not strengthened against those of other factors of production.

Finally, we examine effects of the income tax on the percentage share of inner-city income accruing to households in the nine household income categories moving from the most affluent to the poorest. Table 26.13 depicts the distribution of income to inner-city households, before and after tax. A given percentage share is interpreted as follows: in inner-city New Haven, 2 percent of the pretax income accrues to households earning at least $5,000 but no more than $10,000, while 3 percent of after-tax income accrues to households in this income category. Thus, the tax effected a redistribution of 1 percent of income to households in this income category.

The tax has a relatively small effect on the distribution, as a whole. The tax effected a redistribution of 1 percent of annual income to households earning less than $20,000, as well as a redistribution of 1 percent to households earning at least $20,000 but no more than $50,000. In addition, the tax effects income reductions of 1 percent to those households earning at least $50,000. The relatively small redistributive impacts may be due to the inability of the tax system to redistribute income to the poorest, or to the large number of individuals in the community receiving unemployment compensation and other transfer payments from government.

Conclusion

We emphasize that our long-term strategy for inner-city development is to transform a vicious cycle into a virtuous dynamic. Efficacy of our alternative policy may be determined by appraising the extent to which this transformation can be effected by implementation of the measures proposed. To begin with, skill endowment of inner-city labor transforms the occupational structure and skill mix of the inner-city labor force. Indeed, Table 26.14 depicts the occupational structure of total employment effected by provision of procurement contracts to inner-city entrepreneurs. The last row gives total employment generated. Subsequent to procurement contracts, approximately 3 percent of the employees are in managerial and administrative occupations, while about 3 percent are professionals and paraprofessionals. Occupational category VII accounts for the largest component of employment generated. Previously, we stated that this category encompasses a number of occupational subsets, including supervisors, managers, inspectors, and a variety of skilled personnel as well as workers performing various unskilled activities. Provision of procurement contracts to inner-city entrepreneurs, along with skill transformation of the labor force enhances labor productivity, and thus increases demand for skilled labor.

With respect to income, owing to procurement contracts, aggregate annual labor income for the inner city is augmented by $122.8 million.[82] This increases consumption demand and at once raises the living standard of a large subset of the populace. In addition, this income enhancement will effect reduction in crimes associated with unemployment, income deficiency, and substance abuse. Nonetheless, our policy measures must be accompanied by provision of medical and other therapeutic facilities for afflictions associated with long periods of joblessness, such as drug and alcohol abuse, depression, and anxiety.[83]

Investment in development of entrepreneurial and labor skills makes for investment in human capital. This is further enhanced by investment in complementary physical capital, an input required by entrepreneurs to supply

Table 26.14. Occupational Structure of Employment Created Owing to Procurement Contracts in New Haven

I. Managerial and Administrative Occupations	3%
II. Professional, Paraprofessional, and Technical Occupations	3%
III. Sales and Related Occupations	5%
IV. Clerical and Administrative Occupations	5%
V. Service Occupations	10%
VI. Agriculture and Related Occupations	—
VII. Production, Construction, Operating, Maintenance, and Material Handling Occupations	24%
Jobs Generated	10,609

contractual services to government institutions. In addition to investment in physical and human capital, government must also undertake investment in social overhead capital, which includes transportation and communication systems, educational and power facilities, physical structures, and so on, upon which this enhanced economic activity depends. The better and more complete the inner city's social overhead capital, the more effectively its economic activities can be carried out. Furthermore, if a community has considerable employment of highly skilled manpower and a number of the better jobs, it is likely to have schools of high academic standing (and, by extension, very good students). This may not occur without additional positive intervention. To be sure, very high employment in skilled occupations provides an environment conducive to good schools, which is also complementary to policies for provision of better schools, and by extension, adequate social overhead capital.

Moreover, awarding procurement contracts to inner-city entrepreneurs enhances government tax revenue and thus benefits the city at large and the nation as a whole. Indeed, as a result of meaningful participation of blacks and Hispanics on a large scale, total government revenue is augmented. For example, provision of procurement contracts to inner-city entrepreneurs increases federal tax revenue by approximately $19.3 million and state and local government tax revenue by about $9.7 million. Therefore, as time elapses, the alternative policy recommended in this chapter enlarges the public purse.

Over time, as inner-city household income grows, household expenditure patterns change, and the community will grow attractive to investors. Thus, private investment will be made in the inner city and its periphery, without the necessity of tax concessions, to satisfy growing household demand. Furthermore, setasides are already in place and facilities for employment and job training are readily available and may simply have to be modified to provide training in skills specific to provision of given contractual services. The alternative policy presented here avoids "unscalable political" hurdles, which would be encountered if proposals advanced by Kain and Persky[84] and by Hughes[85] were implemented. Moreover, it avoids the results observed in enterprise/empowerment zone programs, in which most of the benefits actually accrue to nonzone residents.

Finally, our policy alternative not only changes the occupational and skill composition of the inner-city labor force. It also fosters establishment and development of an entrepreneurial class among the racially disadvantaged. This has significant implications. First, development of meaningful black and Hispanic entrepreneurship is an effective means of reducing the wealth gap between blacks and whites. This development will reduce differences in intergenerational transfers for defrayal of costs of college education, down payment on a home, and seed money for establishment of enterprise. Indeed, intergeneration transfer of household wealth can be made only if there is wealth in the family to be transferred, hence the relatively large wealth gap observed between blacks and whites.[86] Equally important, moreover, creation of a black and Hispanic entrepreneurial class, which hires labor, will not eliminate the prevalence of racial discrimination in the job market, but *will* reduce it, since negative racial stereotypes will not be a consideration in employment decisions by these entrepreneurs. This also holds in regard to consideration for promotion and advancement on the job.

The total effects of policy measures proposed in this chapter are quite substantial. Clearly, if we quadrupled the number of sectors in which procurement contracts is awarded to inner-city entrepreneurs, the impact on employment, income, tax revenue, and the occupational structure of the inner-city labor force would considerably enhance the standard of living and quality of life in these communities. And these effects, coupled with those of concomitant measures, will readily transform the prevailing vicious dynamic into a virtuous one.

Appendix 26.1. Panel A Schematic Social Accounting Matrix

Disbursements	1	2	3	4	5	6	7	8	9	10	11	12	13	14	15	16	17	18	19	20	21	22	23	24	25	26	27	28	29	30	31	32	33	34	35	36	37	38	39	40	41
Production Account:																																									
Household Furniture																																									
Laundry and Cleaning																																									
Distilled Liquor																																									
Building Maintenance																																									
Janitorial Services																																									
Textile Goods																																									
Tobacco Products																																									
Stationery Products																																									
Prepared Seafood																																									
Auto Repair Services																																									
Consumption Account:																																									
Household, Low Income																																									
Household, Med Income																																									
Household, High Income																																									
Federal Education																																									
Federal Other																																									
State Education																																									
State Other																																									
Local Government																																									
Value-Added Account:																																									
Employee Compensation																																									
Proprietors' Income																																									
Capital Consumption																																									
Indirect Taxes																																									
Occupational Account:																																									
Professional																																									
Technical																																									
Administrative Support																																									
Sales																																									
Service Workers																																									
Unskilled																																									
Institutional Account:																																									
Households, Low Income																																									
Households, Med Income																																									
Households, High Income																																									
Businesses																																									
Government, Local																																									
Government, State																																									
Government, Federal																																									
Capital Account:																																									
Residential																																									
Commercial																																									
Industrial																																									
Rest of World Account:																																									
Imports																																									
Total																																									

Appendix 26.1. Panel B Schematic Social Accounting Matrix

	Production		Consumption	Accumulation	Trade	Total
	Activities	Factors				
Production						
Activities	$T_{1,1}$	0	$T_{1,3}$	$T_{1,4}$	$T_{1,5}$	q_1
Factors	$T_{2,1}$	0	$T_{2,3}$	0	$T_{2,5}$	q_2
Consumption	0	$T_{3,2}$	$T_{3,3}$	0	$T_{3,5}$	q_3
Accumulation	0	0	$T_{4,3}$	$T_{4,4}$	$T_{4,5}$	q_4
Trade	$T_{5,1}$	0	$T_{5,2}$	0	0	q_5
Total	q'_1	q'_2	q'_3	q'_4	q'_5	

Appendix 26.2. Schematic Social Accounting Matrix: Structure of Social Accounting Matrix

Receiving account	Production 1 Sectors 1 to 10	Consumption 2 Sectors 11 to 18	Value Added 3 Sectors 19 to 22	Occupation 4 Sectors 23 to 28	Institutions 5 Sectors 29 to 35	Capital 6 Sector 36 to 38	RestWorld 7 Sector 39 to 40	Total 8 Sector 41
1 Production	T_{11}	T_{12}	0	0	0	T_{16}	T_{17}	T_1
2 Consumption	0	0	0	0	T_{25}	0	0	T_2
3 Value Added	T_{31}	T_{32}	0	0	0	0	0	T_3
4 Occupations	0	0	T_{43}	0	0	0	0	T_4
5 Institutions	0	0	0	T_{54}	T_{55}	0	0	T_5
6 Capital	0	0	0	0	T_{65}	0	T_{67}	T_6
7 Rest of world	T_{71}	T_{72}	0	0	T_{75}	T_{76}	0	T_7
8 Total	T_1	T_2	T_3	T_4	T_5	T_6	T_7	T_8

Appendix 26.3. *Sectoral and Industry Impacts of Selected Activities on the New Haven Inner-City Economy Prior to Procurement Contracts*

	Industry Total	Sector				
		Security Services	Maintenance and Repair	Laundry and Cleaning	Janitorial Services	Auto Repair Services
(a) Output						
Direct	163,046,594	4,148,057	89,023,312	22,964,870	5,959,059	40,951,296
Indirect	36,723,542	153,455	736,832	4,857,874	129,712	656,096
Induced	33,056,429	42,180	423,655	235,528	61,857	623,053
Total	232,826,565	4,343,691	90,183,800	28,058,272	6,150,628	42,230,444
(b) Employment						
Direct	2,768.7	146.3	1,227.5	585.8	249	560.2
Indirect	493.3	5.4	10.2	123.9	5.4	9.0
Induced	486.3	2.6	5.8	6.0	2.6	8.5
Total	3,748.3	257	1,243.5	715.7	257.0	577.7
(c) Value Added						
Direct	75,215,789	3,300,508	52,847,952	6,702,309	5,568,228	6,796,792
Indirect	20,863,507	122,100	437,414	1,417,773	121,205	108,894
Induced	20,607,332	33,561	251,499	68,739	57,800	103,410
Total	116,686,630	3,456,169	53,536,868	8,188,821	5,747,233	7,009,096

Appendix 26.3. Continued

(d) Employee Compensation

Direct	44,465,556	1,866,466	35,028,436	2,960,899	1,902,757	2,706,999
Indirect	10,585,887	69,049	289,925	626,334	41,418	43,370
Induced	12,848,861	18,979	166,697	30,367	19,751	41,186
Total	67,900,302	1,954,494	35,485,056	3,617,600	1,963,925	2,791,554

(e) Proprietor's Income

Direct	20,388,452	1,165,969	14,789,010	1,737,105	1,473,893	1,222,474
Indirect	2,558,350	43,134	122,406	367,459	32,083	19,586
Induced	1,850,366	11,856	70,380	17,816	15,299	18,599
Total	24,797,167	1,220,960	14,981,796	2,122,380	1,521,275	1,260,659

(f) Labor Income

Direct	64,854,006	3,032,435	49,817,444	4,698,004	3,376,650	3,929,473
Indirect	13,144,237	112,183	412,331	993,792	73,500	62,956
Induced	14,699,227	30,835	237,077	48,183	35,051	59,785
Total	92,697,470	2,175,454	50,466,852	5,739,980	3,485,201	4,052,213

(g) Indirect Business Taxes

Direct	3,635,433	59,484	420,738	951,412	1,036,493	1,167,307
Indirect	2,249,726	2,201	3,482	201,257	22,562	18,702
Induced	1,695,254	605	2,002	9,758	10,759	17,760
Total	7,580,414	62,289	426,222	1,162,427	1,069,814	1,203,769

Appendix 26.4. Economic Impacts of Skill Formation and Procurement Contracts on Inner-City New Haven

	Industry Total	Security Services	Maintenance and Repair	Laundry and Cleaning	Janitorial Services	Auto Repair Services
				Sector		
			(a) Employment			
Direct	4,070.2	498.9	1,365.3	840.9	666.8	697.0
Indirect	643.2	10.3	13.6	172.8	7.4	11.4
Induced	644.6	2.0	7.7	8.0	3.4	11.3
Total	5,358.0	511.2	1,386.7	1,021.6	677.5	719.7
			(b) Output			
Direct	213,254,600	14,148,105	99,023,312	32,965,328	15,959,118	50,952,888
Indirect	47,449,144	291,779	989,712	6,774,700	176,121	830,120
Induced	43,806,457	55,928	561,638	312,355	81,974	825,946
Total	304,510,203	14,495,812	100,574,664	40,052,384	16,217,213	52,608,952
			(c) Employee Compensation			
Direct	58,081,797	6,366,104	38,963,184	4,250,275	5,095,825	3,368,133
Indirect	13,494,474	131,289	389,427	873,473	56,236	54,873
Induced	17,028,529	25,166	220,990	40,272	26,175	54,597
Total	88,604,803	6,522,559	39,573,604	5,164,021	5,178,236	3,477,603

Appendix 26.4. Continued

(d)

Direct	28,394,197	3,976,863	16,450,261	2,493,559	3,947,274	1,521,041
Indirect	3,359,342	82,016	164,416	512,451	43,561	24,781
Induced	2,451,765	15,721	93,302	23,627	20,275	24,656
Total	34,205,305	4,074,599	16,707,979	3,029,637	4,011,111	1,570,477

(e) Indirect Business Taxes

Direct	6,269,813	202,885	467,999	1,365,721	2,775,861	1,452,400
Indirect	2,881,678	4,184	4,678	280,669	30,634	23,662
Induced	2,264,334	802	2,654	12,941	14,258	23,543
Total	11,397,825	207,871	475,331	1,659,331	2,820,752	1,499,606

(f) Total Value Added

Direct	103,092,879	11,257,302	58,784,368	9,620,947	14,912,423	8,456,782
Indirect	26,862,959	232,161	587,534	1,977,199	164,570	137,777
Induced	27,308,038	44,501	333,411	91,161	76,598	137,084
Total	157,263,878	11,533,964	59,705,316	11,689,307	15,153,591	8,731,643

(g) Labor Income

Direct	86,475,9912	10,342,966	55,413,444	6,743,833	9,043,098	4,889,173
Indirect	16,853,816	213,305	553,843	1,385,924	99,797	79,654
Induced	19,480,295	40,886	314,292	63,899	46,450	79,253
Total	122,810,103	10,597,157	56,281,580	8,193,657	9,189,345	5,048,081

Appendix 26.5. Inner-City New Haven Encompasses the following zip code areas: 06511, 06513, 06515, 06509

Appalachian *Appendix 26.6. Inner-City New Haven: Tax Impact of Procurement Contracts*

		Employee Compensation	Proprietary Income	Household Expenditures	Enterprises (Corporations)	Indirect Business Taxes	Total
Enterprises (Corporations)	Transfers	76,634					76,634
	Total	76,634					76,634
Federal Government NonDefense	Corporate Profits Tax				2,110,047		2,110,047
	Indirect Bus Tax: Custom Duty					283,307	283,307
	Indirect Bus Tax: Excise Taxes					824,835	824,835
	Indirect Bus Tax: Fed NonTaxes					286,258	286,258
	Personal Tax: Estate and Gift Tax			274,111			274,111
	Personal Tax: Income Tax			10,445,964			10,445,964
	Personal Tax: NonTaxes (Fines-Fees)			40,725			40,725
	Soc Sec Tax-Employee Contribution	4,348,609	1,642,521				5,991,130
	Soc Sec Tax-Employer Contribution	5,548,343					5,548,343
	Total	9,896,952	1,642,521	10,760,800	2,110,047	1,394,400	25,804,720
State/Local Govt NonEducation	Corporate Profits Tax				572,703		572,703
	Dividends				174,061		174,061
	Indirect Bus Tax: Motor Vehicle License					81,627	81,627
	Indirect Bus Tax: Other Taxes					262,194	262,194
	Indirect Bus Tax: Property Taxes					4,654,598	4,654,598
	Indirect Bus Tax: S/L NonTaxes					135,415	135,415
	Indirect Bus Tax: Sales Tax					4,869,591	4,869,591
	Personal Tax: Estate and Gift Tax			288,761			288,761
	Personal Tax: Income Tax			678,799			678,799
	Personal Tax: Motor Vehicle License			228,562			228,562
	Personal Tax: NonTaxes (Fines-Fees)			439,464			439,464
	Personal Tax: Other Tax (Fish/Hunt)			47,338			47,338
	Personal Tax: Property Taxes			79,599			79,599
	Soc Sec Tax-Employee Contribution	432,277					432,277
	Soc Sec Tax-Employer Contribution	1,053,915					1,053,915
	Total	1,486,192		1,762,523	746,763	10,003,425	13,998,903
	Total	11,459,778	1,642,521	12,523,323	2,856,811	11,397,825	39,880,257

Appendix 26.7. Aggregate SAM (Aggregated Industries, Aggregated Rows)

Institution Receipts	1001	2001	5001	6001	7001	8001	10000	11001	11002	1103	12001	12002	12003	13001	14001	14002	25001	28001	Total
1001 Industry Total	0.0	2,672.1	0.0	0.0	0.0	0.0	0.0	0.0	0.0	0.0	0.0	0.0	0.0	0.0	0.0	0.0	268.2	2,232.9	5,128.2
2201 Commodity Total	878.6	0.0	0.0	0.0	0.0	0.0	1,218.7	25.7	25.4	1.8	198.9	144.0	31.9	0.0	118.9	15.4	0.0	0.0	2,659.3
5001 Employee Compensation	2,031.4	0.0	0.0	0.0	0.0	0.0	0.0	0.0	0.0	0.0	0.0	0.0	0.0	0.0	0.0	0.0	0.0	0.0	2,031.4
6001 Proprietary Income	221.9	0.0	0.0	0.0	0.0	0.0	0.0	0.0	0.0	0.0	0.0	0.0	0.0	0.0	0.0	0.0	0.0	0.0	221.9
7001 Other Property Income	771.3	0.0	0.0	0.0	0.0	0.0	0.0	0.0	0.0	0.0	0.0	0.0	0.0	0.0	0.0	0.0	0.0	0.0	771.3
8001 Indirect Business Taxes	154.4	0.0	0.0	0.0	0.0	0.0	0.0	0.0	0.0	0.0	0.0	0.0	0.0	0.0	0.0	0.0	0.0	0.0	154.4
10000 Households	0.0	0.1	1,768.6	0.0	291.0	0.0	74.2	528.5	0.0	0.0	127.3	0.0	0.0	117.3	0.0	0.0	9.0	313.0	3,510.3
11001 Federal Government NonDefe	0.0	0.3	226.9	10.7	0.5	18.9	312.1	0.0	0.0	0.0	0.0	0.0	0.0	74.2	79.2	0.0	0.0	0.0	722.8
11002 Federal Government Defense	0.0	0.0	0.0	0.0	0.0	0.0	0.0	27.2	0.0	0.0	0.0	0.0	0.0	1.4	0.0	0.0	0.0	0.0	28.6
11003 Federal Government Investme	0.0	0.0	0.0	0.0	0.0	0.0	0.0	5.0	0.0	0.0	0.0	0.0	0.0	0.0	0.0	0.0	0.0	0.0	5.0
12001 State/Local Govt NonEducati	0.0	23.6	34.1	0.0	2.7	135.5	52.6	119.6	0.0	0.0	0.0	0.0	0.0	26.3	156.7	0.0	0.1	19.1	570.3
12002 State/Local Govt Education	0.0	0.0	0.0	0.0	0.0	0.0	0.0	0.0	0.0	0.0	135.6	0.0	0.0	0.0	33.0	0.0	0.0	0.0	168.6
12003 State/Local Govt Investment	0.0	0.0	0.0	0.0	0.0	0.0	0.0	0.0	0.0	0.0	51.3	0.0	0.0	0.0	12.5	0.0	0.0	0.0	63.7
13001 Enterprises (Corporations)	0.0	0.0	1.8	0.0	290.6	0.0	0.0	13.0	0.0	0.0	0.2	0.0	0.0	0.0	0.0	0.0	0.0	0.0	305.4
14001 Capital	0.0	6.3	0.0	0.0	324.4	0.0	361.2	0.0	0.0	0.9	0.0	0.0	0.0	87.7	0.0	0.0	26.2	4.7	811.4
14002 Inventory Additions/Deletions	0.0	1.9	0.0	0.0	0.0	0.0	0.0	0.0	0.0	0.0	0.0	0.0	0.0	0.0	13.8	0.0	1.7	7.5	24.9
25001 Foreign Trade	85.4	0.0	0.0	0.0	3.0	0.0	163.7	2.3	0.6	0.9	4.3	1.9	3.5	0.0	38.1	1.6	0.0	0.0	305.3
28001 Domestic Trade	985.1	0.0	0.0	0.0	−140.9	0.0	1,328.0	1.6	2.6	1.4	52.7	22.7	28.3	0.0	287.9	7.8	0.0	0.0	2,577.2
Total	5,128.2	2,659.3	2,031.4	221.9	771.3	154.4	3,510.3	722.8	28.5	5.0	570.2	168.5	63.7	305.4	811.4	24.9	305.3	2,577.2	20,059.9

Note: All values are in millions of dollars.

Notes

This chapter is a revised and extended version of a presentation to the ISPS faculty seminar on Inner City Poverty. I thank Shawn Cole and Richard Thompkins for excellent research assistance.

1. For excellent analyses of these hardships among blacks in the contemporary period, see chapters, by Orfield, Massey, Hochschild and Danielson, Williams, Anderson, and Myers in this volume.

2. See Helen Ladd, "Spatially Targeted Economic Development Strategies: Do they Work?" *Cityscape: A Journal of Policy Development and Research,* Proceedings of the Regional Growth and Community Development Conference, November 1993, Washington, D.C. (August 1994), pp. 193–218. See also Sara A. Levitan and Elizabeth I. Miller, "Enterprise Zones Are No Solution for Our Blighted Areas," *Challenge,* 35, no. 3 (1992), pp. 1–6.

3. Prolonged periods of unemployment among low income groups have led to serious social problems such as petty crime and violence, and result in overburdened the courts and overcrowded prisons, to name a few consequences.

4. With respect to households, income deficiency may understate the level of living of a given household since a household may dissave or borrow and thus its current level of living may not be constrained by current income, in which case expenditure is a more appropriate index. Conversely, income may overstate levels of living in cases where money income alone is inadequate to purchase goods and services, for example, where rationing or a shortage of goods prevails.

5. For elaboration on the vicious and virtuous dynamic, see C. Michael Henry, "Application of a Social Accounting System to Inner Cities: An Alternative Approach to Inner City Development" Discussion Paper, Domestic Research Department, Federal Reserve Bank, New York, 2000.

6. Black poverty is engendered, in part, by racial inequality. Hence, alleviation or eradication of poverty will not necessarily eradicate racial inequality. For example, racial inequality is exemplified by lack of economic wherewithal, equity in the courts, equal police protection, representation in government relative to whites, etc. Thus, provision of substantial economic wherewithal per se to blacks will not eradicate racial inequality.

7. Details of these inimical forces may be found in: Gunnar Myrdal, *An American Dilemma: The Negro Problem and Modern Democracy* (New York: Harper and Row, 1944); Robert A. Margo, *Race and Schooling in the South, 1880–1950* (Chicago: University of Chicago Press, 1990); W. E. B. DuBois, *The Philadelphia Negro: A Social Study* (New York: Schocken Books, 1967); Franklin Frazier, *The Negro Family in the United States,* rev. ed. (Chicago: University of Chicago Press, 1966); St. Clair Drake and Horace R. Cayton, *Black Metropolis: A Study of Negro Life in a Northern City* (New York: Harcourt, Brace, 1945); C. Vann Woodward, *The Strange Career of Jim Crow* (New York: Oxford University Press, 1955); Elliot Liebow, *Tally's Corner: A Study of Negro Streetcorner Men* (Boston: Little, Brown, 1967); Claude Brown, *Manchild in the Promised Land* (New York: Macmillan, 1965); and Kerner Commission, *Report of the National Advisory Commission on Civil Disorders* (New York: Bantam, 1968).

8. For example, given government historical acquiescence in denigration of blacks,

the federal government should have advanced intellectual, professional, and skill development of blacks by fully financing historically black colleges. This would have ensured that competitive remuneration would have been offered to attract highly qualified faculty and staff, defray tuition costs of students, and adequately equip libraries, laboratories, and other facilities. The same approach should have been undertaken at secondary, primary, and earlier levels of schooling for children of these citizens. And, the black workforce should have been endowed with skills and trained for gainful employment in the public sector, since given the prevailing racial barriers, in general, blacks would be either rejected or given low-paid, dirty jobs. In short, the government should have committed itself unstintingly to this cause. Indeed, government historical participation in black degradation was an abrogation of its role with respect to the well-being of these citizens.

9. Sen provides an interesting and persuasive critique of the traditional *economistic* approaches to defining the standard of living, arguing in particular, that utility cannot provide an adequate basis for evaluating living standards. Part of the problem is that utility (whether defined as pleasure, desire, fulfillment, or choice) is too subjective. But he also rejects the more objective measures of "commodity possession and opulence" because, by themselves, these fail to take into account needs, circumstances, choices, and constraints. Thus, he argues, the standard of living "must be directly a matter of the life one leads rather than the resources and means one has to lead a life" (chapter 1, this volume). For Sen, therefore, the standard of living consists of our "functionings" — our living conditions and our "capabilities" — our ability to achieve those living conditions.

10. This view has been suggested by Petersen. For details, see Timothy Noah and Rick Wartzman, "Hope or Hype?" *Wall Street Journal* (February 19, 1993). Finance, entrepreneurial and labor skills, and a viable market are all essential for minority development.

11. The extension officer is a member of our suggested enterprise extension service, details of which are elaborated below.

12. See *Wall Street Journal*, May 7, 1997. In 1996, federal government contracts awarded under "racial preferences" amounted to $10.9 billion, an increase of $2.4 billion since 1992. Our proposed framework suggests that such contracts be awarded to create jobs for and skills among inner-city labor and to develop minority entrepreneurship.

13. Access may be created for minority entrepreneurs to a larger market for contractual services through contractual arrangements between minority enterprises and private sector firms for processing raw materials, etc., as is common in some less developed countries, such as South Korea, Taiwan, and Sierra Leone. In this essay, our focus is provision of services to government.

14. See Timothy Bates, "Analysis of Korean Immigrant-Owned Small Business Startups with Comparisons to African American and Nonminority-Owned Firms," *Urban Affairs Quarterly* (December 1994).

15. See Michael Porter, "The Competitive Advantage of the Inner City," *Harvard Business Review* (May–June 1995), pp. 55–71. Cf. C. Michael Henry, "The Porter Model of Competitive Advantage: An Appraisal" in *The Inner City: Urban Poverty and Economic Development in the Next Century,* ed. Thomas D. Boston and Catherine L. Ross (New Brunswick, N.J.: Transaction, 1998). This volume includes a number of excellent critiques of the Porter model.

16. Quotations in text are cited in Martin Vander Wyer's review of *Michael Young, Social Entrepreneur* by Asa Briggs, *Daily Telegraph*, June 18, 2001.

17. Actually, the term *enterprise zone* was coined by British geographer Professor Peter Hall and subsequently proposed as a policy instrument by Sir Geoffrey, given the success of its implementation in Hong Kong and Taiwan. See Marylyn Rubin "Urban Enterprise Zones: Do They Work? Evidence from New Jersey," *Public Budgeting and Finance,* 10, no. 4 (Winter 1990), pp.4–5.

18. See Stuart M. Butler, *Enterprise Zones: Greening the Inner Cities* (New York: Universe Books, 1981), p. 2.

19. Rural areas were also designated as enterprise zones, but we focus on urban areas.

20. See Stuart Butler, "The Conceptual Evolution of Enterprise Zones," in *Enterprise Zones: New Directions on Economic Development,* ed. Roy E. Green (Newbury Park, Calif.: Sage, 1991), p. 35.

21. See Katherine M. O'Regan and John M. Quigley, "Labour Market and Urban Youth," *Regional Science and Urban Economics,* 21, no. 2 (1991), pp. 277–94; Katherine M. O'Regan, "Family Networks and Youth Access to Jobs," *Journal of Urban Economics,* 34 (1993), pp. 230–48, and Jens Ludwig, "Information and Inner City Educational attainment," paper presented at APPM Research Conference, Washington, D.C., October 28–30, 1993.

22. See Butler, "The Conceptual Evolution of Enterprise Zones," p. 35, and Barry M. Rubin, "Are Enterprise Zones Effective Tools for Urban Economic Development?" unpublished paper, School of Public and Environmental Affairs, Indiana University, 1993.

23. See David L. Birch, "Who Creates Jobs?" *Public Interest,* 65 (Fall 1983), pp. 3–14, and David L. Birch, *Job Creation in America: How Our Smallest Companies Put the Most People to Work* (New York: Free Press, 1987).

24. Charles Brown, James Hamilton, and James Medoff, *Employers: Large and Small* (Cambridge, Mass.: Harvard University Press, 1990). See also Steven J. Davis, John C. Haltiwanger and Scot Schuh, *Job Creation and Destruction* (Cambridge, Mass.: MIT Press, 1997).

25. See John F. Kain, "The Spatial Mismatch Hypothesis: Three Decades Later," *Housing Policy Debate,* 3, no. 2 (1992), pp. 371–460.

26. See John F. Kain and Joseph J. Persky, "Alternatives to the Gilded Ghetto," *Public Interest* (Winter 1969), pp. 74–88.

27. For example, see the essays by Massey and by Hochschild and Danielson in this volume.

28. Mark A. Hughes, "Emerging Settlement Patterns: Implications for Antipoverty Strategy," Center of Domestic and Comparative Policy Studies, Woodrow Wilson School, 1991.

29. See Ladd, "Spatially Targeted Economic Development Strategies," p. 195.

30. See Rodney A. Erickson and Susan W. Friedman, "Comparative Dimensions of State Enterprise Zone Policies," in *Enterprise Zones: New Directions on Economic Development,* ed. Roy E. Green (Newbury Park, Calif.: Sage, 1991), pp. 155–76.

31. See Ladd, "Spatially Targeted Economic Development Strategies," p. 199.

32. See Levitan and Miller, "Enterprise Zones Are No Solution."

33. See Jane G. Gavelle, "Enterprise Zones: The Design of Tax Subsidies," CRS Report for Congress (June 1992).

34. Leslie E. Papke, "What Do We Know About Enterprise Zones," in *Tax Policy and the Economy*, ed. J. M. Poterba, vol. 7. National Bureau of Economic Research (Cambridge, Mass.: MIT Press, 1993).

35. See Richard E. Elling and Ann Workman Sheldon, "Comparative Dimensions of State Enterprise Zone Policies," in *Enterprise Zones*, ed. Roy E. Green (Newbury Park, Calif.: Sage, 1991).

36. This relates to public-private partnerships established in some zones. They termed this strategy interventionist.

37. Levitan and Miller, "Enterprise Zones Are No Solution," p. 5.

38. Ibid., p. 4.

39. Ibid. For detailed evaluations of specific zone programs in New Jersey, Indiana, and Maryland, see C. Michael Henry, "Application of a Social Accounting System to Inner Cities: An Alternative Approach to African American Development," discussion paper, Domestic Research Department, Federal Reserve Bank, New York, 2001.

40. The Minnesota Implan Group (MIG) provided inter-industry and other data on economic activities of inner-city New Haven. Details on the data are given below.

41. Final users include household, government, and investment expenditures.

42. With exception of transactions in the underground economy, which, of course, also holds for the national economy.

43. In developing the SAM model, we draw on works by W. A. Leontief, *Studies in the Structure of the American Economy, 1919–1939* (Cambridge, Mass.: Harvard University Press, 1951); Hollis B. Chenery and Paul G. Clark, *Interindustry Economics* (New York: John Wiley, 1959); V. Bulmer-Thomas, *Input-Output Analysis in Developing Countries* (New York: John Wiley, 1982); Richard Stone, *Input-Output and National Accounts* (Paris: OECD, 1961); Richard Stone, "The Disaggregation of the Household Sector in the National Accounts," Paper presented to the World Bank Conference on Social Accounting Methods in Development Planning," Cambridge, England, 1978; Graham Pyatt and J. Round, "Accounting and Fixed Price Multipliers in a Social Accounting Framework" *Economic Journal* 89 (1979), pp. 850–73; Ronald E. Miller and Peter D. Blair, *Input-Output Analysis* (Englewood Cliffs, N.J.: Prentice-Hall, 1985); and, C. Michael Henry (1989) "Classification and Disaggregation of the Household Sector in Social Accounting Matrices: An Appraisal," occasional paper, Institute for Economic Analysis, New York University.

44. For example, of the total available product of the basic industry (170), 10 units are used by the janitorial sector, 25 are used by laundry and cleaning, 45 by establishments in the basic sector and 40 by "other" services. Total intermediate use is therefore 120. The remaining uses for consumption, government and investment are for "final use."

45. The average ratio of intermediate to total use shown here is 605 out of 1,230 or .49.

46. In this chapter, the terms *activities, sectors*, and *industries* are used interchangeably.

47. Since imports are omitted, total value added equals total use.

48. Or, in real terms, that is, all values are expressed in prices which prevailed in a given base year.

49. We should note that when output is valued at market prices, indirect taxes must

also be treated as a primary input to make the accounts balance. Total payments for primary inputs by each sector correspond approximately to value added in production.

50. That is, the processing sector has the same number of rows as columns.

51. Equation (1) is written as an identity because this relationship must always be satisfied.

52. Prices are suppressed on assumption that (a) skilled labor is the only scarce factor hence, there is only one thing on which to economize; and (b) all cross-price elasticities are zero while own price elasticity of demand is unity. Hence, a 2 percent change in price will produce a 2 percent change in quantity; therefore, the relationship between inputs and output will be stable in value terms. With everything reduced to its value in terms in labor time, relative prices cannot change because the numerator and denominator will always change in the same proportion. Accordingly, there is no need to include price in equation (1). This is often referred to as the Samuelson no-substitution theorem. See Paul Samuelson, "Abstract of a Theorem Concerning Substitution in Open Leontief Systems," in T. Koopmans, ed., *Activity Analysis in Production and Allocation* (New York: John Wiley, 1951). Additionally, relationships in equations (1) and (2) are expressed in physical terms. But by choosing a quantity unit in the base year such that price equals the unit of account, value data in the base year can be used they referred to physical quantities.

53. Assuming constant returns to scale (CRS), hence, the linear proportional relationship between inputs and output:

$$(3) \quad \omega_{ij} = \alpha_{ij} x_j$$

Substituting equation (3) into equation (1) gives the input-output system as:

$$(4) \quad \begin{aligned} x_1 &= \alpha_{11}x_1 + \alpha_{12}x_2 + \ldots + \alpha_{1N}x_N + f_1 \\ x_2 &= \alpha_{21}x_2 + \alpha_{22}x_2 + \ldots + \alpha_{2N}x_N + f_2 \\ &\vdots \qquad \vdots \qquad \vdots \qquad \quad \vdots \qquad \vdots \\ x_N &= \alpha_{N1}x_2 + \alpha_{N2}x_2 + \ldots + \alpha_{NN}x_N + f_2 \end{aligned}$$

Thus, output of each sector depends on final demand for that sector and the output of all sectors. Equation (4) may be rewritten by separating the input-output coefficients (α_{ij}), to form a matrix A.

54. See I. Ozaki, "Economies of Scale and Input-Output Coefficients," in A. Carter and A. Brody, eds., *Applications of Input-Output Analysis*, Vol. II (Amsterdam: North-Holland, 1970) This suggests the following relationship:

$$(5) \quad \lambda_j = \delta_j x_j^{\beta_j}$$

where λ_j is employment in the jth sector and β_j, the elasticity of employment with respect to output is assumed to be less than unity. The parameters of this expression can be estimated in log linear form:

$$(6) \quad \log \lambda_j = \log \delta_j + \beta_j \log x_j$$

Equations (5) and (6) may be estimated to predict employment, once gross output of the jth sector, janitorial service, is known. And, since the latter is obtained from equation (8), there is no necessity for imposition of the untenable assumption of CRS on employment and other primary input functions. Hence, with respect to labor, the assumption of linear proportionality between labor and output does not obtain.

55. Alternatively, the social accounts for a given inner-city economy, as depicted in Appendix 26.1, below, can be treated as a partitioned matrix with each submatrix represented by $T_{i,j}$. For example, in Appendix 26.2, $T_{1,1}$ denotes transactions between producing and using sectors, $T_{2,1}$ payments to factors by activities, and $T_{1,3}$ payments to producers by households for goods and services. The balance equations for activities are:

$$(7) \quad x = y_1 = T_{1,1} + T_{1,3} + T_{1,4} + T_{1,5}$$

In the simplest form of the inter-industry model, $T_{1,1}$ is related to y_1 through the input-output coefficient matrix $(A = T_{1,1}\, \hat{y}_1^{-1})$ whereas the other terms $(T_{1,4}$ and $T_{1,5})$ on the right hand side of equation (7) are included in the exogenous vector of final demand.

56. Called the intra-group effect by Stone. See Richard Stone "The Disaggregation of the Household Sector in the National Accounts," paper presented to the World Bank Conference on Social Accounting Methods in Development Planning," Cambridge, UK, 1978.

57. Equation (8) $P = T_{ij}\, \hat{y}_j^{-1}\, i, j = 1,2,3$.

58. Referred to as the intergroup effect.

59. Referred to as the extragroup effect.

60. Type I multiplier, as opposed to SAM multiplier, treats payments to households as leakages. Type I multiplier is given by the ratio of the sum of direct and indirect effects to the direct effect whereas, the SAM (Type II) multiplier is given by the ratio of the sum of direct, indirect, and induced effects to the direct effect.

61. With respect to the relationship between raw material input and output.

62. See, for example, Graham Pyatt and J. Round, "Accounting and Fixed Price Multipliers in a Social Accounting Framework," *Economic Journal* 89 (1979), pp. 850–73; and Graham Pyatt, "Fundamentals of Social Accounting," *Economic Systems Research*, 3, no. 3 (1991), pp. 315–41.

63. Zip codes for inner-city New Haven are as follows: 06511, 06513, 06515, 06519.

64. Implan denotes IMpact Analysis for PLANning.

65. MIG collects data at the national level, converts it to Implan data format and then derives the national input output matrices (that is, "use," "make," "byproduct," "absorption," and "market shares" matrices) and national tables for deflators, margins and regional purchase coefficients.

66. MIG's data sources are: the Bureau of Economic Analysis Regional Economic Information System, the Bureau of Labor Statistics, the Bureau of Economic Analysis' Benchmark Input-Output Study, County Business Patterns, the Bureau of Census Annual Survey of Manufactures, Internal Revenue Service Quarterly Payroll file, the Bureau of Census Economic Census and ES202 Data.

67. For example, 1–4 employees, 4–9, 10–19, 20–29, 30–39, etc. By omission of employment counts, the CBP does not disclose the exact number of employees in a firm.

68. These ratios are derived by dividing the desired region's zip code employment by the county's zip code employment for each Implan sector.

69. The measure of labor intensity may be given as follows:

$$\lambda_0 = \frac{\Sigma \, L_i \, w_i}{\Sigma \, L_i \, w_i + \Sigma \, k_i \, r_i}$$

where k, L, w, and r denote capital, labor, and their respective prices. See D. Morawetz, "Employment Implications of Industrialization in Developing Countries," *Economic Journal*, 84, no. 355 (1974).

70. For a clear outline of an agricultural extension system, see Daniel Benor and James Q. Harrison, *Agricultural Extension: The Training and Visit System* (Washington, D.C.: World Bank, 1977), pp. 55.

71. From Table 26.4, panel (a), 643.2/4,070.2 = .16

72. From Table 26.4, panel (a), 644.6/4,070.2 = .16

73. From Table 26.4, panel (a) 5,358/4.070.2 = 1.32

74. All values are given in millions of dollars.

75. The use matrix gives the dollar value of intermediate inputs used by each industry in production of output.

76. Other columns accounted for include the following: Column 5 gives the distribution of property type income. The payment of $291.0 million to households comprises four different types of payment: (1) rental income; (2) business transfer payments; (3) net interest from industries; and (4), net interest paid by households to the rest-of-the-world. Payments to federal (nondefense) ($.5) and to state and local ($2.7) governments comprise government enterprise surplus less government subsidy. The payment of $324.4 million to capital represents capital consumption allowance, while the payment of $290.6 to enterprises represents purchase of corporate stocks and bonds. The entry for foreign trade includes business transfers to the rest-of-the-world, e.g., corporate gifts. This entry also includes net factor payments and payment of dividends to the rest-of-the-world. Similar payments to domestic trade are indicated in the entry for domestic trade. The entry of $140.9 million to domestic trade represents net inflows to other property income from domestic trade. Column 6 gives the distribution of indirect tax receipts to federal ($18.9 million) and state and local governments ($135.5 million). Payments to the federal government consist of excise taxes and customs duty.

77. The distribution of household expenditures is given in column 7. The sources of household income are given in row 7. The first household expenditure is for purchase of commodities ($1,218.7 million). The next entry represents household payment of interest ($74.2 million) to households—an intra-institution transfer. The payment of $312.1 million to the federal government includes gross interest, income tax payments, estate and gift taxes, and nontaxes, which represent fines and forfeitures. With respect to state and local government, these payments are similar to payments made to the federal government; in addition, state and local government receive motor vehicle licenses, property taxes and other taxes. The payment of $361.2 million to capital represents household savings. The penultimate entry of $163.7 million represents household purchase of imported goods and transfer payments to the rest of the world. The payment of $1,328.0 million to domestic trade represents domestic commodity imports. Column 9 gives the distribution of defense-related expenditures. The payment of $25.4 million represents payment for commodities produced locally, while the payment of $2.6 million to do-

mestic trade represents purchase of commodities produced outside the local economy. The payment of $0.6 million to foreign trade represents purchase of foreign goods and services.

Column 10 gives the distribution of federal investment expenditures. The first payment of $1.8 million represents purchase of capital goods while the payments of $0.9 million and $1.4 million represent purchase of capital goods from the rest-of-the-world and domestic capital imports, respectively. The distribution of state and local government (education) expenditures is given in column 12. The first expenditure of $144.0 million is for domestic commodity purchases. Expenditures of $1.9 million and $22.7 million represent foreign and domestic imports, respectively.

State and local government investment expenditures are given in column 13. The first purchase of $31.9 million is for capital goods. Expenditures of $3.5 million and $28.3 million, respectively, are for foreign and domestic imports of capital goods.

78. Domestic because, at this point, exports are excluded from the make mix.

79. Inner-city New Haven records no factor income payments to foreign workers.

80. Contributions to social security are not considered part of household income.

81. Interest payments include payments to holders of government bonds and other securities, while transfers to households include social security, veteran benefits, food stamps, direct relief, earned income credit, and "other," which includes payments to nonprofit institutions, student aid, and payments for medical services for retired military personnel and their dependents at nonmilitary facilities.

82. Labor income includes employee compensation, proprietor income, and other labor income.

83. For elaboration of this point, see C. Michael Henry, "The Porter Model of Competitive Advantage: An Appraisal," in *The Inner City: Urban Poverty and Economic Development in the Next Century,* ed. Thomas D. Boston and Catherine L. Ross (New Brunswick, N.J.: Transactions Publishers, 1998).

84. Kain and Persky, "Alternatives to the Gilded Ghetto."

85. Hughes, "Emerging Settlement Patterns."

86. See Francine D. Blau and John W. Graham, "Black White Differences in Wealth and Assets Composition," *Quarterly Journal of Economics* (1990); James Smith, *Closing the Gap: Forty Years of Economic Progress for Blacks* (Santa Monica, Calif.: Rand Corporation, 1986); Lee Soltow, "A Century of Personal Wealth Accumulation," in *The Economics of Black America,* ed. H. G. Vatter and T. Palm (New York: Harcourt Brace Jovanovich, 1972); Terrel S. Henry, "Wealth Accumulation of Black and White Families: The Empirical Evidence," *Journal of Finance* 26 (1971); and C. Michael Henry, "A Framework for Alleviation of Inner City Poverty," in *A Different Vision: Race and Public Policy,* ed. Thomas D. Boston (London: Routledge, 1997), pp. 82–102.

Contributors

ELIJAH ANDERSON, Department of Sociology, University of Pennsylvania

TIMOTHY BATES, Department of Urban Affairs, Wayne State University

REBECCA M. BLANK, School of Public Policy and Department of Economics, University of Michigan

SAMUEL BOWLES, Professor Emeritus of Economics, University of Massachusetts, Amherst, and Director of Economics Program, Santa Fe Institute

GARY BURTLESS, Brookings Institution, Washington, D.C.

GLEN G. CAIN, Department of Education, University of Wisconsin, Madison

CECILIA A. CONRAD, Department of Economics, Pomona College

MICHAEL N. DANIELSON, Woodrow Wilson School, Princeton University

SHELDON DANZIGER, National Poverty Center, Gerald R. Ford School of Public Policy, University of Michigan

WILLIAM A. DARITY, JR., Department of Economics and Institute of African American Research, University of North Carolina, Chapel Hill, and Departments of Economics and African American Studies and Public Policy Studies, Duke University

REYNOLDS FARLEY, Department of Sociology, University of Michigan

GEORGE GALSTER, Department of Urban Affairs, Wayne State University

ARLINE T. GERONIMUS, Department of Health Behavior and Health Education, University of Michigan

MARTIN GILENS, Department of Political Science, Princeton University

HERBERT GINTIS, Professor Emeritus of Economics, University of Massachusetts, Amherst

PHILIP M. GLEASON, Mathematica Policy Research, Princeton, N.J.

JAMES J. HECKMAN, Department of Economics, University of Chicago

C. MICHAEL HENRY, International Development Centre, University of Oxford

JENNIFER HOCHSCHILD, Departments of Government and Afro-American Studies, Harvard University

JEFFREY LEHMAN, President, Cornell University

FRANK LEVY, School of Urban Studies, MIT

DOUGLAS S. MASSEY, Department of Sociology, Princeton University

RONALD MINCY, Department of Social Policy and Social Welfare Practice, Columbia University

RICHARD J. MURNANE, School of Education, Harvard University

SAMUEL L. MYERS, JR., Herbert H. Humphrey Institute of Public Affairs, University of Minnesota

GARY ORFIELD, Department of Education and Social Policy, Harvard University

LADONNA PAVETTI, Mathematica Policy Research, Washington, D.C.

HAROLD POLLACK, Department of Health Management and Policy, University of Chicago

AMARTYA K. SEN, Master, Trinity College, Cambridge, England

SARAH SIEGEL, Department of Economics, MIT

ROBERT SZARKA, Department of Economics, University of Massachusetts, Amherst

MITCH TOBIN, Department of Political Science, University of California, Berkeley

DANIEL H. WEINBERG, U.S. Bureau of Census, Washington, D.C.

JOHN B. WILLETT, School of Education, Harvard University

DAVID R. WILLIAMS, Department of Sociology, University of Michigan

TUKUFU ZUBERI, Department of Sociology, University of Pennsylvania

Index

Abramson, Alan J., 179–81

advertising, 325–26, 339

affirmative action, 41, 271–72, 277, 307–8, 733–34

affluence, 173, 179–83. *See also* geographic inequality; socioeconomic segregation

affordable housing. *See* housing

AFL-CIO, 7

AFQT. *See* Armed Forces Qualification Test

African Americans: and assimilation, 38–39, 157–58, 165–69; cost of living, 319; death rates/causes, 311–12, 323–24; educational achievement, 4, 277–79, 411–12*tt* (*see also* education; educational achievement); education funding, 769–70(*n8*); employment discrimination, 5–7, 93, 194 (*see also* discrimination); employment hours, per capita, 287, 288*f*; employment rates, 193, 279–81 (*see also* employment); entrepreneurship (*see* entrepreneurship); E/P ratios, 285–87; family strengths, 327–29; health, 41, 312*t*, 314–20, 322–26, 486, 495 (*see also* health disparities; health

spending; life expectancy); immigration views, 167, 171(*n29*); incarceration, 172(*n32*) (*see also* incarceration); income and earnings, 2*f*, 281–83, 295–97, 411–12*tt* (*see also* wages); infant health and mortality, 486; inner-city life (*see* inner cities; street culture; violence, inner-city); interracial marriage, 166–67, 273, 301–3 (*see also* interracial marriage); life expectancy, 36, 62–63, 64*f*, 65*f*, 76(*n8*), 311, 492, 493*t*; media coverage (*see* news media and poverty perceptions); mental health, 327–28, 330; metropolitan distribution, 174–75, 176*t*, 350–51, 360(*n18*), 470(*n2*) (*see also* inner cities; metropolitan distribution; urban-suburban divide); middle class, 181, 328 (*see also* subhead suburbanization); police, attitudes toward, 671–72; political power, 326; population, 161*f*, 162–63, 164*t*, 167, 274*f*, 275; poverty change rates, 195–96; poverty concentration, 178–79, 181–82, 189–90, 350–52 (*see also* geographic inequality); poverty dis-

779

Touch of Silver

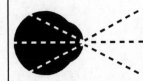

This Large Print Book carries the
Seal of Approval of N.A.V.H.

TOUCH OF SILVER

SHARON MCANEAR

THORNDIKE PRESS
A part of Gale, Cengage Learning

GALE
CENGAGE Learning·

Farmington Hills, Mich • San Francisco • New York • Waterville, Maine
Meriden, Conn • Mason, Ohio • Chicago

GALE
CENGAGE Learning®

LIBRARY OF CONGRESS CATALOGING-IN-PUBLICATION DATA

Names: McAnear, Sharon, author.
Title: Touch of silver / by Sharon McAnear.
Description: Waterville, Maine : Thorndike Press Large Print, 2016. | © 2008 | Series: Thorndike press large print Christian historical fiction | Series: Hometown Texas girl trilogy ; 2
Identifiers: LCCN 2015040077| ISBN 9781410485700 (hardback) | ISBN 1410485706 (hardcover)
Subjects: LCSH: Young women—Texas—Fiction. | Nineteen sixties—Fiction. | Texas Panhandle (Tex.)—Fiction. | Christian fiction. | Large type books. | BISAC: FICTION / Christian / Historical.
Classification: LCC PS3613.C2659 T43 2016 | DDC 813/.6—dc23
LC record available at http://lccn.loc.gov/2015040077

Printed in Mexico
1 2 3 4 5 6 7 20 19 18 17 16

DEDICATION

For
Dwight

LIFTED

Dance now in sunrise or moon-cast
    shadow,
Music sprung from love — a sweet melody.

Be lifted to the stars, my one and only,
And fret not of melodies unsung for me.

To far constellations, I shall whisper no
    sonnets,
Nor secrets — my dear, my dearie thee.

For you are with me always — the
    brightest star,
And forever the best part of me.

— Jemmabeth Forrester

The charming Jemmabeth Forrester
has painted her way
into the hearts of two men.

One she tries to avoid.
The other she's hoping will offer her
"The Ring."
Neither will be an easy task. . . .

Chapter 1
Blessings

Paul Turner wedged the quart of milk between the other containers of liquid refreshment in his fridge. He tossed off his Stetson and ran his hand through his thick black hair. He wasn't all that hungry anyway. His dad's parting words as they had left the office still hung in his ears. "You're one sorry disappointment, son," he'd said, without humor. Not exactly something a grown man wants to hear, but it was better than some of the things his dad had called him in college. He knew the old man wasn't talking about his work in their legal practice because Paul was carrying that off with style. His dad was referring to Paul's private life, and he was right — it was slime.

Paul had considered buying a few more groceries so he didn't have to eat all his evening meals out or maybe taking his little sisters up on their constant offers to cook for him. Neither of those options was ap-

11

pealing. If he went to one of their places in Dallas for supper, it would haunt him for a month. They were both married with kids, and that was the root of the disappointment he'd brought to his dad.

Paul settled for cold cereal. He pitched his boots at the front door, then parked himself in front of the television to eat. He hadn't been to the Best Burger Stop in Texas since Jemma had left Wicklow. It was their place, and he wouldn't go back without her. He didn't need his dad to tell him what he'd lost when he had messed up with Jemmabeth Forrester. She had been his one treasure in life, and he had botched that relationship at every turn. She most likely was with that puppy love of hers right now in France. Maybe the kid would get drafted and shipped off to Vietnam.

Something solid shifted through the couch cushions. Paul felt around and pulled out a gold bangle bracelet. It probably belonged to the loudmouth redhead from the night before or one of the crazy blonds from the past Saturday. He sailed it across the room and into the trash can. "Bingo," he said aloud and returned to his cereal. If his mother had lived, he might've turned out different. She was spiritual and smelled like flowers, too, like his darlin' Jemma. But God

12

had other plans.

The painting Jemma had made for him hung behind his desk at the office. Most days that was his sole motivation to go in to work. He liked to imagine that they were together again, back in the hill country, watching that very spot from the riverbank, and that Jemma was safely in his arms.

Paul set his bowl in the sink. He needed more of her paintings so he could have some at the office and others at home. Her art gave him hope and a chance to look into her pretty head. He stared blankly at a sparrow scratching at the fresh leaves on his lawn, then wiped his eyes. She was bound to come back to her school in Dallas some-time, and then he would have a chance to prove his love to her in ways that really mattered. Until that day, he would fill his evenings with whatever came along, because nobody could ever fill his heart like Jemma did.

He could wait forever for her because she was his solitary blessing from God. She was inside him, in his bones, and there was nothing anybody could ever do about it.

In the golden bath of dawn, a pigeon with feathers the color of rust and wings striped with red, moved around the great gargoyle.

A shimmering white female caught his eye as she spread her wings and glided, embracing the cool air, to feed on the ground below. The male followed, settling near a bench. Puffing out his neck feathers, he circled her, then lowered his head and bowed. She would be his mate for life.

Jemmabeth watched the feathered dance as she and Spencer sat on the bench outside the grand Notre Dame Cathedral, holding hands. They had walked the streets of Paris all night, catching up on their lives since their hard parting five months earlier in Texas.

Jemma rested her head on his shoulder. "Do you think pigeons ever make stupid mistakes?"

"I guess if one showed up in a pie, he would have made an error in judgment somewhere along the way."

"Yuck, but I bet even a pigeon knows the difference between real love and infatuation. Look at that pigeon couple there. Do you think she's cooing to him while all the time that one over there is her true love? I doubt it. That makes me dumber than a pigeon. I'm the ultimate birdbrain," she said, then jumped up. "Dance with me."

"Fast or slow?"

"Roy's 'Candy Man.' We'll make our own

music." She took right off on the song.

The pigeons flurried skyward as a gardener began his work near them. Jemma's golden eyes were fixed on Spencer's as they worked out their own version of the Chillaton Stomp — the dance that had made everybody in high school know they would get married someday.

When they'd sung their last note, the gardener applauded. Jemma bowed, not at all embarrassed, then stepped up on a bench and made an announcement to the returning birds. "As of today, October 15, 1966, I publicly declare that I never loved Paul Turner, not even a little bit." She gestured toward Spencer. "This man is my dearest and best cowboy. He's my hero and my one true love."

The pigeons ignored her, but Spencer didn't. He grinned and helped her down. "Enough adjectives. Those were just half truths anyway, because if there's one thing I'm not, it's a cowboy."

Jemma danced circles around him as they toured the grounds. "So, this Michelle person from New York, was she a good kisser?" Her voice came out like she was still in the first grade when she gave him her answer, that yes, she would be his girlfriend. "Everybody in Chillaton thought

15

you were about to propose, and I know you wouldn't marry someone who couldn't kiss."

"I assume this information about proposing came from Nedra's Beauty Parlor & Craft Nook."

"How else? You know her motto: *Hair's where it all begins!* Gram saw the pictures and Twila saw them, too. Twila said that Michelle was completely gorgeous, whatever that means."

"Pictures don't mean anything," he said. "Who knows what Mother was flashing around?"

Jemma wasn't through with it. "Then why did you go out with her for nearly five months?"

"Jem, what else was I going to do? For all I knew, you were making wedding plans with the cowboy."

They leaned against the Pont au Double. The sunlight filtered through Spencer's blond hair, creating a halo of sorts and making her smile. "I know it was stupid the way I handled it, but I didn't want to have him floating in my brain when we were together. I needed to get rid of Paul, like a toothache, and I had to see him to do that."

"So, is the great Paul out of the picture forever?"

"He is gone. Complete history."

The cathedral bells tolled, adding a nice touch. She took the wilted rose from her long, auburn hair. Her cousin had given it to her the night before, for her first exhibition as the only American art student ever to be named the Girard Fellow at Le Academie Royale D'Art in Paris. She dropped the white petals, one by one, into the Seine. "I want to mark this night. It is the best one in my life."

"Nope, you just wait, baby. I have plans for when we finally say 'I do.' "

Jemma put her arms around him and looked into his eyes, black-rimmed pewter. "Should I be feeling guilty about that girl?"

"I didn't make any commitments to Michelle, but I suppose you could manage a little guilt about making me wait while you made up your mind."

"Hey, I'll never let you go again." She yawned. "But right now I'm ready for bed."

"What about our eighth-grade promise?"

She giggled. "Silly boy. I'm exhausted and I need some rest. Did you sing 'Michelle' to her?"

"She sang it to me, I think," Spencer said.

"Rats. I love that song; now I'll always associate it with her."

"She's not the French type, baby. Don't

worry about it." He pulled the collar up on his jacket that she had been wearing since midnight. It almost fit her. Their kids would be basketball players, for sure.

They walked along the Seine as shopkeepers opened their doors and set up for the day. He got a cab as she continued her interrogation.

"Was she as pretty as everybody said?" she mumbled.

"Nah, she was nowhere near as beautiful as you, inside or out, and she can't even kiss as good as Missy Blake."

Jemma woke up. "What? The Cleave entered your brain as the pinnacle of kissers? Now I'm mad!" She folded her arms and set her mouth into a Shirley Temple pout.

Spencer was still laughing as the cab pulled up in front of the hotel where her family was staying. "Hey, time out. You know you're the best. I just thought maybe the solid way to your heart would be to bring up Missy."

"The way to my heart is a straight line from yours, Spencer Morgan Chase. My Scarlett O'Hara days are behind me." Jemma wrapped her arms around him and kissed him until even the passing Parisians took notice.

■ ■ ■ ■

Lester Timms was having himself a good laugh at one of his own jokes when a hefty gust of Texas Panhandle wind showered him with sand and lifted his straw hat off his head. He had to spit. "Them flowers just keep on bloomin', don't they, Miz Liz?" he asked through a gritty smile. "Don't see that on nobody else's grave. I think it's 'cause your Cam had a way with plants." He picked up his hat and waited for her to look away and she did, just in time, too. He wiped his mouth on his sleeve.

Lizbeth Forrester dusted her hands, then shaded her eyes to check around the cemetery. "I suppose you're right, Lester, but there's not much glory in farming from the grave, now is there?"

Lester planted his feet in case she needed help getting up, but she didn't. She was a tall, slender woman, and limber for her age.

Lizbeth smoothed her dress. "Why don't we drop by your wives' resting places? I'm sure there's work to be done on those graves, too." She retied her headscarf to keep the Panhandle wind from fiddling with her fresh hairdo.

"Well now, that would take us a few days,

Miz Liz, seeing as how I got me three of 'em fillin' graves out here. That old Zippy could be passed on somewheres, too, for all I know. 'Course she run off and I didn't have to bury her."

Lizbeth patted her husband's headstone. Lester knew that meant to hush up while she prayed.

"Lord, I give You thanks for Cameron Forrester. He was my best blessing, and I praise Your name for the years we had together and the children we raised. I ask now that You have mercy and help me, Lord, to keep on working to Your glory. Amen, sweet Jesus."

They walked to Lester's black-and-white '62 Buick. He always waited for her to start talking again. She was the finest woman he knew, but he didn't have a lick of a chance with her. He considered himself lucky to be her neighbor and that she let him bring over her mail and give her a ride now and then. She'd been married to Cameron for fifty-five years and she still grieved over losing him to a heart attack the same year Lester had bought the Buick, fresh off the delivery truck in Amarillo.

"Thank you for bringing me out here today," Lizbeth said as they reached the cemetery entrance arch. "My car should be fixed by tomorrow. It's just a broken head-light."

"It's never a problem, Miz Liz, you know that. No offense, but if you'd let me drop you off at Nedra's like you used to, maybe your car wouldn't be in the shop right now." Lester glanced at her as he turned down the county Farm to Market Road. That could have been a dangerous comment he'd just made.

"What's that supposed to mean — that I'm not a good driver? I'm as good or better than any other new driver in the county." Lizbeth shot him a look then watched out her window as a dust devil whipped through Myrtle Gist's white sheets hanging on her clothesline. Myrtle would have to wash them again.

Lester tapped his fingers on the steering wheel, thinking fast. "Well, sir, I reckon the city ought not to keep them old hitchin' posts on the sidewalk anyhow. Nobody ties up horses these days." He faked a chuckle. "I was fixin' to ask you how Jemmerbeth is doin'. Wasn't her big art show in Paris last night? We should've heard somethin' about it by now."

"It's no use to change the subject, Mr. Timms. You know good and well that it was last night and you know also that it costs too much money to call from France. Alexandra will phone me when she gets back to Arizona." Lizbeth hummed the chorus of a hymn as they entered the city limits, a further sign that he had irritated her. "Jemmabeth didn't know that Alex was coming to Paris," she volunteered. "The Lillygraces bought tickets so their whole bunch could attend. Too bad Jim and little Robby couldn't have gone, but it should cheer Jemmabeth up to have her mother there. Alex is so full of fun. I do hate it that Jemma's been depressed, but it seems Spencer's in love with that New York girl in his architecture class."

Lester jumped on the topic. "I've got my money on Spencer. He's known that Jemmer is the sweetest and the prettiest gal he could find ever since they was young. Not to mention she's gonna be famous someday, like Cam said. She's twice as good as Norman Rockwell and that's saying a lot."

"She is, Lester, but all the same, Jemma didn't do right by Spencer and we have to keep that in mind."

"The way I see it, Jemmer never should've give that lawyer the time of day. He was a real good-lookin' feller, but smart-aleck. I sure didn't cotton to him. Lawyers do make a right good livin', though. I always heard that money don't buy happiness, but it sure helps iron out the rough spots. 'Course them Chases have got more money than all the rest of Chillaton put together." Lester stopped the car in the middle of the road. "Would you like to drive out to your old home place and check on your renter's cotton crop?" He knew she couldn't turn down such an offer.

"Why, yes, Lester, that's a fine idea."

Lester backed up and turned onto the graveled shortcut through Windy Valley. His description of Jemmabeth was easy to come by because her grandmother Lizbeth had the same golden eyes, and was sweet, too . . . at least when she was in a good mood.

That evening, Lizbeth set out two fruit pies and two lemon custards for the North Chillaton Quilting Club to enjoy the next morning. She would have to hide them before Lester came over for *Bonanza*. He ate twice as much as her Cameron had ever eaten, but you couldn't tell it by Lester's scrawny frame. Cam loved desserts. He liked to sneak a slice of fruit pie before breakfast but always denied it. She could look in those twinkling blue eyes of his, though, and know what happened.

Their three boys and her baby sister had

23

enjoyed her lemon custard meringue pie the last time they were all together. They had sat in the home place kitchen, laughing and kidding around. That same day at the train station was the last time she had seen her Matthew and Luke. Only Jimmy had returned from that awful war.

Now she baked for what was left of her family on holidays or for old quilters like herself and shut-ins. Sometimes Lester would get the last piece, if he was lucky. He talked so much that he gave her a headache, but just as often, he made her laugh. Nobody could get her tickled like Cam could, but he had passed on without ever uttering a word one morning while she was making biscuits. His heart just played out.

"Sure smells like heaven in there," Lester said outside the back screen door.

"Aren't you early?" Lizbeth quickly laid a cloth over the fruit pies but left the meringue ones exposed.

"Nope. It's eight o'clock, on the nose." He checked the gold pocket watch given him by the Santa Fe Railroad Company. "You're cookin' awful late."

"Now don't get your hopes up for any pie. These are all for my club tomorrow. Go ahead and get *Bonanza* going. I'll be there directly." She could hear Little Joe throwing the first punch in an all-out brawl when her telephone rang in the good bedroom. She took off her apron and picked up the phone.

"Gram? It's Jemma."

"Jemmabeth, honey, how was your art show? Did your mom surprise you?"

"Yes ma'am, she did, and the exhibit was fantastic. I have someone else who wants to say hello."

"Hi, Gram. This is Spencer."

"Spencer, help my life. Are you in Paris? I thought you were in Italy."

"Well, I'm in Paris with my girlfriend."

"Oh." Lizbeth's heart sank. "We heard about the girl in your architecture school. Your mother had photos at Nedra's Nook."

"Well, my real girlfriend is the famous artist from Chillaton, Texas. You know her, don't you? We want you to do us a favor. Make it a point to tell everybody at Nedra's the next time you get your hair done that we are back together. Talk loud and long, especially if my mother is there. Dig out some old pictures of us and pass them around."

Lizbeth laughed. "I will indeed. Goodbye, you two. Blessings." She turned to Lester, who stood in the doorway, hat in hand.

"Good news, Miz Liz?"

"Lester, let me cut you a piece of pie. Do you want lemon custard or fruit? How about a piece of each?"

"Them young'uns seen the light, huh? Well, sir, I was hopin' that would happen. I expect I'll have me a slice of your lemon custard."

Lizbeth cut them both generous pieces and made coffee in the percolator. They sat across from one another at the yellow and chrome kitchenette because Lester made it a point to never sit in Cameron's chair.

"Do you think there'll be weddin' bells for them two?" he asked.

Lizbeth's smile widened. "I do indeed. It could be this summer or the next because they both have their schooling to finish. I'm just glad that Jemma got her heart still, long enough to listen to the Lord."

"Well, sir, He's blessed her with the Chase boy and a whole lot of talent to boot." Lester ran his fingers across his upper lip. "Not to change the subject, but do you hear much from that Englishwoman friend of yours?"

"Helene calls once a week. Why do you ask?"

"I wondered if she's ever comin' back to the Panhandle to see you again."

"Are you hoping to show her your new

moustache?"

His ears turned cherry red. "Why, no, Miz Liz, I just think she's a fine lady, and a nice complement to your company. I know she'll want to know about Jemmerbeth and Spencer, since Jemmer lived with her for a good while."

Lizbeth gave him a sidelong glance. "If Helene decides to come, I'll let you know." She ate a bite of pie. "Do Dah is coming in about a month."

"Well, sir, truth is, your baby sister gives me the same looks that Zippy was prone to givin'. I try to steer clear of her, no offense."

"Lester, any man who's been married as many times as you have should be able to handle Do Dah."

"Well, sir, have I ever told you about the time that Zippy shut me up real good? She'd been actin' peculiar all week, so I excused myself to the privy after supper one night, just for a little peace and quiet — no offense, Miz Liz. I was readin' the Roebuck catalog and come hence to hearing shufflin' noises outside. I give a yell and nobody answered. The next thing I knew, there was a good bit of poundin' on the door. I kept on sayin' that the privy was occupied, but it didn't make no difference. The poundin' went on until I give the door a shove, but it wouldn't budge. Zippy had nailed 'er up good and tight." Lester tapped his foot on the black-and-white-checkered linoleum.

"Well? What happened next? You always do this to me, Lester. You consider yourself to be such a storyteller, but you leave your audience hanging about half the time."

"My apologies, Miz Liz. You're as right as rain. I shouldn't have started this one because it gets to me every time."

"Meaning what?"

"I never saw Zippy again. She up and left me in the outhouse and took off to parts unknown. The only good thing is, that if The Judge hadn't said he figgered her for a goner, I'd never had my number four, pretty Paulette."

"I suppose there's more as to how you escaped a nailed-up outhouse."

"Well, sir, I was in there a good while, but I got my neighbor's attention when he come out to his own privy. That would be the feller who sold you and Cam this house. He got his hammer and pulled them nails out. It took him awhile, too, seeing as how he was up in years. He like to have had himself a stroke for laughin' the whole time, too. I failed to see the humor in it myself, but then, like I said, if Zippy hadn't took off, I wouldn't have married my Frenchy. The very next year the town council passed a rule that everybody on this side of the tracks had to have indoor plumbin'. Old Zippy would have a hard time nailin' me up in the indoor privy that I got now."

Lizbeth had stopped listening to him. She moved to the window and looked out toward the tracks where Jemma used to dance on the rails. She had taken pure joy from their news but was troubled with another feeling, too. She went to the closet in the good bedroom and took down the quilt top that she had made last spring. It was the wedding ring pattern. In the middle she had added a heart with their names on it. When she knew the date, she would add that as well, but for now, it gave her the comfort that she needed just to touch it. "Thanks be to You, good and gracious Lord." She replaced the quilt and returned to Lester, who was still talking.

Alex was absorbed in a French magazine when her daughter woke up. They looked enough alike to be sisters.

"Good afternoon, sweet pea," she said. "How are things?"

"Things are perfect. Spencer is perfect."

"Jem, don't put that burden on him."

"I know, but he's close." Jemma stretched

29

and sat up. "I think I've ruined my new dress by walking around in the rain all night."

Alex picked up the blue satin gown. "There's nothing here that a good dry cleaner can't fix. Let's see what I have that you could borrow for the airport."

Alexandra was a fashion queen, but not on Jim's coaching salary. Her high-society parents were always generous to their daughter even though they still felt she had married beneath herself when she'd married a farmer's son. Jemma watched her mother search through the neatly packed suitcase.

Alex held up her choice. "Try this on. Everybody needs a simple black dress. It'll be short on you, but miniskirts are the style these days."

Jemma took her mother's hand. "I'm glad you were here for all this good stuff, Mom. I've been a fool."

"No. You've been foolish, but all is well now."

"I sure hope so." Jemma touched the gold heart on her necklace.

"You made your mark on Paris with your show, cousin," Trent said as her extended family waited at the airport. "I should have bought a painting myself, as an investment, like Grandfather did."

Her Grandfather Lillygrace perked up at the mention of the show. "I assume the gallery will retain some of the proceeds, but you should have a nice nest egg," he said, all business. "We are very pleased with our purchase." Her prim grandmother nodded in agreement.

Jemma didn't care. She only wanted to be alone again with Spencer. They couldn't keep their eyes off each other. The flight was announced, and Jemma passed out hugs and kisses. "I love y'all. Mom, give Daddy and Robby my love," she said as Alex waved and vanished down the gate corridor.

Spencer didn't waste any time. He cornered Jemma in the waiting area like they were already alone. They headed to her apartment. Jemma thought she was going to die before they could get there. She could barely get the door unlocked.

"Wait," Spencer said with his hand on the knob, "how are we going to stand this? I don't know if I can be in this room with you, baby."

"Spence, I have to be alone with you without Paris. That's all I ask. I need to hold you and tell you some things, okay? Just five minutes."

"I could go berserk in five minutes."

She giggled. "I won't allow it."

"Let's go to that little courtyard I saw as we came in. I don't want to lose control after all these years."

She grinned at him, at the idea that he would lose control, then relented. He was the most composed human she had ever known. "Okay. Good grief. Do you realize that I've loved you since the first grade? What would that be in dog years?" she asked as they smooched and talked under the trees.

"About one hundred and five years."

"That's too old to get married, huh?"

"Hey, you promised Papa that you wouldn't marry until you got out of college. Do you think he would hold you to that if he were still alive?"

"No, but can we make it a whole year, being over here in Europe, all by our lonesome?"

"I can if you can," he said. "Now, let me show you my favorite things about Paris while it's still daylight."

They crammed his favorites into an afternoon, and he saved the best for last. They entered the lower level of Sainte-Chapelle while it was still light. Jemma was already impressed, thinking that they were in the main chapel.

Spencer led her up a small stairwell in the corner. "Close your eyes," he said when they neared the top. He held her hand and took her to the center of the chapel. "Now open."

Jemma caught her breath. "Whoa. It's like being inside a kaleidoscope. I can't believe this." She walked around him, captivated by the brilliant stained-glass windows. "I don't know where to look."

"This is the best of Gothic architecture." He scanned the windows. "Louis IX had bought what he believed was the Crown of Thorns and a piece of The Cross, so he had this chapel built to house them and probably to show off. The relics cost him three times more than what the chapel cost to build. During the war, they actually took all the stained glass out and stored it so it would be safe. Extraordinary, huh?"

They sat on the floor in the bare room, soaking in the panorama of color and light. The sun went down, leaving them still absorbed in the jeweled walls. They stayed until workers began to set up for a concert.

"Jem," he said, looking up at the windows, "do you know Psalm 37?"

"No." She barely knew any scriptures by heart.

"It's been my hope."

"I'll look it up. You're a better Christian than I am, Spence. I have all those Sunday school perfect attendance certificates, but I've never just hung on to a scripture because that's sort of scary and hard. Nobody ever tells you that."

"I'm not a better Christian than you are. I'm just older and wiser."

"Oh brother. You're right though, about the wiser part."

He drew her close.

"Good-bye, beautiful place," Jemma said as they turned to go. "I had a chance to attend a concert here last month, but I wanted to wait and see if you still loved me so we could come together."

Spencer stopped on the stairs. "Jemmabeth, did you read the back of that necklace you're wearing?"

"I know," she said. *"Always."*

"I meant it."

"I'm so glad."

They ate ice cream and took a tourist boat down the Seine.

"You know I have to go back to Florence tonight," he said. "I'm on the last flight."

"When will I see you again?"

"I'll be right here every weekend, unless you want to come to Florence."

"I don't want to see her, Spence. What do you think she'll do? Does she know about me?"

"She knows. I told her on our first date. I wasn't looking for a girlfriend, Jem, just entertainment. Michelle has her own plans, and I came along at the right time. I'll take care of things. Don't worry."

"Speaking of worrying, what do you think about Vietnam? Sandy says it's quicksand. Martin is convinced that he'll get sent there. You don't think they'll draft you as soon as you graduate, do you?"

"I don't know. We'll take what comes. Maybe I'll get a master's degree, but even graduate school doesn't guarantee a deferment."

"Should I be worried about the draft?"

"You should worry that we can keep our eighth-grade promise." He stopped at the hallway phone in her building. "Here's the plan, Jem. I'll call this number and let it ring just once and hang up. Then you'll know that I made it back okay or maybe that I'm thinking about you, but then I guess I'll be calling all the time."

"I'm at the Academie from seven in the morning until about nine at night."

"You keep long hours."

"Well, I have classes, then I paint — a lot."

"I really have to go, baby. I'll see you next Friday night. The best day of my life will be our wedding day," he whispered. "It's been an unbelievable weekend." He skipped down the stairs, two at a time.

She couldn't stand it. She ran down the steps and caught him on the last landing, almost knocking him to the floor. They held one another until the taxi took him away. She had never kissed so much in twenty-four hours.

Jemma returned to her room and looked up the verse he'd mentioned. "Delight thyself also in the Lord; and he shall give thee the desires of thine heart. Commit thy way unto the Lord; trust also in him; and he shall bring it to pass." She looked toward Sacré-Coeur, then got on her knees. "Lord, only You could have kept Spencer loving me all this time. I'm glad You and I are finally on the same track. Amen." It was probably a weird prayer, but it was to the point.

She sat on the floor in the hallway sketching park benches, pigeons, gothic churches, kaleidoscope windows, and him. A few minutes before midnight the phone rang once. She caught it before it finished ringing. "Spence?"

"Hey, you aren't supposed to answer, but I'm glad you did. Go to sleep and dream about us trying to catch those minnows in Plum Creek."

"You dream about our names carved on the cottonwood tree there."

"I love you," he said.

She hung up the phone and danced down the hall to her room. As was her habit, she wound the Starry Night music box Spence had given her on her twenty-first birthday and got in bed. She was asleep before "I Will Wait for You" wound down.

CHAPTER 2
SHICK

Their weekends were crammed with fun, and they took advantage of all the nooks and corners in Paris. It wasn't quite the same as their special spot at the Salt Fork of the Red River or their parking place on The Hill back in their Texas Panhandle hometown, but it served the purpose. She quit asking about Michelle Taylor, Miss Completely Gorgeous, as Spence's mother had called her, but she still wondered.

Since the exhibition, Jemma had painted several pieces. Her favorites were of the café owner standing in his doorway near her apartment, and a couple arguing in the foreground of the tangle of buildings visible outside her window. Spencer was so good for her. Gram was right. Love could clear muddy waters.

She was working on the third painting when the Academie's gallery manager came to visit her workspace. "Mlle Forrester, a word with you, please."

"*Oui,* madame." Her French was inching along.

"It is about the proceeds of the exhibition. You have not yet inquired as to the sales. The patrons paid a total of 31,375 francs. The Academie retains a small portion of those funds, but the majority of it is yours. We have set up a bank account for you with this money. When you wish to withdraw funds, all you need to do is notify Peter. He will take care of it for you. Your work sold exceptionally well. Our congratulations."

"*Merci,* ma'am, but how much money is that in American dollars?"

"Perhaps about seven thousand dollars."

Jemmabeth whistled. The last time anybody had paid for her art was in the third grade when her best friend, Sandy Kay Baker, gave her a nickel to paint a picture of her mean cat.

Lizbeth sat at the kitchenette with Julia, looking at brochures of Europe.

"You know that I'm scared to death of being in an airplane, Do Dah," Lizbeth said.

Julia yawned. "You have never been in one, my dear. Furthermore, please don't be calling me that silly name all over Europe."

Her red-orange hair stood out a little funny on one side.

Lizbeth smiled at her. "I'll try to remember, but I'm the old one, so keep that in mind."

"You are also the one with the college degree, so you can remember things."

Lester knocked on the door with his hat pulled low over his brow.

"Mr. Timms," Julia said as she opened the door, "I never see you around much when I visit. Why is that?" Julia never beat around the bush about anything.

"Well, sir, I figured y'all would like to have your time alone to hash out one thing or the other. I ain't good for nothin' but bringin' the mail."

"Sit down, Lester, and have some coffee." Julia pulled out a chair, then ushered him to it.

"Here's something for you," Lizbeth said. "Just look at those pretty French stamps."

Julia opened the letter and took a money order from its fold.

Paris, November 11, 1966

Dear Do Dah,

Gram said you were coming to Chillaton, so I hope this gets to you in time. I am sending part of the money that I got from the art show, and I want you to do something for me.

Julia finished the letter and disappeared into the bathroom, just off the kitchen, and blew her nose. Lizbeth and Lester stared at one another until she returned, sniffling.

"What did Jemma have to say?" Lizbeth asked, eyeing her sister.

Julia cleared her throat. "Jemmabeth and Spencer are coming home for Christmas, and she sends her love. Anybody need a refill?" she asked, bringing the coffee percolator to the table.

Lizbeth decided not to press. "Lester, you've been to Europe. Am I wrong about the plane ride being just awful?"

"Miz Liz, that plane ride was about the least scary thing that happened to me in the Big War. I wasn't thinkin' about nothin' but keepin' body and soul together long enough to see a cotton field again."

She sighed. "I suppose that wasn't a fair question."

"The main reason we're going is to visit the boys' graves, Lizbeth Forrester. You keep that in mind when you start turning chicken on me." Julia drank her coffee at one of the tall windows, looking toward the train tracks

41

that ran just beyond the alley.

"Well, I guess if I'm going to go, I'd best hush up, but sometimes I wonder if I shouldn't just wait and see my boys in heaven."

"I'm thinkin' the Bible says we won't know our family in heaven, Miz Liz. I'm bankin' on that, seeing as how I've got me three or four women waitin' up there," Lester said.

"Lizbeth, you're going and that's that. It's high time that you see the rest of the world. There are actually places where cotton is not the main topic of the day." Julia poured what was left of her coffee in the sink and resumed her seat at the kitchenette.

Lester shook his head. "No, sir, I don't think we'll know family in heaven. We're gonna be there just to worship the good Lord forever. I've heard many a sermon on that in more than one denomination."

"Where were you in the war, Lester?" Julia asked. She was well aware of Lester's penchant for telling long tales. Cam's nickname for Lester was "Windy." Cam should have known, too, since he could tell a few tales himself.

"In France, mostly — Battle of the Marne, the second one. It was there that I met up with the gypsies. Now they were a fearsome lot. I was more afraid of them than any airplane. Not meanin' to change the subject, but I keep hearin' about this Vietnam War havin' gorilla warfare. Now what in the Sam Hill could a gorilla do in a war?"

Julia laughed. "Y'all are going to have to excuse me. I need to say hello to Willa and Trina; I'll be back shortly. Don't get up, Lester. You keep on with your story." Julia slipped on her fur coat and walked over the tracks to what many still called "Colored Town."

Lizbeth and Lester watched her make her way through the little trail that had been worn through the weeds.

"That's what I was talking about, Miz Liz. Zippy would up and walk out, just like that, while I was talkin'."

"Don't let it bother you, Lester. We have to keep in mind that she's from Houston, and that she and Arthur are money folk."

"That looked like a chinchiller coat she's wearin'. See, if that old twister hadn't tore up my chinchiller ranchin' business, I could've been livin' in high cotton by now. Exceptin' for Bruno. I couldn't have parted with him for his fur. He was my sleepin' buddy. How come your sister got to be called that strange name when you and Annabeth and Sarabeth and Marybeth all sound alike?"

"She's wearing a mink coat, Lester, and her nickname is a family joke. Her real name is, of course, Julia. They tacked *beth* onto our names to make up for no middle name. The joke has it that my father wanted a boy so much that he just ran out of 'beth.' When my dear mother died giving birth to her, Cam and I took Julia to raise. We already had Matthew, and the other boys came along right afterward. They couldn't pronounce Julia, and it came out Do Dah. She is not fond of it, as you can tell, and I do believe we've had this conversation before."

"She's sure bossy. No offense, Miz Liz," Lester said, taking a chance since Lizbeth was in a talkative mood.

"Julia has her own way of doing things. That girl nearly was the death of Cameron. I don't know how she got to be so stubborn and sassy. We loved her, though, like she was our own little girl."

"How'd she come to meet up with a big shot like Mr. Billington?" Lester asked. "She have that kinda hair then, too?"

"Julia was so downhearted after we lost the boys, Cam thought it might do her good to visit my sisters in Houston for a while. She lived with Annabeth, Marybeth, and

44

Sarabeth for a short while, but she couldn't get along with them. She talked about going to college, too, but she didn't have the funds. That's when she got a job at Billington's. They only had the one store back then, and she worked her way up to being a manager in the cosmetics department. That's when she changed her hair color and that's how she met Arthur. She's sharp and always about ten steps ahead of everybody else. She got that from our mother, too, even though she never knew her."

"Mr. Billington bought some hair color from her? Ain't that kindly odd?"

"Lester, really. Julia wanted to make some changes in the merchandise, so she made an appointment with him. He says it was love at first sight. He liked her spunky ways. Of course she was a cute little thing in those days, too, before she got that front porch around her middle."

"Why didn't they have young'uns?"

"Art is twenty-odd years older than Julia. Besides, I think they like being free to trot around the globe. Now help me pick out someplace to visit in Italy before she gets back."

"Wherebouts is your boy buried in It'ly?"

"Near Florence, that's Matthew, bless him. Luke is buried in Africa at a place called Carthage."

"Africa? Miz Liz, I don't know nothin' about Africa."

"All I know is that I'll get to see their names chiseled into those crosses, and I can stand on the same dirt that they gave their lives for."

"Yes, ma'am. You deserve that, Miz Liz, at the very least."

"Miz Julia, come on in this house." Willa Johnson opened her door wide and gave Julia a hug. She cleared a basketful of ironing off a chair and smoothed her starched apron over her own generous middle. "Latrina, we got company. Stop that sewin' machine for a minute and get on in here."

Latrina, a tall girl with dimples and almond-shaped eyes, emerged with a big grin for Julia, who had made her laugh since the first time she met her, a little less than a year ago. "Hi, Do Dah. Have you heard from Jemma?" she asked with a hug.

"I just got a letter from her, and I need to talk to you two," Julia said.

"Well, set yourself down." Willa pointed at the table with her cane. "There's not trouble again with them two lovebirds? I'm gonna give that girl a spankin' myself if she's done

46

gone and fiddled with that boy's heart again."

"No, no, I think we'll be hearing wedding bells before we hear of anything like that ever again. Jemmabeth has learned her lesson."

"What's going on then?" Trina asked.

"Jemma sold most of her paintings at that art show in Paris. She got a pretty penny for them, too, and she wants to use some of it to send you two to Europe with Lizbeth and me."

Their jaws dropped. Julia might have just as well announced that Lady Bird Johnson was coming for high tea at their house.

"That girl is plain crazy," Trina said.

Willa rubbed her face. "Now I know for sure that Jemma's gotta be the sweetest white child in this world. How come her to think of such a thing, Miz Julia?"

"Jemma *is* the sweetest white child in the world, and she won't take no for an answer. She got that from my side of the family."

"What would become of my ironin'? Folks would find somebody else to do it, and I'd be out of business."

"Oh Mama, they'd come right back to you. Nobody else can please them," Trina said. "I can't believe that Jem. She'll be home Christmas, right?"

"Yes, but she wants this all settled before she gets back. She figured on Willa giving me trouble. Are you going to give me trouble, dear?" Julia asked.

Willa moved around the table, her heavy steps accentuated by the tapping of her cane. In the distance, the noon whistle blew at the fire station. "Law, law, Miz Julia. You reckon a plane could get off the ground with this big old caboose inside?"

Julia laughed. "I reckon. Now you two will need a passport. I'll take care of that, but I'll need your birth certificates."

"Trina's grandpap got her a birth certificate, but I ain't got one. I got my Pap's Bible with my name in it. He had the preacher to write it."

"Good. We'll get you passports one way or another," Julia said.

"When are you going, Do Dah?" Trina asked, her heart thumping.

"You mean, when are *we* going? I like to go in the spring. Things will be so pretty over there. Does that sound okay with you?"

Willa and Trina looked at each other and shrugged, still in shock.

"I need to get back to Lizbeth for now. I'll come over and get you girls, and then we can sit down and do some serious planning at her house. Would this evening work for y'all?"

"We'll be ready after supper. Thank Jemma for us and tell her I said that she's too much." Trina walked Julia to the door, then ran back to throw her arms around her mama's neck. "Wait 'til I tell Nick. He's gonna flip."

"Sugar, do you know what a pass the port is?" Willa asked, wide-eyed, as Trina skipped away.

"Don't worry, Mama," Trina hollered from her room, "it's just a way to identify us as Americans." She took down the yellowed postcard that had been thumb-tacked to the wall beside her bed. She had never imagined that she might someday see Europe, and maybe even the Eiffel Tower that was on that card. God was so good to her.

Jemma left school early on Friday to get ready to meet Spencer at the airport. She had already laid out the clothes she was going to wear for the evening and was gathering things to take a bath when she heard the phone ring. She waited to see if it only rang once, his signal that he was about to leave Florence. It kept ringing, though, and she answered.

"Jemmabeth Forrester, please," requested

49

a male with a distinct English accent.

"This is Jemma."

"I am a friend of Spencer Chase's. He wanted me to call because he is ill and will be unable to come to Paris."

Her pulse rocketed. "What do you mean, ill? Is he in the hospital?"

"No, actually, he is in his flat. It's most likely a nasty bug he's picked up."

"Thank you for calling me. What's your name?"

"Lawrence. Lawrence Miles."

"I'll be on the next train."

"Our flats are only two blocks from the School of Architecture, and I'm in number eleven. Just ring for me."

Jemma threw some clothes in her bag and called Peter, her liaison with the Academie. At his suggestion, she bought a ticket to fly to Florence. Peter and his wife, Ami, drove her to the airport. Rather than thirteen hours on the train, the flight only took three. She took a cab to the apartment house. Lawrence, a slender, pale young man, answered.

"Is he any better?" Jemma asked as they went upstairs.

"He seems the same to me. Just a warning; he has company. It's Michelle. She has been with him since Wednesday."

Her insides turned to ice. "Oh? How did she know Spence was sick?"

"Our classes are quite small and Spencer is, of course, a dynamic component. I know that you and he are, shall we say, a couple. Michelle is tenacious, though. If you need me, I'm right downstairs. Where are you staying?"

"I'll be staying in Spence's room, on the floor, if necessary."

"I see," Lawrence said with a smile. "Good luck, Jemma. Lovely meeting you."

Jemma didn't even knock; she opened the door and walked right in. Spencer was asleep, his face glistening with perspiration. In an armchair, curled in slumber, was Michelle. Her blond hair was pulled back with a clip. She wore slacks and a sweater. Her shoes were on the floor beside his bed. She was completely gorgeous, as advertised. Rats. Jemma's heart pounded as she sat within inches of the woman who had almost stolen Spence's heart.

His room was organized and light. Her first self-portrait and the photos he had taken of her at Plum Creek were framed and on his desk. Papa's portrait was propped against the wall, atop his dresser. The place reeked of sickness. Spence turned

51

over, moaning. She touched his burning cheeks.

Michelle awoke and vaulted out of the chair. "Hey, what are you doing in here?"

"I might ask you the same thing," Jemma said, rising to her full height, which was at least three inches above Michelle. "I'm Jemma, Spencer's girlfriend, and you are . . . ?"

Michelle stared a hole through her, then smirked. "Let's just say that I'm the one caring for him so you really aren't needed."

"I am here, though, aren't I? So probably you're the one who's not needed." Jemma chewed on her lip and checked out Michelle's bluish-green eyes. Cat eyes.

Michelle took out the clip and shook her hair. "Spency and I have a relationship, and it's very special. I don't know what he's told you, but things haven't changed between us even if he does see you in Paris."

Spency? Jemma's nose burned. "Really? Are you napping with him while he is passed out with a fever?"

"His temperature does rise with me, but not because he is ill." Michelle raised her chin.

Jemma raised hers as well. "Look, I'm not buying this at all. You're wasting your breath." She could take her down with one good *Saturday Night Wrestling* move.

Michelle shifted her weight. "What *are* you anyway — one of the Harlem Globetrotters? You must descend from giants. Are you familiar with the term *shick*? It's what we call a she-hick like you where I come from."

"Are you familiar with the French term *imbécile de New York*? That's what we call New York smart alecks where I come from."

Word had it at Nedra's Nook that Michelle spoke several languages. Apparently, French was among them. "Amazing that you know a few words in a language other than your native hillbilly. Look, I'm not leaving and I don't think you want to share Spency with me, do you?" she asked in simple English.

"Well, then, are you going to carry me out? Because I'm not going anywhere. *Spency* would prefer me to stay, I guarantee," Jemma said, thinking that maybe The Claw would be the best move, to get her attention.

"Michelle," Spencer whispered, "thanks for your concern. I'll see you around."

Jemma smoothed his damp hair.

Michelle's face twitched, but she picked up her purse and her leather jacket. "Goodbye, Spency," she said, stroking the blanket where it covered his leg. She shot Jemma a look with her feline eyes. "Remember, he's with me five days a week, shick, and we share much more than the same architectural philosophies."

"Watch where you put your paws on my man and get out." Jemma raised her hand in The Claw formation.

Michelle slammed the door behind her. Jemma turned back to Spencer, who opened one eye and smiled weakly at her.

"That was almost worth having this crud, you little spitfire," he said. "I wish I could laugh, but right now I'm feeling a little shick myself."

Jemma found a washcloth and went down the hall looking for water to cool his face. When she got back he was asleep again. She opened the windows a little and picked up a book about architecture that was on his desk. Lawrence came by and brought some food for her and soda water for Spencer.

"Try to get him to drink some tea. There is a kettle and hotplate in his room. Did you meet Michelle?" he asked with an odd grin.

"You could say we met, I guess. It was more like a sparring."

"She's nice to look at, but not worth the bother. I went out with her for a while last year before Spencer came. She is relentless."

"Thanks for the food. Surely he'll be better by tomorrow," Jemma said.

"Yes, well, I know he's glad that you are here. I'll be off now."

She curled up in the same chair where Michelle had been, but awoke to more groaning. "What are you doing?" she whispered.

"If you are going to make me drink all that tea, I have to go to the bathroom." He shivered in his pajama bottoms and undershirt.

"Let me help you," she said. "Here — put on your robe so you won't freeze. It's cold in that hallway." Spencer looked like a little boy again, but his breathing was easier and his skin felt cooler to her touch.

"Is this our first whole night together?" he asked when she put him back in bed.

"I hope not."

"If you get sick, too, I'll never forgive myself," he said, his eyes already closed.

"I wasn't with you the first few days, so maybe I won't get it."

"Michelle was. She'll probably catch it and sue me."

"Yeah, especially since she was sleeping with you in the bed."

"Was she? I hope I didn't hallucinate and think it was you."

"Are you serious?"

Spencer smiled. "I'm very serious. I heard that whole conversation you had with her. I like your French comeback. When did you learn the word for *fool*?"

"When I thought I had lost you."

"You will never lose me, baby, ever," he mumbled, then drifted away.

The next morning Jemma opened the windows wide, changed his sheets, and sent him off to shower and shave. He was on the mend. In two weeks, they would be in Chillaton for Christmas. They talked about art and architecture, music and love, being careful to keep an arm's length apart. Lawrence appeared with more food.

She got up her nerve. "Spence, I saw a motorcycle parked outside, and it hasn't moved since I came. I don't suppose you know anything about that."

He rubbed his chin.

"Well?"

"I have to have some transportation, but it doesn't get used every day. Italians love their cycles."

"Spencer Morgan Chase, you know my feelings about those machines. You have no protection whatsoever when you ride it. I can't believe you haven't told me before."

"I wonder why."

"If you'd seen the Kelseys lying in the road like Mom and I did, you'd never get on one again."

He sighed. "I'm sorry, baby. I just happen to like motorcycles. It's like your cowboy thing."

"I gave that up."

"I'll be careful. It's just a rental."

"Thanks." She took his hand. "I called the Grasso family and they invited me to stay with them tonight. They're friends with Professor Rossi in Dallas. I don't want people getting the wrong idea about us."

"Could we at least hug before you leave?"

"I suppose so, but that's it. I'll come by in the morning with breakfast."

"I love you, Jemmabeth. I dreamed you were running the bulls again. That won't happen, will it?"

She was not expecting this topic. "Babe, I promise that I'll never go back to the rodeo dance and walk through the cowboys to get a thrill. I have no desire to do that. Remember, you're my cowboy now. You're my dearest, my only one." She meant to give him a small kiss but had to pull away. He was getting well. "Don't you let Michelle in this room. Promise? I don't want to have to put The Claw on her, *Spency.*"

He laughed. "I keep it in mind," he said,

using a line from a Paul Newman movie that had become their private joke.

CHAPTER 3
STETSON SUNRISE

It seemed to her that half of Chillaton was waiting for them at the Amarillo airport, and it was a giddy Jemma who flung herself into their waiting arms. Everything and everyone seemed fresh and beautiful to her. She was pleased and surprised that Helene, her former English landlady, had come to share the holidays with them. Neither of Spencer's parents showed up, but he was used to that. Lizbeth's house was all decked out with lights, cedar boughs, and ribbon. Helene was sharing the culinary duties, and beautiful pies were stashed all over the house. It was a curious mixture of English and Texas Panhandle fare.

Jemma's eight-year-old brother, Robby, hung on to Spencer like a magnet, and it was difficult to say which one of them enjoyed it more. The three of them sat on the cold wrought-iron bench beside Cameron's tombstone while she told some funny

Papa stories. Jemma's giggle was the same one she'd had all through grade school that had gotten her into trouble more than once.

"Let's visit your grandparents' mausoleum," she said.

The Chase mausoleum was a smaller version of the Parthenon and stood out somewhat in the Chillaton Citizens' Cemetery. Robby was off, running down the hill to the pond to see the very much alive cemetery ducks.

"Tell me about your grandparents again," Jemma said as they sat inside the pillared, marble extravagance, overlooking the pond.

"I don't remember my grandmother much at all," Spencer said. "She died when I was little, but I went with Granddaddy to church every Sunday. We had lots of fun together. When he died, I was ten years old and he left his estate to me — the ranches, the office buildings back East, trusts, stocks, cash, the banks . . . everything except his house and one hundred acres surrounding it. That place was all he gave my dad because his womanizing embarrassed Granddaddy, especially since he was a state senator and an elder in his church. I don't get into that business much. His lawyers in New York take care of everything for me, but now that I'm over twenty-one, I guess it's time I started learning about it."

"Whoa. You'd make a good catch for some lucky girl. Was your grandmother really on the *Titanic*?"

"Yeah. It left her kind of strange, but then, my whole family is strange. That's why I want in your family, and why I want to have a family with you."

Jemma's scalp tingled at that thought.

Robby burst inside, skidded to a stop, then crept around the mausoleum. "Hey, this is cool. It looks like the place where the gladiators fought."

"I think that was the idea." Spencer grabbed Robby and put him on his shoulders. "Let's go. I have to meet my dad."

Jemma dropped Robby off at home, then took Spencer to his dad's car dealership to get his Corvette. Mr. Chase came out grinning and shook his hand. "Welcome back, son. I guess you and Miss Forrester are riding double again, huh? I thought you had yourself a New Yorker there for a while, but I guess hometown girls are best," he said, winking at Jemma. He lowered his voice. "Your mother still thinks that other girl is coming with you for the holidays. You'd better get home and straighten her out." He lit a cigarette and went back to his office.

Spencer kissed Jemma and walked to his

car. Just as he opened the door, she yelled at him. He came right back and leaned in the window, but she couldn't look up. "Now don't give me a lecture, but I have to know," she said. "You didn't have anything going with Michelle, did you? She acted like y'all were messing around, but I assume that was a lie."

Spencer exhaled. "Baby, we made a promise in junior high to not fool around before we married. Do you think that I would waste my promise on anybody but you?"

She halfway shrugged.

"Did I ask if you and that old cowboy broke our promise? No, because I trust you."

She sniffed, then started to cry, full steam. He opened the door and held her. She was talking and crying, but he was used to it.

"I didn't want to believe her, but she made me doubt. I was so mean to you last spring and she was so sure of herself. I'm sorry, babe. Really, I am. I do trust you. Please forgive me. Say you do." There she was, sounding like Miss Scarlett O'Hara again.

He smiled at her, at those golden eyes full of tears and those pouty lips contorted in remorse. She was the love of his life, his only love, and the only one he would ever give himself to — the only one.

Jemmabeth waited until everybody was asleep. She put on her wool coat, hat, and mittens and walked up to the tracks. A freight train was due soon. She just knew it. A freighter wouldn't be as good as the Zephyr, but it would have to do. The wind whipped around her legs as a dog across the tracks spotted her and wouldn't hush. The last time she stood there, it was to grab some stones from the rail bed to keep with her on a journey to St. Louis. Now those stones were in Europe, thrown in rivers to mark her presence. She picked up a few more in case she visited another water of some significance.

She heard the train coming, but it did not have the smooth, pulsating sound of the passenger train. It was a wobbling dissonance that smacked of empty cars and sluggish, grinding connections. The light from the engine shone yellowish white like a jar full of fireflies. Jemma stood her ground and waited for it to pass, blowing its irreverent horn. It was a poor substitute. She needed the Zephyr to make her feel that all had come full circle and she was truly forgiven.

Early the next morning, she walked across Chillaton to her parents' former home, where she had lived most all her days. She leaned against a big elm tree next to the sidewalk. It wasn't too long ago that she didn't know which end was up in her life. Back then, she had sat on that very curb and cried, but now Spencer's enduring love had changed all that.

The house looked much the same as it did when her parents sold it and moved to Wicklow, Texas, for a while. They had fixed the place up over the years, and Jemma hated moving away from it. One Christmas, the Lillygraces had sent documents showing that they had paid off the loan on the house as a gift. She would never forget the look on her daddy's face that morning — a mixture of gratitude and hurt pride.

She wasn't close to the Lillygrace family. Her mother's folks had never paid much attention to her or Robby, until now that she'd won the Girard Fellowship in Paris. It always puzzled Jemma that her mom was such a generous, kind, and unaffected person because her mother's parents were cool, formal, and very rich. Not that being rich was necessarily a bad thing. Spencer probably had a bigger bank account than they did.

She went to see Willa and Trina and straightened the crooked shingle on Willa's porch post that served as her business sign: DOES IRONING AND GUARANTEE HER WORK. It swung right back like it was.

Willa unplugged her iron. "Jemmabeth Forrester, you and I are gonna go round 'n' round until you quit being such a sweet child to Latrina and me. You shouldn't be givin' up your paintin' money like this. You're throwin' away money so's an old fool like me can get on a plane and fly to kingdom come and back. What do you have to say for yourself?"

"I say that people pay way too much money for art, and I want to spread my little fortune around as it pleases me. I want y'all to go, and it'll hurt my feelings if you don't."

"Does your mama and daddy know that you're gonna do this?"

"Yes, ma'am, and they like the idea."

"You really are something else, girl." Trina hugged her. "Nick says I better not come back with a Frenchman."

"I don't know; those Frenchmen are very debonair," Jemma said.

"Now don't you be coming home with

65

that kind of talk," Willa chided.

Jemma laughed and went with Trina to see her latest dress designs. "How are things with you and Mr. Fields?"

Trina laid out her sketchbooks on the bed. "The same. Nick has to get through his internship before anything can change."

"Have you written to any design schools yet?" Jemma flipped through the multitude of pages.

Trina lowered her voice. "I can't leave Mama. She still can't walk good from breaking her hip. Besides, it would tear her up if I left."

"You left once before to go to junior college. You are talented, Trina, and you should be given a chance to have a career at what you are good at. If you don't write to schools, then I will, and I'll sign your name."

"And mail them from Paris? Yeah, right." Trina laughed.

"We'll see," Jemma vowed.

"I can't trust you, girl. You would just as soon do that as to look at me."

"That's right. C'mon, I want to walk the tracks and play some hoops."

They walked down the rails to Main Street and up the brick-paved Boulevard to the high school tennis courts and its single, net-less basketball hoop. Jemma had her eye on Judge McFarland's house. It was dark and dreary, like The Judge's personality. As such, it stood out from the neatly kept Queen Anne–style homes that lined both sides of the street. Jemma had tried her best to bring some joy into the old place for a while when she was a day companion to Carrie, his invalid daughter.

"I was thinking about that sulky Weese kid that your mama tried to reform," Jemma said. "Remember when we talked about putting him into Carrie's iron lung? What-ever happened to the burglary case they had against him, anyway?"

Trina rolled her eyes. "A judge in Amarillo gave him the choice of the army or jail, and he picked the army. So it was just like we figured — Vietnam. I know in my heart he stole that money, but they never found it. Mama got a letter from him a while back."

"Have you heard from Carrie?"

"Last week. She's still in love with her physical therapist in Houston."

"Good. Let's go see The Judge."

Trina shook her head. "I'll shoot some free throws until you get through with him. Remember, that old geezer tried to kiss me when I was working for him."

Jemma walked to the front door and

knocked. She hadn't been to his house since he sent Carrie to Houston for rehabilitation and fired Jemma as her caretaker for being more trouble than she was worth. The Judge opened the door and drew back when he saw her.

"Miss Forrester. What brings you here?" He stroked his beard.

She could smell whiskey. "I just wanted to say hello and tell you that I'm sorry."

"An apology coming from you? If it's about the portrait you painted of her, I've changed my mind about that. Carolina loves it and whatever she loves, I have to tolerate, somehow, but that doesn't mean I agree with your interpretation."

"No, sir, I want to apologize for not shaking your hand when you offered it on the day you fired me. I wondered if you might give me a second chance. My aunt Julia says that you were well mannered in your youth."

A smile worked its way around The Judge's mouth. He considered Jemma's outstretched hand, then clasped it. "Apology accepted. Now you can go on with your life, Jemmabeth. Give my regards to your aunt Julia and your grandmother."

Jemma turned toward the street. She heard the door close as she was nearly to the gate. Carrie would like the fact that

Jemma had the guts to apologize to her father, the meanest judge in the Panhandle. She would also be interested to know that he had to tolerate whatever Carrie loved. Surely that must extend to boyfriends as well as paintings. She would call her as soon as she got home.

"Jem, I never have told you this, but when we were in junior high, I used to see you dancing around on these tracks," Trina said as they walked home. "I know for a fact you still do it."

"Really? You should've joined me." Jemma stretched out her arms and lifted her face to the sky. "You might have liked it."

Trina smiled at her friend. There was no way on earth that she could have joined her back then. Jemma wouldn't have cared, but Trina wouldn't have had the nerve to share something so free-spirited with a white girl. Besides, the tracks made her nervous even now, and in more ways than one.

Twila Baker called to invite Jemma and Spencer to a party at their new trailer house. It was a used one, but new to them. Twila worked as a helper at Nedra's Nook. Her husband, Buddy B, as everybody called him, was not only Sandy's big brother, but head mechanic at Chase's Chevrolet & Cadillac and lead singer in the Buddy Baker Band. Nedra's Beauty Parlor and Craft Nook offered the women of Connelly County a choice of two hairstyles: the bubble (a.k.a. Nedra's helmet), or a French twist. Both were guaranteed to last a week. She also offered an outlet for local handicrafts, on consignment, of course. Most of her crafty customers never sold anything because nobody wanted to part with their hard-earned money for stuff that they could make just as well or better. Juicy bits of gossip, however, were Nedra's real handiwork, and those outlasted her hairdos.

Jemma was relieved that Missy Blake wasn't at the party. Missy was at the top of Spencer's dating list the first time Jemma broke up with him which, at the time, seemed like a clever move on his part. In high school, Missy was known as The Cleave, due to her abundant bosom. Every boy in town had been out with her, and now even Spencer had joined that dubious club. Missy's family owned all the rural movie theaters across six counties, so she got in free on dates, but the boys always had to pay. She was also Jemma's rival in every high school election, and her well-publicized dream was to have Spencer for her very own. Quite aware of that fact, Jemma had just picked up some fresh moves from *Saturday Night Wrestling* on Lizbeth's TV.

"Missy is comin' with her new boyfriend," Twila whispered as she set out chips and dip. Jemma sucked in a pout as Buddy B put on some records and she and Spencer started dancing. They were taking a break when The Cleave and her date arrived. Missy's dress was so low-cut that if she were to lean over, every male who knew what was good for him would shut his eyes. She went straight to Spencer and surprised him with an embrace and a pucker that landed right on his lips, not to mention that she had to lean over to do it. Her skirt was extra short to show off her drum majorette legs.

"Spence, how are you?" she purred. "I haven't seen you in forever. I heard that y'all were back together. How long do you think this will last? Here, meet Kent Hall, my fiancé. He's a medical student at UT. We might get married sometime, or not," Missy said, shaking back her mane of lustrous blond hair. She looked Jemma up and down. "Hello, Jemmartsybeth. I see you're still going for the bohemian look and creeping across the tracks to find friends. How low can you go?"

"Well, I suppose I could call you one of

my friends," Jemma said.

"I don't think so. We are like people who know each other, but would never be friends . . . you know that word . . . appli . . . admi."

"Acquaintances?" Kent said.

"Yeah, that's it. Here, take care of this."

Missy handed Jemma her black mouton jacket. Rather than hang it up, Jemma let it fall on the floor and stared daggers at Spencer.

He knew that look, and he would have to do something about it, quick. Buddy started the next stack of records.

The Cleave wasn't finished. "C'mon, Spence, let's dance, for old times' sake," Missy said, pulling him out of his chair like a loose tooth.

Jemma choked on her chip. By the time they were on the floor, she was fuming.

Spencer gave her a helpless look.

"I guess that leaves you and me." Kent offered his hand. Kent could certainly dance and Jemma took full advantage of it. "Devil with a Blue Dress On" was playing, and the two of them rocked. Jemma hoped that Spencer was watching, but she never looked at him to see. When the song was over, The Cleave was ready to go in for the kill, but Spencer's attention was on Jemma. Kent held on to her for "Wild Thing," and they were moving on when Spencer cut in. He was out to prove who was the better dancer and the luckiest man. When the song was over, he dragged Jemma into a bedroom. His shirt stank of Chanel No. 5. A skunk might as well have sprayed it as far as Jemma was concerned.

"I know what you're going to say, and you are absolutely right. I should have defended myself, okay? She tackled me, but you got me back good because I was dying while you danced with that guy. I got what I deserved."

"You give in to pushy women and even after what she said about Trina and Willa! Aren't you tough enough to resist the strong arms and loud mouth of The Cleave? You were the bigshot quarterback. Maybe Missy should've been on your team, and then we might have won more games. Don't try to make me smile, either." Out came the pout. After all, she had the lips for it.

"You know, she does remind me of a fullback. I think she's packed on about ten pounds since high school, don't you?" It was a nice pass, but not as well received as he would have liked.

"Why did you let her kiss you like that? Good grief."

"I knew she was leaning toward me, so I shut my eyes. I didn't see the kiss coming, baby."

After about ten minutes, he'd talked himself out of trouble and made her laugh. She was never any good after he got her tickled.

Buddy B probably did it on purpose to help Spencer, but their song was up next on the stereo. As soon as the harmonica played, everybody moved back. It was a tradition to let Jemma and Spencer start this one alone. Roy Orbison sang the first line of "Candy Man" and Spence curled his finger at Jemma, and their version of the Chillaton Stomp was rolling. The best part was when somebody said "umm-humm" low and soft on the record because Jemmabeth always sang that part along with the music and all the boys waited for that to happen. They still had the electricity, too. Spencer was forgiven. He could see it in her eyes. They ended with a kiss since there were no football coach chaperones in sight.

"You two are good together," Kent said at the punch bowl. "I think y'all must be in love."

"Yeah." Jemma watched Spencer talk to a group of laughing guys. "We've been in love for most of our lives."

"Time to get married then," Kent added as Missy yanked him away.

Jemma and Spencer went to their parking spot at the river. They got their old quilts and climbed on the hood of the Corvette to watch the stars as they had done for years, no matter the season. They kissed, then leaned back on their arms.

"I'm really sorry about Missy tonight. I should have spoken up when she made the reference to Trina, too. That was pathetic of me."

"Yeah, well, I forgive you, but keep your guard up around her. I know her better than you do."

"You said that I am a better Christian than you, but I've never made an effort to get to know anyone in Chillaton who's been treated like third-class citizens. That was you, Jem. I followed your lead."

"I've done nothing special. All I want is to make up for lost time and missed friendships. That's it."

They listened to the night sounds for a while, thinking about the past.

"Tell me why you always liked cowboys so much. I know those days are behind you, but I'm curious."

"Rats. I wish you'd forget all those times

when Sandy and I flirted with the buckaroos on the Fourth. I don't know. Cowboys were like forbidden fruit, so I guess I was intrigued. They stood around like wild horses, pawing at the ground."

"Hmm. Why do you love the train tracks?"

She paused. "A long time ago, I used to pretend that the trains would only come if I danced on the rails. Sometimes I still feel that way. It's like a blank canvas before I touch it with my brush. The tracks just sit there, waiting for me to bring them to life."

He leaned on his elbow to look at her. "I know you have a thing about Missy, but she really did catch me off guard tonight."

"I suppose that after all I've put you through the last two years, dancing with The Cleave was a drop in the bucket." She grinned at him. "Just don't ever do it again."

They watched the heavens, but she couldn't help but remember a comment made to her in the ladies' room at a bar, of all places, about drinking from the devil's cup. She had no call to get high-and-mighty with him. "Spence," she said, reaching for his hand, "promise you'll never, ever leave me, no matter how bad I am."

He kissed her hand, palm up. "Promise already made."

■ ■ ■ ■

Christmas Eve night, Lizbeth's house was packed and noisy. Lester played his harmonica, and Willa led Christmas carols in her booming voice. Spencer wanted to wait until Christmas Day to exchange gifts with Jemma, who had bought presents in Paris and was dying for him to open his. She'd found an ebony cuff link box that played "Yesterday," his favorite Beatles' song.

Christmas Day began, as always, with Robby waking Jemma up to dig in to her stocking before dawn. "No, Robby, not this year; have mercy. Wait two more hours," Jemma said into the pillow, but it was useless to try. He was using the bed as a trampoline. "Okay, okay. You're going to break this old thing."

"I got a magic set. Look." He showered the whole works on the bedspread.

She snickered at his attempts to do some of the tricks. "Merry Christmas, Robby," she said, giving him a peck on the cheek.

"Daddy says it's time for you and Spence to get married."

"Aren't you the little tattletale?" she asked, sitting up with her stocking.

"Show me what you got."

"Well, let's see. Here's a candy cane and another candy cane and another. What's the deal? It's full of them."

Robby made a face. "That's no fun. I like my magic set better," he said, running off to practice in the living room.

Jemma poured the stocking out on the bed. It was full of peppermint canes and a note at the bottom:

Meet me on the tracks at eight.

Always,
Your Candy Man

Racing to the kitchen window, she looked toward the tracks. The sun wasn't quite up, so she couldn't really see anything. She took a bath and heard the 6:23 Zephyr blow its horn. After changing clothes twice, she finally settled on her white turtleneck and a long paisley skirt and boots. She brushed her hair and checked herself out in the mirror. Not everybody could be blond and have a gigantic bosom.

She watched Robby practice his tricks. Her family got up and she set the table for breakfast, then began to pace. Papa's clock was about to chime as she went out the back door and walked up on the tracks. She didn't see him anywhere, but there was a box wrapped in gold foil paper and tied with a red ribbon in the middle of the cross ties. She opened it to find another note.

Look to the East.

She turned to see a handsome cowboy wearing a gray Stetson pushed back on his head, a long black duster, a red scarf at his neck, and shiny new boots. He was walking toward her.

"Spence?" She shaded her eyes.

He grinned. "Care to dance?" His eyes shone like sterling silver. She giggled at first as they danced down the tracks and back again to their phantom waltz. Eventually, the only sound was the shuffle of their feet on the wooden ties and packed earth. Their gaze was set on each other. The dancing stopped when Spencer took the blue velvet ribbon out of his pocket that Jemma had worn in her hair the day he told her that he wouldn't be back. He was back, and now the ribbon was threaded through a ring, the likes of which Jemma had never imagined.

Spencer put his Stetson on the ground and got on his knees. "Jemmabeth Alexandra Forrester, you mean more to me than my own life. I have loved you since the first time I saw you, and it's my life's joy just to be with you. The only way that I could be happier is if you would marry me. What say ye, Jemma?"

Jemma knelt with him and cried. It took her a minute to get her voice back. "Everybody knows that I don't deserve you, Spence. I realize that it's an honor being loved by you all these years, but it will be my life's greatest blessing to be your wife."

They kissed, amid tears and shouts of joy from Lizbeth's backyard and Willa's front porch.

CHAPTER 4
MURMURINGS

People she hadn't heard from since high school showed up to see her ring. It was as though they could all now move on with their lives because Spencer and Jemmabeth were getting married. Jemma considered that fact every time she looked at him. How did she ever get so involved with Paul? It must have been the way he twisted words around. Who was she kidding? It was his eyes. He had snake-charmed her. Rats on him. Nobody would ever come between Spencer and her again.

"The Ring," as Alex called it, was a rare, purple diamond set between radiant blue sapphires with a row of tiny white diamonds encircling the band. Spencer had had it made in Italy. Jemma didn't even know there were colored diamonds. Lester said it must have been hijacked from royalty.

"I want you to feel like you are at Sainte-Chapelle every time you look at it. It had to be extraordinary, like you," Spencer said as they sat on the floor in the cramped pouting room where Lizbeth used to go when she was upset with Papa. They kissed until they heard Jim and Alex in the kitchen, then emerged amid grins from her parents.

"Well, I guess we'll have to rename it the smooching room," Jim said.

Spencer blushed. "Sorry; we just needed to be alone."

"Why don't you kids go for a walk?" Alex asked. "We'll have supper ready by the time you get back."

"I want to help," Jemma protested. "I don't want to be called a princess or something."

"Off with you, Princess Jemma," Helene said, bursting into the room as she tucked her silver hair into a bun. Jemma loved the way she said her name — *Zhemma*. Helene winked at Spencer. "We have too many cooks in here already," she added. She and Lizbeth set to work on their latest culinary project.

Alex handed them their coats.

"When you get back, will you watch my magic show, Spence?" Robby asked. "I'll turn Jemma into a toad," he said, then escaped into the living room, laughing.

They walked across town to the park and

sat on a chilly concrete picnic table. A rusty old pickup rolled past and honked. In the bed of the pickup was a blue spruce tree, lit up with Christmas lights. Shy Tomlinson, the driver, had grown the tree for decades in the dirt-filled back of his truck.

"Merry Christmas, Shy," they shouted. He yelled back, then turned the corner.

Jemma leaned on Spencer's shoulder. "Things are too perfect. It's like when the camera moves in behind the actor in a scary movie. I have this feeling that something bad is going to happen."

"It's just the season. They say that more people get down at Christmas than any other time."

"What do your parents say about us being engaged?"

"Well, Mother hasn't been sober long enough for me to tell her, and Dad slapped me on the back, then asked if we needed to have a little talk about the birds and the bees."

"Your mom hates me, Spence. Remember last New Year's Eve? She cussed at me for breaking up with you, and don't say it was only the liquor talking."

"None of that matters because it's just you and me now. I'm closer to Harriet than I am to my parents, anyway."

Jemma jumped off the table. "Then let's go see Harriet. She lives around here, doesn't she? I want somebody from your family to be as happy as we are."

Harriet O'Connor lived a block west of the park. She was a small woman with delicate features and a twinkle in her eye. She had a high, light voice, quite Irish. "Spencer and his lady," she said, untying her apron. "How good to see you. Are things all right at home? Your father gave me the holidays off, you know, but I did so want to see you two. How are you, Miss Jemmabeth?" She took their coats and served them pumpkin pie and cider.

"We wanted you to know our good news." Spence held Jemma's hand.

"Now, let me guess. I don't have to wonder too much since that stunning ring is on your finger, dearie," she said with a sweet smile. "My congratulations to the both of you." She embraced Spencer, then moved to Jemma, taking her hands. "Of course I always hoped that my boy would marry you, since that's all he's ever wanted, so now I can call you my girl, if that's all right."

"I would love that," Jemma said.

"Spencer is like my son, you know. My husband died in Korea and I never remarried. Taking care of Mrs. Chase and Spencer has been my life."

"Then you have outdone yourself," Jemma said.

"Well, I grew up on a ranch, and I tried to bring this boy up under the cowboy code. I think he's turned out to be a fine young man. You probably agree with me, don't you, my girl?"

Jemma beamed at him. "There is nobody finer in the world than your boy."

"I think I've heard about enough of all this," Spencer said. "We're supposed to be home by now."

"Do come back to see me, won't you, dearie? Spencer, I expect to see you tomorrow at your folks' place."

"I guess I'll be there," he said.

Harriet raised her brow at him.

Spencer closed the gate in front of Harriet's house as a '57 Chevy rolled past, then backed up. Wade Pratt stuck his head out. "Where's your 'Vette, Spence?" he asked, flicking cigarette ashes.

"I'm trying to get it in shape so I can take y'all on if I have to," Spencer said.

Dwayne Cummins, the driver, got out and came around to shake Spencer's hand.

"I see you've still got the most beautiful girl to ever come out of this town." Dwayne nodded toward Jemma. "I'm available, ma'am, if you ever need a backup."

Spencer laughed. "I know, I'm a lucky guy. How are you boys doing since you got out of the army? Are you still playing in Buddy B's band?"

Wade answered. "Shoot, yeah, but we could sure use your girlfriend's voice if you could spare her sometime."

Dwayne leaned against his car. "We tried to get on at the power plant. Leon Shafer's makin' some big bucks over there, but they ain't hirin' now. So, we've been doing this and that. Wade's been pumpin' gas at old man Sykes station, and I'm helpin' my daddy get in his crop. How about you? You still gonna be a . . . architecture or whatever you call it?"

"I'm working on it," Spencer said.

"Maybe you'll get famous someday and give us a job, you know, rememberin' the little people that helped you along," Wade added.

"Wade, you never did nothin' to help nobody along, unless you mean runnin' off good-lookin' women . . . am I right about that, Jemma?" Dwayne clicked his tongue at her, then turned to Spencer.

"Me and Wade were about to whup up on old Chubs Ivey the other day for sayin' y'all was gettin' too thick with the coloreds."

Spencer scowled. "What do you think he meant by that?"

"Same thing everybody in town thinks. Y'all are overstepping the friendly churchgoer thing," Dwayne said. "Coloreds is coloreds, and whites is whites. That's the way God made us."

"We ain't agreein' with you or nothin'," Wade added quickly. "We just didn't want your good-lookin' girlfriend's name to be thrown around."

Jemma raised her chin. "I can take care of my own name, thank you. And skin color doesn't have anything to do with brain size or personality. Did y'all know that?"

"Now don't be pickin' on Wade 'cause he's got a small brain and a bad personality. He can't help it." Dwayne punched Wade's shoulder, then turned to Jemma. "You give us a call if you ever dump Spence."

"Yeah, I'll do that," Jemma said. These two yahoos had been flirting with her since she was in the seventh grade and her daddy was coaching them in high school football. Their claim to fame was that they hid in the high school boiler room one night in order to sneak into the social studies classroom and steal test answers. They used them the next day on their sophomore civics exam. The answers were to a senior world history test. What a pair.

Spencer, ever the diplomat, suggested they stop by to see him at his dad's business later in the week. "I've got to get Jemma home. Y'all take care."

"Tell Coach that we said howdy," Wade shouted as the '57 spun out.

Jemma and Spencer walked at a brisk pace to get home before dark.

"Do you think the whole town thinks like Chubs and those two?" Jemma asked.

"I don't really care, do you?"

"Nope. At least they didn't offer us a ride. My hair would've smelled like cigarettes for two days," Jemma said. "Hey, it's faster if we walk down the tracks."

"Let's go, then." Spence took off ahead of her.

"You were in the Gene Autry Club, weren't you?" Jemma asked, running to keep up.

"Yeah, and you were in Roy Roger's," he replied over his shoulder.

"Do you think that was the cowboy code that Harriet was talking about? I think it's funny that Harriet raised you by the cowboy code, then you looked so handsome when you proposed to me in your Western outfit, but you've never even been on a horse."

"Well, don't get your hopes up. That was

a once-in-a-lifetime deal just for you, baby. Now come on, before the chuck wagon runs out of vittles and we miss the magic show." He took off in a sprint with Jemma, ever the competitor, close behind.

"I know, let's decorate a little tree and put it by old Shorty Knox's dugout. I bought some socks and gloves for him," she yelled. "I still owe him."

He grinned back at her, at his sweet love. "You bet. Someday, though, I'm building Shorty a real house."

Helene was due to return to her home in Wicklow. Jemma sat with her on the sofa in the living room.

"This has been delightful, my dear," Helene said. "Your parents are charming, and I would take little Robby home with me if they would allow it."

"Helene, could I stay with you again next year when I return to Le Claire?"

"Of course, dearest, I would like nothing more, but I assumed that you and Spencer would be getting married before then."

"I know. That's what we would like, but I promised Papa I wouldn't marry until I got my degree, and I always keep my promises."

"Have you discussed this with Lizbeth?"

"No, ma'am. It was a promise between

Papa and me."

"From what I know about your papa, he was a compassionate man. To see you and Spencer together, dear, would surely have brought him great joy. One has to believe that he would advise to carry on with your wedding plans. Now, I must see your sketchbook. I do so regret that I was unable to come to the exhibition in Paris." Helene went over each page with her.

She left on the Zephyr that afternoon, headed to Dallas, a short drive from her home.

"Y'all come on," Jim shouted. "We're going out to the old home place, and Mama's driving!"

Robby cut short his magic show matinee, and they all piled into the Rambler.

"Now, let me get acquainted with this." Lizbeth frowned at the gearshift.

"It's easy, Mama. Just pull it down for forward and up for reverse," Jim said.

Lizbeth started the car. "The last time I took a group for a spin, the car ended up in the cemetery pond."

Alex giggled, but Jim gave his mother a dubious glance. She did fine, though, and soon pulled into the driveway of her old farmhouse.

"Boy, the house sure looks run-down,

Mama. Why don't you lease it out and let the renter provide some maintenance?"

"I couldn't do that. Renters would just tear it up."

"Well, it couldn't look much worse than it does now," Jim said.

Alex and Jemma sat in the car while the rest went on an inspection tour of the place. "Your daddy is so happy for you, honey."

"He's happy for himself, too, Mom. He's always wanted me to marry Spence."

"Can you blame him?" Alex asked. "Tell me about living in Paris."

"It's different. I long to hear more English and eat Mexican food. I don't think I have picked up much French, but I love to hear it. I mostly paint and wait to see Spencer on the weekends. As far as my work goes, I know that I have grown as an artist because I see things with a different eye."

"We're concerned about Spencer getting drafted, Jem. Does he talk about it?"

"No, but surely that won't happen. What would they do with an architect in this thing that's not even called a war?"

Alex looked out at the harvested field. Scraps of the cotton still clung to the stalks. "I assume they would put a gun in his hands and push him out the door."

Jemma's face flushed at that thought.

"Spencer is about the least aggressive person I know."

"That doesn't matter when Uncle Sam calls, sweet pea. Your daddy's brothers were gentle, sweet young men, too."

"Mom, don't say that. Look at what happened to them."

"I'm sorry, honey. I just have a bad feeling about this war."

The sun slipped behind a solitary cloud in the sky.

"I know," Jemma whispered.

"Well, baby girl, looks like I'm going to be walking you down the aisle soon, huh?" Jim pulled onto the highway, giving Lizbeth a rest from driving.

"I don't know, Daddy. I promised Papa that I wouldn't marry until I graduated from college."

"Well, Papa didn't know that you were going to drop out for a whole year like you did." Jim adjusted the rearview mirror.

"I painted the whole year, Daddy. That's how I made all that money from the show."

"Yeah, Jemma's loaded," Robby said, not even looking up from his comic book.

Jim pointed at her. "All I know is that you don't want to wait too long."

"What does that mean?"

"It means that Uncle Sam is going to be knocking on Spencer's door, baby girl. He'll be out of school and available," Jim said in a voice tinged with old pain.

"James," Lizabeth began, "the time that Jemmabeth stayed with me in Chillaton was a gift from the good Lord. It was part of His great plan for me and for her. I don't want any more talk that insinuates otherwise." Her voice was clear and strong. "Jemma, your papa loved you and he loved Spencer. If he concocted that promise, it was only because he wanted you to be a success. Look at what you have done with your art, sugar. He would be proud and satisfied. Of course he would want you to finish your degree, but he wouldn't want your hearts to suffer because of it. Married women go to school. There's too much pain in this old world as it is, for you to feel it coming from Papa's grave. He would want you to be happy. I know that for sure."

The rest of the way home, the only sound in the car came from Robby's comic book as he turned the pages.

Lizbeth and Jemma sat on the bed in the side bedroom that was once a shed. Their long legs were drawn up under their chins, and their arms were folded around them.

"I read the Bible that you gave me every night, Gram, and I'm trying to let the Lord lead my life, honest."

"Memorize some verses, sugar. If you have them right up there in that pretty head of yours, they can carry you through hard times. I meant what I said in the car today. I know how you feel about promises, Jemmabeth, but this is one you can let go. I speak for your papa."

Jemma hugged her. "I miss you so much."

"I miss you, too. It'll be hard when everybody leaves. For some reason, an empty house gets me to thinking about the brevity of life. Now, don't tell your daddy that."

"You have Lester to cheer you up."

"Oh, he's a good man, but he's even older than I am and he'll be gone one of these days. I do have the trip with Julia to look forward to. I suppose it'll be good to see the boys' resting places."

"Gram, if Spencer gets drafted, I don't think I can stand it. Marty says that Vietnam is not like other wars. He says it's not a winnable war."

"You'll bear whatever comes your way, sugar. You're a strong woman. It's in our Jenkins's blood. Let's not dwell on this war talk. You should be thinking about wedding dresses and such. You may need Julia to manage things for you. She knows all the right people."

"Did you know that Do Dah, I mean . . . Julia, came to my show the second week? She was disappointed that all the paintings on display were already sold. She's so much fun. Everybody has us planning the wedding, and Spencer and I haven't even had a chance to discuss anything."

"Well, you'll have lots of time to talk about it on that plane ride over the ocean. Oh, I do dread that."

"I love you, Gram. You're always in my prayers."

"It's the same with me, sugar. Now, let's see what's going on in the kitchen."

"Baby girl, I'm sorry if I came down on you too hard yesterday," Jim said as the Rambler idled in the driveway, ready for their trip home to Arizona. He hugged her to him. "I just want you and Spence to be happy and have a good life. I wish Matt and Luke could've had that. I think Mama is right, though; Papa wouldn't hold you to the promise. You were probably ten years old when you made it anyway."

"Actually, Daddy, it was the year he died, so I was almost seventeen. I think that's part of my problem. I made him that promise, and he died the next week. It's hard for me to let it go."

Jim held his daughter's shoulders and looked her in the eye. "Papa didn't know there was a war coming where boys like his own would give up their free will and go fight. You can explain yourself to Papa in heaven, Jem, but you have to grab this blessing of a happy life while you can get it."

Jemma nodded and stared at the floor, but if she didn't keep this promise, then what good were others she had made in her life?

She held Robby in her lap for as long as she could, even though he was half asleep. Alex cried with her, and then they were gone, just as though they had never come. But they had come, and her life's direction was taking a joyous turn, straight to Spence. Jemma couldn't shake off the melancholy from the change, though, nor could she shed the thought that her Candy Man might leave her to go carry a gun. Roy Rogers had guns in his pretty holster, but it was only to wing the bad guys, not to kill or be killed.

Buddy B took them to the airport because it was snowing and Spencer didn't want just anybody driving. Buddy ran Chase's tow service, too, in a four-wheel-drive truck. Today he had a full load of people.

"Hope y'all don't mind Dwayne and Wade hitchin' a ride," Buddy apologized. "Dwayne's car broke down in Amarillo and they need to pick it up."

Wade snickered. "Y'all two lovebirds probably wanted to be left alone, huh?"

"This is fine with us. Jemma will just have to sit in my lap." Spencer winked at her as they all crammed into the front seat.

"Your daddy had to fire Wade's little brother last week," Dwayne said.

"Yeah, they don't come any dumber than him." Wade cleaned his teeth with a guitar pick. "Buddy got him a job washin' and polishin' the cars on the lot, but the genius took a nap in one of 'em. Your daddy was showin' it to some old people and they opened the door on him, snorin'. Like to have scared 'em to death."

Dwayne shook his head. "Old people get scared too easy."

"Not them old people — he scared my brother. Remember that time we shut him up in your locker and he lit a cigarette while he was in there?" Wade snorted at the memory.

"Yeah, yeah." Dwayne slapped his leg. "The principal saw smoke coming out of the locker and called the fire department."

"He lit up all your biology cheat notes.

That's what was making most of the smoke."

"That makes me wanna light up." Dwayne reached for his cigarettes.

"Not in my truck, you don't," Buddy B said and turned up the radio. Jemma was more than glad to sit in Spencer's lap even if it had meant stinky, cigarette-smoke hair.

On the flight to Paris, they talked at last.

"We don't have to rush, Jem. If you want to keep your promise, we'll wait."

"You and I are the only ones who feel that way. I didn't listen to anybody's advice about us last year and I'll regret that forever. I want to marry you on this plane," she said. "I just feel funny about Papa."

"And I want you to have the wedding you've always talked about. I would marry you in Shorty Knox's dugout, but whatever you decide is fine with me. You think you're the lucky one; wrong. I am that person."

She kissed him behind the airline emergency instructions card. "Let's get married this summer." She got goose bumps just saying the words.

Spencer grinned and shoved his fists in the air. "Yes!" he yelled, causing a stir among the passengers. It was the only excitement on the whole flight . . . for them, at least.

She was jet-lag weary, but she had to at least start the painting. She'd missed the smell of the studio and the light that poured in from everywhere. She found the largest canvas in the workroom and put the base coat on it. It was a luminous palette with the sun bursting up from the vanishing point of the tracks. She sketched him in with life-sized proportions. His hands were on his hips, the long fingers curved slightly. She didn't need a sketch for reference. Every detail remained in her heart.

The night janitor was arriving just as she had the basics done. She stood back and the janitor joined her. He smiled and nodded toward the painting. "Zee Duke?"

Jemma laughed, assuming he meant John Wayne. "No, it's my own cowboy."

He shrugged and went about his business. Jemma yawned and held her hand up to see his ring of love sparkle in the studio lights.

Spencer wanted to show her Florence, but she was still nervous about another encounter with Miss Completely Gorgeous. He assured her that Michelle was after a new guy, an Italian. Jemma stayed with the Grasso family at night and with him all day. Listening to him as a tour guide was all she wanted to do, but the city was distractingly beautiful. Spencer rented a car so they could see the countryside and so he could try out his new travel rod and reel. As they drove alongside the River Arno, he found a spot he liked.

"I've wanted to fish this river ever since I came here," he said.

"I don't have to clean them, do I?"

"Nah, I'll let them go."

"Do you want me to wait in the car?"

"Are you kidding? You are going to be my good-luck charm."

Even so, she followed him at some distance, remembering her daddy's admonitions to "stay back" when she went fishing with him. Spencer walked quickly through the narrow meadow that ran down to the river. She loved the way he moved, like he was in high school again, keeping the ball and running across for a touchdown. How did she ever even think of loving anybody else?

To see him from afar, independent of her, and so focused on the moment at hand, gave her a peek at his life all those months with Michelle. A sudden weight in her chest changed her breathing. Guilt. Her eyes filled with tears. Those were lost months that she could have been sharing his sweet company instead of making him wait. Rats.

A few grazing cattle raised their heads as Spencer passed. Jemma clamped her hand over her mouth when he slipped at the river's edge, but at least he didn't fall in. Rising up from the wet mass of undergrowth, he threw out a practice cast. There was a soft whirring of his reel and then the lure floated perfectly in the water. Jemma climbed a small knoll to watch. He lifted the rod a little and she could see his shoulders and biceps tense up, then relax through his shirt. Did he ever go fishing with Michelle? Or for a long walk? Did he kiss her four or five times in a row? Double rats. All her fault.

He reeled in the line, then cast it again. No sooner than the hook broke the surface, it was grabbed by a gray, splashing streak. A tug at the line brought the realization that a fish was ready for a fight.

"Got one," he yelled. In a flash of energy, he swept the rod and line upward and toward the bank. The fish lurched out of the water, then back in again. He repeated the move while taking the slack out of the line. This time it worked. The fish lay just beyond his feet, glinting and flopping in the sunlight. Spencer was breathless but smiled up at her. He dangled his catch before him. Jemma wiped at her tears, then applauded and whistled. This would become a painting, for sure. He tossed the fish back into the water and motioned for her to join him. After he washed his hands in the river, he kissed her.

She covered her nose. "You smell like a fish."

"Yeah, it's great, isn't it?"

She turned to the water and reached in her pocket. "There," she said, plunking a small pebble into the Arno. "From Chillaton to Italy, with love."

They visited the American cemetery just outside Florence where her uncle Matthew was buried. Without Spencer's encouragement, she wouldn't have made it to see his grave, one of many in the rows of white crosses. It was too sad. They laid a bouquet of flowers on it and stood in silent prayer for her daddy's gentle big brother and all the others laid to rest so far from home. Jemma could only think of her great-grandfather's Bible with Matthew's study notes tucked inside, and the yellowed telegrams sent to Papa and Gram telling them of their sons' deaths. She could not imagine enduring that pain. She squeezed Spence's hand extra hard.

Jemma sat in the Grassos' conservatory, much like Helene's in Wicklow, eating Italian ice cream.

"I've never tasted anything like this in my life," she said with a mouthful.

Spencer grinned. "It's like your kisses — sweet and habit-forming."

She gave him The Look, cutting her eyes in his direction, then turning her head to look at him.

"Hey, when are the ladies coming from Texas?" he asked.

"In April. Oh, and Helene is coming, too."

"That's going to be hilarious. Do Dah will be bossing Gram around, and the others will be trying to keep peace. Willa is going to have the time of her life."

"I almost forgot. Sandy and Martin want us to meet them somewhere. Do you have time to travel?"

"You are the one with the big art show coming up. Are you ready?"

"Of course I am. What do you think I've been doing until midnight every night? Sandy wants to get away, and Marty has a few weeks coming up so they want to meet us in Brussels. I think his folks sent them some money. He's about to get shipped out to Vietnam and the military is giving him some time off. Big gift, huh?"

"Brussels it is. I'll fly to Paris and we'll go together."

Jemma and Sandy had been friends since they were toddlers. Sandy was always on the honor roll and won the state typing contest and the Sew It with Wool contest their senior year. Sewing with wool in cotton country didn't get much respect, but Sandy's parents kept her trophy on their mantle even after she got married. Jemma always thought that Sandy resembled her final doll that Santa had brought: pale skin, blond hair, hazel eyes, and extra-long lashes. She was famous for her makeup that she had been allowed to wear since the sixth grade. It was fun to see it smear during basketball games. Due to that fact, Sandy wouldn't put out the extra bit of hustle that could keep her a spot on the starting squad. They never talked about the makeup, though. It was one of those things friends let go about one another.

Martin was in the best shape he'd been in since high school. He was a stocky gorilla guy with curly hair. His brown eyes, normally looking for trouble, seemed to have lost their zip. He'd been in and out of dilemmas in high school and was rarely in good standing with Sandy's family. He was two years older than Spencer, but they had played sports together, at least when Martin was not on probation with the coach for one thing or another.

Sandy squealed when she saw The Ring and the girls giggled like they were in elementary school again. They spent the day touring the city. Spencer and Jemma were engrossed in the art and architecture. Sandy and Martin were happy being off the base. The girls practically had the wedding planned by nightfall. As if Jemma needed any help.

"So, are you guys, you know, going to stay in the same room tonight?" Sandy asked at supper.

"Hey, that's their business." Martin shot her a hard look.

"Well, I just wondered since you are way over here on another continent. Nobody would know or care." She shrugged. "Unless you're still keeping your junior-high vow of celibacy. You are, aren't you! Cheezo, y'all are grown-ups now, in case you haven't noticed."

Spencer took Jemma's hand. "It's our choice, Sandy. It's all about anticipation." He kissed Jemma right in front of them, and it was no junior-high peck.

"Spence, are you going to call on some of your family's old friends in D.C. to get a deferment when you graduate?" Martin asked, clearing the moment, but with a suspicious eye.

"I'll take whatever comes my way. I don't want to, but I will."

"Man, this southeast Asia mess scares me," Martin said. "I'm just hoping to come out of it alive."

Sandy frowned. "I don't want to talk about it. I want to go dancing. Have you been running the bulls anymore, Jem?" She never did know when to shut up.

Jemma bugged her eyes at Sandy. "Not recently," she said through clenched teeth. "Actually, I gave it up for my own cowboy." She batted her eyelashes at Spencer.

"Spence's no cowboy," Sandy said. "Anyway, let's go somewhere and watch Jemma get crazy."

They found a discothèque playing British pop music. Jemma and Spencer got going and couldn't stop. "You Really Got Me" by the Kinks was blasting out when Sandy and Martin decided to join them on the dance floor. Jemma had observed a few things about disco dancing and was springing them on Spencer. He already knew them, making her wonder about Michelle again. The four of them were representing Chillaton quite well, so well, in fact, that an overexuberant French tourist cut in to dance with Jemma. He was singing along, in loud French. Spencer cut back in front of him, shouting over the music, *"Prends ta proper femme, celle-ci est la mienne prenez votre proper femme."*

"What did you say to that guy?" Jemma yelled. "How did you get so good at French for a CHS graduate?"

"I told him he had a nice voice."

"You did not. I caught one of those words."

"I told him to find his own wife, that you are mine."

"I don't recall us getting married yet, big boy."

"It happened the first time we kissed, baby. The deal was sealed."

They slept in separate rooms and Sandy never gave up talking about it, either. She wasn't known as the class blabbermouth for nothing. The next morning was cold and rainy, so they headed for the museums.

Sandy whispered in Jemma's ear at lunch, "Jem, pray for Marty and me, and not just about Vietnam." She drew back and said in a perky voice, "I'll be coming back to Chillaton, so I guess I'll see you there. I can help you with the wedding. What's the timeline?"

Jemma gave her the schedule and a perplexed look. "Spence graduates in the middle of May, but my term isn't over until June. The wedding is at the end of July."

"The hottest time of the year in Texas?"

"That's the only time Daddy can get off. He has one weekend between the high school football camps he hosts and his own college fall training camp. Don't worry; it will be a morning wedding, before it gets too hot." She didn't mention that it would be early enough that Sandy's makeup wouldn't run.

"Pray for us. Don't forget," Sandy said when the guys were paying the bill. "Marty's not himself these days."

Actually, Jemma thought he was a good deal nicer. "I will pray for y'all, I promise, but you practice keeping a civil tongue for our wedding. No more talk about sleeping together and running the bulls. Got it?"

"Yes, ma'am," Sandy said.

Only two weeks to go before the Academie's spring exhibition. She'd sold three more paintings since the opening exhibition in the fall and was saving that money for the wedding. Most of the pieces for the spring show were portraits of people she didn't know personally but had seen on the streets between her apartment and the Academie. There were twelve paintings in all. Her favorite, of course, was of Spencer on the tracks. *My Cowboy* she had named it. After their trip to Brussels, she painted her second favorite, a watercolor of Sandy and Martin sitting on a bench — Sandy leaning on his shoulder and Martin in uniform. Marty was hunched over, arms on his knees and hands clasped, staring at the ground.

Another was of two small children feeding pigeons below the rose window of Notre Dame. She worked through Friday night on a watercolor of Spence fishing in the River Arno, then she was done. They were due at the gallery the next morning, so she went home for a couple of hours of sleep, repeating a Bible verse as she walked. She was trying to memorize scriptures, like Gram had suggested, by Easter. She'd learned eight so far, unlike when she was in vacation Bible school and could learn two or three a day. She said her prayers, wound the music box, and went to bed. Spencer would be on the first flight out of Florence in a few hours to help transport the paintings.

■ ■ ■ ■

"I'm having weird feelings about this show," she said to Spencer. "Some sort of anxiety about you, like at the fall show, I guess, when I thought I'd never see you again."

"Ah, but this time I will be here before the doors open. There will be no drama, just art," Spencer said as they wrapped her last painting for the trip to the gallery.

"Spence, I want to send Trina to design school. I have been putting money aside for her, but she would have a hissy fit if she knew. How can I do it so she won't know?"

He smiled. "You're always surprising me. We'll figure something out."

Spencer watched her at the gallery, talking with the staff. Her conversations were animated, like an Italian's. The way she closed her eyes when she laughed, which was often, enchanted him. It always had. She could be stubborn one minute and then give in completely the next. He knew her better than she knew herself. He could have told the gallery manager that the portrait of her cowboy would have to be the focal piece. Jemma was not budging on that point. The manager wanted a painting of two elderly women laughing on a park bench in that spot, but Jemmabeth won. She usually did when it came to her work. The cowboy piece was too near her heart. Spence just hoped it wouldn't hang in their living room someday with a spotlight on it. He had only bought that Western stuff to make her smile and maybe get it out of her system at last, but that procedure could be a challenge. When Jemma was six years old, her papa had given her a pair of red cowboy boots. She had worn them every day for a year, even when they pinched her toes. Now she used them to hold her brushes. Spencer wondered if she would ever recover from cowboy fever.

He had decided a long time ago that watching her move was even better than watching her talk. She walked with such grace and self-confidence, probably because she was a dancer at heart. Her hair swung when she walked, and she was constantly looking around for something new to paint. Seeing her dance, though, was the ultimate. Movement came to her like her art — smooth, creative, and elegant in detail. It wasn't provocative; it was captivating. He knew all the guys liked watching her when she danced, too, but they knew better than to say it around him. He had missed her so much that to be with her now and to enjoy her company without giving himself to her was maddening, but that was the way it was going to be. He didn't know how he would feel toward any other woman. He had never had the desire to find out, nor did he care. Jemmabeth Forrester was worth waiting for.

She wore a purple silk dress to match her ring of love, the sweet pea earrings, and heart necklace, all gifts from Spence. Once again, the art patrons of Paris were delighted by her work. She was the most talked about artist in town. Her work was "in." Every piece, except the one of Spencer, which was reserved, sold to high bids. The total came to over eight thousand American dollars. Jemmabeth was amazed that people would pay that kind of money for her art, but she was glad of it since she had two more projects to fund. She explained them to Spencer as they sat in her favorite bakery for breakfast.

"I'll never forget the look on Willa's face when we came out of the storm cellar and their church was nothing but scattered splinters and rubble. This money is going to repair some of the pain caused by that tornado. When the new church is done, I want to build a chapel onto the old rest home in honor of Kenneth Rippetoe. Re-

member how he wanted to run a nice nursing home? At least the chapel will smell
good and it will be a place of hope."

Spencer sighed. "What a way to go — in a
tornado. I'll have some time in May and
June to finish up the design for the church
and then I'll get started on the chapel. Have
I ever told you how much I like you?"

"Yup, but I like you more. You're my hero.
Remember?" She melted him with a smol-
dering, movie-star kiss.

"Are you sure your dad can't get off any
sooner than the end of July?" he asked, out
of breath.

"You told me that you liked the wait," she
said, giving him The Look. That was one of
the best things about Paris. Nobody cared if
you kissed like crazy anytime, anywhere.
And they did.

Chapter 5
Reckonings

Lizbeth settled into Cam's chair. She moved her fingers over the worn patches of maroon velvet where his arms had rested. They had bought it just before Pearl Harbor and their plan was to save up for the matching sofa. The war helped them decide to use the money for Matthew's seminary fund instead. Cam would like it that she was taking this pilgrimage to the graves. It never occurred to her that she might fly across the ocean, but she'd learned to drive last spring, hadn't she? Still, she had no idea how she could get on a plane and stay on it for more than a minute. Julia would be watching her, though, and despite the fact she had raised her like a daughter, Julia remained her little sister and a teaser. Flying was for birds, but then surely the good Lord wouldn't have given the idea for humans to build airplanes if He didn't approve. Julia had said she could give her a pill to go to sleep. Perhaps, then, they could carry her on like a suitcase.

"Miz Liz?" Lester shouted from the back door.

"I'm at the front of the house," she yelled back, adjusting her hat. Her bags were packed and on the porch.

Lester was in his Saturday khakis. "We'd better get along to Miz Johnson's. Is this all you're taking? I thought you were gonna be over there two weeks."

"That's none of your concern, Mr. Timms. You just make sure that Cam's flowers get watered and my ivy doesn't die. I'm expecting an important letter in the mail, too, so take care with it."

"Yes, ma'am," he said, recognizing her tone as one not to be trifled with.

They picked up Willa and Trina, who had even less luggage than Lizbeth. Lester chattered the whole hour to a solemn audience. Silence prevailed in the waiting area at the Amarillo airport, too.

"So you'll pick up the rest of your bunch in Dallas?" Lester asked, hoping for some kind of conversation.

"Yes, sir," Trina obliged. "Helene and Do Dah will meet us there."

"Well, all I know is that when you ladies step off that plane, it's gonna look like heaven has done taken itself a recess."

"How's that, Lester?" Trina asked.

"Why, 'cause all the best angels will be vacationing in It-ly." He grinned. He had been waiting to pull that one all morning. A wobbly chuckle made its rounds with the ladies.

Lizbeth remained in continual prayer before takeoff. She tried deep breathing like Jemmabeth had recommended. Willa and Trina were like swivel-headed owls. Trina had made them both several new outfits for the trip. They looked good, but that was of little consequence to their jitters.

A stewardess, pasted-on smile intact, came by to assess their anxiety level. "It's a perfect day for flying, and our pilot has twenty years' experience."

"Doin' what?" Willa asked, making Lizbeth and Trina shake with laughter.

It was a good start to uneventful flights. Lizbeth even managed to look out the window a few times. She closed her eyes and tried to visualize a field of white crosses by the Mediterranean Sea, and another field near a wooded hillside in Italy. Jemma had been there with Spencer and she said it was beautiful. Even if Lizbeth survived these airplanes, she feared she might not hold up to those fields of white.

The five of them, wilted and weary, stepped away from customs.

"I don't know about you ladies, but I need me some food," Willa said.

Trina rolled her eyes. "Mama, you just ate on the plane."

"Nobody could make a meal outta them scraps." Willa eyed a pastry shop in the Rome airport.

"Do Dah, how far are we from Nettuno?" Trina asked.

"About forty miles. Remember, I'm only answering to Julia on this trip."

Lizbeth exhaled. "I am so glad to have my feet on the ground. I was getting restless there toward the end."

"But you made it, dearest. I knew you would," Helene said.

Julia put on her glasses and took a list out of her purse. "Here's the plan. We eat something, grab a short nap, then we'll do a quick tour of Rome."

"Now just hold on, Miz Julia," Willa said. "I don't do nothin' quick. My caboose will only go so fast." She patted her behind.

"Mama and I'll do what we can," Trina said. "Y'all just go on."

Helene raised a brow. "Nonsense. We shall

take a cab to all the sights, and you may move about at your own pace, dear."

"That's right. Nobody is going to be left behind. We are the five musketeers," Julia shouted, gathering their hands.

"Are you talkin' about them Mickey Mouse kids?" Willa asked. "I ain't wearin' no funny hat," she said, adjusting her own Sunday best that had gone askew on the flight.

They checked into a lavish hotel overlooking Rome, courtesy of Julia and Helene. Trina felt like she had stepped into a movie, and Willa thought she had stepped into heaven. Lizbeth commented it was way too extravagant, but enjoyed the fuss over the least little thing. She was ready, though, to get on with the reason for the trip.

They barely fit into the cab that was to take them to the Sicily-Rome American Cemetery. Helene spoke fluent Italian so there was no trickery on the fares with the taxi drivers. Upon arrival, Julia and Trina went to ask the location of the grave. Willa was already breathing hard.

"Are you doing all right?" Lizbeth asked as she put her arm around Willa's broad shoulders.

"Would water help, dear?" Helene asked.

"No, ma'am," Willa said, her voice breaking. "I just need that man who's out there somewhere in this I-talian dirt. The closer I get to him, the bigger my hurt."

Lizbeth turned away and closed her eyes. Willa's pain would soon be her own. Already, she could feel it tugging at her heart. The dread of those crosses with her sweet boys' names on them was strong. Trina and Julia returned, cemetery map in hand.

"Are you ready, Mama?" Trina asked quietly.

"I'm as ready as I'm gonna get, child. Your daddy's been waitin' long enough for us to say a prayer over him. Let's go." Willa and Trina moved slowly along the path to the main group of graves. Trina looked over her shoulder at Lizbeth.

"Oh my." Helene drew a deep breath. "What we do to one another in times of war."

"Jemmabeth did a fine thing, arranging it so they could come here," Julia said.

Lizbeth walked to the edge of the path, shading her eyes to see them. They had stopped, most likely to let Willa rest.

Helene and Julia went for a walk in the garden, leaving Lizbeth alone on the bench. She could barely see Willa and Trina, but she could see plain enough that they were at his cross. She couldn't help but cry, knowing how Willa must feel at the sight. Trina would weep, too, even though she had never chopped weeds out of some white man's cotton with him or pulled a lead-heavy sack of the stuff down a row next to him until their fingers bled from the burrs. Lizbeth was afraid that when it was her turn to say prayers and touch the letters in the stones, her façade might crumble and she herself would come completely undone.

They were there for a couple of hours, but nobody cared about the time. It was Italy and it was a glorious day, despite the sadness. Julia had convinced Lizbeth to walk with them to the museum. It was a place of honor paid to lives lost, but never forgotten.

When Trina and Willa rejoined them, it was Helene who greeted them first, arms outstretched. "My friends, please know that no one will ever forget what your Samuel did for freedom in that hideous war."

Willa wiped her face on a well-used handkerchief and Trina stared at the path. "Yes ma'am," Willa said. "I ain't never been one to question the good Lord's business, but I sure wish He would've took me before He took my man." Her lip quivered. "I guess, though, my Latrina wouldn't be here, would she? Sam never got to see our baby. He wrote to her but never got to hold her."

Lizbeth put her arms around them. "Bless you," was all she could say.

"We'll be staying in the village tonight, Willa, so that y'all can come back this evening and again in the morning, if you've a mind to," Julia said.

"Thank you, Miz Julia; I'll do that."

Lizbeth withdrew from the rest of the group on the long train ride to Sicily. Julia wanted them to fly, but she was voted down. Trina and Helene read while Willa napped. Julia sat by her sister, holding her hand. They took a boat from Palermo, Sicily, to Tunis, on the tip of Tunisia in Africa. How odd, thought Lizbeth, to float on waters that the apostle Paul had traveled. She recalled that he was in Malta, below Sicily, and Syracuse, before traveling to Rome. She had taught about his journeys in Sunday school. Surely his eyes must have looked upon some of the very same Mediterranean coastline, and she took some comfort in that.

The American Military Cemetery in Carthage overlooked the sea. The seabirds dipped and called around the fountains. It was a beautiful, serene place. They went first to the visitors' center, then Lizbeth and Julia walked to the first white cross of their journey.

Lizbeth clenched the paper. How peculiar it was to need a map in order to find her baby with the bright blue eyes of his papa. She read it again:

S Sgt Luke J. Forrester, Plot D, Row 1, Grave 8.
68th Bomber Squadron, 44th Bomber Group, Heavy.

It listed all those medals that she had kept in the Soldier Box. When the telegram came to them on that hot August morning in 1943, it was the beginning of the pain that had shut her heart to grief. She had promised to stand with Cameron through everything, but he had left her to walk this hard row without him. Julia was beside her now, holding her arm like Jimmy did when Cameron died.

The briny scent of the Mediterranean wafted on the cool breeze. Only a few hours earlier, she had been on the deck of a ferry with that wind in her face, dreading this passage. She considered for a moment that the salty air would eat away at his name over the years. Lizbeth read each cross as they walked, thinking it might soften the sight of his. There were no references to birthdays or carefully worded sentiments, only names, numbers, states, and dates of passing. All were equal in death.

Julia's arm twitched when they reached it. A sudden calm spread over Lizbeth and she knelt, feeling the warmth of the earth under her. She traced the letters in his name with her finger, to make them her own doing, and then embraced the cool marble. Julia stood over her, crying. Lizbeth could not weep the day that telegram came, but now tears fell from her chin in clusters. He was her artist — nothing like Jemma, but good enough.

His mischief had often caused her to hide her laughter as best she could in order to discipline him. He was much too handsome for his own good, and the girls had chased after him in a time when it wasn't done. All that love and joy bundled up and sent to Europe to die in the clouds. It had to be a part of God's Great Plan, as her own father had said in his sermons. Luke and Matthew were born to give their lives in the name of liberty.

She reached for Julia's hand. Her baby sister had helped them keep their sanity when the boys had died and was with her now, within six feet of one of them. She drew a long breath. "Will you pray with me, Julia?"

Julia got on her knees beside her.

"Father God, I give my son, Luke Jenkins Forrester, into Your holy hands, at last. I trust he is as much a joy to You in heaven as he was to us on this earth. Thank You for allowing his papa and me to love him for a while. Amen, sweet Jesus."

Lizbeth took an old pill bottle out of her purse. She removed the lid and fished out a slip of paper. Clearing her throat, she read as her father had done at the pulpit, "From the book of Luke, chapter 11, verse 36, 'If thy whole body therefore be full of light, having no part dark, the whole shall be full of light, as when the bright shining of a candle doth give thee light.' " She rolled it up and replaced it in the bottle, snapping the lid.

Moving back the grass with her slender fingers, she dropped the bottle between the base of the cross and the earth. It was Luke's scripture. It was the one that she and Cam had picked for him before he was born, and it should remain with him in this foreign land. She dusted her hand and stood, with Julia's help, then kissed her fingertips and touched the cross. He was their bright candle. "Come, Julia," she whispered, "I have nothing left to give this place."

Lester reshuffled the papers. He had not planned on so much work for himself. Nobody ever asked him such questions. Everybody in three counties knew he was a Democrat. What in the Sam Hill did that have to do with getting a wife? He looked at her photo again. She sure was a beauty. Maybe the Republicans that ran the magazine would switch her out with somebody on the homely side, seeing his strong stance in the Democrat Party. No, surely even a Republican wouldn't pull that kind of business.

There couldn't be any harm in a man his age taking on a new wife. He laid down his pen and went to the front porch to sit a spell. Miz Liz's petunias looked better than usual. She had been his hope for a companion. That dear woman would have been his crowning glory, but he couldn't see clear how to make her turn his way. She was still set on Cam, her dearly departed. Lester had tried every trick he knew, too. He wanted someone to cozy down with at night, but that was never going to happen with her. The closest he had ever come to even touching her was when she almost slipped on the ice getting out of the car at Nedra's Nook. Even then, she had grabbed the door handle and not his arm. No sir, it was going to have to be a foreigner, a woman who came in the mail, just like his pension check.

He went to the pantry. He had stocked up on pork 'n' beans, Vienna sausage, Spam, and canned tamales. He grabbed himself a handful of store-bought cookies. That was the best he could do since Lizbeth was over to Europe. He hoped that foreigners ate baked goods and that this woman knew how to make them. Maybe he'd give Tillie Shepherd a call and order some fancy Avon perfume as a welcome present for his bride-to-be. He poured himself a glass of cold milk and resumed his paperwork with fresh vigor. The advertisement said eight to ten weeks and he would be in matrimony once again. It had to be better than cuddling up to a now-absent chinchilla.

"Spence, where are you?" Jemma pressed the phone to her ear. "I can barely hear you."

"I'm about to leave Venice. I just wanted to say hello. Are you sure you can't come?"

"I can't, babe, my class leaves in the morning for Giverny, and I am required to go. Do Dah called and said they will meet you in Florence tonight. I talked to Gram about it, and I think she's okay. I'm so sorry."

"Don't worry. I'll take care of her. You have fun in Monet's garden. I know you've always wanted to see it. Be sure and throw a Chillaton pebble in his lily pond. I'll miss you this weekend."

"I miss you right now. Is Michelle with you?"

"Jem, she's in the same program with me. Don't worry. She has a boyfriend. All she does now is give me dirty looks."

"Tell her the shick says hello. No! Don't talk to her."

He laughed, and she did love it when she could make him laugh. She closed her eyes and thought she could smell his aftershave.

Willa did not know that such beautiful things existed as she had already seen in Europe, but she wasn't quite sure if she liked them. "Them statues is all so old. These I-talians need to get some new stuff. I sure did like that big David, though. He's my kind of man."

"Mama." Trina giggled along with the rest of the group as they waited in the Piazza.

"Spencer said five o'clock, and it's five thirty," Julia said, always the dutiful guide.

Lizbeth wasn't worried. "He had to rent a car and drive from Venice. His class has been studying there."

"Looks like they could just go to the library. Ain't that what it's for?" Willa asked.

Helene liked all of Willa's jokes. She knew Willa was a sharp cookie behind all that kidding around. "There he is now." Helene waved.

Spencer gave each lady a good hug. He was the darling of the evening. They ate at a bistro and finished with the gelato that Jemma so relished.

Lizbeth walked with him as they headed back to their hotel. "Son, would you go with me tomorrow? Julia doesn't think she can. She was very close to Matthew and took it real hard when he left us."

"Yes ma'am, it'll be an honor," Spencer said.

Lizbeth sighed. "Since Tunisia, I know what's coming."

Spencer put his arm around her. He was a strong young man. Maybe he could hold her up when she had to face the cross of her firstborn.

A steady drizzle accompanied them as they rode to the cemetery. Julia sat in the backseat, silent. Lizbeth could not remember a time when her sister had spoken as little as she had in the last twelve hours. It had rained the day they buried their father, too. Matthew was so like him. Her boys were all tall like their grandpa, but it was their grandmother who had given Matthew and Jimmy their golden eyes. Matthew had gotten his degree on a basketball scholarship, and his plan was to enter the seminary when the war was over. She still had all his Bible study notes at home. His fiancée had her teaching degree, the wedding plans were set, but God's plan was otherwise.

It was a short trip from Florence to the impressive gates of the cemetery. Just as Jemmabeth had said, it truly was a field of white, like cotton ready for harvest. Lizbeth gripped her Sunday purse. Matthew had spent every summer helping Cam in the fields. He had come home from college on weekends during the picking season to help get the crop in. Acres of solid white could mean a bale and a half of cotton to the acre, making life a little easier through the rest of the year. This sight, however, turned her stomach. The windshield wipers came to a sudden stop as Spencer turned off the engine at the car park. "I'll stay here for a while, Lizbeth; you two go on ahead," Julia said.

"Are you sure, Do Dah?" Spencer asked.

"I'm sure," she said, not correcting her nickname.

Spencer came around to Lizbeth's door with the umbrella. The map was easy to follow. They walked for about five minutes, then stopped at his row. She shivered and turned away toward the lush crepe myrtles, heavy with sodden blooms, along the path. Matthew had brought her a bouquet of pink cotton blossoms when he was old enough to know that girls liked flowers. She never saw another one without thinking of him. Walking out from under the umbrella, she broke off a cluster of blossoms from a bush. The grass was standing in water. Every step they took splashed up on her legs and the cuffs of Spencer's trousers.

Lizbeth saw his name on the cross before she realized how far they'd gone. It didn't help at all that she had seen Luke's grave already. The choking sound that had rolled up through her almost a year ago, when she had first been able to weep over her boys, rose again.

Spencer dropped the umbrella and covered her with his raincoat. She laid her head on his shoulder and wept for gentle Matthew. She'd had this dear child inside her before she'd really understood about life.

With him, she came to know the sting of birth and the joy of mothering. Without him and his brother, she had come to endure all the dark sorrow a mother's heart can stand without giving out altogether. She had nursed them from her own body, only for them to become warriors, filling early graves in foreign lands.

Yet knowing that fact earlier would not have changed anything. She still would have read them poetry and taught them how to sew on their own buttons and make scratch biscuits. She had told Cameron that she would stand before God and man and say that she'd love him forever and always. She did not say that she could stand to bury all but one of her menfolk.

Lizbeth sensed that Julia had joined them. She reached for her hand and Julia grasped it. "I have something I must do," she said, kneeling in the wet grass.

Spencer knelt with her, as did Julia.

"Father, here lies my boy, Matthew Cameron Forrester. I give him up to You in the same way You gave him to me, in great pain. You are our Lord, and we love You and trust in Your ways. I pray that my life will be as great a blessing to You as this child was to his father and me. Amen, sweet Jesus."

She took out a second small bottle and

removed the slip of paper, taking care to keep it dry, and read Matt's scripture. "From the fifth chapter of Matthew, verse 8, 'Blessed are the pure in heart: for they shall see God.' "

Julia could not hold back her pent-up grief any longer. Spencer held both of them as the drizzle turned to rain, making dull thumping sounds on the upturned umbrella. Lizbeth pushed the bottle into the narrow space between his cross and the sod. She embraced the stone, leaving the crepe myrtle blossoms to wilt under his name.

"Good-bye, sweet Matty," Julia whispered, and they walked away.

"Gram," Spencer said as they shook off the rain at the chapel door, "Jemma wanted you to see something." He led them inside to the mosaic behind the altar. "She thought this was very peaceful and that you would like it."

Lizbeth nodded at the beautiful artwork and smiled, thinking of her granddaughter. They sat in a pew for a while. "I have to show you this, too. It's from an ancient poem," Spencer said as they left the chapel by way of a courtyard. He read an inscription — one of several — on a granite panel: *"The love of honor alone is not staled by age and it is by honor that the end of life is cheered."*

Lizbeth had never been convinced in her heart that their passing was truly an honor. She read the words again and considered if *honor* crossed their anxious thoughts on the mornings of their deaths. Knowing her boys, it did.

The rain had lessened somewhat as they eased past Matthew's row. Lizbeth wiped her eyes and touched Spencer's arm. He stopped the car and she walked alone to the cross once more, turning to face the east. This would be the closest she would ever be to him in this life. If the Lord came tomorrow, she wanted to look with her own eyes at what her eldest son might see when he rose up from this place so far from home. She traced his name in the stone and gathered a few pink petals from the ground. The seeds of honor had been planted in her heart.

Chapter 6
Postcards

"Mama, you better hurry up and pick out someplace you want to go or everybody else is gonna do it for you," Trina said as the train rocked along near Paris. The women had been writing postcards for the last half hour.

"Child, I'm just glad to be here," Willa said. "If we were home, I'd be sweatin' over a pile of clammy shirts, then hurryin' to iron 'em before they 'dewed. It don't make me no never mind what we do. I'm ready to see Jemma and thank her again for makin' it so I could pray over your daddy's grave."

"Willa, what did you like best about Italy?" Spencer asked as he played cards with Trina and Julia.

"I'd have to say that old statue of David. What I can't get shed of is why that fella made him so big 'cause, in the Bible story, Goliath was the giant, unless everybody in them days was big."

134

Julia piped up. "Maybe he was showing us that David's faith made him bigger than life, and it gave him power."

"It is an impeccable sculpture," Helene proclaimed. "I first saw it with my husband many years ago. Nebs was a great admirer of Michelangelo. He told me that the statue was originally designed to be on top of a building; that's why it is so large."

"Is that a fact? I think I like Miz Julia's story better," Willa said.

"Oh my," Lizbeth whispered. They all turned to see the top of the Eiffel Tower coming into view.

Trina's eyes were glued to it. "I can't wait to get there."

Lizbeth knew it was time for her to put the sorrow aside and enjoy the days ahead. She studied Julia's face. She seemed like her old self again, laughing and bossing. Most likely, she needed to shop, and Paris was probably a good place to do it.

Jemma met them at the train station. She lined the group up like kindergartners and hugged each one. Spence, she hugged twice and kissed him on the lips in front of them all. It was going to be a good week.

The Hotel Lutetia in the Saint-Germain des Pres District was a great hotel in the

Art Deco style, as Spencer pointed out. Only the under-forty crowd was hot to go out that night. They set off to find a bistro with a band, and that was an easy chore. The girls took turns dancing with Spencer, so whoever was sitting out was asked to dance by Frenchmen. Jemma always declined. Trina was shy about it at first, but then she gave in and had her own partners, probably just to let Jemma and Spence dance every dance together. They ended the evening with a soul group that played some good Pickett and Redding.

Trina didn't say a word on the walk home until prodded.

"How's Nick doing?" Jemma asked.

Trina grinned. "He's good. I don't think he really believed me when I told him we were coming over here. He's such a nice guy."

Jemma leaned her head on Spence's shoulder. "We both have nice guys."

"What are your plans, Trina? Are you going back to school?" Spencer asked.

"I don't know. I want to get my degree, but the only thing I'm interested in is fashion design. The schools I can afford don't offer that."

"Have you thought about scholarships?"

Trina shook her head. "I don't want

money for my education to be paid for by somebody who doesn't know me from Adam — like blind charity. I'd rather not go. That sounds crazy, but it's the way I feel. I'll just keep sewing for folks and cleaning houses until Nick gets enough money for us to get married."

"Did you bring your sketch book with you?" Jemma asked.

"Don't you take yours everywhere, girl?"

"Let me look, then."

They went to a coffeehouse and talked about college and life in general, until it closed. They walked Trina to the hotel, then Spencer took Jemma to her apartment. They sat on the floor in the hallway.

"We'll tell her it's a loan. I think her pride would allow her to accept that idea, don't you?" Spencer asked.

"Maybe. At least I hope she will, but enough of finance. I didn't give you a proper hello yet." She pulled him by his shirt and left him breathless. "I liked dancing with you tonight," she said with a grin.

He inhaled. "Whoa. Me, too. You were such a good girl, not taking any offers to dance with anybody but me."

"I told you that you are my last cowboy, sir. You are permanently in my heart, got it?"

"I keep it in mind. I'll see you in the morning."

"You keep this in mind," she said and laid another smacker on him.

They spent the next day at The Louvre, waiting almost an hour to see the *Mona Lisa.*

Jemma led a discussion over it during the evening meal. "What did you think about da Vinci's masterpiece, Willa? He painted it on a thin piece of wood, but it's probably the most famous painting in the world."

"All that fuss over a paintin' that you could've done a whole lot better," she said.

"Why, thank you. Did you notice how her skin looked real, like it changed as you moved, sort of transparent? It is a technique of blurring the lines in a painting by blending tones. He did it with layers of glaze and turpentine. It's called *sfumato.*"

"Very interesting," Helene said. "How do you pronounce that again?"

"Ss-foo-mah-toe." Jemma stretched out the word.

"Sounds like dessert to me. Anybody interested in some French pastry?" Julia asked.

Jemma and Spencer gave them the grand tour of Paris. Willa, her Sunday hat perched just so on her head, enjoyed much of it from a taxi. Lizbeth began leaving her hat at the hotel. She didn't want it to get wet, and it seemed to rain every day. Helene and Julia left the group periodically to duck into various odd little shops. They all rode the tourist boat for an hour down the Seine, telling Jemma the details of their trip.

Back on land, Lizbeth, Trina, and Willa got lost looking for a public bathroom. After finding one, they took a wrong turn and ended up in the opposite direction from the meeting place. Willa was tuckered out.

"I'll just ask in this store," Lizbeth said. "Surely somebody can speak English."

Willa and Trina waited outside.

"No luck. Those folks acted like I was speaking a foreign language or something," Lizbeth said, giving the storekeeper a look from the sidewalk.

"I'll try." Trina disappeared into the shop but came out just as fast.

"We'll all try this one." Lizbeth arched her brow and led the way into a stylish shoe salon. "Pardon me, but we are trying to find the Eiffel Tower," she said with a Texas smile.

Two mannequin-faced saleswomen looked at each other, shrugging. *"Veux-tu acheter des chaussures voulez-vous acheter?"* one woman said, then they both laughed and made faces like they had no clue what Lizbeth had asked.

Willa drew back as though they were cussing at her.

Lizbeth asked again, with exaggerated enunciation. She was careful to say *towhwer,* not *tire* like Lester would have as she built a tower in the air with her hands.

The salesladies again snickered behind the counter.

Willa was hungry as well as sick of hearing French. She suddenly raised her cane and smacked the top of the lacquered counter. The sound bounced off the walls. The women shot up out of their seats.

Willa leaned forward, her Sunday hat quite near their slack-jawed faces. "Ei–full–Tie–er–now! Please," she threw in. Both women pointed across the street. The three weary travelers made their way through the traffic to investigate the spot. Between the buildings, Trina spotted it. The landmark could not have been more than two blocks away. The rest of the crew was waiting for them on the steps.

Trina's heart pounded. It was just like the postcard that her mama had kept pinned up on her bedroom wall all her life, and that she had brought with her from Chillaton, tucked in her purse. She took it out and

140

compared it to the real thing, then turned it over. It was postmarked August 15, 1944. She read the words for the millionth time. *We will be together soon. Love, Your Daddy.* There were things worse than never knowing your daddy, but she hadn't lived through those. She kissed the handwriting and put it back in her purse.

Willa dabbed at her eyes with her hanky. She knew the postcard had been taken off the wall. The spot where it had hung was now a small, bright rectangle. The card was about all that her baby had of her daddy — that, and his almond-shaped eyes and dimples.

Spencer treated them to an elegant farewell meal, and Willa had a thing or two to add about the stingy French food. A violinist came to their table and played for Lizbeth's early birthday celebration. They had all pitched in, some more than others, and bought her an antique sewing basket, most likely found by Julia and Helene on their shopping sprees. Lizbeth would miss her old cigar boxes, though. Cam had gotten them for her from the drugstore for as long as she had been a Forrester.

The concert began at eight. They arrived at

Sainte-Chapelle an hour early, since that was the Chillaton style. The changing light on the stained-glass panels was an awesome sight.

"It is truly a moving experience," Helene whispered. "I am not a religious person, but I could become so, under these circumstances."

"Now, what's that supposed to mean, 'not a religious person'?" Willa whispered back, giving her the eye. "Are you telling us that we've been sleepin' in the same room with a heathen?"

"I wouldn't call myself that, dear." Helene adjusted her hearing aid.

"Well, either you join up with the believers or you join up with the heathens. There ain't no middle section in that choir, sugar."

Trina and Jemma exchanged glances.

Lizbeth could see it coming, too. "I think what Helene means is that she's a believer, but doesn't get to church as often as she would like."

Julia smiled behind her program. Her big sister was very good at being a peacemaker when she wanted to. Even so, Willa gave Helene only the slightest benefit of a doubt.

Spencer missed out on that repartee. He was watching the light from the windows reflecting in Jemma's eyes — those golden eyes created with *sfumato* from heaven.

After the concert, Spencer and Jemma said their good-byes and rode home in a taxi, necking in the backseat. The driver smiled and adjusted his mirror so he couldn't watch.

"We have a date next weekend to celebrate your birthday," Spencer said.

"Where do you want to go for our honeymoon?" she asked.

He grinned. "I was thinking about the That'll Do Motel in Chillaton."

"We can't put that on the society page of the *Chillaton Star.*"

"It has a society page?"

"It's on the page with the high school sports and beef prices. Anyway, I have a honeymoon place in mind."

"I hope it's on a beach. I want to see you in a bikini every day."

"Nope. Scotland."

"Scotland? Doesn't it rain there every minute of the year?"

"I don't know, but I want to do it for Papa since I'm breaking my promise to him."

"No bikini then?"

"Maybe in our room."

"Deal," he said and kissed her with a thrashing heart.

The next morning the kissing resumed, but only with their eyes and at the waiting area of the airport.

Lizbeth cleared her throat as she approached them. "Thank you for everything you did for us on this trip. You'll have to let us give you both hugs now."

Willa gave Jemma an extra-long one. She pulled back and started to speak. She just couldn't because her lip began to tremble.

"Thanks, Jem," Trina said, "from both of us."

Good-byes over, they boarded the once-dreaded plane, bound for Texas.

Spencer's idea of a birthday dinner date was at the restaurant at the *Tour Eiffel* — the Eiffel Tower. She wore a red dress, and Spencer looked like Prince Charming again, like he did when he took Carrie out of her wheelchair and waltzed her around The Judge's study. He didn't have to dress up to look that way to Jemma anymore. They held hands across the table, eating now and then.

"Jem, I couldn't bring your present. It's being shipped home, but here's a picture of it."

She took the tissue off the photographs. There were two circular stained-glass windows, looking much like kaleidoscope designs. "You said you felt like you were inside a kaleidoscope when you first saw Sainte-Chapelle, so I thought you would like to put one in the little church and another in the chapel for the nursing home."

Jemma clapped her hands. "What a fantastic idea and a beautiful present!"

"Actually, I have one more thing," he said, giving her an envelope. She slid her finger under the flap and took out the documents.

Her jaw dropped. "Ten thousand dollars to build the church and the chapel!"

"I think we can do something really special if we put our money together. Happy birthday."

"Thank you." She lowered her head and blinked out fat tears. "How do you keep doing these things, Spence? God made you perfect and I am not worthy of you."

He lifted her chin. "I am not perfect. Now hush, and let's see if we can stargaze from this place." They moved to the observation deck.

She kissed him under a cloudy Paris sky. "I've missed finding Orion with you, but seeing all these city lights is kind of like watching the stars from your car, isn't it?"

she asked.

"Yeah, in a topsy-turvy world," he said. "After we get married, I was thinking we could move into Nedra's rental apartment above her shop . . . you know, to give her something to talk about. What do you think?"

She laughed. "I would live anywhere with you, Spence, even your parents' house, and that's saying a lot. Just tell me that you won't get drafted."

The breeze fluttered her hair across her face. He didn't answer but tucked her hair behind her ear and kissed her neck. She tilted her head a bit to make it easier for him and because it felt so good, like everything was going to be all right.

The graduates walked through the streets of Florence in their caps and gowns and congregated at the University Plaza. Each school then paraded to its respective area and the graduates' names were called out. There were no long speeches, only long celebrations. Spencer Morgan Chase was officially a graduate of Syracuse University via Florence. He left for Chillaton a week ahead of Jemma. The beginning of the end of Jemma's sojourn in Europe had begun. It would be a busy, happy summer, at last.

Le Academie Royale D'Art had opened her mind to subtleties, nuances of perspective and technique, and unparalleled joy — or maybe that part was just Spence. She had developed a close friendship with Peter and his wife, Ami. Her studio partner, Jean-Claude, spoke very little English and Jemma's French was spotty, at best, so their relationship was one of mutual respect as artists, shared glories as well as frustrations, and food. They made each other laugh trying to communicate in charades.

Her final pieces as the Girard Fellow were six nighttime watercolors. Jean-Claude had given her some suggestions since she had helped him with his portraiture efforts. Peter and Ami dragged them away from the studio for a farewell dinner at a lively bistro that Jemma had never heard of before. It served American burgers and shakes along with a rock-and-roll band. Jemma vowed to bring Spencer here if they ever came back to Paris. She was dying to dance. She knew Spence wouldn't care if she danced with Jean-Claude as long as he didn't have to watch. Jean-Claude was not a great dancer, but he had fun, and he was fascinated by

Jemma's style on the dance floor. It was a good way to bring her journey to a close, dancing her way out.

Jean-Claude and Peter shared a laugh. Ami interpreted for her. "Jean-Claude says that if you grow weary of painting, you could work as a go-go dancer."

Jemma rolled her eyes. "That might be a way for a starving artist to eat."

"*Au contraire.* You will never have this worry with your art," Ami said.

Peter winked at his wife. "I think we should take you home, Jemmabeth, before a queue forms to enjoy your company," he said, nodding in the direction of several young men looking her way.

Jean-Claude spoke again.

"He says that it is a good thing that you are leaving for America or he might try to steal you away from your fiancé," Ami said.

"Nope, that's not possible." She gave Jean-Claude a gentle shove.

"We shall miss your cowboy talk," Peter said, "and your élan."

"Well, I'll miss y'all, too, podnuhs," she said, flattening out the vowels.

They tried repeating her words. Jemma laughed so much it hurt.

She was early for an appointment with her

advisor, Louis, the next morning to discuss her progress during the term.

"I asked Louis to meet in my office because I have some exciting news for you," Monsieur Lanier, the Academie director, said as he opened the blinds in his art-filled office. He handed her a magazine.

"*Nouvelle Liberte?*" She stumbled around the words.

"It means New Freedom," Louis said. "It is a very respected publication here. You may not be familiar with it in America."

"I think I've seen it at the newsstand down the street," Jemma said, puzzled.

Monsieur Lanier came around from his chair and sat on his desk near Jemma. He was a small man, balding and fond of playing with his moustache. "My dear," he said, "the magazine bought one of your paintings. They wish to use it as cover art for an issue."

Jemma shrieked. "Fantastic! Which painting?"

"As you might imagine, it is the watercolor of the couple on a bench. The young man is in an American military uniform."

"Oh, the one of Sandy and Martin, my friends. Wait 'til she hears this."

"It is customary to get the artist's permission to reprint the painting, even though

149

they now own it," Louis explained.

"The Academie's legal representative read the document and sees nothing improper about it," Monsieur Lanier said. "It is a mere courtesy to you."

"Sure, I understand. Just show me where to sign. When I was a little girl, I liked looking at the *Saturday Evening Post*'s cover art. They used lots of Norman Rockwell's work. I would draw them, too, and have a completely different perspective than his."

"Ah, but your perspective elicits many emotions, Jemma," Louis said. "It has been an honor to explore your thinking this year. I cannot tell you how much I admire your work. You have been the, how do you say it? Aha — the icing on my cake. I will refer to your art for many years to come with my pupils." Louis kissed her cheeks in the French way.

Monsieur Lanier kissed her hand. "In my years at the Academie, Jemmabeth, I have not enjoyed watching a pupil work as much as I have you. Your passion and concentration are as remarkable as is your gift. We wish you well, but your presence in these halls will be missed. I shall see to it that you are posted several copies of the magazine when it is issued. Enjoy the honor."

She smiled. "I have loved being here. You

have made me reflect and consider other interpretations and techniques. I'll always be grateful to you and your staff. If you ever come to America, please find me. I will have a new name then, Jemmabeth *Chase*." She smiled again. It was the first time she had said it aloud to anybody except Spence, and she liked it.

Her paintings were ready for shipping in Lester's fine crates. Jemma said her good-byes. She took a break from her packing and stood at the window, thinking of her prayerful pilgrimage to Sacré-Coeur almost a year ago. She had begun her time in Paris in sadness, but those days were gone. The Great Plan was with her and with Spencer.

Lizbeth sifted through the mail that had collected while she was gone. The letter that she had hoped to receive was at the bottom of the stack. She read it twice.

Thank you for your interest in this matter. We suggest that you contact your congressman for advice concerning posthumous awards.

So be it. She knew who her congressman was and she would not give up. Just as she sat down to write the letter, Trina appeared

151

at the door to use the telephone.

"I need to call Spencer," Trina said.

"Help yourself, sugar." Lizbeth hid her mail.

Trina dialed the number. "Spencer, what's up? Mama said you came by the house to talk to me. Is Jemma okay?"

"She's great. I just got off the phone with her. How about a burger for lunch? Could you spare a few minutes? I could swing by and pick you up."

"Sure. I have to clean a house at two o'clock, so I'll just wait here at Gram's."

Spencer was his usual charming self, but Trina couldn't help but notice there was a hint of sadness about him, plus he left his cheeseburger half eaten. He was most likely missing his fiancée.

"I need to talk to you about somebody we both know and love," he said.

"Let me guess. Is she out of the country right now?"

"Slightly. Jem wants you to go to design school. She has more money than she's ever had in her life, and she has her heart set on paying your tuition. I don't think you can change her mind. We both know how stubborn she can be. What do you say?"

Trina exhaled. "Wow. This is a surprise.

Well, I have all these ideas in my head, and I'm dying to learn how to make them sell. What can I say? I want to go to design school real bad. Did I talk too much in Paris and sound like a charity case or something? I'm so sorry if I did."

"Nothing like that would enter Jem's head. She wants you to do what you love, like she and I are able to do. Look, Trina, if Jemma didn't do this, I would. She just beat me to it. When money will buy some joy, don't mess with the plan. It will make both of you happy. Let her do it."

Trina's eyes glistened. She looked out her window as the wind gave flight to litter along the train tracks. "Jemma is the best friend I've ever had. I know her pretty well now, and how she feels guilty about being a white girl. But I know also that her heart's in the right place. This is a real sweet thing she's doing. You don't suppose she's one of God's angels, do you?"

Spencer smiled. "I've occasionally wondered that myself, but then you've never seen that temper of hers."

"Nah, but Mama always says that when waters run really deep they're bound to kick up some rocks ever once in a while. I guess that just means she loves you a lot."

He nodded, and Trina thought she saw a

glimmer of a tear in his eye, too.

"So, what's your answer?" he asked.

"That girl just gets crazier all the time, so I'd better take her up on this before we have to put her away." Trina sniffed. "Tell her that I love her, Spence, and I'll make sure her money doesn't go to waste," she said, then flat-out bawled into her napkin.

Jemma's flight was over three hours late. He held her so tight that she knew something was wrong. She drew back to look him in the eye and realized the problem as soon as she did. Her heart sank. She leaned against the wall and cried. He had gotten his draft notice. They sat on the floor at the airport and talked, oblivious to the crowded terminal.

"Why did they jump on you so soon?"

"Who knows, but it doesn't matter now. We can still get married. It's not the end of the world. You can live with me on the base, I think, like Martin and Sandy did."

"You mean until they ship you off to Vietnam?"

"We don't know if that's what will happen."

"Oh, come on, Spence." She didn't mean to sound so sharp. "How long do we have before you go?"

"I have to report for my physical in three weeks."

She pitched a wad of tissues in the trash then turned to him. "I hate this stupid war. It makes no sense. Rats! They don't even call it a war, for Pete's sake."

There was no sparkle in Spencer's eyes. He was suffering enough without her pitching a wall-eyed fit. Willa had told her once to get some backbone. She could, now, and help her sweet man. She just didn't want to lose him like Gram did her boys, but then she didn't even want him to go, period. She eased her arms around him and felt the veins in his neck pulsing against her cheek. This war could not take life from him.

"I have to do this, baby, it's my duty," he whispered.

She could not stand to hear the words. She laid a finger on his lips, then shook her head. They walked to the car, arms full of luggage. She saw the letter on the dashboard and turned away. He drove straight to the river, and they lay under the full moon and searched the starry heavens for consolation. Jemma tried to recall the scriptures she had memorized. The only one she could think of was Psalm 46:10: *Be still, and know that I am God.*

She couldn't let him go to his house and

be away from her. Lizbeth made up the bed in the little side room, and he stayed the night. They talked until Papa's clock chimed three and she woke up again at dawn, her body still in Paris. Everyone else was snoring. She went outside to hear the early morning sounds of late spring in the backyard.

She heard it coming and ran to the tracks. It raced by, blowing its familiar horn. Jemma held down her robe and walked up on the rails to watch the Zephyr disappear into the sunrise. How dare the government take him from her! Spencer would go, too. He would not run off or plead some defense. He would go and let them give him a gun, put him in harm's way, and teach him to kill or be killed. Her dear Spence. She had to choose, though, whether to become a part of his burden in all this, or to be his refuge and joy. She closed her eyes and danced as the wind rustled the tall grass by the tracks.

Trina was ironing Mrs. Lacey's new dress when she saw her. She grinned and slapped the iron down on its stand, ready to squeeze Jemma to death for giving her the money and to say that she had applied to Le Claire, but something told her to leave her friend be. There was no joy in her dance this morning. Trina saw the sadness instead and sat on the porch, hoping it was not what everybody had feared.

Somehow, though, she knew that it was.

CHAPTER 7
WHISPERS

She vowed to buck up and be his joy. After all, they had their wedding and marriage to look forward to. Jemma spent every waking minute with Spencer, drinking up any detail that she thought she might have missed in all years she had known him. She watched him work on the church plans. He was so detail-oriented, like her.

The Bethel Church congregation had approved his design for the building wholeheartedly and offered the muscle to build it. Willa had lifted Spencer off his feet to give him a big smacker kiss, and Brother Cleo, the pastor, wrote Jemma and Spencer a touching letter of appreciation.

Spencer passed his physical and was to report for basic training at Fort Bliss two weeks after the wedding. Jemmabeth would miss another of his birthdays. The wedding was less than a week away. Alex, Julia, and Helene were camping out at Lizbeth's house, as would Jemma's Le Claire friend, Melanie Glazer, when she got there. Rollaway beds and old army cots were in every room. Lester already had Robby at his house, but he was prepared for the second crew that was scheduled to arrive in two days. Jim — Jemma's daddy, cousin Trent, and Uncle Ted — Alex's brother, would stay with Lester, but Uncle Arthur — Julia's husband, wanted to stay at the That'll Do Motel. He thought it would be fun. Julia told him that he would be sleeping alone. The Lillygraces, of course, had reservations in Amarillo. Lizbeth's sisters, the *beth* ladies, would fly in the day of the wedding.

Blabbermouth Sandy was back in town. She threw Jemma a bridal shower for the younger set and another was hosted by some of Alex's friends.

Trina had gotten up her nerve and made an appearance at Sandy's shower. Jemma ignored the whispers and stares as she introduced her newest friend to her lifelong friends. Trina wasn't oblivious to the reserved politeness, but she kept up a good front for Jemma's sake. She had designed the wedding gown and veil from sketches Jemma had drawn in high school. They had gone through every bridal magazine and didn't find anything more perfect. It was waiting for her when she got home.

The only things left to be done were the finishing touches on the bridesmaids' dresses, and Jemma needed to pick up some last-minute items including the reception souvenirs in Amarillo. Buddy B had all the portable equipment he needed for his band, and Spencer had hired a caterer from Amarillo to feed everybody. Jemma planned to make the bouquets herself. She just needed ribbon, florists' wire, and tape. Only the good Lord could provide some decent weather and a windless morning.

Sandy finished her soda and tossed the can in the trash as they cut voile squares for the rice packets. "I hate to tell you this, Jem, but nobody goes to Scotland for their honeymoon," she said. "People go to Padre Island or Colorado or even Hawaii, but not a dreary place like Scotland. Is Spence going to wear a kilt?"

"I think he's all English, but Scotland will be a beautiful place for a honeymoon. I've seen pictures. We're going to a Highland village near the Isle of Skye where Papa's family lived."

Sandy lowered her voice. "Okay, nobody can hear us. You have to tell me what the rules were for 'no fooling around.' "

"Nope. Private."

"Cheezo, you'll be married in three days. Tell."

"I love you, Sandy, but you're a Big Mouth and you don't even realize it."

"I won't tell this. I have my scruples. Just tell me part of it, and I promise I won't say a word to anybody."

"You've had a bad attitude about it ever since we decided to make the promise."

"I just didn't see how you could keep it. What good is a vow if it is doomed before you even make it?"

"Ah, but we lasted to the end, so you were wrong."

"Tell me, or I won't be in the wedding."

"Oh, all right. Swear you will never speak of this again. You can't even tell Marty."

"You don't have to worry about that."

Jemma leaned toward her and whispered in her ear, "I'm never going to tell you because it's just between Spence and me."

Sandy rolled her eyes. "Well, thanks for that news flash. So, you won't even tell your best friend. All I know is that nobody else could've kept whatever those rules were."

"I'm dying for it to be over."

"Never an infraction?"

"Nope."

"Not even with the cowboy? I can't believe

that. Wasn't he like ten years older than you?"

"Yeah, but I've never let anybody break the rules. It's all in the hands. You have to be faster than they are and always on guard."

"Cheezo. I don't know how you did it or why. I hope it was . . . you know . . ."

"Worth it? Yeah, it was. We're moving to a whole new level of love."

Sandy put the last of the rice in the squares. "Maybe it'll help with the fights, and there will be plenty of those, believe me."

"Nah. It will help with the making up," Jemma said, tying the final ribbon.

"Spence was my second choice, remember?" Sandy said with a little too much pride.

"You say that all the time, but I don't remember you picking him second. I think he was your first choice, too."

"Who was your second choice?" Sandy asked, skipping the inference.

"I picked Spencer for all the slots. I can't believe that we will be married in three days. I'm scared now that Uncle Sam has him."

"Marty says Spence will get a desk job or something noncombatant. It's not like they will take an architect and teach him to fly a helicopter or something."

"Good grief, Sandy; I hadn't thought of a helicopter pilot. That has to be the most dangerous job in Vietnam."

"Marty calls it the suicide assignment, but then Marty says that about everything over there."

Jemma wasn't listening. She pushed open the screen door and stood on the porch. A cluster of sparrows darted around the telephone wires, then disappeared into the clear summer sky. She would feel better about everything in only three short days.

Jim, Robby, and Spencer decided to get out of the way by taking a fishing trip to Pearl Lake — a man's day out the day before the wedding. They were to leave before the sun came up and get back before it set, scouts' honor.

Spencer took Jemma for a moonlight picnic at the river the night before. "They are making good progress on the church. Have you been over there?" he asked.

"No, but I'll go tomorrow. I have to run up to Amarillo and pick up some things. Spence, why did you give me a power of attorney?"

"So you could use my bank account for the church or something."

"You aren't having a premonition, are you?"

"Yeah, it's about you and me in a Scottish hotel room."

She giggled. "What's the latest? Are your parents coming or not?"

"Dad says he's coming, and he's going to make a speech, heaven forbid. I don't know about Mother. She could wind up making an embarrassing scene."

"Your mother still hates me for breaking up with you."

"Mother is a pitiful person, Jem."

"Well, nothing can spoil the next two days."

Spencer touched her cheek. She hadn't mentioned the army much since the night he told her, but he knew her better than that. He could see it in her eyes. He only had to keep his hands off her for forty-eight more hours, then their deal was history and she was his, forever. Every dream he ever had was about to come true.

"Come here," she said, lying back on the car. "Spence, if I could, I would erase some things."

"It's okay, baby," he murmured, before she put her fingers on his lips.

"No, hear me out. I would erase in the seventh grade when I said that you just liked me because my daddy was the high school football coach. I would erase running the bulls with Sandy every Fourth of July and dancing with Martin's wild cousin at his graduation party to spite you. I would get rid of that year when I was lost in space thinking that I needed to find out if I really loved you. But most of all, babe, I would wipe out Buddy telling you about Paul right before our disastrous trip to the airport last year. If ever there was a fool on this planet, you are looking at her, and I apologize from the bottom of my heart." She choked up. "You are the only, only one I have ever loved."

He held her. "I just pretend it was research, Jem. You measured me up against the masses and I put them all to shame. Think of it like that."

"I keep it in mind," she said.

Spencer got off the car, humming a little of "In the Still of the Night." She smiled and joined him. They sang and danced like ghost lovers in the moonlight on the banks of the Salt Fork of the Red River.

Her last stop in Amarillo was to pick up the New Testaments from the bookstore. Each one had their wedding date on it. Papa would have approved, and she liked to think he was watching from some fluffy cloud. The Testaments were white with gold foil edges on the pages. Jemma stopped at a filling station just outside Amarillo and bought gas and a Dr Pepper.

After a couple of tries, she got the cantankerous Dodge going, then pulled onto the highway where blasts of Panhandle wind buffeted the car. She hoped the wind would blow itself out and calm down by morning. Across the train tracks, an old green pickup stirred up a cloud of dust as it sped down a dirt road alongside a wheat field. "Try a Little Tenderness" was playing on the radio, so she turned up the volume, then pulled the ring on her drink. The cold liquid spewed everywhere, and she dropped the can.

"Rats," she yelled as it sprayed over her legs like a volcano until the can tipped and rolled under her feet. As she groped around for it, her hair blocked her vision for a fraction of a second. She blew it out of her eyes just as a semi loomed up in front of her. She jerked the steering wheel to get back in her lane, but it was too late.

The eighteen-wheeler careened across the highway, its cab slamming into the Dodge. The sound of the big rig's brakes and crumpling metal blended into her scream.

■ ■ ■ ■

A shiny hubcap spun wildly, then wobbled to a halt on the blacktop just as the truck driver crawled out of his steaming cab. The stench of burned rubber filled the air. He stumbled to his feet and blinked. The other vehicle lay upside down in the ditch with its wheels still rolling. He couldn't see anybody as he scrambled on his knees, shouting for help from the crowd of people who had stopped to look.

"Over here!" a teenage boy yelled, running down the embankment.

The truck driver knew as soon as he looked at her. "Don't touch her 'cause she's hurt bad. I'll get an ambulance."

He ran to his cab and placed a call for help, grabbed a blanket, and went right back to her. She was barely breathing and stone-still. He put the blanket on her real easy and checked to see if all the blood was just from the gash on her head. He found another ugly wound on her arm, not to mention all the smaller cuts and scrapes everywhere else.

"Is she dead?" the young man whispered.

"I don't think so." The driver took off his shirt, ripped it apart, holding the plaid bandages in place with solid pressure on her head and arm. He touched her cheek to get rid of the tiny pieces of dirt and rocks that were stuck there.

The boy stood over them, out of breath and staring at Jemma's face. "Are you hurt, mister? I saw the whole thing. She went right over the line in front of you."

"I've got a couple of scratches . . . nothing like her, though. Man, she's messed up. I need you to double-check inside the car to make sure nobody else is in there," he said.

The kid went straight to the Dodge, his shoes crunching the shards of glass that littered the area. "Nobody," he yelled.

The wind ruffled her auburn hair as it mingled with sunflower petals, now smashed and saturated with blood. There were dozens of little white books strewn between her and the car. Some of them were open, their pages flipping and glinting in the wind.

The truck driver was feeling light-headed. "Bring me one of them little books, would you, young feller?" he said to the kid.

It was a New Testament with the next day's date stamped in gold on the cover. He had one similar to it that he kept in the truck. He took a breath, then leaned down close to her, whispering his favorite verse in her ear. It just seemed like a good idea.

Buddy B stood on the porch, his face drained of color and his tow truck still running in Lester's driveway. He blew out his breath when Julia opened the door. "Ma'am, I need to talk to the toughest person in this family."

"Let's say you're looking at her right now," she said, her mouth going dry.

Tears trailed down his cheeks. "It's our Jemmabeth, ma'am. She's been in one horrible wreck outside Amarillo. And, well, things look real bad."

Chapter 8
A Lit Candle

The Golden Triangle Hospital was sixty-eight miles from Chillaton. Julia Billington drove it in thirty-five minutes with a car full of silent passengers. Sheriff Ezell, his patrol car lights flashing, had to step on the gas to stay in front of her and the others. The group filled the emergency room waiting area. Trent and Ted headed to Pearl Lake to break the news to the rest of the men.

Every time a door opened, they all rose up like a choir in case it was somebody who knew something. No tears yet, not even from Alex. She wouldn't sit down, but paced, as though suspended in a surreal nightmare. A nurse came out and told them that it might be another half hour before they could talk to anyone.

Lizbeth stood at the bank of windows, staring vacantly at a group of crows pecking at the lawn. She had memorized "The Raven" by Edgar Allan Poe in her high school English class and recited it in an assembly. She had learned it because Rachel Moore said the poem was too long for anybody to memorize, but she had done it. Sometimes the lines crept into her thoughts, like wayward sheep. *And my soul from out that shadow that lies floating on the floor shall be lifted — nevermore!*

The Lord would surely hear her prayers and lift this shadow from Jemmabeth. She herself could not stand to lose another piece of her heart to fill an early grave.

The doctor came to them at last. Lester stood close so as not to miss a word, as he molded and remolded the brim of his hat.

"Who is the next-of-kin here?" the doctor asked in a crisp manner.

Alex moved forward. "I'm her mother," she said, trying to read the doctor's face.

"Your daughter is alive, but she has lost a considerable amount of blood. She is undergoing a transfusion and a second one may be necessary. Our gravest concern is that she has a fractured skull and is not responding to stimulation at this point. We are doing all that we can for her."

Alex shuddered and held on to Lester's arm to keep her balance. "May I see her?"

"Her face is swollen, she has multiple abrasions, and we had to shave part of her

171

head to examine and treat the injuries. Perhaps you should wait. The next twenty-four hours are critical."

"I want to see her," Alex said firmly.

"Very well. We'll send for you."

"I need to come with her," Julia announced. "I'm her great-aunt."

"Only two from the immediate family may come and only for five minutes."

Julia stiffened. "She can't go alone. Look at her."

"Only this once." The doctor disappeared into the emergency room complex. Collective sighs spread across the room.

"This just can't be." Lester blew his nose and headed outside.

Buddy B arrived with more of the wedding party. Trina knew from the hushed group how bad things were. Willa dropped in a chair and cried. It was as though the traffic light had turned green because everybody let loose. Sandy sat away from the group, her streaked makeup even paler in the hospital lights.

The Lillygraces kept near their daughter, not knowing how to console her except for cups of water that Robert Lillygrace relentlessly provided. The ICU nurse led Alex and Julia out of the waiting room and down the shiny hallway to the room where Jemma lay, comatose. They put on surgical masks and went in. Alexandra took one quick glance and fainted. Julia tried to hold on, but she staggered out of the room as soon as she entered. They should have waited like the doctor said.

The sheriff pulled into the emergency entryway again, this time with Jim right behind. Spencer jumped out of the moving car, leaving the door open, and burst into the waiting room. Trina threw her arms around him, but everyone else had moved to the Intensive Care area. He listened, wild-eyed, as she told them everything the doctor had reported. Then he turned to the ICU desk. "I need to see Jemmabeth Forrester. I am her fiancé."

The nurse got Jemma's chart and shook her head. "Hon, you don't want to see her. It'll break your heart. Just let us take care of her."

Jim and Robby stood next to Spencer. "I'm her father, and we want to see her now, if at all possible," Jim insisted.

The nurse tapped her pencil on the desk, looking at Spencer. "Let me check, but the boy's too young." Trina took Robby's hand, and they left.

Jim and Spencer still smelled of fish and bait. The nurse came back and had them scrub up and put on masks and gowns. "Only five minutes, gentlemen," she said and took them to her.

They stood by the bed, holding on to one another, weeping into their masks. It was plain to see that she was full of tubes and monitors that couldn't be covered up with sheets. He closed his eyes and pictured this beautiful body moving like silk when she danced. He would look nowhere but her face, so swollen that he could not see any part of her eyes. There were tubes in her nose and in her battered mouth. Crimson fluid oozed into her from a bag overhead and wheezing from a respirator filled the room. The wavy hair that had tickled his nose the night before had been partially shaved into a grotesque Halloween wig. This could not be his Jem because she was going to be his wife in twenty-four hours. He swallowed the urge to throw up.

"Is she going to make it?" Jim whispered to the nurse.

"She's in a real bad way, hon. I'd be calling the prayer hotline if I were you. Your time's up now. Go get some rest. It will be a long shot for this child to live through the night."

"May I wait in the hallway?" Spencer asked.

"No, sugar," she said, looking into his gray eyes. "The rules in here are real strict. We need to move fast sometimes and you'd be in the way." She lowered her voice. "I'll come talk to you on my break, okay? I'll watch her real good." She patted his shoulder.

"Could we say a prayer before we go?" Jim asked.

The nurse hesitated. "Hurry, then. You really do need to leave."

Jim put his arm around Spencer and prayed aloud for his baby girl. He didn't make it through the prayer, and Spencer couldn't finish it for him. It just hung in the air without an "Amen."

Jim left, ashen-faced, but Spencer lingered. He touched his fingers to hers, and his eyes followed the delicate path of veins on her arms. Her sweet, stubborn heart was doing its best to keep her with him. He longed to see her smile like she did in grade school. It was her special grin that always made his heart jump.

He went straight to the nurses' desk. "Jemmabeth Forrester and I are the same blood type. I want to donate the blood she uses."

"We use the blood bank for emergencies, but we never turn down donations," the nurse said.

He looked her in the eye. "This is important to me."

"I'll try, sir, but I can't guarantee it." The nurse left him standing at her desk, but he wasn't moving until he got an answer. He pulled out his wallet and removed his Red Cross blood donation card. The nurse came back with a form.

"If you want to be a directed donor for your fiancée, we'll need proof of your type," she said. Spencer gave her the card and filled out the form. She called the hospital blood bank. He leaned against the wall until a young woman about Jemma's age came to get him. He lay on the table and watched the bag turn red. It was the only thing he could give her for now.

About midnight, the ICU nurse came out. Nobody had left.

"Her heart signs are steady and the second transfusion is underway. Other than that, you will have to talk with the doctor."

"Has she moved?" Alex asked.

The nurse shook her head. "No, sweetie, that's not happening."

"Does she . . ." Spencer stopped.

The nurse smiled at him. "She has your blood in her veins, son."

"May I see her?" he asked.

176

"Let me talk with my supervisor," she said and disappeared through the swinging doors.

"I don't see how you can stand to look at her, Spence." Alex put her head on his chest. "I'm not sure I can go back."

"Do you need me to go with you, son?" Jim asked. "I think I can."

"I would like to go by myself, if that's okay. I need to suffer with her," Spencer mumbled.

Lizbeth held Robby's head in her lap. He had cried himself to sleep. It wasn't this way for her boys. She didn't even know they were hurt until they were gone. Jemmabeth was not going to die. Lizbeth could feel the Lord in this place.

Brother Cleo and his wife came in the room, his booming voice attracting everyone's attention. The atmosphere changed to one of hope as soon as he organized them into a circle and led a hand-holding prayer. Lizbeth watched Jemma's Lillygrace grandparents clasp the hands next to them with awkward reluctance. Jemma would have appreciated that scene.

Brother Cleo's voice demanded that even the angels listen. "Almighty God, we come to You as sinners, pardoned through the blood of Jesus. Hear our prayer of intercession for the life of Jemmabeth Forrester. She is a worthy child, Lord, and we look to You to spare her to us, full of joy, as she was before, if it could be Thy holy will. Be to us like a lit candle in this cavern of anguish. Amen and amen."

The nurse motioned to Spencer, and the room fell silent again, as everyone considered what he would have to endure. He scrubbed up and put on the mask. She hadn't changed. He held her fingers this time and bent to kiss them. His blood would make her stronger. She would live and smile at him again. He kept his eyes on her face because it would be a sacrilege to look at the rest of her like this, plus it would make her mad, and it would be breaking their promise. He squeezed her fingers, hoping otherwise, but knowing that she couldn't respond.

Her fingers were slender and delicate, like Lizbeth's. They were stained now with antiseptic solution. Since the third grade, they were always stained with bits of paint. He related the smell of paint and turpentine with her, but she also smelled like flowers. This was where he wanted to be, not down the hall where he couldn't tell if her fingers were warm. He shouldn't have been at Pearl Lake. He should have gone with her to

Amarillo. He was probably laughing with her daddy and her little brother when something cracked her skull and stole her away from him.

"Time to go now," a new nurse said, checking the monitors and changing things around. "Is she your wife?"

He shook his head. "She would have been today."

The group remained all night, crumpled up in chairs and on the floor. The Lillygraces had gone to their hotel in the early hours. Only Spencer and Alex were awake all night. He saw Jemma every time they would let him. No changes, but she was still alive.

Robby came to sit in his lap. "Is Jem going to die?" he asked, looking up at Spencer with eyes just like Papa's.

Spencer took a breath. "Only God knows that. We can only ask Him to see things our way."

"Why would He take her to heaven?"

"His ways are not our ways."

"Probably so she could paint stuff for Him. Did you see the monkey she painted me for my birthday? It's so cool. He looks like he is gonna jump on you."

The doctor appeared and everyone stirred at her voice. "Things are stable for the first twelve hours. The tests show that there is swelling in her brain, which is normal for a fracture of this type. We are watching now for blood clots or any leakage of brain fluid, which would require surgery."

Spence did not like the way she talked about Jem in a textbook tone. Her incredible brain would not leak.

"Has she moved?" Alex asked again.

"No, she isn't responding, but that is to be expected in this situation. I know that seems frightening to you, but the most important thing right now is that we are aware of complications. I suggest that all of you go home and get some rest. We will give her the best of care," she said in her monotone.

"Ma'am, many of these fine folks are here for her weddin'. Do you think there's gonna be a buryin' instead?" Lester asked when no one else would.

The doctor blinked and looked at Spencer, realizing the situation. Her voice softened. "If there are no complications by tomorrow evening, I think she'll survive."

"So there's hope. I'm obliged, ma'am," Lester said. "Praise the Lord."

Nobody took the doctor's advice. They did take turns going to a nearby hotel room that Julia rented just to shower and nap, and they rotated to the cafeteria for food. Spencer wouldn't go anywhere and he couldn't sleep. Alex finally went to see her with Jim and didn't faint. Lizbeth wouldn't go, but she and Brother Cleo kept a prayer vigil in a far corner of the room. Carrie arrived about noon with her boyfriend and stuck with Trina.

Melanie Glazer had not seen Jemma in months and was prepared for a joyous occasion. Instead, she took her violin to the cafeteria and played for an hour to honor her friend. The diners had no idea a world-class musician was entertaining them. They just knew she was incredibly good, and that her long red hair was like the flame atop an exquisite candle when she played. She visited with each member of the family, giving special attention to Spencer, whom she had never met.

"Jemma was so worried that you were in love with someone else last year," she said.

"I could never love anybody but her," Spencer said, his voice raspy.

"She's a creature of the arts, and we don't think like other people. Jem has been so good to me, and I've really missed her. I believe it will all work out."

"Do you?" Spencer asked, looking up at such optimism.

"I do." She could see why Jemma didn't want to lose him. She saw honest compassion and uncommon goodness, despite this torment, in his eyes. Such qualities had to stem from a heart overflowing with love.

Lizbeth kept a curious eye on Alex's parents. She thought they might break down and cry like everyone else, but not so. She herself was well acquainted with hiding pain, and wished she had the nerve to talk to them about it. Instead, she went to sit with Lester, who tapped his foot and stared out the windows at a man mowing the hospital lawn.

"Lester, I need to have a word with you."

He stirred in his chair and straightened himself. "Help yourself, Miz Liz. Is there news about Jemmer?"

"No, but I want to apologize to you for the way I acted about your chinchilla business last year. It was downright mean of me to poke fun at you about it. Will you forgive me?"

"Oh Miz Liz, no need to ask that. Didn't never take off anyhow, did it? I kinda liked the critters, though, and I might could've made me some spendin' money if that twister hadn't scattered 'em all over town. It's just as well. I ain't sure I could've stole their hides off 'em anyway. I heard just the other day that one showed up in the basement of the Catholic Church. Don't that beat all, considerin' my feelings toward the pope?"

"You've been a fine neighbor, Lester. I know that Jemma loves you, and I'll be sure she knows that you stayed up here all this time, worrying about her. You're a sweet man." She patted his arm and went back to her seat.

Lester blushed. Maybe he was too hasty when he sent off for the mail-order bride. He should've heard back from his application by now but hadn't for some reason. None of that foolishness mattered now that Jemmerbeth was at death's door.

He held on to the arms of his chair as he stood and stretched. He crossed the room and got a drink from the water fountain. A Mexican family nearby bowed together in prayer, most likely over their own loved one.

Life is full of worries. Don't matter who you are, Lester thought. He had a sudden urge to talk to young Mr. Chase.

Spencer nodded off and awoke with a gasping breath. He looked around the room. Carrie was in a far corner of the room talking with Trina. She had avoided him since their initial conversation, but he was too drained to get up and see why. He sat on the floor, watching the clock.

Lester laid his hand on Spencer's shoulder. "Son, I wonder if you mind taking a little stroll?"

"I don't know if I can, Lester. I'm not feeling too hot. Could you sit with me instead?"

"Sure thing." Lester didn't know when was the last time he'd sat on the floor, but he couldn't turn down this pitiful young man. He eased his way down beside Spence. "Son, I wanted to share a tale with you that I'm hopin' will give you a ray of sunshine."

Spencer rubbed his unshaven face and looked at Lester. "I'd appreciate some sunshine right now."

"Well, sir, you know I sure liked Cam Forrester. He was about the best man I ever knew. Had them crinkly blue eyes and a big old belly laugh. He was right proud of Jemmer, as he should've been. Him and me was sitting on my porch one day and he come hence to tellin' me about a dream he had the night before. Now, mind you this was before y'all was in high school, probably around '58 or so. Anyhow, in Cam's dream, the president of the U. S. of A. asked Jemmerbeth to paint his official picture. She did, and it was hung in the capitol buildin' way up to D.C."

"That's a great story," Spencer said.

"Jemma could do it, too, if she gets through this. Who was the president?"

"Well, sir, that's the spooky part. When he told me, I didn't think much of it. Truth of the matter is, we had a good laugh over it."

"Why's that?"

"The president that she painted was that actor feller, Ronald Reagan, the one who just got to be the governor of California. In 1958 he was still making them silly drive-in movies. Don't that beat all?"

A chill spread over Spencer. "Papa was a man of God, Lester. Maybe his dream meant more than he realized."

Just before one in the morning, Carrie McFarland rolled over to a sleeping Spencer with Philip, her boyfriend, at her side. They put a blanket from a nearby chair over him. Carried tucked in the corners as best she could. Then they left.

Spence woke up a couple of hours later and scrambled to the nurses' station, behind the sacred doors. His heart was pounding. "Anybody here?" he asked.

A familiar nurse appeared. "You aren't supposed to be in this area, young man."

"I have to know how she is. I fell asleep."

"She is the same — no better, no worse."

"May I go in?" Spencer asked.

The nurse sighed. He was a hurting man and she had seen them before, but this was such a heart-wrenching case. All the staff was talking about it.

"I tell you what. Let me get somebody to take you to the hospital locker room. You take a shower, put on some surgical scrubs, have a little breakfast, and maybe I'll let you see her. You're a sight right now. If she were to wake up, you'd scare her back into a coma."

Spencer was in no condition to argue. He did as he was told. When he came back, she smiled. "Now, she doesn't look any better, but it's been almost thirty-six hours and there are no complications yet, so that's good. You scrub up and get that mask on."

The nurse was right. In fact, Jemma looked worse in some places. There were purple bruises on her face that he hadn't noticed before. He held her hand in his and stroked her palm. She was so ticklish there. Maybe the next time she would respond to it. He went back to his spot by the door even though his tailbone hurt.

Jim came over, yawning. "I'm going in. Any change?"

Spencer shook his head and looked around the room. It was like an airport with major flight delays. Even Willa was flat-out on the floor, two blankets covering her hefty frame.

The wedding seemed so frivolous now. They should have eloped; at least that way he could have kept her safe. Her uncle Ted and Trent were helping Buddy B get the wedding stuff returned to the rental places. They had such good friends and family.

"Spence?" Trina whispered.

His body jerked to attention. "What? Has something happened?"

"No, no. I just wanted to sit here."

Spencer nodded. "How are you doing?"

She started to say something but choked up. Spencer put his arm around her.

Jim passed through the waiting room and headed straight outside.

Spencer turned to Trina. "Follow me," he whispered. He held out his hand and she took it, glancing around as he pushed open the doors that led down the hallway toward Jemma's room. No nurses were in sight. She stayed right behind him, her pulse thumping against her temples. Spencer pulled a mask out of his shirt pocket and handed it to her. She put it on and entered the room. Unprepared for what she saw, Trina reached for the side rail of the bed. She touched Jemma's hand just as a nurse appeared in the doorway.

"Hey, only immediate family or special permission. Out."

The nurse's sharp tone drew a response from Spencer. "I'm sorry. It was my idea."

Trina glanced at Spencer and turned to the nurse. "I'm her sister," she said through the mask.

The nurse snickered. "Oh really, and I'm the pope's daughter."

Trina looked her in the eye. "I'm adopted."

A Texas State Trooper was in the waiting room when they returned. A nurse pointed to Alex and Jim, but Spencer met him at the desk. "Sir, are you here about Jemmabeth Forrester?"

The officer removed his hat. "I just need to ask a few questions. Are you related to her?"

"She is my fiancée. We were to be married last night."

"I'm sorry, son." He got out his pen and clipboard. "Let's have a seat over here."

The officer gave them the details of the accident, according to witnesses. He also told them about the truck driver, his kindness, and the first aid he administered to Jemma. Jim told him to take the old Dodge to the junkyard and send him the bill. He never wanted to see it again.

The Lillygraces came to say good-bye. Alex had asked for special permission for them to see Jemma.

"I cannot, Alexandra, I have a bad heart, you know, and I don't think I should risk it," her father said. Alex hadn't heard much about his bad heart until this.

"Mother, would you go with me?" she asked.

Her mother cleared her throat. "Yes, I'll go," she said, surprising them all. "I am quite fond of Jemmabeth."

They put on the required apparel. Alex and her mother held hands as they approached the room. The nurse gave them the usual warning.

"Oh, my sweet girl." Catherine Lillygrace covered her face with her hands and wept. When it was time for them to leave, she kissed her fingers and moved them across Jemma's arm. Alex could not remember the last time her mother had let anybody see her cry.

Catherine hugged everybody in the waiting room like she meant it. "She's going to be all right. Look at all these good people praying for her," she said.

Then they left in a waiting taxi.

The group began to shrink. People had to go about their lives. Jemma remained the same and Spencer stayed at the hospital, as did Alex. Ted and Trent took the older ones back to Chillaton, even though Lester didn't want to leave, and Lizbeth would only go to change clothes.

Carrie and Philip came to the hospital before flying back to Houston, and she went straight to Spencer with a long hug. "Spence, I'm sorry I didn't talk much to you the other day, but I didn't know what to say. I was so upset and it broke my heart to see you in such pain. You know how I feel about Jemma. She was my salvation, and I owe her for having a semi-normal life." She gestured toward her boyfriend. "I want you to meet my own long-awaited Prince Charming, Mr. Philip Bryce. Phil, this is my first Prince Charming, Spencer Chase."

Philip was a slight man with thick reddish hair and green eyes. He looked at Spencer and smiled. "First Prince, huh? Should I be jealous?"

"He has been in my bedroom more than once and carried me up the stairs to get there," Carrie added.

Spencer smiled weakly. "Carrie and Jemma say a lot of things just for the dickens of it, Philip. You'd better straighten him out about that, Carrie, or else he might want to have a duel or something."

A nurse, accompanied by a heavy-set, black cowboy, interrupted. "Excuse me. This man would like to talk to Miss Forrester's family."

The cowboy put out his hand. "Name's Joe Cross. I'm the driver of the truck that hit your girl. I'm sure sorry, but there just wasn't nothin' I could do. She came right at me." Cuts on his face and arms were stitched up, and he had a bandage on one hand.

"We're sorry, too," Alex said. "The trooper told us that you took care of Jemma until the ambulance got there. I can never thank you enough for that. Did she say anything to you?"

"No, ma'am, she was out when I got to her. How's she doin' now?"

"She's in a coma," Spencer said.

"Man, I knew it was bad. I was afraid she'd broke her neck. At least that's not the case. I brought some things that I thought you folks might want. I'll go get 'em."

He brought in a couple of large paper bags. "Yesterday must have been a special event for somebody."

"It was supposed to be our wedding day,"

Spencer said quietly.

"Well, that explains it. Bless her heart. These were scattered around the wreck, and I know how people will just steal things . . . it's kinda sick like, but they will. These looked important, so I gathered up all I could. Listen, I've got to hit the road now. I'm headin' home to Sweetwater. God bless."

Neither Spencer nor Alex wanted to look inside the bags. Carrie rolled her chair over to one and reached inside. She held up a dusty little New Testament stamped with the wedding date. She quickly replaced it. The second bag held more of the same, but there was also a leather-bound King James Bible, still in its box, on top. Carrie reached for Philip's hand and read the inscription.

To Spencer from Jemmabeth
July 23, 1967
Philippians 4:13

Spencer took the Bible from her and traced his finger over the gold letters. He took it with him to his spot on the floor and read the scripture. "I can do all things through Christ which strengtheneth me." It was appropriate now, even though she was probably thinking about Vietnam when she placed the order. He went to the nurses' desk and asked if he could go in. He had to touch her.

CHAPTER 9
THE HARDEST THING

After a week, they moved her to a room crammed with flowers. Even The Judge had sent roses. Spencer's father brought an elaborate arrangement in person and hugged Alex, albeit a little too long for her comfort. Alex slept in a recliner and Spencer was in a sleeping bag on the floor. Jemma looked somewhat better. The swelling was down and they had cleaned her hair, but she was still unresponsive. Spencer didn't know how he could leave her, but he did know that he would be on some kind of military transport in nine days to report for basic training.

"Jem," he said, close to her ear, "are you in there, baby? Let me know. Hit me, yell, wrinkle your nose, do anything." He had tried so many things, but he again massaged and kissed her hands, tickled her nose — nothing worked.

Alex sang to her and read works by her

favorite poet, Emily Dickinson.

"She will come around when her brain is ready, but it is good for you to keep trying," the doctor had said. Alex and Spencer suspected that she was giving them busy-work. Jim and Robby came to take Alex out for supper since they were leaving for home, Flagstaff, the next morning.

Spencer held Jemma's hand, and just for himself, started humming "Candy Man," their song, the one that she could dance to like a wild woman. He started out low, but closed the door, took her hand again, and sang loud enough for anybody to hear him. He sang it three times and started on the fourth when he felt her fingers curl inside his own. His heart leaped.

He slipped his little finger into the curl and let her squeeze it. "Do it again, Jem," he said, and she did.

He pressed the call button and a nurse came running. Jemma did it for her, too. He tried her other hand and she did it again, even though the doctor had warned there might be some nerve damage where the lacerations were on her arm. Spencer was half crazy with joy.

Her folks were thrilled, too. Robby drew a happy face in the palm of her hand, making her fingers twitch. Jim talked to his daughter alone for a while, then Alex walked them to the car to say good-bye. It was an encouraging sendoff. While they were gone, Spencer did what he'd wanted to do since he left to go fishing; he kissed her lips. He thought he heard her make a sound. "Jemma, it's me. I love you." He saw her eyes move under her lids. He called for the nurse again. A couple of them came and checked her out.

"These are all good signs, right?" Spencer asked. "She's waking up?"

"They are good signs, but it is a slow process," one of the nurses said. "Take it a day at a time."

"You don't know my girl. She's quick," he said. "She was all-state in basketball."

Alex came back as the nurses were leaving. "What's happened?"

Spencer opened his mouth to answer, but froze. Jemma was looking right at him.

"Jemmabeth!" Alex screamed.

Spencer walked around the room, and she followed him with her eyes. That was it for the night, but what a night. They couldn't turn off the light as long as her eyes were open. Just before midnight, she began mumbling in her sleep. It was the most beautiful sound they'd ever heard.

The scriptures started a couple of days later, and Lizbeth was there when it happened. The first was the inscription on his Bible and she repeated it like a religious robot, as well as Psalm 37. Then the others came like a waterfall. "Let not your heart be troubled, neither let it be afraid."

There was no emotion, just the Word of God. "Be still, and know that I am God" was a particular favorite. "Blessed are the pure in heart, for they shall see God . . . My brethren, count it all joy when you fall into various trials, knowing that the testing of your faith produces patience."

Lizbeth smiled. She knew what her girl was doing, and now it was healing her broken head. "If thy whole body therefore be full of light, having no part dark, the whole shall be full of light, as when the bright shining of a candle doth give thee light."

In the midst of all the scriptures, she whispered his name, and Spencer cried like he was six years old again when he heard it. On the fifth day since she first opened her eyes, the doctor sent her home. She could move her head and say "yes" and "no" when asked a question. She was still taking medication and looked ghastly, but they let her go.

Spencer's dad drove up to get him. It was the second nice thing that he'd done since the accident. Spencer didn't say much until they approached the spot where the wreck had been. "I need to stop here, Dad."

Deep ruts remained in the ditch. Spencer plucked a strand of ribbon that was caught on a barbed wire fence, then walked around the area where he thought the Dodge might have come to rest. He sat on a protruding stone, trying to get a sense of peace for all that had happened to her beside this nondescript asphalt. A dark-stained area near a clump of droopy sunflowers caught his attention. He squatted beside it, then went to his dad's car and opened the trunk. There wasn't much there, except a roadside tool kit. He opened it and took out an ice scraper.

The window hummed as Max opened it. "What's wrong, son? Do you need some help?"

Spencer shook his head.

Max watched his boy go down the embankment and get on his knees, pounding the ice scraper into the dirt. Spencer worked for fifteen minutes making a hole and burying the dark soil in it. It finally dawned on Max what his only child was doing. He hadn't cried since his own father died, but he let the tears come on down his face. He would have to have a heart of bricks to have done otherwise.

With only a few days of freedom left, Spencer slept on the couch at Lizbeth's house. Trina sat with Jemma through the first night. The next day, Jemma drank seventeen big jelly glasses of water and had spent most of the day with the covers drawn up over her head. Alex was worried and called the hospital. The doctor assured her that such behavior was not abnormal after a brain injury. All that water had to be dealt with, so she was back and forth to the bathroom, but at least she was walking, with help.

She became obsessed with her hair, and repeatedly braided it, then unbraided it. Alex combed it as best she could, but her thick hair needed to be properly washed and she wouldn't be still long enough to let them. They were all in her bedroom when she suddenly perched herself on the side of the bed, then stood, wavering in the process. Everybody sprang into action. She ignored them and braided her hair.

"Let not your heart be troubled, neither let it be afraid," she said.

Spencer was exhausted.

"How on earth are you going to start basic training like this?" Alex asked.

"I don't know. Maybe they'll send me home," he said.

Jemma stood again and took a couple of steps toward the door. They let her go. She ran her hands over the door and spoke, her head resting on it. "Each day I go to my studio full of joy; in the evening, when obliged to stop because of darkness, I can scarcely wait for the morning to come . . . My work is not only a pleasure, it has become a necessity. No matter how many other things I have in my life, if I cannot give myself to my dear painting, I am miserable."

Spencer stared at her, a shiver running through his body. It was a quote by a French artist, Bouguereau, from an art history paper she had written two years earlier. She drank more water and stared at the glass as though it were a new concept, turning it over in her hands. What was going on in that precious head of hers? He had hoped that she would at least recognize him before he had to leave, but that was wishful thinking on his part. She unbraided her hair and quoted Emily Dickinson.

He went for a walk. He was going about this all wrong. How could he forget that her first love was her art, and, most likely, her second was to dance, third would have to be the Zephyr. He was lucky to even be on the list.

Spencer and Alex led her to the alley and stood waiting with her, at sunrise.

Jemma played with her hair until she heard the horn zipping past the station. She stopped for a second, then went back to her braiding. As the Zephyr approached, Jemma took them off guard and bolted up to the tracks on her own. They grabbed for her, but she was gone, adrenaline propelling each step. She stopped short of the rail bed.

Spencer was there, too, his feet firmly planted and his arms around her. She lifted her chin and closed her eyes. Spencer had never been this close to a moving train. He held on to Jemma like a child on the edge of a cliff. Her mouth curved into a half smile as the last car had passed.

"Jem?" Spencer asked, hoping for a further response.

She opened her eyes and looked down the tracks to the fast disappearing train, then went back to her hair.

"What did she say?" Alex shouted from the alley.

"Nothing," Spencer said.

They put her to bed, thinking she might be tired from the run to the tracks, but she was out as soon as they turned their backs.

She went to the living room and sat in Papa's chair, rubbing the cut velvet arms.

"I think this is progress," Lizbeth said. "What if we showed her some of her art?" Lizbeth guided Jemma's fingers over the grand *trompe l'oeil* she had painted in the kitchen and over the painting of the cardinals in the good bedroom while Spencer raced to his house and got Papa's portrait that she had made for him when he was in Florence. He went to Trina's, too, and got the painting of the three friends as children and brought it back, along with Trina. Jemma was asleep by then. He paced the floor under the empathetic eyes of the women.

"What if this doesn't work?" Alex asked.

"Play 'Candy Man.' If anything could bring her back, that would be it," Trina suggested.

Jemma stirred in her sleep, bringing them to the foot of her bed. She sat up and drank a glass of water. Spencer brought the paintings to her. She reached for the one of Papa and felt the canvas like a sightless person, then gazed past them to the curtains waving in the breeze. "Let not your heart be troubled, neither let it be afraid," she said and covered her head with the quilt again.

Spencer, for lack of a better idea, stuck

his head under the quilt with her. They all heard the faintest giggle before she conked out again.

Spencer emerged from the quilt. "At least she can laugh," he said and went to the couch. "Maybe she would like to see the cardinals in the pecan tree."

When she woke up, he led her to the trunk of the old tree and pointed out a red bird hopping amongst the leaves. Jemma never even looked up; she was too fascinated by the tree bark.

Sandy came over to join the vigil. "She and I used to say that amnesia was fake, something created by desperate soap opera writers. I wish I could make a movie of this because she won't believe it," she said to Spencer. "If it weren't so pathetic, it would be hilarious."

He drilled her with a hard look, then went out to the porch swing and sat with his head in his hands.

Trina joined him. "Spence, Brother Cleo would like to pray over her, but only if you want him to."

"Sure, tell him that would be nice. Jem would like that."

"I'm serious about the 'Candy Man' dance. I'll make everybody leave. Jemma loves dancing with you. Have you tried letting her paint or draw?"

Spencer sat up. "I should have thought of that. Her art supplies are all in her suitcase, ready to take on the honeymoon." He went inside and got out the brushes and watercolors she had so carefully packed for the honeymoon. Jemma was back in Papa's chair, running her hands over the arms again. Spencer set up her easel and a sheet of watercolor paper. He filled the little containers with water and mixed the colors as he had seen her do so many times.

"Jemmabeth?" he asked. "Would you like to paint?"

She looked at him, expressionless. "Yes."

Alex put the paintbrush in her hand and held the big palette for her. Jemma stood in front of the blank paper. Spencer guided her hand to a rosy red on the palette and dipped the brush, then took her hand to the paper. Jemma turned her gaze on the brush that was in her hand. She moved it in a circle on the paper and stared at her creation. Dipping the brush first into the water, then another color, she filled in the circle with geometric shapes. She sat back in Papa's chair, still holding the brush.

"It's the kaleidoscope window." Spencer smiled at her, even though it looked like the work of a preschooler.

Lizbeth left the room. She could not bear to see her Jemma like that. The artist who had won a coveted fellowship in one of the world's best art schools was painting like she did when she was three years old. Lizbeth was glad that Cam at least did not have to suffer through this ordeal. He would have been devastated. Jemmabeth would come out of this; she had survived that wreck for a reason.

The kitchen had overflowed with casseroles and baked goods from folks all over the county since the accident. Lizbeth had given most of them to Willa for distribution at the Bethel church. The flower garden and home place mural that she had painted on the kitchen walls, the *trompe l'oeil,* served as a daily reminder of Jemma's spirit.

Lizbeth sighed, then went through the mail. She hadn't paid it any mind since the accident. There were so many cards for the family and a large package from Jemma's school in Paris. She took it to Alex, who promptly opened it and caught her breath. It contained several copies of a French magazine with a perfect likeness of Sandy and Martin on the cover. Alex gave a copy to Spencer, who took it to the hollyhock patch, where he stayed for a while.

Spencer walked to the tracks. Jemma had such an affinity for them. He didn't even try to understand it. Everything she did fascinated him. Melanie had said it well. *"She is a creature of the arts, and we don't think like other people."* God had spared her life, and it was selfish of him to want more at this point. The doctor had said it could be a long process, so maybe he should be praying that there was no permanent damage. She had to love him, under all those scriptures and quotes.

"Spencer. How's our girl doing?" Brother Cleo's voice carried across the tracks.

"Come on over," Spencer said, waving.

They went to Jemma's room. She was out from under the quilt, but braiding again. Everybody but Spencer sat at the kitchenette. He paced around the backyard.

Brother Cleo opened the door after a full hour had gone by. Nobody knew what to expect. They did not expect a miracle, only encouragement.

Alex hugged him. "Thank you."

"She's a sweet child with a heart for the Lord, and He's gonna take care of her. She sure does like to quote the Scriptures. You call me anytime, and I'll drive down from

Amarillo. Now, I mean that."

Sandy went to get Spencer. "You need some rest. They're going to eat you alive at boot camp."

"So be it. I won't leave her," he said stiffly.

"Look, with Soap Opera Amnesia, Jem won't know whether you are here are not. You might as well be sleeping on your own bed and having your last bit of freedom. Go on home. When she gets well, you can say you were here the whole time."

Spencer stared her in the eye. "Sandra, now is not the time for your flippant attitude. I know you're hurting like the rest of us, so just cut it out." He walked past her and into the house.

Sandy went behind the little building that Jemma's grandpapa always called his "car house" and cried. Not because Spencer had chewed her out — she probably deserved that — but because her best friend was not right and her own life was about as far from perfect as it could get.

Spencer sat with Jemma, reading a depressing book he had bought about brain injuries. It put him to sleep. He woke up to see Alex and Trina in the corner of the room, setting up Jemma's old portable stereo and a few records.

Alex came to his chair and whispered in his ear. "You go eat supper. I'll stay with her. When she wakes up, see if she'll dance with you, okay?" Alex patted his arm. It was his last night in Chillaton. He had to be in Amarillo at eight sharp the next morning.

An hour went by before they appeared in the kitchen, headed to the bathroom. Spencer went to her room to wait. Alex brought her back and closed the door.

Jemma sat on the side of the bed. Her old chenille robe was knotted at her waist and she was barefooted. She undid her braids and redid them. Spencer sighed and sat next to her. He was dying to kiss her.

"Jem, would you like to dance with me?" He moved a stray lock of hair out of her eyes.

"Yes," she said in a monotone.

He put on "True Love's Ways." He helped her up and put his arms around her. She was so thin and moved like a junior-high boy at his first dance, not exactly the satiny smooth girl who could dance all night. The song ended and she stood there, seemingly unaware of anything. The next record dropped. It was their song. At the first notes of the harmonica, she looked right at him, like she did at the Zephyr when it moved down the tracks. His heart jumped. He held his hand out to her and she took it.

They danced out of sync with the rhythm, but at least she moved and kept her eyes on him. When the song finished, they stared at each other until Spencer had to look away. She was sweating, and the water pitcher was empty. He opened the door to see the faithful three peering at him from the kitchen. Jemma was still sweating in the center of the room, so he went to fill the pitcher for her.

"Listen," Alex said, over the sound of the water spilling out of the faucet.

Spencer turned it off. "Candy Man" was playing again. He dropped the pitcher and raced to the room. Jemma turned to him and held out her hands. He ran to her and kissed them, then started their dance. They danced again and again, and each time she moved a bit more like herself.

He looked her in the eye. "Jemmabeth Alexandra Forrester, I love you."

She looked down, breathing hard, then raised her chin. "I keep it in mind?" she said, and went back to bed, drawing her quilted shroud over her head.

Spencer turned to the doorway and smiled. She was on the right track.

Lizbeth went to her at sunrise. The head wound was healing and the downy hairs that had sprung up around it would perhaps cover the area. Nobody would ever notice unless it was Nedra, scrutinizing her hair. It was Lizbeth's prayer that she would come back to them, that she would again paint like the masters, dance on those tracks, laugh at Lester's stories, and move like satin when she danced with her love. She touched Jemma's hand. "Sugar, Spencer is coming to tell you good-bye. I thought you might wear something besides that old robe."

Jemma sat up in the bed, picking at the Lone Star quilt that was spread over her.

Alex came in. "Good morning, sweet pea. I've got a wonderful bubble bath ready. You'll like it."

She let them get her ready, then sat in Papa's chair, chewing on her upper lip. Spencer arrived and sat on the couch while Buddy B waited in the Corvette to drive it home.

"I have to go away, Jem," he said, holding her hand. "While I'm gone, I want you to get better. I want you to paint me a picture, and I want you to wear your ring again," he said, slipping it on her finger. She raised her hand to the light and the stones glittered. Suddenly, she left the room and he followed her outside. She sat on the porch swing, hiding something in the folds of her skirt.

They had spent many hours in that swing ever since Lizbeth and Cam had moved into town. He pushed off and let the clinking of the extra chain fill the silence as the honeysuckle blossoms sweetened the air around them. He knew she loved that fragrance. "Here, baby, can you smell it?" he asked, breaking off a few blossoms and tickling her nose with them.

She giggled, making him grin, so he did it again. She wrinkled her nose and sniffed, then put the blooms in her pocket. "What do you have there?" he asked, pointing where her skirt was clutched in a knot. She shrugged but moved her hands away to reveal the Starry Night music box.

"Would you like for me to make it play?"

"Yes," she said and let him take it. He wound it and opened the lid. Jemma closed her eyes and smiled at the familiar sound of "I Will Wait for You." She looked at Spencer from the corner of her eye, then turned to face him. "I think of thee."

He caught his breath. She returned the music box to the folds of her skirt and stared down at it again.

He turned her chin. "Jem, do you remember other things?"

"No."

He was accustomed to that answer. "Do you remember love?"

"Yes."

"Do you remember us?"

"I remember a cowboy."

Spencer's face fell. Surely Paul was not stuck in her head. "What was his name?" he asked, not really wanting to hear the answer.

"Candy Man."

He kissed her and she warmed to it, but not like the old Jemmabeth. She looked aside, embarrassed.

"I have to leave, Jem."

"No."

"I have to serve in the army for a while, and I will be away from you. I'll miss you so much."

She touched her fingers to his lips. "Are we married?"

"No, baby, not yet."

"Oh."

"I have to go now. Buddy is here to take me to Amarillo."

"Will you kiss me again tonight? I like it."

"I will come back and kiss you."

"Deal," she said, nodding.

No matter what else had been tough in his life, this was the hardest thing he had ever done. He stood in front of her and held her hands, palms up, and kissed them.

She concentrated her gaze on the little scar on his chin, and chewed on her lip. "Don't leave. Stay and kiss."

"I love you, Jemmabeth," he said, no longer able to control his voice. "Good-bye." He kissed her one last time, then turned toward the truck.

"No!" she yelled, stamping her foot. He ran back.

"Love you." She gave him the honeysuckle bloom, wilted and crushed from her pocket. She kissed his hands the same way he had kissed hers, then whispered, "Spence."

CHAPTER 10
THE BRIDE

Jemmabeth stayed in bed for two days, covering her head with a quilt even though, like Sandy said, the summer heat was bad enough to make her own mascara run. Neither Alex nor Lizbeth could coax Jemma out. There were no more scriptures or quotes, she wouldn't eat, and they were worried sick about her.

It was before dawn on the third night that she noticed Jemma was gone, but Alex did her best to keep her wits. Not wanting to wake Lizbeth, she maneuvered in the dark, searching each room and the front porch. She went to the backyard, hoping to find Jemma in the hollyhock patch, but then she saw her. She should have known. Jemma sat on the rails, huddled like a beggar. Alex was about to call out to her when she heard the sobs.

"Sweet pea," Alex said softly, moving to the cool steel rails next to her. "It's Mom."

Jemma reached for her hand. "Spence is gone, isn't he?"

Alex nodded.

"Mom, what has happened to me?"

Alex exhaled. "You were in a serious car accident, honey. We nearly lost you."

"Was I alone?" she asked, searching her mother's face.

"Yes, honey, you were alone."

"Did I hit somebody?"

"You hit a truck, but the driver wasn't seriously hurt." They heard the train and stood up. Alex stepped away, down the embankment, but Jemma turned toward the light coming down the tracks.

"Jem, come on. This is dangerous," Alex said.

Jemma moved off. "I'm all right, Mom. I'll be there in a minute."

Alex took a few steps, then waited. The Zephyr sped past, picking up speed as it left town. Jemma's hair and nightgown fluttered in its wake. She watched until it was out of sight, then turned and walked back to the house with her mother.

Later, when Jemma was alone, she opened her dresser drawer and took out the velvet box containing his wedding ring. She'd had it specially engraved with Scottish thistles twining around the white gold band. It was beautiful, like him. She laid it carefully in the music box as the last few notes played. Now it was her turn to wait for her man like he had always waited for her.

The artist's brain began to function properly. She had yet to paint, but she began to see things with an artistic eye again. She spent time alone with people she loved, just to reassure herself that she was becoming who she used to be. Trina took her out to Plum Creek and they talked under the cottonwoods. Nothing, though, could fill the void left by Spencer's absence. Nobody could tell her exactly how they parted. She had some memory of it, but that was not good enough. Rats. She needed to look him in the eye and make sure that all was well between them.

"Jemmerbeth," Lester said as they sat on his porch, "do you have any recollection about that old wreck you was in?"

"I remember picking up Bibles at the bookstore and that's it."

"That young Buddy B told us that he figures the Dodge helped save your life, it being so heavy and all."

"Where is the Dodge now?" she asked.

"Your daddy had it hauled off as far away

as they could get 'er, I reckon. That's a fine little car that Spencer got for your gram, though."

Jemma stared blankly at the vacant lot across the street.

Lester shifted in his chair. He still wondered if she was all right in the head. Alex must have thought so, or she wouldn't have gone back to Arizona.

"Are you gonna be headin' down to Dallas soon?" he asked.

"I don't know. Mother and Daddy don't think I'm ready."

"What are you thinkin'?"

"I haven't started painting yet, Lester. How dumb is that? I can't go to art school and not be able to paint."

"Have you give it a try?"

"No. I'm scared. Even my new sketchbook is empty."

He wished he hadn't asked about Dallas. "Have you heard from Spencer?"

"Not yet, but I'm hoping he can call next weekend."

Their conversation was interrupted by a shout from the street. An oafish woman with bulging tapestry bags yelled at them as she approached.

Lester stood and cupped his hand behind his ear. "What's that?" he yelled back.

"Timms?" she shouted and lumbered nearer his driveway. Her hair flew around her head like a rusty wad of steel wool and her heavy, dark dress could easily carpet Lester's living room.

"I'm Lester Timms. What can I do you for?"

"Hanna," she said, jabbing her thumb toward her chest. "Your bride." She scowled at Lester. Lester turned three shades of maroon and walked out to meet her.

Jemma watched with great interest from the porch.

"Who iss she?" the woman asked, pointing at Jemma. "You got kids? No kids." She waved her finger in Lester's face.

Jemma leaned on the porch rail, straining to catch every word. The woman outweighed Lester by at least a hundred pounds. Lizbeth came out on her porch to see what the hubbub was. Lester started toward the house and tried to take one of the bags.

The woman jerked it back and rutted her head at him. "You go. I got bags."

Lester's face was a mixture of Elmer Fudd's and Wile E. Coyote's on a bad day.

"What iss this girl?" She wiped her forehead on her skirt, then set her bags on the porch and walked up to Jemma. "You are his?" she asked, jerking her head toward Lester, who was stammering explanations. Her heaving bosom rivaled that of Eleanor Perkins, who, up until this moment, had the most ample in town. The buxom newcomer was in dire need of deodorant.

"I am Jemmabeth Forrester, and I live next door. Who are you?" Jemma offered her hand. It might as well have been a toad the way the woman looked at it.

"Hanna Fitz," she said. "I am to be his bride. I am from the old country."

"Ah." Jemma swallowed her giggle.

"I've been meanin' to tell y'all about my mail-order bride," Lester said. His ears were the same color as Hanna's hair. He turned to the woman. "Come on in, Hanna, is it? That ain't the name on the picture I got." Lester strained to lift one of the bags. Jemma set it inside.

"So you will go now," Hanna said, with her hands on her hips and brown eyes peering into Jemma's. "I have business with this Timms." Her upper lip glistened and massive beads of sweat had collected at her hairline and on her nose.

"I can see that you do." Jemma winked at Lester, whose knuckles were white against the porch railing. The breadth of his body would be no match for even one of her legs.

Jemma skipped down the steps but not before she had one last look at the mail-order surprise who retreated into Lester's house with her navy wool dress undulating behind like a defective parachute. She was a sight.

There was no rest for Lester. He didn't even pick up his own mail. Lizbeth and Jemma had to pick up his and theirs as well as the *Chillaton Star,* but they were having a high time listening and watching. Hanna charged from room to room like a freight train and her voice carried like the fire station's noon whistle. Lester was seen off and on as he emptied buckets, boxes, and carried stacks of newspapers and magazines to the trash barrel. After a few days observing this hard labor, even Jemma and Lizbeth were exhausted.

Trina came for a visit. "Do you think he'll really marry her?" she asked as Lester hung out gigantic undergarments on the clothesline.

"Not if he knows what's good for him," Jemma said.

"Poor Lester. How humiliating. I'm not sure he got what he bargained for," Lizbeth empathized. "I hope she's feeding him."

Jemma giggled. "There may not be much

left when she finishes with a meal."

"Do you know that is the first time I have heard you really laugh since the wreck?" Trina said.

"Maybe I'm getting back to normal. Have you heard from Le Claire?"

"That's why I'm here." Trina grinned and held up a letter. "I have been accepted and classes start September third. Nick is nearly as excited as I am."

Lizbeth and Jemma jumped on her with hugs.

"I *will* pay you back someday, girl. I promise. Are you going to be able to go by the end of August?"

"Obviously, there's no use in me going if . . ." Jemma couldn't say it.

"What?" Trina asked.

"I'm too scared to paint, but at least I have an idea for a new piece. Maybe I'll work up a sketch to see how it feels. You can stay with Helene even if I can't go. She's anxious for the company."

Trina looked to Lizbeth for help.

Lizbeth lifted her granddaughter's chin. "Sugar, you are going to be back to normal in every way. I believe that. The good Lord will not allow the gift He gave you to be wasted. His plan will unfold. You just remember that scripture about strength."

"What scripture?" Jemma asked.

"You gotta be kidding me," Trina said. "You pounded us with Bible verses all this time, but now you don't know one?"

"Maybe you needed to hear them." Jemma laughed again. "I'm sorry, Gram. I just don't remember."

"I can do all things through Christ, which strengtheneth me," Lizbeth said.

Jemma looked out the window. The verse roused her memory. "I will paint tonight. I feel it in my heart, but I hope I can put it on canvas."

The sketchbook had been an albatross for her. If she messed up in that book, she would not touch her brushes. She closed the door to the car house and switched on the lights. She walked in circles around the big canvas. Her old red cowboy boots sat side-by-side, full of brushes. It was too much.

She opened the door and went up to the tracks. She lifted her face to the starry sky and whispered the verse again, then gathered her hair on top of her head and took a deep breath. Tomorrow could be the day she'd hear her sweet man's voice again. He should be her husband now, rather than her boyfriend. Rats. She knew he must have suffered after the accident. Everybody said that he was there every minute they would allow. Bless his heart.

Her brainwaves seemed retrievable tonight, unlike many times since the wreck when complete thoughts seemed to float away from her. It was time for her to put it to use before it left her again. She had missed the exhilaration of passion, in her work and in her heart. She missed him. She looked down at the car house. Spencer had it all redone after the tornado ripped it in two, and now the lights were shining, ready for her to begin again.

Lizbeth awoke to the sound of water running in the bathtub. She sat up and called Jemma's name as the clock chimed five times, blocking out her voice. She pulled her robe over her nightie. A dim light shone under the bathroom door.

"Jemmabeth, are you all right?" she asked with some concern.

"I'm sorry, Gram. I just wanted to relax and get the paint off me," Jemma said. "I didn't mean to wake you."

Lizbeth dared not ask more. "That's fine. I needed to get up and read my Sunday school lesson again." She switched on the kitchen light.

"I'll go with you to church, but this evening I want to hear Brother Cleo," Jemma said.

"That's fine. I'll go with you tonight." Lizbeth lit the burner and got the percolator going on the stove. She sat at the kitchenette, reading her lesson. A light came on at Lester's house. It was in the back bedroom, his room. She knew they were sleeping in separate beds because Hanna never pulled her shades. She watched as Lester slipped down his back steps and out of sight behind his garage.

Jemma emerged from the bathroom in her old robe with a towel wrapped around her head. She gave Lizbeth a hug. "I did it, Gram. I painted all night. I want to see what you think. C'mon." She tugged at her arm.

"Sugar, I'm not even dressed, and you are barefooted. You could step on a goat's head sticker or a snake out there."

But Jemma was determined and coaxed her to the car house. She unlocked the door and turned on the lights.

Lizbeth's heart skipped a beat. "My goodness, sweet child of mine. Where did you ever get this gift to paint but from the Lord?" Lizbeth studied the piece. "Why did you choose to paint him?"

"It's burned into my head."

"My, my. Brother Cleo spent a good amount of time on his knees with you, and it's fitting that you paint him like that."

The door behind them creaked, sending them both a few inches off the floor.

"Lester!" Lizbeth yelped. "What are you doing in here?" She gathered her housecoat around her like a mummy.

"Shhh," Lester whispered, "that woman will hear you. Listen, I gotta talk, and I ain't got much time. Mornin', Jemmerbeth. Well, I'll be Uncle Johnny. I see that you are gonna be goin' back to school in Dallas with that fine paintin'. Did Miz Liz tell you that we had us a circle prayer for you?"

"No, but I remember Brother Cleo and his words from someplace."

Lester walked closer to the canvas. "Well, if that don't beat all. You've still got it, Jemmer. You've got it even better, if that's possible."

Lizbeth sneaked to the door. "I need to get dressed, so if you'll excuse me," she said, pulling on the handle.

Lester was against it in a flash. "Oh no, Miz Liz, you can't leave me in my hour of need. Brother Cleo'll be havin' another circle prayer — only it'll be for me this time."

"Let's go around the other side of the

225

house," Jemma said. "I don't think she can see us if we come in the east door, through the hollyhock patch."

"That woman can see through brick and steel," Lester said, his eyes still like Elmer Fudd's.

They crept around the dark side of the house and into the east door, as planned. Lizbeth and Jemma dressed while Lester hid in the quilt closet.

Lizbeth cleared her throat. "Come out, Lester. I'm not going to talk with you in there."

"It would mean a lot to me if you would, Miz Liz," Lester said, his voice muffled into the stacks of quilts.

"I'll stay in there with you, if y'all want me to," Jemma said. "Just so I can hear the phone."

She went to the kitchen and got chairs for them. The closet was long and narrow, so they had to sit facing each other. Jemma sat on the floor. Lester's face had taken on a pink tone ever since Hanna's arrival. It didn't really suit him. Something else was different, too.

"What became of your moustache?" Lizbeth asked.

"That woman," he said.

"Lester, did you send off for her like a

packet of flower seeds?" Lizbeth narrowed her eyes.

He nodded. The tips of his ears changed from pink to red.

"Where did you find her?"

"In the back pages of that *Ring of Truth* magazine. The ad said, 'The woman of your dreams.' Well, sir, I didn't plan on no nightmare. Her name's different, plus she don't look nothin' like her picture."

"Isn't that a political magazine?" Jemma asked.

"It's how I keep up with the Republicans. 'Know the enemy,' is what I always say. That could be in the Good Book, too."

"Looks like the Republicans pulled one on you," Lizbeth said, trying not to laugh.

"I paid three hundred dollars to bring her over. My old truck cost less than that, and she's grieved me a hundred times more than that pickup. I ought to sue somebody, but I ain't sure who. Probably the Republican Party."

"Maybe she just doesn't know how things are done in America," Jemma said.

"All she does is give me work to do and chew me out. She's got Beelzebub's temper on her. We ain't even talked about our future, heaven help me."

"Your future?" Lizbeth asked. "It seems to

me that when you send off for a mail-order bride, you have set your course for the future."

Jemma yawned. "I think we should get to know her better. Maybe she's scared or lonely."

"Well, sir, I don't know about the lonely part, but that woman ain't scared of nothin'."

"I think you're right, Jemmabeth. We'll have her over for supper tonight. You make sure she comes, Lester."

Lester tapped his foot on the wood floor and scratched behind his ear. "I ain't sure that I want to keep her. No offense, Miz Liz."

"You will make good on your promises, Mr. Timms," Lizbeth said without hesitation.

Lester rose slowly. "I should've been happy just gettin' your mail, Miz Liz, and drivin' you to the post office and whatnot. Once you up and got your own license, I couldn't even do that for you. Now all I've got is my tales, and she's probably gonna put the quietus on that. At least my chin-chillers was good to cozy down with at night, but I ain't even interested in sharin' a meal with this big 'un. She's fixin' to put me in the ground." He picked up his chair and left.

Lizbeth stared after him. "I suppose I'd better get ready for church. I'll have to come right home and get busy since we're having company tonight."

Jemma sat by the phone, half asleep. The stupid wreck had stolen their wedding from them. Was that a part of God's Great Plan, or was it her punishment for falling for Paul? When the phone did ring, she was dreaming that the Zephyr was in a race with Spencer. She fell back on the bed at the sound of his voice.

"Hi, Jem, do you know who this is?" he asked, not sure if she would have the answer.

"I sure do. Hi, Daddy," she teased.

Spencer was silent.

"Oh Spence, I'm sorry. I'm so bad. I love you, I love you, and I miss you."

He laughed. "I love you more. Now you sound like yourself."

"My head is better, but my heart's in bad shape. I wanted to be your wife by now, babe. It's another thing for you to forgive about me."

"Jemmabeth, don't ask me to forgive you for nearly dying. I'm just glad that you know who I am and remember loving me."

"I not only remember, I think about you

and dream about you day and night. Are they being mean to you and teaching you how to shoot?"

"It's about like you would imagine — kind of like an evil football camp with guns. I don't want to talk about it. I want to talk about you. Are you painting?"

"Yes, sir. I finished my first piece this morning."

"Not another one of me, I hope."

"Hey, I love to paint you, but this one is of Brother Cleo, praying for me, I guess. It came from some fuzzy place in my head. Spence, we need to see each other. I know that I wasn't right when you left."

"You're telling me. I need to hold you and kiss you and dance with you. I need to look in your eyes and see if you are really okay."

"If I'm not 100 percent, I'm close. Hey, Trina got accepted to Le Claire. Now if I can just convince Mother and Daddy to let me go back there myself."

"That's great! How's the church coming?"

"It's really nice. Your design is beautiful."

"Next will be the chapel for the nursing home. I guess that'll have to wait until I get out. I'd better go because I'm getting looks from people in line here."

"Oh Spence, kiss me through the phone. I love you."

"I love you, too. You be careful. Don't get a second concussion. You know that the Corvette is waiting for you when you are ready to drive again. Just call Buddy B. Is Sandy still there?"

"You're too good to me. Sandy left today to be with Martin's parents in Tyler."

"Well, maybe you will get well fast enough to go to school next month. Gotta go. Love you. Here's your kiss."

"Bye, babe," she whispered.

Then she ran to her room and cried. Again.

Hanna came early, without Lester. "Timms, he iss working. He will not be here."

"Really?" Lizbeth turned a suspicious eye on their guest. "That's too bad. I made his favorite dessert, too."

Hanna lifted lids off the pots on the stove. "More salt," she said, dipping a stubby finger in the potatoes. "Too much onion," she said as she sampled a corner of the meat loaf, fresh out of the oven.

Lizbeth pulled herself up to her full height. Nobody had ever criticized her cooking before. Ever. "We might as well begin. Let's bow our heads for grace."

Hanna frowned. "Who iss this Grace? Too many women around Timms. Iss not good."

This could be a fun night, Jemma thought, as she struggled to concentrate on the blessing. Hanna's lack of deodorant deserved a prayer, for sure.

"Hanna, what old country are you from? I have a friend who was stationed in Germany." Jemma smiled like sweet cakes.

"You haff no need to know this." Hanna took an extra portion of Lizbeth's homemade rolls.

"I think my granddaughter is being polite, Miss Fitz, is it? Good manners are the mark of a lady in this country."

"Too much talk in this country. Not enough work. I will teach Timms this."

"We thought it would be nice to get to know you a little better since we will be neighbors," Lizbeth said, her lips forming a sickly smile.

Hanna's head was bowed low over the fried okra while Lizbeth spoke of the variety of churches, a choice of the North or South Chillaton Quilting Clubs, the library volunteer group, and all the amenities offered a new female resident of Chillaton. Jemma ate her corn on the cob and wiped the butter off her chin. Hanna did not bother to clean hers. It was a stretch to imagine her volunteering for library duty.

"In the old country, I haff eight sisters

older than me. My mother, she had a sickness. I take care of her until she died. Now it iss my turn to go the ways of the worlt. Timms iss to be my husband, no? He iss not your husband. You find your own. I go home now to see if Timms has done his work. No more talk."

Lizbeth planted her tea glass with a thud that reverberated down the metal legs of the kitchenette. "Miss Fitz, you are in America now. That alone is a privilege. How you got here is another story. I don't know all the details about mail-order brides, but I do know this. Lester Timms is a fine man. He brought you here with his own money. You should be grateful for that. If you don't know how to show gratitude to another human being, then I will be glad to help you. I have no romantic notions about Mr. Timms, but he is a good friend to me, and I will not tolerate him being mistreated. We can live as good neighbors, or you can go back to where you came from." She took a breath. "Would you please pass the potatoes, Jemmabeth?"

Hanna dipped her tongue to her chin and cleared the last bits of butter from it. She maintained a steady gaze at Lizbeth. "You haff the big talk. I do not hit this Timms with pots. It iss not as you say. You and I will not be this good neighbor. We will liff in the big city. I am going the ways of the worlt. Timms will be my husband and not your friend. Good-bye, American old lady." She rose and left, slamming the screen door, but not before she scrounged the last of the rolls.

Jemma exhaled and turned to Lizbeth. "She has to go."

Lizbeth finished her meal in silence. Jemma wasn't quite sure what to make of it, but she cleared the table and did the dishes. Lizbeth sat in Papa's chair and read her Bible, marking certain pages with dainty, crocheted crosses.

"Gram, are you all right?" Jemma asked when she could stand it no longer.

"Oh sugar, I'm sorry to have neglected you since supper, but I had to collect my thoughts and prepare my heart."

"For what? Hanna?"

"For battle. I was angry with her, as you could probably see. I needed God's Word to calm me down. Now I know what I must do."

"Do you need an assistant?"

"The battle will be with my temper, Jemmabeth. I am going to follow the Scriptures to deal with that woman. We must stand by Lester, but we cannot lose sight of the fact that he brought her here and she is God's child, just like the rest of us."

"You're a better Christian than I am, Gram. I'd send her back."

"I would, too, but that's not an option. The Word says to love your enemies, do good to them that despise you. Now that should be a hefty goal in this case. No pun intended, mind you."

Jemma leaned down to kiss Lizbeth's cheek. The Moonlight Over Paris perfume she always wore, especially with company, was wasted this evening.

Lizbeth patted her hand. "You run along and paint. I'm going to work on a quilt."

Jemma went to the car house and sat on the stool, staring at the floor. She had chosen to take the Christian walk when she was in the third grade, but she really didn't know anything about it. She was on more of a Christian crawl. It seemed to her that almost everyone was better at living their faith than she was. She sighed and placed a blank canvas on the easel. Lester had made her so many while she was in the hospital. He did not deserve to be treated like dirt. Gram had a plan and she always carried through on things. Jemma should stick to painting now that she knew she could still do it.

■ ■ ■ ■

A week later, Lester rapped at Lizbeth's front door in the dark of night, his face plastered against the oval glass.

Jemma got out of bed and put on her robe. "Lester, did you fall or something?"

He had a hefty bruise on his cheek and a black eye.

He shuffled inside. "Could I sleep on the couch, Jemmerbeth? That woman is after my hide. No offense, but she got in my bed tonight. I don't even know when she did it, seein' as how I was dog-tired from my chores. First thing I knew, I had rolled plumb to the other side of the bed. I dreamed that I was helpin' push the Dodge out of a ditch when I woke up and found myself next to her big backside. Imagine the gall of her invadin' my sleepin' quarters without matrimony. I ain't goin' back to my own house until she's gone, and you can bank on that."

Jemma got a pillow and some quilts. She spread them on the couch and kissed Lester on the forehead. The bruises were plentiful. Papa's clock struck three as she lay in bed. The woman was a criminal to do that to Lester. Rats on her. Surely Gram would see that now. She dozed off thinking about Spencer and how much she would love to invade his sleeping quarters.

Lizbeth did not know what to do. She thought her plan had been going well until this.

"Miz Liz, I know you had a fancy to wear her down with good deeds and kind words, but all it's doin' is making her think you're, no offense now, 'an old American donkey,' to use her exact words. I figgered you was goin' by the Good Book, but the way I see it, the good Lord never had no notion of that woman. I'm thinkin' she's a twin to old Beelzebub himself."

Lizbeth poured herself another cup of coffee and sat at the kitchenette next to Jemma. "Where do you suppose she thinks you are now?" She eyed the bruises on his face.

"I left the car down by the Ruby Store. I'm supposed to be buyin' groceries this mornin'. She's got the place stocked up with vittles. You'd think the Russians were comin' tomorrow."

Lizbeth shook her head. "I have been praying for Hanna's heart to soften and for her to open up to friendship. Maybe it hasn't been enough time."

"No offense, Miz Liz, but I don't know how much longer I can hold on," Lester

237

said, his shoulders sagging and his neck slung out like a vulture's. "I can't even conjure up a good tale to tell these days. 'Course there ain't no time to tell one anyway. I thought I put in my fifty year down to the station. I didn't know that I was gonna have to start toein' the work line like this in my sunset years with a big ol' rhino breathin' fire at me."

"What would she do if you pretended to be sick?" Jemma asked.

"I already tried that. She poked me with a broom handle until I had bruises all up and down my ribs. I'm tellin' you, she's a mean one. Yesterday she smacked me so hard that I fell plumb off my chair. I got this shiner from workin' too slow to suit her."

Lizbeth went to the window, her jaw set.

"She hit you with a broom?" Jemma asked, just to reiterate.

"Yes ma'am, then come hence to usin' her fist right across the back of my head. Give me a headache, for sure." Lester rubbed the back of his neck. "There's been other things, too." His voice cracked.

"She told us that she didn't hurt you," Lizbeth said. "She's a liar to boot."

"She said she didn't hit him with pots, Gram. Maybe we didn't ask the right questions. I say we call the sheriff on her."

"Well, I know the good Lord would not want this to continue." Lizbeth's lips were in full pucker. "What do you say, Lester?"

"I ain't one to go whinin' to the law, but I don't know what else to do. I got my own self into this pickle, but I thought I'd get me some company. Instead I got me a rattlesnake from the *old country,* wherever the Sam Hill that is."

Lizbeth smacked her hands on the table. "Lester, we are going to go see Dr. Huntley first, then we'll go to the sheriff with this. I think your safety is in danger, and Hanna needs help as well."

"It will take forever for a trial or some other legal action. I'd like to try something else," Jemma said.

"What's that, sugar?"

"Well, Hanna was so concerned that first day about Lester not having any kids. We might run her off if we convinced her that he does have kids. Have you told her that you don't have any children?"

Lester shook his head. "We haven't talked about nothin', except my chores and my money."

Lizbeth frowned. "These are serious charges we'll be making against her. I don't know as she needs to be run off to harm someone else."

"Nobody else would be thickheaded enough to take up with her," Lester said, feeling his ribs.

"Let me just try this, Gram. I could get things started today," Jemma said. "Lester could stay at Willa's house because Hanna would never look for him over there."

Lizbeth nodded. "I suppose we have to be the Lord's hands on earth. If Hanna's goal was to come to America, she has done that much."

"Her goal is to *go the ways of the worlt*," Lester said, "and I'm ready for her to take off."

"The ways of the world are sinful, right, Gram?" Jemma asked, hopeful that her grandmother was lending her full support to this.

Lizbeth twisted her wedding ring. Cam would have tackled this predicament with a cool head and a Christian heart. She had to do the best she could without him. "All right; I'll take him to Willa's myself. Lester, I'm going to hang some sheets on the line for cover. Then you sneak around the hollyhock patch and out to the car. I'll be along directly. First, though, I'm calling the doctor for an appointment for you."

Lester exhaled. He stood and put his arms around her neck. It was a first. "No offense,

Miz Liz, but I had to give you a hug of appreciation. I've been kindly in a bad way lately, and I hope you don't mind the gesture."

Lizbeth recovered quickly and lowered her voice. "Since Jemmabeth is here with us, I find nothing wrong with a hug once every few years between old friends. You're a good man and a good neighbor to me. I've told Jemma how you sat up with us while she was in the hospital. We all care for you very much, and we'll see this through. Don't worry about Hanna any more. Now I've got a call to make and some sheets to hang."

"Lester, get in the closet and read the *Star*. I have some business to take care of myself." Jemma ushered him out of the room. She made her list and timetable. It had to be perfect because Lester didn't have a phone so Hanna would have to come to Lizbeth's house to take the call. She waited until Lizbeth took Lester to the doctor's office before making the first one. "Sandy, I need you to do me a favor," she said.

Sandy was quite willing to participate.

Jemma went to Lester's house and knocked.

Hanna lumbered to the door, wiping her forehead on her arm. "I'm too busy for you," she said, stopping short of the screen door. "Timms iss not here. Go away."

"You have a phone call at our house," Jemma said, her voice like an angel's.

"Phone call? I haff no calls." Hanna frowned. "Iss it the government of America?"

"Could be. It sounds important. I think you'd better take it."

Hanna made a disgusting noise in her throat, opened the door, and spat just past Jemma's foot. "I haff no time for this telephone." She grunted her way down the steps toward Lizbeth's house. She picked up the receiver and yelled into it, "It iss Hanna Fitz."

Jemma could imagine Sandy's response on the other end.

"What iss this? Timms iss not missing. He iss here. He iss getting food." Hanna's face changed from ruddy to fire red as the fury rose and settled in the shafts of her hair. "Daughter? No. No visits. I go now. No visits." She slammed down the receiver and made for the back door, ignoring Jemma and squawking in a foreign language.

Buddy B and Twila came by right as the noon whistle blew. Twila had borrowed six little nieces and nephews, as instructed. Jemmabeth watched from the porch swing. The crew stood on Lester's porch waiting for Hanna to answer the door.

"What iss it? Go away. Timms iss not here," Hanna shouted from inside.

"Hey, we need to see Granddaddy. He hasn't called in weeks and he was supposed to babysit tonight," Buddy yelled in the door. Twila's nieces and nephews pressed their faces to the screen. Perfect.

"Shoo, shoo!" Hanna poked at them with her infamous broom. "No babies, never."

"Oh yes, he keeps them all every Friday and Saturday — both nights, too," Buddy shouted. "We've got the baby in the car. She fixin' to need a diaper change real quick."

"Granddaddy takes care of his great-grandkids," Twila said, getting into it.

Hanna slammed the door in her face. Twila, Buddy, and their entourage went to the back door and started up again. Hanna pulled all the shades.

Jemmabeth watched Lester's house like a real-life Nancy Drew while Lizbeth drove over to Willa's with a couple of pecan pies. She walked home because they would need the car for the next phase.

Hanna stayed in the house until bedtime, then appeared. "Old lady!" Hanna yelled in the back door.

Lizbeth was already in bed, and Jemma was writing to Spencer at the kitchenette.

"Are you talking to me?" Jemma asked.

"I need that old one," Hanna said, coming in the door, uninvited.

"That's a rude way to talk about my grandmother, Hanna. I won't get her until you show a respectful tongue in your head."

"Where iss Timms? You are hiding him." Her beady eyes darted around the room.

"Did you hit Lester?" Jemma asked.

Hanna stopped and looked Jemma up and down. She puffed out her cheeks and folded her arms. "Timms iss my business. I am to be the wife."

"You may have to marry him in jail because that's where you will be living if you ever touch him again. We have laws in America to protect people from being beaten."

"Iss my business, not yours." She returned Jemma's glare.

"No, it is the business of the great state of Texas and her people," Jemma said, widening her eyes at Hanna. "I suggest you go home and think about that."

Jemma couldn't sleep. She heard Hanna running bathwater before the 6:23 Zephyr came through. Jemma got dressed and waited in the hollyhock patch. At promptly seven o'clock, Trina drove up with Willa in the backseat of Lizbeth's car. After some maneuvering, Willa was up the steps and standing tall on Lester's back porch. She knocked hard with her cane.

Hanna came to the kitchen window and peeked out. Spying Willa, she ducked into the shadows.

Willa knocked again. "Ain't no use in hidin'. I ain't leavin' 'til you open this door."

Jemma was impressed with her tone.

Hanna cracked the door open. "Timms iss not here. He has run away."

"Is that so?" Willa leaned into the screen. "It don't matter anyway because I've got a piece of paper here that says him and me are legally man and woman. I heard around town that you was movin' in. Well, if you know what's good for you, you'll hightail it out of this county, maybe out of the state. I've got Lester Timms just where I want him. C'mon out here now and show your-self."

Hanna ventured a longer look. Willa peered in the glass at her, too, her generous caboose sticking way up in the air. Trina sat in the car, mesmerized, as was Jemma.

"Enough pussyfootin' around. Either you show yourself, or I'm callin' the sheriff on you," Willa said.

"I am not knowing that Timms has a woman. He iss a liar to me. I come to this place to go the ways of the worlt, and I find nothing but talk and lies. Americans are all the big liars," Hanna said from behind the door.

"Enough said. I'm comin' in. There's just so much of this hogwash that I can take." Willa pulled back the screen and twisted the doorknob. It was locked. She blasted the door with her cane. Just as she did, Lizbeth came across the driveway.

"Help my life, Willa, what are you doing? You're going to scare poor Hanna to death," she said, her tone like butter frosting.

"This woman is insultin' the U.S. of A. and tryin' to commit a crime by marryin' Lester. She can either get herself on the next train out of town, or I'm fixin' to have a go at her right now."

Hanna appeared in the door again. "This crazy woman goes away. I do nothing wrong. It iss Timms that goes to jail!"

Jemma joined them on the little porch. "Hanna, I'll take you to the train station. You can catch the next train to California. There are lots of jobs there and it's on the ocean, too." They heard words in a foreign language that didn't sound complimentary to anyone. "I will give you some money for the trip," Jemma offered.

All became quiet on the other side of the door. "Money iss good," Hanna said.

"You get your things together, and I'll be back in an hour." Jemma saw a few frazzled copper hairs emerge from around the corner of the glass.

"Crazy woman go first," Hanna said.

They all left, not knowing which one she thought was the craziest. Jemma and Trina sat in the metal chairs in the hollyhock patch. When Trina could stand it no longer, she erupted in laughter.

"Shhh. She'll hear you," Jemma said, barely able to hold it in herself.

"I can't help it, girl. Mama should get an Academy Award for that. I don't know how she did it."

"I know. She was perfect. Everybody was, except you. You didn't have to do squat."

"Hey, I had to sit in the car and pinch myself to keep from laughing the whole time."

"Well, it was worth it to protect poor Lester. Did you see all those bruises on his face? She could be in jail for that."

"Yeah, I'd like to chase her around with her own broom."

"What's he doing at your house? Where did he sleep?"

"I gave him my bed, and I slept with Mama. She snored all night long. Creepers, it was bad. When we left, he was doing some hammering around on the porch. It could use some handyman work, that's for sure."

"Oops, there she is. I'll see you later."

Hanna was early, and the same two bags that she came with were bulging in her grip. Jemma went for a tour of Lester's house. She didn't see anything out of place, but then she didn't know his things all that well, either. "You had better not be taking any of Lester's belongings because I would have you arrested as a thief, too," Jemma said in a bold move.

Hanna begrudgingly unbuckled one of the bags. She took out a silver cup, a lace collar, two teacups, and an ivory shoehorn. "There. We go now."

"Open up the other one, too."

The big woman snarled but unfastened the second bag. She took out a small satin purse, a porcelain doll, a painted fan, and a book. "You are this mean woman," Hanna said.

"Why am I the mean one? I did not beat a helpless old man and then steal from him. Go on — get in the car before I change my mind."

"You giff the money now," Hanna said

with an evil eye.

Jemma had seen the evil eye before, and it had no effect on her. "You get in the car *now.*" She pointed the way.

Jemma waited at the station until she saw Hanna seated on the moving train. She had bought a one-way ticket to Los Angeles and had given her plenty of her own money to eat and sleep for two months. She thought that Spencer would approve of spending her money that way. If she didn't have Lizbeth's car, she would have danced down the tracks to get home. Lester had been spared the misery of being painted into a corner with no recourse. Jemma knew that feeling to some extent from her summer fling with Paul. Now she couldn't wait to get home and wait for her soldier man to call.

CHAPTER 11
SUNFLOWERS

"Spence!" She closed her eyes and fell back on the bed, propping her feet on the headboard. "I thought you'd never call. I miss you so much."

"Hey, baby. I am dying to see you. Are you still making progress?"

"Yup. In fact, I talked with Mom and Daddy, and I'm going to Le Claire next week. I can't wait. I've done two paintings since you left."

"I'll come to see you in Wicklow then. Can y'all get everything in the Corvette?"

"I'm shipping most of our stuff, but I'm about to run out of money. I think I'll have to get a job when I get there."

"I'll take care of you, Jem. You just write checks on my account. You don't need to work."

"You're sweet to do that, but we aren't married yet. I want to use my own money, unless I have an emergency. Remember, my grandparents are paying all my expenses this year. So I'll pay Trina's tuition and her books out of my savings. I've kept that much back, but I gave some of it to Lester's mail-order bride."

"His what?"

Jemma told him the whole story. He laughed at first, then like everybody else, got serious. "She should have been reported, but I guess it's too late for that."

"I decided this called for quick action. Besides, Gram felt kind of sorry for the woman. I think she must have been raised the same way she treated Lester."

"She needs help then," Spencer said.

"They wouldn't have done anything but keep her in the county jail. Then when she got out, she would have been right back on Lester's doorstep with a vengeance."

"Well, what's done is done. You did well. Brains and beauty all rolled into one. Your picture gets lots of comments around here. Most of the guys think I have a movie star's photo. They can't believe that I have a fiancée who looks like you do."

"Oh brother. I don't look too hot with this weird spot on my head. I have to figure out a way to comb my hair over it. Rats. A comb-over at my age."

"You could be bald and look good."

"Spence, when are we going to get married? I want to invade your sleeping quarters."

"You have no idea how much I want you to do just that."

"So let's get married."

"Jem, you know that I will probably wind up in some foreign place."

"How will they decide that?"

"They gave us a bunch of tests, so I'm sure those scores determine placement."

"Well, that's no help. You ace all tests."

"When do you think we should try the wedding again?" he asked.

"Sandy said they give you some time off between your first year and your second year."

"Maybe I'll get stationed in Europe like Martin did. We could live on a base there." He didn't sound too convincing.

"You really think you might go to Europe? That'd be fun."

"Baby, we have to face the fact that I may get sent to Vietnam."

"Oh Spence, I can't think about war, not now, when we're almost happy." Uh-oh. Was that Miss Scarlett talking? At least she didn't add *fiddle-dee-dee.*

"I have to go now. I'll call you next week."

"I'll be at Helene's. I love you."

"I love you, too. You are everything to me. You take care. Bye."

Jemma sat in Papa's velvet chair, eating pie with Lizbeth. "I can't imagine what it was like for you to have all three of your sons in uniform at once. How did you stand it?"

"We simply went on with life and worked harder and longer. Your papa and I consoled each other and, of course, Julia was a distraction, but I would have crumbled without Cam."

"I don't have Papa."

"You will hold up, honey. You have to trust in the Lord."

"I just don't understand how God could let Luke and Matthew be killed. I know you must have prayed every minute for their safety. Doesn't God hear the prayers of righteous people?"

"I am not that righteous, Jemmabeth, and His ways are not always our ways. We have to pray for strength to endure whatever answer comes."

"Then why pray?"

"We pray because the Word says to never give up and bring all our needs to Him. We are told to believe that we will receive what we ask for. In my heart of hearts, sugar, I knew that my boys wouldn't come home.

That's not to say that it wasn't a shock when we lost them, and goodness knows we still grieve over them. When I prayed for their safe return, it was with a heavy burden of doubt. We loved those boys and they brought us great joy, but when they left, I had a gnawing feeling that they were part of a much greater plan of sacrifice and justice. I tried to take some comfort in that thought, but it was small."

"Maybe Spence is part of something bigger than our plans for the future. But I don't get it. I tried to have a good attitude about him being drafted, but Vietnam seems like a trap."

"God doesn't give us more than we can handle. We may struggle, but that is part of living on this old earth."

Jemma moved on the couch with her grandmother. "I want to be with Spencer as his wife, Gram. I want to love him in that way."

"I know you do, honey, and that's good because it's the way God made us. It will happen."

Jemma gazed into her grandmother's eyes, so like her own. "Do you have that heavy feeling of doubt about Spence? Please tell me."

"I believe you and Spencer will have a life

together. He is not my flesh-and-blood child, and I don't mean to sound like one of Lester's gypsy fortune-tellers, but I have a good feeling about things."

"I don't see why I had to have that wreck. All things are supposed to work together for good for those who love the Lord. Where's the good in an accident?"

"Sometimes we never know the good that comes of bad. I do know that joy often follows pain, and Helene told me once that joy follows you around. I believe that, too." She stroked Jemma's hair, making sure not to touch the area that had been shaved.

Jemma drew a long breath and stood. "Enough of this sad talk. I have to get busy packing and painting. We need to have some fun around here before Trina and I leave. Should we go out to Plum Creek or the Salt Fork?"

"Let's go to the river," Lizbeth said. "I heard that Plum Creek is not running just now. We need rain."

They heard a loud engine roar out front and then the little *doink* knob sounded on the front door. Lizbeth peeked out. "Who on earth could that be?"

"Just so it's not Hanna, that's all I can say," Jemma said.

A heavy-set black man stood in front of

them, cowboy hat in hand. "Ma'am, my apologies for showin' up like this. I'm Joe Cross from down Sweetwater way. I'm the truck driver that was in the wreck with Miss Forrester. I wanted to stop by and see how she's comin' along."

Jemma moved in front of Lizbeth. She opened the screen door and looked into Joe's eyes. She slipped her arms around his neck, and he returned the embrace. They stood like that for several minutes, interrupted only by an occasional sniff.

"Thank you for coming," Jemma said.

Joe took out a bandana scarf and wiped his eyes. "I'm on a run to Los Angeles, but I'm real glad to see that you are up and at 'em. You sure had everybody worried there for a while."

Lizbeth shook his hand. "It's very kind of you to check on Jemmabeth, Mr. Cross. Promise me that you'll come by for a meal on your way back. Jemma is leaving for school this Friday, but I'll be here and I'd love to visit with you."

"Yes ma'am, I'll make it a point to do that. I'll call first, though." Joe shifted his weight and looked down at his hat. "I have a confession to make. I kept one of them little New Testaments. I hope you don't mind. It was the one that I had near me before the

256

ambulance got there. It sort of inspired me to speak a scripture in your ear."

Jemma had a sudden chill. "What scripture?"

"My own favorite, John 14:27: 'Let not your heart be troubled, neither let it be afraid.' "

Jemma joined him after the first word. It was the verse she had repeated more than any others. "Mr. Cross, I never tried to learn that verse; you taught it to me out in that ditch."

The three of them stood in awe for a moment.

Joe shook his head. "Well, it was no more than anybody else would've done. I brought you somethin', though. Hold on." He walked to his big rig and came back holding a coffee can full of sunflowers, still on their roots. "I dug this clump up close to where it happened. A batch of 'em were sort of like a pillow for your head when I found you."

"Mr. Cross, you are an uncommon man," Lizbeth said, tears brimming. "We are eternally grateful to you. We'll pray for your safety on the highway and for your family."

"Please, call me Joe. I live with my mother, but she's in real poor health. I have to leave her with my sister when I'm drivin'. I suppose it's worth it because I make good money on the road. Speakin' of which, I'd best be goin'." He turned to Jemma and nodded. "Good luck at your school."

Jemma kissed his cheek. "Thank you."

"Bye, now." He started up his truck and pulled away, leaving the two women standing on the porch.

Jemma spoke first. "Let's plant these on Papa's grave."

"Your papa would've liked that. I'll water them now and then, and Scotty will take care of them, too."

Willa was wallowing in the dumps. She wanted Trina to go to school, but she wanted her home more. "You'd better figger out some way to come home once a month, you hear me?" she said as they laid out the food at their river picnic.

"I know, Mama, I'll do the best I can," Trina promised.

"I'll look after your mama," Lester said. "I owe all you ladies for rescuin' me in my hour of need."

"Willa, what exactly was that piece of paper you were waving around in front of Hanna?" Jemma asked.

"Yeah, Mama, the one that supposedly said you and Lester were man and woman, whatever that means." Trina giggled.

"That was some paper I found on the seat about Lizbeth's new car. It worked good, though."

Lizbeth lifted a brow. "I didn't know you could stretch the truth so well."

"It wasn't no stretch — we are a man and a woman. All I had to do was think about how that creature had beat Lester's old bones around. She's lucky I didn't snatch her baldheaded."

Lester considered that a compliment and took an extra-big spoonful of potato salad. He hadn't eaten this well in a month.

"Are you all packed up, girl?" Trina asked as they dished up Lizbeth's homemade ice cream for dessert.

"Yeah, just about."

Trina gave her a sidelong glance. "Have you driven a car yet, Jem?"

"I made it fine to the cemetery and out to the home place. I'm okay. Maybe we could take turns."

Trina grinned. "Ooh. I get to drive a Corvette."

"Of course they say that the police are attracted to red cars. You'll have to watch out for that lead foot of yours." Jemma looked out at the Salt Fork of the Red River, recalling other times and another someone who liked to drive a little too fast. Maybe he could be a driver for the big brass in the military. Surely *they* didn't get shot at.

CHAPTER 12
HARBINGERS

Jemmabeth and Trina whipped out of Chillaton as the sun was coming up. Spencer's Corvette was packed solid, and the girls were ready for school in Big D.

Helene was waiting at the garden gate with Chelsea. She had fresh flowers in their rooms and lunch on the table. Jemma ran to call Lizbeth to say they had arrived in one piece.

Trina was one big smile. "I can't believe I'm gonna be living in this beautiful house."

"Thank you, dear. I am delighted to have you girls here. I'm sure you haven't eaten a bite on the road, so let's be seated, shall we?" Helene put the final touches on the table setting, then fiddled with her new hearing aid.

"Come here." Trina beckoned, then lifted the fat, white glob of fur into her lap. "So this is the famous Chelsea. I always wanted a cat. We seemed to only collect stray dogs and kids at Mama's."

"Well, a certain spoiled feline has the run of things around here." Helene lowered her voice. "Tell me about our Jemma."

"I think she's back to normal," Trina whispered.

"Good," Helene said. "I was so concerned."

"Everybody was, but she's ready for school, and she drove most of the way here."

Jemma came back into the room. "Okay, stop talking about me. Let's eat, then I'm looking in the *Wicklow Weekly* for a job."

"Me, too," Trina said. "Do you think there's any housecleaning work in Wicklow, Helene?"

"Most assuredly. This town is growing way beyond my liking. Will you be sharing transportation?"

"I don't know how that'll work," Trina said.

They didn't have to spend much time on the few want ads in the local paper. Helene suggested they place their own advertisement for cleaning services. Trina jumped at the idea, but Jemma hoped a certain lawyer would not be looking in the classifieds. They got plenty of calls and worked out a schedule so that they could clean houses on Tuesday and Thursday afternoons, when neither had classes.

Jemma's former garage apartment once again became her studio, and she wasted no time getting to work.

Spencer was due out of basic training in two days and she could barely stand the wait. He would be flying into Love Field at ten thirty. She was there at nine o'clock with flowers and a smile that wasn't about to leave.

Spencer craned his neck to see the airport coming up. Landing at Love Field always seemed as though the plane was going to touch down on a freeway. They had to circle a few times as they waited their turn, then made the final approach, flying low over a small lake. She would be there, looking out the window of the arrival gate. He was nervous. There was a lot to talk about. He had left her when she was barely lucid, yet she seemed fully recovered now. She was back in school and back in the town where her cowboy boyfriend of two summers ago lived. He couldn't worry about that. He walked down the ramp and saw her.

"Spence!" She ran to him and he picked her up, much to the enjoyment of the other passengers. Their kiss lasted from the arrival gate, down the corridor, and to the escalator. "I love you," she said.

"You look fantastic. Let me see the scar." He lifted her hair. "That'll heal up and be gone before you know it." His eyes were fastened onto hers, and they both tripped off the escalator at the bottom.

"Let's get married, right now," she said.

"Okay. First let me get my bags."

"I mean it. I want to go on the honey-moon," she whispered. "This engagement is too long."

"You think I don't agree?" Spencer's heart hammered at the idea.

"Couldn't we just get married, not tell anybody, and then get married again when you are discharged? By the way, you do look good in that uniform," she said, playing with the buttons on his jacket. "C'mon, let's say 'I do.' "

"Would you really want that?" Spencer asked. "To get married in secret?"

Jemma drew back. "Yes, I would."

"If we do, then everybody will know it is for one reason and one reason only."

"Nobody would care."

"I care. Marriage is not just a license to go to bed."

"Whoa. Did you become a prude on me at boot camp?"

"Not quite, but I've heard nearly every

seamy joke known to man."

"Tell me one," she said, taking off his cap to check out his crew cut.

"I will not. Your cute ears are way too precious. We'll make our own stories in our own time, Jem. I don't want you to think for a minute that this wait will not be worth it."

She pouted for a second, then suddenly hummed the birthday song to him. "Happy birthday, late, again, but I hope you got my package."

"You bet. Thanks. That was your gram's divinity, wasn't it?"

Jemma raised her chin. "It's mine now because she showed me how to make it. Did you like the sketchbook?"

"I do. It's like looking into your mind."

He drove the Corvette to Wicklow. They kissed at every traffic light and stop sign. After Spencer was settled in at Helene's, they sat in the conservatory with her. "I'm sorry I ran Trina out of the house," Spencer said.

"I don't believe it was a problem, was it, Jemma?" Helene asked.

"Are you kidding? She was excited to stay with Nick's parents. She's been working hard at school. I told her to slow down, or she was going to burn out."

"Show me your paintings," Spencer said. They went to the garage apartment and she showed him Brother Cleo, a pickup kicking dust alongside a wheat field, and a large piece, in progress, of Joe Cross. "How do you know him?" he asked.

"He came by Gram's before I left. He said a scripture over me when I was unconscious, and I guess it was one of the scriptures I said when I was coming back to earth. I know that I hadn't learned it before because I checked my Bible to make sure. I had underlined all the verses I memorized in my Bible; that one was not one of them."

"Amazing."

"He brought me sunflowers, too. They still had roots, so we planted them at Papa's grave. He said I was lying on a clump of sunflowers when he found me."

"What a sweet thing to do for my girl," he whispered.

"I can't believe you're in this apartment. I'm so glad to just touch you. Come over here to the daybed. I want to wrestle with my military man."

Spencer couldn't turn her down. The little daybed creaked as they sat on it. "Are you sure this thing can stand us both on it?"

"Yeah, are you sure you can stand this?" She jumped on him with a wrestling move.

"I call this one The Cinderblock. What do you think?" She held on to the mattress with her hands on one side, and hooked her feet underneath it on the opposite side. She was dead weight across his chest.

He laughed until he couldn't breathe. "Time out, woman. Let's have a little respect for the military."

They sat in the garden by the Tiffany rose with its pungent fragrance. He decided to go for it. "Jem, I want you to know something. I think we should marry when I'm not under any pressure by the United States Government to be somewhere at any certain time, and when we're not worried about whether I'm going to be shot at. My life is not going to be my own for a while."

She assumed a pout, full-blown. "I think that I want to have you as my husband and all the privileges that go with it. If that means a weekend honeymoon, that's okay with me."

He turned her chin. She knew that was a signal of serious business.

"Jemma, I want you more than any man has ever wanted a woman on this earth. Do you understand that?"

She nodded.

"I'm saying that if we get married just so we can have sex, that would defeat our honor in a way. When we made this promise, we didn't even know what we were doing. Now we know that it was right, and we should also know that sex is not a good reason to marry. Call me a prude if you want to."

"You're different, Spencer. You've changed."

"I haven't changed when it comes to you. When you were in the ICU, I had a lot of time to think. Loving you has been my life's joy. Sex is only a part of married love, Jem. I want to sleep next to you and feed you when you're sick and take turns rocking babies with you. I know that I still haven't recuperated from your accident, and I've just been through some intense stuff that's only going to get worse, but I am committed to this ideal. As far as setting another date goes, well, when we have our wedding night, I want to concentrate on you and on our life together as a couple. I don't want to have all this military stuff in the back of my mind. Maybe I'm wrong, but just think about it, okay?"

"Okay," she mumbled, knowing that she would do whatever he said. She reached for his hand. "Right now I want to have some fun with you. Let me show you my school, then we can go dancing. What do you think?

I'll wear the dress you like."

"I like all your dresses," he said, exhaling, "but I need out of this uniform."

"Are you going to slip into something more comfortable?" she asked, giving him the look he loved.

He pulled her close. "I love you, Jemma-beth. Thanks for listening to me."

They toured Le Claire. She showed him every little nook on the campus. He couldn't help but feel somewhat jealous of all the places. It was there, after all, that she had gotten it in her head to break up with him in the first place. He didn't mention it, but it was on his mind.

"What kind of music do you want?" she asked.

"You choose. I like it all with you."

"Even country?" She drew the vowels out.

He laughed. "Well, almost all."

Jemma had heard about a place on a lake with an outdoor dance floor. It was already rocking when they got there. Lanterns were strung all around, casting a subtle glow on the dancers. There was no band, just a disc jockey in a covered booth above the crowd. They danced to every song, working out their tension on the floor. Stevie Wonder sang "I Was Made to Love Her," and next was "Light My Fire." The accident hadn't taken any edge off her ability to dance like the old days, but they had moved way beyond the Chillaton Stomp.

Two hours had passed before Spencer even checked his watch. Finally, they had a slow dance so he could hold her to him: "I Never Loved a Man" was the one to end on. He wanted to make her his wife and be alone with her, but he had already voiced his opinion and she had agreed to it. He had spoken from his heart, but the rest of him dissented.

Helene was asleep. He knew it would be so easy to bend the rules with Jemma. He knew he wasn't the only one thinking about it because she had the same look in her eyes.

"Spence," she said, holding his hands, "it's hard having you in the room next to me. Remember when I told you that I wanted to invade your sleeping quarters like Lester's mail-order bride did? I still do, even more now, but I know we have to keep our promise." She kissed him, and her breath was warm against his neck. They had never broken their vow even just a little. Nobody would know. She pulled away and looked in his eyes. "Besides, we would be different, wouldn't we? We would always know. Is that what you're thinking?"

"Baby, I am thinking the same things you are, despite my principles, but I need to have the hope of marrying you to keep me focused, no matter the situation. You told me that you had to get that cowboy out of your mind because you were just made that way. Well, I am just made this way. I need to wait to marry you to keep me going. You're right; when I almost lost you in the hospital, it did something to me. We've waited so long that now I want to see it through as an honor to you and to our love. I want to do what's right by God's Word. If we are to walk in the Spirit and lead Christ-centered lives, we have to try to be righteous and pure."

She touched his face. "Spencer Chase, you must be the only man on earth who would say that. I'm pushing you into a corner with my hormones. Okay, when is the earliest that we can marry? Tell me and I'll do it."

"Don't throw a fit, but, like I said, I would like to be free of the military. That means the end of next year."

It was instant. She threw up her hands. "Next year! Rats! Why did I have that wreck, why? It ruined everything for us." She stamped her foot like she was two years old.

"No. It delayed things, but it didn't ruin things. We may never know why, Jem. I know that two more years will be tough. Look at me; I'm shaking right now."

"That means we will be twenty-four years old. Everybody will make fun of me for being an old maid."

"They wouldn't dare. You could marry anybody you want, anytime."

"I don't want anybody but you, and it looks like I'll be an old maid until then."

"Well, it's not like we don't have some good times. I know a few things that still give you a thrill, old maid." Spencer threw her down on the leather couch and proceeded to prove his point. She giggled and kicked off her shoes.

The next day they went to Six Flags Over Texas and stayed until dark. It felt like they were in junior high again. Jemmabeth was fearless, and Spencer tried to keep up with her. They were such goofy pranksters. He told the staff at the Jamboree that it was her birthday. They called her up on stage and sang to her. She got him back by turning his name in as a lost child, and it was promptly announced over the park's public address system.

She told him about her delivery girl

disaster at the flower shop and pointed the building out. He got a big kick out of it, as she knew he would. He went in and bought a similar ceramic deer and some roses for her while she sat laughing in the car. They ate a burger at The Best Burger Stop in Texas. It didn't bother Jemma at all that she and Cowboy Paul used to hang out there. She knew the owner recognized her by his smart-aleck smile.

They took Helene out to dinner, but mostly just sat around and talked. She painted, and he watched her. They went for walks around Helene's property, which was no short stroll.

"Where would you like to live?" Spencer asked as they sat in the garden that night, trying to see the stars.

"It doesn't matter to me. I can paint anywhere. You'll be the one with the career choices."

"I guess we'll have to live wherever I can get a job. I'd like to be close to your family, but who knows?"

"I thought you wanted to live in Europe."

"That was before your wreck. Now I think family is everything."

"You've never had a desire to be famous, have you?"

"I think everybody wants to create something fantastic."

"I suppose. I never really thought about it. You aren't going to open up an architectural firm in Chillaton, are you?"

He laughed. "Maybe you and I should go into business together. I could design buildings, and you could paint murals on the ceilings."

She had waited long enough. "When will you know your assignment for the next year?"

He took a deep breath. "I already know it, baby," he said and bit his lip.

"Well, let me have it."

"Fort Wolters, near Mineral Wells."

"What happens at Fort Wolters?"

He held her hand. "They train helicopter pilots, Jem."

CHAPTER 13
HEART PIECES

The Le Claire senior art students were eager for their first exhibition. It was to be held at the Dallas Museum of Fine Arts. She was glad to have something to pour her heart into. It took many soothing words from Spencer to calm her down after he broke the news to her about his assignment. They both knew he wouldn't be flying helicopters in Europe. She was trying to put it out of her mind, for now.

She had six paintings for the exhibition: *Joe Cross; Brother Cleo; Mirth* — the name she had given the watercolor of Carrie, Trina, and herself as little girls; *Dusty Business* — the pickup on the road by the wheat field; *My Cowboy* — Spencer on the train tracks; and *The Ways of the Worlt* — Hanna holding her tapestry bags.

Professor Rossi, her favorite teacher at Le Claire, was pleased with her choices. "You should be having your own show, Jemmabeth. It will happen after this . . . you wait and see."

"I am working on a painting of your friends in Florence," she said, frowning at a brushstroke of copper in Hanna's hair.

"The Grassos? Ah, they will be happy to hear of this. We will have to send them a photograph when it is complete. Are you working on it at your home? I have not seen it at your station."

"Yes, at home. The one at school is of my mother. Do you like it?"

"She is *bella*. Now I see where you learned that smile. Who is this creature with the fiery mane?"

"She is from the old country. She came to America to go the *ways of the worlt.*"

"It appears she is looking for trouble."

"It's a long story, but it ended well. I'll have to tell you sometime, but right now I have to help clean a house in Wicklow."

The professor clicked his tongue. "It will not always be so with you, Jemmabeth. Someday you will be living like royalty."

She smiled. "I'd just like to be living on a military base right now, but that's not going to happen." She waved and ran to meet Trina.

"Check this out," Trina said, showing deep

dimples as she handed her a letter.

"Wow! That is terrific. You'll have to call Gram tonight so she can tell your mom. How did you get to be a featured designer so fast?"

"They pick somebody from each level. I represent the first level students."

"I knew you had it in you. Congratulations."

"Is Spencer coming to the show?"

"Yeah. I'm picking him up Friday night."

"I hope Nick can come. He and I don't get to see each other much."

"That's the pits. You move to the same county, and you still don't see him."

Trina shrugged. "He doesn't have a car, and I don't either."

"Well, that needs to change." Jemma started thinking. "What happened to his uncle's car?"

"He hates to ask for it. Nick has a lot of pride, so I guess we're a team in that department."

Jemma slammed on the brakes and made an illegal U-turn. "We'll go by his place right now."

Trina held on to the dashboard. "Creepers. You're nuts when you get an idea. I wish Nick and I could afford to get married, but he won't discuss it. You're so lucky to have

Spencer. He was so worried about you in the hospital. When you were in the ICU he went in to see you every hour, around the clock. He even asked if he could sit outside your door. Mama said that the nurses didn't let him, though. Hey, did you know that you were naked in the ICU?" Trina grinned.

"What?" Jemma jerked the steering wheel to get back in her lane.

"I saw you, girl. They couldn't cover you up completely because of all the monitors."

"Spence saw me like that?" Jemma blushed at the thought.

"Come on, you'd just been in a head-on collision with a semi. Even Miss America wouldn't look good after that."

"Even so, he's not supposed to see anything until we get married," Jemma said, without joining in the laughter. In fact, she was getting a little ticked off about it.

"Maybe that's why he kept going in so often." Trina giggled. "Oops, I'm sorry. That was a tacky thing to say."

Jemma was in a snit, and Spencer had better have a good defense.

"Okay, sir, tell me how to fly a helicopter in ten words or less," Jemma said as he pulled out of the base.

"Nah. Tell me how to paint." He leaned

over for another kiss. "I'm starving. Let's stop at the first restaurant we come across."

"You're the boss. Just so I'm at the museum by six o'clock tomorrow night."

They stopped at a Mexican food place. Jemma played with her food, thinking of how to ask. Finally she rolled her eyes and simply said it. "Spence, did you or did you not see me naked in the hospital?"

He glanced at her. She was serious. "Maybe. What's it worth to you?"

"Spencer! That's not fair. You take off all your clothes right now and let me have a look."

The diners in the next booth bugged their eyes at them.

"I have to have more suitable surroundings," Spencer said. "You'll have to come up with a better plan than that."

"Did you see me or not?"

"I'll never tell."

"You will tell me right now, or we'll never leave this place."

He looked at her out of the corner of his eye.

"So, you did see me. Quintuplet rats. I can't believe you did that. You should've covered your eyes. I was unconscious, for Pete's sake. Aren't you ashamed?"

Spencer went nose-to-nose with her. "Jem,

279

I'm teasing you. Yes, you were naked, but when I walked in the room I almost threw up when I saw you. Your sweet body had been laid bare to help save your life, but I only looked at your face, I promise. Your daddy and I stood over you and said a prayer. Every time I went in, I was in such an emotional state that you could have had Roy Rogers and Trigger in the bed with you and I wouldn't have noticed. Now there. Okay?"

Jemma backed off but was pouting. "I didn't want you to see me until we got married. I didn't want you to see any naked women until we get married."

"I don't buy girlie magazines, if that's any consolation."

She couldn't help but smile at him. "I'm sorry. I know you're a good boy, but I bet you saw something."

Spencer finished his meal. "Well, you do have a cute belly button," he said, laughing and dodging her punches. "Just a joke, wild woman."

The senior show was a success. Professor Rossi was right. An art gallery manager in Highland Park Village called and scheduled a meeting for Monday afternoon right before they left to go back to Fort Wolters.

She was to bring her portfolio. Jemma was radiant with the thought of her own show. Helene was on the phone, telling Lizbeth and Julia within minutes, and Spencer was content to listen to her talk about it all the way back to the base.

Jemma bought groceries and went to the post office to pick up stamps for Helene. She stuffed them in her purse and started out the door, still fiddling with her purse.

"Well, hello, darlin'."

His voice made every hair on her arms rise at full attention. She gazed right into the clover green eyes of Paul Jacob Turner, the embodiment of her "summer of the wild cowboy fling," and the source of all her heartache with Spencer. He was taller than Spence and as handsome a cowboy who ever drove a pickup truck. English Leather cologne trickled inside her head.

Her voice came out silly, like it always did when she was around him. "Hi, Paul. How are you?" She looked away toward the Corvette, as though Spencer could be watching.

He stood way too close. "I'm much better, now that I've seen you," he said, always the charmer. "I heard you were back in town. How about going out for a burger sometime?"

"No, thanks, I'm engaged." She flashed The Ring.

"That's some hunk of jewelry," he said, looking her over. "I assume it's the high school kid, huh?"

"He's graduated from college and is in the military now." Jemma narrowed her eyes.

"Is he far, far away yet?" His beautiful smile had not changed one bit.

"What does that mean?" she snapped.

"It means maybe you and I could hang out sometime — you know, just talk."

"Excuse me, Paul, but you and I were supposed to talk at the coffee shop at Love Field over a year ago. Remember? You went to Las Vegas instead."

"You're not holding that against me, too, are you?"

"I'm not holding anything against you. I never think about you anymore."

"Well, I bet you will tonight, darlin', because I'll be thinking about you." He touched her chin. "Looking into those golden eyes has lifted my spirits like nothing else could. You're still the one, Jemma."

She left and didn't dare look back. It was as though she'd seen a rattler up close. Paul Turner knew how to quicken her pulse. She wiped her chin where he had touched it and sat in the Corvette for a minute. He would not weasel his way into her life ever again.

Paul watched as she drove away, his heart pounding. He'd never realized how much he had missed her. Even his bones ached. As long as there was a breath in his body, he would try to win her back. He had wanted to see her smile, hear her laugh, and talk about her art. That might take some doing, but she had reacted to his presence. He knew when a woman did that, and this was no ordinary woman. This was his one and only, his joy, his darlin' Jemmabeth. To hold her and kiss those sweet lips, that would make him feel good about life again. She was the only woman who had ever done that and the only one decent enough for his father to hound him about. There was always hope that she might forgive him and allow his love back into her heart. He lifted his Stetson and ran his hand through his hair. He was too old to cry anymore.

He cranked up the eight-track tape. If she'd known how many hours he'd spent grieving over her, maybe she would've come back to him long ago. They might even have babies by now. He opened his eyes wide and blinked back the tears that had cropped up behind his lashes. He couldn't help it. He loved her from an innocent and gentle place way down deep inside himself — a place where nobody else had ever been and where love lasts a lifetime.

The Gallery at Highland Park was just as exclusive as the shops along the Champs Elysees in Paris, but the owner, Annette Lawson, had a definite Texas accent.

"Please, call me Anne. We are excited at the possibility to showcase your art, Miss Forrester. I understand that you were the Girard Fellow at Le Academie Royale D'Art in Paris last year."

"Yes, it was a fascinating experience." Jemma watched as Anne thumbed through her pieces.

"I was told that most of your work was sold at the Academie exhibitions, but I am very impressed with what's left. These are amazing. You're very prolific."

"I paint every day."

"Do you have other pieces like the one used for the cover of *Nouvelle Liberte*?"

"How did you know about that? I've never seen that magazine in Texas."

"Carlo Rossi told me. He is an enthusiastic admirer of your work."

Jemma smiled. "I have others in that

mood, but I don't include them in my portfolio."

"Oh, and why is that?"

"They are very personal reflections and not for sale."

Anne's eyes brightened. "I want to see them. We can price them so that they won't be sold, but it will enable clients to gain a deeper perspective of your work."

"I suppose I could bring them by tomorrow after classes." She regretted the idea already. Rats.

"Bring everything. These are excellent, and it will be a fabulous show. Simply fabulous."

She was back the next day with her private watercolor collection, pieces that she had never shown anyone. Anne examined each one as though she considered buying it for herself. "These are exactly what I'm looking for. You have bared your soul with them."

Jemma didn't respond. Most of them were too close to her heart for display. She wasn't sure that she wanted to share them with the world.

"I have catalogued the pieces you brought yesterday. Please look over the list and sign at the bottom. I assigned a value to each, subject to your approval, of course. The gallery's commission is included and defined in the paragraph above your signature. Now, let's just quickly title these. A brief description will do. We should begin with number nine."

Jemma flipped through them, heavy-hearted. "Number nine is a girl laughing. Number ten is a girl holding a firefly in her hands. Eleven is a boy and girl kissing. Twelve is a girl looking in a mirror as she brushes her hair. Thirteen is a boy and girl dancing in the moonlight. Fourteen is a girl crying in bed. Fifteen is a boy in a scout uniform. Sixteen is a girl walking on a train track. Seventeen is a bride. Eighteen through twenty-two are all of a soldier."

"Exquisite. Why haven't you exhibited them before now?"

"Personal reasons," she said, staring at them.

"I see. Rest assured, we shall do something special with them. It's such a pleasure to see your work."

"Yes, ma'am. When will the exhibit begin?"

"In five weeks. Is that good for you? I'm having to make some schedule changes, and I need time for advance publicity, etcetera."

"Sure. You said that you would overprice my private collection. Why price them at all? Can't they just be exhibited?"

Anne flashed a patronizing smile. "It is a policy of the gallery that all the pieces in a show be available for purchase by our clientele. Otherwise, we would be a museum. This is a profit-making venture for all of us, Jemma. It protects both your best interests as well as ours. I'm sure that you understand the business side of art. Have you ever considered hiring an agent?"

Jemma shrugged, having forfeited her options by bringing them in the first place.

"Besides," Anne continued, "you can always paint more."

She left the gallery feeling as though she had just forsaken part of her heart and truly bared her soul, like her body in the ICU. She hit the steering wheel with her fist.

She drove back to Le Claire to pick up Trina. They went straight to their house-cleaning job and didn't get home until six o'clock. Jemma flew up to her studio, reached under the daybed, and took out a portfolio case. She removed three watercolors. The first was of Gram, sifting the earth of the home place through her hands as it blew back against her legs. The second was of Spencer as she remembered him in the first grade, front tooth missing and holding an Easter basket. The third was of Papa playing his fiddle. Those would never leave her.

Lizbeth sipped her coffee, eyeing the folded quilts in the oversized closet. There were thirty of them, at least. She had no room left on either side of the narrow, high shelves, and she had no specific plan for any of them. As soon as she finished one, she began another, like Robby reading his comic books. There were even more quilts under the good bed and in the top of Cam's closet. She was no different than the squirrels that ran around the backyard, storing up nuts. At least they planned on eating them to keep from starving through the winter. She had no such excuse, and it was a sin to keep these useful creations folded in plastic.

She was never one to brag, but the quilts were of the highest quality and very pretty. She was a master quilter, one of the best in the Panhandle, and consistently voted president of the combined North and South Chillaton Quilting Clubs. Alex always wanted her to enter some in the county fair, but Lizbeth never had the desire to enter a competition, unlike Julia's compulsion to enter any and all contests. Sewing the pieces to create a pattern had kept her mind busy.

She was blessed that arthritis had not hampered her work as it had some of the club members. Now it was time for her to put these cotton creations to good use. They were not pieces of her heart, like some quilts she had made.

As she walked over the tracks to Willa's house, she was struck by another, even more exciting idea. It made her smile, then grin, much wider than she had in a good while. The sign that read DOES IRONING AND GUARANTEE HER WORK was hanging straight, thanks to Lester. She knocked on the door. Willa's radio was playing.

"Miz Liz, come on in here. I'm glad to see your smilin' face. We gotta stick together since them girls left us."

Lizbeth sat at one of the kitchen chairs and Willa plopped down across from her. "I don't know what I've been doing since Jemma left, to tell the truth," she said. "The days blend into one another. It takes me a while to get over her leaving because I've come to think of her as my own. I don't know if that's good or bad."

Willa nodded. "My baby sure is havin' fun at that school. She took to that dress-makin' right away. I hope she'll like it in that fancy pants world."

"She will. Trina has spunk and talent, just

like Jemma. It's funny how those two came together when they did. I believe that's all part of God's Great Plan, don't you?"

"I do. I believe just that. Now if she can get her man worries out of the way, she'll be doing all right."

"I thought Trina and her young man were practically engaged."

"Well, you and me both thought that, but I think old St. Nick has cooled his heels in that department. I told her to get some backbone. Women go through all kinds of misery in this old world, and she'd better start buckin' up for it."

"Willa, I have an idea and I'd like your help, if you don't mind."

"You ain't needin' me to scare off another one of Lester's women friends?"

Lizbeth laughed. "No, not quite. I do want to get some things out of my house, though. I'd like to offer most of my quilts to folks that are in need. I wondered if your church has a system for that kind of thing. My church has a fund set aside, but no real goods for helping out."

"It'd be nice to keep folks warm this winter. I'll talk to Brother Cleo when he comes down Sunday. I'm sure we can work somethin' out."

"I'm sorry I didn't think of this sooner. I

thought I would give half to my church and the other half to yours."

"Well, poor folks is the same, no matter the color. It's mighty fine of you to use your talent for good deeds, Lizbeth."

"I don't know what I was thinking when I put them away. You'd have thought I was outfitting a small army."

"Speakin' of which, how is Spencer doin'? I sure do hate it that he's gonna be flying them old whirlybirds in that nasty mess. I know Jemma is gonna go out of her mind worryin' over him."

"I think she'll be coming back to Chillaton while he's in Vietnam. I don't know if I can be any consolation to her, Willa. I prayed for my boys to come home safe and sound and it wasn't in God's Plan. You'll have to help me take care of her."

"Spencer'll get through it. Them poor children have had a time of it tryin' to get together."

"That's true. I guess I'd better run. I'm going to talk to Brother Hightower at my church about the quilts. Oh, by the way, come over for dinner on Sunday. Lester will be there, as well as a new friend of ours that I want you to meet." Her heart beat a bit faster as she said the words.

"I'll be there if you cook roast beef," Willa

said, laughing.

"I'll have Lester come over to get you."

"See you Sunday, then. I'll bring cobbler."

Lester was right on the dot to pick Willa up. He was a punctual man. He'd run most of his life by the clock at the train station. To most folks, a minute here and a half minute there might not matter much, but it did to a stationmaster.

"What's that big truck doin' here? Did Lizbeth order somethin' special for dinner?" Willa asked as they pulled into his driveway.

"That would be Mr. Cross's rig. He's the man who was drivin' the truck when Jemmerbeth had that wreck. He's a right nice feller," Lester said. "He could be one of them angels folks talk about."

Lizbeth met them at the door and was very talkative. "Come right in, Willa. I'm so glad you could make it. Let me take that cobbler. Hmm, it's still warm. I'd like for you to meet Mr. Joe Cross. Joe, this is my good friend, Willa Johnson. She makes the best cobbler anywhere."

Joe grinned as he shook her hand. Willa smiled and raised her brow. "I'm thinkin' I need to give you a hug instead of a handshake, Mr. Cross. You saved our girl's life from what I hear," she said and gripped him with a bear hug. Joe, somewhat surprised, hugged her back. They exchanged a number of glances as the meal progressed.

"Well, now, Mr. Cross, I never knew nobody who drove a truck for money. Tell us about the truckin' business," Willa said.

"Please call me Joe. Ain't much to tell. I drive my rig across the country and back, east to west, but mostly west these days. It's a good livin', but it's kinda lonely, too."

"Joe lives in Sweetwater." Lizbeth passed the rolls but avoided Willa's eyes.

"I had me a time in Sweetwater once," Lester said. "I went down for the Rattlesnake Roundup. That was about the wildest time I ever had without the company of a lady friend."

"Lester . . ." Lizbeth gave him the schoolmarm eye.

"No offense, Miz Liz, I just mean that I wouldn't dream of takin' a lady to no rattlesnake hunt."

"I can understand that, Lester," Willa agreed. "No lady I know would be hankerin' to go, neither."

Joe shook his head. "I reckon it's a good idea to get shed of as many rattlers as possible, but I ain't never been to it. I'd rather ride to Los Angeles with a load of hogs in the back and a couple more in the cab than to try and catch a rattler."

Willa laughed. "What do you do for entertainment in Sweetwater?"

"I'd have to say that I like to play my daddy's fiddle just about as much as anything."

"You're a fiddler?" Lester perked up. "I'm a French harp man, myself. Miz Liz's dearly departed husband and me were mighty good for a back porch duet. He was a fiddler, too. Do you have yours with you?"

"I take it everywhere I go. It's good company. It never gives me any back talk and stays put, too," Joe said with a laugh to rival Willa's.

"Maybe you two could give us a concert after we have some of Willa's cobbler," Lizbeth said as she cleared the table. "Wait until you taste it."

"I'll just run over and get my harmonica," Lester said. "If you ladies will beg pardon."

Willa watched as Joe helped Lizbeth with the dishes. He was a good-sized fellow, tall, with big bones. She liked that in a man. "Are you a churchgoin' man, Joe?" she asked, surprising herself.

"Yes, ma'am. Sometimes I'm out of pocket, you know, and I can't get to my own church, but I can usually find some place to stop about church time and read my New

Testament and spend some time with the Lord."

"Lizbeth told me that you said some scriptures over Jemma. That was real Christian of you. Not many folks would have seen clear to do that." Willa was recalling anything she'd ever heard about him, and putting that with what she was seeing right then, too. It was an impressive combination.

"That poor child had New Testaments flung all over the place that day. It reminded me of one of my favorite verses. The good Lord impressed me to say it out loud while I was bearin' down on her wounds. I expect He heard a lot of prayin' that day."

"Well, all the same, we are grateful for everything you did, Joe," Lizbeth said.

"Were you in that old war?" Willa asked.

"I served in the Second World War and Korea, too, ma'am. I was a cook in the Coast Guard. I've made more meals on water than on land." He laughed and dried the last of the pots and pans.

Lester came in the door warming up on his harmonica in the living room. Joe excused himself and went to his truck to get his fiddle, leaving the two women alone.

"I'm surely glad to get all those quilts into needy hands, Willa. Thank you for helping me do that. It was so silly to have them collecting dust all these years — a sin, really." Lizbeth kept her eyes on the broom as she swept. "I'd like to do more along those lines, but . . ."

Willa cleared her throat, putting a halt to the speech. "Miz Liz, I ain't no fool, and I can see plain what you're doin' here."

"Oh?" Lizbeth banged the silverware as she placed it in a drawer.

"I just want to say that I think you've got a good eye for menfolk," Willa said.

Lizbeth dried her hands on her apron and held her arms out to Willa. They hugged each other tight.

Willa stepped back and grinned at her. "Now let's go see if he can play as good as he looks."

Trina bent down to get a better look at the newspaper clipping on Helene's bulletin board. "Do you ever look bad in a picture, Jem?"

"Yuck. I look like I'm mad."

"Nah. You look like Bridgette Bardot with brown hair."

"That's the second time somebody said that to me. Doesn't she have buckteeth? Anyway, I'm glad to get that interview over with. I don't like talking to reporters. They can leave out part of what you say and give it a totally different meaning."

"I thought the article was quite nice, Jemma," Helene said from the dining room.

"She can really hear with her new hearing aid, huh?" Trina whispered.

"By the way, dear, the gallery owner called about half past four. She needs to speak with you before she closes." Helene handed Jemma the note.

Her show had just opened, so the owner couldn't have much to say.

"Hi, Anne. This is Jemma Forrester. Did you need to talk with me?"

"Jemma, yes. I . . . ah, hope this is not too upsetting for you, but my assistant sold two of your watercolors this morning."

"Really? That's great! Now I've sold three pieces and the show has just been open for two days. I guess the newspaper article helped."

"Actually, the two watercolors were from the group that we had overpriced, hoping that no one would buy. The client paid two thousand dollars for them."

Jemma's smile evaporated. "What? You have to be kidding. Which two were they?"

"Number nine and number ten were sold, and the client put a hold on number twelve."

"I don't remember the numbers. What were the titles?"

"Let's see. Number nine is a girl laughing, number ten is a girl holding a firefly, and number twelve is a girl looking in the mirror as she brushes her hair. They are all self-portraits, I assume. I hope the sale is acceptable with you. You have my apologies."

Her stomach rose to her throat. "May I ask the name of the client?"

"Of course. I have that right here. His name is Paul J. Turner."

CHAPTER 14
SECRETS

Jemma hadn't said much since they left Helene's, and Trina knew why. "So what's your plan, girl? Are you going to let him keep the paintings?"

"What I can do about it? He paid the asking price. I guess he's just like any other buyer, even though I don't want him to have them, and I dread telling Spence about it. Good grief."

"Paul's after you, huh?"

"He just wants my art as a trophy."

"Maybe he really loved you. Even cowboys gotta have somebody to love."

"I don't want to think about it now. Tell me about you and Nick."

"Same old, same old. We never get to see each other. I think Nick must be overwhelmed with his internship. He's keeping some crazy hours. We never go out because there's the car thing."

"I'm sorry, Trina. I'll take you to see him

right now." She made her famous U-turn at the next block.

Trina held on to the dashboard. She already knew that Jemmabeth Forrester was about the best friend anybody could have. Now she thought she might also be the craziest.

Nick lived in the shabbiest side of Dallas. Kids played in the litter and discarded furniture that dotted the premises. Young men leaned against buildings, engaged in suspicious conversations while old men clumped together, laughing and arguing on tumbledown steps.

"I'll wait here," Jemma said.

"No, you come with me and say hello. You haven't seen him in a long time."

His apartment was like all the others except for a card, neatly thumb-tacked to the door that said NICHOLAS FIELDS, ALMOST AN M.D.

Jemma laughed. "Some of your work, huh?"

"Yeah," Trina said. "I hoped it would cheer him up, but like I said, he's too serious." She knocked on the door that appeared to have been in several fights of its own and lost. Nick came to the door, his glasses perched on the end of his nose.

"Trina, honey! Oh hi, Jemma. You

should've told me y'all were coming. This place is a mess."

Trina kissed him. "I wanted to see you, so Jem brought me by. We can leave if you want."

"No, no, come in. I'll get these papers cleared off so y'all can sit down. I'm glad you came."

Jemma didn't really know Nick very well. She had been around him a few times and liked him. He was a veteran, but before Vietnam, and now he had graduated from Southwestern Medical School and was an intern at Parkland Hospital. The apartment was bare, but neater than she expected for a bachelor. It was organized and functional, like Spencer's room in Florence. "How's the internship going?" she asked.

Nick pushed up his glasses. "I'm working myself to the bone."

"I was thinking that when Spence comes this weekend, maybe we could all go out. You know, on a double date."

"Yeah, that would be nice, but I may be at the hospital all weekend."

Trina put her arm in his. "Oh, c'mon, Nick. We never get to do anything."

"Well, think about it," Jemma said. "It's going to be girls' treat night. Maybe we'll cook for you guys and watch a TV movie.

How does that sound?"

"I might be able to do that. I'll see what my schedule is like."

"Listen, y'all, I need to run to the drug-store a minute. I think I saw one down the street."

"Yeah," Nick said. "It's about two blocks north of here."

Jemma winked at Trina and left. She drove around a while and stopped at Walgreen's, just to stay honest, and bought some bubble gum. It wasn't the sort of neighborhood for taking a stroll or she would have stayed gone longer. She drove back to the apartment parking lot and read a chapter in her *Great Masters* book.

It took a while for someone to answer the door, and she saw that as a good sign. It was. Nick had his glasses off and was grinning at Trina. "I'm sure grateful you brought my girl by. I'll check the hospital schedule and try to get over to Wicklow whenever you say."

"I say as soon as the sun comes up on Saturday," Trina said and waved Jemma out the door ahead of her.

The foursome sat down to a splendid meal in Helene's dining room, complete with candles and cloth napkins.

"This is quite a feast, ladies." Spencer grinned at his favorite chef.

"We eat like this all the time." Jemma gave him The Look that drove him crazy.

"So, Nick, how are things in the world of interns?" Spencer asked.

Nick nodded with a mouthful of steak. "It's okay. I think I'm wearing a little thin on sleep and energy. Maybe this meal will fix me up. What's the latest with your bird training?"

"He won't talk about it." Jemma shoved Spencer's arm. "It's all hush-hush."

"It's no secret. But I need a break from it when I'm with you."

"Do you think you'll be seeing a lot of combat?" Nick asked.

"I think I'm going to be flying Medevac."

Nick folded his arms on the table. "The Dust Offs are unbelievable."

"Explain, please." Jemma frowned at the new terminology.

Nick pushed up his glasses. "The Dust Offs are the medical evacuation team. They fly in and pick up the wounded. I guess there's no sweeter sound than a Dust Off coming when you're down."

Spencer kept eating. He could feel her eyes on him.

"Where'd they come up with that name?"

Trina asked.

"The blades kick up a lot of dust," Nick said.

"Is it the worst job in Vietnam?" Jemma asked.

"Baby, I don't think there are any good jobs there." Spencer reached for her hand.

Jemma and Trina cleaned up the kitchen while Spencer showed Nick around Helene's place. She insisted they take her husband's red, classic MG roadster out for a spin.

"Got a question for you, Nick," Spencer began.

"I can't give medical advice yet," Nick shouted over the wind.

"My dad has a car dealership in our hometown. I'd really like to help Trina with her own transportation, but I don't think I can do it without your help."

"What do you have in mind?" Nick leaned in for the explanation.

"I want you to let her think that it's yours, but that she can use it whenever she has the need. She and Jemma are not going to always have the same schedule, plus Jem will be graduating in the spring. She will probably stay with her grandmother in Chillaton."

Nick shook his head. "You two have done so much for Trina already. She'd have a fit if she knew about a car."

"I'm not going to be the one to tell her."

"I don't want to lie to her," Nick said.

"Then just tell her that I loaned you the money for a car and that will be the truth."

"Man, you don't need to do that. I can make it with the bus and my uncle's car."

"Nick, I have the money, and I have a father in the business. We can get it at cost. Please let me do this for y'all. It's a loan, remember."

"Trina told me that you were a nice guy, but this is too much." He exhaled. "I sure would love to be able to see her more often and not stand around waiting for the bus to get to Parkland."

"Then it's a deal." Spencer pulled into the Wicklow Piggly Wiggly parking lot.

"Some deal, all right." They shook hands. "Thank you, Spencer. I'll pay you back as soon as I can."

"Forget it. C'mon, it's your turn to drive this beauty," Spence said and changed seats with him.

The night was cool and clear when they stopped to watch the stars on a lonely dirt road outside of Mineral Wells. They spread their quilt on the hood and found Orion.

"Do you think we have guardian angels?" Jemma asked, pulling another old quilt up over them.

"What does the Bible say about that?" Spencer wrapped his arms around her, and they gazed at the sky.

"I don't know. I'll have to look it up, I guess. If we do, I'll feel better about this Dust Off thing."

"Baby, don't worry about that. I have to do my job — whatever it is. Maybe I will be able to help somebody. God is going to bring me home to you. I really believe that."

Jemma looked him in the eye. "Spence, I love you so much, but it scares me that I had the wreck and we didn't get married. Why did that happen if we are supposed to get married?"

"All I know is that I'll come home to marry you."

She had to get it out. "Babe, I have to tell you something."

"Okay, shoot."

"Paul bought two, maybe three of my paintings. He spent two thousand dollars for them. If he buys the third, it will be three thousand."

Spencer wasn't expecting such an announcement. It took him a minute to recuperate. "Which paintings?"

"They're all of me," she whispered.

"Of course they are. I should've known."

"The gallery thought they wouldn't sell at those prices."

"Looks like he wanted them really bad."

"I'm not going to paint myself anymore."

"I thought I had your first self-portrait. You gave it to me in Flagstaff, remember? Never mind. Just so he doesn't try to get the real thing. That's not something we have to worry about, right?"

Jemma pressed her nose against his. "I said I'd done some other self-portraits, but no one had ever seen them, until now. I have no interest in that man. If you want me not to worry about you coming home from this war, then you have to promise me that you will not worry about Paul Turner."

He liked it when she got heated up. "Hmmm. You have to keep your end of the bargain, though." They resumed their stargazing and talked about their future, after Vietnam, after he came home.

Paul bought the third painting and the Gallery exhibition earned Jemma enough to forget all about cleaning houses. She also received advance commissions for three portraits. They couldn't be any harder than her Lillygrace grandparents' portrait had been. The first portrait was scheduled for a sitting at The Adolphus Hotel in downtown Dallas. She'd never been there before. She did know that if someone had permanent residence in a ritzy hotel, they were loaded. The arrangements had all been made through the Gallery staff. The patron was a rich old foreigner, she assumed, a Mr. Laup Renrut. She thought that was the funniest name she had heard lately, and had one last giggle over it in the elevator. She knocked on the door, and it opened at her touch into a luxury suite.

"Hello. I'm Jemmabeth Forrester, here to do some sketches for a portrait," she called to the empty room.

"Hello, darlin'," a familiar voice said from the bar.

Jemma's heart stopped. Paul was sitting on a bar stool, his green eyes drilling a hole in her from across the room.

"What are you doing here?" she asked. "I'm supposed to meet someone for a portrait sitting." Her jaw hung open.

He grinned and sauntered to the door, all six foot five of him, and shut it. "Mr. Renrut, I presume? C'mon, Jem, it's me, backwards. I want you to paint my portrait. No harm in that, right?"

Jemma was frozen to the spot. He slipped his big arms around her and halfway kissed her. She jerked back from him and wiped her mouth. "How dare you, Paul! How dare you. This is inexcusable. You tricked me."

"I thought you would get a kick out of this. Have you lost your sense of humor? You always did look good when you were ticked off, Jem. Now come back over here and let me finish what I started." He sat on the tapestry couch and patted the cushion next to him. He looked trimmer than he did when he came to see her at Lizbeth's. Nobody could deny he was a sensational buckaroo, and clearly he knew it.

"Forget it. You've gone to a lot of trouble for nothing. I am not going to paint your portrait so that you can seduce me into your little trap. I'm in love with Spencer, and we're getting married."

"Not any time soon, honey. He's gonna be in another world before long." He relaxed on the couch and stretched his long legs out over it. His boots hung over the arm. "Have you forgotten what it was like between us? Well, I haven't. Every time I look at those paintings of you, I want you even more." He pulled his hat down low over his eyes and moved his hands as though directing oncoming traffic. "You aren't married yet, and I'm giving it all I've got. This old boy's back in the saddle again."

Jemma turned on her heel and flew to the door. He had locked it every which way, but she managed to get them all undone. Paul was off the couch like he had roped a calf, though, and leaned against the door, making it impossible to open.

He touched her cheek. "It's only me, Jem. Won't you let me see if your hair still smells like flowers? I miss you. You're my destiny."

She shook her head to move his hand. "Get away from this door, or I'm going to scream. I mean it."

He looked down at her through his thick, black lashes. "Jemmabeth, I love you. Just give me a chance. You loved me once. We both know you did. It was that night of no mercy that messed us up."

She looked him in the eye. "I was swept away by you, yes, but I didn't love you. We had a great time, but you lied to me. I love Spencer with every part of my being." He traced around her lips while she spoke, further getting on her nerves. She swatted at his hand. "There is no hope for you and me. You'll find someone else if you look in the right places. I'm sorry. I don't want to hurt your feelings, but you'll have to get on with your life."

He touched her forehead with his lips. She wiggled around and plastered her back against the doorknob. He moved a stray lock of hair off her forehead. "You are a thing of beauty, darlin'. I would change my life for you."

"Change your life by going to church, Paul. Then good things will come your way."

"Didn't come here for a sermon. I want you in my life, nothing else." He couldn't keep his hands off her. "Give me one more chance," he whispered and moved his hand to the back of her neck.

Jemma eased her hand behind her and yanked on the doorknob. He held it shut with one snakeskin boot. She gritted her teeth. "There *will* be somebody else. You won't find her at the Handle Bar, though."

He looked right into her eyes. "Would you at least let me have a good-bye kiss?"

"No." He was way too big for any of her wrestling moves. "All my kisses are for Spencer."

"There's bound to be a spare one for old Paul." With that, he pinned her arms to the door and pressed his lips to hers. Jemma's ears were ringing, she was so mad. There was a time when she would have melted with that kiss. It was that good.

Paul pushed his hat back. "Now tell me.

What's he got that I haven't got?" He was so close she tasted English Leather.

Jemma blew out his kiss. "My heart, Paul. Spence has my heart."

"I hope he knows what he's got."

"He knows that I love him. I always have and always will." She reached for the doorknob again, and he laid his hand on hers as she opened the door.

"If you ever need anything, anything at all, darlin', I'll be there for you. I mean that."

"I need you to leave me alone!" She flew down the hallway.

"Good-bye, Jemmabeth Alexandra Forrester," he said, leaning against the doorway, *Hud* style.

Jemma did not look at him again. "Good-bye, Mr. Renrut," she hissed. "Maybe you should get a kiss from your ex-wife."

"I'll be seeing you," he whispered and watched her disappear into the elevator. He went back into the suite and slumped in a chair. What a stupid move this had been. It only served to make her mad again, exactly the opposite of what he had hoped for. In the future, maybe he should plan these things in a sober state of mind, but it hurt too much that way.

■ ■ ■ ■

She chewed on her lip all the way home. How could she have been duped like that, and how on earth could she tell Spencer? She had just told him not to worry about Paul. He had enough to worry about, but she also didn't want to keep any secrets from him. She needed to talk to somebody. She wanted to call her mom, but her parents didn't know the whole story about Mr. Turner. They didn't know that he was not quite divorced while he was dating her. Jemma hadn't known that particular part of the story either, until it was almost too late and the guilt nearly broke her in two. Then it dawned on her how to get some straight talk.

"It's about time you called your old aunty. How are you, and how is that sweet Spencer?"

"Do Dah, I need your advice." Jemma told her the latest. Julia knew everything that had happened with Paul. She had even hired a private investigator to check him out before the whole thing was over that summer.

"A sore loser," she said. "He can't stand it

313

that he wasn't the better man. I see your predicament, sugar. I'll tell you this much. It never pays to harbor a secret, even if it's tough in the telling, but the jolt won't last long. Now, I can't make this decision for you, but I know from experience that each secret is like a brick and the withholding of it is the mortar. After a while you have yourself a wall built up between you and your man, and that's a wall you don't need. Tell Spencer what happened. If you don't, you'll start thinking that you did something wrong. You've already been down that road — feeling guilty when you were completely innocent."

Jemma sighed. "Thank you, Do Dah. You're a wise woman."

"Call me Julia, and I'm not a wise woman. Your gram is a wise woman. I've made so many mistakes that it's like opening a file cabinet to ask me for advice. Don't sell Spencer short, honey. That boy has grit and he can handle this. Let me know how it goes, and I'll be seeing you in a couple of weeks for Christmas."

"You're coming to Chillaton? I thought you always went to England for Christmas."

Julia coughed. "I'll see you, sometime, sugar." She hung up, leaving Jemma alone on the line.

■ ■ ■ ■

"Let's go to Dallas tomorrow morning. I need to do some shopping," Spencer said as they drove away from the base.

"Sure. That'll be fine." She had already chewed several antacids.

He caught on immediately. "What's happened?"

She bawled like a two-year-old. "I'm so sorry. Rats. I didn't want this to happen."

Spencer pulled into a roadside park. They stood beside the car, holding one another until she stopped crying. "Is it your health?" he asked.

Bless his heart. If only it were that simple. "No, I'm fine. It's Paul."

Spencer made no remark as they sat on a picnic table and she spilled the story. He held her hand the whole time, staring at the highway and chewing a hole in his lip. "It's cold, baby. Let's go home," he finally said.

He turned on the radio. Jemma watched him out of the corner of her eye and knew that he was livid. The Corvette fairly flew along the highway. Spencer liked to drive fast, but this was angry fast. The red and blue lights rotated behind them. Neither said a word until the officer left him with a warning ticket in his hand. It was a good thing Spencer had on his uniform.

Jemma spoke first. "If you are mad at me, I'll just die."

He put the ticket in his wallet because it was the least of his worries. "I'm not angry with you, Jem. I love you."

"You look mad."

"Yeah, well, that may be true. Let's take Helene and Trina out to dinner tonight."

"Trina is in Dallas, as usual, now that Nick has a car, and Helene has gone to the opera with a friend tonight."

"Then you and I will have peanut butter sandwiches and snuggle on the couch."

She grinned at his ability to move on from sticky issues. "It's a date," she said, but noticed the change in him.

"Good morning, Jemma," Helene said. "I see that the Corvette is gone. Where is Spencer?"

"I don't know. We're supposed to go shopping in Dallas this morning. Maybe he went to get gas or something."

"I've been up for an hour and I have yet to see him."

Jemma went to the conservatory and stood in the door. He was not altogether himself last night.

Helene took her hand. "Come along, dear, let's have a cup of tea and visit. Tell me about your latest painting."

He had gotten the address from another Turner in the phone book, claiming to be an old military buddy who wanted to see Paul. At least part of that was true. Jem had said he was in the army. He just hoped that he could recognize the guy from Jemma's sketchy, year-old description. It was getting chilly in the Corvette, so he started the engine again to warm up. As he did, a tall, good-looking man emerged from the house and retrieved the newspaper from the lawn. Spencer decided to take a chance.

"Hey, how's it going? Aren't you Paul Turner?" Spencer asked, approaching him.

"Yeah. What's up?"

Spencer extended his hand. "I'm Spencer Chase, Jemmabeth's fiancé, and I think we need to talk." Paul was taken aback. He stammered as he repeated his name and sheepishly clasped Spencer's hand.

"You're going to get cold out here, man. Why don't we go inside?"

"No, uh, whatever you have to say, you can say out here," Paul said, looking past Spencer toward the Corvette. "What's on your mind?" He folded his arms across his

317

bare chest.

"Well, Jemma is on my mind most of the time, and from what I've heard, she's on yours, too. The thing is that she has made a choice here, between you and me. I think we need to respect that choice, don't you, Mr. Turner?"

Paul leveled his eyes at Spencer. "I think all's fair anytime, anywhere, Mr. Chase."

"No, that's where you're wrong. Since you care so much for Jemma, I would hope that you would honor her happiness. We both know that she is worth risking everything for."

Paul looked away.

"What you may not know is that she almost died last summer in a car wreck. She was in a coma for almost two weeks. When she was semi-conscious, there was only one name she said and that was mine. If she had said yours, sir, I'd say that we have a fair race on our hands, but she didn't. I fully realize the pain that losing her can cause, but I'm asking you to be a gentleman, and back off." Spencer always did have a way with words.

The news of Jemma's accident clearly took him by surprise. Paul shifted his weight and looked Spencer over, checking to see why he was the preferred one. "I respect what you've said, but Jemma was the best thing that ever happened to me. I don't see what you have to lose by a little competition. If she still feels the same way when you get back from 'Nam, maybe I'll back off then."

Spencer clenched his jaw. "If you continue to bother Jemmabeth and make her uncomfortable, uneasy, or in the least bit upset, I will insist that she gets a restraining order against you. I'm sure you learned about those in law school."

Paul turned toward the house. "You, sir, are on my property. Get off," he snorted over his shoulder.

"You are on my fiancée's nerves. You get off, Mr. Renrut," Spencer said, standing his ground.

Paul slammed the door, but not before Spencer saw one of Jemma's paintings hanging on the wall inside.

She met the Corvette as he pulled in Helene's driveway. Spencer got out and leaned against the car. She put her arms around him. "Where have you been? I was about to start looking for you."

"I had some business to take care of," he said, then kissed her with a healthy dose of enthusiasm for the early morning hour.

"I could take some more of that." She

319

nuzzled his ear.

"Let's eat and get going on our shopping." He didn't elaborate on the exact business he had before breakfast and she didn't ask. She told herself that it must have had something to do with Christmas gifts. He was so good at surprises.

They spent the day in Dallas and stopped at a pizza place before driving back to Wicklow.

"So where were you this morning, Spence? Is it a secret?"

"I went to see Mr. Renrut."

She bugged her eyes at him. "You didn't. You confronted Paul?"

"Nothing happened. I just told him the truth. That you chose me over him, and that he had better leave you alone or else."

"Or else what? Did you go fisticuffs?"

"Or else we're getting a restraining order against him."

"Wow! I wish I had been there. Why didn't you let me go with you?"

"This is between him and me. You are the victim."

"I love you, Mr. Chase. You are my hero once again."

"Yeah, well, he'd better leave you alone, and I'm serious."

"I'm sorry, babe. He's a nice guy. He just can't help himself, I guess."

"Whose side are you on?"

"I didn't mean it like that, Spence. I simply mean that he may have loved me."

Spencer gave her a look she hadn't anticipated and ate his pizza.

"Now wait." Jemma turned his face toward hers. "I love you. Maybe I shouldn't have told you about this."

Spencer shrugged. "I guess you could have kept it a secret if that's the kind of relationship you want to have."

Jemma put her hands on her hips. "What does that mean? I want to be with you as your wife. I want to have your babies and grow old and wrinkled with you and watch the stars from our rocking chairs. That's the kind of relationship I want to have with you."

A little boy in the next booth peeked over at them.

Spencer puffed out his cheeks. "I misspoke — big-time. I didn't realize how jealous I am of him. I just wish that he had never kissed you or whispered sweet things in your ear or even looked at you with those green eyes of his. Forgive me, Jem. I didn't know he would affect me this way. I think it makes me feel like that song of Roy's. Remember

'Running Scared'? Plus, I saw one of your paintings hanging on his wall and that got to me. His idea is to try and win you back while I'm in Vietnam. That was too much for me to handle."

Jemma held him close. "Let's go home, babe. I want to hold you without an audience."

"Miz Liz, I got them lights strung all across the porch, but when I plugged 'em in, they didn't work," Lester said, his ears the color of frozen eggplants.

"Well, that's okay. Those lights are older than electricity anyway," Lizbeth said as she iced Spencer's favorite cake. "We'll make do with what we have."

"Did I ever tell you about the time that the sheriff let the jailbirds decorate the courthouse for Christmas?"

"No, I don't believe I've had the privilege of hearing that story." She probably had, but it was of no use to tell him.

"Well, sir, it was during the second war and the county didn't have much money to spend on decoratin'. The sheriff had the inmates stringin' popcorn with needles and thread. Old Mrs. Chase, Spencer's grandma, donated about five bushels of cranberries, so they had to string them, too.

It sure was a sight 'cause back then them fellers had to wear them black-and-white-striped suits. It was real funny to watch. The Callister twins was doin' time for makin' moonshine out to their daddy's old Windy Valley place. 'Course their daddy was as guilty as they were, but he took off to the next county on a horse and the sheriff didn't have enough gas to chase him. Chancy and Chauncy was them twins' names. They were about as ugly as sin, poor things, and flat-out had no sense at all. Them boys ate half of the popcorn and hid most of the cranber-ries in their cells and kept them there for weeks."

"What on earth for?"

"Moonshine. Their old daddy started visitin' them real regular like. What nobody knew was that he was slippin' things to them, ingredients and stuff for brewin'. They even had themselves a hot plate and whatnot in their cell. Them boys whipped up a batch of cranberry moonshine in a mop bucket. They kept it hid in a contrap-tion down the commode tank, no offense, Miz Liz. Ever one of them inmates was drunk and sick when the sheriff got to work one mornin'. The twins got themselves another six months for that mischief."

Lizbeth sprinkled the remainder of coconut on top of the cake. "Lester, how do you remember all these stories?"

"Well, sir, after that incident, the sheriff hired me to check out the cells one night a week for mischief makin'. I could sniff out that sort of thing. That's how I got enough money to buy my cuckoo clock. Had it on layaway down to the Household Supply for a long spell. It still works, even after makin' that cuckoo racket all them years."

She stood back to look at the cake. It was her best recipe — coconut crème. Spencer could almost eat the whole thing by himself.

"Jemmerbeth and Spencer still don't know what's going on around here?" Lester asked.

"I hope not. Julia said she almost slipped and said too much to Jemma. I imagine Jemma might smell a rat if she was paying attention. Everybody should be coming in tonight. Trina and Helene will be on the last train from Dallas. You can still pick them up, right?"

"Yes ma'am. I'll be there right after I pick up Willer, but if them young'uns are flyin', they could get here right fast."

"They can't leave until Spencer gets in from Mineral Wells. He's meeting Jemma in Dallas, then they'll fly here together."

"What else do you want me to do?"

"Sit down and have a cup of coffee with

me, Lester. You've been working hard all week. The place looks good, thanks to you."

"My pleasure, Miz Liz, always a pleasure."

Lizbeth poured them each a cupful from the percolator. "What do you think about Willa and Joe?"

"I like him a lot. He's right good on that fiddle, not as good as Cam, of course, but downright decent."

"I bet he shows up here during the festivities. I think he's pretty sweet on Willa, and I think the feeling is mutual."

"She's a good woman, and he saved our Jemmer's life. I think they'd make a nice couple." Lester reached for a cranberry muffin. "How do you think her girl is gonna take it?"

"Trina will be fine. She wants her mama to be happy. Then she won't have to worry about her so much."

Lester took a big sip of coffee and tapped his foot on the linoleum. "Now don't be takin' this wrong, Miz Liz, but ain't it kindly peculiar how you and me took up with Willer and Joe, them being colored and all."

Lizbeth set down her cup. "Where are you heading with this, Lester?"

"Not sure where I'm headin'. I just was thinkin' that in our younger days, shoot, probably even when Cam was alive, nobody our age would've mixed with colored folks."

"I suppose you're right about that. Of course that doesn't mean it was the right thing to do."

"Well, sir, I've come around to that way of thinkin' myself. We all got the same innerds and the same laugh and the same sense about what's right and wrong. There's bad white folk and real nice colored folk and vice versa. I get teased down to the barber shop about bein' friends with Joe and Willer, but I'm to where it don't bother me none."

Lizbeth smiled at him. "I think the next step for you and me is to stop calling folks 'colored' and learn to say 'black.' "

"That's nothin' but fair. Our bunch has picked 'white' for a color and their bunch can have 'black.' I reckon the whole caboodle of us could be called 'colored.' "

They both chuckled at his assessment.

"Oh my, I hear a car," Lizbeth said.

"Gram!" Robby ran in the back door, his blue eyes shining.

"Help my life, child, what are you doing here so early?"

"We left last night. Mom and Daddy took turns driving. Hi, Lester. May I have a muffin, Gram?"

"Help yourself, honey."

"Merry Christmas!" Jim strode across the room to give his mother a hug.

Alex was right behind him, hugging Lester. "We couldn't stand it. We had to get here and help."

"Let me look at you. Aren't you worn out from driving all night?" Lizbeth asked, taking their coats.

Robby took a second muffin. "They took turns snoring in the car, too."

"I did not snore," Alex said. "Have you heard from Jemmabeth?"

"She called last night. Spencer arrives in Dallas about 5:30 and their flight to Amarillo gets in around nine o'clock."

"I made a big sign for Jem and Spence," Robby said, running back to the car.

"Do you think she knows?" Jim asked.

Lizbeth raised her brow. "If she does, we have Julia to thank. She slipped and told Jemma that she would see her this weekend."

"What got into her? I thought she was the big secret keeper in the family," Jim said.

"She's getting old, like the rest of us, I suppose. She thought Jemma was distracted and may not have noticed."

"Oh, Jem notices everything." Alex rolled her eyes.

Robby came in with a bang from the

screen door and flopped a roll of butcher paper on the floor. "See? Jem's gonna love it." He began unrolling the paper, revealing large, red letters — *SURP.*

"Let's wait, son, and I'll help you tack that up." Jim set down his coffee and helped Robby reinstate the noisy paper.

"It says, 'Surprise Jem & Spence!' " Robby grinned. "It's big, too."

"I can see that," Lizbeth said. "You did a fine job."

"Hey, young'un, you want to go with me to buy some popcorn?" Lester asked. "Maybe we'll stop by the drugstore for some comic books and a shake."

"Yeah! Let's go. Okay, Mom?" Robby turned puppy dog eyes on Alex.

"A milk shake this time of the day?" Lizbeth asked.

"Sure, Robby, you go have some fun. It's been a long trip." Jim winked at Lester. "I know what you're thinking, Mama." Jim put his arm around Lizbeth as they watched Robby grab Lester's hand. "He is the spitting image of Luke, right down to that giggle."

She smiled. "He is indeed."

Julia and Arthur were the second to arrive. She was certain that Jemma hadn't caught on to the party plans. Arthur immediately went shopping. When he came back, the kitchen was overstocked with food. He also bought every string of Christmas lights in town. Jim and Lester were busy all day. Carrie and Philip dropped by for a quick visit before heading to The Judge's, and Alex went so far as to extend an invitation for The Judge to join them. Arthur had a few words to say over that idea, quoting Shakespeare's *Macbeth* concerning his wife's high school flame. Alex even called Max and Rebecca Chase, too. Rebecca was almost gracious, if not somewhat inebriated, but declined. Max, however, accepted their offer and promised to bring flowers and something for the punch. Alex assured him that the punch was fine as it was, but that flowers would be very nice.

Ted and Trent Lillygrace had just returned from a month in Europe. They were tanned and fit, like country club men. It was easy to see that Ted and Alex were siblings, but Trent resembled his mother, who had deserted him as an infant for money. Robert and Catherine Lillygrace, completely overdressed and oblivious to it, stayed in the living room visiting with Arthur. The Christmas tree in the living room was inundated with gifts, and Robby had inspected each one. His banner was strung across the ceiling and went the length of the room. The air was filled with the sweet smells and sounds of the holidays and the excitement of a surprise party for everyone's favorite couple.

Jemma and Spencer would have to rent a car in Amarillo, then it would take them an hour to drive to Chillaton, so they were expected around ten thirty. Cam's clock had just chimed ten when Lizbeth finally sat in Cam's chair. She had been in the kitchen for a week, but now she could relax and wait like the rest.

"What if they stop to eat?" Trent asked.

"Jemma will be hot to get home. They won't eat," Trina said.

"I hope they don't come in the back. It looks like a parking lot in the alley," Ted added.

"Spencer always pulls in front," Lizbeth assured them all.

"I hear a car now." Alex moved to the front door. "My goodness. It's a semi-truck. Why would a big truck be coming here?"

"Oh mercy," Willa said and moved to the door. Trina joined her, and Lester was not far behind.

"What's going on?" Jim bent his head to peer out the oval window in the door.

"Willa, I think maybe you'd better have Joe move his truck out back," Lizbeth called out from the living room.

"I'm two jumps ahead of you, Miz Liz. Trina, come on and help me to the gate." Willa opened the door and stepped onto the front porch.

Alex turned to Lester. "Is that the truck driver that Jemma hit?"

"Yes, ma'am," Lester said. "That's him all right, and he's a good'un."

"I'd sure like to meet him," Jim said.

"You'd better ask Miz Liz about Joe. I'm not sure what all I can say at this point," Lester said and ducked back into the good bedroom.

"What's going on, Mama?" Jim asked.

"I think you'll find Joe Cross is one of the nicest men around. I'm sure you'll see plenty of him this week."

The big rig started up again and moved down the block. They heard it pull to the alley behind Lester's house. It wasn't long before the group came in the back door. Trina's eyes were on Joe, and his were set on Willa. He took off his cowboy hat and shook hands all around. "Sounds like we've got us a party tonight."

"Thanks to you and the good Lord." Jim patted Joe's back.

Joe grinned. "No, sir, I didn't do nothin'. It was all the Lord's doin's."

"Car coming!" Robby yelled. "Should we turn the lights out?"

"Are you sure it's them?" Carrie asked. "I can't see."

"It's a big car," Robby said. "It looks like old people, though."

All was quiet as someone rapped on the oval glass.

"Why would they knock?" Trent asked.

Alex opened the door. "Come in. We're so glad that you decided to come. Max, would you mind moving your car to the back of the house? We want to surprise the kids. Thank you."

Lester melted into the woodwork. He and Max Chase had history over a used truck, and Lester wasn't keen on making small talk with him. Spencer's mother, Rebecca, once a beauty herself, had on way too much makeup, and it was not applied quite right. Reeking of alcohol, she snickered and smirked at the introductions. Alex offered her coffee and a chair, both of which she accepted.

"Car!" Robby yelled again. "Oh boy, it's them."

The gathering held its collective breath. Through the lace curtains, most could see

Jemma and Spencer walk to the front porch in the glow of the new Christmas lights. Spencer was still in uniform, and Jemmabeth was full of giggles.

"When they open the door, count to three, then yell," Alex whispered.

"Yuck, they're kissing," Robby whispered, causing stifled ripples of laughter through the house. The doorknob turned, and the door creaked open.

"Good grief, it's so dark in here," Jemma said.

"*SURPRISE!*" came the thunderous response, along with every light in the house being turned on.

Jemma shrieked and the house went dark.

"Way to go, Jem," Robby yelled back. "Now you ruined Christmas."

"What's going on?" Jemma asked.

"Somebody get a flashlight. I think we've blown a fuse," Jim shouted.

"Daddy? Where are you?"

"Just a minute, sweet pea," Alex said, laughing. "We'll have to try this again."

Mumbles and laughter rose up from various rooms.

"I think I saw Carrie," Spencer said.

"I'm over here," Carrie called.

"So am I," Trent added in a falsetto.

"Me, too," Robby said. "I can smell your

stinky perfume, Jem."

"I can smell your stinky socks," Spencer countered, causing another round of laughter. The lights flickered, then went off again.

"Turn off the outside Christmas lights. That'll help," Trent suggested.

"Leave it to an engineer," Alex said.

Lester could be heard fumbling for the front door. At last the house lights all came on. Spencer and Jemma were speechless. They were surprised for real.

"Mom, was this your idea?" Jemma asked as they ate Lizbeth's cake.

"I'm guilty." Alex gave Spencer a hug.

Spencer watched his own mother, whose glazed eyes were on Jemmabeth everywhere she went.

"We all wanted to be together before our favorite soldier takes off for parts unknown," Julia said.

"As well as fatten him up," Helene added.

"There's going to be another soldier in the family now," Ted said with his arm around Trent.

Spencer sat back. "Oh man. You got yours, too."

Trent shrugged. "Yeah. Crazy, huh?"

"I'm being transferred to a different base," Spencer said.

Ted nodded. "Getting you ready for night-time and bad weather."

Alex cleared her throat. "So, did we surprise you kids?"

"You did. Y'all are good." Jemma said, still thinking about Spencer flying in bad weather.

"We hoped Sandy could come, but she is meeting Martin in Hawaii right now," Alex explained.

"Yeah, she called me last week. He's almost done over there. Would you like some more cake, Mrs. Chase?" Jemma asked, still on Spencer's lap.

"No." Her volume made everybody jump. "Can't you find your own chair to sit in?"

Jemma hopped off and Spencer stood. "Maybe you would like some more coffee, Mother."

"Let's go home, son," she said. "We have plenty of chairs there."

Alex intervened. "I wish you could stay longer. You know what? Jim and I would love to take you home, if that's okay. I'd like to see your antiques. We'll be right back, sweet pea." She touched Spencer's hand. "I know you are tired, Spence." Alex was so smooth and thoughtful that the devil himself would have a hard time resisting her.

■ ■ ■ ■

Spencer's dad was working the crowd, and he had cornered Ted Lillygrace. During the Second World War, Max Chase had never left the United States while Ted had flown missions over half of Europe.

"That was the last time anybody had to tell me what two paper clips in a coffee cup meant. You have to learn the pet peeves of the commanding officer, that's for sure." Max laughed harder at his story than his audience did. Lester had sidled up while Max was telling his tale. His beady eyes reminded Lester of a pet mouse he'd had as a youngster, only the mouse wasn't nearly as obnoxious. Finally he couldn't stand it anymore.

"So, are you still passin' off junkers as fine automobiles to elderly folks and then lyin' about it?" Lester said.

"Mr. Timms." Max hustled him aside. "I'm learning more about you every time I see you."

"Well, sir, I'm learnin' more about the devil every time I see your sorry hide around town." Lester's ears colored up.

Max looked around, maintaining a smile. "Mr. Timms, I made that little mistake up to you. Now, it's time to forgive and forget. Let's be upstanding about things."

"I just want you to 'fess up and say you were wrong and that you're sorry. You can take them last few words any way you want."

"I sent you the money back and gave you the truck. I don't want you interfering in my social life like you did. People don't know all the facts when you say things like that."

"I'll be happy to oblige them. I can do it right now, if you like."

"No. Look, I'm sorry that I misrepresented things to you. I probably got them down wrong to start with."

"I didn't hear the word *lied* in there anywhere." Lester clicked his dentures.

"Okay, okay. I'm sorry that I lied to you about that old truck. Now, are you satisfied? Let's not spoil the kids' party over this."

"Mr. Max-a-million Chase, I forgive you," Lester said and put out his hand.

Max drew back at the sudden change of attitude, but he shook Lester's hand.

"The Good Book says to forgive so you will be forgiven. That's what you should do, too, Max-a-million. You need to ask forgiveness from the Lord and forgive yourself for all your skirt chasin' and lyin'. You need to forgive your good wife for drinkin' herself into a hole over you, and you sure enough need to forgive yourself for bein' such a pitiful excuse for a father to that fine boy in there. My pa used to tell us young'uns to straighten up and fly right, and I suggest you do the same. I'll be prayin' for you, mister." Lester turned to join Joe Cross, who was tuning up his fiddle.

Max Chase, who never considered himself as the object of anybody's kindly prayers, stared after Lester. His mouth had gone dry, and his throat seemed to have knotted up under his necktie. He looked around for Spencer and found him in the kitchen, talking to Robert Lillygrace. He stood next to him and, for once, did not enter the dialogue. Instead he slipped his arm around Spencer's shoulders.

Spencer looked at his father, smiled, and then carried on with his conversation. Max admired the way his son spoke. He never had heard him curse, and he could throw nickel- or five-dollar words around as needed. People liked Spencer and he was, unlike himself, a prince of a man. That's what people used to call Max's father, too. Max took a deep breath. Lester had rattled him. At least he hadn't yelled at him like he did that day at the dealership and called him Max-a-million-skirt-chaser, but Rebecca still did, upon occasion.

Joe Cross fired up his fiddle. Lester pulled out his harmonica and the group sang along. Only Papa's presence could have made Jemmabeth happier. She stood between Spencer and Carrie as they all sang "White Christmas."

Around one o'clock, the older ones got sleepy and headed off to the That'll Do Motel. The Lillygraces insisted on staying in Amarillo, so they had an hour's drive ahead of them. A few sturdy souls stayed up talking even later. Spencer and Jemma sat in the living room with Trina.

"Do y'all think Mama's in love with Joe?" Trina asked point-blank.

"She acts like it to me," Jemma said. "What do you think, Spence?"

"I like Joe, and if he can make Willa happy, why not?"

"It just took me off guard, you know." Trina yawned. "I'd better get home. I'm beat. I'll see y'all tomorrow."

"I'll take you home," Spencer offered. "I need to go, too. Who knows what's going on at my house?"

Trina stood with her hands on her hips. "I

think I can walk across the tracks. Sit down, soldier." She gave him a gentle push. Spencer landed in Jemma's lap, quite on purpose. Trina sneaked out while they were giggling. Robby was sound asleep in Papa's chair or he would have protested. They watched the lights on the Christmas tree. Papa's bubble lights were Jemma's favorite.

"Do you think we'll have our own little tree year after next?" she asked.

"Yup. It probably won't have that many presents under it, though."

"I won't care; just so we are married."

"It will happen. Give me a kiss because I want to go home and talk to my dad. Did you see him put his arm around me tonight? I don't remember him ever doing that."

"No more lovey-dovey stuff," Robby mumbled. "Go home, Spence."

"You little wart. I'll take care of you tomorrow," Spencer said, rolling him onto the floor. Robby wandered off to the kitchen, where his parents and uncle were still talking.

"Good night, babe. I love you," Jemma said, then watched his car lights disappear down the street.

"Uncle Art, how do you like it at That'll Do?"

"It's completely underrated, Jemma, and I think your aunty is quite taken with it, right, Julia?"

"Heavenly days. We have a cigarette burn on our blanket, we almost had to build a fire in the bathtub to heat the place, and don't get me started on the bathroom."

"We'll survive. You're looking fit, Jemmabeth. Are you feeling your usual perky self these days?" Art asked.

"I had some headaches for a while when school first began, but they went away."

"I didn't know about that, young lady. You should have told me," Alex said as she distributed orange juice.

"I had Trina's boyfriend do some research. He said if they didn't go away that I should see a doctor. Good advice, I thought."

Everyone laughed.

Julia drank her coffee and looked toward the tracks. "I think we have a wedding coming up. Willa and Joe make a real cute couple."

"What's this I hear about Spencer being transferred to another base?" Arthur asked. "Where will he be going?"

"Fort Rucker, Alabama," Jemma replied. "That means I can't see him every weekend. We've been lucky that he has been so close to Dallas."

"You'll make it, dear," Helene said. "War is a horrid mess, but many soldiers come home. I know that is a constant worry, but you must carry on."

Arthur loaded up his plate with biscuits and gravy, then paused. "There is a quote, Jemmabeth, from my favorite wise man, Mark Twain. 'All war must be just that — the killing of strangers against whom you feel no personal animosity; strangers whom, in other circumstances, you would help if you found them in trouble, and who would help you if you needed it.' Tell that to your young man so he can remember it in times of need."

Jemma wrote it in her sketchbook.

"Don't you love Art's photographic memory?" Julia whispered to Jemma. "It comes in handy for so many things — except my checkbook balance." She kissed her husband on the top of his balding head.

"At least Spence won't be shooting at anybody if he's flying a helicopter to rescue people."

Jemma's comment was met with silence.

The rest of the men came in the back just as Spencer came in the front door, and everyone rallied to change the subject. Jemma, however, wanted reassurance that her dearest would not be killing people, nor would anyone try to kill soldiers in an aircraft with a red cross painted on both sides.

The Negro Bethel Church had another surprise for Spencer. The congregation gathered to thank him and have a blessing to officially open the doors to their new building.

After the reception, Spencer and Jemma stood in the church holding hands. "It's beautiful," she said.

"It's nice, really nice. I would make a few changes if I had it to do over."

"I always think that about my paintings."

Spencer walked around, touching the wood and examining the stained-glass window. "I like it. It has the feel that I was hoping for."

They talked, sharing ideas and enjoying the solitude of the church. It was Spencer's first real project as an architect and it was built to God's glory.

Family and friends dined and laughed their way through four days of glorious Christmas celebration. Carrie and Philip took the opportunity to announce their engagement. On the last day of his leave, Jemma and Spencer went for a drive to Plum Creek in his new black Sting Ray convertible. It was a safe and easy thing for Max to upgrade his son's Corvettes, but the gesture was sorely lacking as a relationship builder.

They had spent many precious hours at the creek with Jemma's family. In December there was no water left to qualify it as a creek. Only a dry bed remained, packed with rippled sand where the water had marked its course. They sat under their favorite tree and exchanged Christmas gifts. Jemma placed a sterling silver cross on a chain around Spencer's neck. Spencer gave her a new watch to mark the time until he came home and a rare copy of Emily Dickinson's poems. They took turns reading the poems aloud until the cold evening air engulfed them, forcing them home.

It was a quiet ride to the airport. Jemma sat as close to him as she could. "You'll tell me when I can come, right?" she asked as they neared the Amarillo city limits.

"I'll call you tonight and every night that I can. I just don't know how long I'll be in Georgia. They are training us to fly tactically."

"What exactly does that mean?"

"It means low level, instrument flying, combat-type training."

"Combat? I thought you were going to be rescuing people."

"Jem, they have to train me for any circumstance. I have to be ready to defend myself. You don't want me ignorant about that, do you?"

"I guess not."

"When I leave Alabama, I'll have my wings."

"You already have wings because you are my angel." She traced around his ear and played with the short hairs at the back of his neck. "My sweet dearie thee. I think I'll write a poem to you and use that."

"Sweetness is in the eye of the beholder, my dearie."

"Is that why you called me a mean woman all those times?"

"Mean can also imply average, you know."

"Hey, that's not sweet talk coming from an angel. Look, it's snowing," she said.

"You be careful driving back. Don't take any chances, okay?"

"It's melting as soon as it hits the road. I'll be fine."

Spencer found his seat on the plane and peered through the window. He couldn't see her through the snow. But as the aircraft rose into the sky, he knew she was watching. He touched the silver cross through his shirt. He would see her again soon, but never soon enough.

CHAPTER 15
CHANGE OF HEART

Max Chase's car was in Lester's driveway when Jemma got home. "He's been here for an hour already," Alex whispered as her daughter came in the back door.

"What does he want?" Jemma asked.

"Nobody knows. He keeps asking when you'll be back."

Jemma went to the living room, where Max was visiting with Uncle Art. He cut his conversation short and took Jemma into the foyer.

"I need to talk with you, if that's okay," he said, his eyes looking right into hers. They were not the pewter gray of Spence's. They were dark and shifty, like his wife's.

"Sure. We could go to the porch if you want." Jemma put her coat back on.

Max, the glad-handing car dealer, stepped outside and shoved his hands in his pockets. He studied the porch floor like it was of the greatest interest to him.

"Someone told me the other day that I have been a pitiful father to Spencer. Has he ever said anything like that to you?"

Jemma blinked. Her first thought was to tell him the truth, but she decided on a different approach. "Spencer is a man of great conviction and character. I'm not sure where he learned those traits."

Max raised his eyes to hers again. "What does he say about me, Jemmabeth? I need to know."

She spoke without hesitation. "Spencer feels that he has been raised by Harriet. I don't see how you could argue with him on that point. He's a precious man, so someone has done right by him."

Max exhaled and rubbed the back of his neck. "I know he is a good boy and I had nothing to do with it. I'm scared spitless for him now. I never thought he'd be put in this kind of danger." He walked to the porch swing and sat down, holding his head in his hands. "I don't like it, but I don't know what to do. You're a good Christian girl. Tell me this. Will God punish me for my sins by taking Spencer away from me?"

Jemma's face flushed, despite the temperature. She had never considered such a thing. "What makes you say that?"

"I don't know much about the Bible, but

I do remember a verse that goes, 'The sins of the fathers will be laid on the children.' That's what scares me. It's not that boy's fault that I've lived a feckless life, and I don't know what I can do about it at this point."

Her stomach hollowed out. This could not be right. Spencer had too much faith in his safe return. "Maybe you should visit with my friend, Brother Cleo. He knows a lot about the Bible."

"You mean that colored preacher?"

"I mean Brother Cleo. If you don't want to talk with him, then talk with the Presbyterian minister. I don't know his name."

"Surely you don't think that I know him." Max sniffed. "I barely know where the church is. I'm not too sure about talking to a colored preacher, though." Max studied the porch floor again. "Where is this Brother Cleo anyway?"

"He's in the kitchen," Jemma said, her mind a swirl of scriptures and conversations she'd had with Spencer about his dad over the years. She felt sorry for Max, though, and sat beside him on the swing. "Spence has such faith that his future will be with me."

Max's shoulders began to shake, and Jemma put her arm around him.

"That boy is all I have," he mumbled into his hand. "He was such a cute little guy. All I can think about now is how I missed all those years with him. I was out running around on his mother. Now it's too late."

Jemma lowered her voice. "There is also a scripture that says: 'With men it is impossible, but not with God — for with God all things are possible.' "

Max drew a quivering breath. "Do you think God knows that I'm sorry?"

"I know He would hear your prayers."

"It's been over twenty years since I prayed. I don't think I can."

"Sure you can. Just talk to Him. Get on your knees somewhere private and talk like you are talking to me."

He shook his head. "My father told me that I was going to regret my life someday, and he was right, as usual. No matter what happens to me, I don't want to hurt my boy."

"You pray about it. When Spence comes back, you can build a whole new relationship with him. I know for sure that he is a forgiving person. In the meantime, you might try to talk to your wife and ask for her forgiveness, too. She has suffered all these years just like Spence." Jemma hoped that the woman had a forgiving bone in her body.

Max didn't respond to that idea. There was too much pain already on the table with his alcoholic wife. "Spencer has been lucky to have you and your family all these years. I think I would have lost him if you had died in that wreck." Max studied her face, then reached for her hand and patted it. "Thanks for talking to me. Maybe we could we do this again sometime."

"I'll look forward to it, Mr. Chase."

"You call me Max. Maybe someday I can become likeable to good people like you. It might make Spencer proud of me."

"I'll pray for you."

"Now I've got two people praying for me. I guess I'd better go do some praying of my own." He stepped off the porch. Jemma followed him, pulling her jacket around her in the sudden cold wind. He turned to her and smiled, a little like his son.

She watched him leave and marveled at how quickly she had fed him spiritual advice. Maybe she was learning to walk. She went inside and rubbed her hands together in front of the heater.

"What was our Mr. Chase up to, Jemma-beth?" Arthur looked up from his book.

Jemma sat on the couch next to Papa's

chair. "He is worried about a scripture and what it could mean to Spencer's safety."

"Oh, and what's that?" Arthur leaned forward.

"The sins of the fathers are to be laid on their children."

He took a quick draw on his pipe. "A similar reference would be from Exodus, part of the Ten Commandments. It was a warning to those people who hated God and worshipped graven images instead. God said that He would hold that sin against even the third and fourth generation. I think our Mr. Chase is actually quoting the Bard."

"What do you mean?"

"Shakespeare used that line in *The Merchant of Venice*. Act three, I believe."

"Uncle Art, you are too much." Jemma jumped up to hug him.

"Think nothing of it, my little artist. By the way, I haven't seen your portfolio in a long time. I've missed all of your shows and I need to make it up to you and to me. What say Julia and I come to Dallas and see your work this spring?"

"Deal. I'm working on some things now for my senior exhibition. I would love for you to come. Thanks, Uncle Art."

"Whatever for, dear girl?"

"For keeping up with the Bard and knowing the Old Testament."

"Baby girl, come here and talk to me," Jim said.

Jemma closed her sketchbook and went to sit by her father in the living room.

"What or whom are you drawing?" he asked, putting his arm around her.

"Spencer, of course. I probably have five hundred sketches of him. I miss him so much."

"I know. Hey, just remember that I went overseas and I came back."

"I also know that your brothers didn't."

He watched the bubble lights on the tree. "He's going to be all right, honey. I know it, in here," he said, laying his hand on his chest. "Sometimes . . ."

The telephone rang, and she was off the couch before Jim could finish his sentence. He smiled when he realized that it was Spencer. Her hushed conversation brought tears to his eyes. He asked God to cover Spencer with His protection and to have mercy that he would not meet the same fate as his brothers. That thought shrouded all optimism.

Ted poured himself a cup of coffee. "Lester,

thanks for letting all of us invade your house."

"I didn't have to do nothin'," Lester said. "Miz Forrester here done all the work. You'd better sit down, Miz Liz, or you're gonna give out before breakfast."

She frowned. "You just drink your coffee, Lester. I'm having fun. Would you care for some more biscuits, Trent?"

"No thanks, I'm doing fine. Jemma, when will you see Spencer again?" Trent tapped his fingers on the table in the same way he had fidgeted through the weekend.

"I don't know. He said that he might not have much time off from now on. He's heard that something big is about to happen in the war."

Trent shook his head. "Too bad that doesn't mean we are withdrawing."

Ted laid his hand on Trent's shoulder. "I'll warm up the car so we can get going. Thank you, Lizbeth, for the best home cooking I've ever had. It was great seeing you, Jim. Don't work too hard." He grasped his brother-in-law's hand. "We really need to do this again. I have that beach house going to waste in California. Do you think we could get this bunch out there?"

"Sure we could. You just set the date."

"Jemmabeth, keep your spirits up and

paint. I'll be thinking about you." Ted kissed her cheek and walked to the car with his sister.

"Trent, do you think a monkey would be a good pet?" Robby leaned on his arm with a new book about primates.

"Well, you turned out okay. I don't know what kinds of stuff your parents had to put up with to train you, though." Trent laughed and dodged Robby's good-natured jabs.

"When do you report for basic training?" Jemma asked.

"January 15." Trent pinned Robby's arms to his side.

"Where?" she asked.

Robby ran off and Trent exhaled. "Fort Drum in upstate New York."

"I'll be praying for you, too." Jemma hugged him good-bye. She was going to have to make a prayer list the way things were going.

Jemma and Alex went to Lester's to clean and strip the beds after everybody left. Lester followed them around in protest. "I was fixin' to do that. I'm a good house-keeper."

"We want to help, Lester. You did us all a big favor, and now we want to return it." Alex kissed his forehead. He blushed and sat down in the nearest rocking chair to watch. He put his fingers on the spot where she kissed him and grinned.

"I'll work on the front room; Jem, you work on this one," Alex called from the hallway.

"Lester, have you ever heard anything from Hanna?" Jemma held a pillow with her chin while she peeled off its flannel case.

"No, sir, I never have. Good riddance, I say. I don't know if I've ever thanked you, proper like, Jemmerbeth."

"No thanks needed. She's lucky that we didn't turn her in." Jemma said, still second-guessing the decision to let her go. "Did you notice anything else missing?"

"Oh, this and that, but nothin' to fret over." Lester folded his hands in his lap as the rocking chair made soft thumps on the linoleum. "Jemmer, I had me a talk with our friend Mr. Chase the other night."

Jemmabeth stopped her work for a second, then continued. "Really? What kind of talk was that?"

"Well, sir, I've had a few things stuck in my craw for a good while, and I sort of told him how the cow ate the cabbage. You know, how he needed to get right with the Lord."

"What did he have to say?"

"Nothin' much. I didn't want to go to my

356

grave without tellin' that man to make amends."

Jemma smiled and leaned over the back of Lester's rocker. She rested her head on his. He smelled of shaving soap and Brylcreem. "Lester Timms, I love you," she whispered.

Lester reached for her hand and patted it, much the same as Max Chase had done.

"I'll miss you, Mom," Jemma said as they packed Alex's suitcase.

Alex didn't want to start crying too early. She fanned her eyes. "After you graduate, we want you to come to Flagstaff for a while, okay?"

"Sure. I think I'll spend part of the year with Gram, though. I want to try to help Spencer's mother. I don't guess I'll ever get to call her by her first name."

"Don't worry about that, honey. She's not responsible for her actions, poor thing."

"Where did Max meet her? Spencer never talks about his mother."

"They met at college. Neither graduated, but they went to Rice a couple of years."

"Rice? I thought that's where the smartest of the Texas smart go?"

"According to your daddy, Max qualified for that honor, but he's never applied himself to anything. Of course he didn't last at Rice. He did, however, meet Rebecca. I think she is the oldest one in a family of girls. She's a Houston native. That's about all I know. You'll have to ask Spencer the rest."

"I'll ask Harriet, their housekeeper."

"I think Harriet is more than a housekeeper around there, honey. She has kept that family together and raised Spence."

"I know. I should visit her. Maybe tomorrow, after you leave. It will help me keep my mind off missing y'all. Something else I want to ask you: why has Uncle Ted never remarried?"

"I think he's had lots of lady friends, but he got burned with Trent's mother and he's never gotten over it."

"He's so good-looking and sweet. Maybe I'll have to fix him up sometime."

"Good luck. I've tried and it's never worked out. Some men keep trudging along as bachelors and, pretty soon, they're too old to find anybody. Those were my exact words to him before they left."

"Yeah, I know the type." Jemma thought of Paul. For the first time ever, she felt sorry for him.

Jemma and Robby stayed up way past his bedtime sketching monkeys. That's all he wanted to talk about. Jemma showed him how to keep the proportions right, but it didn't matter. After all, they were drawing primates.

It seemed that just as she went to sleep she heard the alarm go off in the good bedroom. She heard her daddy talking in the kitchen about snow. Jemma stretched and woke up Robby, who was asleep on the old army cot beside her bed.

"I don't like the looks of this," Lizbeth said. "The highway can be treacherous when it's this cold. Son, you be extra careful. Maybe you should wait awhile."

"We'll be all right, Mama. Don't forget I grew up in this country. Besides, once we get to the New Mexico line, they actually try to clear off the roads. It's only between here and there that I'll have to watch it."

Alex shivered. "When did it turn so cold? I don't remember it being like this last night," she said, hugging Jemma to her side. "Robby, do you have all your stuff in your duffel bag? All your Christmas gifts and books?"

"Yes ma'am." He yawned.

A light came on in Lester's house. He knocked on the window and waved. He had on his big white nightshirt, and his hair was sticking up in the back.

"Bye, Lester," Robby yelled. He scraped together a nice snowball and tossed it at Jemma as she helped load the car.

"You little monkey," she shouted, chasing him around the car with a snowball of her own.

"Just like old times." Jim grinned. "Come on, Robby. Let's go."

"Dust that snow off before you get in the car," Alex said. "We love you two. Sweet pea, we'll see you at graduation."

Lizbeth retreated to the porch, and Jemma waved from the driveway as the swirling snow became more evident in the headlights of the Rambler. Jim honked and they drove away.

Jemma's heavy heart couldn't stand many more good-byes. "Are you going back to bed, Gram?" she asked as they stood, helpless, in the kitchen.

"No, sugar, I like to read some scriptures and have a quiet prayer time when family leaves. You go on and get some rest."

"I think I'll read, too. I'm a little worried about this storm."

The two women went to their separate rooms and opened their Bibles. Jemma turned to the scriptures she knew best for comfort. Lizbeth began, as always, on her knees, confessing her sins and praising God for the precious gift of her children, her grandchildren, and her beloved husband. Despite her admonitions, she had faith that her little family would make it home safely.

"I think Mama is going to get married before I do," Trina said, drying the dishes. "Have you seen how they look at each other? Even Brother Cleo has been teasing her."

"I hope it doesn't really bother you," Jemma replied as she washed the last of the pots and pans. "I guess they just hit it off."

"Well, the way Mama tells it, she didn't have a choice. Somebody fixed her up with Joe." Trina rolled her eyes toward Lizbeth, who was busy paying bills.

"Is that right, Gram?" Jemma asked. "Did you get things started with Willa and Joe?"

"I think they make a nice couple. Joe Cross is a good, Christian man." Lizbeth tore out a check and carefully addressed an envelope, making the girls wait for more information. She marked *paid* on the bills, closed the Hoosier cabinet drawer, then turned to face them. "Now, who can say otherwise?"

Trina shrugged. "Not me. He's a real sweetheart. I just never thought Mama would find somebody that she would get so silly about."

"Love changes people sometimes." Jemma smiled. "Have you and Nick talked about a date yet?"

"Nope, but Carrie's beating both of us to the altar."

"I wonder what The Judge thinks about that."

Trina shrugged. "Carrie told me that he's gonna give her away at the wedding, but I'll believe it when I see it."

Jemma bit her lip. She'd believe her own wedding when she saw it, too.

Chapter 16
Good-Bye Again

"I was beginning to wonder if you had a new girlfriend or something." Jemma pouted into the phone in Helene's conservatory.

"If I had a spare minute, Jem, you would have been the first one to know it."

"You sound exhausted. I bet you could use a good backrub."

"Don't even mention that to me. I'd love one."

"So, when can I come?"

"I'm in a unit that is on a fast training track. They are giving us a double dose of everything. I only get half a day off on the weekends. When I'm not flying, I'm studying. I don't see how we could work it out."

She couldn't respond for a minute, because she was about to cry. Then she managed, "Why are they rushing your training? Are they going to send you over there sooner than we expected?"

"I don't know what they're thinking. It's a

military mystery."

"It's because of those test scores. They think you can handle anything."

"You know how sorry I am about this, baby."

"I know. I had a bad feeling about this move anyway. You don't think your next trip will be to Vietnam, do you?"

"I think they'll send us to Fort Sam Houston next. That's where we'll get the Medevac training."

Jemma brightened. "I could go there and stay with Do Dah and Uncle Art. We could even see Carrie."

"It's not in Houston, baby. It's close to San Antonio."

"Oh. How long?"

"Four to six weeks."

"Then doomsday."

"I don't know. My tour of duty in Vietnam should only be a year, but I guess they'll do whatever they want."

"I'm telling you, Spencer, it's all because you are so smart. I didn't know your parents went to Rice."

"Yeah, well, they didn't stay long. Why the sudden interest in my parents?"

"Mom told me. Everybody says hello and that they all miss you."

"I miss you more than anything on earth.

Tell me what you were doing when I called and what you're wearing. Then I have to go. There's a line waiting behind me to use the phone."

"I was painting, and I'm wearing your old gray sweatshirt and a pair of jeans."

"I bet you look beautiful. Is your hair in a ponytail?"

"Yup. I love you, Spence. Be careful."

"I love you more. Good-bye."

He didn't call often. She got up earlier in case he was flying at night and could call when he got in. It was before six, though, on a Saturday morning when she heard it ringing. She grabbed it, hoping the noise didn't wake anybody else up. It was Sandy. Jemma almost didn't recognize her voice.

"Sandy?" Jemma asked. "You sound weird."

Sandy cleared her throat. "I'm okay. I just wanted to say hi."

Jemma yawned. "Before six in the morning? I can barely hear you."

"Sorry. I'll let you go back to sleep." Sandy sniffed.

"Don't worry about it. I need to paint anyway." Something was up. Jemma just knew it.

"I'm sorry I gave you such a hard time in

365

Brussels, you know, about y'all sleeping in separate rooms. More people should try that. It might help even after the wedding."

"What's going on with you and Martin? Are you pregnant or something?" Jemma asked. The awkward prayer request Sandy made in Brussels had never been brought up again.

"NO. I am not pregnant."

Jemma held the phone away from her ear. Sandy had her old cheerleader volume going, and went on about not being like everybody else and having babies so soon. There was no need to yell because Jemma totally agreed. She was certain that she didn't want to divide her attention with a new baby as soon as Spencer got out of the army. She wanted him all to herself for a long, long time.

Sandy talked nonstop, then the call was over. There was definitely something wrong in Martyland.

She unlocked the door to her studio above Helene's garage. This was her evening and weekend refuge. She inhaled the fragrance of her tools. Propped against the walls were six paintings ready for the show. Two sisters from the local flower shop were staring a hole through her from one canvas, so she turned that painting to face the wall. A sleazy guy leaned against an angelic fountain while he smoked a cigarette. Mr. and Mrs. Grasso, on the other hand, sat smiling as they ate gelato. Just for the memory, she had painted a section of Monet's garden at Giverny. She had given it considerable thought before doing the painting because his garden had been done to perfection by its owner and numerous others. Jemma had kept this one small and detailed, showing a single flower as the focal point.

Her favorite piece this time around was of two pigeons at Notre Dame engaging in a courtship dance. The sunrise cast a golden light on the male's rust-colored feathers. The last one she had finished before Christmas was of Papa reading the Bible in his maroon velvet chair. She was almost finished with a large portrait of her daddy in his uniform as a young soldier. It reminded her of Spencer as he boarded his flight to Georgia. She sat on the daybed and cried until she could pick up her brushes and begin again.

It was almost suppertime when she decided to take a break. The room was losing natural light anyway. Thunder rumbled in the distance and the distinct fragrance of wet earth wafted in the window as she closed it. Caruso blared from Helene's gramophone in the conservatory. Jemma cleaned her brushes, capped her paints, and grabbed her keys in a hurry to help Helene with the evening meal. She heard the crunch of tires on the graveled driveway and assumed it was Trina coming home from her cleaning job. It wasn't.

She recognized the baby blue pickup immediately. *Paul.* Jemma raced back up the stairs. She left the lights off and hunkered down inside. Helene would handle the situation when he knocked on the door *if* she had on her hearing aid and *if* Caruso's song had ended. Jemma's temples thumped. It wasn't as though Paul would do her harm. No, he was a loving cowboy. Rats.

The rain brought the wind with it. The accelerating patter on the roof camouflaged his footsteps on the stairs, but not for long. She caught her breath.

"I know you're in there, Jemmabeth Alexandra. I just want to talk," he said. "Come on, I'm getting wet out here."

Realizing she hadn't locked it, Jemma reached for the dead bolt just as he pushed the door open. She smelled liquor as soon as he stepped inside. "What are you doing on the floor, you sweet thing?" His sleeves were rolled up, and his black hat was low over his eyes.

"Paul, I'm expecting someone any minute."

"Ah, that must be why the lights are off. You wouldn't be hiding from old Paul, now would you?" He braced himself against the door and folded his arms across his drenched chest.

"Why would I do that? We used to be friends."

"Friends?" He laughed. "No, my love, we were more than friends. I'm sorry you got hurt in a wreck, darlin'. If I'd known about it, well, I don't know what I would've done. Right now I really need to talk to you about my feelings. I've been lonesome for you."

"We could talk, I guess, but I don't want to do it here. Let's go to your truck," she said. Dumb, dumb. He wouldn't fall for such an obvious trick.

"Nah. Here's good. Let's start off with a little sugar, though," Paul said as the dead bolt thudded at his touch. He started toward her, pushing his hat to the back of his head. His soaked white shirt clung to his skin and he needed to shave. A smile spread across his perfect lips, and he reached for her.

She dodged him, knocking off his hat in her dash for the door. They scuffled and he picked her up. She was kicking like crazy as he laid her on the daybed and fell over her. She was helpless.

A flash of lightning lit up his emerald green eyes. His hot beer breath was all over her and his mouth was against her ear. "Jem, all I do is think about us. I was so happy with you. Just give me something to hang on to. I need you. I keep you in my mind and in my heart, but I want the real thing." His stubble scraped against her skin.

She turned her head to stop him, but it was useless. He kissed her. and she could taste the devil's nectar.

"Does that kid know how beautiful you are?" he asked, slurring the words. "I've missed those honey-colored eyes. I do love you, Jemmabeth Forrester. I love every single thing about you. If only I hadn't messed up so bad I could've been your husband by now."

The sad thing was that he was right.

"I can't breathe, Paul. Please get up. I don't want to have to scream."

He faked a pout. "You're always threatening me. I just want to hold you." He traced around her lips. "Besides, I don't think anybody could hear you, my darlin'. I may have had a few too many, but I know thunder and hard rain when I hear it. It's kinda romantic. Doesn't it make you want to snuggle, Jem? You were a good snuggler." He kissed her again, holding her wriggling chin.

"Get off me. I have something to tell you." Jemma held her breath, hoping she took him off guard.

"A secret? Later. I don't want to talk now." He buried his nose in her hair and inhaled. "You still smell like flowers."

She coughed and pushed on his broad shoulders. "If you love me, you'll stop this."

He nuzzled her neck because he knew that always got her tickled, but not this time. She turned her head and ground her teeth. If she ever smelled English Leather again, she would throw up.

Paul propped himself up on his elbow and touched her face. He eased off the daybed and ran his hand through his hair. She had seen him do that a hundred times when they were dating.

Jemma stood, trembling.

"See, now you're cold. Let me warm you up," he said, holding her to him. His wet shirt had soaked into her own. Footsteps on the stairs startled them both.

"Jemma!" Trina's voice was loud and clear from the landing. "Let me in." She yelled again and pounded on the door. Jemma glanced at Paul, who looked like he had just dropped his triple-dip cone on the pavement.

"You said we could talk," he pleaded. "If nothing else, give me a good-bye kiss and I'll go. I don't want to have to steal it from you."

The clatter from the door was constant. Jemma's face was hot, but she wouldn't kiss him. He sensed it and wrapped his arms around her like a python, kissing her sweetly. She wiped her mouth and looked him in the eye. "Now *go.*" Her words sprayed across the room as she unlocked the door and heaved it open. Trina stepped in, with wild eyes darting from Jemma to Paul.

"What's going on here?" she asked, standing next to Jemma, who stared at the floor, breathing hard.

"Not a whole lot, thanks to you." Paul squared his hat, then tipped it to Trina. He moved again to Jemma, lifting her chin and wiping the tears with his finger. "Sorry, darlin'," he whispered. "I just want you to love me again. Don't hold this against me. I need you to make me a better man." He ran his finger down the bridge of her nose and left.

The door stood open, allowing a rainy mist to creep into the room. Jemma sat on the daybed and sobbed.

Trina held her. "If he hurt you, I'm calling the police."

"Let him go. I'm okay."

"Helene will be worried if we aren't there for supper."

"I can't let her see me like this." Jemma wiped her eyes.

"Helene's a sharp cookie, Jem. She's gonna know. C'mon, you're freezing. Put this blanket over you." Trina helped her up. "You sure he didn't hurt you?"

"No. He just made me mad."

"Spence will have him thrown in jail when he hears about this," Trina shouted over the storm as they descended the stairs. Jemma stopped in front of her and took the blanket off her head.

"Spencer doesn't need to hear about this, Trina." The rain ran down her face and dripped off her chafed chin. "Okay?"

Trina shrugged. "He's your man, but you'd better think about it, girl. You don't want to keep little secrets. I've heard you say that."

Helene opened the back door. "You two look like sodden pups. Come inside this minute," she yelled over the storm. "Was that Mr. Turner's automobile I saw pulling away just now?"

Trina raised her brow and looked at Jemma.

"Paul paid me a visit, Helene," Jemma said, the tang of his kiss still in her mouth.

"Oh my. Whatever for?" Helene turned her attention to Jemma's downcast eyes. "Has there been trouble afoot while I was singing with Enrico? I think perhaps you should get out of those wet clothes, the both of you. We shall take dinner by the fireplace. Run along now."

They ate in the study. Helene knew how to put problems in perspective and how to ease Jemma's heart and mind. The three of them talked into the night. Jemmabeth knew that Paul never intended to harm her. What she didn't fully realize, until that night, was how truly desperate he was for her love. It was more than a contest for her affections or a practical joke. Helene sensed it, and Trina saw it firsthand. The one thing Jemma knew for sure was that she longed for Spencer.

Monday evening, Jemma and Trina drove home from Le Claire just as the Granny's Basket station wagon was exiting the driveway. Jemma recognized Sister, the co-owner, at the wheel. Helene met them at the door.

"You have some flowers, dear," she said to Jemma.

"Oh wow." Trina gaped in disbelief at the display in the kitchen.

Jemma joined her, and the three of them admired the elaborate arrangements of flowers. "Rats," she said to herself, knowing exactly who'd sent them.

"Here is the card, dearest." Helene handed her the small envelope.

It didn't take Jemma long to read it. She passed it to Helene with Trina looking on.

Once again, I've played the fool.
Forgive me for loving you.

Paul

"That boy's got a big problem." Trina sniffed one of the lilies.

Jemma played with her engagement ring. "Let's take these to the nursing home."

"Sure," Trina said.

The three of them loaded the flowers into Trina's car and drove across town to the Wicklow Sunshine Center. Then, at Helene's suggestion, they ate supper at the Catfish Hut by the lake.

Jemma fell asleep as soon as she laid her head on the pillow that night. Her dreams were filled with a golden-haired soldier

375

dancing like velvet with her in the moonlight, and there were no secrets between them.

At Fort Rucker, Spencer flew at night as much as he did in the day. Sometimes he wound up talking with Helene because she was the only one at home, but it was Jemma's voice he wanted to hear. Having photos of her and wearing the cross she gave him were not enough. He concentrated on the work at hand. The sooner he got to Vietnam, the sooner he could come home to her.

"I got my wings, baby," he said on the phone. "I know you are just jumping for joy, aren't you?"

"I am proud of you, Spence. I know you've worked hard, and I'm glad you made it through all that training. I really am sorry I wasn't there to see you get your wings. You should have told me."

"I want to see you. I'm off for three days, so pick me up at Love Field tonight. I'm coming in at ten thirty."

"I'll be wearing a black dress. Trina made it for me."

"I'll be wearing my wings. Love you."

Jemmabeth knew that it was time for her to tell him or save the story for after Vietnam. They didn't need any brick walls.

She decided not to tell him. Things were too perfect to distract him with another Paul story. Every minute was precious because they knew there was only one more step to go before quicksand.

They sat by the pond behind Helene's house. "Spence, I can't even imagine how hard it must be to fly a helicopter. I hope you know how much I admire you. That your superiors must have recognized your smarts and your calm, cool self is no surprise to me. I've known that since the first grade."

His eyes were the same color as the old gray sweatshirt he was wearing. He smiled. "Thank you, ma'am. Flying is actually fun. I know it won't be fun once I get in the thick of things for real, but it comes easy to me now. You have to use your hands, your feet, and you are constantly making decisions."

"Maybe you are descended from weavers or something like that. My freshman year we visited a weaver and saw a demonstration of an old, hand-operated loom. The guy's hands, feet, and eyes were in motion all the time and his coordination was incredible."

He smiled at the innocence of such a

comparison. "I guess you could make that association with flying a helicopter. Experienced pilots are the incredible ones, though. It's an honor just to be around them. They have a lot of intestinal fortitude because rescue helicopters are easy targets." He knew he shouldn't have said it as soon as the words spilled out.

She gave him a wild look. "I thought that was why they painted that big red cross on rescue helicopters, so they wouldn't get shot at. Now you're telling me they are easy targets?"

He tried to back out of it, but the damage had been done. She pouted for a while, then changed the subject, even though it took a lot of effort for her to move away from the topic.

"Lie down so I can give you a backrub," she said. "Are you going to give up architecture for aviation?"

"Yeah, right." His voice was muffled in the quilt. "I can't wait to get back to the drawing board. How about you? What have you been painting? C'mon, let's go look at your work." Spencer took her hand in his and held it all the way to her studio.

Queasiness gripped her as she unlocked the studio door and they stepped inside. She felt the weight of Paul's body that rainy evening, and she could still taste his devil kisses. Spencer's presence was an even heavier weight on her conscience. She did not want to keep this secret from him, but she did, and they discussed her paintings instead.

"It seems like you just got here," Jemma said as they drove back to the airport.

"Time goes by too fast when I'm with you. You look so good, Jem. I think you are back to your old self now. I see the difference in the way you walk and dance."

"Really? I didn't know that I was ever any different. I've sure gained all the weight back that I lost. I'm ready to arm-wrestle any of your old girlfriends." Jemma flexed her biceps.

"Then you will have to wrestle yourself. I don't have any old girlfriends, unlike you, with your old boyfriend hanging around."

A twinge ran through Jemma's stomach and darted into her throat.

"Has he bothered you any more?" Spencer asked.

She didn't know what to say. She had decided not to bring it up. She hadn't considered that he would.

"Jem, has Paul shown up again?" Spencer could barely keep his eyes on the road as he tried to read her face. "He has." He took the next exit and pulled off the road. He held her hands in his. "Tell me right now. We're not having secrets. I know he's a desperate man because I understand the stakes."

She broke down and couldn't say a word.

"Okay. I'll call an attorney and check on a restraining order," he said.

"Spence, don't call an attorney. I think he's going to leave me alone now. I really do. He's not a bad person."

"He wants you, baby, and I don't want him harassing you. If you don't tell me exactly what happened, I'll assume the worst."

"Which would be what?" She wiped her nose on the back of her hand.

"That he tried some other stupid stunt to see you. Am I right?"

Jemma didn't know what to do. Spencer was much too smart and perceptive to let it drop, plus he loved her too much to do that. If Paul was going to continue with this obsessive behavior, maybe he did need a restraining order slapped on him, but then it could ruin his career and that was about all he had. She didn't hate him, and she knew that he loved her, still.

She could not look Spencer in the eye.

"He came to Helene's and wanted to see me. We talked about him leaving me alone. He apologized and left."

"Look at me, baby." Spencer turned her face toward his.

"You don't need to know all the details, do you? He didn't scare me or anything."

"What exactly did he do?"

She looked him in the eye. "Spencer, you are about to go to the other side of the world and spend a year tackling the worst thing you have ever done in your life. Let me handle this situation. If you can fly into jungles and pick up wounded soldiers while the enemy shoots at your helicopter, I think I can take care of Paul. He's not a mean person, and I don't want you to worry about this anymore." She swallowed, hoping her bravado had convinced him.

Spencer looked out the window, then turned to her. "Jem, if anything should ever happen to you, I'll never forgive myself, and I don't say that lightly. You know this guy better than I do, I'm sorry to say, but I don't want him touching you. I trust you, but I don't trust him at all."

"I'll be all right. I only have a few more months left. Then I'll be going home."

"That's when things happen, baby, when you are about to go home."

"I hope you are not speaking self-fulfilling prophecy."

"I don't believe in that, but I do believe in you."

She exhaled. "I can handle Paul."

Spencer paused, then slammed the car into gear and peeled out. Only the good Lord kept the highway patrol from seeing him fly the Corvette to the airport.

"This is not going to be like Alabama, is it?" Jemma asked as they sat on the floor, waiting for his flight to be called. "We will get to see each other, right?"

"I'll be up here every weekend that I can," Spence said, his head resting in her lap. "I wish we were back in Paris so we could neck right here."

Jemma suddenly threw her sweater over them and kissed him until she got tickled. Spencer sat up and tossed off the sweater. "We'll never see these people again," he said and kissed her like they were still on Pont Neuf, over the Seine.

The Senior Spring Exhibition was crowded, and Spencer was on his way. Trina and Nick volunteered to pick him up at Love Field. The Exhibition was a formal affair, so Trina had designed Jemma a new white satin dress. It was very sleek and sophisticated; she was just glad she could fit into it. She wore her hair up and put on as much makeup as she could stand. She watched the doors for Spencer, but Paul got there first. Helene saw him and went straight to tell Jemma, who was talking with Professor Rossi and the Dean.

"He has a date," Helene whispered. "Just carry on." That was some consolation. At least he wouldn't be cornering her and demanding affection that she had no desire to give. That would be the least of her worries if Spencer saw him.

She had ten paintings on display. A *Dallas Morning News* reporter asked Jemma for comments about her art and took a few photos. "Who's your favorite artist?" the reporter asked.

Jemma hated that question. "I don't have one."

The reporter nodded and walked away.

"She has so many that it's hard for her to say," Paul offered from behind her. She turned and was practically in his arms. "Hello, darlin'. You're looking like a movie star tonight, and I don't mean Trigger, either." He grinned and put his finger on the tip of her nose. He was dressed in expensive cowboy duds, complete with a black Stetson that he took off and held at his side. He was definitely movie-star material.

"Aren't you with a date?" Jemma whispered, looking around for Spencer.

"Oh yeah, she's here somewhere. Look, Jem, I apologize for my behavior at your place the other day. It was pathetic and inexcusable. I don't know what came over me." His long, black lashes masked those green eyes as they roamed all over her. "That's not who I am, and you know it."

"Paul, we are over, done, finished. I'm going to marry Spencer as soon as he gets back from Vietnam," she said through a stiff smile.

"Assuming he comes back, you mean," Paul said, tight-lipped.

"Just go, please. Spencer will be here any minute, and it's not fair for you to spoil things for us."

"I thought this was open to the public. I want to buy one of your new pieces." He scanned the crowd.

"Don't do this to yourself. Find somebody else and love her."

"I love you. I've been out there looking for a long time, and you are my heart's desire. There will be nobody else — ever."

"If you love me, leave me alone. Spencer

is everything to me. There is no room for anybody else in my life. Now go, please, before he gets here."

A curvaceous redhead swaggered up next to him and slipped her arm in his. "And who might you be?" she asked Jemma with a syrupy smile.

Paul never even looked at her. "This is the famous artist, Jemmabeth Alexandra Forrester. She and I go way back, don't we, darlin'?"

"Really? I like your paintings," the redhead gushed, still smiling. She turned to Paul, brow raised. "I think Paul already has some of your work."

"Christy likes art. She used to be a model herself," Paul said, not taking his eyes off Jemma. "Now she's a photographer."

"That's nice. If you'll excuse me, I need to meet some of the other patrons," Jemma murmured.

Christy squealed like a stuck hog at Paul's well-placed hand on her derrière. He always did have wandering hands, but Jemma was quicker than Christy, motivated by a certain promise. Of course this particular squealer may have liked his octopus hands.

She moved as far away from him as she could get and kept her eyes glued to the entrance area. Spencer should have been there by now. She could only assume that his flight was delayed or the traffic was heavy. Maybe they would get kicked out if Christy got any louder. Anything to keep Mr. Turner away from Mr. Chase.

"Hey, good looking." Spencer had sneaked up on her. He dipped her back and kissed her. Jemma recovered completely with that.

"I didn't see you come in," she said. "You look great. What took you so long?"

"Dallas traffic," Nick explained, studying Jemma's work. "You're some artist. Wow." He and Trina took off to tour the exhibition.

"Whoa, did you say Trina designed that dress?" Spencer asked. "You're going to give me a heart attack just standing there."

Jemma gave him The Look. She drew a deep breath and sputtered it out. "Spence, don't get upset, okay? Paul is here with a date. Now don't do anything. But I wanted to forewarn you."

Spencer's jaw twitched. "Where?"

"I don't know. They wandered off. Please don't talk to him."

Spencer looked around the room, then straight into her eyes. "You said you would take care of it, and I trust you to do that. He'd better keep his hands off you, though."

"Spence, I don't want this to spoil our

evening. Maybe he left. C'mon, let's look at my work." She hooked her arm in his and turned, smiling, toward the main gallery.

"I'd follow you anywhere," he whispered in her ear. Every eye was on her as she passed. To have her love was a precious gift for this earthly life and he knew it. He also knew that Paul Turner coveted that gift for his own.

Professor Rossi appeared out of nowhere with his slender, quiet wife, Carlina. "Hello, Mr. Chase. What do you think of your Jemma's work this season? *Perfezione, sì?*"

"*Ami l'arte, ami l'artista,*" Spencer said and kissed Jemma's hand, palm up.

Carlina Rossi blushed and glanced at her husband. Jemma wondered if the professor ever did such a thing to her.

"Hey, stop that fast Italian. You know I can't keep up with y'all." Jemma grinned at them, then scanned the crowd for Paul and his model friend.

Professor Rossi embraced them both. "We will pray for your safe return, Spencer. You both will be in our hearts."

Jemma saw the glistening in his eyes as they walked away.

"These pieces are amazing, Jem. Just when I think you can't get any better, you add a new dimension to your style." Spen-

387

cer held her close.

"What did you say to Professor Rossi?" she asked.

"I said 'love the art, love the artist.' "

"Let's run away and get married tonight," she said, meaning it.

Across the room, Paul watched every move Jemma made with a heavy heart. She might never be his again. He could still afford to look at her, though, and buy her work. To have, for his own, the canvas she had touched with her heart and hand was better than nothing at all. "Christy," he said, grabbing her tanned arm, "let's get out of here. How about we stop off for some refreshment before we head home?"

"You got it, cowboy," she schmoozed. "Whatever you want."

"Nope, darlin'," Paul muttered, looking back at Jemma. "I blew that chance a long time ago."

The family began arriving on Thursday evening. Even though Helene rented roll-away beds and put them all over her house, Trina opted to stay in Dallas with Nick's parents — to get to know them better. Spencer bought tickets for the Arizona bunch to fly down. Lizbeth, Lester, and Willa came on the train. Lester had not been to Dallas since he worked for the railroad company. The train was not punctual enough to suit him, but he soon got over it as he admired Helene's estate. "You could run yourself a small herd of cattle in here and not find 'em for a week," he announced at the supper table.

"I thought you were just a chinchilla rancher, Lester," Jemma said. "I didn't know you were a cattleman."

"Don't bring up Lester's chinchilla ranching days," Lizbeth replied. "He ran into some back luck with that venture."

"No, sir, it wasn't no bad luck. It was the weather. I knew it could ruin a farmer's whole crop, but it never occurred to me that the weather could wipe out my herd."

"We have tornadoes in this part of Texas, too," Helene said. "I don't see the point of the nasty things."

"The point is that the devil himself is throwin' his weight around on this old earth until the good Lord comes back." Willa pointed her finger toward heaven for emphasis. "Have you decided to become a full-fledged believer or not?" Willa pursed her lips in Helene's direction. Only the lovebirds in the conservatory dared make a sound.

Helene smiled. "Jemmabeth and Trina

have been diligent missionaries. I cannot say that I have any argument with their message. I'm not quite certain, however, that I want to join a church yet."

"Well, when? You ain't exactly gettin' any younger. None of us are. I'd sure hate to attend your funeral at the undertaker's place of business. That would be a downright shame."

"Helene, maybe you could visit our church in Chillaton the next time you're there," Lizbeth suggested as a little peace offering.

"I shall do that. Thank you, Lizbeth," Helene said.

"Hmmph," Willa growled. "Visitin' don't mean nothin'. Anybody can visit. You gotta get your name on the roll."

"I know a kid that has Babe Ruth's name on a baseball," Robby said, much to everybody's relief.

"Really?" Jim asked. "Where did he get that?"

"His daddy met Babe Ruth when he was a teenager. They drew his name out of a big barrel and he won the ball. Cool, huh?" Robby, who wasn't worried in the least about Helene's church status, helped himself to more cheesecake.

"When does Spencer's flight get into Dallas?" Alex asked.

"Seven thirty. Why?" Jemma cast a suspicious eye toward her mother.

"I thought we might go shopping. Since Mother and Dad are in Europe and can't get back for your graduation, they sent a very fat check for us to find you something. I know there are some great shops in Dallas."

"Sounds good to me. Just so we are at the airport in plenty of time. This is the last weekend Spence will have off for a while. He's training with medical evacuation specialists now. How's that for scary?"

They offered to take Willa to meet Nick's family on their way to the shopping malls. Willa was quiet, for once in her life. Alex and Jemma made small talk in the front seat.

"I bet you're excited to meet Nick's family," Jemma said.

"*Excited* ain't the word for it." Willa stared out the window.

Alex took her turn. "I know you must be happy for Trina."

"Trina and Nick have been havin' one of them long-distance things for a while now. I guess comin' down here to school stirred up their feelings again. Now they want to hurry things up."

Jemma decided to risk it. "Are you and

Joe getting serious?'

Willa coughed and adjusted her hat. "I think Joe Cross is about the sweetest man I've been around since Trina's daddy. Could be that I've given a serious thought or two about marryin' him."

"Then what are you fretting about? I've never seen you so grumpy." Jemma turned in her seat to look Willa in the eye.

"Grumpy? What's that supposed to mean?" Willa shook her head and returned to her preoccupation with the scenery.

They were in Dallas before she spoke again. "I don't reckon I've been listenin' to myself. You're right. I am actin' like a mule-headed old woman. I think I miss Joe. He's been gone for a week on a cross-country run. I worry when he does that." Willa leaned over the front seat. "It's true what the Good Book says about 'out of the mouths of babes.' 'Course you ain't much of a babe anymore, Jemma, but I thank you for pointin' my problem out to me. It's a good thing you did, too, or else Nick's folks would take me about as well as a dose of castor oil." Willa threw back her head and laughed. Her hat tumbled off her head. She laughed even harder and pitched it in the back of the Rambler. "That old thing needs to go to the trash. I think I need me some new clothes, too. Maybe Trina could whip me up a few dresses, if we can find enough feed sacks to cover this big caboose."

By the time they dropped her off at Trina's prospective in-laws' house, Willa was back to her genial self. Jemma and Alex knew exactly what they were going to buy and it wasn't feed sacks, either. Willa would get her new dresses.

"Thanks for today, Mom. You are such a good shopper." Jemma held up one of her purchases, a cerise linen blouse, as they pulled into Wicklow. "Oh yeah, please stop up here at the post office so I can buy some stamps. I have to get my thank-you notes in the mail."

Alex parked the Rambler across the street from the post office. "What are you doing?" she asked as Jemma took a dive into her seat.

"Rats! It's him — Paul. He just went in the door. Let's get out of here." Jemma covered her head with her new blouse.

Alex turned off the engine and fixed her sights on the post office door. "The famous Paul, huh? This I have to see. I wouldn't miss a chance to see who could steal you away from Spencer."

"Mom. He'll spot me. He has issues.

That's his truck parked next to the building. C'mon, you can see him some other time."

"No way. I live in Flagstaff, so hush. Is that him?"

Jemma peeked out. "No, good grief. He's not that old. Wait, that's him with the cowboy hat on."

Paul held the door for an elderly couple and then walked to his truck. He paused, then took off his shirt, pitching it across the seat. Standing beside his pickup, he ran his hand through his hair, put his hat back on, and got in.

Both women watched as he pulled out of the parking lot with Otis Redding blasting from his eight-track tape. He passed within ten feet of them.

"Mama mia." Alex looked straight ahead, her mouth hanging open. She whistled. "My goodness, Jem. My goodness gracious. He's some looker. Anybody could get caught in that web. It's no wonder you lost your senses." She sighed. "Now, go get those stamps."

Alex watched as Jemma crossed the street. She clicked her tongue. Paul could tempt any woman, and her beautiful daughter would be hard for a good-looking cowboy like that to pass up.

As soon as Jemma got back in the car, Alex was ready. "What did you mean by Paul having 'issues'? What's going on?" Alex asked, not starting the engine. Her mouth was set.

Jemma rubbed her forehead. She knew when her mother meant business. Alex didn't know the whole story. Jemma hadn't lied to her parents about Paul, but she hadn't told them everything, either. Maybe now, with her life set for marriage with Spencer, it would be safe to tell.

"Mom, the reason I broke up with Paul was because I found out he had a wife, and I never even knew he'd been married. I was humiliated and ashamed, so I didn't tell you and Daddy about it. Paul loved me and wanted to get married. He still does. He's divorced now and buys my paintings, plus he keeps trying to get me to change my mind about Spence."

Alex was stunned, but she reached for Jemma's hand and squeezed it. "Oh, sweet pea. I'm so sorry that you felt like you couldn't tell us. That must have hurt to keep it inside. Does Gram know?"

Jemma nodded but kept her head down, feeling the unwarranted guilt rising up again.

"I assume Spencer knows?"

"Yes. I wasn't the one who told him, though. Buddy B told him, and he was devastated. That's why we sort of broke up again when he left for Italy. It was such a mess."

"Is Paul harassing you?"

"He's harmless, Mom. I think it's over now. He's not a bad guy, just a ladies' man."

"Well, I can certainly see why." Alex lifted Jemma's chin to look her in the eye. "You were afraid to tell your daddy."

Jemma nodded again.

"I'll tell him sometime after you and Spencer are married. Leave him to me, honey, but you watch your step around this guy. He's magnificent to look at, but that doesn't mean he's not dangerous."

Jemma looked out the window. Life could move so fast. Within ten minutes she had confessed the dreaded truth to her mother, and she'd seen Paul Jacob Turner with his shirt off. Good grief.

Her family was seated together in the concert hall. It was filled with happy graduates and guests. Jemmabeth sat on the stage with the faculty as the dean gave a welcoming speech. She was nervous, but kept her eyes on Spencer, who grinned at her the whole time. Nobody knew she was going to speak until they saw it in the program. The dean introduced her as the only American to ever receive the Girard Fellowship, and only the second woman to win in seventy years. She had practiced and rewritten this speech for two weeks. Jemma took a breath and began:

"Ladies and gentlemen, distinguished guests, parents, faculty, and fellow students of the arts — rejoice! We have much to celebrate. It is not specifically this ceremony of which I speak, though. It is life itself. It's the air we breathe, the birds we hear, the warmth of a beloved's kiss, the chord struck in perfect tone, words that move the heart, and the subtle blend of pigment to reflect sunlight on a child's silken hair. The very first time you put on your ballet slippers, memorized your lines, rested your bow on the strings, picked up your sketchbook, or loaded your brush, you were commencing on life's unique journey into the finer arts. It's an uncharted journey and not meant for just anyone. Whether we become famous for our skills or fade into a personal world of creativity, what matters most is that we celebrate life by bringing joy or by expressing emotion on behalf of others.

"To connect with one another on a level beyond the mundane is a gift for which we must be thankful. Today, I offer you a challenge. We will never neglect to strengthen the collective spirit of mankind through the arts. Whatever joy or sorrow unfolds in this lifetime, your talent is a vessel for those emotions. Whether your goal is self-expression or shared reflection, you are compelled to create and thereby to engage your talent. We have been blessed, and it is required that we enrich what little time we have on earth with those blessings.

"We must practice our craft, regardless of our personal circumstances, in order to uplift or calm the beleaguered spirit. The world affords breathtaking and heartbreaking moments, but in between, people carry on. All beings must be able to honor each and every aspect of life either as the artist or the audience. However, we, as artists, are compelled to accept such a task because we are the eyes, the ears, the voices, and the wings of the spirit. As I see it, graduates, our next homework assignment lies before us. Carry on with joy. Thank you and congratulations."

Her family may have started the ovation, but it progressed with vigor. Professor Rossi shouted above the rest. Spencer and Jim competed for the loudest whistle. Jemma, somewhat embarrassed, returned to her place on the stage.

She wasn't seated long until she was recalled to the podium to accept the Miriam Beach Chapman Award for Outstanding Contribution to Fine Arts. She held the crystal statue to her heart and graciously accepted the check from Mrs. Chapman's elderly descendant. It was a prestigious award, open to professionals and students, in all fields of the arts and from all states west of the Mississippi.

The families gathered outside the concert hall, waiting for the graduates. Jemma ran up to them as she took off her graduation gown.

"Your speech was fantastic!" Spencer picked her up and kissed her. "Congratulations on the award, too. The audience wouldn't have paid any attention, though, if they could have seen you in that dress." Her graduation dress, a swirl of lavender and white chiffon, had cutaway arms and a draped neckline. It was miniskirt length. Gram pursed her lips and Jim drew back when he saw it, but Spencer loved it. Everybody crowded around her and talked at the same time.

Toward the edge of the crowd, Paul shaded his eyes to see her, his Jemmabeth, his only true darlin'. She was the eyes, ears, voice, and wings to his spirit and more. How could he *carry on* without her? He exhaled, folded his program in his suit coat pocket, and walked away. He stopped, though, and looked back at the sound of her laughter. It nourished his very bones. How he longed to hear that again and have it meant for him only.

Spencer had rented a room at the best seafood restaurant in Dallas. Jemma ate hush puppies until she was about to choke.

He leaned over to her. "Baby, that dress will give me something to think about when I get back to the base."

"I'll give you something to think about when we're alone," she whispered.

"Hey, watch it. I'm a pilot now. I get to be in charge of the flight plan."

"Maybe so, but we're still on the ground, sir."

"Jem, your speech was so bad it made Mom cry." Robby wrinkled his nose at Alex.

"Those were some awful fine things you said, Jemmerbeth," Lester said. "It'll take a while for them words to sink in, but they'll get there."

"How much money did you get?" Robby asked. "Could you loan me enough to buy a monkey?"

"I think you need to talk to Daddy, mister," Jemma replied. "The award was five thousand dollars."

"No way," Robby said. "Monkeys don't cost much, and you'd have lots left over."

"You talk to Mom and Daddy first, then come to see me." Jemma smiled at his serious tone and the thought of their classy mother hosting a monkey.

Helene had a tent set up on her front lawn, and the group danced until midnight. Even Willa and Lester joined in the Bunny Hop. Jemmabeth and Spencer were the last ones to go to bed. They sat in the conservatory with the caged lovebirds.

"What's this?" she asked. "Another present?"

"Yup." Spencer laid a gold foil–wrapped box tied with a blue velvet ribbon in her lap. "This is for our wedding night."

"Our wedding night? Are we going to elope right now? Oh, it's beautiful, Spence." She drew out the long, light gold nightgown. "It's silk, too. I don't think you are supposed to give me lingerie until we are married." She held it up to her dress.

"I don't care about etiquette after all we've been through."

"Yeah." She smiled at him. "I know."

"Now I can dream about you in this gown. It's almost the color of your eyes," he said.

Jemma pulled the gown over her dress and twirled, grinning at him.

He blew out his breath. "On second thought, we'd better go by the etiquette rules. You want me to survive the night, don't you?"

"I keep it in mind," she said.

Everybody left on Sunday except Spencer. He had one more night. The time had pleasantly slipped away from them. They kissed good night and went to their separate rooms, but he couldn't sleep. She was on the other side of that wall, probably two feet from him. He was the one who chose to wait on the wedding. It was his big idea. She would be taken care of financially — he had seen to that — but she wouldn't have his name, though, and he would never have her, completely, if he didn't come back. The thought of coming home to her would be his goal. He had meant this vow to honor her, but he ached, wanting to love her tonight. He stared up at the canopied bed. He had heard all the horror stories about Vietnam. He knew it was going to be worse than he could imagine. She would worry constantly, and he could only dream about her and do his best to survive.

The knock was so soft that, at first, he thought it was the wind. Then he heard it again. He pulled on his jeans. There was no light coming from under the door. He opened it to find Jemma standing in the doorway, her silhouette lit only by the moonlight. His whole body tingled at the sight of her.

"Spence," she whispered, "thank you for this gown."

He drew her to him. The warmth and softness of her body under that honeyed, silken gown was against his skin for an instant, making him weak. She pulled away from him as soon as they touched.

"I love you, and I want you to remember this moment forever. I had to give you something tonight, my sweet Candy Man, my hero." She disappeared into her room and shut the door. He stood in the hallway for a while in case she returned but knew that she would not.

CHAPTER 17
CEREMONIES

"When I worked for the Burlington Line, we kept things runnin' on time. There wasn't none of this business about 'mechanical delays' and whatnot. If there was a breakdown on the line, another engine was roped in to take care of it. No sir, we didn't have late troubles." Lester slurped his coffee from the saucer, vexing Lizbeth, and tapped his foot on the linoleum.

"Hold it right there, Lester. I recall plenty of times during World War II that the trains ran behind schedule." Lizbeth set a plate of biscuits and dewberry jam in front of him.

"Well, sir, you could be right. I forgot about that. We had us a shortage of help and a few other problems then, but most days the train run on time. Everybody suffers during a war. I ain't sure them times should count, no offense."

"I don't think enough folks appreciate what our boys are going through in Vietnam right now. If something were to happen to Spencer . . ." Lizbeth sat down and unfolded her napkin.

"Could I say grace, Miz Liz?"

"That would be very nice."

"Lord, for this food and the hands that prepared it, we give our thanks. Amen."

"Amen," Lizbeth added. "Thank you, Lester."

They ate their meal without further discussion. Lester knew that Cameron and her sons were on her mind, and he didn't want to interfere. He surely didn't want her to get down about it, either. He decided to take a chance and break the quiet.

"Did I ever tell you about them gypsies that I met over to France? I've been meanin' to bring it up. I'm kindly worried about it."

"Hmm . . . I don't believe I've heard that one," Lizbeth said as she put the dishes in the sink. "Surely you aren't worried about something that happened so long ago."

Lester leaned forward and pulled a tattered coin purse out of his hip pocket. He opened it and fished out a scrap of something, which he handed to Lizbeth.

"What's this?" It was only a pinch of paper with more cellophane tape on it than writing.

"See for yourself." Lester nodded toward

the scrap.

She could barely make out two smudged numerals in pencil. "Are these numbers?"

"Yes ma'am. Them's gypsy fortune-tellin' numbers."

"Who wrote this?"

"A little French woman."

"Your wife, Paulette?"

"No, lawsy mercy, no. This here was a French gypsy fortune-tellin' woman. She was a scary one, too. Had them eyes that look like a couple of shooter marbles. 'Course this was over to France. Like I've said before, I walked all over France. It was at the second Battle of the Marne, toward the end of July. Me and another old boy were on patrol and we come up on this here band of gypsies. They were right smack-dab in the middle of a battlefield that our boys had just finished cleanin' up. Had one of them little outhouse-lookin' carts all painted up fancy with a skinny mule pullin' it. They couldn't speak American and we sure couldn't speak gypsy French, but this wild-haired woman come hence to motionin' for us to sit down on some kegs. We did and she grabbed ahold of our hands and oohed and aahhed and babbled on about somethin'. Gypsies scare the piddlywinks out of me anyway — no offense, Miz Liz. Don't they worship the devil or somethin'?"

Lester wrung his hands under the table but went ahead with it. "I know gypsies claimed to be acquainted with the future; I seen one in a travelin' show once. So I says, 'Are we gonna make it through this here war? How much time have we got left?' She stared at us for a bit with them spooky eyes, then handed me this note with what used to be a sixty-eight on it, just as plain as day. I took it to mean that was how long I had to live. I even asked her, 'Is this how long I have to live?' You, know, we were plumb scared that we weren't even gonna see the next hour."

"Why did you ask her if she didn't speak English?" Lizbeth asked, her head cranked to the side.

"Well, now, she understood somethin' because she pointed at the writin'. I've sweated through everything it could've meant up until now, and this here's the last straw. Nineteen hundred and sixty-eight — not months, not days, hours, or minutes."

"Did you give her money?"

"Nope. Didn't have no money on us."

"Maybe this figure is how much she wanted for her fortune-telling services."

"How come she didn't give my buddy the note?"

"Maybe you looked like a man of means or like you were in charge."

"No, sir, it's doomsday for me, and that's all there is to it. My time's comin' this July. I just know it."

Lizbeth exhaled slowly. "Of all the foolishness that you've come up with, Lester, this is the most harebrained. How can you ask grace with one breath and profess belief in a gypsy curse with the next? It's hogwash. No wild gypsy woman in 1918 had any more idea about the length of your life than I do this very minute. Now you get out of that chair, throw that silly note in the trash, and go get our mail. I am surprised at you, Mr. Timms. The good Lord is the only one who knows our future."

Lizbeth scooted her chair back and stalked to the front of the house, leaving Lester staring cow-eyed at the table. He whistled under his breath and headed for the door, picking up his hat on the way out. Maybe he got her mind off her men for a while. He wasn't known as the best storyteller in Connelly County for nothing. Besides, he liked it when Lizbeth got riled up. It reminded him of Paulette . . . only she chewed him out in French.

It was almost her bedtime when Lizbeth

heard the noise at the front door. Someone pulled the little *boink* knob three times in a row. Only Robby could get away with that. She put on her housecoat and slippers and went to the door. "Willa and Joe, come in this house," she said.

"Sorry to be callin' so late, Miz Liz, but we wanted you to be the first to know," Joe announced, holding Willa's hand.

"Since you played Cupid for us, we figgered you had a right." Willa was grinning like a toothpaste commercial.

"Let me guess," Lizbeth said. "Joe, you got some new tires for your truck?"

They laughed, and Willa put out her hand. "This don't look like no truck tire to me." A diamond ring sparkled on her wedding finger.

"Bless your hearts." Lizbeth hugged them. "When is the wedding?"

"Soon as Trina can get herself up here this weekend." Willa's smile was as wide as Joe's.

Joe shrugged. "I don't believe in waitin' around. Willa might change her mind."

"This calls for a celebration. How about supper tomorrow? I'll invite Lester. Will Brother Cleo be in town by then?"

"Yes, ma'am. We're meetin' tomorrow afternoon to talk about the weddin'. It'll be real simple, though. Just a few folks."

"Well, I'm really happy for y'all. I knew that it was meant to be. I'm glad you came into our lives, Joe. God bless the both of you," Lizbeth said, tickled at the Lord's work.

Willa leaned toward Lizbeth. "We want you to stand with us, and we won't take no for an answer."

"It'll be an honor. Now let me see this ring again."

Before she went to sleep, Lizbeth knelt beside her bed and thanked her heavenly Father for Joe Cross and Willa Johnson. Joe, for saving her baby girl's life and Willa, for being her dear friend who had lived so near, yet was a world apart from her for such a very long time. She prayed that the good Lord would forgive her sins of omission, one of which was not looking beyond those train tracks, drawn like a thin line of demarcation in a town that professed to be filled with Christians. It had been her sin and her loss to honor that line, if not in word, at least in deed.

Spencer had two weeks off before he was to ship out. They decided to spend a few days in Flagstaff with her family and the rest of the time in Chillaton. It was Jim that suggested they all go camping. They hiked, played board games, and sat around the campfire talking. Robby kept them laughing. Spencer and Jemma got in plenty of stargazing, too.

When it was time to leave, Alex fell apart at the airport. Spencer had been like a son to them for most of his life. She and Jim wanted to believe otherwise, but they couldn't be certain that they would ever see him again.

Robby said it for all of them. "Spence, you are like my big brother. If you croak in Vietnam, I'll miss you a lot. Maybe you could hide somewhere."

"I'll be careful, I promise, Rob. You write to me and tell me about all your girlfriends."

Robby grinned and nodded. "I only have two, but I'll write if you will."

"I've heard that deal before," Jemma said, "and you don't keep your end of it."

"You aren't a soldier, though. You're just a sister," Robby said in his own defense.

Jim took Spencer aside and talked in hushed tones until their flight was called.

"Good-bye, Spencer. We love you." Alex was crying again. "We'll see you soon."

"I'll be back," Spencer said. "Look what I have to come home to."

■ ■ ■ ■

Lizbeth tried to give them all the privacy she could at her house. Spencer spent the mornings with his mother and once he went with his dad to pick up a car in Lubbock.

"I think my dad is changing," he said. "He actually listens when I talk, and he keeps hugging me. What do you suppose caused this sudden interest?"

"Maybe he realizes what a treasure you are," Jemma suggested.

"Maybe he wants something," Spencer said.

"I want something," she said and kissed him.

They went to pay their respects to Papa. The sunset was always more vivid from the cemetery, and they lingered on the wrought-iron bench next to his grave.

"We're going to be buried together even if we're not married," Jemma said. "I'm going to have them write our story on the tomb-stones."

"We *will* be married, Jem. I'll come home."

"I bet a lot of guys have said that to their sweethearts down through history." She rested her head on his shoulder. "Not all of them could keep their promises. It's out of

412

a soldier's hands."

"I know I will, baby, I feel it here." Spencer took her hand and put it on his heart. "Remember to check on my mother for me now and then."

"Spence, she can't stand me."

"She'll come around. Remember, it's usually the liquor talking when she's mean. Go see Harriet, too. She's taking this really hard. I don't want you to sit around and be sad for a year, either, so I told Buddy B that maybe you would be in his band if he asked you really nice."

Jemma sat upright and blew her hair out of her eyes. "You what? I'm not going to be in a band. That'll be the day."

"When you say good-bye, yeah," Spencer sang and grinned at her.

"Oh funny. Don't be throwing old Buddy Holly songs at me. How could you even consider such an idea as me singing with his band?"

"It might be fun for you. You could laugh at Wade and Dwayne's stories. That's always worth something. I want to think of you laughing and singing and dancing. I don't want to picture you moping around and crying while you try to paint. See, you're pouting right now." Spencer tickled her until she smiled.

Jemma ran her hand over Papa's marble stone. "Papa would be sad that you're going off like his sons did. Gram said he never got over that, but he never talked about it. She thinks it would have helped them both if he had."

"We are going to talk about everything, okay, baby? No secrets."

Jemma winced as that rainy afternoon in Wicklow slipped across her mind.

"Hello?" Spencer waved his hand in front of her face.

"I agree." She closed her eyes and listened to a meadowlark in the pasture next to the cemetery, then jumped up. "Let's go see the ducks."

They walked down the steep slope to the pond.

Jemma shared her sunflower seeds with the flock. "I don't think I can stand to see your plane leave, Spence. It's bad enough seeing you walk through that gate and disappear." She pounded her fist into her leg. "I hate this war."

"I hate it, too, but there's nothing we can do about it."

"I've already written so many letters to congressmen. I guess now I'll have to start making speeches and leading protest marches."

"You do whatever your heart tells you to. Of course you might do more good by coming up with ideas to rejuvenate the neighborhood across the tracks. That's just a thought."

Jemma looked at him and smiled. "You are a sly one, aren't you? You have a smooth way about you, Spencer Chase. I'm just glad you use it for good and not to get women."

"You are the one I wanted, and you are the one I got," he whispered and kissed her, gentle and sweet.

They went to Plum Creek. There was water running, but enough to go wading. No minnows were to be found, though, so they resorted to their cottonwood tree.

"Pray with me, Spence." Jemma held his hand, and they knelt on the sandy bank where she had danced the first time he had played his guitar for her.

"Heavenly Father, I give You praise for Spencer, Lord, and I ask that You watch over him and bring him home to me. I ask this in the name of Jesus. Amen."

"Let's marry ourselves right now," he said, and took her face in his hands. "Jemmabeth Alexandra Forrester, you have always been my adored one, and I take you now to be my beloved wife. Before God, I give you my heart and my life. I will cherish and honor you above all women as long as we live on this earth."

Jemma did not look away as she collected her thoughts. "In the presence of our dear Lord, I promise you, Spencer Morgan Chase, that I will love you and adore you as my husband from this moment until I breathe my last. No one but you will ever fill my heart and my life." Her voice, soft with emotion, came out as a whisper. "I promise to cherish and honor you above all men, as my only and dearest love."

They embraced under the tree that held their names, carved long ago in childish fervor.

S M C + J A F

It was his last day. They went to Willa's church and heard Brother Cleo's sermon on God's mercy. Afterward, Brother Cleo called them up front and the congregation had a prayer circle for Spencer's safe return. Brother Cleo gave him a pocket Bible study guide with notes in his own hand.

After lunch, they sat on the grass at the city park. "I used to play here when I was little," Spencer said. "I stayed at Harriet's house a lot then, and she would let me walk over here by myself. I looked for horned toads. When it rained, this ditch was full of water, and that's why these little bridges are scattered around the park." He tossed a stone in the direction of one of the small stone structures. "I bet the WPA built them when they built the high school stadium."

"Hey, you take one of these little stones and throw it in a river over there, so Chillaton will make a mark in Vietnam." Jemma folded his hand over a pebble shaped like a jelly bean. "I remember the Easter egg hunts our class had. Have I ever thanked you for sharing your eggs with me?" she asked, twirling a long-stemmed cloverleaf under his nose. "Have you ever seen a four-leaf clover?"

"I bet the odds of finding one of those are slim to none," Spencer said as he tuned his guitar. "If you find one, I'll take it with me to Vietnam and then I'll bring it back home to you."

"Deal. You play, and I'll look." She crawled to a new spot and began her search.

Spencer was on his fourth song when she screeched. He stopped and joined her on the ground. She held it up. "Ta da! Now you owe me, big boy, and I'm going to collect."

"I think you cheated. I've never seen one

except on a greeting card." He touched the delicate leaves. The veins reminded him of hers that night in the hospital. "Incredible. Okay, little Miss Lucky, I'll keep my end of the bargain. When I bring it back to you, we'll frame it and set it out to tell our grandchildren this story."

She smiled at him. "Do you want seven letters a week or one really long one?"

"Whatever you send me will be perfect."

"I want to know what you want. I'll be all cozy at home. Who knows where you'll be. Tell me, please."

"One long, long letter. It will give me something to look forward to."

"You know I'm going to go crazy, don't you? I'll start feeling guilty about old stuff, and you won't be here to forgive me for the thousandth time."

Spencer took her sketchbook away from her and flipped to a blank page. He scribbled something and handed it back to her. "There. Every time you bring that junk up in your brilliant brain, read this, but wait 'til I leave to read it the first time."

She gave him The Look and smiled. "Sometimes I think you are not of this world, Spence. I do believe you are an angel."

"Baby, I'm no angel. If you knew what

418

goes on in my head when I'm thinking about you, the angel idea would be out the window."

"Play some more. I want to remember everything about this day," Jemma said, lying back on the grass. She opened the sketchbook and carefully placed the clover inside. She closed her eyes while Spencer played "Dream Baby."

He watched her every move because she was the baby of his dreams.

"I think God made the stars just so you and I could look at them," Jemma murmured as they lay on the hood of the Corvette at the river that night.

"Maybe. I think He might have also wanted to give us a map to get around in the dark. Remember, Jem, when you look at the stars, no matter where I am, I'll watch them, too."

"Did you pack the moon I made for you? Can you say the words on the back?"

" 'Near or far, I am where you are.' "

"Good. I wish I could send you messages in the stars. Wouldn't that be cool?"

"Make up one now and choose the star. When I look up, I'll remember the message."

"I choose the star of love, Venus. That's

what Charlotte Brontë called it."

"The morning and evening star. Good. Give me a backup."

"Orion, our old standby."

"What's the message?"

"I think of thee." She turned to him and touched his cheek. "Of course."

He smiled. "Let's dance."

She took his hand. They moved to the music of crickets and bullfrogs and the beat of their hearts. She could not look at him; instead she watched as the moon cast their shadow onto the hard-packed earth. It was the same earth that Papa coaxed a life out of with his cotton crops. It was the same earth that held Papa now. She could not bear for her life's greatest blessing to join Papa in that dirt before their time together had even begun.

"Please don't leave me and be lost to the stars," she whispered.

He lifted her chin. "Jemmabeth, if I ever leave you, it will be to become the stars for you."

"No," she said, her voice quavering. "Surely that cannot be in God's plan."

They slipped the clover between two sheets of plastic cut from a cheap wallet they bought at the airport gift shop. Spencer taped it on all four sides and put it in his own billfold. He knew what she was thinking. "I'll bring it home. You just paint, okay?"

She looked away.

"Remember, in six months, I'll get R&R. So you get a bikini. We'll be in Hawaii before you know it." He was trying hard to get her to smile because that's how he wanted to remember her, but he couldn't even get her to talk. "What is your next painting going to be?"

She shrugged and pouted.

"Jemmabeth, talk to me. You don't want me to go away thinking you were mad, do you?"

She looked at him like a cornered kitten. "I'm not mad. How could I ever be mad at you? I'm just trying not to cry."

"We're both going to cry. So talk to me, please. Tell me that you will think about singing in Buddy's band."

"Spence, I am not going to sing in a silly band with Wade Pratt and Dwayne Cummins while you are risking your life in Vietnam."

"I only ask that you think about it. It would make me happy to know that you're full of life. Besides, it's a decent band."

"I'm full of life all right. I wish we were

married so I could show you."

"I know you are. All you have to do is stand there and I know it. Remember, don't open your birthday present until the real day."

"I won't." She twisted The Ring. The first call for boarding was announced and panic set in. "Do you have everything?" she asked, just to have something to say.

"No, but I can't stuff you in my bag," he said in an attempt at humor. "I love you, Jemmabeth." He kissed her palms, the way she liked.

She clamped her hand over her mouth before it contorted into misery, but then she moved it away and grabbed his face. "Don't die, Spence. If you do, I'll never marry anybody else. I want you to know that. You are my only husband, and I'm so sorry that I ever caused you pain. Remember that I love you."

He kissed her one last time. Jemmabeth let him go, then closed her eyes so she could not see him disappear, but relented. He turned to the gate and looked back, straight into her golden eyes. She forced a smile, and he winked at her.

She ran outside and watched his plane taxi down the runway and wait for clearance to take off. The jet lifted off and glinted in the morning sun. Jemma waved both arms. She knew that she was nothing more than a speck on the ground, but it gave her something to do besides cry.

She trudged back to the car and sat there. The corner of her sketchbook stuck out of her purse. She opened it to the page where he had written. She read aloud:

"My dear Mrs. Chase,

I'm glad you checked the competition because you will never have to wonder again. We were meant to be together, and so it shall be.

With all my love,
Your Mr. Chase"

August 16, 1968

Dearest Jemmabeth,

I have arrived on the other side of the world. By the time you get this, I will probably be doing what they brought me over here for. This is a busy place. We can hear artillery in the distance. I hope it stays there, but I think we'll be flying right into the thick of it. Don't spend all your days worrying about me. All will be well.

I want to get this in the mail, so I'll

write again when I have more time. Say hello to Gram and Lester. If you have a chance, please visit Harriet.

I hope my father doesn't become a problem for you. He must be operating on guilt these days. Think about the band because I promise those nuts will make you laugh if nothing else. Remember, I'd like for you to give it a try.

Here's what I have to keep me company: my Bible and the pocket study guide, your old sketchbook, the lock of hair you gave me in Italy, the ribbon I took from you at the airport that bad summer, the four-leaf clover, my silver cross necklace, the blue moon you made me, and twenty photos of you. Oh yeah, and the pebble from the park. I'll be glad when it's you keeping me company, all night long.

I tried to see you in the parking lot at the Amarillo airport, and I think I did.

Watch the stars tonight, baby. I think of thee always.

Love you, Spence

Spencer got his fat letters and there were surprises in every one. His favorite was the letter that was written on a life-sized picture of her on butcher paper. She had Lizbeth trace around her, then she painted her form with watercolors, cut it out, and wrote him love poems all over the back of it. She wrote like she talked — full of fun and in a stream-of-consciousness. He knew she was going out of her way to be cheerful. The letters always ended in words of abiding love. She was a brilliant artist, an irresistible woman, and she was almost his wife. He was about to doze off when Paul suddenly crossed his mind. If something happened and Jemma were left alone in the world, would he step in and take care of her? She had said she wouldn't marry anyone else. Spencer fell asleep with that bittersweet thought.

Carrie's wedding was small, informal, and pretty, like her. There were staff members from the physical therapy center and two of her mother's sisters from out of state. Eleanor, Carrie's longtime caregiver, wouldn't travel to Houston because the humidity bothered her sinuses. Jemmabeth and Trina wore tailored, matching dresses of periwinkle shantung silk and each carried a white rose. Carrie's dress and veil were lace-covered white satin, worn by her mother when she married The Judge. A dozen cornflowers, the color of her eyes, made up her bouquet. Philip never took his eyes off her throughout the ceremony. Jemma watched The Judge because she knew he was struggling. She had exchanged hot words with him when he fired her, but now her heart went out to him. Probably he would become even more attached to the bottle after the wedding.

Carrie was radiant. When Jemma had first met her, Carrie had no life at all. Even her appearance was an afterthought back then. Now her long, blond hair was pulled back into a French twist, and she had learned to use makeup nearly as well as Sandy. She had come to look like her mother's portrait, but with an added measure of impishness.

"Well, girls, who would've ever thought this would happen?" She grinned at her husband.

Jemma gave her a hug. "I'm so glad that you came to Houston, Carrie. At the time, though, I was majorly ticked at your father for sending you." Everyone took a sudden interest in the punch, and someone faked a cough. Jemma turned to find The Judge standing at her elbow.

"I agree with that," The Judge said. "Coming to Houston gave you new life, Carolina. Just look at what Philip has done for you. You are out of your wheelchair."

Jemma turned to Carrie and crossed her

eyes in amazement. For The Judge to agree with her was an astounding event on its own, but for him to compliment someone in the same breath was unheard of. Maybe he did have to love whatever and whomever his daughter did, like Carrie had once told her.

Philip was enjoying the moment. "She has a long way to go, sir, but we'll get there, won't we?" Carrie agreed by kissing him and it wasn't a peck, either. She held her arm out to her father and balanced herself between them.

"Who needs wheels when I've got my two favorite men to hold me up? Now, let's get on with the honeymoon." Philip scooped Carrie up and The Judge followed behind and carried her walker to a waiting limo. Trina and Jemma tossed rice as it pulled away. The Judge waved on even after the limo disappeared around the block. He finally let his hand drop and it hung at his side.

Jemma turned away. She wanted to be in that car with Spencer.

He got her letters and stretched out on his cot. Just seeing her handwriting made him feel good. In junior high, she slanted her words so much that they all looked as though they were sliding into home plate. Their freshman year in high school, she had dotted her *i*'s with little circles, but now her words were flowing and clear, free of embellishment, just like her. He liked reading the letters until he had them memorized.

November 14, 1968

My dearest Spence,

Gram and I have a kitten. Lester found a whole litter in his garage. This one is black with little white patches on its nose and feet, and I've named him Vincent (Van Gogh) because one of his ears got a chunk bitten out of it by something. We need one around here because you know how Gram hates mice.

Do you think that we could have our studios in the same room? I don't want you to work in an office. I want you to work at home with me, unless you could give me a corner in your office so I could paint. I suppose oil paint and brush cleaner fumes might bother your clients, so maybe I will only use acrylics and watercolors in your office. It's just an idea.

I hope you are getting enough sleep. I read an article the other day about how lack of sleep affects your decision-making and motor skills. Please go to sleep right now instead of reading this letter.

It occurred to me that I haven't seen your mother in a long time, so I am going to get up my nerve and pay her a visit. I'll let you know how it goes. (It probably won't.) I'm glad you liked your birthday divinity and it wasn't ruined. I hope they don't open all your packages. They probably ate some of it.

You don't really think that I am going to buy a bikini, do you? I wouldn't wear it anyway. I never liked changing clothes in the dressing room for basketball, so I doubt that I would feel comfortable in a bikini on a beach. You'll just have to be satisfied with my old one-piece in Hawaii.

Spencer stopped reading when he got to that part. Seeing her in a bikini right now was something he wanted to think about because he was weary of war. He rolled over to take her advice and catch some sleep before they got called out again. It was a heart-wrenching, never-ending cycle.

Jemma was in Flagstaff for most of November, but it didn't feel like she was home. She missed Chillaton, and Alex could see it.

"We are so glad that you came, sweet pea. It's good to see your head on the pillow in the mornings. Robby is so happy to be around his big sister."

"I know, Mom, and I'm sorry to be such a drag. Maybe I just need to be where I was with Spence last. I love y'all so much, but something's missing."

"You've grown up, and you're ready to build your own nest." Jim poured himself a last cup of coffee before heading off to work. "Don't worry about it because we'll take what we can get. Right, honey?" He gave Alex a good kiss for an old married couple.

Robbie squeezed his eyes shut. "Are they done yet? Monkeys don't kiss like that. They are way cooler than people."

Jemma visited Robby's class to talk with them about art. He wore a Sunday shirt for the occasion. She demonstrated background, foreground, horizon, and vanishing point. They went outside and sketched a scene, then painted it with water paints. She watched Robby to see if he had the artistic spark she had at his age. He had a spark all right, but it didn't seem to be for art. It was for sports and talking. She should have known that anyway. He was the junior team manager for their daddy's football team, he could keep up with an adult conversation, and could match wits with anybody. She loved being around him. He made her think everything was going to turn out fine.

"I want to be called Rob now," he announced at the supper table one evening.

"Really?" Alex asked. "What brought this on?"

"Spence calls me Rob and since he's not here right now, I want everybody else to do it until he gets back."

"I think Spencer would like that. You should write him and tell him about your name change. I'm mailing him a big letter tomorrow," Jemma said.

"How does he like army food?" Jim asked, passing the roast beef.

"I don't know. We've never talked about it," Jemma said.

"Yeah, they only talk about kissy stuff. 'Oh Spencer, you are so handsome and strong. I hope you don't have a new girlfriend in Vietnam,' " he said in a high-pitched voice.

"You little rat. You've been reading my letters." Jemma put down her fork in mock indignation.

Robby looked at her and grinned. "I wish. Then I could have some really juicy stuff to tell everybody."

"Maybe I should tell who you sat next to — every chance you got — at school the other day, *Rob.*" Jemma gave him a *hardee-har-har* look, bringing a little color to his cheeks.

"Well, now I have to know," Alex said. "I thought you still liked the little Wilson girl."

"Nope. Things change, Mom. I don't want to get tied down. If the right girl comes along, I want to be available." Robby ate another roll in two bites.

"Available in the fourth grade?" Jim asked. "Are you even chewing your food, young man?"

"Yes, sir," he said and gulped. "Jemma and Spence were boyfriend and girlfriend all their lives, except for that old guy she liked. I have to be ready."

They all laughed at that, except Jemma, who winced at the reference to Paul. Would he never go away?

She returned to Chillaton and tried to get back into her routine. Lizbeth still allowed Lester to bring the mail, and Jemma received a very belated letter from Robby. She smiled at the drawing of a saguaro cactus on the back.

October 28, 1968

Dear Jem,

How are you? How is Spence doing? I am writing Gram a letter, too. We are getting stuff ready for your visit next week. Do you think it is okay to pray for a monkey? I have been learning about jungle animals at school. You know that my favorite animal is a monkey and I want one really bad. On the back of one of my comic books it says I can order a monkey for $12.00. I have been saving my money and I have $9.00 so far and Mom owes me $3.00. I am going to order one because they are so cute. I have to go now. Write me back. I am helping Daddy for 25 cents.

Love,

Your Bother (crossed out) Brother

P.S. Don't tell Mom or Daddy. I am going to keep the monkey in my room. I have made him a bed. I am going to call him Ro Ro, the way I said my name when I was littler.

P.S. Again. Do you know that money and monkey are kind of spelled the same? This is a long letter, huh?

Jemma laughed until she couldn't any more. He hadn't mentioned the monkey idea at all when she was there in November. She considered whether or not she should tell her mother about the monkey plans or let it slide, in the hopes that it would never happen. She read the letter again and saw the date on it: *October 28th.* She checked the postmark — *December 14th* — five days ago.

"Gram, I just got this letter from Robby and I think it deserves looking into."

"Oh yes. I got a cute letter from him, too," Lizbeth said. "He wrote it in October, but your daddy jotted a note on the back of the envelope saying that he just found it the other day and stuck it in the mail."

Something told her to call home. She gave Lizbeth the letter to read while she dialed long-distance and gave her parents' number to the operator.

"Daddy. Hi, it's Jem. What? Uh-oh. I hope Mom is okay. Good grief. The Christmas tree and the presents, too. Yuck. Her new curtains, the ones she had specially made? Poor little guy. No, no, I meant Robby. Sure, I'll talk to him. Love you, too, Daddy. Hi, Rob. I'm so sorry. Well, I'm sure he'll be happy at the zoo. I miss you, too, sweetie. So, Santa is bringing you new curtains for the living room." Jemma winked at Lizbeth. "Okay. Tell Mom I love her when she wakes up tomorrow."

"What on earth happened?" Lizbeth asked.

Jemma hung up the phone. "Ro Ro, the monkey, arrived yesterday. Robby wasn't home so Mom opened the shipping box and the little thing bit her, climbed up the Christmas tree, and swung over to sit on the light fixture until it got too hot. His next perch was her new valance and curtains, which he tore up and pooped on. Finally, he ripped into the Christmas packages and started throwing poop at Mom. He went into the kitchen and hid in the cabinet until Robby got home and tried to catch it. When he did, Ro Ro bit him, too. Daddy came home and the police were there with a cage and asked Robby all kinds of questions about his comic book. The monkey bit a policeman, too. I guess everybody but Daddy and the monkey were crying all the way to the emergency room. They have to make sure that the monkey doesn't have rabies. If he doesn't, he'll be sent to a zoo somewhere. What a mess. I feel sorry for everybody, including the monkey, but it is hilarious."

Lizbeth snickered, then shook her head

and laughed, long and loud. Jemma did love to see her laugh.

Spencer had saved the package until Christmas Day. Opening it would be his celebration. He had just returned from a candlelit service attended by a lonesome crowd of soldiers. Inside the box was a Christmas tree made from small strips of green fabric meticulously tied together on a wire, tree-shaped frame. She had tied red bows on every branch. He could see Lester's handiwork in the wooden base. He set it next to his photos of her. She also sent him a ukulele "to practice for Hawaii." At the bottom of the box was a small photo album filled with pictures of Thanksgiving and a snowy mountain scene in Flagstaff. Jemma and Robby had made a giant snowman, and the Flagstaff newspaper put a picture of it on the front page. The clipping included a short interview with Robby. His comments made Spencer smile, but the picture of Jemmabeth made him ache to hold her.

CHAPTER 18
PEACE

Gram handed her the phone, "It's for you, sugar."

"Jemma, it's Buddy B. Hey, remember in high school when you and Sandy sang backup for me at the talent show?"

She'd wondered when he would call. "Nope. I don't remember that." She did, but it was more fun to say she didn't.

"Spence said you might like to do it again."

"We were freshmen and you were a senior. You know that you intimidated us into doing it because you're her big brother."

"That's true, but this is my side business now, and I can pay you. We do gigs, you know, all across the Panhandle and over in Oklahoma and New Mexico. Next Friday, it's a dance at Lido, then we've got the Travis High School Valentine's dance in three weeks, and a junior college ball in March. This summer we've got the Goodnight Trail dance. Oh yeah, and the King Cotton Days festival next October."

Jemma sat on the bed. "Whoa. Busy schedule, but I have things to do on Friday nights. Besides, Spence will be home next August."

"C'mon, Jem, help me out here. Sometimes it's a Saturday night. I'm talking cash, and Spence wants you to do it."

Jemma lay back on the bed and put her bare feet on the headboard. "All Buddy Holly songs, I presume."

Buddy snickered. "Shoot. You're way behind. We're doing everybody's stuff now."

"Why do you need me so bad?" Jemma asked. "I thought you had Leon singing backup."

"He's sick of it. Besides, I need a little spice in the show."

"You think I'm going to add some spice for you? Wait until Spencer hears this."

"If I didn't have Spence's blessings, I wouldn't be calling." Twila yelled something in the background. "She wants you to wear that dress you wore in Sandy's wedding. You were a knockout in it."

"If you want spice, find The Cleave. I don't think Spencer knew that you wanted spice."

Buddy exhaled. "Just say you'll do it. At

least try it once. Remember, I gave Carrie her big break. Just come to one rehearsal. That's all I'm asking. Come over to the house tomorrow night for supper. You've got that certain something that will bring in the guys."

"You're scaring me, Buddy."

"Just kidding. I'll see you tomorrow night, okay?"

"Maybe."

She knew it was going to be a bad day when she saw the mass of hair coming down the sidewalk by the post office. The Cleave was home from Europe.

Missy Blake flashed her most spiteful smile at Jemma, like she'd been saving it up. "Jemmartsybeth, how weird to see you because I dreamed about Spence last night. I hope he's not getting shot at or something. I've been thinking about writing him, so I got his address from his mother. My letters will be like a . . . something . . . of hope to him in his . . ."

"Trash can?" Jemma suggested. "Write all you want. I don't think you'll be getting an answer, though. Spence and I are engaged, as in to be married." Jemma held up The Ring.

Missy rolled her eyes. "Really. Engagement rings are ho-hum these days. Couples live together first. That way there's none of that crybaby stuff if something better comes along. Oh yeah, like a *beacon* of hope to him in his . . . what's a word for, you know, being sad and scared all at the same time? I heard it on the radio the other day."

"I'll see you around." Jemma turned toward the post office.

"I just got back from a year in Madrid. That's in Spain."

"I know where Madrid is, Missy. I didn't know you spoke Spanish. You barely passed Mr. Smalley's class in high school."

"I didn't have any problems. The guys there are all hunks and talking wasn't exactly at the top of our list, if you know what I mean."

"Yeah, I know exactly what you mean." Jemma shoved open the door to the post office.

"Tell Spence to write me back. I'll send him a care package with some surprises in it," The Cleave yelled.

Jemma didn't look back, but she did chew on her lip. She knew The Cleave's idea of surprises. Their junior year at CHS, Mollie Sykes threw a "come as you are" party and Missy showed up in skimpy baby-doll pajamas. The boys went cuckoo until Mrs.

Sykes called Missy's father to come and get her. Nobody believed that The Cleave was dressed for bed at six thirty at night, anyway. It put quite a damper on the party for the rest of the girls. Spencer, bless his heart, never left Jemma's side to check out Missy's arrival and further antics. He was truly every girl's dream boyfriend. Now he was fighting in a war a world away from her. *Misery* or *despair* — either word might have been what The Cleave heard on the radio. She was never known for her vocabulary, but she was remembered for those baby-doll pajamas. Rats.

The Buddy Baker Band consisted of: Buddy B — vocals and rhythm guitar; Leon Shafer — lead guitar; Dwayne Cummins — bass guitar; and Wade Pratt on the drums. They weren't too bad and had played for many dances at Chillaton High School before branching out. Buddy was probably right, though: it was time to add something to the group.

Leon, Dwayne, and Wade were already there when Jemma arrived at the Bakers' house. The prospect of a meal was always a good incentive for single guys.

"Hi, Jemma, come in." Twila gave her a hug and shoved Wade's feet off the coffee

441

table as she walked by. The boys were too busy wolf-whistling at Jemma to say hello. She didn't mind because she had known them all her life, and they had yet to make a good impression. They were a scraggly bunch with good hearts. Dwayne and Wade had barely scratched their way out of CHS. Now they were hanging out together just like they were still in junior high. If they hadn't joined the military right after graduation, they'd be in Vietnam, like Spencer. Instead, they were looking for wives and eating greasy food from the truck stop and still wearing crew cuts, except for Leon, the smartest one, whose blond hair was fast becoming a ponytail. "Come on back here in the kitchen and talk to me," Twila said.

"Did you guys come early for the free food or to get in some extra practice?" Jemma asked the crew. "You probably need it."

"We just came to see you, sweet thang." Dwayne made kissing noises at her and bugged his muddy blue eyes.

"Where's Buddy?" she asked.

"He's running late from work, as usual," Twila said from the kitchen. "He called from the dealership about ten minutes ago and said he has to finish up a job, then he'll be right home."

Jemma set the table while Twila talked

about her day at Nedra's. The most interesting conversation, though, was coming from the living room between Dwayne and Wade. Leon, a man of few words, was watching television. Jemma needed a good laugh and Spence said these two would provide it. It really didn't matter who was saying what. The story was the thing.

"Were you at the game last night? I tell you what, we got ourselves a ball club this year," Wade said, jabbing his finger into the air for emphasis.

"Shoot yeah, we got us some neegroes," Dwayne shouted toward the kitchen.

Jemma gave him a dirty look.

"This is the best team I've seen in thirty years. What we been needin' all along is some colored boys to rebound," Wade added.

"That is so pathetic," Jemma replied. "Are you a bigot or what? Besides, you aren't even thirty years old. How could it be the best team you've seen in thirty years?"

Wade took a big drag on his cigarette and pondered this new word she'd thrown at him. "Bigot? Are you talking about my height or somethin'?"

"Oh brother. You both sound like you just fell off a turnip truck," Jemma yelled.

Dwayne stubbed out his cigarette. "You

443

been spendin' too much time with the coloreds. Nobody that I know grows turnips, at least not on this side of the tracks."

They fell silent, turnips having no hold in cotton country. Turnip greens, maybe.

"I like to have fell off my seat at the game Friday night when somebody said Lorena Hodges was goin' to stewardess school. You remember her?" Wade asked.

"Oh yeah," Dwayne said, "but you gotta be kiddin' me. What airline would take her on?"

"One of them big ones. Braniff, maybe."

"Man, I hope the people that hired her ain't the same ones flyin' the planes. They gotta be hard up for help."

"Remember when we set her up with Jeeber McCleary for a homecomin' dance?"

"You know, she didn't look half bad that night."

"Maybe if you were comin' toward her and not behind her."

"That'd be like watchin' two pigs fightin' under a blanket." Wade hooted at his own perceptiveness, then they were both quiet, reflecting on his exquisite example.

"Whatever become of Ethan Sears?" Dwayne asked. "I'll never forget him claimin' he roasted a mouse once down at the park, then ate it."

"He made a preacher," Wade said. "Then he come up sellin' vacuum cleaners and made good money at it so he gave up the preachin' business right quick."

"Did the devil get at him?"

"Somethin' did. Maybe he figured his name would help him get rich."

"In the preachin' business?"

"No, dummy, in the vacuum cleaner business. You know, Sears. As in Sears & Rareback."

"Oh, like Monkey Wards. I get it. How's that help?" Dwayne's upper lip curled in puzzlement.

Leon stood and faced them. "If you're gonna buy an appliance, you might come nearer buying it if you thought it was from Sears." He went outside.

"Yeah, yeah, I see what you gettin' after. Reputation," Dwayne said.

"I hadn't seen Ethan since high school."

"Me neither. All I know is that Lorena must've lost a whole lotta bohunkus to be making a stewardess or else some plane is gonna be flyin' low with her on it."

The door flew open and Buddy B entered. His voice boomed when he was excited, just like Sandy's. "Supper about ready, hon?" he asked and gave Twila and Jemma each a peck on the cheek.

445

Dwayne leaned back in his chair, stretching and shouting. "What are we havin' tonight, little woman?"

"Turnip casserole," Twila shouted back, much to Jemma's delight.

Buddy B gave her a list of all their songs. There were check marks by those that she was to sing harmony with him, and stars by those that she was supposed to sing dumb backup lyrics.

"Hold it, Buddy," she began. "I'm not doing that bop, bop, bop, bop business on 'Fade Away.' I'm sorry, but I think it's stupid."

"Hey, you're not the star here, Miss Priss," Wade said.

Buddy filled his plate. "That's okay; you don't have to do the bop part. Just hit the tambourine, but when you are singing harmony, don't step on my speci-alities."

"Your what?"

"My speci-alities. Like when I break my voice like Buddy H did. You know, like ah-hoo on 'It Doesn't Matter Anymore' and way-uh-hay-hay-hay on 'Everyday.' "

"Oh brother," Jemma said. "I thought you weren't doing just his songs anymore."

"I've kept a few of the best," Buddy said.

"Yeah, Jemma, it's his signature stuff and

it's his band," Dwayne said in a sing-songy voice.

Buddy winked at her.

"Do I get a break when I'm not singing?" she asked.

Everybody laughed.

"No, sweetness, don't ever leave the stage. We take a break halfway. Just move around to the music and that'll drive 'em wild. Now, when I sing the part about Cupid shootin', you act like you just got shot — in the heart."

Jemma stared at them cockeyed and started to laugh but thought better of it when she saw Buddy's deadpan face. "Show business," she said under her breath.

She was chewing a hole in her lip as she watched the Lido High School gym fill up. She wiped her damp hands on her poodle skirt. Buddy B came over and gave her a pep talk. He had on his black, horn-rimmed glasses that had no lenses. "Don't worry about anything, Jem," he said as he combed his recently dyed hair. "You've nailed every song at rehearsals so relax and have a good time. The girls are all gonna be wishin' they were you, and the guys are all gonna be wishin' they were your boyfriend. Just sling your hair around and do some of those

447

moves you've got." He grinned. "They'll be hollerin' for more."

Jemma considered what her own boyfriend might be doing at the moment. Whatever it was, it couldn't be much fun. This was his idea, for her to sing with Buddy's band, so if it would give Spence a little happiness, she'd better do it and do it well. Buddy would most likely be giving her boyfriend a report.

Buddy's list was unnecessary now, but she laid it on the floor by her microphone anyway. Buddy could read the audience and give them what they wanted and what they had paid for. The lights came up on the stage, and he started his introduction to the crowd.

"Jemma," Leon whispered, "turn on your mike."

She did and bumped it at the same time, but nobody seemed to notice. Buddy wailed out, "Well-ll-ll . . ."

The night was crazy. Jemma added the spice, as Buddy had predicted, and the audience loved her. She had to admit it was fun. If Spencer wanted her to do it, she'd give it a try because there wasn't much else to do in Chillaton when your man was far away. The so-called Peace Talks in Paris didn't make her think that he'd be coming home sooner than expected, either.

Her flight was late into the Honolulu Airport. Spencer paced from one end of the terminal to the other. He stopped at the big window and peered skyward, but it was too foggy to see anything. What if her flight was cancelled or the plane ran into trouble? No. This trip could not get messed up for them, like other times, other places. His nerves were just like they were on his first solo flight. He was very good at what he did, but he was not cut out for the emotional strain. Dealing with the continual agony of the wounded, and the gory aftermath of weapons inflicted on the human body was too much.

Transporting young men his own age, or even younger, in plastic bags was slowly killing him. It had taken a toll on his spirit and he couldn't let it go. He wanted to help save as many lives as he could, but he also longed for the peace of his childhood with happy playmates and Harriet reading him a story until he fell asleep. Now scenes of an especially horrific nature had left a permanent imprint. The hideous sound of gunfire and the sickening smells of combat were becoming the norm for him. He didn't know if he could ever speak of this time, even with her. He needed joy, light, enchantment, warmth, and peace. He needed his Jemmabeth.

His heart pounded as the passengers finally began filing through the gate. She was in the middle of them. She didn't cry like he thought she might, but instead dropped her bags and ran to him, yelling his name the whole way. They embraced and kissed in the center of the crowd until nobody was left but them. "Aloha, baby. Welcome to Hawaii." He took the lei off his neck and put it around hers.

"Let's go to the hotel," she said. "I want to hold you for a week."

They checked into the Ilima Hotel near Waikiki Beach. Each had their own room, but he had filled Jemma's with bouquets of flowers.

"They are beautiful, Spence, thank you," she said. "Now, this is what I came for." She dove at him, knocking him flat on the sofa. He was ready. They were on the couch for an hour before Jemma sat up. "Whew. I've missed you. Let's get married right this minute."

Spencer pulled her to him. "Nope. In six months, I'll be home and we'll have our big wedding with family and friends."

She rested her head on his chest and

pouted. "Please, Spence, I want to get married. Willa's married, Carrie's married, Sandy is married, and here we sit in a hotel in Hawaii, going insane. Give me the speech again."

"I need to wait to get me through this."

"If we were married, though, you would have us getting together when you get out to look forward to. Am I going to lose my irresistible charm once you marry me?"

"You will be even more irresistible. It's just the way I am, baby. Remember your old cowboy theory?"

"Of course I remember that theory, but you are my only cowboy now."

"You had to get him out of your mind, though. You said it was just the way you were made. Well, I have to have the most important event of my life and the big prize that comes with it as my reward for finishing this job. It's just the way I'm made."

Jemma banged her head on his chest in exasperation. "Aarrgghh! Okay. I'll drop that idea for now, but I had to try. So, how does this fit into your little plan?" She whispered something in his ear and then nipped it. She jumped up, giggled, and ran to the opposite end of the room.

"You're a mean woman, Jemmabeth Alexandra. I'll show you what I think of your idea." Spencer chased after her, but she crawled over the top of the bed. He grabbed her foot and there they were, on the bed, in a heap. Spencer caught his breath and looked into her eyes that were the same color as a tiger's. She gave him a half smile and he couldn't help but kiss her. "C'mon, get up. I know when I'm being lured into your trap." He stood. "Let's go for a walk on the beach."

"Spoilsport," she said. "This beach can't be any better than Plum Creek."

The beach at Waikiki was not Plum Creek, but it would do. They felt the sand under their bare feet for an hour. Not until it began to rain did they decide to go back to the hotel. Their days were spent talking and walking. Their nights were filled with dancing and necking, but they slept in their respective rooms.

On their last day, they rented a car and drove around the island. A spectacular sunset materialized and waves pounded the shoreline. He played his ukulele for her and they watched the stars. It was a heavenly night that would be over much too soon.

"Spence," Jemma said as they sat in her room, "I want to ask you a favor."

"Anything."

"I want you to sleep with me tonight," she

said, smoothing his hair.

"Jem, don't do this."

"Now just listen to me. I really mean sleep, to be together while we sleep. It will be the same as stargazing on the hood of the Corvette. Nothing will happen, I promise. I want to have that memory for the next six months. I want to wake up in the night and kiss you. I'll be good, really, I will." She hoped that didn't sound like Miss Scarlett.

Spencer walked around the room. He came back to the sofa, looked at her, then smiled. "Let's brush our teeth together, too. We've never done that."

"Thank you, thank you." Jemma jumped up and got her toothbrush and loaded it with toothpaste. He went next door and got his.

They said their prayers, then curled up on the couch in their jeans with their shirts tucked in, and made plans for their wedding and their future as man and wife. It was the most peaceful feeling that Spencer could remember. It wouldn't be easy for him to have her perfect body against him all night, but it would be worth it to have her breath intermingle with his. It was about as far away from a battle zone as he could get.

"I'm always amazed that I can love you more than the last time I was with you,"

Spencer whispered, long after she thought he was asleep.

She snuggled even closer until her hair tickled his chin. "I adore you, Spencer Chase. Good night."

"Sweet dreams, baby." He closed his eyes and prayed that the good Lord would bring him home so that he could spend tens of thousands of nights with her.

At daybreak, Jemma turned to see if he was awake yet. He wasn't. She wanted to touch him but knew he needed the rest. From the instant she saw him at the airport, she knew that he was stretched to his limit with this job. He wouldn't say so, but she could tell that he had been living with terror and it was consuming him. She was so grateful that he had given in to letting her rest beside him. Jemma laid her hand on his arm and asked God to keep him safe until they could hold one another again on their wedding night. She memorized every detail about him as she watched him sleep until the sun was in the sky.

Only a few hours later, Spencer watched the plane take her away and leave him to face the months that lay ahead.

Lizbeth and Jemma had been looking forward to Julia's visit for weeks. Having her

454

around brought a burst of excitement to everybody's world.

"I wonder if Julia knows that the revival starts Sunday," Lizbeth said. "I don't think I'll go. That Ryder fellow is the evangelist, and I don't care for his style at all, not one bit."

"It's that slick hair and all the jewelry," Jemma said with a mouthful of biscuit and jam.

"Well, he brings in crowds of backsliders, plus he fills up the pews and the offering plates. My father would have called him a Soul Tinker."

"Mom said that he was tinkering around with Paula Sharpe the last time he held a revival here."

"I heard about that at the beauty parlor and I hoped that wasn't true. I hate to see a man who claims to be doing the Lord's work doing his own dirty work instead."

There was a shuffling at the screened-in porch as Lester laid the mail inside the back door, then shut it. "Get in here and have coffee with us," Lizbeth shouted, still peeved with Brother Ryder.

"Is your sister up yet?" he asked, peering through the screen.

"No, it's safe." Jemma grinned. "You aren't scared of Do Dah, are you, Lester?"

"I just like to give that woman a clear track."

"Tell us what's going on downtown," Jemma said.

"Well, sir, Son Wheeler is down in the dumps. Seems that his two full-growed daughters have up and started their own restaurant where the old feed store used to be."

"How nice," Lizbeth said. "I wondered what was going in there."

"It may be nice for the town, but Son don't look at it that way. He's got a good business goin' for hisself at the drive-in burger place. He was down to the post office this mornin', and he looked like he'd been shot in the foot." Lester took a slurp of coffee.

"And?" Lizbeth pressed.

"Seems that these gals are from his first marriage and they've both been livin' down to Corpus. The wife, she passed on, and left them all the alimony money that Son has been sendin' her for all these years. They decided to move here and start up a restaurant to give Son some competition. Appears they don't much cotton to him and the way he done their mama."

"What kind of restaurant is it?" Jemma asked.

"It's a sit-down place with menus at every table."

"Well, I think it's good that we can go somewhere to eat besides the truck stop," Lizbeth said.

"Son ain't happy about none of it, but especially since them gals is plasterin' up a big billboard advertisement right next to his burger joint and it's even got lights on it. The place is supposed to open tomorrow."

"What's the name of the new restaurant?" Jemma asked.

"Daddy's Money." Lester shook his head. "Ain't that a fine howdy-do name for a eatin' place?"

Lizbeth was distracted by a letter with an official-looking return address. She took it to the living room and opened it. Her face softened into a smile. At long last, good news.

Jemma's twenty-third birthday came and went like an empty passenger train. Everyone tried to make it special, but they all knew what she really wanted. She got out all his letters and read them again, then went to her dresser and picked up the pretty package Spencer had given her at the Amarillo airport. She sat in the porch swing and opened it with care, afraid that even tearing the paper could somehow cause him harm. She knew better, but lately she had become weird about such things. Spence's hand had last touched the box inside, making even that dear to her. It was small, so her guess all along had been that it contained jewelry, and she was right. A gold bracelet lay curled inside the velvet liner. The delicate chain flanked a design just like the heart necklace he had given her, only this one did not have a diamond in the center. Instead, it had initials — JAC. She smiled and traced it. He not only had a way with words, but with initials, too. She put it on her wrist and leaned back to admire the combination of letters. How she ever got so lucky to have him love her, she would forever wonder.

Jemma caught up with Twila in the grocery store. "Hey, I haven't seen you at Nedra's lately."

"I quit," Twila said flatly. "Nedra wanted me to work on the hairpieces, and I tried my best. She didn't tell me that you couldn't wash the fake hair like you do real hair. I guess I ruined a bunch. They looked like cow patties when I was done with them. Nedra had a hissy fit at first, talkin' about all the money I had wasted and how those old ladies were going to look half bald until she could order some more, 'specially that old Gramma Knuckle. She yelled at me in front of everybody and said that it didn't take a genius to wash a wig. Then she told me to stick with sweepin' and runnin' the cash register if I wanted to keep my job. When I told Buddy B, he said to quit."

"How are y'all going to make it on his salary?"

"Eat beans, I guess. I'm gonna go talk to Dr. Benson today and see if he'll hire me for that dental helper job he's got in the *Star*."

"Don't you have to go to school for that?"

"I don't know. He said he would use me for little stuff until he gets a real nurse or whatever you call 'em."

"Good luck, Twila," Jemma said. "Call me whenever you want to talk."

She called that night. "I didn't understand some of the questions on the application, Jem. Like, 'Does your spouse work?' I took it up to Dr. Benson and said I didn't know I had one, so how would I know if it was workin' or not?"

Jemma clamped down on her tongue. "Oh Twila. Did Dr. Benson laugh?"

"He liked to have died laughin'. I was so embarrassed. I still don't know what was so funny. I'm not askin' Buddy, though, because he'll laugh at me, too."

"Buddy B is your spouse, Twila."

"He is? Oh. Well, he'd better be workin'. See, Jemma, I need you there when I take these tests."

"Did you get the job?"

"I'm workin' tomorrow. He showed me what I have to do. It's kind of like workin' at Nedra's, only it smells funny, like the hospital."

"You'll do fine."

"I hope so. Otherwise I don't know where else I can find a job."

Twila called again during lunch the next day. "I got sent home."

"Oh Twila," Jemma said.

"I fainted. Dr. Benson wanted me to hold this little doodad in this old man's mouth to suck out the blood and spit while he yanked out a tooth. I started out okay with my eyes shut, but he told me to watch what I was doin' and as soon as I opened my eyes, there was blood and yucky spit and he was pullin' with these pliers and I couldn't help it; I just went down. I fell right across the old guy's chest. I guess they had a hard time pullin' me off him."

"I'm sorry. Are you fired?"

"He didn't say that in so many words, but

I got the feelin'. I did okay before that happened. You remember the old guy that used to run the hardware store? He wears false teeth and I guess one of the teeth was loose, so he tried to fix it at home with something real strong. He glued his uppers to his hand and had a hard time drivin' to the office. It was real funny but I didn't laugh, honest. I was professional with him. Dr. Benson gave me some stuff to get rid of the glue then I cleaned him and his teeth up good as new, and he left happy. Now I have no job."

"Talk to Nedra. I bet she would take you back. She didn't fire you."

"I know. Buddy's gonna blow his stack when he hears about me faintin'. That would've been a nice job except for the icky parts."

"He'll be okay. Buddy's a good guy."

"I'll go see Nedra. Thanks, Jem."

Jemma hung up the phone and collapsed into laughter. She had never heard Twila talk so much in her life, but it was worth every word. She couldn't wait to write it all down for her own, soon-to-be spouse.

The revival banners were hung from tree to tree and the church was packed. The newest member of the revival team came down the aisle and sat at the organ. He played a chord, then hushed up the congregation with a hopping rendition of "When the Saints Go Marching In." At the last note, Angel Ryder appeared at the pulpit, Bible in hand. The mood in the sanctuary was much the same as right before the referee blows the whistle at the kickoff in a football game.

Lizbeth opened her Bible and read to herself. Julia looked around the sanctuary.

A dazzling smile spread across Angel's face. "Welcome to the Lord's House. Praise God! Yes, yes. How y'all doing tonight? Let me hear you say amen," Angel thundered.

The congregation wasn't quite revived. They were used to Brother Hightower's mild-mannered sermons. It had been a year since Angel Ryder had held a revival in Chillaton. He lifted his Bible above his head and leered out at the pews and did a double take, like nobody was there. "Let-me-hear-you-say-*amen*," he repeated, with gusto.

The congregation obliged, somewhat more enthusiastically. Lizbeth and Jemma exchanged glances. Julia closed her eyes.

Angel nodded approval. "Now let's get started with a song that everybody knows. Brothers and sisters, leading the music this week will be a good friend of the Lord's, Frankie Franco."

Julia stretched her neck a little toward the action.

Frankie stood and bowed, then moved to the piano.

Angel looked thoughtful. "Say, Frankie, I've been wondering, what kind of name is Franco, anyway?"

Frankie leaned into the microphone that was rigged up on the piano. "A-mer-i-can." The words oozed out of his mouth like an announcer at the Fourth of July bingo tent and resounded into the street.

"Well, that's what we all are this morning — Americans. If you love your country, raise your hand. Good. If you love your family, raise your hand. Yes, yes. Now, if you love the Lord, rise up, brothers and sisters, and start singing page 153 in your hymnal."

Frankie crooned the hymn into the mike. He sounded a little like Dean Martin. Lizbeth stood and began singing in her sweet soprano and Jemma sang alto. Julia didn't sing, but held her hymnal high and kept her eyes on Frankie.

Angel made a sizable impression on the congregation with his sermon on the sinful ways of man. Three humble souls went down to the front of the church wanting to be saved, and a half-dozen more went down to rededicate their lives to the Lord. He

463

closed with the announcement that he would be preaching on a different sin every night that week. He emphasized that it was each person's Christian duty to bring at least one sinner, each preferably linked to the sinful topic of the evening. When the offering plate was passed, it was already brimming over by the time it reached Lizbeth's pew. One of the deacons got a fresh plate to pass to the next row. Julia, who normally dropped in a large bill, didn't. The service had gone on for over an hour, and, after the final hymn, Julia asked them to wait for her on the front steps.

"What's she up to?" Lizbeth whispered.

"Maybe she's making sermon suggestions to Angel."

"I wouldn't put it past her."

They waited as the revived filed out of the church, shaking hands with Brother Hightower and squinting into the sunlight. Several men clustered under the trees and fired up their cigarettes, inhaling deeply after the long sermon. Most children ran around under the big elms while others clambered up the brick railings that flanked the steps so they could jump off before their parents yelled at them. Almost everyone paused to say hello to Lizbeth and visit for a few minutes. Finally, the only conversations to be heard were chirps high in the branches of the old trees, and only a couple of cars remained.

"Jemmabeth, would you go check on her?" Lizbeth asked, more suspicious than worried. Jemma turned to go inside but was met by Julia, Frankie, and Angel. Lizbeth caught her breath and looked skyward.

"Sorry, y'all, that it took me so long, but I've invited these gentlemen out to eat with us girls," she said, smiling at the slick-haired duo. Their white suits and wide, loud ties made them ready for carnival work at best.

Angel extended his hand to Jemma. "And who might this be?"

"This is my great-niece, Jemmabeth, and this is my sister, Lizbeth."

"Well, beauty runs in this family, isn't that a fact, Frankie?" Angel said, laying his other hand over Jemma's, too.

Frankie nodded, giving Jemma a thorough inspection. "C'mon, let's go. I'm starving."

They all climbed in Julia's Cadillac DeVille. Lizbeth and Jemma got in the backseat. Lizbeth sat wooden-faced. "You can just drop me off at the house," she said.

"No, you are going with us, Lizbeth." Julia rounded the corner heading toward Daddy's Money. "We are going to have a good time." She winked at her niece in the

465

rearview mirror.

Daddy's Money was full of the after-church crowd, mostly Methodists and Presbyterians. The Baptists still had not warmed to the thought of going out to eat after Sunday morning services. Lizbeth puckered her lips and folded her arms across her chest. They got the last big table, a corner booth.

"Well, now," Angel said, "tell us all about yourself, little Miss Jimmybeth Foster."

"Forrester," Lizbeth corrected, "Jemmabeth Forrester."

"Ah." Angel nodded.

Julia put on her reading glasses and looked over the menu. "Jemma is an artist. You would be wise to invest in her work someday, if you can afford it."

The waitress brought water to the table and took an immediate liking to Angel and Frankie. "How are y'all doin' today?" she asked, cutting her eyes at them.

"The question is," Angel said, "how are *you* doing?"

"I'm just great, what can I get for y'all?" She concentrated her attention on the sullen Frankie.

"We'll all have the special, sweetheart, and I'm paying," Julia said. "Bring us some iced tea, and for dessert, we'll try your Mama's

Fudge Pie."

Angel leaned back in the booth and loosened his flashy necktie. "I can see that you are a take-charge woman, Miss Julia."

"Mrs. Billington," Julia said, putting her glasses away.

"Ah."

"So, Mr. Franco," Julia said, "what do you think of our little town?"

Frankie waved to the waitress for a refill. "I prefer Brother Franco."

"Is that so," Julia said.

"We consider it an honor to be called *brother* in the good Lord's service. It keeps us humble," Angel said. He was still hot from the pulpit and gave a brief, yet disquiet, sermon on the rigors of circuit evangelism. Jemma was sure that some of the Methodists left before their desserts were served because of it.

Lizbeth cleared her throat and shifted on the slick plastic seat.

"How long have you been preaching?" Jemma asked.

"Thirteen years." Angel pushed back a twirl of hair that had somehow escaped his Brylcreem. "The time has flown by, praise the Lord." The stone in his ring was the same size as Julia's.

"Brother Franco, how long have you been

467

in the good Lord's service?" Julia asked.

"We started out in this business together," Angel answered, giving Julia a pious look.

The waitress arrived with five plates of chicken-fried steak lined up both arms.

"Now that's a real talent you've got there, girly-girl," Frankie said.

"Help my life," Lizbeth said, looking at her plate. "That's enough to feed Cox's army."

"A toast." Angel raised his glass without response from the odd assemblage. "To the fine-looking, generous women of Texas."

"Hear, hear," said a man in the next booth.

Jemma nudged Lizbeth's foot with hers. A smile played in the corners of Julia's mouth, but the men concentrated on the meal before them.

Julia picked at her steak. "You know, my husband is Arthur Billington," she began. "We own several retail stores around Texas. Maybe you have heard of Billington's in Houston, Dallas, or maybe San Antonio?"

Angel shook his head. "Can't say as I have, but I don't shop much on the road."

"Where's home for you, Brother Franco?" she asked.

Frankie frowned. "Are you a reporter or something?"

"I'm trying to satisfy my curiosity," Julia said.

"I'm not much on curiosity." Frankie dabbed at his chin with a napkin.

Julia continued. "Arthur and I were in Las Vegas last summer for a buyers' convention."

Angel winked at Jemma. "The devil's playground."

"We stayed away from the playground, Brother Ryder, but I do remember a poster in the convention center elevator advertising a Frank Franco and Frankie's Naughty Mamas performing nightly in some casino bar."

Angel's fork slipped and hit his plate. Frankie swiveled and faced Julia, who dabbed at her mouth with her napkin.

"What are you up to, lady?" Frankie was on the edge of the booth, one leg bouncing wildly.

"Now, let's not get upset." Angel lowered his voice and looked around. "Nobody wants trouble." He shook his head slightly at Frankie. "Maybe we should call a cab."

"This is not Vegas. If you don't have a ride in Chillaton, you walk," Julia said. "You two are fixin' to have some bumpy roads ahead of you if you don't watch out."

Jemma realized that she had been holding

her breath and she suspected Gram had, as well.

"What are you suggesting?" Angel asked with a maniacal grin.

"I suggest," Julia said, "that you give every penny of the offerings that you collect this week to the church's fund for the poor. What do you think about that, Brother Ryder?"

"I think you are out of line, sister," Frankie spewed through clamped teeth.

"I believe that the Lord has His own ways of taking care of the poor." Angel eased his way toward Frankie, who was already standing, cracking his knuckles. "Let us take this situation to the Lord in prayer, sisters." He quickly knelt on the linoleum with his hands folded on the booth's plastic upholstery. "He'll reveal His divine consideration to me real quick, always does."

"No consideration required," Julia said. "I've already told the good pastor and the head deacon that those are your wishes. The pastor will announce it tonight at the evening service. He was very impressed with your generosity. Good afternoon, brothers." She spread a hot roll with the melting pat of butter beside her plate. "Now, I'm about ready for some of Mama's Fudge Pie. Aren't you, girls?"

Angel stood, adjusted his suit coat, then wiped sweat off his upper lip before moving toward the exit. Frankie eased out the door and onto the sidewalk. Jemma watched as Angel and Frankie gestured wildly at one another before slithering down the street.

Lizbeth blew out a low whistle. "Julia, you never cease to amaze me." She began to chuckle as the waitress plunked down five dessert plates.

"I told you this was going to be fun." Julia closed her lips around her first bite of pie.

"Do Dah, I wish I could be you for just one day." Jemma giggled with relief and admiration.

"The feeling is mutual, sweet girl. I'd like to be your age again. Let's get going on this dessert. We've got extra now."

Buddy's band was waiting to rehearse for the next dance.

"So, Jemma, are you fixin' to have your own act?" Wade asked. "That was some heavy stuff you were layin' on the other night."

"Excuse me, my own act?"

"Yeah," Dwayne said, "I didn't know good little church girls knew how to dance like that."

Wade added a *ba-dump-bump-chhhh* on

the drums.

"We know a thing or two," Jemma said, a tad embarrassed.

"Y'all shut up and leave her alone," Leon yelled. "You done real good, Jemma. You've got that Peggy Lee kinda voice. You've got the moves, too. It's all in the shoulders, isn't it?" He took his eyes off the television momentarily. "I'm sure sorry that Spencer had to go to 'Nam."

Jemma was somewhat taken aback by this sudden display of chivalry and compliments. "Why, thank you, Leon."

"No thanks needed," he said, going back to his TV show.

"Didn't you go to some fancy-pants school in Dallas?" Dwayne asked. "Did they teach you how to fold napkins like birds and stuff?"

Jemma went in the kitchen to say hi to Twila, ignoring him.

"I just want to know if they really have buck-naked girls for you to draw," he shouted, then snorted.

"You'll have to get accepted to art school to find that out," Jemma yelled back.

Twila stopped laughing and leaned in close to Jemma's ear. "Do they have naked men, too?"

"Yeah, but things are sort of covered. You

couldn't pay me enough money to model for an art class," Jemma whispered.

"Hey, what's going on? Y'all ready to hit it?" Buddy B burst in, smelling like axle grease. "Hi, hon," he said, giving Twila a peck on the cheek.

"Is that the best you can do?" Jemma asked, hands on her hips.

Buddy took off his jacket. "What'd I do wrong? I just got here."

"Where's the romance? Is that what becomes of married couples?" Jemma asked.

"Oh, that was just the warm-up." He dipped Twila off her feet and laid a huge smacker on her. Twila looked as though she'd been dunked in a tank at a carnival game.

The boys all whistled.

"Now that's more like it," Jemma said.

"Let me grab a bite to eat and I'll be right out. Y'all go ahead and warm up with 'Mustang Sally.'"

"You sure got Twila all warmed up," Dwayne said on his way to the garage.

Wade got a chuckle out of that and raised his brow at Twila, who threw a wet dishrag at him. Leon went outside for a smoke.

"Jemma, can you come here a sec? I've got an idea that I want to run by you." Buddy B motioned her into the kitchen. He heaped his plate with corn bread and black-eyed peas. "Looks good, hon," he said and dug in.

"Here, I'll clean up the dishes; you go eat with your husband," Jemma said as she pushed Twila into a chair. "Buddy, you were great on 'Candy Man' the other night. You should do more Roy Orbison."

"I just might do that," he said. "Listen, I thought we might try you comin' up to my mike for harmony on 'That'll Be the Day,' and 'He Will Break Your Heart,' then we'll take turns on 'Stand by Me.' I want to work on some Aretha stuff for you to try solo, too."

"Solo?" Jemma whirled around from the sink. "You want me to sing solo?"

"You've got the voice for it. What do you think?"

"Good grief."

"I think it'll go over real nice. Like you and me are in love or somethin'." Buddy jabbed at Twila with his elbow.

Twila elbowed him back. "Hey, if you were singin' with anybody but Jemma, I'd fix your clock."

"I'm going to the garage." Jemma dried her hands on her jeans. "Y'all need some time alone."

Wade and Dwayne were already out there,

relaxing and catching up on Chillaton cave-man gossip, which was Jemma's exact reason for leaving the kitchen. Leon was outside, still smoking. Jemma picked up a year-old *Chillaton Star* and pretended to read it.

"So, did you hear about old man Huff?" Wade asked.

"I thought I went to his funeral," Dwayne said.

"What? He was pullin' a trailer full of hogs to Amarillo last Friday. You know that hill right before the big house where they made that movie?"

Dwayne frowned. "You mean on the highway with the cotton gin on the left or on the Farm to Market that's on the right?"

"The highway. Anyway, old man Huff is coming down the hill when his own trailer passes him, just as smooth as you please. Whole thing come unhitched and rolled right on by him in the other lane."

"What about the hogs?"

"They were givin' him the pig eye as they went past. He liked to have had a heart at-tack. He slammed on the brakes first, like that would do a lot of good. Then he chased the trailer down the highway until it rolled into that big windbreak on the old Davis place."

"Man. Was anybody else on the road?"

"Highway patrol car. Threw the book at him."

"Old people shouldn't pull trailers."

Jemma had moved to a stack of magazines, discards from Nedra's Nook, and thumbed through several. Spencer was right — these two made her smile.

The next night, Buddy B was on time for rehearsal. "I've got about the best news we could get," he said with a grin.

"We're splittin' up?" Dwayne asked. He and Wade enjoyed guffaws over that.

"Western State wants us to play for their weekend homecomin' dances next fall. We could headline. It's somebody's big re-union."

"How much are they payin' us?" Wade asked.

"Five hundred bucks."

"American money?" Dwayne asked amid whistles of disbelief.

"There's a hitch, though," Buddy B said.

"They don't want you to sing." Dwayne cracked another one.

"Some of them are comin' to Chillaton to hear us play for the prom."

"We're auditioning?" Jemma asked.

"Looks like."

"Then let's get goin.' I got me some TV to watch later," Leon said.

Leon and Buddy worked out some new arrangements while Jemma caught the Dwayne and Wade Show.

"Hey, did you hear about Sherman Ray?" Dwayne began.

"Nelson or Fisher?"

"Nelson. He wrecked his car. It went airborne out by the bridge in Windy Valley."

"Is he dead?" Wade sat up with renewed interest.

"Too dumb to die. He never knew what hit him until he woke up in jail the next day. His face was all swoll up, though."

"They put him in jail?" Wade asked.

"Problem was they didn't know what to do with him because he had about five fake driver's licenses on him. The deputy couldn't figure out who he was to call his folks. He had just made one for Donna Sitton, so I guess they knew that wasn't his name."

"How's that?" Wade raised his brow.

Dwayne lowered his. "Donna is a girl, bonehead. What's the matter with you?"

"Oh yeah. I heard she was datin' old Chick Mason."

"Chick's in the doghouse right now. He

won't be datin' nobody for a while," Dwayne said.

"The doghouse? I heard he'd been sleepin' in the outhouse again." Wade snickered. "That was about the funniest story I ever heard. How did Chick get to be so ignorant?"

"Same way you did," Leon said, ready to rehearse.

Wade looked up. "How's that?"

"All the brains get used up in the first few kids born." Leon winked at Jemma. "Everybody knows that."

Wade and Dwayne considered the possibility of that being a scientific fact, since neither was the oldest in their families.

The Cleave leaned against the bank teller's window where Jemma waited for her deposit receipt. "We keep bumping into each other. It must be bad . . . uh . . . that stuff. I've been studying other religions. Spencer is probably our connection. I know he loved my care package because I sent him lots of expensive chocolate and a girlie magazine that I know soldiers always crave. One of my sorority sisters is in it. I could've been in it, too, but I was in Madrid."

Jemma's scalp prickled. "He hasn't mentioned it."

"Well, of course not, silly. Why would he tell you how much he's enjoying looking at Shelia Thompson? She's got plenty to look at, too — not like me, but okay. I'm expecting a letter from him any day."

Jemma took her deposit slip and walked away. Her face had to be the same color as Missy's fingernail polish. Spencer wouldn't open anything from The Cleave. He just wouldn't.

"Karma!" Missy yelled from the teller's window.

She turned back to the cashier, Durinda McAfee, and flashed her perfect smile. "I've been studying other religions."

Durinda popped her gum. "That so? Well, now, I bet the angels are singing an extra hallelujah chorus to hear that. Next, please."

CHAPTER 19
DEAREST

July 22, 1969

Dearest Jemmabeth,

I'm looking at the watercolor you sent of Plum Creek and thinking about the vows we said there. Let's use them in our real wedding. The words came right back to me. I miss your laugh and your kisses, but I think I've fallen for this tempting girl who lives under my bed. She's getting premature wrinkles, though, from spending most of her life all folded up.

Your letters are the carrot that gets me through the week. I read an old one again each night. I told you way back about the guys over here calling me "cowboy." Now somebody has painted a cowboy boot kicking the VC on the side of our chopper, and the other day there was a sign taped to the chopper door that said DO NOT DISTURB — COWBOY AT WORK. It's good to have some humor around this place because there is an overload of suffering and death. We're all wound tight. This is a world I hope our sons never have to know, Jem. There are some real heroes over here. My crew is incredible. I don't know how they keep it together, but they do. We fly all hours of the day and night. Many of the wounded are in such bad shape that they don't make it. It's hard, really hard.

I hope you're painting. I'm expecting a twenty-piece show when I get home. That's great news about the Girard Fellows exhibition in Paris and the commission for another magazine cover, but it had better not be of me. Just think, we'll be married the next time we visit Sainte-Chapelle. By the way, I tossed that little pebble into the Mekong River while we were on a mission. Chillaton has landed, just like Neil Armstrong on the moon! What did you think about that event? Everybody got quiet around here as we listened to the radio. It's as though part of life's mystery has come undone now that we've touched the moon.

Keep knocking their socks off in the band! I would love to hear you. I'm so glad that Dwayne and Wade keep you laughing. It won't be long until I'll be home. I just know that everything will be all right. God is with me every step. I watch the silvery stars every night as I think of thee, my beautiful love. You are more than in my heart. You are the marrow, the strength in my bones, Jemmabeth, and that's what keeps me going.

Always,
Spence

Jemma sat in the Corvette in front of the Chase castle reading his letter again. She put it in her purse and stared up at the turrets that Spence so disliked. Spencer's grandfather had built the house to please his grandmother. For her own part, this was Jemma's third visit to check on Mrs. Chase like Spencer had requested. On the first visit, Rebecca Chase opened her bedroom door just enough to hear the conversation in the foyer below. It was almost humorous, as though nobody could see her through the crack. The second visit proved no better. Jemma told herself she was doing this for Spence, but she knew in her heart that she was doing it for her own reasons. She couldn't bear for his mother to dislike her.

She went up the steps and looked back

toward town. The crows on the barbed-wire fence stared back at her like some Shakespearean omen.

Max answered the door. They were equally surprised to see one another. "Jemmabeth, come in. Is everything okay?"

"I was about to ask you the same thing. I thought you would be at work."

"If you're looking for Harriet, she has the day off." Max glanced toward the kitchen as dishes clattered to the floor. "Have a seat, hon. I'll be right back."

He disappeared into the dining room, and Jemma looked around at the furnishings and décor. The house had been featured in *Southern Comfort* magazine a few years back, which further embarrassed Spencer. She turned at the onset of an argument followed by shouted obscenities blasting out of the kitchen. Max reappeared, pulling Mrs. Chase behind him.

"Becky, come say hello to Jemmabeth. You two need to get to know each other since we are going to be family pretty soon," Max said, like there was no history between them.

Jemma looked away. Mrs. Chase was still in her nightgown. Her hair hadn't seen a comb in some time, and she had spilled something down the front of her gown.

"Hello, Mrs. Chase," Jemma said, unable to look directly at her. Rebecca protested with no small amount of profanity to Jemma's presence and stumbled toward the stairs. Max ignored her and tried to engage in polite conversation about Spencer. Rebecca inched her way up the stairs, holding onto the handrail. She was almost to the top when she lost her grip. She slipped and plummeted back down. Jemmabeth screamed and raced to the bottom of the steps.

"Becky!" Max shouted, touching her shoulder.

"Don't move her," Jemma said. "I'll call Sheriff Ezell; he'll get an ambulance. Don't move her." She darted around the room, looking for a phone.

"There's one in the kitchen," Max yelled, still hunched over his wife's body.

The ambulance took her to Amarillo, to the same hospital where Jemma had been in a coma. Mrs. Chase was not in a coma, but she had broken her arm and dislocated her shoulder. She wouldn't be drinking for a while.

"You don't need to take me home. I'll hop on the Zephyr and be there in no time," Jemma said to Max in the waiting area.

"I'm sorry this all happened. I should have

paid more attention to her. It's just another example of my useless life." Max looked out at the courtyard and rubbed the back of his neck. "You know she was a beauty in her day. Of course you couldn't tell it now, but that's where Spencer got his good looks."

Jemma had been waiting for the right moment. "You know, Mr. Chase," she began.

"Please, call me Max. I'd really like that." She noticed that his hair was getting a little gray around the temples.

"Max, this might be the perfect time to get Mrs. Chase into an alcohol rehabilitation program. It could be a blessing that she's in this situation. I'm sorry she got hurt, but maybe you could use this time to get her some help. She could become that beautiful person again."

"Yeah, I've thought about that a lot lately. Spencer has been asking to get her some help for years, but I don't want him to know that she's in the hospital now. The doc says that she'll recover, so let's not worry him, okay?"

"Of course. I totally agree, but please consider taking her straight from here to a treatment center. That would make Spence very happy."

"There's a good one in Waco. I checked it out a couple of months ago. I'll make some calls." He smiled at her. "C'mon, at least let me drive you to the train station. I don't know when the next train will be heading to Chillaton."

"There's one that gets into town at 9:04," Jemma said. "Max, thank you for taking care of Spence's mother."

"Well, before she was his mother, she was my wife. We had a lot of fun . . . until the drinking started. It's time I did something for her."

Jemma and Lizbeth went to the cemetery to work on Papa's grave. Afterward, Jemma walked to the pond below the Chase mausoleum. The ducks weren't there. Maybe they were hiding in the cattails. As she started back up the path, a helicopter flew overhead. Jemma's heart stopped. For one crazy second, she thought it might be Spence. She didn't cover her ears as it passed; she wanted to hear the sounds that he might hear. It wasn't a fat Huey like he flew, but its blades made a whirring, chopping sound and it moved through the sky like an ugly dragonfly. She closed her eyes and strained to listen as it faded away. He would be home soon.

The sun was low and a thin drizzle chilled

the air as Spencer and his crew ran to their chopper for the fifth time in sixteen hours. He pulled the trigger and waited for the engine to take hold. The wind was off their tail because he could smell the burnt jet fuel. Thirty more seconds and the turbine engine, with its increasingly loud whine, would spin up to full rpm. Spencer preferred to wait several minutes to make sure everything was working right, but with guys down and waiting for them, he could be ready to pick his bird up and fly in much less than that. The crew was exhausted. His co-pilot was John Davis from Pennsylvania. The crew chief was Allan Porter, whose hometown was Milwaukee, and Shelton "Skeleton" Taylor, the best flight medic in the army, was born and bred in Kentucky. They had flown enough missions together to be like family. Now they were concentrating on getting in and out of this hot landing zone as quickly as possible and bringing back as many soldiers as they could hoist.

Spencer picked up the Huey slowly, stopping just above the ground to check things out, then hovered to the take-off pad. He got clearance and took it up to altitude.

"Giddy up, cowboy." Skeleton gave a thumbs-up and a weary grin.

Spencer made contact with the troops in

the landing zone for an estimate of casualties and to see where Charlie, the Viet Cong, was concentrated. The gunship team assigned to cover them was also on the radio. In a half hour they were both over the pickup point. The ground unit was in a wooded area flanked on one side by a field of tall grass. Porter began lowering the hoist cable through the canopy of trees. The gunship radioed that a hostile missile launch pad had been spotted.

Spencer was scanning the area and talking to the gunship pilot when, like a bolt of lightning, a massive fireball lit up the sky right in front of his chopper. Instantly, all contact ceased from the gunship. Spencer gasped and Skeleton called on the Almighty. They shuddered as the gunship debris pelted their chopper and its fiery smoke left sinister trails in the twilight. John called in the hit while Porter continued with the cable.

Spencer drew a quick breath and talked to the guys on the ground. "The cable is still coming. Get ready."

As the words came out of his mouth, a large volley of small-arms fire penetrated the engine. The big bird reacted to the hit, shaking violently, then dropped in altitude like a giant boulder.

Spencer held it as best he could. There was no time for a May Day call. An RPG round blasted through the cockpit window. Flames burst into the cabin as the crippled Huey slammed into the trees, nose down. Within seconds, the only sounds that remained were the sickening shift of metal against metal and the hiss and crack of an inferno. Thick, black smoke curled upward to the heavens, its tentacles clawing at the stars.

CHAPTER 20
IN THE STARS

Jemma stopped by the post office to mail Carrie a letter.

Paralee Batson, the postmistress, stubbed out her cigarette and leaned over the window. "Spencer sure has dropped off in the mail department. You two are still an item, aren't you? That Blake girl has been sendin' him a right smart amount of letters and packages. I had half a mind to lose them in the trash barrel." Her cat, H.D., lifted his head and twitched an ear for Jemma's response.

"Oh, you'll never have to worry about that again, Paralee," Jemma said and gave H.D. a pat. He stretched and jumped off the counter. "I guess Spence is really busy now. It's almost time for him to come home. Then you'll get to come to our wedding."

A right smart amount of letters and packages, huh? Rats. She was considering a few wrestling moves that The Cleave could sure write about.

Paralee raised her Joan Crawford brow. "I'd better be findin' me a dress to wear, then. The mister and me might go up to Amarillo next week after he gets his social security check. Don't let Spencer get in a rut of watchin' too much TV. That's about all my mister does these days. He likes them game shows. If it weren't for the beauty parlor, I wouldn't have nobody to talk to at all. Not countin' folks who come in for their mail, of course. On the other hand, hon, you can get some good ideas for fashion off them soaps. I got my little TV in the back, you know. Just the other day, I told Nedra about a new hairdo that I saw on 'As the Stomach Turns' — that's what the mister calls it. She's gonna fix me up just like that actress for your weddin'."

Jemma had never seen Paralee's hair combed out in her life. If not tightly wound in brush rollers, her silver locks were frozen in the same shape as the rollers and corralled under a hairnet.

"I bet you'll look very pretty at our wedding. I'll see you, Paralee."

"If you get a letter from Spencer, I'll give you a call," Paralee shouted.

Jemma went next door to buy her favorite shampoo at Nedra's Nook. Twila, recently rehired, waited on her.

"Come outside," Twila said and pulled her to the sidewalk. She glanced around and lowered her voice. "I need your help with somethin'. I'm tryin' to get p.g."

"Well, don't look at me," Jemma said, laughing.

"Ow." Twila's face contorted into a knot. "Hold on a minute."

"What's wrong with you?"

"Sorry. I was ovulatin'."

"You can't tell when that happens. You were in pain just then."

"I get this little twinge in my side."

"Left or right?"

"Sometimes it's both sides, so I'm thinkin' that would be twins."

"Twila, have you talked to your doctor about this?"

"No. I read about ovulatin' in a magazine here at Nedra's."

"I think you should check with your doctor and not a beauty parlor magazine. That isn't the way things work. I'm a girl, and I've never had twinges like that."

"Well, it's gotten stronger right after Buddy and me started tryin' to have a baby."

"How long has that been?"

"Almost two months."

"You don't have to get twinges to get

pregnant. You don't even have to be married to get pregnant."

"All I know is that you can't get p.g. without ovulatin'. I'm ovulatin', but I'm not p.g. yet."

"All the more reason why you should see a doctor."

"I was hopin' that you would ask your doctor for me," Twila said, grimacing again.

"You need to see Dr. Huntley now."

"I'm not going to a man doctor for this kind of stuff."

Jemma took Twila's hand. "Twila, those pains in your side could be something else. My doctor is a man and he's very nice."

"Is he an old man?"

"He's not as old as Dr. Huntley."

"How much does it cost to see him? We've been savin' up for a baby for five years."

"Don't worry, I'll pay for it."

"I don't want Buddy B to know about the twinges. He's already worried why I'm not p.g."

"I'll get an appointment for you, and it'll be our secret, okay?"

Twila winced again.

"I'll call today," Jemma said firmly.

They went to Amarillo that week. Twila had a monster bladder infection that had gone on far too long, and she was pregnant.

Twila rode home with her hands on her belly and a silly little smile.

Jemma grinned at her. "Now aren't you glad we went? You wouldn't have known about the infection, and it might have hurt your baby."

Twila nodded. "Buddy is gonna be so happy. I can't believe I'm p.g. If it's a girl, we'll name her after you and my mother."

Jemma dropped Twila off, thinking of Buddy's reaction to the great news, and headed home to see if there was any mail from Spencer. There wasn't. She hadn't heard from him in two weeks. Max was due back soon from an auto show in Detroit and a visit to see Mrs. Chase in Waco. Harriet was in North Carolina, visiting her sister. Jemma assumed that the army was getting all they could out of Spence before he was discharged. He only had two weeks left until he would be coming home to her. Then they could have their wedding at Plum Creek before it went dry and the trees lost their leaves.

Jemma had the feeling that maybe Shorty Knox had been peeking in the car house window for a couple of days, but she hadn't seen him. It was nothing to be frightened about, but she knew that Spence wouldn't like the idea of the town peeping Tom watching her paint again. The last time he'd hung around, it was to rescue Jemma's paintings before a deadly tornado swept through Chillaton. Spencer had made it up to Shorty by installing a color television with its own generator at his dugout. He had all but given up his peeping career after that.

She saw him on the fourth night. He grinned at her and she waved at him, then went outside to say hello. He was nowhere to be seen, but under the window was a dirty scrap of cardboard held down by a rock. She got goose bumps when she saw the crude stick drawing of a girl with a paintbrush in her hand. Spence would have to hear about this.

That same evening, besides her usual bags of groceries, she carried a giant box full of Big Chief tablets, pencils, and crayons to Shorty's dugout and left them next to the generator. There were other things to do in life besides watch television and peek into people's windows. There was art.

It had rained for three days in a row. Lizbeth had used the dreary weather to bake. "Sugar, I'm going to make some fruit pies for the wedding and freeze them in that new chest freezer that Julia bought me. What do you think? Is it tacky to serve thawed pies?" she asked.

"It might be tacky if they were still frozen." Jemma laughed and put her arm around Lizbeth while she went through the mail. "I don't know why I haven't heard from Spencer. He's so faithful to write every week and I sent him that big birthday package."

"Maybe his letters got misdirected. You'll hear soon, I'm sure."

Lester came in the back door for his mid-morning coffee. "That kitty cat dragged up a snake this mornin'."

Jemma drew back, big-eyed. "I'm not going out the door if there's a snake around."

"It's just a garter snake, no more than a cat's plaything." Lester helped himself to a cold biscuit with his coffee. "It's pretty much dead now. 'Course you can't be too careful when it comes to dead snakes. Ask Bernie Miller about that. Here 'while back, he was movin' some old lumber at his mother's house and uncovered a rattler. He picked up a two-by-four and give it a wallop. It was a big 'un, too, about this long, accordin' to Bernie." Lester held his arms out as far as he could reach. "Anyway, he was gonna skin it for a belt, so he put it in a gunny sack in the back floorboard of his

Hudson. He come hence to drivin' back into town when he heard a rattlin' sound. Bernie thought it was the old Hudson, but it turned out to be the rattler. It was coiled up in the front seat floorboard until it struck at him and nipped his boot. Bernie slammed on the brakes and jumped outta the car while it was still rollin'. Got himself all scratched up. Never did find the rattler."

"How did it live through a hit by a two-by-four?" Jemma asked.

"I expect he just winged the critter. It most likely woke up in the sack, kinda woozy. Bernie could've been a good inch or so off since he's just got the one eye. I never could figure out how he cuts hair so good. 'Course all them young fellers get crew cuts. He just has to aim his electric shaver at their heads."

Jemma peeked around the screened-in porch. "I have to work in the yard today, too. I hope Vincent doesn't find any more reptiles." She shivered. "I hate snakes. They are evil."

"I got some other news, too. The Burlington Line is droppin' the Zephyr passenger service startin' New Year's Eve. Not enough folks ridin' these days. I know how much you love that train, Jemmer, so I thought it was best that you heard it from me."

Jemma stared at Lester, hoping he was joking, but he looked at his coffee cup and tapped his foot.

"I've seen that train come and go a thousand times. It won't be the same without it," Lizbeth said, watching her granddaughter.

Jemma went outside and wandered to the tracks. Since she was old enough to point, she had loved that train. The Silver Zephyr was beautiful and powerful. It held such mystery, anticipation, and exhilaration. What would all those strangers do now? Looking down on life in miniature from a jet wouldn't be the same as seeing into the eyes of the people who lived in those towns below. Blurred glimpses of unfamiliar faces would be no more. There would be no reason to dance on the tracks because nothing special would happen if she did. Freight trains offered no romance or mystery. Jemma sat on the rails and cried. The world was changing, and their sweet kitty had touched evil, all in the same day.

She was pulling weeds around Papa's rosebushes when she heard the car drive up. It was Harriet. She broke down as soon as they embraced. Jemma saw the mustard-colored envelope in Harriet's hand. Every muscle in Jemma's body tightened and her stomach rose to her throat. Lizbeth came outside and searched their faces, then put her arms around them.

Harriet could barely speak. "I'm sorry to bear this news to you, my girl. I just now got back in town, and found this in the Chases' front door." She held out the envelope with *Western Union* on the front. Jemma recoiled, letting it drop to the ground. She clenched her fists inside Papa's big work gloves and they fell to the grass beside the letter.

Lizbeth picked up the telegram and slipped her arm around her granddaughter's waist. "We'll read it together, honey. Come over to the porch swing."

"I can't," Jemma whispered.

"You have to, Jemmabeth. You owe it to Spencer."

Harriet sat in a wicker chair next to the swing, her hands covering her mouth.

Jemma's hands trembled as she unfolded the telegram. She scanned it in silence, then threw it on the swing and bolted inside the house.

Lizbeth read it.

THE SECRETARY OF DEFENSE REGRETS TO INFORM YOU THAT YOUR SON, WO1 SPEN-

CER M. CHASE, FAILED TO RETURN FROM A RESCUE MISSION 23 JULY, 1969. WO1 CHASE IS NOW CLASSIFIED AS MISSING IN ACTION. THERE WERE NO OTHER SURVIVORS IN THE INCIDENT.

Lizbeth took Harriet's hand and led her inside. The two of them sat on the couch and cried. She heard Jemma being sick in the bathroom, then the slam of the back screen door. Lizbeth excused herself and looked out the kitchen window toward the tracks and saw Jemma. Her first instinct was to go to her, but decided instead to give Jemma some privacy. That's what she had needed when her telegrams had come about her dear boys. She said a quick prayer, then returned to the living room to comfort Harriet.

Jemma was blank. She turned east on the rail bed and ran to the city limits and stopped. On the horizon she could see the Chase castle and felt the bile come up in her throat again. She screamed his name and planted herself in the middle of the tracks until she heard the 3:37 blow its horn. The steel rail was blistering hot in the August sun, but she ran her hand along the smooth metal surface. She didn't turn even when she felt it coming. She didn't care what happened to her. It blasted its horn. A rabbit, startled by the shrill whistle, paused in the rail bed not far from her, and then hopped off. Her own life didn't seem all that important, but when the rails vibrated hard against her hands, Jemma moved off, too. The engineer yelled at her, but she didn't even look up.

Lester and Lizbeth made their way down the tracks after Jemma had been gone for over two hours.

"I should have comforted her," Lizbeth said, picking her way through the rail bed. "I thought she needed some time alone, and I surely needed to collect my composure. That was downright foolish of me."

"She's gonna be all right, Miz Liz. Jemmerbeth is rock-solid." Lester sniffed. "What are you thinkin' about Spencer?"

"Well, at least they haven't found him, but I know the pain of hoping against hope, only to get the next telegram with the worst of all news."

"I know you do, Miz Liz. I can't see the good Lord lettin' this happen to your family again. No sir, I just can't figger on it."

Lizbeth gasped. "There she is, Lester. Oh my." Jemma was curled up like a ball of yarn on the rails.

The three of them talked through suppertime. Lizbeth pleaded with her to eat something.

"I'm not hungry," Jemma said. "I'll sit outside for a while."

"Jemmabeth, you must at least drink some water. It's not good for you to go without fluids." Lizbeth filled a tall glass for her.

Jemma sat on the steps, holding the glass in her hands. She had to make him drink fluids when he was sick in Florence. What if he were thirsty now? She could not get the date out of her head — it was July 23, exactly a year after their wedding date that had ended in disaster. It could not be in God's plan for him to lose his dear life on that same date. It hurt her heart that she had not known for all this long time. Jemma bit her lip thinking of conversations where she had laughed or made jokes or times she had neglected her Bible study. Spencer could have been fighting for his life while she was thinking of wedding cakes.

She had forgotten to look at the stars tonight, and she had a dumb thought. If, in God's mercy, Spencer was safe, he might send her a message there. Jemma moved to the grass and searched the heavens. There was the moon with a part of its mystery now gone, like he'd said. She found Venus, then prayed to the good Lord that she would not have to inscribe *I Think of Thee* onto a cold marble stone. Before she could finish her prayer, a Cadillac slammed to a halt in front of Gram's gate. Max Chase jumped out, leaving the door open and the car running. He didn't see Jemma sitting in the grass as he barreled up to the front door.

"Max," Jemma said, getting up slowly. "Bad news?"

He turned and collapsed in her arms. "I just got home and Harriet was waiting with the news. How could this happen? He was so close to coming home. I thought maybe the Lord was going to spare my boy," he said, sobbing without shame. "I've been praying hard for it."

"The letter said that he is missing, though. They have not found him, and that should give us hope."

"I remember when your daddy's brother was missing in action. They even had prayer vigils at the church. Look what happened to him, to both of those boys. Families all over the country have prayed for their kids in wars. This is my fault. I told you that the sins of the fathers would come out on the children. That sweet boy of mine could be suffering some kind of torture because of me, if he's still alive."

"We don't know that he's a prisoner, Max. We don't know anything, really. He told me in his last letter that he was sure he'd make it home. I've decided to believe that, too."

Max shook his head. "It's my fault."

"Does Mrs. Chase know?"

"Oh no, hon. She doesn't need to know anything about this. They evaluated her and put her right into rehab. She's got enough worries."

Jemma wiped her cheeks. "He told me once that things happen just when you think you're safe."

"What are we going to do?" he asked.

"Pray. That's all we can do. Spence is smart and he wants to come home more than anything. I know that even smart people get killed and captured, but we have to trust that God's Great Plan includes him coming back to us."

"He can't be dead." Max tilted his head back and groaned. "My mother always called dying being *lifted* — such a funny thing to say, huh? But Spencer can't have been lifted. He's got to know that I'm trying to change."

Jemma put her arm around him. "Let's think of Spence being lifted by angels, Max, but only to safety for now."

Lizbeth opened the front door. "Jemma-beth, there you are, sugar. Your folks are on the phone. Come in, Mr. Chase, and have some coffee with us." Much to Lizbeth's surprise, he did. Lester was even more surprised to see him, and he was especially shocked to get a hug from Max-a-million Chase.

Jemma went to bed just before dawn. She had talked with Max until they were hoarse. She searched his face for Spencer, but Max had none of Spence's mannerisms or wit, but he was suffering, and he was his father. It gave her strength to offer him hope.

She had read so many stories of inhumane treatment for Americans held captive by the Viet Cong and their allies. She prayed that Spencer be spared such horror. In fact, each breath became a prayer. Jemma's head ached and her nerves buzzed as she crumpled across her bed. She was still wearing her gardening clothes, Papa's old overalls, but she didn't want to get under the covers anyway. The lace curtains billowed out with an early morning breeze and touched her face. He could not be dead. She would have felt something when his life left him, and she would have seen him in the stars.

■ ■ ■ ■

Lizbeth stood in the pouting room with the door shut. She had been on her knees for an hour. It had been the same when they had gotten the telegram with the news that Matthew was missing. She had spent almost every waking minute in prayer then, too, but Matt's death didn't mean that she shouldn't pray for Spencer's life. It was different to be the mother, but it was all agony of the heart. She wanted to lift this burden from Jemmabeth and take it upon herself . . . if only that were possible. Jemma had shown great faith for one so young, but nobody should have to go through this sickening wait.

She closed up the pouting room and set about cooking breakfast. She could make it in her sleep. Now her hands worked at it without a single thought propelling them. Jemma wouldn't eat anything, but Lester would. Since they got the news, Lester was with them most of the days and into the evenings, as were Willa and Joe . . . bless their hearts.

Cameron would have grieved himself sick over this. He loved Spencer, and Jemmabeth was his jewel. She held fast to the countertop and said one more prayer that the good Lord would have mercy on this sweet boy. She asked that it could be within The Great Plan for him to come home in one piece and, most assuredly, not in a box. She heard Jemma playing that sad song again on her stereo: "Praeludium and Allegro" was the name on the record. Lizbeth sat at the table, her head in her hands. She wasn't sure that Jemmabeth was the only one who might fall apart if they got that second telegram. Cam had kept her from crumbling before, but she would have to be the strong one now.

As had become her habit the past week, Jemma spent part of her day praying in the chapel that Spence had designed. She prayed for Harriet and Max, too. Max had taken a week off from work to stay in a motel in Waco. He was taking this hard. Jemma prayed that God would heal Mrs. Chase and that she and Max could start over, somehow. Most of her prayers were for her beloved. If she didn't have faith about this, she was still on her Christian crawl, rather than her walk.

This particular evening, she sat in the hollyhock patch and read Emily Dickinson's poem that compared hope to a little bird that never gives up and is a constant comfort to all. Emily always spoke to her heart.

It had been weeks since the crash, but Jemma's faith rested in the God of the universe, the author of The Great Plan. Her everlasting hope lay with Spencer and his determination to return to her. Spence was her hero, whatever happened. She laid the book across her lap. The hollyhock stalks bobbed and swayed, heavy with white, pink, and maroon blossoms. She had been there so many times with Spencer, laughing and flirting. Flowers might be blooming where he was, too. The little scar on his chin came to her mind. It had taken forever to heal when it happened, but it was smooth against her fingers in Hawaii. She had caused it at recess in the fifth grade when she went up to knock the basketball out of his hands and came down with a bit of his chin instead. He had teased her about scarring him for life. She wondered what deeper scars he bore now.

She wanted to walk with Spence in Papa's cotton fields when the plants were loaded with pink and white flowers. Someday they could pick just enough cotton at harvest for a little quilt to lay their babies on. Their children should be like him, steady and even-tempered. The boys might all have gray eyes like their daddy. The girls could be a little like her. No. None should be so stubborn, wishy-washy, and prone to pouting. She did not pout their last night in Hawaii. That memory, tucked in her heart, could not be their only time together.

Jemma looked at her watch. The Zephyr would be coming soon in the early autumn twilight. She would miss seeing its passengers as they lingered over an evening meal when the Burlington big shots closed it down. Those diners were the subject of her latest painting. She walked up to the tracks and sat on the rail. Joe's dog barked a couple of times, then gave up. The lights from the football field cast a faint glow in the western sky. The CHS band was playing the fight song. How could people around her carry on without knowing if Spencer had breath? The Johnson grass by the tree row had gone to seed, and the evening breeze ruffled through it, stirring the heads into a raspy chatter. Jemma gathered her skirt around her legs. She picked up a twig, twirling it between her thumb and finger, then drew a heart in the dirt.

When she and Sandy were younger, they had danced on the tracks to see who would be the last to jump off before the train got too close. She hadn't danced since the telegram came. It hadn't even occurred to her. The 9:04 blew its whistle at the station, and she moved off the tracks to wait for it.

The Zephyr passed by, picking up speed. Its horn changed tones as it moved past. Jemma returned to her seat on the rail, now hot through her skirt. A grasshopper flew up from the sunflowers and landed on her. She brushed it off and watched it recover. Gram would be home soon from her Bible study circle. Jemma dusted the back of her skirt and faced the breeze. The gentle wind parted her hair, and she felt a slight prickle where the scar remained from her wreck.

She closed her eyes and hummed "Candy Man," moving like the hollyhock stalks with their heavy burdens. Crickets had begun their night rhythm and a flock of birds resting on the telephone lines overhead kept curious eyes on her. She could almost hear Spencer saying her name on the warm wind. It gave her a chill to think that he could be calling out to her somewhere. She stopped and peered into the dim horizon, then closed her eyes and resumed her solitary dance.

It came to her again, but his voice was not in her head. It was drifting down the track. Her eyes popped open and her body tingled at the familiar form heading toward her.

"Spence!" she screamed. She ran, her feet flying over the rail bed.

The flock of birds took flight, too. Spencer, sprinting full speed, dropped his bag somewhere along the last fifty yards. They collided, like two shooting stars whose collective radiance overshadowed Venus and dazzled the heavens. He held her, breathless, and they peered into one another's eyes — golden and pewter, fastened together for life. They trembled, first in disbelief, then in laughter.

He was not lost among those stars, not while she could hear the beat of his heart above her own. Praise God.

CHAPTER 21
THAT'LL DO

The Cotton Festival and Fourth of July committee members sprang into action to celebrate the return of Chillaton's native son. Spencer would have none of it, though, unless all the veterans in the county were honored as well. The cars in the parade were courtesy of Chase's Cadillac & Chevrolet. The Lion's Club served hot dogs and cherry pie to every citizen who could get to the courthouse lawn and delivered to those who couldn't. Congressman Cyrus Millsap made a speech and, to everyone's surprise, presented Willa with a posthumous Purple Heart to honor Sergeant Samuel Augustus Johnson, 92nd Infantry, for his actions in WWII. The crowd became suddenly quiet at this honor for a brave Buffalo Soldier who was born and raised just across the tracks, and whose widow had, at one time or the other, ironed their clothing.

A tearful Willa embraced Lizbeth. "I know

this come from your doins', Miz Liz, but my words ain't good enough to thank you."

Trina couldn't manage to say anything. The moment was too close to her heart.

Spencer told his own story with his usual good-natured poise and humor at least twenty times. The Amarillo television stations and newspaper were there. The Judge showed up and was in line for hot dogs right alongside Shorty Knox.

When they got back to Lizbeth's house, the phone was ringing. It was the Lillygraces.

"Dear boy, you must tell this story once more. I know you are weary of it, but we want to know all the details. Everyone was so worried," Robert said.

Spencer clasped Jemma to his side, where she had been since he came home, and they sat on the floor in the good bedroom. "I don't mind telling you my story, sir. We were on a mission to hoist some wounded who were pinned down by snipers in a wooded area. We were at the LZ, the landing zone, but a missile hit the gunship that was supposed to cover us, wiping it completely out. We were continuing with the rescue when our chopper took a major hit in the engine and dropped about the same time that another missile exploded in the cabin. I lost

513

my whole crew."

Spence exhaled and there was a long pause before he continued. "My leg had a gaping rip in it, but I could still move. I felt around in the smoke for the hoist cable and inched my way down it until I couldn't hold on anymore and fell into some bushes. By some miracle, I was able to crawl into a big field of elephant grass and hide. I just kept crawling and praying. I heard shots again and knew that they were still in the area so I sweated it out in the grass until right before dawn. It was quiet because I remember hearing birds, then I got it stuck in my brain that we'd heard of guys encountering cobras in elephant grass. I thought that would be a great way to die in 'Nam. I was in shock, for sure.

"My plan was to get back across the field where we went down and get with any unit that was still in the woods. My arm throbbed and was so swollen that I figured it was broken. I made a sling with my belt, and I had gone about a hundred yards when I heard the VC yelling in the woods where I was headed. I got out my map and went the opposite direction for a couple of hours. I crossed a stream and came up on a cluster of shacks, a village of sorts. There were women cooking outside and little kids running around, but I didn't see any VC. The villagers were eating, so I decided to stay put. My arm was giving me fits, and I had lost a lot of blood from my leg wound. I thought that if my unit was looking for me, I needed to stop moving. The whole day, I never saw any men around the area, so I got my nerve up and moved closer to one of the shacks. I could smell food, and I would have eaten anything at that point, believe me.

"The last thing I recall was watching the sunset. When I woke up, some little kids had found me. I kept thinking about Gulliver and the Lilliputians and cobras. I was out of my head. I just knew they were going to turn me in to the nearest VC, but I was wrong. One of them went to get an elderly woman and a skinny teenage girl. They helped me into her hut and put me on a floor mat. The old woman was in charge of the whole village, or so it seemed to me. They fed me and made a splint for my arm and dressed my thigh. I drank some hot tea or something and fell asleep. The next morning the hut was full of women and children watching me. There was one man there, though. He was probably ninety years old. He came to check me out, too. I guess I must have been out of it for a week."

"How did you communicate?" Robert asked.

"My crew's *mamasan,* who cleaned our quarters, taught me some of her language. Anyway, I tried to explain to the teenage girl that I needed to get back to my people. I could hear choppers in the distance off and on, and sporadic gunfire, so I knew we had a unit around the area. I guess I was at the village about three weeks. They were very kind to me. I taught the kids some songs that we used to sing in Sunday school. The grandma really liked the silver cross that Jem had given me before I left home, so I gave it to her. Then one morning she woke me up before sunrise and walked with me to the woods on the other side of their village. Grandma waved me off with the girl, and I just hoped we weren't walking into a trap.

"The girl walked for about an hour with me, then pointed toward the hills and said for me to go over them. I took off my boot and gave her all the money I had hidden there. She disappeared into the jungle. I got out my survival map and tried to figure out where I was. I made my way across a river and got up in the hills. It seemed to take forever. About dusk I was sighted by one of our assault helicopter units. I was never so happy to see a Huey aimed at me. They picked me up and took me to their camp. The doctors checked me out and said nothing was broken. Two weeks later, I was running down the tracks to my beautiful fiancée."

"It's a shame the army didn't tell Jemmabeth that you were safe," Catherine said.

"Yes ma'am. Jem and I talked about that, and I think there was some military miscommunication."

Jemmabeth reached for another tissue and blew her nose.

Robert cleared his throat. "I see. To what do you attribute this fascinating survival story, Spencer?"

Spence rested his head on the edge of the bed as he considered the question. "There was a scripture from Isaiah that stuck in my mind. 'When you pass through the waters I will be with you; and through the rivers, they shall not overflow you: when you walk through the fire, you shall not be burned; neither shall the flame kindle upon you.' Brother Cleo used that verse in his sermon the last Sunday before I left. Now that I'm home, I recall an appropriate quote from Mark Twain, too, about war and strangers helping you. Those women helped me survive, and I'll never forget them. Oh, and

I also had a four-leaf clover that my fiancée had given me." He grinned at her.

"You are an intrepid young man, Spencer. We are so grateful that you are home. Jemmabeth has been distraught, as we all have. We shall be seeing you in a few days for the wedding. Until then."

"Yes, dear. We are anxious to see you and give you a proper welcome. Do give Jemmabeth a hug for us," Catherine said. "Godspeed."

Spencer and Jemmabeth stayed on the floor by the good bed and relaxed in one another's arms.

"I didn't tell your grandfather one other thing, Jem," Spencer said.

"What's that?"

"You have the most delicious lips and eyes the color of honey."

"Is that what you didn't tell him?"

"Nope, but it's true. I also didn't tell him that I kept thinking about holding you in that silk nightgown, and how that thought helped carry me out of the jungle."

"I'm glad I could be of service, sir." She saluted.

"You'll never know, Jem. You'll just never know," he said and kissed her. "That first night, when the smoke lifted, the stars were brilliant. I was so shook up about my crew, the gunship team, and all those wounded that we didn't get out. Those images will always be in my head, I suppose. I had to concentrate on you to keep my wits. I went through our whole conversation we had at the river, the night before I left. *I think of thee,* remember? I know this sounds crazy, but I saw it in the stars, baby, I really did."

She cradled him, like she did in Hawaii. He was thin, but he was home.

"The earth is a big place and there are lots of good people on it," he said, his cheek buried in her hair. "Somewhere there's a little grandma who made this day possible. I honor her tonight, too."

"Maybe she was an angel."

"Maybe so." It had crossed his mind.

The wedding plans were easy. All they had to do was get out the old list and follow it. This time, though, Spencer went with her everywhere. There were no hitches. Everything was perfect and everybody came, right down to Uncle Arthur and all the Jenkins sisters.

On the eve of the wedding, the sunset was all Hollywood. There were no fishing trips, just one big party. Lizbeth presented them with the wedding ring quilt that she had made two years before. It was in shades of yellow and gold on a tiny blue floral background. The fabric in one corner was solid cornflower blue. Jemmabeth knew it was meant to be for Papa's twinkling eyes always watching over them. She draped it over herself and Spencer as cameras snapped.

In the early morning sunshine, Jemmabeth appeared under the cottonwoods on her daddy's arm. Melanie played "Morning Has Broken" as they walked along the creek to the old cottonwood tree. The sight took Spencer's breath away. Jemma and Trina had designed her two-piece wedding dress of vintage French lace over cream-colored Italian silk. It was nothing like the gowns Miss Scarlett wore. The skirt was slender, encircled by burgundy and pink beaded flowers and golden leaves, and a long, silky train was attached at her waist. The strapless bodice was fitted and the scrolled neckline showed off Spencer's wedding gift — a double strand of pearls embracing a ruby heart. Her auburn hair cascaded over her shoulders and was crowned with a wreath of rosebuds and forget-me-nots attached to the veil that flowed behind her like a misty lace confection. She carried a bouquet of fragrant roses, sweet peas, cornflowers, and one small sunflower. Her great-grandmother Forrester's lace handker-chief was tucked inside the bouquet.

Trina, her maid-of-honor, was "looking fine," as Nick put it, in the gold crepe silk dress of her own design. The fabric was embroidered across the bodice and hem with burgundy and pink rosebuds. Sandy's matching one was pewter, the same as Spencer's eyes, and Carrie's was the color of Scottish heather. Each carried a cluster of heather, tied with an ivory velvet bow. Robby was Spencer's best man. He didn't try any monkey business, and he looked quite handsome in his tux.

When Jim gave her to him at the rose-bedecked altar, Spencer whispered some-thing in her ear, then they repeated the vows from their private ceremony. Brother Cleo said, at last, "I now pronounce you man and wife."

Spencer picked her up and spun her around. The guests clapped and yelled like it was the winning touchdown at homecom-ing.

Melanie played "Josefin's Waltz" and "Archibald MacDonald of Keppoch" — Papa's favorite songs. Jemma and Spencer danced the first dance alone as Melanie played "I Will Wait for You." Nobody said a word, but there were constant sniffles from the crowd.

Things lightened up when Buddy took over. The band was cookin'. Buddy played his harmonica and sang "Candy Man." The fire that had glowed for almost eighteen years was burning its brightest when the newlyweds danced.

After a few more songs, Spencer took the microphone. "This one's for Jemmabeth Alexandra Chase." He sang "Pretty Woman." Jemma laughed and danced with Robby, cutting her eyes at Spencer, whenever she could, to give him The Look.

The band got a big kick out of Spencer singing to her, especially Leon, who nodded his approval. Spencer, looking like Prince Charming once again, danced with every woman there, so it was a good thing that Missy Blake wasn't invited. Jemma did the same with all the guys. Uncle Art knew how to move for a man his age and Max showed her where Spencer got his dancing skills. Helene and Lester waltzed solo when Melanie played *Un Coin Tout Bleu,*" a French song that Helene liked. Nobody knew Lester could dance like that. Lizbeth assumed he had learned with his Methodist wife.

"Jemma," Paralee Batson yelled, "if the U.S. of A. government would use its own postal service instead of Western Union, I could've got the news about Spencer to you quicker. You know that, don't you?"

Jemma waved.

Paralee sniffed and touched her hair. Nedra had combed it back behind her ears, just like the twin on *As the World Turns* who showed up after eight years of amnesia. It was perfect, just like her new dress and this wedding, which would be the hot topic at Nedra's until Christmas.

Lester was keeping Lizbeth company when Jemma came to say good-bye. "Bless you two, in your new life. I don't suppose you'll be comin' back to live with your gram anymore, but we'll sure miss you," he added, giving her a hug.

"Thank you, Lester, I'll miss you, too." She took Lizbeth aside. "Gram, you know that nobody in this world is more precious to me than you. Of course, that's not counting my husband." She saw him across the crowd and blushed a little.

"I know, sugar, the feeling is mutual. I see that you gave him a new Bible."

"Yes ma'am. I wanted it to have the right date on the cover. I also gave him a new silver cross to wear."

Spencer came to get her.

"Gotta go," Jemma said, kissing Lizbeth's

soft cheek that was laced with an extra dose of "Moonlight Over Paris" perfume. "We'll be back in three weeks. Maybe you can live with us someday! You, too, Lester, because you never know what The Great Plan has in store," she yelled as Spencer tugged her away from the happy group. Jemma got inside a makeshift tent and changed into her traveling outfit.

She threw an extra bouquet into the clump of hopefuls and Lester caught it, but promptly handed it over to Trina. They escaped ahead of the rice in their new silver Corvette, a gift from Max, and drove to the cemetery. They walked to Papa's grave, holding hands. The sunflowers were in full bloom this year.

"Here we are, Papa — Mr. and Mrs. Spencer Chase," Spence said.

"We just wanted to introduce ourselves," Jemma whispered and laid some of the flowers from her bouquet at the base of his headstone. She kissed her fingers and touched his name.

"When does our flight leave for Scotland?" Jemmabeth asked, turning her attention to other things in the car.

"Not for four hours," Spencer answered, trying to concentrate on the road.

"Four hours? It just takes an hour to get to Amarillo."

"I know," he said.

They had just passed Main Street when he suddenly made a left turn and pulled into the driveway of the That'll Do Motel. He parked, jangling a room key in front of his giggling wife. He opened her door and stood for a moment as a breeze swirled her hair around her face. He growled, then lifted her out of the car and carried his bride inside, closing the door behind them. He opened it once again, just wide enough to hang a ragged, handmade sign on the doorknob.

Do Not Disturb — Cowboy at Work

ABOUT THE AUTHOR

Sharon McAnear, author of the Jemma series and Stars in My Crown series, was raised in the small towns of the Texas Panhandle, where anybody and everybody helped a child know who she was and what was expected of her. Her Jemma series, which introduces some of the lively Chillaton residents, is "more than a love story," Sharon says. "It rekindles a sweeter time when family and friends were everywhere, and you were frequently glad of it. When needed, the good citizens of Connelly County stood ready to help out with chores, form a prayer circle, or stretch the truth about your situation. Take your pick. It was a place where sweet companionship soothed lonely hearts and 'porch company' abounded." Her Stars in My Crown series covers the eventful, exciting lives of Jemma's three children: Annalisa, Drew, and Betsy.

Sharon now lives in Colorado with her

very patient husband, and her periodically dramatic family is scattered around the country. As a writer, she has come to rely heavily upon the frozen talents of Marie Callender and the Grace of God. Well, perhaps only a couple of times a week for Marie.

May 14,1.5 2016